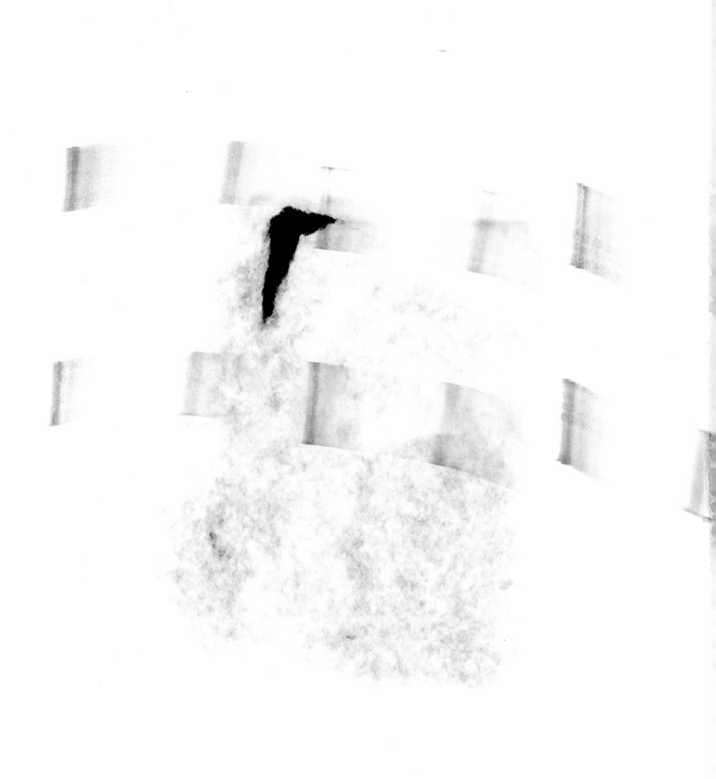

GREAT AMERICAN COURT CASES

GREAT AMERICAN COURT CASES

COURT CASES

Volume II:
Criminal Justice

FIRST EDITION

Mark Mikula and
L. Mpho Mabunda,
Editors

Allison McClintic Marion,
Associate Editor

The Gale Group

DETROIT • SAN FRANCISCO • LONDON • BOSTON • WOODBRIDGE, CT

Staff

Mark F. Mikula, L. Mpho Mabunda, Editors

Allison McClintic Marion, Dawn R. Barry, Rebecca Parks, Dave Oblender, Associate Editors
Elizabeth Shaw, Brian J. Koski, Gloria Lam, Catherine Donaldson, Assistant Editors
Linda S. Hubbard, Managing Editor, Multicultural Team

Susan Trosky, Permissions Manager
Margaret A. Chamberlain, Permissions Specialist

Victoria B. Cariappa, Research Manager
Barbara McNeil, Research Specialist

Evi Seoud, Assistant Production Manager

Cynthia Baldwin, Product Design Manager
Eric Johnson, Art Director

Barbara Yarrow, Graphic Services Manager
Randy A. Bassett, Image Database Supervisor
Robert Duncan, Imaging Specialist

Theresa Rocklin, Manager, Technical Support Services
Jeffrey Muhr, Technical Support

Library of Congress Cataloging-in-Publication Data

Great American court cases / Mark F. Mikula and L. Mpho Mabunda, editors;
Allison McClintic Marion, associate editor. -- 1st ed.
p. cm.
Includes bibliographical references and index.
Contents: v. 1. Individual liberties -- v. 2. Criminal justice -- v. 3. Equal protection and family law
-- v. 4. Business and government.
ISBN 078762947-0 (set).
1. Law--United States.--Cases. 2. Civil rights--United States-Cases. I. Mikula, Mark F. II. Mabunda,
L. Mpho., 1967-. III. Marion, Allison McClintic.
KF385.A4g68 1999
349.73--dc2

99-11419
CIP

Copyright © 1999
The Gale Group
27500 Drake Road
Farmington Hills, MI 48331-3535
http://www.galegroup.com
800-877-4253
248-699-4253

ISBN 0-7876-2947-2 (set) Vol 1 ISBN 0-7876-2948-0; Vol 2 ISBN 0-7876-2949-9;
Vol 3 ISBN 0-7876-2950-2; Vol 4 ISBN 0-7876-2951-0

10 9 8 7 6 5 4 3 2

CONTENTS

Volume II

CONTENTS

Volume I, III, IV

This abbreviated view shows just the issues covered in the other volumes. Consult the Cumulative Index that appears in each volume for all the cases, people, events, and subjects in all four volumes.

PREFACE

U.S. citizens take comfort and pride in living under the rule of law. Our elected representatives write and enforce the laws that govern everything from familial relationships to the dealings of multi-billion-dollar corporations, from the quality of the air to the content of the programs broadcast through it. But it is the judicial system that interprets the meaning of the law and makes it tangible to the average citizen through the drama of trials and the force of court orders and judicial opinions.

The four volumes of *Great American Court Cases* profile nearly 800 judicial proceedings. The editors consulted textbooks, curriculum guides, and authoritative Internet sites to identify cases studied for their influence on the development of key aspects of law in the United States. Although the majority of the cases resulted in decisions by the U.S. Supreme Court, nearly 60 cases from state courts or lower-level federal jurisdictions are included because of their impact or their role in an emerging point of law. Comprehensiveness requires that fundamental cases from the nineteenth century and earlier, such as *Marbury v. Madison* (1803) and *Swift v. Tyson* (1842), are included. This is especially true in Volume IV, which covers how laws have shaped the government. Nevertheless, to serve the information needs of today's users, most of the cases are from the twentieth century, with emphasis on the last three decades.

Scope and Arrangement

The case profiles are grouped according to the legal principle on which they reflect, with each volume covering one or two broad areas of the law as follows:

- *Volume I: Individual Liberties* includes cases that have influenced such First and Second Amendment issues as freedom of the press, privacy, the right to bear arms, and the legal concerns emerging from the growth of the Internet. Libel, the Establishment Clause, and other important facets of freedom of speech and freedom of religion are treated in separate essays with their own cases.

- *Volume II: Criminal Justice* covers cases that establish the rights of the accused before, during, and after trial, or address criminal law and procedure, search and seizure, drug laws, the jury, damages, and capital punishment.

- *Volume III: Equal Protection and Family Law* includes cases related to two broad areas of law. Equal protection issues covered in this volume include the broad range of civil rights related issues, from affirmative action, segregation, and voting rights to the special concerns of immigrants, juveniles, the disabled, and gay and lesbian citizens. Family issues covered include child support and custody and reproductive rights. Sexual harassment and the right to die are also represented in this volume.

- *Volume IV: Business and Government* also encompasses two major spheres of the law. Consumer protection, antitrust, and labor-related cases supplement the business fundamentals of contracts and corporate law. The government cases document the legal evolution of the branches of the federal government as well as the federal government's relation to state power. Separate topics address environmental law, military issues, national security, taxation, and the legal history of Native American issues. Appendixes in this volume also present the full text of the U.S. Constitution and its amendments and a chronological table of Supreme Court justices.

Coverage

Issue overviews, averaging 2,000 words in length, provide the context for the case profiles that follow. Case discussions range from 750 to 2,000 words according to their complexity and importance. Each provides the background of the case and issues involved, the main arguments presented by each side, and an explanation of the court's decision, as well as the legal, political, and social impact of the decision. Excerpts from the majority, concurring, and dissenting opinions are often included. Cross-references lead the user to related cases, while suggestions for further reading launch in-depth

---

Deciphering Legal Citations

Great American Court Cases includes citations for the cases covered in the profiles. Three sources, *United States Reports* (U.S.), the *Supreme Court Reporter* (S.Ct.), and the *Lawyers' Edition* (L.Ed.), all cite Supreme Court cases in separate series, resulting in three distinct citation numbers for each case. The citations for *Great American Court Cases*, in most cases, are drawn from *United States Reports*. On rare occasions, because there is a lag between the time that a case is heard and the time that its companion volume is published, the citation has been drawn from another reporter, usually the *Supreme Court Reporter*. In all cases, the structure of the citation is as follows: the volume number precedes the abbreviation for the reporter and is followed by the page number. For instance, *Davis v. Bandemer*, 478 U.S. 109, is included in volume 478 of *United States Reports*, beginning on page 109. Citations for cases tried below the level of the Supreme Court follow a similar structure with an abbreviation for the reporter associated with the lower court falling between the volume and page number. The case *In re Quinlan*, 355 A.2d 647, is covered in volume 355 of the *Atlantic Reporter*, second series (cases for states in the East), beginning on page 355.

---

research. Within each issue section, the cases are arranged from earliest to most recent to indicate the evolution of precedent.

The editors have had to make hard choices when a single case has bearing on more than one issue, as often occurs. The landmark reproductive rights decision in *Roe v. Wade,* for example, is based upon an assertion of privacy rights, so the case could have been placed with either issue. Also, the case of *Marbury v. Madison,* while establishing the concept of judicial review, dealt foremost with a separation of powers issue at the time that it was decided, meriting its inclusion in the separation of powers section of Volume IV. Users should consult the cumulative index that appears in each volume to find cases throughout the set that apply to a particular topic.

A small percentage (under 10 percent) of cases were previously covered in *Women's Rights on Trial* or *Great American Trials,* both Gale products. Selection criteria for each publication were different, but the *Great American Court Cases* editors preferred this slight overlap to omission of landmark cases. Entry elements particular to *Great American Court Cases,* such as the Supreme Court justices' votes, have been added to the material, along with updating as appropriate.

The editors determined that with the focus on constitutional law, sensationalistic cases, such as the O. J. Simpson trial and the trial of Ted Kaczynski, were more appropriately covered in the sidebars that complement the main text rather than receiving full treatment in the main body of the text. Also, at the time of publication, the impeachment trial of Bill Clinton had not reached its conclusion. It, therefore, does not receive coverage in this series.

Additional Features

Great American Court Cases has several features to enhance its usefulness to students and non-professional researchers:

The **legal citation** appears at the head of each case profile, enabling researchers to access the authoritative records of the court action. The "Deciphering Legal Citations" sidebar that is part of this preface explains the elements that make up the citations and remarks on the abbreviations for the various series, called "reporters," where records are published.

Each case opens with a **factbox** so the user can quickly scan (when available): the names of litigants; the initiating litigant's claim; the names of chief lawyers on each side; the name of the judge or justice who wrote the majority opinion or decision, as well as names of those who concurred or dissented; the date and location of the decision; the summary of the decision and comments on the decision's significance.

Sidebars in the case profiles highlight interesting aspects of the legal process or arguments, key participants, or related facts and incidents. Some outline the arguments for and against a particular issue or line of reasoning, which will promote critical thinking as well as fuel debates or mock-trials. Some also discuss related cases that did not warrant their inclusion as a main case in the text.

Approximately **300 photographs and graphics** depict individuals and events related to the cases.

A broad overview of the court system and the disciplines of law is presented in a general essay regarding the structure of the legal system.

Contributors have tried to present the issues and proceedings in language accessible to high school, college, and public library users. Legal terms must sometimes be used for precision, however, so a **glossary** of more than 600 words and phrases appears in each volume.

Users interested in a particular case can locate it by name (e.g., *Brown v. Board of Education*) in the **Alphabetical Listing of Cases** in the back of each volume. Those who wish to trace the changing focus of legal interest and opinion over time will find the **Chronological Listing of Cases** in the back of each volume helpful.

A **Cumulative Index** to cases, people, events, and subjects appears in each volume. The Cumulative Index is repeated in each volume to ensure that multiple users of the set have simultaneous access to its complete contents.

Audience for Great American Court Cases

The four volumes of *Great American Court Cases* cover more U.S. Supreme Court and state or lower federal court cases in greater depth than other works for a nonprofessional user. The selection of issues and cases, the consistent treatment, and the minimal use of legal jargon were designed with the student user in mind. Court cases bring important issues into focus in a dramatic way. They are increasingly used in curricula for studies of U.S. government, civics, history, and journalism. Law magnet school and pre-law courses can use *Great American Court Cases* to introduce important content in an accessible manner, while mock court programs will find a wide range of source material here. Students with interdisciplinary writing assignments and exercises in critical thinking will also find inspiration. Beyond the classroom, a broad range of people from activists to history buffs and Court TV watchers, will find the set compelling and useful.

Acknowledgments

Leah Knight, Meggin Condino, and Linda Irvin conceptualized *Great American Court Cases* and solicited feedback from potential users. A number of public and school librarians as well as teachers contributed to the development of the set. While several provided early input, Hilda Weisburg of Morristown High School in New Jersey continued to answer questions to help shape the product through its development. Kathy Nemeh and Diane Carter reviewed selected material for legal accuracy.

Two websites, which are freely available to the public, proved indispensible as resources for fact gathering and checking. These websites are the Findlaw site located at http://www.findlaw.com and the Oyez Oyez Oyez site located at http://court.it-services.nwu.edu.oyez.

Suggestions Are Welcome

The editors welcome suggestions on any aspect of this work. Please send comments to: Editors, *Great American Court Cases,* Gale Group, 27500 Drake Rd., Farmington Hills, MI 48331.

THE AMERICAN LEGAL SYSTEM

The most basic function of the American legal system is to maintain peace by resolving disputes. Federal and state courts, tribunals, and administrative bodies do this by applying laws to cases between specific individuals or organizations.

The primary sources of applicable law are federal and state constitutions, statutes, and administrative regulations. Constitutions establish the structure of government, define and limit its power, and seek to protect individuals from unreasonable or unlawful exercises of that power. Legislatures enact statutes—criminal laws, for example—that govern a wide variety of conduct. Administrative bodies promulgate regulations to govern specific areas of business, such as telecommunications and securities.

In theory, courts apply these existing laws rather than creating new law. The legislatures and administrative bodies, however, cannot always anticipate every possible set of circumstances, and the laws do not clearly dictate a result in every case. Frequently, too, the law is intentionally vague to give the courts flexibility to interpret it in ways which serve general public policies rather than to accomplish specific results. There are, however, constitutional limits on how vague a law may be. In general, it must fairly apprise individuals of behavior that it prohibits or compels.

In practice, then, American courts often make law when they decide cases. Under the doctrine of *stare decisis,* courts at the same or lower level in the judicial hierarchy must follow the first court's interpretation of the law in subsequent cases with similar facts. Higher courts in the judicial hierarchy may either accept the lower court's interpretation or reverse it by interpreting the law differently. Courts in other states may rely on the first court's interpretation as persuasive authority concerning the application of similar laws in their states. This tradition of binding and persuasive authority is a by-product of the American judicial system's origins in the common law system of England.

Origins of the American Judicial System: State Judicial Systems

When America declared its independence in 1776, the 13 original colonies had largely informal judicial systems based loosely on the English system of common law. Common law is the body of law that developed in English courts on a case-by-case basis. Under the common law, judges placed great reliance on decisions in prior cases with similar facts. Although state courts today apply laws enacted by legislatures and administrative bodies, they continue the common law tradition of case-by-case interpretation of these laws and reliance on prior judicial decisions.

As the United States expanded southward and westward, it acquired Mexican, Spanish, and French territories, which had legal systems based on the European civil law tradition. Under that tradition, courts in Europe applied detailed civil codes that the legislatures had designed to resolve all potential disputes. Civil codes reflected the natural law concept that there are unchanging, God-made laws that govern human behavior. Unlike in common law systems, civil law courts were not supposed to interpret the law beyond what was provided in the civil codes—they simply resolved disputes by applying the appropriate portion of the code. While the English common law tradition dominated the formation of American state legal systems, remnants of the civil law tradition exist even today, most notably in Louisiana, which based its legal system on the civil law of France.

Origins of the American Judicial System: Federal Judiciary

The federal judiciary was born in 1789 upon adoption of the U.S. Constitution, which vested the judicial power of the United States in "one supreme Court, and in such inferior Courts as the Congress may from time to time ordain and establish." The Constitution created a judicial system that contains elements of both the common and civil law traditions. The latter is evident in one of the purposes expressed in the Constitution's preamble—to "secure the Blessings of Liberty." The

Constitution, however, is subject to case-by-case interpretation by the U.S. Supreme Court, which usually limits itself by the principle of *stare decisis.*

Origins of the American Judicial System: Federalism

The existence of separate federal and state judicial systems in the United States is a hallmark of federalism, which means these systems share authority to resolve legal disputes in their geographic boundaries. Federal and state courts sometimes have concurrent jurisdiction to resolve disputes arising from the same set of circumstances. For instance, federal and state authorities both took judicial action following the bombing of the Alfred P. Murrah Federal Building in Oklahoma City in 1995. Federal and state courts occasionally have exclusive jurisdiction over certain areas of the law. State courts, for instance, typically have exclusive jurisdiction to handle child custody disputes, while federal courts exclusively handle bankruptcy cases. The U.S. Constitution determines whether state and federal courts have concurrent or exclusive jurisdiction over a particular issue.

Structure and Operation of the Courts: Judicial Hierarchy

American state court systems are hierarchical. Most states have trial courts of general jurisdiction where the judges preside over all types of cases, both civil and criminal. Most states also have special courts of limited jurisdiction that hear only certain kinds of cases—domestic relations and family court, juvenile court, and courts for the administration of wills are typical examples. There also are state courts of inferior jurisdiction, such as justices of the peace, small claims court, and traffic court, that handle petty matters. Appeals from all lower courts usually go first to an intermediate appellate court, often called the court of appeals, and then to the state's highest court, often called the supreme court. When a case involves application of the U.S. Constitution or federal law, the parties sometimes may appeal from the state's highest court to the U.S. Supreme Court.

The federal judiciary is similarly hierarchical. Federal district courts handle trials in civil and criminal cases, and appeals from some federal administrative agencies. The federal judiciary also has special courts of limited jurisdiction, such as the Court of Federal Claims, the Court of International Trade, and the Tax Court. Appeals from federal district courts go to one of 11 numbered circuit courts of appeals covering different geographical regions, or to the District of Columbia Court of Appeals. Appeals from the Court of Federal Claims and the Court of International Trade go to the Federal Court of Appeals. Parties may appeal a case from the appellate courts to the U.S. Supreme Court.

Structure and Operation of the Courts: Criminal and Civil Procedure

The progress of a case through the court system is governed by rules of procedure. There are separate rules of civil and criminal procedure because criminal cases require special constitutional safeguards for the accused. The following illustration explains the procedure in a civil case, which generally is a dispute between private individuals. Some of the notable differences between civil and criminal procedures are noted in this discussion.

Rules of civil procedure define and limit the roles of the various persons in a case. The party who brings a case is called the plaintiff, and the person being sued is the defendant. (In criminal cases there is a prosecutor instead of a plaintiff.) As the American legal system is adversarial, the parties are represented by lawyers who must zealously protect their clients' interests. A jury typically hears the evidence and determines the outcome under the substantive law as instructed by the judge. The judge acts as a referee to enforce the rules and explain the applicable law.

While the federal and state courts each have their own rules of civil procedure, the federal process is fairly representative. A federal case begins when a plaintiff files a complaint and summons in a federal district court. The complaint explains the nature of the plaintiff's claim against the defendant. The summons notifies the defendant to appear and to answer the complaint by either admitting or denying the plaintiff's allegations. If the defendant fails to appear and answer, the court may enter a default judgment against the defendant and order the relief sought by the plaintiff. If the defendant appears, he typically files an answer that denies the plaintiff's allegations. The plaintiff's complaint, the defendant's answer, and any reply by the plaintiff are called the pleadings.

The defendant next may file a motion to dismiss, which argues that even if the plaintiff proves everything in his pleadings, the law does not provide any relief. If the judge grants this motion, she dismisses the case. If not, the parties proceed to the discovery phase.

The purpose of discovery is to help the parties identify and narrow the issues for trial, and to require the parties to disclose all of their evidence. The parties begin discovery by making mandatory disclosures containing basic information, such as the identity of persons and documents with evidence related to the pleadings. The parties then answer interrogatories and take depositions. Interrogatories are written questions that a party must answer in writing under an oath that acknowledges a penalty for perjury. Depositions are oral, transcribed proceedings by which a prospective witness, who also is under oath, answers verbal questions posed by the lawyers. Interrogatory answers and deposition transcripts may be used at trial as evidence or to impeach a witness's testimony if she contradicts what she said during discovery.

After discovery, the defendant may make a motion for summary judgment, which argues that even with everything that discovery has revealed, the plaintiff is unable to prove a violation of law warranting relief. If the judge grants this motion, she dismisses the case. Otherwise the case proceeds to trial.

The trial begins when the judge and parties pick a jury. (In civil cases for which there was no right to a jury trial upon adoption of the U.S. Constitution, or when the parties do not want a jury trial, the parties have a bench trial before a judge without a jury.) In some cases a grand jury, consisting usually of 23 members, is called to determine whether grounds exist for a criminal proceeding to be initiated by the state. To pick the jury, the judge or lawyers pose questions to prospective jurors. After hearing the answers, the parties may dismiss a set number of prospective jurors for any reason, although they may not discriminate unlawfully. The parties further may dismiss an unlimited number of jurors for good cause, such as bias in the prospective juror's responses.

Once they have selected 12 jurors, the lawyers present opening statements, which give the jury a roadmap of what the evidence will prove. The plaintiff then presents his case by the testimony of witnesses and the admission of documents into the record of evidence. The presentation is governed by rules of evidence, which the judge enforces to determine what the jury can and cannot hear. The rules of evidence are supposed to give the jury only the most reliable evidence. The defendant is allowed to cross-examine the plaintiff's witnesses to challenge their accuracy, truthfulness, and bias. The defendant presents his evidence after the plaintiff, who then may cross-examine the defendant's witnesses.

At the close of the evidence, each party may ask the judge to enter judgment in his favor on the ground that a reasonable jury could only reach one verdict under the evidence presented. If the judge denies this motion, she instructs the jury about the applicable substantive law, the lawyers make closing arguments to explain the result their clients seek, and the jury retires to deliberate and reach a verdict. After the jury (or the judge in a bench trial) delivers its verdict, each party may ask the judge to reverse the verdict or order a new trial based upon errors the judge made applying the rules of procedure, rules of evidence, or substantive law. If these motions are denied, the parties may file a notice of appeal to the proper circuit court of appeals. Notably, if a person is found not guilty in a criminal proceeding that is not declared a mistrial, that person cannot be tried again for the same crime. This concept of dou-

ble jeopardy has its origin in the Fifth Amendment, which prevents people from being placed at risk of conviction more than once for a single offense.

Cases in the courts of appeals are heard by a panel of three judges. The parties file briefs that explain the errors they think the trial judge made under the rules of procedure, rules of evidence, or substantive law. The court of appeals does not hear the evidence anew, but relies on the record—the trial testimony and documents entered into evidence before the district court. The court also might hear oral argument, during which the parties' lawyers may respond to questions posed by the judges on the panel. The judges then study the record, briefs, and oral argument, discuss the case among themselves, vote on the result, and issue a decision based on the majority vote.

Dissatisfied parties may appeal to the U.S. Supreme Court, which is composed of nine justices. The procedure is similar to that in the courts of appeal, with one major exception: a party first must file a petition for a writ of *certiorari* to convince the Supreme Court that the case is important enough to warrant consideration. The Supreme Court grants the writ—by a vote of four or more justices—for only approximately five percent of the thousands of petitions it receives each year. These lucky few file briefs and engage in oral argument as they did before the court of appeals. After the justices vote, one of the justices voting in the majority writes an opinion explaining the Court's decision. Dissatisfied parties have no further avenue of appeal from this court of last resort.

Structure and Operation of the Courts: Alternative Dispute Resolution

The procedure for pursuing a case, especially a civil case, from trial through appeal is time-consuming. It can take one or more years to get a verdict in the trial court, and five or more years for an appeal to the court of appeals and the Supreme Court. The legal fees and other costs can amount to hundreds of thousands or millions of dollars. The vast majority of civil cases thus settle before going to trial, which means the parties resolve their dispute by agreement. Most criminal cases also settle, a process called plea-bargaining.

Efforts to reduce costs in civil cases have popularized an area of legal procedure called alternative dispute resolution, or ADR. Arbitration, the best known form of ADR, is an informal, abbreviated trial where one or more neutral arbitrators hears and decides the case like a judge and jury. Conciliation, a less common form of ADR, involves submission of the dispute to a neutral third party for her investigation and recommendation. With mediation the parties try to negotiate a resolution with the assistance and guidance of a neutral mediator.

Today many contracts include a clause that requires parties to use ADR to resolve their disagreements. Whether or not they have a contract, many parties voluntarily pursue ADR before going to court. State courts increasingly require parties in certain types of cases to try arbitration or mediation before proceeding to trial. The American Arbitration Association and other organizations support these efforts by designing ADR systems and procedures.

Types of Law

In the United States, where most courts hear cases concerning all areas of law, categorizing the laws is largely arbitrary. In *An Introduction to the Legal System of the United States,* Professor E. Allan Farnsworth suggested a useful distinction between public and private law. Public law generally concerns disputes between the government and individuals. Private law concerns disputes between private individuals.

Types of Law: Public Law

Public law, as described by Professor Farnsworth, includes constitutional, criminal, trade regulation, labor, and tax law. Constitutional law is embodied in the decisions of the U.S. Supreme Court that interpret the federal Constitution. Many of these cases concern whether conduct by the legislative or executive branches of the federal government violate constitutional definitions or limitations on their powers. Under the "political question" doctrine, however, the Supreme Court will decline to decide such a case if the Constitution reserves the issue for the legislative or executive branch without judicial interference.

A large majority of constitutional law cases concern the protection of individual rights from unlawful federal conduct. The Bill of Rights, which comprises the first ten amendments to the Constitution, is the primary source of these rights. For example, the First Amendment protects the freedom of speech, while the Fourth Amendment protects the right to be free from unreasonable search and seizure. The Constitution also protects individual rights from unlawful state conduct. The most important source of this protection is the Fourteenth Amendment, which contains the Due Process and Equal Protection Clauses. By interpretation of these clauses, the U.S. Supreme Court has applied the rights and protections found in the Bill of Rights to state conduct.

Criminal law mostly appears in state penal codes. These codes, while largely based on the common law of England, reflect an effort to arrive at uniform, reliable definitions of crimes. The codes define everything from felonies, such as murder and rape, to misdemeanors and petty offenses. There also are federal sources of criminal law, most notably relating to interstate conduct, such as drug trafficking and fraudulent use of the mails. Another important source of federal criminal law is the statute that protects civil rights, such as the right to be free from discrimination on the basis of race, color, or creed. Criminal law cases also can involve issues of constitutional law, such as the rights of the accused to remain silent and to be represented by an attorney.

Trade regulation includes antitrust law, which seeks to prevent monopolies and other restraints of trade under America's system of free enterprise. It also includes laws designed to prevent unfair competition among businesses. Labor law protects the well-being of employees and the rights and duties of labor unions. Tax law primarily concerns the federal income tax.

Types of Law: Private Law

Private law, often referred to as civil law, includes tort, contract, family, commercial, and property law. States are the primary source of private law. Tort law is a system of providing compensation between individuals for private wrongs, such as battery and defamation. The enforcement of promises or obligations between individuals is the subject of contract law. Family law deals with the relationships between husband and wife or parent and child: marriage and divorce; spousal abuse and support; and child custody, abuse, support, and adoption. Commercial law, derived primarily from the Uniform Commercial Code, governs the sale and lease of goods. Property law governs transactions in real estate.

The Appointment of Judges

The process for appointing state judges varies from state to state. Most state trial judges are elected by popular vote or by the state legislature. The supreme court judges in most states are appointed for a fixed term by the governor, and then periodically stand unopposed for reelection based on their records. In some states the judges of the highest court are elected by popular vote. State judges usually serve for a fixed term of years or for life, and can be removed only for gross misconduct by formal proceedings.

Federal judges are appointed by the president with the advice and consent of the Senate. This process typically results in the appointment of judges who are members of the president's political party. If the Senate judiciary committee is controlled by the president's opposition party, the confirmation process can be hotly contested. Federal judges are appointed for life, and can be removed only by impeachment and conviction by Congress.

The Role of Judges

State and federal judges perform various important roles in the American legal system. Trial judges referee cases under the rules of procedure and evidence. The trial judge also instructs the jury concerning the substantive law that is applicable to the case. In bench trials, the judge determines the facts, law, and result without a jury. The role of appellate judges is to review the record of evidence before the trial court, decide the applicable substantive law, and either affirm or reverse the result below. In doing so, the appellate judge may announce principles of law for application by trial judges in future cases.

Limitations on Judicial Power

In *Marbury v. Madison* (1803), the Supreme Court said "[i]t is emphatically the province and duty of the judicial department to say what the law is." Judicial power, however, is not unlimited. The U.S. Constitution is the primary source for limitations on federal judicial power. The Constitution constrains federal courts to hear only "cases and controversies," which means actual cases rather than hypothetical situations or stale disputes. Under the political question doctrine, federal courts will not address issues reserved to the legislative or executive branches of the federal government. Congressional authority under the Constitution also limits judicial power. Congress may impeach and convict federal judges for "Treason, Bribery, or other high Crimes and Misdemeanors." If Congress is dissatisfied with a court's interpretation of a statute, it may pass legislation to correct the interpretation, as long as it acts within the constitutional limitations on its own power.

Similarly, state judicial power is restricted by state constitutions, the process for selection and removal of state judges, and the ultimate supremacy of the U.S. Constitution over both state and federal statutes and case law.

Bibliography and Further Reading

Calvi, James V., and Susan Coleman. *American Law and Legal Systems,* 3d ed. Upper Saddle River: Prentice Hall, 1997.

Farnsworth, E. Allan. *An Introduction to the Legal System of the United States,* 3d ed. New York: Oceana Publications, Inc., 1996.

Fowler, Michael Ross. *With Justice for All? The Nature of the American Legal System.* Upper Saddle River: Prentice Hall, 1998.

Van Dervort, Thomas R. *Equal Justice Under the Law.* Minneapolis/Saint Paul: West Publishing Company, 1994.

CONTRIBUTORS

Shannon Armitage

Beth Babini

Holly Barton

Daniel Brannen

Carol Brennan

Michael Broyles

ByLine Communications

Holly Caldwell

Jo-Ann Canning

Diane Carter

Richard Chapman

Chapterhouse

Linda Clemmons

Amy Cooper

Richard Cretan

Julie Davis

Michael Eggert

Grant Eldridge

Robert Gluck

Joel Golden

Carrie Golus

Nancy Gordon

Connor Gorry

Bridget Hall

Richard Clay Hanes

Lauri Harding

James Heiberg

Karl Heil

Robert Jacobson

Constance Johnson

Lois Kallunki

John Kane

Christine Kelley

Edward Knappman

Judson Knight

Paul Kobel

Jacqueline Maurice

Olivia Miller

Nancy Moore

Melynda Neal

New England Publishing Associates

Helene Northway

Carol Page

Akomea Poku-Kankam

Debra Reilly

Mary Scarbrough

Robert Schnakenberg

Bryan Schneider

Maria Sheler-Edwards

Elizabeth Shostak

Ginger Strand

Karen Troshynski-Thomas

Katherine Wagner

Linda Walton

Michael Watkins

Daniel Wisher

Susan Wood

Lisa Wroble

CAPITAL PUNISHMENT

Capital punishment, also known as the death penalty, is the lawful imposition of death as punishment for crimes. Thirty-eight states, as well as the federal government, recognized capital punishment as of 1998; Maine, Massachusetts, Rhode Island, Vermont, Iowa, Michigan, Minnesota, North Dakota, Wisconsin, the District of Columbia, West Virginia, Alaska, and Hawaii did not. Lethal injection, electrocution, lethal gas, hanging, and firing squad were the methods of execution, from most common to least common, respectively. Although federal law authorizes lethal injection, the state law where the crime was committed applies for offenses under the Violent Crime Control and Law Enforcement Act of 1994.

The United States stands apart from Western Europe's clear opposition to the death penalty. Nevertheless, the United States is one of 94 countries and territories in the world that use the death penalty. Most Eastern European nations retain the death penalty. Fifty-seven countries prohibit capital punishment for all crimes; 28 recognize capital punishment but do not use it. Another 15 retain it only for exceptional crimes such as crimes committed in violation of military law or certain wartime circumstances. Closer to the United States, Canada abolished the death penalty and Mexico retains it but does not use it.

History of Capital Punishment in the U. S. and the Abolitionist Movement

The first colonists, based upon long-standing English tradition, brought the idea of capital punishment with them. Until the nineteenth century in England, the death penalty could be imposed for more than 200 different crimes, ranging from the obvious, such as murder, to the inconceivable including theft of linens from a bleaching ground. The first recorded use of capital punishment occurred in 1608 in the Jamestown Colony, Virginia. Laws drawn by the Massachusetts Bay Colony in 1636 identified idolatry, witchcraft, blasphemy, murder, assault in sudden anger, adultery, statutory rape, sodomy, manstealing, perjury in a capital trial, and rebellion as offenses punishable by death; an Old Testament reference accompanied each listing.

Following the Revolutionary War, 11 colonies adopted new constitutions. Nine of the colonies prohibited cruel and unusual punishment, but all permitted capital punishment. The First Congress passed a 1790 law authorizing the death penalty for robbery, rape, murder, and forgery of public securities. Over 160 known executions took place during the eighteenth century. For centuries to come, the Fifth and Eighth amendments to the Constitution became the focal point of ensuing controversies over the death penalty.

Opposition to the death penalty in America has existed since the seventeenth century, gaining momentum around the time of the Revolutionary War and shortly thereafter. Dr. Benjamin Rush, Judge William Bradford, the Philadelphia Society for Relieving Distressed Prisoners, and the Philadelphia Society for Alleviating the Miseries of Public Prisons incited the early movement. In 1847, Michigan became the first state to abolish capital punishment. By 1850, nine states had abolition societies. However, the Civil War slowed momentum of the abolitionists. One key victory of the nineteenth century abolition movement was elimination of mandatory capital punishment sentences.

Despite the sometimes vigorous opposition and gains made by the abolitionists, the use of capital punishment grew along with the country. Nearly 1400 documented executions took place during the nineteenth century. Early in the twentieth century, the Prohibition Era and Great Depression brought the abolition movement to a near stand-still. As a result, the 1930s and 1940s saw the highest levels of executions with between 100 and 200 prisoners executed annually. The 1950s and 1960s began to witness a decline in executions, due partly to increasing appeals in courts following initial convictions and sentencing. From 1930 through 1997, 4,291 executions occurred of which over 3,800 took place between 1930 and 1964. Support for the death penalty declined slightly in the 1960s, but grew again by the late 1970s. By 1996 over 70 percent of Americans supported the death penalty according to polls. By the close of the twentieth century, the abolitionist movement remained a vocal minority unable to sway public opinion or make significant legislative gains.

Constitutional Challenges to the Death Penalty

The notion that the death penalty constituted cruel and unusual punishment would seem integral to the abolitionist argument, but the constitutionality of capital punishment was virtually unchallenged until late in the twentieth century. For many years, the Eighth Amendment's prohibition against cruel and unusual punishment was associated with torture and barbarous punishments, not capital punishment. In 1967, a nationwide moratorium on capital punishment gave the courts time examine its constitutionality. Finally, the U.S. Supreme Court in *Furman v. Georgia* (1972) found that certain capital punishment laws did constitute cruel and unusual punishment because of the arbitrary way they were applied.

The Fifth and the Eighth Amendments hold the key to the constitutionality debate. The Eighth Amendment, the most frequently cited in arguments against the death penalty, prohibits cruel and unusual punishment. The Fifth Amendment provides that no person shall be "deprived of life . . . without due process of law." It also provides that no person "shall be held to answer for a capital . . . crime" without indictment by a grand jury, and prohibits a person from being "twice put in jeopardy of life" for the same offense. This language, in addition to the limited record of debates on the subject while writing the Bill of Rights and its common use at the time, strongly suggests the framers intended capital punishment to be lawful when due process rights were respected. Indeed, the Eighth Amendment, at the time of passage, was understood to only prohibit such disturbing forms of capital punishment as crucifixion or burning at the stake. Chief Justice Warren Burger's dissent in *Furman,* in essence supporting use of capital punishment, was based upon his reading of the lenient language in the Fifth Amendment.

Furman was not the death knell for capital punishment laws, however. Although an unusual victory for abolitionists, the ruling did not declare all capital punishment unconstitutional, *per se.* Several states quickly drafted new laws correcting the deficiencies highlighted by *Furman.* The new laws were quickly put to the test. In 1976 the Court abruptly ended the execution moratorium by upholding some of the new capital punishment legislation. The state statute upheld in *Gregg v. Georgia* became a model for later death penalty laws. As described in *Gregg,* a typical death penalty should include a two-part trial. The first part determines guilt, the second is a sentencing phase. During sentencing the jury weighs mitigating and aggravating factors to determine whether the death penalty is appropriate, or whether a lesser sentence, commonly life imprisonment, should be imposed. Florida adopted a three-part system in which an advisory jury makes recommendations to a judge, who then decides the punishment after weighing the mitigating and aggravating factors.

Although executions were restricted only to murder convictions after 1964, rape accounted for a large number of executions between 1930 and the 1960s. In 1977, the Court ruled out the death penalty for rape by finding that the punishment was too excessive for the crime and therefore unconstitutional. By the close of the twentieth century, capital punishment was constitutionally appropriate only for criminal homicide. The death penalty was even determined unconstitutional for an individual involved in a felony crime during which a murder is committed by someone else. In other rulings, the Court also ruled that the Eighth Amendment does not prohibit execution of a mentally retarded person, although the retardation is a mitigating factor for the jury to consider. Moreover, the Court also upheld a death sentence for a juvenile who was at least 16 at the time of the crime.

Racial Bias

One persuasive argument against the death penalty is that its is racially biased. According to the U. S. Department of Justice, Bureau of Justice Statistics, 42 percent of the death row population in the nation were African American in 1997. Yet less than 15 percent of the general population of the United States was African American. Until the latter half of the 1970s, most death row inmates were African American. Aside from the minority affiliation of the executed was the even more striking minority affiliation of the victims whose assailants were sentenced to death. Between 1977 and 1995, whites accounted for over 80 percent of the murder victims of death row inmates. It appeared that lesser sentences were assessed for the killing of African Americans. The Court, examining the racial disparity issue in *McCleskey v. Kemp* (1987) ruled that a racially disproportionate executions did not violate the Eighth and Fourteenth Amendments of equal protection if the disparities were not resulting from intentional discrimination against a particular defendant, or did not demonstrate "irrationality, arbitrariness, and capriciousness."

Opponents also charged the death penalty is discriminatory because it is imposed far more often on the poor and uneducated than on wealthy or well-educated Americans. Court-appointed lawyers for indigents are often over-worked and have little experience in capital cases. Also, court-appointed lawyers are usually only involved in the trial and first round of appeals. After that, inmates are frequently hard-pressed to find an attorney to handle their case on a volunteer basis.

Expense and Length of Process

Though an execution itself is inexpensive—less than $1,000, according to one estimate—the legal process itself is extremely costly. The state often pays expenses for both the prosecution and the defense. Because of the two-part process, capital trials are more expensive than others. Death sentences undergo a mandatory review in the state appeal process, and often this step is only the beginning of a sequence of delays as defendants file multiple appeals. In 36 of the states condoning capital punishment, automatic reviews of the trials are required. Prisoners also frequently file petitions for writ of *habeas corpus* in federal court to challenge the constitutionality of their convictions.

The average time for an inmate on death row is 11 years. The Supreme Court has consistently declined to determine whether an extremely lengthy wait on death row constitutes cruel and unusual punishment, although in a 1995 case two justices noted concern regarding an inmate who had awaited execution for 17 years. The Supreme Court did rule the government must supply counsel to indigent death row inmates seeking *habeas corpus* review. But a shortage of available lawyers commonly added further to the delay.

In 1996, the Anti-Terrorism and Effective Death Penalty Act went into effect, significantly curtailing *habeas corpus* appeals. The law generally required state death row prisoners to file their petitions within six months after exhausting all state appeals. In addition, the law instructed federal judges to defer to state courts on constitutional and other issues, unless the ruling by the lower court was "unreasonable." Previously, federal courts often intervened when constitutional issues were presented in *habeas corpus* petitions. An estimated 558 death sentences were found unconstitutional between January of 1973 and May of 1990.

Deterrence

Many studies attempted to determine the deterrent effect of the death penalty. No consensus emerged. Several indicated some deterrence while others concluded otherwise. However, many death penalty supporters focused more on the retributive nature of the punishment as justification for its use, rather than any deterrent effect.

With only 131 prisoners on death row in 1953, the number first topped 500 in the late 1960s and grew sharply after 1984. By 1998, 3,335 inmates were under a sentence of death. Whites comprised a slight majority of that number (1,876), and fewer than two percent were female. According to Amnesty International, at least 47 juveniles were on death row in 15 states in 1996 for murders committed at age 16 or 17. Despite the large number of inmates on death row, only 193 executions actually took place during the first half of the 1990s. However, the number of executions began to increase later in 1990s. A total of 76 inmates were executed in 1997, the most since 76 in 1955. Eighteen states executed 68 prisoners in 1998. Forty-eight of those executed were white, 18 were African American, and two were women, the first since 1984.

See also: **Criminal Law, Criminal Procedure, Jury, Juvenile Courts, Rights of the Accused Following Trial**

Bibliography and Further Reading

Arriens, Jan. *Welcome to Hell: Letters & Writings From Death Row.* Boston: Northeastern University Press, 1997.

Cook, Kimberly J. *Divided Passions: Public Opinions on Abortion and the Death Penalty.* Boston: Northeastern University Press, 1998.

Haines, Herbert H. *Against Capital Punishment: The Anti-death Penalty Movement in America, 1972-1994.* New York: Oxford University Press, 1996.

Hood, Roger G. *The Death Penalty: A World-wide Perspective.* New York: Oxford University Press, 1996.

Mello, Michael. *Against the Death Penalty: The Relentless Dissents of Justices Brennan and Marshall.* Boston: Northeastern University Press, 1996.

Schabas, William. *The Death Penalty as Cruel Treatment and Torture: Capital Punishment Challenged in the World's Courts.* Boston: Northeastern University Press, 1996.

Winters, Paul A., ed. *The Death Penalty: Opposing Viewpoints.* San Diego, CA: Greenhaven Press, 1997.

HURTADO V. CALIFORNIA

Legal Citation: 110 U.S. 516 (1884)

Appellant
Hurtado

Appellee
State of California

Appellant's Claim
Because he was tried, found guilty, and sentenced to death without having been indicted by a grand jury, he was deprived of his right to due process of law under the Fifth and Fourteenth Amendments.

Chief Lawyer for Appellant
A. L. Hart

Chief Lawyer for Appellee
John T. Cary

Justices for the Court
Samuel Blatchford, Joseph P. Bradley, Stephen Johnson Field, Horace Gray, Stanley Matthews (writing for the Court), Samuel Freeman Miller, Morrison Remick Waite, William Burnham Woods

Justices Dissenting
John Marshall Harlan I

Place
Washington, D.C.

Date of Decision
3 March 1884

Decision
The Fourteenth Amendment's requirement of "due process" cannot be held to include the rights specified in the Fifth Amendment, and that therefore Hurtado's conviction and death sentence should stand.

Significance
Hurtado v. California is part of a long-standing debate over which rights constitute due process of law and over whether those rights are spelled out in the Constitution or are to be gradually discovered as the Supreme Court hands down various decisions.

The Fourteenth Amendment was passed in 1868, one of several "Reconstruction" amendments designed to assure that the people who had formerly been slaves had full legal rights as U.S. citizens. According to the Fourteenth Amendment, no state had the right to "make or enforce any law" that deprived any person "of life, liberty or property, without due process of law . . ." Previously, the Constitution had focused on what the federal government could or could not do. Now, the Fourteenth Amendment was specifying limitations on state governments.

Because the Fourteenth Amendment opened up a whole new area of law, it gave rise to many court cases. Over the second half of the nineteenth century, the Supreme Court handed down many decisions that helped to define what the Fourteenth Amendment meant by "due process of law." One of the most significant of these decisions was *Hurtado v. California*.

The Right to Be Indicted

On 20 February 1882, California resident Hurtado was charged with the murder of Jose Antonio Stuardo. A murder charge often results from an indictment by a grand jury—a process whereby a jury of 13 to 23 citizens hears evidence and decides whether enough cause exists to charge someone with a particular crime. Under this system, a grand jury indictment is needed in order to try someone for murder.

The right to a grand jury for capital crimes (crimes that might result in the death penalty) is actually spelled out in the Fifth Amendment. However, the Fifth Amendment only covers federal courts. Murder trials generally take place in state courts.

That was the case with Hurtado, who was tried in a California state court. According to California law, Hurtado was examined by a magistrate who decided, based on the information presented to him, that there were indeed grounds to try Hurtado for murder. The trial was held, Hurtado was found guilty, and on 5 June 1882, he was sentenced to death.

At this point, Hurtado claimed that he was not being treated fairly. He pointed out that he had never

Is There Such a Thing as Justifiable Homicide?

The idea of "justifiable homicide," in legal terms, is usually considered in terms of self-defense. English common law dictated that a person who killed in self-defense was liable for conviction, but usually he would be pardoned by the king.

There are instances where homicide is clearly justified in self-defense, but the legal system takes great care regarding three issues: was the determination on the part of the accused that killing was necessary to defend himself a "reasonable" decision? Was the attack "imminent," therefore justifying an act of self-defense? And did he use a level of force necessary in repelling the attacker, or was it excessive?

On some levels, it is easy, when confronted with the situation of a woman who kills her rapist or a man who shoots a home invader, to automatically agree with the self-defense plea. However, American justice attempts to take account of other contingencies. One of these is a concern regarding vigilantism: when Charles Bronson in the *Death Wish* movies goes out and looks for muggers to rob him, so that he can shoot them, this may feel justified—but it is legally indefensible.

Source(s): Kadish, Sanford H., ed. *Encyclopedia of Crime and Justice.* New York: Free Press, 1983.

received a grand jury trial which, he charged, violated his Fourteenth Amendment right to due process of law.

"Ancient Established Law"

In an 8-1 decision, the Supreme Court ruled against Hurtado. Justice Matthews, writing for the majority, explained that the Fourteenth Amendment's notion of due process did not necessarily include the right to a grand jury proceeding. He went on at great length to explain why, offering an argument that was to shape the way that due process was interpreted for many decades to come. Justice Matthews began by taking on Hurtado's argument:

> . . . that the phrase "due process of law" . . . has acquired a fixed, definite, and technical meaning; that it refers to and includes, not only the general principles of public liberty and private right, which lie at the foundation of all free government, but [also] the very institutions which . . . have been . . . the birthright and inheritance of every English subject . . . [and] that one of these institutions is that of the grand jury . . . in order that he may not be harassed or destroyed by prosecutions founded only upon private malice or popular fury . . .

In other words, Matthews said, Hurtado was arguing that the right to a grand jury proceeding was a very ancient right indeed, one that had belonged to every English subject centuries before the United States was ever founded. In fact, the Supreme Court had long thought of "ancient established law"—the rights traditionally granted to British citizens—as the very basis for American law.

"Incapable of Progress or Improvement"

Matthews, however, was about to introduce a new concept into the American legal tradition. As so many Supreme Court justices had done before him, he acknowledged the importance of tradition—but then he cautioned that innovation was also important:

> The Constitution of the United States was ordained, it is true, by descendants of Englishmen, who inherited the tradition of English law and history; but it was made for an undefined and expanding future, and for a people gathered and to be gathered from many Nations and of many tongues. And while we take just pride in [English] . . . common law, we are not to forget that in lands where other systems . . . prevail, . . . justice [is] . . . not unknown . . . [W]e should expect that the new and various experiences of our own situation and system will mold and shape it into new and not less useful forms . . .

Therefore, Matthews argued, if the only test that the Court had for due process was "settled usage"—what had always been done—the law would be "incapable of progress or improvement." And from that point followed his decision: California had the right to try out a new system of due process. If the state of California wanted to try people for murder without going through a grand-jury proceeding, why should it not have that right? Who was to say that due process could not take on a new definition from the one that English citizens had enjoyed for hundreds of years?

From Justice Harlan's mouth to the Warren Court's ears

The lone dissenter to the Court's majority ruling was Justice Harlan. In his view, if the right to a grand jury had not been a "fundamental" component of due process, it would not have been guaranteed by the Fifth Amendment. Certain rights, including the right to a grand jury, "were of a character so essential to the safety of the people" that they had been specifically written into "the early Amendments of the Constitution . . ." Harlan, as a minority of one, did not prevail. Instead, the majority decision meant that the Court spent much of the next few decades hammering out its notions of due process, by means of ruling on various cases.

In 1953, Earl Warren became the Supreme Court chief justice. Under his leadership, virtually every right guaranteed by both the Fifth and the Sixth Amendments was incorporated into the legal understanding of due process: the right to counsel, the right against self-incrimination, the right of the accused to confront his or her accuser, the right to a speedy trial, the right to trial by jury, and the right to protection against double jeopardy (being tried or punished twice for the same crime).

Many legal commentators saw the decisions of the Warren Court as a departure from the Court's previous cautious approach to establishing rights. However, some commentators have had the opposite reaction. They see the so-called activism of the Warren Court as returning to the traditional understanding of rights, the one that existed before *Hurtado*. In that view, *Hurtado* was the departure, the case in which, for the first time, the U.S. Supreme Court ignored the traditional English common law provisions spelled out in the Bill of Rights in favor of the possibilities of "progress and improvement."

Related Cases

Duncan v. Louisiana, 391 U.S. 145 (1968).

Goss v. Lopez, 419 U.S. 565 (1975).

Ballew v. Georgia, 435 U.S. 223 (1978).

Lockett v. Ohio, 438 U.S. 586 (1978).

Bibliography and Further Reading

Bartholomew, Paul C. *Summaries of Leading Cases on the Constitution.* Totowa, NJ: Littlefield, Adams & Co., 1976.

Bodenheimer, Edgar. *"Hurtado v. California." The Oxford Companion to the Supreme Court of the United States.* Kermit L. Hall, editor in chief, New York: Oxford University Press, 1992.

Cushman, Robert, with Susan P. Konick. *Leading Constitutional Decisions.* Englewood Cliffs, NJ: Prentice Hall, 1987.

Skeels, David. "The Massachusetts Concept of Due Process of Law and the Incorporation of the Bill of Rights into the Fourteenth Amendment to the United States Constitution." *Boston Bar Journal.* November-December 1991, Vol. 35, No. 6, pp. 21-24.

CHAMBERS V. FLORIDA

Legal Citation: 309 U.S. 227 (1940)

Petitioners
Isiah (Izell) Chambers, Jack Williamson, Charlie Davis, Walter Woodward (Woodard)

Respondent
State of Florida

Petitioners' Claim
Four black men sentenced to death for the murder of a white man claimed their convictions were obtained "solely upon confessions and pleas of guilt extorted by violence and torture" in violation of the Fourteenth Amendment.

Chief Lawyers for Petitioners
Leon A. Ransom, S. D. McGill, Thurgood Marshall

Chief Lawyers for Respondent
Tyrus A. Norwood

Justices for the Court
Hugo Lafayette Black (writing for the Court), Pierce Butler, William O. Douglas, Felix Frankfurter, Charles Evans Hughes, James Clark McReynolds, Stanley Forman Reed, Owen Josephus Roberts, Harlan Fiske Stone

Justices Dissenting
None (Frank Murphy did not participate)

Place
Washington, D.C.

Date of Decision
12 February 1940

Decision
The unanimous Court threw out verdicts of murder against the four black men handed down by two juries.

Significance
Chambers v. Florida was the first case in which the Court unequivocally declared the Fourteenth Amendment meant state courts would have to observe due process of law. Henceforth, state prosecution methods used in obtaining convictions would be subject to Supreme Court review, and the Fourteenth Amendment would be used to further individual rights for all.

On 13 May 1933, Robert Darsey, an elderly white man, was robbed and murdered. Within 24 hours, between 25 and 40 African Americans—the exact number was never determined—were arrested without warrants and held in the Broward County jail. Over the next six days, the men were individually questioned by teams of four to ten police officers without any opportunity to talk to lawyers, relatives, or friends.

By 20 May, police attention focused on Isiah Chambers, Jack Williamson, Charlie Davis and Walter Woodward. "Sometime in the early hours of Sunday, the 21st, Woodward apparently 'broke,'" Justice Black wrote in his summation. So did the others "one right after the other," and the state's attorney was summoned from bed. When, however, he read Woodward's confession, he said, "Tear this paper up, that isn't what I want, when you get something worthwhile call me." State officials renewed the questioning into the next morning. That's when they got "something 'worthwhile' which the state's attorney would 'want,'" Justice Black wrote.

For six days, the four had been questioned under circumstances "calculated to break the strongest nerves and the stoutest resistance" and to "fill petitioners with terror and frightful misgivings." Black observed:

> The haunting fear of mob violence was around them in an atmosphere charged with excitement and public indignation.

The four "broke" only under "the relentless tenacity" of their interrogators. Judge Harlan was:

> . . . not impressed with the argument that law enforcement methods such as these are necessary to uphold our laws. The Constitution proscribes such lawless means irrespective of the end. And this argument flouts the basic principle that all people must stand on an equality before the bar of justice in every American court.

Then, at a time when news of Nazi victories were daily headlines, Black concluded:

> Today, as in ages past, we are not without tragic proof that the exalted power of some governments to punish manufactured crime dictatorially is the handmaid of tyranny.

Under our constitutional system, courts stand against any winds that blow as havens of refuge for those who might otherwise suffer because they are helpless, weak, outnumbered, or because they are nonconforming victims of prejudice and public excitement. Due process of law, preserved for all by our Constitution, commands that no such practice as that disclosed by this record shall send any accused to his death. No higher duty, no more solemn responsibility, rests upon this Court than that of translating into living law and maintaining this constitutional shield deliberately planned and inscribed for the benefit of every human being subject to our Constitution—of whatever race, creed or persuasion.

Black later recalled, "There's been no case which I put more work in." He did not want to write the decision and had even voted against the Court hearing it, fearing the decision would go the wrong way. Chief Justice Hughes assigned the case "to me because I was a Southerner," Black said:

And there were these Negroes here who were so mistreated. He forced me to write the case. At first I didn't want to. He said, "Don't worry, I'll get the Court for you." So I saved all my views and wrote them since I knew I had the whole Court with me.

Black wrote his opinion within two weeks after oral arguments were heard on 4 January 1940, and circulated it among his fellow justices. Justices McReynolds and Reed had considered dissenting, but changed their minds. Chief Justice Hughes rescheduled the announcement of the decision from 5 February to 12 February. On Lincoln's Birthday, 1940, the former member of the Ku Klux Klan delivered his opinion in open court— "one of the enduring utterances in the history of the Supreme Court and in the annals of human freedom," Justice Frankfurter wrote in a letter to his wife.

Florida officials scheduled another trial for the four prisoners, but they made what the same Florida officials called an "escape" and were never recaptured.

Impact

The decision was written by a justice whose appointment to the Supreme Court had been hotly controversial because of his membership, as a youth, in the Ku Klux Klan. But after *Chambers v. Florida,* Justice Black emerged as perhaps the Court's most forceful defender of civil rights.

The decision was "far and away the most direct, sweeping and brilliantly written application of the Fourteenth Amendment to human rights that has come from our highest Court," the *New York Times* declared at the time. The appeal, one of the first brought by the newly established Legal Defense Fund of the NAACP headed by Thurgood Marshall, "will ring with power as long as liberty and justice are cherished in our land." So said the usually cynical historian Charles Beard. A gratified Franklin Delano Roosevelt, still smarting over criticism over Black's appointment, slyly suggested the press should not just "give a little praise," but add a "modicum of apology for things they have said in the last two years. Is that fair enough?"

Related Cases

Gallegos v. Colorado, 370 U.S. 49 (1962).
Miller v. Fenton, 741 F.2D 1456, (3rd Cir. 1984).

Bibliography and Further Reading

Davis, Michael D., and Harlan R. Black. *Thurgood Marshall: Warrior at the Bar, Rebel on the Court.* Seacus, NJ: Carol Publishing Group, 1992.

Leuchtenburg, William E. *The Supreme Court Reborn: The Constitutional Revolution in the Age of Roosevelt.* New York: Oxford University Press, 1995.

Miller, Loren. *The Petitioners: The Story of the Supreme Court of the United States and the Negro.* New York: Random House, 1966.

Newman, Roger K. *Hugo Black: A Biography.* New York: Pantheon, 1994.

LOUISIANA EX REL. FRANCIS V. RESWEBER

Legal Citation: 329 U.S. 459 (1947)

Petitioner
Willie Francis

Respondent
E. L. Resweber, Sheriff of St. Martin Parish, Louisiana, et al.

Petitioner's Claim
The petitioner, who had been sentenced to die by electrocution, had survived the state's first electrocution attempt; he contended that for the state to try to electrocute him again would be "cruel and unusual punishment" under the Eighth Amendment, double jeopardy (being tried twice for the same crime) under the Fifth Amendment, and a violation of his right to due process of law under the Fourteenth Amendment (since other prisoners only had to undergo one execution attempt).

Chief Lawyer for Petitioner
James Skelly Wright

Chief Lawyers for Respondent
Michael E. Culligan, L. O. Pecot

Justices for the Court
Hugo Lafayette Black, Felix Frankfurter, Robert H. Jackson, Stanley Forman Reed (writing for the Court), Fred Moore Vinson

Justices Dissenting
Harold Burton, William O. Douglas, Frank Murphy, Wiley Blount Rutledge

Place
Washington, D.C.

Date of Decision
13 January 1947

Decision
That the botched electrocution attempt on Willie Francis was not due to any malice or intentionality on the part of the state, and that therefore the decision to repeat the attempt did not constitute cruel and unusual punishment; since Francis was not being retried, the second execution attempt did not constitute double jeopardy; since Francis had not deliberately been singled out to receive two electrocution attempts, the second attempt did not violate his right to due process; therefore, a second attempt at electrocution could proceed.

Significance
In this decision, the Court specified that electrocution in and of itself was not cruel or unusual punishment, a finding that has been used to deny other prisoners' claims that electrocution is a particularly inhumane form of execution. Also in this decision, the Court stressed that the botched electrocution attempt did not result from deliberate action by the state; this finding was used to support a 1991 decision that corrections officials are liable for inhumane conditions in prisons only if the inhumane conditions are the direct result of the deliberate indifference of these officials.

Willie Francis, a 16-year-old African American resident of St. Martinville, Louisiana, was arrested for the murder of Andrew Thomas, the town druggist. Although Francis himself, as well as later commentators, claimed that Francis was innocent and that his counsel did not adequately represent him, Francis was found guilty of first-degree murder by an all-white jury and sentenced to death on 29 March 1946.

The state of Louisiana conducted its executions by means of electrocution, which had first been introduced in 1890 as a supposedly humane alternative to hanging. Defenders of electrocution held that the method offered the prisoner an instantaneous and painless death, so that death itself was the only penalty to be inflicted.

Many contemporary observers have challenged that belief, claiming that electrocution is frequently slow and painful, as well as unreliable, often requiring a second or even a third shock to be administered to the suffering prisoner. Thus, they claim, prisoners executed by electrocution face not only the punishment of death, but also the torture of being shocked and burned.

Execution was both unreliable and painful in the case of Willie Francis. According to official witness Harold Resweber:

> . . . the electrocutioner turned on the switch and when he did Willie Francis' lips puffed out and he groaned and jumped so that the chair came off the floor. Apparently the switch was turned on twice and then the condemned man yelled: "Take it off. Let me breath[e]."

A Cruel and Unusual Punishment?

The first attempt to electrocute Willie Francis had failed. Francis filed suit, claiming both that his original trial had been unfair, and that a second attempt to execute him would constitute cruel and unusual punishment, which is prohibited by the Eighth Amendment. Francis also argued that a second execution attempt would violate the double-jeopardy provision of the Fifth Amendment, which states ". . . nor shall any person be subject for the same offence to be twice put in jeopardy of life or limb . . ." Finally, since no other prisoner was

When the Electric Chair Malfunctions

Executions in the United States have tended to take place according to five basic methods, in chronological order: hanging, firing squads, electrocution, lethal gas, and lethal injection.

The world's first electrocution, of William Kemmler at Sing Sing in 1890, was indeed a horrific affair, but the problem had to do with incompetence on the part of the executioner. The latter sent a 17-second jolt into Kemmler's body, but afterward Kemmler's heart began beating again. As the observers began to panic, the executioner turned on 1,300 volts of current, and sustained it for 70 seconds.

This time Kemmler was truly dead, and the electric chair became a part of the American punitive system. But Kemmler's was not the last case of a failed execution. Besides the instance of *Resweber*, there was Arthur Lee Grimes in Alabama in 1954, whose electrocution took seven full minutes before he expired; and Fred Van Wormer in 1903, who began to move when he was already on the autopsy table. Van Wormer died while guards were waiting for the executioner to return, but just to be on the safe side, they put his body back in the chair and administered another 1,700 volts.

Source(s): Sifakis, Carl. *The Encyclopedia of American Crime.* New York: Facts on File, 1982.

---

subject to two separate electrocution attempts, Francis argued that a second attempt would violate his right to due process of law under the Fourteenth Amendment.

The Supreme Court was sharply divided on this issue. Four justices voted to uphold Francis's execution. Four justices voted to overturn it. The deciding vote was cast by Justice Frankfurter, who wrote, ". . . this Court must abstain from interference with State action no matter how strong one's personal feeling of revulsion against a State's insistence on its pound of flesh." In other words, Frankfurter wished personally to spare Willie Francis's life, but he felt that the state of Louisiana did indeed have the right to execute Francis. With Frankfurter's vote, Willie Francis's death sentence was upheld, and he was electrocuted a second time.

What Is the State's Responsibility?

In upholding the right of Louisiana to electrocute Willie Francis a second time, the Court relied on the belief that the first failure had not resulted from any wrongdoing by the state. The Court compared the failure of the electric chair to another traumatic occurrence, such as a fire in the cell block. Even if Willie Francis's life had been threatened by such a fire, the Court argued, the state would have the right to execute him. It would be irrelevant that no other prisoner would have had to endure the trauma of undergoing first a fire, then an electrocution.

The minority opinion on the Court disagreed. These dissenting justices claimed that the state had a special responsibility to execute Willie Francis properly, a responsibility far greater than their obligation to prevent a fire in his cell block. The dissenting judges argued that if the state could not execute Willie Francis humanely, in one try, they did not have the right to subject him to a second electrocution—regardless of the reason that the first execution had failed.

At the time the decision was written, both the majority and the minority believed that Willie Francis's electrocution had failed for technical, unavoidable reasons. What neither side knew was that in fact, human error was involved. The two men responsible for Francis's execution had been drunk at the time and had improperly connected the electrical cables. As a result of their negligence, the electric chair did not work properly, and Francis was subjected to considerable pain.

A More Humane Method?

Certainly, the history of electrocution is full of instances in which the apparatus did not work properly, and prolonged jolts of electricity were required to kill the prisoner. In some instances, these failures resulted from human error, as apparently happened in Willie Francis's case. In other cases, the difficulties simply resulted from the unreliability of electrocution itself. Human bodies differ, and differing amounts of electricity are required to put people to death.

Because so many people consider electrocution both painful and unreliable, it has been challenged as a method of execution even when the challenger is not questioning the state's right to execute someone. This is based on the Eighth Amendment's guarantee against "cruel and unusual punishment." As the Supreme Court found in an earlier case involving electrocution, *In re Kemmler* (1890), the Constitution prohibits such punishments as burning at the stake, disemboweling, hanging in chains, and breaking at the wheel "because they involve torture and lingering death." Electrocution, on the other hand, was specifically allowed in *In re Kemmler* because it did not seem to involve "more than the mere extinguishment of life."

Opponents to electrocution argued that electrocution does involve "torture and lingering death," and so it should be outlawed, just as burning at the stake has been. As detailed in a 1997 U.S. Department of Justice bulletin, 15 of the 18 states that executed prisoners used lethal injection.

Francis was also cited in a 1991 Court ruling concerning prison conditions. In that case, *Wilson v. Seiter,* the Court found that even if inhumane conditions did occur in a prison, correctional officials could be held responsible only if someone could prove that the conditions were the direct result of those officials' deliberate indifference. Just as in *Louisiana ex rel. Francis v. Resweber,* the state was assumed to be free of responsibility for any cruel or unusual punishment that it did not intentionally cause.

Related Cases

In re Kemmler, 136 U.S. 436 (1890).
Gregg v. Georgia, 428 U.S. 153 (1976).
Proffitt v. Florida, 428 U.S. 242 (1976).
Jurek v. Texas, 428 U.S. 262 (1976).
Stanford v. Kentucky, 492 U.S. 361 (1989).
Wilson v. Seiter, 501 U.S. 294 (1991).

Bibliography and Further Reading

Biskupic, Joan, and Elder Witt. *Congressional Quarterly's Guide to the U.S. Supreme Court,* 3rd ed. Washington, DC: Congressional Quarterly, Inc., 1996.

Cushman, Robert F. *Leading Constitutional Decisions.* Englewood Cliffs, NJ: Prentice-Hall, Inc., 1982.

DeWolfe, Ruthanne. "The view from inside the heads of correctional officials: The Legacy of *Resweber*." *Clearinghouse Review,* Vol. 26, no. 9. January 1993, pp. 1007-1018.

Hall, Kermit L., ed. *The Oxford Companion to the Supreme Court of the United States.* New York: Oxford University Press, 1992.

Hoffman, Lonny J. "The madness of the method: the use of electrocution and the death penalty." *Texas Law Review,* Vol. 70 no. 4, March 1992, pp. 1039-1062.

WITHERSPOON V. ILLINOIS

Legal Citation: 391 U.S. 510 (1968)

Petitioner
William C. Witherspoon

Respondent
State of Illinois

Petitioner's Claim
It is unconstitutional for a penalty of death to be delivered by a jury that is selected through a process of eliminating certain prospective jurors simply because they voiced general objections to the death penalty or expressed conscientious or religious scruples against imposition of the death penalty.

Chief Lawyer for Petitioner
Albert E. Jenner, Jr.

Chief Lawyer for Respondent
James B. Zagel

Justices for the Court
William J. Brennan, Jr., Warren E. Burger, William O. Douglas, Abe Fortas, Thurgood Marshall, Potter Stewart (writing for the Court)

Justices Dissenting
Hugo Lafayette Black, John Marshall Harlan II, Byron R. White

Place
Washington, D.C.

Date of Decision
3 June 1968

Decision
In a death penalty case, it is a violation of the defendant's constitutional right of due process to exclude from the jury persons who have general objections to the death penalty or moral or religious concerns about inflicting it.

Significance
The decision represented an expansion of the High Court's authority to review the regulation and administration of state court death penalty cases. It also served as precedent for the selection of jurors in death penalty cases.

In 1960, William C. Witherspoon was tried in a Cook County, Illinois court on a charge of murder, a crime that carried a sentence of death. In choosing the jury for Witherspoon's trial, the prosecutor was allowed, under Illinois law, to remove any juror who was opposed to capital punishment or possessed "conscientious scruples against capital punishment." Jury selection procedures typically allow attorneys for all sides to exclude a certain number of jurors at their discretion with "peremptory challenges," and an unlimited number of jurors "for cause," or for a reasonable belief that the juror may be biased. Witherspoon was convicted and sentenced to death by the jury.

Witherspoon spent his round of state court appeals without success. Thereafter, Witherspoon petitioned the state courts for post-conviction *habeas corpus* relief. The state courts rejected Witherspoon's requests, and the U.S. Supreme Court denied Witherspoon's writ of *certiorari*. Undeterred, Witherspoon filed another claim for post-conviction relief in February of 1965, this time asking for any form of remedy provided by state law and, for the first time, claiming that his constitutional rights were violated when the prosecutor was allowed to excuse jurors for expressing doubts about the death penalty. Witherspoon lost again in the state courts, but this time the U.S. Supreme Court agreed to hear his case. After oral arguments in April of 1968, the High Court reversed Witherspoon's sentence of death by a vote of 6-3.

Justice Stewart, writing for the majority, began the analysis by noting that almost half of the prospective jurors, or veniremen, in Witherspoon's trial had been excused by the prosecution. These veniremen were challenged for cause and excused during *voir dire* for having expressed "qualms about capital punishment." The question in the case, the majority observed, was "whether the Constitution permits a State to execute a man pursuant to the verdict of a jury so composed." The majority then examined the juror selection procedures in Witherspoon's case, the nature of juries, and public sentiment on the death penalty.

The issue was not, maintained the majority, whether the state of Illinois could exclude prospective jurors who could not make an impartial decision about guilt or innocence. Nor was the issue whether the state could exclude jurors who said they could never impose the death penalty. Those issues had already been decided in the affirmative. The real issue was whether the state had the right to exclude all persons "who indicated that they had conscientious scruples" against imposing the death penalty.

The "tone" in Witherspoon's case was set, the majority opined, "when the trial judge said early in the voir dire, 'Let's get these conscientious objectors out of the way, without wasting any time on them.'" The court then proceeded to allow the prosecution to exclude 47 veniremen on the basis of their feelings on the death penalty. Of these 47, only five had stated that they would never impose the death penalty. Six had stated that they did not "believe in the death penalty" and were summarily excused without further inquiry into whether they nevertheless could, as jurors bound to follow the law, deliver a sentence of death. Thirty-nine veniremen were excused after admitting to conscientious or religious misgivings about the infliction of capital punishment or against its infliction in a certain case.

Witherspoon argued that his conviction was unconstitutional, but the Court dismissed this argument. According to Witherspoon, the jury was unrepresentative of a cross-section of the community and its selection substantially increased his chances for conviction, and these made his conviction unconstitutional. The Court was not ready to say that the jury in Witherspoon's case was too biased to deliver a fair verdict on guilt or innocence.

The majority of the Court was, however, ready to hold that Witherspoon's jury was too biased to deliver a fair and impartial sentence. The state argued that persons who express doubts about the death penalty cannot be relied upon to deliver a verdict of death, even when the law of the state and the trial court's instruction "would make death the proper penalty." The majority rejected this argument, observing that in some states, including Illinois, the jury had broad discretion to determine the proper penalty. "A man who opposes the death penalty, no less than one who favors it," the majority explained, "can make the discretionary judgment entrusted to him by the State and can thus obey the oath he takes as a juror."

The majority recognized the difficulty in determining whether a juror cannot follow the rule of law. Such determinations are based on questions asked by attorneys and judges during voir dire. This difficulty was only natural, the Court observed, given the sympathies of human beings. In a footnote, the Court cited Smith v. State, an old Mississippi case in which the state's supreme court noted that most jurors did not like imposing the death penalty. "Few men would," said the Court. "Every right-thinking man would regard it as a painful duty to pronounce a verdict of death upon his fellow-man." The majority felt that the expression of such feelings by potential jurors should not prevent all such jurors from deciding the sentence in a death penalty case. To hold otherwise, the Court reasoned, would produce "a jury uncommonly willing to condemn a man to die."

In another footnote, the majority cited studies revealing that Americans were split in their opinions over the death penalty for convicted murderers. In a country where a decreasing number of persons supported the death penalty, said Stewart, "a jury composed exclusively of such people cannot speak for the community . . . such a jury can speak only for a distinct and dwindling minority."

The majority closed its opinion by citing a prior case in which the Court held that a state "may not entrust the determination of whether a man is innocent or guilty to a tribunal 'organized to convict.'" By the same token, a state should not "entrust the determination of whether a man should live or die to a tribunal organized to return a verdict of death." Without commenting further on its own attitude toward the death penalty, the Court felt it sufficient to declare that a sentence imposed "by a hanging jury" was unconstitutional under the due process clause of the Fourteenth Amendment.

Justice Douglas, in a concurring opinion, contended that the majority had made the right decision in the case, but that it had incorrectly analyzed the issue. The real issue, Douglas said, quoting Fay v. New York, was whether the jury was "'impartially drawn from a cross-section of the community.'" If the jury was drawn "with systematic and intentional exclusion of some qualified groups," then the jury was not a cross-section of the community and the voir dire was unconstitutional. Douglas saw no constitutional basis for excluding even those persons who would never impose the death penalty on any defendant. "Exclusion of them . . . results in a systematic exclusion of qualified groups," Douglas maintained, "and the deprivation to the accused of a cross-section of the community for decision on both his guilt and punishment."

Douglas felt the Court should have overturned Witherspoon's conviction in addition to his death sentence. The conviction should have been overturned, Douglas argued, because it was reasonable to believe that a jury predisposed to the death sentence would be predisposed to a finding of guilt. Douglas would not have required Witherspoon to make a specific showing of prejudice because, according to Douglas, such prejudice "is so subtle, so intangible, that it escapes the ordinary methods of proof."

Justices Harlan and White joined a dissenting opinion written by Justice Black. Black felt that the Court's opinion would force states to try their murder cases before biased juries. Black hinted that the real reason behind the Court's holding was the majority's personal feelings on the death penalty. "If this Court is to hold capital punishment unconstitutional," Black chided, "I think it should do so forthrightly, not by making it impossible for States to get juries that will enforce the death penalty."

Black reminded the majority that the case had been tried and appealed long before Witherspoon ever raised the issue of jury bias. He also noted that Witherspoon had received above-average legal representation at all stages of the prosecution. According to the dissent, a juror with moral scruples against the death penalty would "seldom if ever" vote for it. "This is just human nature," Black wrote. At the same time, though, Black said he "would not dream of foisting on a criminal defendant" a juror who would invariably vote for capital punishment of a convicted murderer.

Black criticized the Court's holding as an unwarranted entry into the realm of psychology. It assumed, insisted Black, that all persons not opposed to the death penalty were "somehow callous to suffering" and, in the words of legal commentators, "'prosecution prone.'" That assumption represented to Black "a psychological foray into the human mind that I have considerable doubt about my ability to make."

Justice White filed a separate dissenting opinion. White defended the Illinois statute that allowed the exclusion of potential jurors who have "conscientious scruples against capital punishment" and jurors who are opposed to capital punishment. "The legislature undoubtedly felt that . . . if one citizen with especially pronounced 'scruples' could prevent a decision to impose death, the penalty would almost never be imposed." White dismissed the majority's analysis and objected to what he saw as personal politics replacing legal reasoning. In White's opinion, the Court should have "restrain[ed] its dislike for the death penalty" and left the decision about penalties to the duly elected state governments.

Impact

The precise effect of the *Witherspoon* decision has been difficult to quantify. On one level, the decision continues to serve as precedent for the proposition that the federal Constitution protects criminal defendants from being sentenced by biased juries. However, the contours of *Witherspoon*'s meaning were reshaped by the Court in *Wainwright v. Witt*. In *Witherspoon*, the Court had stated that a person may be excluded from a jury only if that person makes it "unmistakably clear" that he or she cannot be impartial or will cast an automatic vote against the death penalty. In *Witt*, the Court held that a juror may be excluded if it appears that her views on the death penalty will "prevent or substantially impair" the performance of her duties.

On another level, the *Witherspoon* decision continues to serve as precedent for the proposition that the federal Constitution protects criminal defendants from being sentenced by biased juries. While the *Witherspoon* Court upheld the right to challenge a juror because of bias against the death penalty, it paved the way for a later ruling in *Morgan v. Illinois* giving criminal defendants the right to challenge jurors for cause based on a bias in favor of the death penalty.

Related Cases
Wainwright v. Witt, 469 U.S. 412 (1985).
Morgan v. Illinois, 504 U.S. 719 (1992).

Bibliography and Further Reading
Belt, John C., "*Morgan v. Illinois*: The Right to Balance Capital Sentencing Juries as to Their Views on the Death Sentence Is Finally Granted to Defendants." *New Mexico Law Review*, winter 1994.

New York Times, June 4, 1968.

Zerman, Melvyn Bernard. *Beyond a Reasonable Doubt: Inside the American Jury System*. Crowell, 1981.

FURMAN V. GEORGIA

Legal Citation: 408 U.S. 238 (1972)

Appellant
William Henry Furman

Appellee
State of Georgia

Appellant's Claim
That the Georgia death penalty constituted cruel and unusual punishment in violation of the Eight and Fourteenth Amendments.

Chief Lawyers for Appellant
Anthony G. Amsterdam, Elizabeth B. Dubois, Jack Greenberg, Jack Himmelstein, B. Clarence Mayfield, Michael Meltsner

Chief Lawyers for Appellee
Dorothy T. Beasley, Arthur K. Bolton, Harold N. Hill, Jr., Andrew J. Ryan, Jr., Andrew J. Ryan III, Courtney Wilder Stanton

Justices for the Court
William J. Brennan, Jr., William O. Douglas, Thurgood Marshall, Potter Stewart, Byron R. White (unsigned)

Justices Dissenting
Harry A. Blackmun, Warren E. Burger, Lewis F. Powell, Jr., William H. Rehnquist

Place
Washington, D.C.

Date of Decision
29 June 1972

Decision
Georgia death penalty statute declared unconstitutional.

Significance
Although *Furman v. Georgia* did not completely abolish the death penalty, it placed stringent requirements on death penalty statutes.

On the night of 11 August 1967, 29-year-old William Joseph Micke, Jr. came home from work to his wife and five children in the city of Savannah, Georgia. He went to bed around midnight. Two hours later, the Mickes were awakened by strange noises in the kitchen. Thinking that one of his children was sleepwalking, William Micke went into the kitchen to investigate. He found William Henry Furman there, a 26-year-old African American man who had broken into the house and was carrying a gun. Furman fled the house, shooting Micke as he left. The bullet hit Micke in the chest and he died instantly. Micke's family promptly called the police, who arrived on the scene within minutes. The police searched the neighborhood and found Furman, who was still carrying the murder weapon.

Furman was charged with murder and was tried in the Superior Court of Chatham County, Georgia on 20 September 1968. Furman was a poor man, and he got a poor man's trial. His court-appointed lawyer, B. Clarence Mayfield, received the court-approved standard retainer for murder cases: $150, which did not include costs. The trial lasted just one day: the jury was selected at 10:00 a.m., the evidence was presented and the judge's instructions to the jury given by 3:30 p.m., and the jury's guilty verdict was returned at 5:00 p.m.

Long before the trial, the court committed Furman to the Georgia Central State Hospital at Milledgeville for psychological examination. Furman had dropped out of school after the sixth grade, and he tested in the lowest four percent of the test's intelligence range. The hospital diagnosed Furman as being mentally deficient and subject to psychotic episodes. Nevertheless, the court denied Furman's insanity plea at trial.

Furman Sentenced to Death

Under Georgia law, Furman faced the death penalty. This was despite the fact that Furman had testified that his shooting of Micke was accidental:

> I admit going to these folks' home and they did caught me in there and I was coming back out, backing up and there was a wire down there on the floor. I was coming out backwards and fell back and I didn't intend to kill nobody

First- and Second-Degree Murder

In 1794, Pennsylvania became the first state to establish a legal distinction between first-degree murder—that is, "willful, deliberate, or premeditated killing"—and a second degree of murder charges, in which the defendant was judged to be less culpable due to a lesser intent or other mitigating circumstances.

Since that time, other states have adopted their own standards of first-degree (or capital) murder on the basis of a variety of circumstances. Some of the factors involved in the determination of first-murder in various states are the use of torture; murdering for financial gain; killing a police officer or other public official; killing during the commission of a felony such as rape, robbery, kidnapping, or the performance of a sexual act with a person under the age of fourteen; use of an explosive; a prior record for murder; and murder that involves—to use a phrase from the 1794 Pennsylvania statute—lying in wait for the victim.

Just as misdemeanors are generally understood as that class of crimes which are not classified as felonies, so second-degree murder is usually any type of murder that does not qualify as first-degree.

Source(s): Sifakis, Carl. *The Encyclopedia of American Crime.* New York: Facts on File, 1982.

. . . The gun went off and I didn't know nothing about no murder until they arrested me, and when the gun went off I was down on the floor and I got up and ran. That's all to it.

Georgia's death penalty statute, however, permitted executions even for unintended killings. So long as Furman had broken into the Micke house illegally, it was irrelevant that his shooting was accidental since that shooting had caused Micke's death while Furman was committing a criminal act. The judge's instructions to the jury made this clear:

If you believe beyond a reasonable doubt that the defendant broke and entered the dwelling of the deceased with intent to commit a felony or a larceny and that after so breaking and entering with such intent, the defendant killed the deceased in the manner set forth in the indictment, and if you find that such killing was the natural, reasonable and probable consequence of such breaking and entering, then I instruct you that under such circumstances, you would be authorized to convict the defendant of murder and this you would be authorized to do whether the defendant intended to kill the deceased or not.

The Georgia Supreme Court affirmed Furman's conviction and death sentence on 24 April 1969, but on 3 May 1969 Chief Justice W. H. Duckworth stayed the execution so that Furman could file a petition with the U.S. Supreme Court. Furman was no longer represented solely by court-appointed counsel: his case had generated some publicity, and several lawyers were now handling his appeal.

On 17 January 1972 the parties argued their case before the U.S. Supreme Court in Washington, D.C. The Court had agreed to hear the case to answer the legal question of whether the death penalty violates the Eighth Amendment to the U.S. Constitution, which states that "Excessive bail shall not be required, nor excessive fines imposed, nor cruel and unusual punishments inflicted."

The Court issued its decision 29 June 1972. By a narrow 5-4 majority, the justices voted to overturn Furman's conviction on the grounds that in his case the death penalty constituted cruel and unusual punishment. The justices were deeply divided over how to interpret the Eighth Amendment, however. All nine justices filed separate opinions stating their legal reasoning, which is highly unusual. For the most part, Justice William O. Douglas' opinion spoke for the five-member majority.

Court Severely Restricts Death Penalty

Douglas reviewed the history of capital punishment under the English common law, from the Norman Conquest in 1066 through the American colonial period and up to the ratification of the Constitution. He noted that English law had evolved to consider the death penalty unfair when applied selectively to minorities, outcasts and unpopular groups. In America, the Court had already held that discriminatory enforcement of the law violates the equal protection clause of the Fourteenth Amendment. Therefore, if a death penalty statute was applied in a discriminatory manner, it was unfair and constituted cruel and unusual punishment. For Furman, the death penalty was unfair because there had not been enough protection for him at trial. He had gotten a quick one-day trial and he was African American, poor, uneducated, and mentally ill:

The generality of a law inflicting capital punishment is one thing. What may be said of the validity of a law on the books and what may be done with the law in its application do, or may, lead to quite different conclusions.

It would seem to be incontestable that the death penalty inflicted on one defendant is "unusual" if it discriminates against him by reason of his race, religion, wealth, social position, or class, or if it is imposed under a procedure that gives room for the play of such prejudices.

The rest of Douglas' opinion reads almost like a professional case study of prisoner treatment throughout the United States. Based on surveys and statistics drawn from a variety of sources, Douglas concluded that the death penalty was disproportionately applied to African Americans, the poor, and other groups who are at a disadvantage in society:

> Former Attorney General Ramsey Clark has said, "It is the poor, the sick, the ignorant, the powerless and the hated who are executed." One searches our chronicles in vain for the execution of any member of the affluent strata of this society.

Justices Brennan and Marshall, who had voted with Douglas, wrote opinions that called for the complete abolition of the death penalty for all crimes and under any circumstances. They were in the minority, however, and so Douglas' opinion embodied the impact of the Court's decision: the death penalty could still be imposed, but only if the law bent over backwards to make sure that people like Furman were protected.

While *Furman v. Georgia* was hailed as a landmark decision protecting minorities and other historically oppressed groups, it did not give the states much guidance on what they had to do to make their death penalty statutes comply with the Eighth Amendment. In the 1976 case of *Gregg v. Georgia,* the Court upheld the death penalty imposed on a convicted murderer under a revamped Georgia statute that required sentencing hearings and other protective procedures. Most states with death penalty statutes have followed *Gregg* and modified their laws so there are procedures to protect the poor, minorities, the mentally ill, and other groups. Further, most states have repealed the death penalty for accidental killings and other crimes less serious than cold-blooded intentional murder.

Furman v. Georgia did not forbid capital punishment, but it did place strict requirements on death penalty statutes, at both the state and federal levels, based on the Eighth Amendment.

Jackson and *Branch*

In the two cases decided with *Furman, Jackson v. Georgia* and *Branch v. Texas,* the petitioners Jackson and Branch were both convicted of rape and sentenced to death. Jackson, an African American male who had escaped from a work gang, entered a woman's home and committed a rape and robbery of that woman. At trial, a psychiatrist testified that Jackson was not schizophrenic and was competent to stand trial, when in fact he was not. The Supreme Court, using the same reasoning as that applied to *Furman,* said that the unequal application of the death penalty that does not protect due process for all citizens is unconstitutional. The facts in *Branch* were substantially similar. Branch was an African American male who was convicted of raping an elderly woman. At trial, it was determined that Branch had a below average IQ and was in the lowest fourth-percentile in his class. He was sentenced to death nonetheless. The Supreme Court, again, said that the unequal application of the death penalty where some prejudices might exist is not constitutional in those cases.

Related Cases

Yick Wo v. Hopkins, 118 U.S. 356 (1886).
Louisiana ex rel. Francis v. Resweber, 329 U.S. 459 (1947).
Reid v. Covert, 354 U.S. 1 (1957).
Trop v. Dulles, 356 U.S. 86 (1958).
Robinson v. California, 370 U.S. 660 (1962).
Gideon v. Wainwright, 372 U.S. 335 (1963).
Malloy v. Hogan, 378 U.S. 1 (1964).
Witherspoon v. Illinois, 391 U.S. 510 (1968).

Bibliography and Further Reading

Aguirre, Adalberto. *Race, Racism, and the Death Penalty in the United States.* Berrien Spring, MI: Vande Vere, 1991.

Horwitz, Elinor Lander. *Capital Punishment, U.S.A.* Philadelphia: J. B. Lippincott Co., 1973.

Johnson, John W. *Historic U.S. Court Cases, 1690–1990: An Encyclopedia.* New York: Garland Publishing, 1992.

Masur, Louis P. *Rites of Execution: Capital Punishment and the Transformation Of American Culture.* New York: Oxford University Press, 1989.

Radelet, Michael L. *In Spite of Innocence: Erroneous Convictions in Capital Cases.* Boston: Northeastern University Press, 1992.

Trombley, Stephen. *The Execution Protocol: Inside America's Capital Punishment Industry.* New York: Crown Publishers, 1992.

Various Contributors. *Congregation of the Condemned: Voices Against the Death Penalty.* Buffalo, NY: Prometheus Books, 1991.

GREGG V. GEORGIA

Legal Citation: 428 U.S. 153 (1976)

Petitioner
Troy Leon Gregg

Respondent
State of Georgia

Petitioner's Claim
That the death penalty, even when imposed under the safe-guards applied in the state of Georgia, violates the Eighth Amendment's ban on cruel and unusual punishment.

Chief Lawyer for Petitioner
G. Hughel Harrison

Chief Lawyer for Respondent
G. Thomas Davis

Justices for the Court
Harry A. Blackmun, Warren E. Burger, Lewis F. Powell, Jr., William H. Rehnquist, John Paul Stevens, Potter Stewart (writing for the Court), Byron R. White

Justices Dissenting
William J. Brennan, Jr., Thurgood Marshall

Place
Washington, D.C.

Date of Decision
2 July 1976

Decision
The Supreme Court upheld the death penalty as imposed by Georgia.

Significance
In 1972, in *Furman v. Georgia*, the Supreme Court had declared that the death penalty was unconstitutional. Over the next few years, a change in justices, as well as the imposition of certain procedures to prevent arbitrariness and prejudice in state trials of capital crimes, resulted in a changed attitude towards capital punishment.

Troy Gregg was charged with two counts each of armed robbery and murder. At his trial, evidence was presented that Gregg, together with a traveling companion, Floyd Allen, had been hitchhiking north in Florida when, on 21 November 1973, they had been picked up by Fred Simmons and Bob Moore. After their car broke down, Simmons purchased another with cash that he was carrying, and the four traveled on together into Georgia, where they stopped at a highway rest stop. The next morning, Simmons's and Moore's bodies were found in a nearby ditch. Allen and Gregg, who were riding in Simmons's car, were picked up the next afternoon by police. Claiming self-defense, Gregg signed a confession admitting he had shot, then robbed, Simmons and Moore. Allen, however, told police that Gregg had first threatened to rob the two victims after they left the car. When they started to climb up an embankment towards the car, Allen said, Gregg climbed up on the automobile in order to improve his aim. After felling the two men, Gregg shot each in the head, execution style, and robbed them of their valuables.

Owing to a U.S. Supreme Court ruling, *Furman v. Georgia* (1972), that had been handed down just the year before, the state of Georgia had implemented new procedures for trying criminal defendants charged with crimes punishable by death. Before *Furman*, in which the Court for the first time struck down the death penalty as unconstitutional, the decision of whether or not to impose capital punishment had been more or less left to the unlimited discretion of juries. The result was often arbitrary, with African-American, poor, or socially disadvantaged defendants being sentenced to death in disproportionate numbers. After *Furman*, all 36 states that authorized the death penalty halted executions while procedural safeguards were put in place.

In Georgia, the legislature adopted the following provisions: 1) in trials for capital offenses, guilt or innocence is determined in the first part of a two-part trial, during which the judge is required to instruct the jury about the possibility of finding guilt for other, lesser offenses, 2) after a verdict is handed down, another hearing is conducted as to the possible presence of mitigating or aggravating circumstances that could affect the sentence imposed, 3) at least one of 10 aggravating circumstances

Caryl Chessman Trial

After eight stays of execution, the convicted "Red Light Bandit," Caryl Chessman, was put to death 2 May 1960, just seconds before a ninth stay of execution was telephoned. The case was significant due to the generation of worldwide attention and sympathy for Chessman's documented struggle against capital punishment and the U.S. death penalty process.

The main point of argument for a new trial had been that after Chessman had been sentenced 21 May 1948, the court reporter, Ernest Perry, died of coronary thrombosis, leaving behind 1,800 pages of shorthand testimony to be transcribed. Under California law, if the court reporter dies before transcribing his notes a new trial must be held. On 25 June 1948, Judge Charles W. Fricke ruled that a new trial would not be given since Chessman's case was criminal and not civil. In September of 1948 the job of transcribing the notes was given to Stanley Fraser, the uncle of the prosecutor in the case who also received three times the standard pay rate to complete the transcription. Other issues of rulings made by Fricke, as well as the unbalanced jury of 11 women and one man in a sexual assault case added to Chessman's plea for a new trial.

Source(s): Knappman, Edward W., ed. *Great American Trials.* Detroit, MI: Visible Ink Press, 1994.

(such as the defendant having a prior criminal record) must exist before the death penalty could be imposed, 4) after the death sentence is imposed, it is automatically appealed in order to determine whether it was fairly imposed and is proportional to the crime, and 5) if the death penalty is upheld by the Georgia Supreme Court, that court must include in its decision references to other, similar cases the court has considered.

The trial judge in *Gregg* followed these procedures. He advised the jury that it could impose either life-in-prison or the death penalty for each of the crimes charged and that it could consider both aggravating and mitigating circumstances. He instructed the jury that the death sentence would apply only if it found beyond a reasonable doubt that the murders were committed under any of three possible scenarios that could be considered aggravating: 1) that they were committed in the course of committing other capital crimes, 2) that they were committed to facilitate robbery, or 3) that they were outrageously inhumane. The jury found that the first two aggravating circumstances applied and sentenced Gregg to death. The Georgia Supreme Court, following the new statutory guidelines, upheld the sentence, finding that it was neither excessive nor arbitrary. It did, however, reverse the sentences for robbery, finding that the death penalty was rarely imposed for this crime. Gregg then appealed to the U.S. Supreme Court.

In *Furman*, the Court had declined to declare the death penalty a *per se* violation of the Eighth Amendment ban on cruel and unusual punishment. The reason given in this case for outlawing capital punishment was that it was improperly administered. With the adoption and application of court rules such as those under consideration in *Gregg*, this objection seemed to have been answered. The Court upheld the decision of the Georgia Supreme Court. Justices Brennan and Marshall were the two dissenting votes; in *Gregg*, as in every death penalty case that came before the Court during their tenures, the dissenting justices found capital punishment a *per se* violation of the Eighth Amendment.

Death Penalty Upheld Under Certain Circumstances

The justices were unable to agree on a single opinion, but Justices Stewart, Powell, and Stevens spoke for the seven-member majority. The Eighth Amendment prohibition against cruel and unusual punishment was not a static concept, they declared. Instead, it was subject to the public's evolving standards of decency. At the time the Constitution and Bill of Rights were drafted, capital punishment was a common practice. Although less common in the latter half of the twentieth century, the ultimate punishment was still endorsed by public opinion as expressed in the legislation of a majority of the states. Accordingly, the Court was obliged to defer to public acceptance of the appropriateness of the death penalty as punishment for certain crimes, provided that it was imposed under strict conditions designed to rule out cruelty and unfairness:

> [O]ur cases . . . make clear that public perceptions are not conclusive. A penalty also must accord with "the dignity of man," which is the "basic concept underlying the Eighth Amendment." This means, at least, that the punishment not be "excessive." When a form of punishment in the abstract (in this case, whether capital punishment may ever be imposed as a sanction for murder) rather than in the particular (the propriety of death as a penalty to be applied to a specific defendant for a specific crime) is under consideration, the inquiry into "excessiveness" has two aspects. First, the punishment must not involve the unnecessary and

The Burger Court, 1976.
© Corbis-Bettmann.

wanton infliction of pain . . . Second, the punishment must not be grossly out of proportion to the severity of the crime.

Subsequent critics have pointed out the disparity between the Court's claim that the Eighth Amendment embodies a concept of fundamental human decency and its endorsement of a wide variety of considerations by state courts in death penalty cases. How, these critics ask, can a single standard for evaluating the appropriateness of the death penalty be squared with a proliferation of rules for its application? Seen from this perspective, *Gregg* gave states permission to continue to impose the death penalty without providing much guidance as to how this should be done. For some Court observers—as well as for Justices Brennan and Marshall—the *Gregg* decision had only succeeded in perpetuating the arbitrariness *Furman* condemned.

Related Cases
Proffitt v. Florida, 428 U.S. 242 (1976).
Jurek v. Texas, 428 U.S. 262 (1976).
Woodson v. North Carolina, 428 U.S. 280 (1976).
Roberts v. Louisiana, 431 U.S. 633 (1976).

Bibliography and Further Reading
Bedau, Hugo Adam, ed. *The Death Penalty in America.* New York, NY: Oxford University Press, 1982.

Costanzo, Mark, and Lawrence T. White. "An Overview of the Death Penalty and Capital Trials: History, Current Status, Legal Procedures, and Cost." *Journal of Social Issues,* summer 1994, p. 1.

Ellsworth, Phoebe C., and Samuel R. Gross. "Hardening of the Attitudes: Americans' Views on the Death Penalty." *Journal of Social Issues,* summer 1994, p. 19

Garnett, Richard W. "Depravity Thrice Removed: Using the 'Heinous, Cruel, or Depraved' Factor to Aggravate Convictions of Nontriggermen Accomplices in Capital Cases." *Yale Law Journal,* June 1994, p. 2471.

Garvey, Karin E. "Eighth Amendment—The Constitutionality of the Alabama Capital Sentencing Scheme." *Journal of Criminal Law and Criminology,* summer 1996, p. 1411.

Haney, Craig, and Deana Dorman Logan. "Broken Promise: The Supreme Court's Response to Social Science Research on Capital Punishment." *Journal of Social Issues,* summer 1994, p. 75.

Johnson, John W., ed. *Historic U.S. Court Cases, 1690–1990: An Encyclopedia.* New York: Garland Publishing, 1992.

Kessler, Daryl I. "Eighth Amendment—Sentencer Discretion in Capital Sentencing Schemes." *Journal of Criminal Law and Criminology,* winter-spring 1994, p. 827.

Murphy, Cornelius F. "The Supreme Court and Capital Punishment: A New Hands-Off Approach." *USA Today (Magazine),* March 1993, p. 51.

Nakell, Barry, and Kenneth A. Hardy. *The Arbitrariness of the Death Penalty.* Philadelphia, PA: Temple University Press, 1987.

White, Welsh S. *The Death Penalty in the Eighties: An Examination of the Modern System of Capital Punishment.* Ann Arbor: University of Michigan Press, 1987.

JUREK V. TEXAS

Legal Citation: 428 U.S. 262 (1976)

Petitioner
Jerry Lane Jurek

Respondent
State of Texas

Petitioner's Claim
The death penalty was cruel and unusual punishment and violated the Eighth and Fourteenth Amendments of the U.S. Constitution.

Chief Lawyer for Petitioner
Anthony G. Amsterdam

Chief Lawyer for Respondent
John L. Hill

Justices for the Court
Harry A. Blackmun, Warren E. Burger, Lewis F. Powell, Jr., William H. Rehnquist, John Paul Stevens (writing for the Court), Potter Stewart, Byron R. White

Justices Dissenting
William J. Brennan, Jr., Thurgood Marshall

Place
Washington, D.C.

Date of Decision
2 July 1976

Decision
Upheld the state of Texas' claim that the death penalty was not cruel and unusual punishment and therefore was not unconstitutional.

Significance
This case determined that the death penalty, if applied fairly and without discrimination, was not considered cruel and unusual punishment, and therefore was not an infringement on an individual's constitutional rights as put forth in the Eighth and Fourteenth Amendments.

In 1976 Jerry Lane Jurek, 22 years of age, was charged by indictment with the murder of Wendy Adams, a ten-year-old girl. The murder was considered quite brutal, Jurek "choking and strangling her with his hands, and . . . drowning her in water by throwing her into a river . . . in the course of committing and attempting to commit kidnapping of and forcible rape . . ." Evidence against Jurek was quite convincing, and included the testimony of several people who saw him with the victim on the day of her murder, technical evidence, and incriminating statements made by the petitioner himself. This evidence indicated that the petitioner, while drinking beer with two friends and driving his truck, had expressed an interest in having sexual relations with some young girls they saw. After his friends stated that the girls were too young, Jurek dropped them off at a pool hall, then returned and was seen talking to Wendy Adams at a public swimming pool. Witnesses stated that a man resembling Jurek was later seen driving out of town at a high rate of speed with a girl matching Adam's description in the bed of the truck; the girl was screaming "help me, help me." According to Jurek's own statement, he took the girl to the river, choked her and disposed of the unconscious body in the water. The girl's dead body was found two days later.

The jury found Jurek guilty. During the sentencing phase of the trial, the jury had to consider two of three specific questions before rendering a judgment that could result in a capital sentence: 1) Was the conduct of the defendant that led to the death of the deceased committed deliberately with death as the ultimate goal? and 2) Should the defendant be considered a threat to society because he was likely to commit other acts of violence? The third question, concerning whether the defendant's conduct was an unreasonable response to provocation by the deceased, was not considered.

Texas statutes maintained that if the jury found that the state proved beyond a reasonable doubt that the answer to each question was "yes," then the death sentence would be imposed. If the answer to any question was "no," then the defendant faced life imprisonment. In the case of *Jurek v. Texas* the jury unanimously voted "yes" for both questions presented. The judge sentenced Jerry Lane Jurek to death.

Types of Capital Punishment

There are five basic types of execution in the United States: hanging, firing squads, electrocution, lethal gas, and lethal injection. Each of the 38 states with a death-penalty statute authorizes at least one of these forms. In addition, lethal injection is the method authorized by the federal government.

Lethal injection is by far the predominant method of execution, with 32 states authorizing it as of 1997. In 1997, 92 percent of all executions took place by this method, as compared with 28 percent in 1987. With 284 lethal injections, it was also the most common method among those administered to the 432 prisoners executed between 1977 and 1997, as compared with 134 electrocutions, nine killed by lethal gas, three by hanging, and two by firing squad.

Sixty-eight of the 74 executions during 1997 were by lethal injection, and six were by electrocution. Texas led the nation in executions, with 37. Virginia had nine; Missouri had six; Arkansas four; Alabama three; Arizona, Illinois, and South Carolina two each; and the remaining nine states one each. Of the 74 men executed, 41 were non-Hispanic white, 26 non-Hispanic African American, four white Hispanic, and one each black Hispanic, American Indian, and Asian American.

Source(s): U.S. Department of Justice, Bureau of Justice Statistics. *Capital Punishment 1997.* Washington, DC: U.S. Government, 1998.

Jerry Lane Jurek was one of the first to be electrocuted after the Supreme Court reinstated capital punishment. © AP/Wide World Photos.

Action and Reaction

Jurek appealed his sentencing, claiming that the death penalty—under any circumstances—was cruel and unusual punishment and represented a violation of the Eighth and Fourteenth Amendments of the U.S. Constitution. Jurek's attorney said that a certain amount of arbitrariness existed in Texas' criminal justice system and that it was also impossible to predict any individual's future behavior. The U.S. Supreme Court took up the task to determine whether or not this was so.

One of the most important elements considered by the Supreme Court was the revision of Texas' capital-sentencing procedure. This revision took place in the mid-1970s, a result of what many justices viewed as an uneven application of the death penalty in *Furman v. Georgia* (1972), *Jackson v. Georgia* (1972), and *Branch v. Texas* (1972). In each of these cases a black defendant received the death penalty for killing a white person. In attempting to pinpoint racial bias as to why these defendants were sentenced to death while others in similar circumstances were not, the Court discovered a certain randomness in the application of the death penalty. It was held that the death penalty in these cases was cruel and unusual punishment, and therefore violated the Constitution. This forced states and the national legislature to reevaluate their capital-sentenc-

ing structures to guarantee that the death penalty would be administered in a responsible manner.

Texas responded to this by narrowing the circumstances in which the state could seek the death penalty. Capital punishment could now be only applied in five situations: 1) the murder of a fireman or a peace officer; 2) murder committed in the course of burglary, forcible rape, arson, kidnapping, or robbery; 3) murder committed for pay; 4) murder of a prison employee by a prison inmate; and 5) murder committed during escape or attempted escape from a penal institution. Texas also adopted the new capital-sentencing procedure requiring the jury to answer three specific questions designed to maintain guilt beyond a reasonable doubt.

When considering the claim that Texas' death penalty was cruel and unusual punishment, the Supreme Court also examined how the death penalty was applied by other states. Georgia and Florida each used a list of aggravating circumstances to justify the enforcement of the death penalty. Each of the five classes of murder stipulated in the Texas statute was represented in these lists by one or more statutory aggravating circumstances. It was found that the primary difference between Texas and the other two states was that the death penalty was available as a sentencing option for a smaller class of murders in Texas.

Constitutional Infringement?

Lastly, the Court considered the requirements of the Eighth and Fourteenth Amendments. The Eighth Amendment states "Excessive bail shall not be required, nor excessive fines imposed, nor cruel and unusual punishments inflicted," while the Fourteenth Amendment essentially guarantees an individual's rights to due process and equal protection under the law. In order for a capital-sentence ruling to be constitutional a jury must consider the case based not only on evidence showing why a death sentence should be imposed, but also on the factors surrounding why it should not be imposed. In other words, mitigating circumstances must be considered. The Texas statute only directed jurors to answer three questions. Did these required questions allow consideration of the mitigating circumstances during the sentencing of Jurek?

In determining this, the Supreme Court focused primarily on the question concerning the petitioner's potential danger to society. It was noted that the jury in this case had to consider various factors concerning Jurek, such as his age, his emotional state-of-mind, and his past conduct. These observations were presented not only by the prosecutor, but also by the defense.

The Supreme Court concluded that Texas' capital-sentencing structure did not violate the Eighth and Fourteenth Amendments. This decision was reached due to the narrowing of the definition of capital murder, requiring at least one statutory aggravating circumstance of five be present before a death sentence can be considered. By allowing the defense to provide testimony as to why the death penalty should not be invoked during the separate sentencing hearing, the Court felt that mitigating circumstances concerning the defendant were brought to light, thus providing the jury with an acceptable amount of guidance to enable accurate sentencing. The substantive crime of murder was defined in a precise enough manner under Texas' revised statute so that the issues presented in *Furman*

v. Georgia, Branch v. Texas, and *Jackson v. Georgia* did not come to bear.

Impact

The verdict of *Jurek v. Texas* confirmed that the death penalty could be invoked without the disruption of an individual's Eighth and Fourteenth Amendment rights. The most important consequence of this pertained to the amount of evidence presented to a jury. It was recognized that there was a significant difference between the death penalty and all other punishments—and therefore "a corresponding difference in the need for reliability in determining whether the death sentence is appropriately imposed in a particular case." This case maintained that the jury must be made aware of all relevant information concerning the defendant whose life is on the line; therefore all mitigating circumstances must be considered in capital-sentencing cases.

Related Cases

Jacobs v. Wainwright, 469 U.S. 1062 (1984).
Branch v. Texas, 408 U.S. 238 (1972).
Furman v. Georgia, 408 U.S. 238 (1972).
Jackson v. Georgia, 408 U.S. 238 (1972).
Gregg v. Georgia, 428 U.S. 153 (1976).
Woodson v. North Carolina, 428 U.S. 280 (1976).

Bibliography and Further Reading

Brown, J. Michael. "Eighth Amendment—Capital Sentencing Instructions." *Journal of Criminal Law and Criminology,* winter-spring 1994, p. 854.

Fagan, Jeffrey, and Martin Guggenheim. "Preventative Detention and the Judicial Prediction of Dangerousness for Juveniles." *Journal of Criminal Law and Criminology,* winter 1996, p. 415.

Plural at the Intersection of Race, Law, and Politics. "Furman v. Georgia, 408 U.S. 283 (1972)." http://www.plural.org/research_dpcases2.html (16 May 1998).

WOODSON V. NORTH CAROLINA

Legal Citation: 428 U.S. 280 (1976)

Petitioner
James Tyrone Woodson, et al.

Respondent
State of North Carolina

Petitioner's Claim
That a North Carolina law establishing a mandatory death sentence for all convicted first-degree murderers constituted a violation of the Eighth and Fourteenth Amendments to the Constitution.

Chief Lawyer for Petitioner
Anthony G. Anderson

Chief Lawyer for Respondent
Sidney S. Eagles, Jr.

Justices for the Court
William J. Brennan, Jr., Thurgood Marshall, Lewis F. Powell, Jr., John Paul Stevens, Potter Stewart (writing for the Court)

Justices Dissenting
Harry A. Blackmun, Warren E. Burger, William H. Rehnquist, Byron R. White

Place
Washington, D.C.

Date of Decision
2 July 1976

Decision
That the North Carolina law was unconstitutional because it failed to take into account the "fundamental respect for humanity" inherent in the Eighth Amendment's requirement that punishment be "exercised within the limits of civilized standards."

Significance
Woodson v. North Carolina tested the Court's resolve with regard to its 1972 *Furman v. Georgia* ruling when it found that a Georgia death penalty law amounted to cruel and unusual punishment as proscribed by the Eighth Amendment. *Woodson* was one of the five "Death Penalty Cases" of 1976, along with *Gregg v. Georgia*, *Jurek v. Texas*, *Proffitt v. Florida*, and *Roberts v. Louisiana*, the latter decided on the same day as *Woodson*. The first three affirmed state death penalties, whereas *Woodson* and *Roberts* struck down mandatory death sentences. Rather that settling death penalty issues for all time, however, these cases raised questions which continued to be debated with increasing passion over subsequent decades.

Woodson's Crime, Carolina's Punishment

According to court testimony, the events involving James Tyrone Woodson and three others on 3 June 1974 took place as follows. Woodson had been drinking heavily when at 9:30 p.m. Luby Waxton and Leonard Tucker arrived at his trailer. Woodson went out to meet him, at which time a belligerent Waxton struck him on the face and threatened to kill him if he did not join the other two in a robbery. Woodson got in the car with them, and they drove to Waxton's trailer, where they were met by Johnnie Lee Carroll. Waxton got his nickel-plated derringer, and Tucker gave Woodson a rifle; then the four men drove to a convenience store in a single vehicle.

Upon arrival, Tucker and Waxton entered the store while Carroll and Woodson remained in the car as lookouts. Inside the store, Tucker bought a pack of cigarettes, then Waxton approached the clerk and also asked for a pack; but when she went to give them to him, he withdrew his derringer from his hip pocket and shot her at point-blank range. Waxton removed the money from the cash register and gave it to Tucker, who rushed past an entering customer to the parking lot. From outside, Tucker heard a shot, and moments later Waxton appearing holding a wad of paper money. The four men drove away.

As it later turned out, the customer had been wounded seriously, but the cashier was dead, making this a first-degree murder case. At the trial, Tucker and Carroll testified for the prosecution in return for lesser sentences. Waxton, who claimed that Tucker, and not himself, had shot the cashier and the customer, also tried to get a reduced sentence. Woodson, on the other hand, held that he had been coerced by Waxton into riding in the car to the store that night, and therefore he refused to plead guilty to any offense. Both Woodson and Waxton were found guilty and, according to a recently adopted North Carolina law that made a death sentence mandatory in first-degree murder cases, were sentenced to death.

When the case came before the Supreme Court, the human-rights organization Amnesty International filed an *amicus curiae* brief on behalf of Woodson and Wax-

Attitudes Toward the Death Penalty for Murderers

According to Gallup polls taken periodically during the years between 1953 and 1995, the percentage of Americans favoring the death penalty for persons convicted of murder was at its lowest in 1966 (42 percent), and its highest in 1994 (80 percent).

The College of Criminal Justice at Sam Houston State University found that in 1996, more than 73 percent of Americans favored the death penalty. Of males, almost 82 percent answered in the affirmative when asked "Are you in favor of the death penalty for persons convicted of murder?"; of females, 65.6 percent.

Several interesting facts emerged from the Sam Houston State materials. The percentage in favor was more or less constant among age groups, varying from 70.4 percent for 18-to-24-year-olds to 77 percent for 40-to-59-year-olds. The lowest education bracket, those who had not finished high school, was as likely to answer in the affirmative as the highest, college graduates. Both were at 67.2 percent, with the highest percentage (80.5 percent) for people who had graduated high school but not attended college. The study, which divided respondents into demographic groups on a variety of lines, revealed that the lowest group support for the death penalty came from African Americans, of whom only 58.6 were in favor.

Source(s): *Bureau of Justice Statistics Sourcebook of Criminal Justice Statistics—1996* Washington, DC: U.S. Government, 1997.

ton. Solicitor General Robert Bork filed an *amicus curiae* brief for the United States on behalf of the respondents.

"A Faceless, Undifferentiated Mass"

The Court concluded that North Carolina's mandatory death sentence violated not only the Due Process Clause of the Fourteenth Amendment, but the less often cited Eighth Amendment, which states in full: "Excessive bail shall not be required, nor excessive fines imposed, nor cruel and unusual punishments inflicted." In a joint opinion delivered by Justice Stewart, a plurality composed of Justices Powell, Stevens, and Stewart held that the Eighth Amendment "serves to assure that the State's power to punish is 'exercised within the limits of civilized standards,'" a stipulation established in *Trop v. Dulles* (1958).

By three criteria, the North Carolina law—which had been adopted only two years before, in 1974—was found wanting. The first of these was the criterion of "contemporary standards," from which the law "depart[ed] markedly." Though at the time of the Eighth Amendment's adoption all states provided mandatry death sentences for certain offenses, the Court held that the Amendment should be viewed in light of changing standards regarding cruel and unusual punishment.

This did not mean, however, that the Court was opposed to the death penalty *per se*. One of the first issues addressed in *Woodson,* as a matter of fact, was the question of whether the death penalty "under any circumstances is cruel and unusual punishment in violation of the Eighth and Fourteenth Amendments." Citing statements made in *Gregg v. Georgia,* the Court rejected this argument. The issue considered in *Wood-*

son was purely that of the mandatory death penalty, and in handing down its opinion, the Court offered a short history of mandatory death penalty statutes in the United States.

Although mandatory statutes existed from the nation's beginnings, "Almost from the outset jurors reacted unfavorably to the harshness of mandatory death sentences." This led to reforms, the most notable of which was a 1794 Pennsylvania statute which limited mandatory death sentences to "murder of the first degree," which it defined as "willful, deliberate and premeditated" killing. This idea of dividing murders into degrees, and of punishing accordingly, caught on. But starting with Tennessee in 1838, a new type of reform emerged: jury discretion in sentencing. By 1963, all jurisdictions in America had some form of discretionary jury sentencing in place of automatic death sentences.

Hence "the reaction of jurors and legislators to the harshness of those provisions [in the Amendment] has led to the replacement of automatic death penalty statutes with discretionary jury sentencing." The North Carolina statute, by contrast, seemed tied more to an attempt by that state to "retain the death penalty in a form consistent with the Constitution" than it did with "a renewed societal acceptance of mandatory death sentencing." Hence the statute, the Court ruled, "is a constitutionally impermissible departure from contemporary standards respecting imposition of the unique and irretrievable punishment of death."

The second criterion involved standards again, but in this case the standards tested were those by which a jury exercised "the power to decide which first-degree murderers shall live and which shall die." Much of *Woodson* referred back to the Court's 1972 ruling in *Fur-*

man v. Georgia. The earlier case had involved a burglary defendant who, while attempting to flee after being discovered by a person whose house he was robbing, tripped and fell and thus caused his gun to go off, killing a resident of the house. He received the death penalty, and challenged this before the Court, holding that the imposition of a death sentence under such circumstances constituted cruel and unusual punishment in violation of the Eighth and Fourteenth Amendments. In one of its longer rulings—some 200 pages of opinions—the Court held that the death penalty was indeed cruel and unusual as applied to Furman and to the petitioners in Jackson v. Georgia and Branch v. Texas.

As a result of Furman, state legislatures had reconsidered their death penalty provisions to ensure fairness in the disposition of death sentences, and North Carolina was among those states. However, in the Court's view, the resulting North Carolina statute "fails to provide a constitutionally tolerable response to Furman's rejection of unbridled jury discretion in the imposition of capital sentences." A central aspect of the Court's ruling in Furman had been its "conviction that vesting a jury with standardless sentencing power violated the Eighth and Fourteenth Amendments." However, North Carolina's solution to the problem of "standardless sentencing power" was in the Court's view no solution: instead of allowing juries too much sentencing power, it had removed all of their power by enforcing a mandatory death sentence, thus achieving the exact opposite result of that desired by the majority in Furman.

The third criterion related to a jury's ability to evaluate the character of an individual defendant before it voted for the ultimate sentence. Again, the North Carolina law failed to take account of an ever-important concept in human affairs: gradations of good and evil. In theory, the state law would apply the same treatment to a serial killer as to a defendant who accidentally shot someone while committing a robbery to obtain food for his family. Whereas

> The respect for human dignity underlying the Eighth Amendment . . . requires consideration of aspects of the character of the individual offender . . . The North Carolina statute impermissibly treats all persons convicted of a designated offense not as uniquely individual human beings, but as members of a faceless, undifferentiated mass to be subjected to blind infliction of the death penalty.

Thus by these three criteria, the Court held the North Carolina statute unconstitutional.

Concurrence and Dissent Intertwined with Other Cases

Toward the end of its opinion, the Court had noted that "Death, in its finality, differs more from life impris-

onment than a 100-year prison term [differs] from one of only a year or two." On this count, at least, all nine members of the Court would most likely have been in agreement. But to Justice Marshall, the death penalty under any circumstance was cruel and unusual punishment; hence he concurred with the Court's opinion while noting his position on the larger subject. Marshall made reference to his dissenting opinion in Gregg v. Georgia, issued earlier that day (p. 231); likewise Brennan referred to his own dissent in that case (p. 227) and stated that for reasons he had given there, he concurred with the Court's judgment in the present one.

Likewise Justice Blackmun, one of the four dissenters in Woodson, cited his own earlier dissent, as well as the dissenting opinions with which he joined, in an earlier case: Furman v. Georgia (pp. 375, 414, 465). Justice White, joined by Chief Justice Burger and Justice Rehnquist, referred to yet another case: Roberts v. Louisiana, which the Court decided along with Woodson, Gregg, and other capital cases on that day, 2 July 1976. Citing his opinion on page 325 of that case, White stated that he disagreed both with the petitioner's claim that the death penalty was cruel and unusual punishment under any circumstance, and with the Court's assessment of the North Carolina statute according to its three criteria.

Justice Rehnquist offered his own dissenting opinion in which he examined the three criteria used by the plurality in establishing the Court's decision. "I do not believe," he wrote, "that any one of these reasons singly, or all of them together, can withstand careful analysis." He found no clear proof that mandatory sentencing was necessarily and always more harsh than discretionary, or that society as a whole was as opposed to the idea of mandatory sentencing as the Court held. As for the second flaw noted by the Court in the North Carolina statute, he wrote that "In North Carolina, jurors unwilling to impose the death penalty may simply hang a jury or they may so assert themselves that a verdict of not guilty is brought in." He stated provisions in the laws of other southern states, including Georgia, Florida, and Texas, whereby juries have considerable leeway in sentencing, but stated that "it seems to me impossible to conclude . . . that a mandatory death sentence statute such as North Carolina enacted is any less sound constitutionally than the systems enacted by Georgia, Florida, and Texas which the Court upholds." As for the plurality's assertion that before the death penalty could be imposed there should be "particularized consideration of relevant aspects of the character and record of each convicted defendant," Rehnquist was again in disagreement. "None of the cases halfheartedly cited by the plurality," he wrote, ". . . comes within a light-year of establishing the proposition that individualized consideration is a constitutional requisite for the imposition of a death penalty."

In conclusion, he stated that the Fourteenth Amendment, "given the fullest scope of its 'majestic generalities' . . . is conscripted rather than interpreted when used to permit one but not another system for imposition of the death penalty."

Impact

Woodson, along with the other capital cases decided on 2 July 1976, just 48 hours before the nation's Bicentennial, was important at least as much for the issues it raised as for the questions it answered. In the years that followed these death penalty cases, numerous others came before the Court, and most made reference to *Woodson* and the other July of 1976 cases. In *Lockett v. Ohio* and *Bell v. Ohio* the Court again considered Eighth and Fourteenth Amendment issues with regard to a state law which, in the Court's opinion, failed to take into account mitigating factors in sentencing. As to whether a person involved in a crime that includes murder can be sentenced to death along with the actual perpetrator, as Woodson had been, that question was examined in *Enmund v. Florida* (1982) and *Tison v. Arizona* (1987). In the first case, the answer was "no"; in the second "yes". This serves to illustrate the complexity of the death-penalty issue, which continues to be debated in the Supreme Court and in many lower courts throughout the country.

Related Cases

Trop v. Dulles, 356 U.S. 86 (1958).
Furman v. Georgia, 408 U.S. 238 (1972).
Gregg v. Georgia, 428 U.S. 153 (1976).
Proffitt v. Florida, 428 U.S. 242 (1976).
Jurek v. Texas, 428 U.S. 262 (1976).
Roberts v. Louisiana, 431 U.S. 633 (1977).
Lockett v. Ohio, 438 U.S. 586 (1978).
Bell v. Ohio, 438 U.S. 637 (1978).
Butler v. South Carolina, 459 U.S. 932 (1982).
Boyd v. North Carolina, 471 U.S. 1030 (1985).
Darden v. Wainwright, 477 U.S. 168 (1986).

Bibliography and Further Reading

Bedau, Hugo Adam, ed. *The Death Penalty in America.* New York: Oxford University Press, 1982.

Biskupic, Joan, and Elder Witt. *Guide to the U.S. Supreme Court,* 3rd ed. Washington, DC: Congressional Quarterly Inc., 1997.

Doyle, Charles. *Capital Punishment in the Supreme Court Prior to Gregg v. Georgia and Woodson v. North Carolina.* Washington, DC: Congressional Research Service, 1976.

Hall, Kermit L., ed. *The Oxford Companion to the Supreme Court of the United States.* New York: Oxford University Press, 1992.

Levy, Leonard W., ed. *Encyclopedia of the American Constitution.* New York: Macmillan, 1986.

Witt, Elder. *Congressional Quarterly's Guide to the Supreme Court,* 2nd ed. Washington, DC: Congressional Quarterly Inc., 1990.

———. *The Supreme Court A to Z. CQ's Encyclopedia of American Government,* revised ed. Washington, DC: Congressional Quarterly, Inc., 1994.

COKER V. GEORGIA

Legal Citation: 433 U.S. 584 (1977)

Appellant
Ehrlich Anthony Coker

Appellee
State of Georgia

Appellant's Claim
That the death penalty for rape violates the Constitution's Eighth Amendment.

Chief Lawyer for Appellant
David E. Kendall

Chief Lawyer for Appellee
B. Dean Grindle, Jr., Assistant Attorney General of Georgia

Justices for the Court
Harry A. Blackmun, William J. Brennan, Jr., Thurgood Marshall, John Paul Stevens, Potter Stewart, Byron R. White (writing for the Court)

Justices Dissenting
Warren E. Burger, Lewis F. Powell, Jr., William H. Rehnquist

Place
Washington, D.C.

Date of Decision
29 June 1977

Decision
In a split decision, the Court ruled that Georgia's death penalty for rape violated the Eighth Amendment of the Constitution.

Significance
Many feminists celebrated this decision, believing the death penalty made juries less likely to convict rapists. They also thought it would discourage the old idea that a woman was the property of her husband or father and became valueless to them after a rape.

On 2 September 1974, Ehrlich Anthony Coker escaped from the Ware Correctional Institution near Waycross, Georgia. He had been serving six separate sentences, including two terms of life imprisonment for assault, kidnapping, rape, and murder. At about 11:00 p.m., he entered an unlatched kitchen door and attacked the married couple he found inside. He tied up the man and took his money and car keys. Then he raped the 16-year-old woman at knife point and forced her to accompany him as he continued his flight in the couple's car. The police caught Coker.

Coker stood trial, and a jury convicted him on all counts. At a separate sentencing hearing, the jury considered whether Coker should receive the death penalty for rape. Georgia's statutes permitted the death penalty when a rape "(i) . . . was committed by a person with a prior record of conviction for a capital felony; (ii) the offense was committed while the offender was engaged in another capital felony or in aggravated battery; and (iii) the offense was 'wantonly vile, horrible, or inhuman in that it involved torture, depravity of mind, or an aggravated battery to the victim.'" The first two aggravating circumstances applied to Coker, and the jury sentenced him to death by electrocution.

On Appeal

Coker appealed to the Georgia Supreme Court, which upheld both his conviction and his sentence of death by electrocution. He then appealed to the U.S. Supreme Court, which agreed to examine just one question raised by the case: whether "the punishment of death for rape violates the Eighth Amendment, which proscribes 'cruel and unusual punishments' and which must be observed by the states as well as the federal government."

On 28 March 1977, Coker's attorney argued that the death penalty was too severe a punishment for rape and therefore violated the Eighth Amendment. Ruth Bader Ginsburg and others filed an *amici curiae,* or friend of the court, brief on behalf of the American Civil Liberties Union and other organizations.

Assistant Attorney General Grindle argued that the death penalty was a punishment commensurate with the crime of rape in certain irritant circumstances and that the Constitution permitted it.

The Verdict

The Supreme Court ruled on 29 June 1977, that Georgia's death penalty for rape was unconstitutional. Justice White, in a plurality opinion joined by Justices Blackmun, Stevens, and Stewart, ruled that the death penalty for deliberate murder was neither too severe nor "grossly disproportionate to the crime."

However, noting that the Court had "reserved the question of the constitutionality of the death penalty when imposed for other crimes," White turned to the case at hand and wrote: "We have concluded that a sentence of death is grossly disproportionate and excessive punishment for the crime of rape and is therefore forbidden by the Eighth Amendment as cruel and unusual punishment."

He elaborated that while the crime of rape was serious, reprehensible in a moral sense, and showing "almost total contempt for the personal integrity and autonomy of the female victim," still "it does not compare with murder, which does involve the unjustified taking of human life."

He continued, "Although it may be accompanied by another crime, rape by definition does not include the death of or even the serious injury to another person . . . Life is over for the victim of the murderer; for the rape victim, life may not be nearly so happy as it was, it is not over and normally is not beyond repair." Therefore, "the death penalty . . . is excessive for the rapist who, as such, does not take human life."

Justices Brennan and Marshall, in separate concurring opinions, concluded that the death penalty was cruel and unusual punishment prohibited in all cases. Justice Powell agreed that the death penalty was a disproportionate punishment in Coker's case, since the victim did not suffer a serious nor lasting injury. He dissented, however, from the view that a death penalty would be unconstitutional in "the case of an outrageous rape resulting in serious, lasting harm for the victim," a question he said he "would not prejudge."

Nothing Left to Lose

Justice Burger, joined by Justice Rehnquist, filed a scathing dissenting opinion. Burger outlined Coker's criminal history, noting that he had raped and stabbed to death one young woman; kidnapped, raped, and beat nearly to death another young woman; and, after his escape from prison, raped, threatened with death, and kidnapped the woman from Waycross, Georgia. The ruling that Coker could not be executed, Burger wrote, "prevents the State from imposing any effective punishment upon Coker for his latest rape . . . [and] bars Georgia from guaranteeing its citizens that they will

suffer no further attacks by this habitual rapist." Burger agreed that he "accept[ed] that the Eighth Amendment's concept of disproportionality bars the death penalty for minor crimes. But rape is not a minor crime . . ." Rather, he wrote later in the opinion:

> A rapist not only violates a victim's privacy and personal integrity, but inevitably causes serious psychological as well as physical harm in the process. The long-range effect upon the victim's life and health is likely to be irreparable . . . it is destructive of the human personality . . . To speak blandly, as the plurality does, of rape victims who are "unharmed" or to classify the human outrage of rape, as does Mr. Justice Powell, in terms of "excessively brutal," versus "moderately brutal," takes too little account of the profound suffering the crime imposes upon the victims and their loved ones.

Burger concluded that "if murder is properly punishable by death, rape should be also, if that is the considered judgment of the legislators."

Ginsburg Revisits Her Brief

Sixteen years later, during the confirmation hearings upon her appointment to the Supreme Court, Ruth Bader Ginsburg discussed her *amicus curiae* brief in the case and her continued support for the decision reached in *Coker v. Georgia*. The death penalty for rape, she said:

> Where there was no death or serious permanent injury apart from the obvious psychological injury—that . . . was disproportionate for this reason: The death penalty for rape historically was part of a view of woman as belonging to the man, as first her father's possession. If she were raped before marriage, she was damaged goods . . . And if she were a married woman and she were raped, again, she would be regarded as damaged goods.

> We've seen . . . in many places in the world, where women in Bangladesh, for example, were discarded, were treated as worthless because they had been raped. And that was what Coker against Georgia came out of, and that's the whole thrust of [my] brief, that this was made punishable by death because man's property had been taken from him because of the rape of the woman . . .

Pressed by Senator Charles E. Grassley (R-Iowa), who was questioning her, to concede that her brief reflected a view that the death penalty itself was unconstitutional, Ginsburg shot back:

> . . . I urge you to read the entire . . . brief. I think you will find it to be exactly what I represented it to be. One of the reasons why rapes

went unpunished, why women who had been raped suffered the indignity of having the police refuse to prosecute, was statutes of that order.

According to Linda Fairstein, director of the Sex Crimes Unit in the Manhattan district attorney's office, the conviction rate in rape cases has greatly increased during the 1980s and 1990s. In addition to the elimination of the death penalty for rape, other measures passed in the 1970s have helped to make this possible. These include the elimination of requirements that a rape be witnessed and its victim use earnest resistance, as well as the passage of rape shield laws which prohibit testimony about a victim's prior sexual history.

Related Cases
Robinson v. California, 370 U.S. 660 (1962).
Furman v. Georgia, 408 U.S. 238 (1972).
Gregg v. Georgia, 428 U.S. 153 (1976).

Bibliography and Further Reading

Brownmiller, Susan. *Against Our Will: Men, Women, and Rape.* New York: Simon & Schuster, 1973.

"Excerpts From Senate Hearings on Ginsburg's Supreme Court Nomination." *New York Times,* July 23, 1993.

Fairstein, Linda A. *Sexual Violence: Our War Against Rape.* New York: William Morrow and Company, 1993.

Goldstein, Leslie Friedman. *The Constitutional Rights of Women,* rev. ed. Madison: The University of Wisconsin Press, 1989.

LOCKETT V. OHIO

Legal Citation: 438 U.S. 586 (1978)

Petitioner
Sandra Lockett

Respondent
State of Ohio

Petitioner's Claim
That the Ohio death penalty statute—which limited the number of mitigating factors that a judge passing sentence could take into account—was unconstitutional.

Chief Lawyer for Petitioner
Anthony G. Amsterdam

Chief Lawyer for Respondent
Carl M. Layman III

Justices for the Court
Harry A. Blackmun, Warren E. Burger (writing for the Court), Thurgood Marshall, Lewis F. Powell, Jr., John Paul Stevens, Potter Stewart

Justices Dissenting
William H. Rehnquist, Byron R. White (William J. Brennan, Jr. did not participate)

Place
Washington, D.C.

Date of Decision
3 July 1978

Decision
That the death penalty is so severe, it requires greater reliability than other penalties, and so statutes that limit the mitigating factors that a sentencer may take into account are indeed violations of the Eighth Amendment and the Fourteenth Amendment.

Significance
Because of this case, many states, including Ohio, rewrote their death penalty statutes to allow sentencers to take mitigating factors into account. Subsequently, several death penalty cases were reversed and some death row inmates received sentences other than the death penalty.

Sandra Lockett was a 21-year-old woman visiting New Jersey when she met Al Parker and Nathan Earl Dew. Lockett, her friend Joanne Baxter, and her brother accompanied Parker and Dew back to Lockett's hometown of Akron, Ohio. Parker and Dew realized, after they had arrived, that they had no money for their trip back to New Jersey. Lockett suggested obtaining money by robbing a grocery store and a furniture store, using a gun from her father's basement. By the time the plan was made, however, the stores had closed and it was too late to rob them.

The group next came up with a plan to rob a pawnshop. Parker, Dew, and Lockett's brother loaded the gun with bullets they had brought in themselves, and used the gun to rob the shop. Lockett was supposed to wait in the car with the engine running while the others were in the shop. But when Parker used the gun for the stickup, the pawnbroker grabbed for it. The gun went off with Parker's finger on the trigger, killing the pawnbroker.

Lockett was waiting with the car when the others came out. When she heard what had happened, she put the gun in her purse. Later she stored it under the seat of a taxicab that she and Parker were taking to escape. When the police stopped them, Lockett told them that Parker rented a room from her mother and lived with her family, and, after checking with her family, the police let them go. Lockett hid Dew and Parker in her attic when the police showed up at her family's house later that night.

Did She Deserve to Die?

This was the extent of the state's murder case against Sandra Lockett. Under an Ohio law, however:

> [One who] purposely aids, helps, associates himself or herself with another for the purpose of committing a crime is regarded as if he or she were the principal offender and is just as guilty as if the person performed every act constituting the offense . . .

Ironically, Parker, who had actually had his hand on the gun, had made a deal with the state. In exchange for a plea that eliminated the possibility of him receiv-

Mitigating Circumstances

Mitigating circumstances, or mitigating factors, are facts which, though they do not exonerate the defendant, may serve to reduce the charge or the punishment. In civil actions, for instance, the defense will often ask the jury to consider mitigating circumstances in order to reduce the damages or the extent of the defendant's liability. Thus the legal counsel for a corporation accused of racist hiring practices may seek to show such mitigating factors as the company's heavy investment in inner-city community development programs.

As for mitigating circumstances in criminal law, these are most often brought to bear in cases where the death penalty is among the forms of punishment available. Mitigating circumstances could include mental illness, the youth of the defendant, economic hardship, and childhood abuse. Though the use of mitigating circumstances often generates little sympathy among the population as a whole, to whom the idea of justifying heinous crimes on the basis of past abuse has become something of a running joke, the Supreme Court has ruled that juries must consider mitigating circumstances in death-penalty cases. The Court has used as its basis the Eighth Amendment prohibition against cruel and unusual punishment, and the Fourteenth Amendment's extension of due process to the states.

Source(s): *West's Encyclopedia of American Law.* St. Paul, MN: West Group, 1998.

---

ing the death penalty, he would testify against Lockett, her brother, and Dew. Lockett, on the other hand, who had done nothing more than help devise a plan for robbery—not murder—and drive a getaway car, was found guilty of aggravated murder. Under Ohio state law, there were only three mitigating circumstances that might allow the sentencer to avoid imposing the death penalty:

(1) If the victim had "induced or facilitated the offense";

(2) If the murderer was "under duress, coercion, or strong provocation";

(3) If the murder was "primarily the product of [the murderer's] psychosis or mental deficiency."

The psychiatric and psychological reports on Lockett showed that she was an excellent candidate for rehabilitation. Although she was of average or below-average intelligence, she had committed no major offenses (though she had a record of several minor ones), and she was "on the road to success" in curing her addiction to heroin. Yet these very factors meant that she was not eligible for consideration to avoid the death penalty. Clearly, she was not psychotic or mentally deficient.

Deciding Who Shall Die

In considering *Lockett v. Ohio,* the Court kept in mind a previous landmark death penalty case, *Furman v. Georgia* (1972). In that case, the Court expressed its dismay at the inconsistency of death penalty sentencing, pointing out that without clear statutory guidelines as to when the death penalty should be administered, courts were prone to discriminate against minority defendants.

As a result, many states enacted mandatory death penalty statutes, laying out the types of cases in which judges were legally required to offer the death penalty. Other states, including Ohio, enacted statutes that listed the factors that a judge might consider in deciding whether or not to offer the death penalty. Indeed, the Ohio state legislature had been in the process of writing a new death penalty statute when *Furman* came down, and legislators revised their new law to conform to the new decision.

Now the Court was viewing another situation with dismay: restrictive laws that kept judges from taking all mitigating circumstances into account when they administered the severest penalty of all. The Court had already struck down several mandatory death penalty statutes. In *Lockett,* it would go one step further: it would require that judges who were administering the death penalty should hear evidence on any mitigating circumstance that the defense wished to present.

The Mitigating Factors

The Court's reasoning was based on three arguments:

(1) The Eighth and Fourteenth Amendments require that "in all but the rarest kind of capital [death penalty] case," the sentence be able to take into account the defendant's character and record, as well as any circumstances surrounding the offense that the defendant offers.

(2) After a person has been sentenced to prison, he or she might be offered probation, parole, or work furlough. Thus, even if the sentence were given without regard to the person's individuality, some mechanisms are available to tailor the sentence more exactly to fit the unique circumstances surrounding the person and

Knapp Brothers Murder Trials

In 1830, brothers John Francis Knapp and Joseph Jenkins Knapp conspired to have their wealthy uncle, Captain Joseph White, murdered. They hired Richard Crowninshield to carry out the deed. On the night of 6 April 1830, Crowninshield slew Captain White in his sleep, while the brothers waited outside on the street, 300-feet away.

The case was significant because it was the first time that accessories to murder had been tried, convicted, and executed. The eloquence of prosecutor Daniel Webster in defeating an old English common law that an accessory to murder could not be convicted without being present at the time of the murder brought the Knapp brothers to justice. Webster in his prosecution redefined the legality of being present during the murder by raising the issue ". . . to constitute a presence, it is sufficient if the accomplice is in a place, either where he may render aid to the perpetrator of the felony, or where the perpetrator supposes he may render aid. If they selected the place to afford assistance, whether it was well or ill chosen for that purpose is immaterial. The perpetrator would derive courage and confidence from the knowledge that his associate was in the place appointed."

Source(s): Knappman, Edward W. *Great American Trials*. Detroit, MI: Visible Ink Press, 1994.

the crime. In the case of the death penalty, however, these "post-conviction mechanisms" are not available. All the more reason, then, that "each defendant in a capital case [be treated] with the degree of respect due the uniqueness of the individual."

(3) A statute that restricts the sentencer from taking into account the defendant's character and record, as well as the circumstances surrounding the offense, "creates the risk that the death penalty will be imposed in spite of factors that may call for a less severe penalty, and when the choice is between life and death, such risk is unacceptable and incompatible with the commands of the Eighth and Fourteenth Amendments."

The Evidence a Defendant Can Present

The Court said that its *Lockett* decision simply recognized the principle that punishment should be individual, fitting both the crime and the person who committed the crime as exactly as possible. But, in fact, *Lockett* considerably broadened that principle. Before *Lockett,* the state got to decide what evidence was relevant to the death penalty sentence. Ohio's statute, for example, listed the three factors that the state had decided were relevant. What *Lockett* said was that the defendant, rather than the state, got to decide what evidence to present to the sentencing judge—and that the defendant's right to make this decision was guaranteed by the Constitution.

The decades since *Lockett* have seen increasing hostility toward people convicted of crimes. The trend has been to call for ever-harsher penalties, often mandatory penalties, and to impose the death penalty more and more often. Yet because of *Lockett,* at least six death penalty cases have been overturned by the Supreme Court, and potentially many more death penalty sentences were not offered in the first place. Ohio itself rewrote its death penalty statute, raising the number of mitigating factors to be taken into account from three to seven, and including as the seventh a "catch-all" provision that reads, "Any other factors that are relevant to the issue of whether the offender should be sentenced to death."

In a climate of increasing support for the death penalty, the doctrine of *Lockett* continues to endure. It reminds sentences and legislators alike that under the U.S. Constitution, even a convicted criminal has the right to "respect [for] the uniqueness of the individual."

Related Cases

United States v. Jackson, 390 U.S. 570 (1968).
Witherspoon v. Illinois, 391 U.S. 510 (1968).
Furman v. Georgia, 408 U.S. 238 (1972).
Smith v. North Carolina, 459 U.S. 1056 (1982).
Jones v. Illinois, 464 U.S. 920 (1983).
Straight v. Wainwright, 476 U.S. 1132 (1986).
Darden v. Wainwright, 477 U.S. 168 (1986).

Bibliography and Further Reading

Bilionis, Louis D. "Moral Appropriateness, Capital Punishment, and the Lockett Doctrine." *Journal of Criminal Law and Criminology,* Vol. 82, no. 2, summer 1991, pp. 283-333.

Domozick, Daniel D. "Fact or Fiction: Mitigating the Death Penalty in Ohio." *Cleveland State Law Review,* Vol. 32, no. 2, spring 1983, pp. 263-293.

Fein, Bruce E. *Significant Decisions of the Supreme Court, 1976-1977 Term.* Washington, DC: American Enterprise Institute for Public Policy Research, 1978.

Gillers, Stephen. "Deciding Who Dies." *University of Pennsylvania Law Review,* Vol. 129, no. 1, November 1980, pp. 1-124.

Herz, Randy, and Robert Weisberg. "In Mitigation of the Penalty of Death: *Lockett v. Ohio* and the Capital Defendant's Right to Consideration of Mitigating Cir-cumstances." *California Law Review,* Vol. 69, no. 2, March 1981, pp. 317-376.

Sundby, Scott E. "The Lockett Paradox: Reconciling Guided Discretion and Unguided Mitigation in Capital Sentencing." *UCLA Law Review,* Vol. 38, no. 5, June 1991, pp. 1147-1208.

BELL V. OHIO

Legal Citation: 438 U.S. 637 (1978)

Petitioner
Willie Lee Bell

Respondent
State of Ohio

Petitioner's Claim
That his conviction of aggravated murder, which resulted in a death sentence under the Ohio death penalty statute, violated his rights under the Eighth and Fourteenth Amendments to the Constitution by preventing the sentencing judge from taking into account mitigating factors with regard to his character and intelligence.

Chief Lawyer for Petitioner
H. Fred Hoefle

Chief Lawyer for Respondent
Leonard Kirschner

Justices for the Court
Harry A. Blackmun, Warren E. Burger (writing for the Court), Thurgood Marshall, Lewis F. Powell, Jr., John Paul Stevens, Potter Stewart, Byron R. White

Justices Dissenting
William H. Rehnquist (William J. Brennan, Jr., did not participate)

Place
Washington, D.C.

Date of Decision
3 July 1978

Decision
That the Ohio death penalty statute does not allow for consideration of all possible mitigating factors in sentencing a defendant, as provided in the Eighth and Fourteenth Amendments to the Constitution; therefore the Court ruled in favor of the appellant.

Significance
Though not as well-known as *Furman v. Georgia* (1972) and other cases related to capital punishment procedure, *Bell v. Ohio* concerned itself with two of the fundamental issues explored in most of the landmark death penalty-related cases: the examination of mitigating factors in sentencing, and the question of whether the death penalty itself constitutes cruel and unusual punishment.

On 16 October 1974, Willie Lee Bell, a 16-year-old, met his 18-year-old friend Samuel Hall at a youth center in Cincinnati, Ohio. After going to Hall's home, Hall borrowed a car, and the two drove around for some time. They pursued a car driven by Julius Graber, 64, and forced him into a parking garage. Using a sawed-off shotgun, Hall forced Graber to give up his car keys, then ordered him to get into the trunk. Hall drove Graber's car, and Bell followed in Hall's car, back to Hall's house; then the two drove Graber's car, with Bell at the wheel and Graber still in the trunk, to a cemetery.

A nearby resident would later testify that he saw Graber's car on the cemetery's service road with its parking lights on. There were sounds of two car doors closing, and a voice screaming, "Don't shoot me! Don't shoot me!" This was followed by two shots. After seeing Graber's car pull away, now with its lights off, the witness called the police. The latter found Graber lying facedown with a wound on the back of his neck, and another on his right cheek. By the time the ambulance arrived at the hospital, he was dead.

Meanwhile, Bell and Hall spent the night with friends of Hall in Dayton, Ohio. The next day, with Bell again at the wheel of Graber's car, they pulled up at a service station, where Hall used the shotgun to force the station attendant to get into his own car's trunk. Now in an apparent repeat of the previous day's escapade, Hall drove away in the attendant's car, with the latter in the trunk, while Bell followed in Graber's car. But this time, a policeman stopped Hall for a defective muffler—and in the course of this, discovered the car's owner in the trunk.

Bell was not caught immediately, having driven on past when the patrolman stopped Hall, but he was apprehended soon after he returned to Cincinnati and abandoned Graber's car. He waived both his right to testify and his right to a jury trial, opting instead for trial by a three-judge panel. In lieu of testimony from the defendant, Bell's counsel presented the court with a statement made by the defendant at the time of his arrest. In it, Bell said that although he had gone to the cemetery with Hall, he had no intention of participating in a murder. Instead, he claimed, he asked Hall what they were going to do to, and was told, "We'll see. Give me the keys." According to Bell's statement, Hall marched Graber into the woods and shot him out of Bell's sight. (Perhaps not surprisingly, Hall claimed that Bell had shot Graber.)

Ohio Sentences Bell to the Death Penalty

The judges were unanimous in finding Bell guilty of aggravated murder, which occurred in the course of a kidnapping—an offense punishable by death under Ohio law. The law required that, before sentencing, the court should order a psychiatric evaluation of the defendant. The investigation of his mental state found him to be of "low . . . intellectual capability." The report noted that he had appeared in juvenile court several times, and stated that he claimed to have been using the drug mescaline on the night of the crime.

In this, the penalty phase, the panel of judges allowed both sides to speak, and now Bell testified. He said that he had been on drugs nearly every day for the three years leading up to the crime, and had been intimidated by Hall to the extent that he was highly suggestible. Hall had been like an "older brother," he said, and he was "scared" not to do what Hall told him to do. Following Bell's testimony, several of his teachers testified to his problems with drugs, his emotional instability, and his mental deficiencies. Bell's lawyer further argued that Bell was a minor, which in itself constituted a type of mental deficiency in that he did not have full understanding of the choices he was making.

The defense contended that not only Bell's youth, but his cooperation with the police and the lack of proof that he had actually participated in the killing, were all mitigating factors that presented a strong case for a penalty less than death. Furthermore, the defense moved that Ohio's death penalty law, which the state had formed in the wake of the Supreme Court case of *Furman v. Georgia*, should be declared unconstitutional. The Ohio statute, it was stated, was in violation of two constitutional amendments: the Eighth, which forbids cruel and unusual punishment, and the Fourteenth, which guarantees a citizen's right to the due process of law. According to the defense, the Ohio statute did not allow for the mitigating factors of Bell's age, his coop-

eration, and the lack of proof to be used as a basis for receiving a lesser sentence.

The judges, having concluded that none of the mitigating factors as defined by Ohio law were present, sentenced Bell to death. Bell's counsel immediately appealed the case and took it to the state supreme court, which ruled that there was sufficient evidence to establish that Bell had aided and abetted Hall—which meant, under Ohio law, that Bell could be prosecuted and punished as though he were the one who had actually pulled the trigger.

The High Court Strikes Down Ohio's Law

In reviewing the case of *Bell v. Ohio*, the Court ruled 7-1 in favor of Bell. In an opinion joined by Stewart, Powell, and Stevens, Chief Justice Burger made two points. First, he said, the two Amendments referred to in Bell's case do indeed require that the sentencing judge not be prevented from considering any and all possible mitigating factors relating to the defendant or the circumstances of the offense. And second, the Ohio death penalty statute precludes such individualized consideration of mitigating factors.

Justices White and Blackmun concurred with the judgment, but for different reasons, both finding causes why the death sentence was invalid in this instance. Marshall, while also concurring with the judgment, announced that he believed the death penalty to be cruel and unusual punishment under all circumstances, and therefore disagreed with "the Court's assumption to the contrary." The lone dissenter was Justice Rehnquist, who ruled, as he had earlier that year in the case of *Lockett v. Ohio*, that federal law can only require that states give defendants fair trials—not that they hear all possible mitigating testimony.

Related Cases

Furman v. Georgia, 408 U.S. 238 (1972).
Lockett v. Ohio, 438 U.S. 586 (1978).

Bibliography and Further Reading

Biskupic, Joan, and Elder Witt, eds. *Congressional Quarterly's Guide to the U.S. Supreme Court*, 3rd ed. Washington, DC: Congressional Quarterly, Inc., 1996.

ENMUND V. FLORIDA

Legal Citation: 458 U.S. 782 (1982)

Petitioner
Earl Enmund

Respondent
State of Florida

Petitioner's Claim
That his death sentence constituted cruel and unusual punishment in violation of the Eighth and Fourteenth Amendments for aiding a felony that ended up a murder, even though he did not participate in the murder or intend for it to happen.

Chief Lawyer for Petitioner
James S. Liebman

Chief Lawyer for Respondent
Lawrence A. Kaden

Justices for the Court
Harry A. Blackmun, William J. Brennan, Jr., Thurgood Marshall, John Paul Stevens, Byron R. White (writing for the Court)

Justices Dissenting
Warren E. Burger, Sandra Day O'Connor, Lewis F. Powell, Jr., William H. Rehnquist

Place
Washington, D.C.

Date of Decision
2 July 1982

Decision
The Supreme Court held that Enmund's sentence violated his Eighth and Fourteenth Amendment rights to fair punishment proportionate to his role in the crime. The Court found that Enmund's deed warranted a serious punishment, but not capital punishment, as the state of Florida argued.

Significance
The Supreme Court's decision in this case stands out as one of the more liberal opinions of the Court for cases involving the death sentence of a person who did not actually attempt or intend to kill the victim. Because the state conceded that it could not prove that Enmund attempted or intended to kill the victim, the Court reversed the lower courts' rulings. However, the Supreme Court ruled differently in later cases, indicating that the Court has grown less lenient over the years.

The Facts of the Crime

The state of Florida charged Earl Enmund, the petitioner, with first-degree murder and robbery perpetrated against two elderly people. The Florida Supreme Court upheld this decision, although it recognized that the court could only infer that Enmund drove the car that helped the killers, Sampson and Jeanette Armstrong, escape. Under Florida law, the state could prosecute Enmund as a constructive accomplice because he drove the getaway car, considering him equally responsible for the homicides.

Based on witness testimony, the court deduced that Enmund had driven the Armstrongs to and from the scene of the crime, although no direct evidence existed. According to the court's theory, Enmund waited in the car while the Armstrongs pretended to need water to stop his car from overheating. Sampson Armstrong then pulled a gun on one of the residents, Thomas Kersey. Kersey called his wife for help, who came out with a gun and shot Jeanette Armstrong, wounding her. After that, Sampson Armstrong killed and robbed the Kerseys. Then the Armstrongs fled in the car driven by Enmund.

The Legal Process

The court charged Enmund with and convicted him of two counts of first-degree murder and one count of robbery. Because Enmund received the death penalty, he appealed his sentence to the Florida Supreme Court, which upheld the lower court's decision. The Florida Supreme Court argued that because Enmund was an accomplice in an armed robbery when the murders took place and because Enmund was previously convicted of a felony involving at least the threat of violence, the death sentence suited the crime.

On 23 March 1983, the U.S. Supreme Court began hearing the case and considering whether states could apply the death penalty without violating the Eighth and Fourteenth Amendments to felons "who neither took life, attempted to take life, nor intended to take life." In the 5-4 decision, the Supreme Court majority contended that the Eighth Amendment ban on cruel and unusual punishment did not allow a capital pun-

Accessory to Murder

Under the system of law passed down to Americans via the English common-law system, guilt is personal and individual, rather than collective. This is the essence of the liberal Western tradition. By contrast, in a country such as China, family members are routinely held responsible for the crimes of a relative.

The only way an American citizen can be held guilty for another person's crime is if it can be proven that they aided or abetted the crime. They may either be an accessory before the fact, if they encouraged, ordered, aided, or advised the commission of a crime; or an accessory after the fact, if they gave aid to someone who they knew was a felon by assisting him in eluding capture or by destroying evidence.

These common-law classifications, which are coupled with principals in the first degree (those who actually commit the crime) and principals in the second degree (those who assist in the commission of the crime) are subject to some variation. For instance, in the case of Charles Manson, whose disciples murdered seven adults in Los Angeles over the course of two nights in August of 1969, Manson was clearly more than an accomplice before the fact, even though he was not actually present at the scene of the murders.

Source(s): Kadish, Sanford H., ed. *Encyclopedia of Crime and Justice.* New York: Free Press, 1983.

ishment sentence in this case, because of previous Supreme Court decisions such as *Weems v. United States* (1910) where a man was sentenced to 15 years of hard labor for falsifying a public document and *Coker v. Georgia* (1977) where a man received the death penalty for raping a woman. With these Supreme Court decisions in the background, the majority also compared the sentences of other jurisdictions with Enmund's sentence and found that of the 36 jurisdictions only 8 permit the death penalty in similar cases. Furthermore, the Court considered jury verdicts for death sentences and the death row population and noticed that accomplices who did not participate in the murder accounted for only a small minority, demonstrating that the general population rejects the use of the death penalty for an accomplice such as Enmund, who do not plan or attempt to kill.

Given this foundation, the Court found that although Enmund's robbery conviction was indeed a serious offense that warranted a stiff penalty, it was not so atrocious that it warranted capital punishment. While the Court admitted that the death penalty can apply to robbers who commit murder in the process of robbing without violating the Constitution, it maintained that in order for it to apply to Enmund's case and ones like it, courts must demonstrate that Enmund's behavior directly led to the murder, thus making him responsible. By studying statistics of robberies in the United States, the Court concluded that murders occur in conjunction with robberies only less than one percent of the time and so it showed that as a robber alone Enmund should not have anticipated murder as a possible outcome. Therefore, the Supreme Court majority reversed the state supreme court's ruling, finding the death penalty in this case a violation of the Eighth and Fourteenth Amendments.

Degree of Responsibility

However, the dissenting justices believed that the majority's decision interfered with the state criteria for determining guilt, relying too much on intent. They also point out that 23 states allow courts to impose capital punishment even when the accused neither kills or intends to kill the victim. Consequently, they reached a different conclusion than the majority. Contrary to the claim that society largely disapproves of the death penalty for cases such as Enmund's, they found that two-thirds of the states that have the death penalty embrace it as an acceptable and appropriate punishment for accessories to felonies that result in murder.

Furthermore, the dissenting justices argued that the Eighth Amendment calls not only for a ban on cruel and unusual punishment, but also for a sentence proportionate to the harm and damage caused by degree of responsibility of the accused. Since Enmund set the crime in motion by planning it and driving the Armstrongs to the Kersey home, he must accept a greater share of the guilt than he or the Supreme Court majority admitted, according to the dissenting justices.

Implications of Decision

Although the Supreme Court majority decided to overturn the lower courts' rulings, its decision did not constitute the final say in the execution of accomplice felons who did not attempt or intend to kill the victim in crimes that resulted in murder. The Court never overruled this decision, but it reached more stringent decisions for similar cases afterwards, reducing the role intent plays. For example, in 1995 the Court denied a man a stay of execution, even though the state admitted that he did not participate in the killing of the victim, whom he helped kidnap in *Jacobs v. Scott.*

The question before us is not the proportionality of death as a penalty for murder, but rather the validity of capital punishment for Enmund's own conduct. The focus must be on his accountability, not on those who committed the robbery and shot the victims, for we insist on 'individualized consideration as a constitutional requirement in imposing the death sentence.'

Related Cases

Weems v. United States, 217 U.S. 349 (1910).
Coker v. Georgia, 433 U.S. 584 (1977).
Cabana v. Bullock, 474 U.S. 376 (1986).

Tison v. Arizona, 481 U.S. 137 (1987).
Gregg v. Georgia, 428 U.S. 153 (1987).
Jacobs v. Scott, 513 U.S. 1067 (1995).

Bibliography and Further Reading

Biskupic, Joan, and Elder Witt, eds. *Congressional Quarterly's Guide to the U.S. Supreme Court,* 3rd ed. Washington, DC: Congressional Quarterly, Inc., 1996.

Camper, Diane. "The Court's Hectic Finale." *Newsweek,* July 12, 1982.

Greenhouse, Linda. "Court Upholds Execute Order Appeal Denied Despite Recant." *Times-Picayune,* January 3, 1995.

PULLEY V. HARRIS

Legal Citation: 465 U.S. 37 (1984)

Petitioner
R. Pulley, Warden

Respondent
Robert Alton Harris

Petitioner's Claim
The failure of the state to provide for a judicial review of the proportionality of his death sentence was unconstitutional and required reversal of the sentence.

Chief Lawyer for Petitioner
Michael D. Wellington

Chief Lawyer for Respondent
Anthony G. Amsterdam

Justices for the Court
Harry A. Blackmun, Warren E. Burger, Sandra Day O'Connor, Lewis F. Powell, Jr., William H. Rehnquist, John Paul Stevens, Byron R. White (writing for the Court)

Justices Dissenting
William J. Brennan, Jr., Thurgood Marshall

Place
Washington, D.C.

Date of Decision
23 January 1984

Decision
The Constitution does not require that a court review a sentence of death to confirm that it has been imposed in similar cases.

Significance
The *Harris* decision described a minimum procedural threshold for statutory death penalty schemes.

The 14-year-long case against Robert Alton Harris began in 1978, when Harris asked his brother, Daniel, to help him rob a bank. In July, the two brothers began to buy materials for the robbery, including pistols, rifles, ammunition, and face masks. After practicing shooting while running and rolling in a rural area near Mira Mesa, California, Harris and his brother staked out the San Diego Trust and Savings Bank on Mira Mesa Boulevard on 4 July 1978. The next morning they decided to steal a car to use for a getaway in the robbery. Spotting 15-year-old John Mayeski and 16-year-old Michael Baker in a car eating hamburgers near the bank, Harris approached the car, hopped into the back seat, pulled out his pistol, and ordered the boys to drive to a rural area.

Although Harris had assured his brother that no one was "going to get hurt," Harris eventually shot Mayeski in the back, fired four shots at the shrieking Baker, and then returned to Mayeski for a pistol shot to the head and, finally, a blast from the shotgun. After killing the boys, Harris ate the boys' hamburgers and then chided his brother Daniel for being too weak to join him. Harris laughed about the murders and, when Daniel remarked that the pistol was covered with fragments of flesh, Harris chuckled, saying as he flicked pieces of Mayeski's brain onto the street that he had "really blown [Mayeski's] brains out." Later that day, Harris and his brother robbed the bank of Mira Mesa Boulevard, but they were quickly apprehended when a witness to the robbery followed them from the bank to Harris' house and then called the police.

Daniel confessed to the police less than three hours after the arrests. Robert Harris confessed shortly thereafter on four different occasions to three different law enforcement officials and one psychiatrist. Both men were charged in a California state court with the murders, but prosecutors offered Daniel a lesser charge of kidnapping in exchange for a plea of guilty to that charge and his testimony against his brother. At his trial for first-degree murder, Robert Harris testified that his confessions were lies, and that he had lied to save his brother, who was the real killer. Harris had done the same thing in 1975, when he was accused and convicted of killing a neighbor; after confessing, Harris attempted to pin the blame on another of his brothers Ken. Harris was convicted of voluntary man-slaughter in the 1975 case. For the 1978 slayings of Mayeski and Baker, Harris was convicted of first-degree murder. Harris admitted to the murders at the penalty phase of his trial and explained to the jury that he had suffered a difficult childhood, but the jury sentenced him to death.

The Supreme Court of California affirmed the conviction and the sentence, and the U.S. Supreme Court denied *certiorari*. Harris filed a *habeas corpus* petition against his prison's warden in state court, but the petition was denied, and the U.S. Supreme Court again denied *certiorari*. Harris then filed a petition for *habeas corpus* in federal district court; the district court denied the writ and refused to stay Harris' execution, but the Court of Appeals for the Ninth Circuit reversed the decision. The appeals court held that, under the Eighth Amendment's prohibition of cruel and unusual punishment, Harris was entitled to a judicial determination of whether Harris' sentence was proportionate to sentences imposed for similar crimes. The appeals court ordered the district court to issue a writ revoking the sentence unless the Supreme Court of California conducted a proportionality review with 120 days. The state of California appealed this ruling to the U.S. Supreme Court through Harris' prison warden, and the High Court, by a vote of 7-2, reversed the decision.

Writing for the majority, Justice White defined proportionality in the context of sentencing as "an abstract evaluation of the appropriateness of a sentence for a particular crime." The Court acknowledged that the lack of proportion in a particular sentence could violate the Eighth Amendment's prohibition of cruel and unusual punishment. The High Court had held, in the past, that the severity of a sentence could be inherently disproportionate to the seriousness of the crime. However, the Court had never engaged in the kind of proportional analysis offered by Harris and accepted by the appeals court. Specifically, Harris was claiming that he was entitled to a judicial review to determine that the death sentence was proportionate compared to the sentences meted out in cases with similar facts.

Harris argued, in part, that the Court's ruling in *Furman v. Georgia* (1972) supported a constitutional right to the so-called "comparative review." In *Furman*, the Court held that the death penalty was unconstitutional under the Eighth Amendment, effectively outlawing the death penalty. The Court ruled the same way in two companion cases, *Proffitt v. Florida* (1976) and *Jurek v. Texas* (1976). The Court ruled in *Gregg v. Georgia* (1976) that certain states had cured the infirmities in their death penalty sentencing schemes, effectively reinstating the death penalty. Still, the *Gregg* Court had not departed from the reasoning employed by the Court in *Furman,* so the *Furman* case remained good law, and the Court was forced to meet Harris' argument.

The *Furman* Court, without a clear majority, essentially had held that the death penalty, at the time, "was being imposed so discriminatorily, so wantonly and freakishly, and so infrequently, that any given death sentence was cruel and unusual." After the *Furman* decision, states changed their capital sentencing statutes to limit the jury's discretion to impose the penalty and to "avoid arbitrary and inconsistent results." States gave to capital defendants the right of automatic appeal of a death sentence to a court with statewide jurisdiction, and they also created a second proceeding, called the sentencing phase, that took place after a guilty verdict in a capital case. The sentencing proceeding allowed the introduction of evidence and testimony and was designed to ensure that the sentencing authority (the judge or jury) had sufficient information and guidance to make a fair decision on the sentence.

Most states did require the reviewing court to determine whether the sentence was proportionate to that imposed in similar crimes, but some states did not require such a comparative proportionality review. According to Justice White and the majority, the Court in *Gregg, Proffitt,* and *Jurek* did not think that such a proportionality review was necessary. Just because some states required a sentence proportionality review in death penalty cases, that did not "mean that such review [was] indispensable." The most important factors that had resolved the constitutional infirmities in the statutory death penalty schemes were the provisions for stricter guidance of the sentencing authority and the availability of appellate review. Comparative proportionality review was not, declared the Court, a factor in the 1976 cases. In 1983, the Court in *Zant v. Stephens* had upheld a death sentence based in part on the fact that the defendant had a right to comparative proportionality review. However, the right to comparative proportionality review was merely "an additional safeguard against arbitrarily imposed death sentences" and was not "constitutionally required."

The majority analyzed California's capital sentencing scheme and found it constitutionally sound. Although California did not provide for comparative proportionality review, it did provide "checks on arbitrariness" by requiring the sentencing authority to conduct a detailed process in deciding whether to impose the death penalty. The Court concluded that it could not "say that the California procedures provided Harris inadequate protection against the evil identified in *Furman*." By reversing the appeals court's decision, the Supreme Court placed Harris back on death row.

Justice Stevens concurred in the judgment, but he agreed with only part of the majority's reasoning. To Stevens, the Court's own precedent indicated that "meaningful" appellate review was required in death penalty cases. Stevens was not convinced, though, that comparative proportionality was "the only method by which an appellate court can avoid the danger that the imposition of the death sentence in a particular case, or a particular class of cases, will be so extraordinary as to violate the Eighth Amendment."

Justice Brennan authored a long, passionate dissent in which Justice Marshall joined. In the estimation of Brennan and Marshall, the minimal procedures that the majority required in capital sentencing were not enough to prevent the arbitrary and capricious imposition of the death penalty. Brennan was concerned mainly about the possibility of racial discrimination in the application of the death penalty. Additional concerns for Brennan included the discriminatory imposition of the death penalty based on gender, socioeconomic status, and location within a state.

Brennan observed that most states required comparative proportionality review in capital case sentencing. This fact convinced Brennan that comparative review "serve[d] to eliminate some, if only a small part, of the irrationality that infect[ed] the . . . imposition of the death sentences throughout the various States." Thus, reasoned Brennan, such review should be required in capital case sentencing. Brennan discussed the teachings of various legal commentators on the topic of the death penalty and cited cases in which men were put to death on questionable grounds. Reviewing the proportionality of a death sentence by comparing it to the sentence imposed in cases with similar facts was "clearly no panacea," but "such review often serve[d] to identify the most extreme examples of disproportionality among similarly situated defendants." To the dissent, there was no reason not to require comparative proportionality review, especially when death sentences were being vacated in states that required it. Even if Brennan and Marshall did not believe that "the death penalty is in all circumstances cruel and unusual punishment," they "could not join in such unstudied decision making."

Harris continued to file *habeas corpus* petitions in an attempt to avert his sentence. His sentence was stayed four times. In April of 1992, the appeals court stayed his execution and ordered the district court to conduct a hearing to determine whether the use of cyanide gas to kill Harris might constitute cruel and unusual punishment. The U.S. Supreme Court vacated that decision too, and Robert Harris died in the gas chamber at San Quentin Prison in California on 21 April 1992.

Impact

Although most states require a court reviewing a death penalty sentence to determine that the sentence is proportional compared to similar crimes, such review is not required because of the holding in the *Harris* case. A later decision in Harris' case also stands for the proposition that use of gas chambers for executions does not violate the Eighth Amendment's prohibition of cruel and unusual punishment.

Related Cases
Furman v. Georgia, 408 U.S. 238 (1972).
Gregg v. Georgia, 428 U.S. 153 (1976).
Proffitt v. Florida, 428 U.S. 242 (1976).
Jurek v. Texas, 428 U.S. 262 (1976).
Zant v. Stephens, 462 U.S. 862 (1983).
Gomez v. California, 503 U.S. 653 (1992).

Bibliography and Further Reading
Caminker, Evan, and Erwin Chemerinsky. "The Lawless Execution of Robert Alton Harris." *Yale Law Journal*, October 1992.

Kaplan, John. "The Problem of Capital Punishment." *University of Illinois Law Review*, 1983.

"The Modern View of Capital Punishment." *American Criminal Law Review*, summer 1997.

FORD V. WAINWRIGHT

Legal Citation: 477 U.S. 399 (1986)

Appellant
Alvin Bernard Ford

Appellee
Louie L. Wainwright, Secretary, Florida Department of Corrections

Appellant's Claim
That because Alvin Ford had become insane awaiting execution on death row, according to the Eighth Amendment, it would be cruel and unusual punishment to execute him; and that the way that Ford's sanity had been determined under Florida state law was a violation of Ford's right to due process under the Fourteenth Amendment.

Chief Lawyer for Appellant
Joy B. Shearer, Assistant Attorney General of Florida

Chief Lawyer for Appellee
Richard H. Burr III

Justices for the Court
Harry A. Blackmun, William J. Brennan, Jr., Thurgood Marshall (writing for the Court), Lewis F. Powell, Jr., John Paul Stevens

Justices Dissenting
Warren E. Burger, Sandra Day O'Connor, William H. Rehnquist, Byron R. White

Place
Washington, D.C.

Date of Decision
26 June 1986

Decision
That executing a person who had become insane while awaiting execution was indeed a violation of the Eighth Amendment, and that Florida state statutes did not offer due process to determine prisoners' sanity.

Significance
This key decision established the constitutional right of prisoners not to be executed once it is determined that they are insane.

In 1974, Alvin Bernard Ford was found guilty of murder by a Florida state court. Under Florida's capital-punishment legislation, he was sentenced to death. At that time, he was presumably sane and competent to stand trial.

In early 1982, Ford was still awaiting execution—but now he was starting to show what was described as "gradual changes in behavior." First he became obsessed with the Ku Klux Klan. Then he began to think he was:

> . . . the target of a complex conspiracy, involving the Klan and assorted others, designed to force him to commit suicide. He believed that the prison guards, part of the conspiracy, had been killing people and putting the bodies in the concrete enclosures used for beds. Later, he began to believe that his women relatives were being tortured and sexually abused somewhere in the prison. This notion developed into a delusion that the people who were tormenting him at the prison had taken members of Ford's family hostage . . . By "day 287" of the "hostage crisis," the list of hostages had expanded to include "senators, Senator Kennedy, and many other leaders." . . . Ford . . . claim[ed] to have fired a number of prison officials. He began to refer to himself as "Pope John Paul III . . ."

Dr. Jamal Amin, who had previously examined Ford, concluded that Ford suffered from "a severe, uncontrollable mental disease which closely resembles 'Paranoid Schizophrenia with Suicide Potential.'" Amin based this conclusion on some 14 months of evaluation.

Amin's conclusions were supported by Dr. Harold Kaufman, who interviewed Ford in November of 1983 after Ford had refused see Dr. Amin, believing him to be part of the conspiracy. Dr. Kaufman found that there was "no reasonable possibility that Mr. Ford was dissembling, malingering, or otherwise putting on a performance." Indeed, the next month, Ford was virtually incomprehensible, making such statements as: "Hands one, face one. Mafia one. God one, father one, Pope one. Pope one. Leader one."

Manslaughter

Manslaughter is popularly—and erroneously—thought of as a form of murder. In terms of its ordinary definition, of course, manslaughter is indeed a type of killing, but legally it is not murder. For an act to qualify as manslaughter in legal terms, a killing may be intentional, but it cannot be premeditated or a product of malicious aforethought.

Thus manslaughter is to be distinguished from a situation in which a person causes death, but is not guilty of intent, negligence, or other wrongdoing. Examples of these situations would be self-defense, or pure accidents, as when a driver obeying all traffic laws hits and kills someone who runs in front of his car on a dark night. Killing in such circumstances is usually not prosecuted; manslaughter, by contrast, is clearly a crime.

Voluntary manslaughter occurs when someone intentionally (but without premeditation) kills another.

Involuntary manslaughter, by contrast, happens without intent, and is divided into two categories, criminal-negligence manslaughter and unlawful-act manslaughter. To use the situation of the driver referred to above, if he were asleep at the wheel when he killed the person running across the road, this would probably be criminal negligence; if, on the other hand, he were drunk, that would most likely qualify as unlawful-act manslaughter.

Source(s): *West's Encyclopedia of American Law.* St. Paul, MN: West Group, 1998.

Ruling on Insanity

Ford's lawyer tried to get the state of Florida to declare Ford insane. Following Florida state law, the governor appointed a panel of three psychiatrists, who met with Ford for about half an hour and then each filed their own reports. Although each doctor came up with a different diagnosis, all agreed that Ford was competent "to understand the nature and the effects of the death penalty and why it is to be imposed on him."

Ford's lawyer tried to submit other written materials to the governor, including the reports of Dr. Amin and Dr. Kaufman, but the governor would not accept the submission. On 30 April 1984, the governor signed a death warrant for Ford's execution.

Ford's lawyers managed to get their client's case up to the Supreme Court. There they found the sympathy they had sought. In a 5-4 decision, the Court ruled that Florida's procedures had violated the due process clause of the Fourteenth Amendment. Five Supreme Court justices held that the execution of any insane person was cruel and unusual punishment and prohibited by the Eighth Amendment.

Cruel and Unusual Punishment?

The broadest significance of *Ford v. Wainwright* is its overall ruling that the execution of insane persons is forbidden by the Eighth Amendment. Although the amendment specifically prohibits "cruel and unusual" punishment, it does not define what such punishment is. But Justice Marshall, in his majority opinion, went a long way towards creating such a definition.

First, said Justice Marshall, we begin with the punishments that were forbidden by English Common Law at the time that the Bill of Rights was adopted. In this tradition, executing an insane man is viewed as a kind of cruelty that should not be allowed in civilized society. First, an insane person cannot help think of reasons why he should not be executed, which means that he or she is deprived of rights to protect himself or herself. Moreover, executing the insane frustrates the two main reasons for capital punishment: that it is a deterrent and that it offers retribution. Executing an insane person will hardly deter anyone, and if the insane person does not understand why he or she is being killed, no retribution has been achieved. In addition, executing the insane offends against religion, for insane people cannot make their peace with God. Finally, execution of the insane serves no purpose, because insanity is its own punishment.

Having considered English Common Law, Justice Marshall went on to point out that we must also consider newer notions of fairness. Contemporary punishments have to be measured against the "evolving standards of decency that mark the progress of a maturing society . . ." Clearly, our "maturing society" has found it repellent to execute the insane, since no state in the Union had allowed such an action.

Deciding on Insanity

Having decided that an insane person should not be executed, Justice Marshall went on to wonder what procedure should be used to decide whether a prisoner was insane. On the one hand, prisoners have the right to the due process guaranteed by the Fourteenth Amendment. On the other hand, states have the right to speedily proceed with legal executions—and they have the right to weed out frivolous claims of insanity by sane prisoners wishing to avoid execution.

Justice Marshall's decision did not spell out what the Court might consider sufficient procedures to guarantee due process. He did list three inadequacies in the Florida law:

(1) Prisoners should be able to participate in the investigation of their sanity.

(2) Attorneys and prisoners should be able to submit information.

(3) The final decision should not be made by the executive branch (the governor or people appointed by the governor), because that is also the branch of government which is responsible for prosecuting the prisoner.

Implications of the *Ford* Decision

Not every member of the Court agreed that executing the insane is a violation of the Eighth Amendment. But seven members of the Court did agree that Ford should not be executed based on the procedure that Florida had actually used to determine that he was not insane. As a result, Ford's case was remanded for further review—and the states were left to develop adequate due process procedures as best they could.

Members of the Court disagreed even among themselves over what procedures would be adequate. Although Justice Marshall said that a full jury trial was not necessary, the decision raised many questions: They were uncertain as to whether the prisoner and his or her lawyer needed to be able to make oral arguments—or if written submissions were sufficient; whether the burden was on the state to prove the prisoner's sanity or on the prisoner to prove insanity; And if insanity kept a death sentence from being carried out, what would happen to the prisoner who recovered from insanity. The newly sane prisoner, rather than being relieved at the healing process, would now face death.

Moreover, the issue of medications was called into question. In these days of antipsychotic drugs, some prisoners who are psychotic or delusional without their medication seem lucid and competent while the medication is in effect. No decision could be made as to whether it was a violation of the prisoner's privacy to compel them to take antipsychotic drugs—merely so that they can become competent enough to be killed. There was also the concern of doctors who would be in violation of their Hippocratic oath to cure a prisoner merely so that he or she can then be executed.

Clearly, *Ford v. Wainwright* raises many knotty questions that have not yet been answered. Meanwhile, by outlawing the execution of those who have no idea what is happening to them, the Court has helped to preserve the decency and humanity on which the American system of justice is supposed to be based.

Related Cases

Louisiana ex rel. Francis v. Resweber, 329 U.S. 459 (1947).
Woodson v. North Carolina, 428 U.S. 280 (1976).
Roberts v. Louisiana, 428 U.S. 325 (1976).
Solem v. Helm, 463 U.S. 277 (1983).
Thompson v. Oklahoma, 487 U.S. 815 (1988).
Penry v. Lynaugh, 492 U.S. 302 (1989).

Bibliography and Further Reading

Bernstein, Sidney. "Death Penalty." *Trial*, October 1986, pp. 85-86.

Lombardi, George, Richard D. Sluder, and Donald Wallace. "Mainstreaming Death-Sentenced Inmates: The Missouri Experience and Its Legal Significance." *Federal Probation*, June 1997, p. 3.

Pastroff, Sanford M. "Eighth Amendment—The Constitutional Rights of the Insane on Death Row." *Journal of Criminal Law and Criminology*, fall 1986, pp. 844-866.

Taylor, Ptolemy H. "Execution of the 'Artificial Competent': Cruel and Unusual?" *Tulane Law Review*, March 1992, pp. 1045-1065.

McCleskey v. Kemp

Legal Citation: 481 U.S. 279 (1987)

Appellant
Warren McCleskey

Appellee
Ralph Kemp, Superintendent, Georgia Diagnostic and Classification Center

Appellant's Claim
That statistics demonstrated that the death penalty was being administered in Georgia in a racially discriminatory manner, thus violating the constitutional guarantee of due process and the ban on cruel and unusual punishment.

Chief Lawyer for Appellant
John Charles Boger

Chief Lawyer for Appellee
Mary Beth Westmoreland

Justices for the Court
Sandra Day O'Connor, Lewis F. Powell, Jr. (writing for the Court), William H. Rehnquist, Antonin Scalia, Byron R. White

Justices Dissenting
Harry A. Blackmun, William J. Brennan, Jr., Thurgood Marshall, John Paul Stevens

Place
Washington, D.C.

Date of Decision
22 April 1987

Decision
The Supreme Court rejected McCleskey's claim and upheld his death sentence.

Significance
In declaring that the remedy for racial discrimination in capital punishment lay with the legislatures and not with the courts, the Supreme Court was, in essence, permitting variable application of the law's ultimate penalty.

In 1978, Warren McCleskey was convicted and sentenced to death for killing a white police officer during a robbery attempt. After his conviction was upheld by the Georgia Supreme Court, McCleskey filed a *habeas corpus* petition with the federal district court. This petition claimed that his sentence was invalid because, in Georgia, the death penalty was being applied in an unconstitutionally discriminatory manner. In support of his petition, McCleskey submitted the report of an extensive statistical study by Professor David Baldus. This study examined 2,000 murder cases that were tried in Georgia during the 1970s. Baldus found that an individual charged with killing a white person was 4.3 times more likely to be sentenced to death than one accused of killing a black person.

On the basis of the Baldus study, McCleskey claimed that the death penalty as administered in Georgia was unconstitutional on one or both of the following grounds: 1) it violated the Equal Protection Clause of the Fourteenth Amendment, granting citizens of the states equal protection of the law; 2) it violated the Eighth Amendment's ban on cruel and unusual punishment. Baldus's petition was rejected, and he pursued it all the way up to the U.S. Supreme Court.

Writing for the five-member majority, Justice Powell also rejected McCleskey's petition. As to McCleskey's equal protection argument, Powell indicated that the Baldus statistics really should be presented to the Georgia legislature, not the Supreme Court:

> It is not the responsibility—or indeed even the right—of this Court to determine the appropriate punishment for particular crimes. It is the legislatures, the elected representatives of the people, that are "constituted to respond to the will and consequently the moral values of the people." [Quoting *Furman v. Georgia* (1972)] . . . Despite McCleskey's wide-ranging arguments that basically challenge the validity of capital punishment in society, the only question before us is whether in his case . . . the law of Georgia was properly applied.

Because McCleskey had failed to demonstrate that in his particular case the Georgia legislature had deliberately acted in a discriminatory fashion, the Court could not agree that his right to equal protection of the laws had been violated

McCleskey's Eighth Amendment argument was equally unconvincing to the majority. The conclusions of the Baldus study were not so extreme as to violate "evolving standards of decency." Fifteen years earlier, in *Gregg v. Georgia* (1976), the Court had ruled that the death penalty did not constitute cruel and unusual punishment if it were imposed after a careful review that avoided arbitrariness and prejudice. In *Gregg*, the state of Georgia demonstrated to the Court that it had instituted procedures designed to prevent precisely the type of discrimination that McCleskey alleged resulted in his death sentence. The Court was not willing, however, to reverse itself on the basis of one statistical survey that did not produce alarming results. As Powell was careful to point out, capital punishment was by 1990 "the law in more than two-thirds of our States." It was neither cruel nor unusual.

For two of the dissenters, Justices Brennan and Marshall, the death penalty was in all circumstances cruel and unusual punishment. In *McCleskey* they were joined by Blackmun and Stevens, who likewise found that there was no need for the Baldus study to prove definitively that Georgia applied the death penalty discriminatorily. All that was necessary to render the state statute unconstitutional was a showing that the procedures for adjudicating capital cases posed a significant risk of discrimination. For these four members of the Court, the Baldus study proved precisely that point.

One year later, the Supreme Court rejected another death penalty appeal from McCleskey in *McCleskey v. Zant* (1991), in which the appellant claimed that he had been forced to make incriminating statements without the assistance of counsel. McCleskey was finally executed on 25 September 1991.

Related Cases
Gregg v. Georgia, 428 U.S. 153 (1976).
McCleskey v. Zant, 499 U.S. 467 (1991).

Bibliography and Further Reading

Alexander, Rudolph, Jr., and Jacquelyn Gyamerah. "Differential Punishing of African Americans and Whites Who Possess Drugs." *Journal of Black Studies,* September 1997, p. 97.

Angeli, David H. "A 'Second Look' at Crack Cocaine Sentencing Policies." *American Criminal Law Review,* spring 1997, p. 1211.

Diamond, Shari Seidman, and Jonathan D. Casper. "Empirical Evidence and the Death Penalty: Past and Future." *Journal of Social Issues,* summer 1994, p. 177.

Garvey, Karin E. "Eighth Amendment—The Constitutionality of the Alabama Capital Sentencing Scheme." *Journal of Criminal Law and Criminology,* summer 1996, p. 1411.

Gorr, Michael J., and Sterling Harwood, eds. *Crime and Punishment: Philosophic Explorations.* Boston, MA: Jones and Bartlett, 1995.

Gross, Samuel R., and Robert Mauro. *Death & Discrimination: Racial Disparities in Capital Sentencing.* Boston, MA: Northeastern University Press, 1989.

Johnson, Sheri Lynn. "Race, Crime, and the Law." *Yale Law Journal,* June 1998, p. 2619.

Mello, Michael. "Defunding Death." *American Criminal Law Review,* summer 1995, p. 933.

Russell, Gregory D. *The Death Penalty and Racial Bias: Overturning Supreme Court Assumptions.* Westport, CT: Greenwood Press, 1994.

Spohn, Cassia C. "Courts, Sentences, and Prisons." *Daedalus,* winter 1995, p. 119.

Stevenson, Bryan. "The Hanging Judges: Once the Court Said, 'Death is Different.' Now It Says, 'Let's Get On With It.'" *The Nation,* October 14, 1996, p. 16.

Sullivan, Dwight. "Military Death Row: Separate, Not Equal." *The National Law Journal,* November 6, 1995, p. A19.

THOMPSON V. OKLAHOMA

Legal Citation: 487 U.S. 815 (1988)

Appellant
William Wayne Thompson

Appellee
State of Oklahoma

Appellant's Claim
That Thompson was a child at the time of his crime and should not be subjected to the death penalty.

Chief Lawyer for Appellant
Harry F. Tepker Jr.

Chief Lawyer for Appellee
David W. Lee, Oklahoma Assistant Attorney General

Justices for the Court
Harry A. Blackmun, William J. Brennan, Jr., Thurgood Marshall, Sandra Day O'Connor, John Paul Stevens (writing for the Court)

Justices Dissenting
William H. Rehnquist, Antonin Scalia, Byron R. White (Anthony M. Kennedy did not participate)

Place
Washington, D.C.

Date of Decision
29 June 1988

Decision
The Oklahoma Court's death sentence against Thompson was overturned and the case was remanded.

Significance
The decision established a national standard recognizing that sentencing defendants under 16 years old to death constitutes "cruel and unusual punishment" which is prohibited by the Eighth Amendment.

A Question of Age

In 1983, when he was 15 years old, Wayne Thompson helped to kidnap and kill his abusive brother-in-law, Charles Keene, who had repeatedly beaten Thompson's sister and other members of their family. Thompson's own life would later be spared in a Supreme Court decision which recognized that both society and the law are works in progress.

Grady County prosecutors charged four suspects with Keene's murder—Thompson, his half-brother Tony Mann, and two friends, Richard Jones and Bobby Glass. The state decided to try the cases separately. Before the 15-year-old Thompson could be tried as an adult, however, the prosecution had to prove the prospective merits of the case and convince a district court that there was no reasonable hope of his rehabilitation. A psychiatric examination found that Thompson was mentally competent to stand trial. Police records showed violent behavior in Thompson's past, including arrests for crimes ranging from shoplifting to assault. Prosecutors successfully convinced the court that he should be tried as an adult.

Keene's murder had been especially gruesome. He had been abducted and savagely beaten. His throat and abdomen had been slashed, he had been shot twice, and his body had been weighted with a concrete block before his killers dumped the body into a river. The prosecution introduced three grisly color photographs of Keene's corpse during the trial, after which Thompson was found guilty. In Oklahoma's justice system, trials to determine guilt are separate from a subsequent phase to determine sentencing. Before the death penalty can be applied, a state statute requires proof that "aggravating circumstances" were involved in a capital crime. During the sentencing phase, the prosecution reintroduced the graphic photographs to demonstrate the cruel nature of the murder. The jury agreed that Keene's murder met the criteria for the death penalty. Like his three accomplices, Thompson was sentenced to die (Glass was later killed in prison, while Jones' conviction was overturned).

Thompson's lawyers appealed the sentence. Oklahoma law held that because Thompson had met the criteria to be tried as an adult, he was eligible to be

Amnesty International on Capital Punishment

According to its own statement of purpose, Amnesty International (AI), sometimes called simply "Amnesty," is "a worldwide campaigning movement that works to promote all the human rights enshrined in the Universal Declaration of Human Rights and other international standards." Among its campaigns are efforts to free "prisoners of conscience" or political prisoners; fair trials for all political prisoners; and abolition of the death penalty.

Amnesty opposes capital punishment for a number of reasons, holding that it is "cruel, inhuman and degrading," and violates the right to life; that innocent people can be killed, and since it is irrevocable, there can be no correction of the error; that it does not deter crime to any greater degree than other forms of pun-

ishment; that by committing an execution, the state is in effect sponsoring violence; and that capital punishment is often used as a weapon against minority groups and those opposed to the government.

The group reports that in 1996, more than 4,200 prisoners were executed worldwide, a staggering proportion of which—3,500—were killed in China. (And those are only the executions that have been reported.) China, the Ukraine, the Russian Federation, and Iran accounted for 92 percent of all executions in 1996. On the other hand, 25 countries have abolished the death penalty.

Source(s): Amnesty International, http://www.amnesty.org.

punished as one. The appeals court accepted Thompson's contention that reintroducing two of the graphic crime photographs during the sentencing phase of the trial was a prejudicial prosecution tactic. In light of the amount of other evidence against him, however, the court found that the jury would have passed the death sentence regardless of whether or not they had seen the inflammatory photographs. The appeal was rejected.

The Consensus of Society

Thompson's subsequent appeal reached the U.S. Supreme Court on 9 November 1987. Briefs were filed in support of the appeal by representatives of the Child Welfare League of America and the International Human Rights Law Group. Attorney Generals of 20 states supported Oklahoma with a brief asking that the judgement against Thompson be affirmed. The state of Oklahoma continued to insist that Thompson had met the criteria to be tried as an adult and should be punished as one, but this time Thompson's attorney's arguments were successful. On 29 June 1988, the Court vacated Thompson's death sentence and remanded his case back to Oklahoma's courts.

The Court's five-vote majority agreed that Thompson's sentence was inappropriate, but their reasoning varied. Justices Stevens, Marshall, Brennan, and Blackmun looked to state laws for a reflection of society's views on the issue. In the written opinion, Justice Stevens quoted the 1958 *Trop v. Dulles* decision, in which the Court looked for guidance to "evolving standards of decency that mark the progress of a maturing society." Stevens noted that 18 states had set the age of 16 as the minimum age for imposition of the death penalty. Furthermore, he noted that most Western soci-

eties and even some totalitarian states like the Soviet Union forbid the execution of juveniles.

Justice O'Connor agreed in a separate opinion that Thompson should not be executed, but disputed that

David W. Lee, 1998 © Photograph by Mike Dere. AP/Wide World Photos.

his particular case should prove the existence of any national consensus on imposing the death sentence on minors. Although 18 state legislatures had barred seeking the death penalty against juveniles and another 14 states had completely dispensed with capital punishment, O'Connor pointed out that the federal government and 19 other states set no rules regarding age in statutes accepting death as a legitimate penalty.

Nevertheless, O'Connor accepted that a national consensus on the minimum age issue "very likely" did exist. Furthermore, O'Connor wrote that the absence of a minimum age statute in Oklahoma law showed a lack of necessary care and deliberation had been taken in drafting state statutes relating to the Eighth Amendment. She noted that laws authorizing capital punishment and providing that minors could be tried as adults had been passed separately by the Oklahoma legislature, as if no serious consideration had been given to the effect one law might have upon the other. Since Oklahoma lawmakers had apparently failed to consider such a possible interrelationship, O'Connor deferred to the "national consensus" that defendants under 16 should not be executed.

Justices Scalia, White, and Rehnquist rejected the idea that a consensus existed on the minimum age issue. In their dissent, Scalia wrote that the Court should not involve itself in setting a precedent in the minimum age issue unless the national consensus and the lack of judgemental maturity in juveniles alluded to by the majority could be established beyond any doubt in every case. Scalia wrote that the Eighth Amendment was not written to ban the execution of juveniles. In the majority opinion, Justice Stevens had cited statistics showing that no defendant under 16 had been executed in the U.S. in forty years and that juries had sentenced fewer than two dozen minors to death in the twentieth century. To Stevens, this implied a national consensus. To Scalia and the dissenters, it implied that juries took such cases so seriously that the death penalty was meted out to minors only when it was deserved.

The *Thompson* decision was a landmark in ongoing controversies over the death penalty and the administration of justice to youthful offenders. In 1997, Amnesty International listed the United States as one of only five nations, including Iraq, Pakistan, Yemen, and Saudi Arabia, which allow the execution of prisoners under the age of 18.

Related Cases
Trop v. Dulles, 356 U.S. 86 (1958).
Furman v. Georgia, 408 U.S. 238 (1972).
Gregg v. Georgia, 428 U.S. 153 (1976).
Penry v. Lynaugh, 492 U.S. 302 (1989).
Stanford v. Kentucky, 492 U.S. 361 (1989).

Bibliography and Further Reading
"Juveniles and the Death Penalty: Executions Worldwide since 1985." Amnesty International Index: ACT 50/05/95.

Taylor, Stuart, Jr. "Justices Put Age Limit On Executions." *New York Times,* June 30, 1988, p. 17.

Tushnet, Mark. *The Death Penalty.* New York: Facts On File, 1994.

Whitford, Ellen. "How A Family Tragedy May Lead To A Landmark Court Ruling." *Scholastic Update,* April 8, 1988, pp. 10-12.

PENRY V. LYNAUGH

Legal Citation: 492 U.S. 302 (1989)

Petitioner
Johnny Paul Penry

Respondent
James A. Lynaugh, Director, Texas Department of Corrections

Petitioner's Claim
That execution of the mentally retarded violates the Eighth Amendment ban on cruel and unusual punishment.

Chief Lawyer for Petitioner
Curtis C. Mason

Chief Lawyer for Respondent
Charles A. Palmer

Justices for the Court
Anthony M. Kennedy, Sandra Day O'Connor (writing for the Court), William H. Rehnquist, Antonin Scalia, Byron R. White,

Justices Dissenting
Harry A. Blackmun, William J. Brennan, Jr., Thurgood Marshall, John Paul Stevens

Place
Washington, D.C.

Date of Decision
26 June 1989

Decision
The Supreme Court reversed Penry's death sentence.

Significance
Penry underscored the point that in capital cases—especially when they involve defendants with diminished mental capacities—factors which mitigate guilt must be taken into account. At the same time, the case stands for the proposition that the death penalty is constitutional in most such cases.

Johnny Paul Penry was moderately mentally retarded. As an adult, he had the mental maturity of a six and a half year old child. Possibly, his brain damage dated from birth; more probably it dated from his childhood, when he had been beaten and abused. On the morning of 25 October 1979, when he was 22 years old, Penry raped, beat, and fatally stabbed Pamela Carpenter in her home in Livingston, Texas. During the hearing of his murder trial, expert testimony was offered as to his mental state at the time of the killing. Dr. Jose Garcia testified that, as a result of his brain disorder, Penry suffered from poor impulse control and an inability to learn from experience. These disorders, said Dr. Garcia, made it impossible for Penry to appreciate the wrongfulness of his acts.

The state introduced expert testimony that although Penry had limited mental capacity, he was not mentally ill and that he knew right from wrong. The jury rejected Penry's insanity defense and found him guilty of capital murder. Finding that Penry had deliberately killed and would probably kill again, the jurors sentenced him to death. The Texas Court of Criminal Appeals affirmed Penry's conviction and sentence, as did two federal courts. The U.S. Fifth Circuit Court of Appeals, however, stressed that it found merit in Penry's argument that the jury had not been allowed to consider all of the mitigating circumstances surrounding his crime. When Penry applied to the U.S. Supreme Court for review, the Court agreed to do so. For the justices, two questions regarding Penry's case remained unanswered: 1) whether Penry's Eighth Amendment rights were violated by the judge's failure to instruct the jury properly as to mitigating circumstances, and 2) whether it was cruel and unusual punishment to execute a mentally retarded person with Penry's capacity to reason.

Supreme Court Finds Application of Capital Punishment to the Mentally Retarded Constitutional

The Court struck down Penry's conviction and sentence in a 5-4 vote. Although they agreed on an outcome, in part because they were obliged to consider two questions, the justices could not agree on an opinion. Jus-

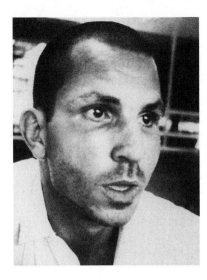

Johnny Paul Penry had his death penalty reversed by the U.S. Supreme Court. © AP/Wide World Photos.

tice O'Connor announced the judgment of the Court and delivered two separate opinions of the Court. In the first, she stated the reasons for reversing Penry's death sentence. In *Gregg v. Georgia* (1976), the case which reaffirmed the constitutionality of the death penalty, the Court mandated that mitigating circumstances be reviewed in each capital case. Here again, the Court stressed the importance of this requirement:

> In order to ensure "reliability in the determination that death is the appropriate punishment in a specific case," [Quoting *Woodson v. North Carolina* (1976)], the jury must be able to consider and give effect to any mitigating evidence relevant to a defendant's background and character or the circumstances of the crime.

Because at Penry's trial the judge had failed to instruct the jury specifically that they could consider mitigating circumstances, Penry's constitutional rights had been violated. His death sentence was overturned.

The justices were even more divided with the regard to the constitutionality, in general, of sentencing the mentally retarded to death for capital crimes. While upholding their decision in *Ford v. Wainwright* (1986) that execution of an insane person is cruel and unusual punishment, they nevertheless held now that mental retardation was not, of itself, a violation of the Eighth Amendment. While stressing that diminished mental capacity was a mitigating factor and admitting that severe retardation may result in acquittal in capital cases, the Court said that not all mentally retarded people who share Penry's level of awareness lack the capacity to appreciate their crimes. Such was the consensus among the framers of the Constitution, and such was the consensus in today's society:

> [A]t present, there is insufficient evidence of a national consensus against executing mentally

retarded people convicted of capital offenses for us to conclude that it is categorically prohibited by the Eighth Amendment.

Impact

The Court's opinion in *Penry* expressed uncertainty about the constitutionality of executing a mentally handicapped individual. O'Connor essentially deferred to the legislative branch suggesting that if a majority of the public opposed the practice that sentiment would eventually find its way into legislative statutes. Although the petitioner offered empirical data suggesting that a majority of people opposed the execution of mentally handicapped individuals, even in Texas where capital punishment is generally accepted, O'Connor was not persuaded to resolve the matter. Since *Penry* the public has decisively weighed in on the matter. Organizations such as the American Association on Mental Retardation (AAMR), the Association for Retarded Citizens (ARC) and the American Psychological Association (APA) have formally adopted positions in opposition to administering the death penalty to mentally handicapped individuals. In addition, some states have adopted legislation prohibiting the practice.

O'Connor's opinion in *Penry* was important because it suggested that the Court should include the "national consensus" on matters in its deliberations. Justice Scalia echoed O'Connor's point in *Stanford v. Kentucky* (1989) stating that the Supreme Court has a "constitutional obligation" to consider the sentiments of the public, or to conduct what he called "proportionality analysis." If the Court is true to its word, it seems likely that the application of capital punishment to mentally handicapped individuals will be prohibited by the Court in due course.

Related Cases

Gregg v. Georgia, 428 U.S. 153 (1976).
Ford v. Wainwright, 477 U.S. 399 (1986).
Thompson v. Oklahoma, 487 U.S. 815 (1988).
Stanford v. Kentucky, 492 U.S. 361 (1989).

Bibliography and Further Reading

Berger, Vivian. "Execution of Mentally Disabled Killer Shames Our 'Civilized' Society." *The National Law Journal,* June 16, 1997, p. A22.

Brown, J. Michael. "Eighth Amendment—Capital Sentencing Instructions." *Journal of Criminal Law and Criminology,* winter-spring 1994, p. 854.

Conley, Ronald W., Ruth Luckasson, and George N. Bouthilet, eds. *The Criminal Justice System and Mental Retardation: Defendants and Victims.* Baltimore, MD: P. H. Brookes Publishing Co., 1992.

Dicks, Shirley, ed. *Young Blood: Juvenile Justice and the Death Penalty.* Amherst, NY: Prometheus Books, 1995.

Haney, Craig, and Deana Dorman Logan. "Broken Promise: The Supreme Court's Response to Social Science Research on Capital Punishment." *Journal of Social Issues,* summer 1994, p. 75.

Masur, Louis P. *Rites of Execution: Capital Punishment and the Transformation of American Culture, 1776–1865.* New York: Oxford University Press, 1989.

STANFORD V. KENTUCKY

Legal Citation: 492 U.S. 361 (1989)

Petitioner
Kevin N. Stanford

Respondent
State of Kentucky

Petitioner's Claim
That the imposition of a death sentence for a murder he committed when he was 17 years old violated the Eighth Amendment ban on cruel and unusual punishment.

Chief Lawyer for Petitioner
Frank W. Heft, Jr.

Chief Lawyer for Respondent
Frederic J. Cowan

Justices for the Court
Anthony M. Kennedy, Sandra Day O'Connor, William H. Rehnquist, Antonin Scalia (writing for the Court), Byron R. White

Justices Dissenting
Harry A. Blackmun, William J. Brennan, Jr., Thurgood Marshall, John Paul Stevens

Place
Washington, D.C.

Date of Decision
26 June 1989

Decision
The Supreme Court upheld Stanford's death sentence.

Significance
In declaring that neither the framers of the Constitution nor contemporary society regarded a death sentence as cruel and unusual punishment for someone who was almost 18 years old at the time he committed murder, the Court lowered the barrier to capital punishment. After *Stanford*, states could impose the death penalty on anyone over the age of 16.

On 7 January 1981, Kevin Stanford was 17 years, four months old. That night, he and an accomplice repeatedly raped and sodomized 20-year-old Barbel Poore during a robbery of the gas station where she worked as an attendant. After taking 300 cartons of cigarettes, two gallons of fuel, and a small amount of cash, Stanford and his accomplice drove with Poore to a secluded area, where Stanford shot Poore point blank in the face and then in the back of the head.

After Stanford was arrested, a Kentucky juvenile court conducted a hearing to determine whether or not he should be tried as an adult. A state law provided that anyone charged with a capital crime, or who was over the age of 16 and charged with a felony, could be tried as an adult. Because of the seriousness of Stanford's crime and his long record of juvenile arrests, the juvenile court certified him for trial as an adult.

Stanford was convicted of murder, sodomy, first-degree robbery, and receiving stolen goods. He was sentenced to death plus 45 years in jail. The Kentucky Supreme Court affirmed this decision, citing the numerous failed attempts to treat or reform Stanford. Claiming that his death sentence amounted to unconstitutional cruel and unusual punishment, Stanford appealed to the U.S. Supreme Court.

Court Declares that Capital Punishment May Be Imposed on Those Over Sixteen Years of Age

Writing for the Court, Justice Scalia held that it was not cruel and unusual punishment to impose the death sentence on those who were juveniles at the time they the committed crimes for which they were later convicted. Putting to death those who had almost reached the age of majority for horrendous crimes did not offend the drafters of the Bill of Rights and does not offend contemporary American society:

> At that time [when the Bill of Rights was adopted], common law set the . . . presumption of incapacity to commit any felony at the age of 14, and theoretically permitted capital punishment to be imposed on anyone over the age of 7 . . . Thus petitioners are left to argue

Juvenile Capital Punishment

As of 1996, there were eight states—Arizona, Idaho, Montana, Louisiana, Pennsylvania, South Carolina, South Dakota, and Utah—that had no statutes governing the minimum age for capital punishment. Fourteen states, along with the federal system, set the minimum at 18 years of age: California, Colorado, Connecticut, Illinois, Kansas, Maryland, Nebraska, New Jersey, New Mexico, New York, Ohio, Oregon, Tennessee, and Washington.

Among Southern states, Tennessee had the highest minimum age for execution. Four states (George, New Hampshire, North Carolina, and Texas) authorized 17 as the minimum age, though in North Carolina a person 14 or older who was incarcerated for murder and then committed another murder could be executed.

The remaining states all had minimum ages of 16 or less. Sixteen was the minimum in Alabama, Delaware, Florida, Indiana, Kentucky, Mississippi, Missouri, Nevada, Oklahoma, and Wyoming. Finally, Arkansas and Virginia authorized the death penalty for persons 14 years old or older.

According to Amnesty International, five nations have executed prisoners younger than 18 years of age since 1990. Of these, the United States is the only non-Islamic country, the others being Iran, Pakistan, Saudi Arabia, and Yemen.

Source(s): U.S. Department of Justice, Bureau of Justice Statistics. *Capital Punishment 1996.* Washington, DC: U.S. Government, 1997.

that their punishment is contrary to the "evolving standards of decency that mark the progress of a maturing society" [Quoting *Trop v. Dulles* (1958)] . . . a majority of the States that permit capital punishment authorize it for crimes committed at age 16 or above . . .

For Scalia, and for four other members of the Court, the fact that a majority of the states permit capital punishment to be enforced against those over 16 years of age proved conclusive: Stanford's sentence was affirmed.

Justices Brennan and Marshall dissented from this view, declining to vote in favor of the death penalty, as always. In his dissenting opinion, Brennan made much of the fact that state prosecutors seldom pursue the death penalty for juveniles. For Brennan, this was proof that capital punishment for anyone under the age of 18 did not conform with "contemporary standards of decency."

The whole notion of juvenile justice is in fact a modern one. The concept originated late in the nineteenth century and was not subjected to constitutional restraints until *Kent v. United States* (1966). In *In re Gault* (1967), the Supreme Court held that juvenile courts must observe the same procedural protections afforded adult offenders. And in *In re Winship* (1970), the Court ruled that prosecutors who charge juveniles with adult crimes must meet the adult standard of proof, "beyond a reasonable doubt."

While these early decisions might seem to have expanded protections for juvenile offenders, *Stanford* demonstrates that the process of bringing juvenile justice in line with the criminal procedure applied to adults has its darker side. *Stanford* made it clear that if an offender is at least 16 when he or she commits a capital crime, the Supreme Court will not intervene to prevent the death sentence from being carried out.

Related Cases
Trop v. Dulles, 356 U.S. 86 (1958).
Kent v. United States, 383 U.S. 541 (1966).
In re Gault, 387 U.S. 1 (1967).
In re Winship, 397 U.S. 358 (1970).
Gregg v. Georgia, 428 U.S. 153 (1976).
Coker v. Georgia, 433 U.S. 584 (1977).
Thompson v. Oklahoma, 487 U.S. 815 (1988).

Bibliography and Further Reading
Dicks, Shirley, ed. *Young Blood: Juvenile Justice and the Death Penalty.* Amherst, NY: Prometheus Books, 1995.

Kraemer, Rita. *At a Tender Age: Violent Youth and Juvenile Justice.* New York, NY: Holt, 1988.

Streib, Victor L. *Death Penalty for Juveniles.* Bloomington: Indiana University Press, 1987.

ARIZONA V. FULMINANTE

Legal Citation: 499 U.S. 279 (1991)

Petitioner
State of Arizona

Respondent
Orestes C. Fulminante

Petitioner's Claim
That the Arizona Supreme Court had erred in awarding Fulminante a new trial for murder.

Chief Lawyer for Petitioner
Barbara M. Jarrett

Chief Lawyer for Respondent
Stephen R. Collins

Justices for the Court
Anthony M. Kennedy, Sandra Day O'Connor, William H. Rehnquist (writing for the Court), Antonin Scalia, David H. Souter

Justices Dissenting
Harry A. Blackmun, Thurgood Marshall, John Paul Stevens, Byron R. White

Place
Washington, D.C.

Date of Decision
26 March 1991

Decision
Affirmed the lower court's decision to grant a new trial, on the basis that the state used an inadmissible, coerced confession to convict Fulminante.

Significance
Although in this instance the Court disallowed a coerced confession, it opened the door for permitting such confessions in the future, ruling they no longer were exempt from "harmless error" analysis. In principle, the Court's ruling meant that the introduction into evidence of a coerced confession did not automatically taint an entire trial and void a conviction, if there was enough other evidence to justify a guilty verdict.

When Orestes Fulminante entered a New York federal prison, he faced greater danger than the typical convict might. Although Fulminante had been convicted on a firearms charge, rumors circulated that he had killed his 11 year-old stepdaughter while living in Arizona. Child murderers and molesters are often targeted for violent attacks by other inmates, but Fulminante found a friend who offered to help protect him—if Fulminate told the truth about his stepdaughter's death. Fulminante's subsequent confession and conviction for murder are the heart of *Arizona v. Fulminante*.

Fulminante's new friend was Anthony Sarivola, a former police officer in jail for extortion. But Sarivola was also an FBI informant pretending to be an organized crime figure. Under instructions from the FBI, Sarivola urged Fulminante to confess. If Fulminante told the truth about the murder, Sarivola said he would protect him from the other inmates. Fulminante agreed, describing how he took his stepdaughter, Jeneane Hunt, to an isolated stretch of Arizona desert. There, he sexually assaulted the girl, choked her, then shot her two times in the head. Based on this confession and another one Fulminante gave later to Sarivola's fiancee, the state of Arizona arrested Fulminante for first-degree murder.

Before his trial, Fulminante asked the court to exclude his confessions, saying they were involuntary or coerced, and thus not admissible evidence. Sarivola had said he would help Fulminante only if he confessed to the murder, and Fulminante never would have told his friend's fiancee about the murder if Sarivola had not been his protector. The trial court, however, ruled the confessions were voluntary and allowable in court. On 19 December 1985, Fulminante was found guilty and later sentenced to death.

Fulminante appealed the verdict, still arguing his confessions were coerced and not admissible under the Due Process Clauses of the Fifth and Fourteenth Amendments. The Arizona Supreme Court ruled that the confessions were coerced, but that their admission was a "harmless error" and not sufficient reason to overturn the conviction. Later, however, the state court said

The Federal Bureau of Investigation

The Federal Bureau of Investigation (FBI) is a unit of the Department of Justice responsible for investigating federal crimes. Its purview consists of all areas of law not otherwise assigned to federal agencies—for example, the Drug Enforcement Agency (DEA). Though it does not prosecute crimes, it provides assistance to federal, state, and local agencies engaged in prosecution.

In 1908, President Theodore Roosevelt called for the development of a special investigative unit within the Justice Department. The following year, Attorney General George W. Wickersham established the Bureau of Investigation, later named the Federal Bureau of Investigation in 1935. During World War I and afterward, the FBI was involved in a wave of investigations regarding subversive activities. The bureau became more prominent during Prohibition, when it faced prominent gangsters, bootleggers, and other criminals. In 1924, J. Edgar Hoover became FBI director, a position he would hold for 48 years. Under his tenure, the bureau concerned itself with civil rights activities and operations of organized crime. In the years since, the FBI has been involved in a number of investigative areas, including background checks, counterintelligence, and white-collar crime.

Source(s): *West's Encyclopedia of American Law.* St. Paul, MN: West Group, 1998.

that, based on previous U.S. Supreme Court rulings, the harmless error standard did not apply to a coerced confession. The Arizona Supreme Court overturned the verdict and ordered a new trial for Fulminante, without use of the confession. The state of Arizona then appealed that verdict to the U.S. Supreme Court.

Harmless Error and the Supreme Court

Under the harmless error analysis, the Supreme Court had said that a trial procedure could be flawed, or some evidence could be illegally obtained, and a guilty verdict could still stand, if the mistake was merely a harmless error that did not outweigh all the other evidence of the case. But in a 1967 case, *Chapman v. California,* the Supreme Court had ruled that admission of a coerced confession was never a harmless error; any time a coerced confession led to a guilty verdict, the verdict had to be overturned.

In *Arizona v. Fulminante,* the Court voted 5-4 to uphold the Arizona court's decision: Fulminante would get a new trial and the confession would not be allowed. But in a verdict Linda Greenhouse of *The New York Times* called "unusually convoluted," the decision was broken into four parts, with justices shifting from the majority to the minority and back again. In the most stunning part of the verdict, the Court, agreeing with a brief presented by the Bush Administration, overturned the precedent set in *Chapman.* Now, the Court ruled, a coerced confession could be allowed as a harmless error under some circumstances.

Writing for the majority on that point, Chief Justice Rehnquist said, "The admission of an involuntary confession . . . is similar in both degree and kind to the erroneous admission of other types of evidence." If other evidence separate from the confession was strong enough to convict a defendant, the verdict should stand. For Rehnquist, only "structural defects," such as a biased judge or a defendant's lack of adequate legal defense, were absolutely excluded from the harmless error analysis.

Justice White strongly disagreed with Rehnquist, and in a rarity for the Supreme Court, White read his dissent in the courtroom. A coerced confession, he wrote, is "fundamentally different from other types of erroneously admitted evidence to which the rule [of harmless error] has been applied." White was dismayed that the Court was ignoring the precedents on coerced confessions. "Permitting a coerced confession to be part of the evidence on which a jury is free to base its verdict of guilty is inconsistent with the thesis that ours is not an inquisitorial system" of criminal justice.

New Direction?

During 1990, one of the Court's most liberal members, William J. Brennan, Jr., retired. President George Bush filled his seat with the more conservative David H. Souter. Souter joined Rehnquist in overturning the harmless error analysis for coerced confessions. Some legal experts believed the Arizona verdict would have been different if Brennan had still been on the Court. Said one lawyer, Joseph L. Rauh, "I bet Bill Brennan is sick this morning."

Observers split in their opinions on the verdict. Some lawyers strongly attacked it, saying it might make police more likely to use threats or violence against a suspect to force a confession. But others said the verdict would have little effect, since coerced confessions are rare.

Related Cases

Chapman v. California, 386 U.S. 18 (1967).

States and the Death Penalty

As of 1998, the following states had no provision for the death penalty: Alaska, Hawaii, Iowa, Maine, Massachusetts, Michigan, Minnesota, North Dakota, Rhode Island, Vermont, West Virginia, and Wisconsin. The District of Columbia also did not practice capital punishment.

Of the 38 states that practice the death penalty, 36 provide for automatic review of the death sentence, regardless of the wishes of the defendant. The only exceptions are Arkansas, which simply lacks provisions for automatic review, and South Carolina, in which the defendant may waive sentence review if he or she is deemed competent by the court. Additionally, federal death-penalty procedures do not provide for automatic review after a sentence of death has been passed down.

Usually the highest appellate court in the state conducts the automatic review. Kentucky authorizes waiver of appeal on the defendant's part. In both Mississippi and Wyoming respectively, the defendant's right to waive automatic review and appeal remained open to question as of the end of 1995. Also, rules regarding automatic review of both the conviction and the sentence (as opposed to just one or the other) vary, with Idaho, Indiana, Oklahoma, and Tennessee requiring review only of the sentence.

Source(s): U.S. Department of Justice, Bureau of Justice Statistics. *Capital Punishment 1996.* Washington, DC: U.S. Government, 1997.

Bibliography and Further Reading

Biskupic, Joan, and Elder Witt. *Guide to the U.S. Supreme Court.* Washington, DC: Congressional Quarterly, Inc., 1997.

Choper, Jess H., Yale Kasimir, and William B. Lockhart. *Constitutional Rights and Liberties.* St. Paul: West Publishing Co. 1975.

Hall, Kermit L., ed. *The Oxford Companion to the Supreme Court of the United States.* New York: Oxford University Press, 1992.

New York Times, March 27-28, 1991.

PAYNE V. TENNESSEE

Legal Citation: 501 U.S. 808 (1991)

Petitioner
Supreme Court of Tennessee

Respondent
Pervis Tyrone Payne

Petitioner's Claim
That the conviction of two counts of first-degree murder and one count of assault with intent to murder in the first degree should be upheld on the grounds that rights under the Eighth Amendment were not violated by the introduction of victim impact evidence.

Chief Lawyer for Petitioner
J. Brooke Lathram

Chief Lawyer for Respondent
Charles W. Burson, Attorney General of Tennessee

Justices for the Court
Anthony M. Kennedy, Sandra Day O'Connor, William H. Rehnquist (writing for the Court), Antonin Scalia, David H. Souter, Byron R. White

Justices Dissenting
Harry A. Blackmun, Thurgood Marshall, John Paul Stevens

Place
Washington, D.C.

Date of Decision
27 June 1991

Decision
The Court affirmed the conviction and the sentence.

Significance
A defendant's rights under the Constitution are a vital safeguard against a miscarriage of justice, particularly in a capital trial. In *Payne v. Tennessee*, the Supreme Court of Tennessee overturned an earlier U.S. Supreme Court ruling that barred victim impact evidence in deciding the death sentence. By allowing victim impact evidence at the sentencing phase, this case caused much debate regarding both victims' rights, and the rights of the defendant under the following: the Eighth Amendment forbidding cruel and unusual punishment; the Fourteenth Amendment demanding due process under the law to all persons; the Sixth Amendment allowing a defendant to confront witnesses; and the Constitution's Equal Protection Clause prohibiting comparative judgments of the worth of victims.

The Crime

On Saturday, 27 June 1987, Pervis Tyrone Payne visited the apartment of his girlfriend, Bobbie Thomas, in Millington, Tennessee, awaiting her return from an out-of-town trip. Across the hall from Thomas lived Payne's three victims, Charisse Christopher, her two-year-old daughter Lacie, and her three-year-old son Nicholas. While waiting for Thomas to return home, Payne spent the late morning and early afternoon injecting cocaine and drinking beer. Later, he and a friend drove around in the friend's car, taking turns reading a pornographic magazine.

Payne returned to the apartment complex around 3:00 p.m., entered the Christopher apartment and made sexual advances toward Charisse Christopher. When she resisted, Payne stabbed Charisse 84 times with a butcher knife. She died from massive bleeding. He also stabbed Lacie and Nicholas. Lacie died next to her mother, but Nicholas survived Payne's attack. The murder weapon, a butcher knife, was left near Lacie.

When she heard screaming from the Christopher apartment, a neighbor phoned the police, who arrived shortly thereafter, and encountered Payne as he was leaving the building. Payne was soaked in blood, and carrying his overnight bag. When confronted by the officer, Payne struck him with the overnight bag and fled.

The Trial

Payne testified at trial he had not harmed any of the Christophers. However, the evidence against him was overwhelming, and jury returned guilty verdicts on all of the three counts against him. During the sentencing phase of the trial, the defense presented four witnesses who testified that Payne attended church, was of good character, treated his girlfriend and her children with loving kindness, had no criminal record, did not use drugs, and, although he had a low I.Q., was mentally normal. Thomas, Payne's girlfriend, stated further that the crimes were inconsistent with Payne's character. The prosecution presented Charisse Christopher's mother, who testified to the effects of the murders on Nicholas. Then, in the sentencing phase, the prosecution argued for the death penalty, using the ongoing psychological burden on the boy as part of his argument. The jury sentenced Payne to death on each of the murder counts, and to 30 years for the attempted murder of Nicholas.

A Defendant's Rights

Payne contended that the victim impact statement of Charisse Christopher's mother violated his Eighth Amendment rights and emotionally influenced the jury against him. In reviewing the trial, the Tennessee Supreme Court rejected the claim, affirming both conviction and sentence.

> [w]hen a person deliberately picks up a butcher knife . . . and proceeds to stab to death a 28-year-old mother, her two and one half-year-old daughter and her three and one half-year-old son, in the same room, the physical and mental condition of the boy he left or dead is surely relevant in determining his blameworthiness . . . [The grandmother's testimony] did not create a constitutionally unacceptable risk of an arbitrary imposition of the death penalty and was harmless beyond a reasonable doubt.

The U.S. Supreme Court was careful to point out in its 5-4 decision, however, that the ruling should be narrowly defined. It emphasized that it did not preclude the possibility of an Eighth Amendment violation, but that "such evidence was *per se* inadmissible in the sentencing phase of a capital case except to the extent that it related directly to the circumstances of the crime."

Discussions of the implications of this case touch on other parts of a defendant's constitutional rights, as well. The Fourteenth Amendment guarantees all persons a right to due process under the law. Justice O'Connor noted that "If, in a particular case, a witness's testimony or a prosecutor's remark so infects the sentencing proceeding as to render it fundamentally unfair, the defendant may seek appropriate relief under the Due Process Clause of the Fourteenth Amendment . . ."

The Sixth Amendment right to confront a witness can also be at issue when victim impact evidence is offered by the prosecution. When a video or taped statement of a dead victim is offered to show the impact of society's loss, the defendant cannot confront a witness to prove the veracity of the statements. When the defendant has been found guilty of a capital crime, the opportunity to confront a witness can become, literally, a matter of life and death. And because the penalty phase of a capital case is considered an extension of the guilt phase, the same protections for the defendant need apply.

The last problem created by *Payne v. Tennessee* deals with the Constitution's Equal Protection Clause. This prohibits comparative judgments of the worth of victims. In doing so, it does the same for defendants. The murderer of a hardworking parent does not deserve a death penalty sentence any more than the murderer of an unemployed itinerant; the killer of a pedophile deserves a death sentence no less than the killer of a wealthy philanthropist. Victim impact evidence can cloud this issue. For example, African American defendants are four times more likely to receive the death penalty than are white defendants, so the matter of equal protection under the law is far more than a legal nicety.

The Future of Victim Impact Evidence

As of 1999, 49 states had some form of a statute permitting the introduction of victim impact evidence. Although a defendant's appeal of a capital case verdict on constitutional grounds may seem spurious in some instances, this federal challenge must be upheld. When a person opposes the state, both verdict and sentence must be able to withstand close constitutional scrutiny. This legal debate is sure to remain heated for some time to come.

Related Cases

Gregg v. Georgia, 428 U.S. 153 (1976).
Woodson v. North Carolina, 428 U.S. 280 (1976).
Booth v. Maryland, 482 U.S. 496 (1987).

Bibliography and Further Reading

Bilionis, Louis D. "Legitimating Death." *Michigan Law Review,* June 1993, p. 1643.

Friedman, David D. "Should the Characteristics of Victims and Criminals Count?: *Payne v. Tennessee* and Two Views of Efficient Punishment." *Boston Law Review,* 1993, pp. 731-69.

Kreitzberg, Ellen. "Capital Cases: How Much *Payne* Will the Courts Allow?" *The Champion,* January/February 1998.

Luginbuhl, James, and Michael Burkhead. "Sources of Bias and Arbitrariness in the Capital Trial." *Journal of Social Issues,* summer 1994, p. 103.

Phillips, Amy K. "Thou Shalt Not Kill Any Nice People: The Problem of Victim Impact Statements in Capital Sentencing." *American Criminal Law Review,* fall 1997, p. 93.

"Sentencing Criminals: The Constitutionality of Victim Impact Statements, *State v. Wise.*" *Missouri Law Review,* Vol. 60, 1995, p. 731-D34.

CRIMINAL LAW

Criminal law is comprised of rules and statutes intended to dictate parameters of conduct that will prevent harm to society. Criminal law differs from criminal procedure. Criminal law is concerned with defining crimes and setting punishment, while criminal procedure refers to the process by which those laws are enforced. For example, substantive criminal law is used to determine whether someone has committed arson. Criminal procedure guides the prosecution of the arsonist, from evidence gathering to trial and beyond. Criminal procedure encompasses constitutional protections such as the right to be free from unreasonable searches and seizures, the right to counsel, the right against self-incrimination, and the right to trial by jury.

In England criminal law arose from case law, rather than from codified laws. Known as part of the common law, these rules formed the foundation of U.S. criminal laws. Some crimes are still defined by their common law meanings, but much of this common law has been codified in statutes. Other crimes, such as embezzlement and receiving stolen property, are wholly statutory creations.

The Necessary and Proper Clause of the Constitution grants Congress the authority to denominate certain conduct illegal. States may make laws prohibiting and punishing certain acts, so long as the law does not contravene the U.S. Constitution or state constitutions, and so long as the conduct prohibited is reasonably related to protecting the welfare and safety of society. Municipalities may also designate illegal behavior, based upon limited powers delegated to them by the state legislature.

Categories of Criminal Conduct

Under federal law and most state statutes, a felony is a crime punishable by death or imprisonment for more than one year. Felonies are usually divided into several classes, grouped by perceived severity and applicable punishment. Misdemeanor offenses are less serious than felonies. They are generally punishable by nonpenitentiary confinement for less than one year, by imposition of a fine, or both imprisonment and fine. Petty offenses are typically crimes with potential imprisonment not to exceed six months, a fine of not more than $500, or

both. If a violation of a statute provides only for the imposition of a fine, the law is called an infraction. Infractions, such as traffic and parking violations, are generally not considered part of criminal law.

Criminal conduct has traditionally been divided into two broad categories: crimes against the person and property crimes. Crimes against the person include murder, battery, assault, rape, kidnapping, and false imprisonment. Property crimes include larceny, arson, criminal trespass, criminal mischief, and burglary, to name a few. Modern-day categories often group statutes according to: 1) those that affect public order, health, and morals; 2) offenses involving trade, business and professions; and 3) offenses against the family.

Elements of a Crime: *Mens Rea* and *Actus Reus*

Most crimes consist of two broad elements: *mens rea* and *actus reus*. *Mens rea* means to have "a guilty mind." The rationale behind the rule is that it is wrong for society to punish those who innocently cause harm. *Actus reus* literally means "guilty act," and generally refers to an overt act in furtherance of a crime. Requiring an overt act as part of a crime means that society has chosen to punish only bad deeds, not bad thoughts.

To constitute criminal behavior, the *actus reus* and the *mens rea* must occur simultaneously. For example, suppose John Doe shoots Bob Roe with the intent to kill, but misses completely. Doe later accidentally runs over Roe, resulting in Roe's death. Doe is not guilty of murder.

Different crimes require different degrees of intent. For example, to prove larceny, the prosecution must establish that the defendant intentionally took property to which he knows he is not entitled, intending to deprive the owner of possession permanently. Negligent homicide, on the other hand, involves thoughtlessness, inadvertence, or inattention in a person's duty to exercise due care toward others. A drunk driver who kills another is often charged with criminal negligent homicide.

Specific intent and general intent are other terms used to describe a person's state of mind. General intent means the intent to do something that the law prohibits; the prosecution does not need to establish that the defendant actually intended the precise result. Specific intent designates a special element above and beyond the *actus reus* of the crime, and generally signifies an intentional or knowing state of mind. For example, in the case of larceny, the prosecution must establish the defendant's intent to steal the property. Statutes frequently employ terminology such as purposeful, knowing, reckless, or negligent to describe differing gradations of intent.

Intent is irrelevant in proving a strict liability crime. For a strict liability crime, a prosecutor need only prove that the forbidden act occurred. Statutory rape is a strict liability crime. Only the *actus reus*, a defendant's non-forcible sexual intercourse with a minor, is needed to establish criminal responsibility. The fact that a defendant might have made an honest and reasonable mistake as to the age of the victim is not a defense. Restrictions on the sale of alcohol are also strict liability offenses.

Intent on the part of the defendant is also often lacking in certain vicarious liability offenses. Vicarious liability offenses occur where a defendant's criminal liability is predicated upon the actions of another, often based upon an employer/employee relationship. For example, a bartender who serves alcohol to minors may, by his actions, make the bar owner criminally responsible. This may be true whether the bartender was acting on orders, or deliberately disobeying orders.

Actus reus requires a voluntary act. An epileptic who strikes another during a seizure has not committed a battery. On the other hand, an epileptic who knows he should not drive but does and causes injury, may be guilty of reckless criminal behavior because he created the dangerous situation. Moreover, a failure to act may also constitute a guilty act. Failure to fill out an income tax return is a violation of law. A lifeguard who allows a child to drown would almost certainly face criminal charges.

Defenses

A person may escape criminal responsibility by successfully tendering a legally recognized defense to conduct that is otherwise criminal. Some defenses, such as insanity, infancy, and intoxication, are based on the defendant's lack of capacity to be held legally responsible. Other defenses such as duress, coercion, or necessity, stem from undue pressure or unusual circumstances outside of a defendant's control. An entrapment defense serves as a limitation on the powers of the government to manufacture criminal behavior.

An insane person may be unable to form the requisite intent necessary to commit a crime. Over the years a number of different approaches have been devised to determine when criminal intent is negated by insanity.

The M'Naghten test is named for a delusional Englishman who believed the prime minister was trying to kill him; he mistakenly killed the prime minister's secretary instead. The psychotic M'Naghten was acquitted by an English jury in 1843 based on his insanity defense. The test requires that "at the time of the committing of the act, the party accused was labouring under such a defect of reason, from a disease of the mind, as not to know the nature and quality of the act he was doing; or if he did know it, that he did not know he was doing what was wrong."

A limited number of jurisdictions employ the irresistible impulse test to determine sanity for purposes of criminal liability. If a person's disease of mind prevents him from controlling his conduct, he may be found not guilty by reason of insanity. This defense may be used even where a person was able to distinguish between right and wrong at the time of the offense. For example, if an otherwise-sane father kills the person who molested his child, the father might claim that he was unable to control his actions because of his outrage at the molester's heinous conduct. The irresistible impulse defense fell into disfavor following John Hinckley's acquittal by reason of insanity for his 1981 attempt to assassinate President Ronald Reagan.

Also used in some jurisdictions is the Model Penal Code test of insanity (first used at large in 1960). It provides that a person is not responsible for his conduct if at the time of the conduct the he lacks the substantial capacity, because of a mental disease or defect, either to appreciate the criminality or wrongfulness of the conduct or to conform the conduct to the requirements of the law. In 1984 in response to Hinckley's acquittal, Congress passed the Insanity Defense Reform Act. The Insanity Act employs language similar to the Model Penal Code test.

Trial must be rescheduled if a defendant is insane at the time of trial. The Supreme Court has ruled that a defendant must have the present ability to consult with a lawyer with a reasonable degree of rational understanding, and must have a rational and a factual understanding of the proceeding against him. A convict who goes insane after imposition of a death sentence is entitled to a stay of execution until adjudged sane.

Infancy is a lack of legal capacity to be held responsible for a crime due to the age of the perpetrator. At common law, a child under the age of seven was presumed incapable of committing a crime. Between ages seven and 14, a rebuttable presumption existed that a juvenile was incapable of committing a crime. This presumption weakened progressively as the child approached age 14. Presently, most states define juveniles as persons under the age of 18, although a some states denominate 17 or 16. Juvenile cases are handled under a different system than adult criminal cases. After a certain age, typically set between 13 and 15, a juvenile who commits a serious crime may have his case transferred to adult court and tried as an adult.

Voluntary intoxication caused by drugs or alcohol is permitted as a defense only in very rare instances. It may be allowed as a defense in some situations where specific intent is required; the intoxication may negate the requisite mental state required to establish the offense. Involuntary intoxication, where a defendant is forced to take intoxicants or imbibes without knowledge or reason to know of the intoxicating character, is treated much like an insanity defense.

Duress and coercion are defenses seldom used. These ask the court to treat an alleged perpetrator as a victim, as when a bank robber says he had to do it or his partner would have killed him. A successful defense usually requires a threat of death or serious bodily harm to oneself (or sometimes to a close relative); most states do not recognize duress or coercion to excuse murder charges. Patricia Hearst unsuccessfully invoked this defense in a widely-followed case during the 1970s. Hearst, daughter of wealthy newspaper owners, was kidnapped by social revolutionaries, then later participated with her captors in an armed bank robbery.

Necessity differs from coercion in that it provides an excuse from criminal liability where, in order to protect life or limb, a person reasonably has no other acceptable choice than to commit a criminal act. For example, a defendant who is fleeing a gun-toting criminal may invoke a defense of necessity if when fleeing, the defendant had to break and enter into the dwelling of another.

Entrapment is a defense developed to prevent government officials from inducing a person to commit a crime, where that person was not previously disposed to commit the crime. Entrapment as a defense does not rule out some deception on the part of the police. A person who was planning or willing to commit a crime may generally not invoke an entrapment defense where officials merely create an opportunity for commission of the crime.

Self-Defense

A person may use the amount of force reasonably necessary to prevent immediate unlawful imposition of harm to oneself. In addition, a defendant generally must not be the provoker. Deadly force may be used to repel someone when it reasonably appears necessary to prevent imminent death or serious injury. Some jurisdictions require a defendant to retreat before using deadly force, if it can be done safely.

Inchoate or Prepatory Crimes: Attempt, Conspiracy, and Aiding and Abetting

Attempt was not recognized in very early common law, but now is universally recognized. It means a substantial but unsuccessful effort to commit a particular crime. It usually requires one or more affirmative steps toward the commission of a crime beyond mere preparation. Attempt typically warrants less severe punishment than would the completed crime.

Conspiracy is an agreement between two or more persons to commit an unlawful act or a lawful act which becomes unlawful when done by the concerted action of the conspirators. Some jurisdictions require an overt act in furtherance of the crime to constitute a conspiracy; other jurisdictions hold that the conspiracy agreement constitutes the *actus reus*. Conspiracy is separate and distinct from any underlying crime. A defendant may be guilty of arson and conspiracy to commit arson if she conspires with another to commit the crime and then does so.

An aider and abettor helps, assists, or facilitates the commission of a crime by words or conduct. An aider and abettor need not be present when the crime is committed, although she must share the criminal intent of the principal (the chief perpetrator). An aider and abettor who is present during commission of a crime may be charged as a principal; otherwise he may be charged as an accomplice before or after the fact.

Limitations on Criminal Laws

Ex post facto laws are laws that work to retroactively make conduct previously legal illegal, retroactively increase a punishment, retroactively change the rules of evidence in a criminal case, or retroactively alter the definition of a crime. *Ex post facto* laws are prohibited by the Constitution. The framers believed it was imperative to provide citizens with some idea of what behavior could be punished, and that it was important to prevent tyranny by those in power.

Criminal statutes also need to be understandable to persons of ordinary intelligence. If a reasonable person cannot determine what a law is trying to command or prohibit, that law will be struck down as being void for vagueness. The doctrine of vagueness comes from the Due Process Clauses of the Fifth and Fourteenth Amendments to the Constitution. Laws prohibiting vagrancy have sometimes come under attack as being void because of language that fails to provide an adequate warning as to the type of conduct that might offend the law.

The Eighth Amendment's prohibition against cruel and unusual punishment prohibits punishment which is cruelly disproportionate to the crime. The Supreme Court has ruled that a sentence of 15 years of hard labor was a constitutionally prohibited punishment for a pubic official who falsified a minor document. Likewise, a death sentence for a convicted rapist has also been ruled to constitute cruel and unusual punishment.

See also: **Criminal Procedure, Damages, Juvenile Courts**

Bibliography and Further Reading

Loewy, Arnold H. *Criminal Law in a Nutshell.* St. Paul, MN: West Publishing Co. 1987.

West's Encyclopedia of American Law (various sections). St. Paul, MN: West Publishing Co. 1997.

PEOPLE V. WHITE

Legal Citation: 117 Cal.App.2d 270 (1981)

Plaintiff
State of California

Defendant
Daniel James White

Plaintiff's Claim
That the murders committed by White were premeditated.

Chief Lawyer for Plaintiff
Thomas F. Norman

Chief Lawyers for Defendant
Douglas Schmidt, Stephen Scherr

Judge
Walter F. Calcagno

Place
San Francisco, California

Date of Decision
21 May 1979

Decision
Guilty of voluntary manslaughter; sentenced to seven years and eight months in prison.

Significance
Celebrity murder trials inevitably attract massive media coverage. What made the Dan White case unique was the volatile mix of politics, revenge, and homosexual intolerance. Many wondered if that intolerance spilled over into the jury room.

On 27 November 1978, 32-year-old Dan White entered the San Francisco City Hall by crawling in through a basement window. He adopted this unorthodox means of access to avoid negotiating a metal detector in the main entrance, for reasons which would soon become clear. Once inside, White breezed through the familiar corridors of power. He was on a retrieval mission. Earlier that summer, this ambitious young politician had impetuously resigned his post as a city supervisor, citing financial difficulties; now he wanted that job back. Only one man could make that possible: Mayor George Moscone. White reached Moscone's office and was invited in.

The two men argued for several minutes. As the exchange heated up, Moscone made it plain that he had no intention of reappointing White, who had become a political liability, whereupon White drew a .38 caliber Smith and Wesson revolver that had been tucked into his belt and pumped four bullets into his former boss. After reloading, White hunted down longtime political foe Harvey Milk, another city supervisor. Five shots ended Milk's life. White ran from the building, only to surrender to the authorities one hour later.

Police guarded White closely, fearing possible retaliation. They had good cause for concern. Milk, one of San Francisco's most militant gay activists, had many supporters, all of whom loathed White and the homophobic attitudes he had espoused when in office. Anything was possible in such a volatile situation.

Double Execution

Prosecutor Thomas Norman sought to diffuse some of that volatility with a calm, orderly representation of the facts when the state opened its case against Dan White on 1 May 1979. He described in simple terms what amounted to a double execution, carried out deliberately and with malice aforethought. It was, he said, a crime deserving of death in the gas chamber.

Few could have envied Douglas Schmidt's task when he rose to make the opening statement on White's behalf; after all, he was representing an admitted double assassin. However, he soon went on the offensive. In a fine speech he skillfully diverted the jury's atten-

George Moscone.
© Corbis-Bettmann.

Harvey Bernard Milk.
© Corbis-Bettmann.

tion away from the crime itself and onto the emotional traumas that White had undergone since relinquishing his position as city supervisor. "Good people, fine people, with fine backgrounds, simply don't kill people in cold blood," said Schmidt, "it just doesn't happen, and obviously some part of him has not been presented thus far." Schmidt claimed that White's crimes had been the product of manic depression, "a vile biochemical change" over which the defendant had no control. As added insurance, just in case this line of reasoning failed to sway the jury, Schmidt rounded out his opening with some very pointed comparisons between Milk's overtly homosexual lifestyle and White's all-American background.

The prosecution responded with a parade of witnesses, each of whom recounted events leading up to and on the fateful day at city hall. Chief among them was recently elected San Francisco Mayor Dianne Feinstein. Mayor Feinstein detailed White's frustration with

the political system, his inability to make a difference, as a major source of his discontent. Schmidt scored heavily on cross-examination when he asked, "Would it be your opinion that the man you knew [White] was the type of man who would have shot two people?" Over strenuous state objections, she was allowed to respond. "No," she said. "It would not."

At this point the prosecution began to unravel. What was supposed to be the high-water mark of their case—a taped confession made by White within hours of the shooting—turned into disaster. The tape should have sealed his fate. It did no such thing. Jurors heard him whine: "Well, it's just that I've been under an awful lot of pressure lately, financial pressure, because of my job situation, family pressure . . . because of not being able to have time with my family." The killings were hardly mentioned at all, and White's only display of remorse came when describing his own predicament. And yet, several jurors wept openly as they listened to the story

---

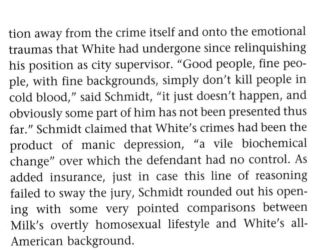

The Blame Game

"The Blame Game" is played by many criminal defendants, and many legal observers believe that the game has spun out of control. Defendants have a right to present arguments in their defense, but some claim that the right is being abused to the detriment of justice.

The first great example of the Blame Game was the Twinkie Defense asserted by manslaughter defendant Daniel White in 1979. What followed has been called "The Abuse Excuse" by legal analysts. Essentially, criminal defendants are asking to be found not guilty, or to have their sentences or charges reduced, based on problems in their past or their own personal short-

comings. With the rise of expert testimony and advances in the psychological and medical disciplines, defendants have more arguments at their disposal than ever before. Some arguments may be more legitimate than others. Women have laid claim to "premenstrual stress" syndrome and men and women alike have defended criminal charges on the basis of "battered person" syndrome. If a criminal defendant suffered any abuse as a child, it is likely that this fact will be presented at trial as mitigating circumstances.

Source(s): *West's Encyclopedia of American Law*, Vol. 7. Minneapolis, MN: West Publishing, 1998.

of a man pushed beyond his endurance. Prosecutor Norman could not believe that—Dan White had been turned into a martyr, an object of sympathy.

Unique Defense

Schmidt capitalized on what had been a lackluster prosecution by turning the trial into an examination of White's mental state. Several psychiatrists testified that the defendant had not really meant to commit murder but had been driven to it by factors beyond his control. Much was made of White's prodigious intake of junk food and candy—what came to be known as the "Twinkies Defense"—in which an abnormally high blood sugar count was blamed for the mayhem that he had wrought. It was a novel but effective defense.

But most effective of all were Schmidt's repeated portrayals of White as an upstanding young man, an ex-fireman and ex-police officer, someone who had been defeated by a corrupt system he was powerless to change. Schmidt cunningly marshaled public resentment against both politicians and homosexuals into one neat package. He found nothing unusual in the fact that White was carrying a gun on the fateful day (As an ex-cop, nothing could have been more natural), or that he had crawled in through a window at city hall to, as one psychiatrist stated, avoid "embarrassing the officer at the metal detector." Dan White, Schmidt said, was acting under an "irresistible impulse to kill," and as such, under California law, was entitled to a verdict of manslaughter.

The jury agreed. On 21 May 1979 they returned two verdicts of voluntary manslaughter. Judge Walter Calcagno handed down the maximum sentence, seven years, and eight months imprisonment. With time off for good behavior, Dan White was looking at freedom in five years.

When news of the verdicts hit the streets, an already incendiary situation exploded. Five thousand gays marched on city hall to protest, and a full-scale riot ensued. Inside the jail, the target of their rage, Dan White, lay on his cell cot, ears plugged against the bedlam.

Over concerted gay protests, White was paroled in 1984. But liberty proved even more onerous than incarceration. Plagued by demons that just would not leave him alone, on 21 October 1985, Dan White wrote the final chapter in this tragedy by committing suicide.

Daniel James White. © Corbis-Bettmann.

The Dan White trial became a rallying call for homosexuals all across America. In their eyes, the jury had semiofficially sanctioned gay murder. Overlooked was the fact that George Moscone was a happily married family man. It is difficult to dispute their firmly held belief that had White killed Moscone alone, he probably would still be behind bars.

Bibliography and Further Reading

Fitzgerald, Frances. "The Castro-II." *New Yorker*, July 28, 1986, pp. 44-63.

Robinson, P. "Gays In The Streets." *New Republic*, June 9, 1979, pp. 9-10.

Shilts, Randy. *The Mayor of Castro Street*. New York: St. Martin's Press, 1982.

Weiss, Mike. *Double Play*. Reading, MA: Addison-Wesley, 1984.

SELECTIVE SERVICE V. MINNESOTA PUBLIC INTEREST RESEARCH GROUP

Legal Citation: 468 U.S. 841 (1984)

Appellant
Selective Service System of the United States

Appellee
Minnesota Public Interest Research Group, et al.

Appellant's Claim
That section 12(f) of the Military Selective Service Act did not constitute a bill of attainder or a violation of the Fifth Amendment protection against compelled self-incrimination.

Chief Lawyer for Appellant
Rex E. Lee, U.S. Solicitor General

Chief Lawyer for Appellee
William J. Keppel

Justices for the Court
Warren E. Burger (writing for the Court), Sandra Day O'Connor, Lewis F. Powell, Jr., William H. Rehnquist, John Paul Stevens, Byron R. White

Justices Dissenting
William J. Brennan, Jr., Thurgood Marshall (Harry A. Blackmun did not participate)

Place
Washington, D.C.

Date of Decision
5 July 1984

Decision
That section 12(f) of the Military Selective Service Act, which denied federal financial assistance to male students between the ages of 18 and 26 who had not registered for the draft, constituted neither a bill of attainder nor a violation of appellees' Fifth Amendment privilege against compelled self-incrimination.

Significance
Selective Service v. Minnesota Public Interest Research Group raised issues which date back as far as the post-Civil War era of Reconstruction, when the 1867 cases *Cummings v. Missouri* and *Ex parte Garland* addressed concerns over the Bill of Attainder Clause of the Constitution. A bill of attainder, as the Court had defined it in *Nixon v. Administrator of General Services* (1977), was "a law that legislatively determines guilt and inflicts punishment upon an identifiable individual without provision of the protections of a judicial trial," thus unfairly subjecting an individual to judgment without the benefit of a genuine legal action. The case also established important distinctions regarding prohibitions against self-incrimination embodied in the Fifth Amendment.

Uncle Sam and Eligible Young Men

Under section 3 of the Military Selective Service Act, the president of the United States is empowered to require every male citizen and resident alien in the country between the ages of 18 and 26 to register for military service under the draft. On 2 July 1980, President Jimmy Carter signed Presidential Proclamation No. 4771, which required all young men to register within 30 days of their eighteenth birthday.

On 8 September 1982, Congress passed the Department of Defense Authorization Act of 1983, thereby adding section 12(f) to the Selective Service Act. Under 12(f), eligible young male students who failed to register would be ineligible for federal financial assistance under Title IV of the Higher Education Act of 1965. Under section 12(f)(2), applicants for such assistance were required to file a statement with their college, university, or trade school showing that they had complied with the draft registration law. Clauses (3) and (4) of 12(f) further required the secretary of education, working with the director of Selective Service, to prescribe methods for verifying statements of compliance, and to issue regulations for implementation. In their final form, as issued on 11 April 1983, these regulations stipulated that no applicant could receive financial aid for higher education under Title IV unless he first filed a statement certifying that he had registered with the Selective Service or that, due to a specified reason such as a physical impairment which would prevent him from military service, he was exempt from the registration requirement. The provision did not require the applicant to state the date on which he had registered.

In November of 1982, an organization called the Minnesota Public Interest Research Group (MPIRG) filed a complaint with the U.S. District Court in Minnesota to enjoin, or stop, the federal government's operation of 12(f). The district court dismissed MPIRG for lack of standing, but did allow three anonymous students to stand in as plaintiffs in the case. The students, still operating under the MPIRG name and in conjunction with MPIRG counsel, held that they resided in Minnesota; that they required financial aid to complete their education; that they intended to apply for such aid; and that though they were eligible

---

Financial Aid Conditions

The conditions that a student must meet to receive financial aid can vary from state to state and from school to school. On the federal level, the United States Department of Education sets various conditions for both schools and students to qualify for federal funds. Registration for selective service by all adult males over the age of eighteen is mandatory for male students to receive financial aid.

The forms of financial aid are many and varied, ranging from loans and grants to scholarships and work-study arrangements. Typically, schools determine what

kind of financial aid a student qualifies for based on need. If a student has more than a certain amount of income and assets, that student may not qualify for need-based grants or scholarships or loans. The most important factor after receiving financial aid is academic performance and progress. If a student is not making satisfactory progress toward a degree, or if the student is not maintaining enough class credits, then the student may lose financial aid.

Source(s): University of Minnesota Office of Financial Aid. 1998.

---

for the draft, they had failed to register with the Selective Service. Later they consolidated their suit with that of three other anonymous young men making essentially the same claim.

In March of 1983, the district court granted a preliminary injunction restraining the Selective Service from enforcing section 12(f). The court's reasoning was twofold. First, it held that 12(f) was a bill of attainder, and thus "clearly singles out an ascertainable group based on past conduct" and "legislatively determines the guilt of this ascertainable group." Second, the court held that 12(f) violated the appellees' privilege against compelled self-incrimination as guaranteed under the Fifth Amendment, because it compelled students requesting financial aid to confess the crime of not having registered for the draft.

On 16 June 1983, the district court issued a nationwide injunction against the enforcement of 12(f), but less than two weeks later, on 29 June, the U.S. Supreme Court stayed that order pending docketing and final disposition of the appeal. Filing *amici curiae* briefs urging affirmance of the lower court's ruling were individuals representing Swarthmore College and the University of Minnesota. The trustees of Boston University filed a brief urging reversal.

Questions of Punitive Intent and Compulsion

By a vote of 6-2 the Court reversed the ruling of the lower court. Chief Justice Burger, writing for the Court, addressed the two issues under debate: the bill of attainder question and the Fifth Amendment question. On both counts, he found 12(f) fully constitutional, an opinion in which Justices O'Connor, Rehnquist, Stevens, and White joined, and with which Powell concurred in part while concurring in the judgment. Justices Brennan and Marshall dissented, and though both filed opinions, the latter's was much longer and more forceful.

A bill of attainder, the Chief Justice held, quoting *Nixon v. Administrator of General Services,* was "a law that legislatively determines guilt and inflicts punishment upon an identifiable individual without provision of the protections of a judicial trial." An example of a bill of attainder was a provision in the post-Civil War Constitution of Missouri, which prevented a person from entering a given profession unless he swore under oath that he had not "been a member of, or connected with, any order, society, or organization inimical to the government of the United States." The law, which was clearly intended to bar former supporters of the Confederate government from any role in public life, was struck down in *Cummings v. Missouri* (1867), and the Court struck down a similar law in *Ex parte Garland* (1867).

Section 12(f), on the other hand, did not single out those who failed to register, or make them ineligible based on that past conduct. It did not require registration within the time period established by the Presidential Proclamation, nor did it deem late registrants ineligible for aid. Rather, it "clearly gives non-registrants 30 days after receiving notice that they are ineligible for Title IV aid to register for the draft and qualify for aid." Nor did it inflict punishment, at least as that term was understood in the Bill of Attainder Clause in the Constitution. "It does not even deprive appellees of Title IV benefits permanently," the Chief Justice wrote, "since it leaves open perpetually the possibility of qualifying for aid." In passing 12(f), Congress had meant simply to "encourage registration" by those who were required to register and had not done so. It was not punitive in nature, but rather was intended to provide "a rational means to improve compliance with the registration requirements."

With regard to the Fifth Amendment privilege against compelled self-incrimination, Burger held that since a student who had not registered with the Selective Service would be bound to know that his application for financial aid would be denied, he was by no means under any "compulsion" to seek that aid. In other words, applying for aid was a choice he would have to make of his own free will, and if he did not want to sign up for the draft, then he would have to accept the consequences of that freely taken action—including the withholding of federal funds. As for the fact that a student who changed his mind and registered for the draft after all might be registering after the 30 day deadline, this too failed to constitute compulsory self-incrimination. The law did not require a student to inform officials at his school whether or not he had registered late, nor would lateness in registering disqualify a student from applying for financial aid. Because the appellees had not attempted to register, they "had no occasion to assert their Fifth Amendment privilege when asked to state their dates of birth . . ." Nor, finally, had the government threatened them with any consequences—short of not receiving a financial aid check—for their failure to comply. "Under these circumstances," Burger wrote, "appellees will not be heard to complain that 12(f) violates their Fifth Amendment rights by forcing them to acknowledge during the draft process they have avoided that they are registering late."

Justice Powell concurred in part and concurred in the judgment. In his view, the bill of attainder issue could be settled much more easily than the Court had disposed of it, simply by noting that 12(f) was not punitive legislation, a distinction established in *Nixon v. Administrator of General Services.* The Selective Service Act—and only that act—provided a punishment for the crime of failing to register for the draft. Section 12(f), by contrast, "authorizes no punishment in any normal or general acceptance of that familiar term." Using much the same logic as the Court, but applying it more directly, Powell was saying that withholding a privilege is not the same thing as conferring a punishment. Far from authorizing punitive actions, section 12(f) "provides a benefit at the expense of taxpayers generally for those who request and qualify for it." No one was compelled to receive it, nor was any minority group forbidden from receiving it. Since he found that 12(f) was not punitive in purpose or effect, Powell held that it was unnecessary to address the other questions the Court had reviewed in examining the bill of attainder issue.

Marshall's Dissent: "A De Facto Classification Based on Wealth"

Justice Brennan issued a short dissenting opinion, wherein he stated that he would affirm the lower court's judgment because in his view section 12(f) "compels those students seeking financial aid who have not registered with the Selective Service in timely fash-

ion to incriminate themselves and thereby violates the Fifth Amendment." For the rest, he deferred to Justice Marshall. The latter, in a much longer and more forceful opinion, took an approach not unlike the one he had used in a very different case, *Beal v. Doe* (1977). In both cases, he held that the withholding of government benefits from a financially needy individual—abortions for young women in *Beal,* college money for young men in *Selective Service*—did indeed constitute a form of coercion or compulsion. Likewise in both dissenting opinions, he attacked a policy of what he judged as special punishment for the poor.

Section 12(f), Justice Marshall wrote, was unconstitutional not only on the Fifth Amendment question, but also from a standpoint not previously discussed in the case: that of the Fourteenth Amendment's Due Process Clause. When Congress enacted 12(f), it was well aware that some 674,000 of the 9,039,000 young men eligible for the draft had failed to register. In using the statute in question, however, it had sought to unfairly coerce the poor to shoulder the burden of national defense. Given his other disagreement with the statute, Justice Marshall wrote, it was not necessary to approach it on the bill of attainder issue; the Fifth Amendment critique was powerful enough. Marshall conceded that 12(f) did not force the student to incriminate himself before his educational institution, but "our inquiry cannot stop here." The statute in Marshall's eyes clearly coerced registration with the Selective Service System, and this led to reporting of self-incriminatory information to the federal government.

Hence a student who registered after the 30 day deadline "provides the Government with two crucial links in the chain of evidence necessary to prosecute him criminally." First of all, his birth date and date of registration offered two pieces of evidence that the student has violated a law; second, and in Marshall's view even more important, the student thus called attention to his technical violation of the Military Selective Service Act. "Armed with these data," Marshall wrote, "the Government need only prove that the student 'knowingly' failed to register at the time prescribed by law in order to obtain a conviction."

As for the Fourteenth Amendment issue, Justice Marshall addressed the fact that it had not been raised by the rest of the Court when he noted "The majority's superficial, indeed cavalier, rejection of appellees' equal protection argument." This, he said, quoting himself in *Flagg Bros., Inc. v. Brooks* (1978), showed a "callous indifference to the realities of life for the poor." It was incorrect to say, as the majority had, that 12(f) treated all young men alike. The fact was, according to Marshall—who quoted a statement by Rep. Moffett during floor debate on the issue in 1982—"Only low-income and middle-income students will be caught in this trap."

Impact

Several authors writing in law journals soon after *Selective Service* responded with alarm. Hence Anthony L. Cogswell concluded a 1985 article in the *Thurgood Marshall Law Review* with the statement "It is possible that *Selective Service System* may have a chilling effect on claims brought under the Fifth Amendment." Cheryl V. Cunningham, writing in the *Loyola Law Review,* sounded a more muted tone: noting that the case "marks a retreat from the course paved in the 1960s by a Court then more prone to expand the privilege against self-incrimination," she went on to say that "Most probably, *Minnesota Public Interest Research Group* will not arouse the concern it deserves." By and large, this statement has proven true, as very few Supreme Court cases in subsequent years have drawn on the Court's judgment in this one. The end of the Cold War in the period from 1989 to 1992 helped to reduce concern about the draft, though subsequent U.S. police actions in Iraq, Bosnia, Haiti, and other locales have served to raise it again.

Related Cases

Cummings v. Missouri, 4 Wall. 277 (1867).
Ex parte Garland, 71 U.S. 333 (1867).
Garrity v. New Jersey, 385 U.S. 493 (1967).
Marchetti v. United States, 390 U.S. 39 (1968).
Lefkowitz v. Turley, 414 U.S. 70 (1973).
Nixon v. Administrator of General Services, 433 U.S. 425 (1977).

Bibliography and Further Reading

Cogswell, Anthony L. "Constitutional Law—Federal Financial Aid and Draft Registration—Males Who Fail to Register With the Selective Service Can Be Denied Federal Student Financial Aid, *Selective Service v. Minnesota Public Interest Research Group.*" *Thurgood Marshall Law Review,* Vol. 10, pp. 585–93.

Cunningham, Cheryl V. "*Selective Service v. Minnesota Public Interest Research Group:* A Serious Constitutional Challenge." *Loyola Law Review,* Vol. 30, pp. 987–1008.

"The Supreme Court Sanctions the Conditioning of Financial Aid for College on Draft Registration: *Selective Service v. Minnesota Public Interest Research Group.*" *Boston College Law Review,* Vol. 26, pp. 1063–1100.

FLORIDA V. RILEY

Legal Citation: 488 U.S. 445 (1989)

Petitioner
State of Florida

Respondent
Michael A. Riley

Petitioner's Claim
It is not unlawful under the Fourth Amendment for a police officer to hover in a helicopter 400 feet above the home of a person and look with the naked eye into the person's property.

Chief Lawyer for Petitioner
Parker D. Thomson

Chief Lawyer for Respondent
Marc H. Salton

Justices for the Court
Anthony M. Kennedy, Sandra Day O'Connor, William H. Rehnquist, Antonin Scalia, Byron R. White (writing for the Court)

Justices Dissenting
Harry A. Blackmun, William J. Brennan, Jr., Thurgood Marshall, John Paul Stevens

Place
Washington, D.C.

Date of Decision
23 January 1989

Decision
An officer's observation, with the naked eye, of the interior of a partially covered greenhouse in a residential backyard from the vantage point of a helicopter positioned 400 feet above the yard does not constitute a search for which a warrant is required.

Significance
The decision gave police officers unprecedented authority to surveil from the sky.

In August of 1984, Deputy Kurt Gell, a police officer with the Pasco County Sheriff's Office received an anonymous tip that Michael A. Riley was growing marijuana at his home, which was situated in a rural area. Deputy Gell surveilled the area on foot and found a greenhouse located near a mobile home. The home and greenhouse were surrounded by a fence, and the only two sides of the greenhouse that were not enclosed were obscured by trees and the mobile home. In order to see what the greenhouse contained, Deputy Gell flew a helicopter over the property at an altitude of approximately 400 feet. As two panels from the top of the greenhouse were missing, Gell was able to see inside, and he identified the plants inside the greenhouse as marijuana plants. Although Gell took pictures of the greenhouse, he testified that he was able to see inside the greenhouse and identify the plants as marijuana with his naked eye.

Based on these observations, Gell went to a magistrate and obtained a warrant to search Riley's property. Forty-four marijuana plants were found in the greenhouse, and Riley was charged with possession of marijuana. At trial, Riley moved to suppress the marijuana evidence, arguing that the aerial search of his property was a violation of the Fourth Amendment and that, as such, the fruits of the search should be excluded from trial. The trial court granted Riley's motion to suppress, but the Florida Court of Appeals reversed. The Florida Supreme Court, however, reversed the appeals court's decision and reinstated the order suppressing the evidence. The state of Florida appealed to the U.S. Supreme Court, which reversed the Florida Supreme Court's decision.

In a close decision, the High Court ruled by a vote of 5-4 that Gell's aerial surveillance was not unconstitutional. In the plurality opinion, written by Justice White, the Court asserted that one of its recent cases, *California v. Ciraolo* (1986), was the controlling precedent. In that case, police officers visually inspected the backyard of a house while flying a fixed-wing aircraft at an altitude of 1,000 feet. After identifying the presence of marijuana from that distance with their naked eyes, the officers obtained a search warrant based on the observations and found marijuana plants. In that case, the High Court held that the search was not subject to the Fourth Amendment and therefore not illegal. Quoting *Katz v. United States* (1967), another applicable precedent, the Court reiterated that "'[w]hat a person knowingly exposes to the public, even in his own home or office, is not a subject of Fourth Amendment protection.'" Generally, a person receives protection from unreasonable searches and seizures by police under the Fourth Amendment if the person has a reasonable expectation of privacy. A reasonable expectation of privacy is an objectively reasonable expectation that a police officer may not search around for evidence of a crime without first developing probable cause to believe that evidence of a crime can be found in the particular place. To determine whether a person has a reasonable expectation of privacy, courts look at a number of factors, including the capacity of persons to see a particular place with the naked eye.

In *Florida v. Riley,* Riley's expectation of privacy was not reasonable because the area for which he sought Fourth Amendment protection was visible to the naked eye from above. Quoting *Ciraolo* and *Katz,* the Court decided that Riley's expectation of privacy was unreasonable because we live "[i]n an age where private and commercial flight in the public airways is routine." Because Riley had left the roof of his greenhouse partially open, it was open to viewing from the air, and, since the police in *Ciraolo* did not need a warrant, Gell did not need a warrant.

That Gell's helicopter was flying at a low level of 400 feet above Riley's home was of no matter to the Court. The case would have been different, the Court allowed, if the police had observed any "intimate details" connected with the use of the home or curtilage, or "if flying at that altitude had been contrary to law or regulation." Because it is not illegal for a helicopter to fly at an altitude of 400 feet, such flights are not rare, and so Riley's anticipation that his property would not be observed from such a height was unreasonable.

Justice O'Connor concurred in the judgment, but only because she agreed that Gell's observation "did not violate an expectation of privacy 'that society is prepared to recognize as reasonable.'" To O'Connor, though, the decision relied to heavily on compliance with regulations of the Federal Aviation Administration (FAA). "Because the FAA has decided that helicopters can lawfully operate at virtually any altitude so long as they pose no safety hazard," O'Connor argued, "it does not follow that the expectations of privacy 'society is prepared to recognize as reasonable' simply mirror the FAA's concerns." O'Connor warned that the basis of the decision on police compliance with FAA standards could eventually erode privacy rights and quality of life. "[E]ven individuals who have taken effective precautions to ensure against ground-level observations cannot block off all conceivable aerial views of their out-

door patios and yards," noted O'Connor, "without entirely giving up their enjoyment of those areas." O'Connor opined that aerial observations lower than 400 feet "may be sufficiently rare that police surveillance from such altitudes would violate reasonable expectations of privacy, despite compliance with FAA air safety regulations."

Justices Brennan, Marshall, Stevens, and Blackmun dissented. In a dissenting opinion joined by Marshall and Stevens, Justice Brennan wrote that Justice O'Connor's opinion "gives reason to hope that this altitude [of 400 feet] may constitute a lower limit." Brennan lamented, however, that "four Justices would remove virtually all constitutional barriers to police surveillance from the vantage point of helicopters." "I cannot agree," Brennan stated, "that the Fourth Amendment . . . tolerates such an intrusion on privacy and personal security."

According to Brennan, Marshall, and Stevens, precedent called for an affirmation of the Florida Supreme Court's ruling. The *Ciraolo* case hinged on the fact that the officers in the plane were flying at an altitude of 1,000 feet, stated Brennan, not the legality of their location. Employing the standard for determining whether the defendant's expectation of privacy was reasonable, the Court in *Ciraolo* held that because plane traffic at 1,000 feet was so common, the defendant could not reasonably expect to keep private any activity that could be visible with the naked eye from that altitude. In Riley's case, though, Officer Gell was flying only 400 feet above the ground, enjoying an extraordinary vantage point and using "a very expensive and sophisticated piece of machinery to which few ordinary citizens have access."

Brennan ridiculed the plurality's emphasis on the absence of wind, noise, and dust. "Imagine a helicopter," wrote Brennan, "capable of hovering just above an enclosed courtyard or patio without generating any noise, wind, or dust at all . . . [or] any threat of injury." Brennan was also puzzled by the plurality's emphasis on the fact that Officer Gell had not seen any "intimate" activity while he was spying. "Where in the Fourth Amendment or in our cases," Brennan wondered, "is there any warrant for imposing a requirement that the activity observed must be 'intimate' in order to be protected by the Constitution?" In Brennan's opinion, the Court was dismissing Riley's case "as a 'drug case' only at the peril of [its] own liberties."

Brennan concluded the dissenting opinion with a quote from George Orwell's novel *1984:*

> The black-mustachio'd face gazed down from every commanding corner. There was one on the house front immediately opposite. BIG BROTHER IS WATCHING YOU, the caption said . . . In the far distance a helicopter

skimmed down between the roofs, hovered for an instant like a bluebottle, and darted away again with a curving flight. It was the Police Patrol, swooping into people's windows.

"Who can read this passage without a shudder," Brennan asked, "and without the instinctive reaction that it depicts life in some country other than ours?"

In a shorter dissenting opinion, Justice Stevens noted that no High Court precedent indicated who had the burden of proving whether a person's expectation of privacy was reasonable. Stevens indicated that he would place the burden of such providing such proof on the prosecution in any case where the police had surveilled from an altitude of under 1,000 feet. In Riley's case, Stevens felt, the prosecution had not carried that burden.

Impact

The decision essentially made it possible for law enforcement personnel to conduct aerial searches without a warrant, so long as such searches do not violate FAA regulations, yield intimate details, pose too much danger, or create too much dust, noise, or wind. An earlier decision, *Dow Chemical Co. v. United States*, decided on the same day as the *Ciraolo* case, approved aerial photography by law enforcement officers. Thus, when combined with the *Dow Chemical* case, the *Riley* decision made it possible for law enforcement officers to take photographs from at least 400 feet in the air.

Related Cases

Katz v. United States, 389 U.S. 347 (1967).
California v. Ciraolo, 476 U.S. 207 (1986).

Bibliography and Further Reading

Epstein, Lee, and Thomas G. Walker. *Constitutional Law for a Changing America: Rights, Liberties, and Justice.* Washington, DC: Congressional Quarterly, Inc., 1995.

New York Times, January 24, 1989.

ILLINOIS V. PERKINS

Legal Citation: 496 U.S. 292 (1990)

Petitioner
State of Illinois

Respondent
Lloyd Perkins

Petitioner's Claim
That Perkins's jailhouse admission of murder to an undercover agent should be admissible, even though Perkins did not receive Miranda warnings before the questioning.

Chief Lawyer for Petitioner
Marcia L. Friedl

Chief Lawyer for Respondent
Dan W. Evers

Justices for the Court
Harry A. Blackmun, William J. Brennan, Jr., Anthony M. Kennedy (writing for the Court), Sandra Day O'Connor, William H. Rehnquist, John Paul Stevens, Antonin Scalia, Byron R. White

Justices Dissenting
Thurgood Marshall

Place
Washington, D.C.

Date of Decision
4 June 1990

Decision
An undercover law enforcement officer posing as a fellow inmate need not give Miranda warnings to an incarcerated suspect before asking questions that may elicit an incriminating response.

Significance
In *Illinois v. Perkins*, the Court recognized limitations to the rule announced in *Miranda*. Perkins was an example of a custodial interrogation that created no compulsion. Since *Miranda* was not intended to protect individuals from themselves, the Court held there was no need to advise Perkins of his Miranda rights prior to his conversation with an undercover police officer. This decision allowed law enforcement to use undercover agents in a jail without necessitating the giving of Miranda warnings to the suspect.

Richard Stephenson was murdered in November of 1984 in a suburb of East St. Louis, Illinois. His murder remained unsolved until March of 1986, when Donald Charlton told police that Lloyd Perkins had confessed to the murder while the two were in jail together at the Graham Correctional Facility. By this time, Perkins was in a different jail on a charge of aggravated battery, not connected to the Stephenson murder. The police decided to place an undercover agent in the cellblock with Perkins and Charlton. John Parisi, the undercover agent, and Charlton posed as escapees from a work release program whom had been arrested for burglary. While in the same cellblock with Perkins, Parisi suggested that the three of them try to escape from the jail. While discussing the escape plan, Parisi asked Perkins if he had ever killed anyone. Perkins described Stephenson's murder. Parisi asked more questions about the murder, including what type of weapon was used.

Perkins was charged with the murder, but before the trial, he asked that the evidence of his statements made to Parisi in jail be suppressed (not allowed in court) on the ground that Parisi had not given him the Miranda warnings before their conversations. The trial court granted the motion to suppress. The Appellate Court of Illinois affirmed the ruling, stating that *Miranda* prohibits all undercover contacts with incarcerated suspects that are reasonably likely to elicit an incriminating response.

A Coercive Atmosphere Is Lacking

In his opinion for the majority, Justice Kennedy wrote that Miranda warnings are not required when the suspect is unaware that he is speaking to a law enforcement officer and gives a voluntary statement. *Miranda v. Arizona*, gave rise to the Miranda warnings that are read to suspects when they are arrested. The warnings state that the person has a right to remain silent and that whatever a person says may be used against him in court. Kennedy noted that in *Miranda*, the Court held that the Fifth Amendment privilege against self-incrimination prohibits admitting statements given by a suspect during "custodial interrogation" without prior warning. Miranda rights were formulated to make sure people did not incriminate themselves while in a "police-dominated atmosphere" which generates "compelling pressures." The Court held that conversations between suspects and undercover agents do not involve such an atmosphere or compulsion; an incarcerated person speaks freely to someone he thinks is a fellow inmate. When a suspect considers himself in the company of cellmates and not officers, the coercive atmosphere is lacking.

Miranda stated that the danger of coercion results from the interaction of custody and official interrogation. Kennedy rejected the argument that the Miranda warnings are required whenever a suspect is in custody and converses with someone who happens to be a government agent. When a suspect does not know that he is talking to a government agent, pressure does not exist. "*Miranda* forbids coercion, not mere strategic deception by taking advantage of a suspect's misplaced trust in one he supposes to be a fellow prisoner." Kennedy quoted *Miranda*: "Confessions remain a proper element in law enforcement. Any statement given freely and voluntarily without any compelling influences is, of course, admissible in evidence." Kennedy noted that ploys to mislead a suspect are not compulsion or coercion and *Miranda* was not meant to protect suspects from boasting about their criminal activities. The tactic used by the police in Perkins's case to elicit a voluntary confession does not violate the Self-incrimination Clause of the Fifth Amendment.

In several past cases the Court held that the government may not use an undercover agent to circumvent the Sixth Amendment right to counsel once a suspect has been charged with a crime. In this case, no charges had been filed against Perkins regarding the subject of the interrogation, the murder of Stephenson, thus the Sixth Amendment precedents did not apply here. Law enforcement officers will have little difficulty putting into practice the ruling that undercover agents need not give Miranda warnings to incarcerated suspects. Miranda warnings are not required to safeguard the constitutional rights of inmates who make voluntary statements to undercover agents. These statements are admissible at trial.

Deception And Manipulation Practiced

Justice Brennan wrote a concurring opinion. He agreed that when a suspect does not know that his questioner is a police agent, the questioning does not amount to "interrogation" in an "inherently coercive" environment and thus does not require the Miranda warnings. However, Brennan felt that the deception and manipulation practiced on Perkins raised a substantial claim that the confession violated the Due Process Clause of the Fifth Amendment. In his opinion, the state was in a unique position to exploit a suspect's vulnerability because it had complete control over the suspect's environment. An undercover agent could barrage a suspect

with questions until he confessed, as in Perkins's case. The deliberate use of deception and manipulation by the police was incompatible with a system that presumes innocence and assures that inquisitorial means will not be used to get a conviction.

Compulsion Includes Police Deception

Justice Marshall dissented. He noted that the conditions that require the police to read a suspect the Miranda warnings—custodial interrogation conducted by an agent of the police—were present in *Illinois v. Perkins.* Because Perkins did not receive his Miranda warnings before he was subjected to custodial interrogation, his confession should be inadmissible. The majority's creation of an exception to the Miranda rule that applies when an undercover agent asks questions that may elicit an incriminating response was inconsistent with the rationale supporting *Miranda,* in Marshall's opinion. It allowed police officers intentionally to take advantage of suspects who are unaware of their constitutional rights.

While Perkins was confined he was subjected to express questioning likely to evoke an incriminating response. *Miranda* dealt with any police tactics that might compel a suspect to make incriminating statements without full awareness of his constitutional rights. The point of the Miranda warnings is to make a suspect aware of the Fifth Amendment privilege and the consequences of foregoing it. "Thus when a law enforcement agent structures a custodial interrogation so that a suspect feels compelled to reveal incriminating information, he must inform the suspect of his constitutional rights and give him an opportunity to decide whether or not to talk."

The compulsion described in *Miranda* includes police deception. The police deceptively took advantage of Perkins's psychological vulnerability by including him in a sham escape plot, where he would feel compelled to show his willingness to shoot a guard by discussing his past involvement in a murder. The pressure unique to custody allowed the police to use deception to compel a suspect to make incriminating statements. The suspect's ignorance of the agent's real identity did not mean compulsion was not used.

The Court's adoption of this exception to the Miranda warnings was incompatible with the principle that the doctrine should be simple and clear. The Court's ruling complicated a previously clear and straightforward doctrine. "Would *Miranda* be violated, for instance, if an undercover police officer beat a confession out of a suspect, but the suspect thought the officer was another prisoner who wanted the information for his own purposes?" The exception created in this case may result in police officers conducting interrogations of confined suspects through undercover agents, getting around the need to administer Miranda warnings. "The Court's adoption of the 'undercover exception' to the Miranda rule thus is necessarily also the adoption of a substantial loophole in our jurisprudence protecting suspects' Fifth Amendment rights."

Impact

Legal scholars have debated the legality and propriety of using cellmate informants. Some scholars find the practice a strategic deception that takes advantage of a suspect's misplaced trust in a person he thinks is a fellow prisoner. Others view the use of cellmate informants as offensive to a civilized system of justice. Law enforcement officers find that the use of cellmate informants is a method that works. *Illinois v. Perkins* answered some questions regarding the constitutionality of using cellmate informants. The case resolved the issue of exactly when Miranda warnings must be given. A suspect's being in custody alone does not necessitate the warnings. The impact on the suspect of both police interrogation and police custody makes custodial police interrogation so corrosive and thus requires "adequate protective devices." This decision paved the way for law enforcement officers to take advantage of using cellmate informants.

Related Cases

Massiah v. United States, 377 U.S. 201 (1964).
Miranda v. Arizona, 384 U.S. 436 (1966).
Mathis v. United States, 391 U.S. 1 (1968).
Rhode Island v. Innis, 446 U.S. 291 (1980).
Berkemer v. McCarty, 468 U.S. 420 (1984).

Bibliography and Further Reading

Alpert, Geoffrey P., and William C. Smith. "How Reasonable is the Reasonable Man?: Police and Excessive Force." *Journal of Criminal Law and Criminology,* fall 1994, p. 481.

Hall, Kermit L., ed. *The Oxford Companion to the Supreme Court of the United States.* New York: Oxford University Press, 1992.

Stuntz, William J. "The Uneasy Relationship Between Criminal Procedure and Criminal Justice." *Yale Law Journal,* October 1997, p. 1.

UNITED STATES V. ALVAREZ-MACHAIN

Legal Citation: 504 U.S. 655 (1992)

Petitioner
United States

Respondent
Dr. Humberto Alvarez-Machain

Petitioner's Claim
That U.S. courts have jurisdiction over internationally abducted criminal defendants when not taken in explicit violation of an extradition treaty.

Chief Lawyer for Petitioner
Kenneth Winston Starr, U.S. Solicitor General

Chief Lawyer for Respondent
Paul L. Hoffman

Justices for the Court
Anthony M. Kennedy, William H. Rehnquist (writing for the Court), Antonin Scalia, David H. Souter, Clarence Thomas, Byron R. White

Justices Dissenting
Harry A. Blackmun, Sandra Day O'Connor, John Paul Stevens

Place
Washington, D.C.

Date of Decision
15 June 1992

Decision
Upheld the United States claim and overturned two lower court's decisions prohibiting the prosecution of a foreign national due to violation of the spirit of an extradition treaty.

Significance
The ruling established that foreign citizens who commit crimes against U.S. citizens outside U.S. boundaries still come under jurisdiction of U.S. courts even when forcibly abducted from their country over official protests of that nation. Abducted defendants can still receive fair trials under the Due Process Clause. Government-sponsored abductions of another country's citizens in absence of explicit treaty prohibitions was approved. The Court, relying solely on U.S. domestic law precedents while ignoring international law, held that international implications were more appropriately the concern of the executive branch. The abduction and Court decision led to an outcry from other nations and efforts in the United States to restrict further foreign abductions.

Treaties between the United States and foreign governments hold a unique place in the U.S. legal system by residing both in American domestic law and international relations. Created by the executive branch of the government rather than Congress, these agreements need only receive Senate approval. Legal disputes often involve conflicts between America's exercise of political independence, domestic law, and international law. A common form of treaty is the extradition treaty that provides a process a country can use to turn over jurisdiction of an individual within their territorial boundaries to another nation. Such treaties commonly seek to establish mutual respect of boundaries and maintain political sovereignty. Abductions without consent are rarely acceptable.

Prior to the 1990s, two landmark cases in extradition and international abductions had been decided by the U.S. Supreme Court, both in 1886. *Ker v. Illinois* involved the forcible abduction by a private individual of a U.S. citizen in Peru wanted on embezzlement charges in Illinois. Ker argued he had a right to be returned to the United States only through the existing extradition treaty with Peru. The Court did not accept Ker's claim of due process violation by ruling that forcible abduction does not prevent a person answering to the charges brought before the court. Furthermore, Peru had not protested the abduction. Also in 1886, the Court ruled in *United States v. Rauscher* that a person extradited under a treaty could only be prosecuted for the crimes for which he was extradited. U.S. jurisdiction did not exist if terms of an extradition treaty were violated.

Years later, in 1952, the Court ruled on a case in which a defendant kidnapped in Chicago by Michigan law officers was brought to trial in Michigan. The defendant argued his rights were violated under the Due Process Clause of the Fifth Amendment. However, the Court again held that "the power of a court to try a person for crime is not impaired by the fact that he had been brought within the court's jurisdiction by reason of a 'forcible abduction.'" Judges were not required to consider how defendants got into their courtrooms. Due process only applied to the defendant being appropriately informed of the charges and given a fair trial.

The Court held that nothing in the Constitution prohibited the government from convicting a person who was brought to trial against his will. Decisions in the *Ker* (1886) and *Frisbie* (1952) cases became known as the *Ker-Frisbie* doctrine recognizing jurisdiction over forcibly abducted criminal defendants.

In 1978, the United States and Mexico signed a new extradition treaty. In February of 1985 U.S. Drug Enforcement Agency (DEA) Special Agent Enrique Camarena-Salazar and his pilot, Alfredo Zavala-Avelar, were kidnapped outside the American Consulate in Guadalajara, Mexico while investigating a drug case. A month later their mutilated bodies were discovered. In the following years several people in the United States and Mexico were charged in connection with the brutal murders and the drug trafficking activities that Camarena had been investigating. Unsuccessfully, DEA officials had informally negotiated with the Mexican government regarding transport of one of those charged, a medical doctor named Dr. Humberto Alvarez-Machain, to the United States for trial. Finally, in April of 1990, Machain was forcibly kidnapped by several armed Mexican bounty hunters from his medical office in Guadalajara and flown in a private plane to El Paso, Texas where he was arrested by DEA officials. Machain was charged in a U.S. District Court in Los Angeles with kidnapping and murder of the agent. The U.S. government charged that Machain participated in the murder by medically prolonging Avelar's life so that the torture and interrogation could continue. The Mexican government immediately requested an official report from the United States describing the government's role in the abduction. Mexico also sent two diplomatic notes the months following requesting Machain's extradition from the United States for prosecution in Mexico and the extradition of individuals involved in Machain's abduction for prosecution on kidnapping charges.

In his trial, Machain argued "the District Court lacked jurisdiction to try him because he was abducted in violation of the extradition treaty between the United States and Mexico." The court agreed with Machain by concluding that DEA agents had orchestrated the abduction therefore violating the treaty. The court, finding it lacked jurisdiction, ordered Machain returned to Mexico. The United States appealed the decision. The court of appeals concurred with the earlier ruling by finding the "purpose" of the treaty was violated by the forcible abduction. The United States then appealed to the U.S. Supreme Court.

Abduction an Option

The primary government argument before the Court was not that the treaty authorized abduction of Mexican citizens by U.S. authorities, but that it did not prohibit such abductions. Machain argued the treaty did not expressly recognize the *Ker-Frisbie* doctrine, and in fact, Article 9 of the treaty allowed for Mexico to deny U.S. extradition requests. The Court, therefore, deliberated which applied, the *Ker-Frisbie* doctrine recognizing jurisdiction over abducted defendants or the *Rauscher* (1886) decision denying jurisdiction if a treaty was violated.

Chief Justice Rehnquist delivered the opinion of the majority in a 6-3 vote. A key finding by Rehnquist was that Mexico had been made aware of the *Ker-Frisbie* doctrine as early as 1906. As to whether Mexico accepted or recognized the legal principle was not an issue. Rehnquist wrote, therefore, the treaty merely established one option available to obtain a suspect in addition to forcible abduction. Rehnquist concluded the abduction may have been "shocking" and may have violated "general international law principles." However, those matters were for the executive branch to address and not the subject of the Court. The Court was only to determine the relationship of the abduction to the treaty. In that regard, the abduction was found not in violation of the treaty and the *Ker-Frisbie* doctrine fully applied. The forced abduction did not negate a fair trial under U.S. court jurisdiction. The court of appeals decision was reversed and the case remanded back to the district court for trial.

A Monstrous Decision

Justice Stevens, joined in dissent by Justices Blackmun and O'Connor, wrote that the majority simply chose to ignore Mexico's interpretation of the 1978 treaty. The treaty plainly stated its purpose was to foster closer working relationships regarding crime fighting and extradition matters. Such neglect by the majority negated the whole purpose of extradition treaties which is to maintain harmonious working relationships, prevent international conflict, and protect nations from invasions by other countries. Based on this general understanding of international law, Stevens concluded, "it is difficult to see how an interpretation that encourages unilateral action could foster cooperation and mutual assistance." Stevens noted that Mexico had already prosecuted several individuals for Camarena's murder. In addition, he found significant differences in this case and the *Ker* and *Frisbie* cases. In *Ker*, the U.S. government was not involved in the abduction and Peru did not protest. The *Frisbie* case only involved state boundaries, not national. Stevens thus noted the "Court's failure to differentiate between private abductions and official invasion of another sovereigns territory" representing "flagrant violation of international law." According to Stevens, the two lower courts had appropriately applied *Rauscher* to this case. They came to the logical conclusion that the extradition treaty with Mexico was intended to establish the exclusive means of transferring jurisdictions of individuals and should be interpreted from the perspective of both countries. In conclusion, Stevens lamented that "most courts throughout the civilized world—will be deeply disturbed by the 'monstrous' decision" of the Court.

Impact

The *Machain* case was a highly publicized international abduction owing in part to the unusual use of bounty hunters by U.S. officials. The United States had directly orchestrated the abduction of a Mexican citizen on Mexican soil against the wishes of the Mexican government.

The abduction and trial severely strained relations between the United States and Mexico and attracted substantial negative international reaction of not only allies, but Iran and China as well, concerning human rights issues. The district court, in the retrial, dismissed the charges against Machain for lack of evidence.

The decision demonstrated the Court's increasing tendency to rule in favor of the United States in foreign treaty disputes and diverge from the international standards of good faith and liberal interpretation. To the astonishment of the international law community, the Court derived its decision in *Machain* entirely from its own previous decisions, avoiding any use of relevant decisions by courts of other nations. As this and the *Itel Containers International Corporation v. Huddleston* (1993) case the following year clearly indicated, foreign governments' interpretations of treaties carried little weight in American courts. Even sections on treaty interpretation in the 1980 Vienna Convention were overlooked. In stark contrast to foreign courts as noted by Stevens' dissent, the Court treated a case with international implications solely as a domestic case with domestic precedents and domestic answers.

Treaty cases heard by the Court in the late 1980s and early 1990s demonstrated the exceptional degree the Court yielded to the wishes of the executive branch. The Court, recognizing the constitutional role of the president in establishing treaties, in effect implicitly applied the "political question doctrine." In other words, international treaty disputes were considered matters for the president and Congress to decide and should not be the subject of court rulings.

Given the Court's position, international kidnapping proved to be an attractive tool for U.S. law offi-

cials seeking to avoid lengthy extradition procedures in obtaining suspects or when dealing with uncooperative governments. At times the abductions were quietly sanctioned by sympathetic governments where extradition was not popular with its citizens. Such abductions were particularly useful in fighting international drug crime.

The *Machain* case raised questions of how the United States should regulate its police activities in other countries, the president's role in foreign relations, and treatment of foreign defendants in U.S. courts. Legislative solutions were immediately but unsuccessfully sought after the *Machain* decision. Legislators introduced a bill in Congress in 1992 forbidding prosecution of persons abducted by U.S. officials in violation of treaty terms or despite government protests.

Related Cases

United States v. Rauscher, 119 U.S. 407 (1886).
Ker v. Illinois, 119 U.S. 436 (1886).
Frisbie v. Collins, 342 U.S. 519 (1952).
Medina v. California, 505 U.S. 437 (1992).
Itel Containers International Corporation v. Huddleston, 113 S. Ct. 1095 (1993).

Bibliography and Further Reading

Bassiouni, M. Cherif. *International Extradition: United States Law and Practice.* New York: Oceana Publications, 1987.

Blackmun, Harry A. "The Supreme Court and the Law of Nations." *Yale Law Journal,* October 1994, p. 39.

Gurule, Jimmy. "Terrorism, Territorial Sovereignty, and the Forcible Apprehension of International Criminals Abroad." *Hastings International and Comparative Law Review,* Vol. 17, pp. 457-78.

Koh, Harold Hongju. "The 'Haiti Paradigm' in United States Human Rights Policy." *Yale Law Journal,* June 1994, p. 2391.

Lonner, Jonathan A. "Official Government Abductions in the Presence of Extradition Treaties." *Journal of Criminal Law and Criminology,* winter 1993, p. 998.

Michell, Paul. "English-speaking Justice: Evolving Responses to Transnational Forcible Abduction After *Alvarez-Machain*." *Cornell International Law Journal,* Vol. 29, pp. 383-500.

CRIMINAL PROCEDURE

Contrasting Perspectives on the Legal System

Many Americans come in contact with the U.S. legal system during their lifetimes, some for just cause and others without sufficient reason. From the "bottom"—that is, from the perspective of the person charged with a crime—the system of criminal justice may seem like a maze through which the individual is processed by means that often appear arbitrary and sometimes seem hostile or discriminatory in nature. There is little that is dignifying about undergoing arrest and incarceration; but under the constitutional system, persons in the United States enjoy a variety of protections against abuses of their basic rights.

Viewed from the "top"—that is, from the perspective of legal scholarship—criminal procedure in America is not so much concerned with the concrete paraphernalia of police activity, such as handcuffs and jail cells, as it is with qualities considerably more abstract. Specifically, criminal procedure is governed by a quartet of amendments to the U.S. Constitution, and by the legal interpretation of those amendments which has developed over the years since their adoption.

Four Constitutional Cornerstones

Much of contemporary understanding with regard to criminal procedure arises from interpretations of the Fourth, Fifth, and Sixth Amendments—adopted along with seven others as part of the ten-amendment Bill of Rights in 1791—as well as the Fourteenth Amendment, ratified in 1868 as a means of securing rights for former slaves freed during the Civil War.

The Fourth Amendment addresses the issue of search and seizure, and limits the power of the government to search the property of an individual—whether that property is a house, papers, effects, or the citizen's own body—without "probable cause." The latter term has undergone varying interpretations, but can be explained in common-sense terms as a reasonable expectation that some form of crime has been committed. For example, if neighbors report that they have heard the sound of machine-gun fire coming from a particular individual's dwelling, the police have probable cause to search the premises for illegal weapons

and, given that such weapons are illegal, to seize them. They do not, however, have the power to search for items not specified in the warrant (e.g., to look for illegal drugs if the warrant is for weapons), or to search parts of the individual's property other than those defined in the warrant. This derives from the guidelines for warrants provided in the amendment: they must be "supported by Oath or affirmation," and must "particularly [describe] the place to be searched, and the persons or things to be seized."

The Fifth Amendment contains several guarantees of rights important in the system of criminal procedure, the most well-known of which is the right against making self-incriminating statements. This means that a suspect charged with a crime is not required to act as a witness against himself, or to provide any information which would lead to his conviction; rather, the burden of proof is on the government.

As for the Sixth Amendment, it guarantees the individual's rights in the courtroom, rights which include a speedy and public trial, an impartial jury, and confrontation by witnesses against the individual (i.e., someone cannot make an accusation without formally presenting themselves as a witness in a courtroom). The individual is also guaranteed the right to "[obtain] witnesses in his favor," as well as the right to legal counsel. In a case where a defendant cannot afford an attorney's fees, the court will appoint a defense lawyer whose fees will be paid by the public. Such was the situation, for instance, in the famous Oklahoma City bombing trial, *United States v. McVeigh* (1997), when accused bomber Timothy McVeigh was granted the services of Stephen Jones, a court-appointed lawyer. Whereas the right to defend oneself is embodied in the Sixth Amendment, however, the right to a court-appointed defense in the absence of other means has only arisen through subsequent interpretation of the amendment.

Likewise the Fourteenth Amendment represents a progressive development of ideas contained in the Fifth. Though the language and the immediate purposes of the two amendments differ greatly, both contain a key phrase: "due process of law." These four words are at the bedrock of America's legal tradition, and whereas the Fifth Amendment guarantees individuals' right to due process with regard to federal proceedings, the Fourteenth Amendment does the same with regard to state proceedings. Because the majority of all legal action takes place at the state or local level, this expansion of constitutional safeguards was one of the most pivotal events in American legal history.

Habeas Corpus and Other Guarantees

In addition to the amendments, the main body of the Constitution provides a number of provisions governing criminal procedure. Among these is a guarantee regarding writ of *habeas corpus*. In Latin, the phrase literally means "You should have the body," the first words of the original Habeas Corpus Act, adopted in England in 1679. Under the writ of *habeas corpus,* a defendant has a right to appear before a judge to determine whether he is being held illegally. During the Civil War, President Lincoln suspended the writ of *habeas corpus* in order to detain suspected Confederate agitators, using as his justification the provision in the Constitution which provides that "The privilege of the writ of *habeas corpus* shall not be suspended, unless when in cases of rebellion or invasion the public safety may require it." The Supreme Court ruled, in *Ex parte Merriman* (1861), that Lincoln had exceeded the powers granted the executive branch of government; however, Congress, in what remains a controversial act, authorized suspension of the writ for the duration of the war.

Other clauses in the Constitution which address criminal procedure include prohibitions against bills of attainder, a law declaring a person guilty without trial; and against *ex post facto* laws, or retroactive laws that attempt to punish someone for something that was not a crime when they did it. Finally, Article III, Section 2, provides for one of the foundational elements of the criminal justice system, trial by jury.

From Probable Cause to Appeal: The Criminal Procedure Cycle

To return to the earlier view of the criminal justice system from the "bottom," the following provides a rough outline of the procedure whereby a suspect is sent through the legal process. The latter term, of course, suggests a factory-like atmosphere, which in turn carries with it negative connotations regarding the attitude of the justice system toward the individual. In fact the establishment of a routine structure for criminal procedure suggests an underlying desire, however imperfectly realized, to treat all defendants the same.

The process begins with the report of a crime, or with the law enforcement officer's direct awareness of a crime in progress. There follows a pre-arrest investigation, at which time the officer may, within strict guidelines which include the requirement of a search warrant, obtain information about the suspect and the crime which may lead to arrest. If a court later determines that the officer obtained evidence illegally at this or any point in the process, then that evidence will have to be suppressed or excluded from the legal record.

The officer having determined sufficient grounds for arrest, he or she reads the defendant his Fifth Amendment rights. This statement, often called the Miranda rights (*Miranda v. Arizona* [1966]), contains words famous to viewers of almost any crime drama on television: "You have the right to remain silent; anything you say can and will be used against you. . . ." Like the Exclusionary Rule which governs the exclusion of evidence obtained illegally, the reading of the Miranda rights is a provision that results from a Supreme Court decision, rather than from a specific stipulation in the Constitution or its amendments.

Police may spend a great deal of time leading up to the arrest, but in accordance with the constitutional guarantee of the right to a speedy trial, the next stages proceed as quickly as possible. The suspect is booked, and usually is placed in a temporary jail cell pending charges. The arresting officer may then make a post-arrest investigation, and assuming that the evidence seems sufficient to do so, will then decide to charge the suspect. The officer files a complaint, under sworn oath, stating that he or she believes that the suspect committed the crime in question. Assuming that the magistrate (or judge) agrees that there is probable cause, the suspect then appears before the magistrate for a bail decision, and to enter a plea of guilty or not guilty.

The case only goes to trial—and hence bail becomes an issue—if the defendant pleads not guilty. Assuming the judge has set bail at levels which the defendant can meet, either through his own resources or through the use of a bail bondsman, the defendant is released pending trial. After a preliminary hearing, the case will be bound over for trial and, assuming it involves violation of a federal statute, will be taken before a grand jury for review. This hearing is called an arraignment and the purpose is for the grand jury to investigate a crime and determine if there is sufficient evidence to indict the accused, sending the case to trial. (State laws regarding grand juries vary.) After arraignment and pre-trial motions, the trial begins. Here a key element is the requirement that guilt must be established "beyond a reasonable doubt." This does not mean that guilt has to be proven beyond all doubt, which in any case would be impossible. To be sure, the phrase "beyond a reasonable doubt" is a vague one—perhaps necessarily so—but is usually interpreted to suggest such a doubt as would cause reasonble men or women to hesitate to convict on the evidence provided.

Assuming the defendant is found guilty in the trial, sentencing—as well as appeals and post-conviction proceedings—will follow. As suggested above, this only a rough and generalized outline of criminal procedure;

in fact the process is an exceedingly intricate one, woven with a rich history of judicial opinions.

Crime Control and Due Process

Criminal procedure places at odds two concepts dearly cherished by most Americans: public safety and order, and liberty. Accordingly, legal scholars have identified two opposing perspectives on criminal justice: the Crime Control model versus the Due Process model. The former places a premium on public safety, and accordingly values the interests of the public (and of the state) over those of the criminal defendant. The latter, as its name suggests, puts the primary emphasis on the due process provisions of the Constitution, and thus favors the rights of the accused. In the past, the Crime Control viewpoint has been associated with political conservatives, and the Due Process perspective with liberals, but these distinctions have tended to blur in the 1990s. Hence in the instance of the Branch Davidians in 1993, an action in which the FBI engaged in a standoff with cult members at their Waco, Texas, compound, many conservative commentators took the side of the Branch Davidians.

Dissenting in *Shaughnessy v. United States* (1953), Justice Robert H. Jackson held that due process ultimately benefits the public as a whole: "It is the best insurance for the Government itself against those blunders which leave lasting stains on a system of justice. . . ." In the same year that Jackson wrote this opinion, Earl Warren became Chief Justice, ushering in an era of increased sensitivity to the rights of the accused. It was during this period, for instance, that the Court extended the Exclusionary Rule—applicable to the federal government ever since 1914—to the states as well. Again, because of the larger number of state and local cases than federal ones, this decision (*Mapp v. Ohio* [1961]) had far-reaching effects. Likewise the decision

in *Miranda v. Arizona* (1966) opened the way for significant change as well.

The question as to whether the reading of Miranda rights constituted more than a mere formal change, however, remained open to debate. Likewise the differing views—Due Process and Crime Control—continued to do battle in the nation's courts. With the appointment of conservative judges, particularly under the administration of President Ronald Reagan in the 1980s, the Court moved toward a Crime Control model. This coincided with increasing public concern and alarm over the spread of crime.

See also: **Criminal Law, Rights of the Accused**

Bibliography and Further Reading

Amar, Akhil Reed. *The Constitution and Criminal Procedure: First Principles.* New Haven, CT: Yale University Press, 1998.

Cortner, Richard C. *The Supreme Court and the Second Bill of Rights.* Madison: University of Wisconsin Press, 1980.

Del Carmen, Rolando. *Criminal Procedure and Evidence.* Gardena, CA: Harcourt Brace Jovanovich Legal and Professional Publications, 1978.

Dressler, Joshua. *Understanding Criminal Procedure,* second edition. Matthew Bender, 1997.

Fleming, Macklin. *The Price of Perfect Justice.* New York: Basic Books, 1974.

Israel, Jerold H. and Wayne R. Lafave. *Criminal Procedure: Constitutional Limitations in a Nutshell,* fifth edition. West, 1993.

Zimring, Franklin E. and Richard S. Frase. *The Criminal Justice System: Materials on the Administration and Reform of the Criminal Law.* Boston: Little, Brown, 1980.

KENTUCKY V. DENNISON

Legal Citation: 65 U.S. 66 (1861)

Petitioner
State of Kentucky

Respondent
William Dennison, Governor of Ohio

Petitioner's Claim
That Governor Dennison should return to Kentucky the man, Willis Lago, who had allegedly helped a slave to escape and who had been indicted in Kentucky for what was a crime under the laws of that state.

Chief Lawyers for Petitioner
John W. Stevenson, Humphrey Marshall

Chief Lawyer for Respondent
Ohio Attorney General Christopher P. Wolcott

Justices for the Court
John Archibald Campbell, John Catron, Nathan Clifford, Robert Cooper Grier, John McLean, Samuel Nelson, Roger Brooke Taney (writing for the Court), James Moore Wayne

Justices Dissenting
None

Place
Washington, D.C.

Date of Decision
14 March 1861

Decision
That although it was in fact Governor Dennison's duty to return a fugitive from justice to another state, as the executive authority of a state, he could not be coerced into doing so.

Significance
At the time, the decision was seen as a victory for Southern states' right to demand that Northern states support the institution of slavery. The decision supported the ability of a governor to refuse to extradite a fugitive from justice to another state until it was reversed by *Puerto Rico v. Branstad* (1987).

The years before the Civil War were full of legal battles between the slave states and the free states. In 1793, Congress had passed a law providing for the return of fugitive slaves. This law drew on Article IV, Section 2 of the Constitution, which read:

> A person charged in any State with treason, felony, or other crime, who shall flee from justice, and be found in another State, shall on demand of the executive authority of the State from which he fled, be delivered up, to be removed to the State having jurisdiction of the crime.

In other words, if a person committed a crime in one state and ran away to another, the second state was supposed to return the person to the first state, where he or she could stand trial. Since running away from slavery was considered a crime in the slave states, a slave who ran away, or a person who helped a slave run away, was supposed to be returned to stand trial.

Of course, abolitionists—people who opposed slavery—objected to this use of the law. Since abolitionists believed that slavery was wrong, they wanted to help slaves escape to freedom. They wanted slaves to be able to remain in those parts of the United States where they could be free.

Who Decides?

In the early 1840s, the main controversy over this question had concerned New York Governor William H. Seward. Seward had refused to send to Virginia three free African American men who had allegedly helped a slave to escape to New York. Virginia, a slave state, pointed out that each state had the right to decide what was legal and what was not. Since helping a slave to escape was illegal in Virginia, Seward ought to respect Virginia's laws and send the men back. Seward agreed that each state had the right to make its own laws, but argued that he was obligated only to enforce the laws of his own state. Since helping someone to escape from slavery was not a crime in his state, he had no obligation to enforce Virginia's laws. Moreover, in his opinion, the section of the Constitution that referred to returning fugitives from justice did not apply to this case. Seward also became involved in a similar controversy with the slave state of Georgia. Several Georgia governors had similar conflicts with governors of the free state of Maine.

When these kinds of conflicts occur between states, Congress often passes federal legislation to clarify the matter. In this case, however, Congress was torn between members from Southern states, who wanted to preserve slavery, and a growing number of abolitionists, who wished to abolish it. By the time of *Kentucky v. Dennison,* feelings were running strong on both sides.

A Slave Girl and the Man Who Helped Her

The *Kentucky v. Dennison* case began when Charlotte, a slave girl who lived in Louisville, Kentucky, was allowed to go with her owner, C. W. Nichols, to visit her mother in Wheeling, Virginia, where Nichols was going on business. (In some parts of the court record, his name is spelled "Nuckols.") The route Nichols chose took him through Cincinnati, in the free state of Ohio. There Charlotte met some abolitionists who helped her escape slavery. They took her to a state court, which ruled that she was free.

Nichols tried to fight the Ohio court's decision. Since slavery was not legal in Ohio, he could not claim that Charlotte was property that had been "stolen." Ironically, he declared that the abolitionists were the ones who had deprived Charlotte of her liberty, which was a crime under Ohio state law.

Meanwhile, Governor Beriah Magoffin of Kentucky demanded that Ohio governor, William Dennison, return a man who was supposed to have helped Charlotte. Dennison had run for office specifically on the platform that he would not allow runaway slaves to be returned South. He had already refused to return one man who had been charged with helping a slave to escape, but when he learned that the man had also stolen jewelry, he changed his mind. In this case, however, he was adamant.

The man whom Dennison refused to return was Willis Lago, a free African American. He had been indicted by a county grand jury for offending "against the peace and dignity of the Commonwealth of Kentucky." Dennison argued that the Constitution only required him to return a person accused of treason or felony. Since Lago was guilty of neither treason nor of a felony under Ohio state law, Ohio had no obligation to send him back to Kentucky.

Governor Magoffin was determined to have Lago returned. He wrote back to Dennison, claiming that the framers of the Constitution had in fact intended for fugitive slaves to be sent back. According to Magoffin, "the Constitution was the work of slaveholders . . . their wisdom, moderation, and prudence gave it to us. Non-slaveholding states were the exception, not the rule."

Ohio continued to refuse, so Kentucky tried a new strategy. It petitioned the Supreme Court, asking for a writ of *mandamus,* which would force the governor to return Lago. The petition was submitted by Thomas B. Monroe, Jr., Kentucky's secretary of state.

On the Eve of the Civil War

By the time the Supreme Court heard the case, most of the slave states had seceded from the Union. The whole idea of the federal government forcing the states to do anything had been put in question. Kentucky, however, was still deciding whether or not to secede. Thomas B. Monroe, Jr., the man who had first argued Kentucky's case, would become a Confederate officer and die in the Civil War. His father, a federal judge, would resign in order to support the Confederate cause. Between the time the case was argued and the time the decision was handed down, Abraham Lincoln traveled secretly through Baltimore to avoid possible mob violence on his way to being sworn in as president.

Moreover, the Supreme Court became quite unpopular in the North after the Dred Scott decision, another case involving a fugitive slave in which the Court had ruled in favor of Southern states' rights to enforce slavery. Chief Justice Taney was known to be highly sympathetic to the South.

Yet the decision in *Kentucky v. Dennison* surprised and angered both the North and the South. Taney, who wrote the majority decision, supported Kentucky's right to expect Governor Dennison to respect its laws. He agreed with the Southern governors who had argued throughout the 1830s and 1840s that they had the right to extradite slaves, those who helped free slaves, and anyone else who had been indicted for a crime within their states.

Previously, lawyers and politicians had argued over whether the seriousness of the crime should be a factor in another state's obligation to return an alleged criminal. Taney went further than anyone had ever gone: he said that a state had the obligation to return even someone indicted for a misdemeanor in another state. In the strongest possible terms, he held that the decision of whether a person should stand trial for a crime should be made by the state where the crime was committed, not by the state to which the person had escaped.

However, Taney struck one final blow for states' rights that offended both the North and the South. He said that in the final analysis, a governor was the executive authority of a state. Congress could authorize a governor to perform a particular duty, but, Taney wrote, "if he [sic] declines to do so, it does not follow that he may be coerced, or punished for his refusal." In other words, although Dennison was wrong not to return Lago to Kentucky, no federal power could force him to do it.

With slavery long abolished, Taney's decision stood for many years as an important ruling in the matter of states returning fugitives from justice. While most of the time such returns were routine, every so often, a governor decided not to comply with another state's demand. In 1987 the Court reversed its position in *Puerto Rico v. Branstad* which dictated governors to enforce requests for the return of a criminal.

Related Cases
Prigg v. Pennsylvania, 41 U.S. 539 (1842).
Scott v. Sandford, 60 U.S. 393 (1857).
Puerto Rico v. Branstad, 483 U.S. 219 (1987).

Bibliography and Further Reading
Bartholomew, Paul C. *American Constitutional Law, Vol. I, Governmental Organization, Powers, and Procedure,* 2nd ed. Totowa, NJ: Littlefield, Adams & Co., 1970, 1978.

Biskupic, Joan, and Elder Witt. *Congressional Quarterly's Guide to the U.S. Supreme Court,* 3rd ed. Washington, DC: Congressional Quarterly, Inc., 1996.

Hall, Kermit L., ed. *The Oxford Companion to the Supreme Court of the United States.* New York: Oxford University Press, 1992.

Swisher, Carl B. *The History of the Supreme Court of the United States, The Taney Period, 1836-1864,* Vol. V. New York: Macmillan, 1974.

GOMPERS V. UNITED STATES

Legal Citation: 233 U.S. 604 (1914)

Petitioner
Samuel Gompers

Respondent
United States

Petitioner's Claim
That the alleged contempt took place more than three years before the proceedings began and therefore beyond the statute of limitations.

Chief Lawyer for Petitioner
Alton B. Parker

Chief Lawyer for Respondent
J. J. Darlington

Justices for the Court
William Rufus Day, Oliver Wendell Holmes (writing for the Court), Charles Evans Hughes, Joseph Rucker Lamar, Horace Harmon Lurton, Joseph McKenna, Edward Douglass White

Justices Dissenting
Mahlon Pitney, Willis Van Devanter

Place
Washington, D.C.

Date of Decision
11 May 1914

Decision
The Court reversed the decision of the lower court based on the statute of limitations to punish contempt was three years.

Significance
In this case the Court settled controversy over whether contempt was actually a crime by stating that it definitely was. It also resolved the issue of a statute of limitations for punishing contempt, settling on a term of three years.

Before 1932, the courts attempted to control the activities of labor unions by issuing injunctions that forbade strikes and picketing. Around the turn of the century labor unions began increasingly to use boycotts against individual employers to force them to provide improved working conditions and higher wages. The courts attempted to stop the boycotts by using antilabor injunctions.

Samuel Gompers served as the first president of the American Federation of Labor (AFL) from 1886 to 1924. Gompers and two other labor leaders were convicted of violating an antiboycott injunction for running a notice in its magazine listing Buck's Stove & Range Company along with other companies under the heading "We Don't Patronize." On 15 May 1911, the Supreme Court ruled on the case *Gompers v. Bucks Stove & Range Company*. The Court refused to reexamine the validity of the injunction issued by the lower court and rejected Gompers' claim that the First Amendment protected his activities. However, the convictions were reversed on the ground that the contempts were civil but the lower court had treated them as criminal in nature. The aim of civil contempt is remediation while the purpose of criminal contempt is punitive.

Although the Court had dismissed the charges in *Gompers v. Buck's Stove & Range Company,* the supreme court of the district retained the power to punish contempt, if any had been committed against it. The day after the decision, the supreme court of the district appointed a committee to see if there was reasonable cause to believe that Gompers was guilty of willfully violating an injunction issued by that court on 18 December 1907.

On 26 June 1911, the committee reported that Gompers was guilty of violating the injunction. Rules to show cause were issued that day requiring each of the defendants to show why they should not be adjudged to be in contempt and be punished for it. Gompers pleaded the statute of limitations and not guilty to most of the charges. A trial took place, the statute of limitations was held inapplicable, and Gompers was found guilty and sentenced to prison for 12 months. The court of appeals reduced the sentence to imprisonment for 30 days.

Samuel Gompers

One of the most influential leaders of the American labor movement, Samuel Gompers (1850-1924) was born in London and emigrated to the United States with his parents in 1863. Like his father, he entered the cigar-making trade. He became a leader of the cigar makers union and eventually became the first president of the American Federation of Labor when it formed in 1886, holding the position until his death in 1924.

Gompers was an advocate of "business unionism," also called "pure and simple unionism." This approach to organizing workers emphasized the basics of collective bargaining and was essentially conservative in its accep-

tance of the prevailing economic order. Government intervention and social reform were not emphasized, as in more radical labor organizations such as the Knights of Labor and the Industrial Workers of the World (IWW). Gompers also favored the organization of labor nationally by trade or craft, as opposed to the "one big union" of the IWW or the vertical integration of all employees of a firm into a single union that was later favored by the Congress of Industrial Organizations.

Source(s): Foner, Eric, and John A. Garaty, eds. *The Reader's Companion to American History.* Boston: Houghton Mifflin, 1991.

The Provisions of the Constitution Are Not Mathematical Formulas

In 1914, the Supreme Court in *Gompers v. United States* looked again at the contempt charges brought against Gompers. Considering the statute of limitations the Court noted that the injunction was made permanent on 23 March 1908. The statute of limitations states that "no person shall be prosecuted, tried, or punished for any offense not capital . . . unless the indictment is found or the information is instituted within three years next after such offense shall have been committed." Gompers treated these proceedings as beginning on 16 May 1911, when the inquiry began, thus barring contempts before 16 May 1908. Gompers also argued that the inquiry was only looking at violations of the preliminary injunction, which expired when the final decree took effect on 23 March 1908. Holmes countered that the report mentioned the final decree and acts later than 23 March and that the order to show cause referred to the injunctions, in the plural.

The charges against Gompers included rushing the publication of the *American Federationist* after he knew about the injunction but before it went into effect. Another charge involved referring to the judge as so far having transcended his authority that even court of appeals judges criticized him and that in such circumstances "it is the duty of the citizens to refuse obedience and to take whatever consequences may ensue."

Holmes noted that it had been argued that the contempts cannot be crimes because they are not within the protection of the Constitution and amendments giving a right to trial by jury. He responded that "the provisions of the Constitution are not mathematical formulas having their essence in their form; they are organic, living institutions transplanted from English soil. Their significance is vital, not formal; it is to be gathered not simply by taking the words and a dictio-

nary, but by considering their origin and the line of their growth."

In discussing the meaning of the statute of limitations, Holmes noted that "the substantive portion of the section is that no person shall be tried for any offense . . . except within a certain time. Those words are of universal scope. What follows is a natural way of expressing that the proceedings must be begun within three years." Holmes stated that the power to punish for contempt must have some time limit and that limit should be three years. The majority of the Court voted to reverse the judgments against Gompers since they were based on offenses that could not be taken into consideration.

Gompers wrote in an editorial in the *American Federationist* that the Court had refused to rule on the great human issues involved in the case, which were free speech and free press. Instead the ideas were lost in a maze of legal technicalities. Gompers felt that since the judiciary would not reform the abuses of the injunction process, the reforms must be gotten by legislation. Through lobbying and campaigning, the AFL attempted the statutory abolition of the labor injunction. The Clayton Antitrust Act of 1914 appeared to prohibit federal courts from barring peaceful picketing or communicative activities connected with labor strikes or boycotts. Gompers felt the Clayton Antitrust Act would bring about a new order of human relations in industry and was fundamental to human liberty. However, the lower courts interpreted the deliberately vague language of the anti-injunction provisions so hostilely that no change came about.

Impact

In 1958, in *Green v. United States*, the Court cited *Gompers v. United States* as a case which discussed the relationship between criminal contempts and jury trial and that had concluded or assumed that criminal contempts are not subject to jury trial. In Gompers, the Court construed that summary trials were permitted in contempt cases because at common law contempt was tried without a jury. Until *United States v. Barnett* (1964), the Court consistently upheld the constitutional power of the state and federal courts to punish any criminal contempt without a jury trial and *Gompers* was cited as precedent for this. In *Bloom v. Illinois,* the Court noted that criminal contempt is a crime in the ordinary sense; it is a violation of the law, a public wrong which is punishable by fine or imprisonment or both. The Court quoted Justice Holmes, writing for the majority in *Gompers v. United States:* "These contempts are infractions of the law, visited with punishment as such. If such acts are not criminal, we are in error as to the most fundamental characteristic of crimes as that word has been understood in English speech." The Court concluded that convictions for criminal contempt are indistinguishable from ordinary criminal convictions, for their impact on the individual defendant is the same. Indeed, the role of criminal contempt and that of many ordinary criminal laws seem identical—protection of the institutions of our government and enforcement of their mandates.

Related Cases
Green v. United States, 356 U.S. 165 (1958).
United States v. Barnett, 377 U.S. 973 (1964).
Bloom v. Illinois, 391 U.S. 194 (1968).

Bibliography and Further Reading
Hall, Kermit L., ed. *The Oxford Companion to the Supreme Court of the United States.* New York: Oxford Press, 1992.

Mandel, Bernard. *Samuel Gompers: A Biography.* Yellow Springs, OH: The Antioch Press, 1963.

FRYE V. UNITED STATES

Legal Citation: 293 F. 1013 (1923)

Appellant
James Alphonzo Frye

Appellee
United States

Appellant's Claim
That the trial court erred when it refused the introduction of a systolic blood pressure deception test and expert testimony on the test as evidence.

Chief Lawyers for Appellant
Richard V. Mattingly, Foster Wood

Chief Lawyers for Appellee
Peyton Gordon, J. H. Bilbrey

Justices for the Court
George Ewing Martin, Constantine J. Smyth, Josiah A. Van Orsdel (writing for the court)

Justices Dissenting
None

Place
Washington, D.C.

Date of Decision
3 December 1923

Decision
Upheld the conviction of Frye by refusing to admit the deception test into evidence.

Significance
The ruling set a standard for the acceptance of expert testimony in court that, by the early 1970s, was adopted by almost all state and federal courts.

In 1923 James Alphonzo Frye appealed his conviction for second degree murder. Frye, who had confessed and later retracted his admission, had been prosecuted by the federal government and convicted by a jury sitting in a Washington, D.C. trial court. At trial, the court refused to let Frye introduce evidence about his truthfulness through a "systolic blood pressure deception test," a crude precursor to what is now popularly known as a lie detector or polygraph test. The court also refused to let Frye introduce an expert witness to testify about the deception test.

The sole basis of Frye's appeal was the failure of the trial court to admit the deception test. In a unanimous decision, the three-judge Court of Appeals of the District of Columbia ruled for the United States in a short opinion that became one of the most notorious opinions written by a federal appeals court.

In the opinion, written by Justice Van Orsdel, the court described how the machine operated and how, when attached to a subject, it supposedly could detect whether a subject was being deceptive. "It is asserted," said the court, "that blood pressure is influenced by change in the emotions of the witness, and that the systolic blood pressure rises are brought about by nervous impulses sent to the sympathetic branch of the autonomic nervous system." Frye argued that systolic blood pressure rose in a predictable curve when a subject was being deceptive and afraid that the falsehood could be detected. The curve, maintained Frye, corresponded "exactly to the struggle going on in the subject's mind, between fear and attempted control of that fear, as the examination touches the vital points in respect of which he is attempting to deceive the examiner."

The court characterized the information offered by Frye as a "theory" holding that "truth is spontaneous, and comes without conscious effort, while the utterance of a falsehood requires a conscious effort, which is reflected in the blood pressure." As there were no prior similar cases for use as guidance, the court was left to make up a rule on the admissibility in court of deception tests. Frye insisted that the deception test could be explained by a witness who was an expert in the field, but the court rejected this with these now-famous words:

The Polygraph

A polygraph machine measures an examinee's rate of heartbeat and blood pressure, perspiration, and breathing with various sensing devices. Questions are asked of the examinee while he or she is connected to the machine, and polygraph examiners claim to be able to detect when an examinee is not telling the truth by analysis of these measurements.

The American Polygraph Association claims that polygraph examinations are highly accurate when properly conducted, citing studies finding an average accuracy of 98 percent. According to the association, most of the controversy regarding accuracy involves differing interpretations of tests that are inconclusive: critics label inconclusive tests as inaccurate, while the association

does not. Some critics claim the polygraph has no validity, however, and that trained persons may easily and consistently "beat" polygraph examinations.

Polygraph examination results may or may not be admissible in court, depending on the jurisdiction; often they are deemed admissible when both parties to a case agree on such admissibility before the test is administered. Some jurisdictions have specific rules on admissibility, and in others admissibility is at the discretion of the trial judge.

Source(s): American Polygraph Association.
http:// www.polygraph.org

Just when a scientific principle or discovery crosses the line between the experimental and demonstrable stages is difficult to define. Somewhere in this twilight zone the evidential force of the principle must be recognized, and while courts will go a long way in admitting expert testimony deduced from a well-recognized scientific principle or discovery, the thing from which the deduction is made must be sufficiently established to have gained general acceptance in the particular field in which it belongs.

In the court's opinion, the systolic blood pressure deception test had not gained enough "standing and scientific recognition among physiological and psychological authorities" to justify its admission as evidence in courts of law. The court approved of the exclusion of the deception test, and Frye's conviction was affirmed.

Impact

For years, lie detector tests were inadmissible as evidence in virtually all courts. However, in the 1970s and 1980s, as the practice of lie detection gradually gained respect in the scientific community, some courts began to admit the evidence in certain situations and for limited purposes in both criminal and civil trials. However, courts in most states continue to prohibit any and all forms of polygraph evidence.

On the topic of the admission of expert testimony, the formula in the *Frye* decision reigned supreme for

70 years. This was especially true in the early 1970s when, just before the Federal Rules of Evidence were adopted, courts across the country began to cite *Frye*. The formula for admissibility of scientific evidence created by *Frye*—whether the practice or procedure was generally accepted in the scientific community—eventually proved too difficult for courts to manage as the scientific community expanded and progressed. In *Daubert v. Merrell Dow Pharmaceuticals, Inc.* (1993) the High Court held that admissibility of expert testimony should be controlled by Rule 702 of the Federal Rules of Evidence, and that it need not be generally accepted in the scientific community to be admitted; rather, expert testimony should be admitted if it rests on a reliable scientific foundation and is relevant to the issue at hand.

Related Cases
Daubert v. Merrell Dow Pharmaceuticals, Inc., 509 U.S. 579 (1993).
United States v. Scheffer, 118 S.Ct. 1261 (1998).

Bibliography and Further Reading
Cushman, Robert F. *Leading Constitutional Decisions.* Englewood Cliffs, NJ: Prentice-Hall, Inc., 1982.

Green, Eric D., and Charles R. Nesson. "Expert Testimony, Scientific Proof, and Junk Science." *Problems, Cases, and Materials on Evidence.* Boston: Little, Brown and Company, 1994.

Lyons, Thomas. "*Frye, Daubert,* and Where Do We Go From Here?" *Rhode Island Bar Journal,* January 1997.

PALKO V. CONNECTICUT

Legal Citation: 302 U.S. 319 (1937)

Appellant
Frank Palko

Appellee
State of Connecticut

Appellant's Claim
That when the state tried him a second time for the same offense, it violated the constitutional prohibition on double jeopardy.

Chief Lawyers for Appellant
David Goldstein, George A. Saden

Chief Lawyer for Appellee
William H. Comley

Justices for the Court
Hugo Lafayette Black, Louis D. Brandeis, Benjamin N. Cardozo (writing for the Court), Charles Evans Hughes, James Clark McReynolds, Owen Josephus Roberts, Harlan Fiske Stone, George Sutherland

Justices Dissenting
Pierce Butler

Place
Washington, D.C.

Date of Decision
6 December 1937

Decision
The Supreme Court upheld the Connecticut law that permitted the state to appeal judgments, and retry defendants, in certain criminal cases.

Significance
Palko was not the first test of the applicability of the Bill of Rights at the state level, but it marked the introduction of a new approach to the problem.

Frank Palko was indicted for first degree murder in Fairfield County, Connecticut. After a jury trial, he was found guilty of murder in the second degree, a lesser crime, and sentenced to life in prison. A state law, however, permitted Connecticut to appeal the outcome of his case, and it did so. The Connecticut Supreme Court then found that there had been three errors in the state's favor during the trial: 1) testimony about the defendant's confession had been excluded; 2) testimony from cross-examination of the defendant which challenged his credibility was excluded; and 3) the judge had erred in distinguishing first and second degree murder during his instructions to the jury. The state supreme court overturned the verdict of the first trial and granted a second. At the second trial, Palko was found guilty of first degree murder and sentenced to death.

During his second trial, Palko had repeatedly objected that his constitutional right not to be subjected to double jeopardy—that is, being tried twice for the same offense—was being violated. The prohibition against double jeopardy appears in the Fifth Amendment, and thus applies only to federal proceedings. Palko, however, cited the Due Process Clause of the Fourteenth Amendment: "No state shall . . . deprive any person of life, liberty, or property, without due process of law." He insisted that this provision made the prohibition against double jeopardy applicable to the states, as well. The Connecticut Supreme Court disagreed, upholding his conviction for first degree murder. Palko then appealed to the U.S. Supreme Court.

Supreme Court Announces a "Fundamental Fairness" Test for Constitutional Limits on State Power

The due process argument Palko made really dates from two dissenting opinions written much earlier by Justice John Marshall Harlan I: *Hurtado v. California* (1884) and *Twining v. State of New Jersey* (1908). Although it was decidedly a minority view at the time, in both of these cases, Harlan advanced the theory that after ratification of the Fourteenth Amendment in 1868, any act that violated the Bill of Rights was unconstitutional both at the federal and the state levels. This interpretation of the Due Process Clause, which came to be known as the incorporation doctrine, was later vigorously championed by Justice Black in the 1940s, 1950s and 1960s. Eventually, all but a few of the guarantees of the Bill of Rights were incorporated into the Fourteenth Amendment.

At the time the Supreme Court heard *Palko,* however, the incorporation doctrine had been only partially developed. In his opinion for the Court, Justice Cardozo acknowledged that some aspects of the first eight amendments to the Constitution had been made to apply to the states. Nonetheless, he said, these developments did not mean that such application was automatic. Instead, he said, only certain rights lent themselves to incorporation:

> [S]pecific pledges of particular amendments have been found to be implicit in the concept of ordered liberty . . . The line of division may seem to be wavering and broken [but] . . . There emerges the perception of a rationalizing principle which gives to discrete instances a proper order and coherence . . . [T]hey are of the very essence of a scheme of ordered liberty . . . "principle[s] of justice so rooted in the traditions and conscience of our people as to be ranked as fundamental." [Quoting *Snyder v. Massachusetts* (1934)]

Cardozo cited such rights as the First Amendment guarantees of free speech, free press, and free religion and the Sixth Amendment guarantee of the right to counsel as the types of fundamental protections that should obviously apply to states as well as the federal government. With regard to the case before them, however, a majority of the justices did not believe that any of Palko's fundamental rights had been violated. Instead, the Connecticut law at issue was intended to rectify substantial errors at trial. And it seemed to the justices that the law had been properly applied in Palko's case. His death sentence stood.

The Court would later overturn *Palko* with *Benton v. Maryland* (1969), an important, if belated, step in the so-called "due process revolution" which realized the theory behind the incorporation doctrine. In its early stages, the due process revolution found its most ardent spokesman in Justice Black. In the later stages of his career Black would grow more conservative, but from the late 1940s through the early 1960s, he championed the incorporation of a range of rights protecting individual liberties—including those of criminal defendants. His opponent in this debate was Justice Felix Frankfurter, who favored the "fundamental fairness" test for incorporation of rights into the Fourteenth Amendment. In the end, Black's more liberal approach

Justice Benjamin N. Cardozo. © Photograph by Harris and Ewing. Collection of the Supreme Court of the United States.

was adopted, and the due process revolution saw its fullest flowering during the tenure of Chief Justice Earl Warren.

Related Cases
Hurtado v. California, 110 U.S. 516 (1884).
Twining v. State of New Jersey, 211 U.S. 78 (1908).
Adamson v. California, 332 U.S. 46 (1947).
Benton v. Maryland, 395 U.S. 784 (1969).

Bibliography and Further Reading
Cortner, Richard C. *The Supreme Court and the Second Bill of Rights: The Fourteenth Amendment and the Nationalization of Civil Liberties.* Madison: University of Wisconsin Press, 1981.

Mykkeltvedt, Roald Y. *The Nationalization of the Bill of Rights: Fourteenth Amendment Due Process and the Procedural Rights.* Port Washington, NY: Associated Faculty Press, 1983.

Stevens, Richard G. *Frankfurter and Due Process.* Lanham, MD: University Press of America, 1987.

BARTKUS V. ILLINOIS

Legal Citation: 359 U.S. 121 (1959)

Appellant
Bartkus

Appellee
State of Illinois

Appellant's Claim
The Supreme Court should void his conviction for bank robbery by an Illinois court. A federal court already had tried and had acquitted him of the same crime.

Chief Lawyer for Appellant
Walter R. Fisher

Chief Lawyers for Appellee
William C. Wines, Latham Castle

Justices for the Court
Tom C. Clark, Felix Frankfurter (writing for the Court), John Marshall Harlan II, Potter Stewart, Charles Evans Whittaker

Justices Dissenting
Hugo Lafayette Black, William J. Brennan, Jr., William O. Douglas, Earl Warren

Place
Washington, D.C.

Date of Decision
30 March 1959

Decision
The Court denied Bartkus' appeal and affirmed his conviction. His second trial after a prior acquittal did not deny Bartkus due process of law.

Significance
The majority declared that the Fourteenth Amendment did not impose upon the states the Fifth Amendment's protection against double jeopardy. However, the Court overruled the *Bartkus* decision only ten years later in *Benton v. Maryland* (1969). In the latter case, the Court held that the double jeopardy prohibition did apply to the states.

Bartkus was arrested under a federal law making it a crime to rob a federally insured savings and loan association. He was tried in a federal court and acquitted on 28 December 1953. On 8 January 1954, an Illinois grand jury indicted Bartkus under a state robbery law. The evidence in the Illinois indictment was substantially identical to that contained in the prior federal indictment. An Illinois court tried and convicted Bartkus and sentenced him to life imprisonment. The Illinois Supreme Court affirmed his conviction.

Bartkus's attorney appealed to the Supreme Court. The Fifth Amendment—referring to the federal government—provides that no person shall "be subject for the same offence to be twice put in jeopardy of life or limb." Bartkus argued that this double jeopardy prohibition had been extended to the states by the Due Process Clause of the Fourteenth Amendment: "Nor shall any State deprive any person of life, liberty, or property, without due process of law."

In January of 1958, the Supreme Court split 4-4, and the case was reargued in October. In March of 1959, by a 5-4 vote, the Court denied Bartkus' appeal and affirmed the lower courts. Justice Frankfurter wrote the opinion for the majority. Justice Black dissented, joined by Chief Justice Warren and Justice Douglas. Justice Brennan filed a separate dissent, which also was joined by Justices Warren and Douglas.

Justice Frankfurter acknowledged that federal and Illinois law officers had cooperated in bringing their separate indictments. For example, the FBI had turned over to Illinois officials all the evidence it had gathered against Bartkus. However, the state officials had brought the case under their own authority. The record did not, Frankfurter argued, show that the state trial was a cover for a second federal prosecution—which would have violated the Fifth Amendment.

The Bill of Rights Does Not Restrict the States

For the first time, the Court explicitly ruled on the validity of a state conviction after a defendant had been acquitted in a federal court. The question was whether the Fourteenth Amendment incorporated the

Fifth Amendment's double jeopardy clause. Justice Frankfurter declared unequivocally that the Fourteenth Amendment did not apply the words of the Bill of Rights to the states. "The Due Process Clause of the Fourteenth Amendment does not apply to the States any of the provisions of the first eight amendments as such."

Frankfurter cited the historical record as well as prior decisions by the Supreme Court and state courts. He began by examining the "original intention" of the Congress and states in adopting the Fourteenth Amendment. In ten of the 30 states ratifying the Fourteenth Amendment, the state constitution contained provisions contrary to those in the federal Constitution's Fifth, Sixth, and Seventh Amendments. These ten states clearly did not intend to incorporate the Bill of Rights in the Fourteenth Amendment. To do so, they would first have had to amend their own state constitutions.

Furthermore, Frankfurter continued, 12 states joined the United States after the Fourteenth Amendment was ratified. In all 12 state constitutions, judicial procedures differed from those in the Bill of Rights. By welcoming them into the Union, Congress attested that a state's powers were not limited by the first eight amendments.

For more than a century, Frankfurter continued, the Supreme Court had accepted the validity of consecutive state and federal prosecutions, and state supreme courts also had tolerated double prosecutions. These decisions, Frankfurter declared, had reaffirmed the statement of law in the nineteenth century decision *Moore v. Illinois.*

> Every citizen of the United states is also a citizen of a State or territory. He may be said to owe allegiance to two sovereigns, and may be liable to punishment for an infraction of the laws of either. The same act may be an offence or transgression of the laws of both.

Double Jeopardy Is Wholly Uncivilized

In dissenting, Justice Black vehemently argued that the *Bartkus* decision should be overturned. Perhaps it did not make the entire Bill of Rights applicable to the states. But the Fourteenth Amendment did incorporate those principles of justice "so rooted in the traditions and conscience of our people as to be ranked as fundamental."

Based on the historical record, Black declared, "Fear and abhorrence of governmental power to try people twice for the same conduct is one of the oldest ideas found in western civilization." Rules against double jeopardy existed in Greek, Roman, and canon law as well as in English common law. Every state prohibits and most foreign nations forbid two trials for the same offense. And, Black continued, the Supreme Court also had barred two trials. The cases cited in Justice Frankfurter's opinion were, Black asserted, really irrelevant to the issue at hand.

In another dissenting opinion, Justice Brennan disagreed with the majority on substantive grounds. Brennan was convinced that the state trial was a sham. The federal officers had solicited the state indictment and prepared and guided the state prosecution. Federal officials participated in the state trial so completely that it was in actuality a second federal prosecution—a second federal try at Bartkus in the guise of a state prosecution.

Related Cases

Benton v. Maryland, 395 U.S. 784 (1969).

Bibliography and Further Reading

Ball, Howard, and Philip Cooper. *Of Power and Right: Hugo Black, William O. Douglas, and America's Constitutional Revolution.* New York: Oxford University Press, 1992.

Biskupic, Joan, and Elder Witt, eds. *Congressional Quarterly's Guide to the U.S. Supreme Court,* 3rd ed. Washington, DC: Congressional Quarterly, Inc., 1996.

BENTON V. MARYLAND

Legal Citation: 395 U.S. 784 (1969)

Petitioner
John Dalmer Benton

Respondent
State of Maryland

Petitioner's Claim
That his conviction and sentencing for burglary and larceny, accomplished in two state court trials after the initial verdict was thrown out due to jury invalidation, was in violation of his constitutional protection from double jeopardy (being tried more than once for the same offense).

Chief Lawyer for Petitioner
M. Michael Cramer

Chief Lawyer for Respondent
Francis B. Burch

Justices for the Court
Hugo Lafayette Black, William J. Brennan, Jr., Warren E. Burger, William O. Douglas, Abe Fortas, Thurgood Marshall (writing for the Court), Byron R. White

Justices Dissenting
John Marshall Harlan II, Potter Stewart

Place
Washington, D.C.

Date of Decision
23 June 1969

Decision
That the second trial did violate Benton's right to freedom from double jeopardy, and that portions of his second conviction could not stand.

Significance
Overturned legal precedent set in *Palko v. Connecticut* and ruled that the double jeopardy clause of the Fifth Amendment to the U.S. Constitution, through application of the Fourteenth Amendment, does constrain the actions of state courts.

John Benton faced trial for burglary and larceny in Maryland state court in 1965. He was convicted of burglary but found innocent of larceny in August of that year, and was sentenced to ten years in prison for his offense. Shortly after his conviction the Maryland Court of Appeals struck down a state law requiring jurors to swear to their belief in the existence God, and Benton's conviction was remanded due to improper jury selection. The state granted Benton the opportunity to have a new indictment and trial, which he accepted. At Benton's second trial he was found guilty of both burglary and larceny, and sentenced to 15 years in prison for burglary and five years for larceny, to be served concurrently. Benton then appealed to the Maryland Court of Special Appeals, claiming that his second trial violated his Fifth Amendment protection against double jeopardy, or being tried twice for the same offense. The Court of Special Appeals rejected Benton's appeal in 1967, and the Maryland Court of Appeals refused to review the case.

The U.S. Supreme Court took Benton's case on *certiorari* in 1968, but stipulated that the Court would limit its consideration to two issues: whether "the double jeopardy clause of the Fifth Amendment is applicable to the states through the Fourteenth Amendment," and whether Benton was put in double jeopardy in his second trial. After hearing opening arguments, the Court rescheduled the case for the following year, as it did not wish the legal implications of concurrent sentencing to complicate its decision of the two issues to be decided in the case. The Court also added a third question to be adjudicated upon reargument: whether concurrent sentencing was still legally valid in light of recent court decisions.

Benton's case was reargued on 24 March 1969. First, the Court considered the matter of concurrent sentencing, ruling that such sentences provide "no jurisdictional bar to consideration of challenges to multiple convictions." Attention then turned to the question of the applicability of the Fifth Amendment prohibition against double jeopardy to state trials given Fourteenth Amendment guarantees of equal protection under the law. In the 1937 case of *Palko v. Connecticut* the Court had ruled that federal double jeopardy standards did

Double Jeopardy

Double jeopardy, being subjected to trial for the same offense twice, is barred by the Fifth Amendment. Until *Benton v. Maryland*, this prohibition applied only to the federal government, not to the states. Under the principle of "dual sovereignty" (the separation of state and federal spheres of authority), however, there is no constitutional prohibition of federal prosecution for an offense after state prosecution for that offense; however, many states have laws barring state prosecution for an offense after federal prosecution has taken place.

An issue in double jeopardy is at what point jeopardy "attaches," that is, when a person may be considered to be in jeopardy. In jury trials, jeopardy attaches with the swearing in of the jury; in trials by judge it attaches with the swearing in of the first witness. The other major issue in double jeopardy is what actually constitutes double jeopardy, since a single incident may result in multiple charges against a person, and prosecutors have great discretion as to what charges they bring in a particular matter.

Source(s): *West's Encyclopedia of American Law*. Minneapolis, MN: West, 1998.

not apply to state courts, and this view had prevailed ever since. Justice Marshall, speaking for the Court in the *Benton* case, announced a change in view:

> this Court has "increasingly looked to the specific guarantees of the [Bill of Rights] to determine whether a state criminal trial was conducted with due process of law" . . . [and has] rejected the notion that the Fourteenth Amendment applies to the States only a "watered down, subjective version of the individual guarantees of the Bill of Rights."

The Court had also recently found that the Fourteenth Amendment did make the Sixth Amendment right to a trial by jury applicable to all states in *Duncan v. Louisiana*. In light of this recent trend in Court decisions, it was clear that the Fourteenth Amendment did extend Fifth Amendment protection from double jeopardy in supersession of state laws. Finally, the Court ruled that, since the Maryland Court of Special Appeals had ruled that Benton had not faced double jeopardy, it had not considered what had become relevant matters in light of the Court's ruling that double jeopardy had in fact occurred. Furthermore, Benton now contended that certain evidence presented in his second

larceny trial, which the Court ruled should never have occurred, may have prejudiced the jury with regard to his second burglary trial. As such, the Court remanded the case to the Maryland Court of Special Appeals for consideration of Benton's evidentiary claims. His larceny conviction was reversed.

Benton v. Maryland represents an extension of Fifth Amendment rights, particularly strengthening the position of the individual faced by state prosecution. By citing the Fourteenth Amendment as a means for applying Fifth Amendment protections in supersession of state law, the Court ensured national review of state statutes and procedures affecting the civil rights of individuals.

Related Cases
Palko v. Connecticut, 302 U.S. 319 (1937).
Duncan v. Louisiana, 391 U.S. 145 (1968).

Bibliography and Further Reading
Holmes, Burnham. *The Fifth Amendment*. Englewood Cliffs, NJ: Silver Burdett Press, 1991.

Israel, Jerold H. *Criminal Procedure and the Constitution*. St. Paul, MN: West Publishing Co., 1996.

WALLER V. FLORIDA

Legal Citation: 397 U.S. 387 (1970)

Petitioner
Joseph Waller, Jr.

Respondent
Earl Faircloth, Attorney General of the State of Florida

Petitioner's Claim
That a prosecution in a court of the United States is a bar to a subsequent prosecution in a territorial court, since both are arms of the same sovereign.

Chief Lawyer for Petitioner
Leslie H. Levinson

Chief Lawyer for Respondent
George Georgieff

Justices for the Court
Hugo Lafayette Black, Harry A. Blackmun, William J. Brennan, Jr., Warren E. Burger (writing for the Court), William O. Douglas, John Marshall Harlan II, Thurgood Marshall, Potter Stewart, Byron R. White

Justices Dissenting
None

Place
Washington, D.C.

Date of Decision
13 November 1969

Decision
The Supreme Court vacated the felony conviction against Waller and remanded the case to the District Court of Appeal of Florida.

Significance
Because the state felony charge was based solely on acts covered in the previous municipal court conviction for the lessor included offenses, the second trial constituted double jeopardy violating the Fifth and Fourteenth Amendments to the Constitution.

In 1967, Joseph Waller, Jr., along with several other persons, removed a canvas mural from the inside of the city hall of St. Petersburg, Florida. As Waller and the others were carrying the mural across town, they were stopped by the police. A struggle broke out resulting in a damaged mural and the arrest of Waller and his compatriots. Waller was charged with destruction of city property and disorderly breach of the peace. Found guilty of both counts, Waller was sentenced to six months in the county jail.

At this point, the state of Florida stepped in and charged Waller with grand larceny based on the same acts that had already gotten him convicted on the city ordinances. Before the circuit court trial began Waller and his lawyers attempted to stop the trial by appealing to the Supreme Court of Florida, but his motion was denied without opinion. Waller was then tried and found guilty in circuit court and sentenced to a term in prison of between six months and five years, less the six months already served.

Waller then appealed his second conviction to the Florida District Court of Appeals which considered and then rejected his claim of double jeopardy stating:

> This double Jeopardy argument has long been settled contrary to the claims of the petitioner. We see no reason to recede from our established precedent on the subject. Long ago it was decided that an act committed within municipal limits may be punished by city ordinance even though the same act is also proscribed as a crime by a state statute. An offender may be tried for the municipal offense in the city court and for the crime in the proper state court. Conviction or acquittal in either does not bar prosecution in the other.

However, the U.S. Supreme Court agreed to hear the case and on 13 November 1969 arguments were made. On 6 April 1970, Chief Justice Burger issued the unanimous decision of the Court "that the Florida courts were in error to the extent of holding that—'even if a person has been tried in a municipal court for the identical offense for which he is charged in a state court, this would not be a bar to the prosecution of such person in

Motion to Suppress

A motion is an official request for a court or judge to issue a ruling or order for some act to be done in favor of the party making the request. Hence, a motion to suppress evidence is a request for evidence to be suppressed or not be admitted in a criminal trial. Motions to suppress evidence usually are filed when a defendant believes evidence was obtained illegally in violation of his or her constitutional rights. A written motion must include the specific request as well as the reasons for the request. In addition, a written motion also may include references to other cases that support the request.

After a judge receives a motion to suppress, he or she has two options. First, the judge may grant or deny the motion as a result of the motion's contents alone. Second, the judge may set up a hearing. A motion hearing permits each party to argue in support of its position and allows the judge to ask questions about the facts of the case.

Source(s): *West's Encyclopedia of American Law.* Minneapolis, MN: West Publishing, 1998.

the proper state court.'" Therefore, the Court stated, the second trial of Waller, which resulted in a guilty verdict, was invalid, the judgement vacated and the case remanded to the Florida District Court of Appeals.

The true importance of this ruling rests not in the striking down of the outdated notion of "Dual Sovereignty" which allowed each level of government its successive crack at the defendant. Rather, it is in the rulings extension of the Fifth Amendment's protection against double jeopardy, from the Constitution's Bill of Rights, to state cases as well.

Related Cases

Palko v. Connecticut, 302 U.S. 319 (1937).
Bartkus v. Illinois, 359 U.S. 121 (1959).
Reynolds v. Sims, 377 U.S. 533 (1964).
Benton v. Maryland, 395 U.S. 784 (1969).

Bibliography and Further Reading

Biskupic, Joan, and Elder Witt, eds. *Congressional Quarterly's Guide to the U.S. Supreme Court,* 3rd ed. Washington, DC: Congressional Quarterly, Inc., 1996.

OREGON V. MATHIASON

Legal Citation: 429 U.S. 492 (1977)

Petitioner
State of Oregon

Respondent
Carl Ray Mathiason

Petitioner's Claim
That the Fifth Amendment right to be free from self-incrimination does not require police to give Miranda warnings to a person who is not under arrest and is not deprived of freedom of action.

Chief Lawyer for Petitioner
W. Michael Gillette

Chief Lawyer for Respondent
Gary D. Babcock

Justices for the Court
Harry A. Blackmun, Warren E. Burger, Lewis F. Powell, Jr., William H. Rehnquist, Potter Stewart, Byron R. White (unsigned)

Justices Dissenting
William J. Brennan, Jr., Thurgood Marshall, John Paul Stevens

Place
Washington, D.C.

Date of Decision
25 January 1977

Decision
Law enforcement personnel need not read Miranda rights to a person before interviewing and receiving a confession from the person provided the person is not under arrest and is free to leave, even if the person is at a police station.

Significance
The ruling limited the scope of Miranda v. Arizona (1966). In that case, the Court held that a person in police custody must be advised of her rights before the police may ask questions. Instead of holding that "police custody" includes questioning that takes place inside a police station, the Mathiason Court held that a person must be arrested or somehow confined before Miranda warnings are required.

In 1966, the U.S. Supreme Court delivered a landmark decision in *Miranda v. Arizona,* holding that a criminal suspect who is in police custody must be advised of certain constitutional rights before a law enforcement officer may question the person. In the primary prosecution that constituted the *Miranda* case, police officers had questioned a rape suspect while the suspect was in jail, without advising the suspect of his right to an attorney. The High Court struck down the suspect's confession and reversed his conviction, making new law in the process. Prior to *Miranda,* courts examined the totality of the circumstances surrounding a confession to determine whether it was made voluntarily. *Miranda* threw out that approach and established that a confession by a person who is in police custody is involuntary and therefore inadmissible in court if the interrogating officers do not advise the person of his or her basic legal rights as a criminal suspect. These rights, by virtue of the case name, became known as "Miranda" rights, and they include the right to an attorney, the right to remain silent, and the right to be free from self-incrimination.

The *Miranda* decision was controversial. Deemed by many in the law enforcement community as hostile to law enforcement, the *Miranda* case was decided by a divided Court, and its import has been eroded by subsequent cases. One of those cases was *Oregon v. Mathiason.*

A Violation of Miranda?

The *Mathiason* case began when an officer of the Oregon State Police was called to investigate a burglary at a home near Pendleton, Oregon. The victim of the burglary named Carl Mathiason as a possible suspect. Mathiason was a friend of the victim's son and was on parole from prison. After the officer tried in vain to contact Mathiason, he left a card for Mathiason, asking him to call on the telephone. Mathiason called the next day, and the officer asked Mathiason to come to the police station to meet. Approximately 90 minutes later, Mathiason arrived at the state patrol office, which was housed in a building with several other state agencies. The officer shook hands with Mathiason and led him to an office, where the two sat at a desk. The officer described the burglary and told Mathiason that he

---

The Whitmore Confessions

On 23 April 1964, George Whitmore, Jr., witnessed an assault on Elba Borrero in Brooklyn and volunteered a description of the attacker to the police. Similarities between the Borrero case and the recent murder of Minnie Edmonds in the same neighborhood prompted detectives to have another talk with Whitmore. After questioning him for 22 hours without the presence of an attorney, detectives announced that Whitmore had confessed to both the Borrero assault and the Edmonds killing. The detectives also got Whitmore to sign a confession that he had committed the unsolved double murder of Janice Wylie and Emily Hoffert in Manhattan.

Whitmore contended that the confessions had been beaten out of him. Even when another arrest was made in the Wylie-Hoffert murders, Whitmore still was not dismissed, causing technicalities in his defense in the Borrero assault case. His guilt was assumed on racist grounds.

On 13 June 1966, when the Supreme Court handed down the *Miranda* decision regarding the rights of crime suspects, they acknowledged that coercive interrogations could produce false confessions. "[T]he most conspicuous example occurred in New York in 1964," stated a footnote, "when a African American confessed to two brutal murders and a rape which he had not committed. When this was discovered, the prosecutor was reported as saying: 'Call it what you want—brainwashing, hypnosis, fright. The only thing I don't believe is that Whitmore was beaten.'"

Source(s): Knappman, Edward W., ed. *Great American Trials.* Detroit, MI: Visible Ink Press, 1994.

---

was not under arrest, but he also said that he believed that Mathiason had committed the crime and that the police had found his fingerprints at the scene. The latter statement—that Mathiason's fingerprints had been found—was a fabrication, but Mathiason did not know that. The officer told Mathiason that he would be best served by telling the truth; Mathiason sat for a few minutes and then decided to confess to the crime.

At trial, Mathiason moved the court to exclude evidence of his confession. Mathiason argued that he was entitled to, but did not receive, notice of his Miranda rights, and that he confessed only because he thought it was to his benefit to do so. Mathiason was convicted in a bench trial and his conviction was affirmed by the Oregon Court of Appeals. However, the Supreme Court of Oregon reversed, holding that Mathiason was in custody and was entitled to his Miranda rights. The state of Oregon appealed the decision to the U.S. Supreme Court, which reversed without hearing oral arguments and without giving it full consideration.

The Court Clarifies Miranda

In a *per curiam* opinion (one that is not credited to any particular justice), the Court recounted the facts and procedural disposition of the case and conducted a quick analysis. *Miranda,* according to the Court, was directed toward police procedures in "custodial interrogations." Citing *Miranda,* the Court explained that custodial interrogation is "questioning initiated by law enforcement officers after a person has been taken into custody or otherwise deprived of his freedom of action in any significant way." In this case, Mathiason was not in custody or deprived of his freedom of action. Math-

iason was free to leave the patrol office, and he in fact did leave the patrol office after giving his confession. The Court acknowledged that the interview may have been somewhat coercive, but "[a]ny interview of one suspected of a crime by a police officer will have coercive aspects to it" because "the police officer is part of a law enforcement system which may ultimately cause the suspect to be charged with a crime." Nevertheless, "Miranda warnings are required only where there has been such a restriction on a person's freedom as to render him 'in custody.'"

Unfaithful to Miranda?

Justices Brennan, Marshall, and Stevens dissented. Justice Brennan disagreed with the Court's decision to deny oral arguments and limit its review of the case. Justice Marshall objected to the Court's strict reading of *Miranda.* Marshall conceded that Mathiason may not have been under arrest, "but surely formalities alone cannot control." If Mathiason "entertained an objectively reasonable belief that he was not free to leave," then he was, under the law, deprived of his freedom of action. Marshall opined that it would have been reasonable for Mathiason to believe that he was not free to leave, considering the isolated, unfamiliar setting of the patrol office.

Marshall called for a more careful reading of *Miranda.* "[F]aithfulness to *Miranda,*" wrote Marshall, "requires us to distinguish situations that resemble the 'coercive aspects' of custodial interrogation from those that more nearly resemble [g]eneral on-the-scene questioning . . . which *Miranda* states usually can take place without warnings." Marshall noted that the Court's decision was based only on the Fifth Amendment to the U.S. Constitution, and he roguishly reminded state courts that they "remain free, in interpreting state constitutions, to guard against the evil clearly identified by this case."

Justice Stevens complained of the Court's cursory treatment of the case and raised an issue that had been ignored by the majority. Mathiason, Stevens noted, was on parole at the time of the questioning. Law enforcement officers have greater power to question parolees than regular citizens, and parolees are, by and large, familiar with police procedures. Considering these factors, the Miranda warning seemed inappropriate. Conversely, Mathiason's parole status may have been a factor requiring Miranda warnings. If a parolee is technically in legal custody, Stevens reasoned, "a parolee should always be warned." The landmark case of *Miranda* had been qualified, said Stevens, and the Court "would have a better understanding of the extent of that qualification . . . if we had the benefit of full argument and plenary consideration."

Impact

The ruling in *Mathiason* gave police more freedom to question criminal suspects and left uninformed persons more susceptible to coercive police interrogations. The decision pared down the significance of *Miranda* and signaled its demise. Preceded by *Michigan v. Tucker* (1974) and succeeded by several other cases, *Mathiason* became part of a string of cases that slowly drained *Miranda* of its precedential value. In 1984, the High Court held in *New York v. Quarles* that Miranda rights are not required if the questioning is prompted by an immediate concern for public safety. Two years later, in *Moran v. Burbine* (1986) the Court appeared to return to the pre-*Miranda* law of police questioning by looking only at the totality of the circumstances. In that case, officers prevented a suspect from seeing his lawyer, but the Court held that under the circumstances the incriminating statements were made voluntarily and did not have to be excluded from trial. However, in *Withrow v. Williams* (1993), the Court reapplied some value to the reading of Miranda rights when it held that, generally, a *habeas corpus* petitioner can base the petition on the failure of police to issue Miranda warnings before questioning.

Related Cases

Miranda v. Arizona, 348 U.S. 436 (1966).
Michigan v. Tucker, 417 U.S. 433 (1974).
New York v. Quarles, 467 U.S. 649 (1984).
Moran v. Burbine, 475 U.S. 412 (1986).
Withrow v. Williams, 507 U.S. 680 (1993).

Bibliography and Further Reading

Kerper, Hazel B. *Introduction to the Criminal Justice System,* 2nd ed. Minneapolis: West Publishing Co., 1979.

New York Times, June 22, 1977, sec. II, p. 4.

Steiker, Carol S. "Counter-Revolution in Constitutional Criminal Procedure? Two Audiences, Two Answers." *Michigan Law Review,* August 1996, p. 2466.

Stuntz, William J. "The Uneasy Relationship Between Criminal Procedure and Criminal Justice." *Yale Law Journal,* October 1997, p. 1.

BORDENKIRCHER V. HAYES

Legal Citation: 434 U.S. 357 (1978)

Petitioner
Don Bordenkircher, Kentucky State Penitentiary Superintendent, et al.

Respondent
Paul Lewis Hayes

Petitioner's Claim
Hayes claimed he had been denied his right to due process when, during plea bargaining, he was faced with either pleading guilty to a lesser charge or, if he entered a plea of "not guilty," facing prosecution under a Kentucky recidivist law that carried a mandatory sentence of life imprisonment.

Chief Lawyer for Petitioner
Robert L. Chenoweth

Chief Lawyer for Respondent
J. Vincent April II

Justices for the Court
Warren E. Burger, William H. Rehnquist, John Paul Stevens, Potter Stewart (writing for the Court), Byron R. White

Justices Dissenting
Harry A. Blackmun, William J. Brennan, Jr., Thurgood Marshall, Lewis F. Powell, Jr.

Place
Washington, D.C.

Date of Decision
18 January 1978

Decision
The Supreme Court overturned the verdict of the Court of Appeals for the Sixth Circuit and upheld the decisions of two lower courts that the Petitioner's right of due process had not been constitutionally violated during plea bargaining when, by electing to exercise his right to trial, he was prosecuted under more stringent sentencing requirements.

Significance
The Supreme Court chose to adjudicate this case in an effort to clarify previous decisions, which had not provided specific criteria under which the plea bargaining process should be conducted. Justices for the majority held that although prosecutors might threaten to pursue harsher sentences if a potential defendant chose to plea "not guilty" and go to trial, such negotiations did not constitute a prejudicial or vindictive act. Instead, the majority opinion ruled that the only requirement was that a defendant had to exercise free will in making a choice to refuse a lesser sentence for a guilty plea.

In 1977 Paul Lewis Hayes was charged for writing a single forged check in the amount of $88.30. Under Kentucky law, the offense was punishable by a term of two to ten years in prison. During plea bargaining, the state prosecutor recommended a sentence of five years if Hayes would plead guilty to the indictment. The defendant was warned that if he did not comply with the offer and "save the court of the inconvenience and necessity of a trial," the prosecutor intended to indict him as a recidivist on the basis of two prior felony convictions. That indictment would bring the defendant within the terms of the state Habitual Criminal Act statute, which at the time of trial, provided that "any person convicted a . . . third time of [a] felony . . . shall be confined in penitentiary during his life."

Although the state did not obtain an indictment under the Habitual Criminal Act (also called the "recidivist statute") until after the plea session had ended, the prosecutor's intention to do so was clearly expressed at the end of plea conference. Thus, Hayes was fully notified of the sentencing possibilities of trial if he made the decision to plead "not guilty." The prosecutor carried out his threat and reindicted Hayes under the state's recidivist statute. The grand jury found sufficient grounds on which to issue an indictment charging the defendant with felonious forgery and triggering prosecution under provisions of the recidivist statute. In proceedings that followed, because the jury found that the defendant had two prior felony convictions, the defendant was sentenced to mandatory life imprisonment (and would only be eligible for parole consideration after serving 15 years).

The Kentucky Court of Appeals rejected Hayes's petition objecting to the enhanced sentence and in an unpublished opinion held that "imprisonment for life with the possibility of parole was constitutionally permissible in light of the previous felonies of which Hayes had been convicted." The court further reasoned that the prosecutor's decision to charge him as a habitual offender was, in the normal course of negotiations, legitimate application of the "give and take" inherent in plea bargaining. Hayes subsequently petitioned for a federal writ of *habeas corpus* to the state District Court for the Eastern District of Kentucky, which denied the

Pro and Con: Plea Bargaining

Accused criminals are often offered opportunities to plead guilty to a lesser charges rather than go to trial and risk conviction under more severe charges. For instance, a prosecutor may offer to charge a litigant with manslaughter as opposed to trying to fight for a murder conviction. In such cases, manslaughter carries with it a lighter sentence. Detractors of plea bargaining claim that it the practice is misguided; that plea bargains result in convictions for crimes other than those that are actually committed. They also believe that innocent people may be pressured to plead guilty to crimes they have not committed. Finally, and perhaps most vehemently, that it is simply unfair, because criminals receive lighter penalties than they deserve.

The defenders of the practice point out that plea bargaining has advantages for the defendant and the state as well. As well as receiving a lighter punishment, the defendant is spared the cost of defense and may also avoid the greater publicity surrounding a case that goes to trial. The state is better able to prosecute more cases within its given budget. This also means that the state is more easily able to fulfill its constitutional obligation to provide a speedy trial. Further, in certain serious cases the intent of the defendant must be determined, which can be extremely difficult. Thus it may be better for a prosecutor to accept a certain guilty plea to a lesser charge than to risk acquittal.

Source(s): Kapsch, Stefan J. "Plea Bargaining." *The Guide to American Law: Everyone's Legal Encyclopedia.* Minneapolis, MN: West, 1998.

writ. The court affirmed the decision of the lower court, confirming that neither the enhanced sentence nor the procedure of the indictment violated the Constitution.

The Court of Appeals for the Sixth Circuit reversed the district court's ruling. The court's position was that while "plea bargaining now plays an important role in our criminal justice system," the state prosecutor's conduct in plea sessions had violated the principles of *Blackledge v. Perry* (1974), which stated that the U.S. Constitution "protected defendants from the vindictive exercise of a prosecutor's discretion." Accordingly, the court of appeals ordered that Hayes be set free after serving a prison term commensurate with a guilty conviction for passing a forged document.

On a writ of *certiorari* (a written order directing a court to forward a case for review), the U.S. Supreme Court agreed to consider the matter because they felt inherent in the case "a constitutional question of importance in the administration of criminal justice." In a 5-4 vote, the Supreme Court overturned the lower court's decision. Writing for the majority, Justice Stewart delivered the Court's opinion. The constitutional question addressed by the Court was whether the prosecutor had violated the Due Process Clause of the Fourteenth Amendment when he carried out a threat he made in the course of plea bargaining to reindict Hayes on harsher charges if he pleaded not guilty.

Even though the prosecutor did not obtain an indictment under the recidivist statute until after the plea session ended, at the outset of the plea bargaining the defendant was fully informed of the sentencing possibilities should he undergo a trial. Further, the additional charge (brought as a result of his prior felonious convictions) was not exclusively related to the original indictment. The appellate court felt that there was "strong likelihood of vindictiveness" in the case. The court of appeals found no such element of retaliation or wrongdoing in the process, however, as long as Hayes was free to choose and knowingly make a decision. In explaining the rationale for its decision, the appellate court cited *North Carolina v. Pearce* (1969), wherein the U.S. Supreme Court held that the Due Process Clause of the Fourteenth Amendment requires that "vindictiveness against a defendant for having successfully attacked his first conviction must play no part in the sentence he receives after a new trial." This case outlined criteria with respect to what constituted prosecutorial vindictiveness. The state prosecutor's newer, more punitive indictment made the stakes higher if the defendant in *Pearce* was convicted. However, the indictment was not retaliation for his having successfully defended himself in a prior action. Thus, because the defendant knew what the possibilities were if he chose to plead "not guilty," the prosecutor's threat to seek a stringent sentence in no way approached what the Supreme Court deemed "vindictiveness." The court of appeals recognized the difference between a possible deal that prosecutor and defendant might reach on the actual indictment, and the threat that a greater sentence would be imposed on the defendant with a new, more stringent charge.

In expressing the Court's majority opinion, Justice Black expressed that "to punish a person (such as the state prosecutor) because he had done what the law plainly allows him to do is a due process violation of the most basic sort." Moreover, the Court rejected the idea that Hayes's constitutional rights would have been infringed had he made a guilty plea to a lesser charge because, as such, that plea would have been involuntary. The Court recognized the choices defendants faced were surely difficult choices but that such was the "inevitable" and legally "permissible" nature of a U.S. legal system that encouraged plea negotiations. In fact, the majority opinion found no fault if, in facing greater punishment, a defendant might be deterred from exercising the right to trial in order to gain a more favorable sentence.

The U.S. Supreme Court found that Hayes was properly chargeable under the recidivist statute because he had two, prior, felony convictions. It was up to the prosecutor to determine what charges to file, within the limits of the recidivist statute, and then present them to the jury. And while selection based on race, religion, gender, and other "arbitrary classification" remained a constitutional violation in itself, selection was permissible if not made upon those criteria. In the *Hayes* case, the prosecutor did not make an "arbitrary classification" but rather made determination that it would be in the public interest to file charges under the recidivist statute.

Justice Blackmun wrote the dissenting opinion. The dissenting justices felt that the Kentucky prosecutor neglected principles set in *North Carolina v. Pearce* and *Blackledge v. Perry*. If a defendant invokes the right of pleading "not guilty," she should not be punished for such an action by facing an exceedingly more stringent sentence as a result of going to trial. Moreover, the justices felt that if, in coming to a new trial, a defendant receives a harsher punishment than would have been meted in the first one, the prosecutor must explain such action. And justification for such actions could not simply be to "discourage" the defendant from exercising rights guaranteed under the Constitution.

Feeling compelled to render an additional, separate dissenting opinion, Justice Powell stated that he was inclined to support the majority opinion. His opinion departed from the Court's findings, however, because he did not share their view that the prosecutors conduct during the plea bargaining process was in accordance with due process. He pointed out that the prosecutor did not offer any explanation for seeking an indictment that carried extreme punishment other than the defendant's refusal to plead guilty to the lesser charge. Accordingly, Powell agreed with the minority opinion that it was constitutionally unacceptable to deter a defendant from using his rights. In discussing *United States v. Jackson* (1968) and *North Carolina v. Pearce* (1969), he charged that the Court had stated in clear terms that "*Jackson* and *Pearce* are clear, and subsequent cases have not dulled their force: if the only objective of a state practice is to discourage assertion of constitutional rights it is 'patently unconstitutional.'" But while the Court had recognized plea bargaining as a vital part of the criminal justice system, the facts of Hayes's case suggested the prosecutor acted in a manner that denied the respondent his right to due process.

Impact

In rendering a decision, the Court was faced with a challenge to their previous decisions that tacitly supported plea bargaining. In order to clarify its position, the Court agreed to hear the case, and in order to provide guidance to lower courts, the justices reiterated and recognized the importance of the plea bargaining process in the U.S. judicial system. The majority held that a prosecutor had full authority to pursue more stringent sentences when going to trial so long as a defendant was able to exercise free will in making a choice to refuse a lesser sentence for a plea of guilty. Prosecutors had to, as did the Kentucky State prosecutor, inform the defendant at the outset of the plea bargaining regarding sentencing possibilities should s/he undergo a trial. The Court also clarified its findings in *North Carolina v. Pearce* (1969) that "vindictiveness against a defendant" in that case was defined as only a result of retaliation by a prosecutor for a defendant's success in another trial. In summing up their rationale for their ruling, the Court gave the plea bargaining process essential full sway. Aggressive prosecutors were given a tool to conduct plea bargaining in a manner that might deter defendants from pursuing trial by accepting lesser penalty in return for a plea of guilty.

Related Cases

United States v. Jackson, 390 U.S. 570 (1968).
North Carolina v. Pearce, 395 U.S. 711 (1969).
Blackledge v. Perry, 417 U.S. 21 (1974).

Bibliography and Further Reading

Biskupic, Joan, and Elder Witt, eds. *Congressional Quarterly's Guide to the U.S. Supreme Court,* 3rd ed. Washington, DC: Congressional Quarterly, Inc., 1996.

Cushman, Robert F. *Cases in Constitutional Law,* 7th ed. Englewood Cliffs, NJ: Prentice-Hall, Inc., 1989.

Jampol, Melissa L. "Goodbye to the Defense of Selective Prosecution." *Journal of Criminal Law and Criminology,* spring 1997, p. 932.

Johnson, John W. *Historic U.S. Court Cases, 1690-1990: An Encyclopedia.* New York: Garland Publishing, 1992.

Misner, Robert L. "Recasting Prosecutorial Discretion." *Journal of Criminal Law and Criminology,* spring 1996, p. 717.

BERKEMER V. McCARTY

Legal Citation: 468 U.S. 420 (1984)

Petitioner
Harry J. Berkemer, Sheriff of Franklin Country, Ohio

Respondent
Richard N. McCarty

Petitioner's Claim
That police officers need not provide Miranda warnings prior to misdemeanor interrogations either at roadside traffic stops, in a patrol car, or at a police station and that McCarty's statements made during questioning at the police station should be admissible.

Chief Lawyer for Petitioner
Alan C. Travis

Chief Lawyer for Respondent
R. William Meeks

Justices for the Court
Harry A. Blackmun, William J. Brennan, Jr., Warren E. Burger, Thurgood Marshall (writing for the Court), Sandra Day O'Connor, Lewis F. Powell, Jr., William H. Rehnquist, John Paul Stevens, Byron R. White

Justices Dissenting
None

Place
Washington, D.C.

Date of Decision
2 July 1984

Decision
Police must inform people of their rights in accordance with the Miranda doctrine when formally arrested or vigorously questioned for any offense, including a misdemeanor traffic violation. The Court also held that the Miranda rule does not apply to routine questioning for a roadside traffic stop.

Significance
This case helped the U.S. Supreme Court determine more precisely when police officers must read motorists the Miranda warnings for traffic stops and violations. Whereas in *United States v. Murray*, the Court found that routine questioning pertaining to a traffic stop does not require the reading of the motorist's rights the Court ruled that police must inform motorists of their rights if they formally arrest them and take them into custody.

Miranda Warnings

Because of *Miranda v. Arizona* (1966), the police must inform people they plan to arrest of their rights, including their right to remain silent because anything they say could be used as evidence against them, their right to have an attorney present, and their right to have a state-appointed attorney, if they cannot afford one. The U.S. Supreme Court imposed this measure to protect people from giving self-incriminating statements while in the often intimidating atmosphere and environment of police interrogations. This decision carefully outlined how police must implement this safeguard when questioning suspects in order to avoid forced or otherwise improperly obtained testimonies and confessions.

The Questioning of McCarty

While driving on 31 March 1980, Richard McCarty's car wove in and out of the lanes on Interstate 270 in Ohio, according to Trooper Williams, who followed McCarty and pulled him over. When Williams asked McCarty to get out of the car, he saw McCarty could barely stand up. Williams concluded that McCarty had been driving while under the influence of intoxicants. Williams made McCarty perform a sobriety test to examine his balancing skills to confirm his suspicion and McCarty failed it. Williams next asked McCarty if he had recently taken any intoxicants and McCarty responded that he drank two beers and smoked some marijuana shortly before driving. After that, Williams placed McCarty under arrest and took him to jail in a patrol car.

The police administered a breathalyzer test at the jail to find out the level of alcohol in McCarty's blood; however, the test showed no presence of alcohol in McCarty, so Williams continued questioning him. While filling out the State Highway Patrol Alcohol Influence Report, Williams asked McCarty if he was under the influence of alcohol and McCarty responded, "I guess, barely." Williams then asked if the marijuana McCarty smoked had been laced with any chemicals or other drugs. Williams wrote on the form, "No ang[el] dust or PCP in the pot." However, throughout the questioning at the roadside and at the police station no one—neither Williams nor any other police officer—informed McCarty of his Miranda rights: his right not to answer the questions, his right to an attorney, and his right to have a state attorney appointed, if he needed.

Were McCarty's Rights Violated?

McCarty and his defense tried to have the court exclude the incriminating statements he made while in custody because the police never informed him of his constitutional rights before questioning him. The trial court rejected his request and McCarty pleaded "no contest," receiving a 90-day jail sentence and a $300 fine. The court reduced his penalty to 10 days in jail and a $200 fine. Nonetheless, McCarty appealed his sentence, maintaining that Trooper Williams violated his rights and that he failed the sobriety test because of a back injury and a limp leg, which made him look drunk or intoxicated. The Ohio Court of Appeals, however, argued that the Miranda warnings did not apply to misdemeanors in accordance with the *State v. Pyle* (1970) ruling. Furthermore, the Ohio Supreme Court refused to hear the case, believing that it did not raise a significant constitutional question. McCarty next petitioned the District Court for the Southern District of Ohio. The district court also dismissed McCarty's request, saying that the Miranda warnings did not apply to traffic arrests.

Finally, the Court of Appeals for the Sixth Circuit sided with McCarty, mandating that the police must provide Miranda warnings prior to any formal arrest, no matter what class of crime, including traffic violations. The court of appeals distinguished between the statements McCarty made before and after his arrest, ruling that those made after his arrest could clearly not be used against him. However, the ruling left some things unanswered, in particular, if all of McCarty's statements prior to his arrest could be used against him and which statements the court could use in McCarty's retrial.

The U.S. Supreme Court began hearing the case on 28 April 1984 in order to resolve the dispute surrounding Miranda warnings and minor violations such as traffic offenses and questioning motorists at traffic stops. Since the Fifth Amendment states that "no person . . . shall be compelled in any criminal case to be a witness against himself," state and federal law enforcement officers must ensure that suspects are aware that they are not obligated to answer their questions, especially if the information is self-incriminating. Out of concern for such situations, the Court decided in *Miranda v. Arizona* that police must inform all suspects of their rights prior to interrogating them.

Although the Franklin County police department argued for allowing them to use the evidence they obtained while questioning McCarty, the Court strongly disagreed, holding that the possibility of coercion and police manipulation of the confession applies just as much to misdemeanors as it does to felonies. The Court reasoned that not only can an interrogation for a misdemeanor escalate into one for a felony, but also the setting of police custody works "to undermine the individual's will to resist," as the Court decided in *Miranda v. Arizona*. Berkemer urged that providing Miranda rights for traffic arrests would impede and slow down law enforcement, but the Court rejected this argument, noting that traffic arrests and interrogations do not occur frequently and reading suspects their rights in such cases would not impose any extra burden since police are already accustomed to giving the Miranda warnings prior to all other interrogations in police custody.

The Court then tackled the more difficult question of the statements McCarty made while interrogated at the roadside. McCarty tried to persuade the Court that the Miranda warnings apply to these questionings as well, because he was "deprived of his freedom of action," as the *Miranda* decision stipulates, while Berkemer maintained that traffic stops lay outside *Miranda*'s scope. The Court decided that since traffic stops usually are temporary and brief and since they typically are not that intimidating, Miranda warnings apply to formal arrests, not to routine traffic stop questioning. Consequently, the Court deemed McCarty's roadside statements admissible. However, the Court also found that if roadside questioning should evolve into more intense and vigorous interrogation, then the questioning should be considered interrogation in police custody and subject to all the Miranda warnings. The Court hoped this additional point would help avert police abuse of the roadside-questioning exemption to the Miranda warnings.

While all the justices agreed with most of the Court's decision, Justice Stevens felt the Court answered more than the case required. The Court's decision covered a broad range of issues surrounding Miranda warnings and Justice Stevens felt the decision resembled blanket legislation rather than resolving a specific legal dispute presented by the two parties. Nonetheless, resting on the distinction between questioning for a routine traffic stop and questioning while under arrest or in police custody, *Berkemer v. McCarty* articulated the general circumstances in which the police need and need not provide motorists the Miranda warnings. "When the police arrest a person for allegedly committing a misdemeanor traffic offense and ask him questions without telling him his constitutional rights, petitioner argues, his responses should be admissible against him. We cannot agree."

Related Cases

Miranda v. Arizona, 384 U.S. 436 (1966).
Terry v. Ohio, 392 U.S. 1 (1968).

Bibliography and Further Reading

National Highway Safety Administration. *Highway Safety Desk Book.* Available from http://www.nhtsa.dot.gov/people/injury/enforce/deskbk.html.

Pagel, Briane F. "Maybe It's Better to Just Leave Earlier: Traffic Stops and Your Rights." *The Badger Herald,* 1996.

COLORADO V. CONNELLY

Legal Citation: 479 U.S. 157 (1986)

Petitioner
State of Colorado

Respondent
Francis Barry Connelly

Petitioner's Claim
The state of Colorado maintained that the statements given by a defendant and admitted during trial were not in violation of the Due Process Clause of the Fourteenth Amendment, although the defendant was mentally ill at the time of his confession.

Chief Lawyer for Petitioner
Nathan B. Coats

Chief Lawyer for Respondent
Thomas M. Van Cleave

Justices for the Court
Sandra Day O'Connor, Lewis F. Powell, Jr., William H. Rehnquist (writing for the Court), Antonin Scalia, Byron R. White

Justices Dissenting
Harry A. Blackmun, William J. Brennan, Jr., Thurgood Marshall, John Paul Stevens

Place
Washington, D.C.

Date of Decision
10 December 1986

Decision
The Court ruled that statements by a mentally ill defendant that were given as evidence did not represent police coercion nor violate the Due Process Clause. Neither were such statements in violation of Miranda rights because the defendant was not coerced or misled into surrendering rights guaranteed under the Fifth Amendment.

Significance
Francis Connelly was mentally ill when he gave police statements which eventually led to his arrest and conviction for murder; however, the U.S. Supreme Court ruled that neither his right to due process nor his Miranda rights were in question. Rather, due process was only concerned with protection of a defendant against police or government coercion. Since police merely recorded statements that were freely given, there was no element of coercion. The Justices held that due process guaranteed under the Fourteenth Amendment did not include the "right" to confess only when a person was rational and "appropriately motivated."

Francis Connelly confessed to two police officers in Denver, Colorado, that he killed a young girl and that he needed to talk to somebody about it. At the time, the defendant seemed to be perfectly rational and to understand what he was doing; nonetheless, during the course of the encounter, the arresting officer learned that Connelly had been treated as a mental patient in the recent past. Police officers warned Connelly of his Miranda rights, cuffed him, and then took him to the Denver Police Station. Upon arrival at the police station, Connelly was again informed about his Miranda rights but he insisted on talking about his crime. He told police officers he understood all of what they told him, but that he had to make his confession because his conscience was telling him to do so. The day after making a confession, the public defender's office interviewed Connelly and discovered he was very much disoriented and did not seem to understand what happened the day before. Connelly was sent to a hospital for evaluation. The court-appointed psychiatrist, Dr. Jeffrey Metzner, found him incompetent to stand trial and incapable of giving his attorney assistance in preparing his defense.

Defendant Heard "Voice Of God"

Six months later, doctors who had evaluated and treated the defendant decided that he was ready to attend his trial. When he appeared at a preliminary hearing, before Colorado State Court, Connelly moved to suppress all of his prior statements. The defendant said that, at the time, he was hearing the "voice of God" and that was what made him confess to murder. Called to testify on the defendant's behalf, Dr. Metzner explained that Connelly was in a stage of chronic schizophrenia at least one day prior to his confession. The "command hallucinations" Connelly experienced interfered with his ability to make independent and rational choices. He further explained that the psychosis Connelly was experiencing could motivate him to confess, and that "voices" he was hearing at the time could be interpreted as the defendant's feeling of guilt. However, while opining that Connelly's psychosis motivated him to confess, Metzner also allowed that even in that state, Connelly's cognitive abilities were

The M'Naghten Rule

The M'Naghten rule is a test for criminal insanity. Under the M'Naghten rule, a criminal defendant is not guilty by reason of insanity if, at the time of the alleged criminal act, the defendant was so deranged that she did not know the nature or quality of her actions or, if she knew the nature an quality of her actions, she was so deranged that she did not know that what she was doing was wrong.

The M'Naghten rule on criminal insanity is named for Daniel M'Naghten, who, in 1843, tried to kill England's prime minister Sir Robert Peel. M'Naghten thought Peel wanted to kill him, so he tried to shoot Peel but instead shot and killed Peel's secretary, Edward Drum-

mond. Medical experts testified that M'Naghten was psychotic, and M'Naghten was found not guilty by reason of insanity.

The M'Naghten rule was adopted in most jurisdictions in the United States, but legislatures and courts eventually modified and expanded the definition. The definition of criminal insanity now varies from jurisdiction to jurisdiction, but most of them have been influenced by the M'Naghten rule.

Source(s): *West's Encyclopedia of American Law*, Vol. 7, p. 233. Minneapolis, MN: West Publishing, 1998.

not affected and his mental state did not interfere with his ability to understand his rights as they were presented by the police.

The Colorado trial court ruled that the petitioner's confessions should be suppressed because they were not voluntary. Citing *Townsend v. Sain* (1963) and *Culombe v. Connecticut* (1961), the court held that confessions were admissible only when the defendant was capable of exercising "rational intellect and free will." While the police did not coerce a confession, Connelly was in a state wherein his mental illness incapacitated him temporarily and rendered invalid his waiver of Miranda rights, especially his right to counsel and the right against self-incrimination. Accordingly, his confession was suppressed at trial.

On appeal the Colorado Supreme Court agreed that rationality and free will were absent since Connelly was mentally ill at the time of his confession. The court further pointed out that police coercion was not the only criteria for characterizing a confession as involuntary. Mental illness was, itself, a way that "free choice may be overborne." Thus, when the state's prosecutor moved to admit his confession during trial, the Due Process Clause of the Fourteenth Amendment was applicable. As such, because Connelly was unable "to make a valid waiver" of his rights, due process was violated and, the Colorado Supreme Court ruled, the lower court was correct in excluding Connelly's statements.

The U.S. Supreme Court granted *certiorari* because the conclusions of the lower court seemed at odds with previous rulings by the Court. Believing that the rules of evidence sufficiently addressed the matter of confessions by a suspect who may have been mentally incompetent, the justices did not consider previous decisions regarding coerced confessions or Miranda rights violations. Those rulings were inapplicable. As

such, the U.S. Supreme Court reversed the decisions of the lower courts.

No Violation of Due Process Rights Found

In formulating the majority opinion, the justices acknowledged that the lower courts were correct in their assumption that the specter of involuntary confession was an important factor in considering the validity of an admission of guilt. Toward that end, coercion by police played a significant role. However, while Connelly's mental incapacity may have also been another "significant factor" with respect to "voluntariness," the justices could find no cause to consider such circumstance as a valid rationale to consider whether due process according to *Miranda* was a matter for consideration. In authoring the majority opinion, Justice Rehnquist postulated that "only if we were to establish a brand new constitutional right—the right of a criminal defendant to confess to his crime only when totally rational and properly motivated—could respondent's present claim be sustained." Just because police took the petitioner's statements and just because the state's prosecutor chose to submit those statements into evidence did not constitute a violation of the Due Process Clause of the Fourteenth Amendment.

While Colorado was required to prove the appropriateness of their evidence under a motion to suppress (according to *Lego v. Twomey* [1972]), the state was only obligated to validate their action through a preponderance of evidence to be granted waiver. Because circumstantial evidence in Connelly's trial overwhelmingly supported the state's case, his confessions, too, were admissible. Thus, the Colorado Supreme Court did not apply a standard of "clear and convincing evidence" in rendering a decision. Moreover, while Connelly's confession might be characterized, according to the petitioner's claim, as coercion from "the voice of God," it was in no way appropriate to consider Connelly's assertion that such a "command" or motivation, however hallucinatory, comprised a challenge to his constitutional right to due process under the Fourteenth Amendment. As such, the U.S. Supreme Court moved to reverse the decision of the Colorado Supreme Court and remand the case back for further adjudication.

Dissenting Justices Not Unified in Opinion

In his dissent, Justice Stevens agreed that simply recording the confession of a suspect who might be mentally incapacitated or even admitting that confession into evidence did not necessarily mean that a confession was involuntary. Neither did such action necessarily constitute noncompliance with the Due Process Clause. However, Stevens believed that a defendant's incompetence to stand trial certainly rendered him incompetent to reasonably waive his Miranda rights as well. Similarly, Justices Brennan and Marshall believed a defendant's mental state was a reasonable consideration when determining the validity of a waiver of Miranda rights. In their opinion, the confession of a mentally ill person was one that was not given of his own volition. As such, the state could not reasonably offer proof that the defendant freely waived his Miranda rights. The justices pointed out that without Connelly's confession, police had not collected evidence which would have led to a sufficiently valid case to charge him with murder. Thus, due process required the independent collection of physical evidence which would, of its own weight, substantially contribute to the merits of the case. Absence of police misconduct, then, required that the evidence gathered had to be the by-product of a free, voluntary confession. As such, all minority justices agreed, the lower courts were correct in their decision to suppress the petitioner's statements made to police because he was unable to make an intelligent decision at the time of his confession.

Impact

In a closely contested decision, the U.S. Supreme Court held that rules of evidence sufficiently covered instances wherein a confession made by a mentally ill defendant resulted in the gathering and admission of evidence into trial. By opting to not invoke the con-

stitutional issue of due process or question the applicability of Miranda rights, the Court sent a clear message to lower courts that rarely did coercion entail circumstances other than those brought about by police misconduct. The mere fact that police recorded a confession made by a mentally ill suspect, collected sufficient evidence to build a substantial case because of leads provided by that statement, and provided the statement for the state to admit into trial did not, of itself, constitute a violative waiver of Miranda rights nor a denial of due process. As such, lower courts were given guidance that so long as statements made during a police interview were given voluntarily and freely, regardless of the mental state of the interviewee, that such statements were constitutionally sanctioned and, therefore, admissible as evidence in a court of law.

Related Cases

Blackburn v. Alabama, 361 U.S. 199 (1960).
Culombe v. Connecticut, 367 U.S. 568 (1961).
Townsend v. Sain, 372 U.S. 293 (1963).
Miranda v. Arizona, 384 U.S. 436 (1966).
Harris v. New York, 401 U.S. 222 (1971).
Lego v. Twomey, 404 U.S. 477 (1972).

Bibliography and Further Reading

Hendrie, Edward M. "Beyond *Miranda*." *FBI Home Page: Office of Public and Congressional Affairs and Office of the Chief Scientist.* http://www.fbi.gov/leb/mar976.htm.

Kamisar, Yale. "On the 'Fruits' of *Miranda* Violations, Coerced Confessions, and Compelled Testimony." *Michigan Law Review*, March 1995, p. 929.

National Association of Criminal Defense Lawyers. *National Association of Criminal Defense Lawyers— NACDL Legislative Policies.* "Fifth Amendment Preservation." http://www.criminaljustice.org/LEGIS/leg09. htm.

Vanderhoof, David J. W. "Professor David's Lecture Notes—Investigation and Police Practices." Dept. of Sociology, Social Work and Criminal Justice—The University of North Carolina at Pembroke. February 27, 1998. http://www.uncp.edu/home/vanderhoof/geolr. html.

Winick, Bruce J. "Reforming Incompetency to Stand Trial and Plead Guilty." *Journal of Criminal Law and Criminology*, winter 1995, p. 571.

PUERTO RICO V. BRANSTAD

Legal Citation: 483 U.S. 219 (1987)

Petitioner
Puerto Rico

Respondent
Terry Branstad, Governor of Iowa, et al.

Petitioner's Claim
That the Governor of Iowa was in violation of the Constitution's Extradition Clause for failing to extradite Ronald Calder, a fugitive from justice in Puerto Rico.

Chief Lawyer for Petitioner
Lino J. Saldana

Chief Lawyer for Respondent
Brent R. Appel

Justices for the Court
Harry A. Blackmun, William J. Brennan, Jr., Thurgood Marshall (writing for the Court), Sandra Day O'Connor, Lewis F. Powell, Jr., William H. Rehnquist, Antonin Scalia, John Paul Stevens, Byron R. White

Justices Dissenting
None

Place
Washington, D.C.

Date of Decision
23 June 1987

Decision
The Supreme Court unanimously held that the federal courts must have the authority to order a governor to comply with the Constitution's Extradition Clause.

Significance
The case allowed federal courts more authority to command compliance from states, overturning the long-held precedent set by *Kentucky v. Dennison* (1861), a Civil War era states' rights case.

The Precedent of *Kentucky v. Dennison*

In *Puerto Rico v. Branstad,* the Supreme Court determined that the Constitution granted federal courts the authority to compel an asylum state to fulfill its obligations under the Constitution's Extradition Clause and deliver fugitives for justice on demand. In doing so, it overturned *Kentucky v. Dennison,* one of the long-standing foundational cases for the principle of federalism—the balance of power between state and federal governments. *Kentucky v. Dennison* affirmed the principle that state and federal governments were always to be considered coequal. This, the Court declared in *Puerto Rico v. Branstad,* was "not representative of current law."

Kentucky v. Dennison dealt with the highly politicized issue of fugitive slaves in 1861. As the nation moved towards the Civil War, northern states refused to hand over fugitive slaves, while southern states refused to release free blacks captured and sold in the South. *Kentucky v. Dennison* was representative. The case involved a free African American man from Ohio, named William Lago, who helped a slave named Charlotte escape from Kentucky. Kentucky's governor tried to force Ohio's governor to extradite Lago. When both the Ohio governor and his successor refused on the grounds that Lago had committed no crime in Ohio, Kentucky's governor appealed in 1861 to the Supreme Court to issue a writ of *mandamus* ordering Ohio's governor, then William Dennison, to extradite Lago. The Supreme Court refused, ruling that, while conformity with the Constitution's Extradition Clause was mandatory, the federal courts had no authority to compel it.

The Case of Ronald Calder

For more than a century, *Kentucky v. Dennison* stood as precedent. In 1981, a federally-employed air traffic controller named Ronald Calder struck two people with his car in San Juan, Puerto Rico. A man was injured; his wife and their unborn child were killed. Witnesses testified that the incident took place immediately after an argument between the two men, and that after having struck the two people, Calder backed his car over the woman's prone body several times.

Charged with first-degree murder and attempted murder, Calder fled to his family's home in Iowa. The

Americans Abroad

When traveling abroad, Americans are subject to the laws of the country they are visiting, which may be quite different from those of the United States. Laws of foreign countries may be quite restrictive compared to U.S. laws, particularly in the areas of free speech and freedom of movement. Guarantees regarding legal procedure and rights of the accused may be completely absent.

When an American is arrested or detained abroad, some help is usually available from the U.S. embassy located in that country. Embassy personnel may visit the detainee in order to ensure his or her safety and fair treatment. They may also notify relatives of the sit-

uation and help obtain local legal representation (the legal assistance of someone familiar with local law is usually necessary). Embassy personnel may also aid Americans convicted of crimes and sentenced to imprisonment in foreign countries by arranging visits of relatives, providing information about pardons, and protesting ill treatment when necessary; in some cases, treaties may allow for transfer of prisoners to U.S. prisons. Embassy personnel may not pay legal fees or fines with U.S. government funds or represent a U.S. citizen at trial.

Source(s): U.S. Department of State (http:travel.state.gov.arrest.html)

Puerto Rican authorities notified Iowa that Calder was a fugitive from justice. Calder surrendered himself in Iowa and posted the bond set by that state. When the governor of Puerto Rico requested Calder's extradition, the governor of Iowa held an extradition hearing where Calder's counsel testified that the accused could not, as a white man, receive a fair trial in the Puerto Rican courts. After attempts to negotiate a reduction of charges for Calder failed, Iowa notified Puerto Rico that the request for extradition was denied.

In 1984, the commonwealth of Puerto Rico filed suit against the state of Iowa and its governor, Terry Branstad, in U.S. district court, seeking a writ of *mandamus* forcing the governor to comply with the Extradition Clause. The district court and the court of appeals both ruled that the Supreme Court's holding in *Kentucky v. Dennison* prevented an attempt by federal authorities to force compliance with the clause. The Supreme Court then agreed to consider whether the decision in *Kentucky v. Dennison* still stood.

A Different Era

According to the Court opinion, written by Justice Marshall, it did not. *Kentucky v. Dennison,* wrote Marshall, was "the product of another time," a time in which states were seceding and "the practical power of the Federal Government at its lowest ebb since the adoption of the Constitution." The reluctance of the federal courts to intervene in state extradition disputes during this time was clearly politically motivated. "Yet," wrote Marshall, "this decision has stood while the world of which it was a part has passed away. We conclude that it may stand no longer." There was simply no reason to exclude extradition from a long list of duties which the federal courts had the authority to compel of state governments.

The Court dismissed Iowa's additional contention that even in the absence of *Kentucky v. Dennison* the state would not be compelled under the Constitution to extradite Calder to Puerto Rico, since the latter was not a state. Puerto Rico, as a commonwealth, wrote

Terry Branstad, Governor of Iowa, 1996. © Photograph by Charlie Neibergall. AP/Wide World Photos.

Marshall, was clearly a territory of the United States, and the Constitution stated that the Extradition Act "requires rendition of fugitives at the request of a demanding 'Territory,' as well as State." The Supreme Court thus reversed the decision of the court of appeals, and overturned its own holding in *Kentucky v. Dennison,* ensuring that no state would become a safe haven for fugitives from the law.

Related Cases

Kentucky v. Dennison, 65 U.S. 66 (1861).

Ashwander v. Tennessee Valley Authority, 297 U.S. 288 (1936).

Bibliography and Further Reading

Biskupic, Joan, and Elder Witt, eds. *Congressional Quarterly's Guide to the U.S. Supreme Court,* 3rd ed. Washington, DC: Congressional Quarterly, Inc., 1996.

DUCKWORTH V. EAGAN

Legal Citation: 492 U.S. 195 (1989)

Petitioner
Jack R. Duckworth

Respondent
Gary James Eagan

Petitioner's Claim
That the respondent's rights were not violated simply because police officers failed to follow the exact wording of Miranda during the interrogation process.

Chief Lawyer for Petitioner
David Michael Wallman

Chief Lawyer for Respondent
Howard B. Eisenberg

Justices for the Court
Anthony M. Kennedy, Sandra Day O'Connor, William H. Rehnquist (writing for the Court), Antonin Scalia, Byron R. White

Justices Dissenting
Harry A. Blackmun, William J. Brennan, Jr., Thurgood Marshall, John Paul Stevens

Place
Washington, D.C.

Date of Decision
26 June 1989

Decision
Respondent's Miranda rights were not violated, even if they were not delivered to the respondent exactly as written in Miranda. The Court held that Miranda rights are not prescriptive inasmuch as they express a means by which law enforcement can ensure that the rights of a suspect are not infringed upon when gathering probative evidence.

Significance
This case was marked by the refusal of some justices to address the appropriateness of Miranda's language. Instead, Justices Brennan, Marshall, O'Connor, and Scalia engaged in a judicial argument concerning whether, under Stone v. Powell (1976), federal review under a writ of habeas corpus should be granted at all to cases involving Miranda rights claims. Ultimately, by ruling that no decision was required regarding Stone because litigants had not raised the issue, the majority decision rendered by Chief Justice Rehnquist gave tacit support to Miranda claims under writs of habeas corpus.

Gary James Eagan contacted a Chicago policeman with whom he was acquainted and informed him that he had seen a dead woman on the beach. Although the woman was stabbed nine times, she was alive when police officers arrived. Upon seeing Eagan she asked him, "Why did you stab me?" The respondent claimed that he was with the woman earlier but that several unknown men attacked them and took the woman away. Subsequent to the incident, Chicago police determined that the case belonged in the jurisdiction of Indiana, and they turned the investigation over to the Hammond (Indiana) Police Department.

On initial contact at a Chicago police station, Eagan again told Hammond police that he was attacked and the woman was kidnapped. After filing a battery complaint, Eagan agreed to accompany Hammond police for a more detailed interview. Before questioning, the respondent had been read and had signed a "Voluntary Appearance: Advice of Rights" waiver form. The rights listed in that form advised that he must understand his rights before any questioning; that he had a right to remain silent; that anything he said could be used against him in court; that he had a right to talk to a lawyer before any questioning; that a lawyer could be present during the questioning; that even if he could not afford to hire a lawyer he had a right to the advice and presence of a lawyer; that a lawyer would be appointed "if and when you go to court;" and that if he decided to answer questions without a lawyer, he had a right to stop answering questions at any time. Eagan proceeded to make an exculpatory statement where he repeated his claim about the way events happened.

After questioning, Hammond police jailed Eagan for 29 hours before he was interviewed again. Before questioning, police read from a form that conveyed his Miranda rights. Eagan read the form back to the interrogating officers and then signed the new waiver form. Eagan proceeded to confess to stabbing the woman and led police to where they could fine incriminating evidence—the knife used in the stabbing and some clothes. Although Eagan objected to admission of evidence and both police interviews at his trial, he was found guilty and the Indiana state trial court sentenced him to 35 years in prison.

Believing his rights were violated under the U.S. Constitution's Fifth and Fourteenth Amendments, the respondent directly appealed his conviction. Failing to gain appeal, the respondent sought legal redress under a writ of *habeas corpus* (a petition that orders determination by a federal court as to whether an individual's detention is lawful). He claimed that the first waiver of rights form misrepresented his Miranda rights. The Federal District Court denied his claim, finding that there was no departure in police routine from a regular presentation of Miranda warnings. However, the U.S. Court of Appeals reversed, finding that inclusion of the "if and when you go to court" statement was misleading and did not conform to *Miranda*. The court held that the only acceptable reading of Miranda rights must contain defined and equivocal warnings that before speaking to police, suspects had the right to be represented and advised by lawyer. The "if and when" statement was confusing and may have led the respondent to believe that only people who had money to hire a lawyer may count on legal counsel during questioning while those who could not afford an attorney must wait for a judge to appoint an attorney "if and when" there is a trial. Accordingly, the appellate court remanded the case to the lower court to determine if the first "defective language" presented by police misled the respondent and, consequently, contributed to a coerced, self-incriminating admission of guilt. On *certiorari,* the case was subsequently presented and accepted by the U.S. Supreme Court.

In presenting the argument before the Supreme Court, the attorney for the respondent claimed Eagan's admission of guilt after a second interrogation was inadmissible because the first set of warnings regarding waiving his rights (given prior to his first, voluntary police interview) did not meet the criteria set forth by the Supreme Court in *Miranda v. Arizona* (1966). The attorney for the respondent argued that the language in the first set of warnings did not make clear that Eagan had the right to appointed counsel during questioning but, rather, led him to believe that the stipulation that the court would appoint an attorney "if and when you go to court" meant that he did not have right to counsel until that time. Eagan did not clearly understand he had a constitutional right to counsel (as established in *Miranda v. Arizona*); therefore, his first warnings were undefined, obscure, and constitutionally invalid according to a similar case, *California v. Prysock* (1981), because appointment of counsel was "linked to the future point in time." The respondent's attorney contended that he had not "knowingly and intelligently waived his rights to an attorney." Moreover, although the second presentation of rights warnings correctly conveyed his rights under the Miranda rule, the second warning did not specifically address or correct the misleading rights warning prior to his first interview with police. Thus, because Eagan still operated under the mistaken belief that no attorney would be available during questioning,

any admission of guilt was, therefore, inherently coercive and the collection of probative evidence gained from such a confession was inadmissible in court.

In a strongly worded dissenting opinion, Justice Marshall expressed his dismay that the majority ruling represented what he felt was a "continuing debasement of this historic [*Miranda*] precedent" that the Warren Court had set in 1966. The first part of the minority opinion (supported by all four minority justices) reasoned that Eagan's admission of guilt was given under duress since, when he was first advised of his rights during his first interview with the police, he did not understand questioning could be delayed pending appointment of an attorney "if and when" he went to court. In fact, there existed a great likelihood that most suspects would be confused as to when they might be taken to court and very "likely conclude that no lawyer would be provided until trial." Marshall explained that for the average person, "going to court" is synonymous with "going to trial" and thus, the implication is that no attorney will be provided unless a person goes to trial. Under such circumstances, dissenting justices felt that because a suspect might be inclined to believe police could defer interrogation for an indefinite period, there also existed a chance a suspect would talk without benefit of attorney believing that to be the only course of action available. Further, the minority opinion believed alleviating the potential for confusion was a matter easily remedied—simply delete the "if and when" stipulation.

The U.S. Supreme Court majority ruled that warnings given to the respondent before his first, voluntary interview with police satisfied the requirements set forth in *Miranda v. Arizona*. First, justices for the majority held that police officers satisfied and fulfilled their duty by referring all basic warnings under *Miranda*. Established "procedural safeguards" under *Miranda* were delivered appropriately and provided Eagan with complete information about his rights. Moreover, the majority held that Miranda rights were never intended as a precise formula which police must follow but, rather, as guidance whereby police could assure warnings would "reasonably convey to a suspect his rights." In the opinion of the majority, the Hammond police warning did inform the respondent he had a right "to stop answering at any time until he talked to a lawyer." After being acquainted with his rights, the respondent signed a form that clearly specified what his rights were. The respondent made a free decision to answer questions without an attorney present.

Authoring a separate, supporting opinion, Justice O'Connor (joined by Scalia) further viewed the respondent's claim as invalid for yet another reason. In *Stone v. Powell*, O'Connor pointed out the Court ruled that if alleged police conduct violated the Fourth Amendment (unreasonable search and seizure) and invoked review of the exclusionary rule by the state courts, there would be no federal *habeas corpus* review. The Court had reasoned that since the purpose of the exclusionary rule was to mitigate police behavior before trial, there was no benefit derived from federal review of such cases if the issue was raised and given "full and fair claim to litigate" by the state courts. Scalia and O'Connor felt this was appropriate because the *Stone* decision held that the purpose of the exclusionary rule was to "encourage" law enforcement into embracing "Fourth Amendment ideals into their value system." Similarly, these two justices reasoned that the purpose of Miranda warnings was to ensure that suspects would not be subjected to self-incrimination "by government coercion . . . in the criminal process." As with the *Stone* decision, the intent of *Miranda* was to promote appropriate behavior by police before trial. Thus, in voluntary confessions (O'Connor called these "nonconstitutional" cases), if Miranda warnings were deficient and resulted in self-incrimination, a "suppression remedy" ruling should not be appropriate for redress under writs of federal *habeas corpus* so long as the issue was adequately litigated by state courts.

In direct response to O'Connor's comments, Marshall (and Brennan) appended the dissenting opinion. They believed the *Stone* decision was wrong in the first place because no part of the *habeas corpus* statute stated "that certain federal claims are more unworthy of collateral protection (i.e. federal review) than others." Moreover, Congress recognized an individual's rights outweighed any need by the judiciary to effect comity between federal and state courts if an individual felt he was "in custody pursuant to the judgment of a State Court . . . in violation of the Constitution."

Marshall categorically addressed O'Connor's reliance on *Stone* to suggest that federal *habeas corpus* not be extended to Miranda rights claims when already litigated by state courts. Marshall pointed out "the explicit premise of *Miranda*" was that no confession is freely given "unless a suspect taken into custody is properly advised of his rights." Moreover, state prosecutors could not introduce statements made in violation of Miranda rights—to do otherwise violated the Constitution. Thus (citing Brennan's written, dissenting opinion in *Stone*), even if challenged at state level, Marshall observed that alleged federal violations do not "suddenly vanish after the appellate process has been exhausted." Furthermore, extending *Stone* was inappropriate, because there would be no way to determine before a court ruled which cases would be found involuntary and which would be found "nonconstitutional" (a confession ruled as voluntary despite *Miranda* violations). Finally, Marshall reasoned *Stone* was misdirected in its evaluation of the purpose of *habeas corpus*. Just as a "suppression remedy" would be (appropriately) triggered under a federal writ of *habeas corpus* if statements were found in violation of *Miranda*, *Stone* should have

recognized that the issue of granting federal *habeas corpus* writs had nothing to do with deterrence but rather was a means of ensuring use of evidence to gain a criminal conviction that was obtained independently and through no coercion.

Impact

On the surface, the issue under consideration appeared to center about whether police had to use specific language from the *Miranda v. Arizona* decision (1966) when advising suspects of their rights. The case at hand seemed to involve fairly routine consideration as to whether Indiana police appropriately advised the respondent of his Miranda rights in a clear manner. What transpired, however, was that four justices of the Court erupted into open conflict regarding the appropriateness of granting federal review to writs of *habeas corpus* for Miranda rights cases. Dissension, on the surface, centered about whether Miranda rights were properly served when the respondent was told he would be appointed an attorney "if and when" he went to court. But the most bickering centered around whether a previously decided case, *Stone v. Powell,* rendered what O'Connor characterized as "nonconstitutional" Miranda rights cases inappropriate for consideration beyond state-court level. (Scalia joined O'Connor who wrote a separate opinion siding with the majority while Brennan joined Marshall in the most contentious part of the minority opinion.) Marshall, not only challenged the wisdom of characterizing any cases involving personal rights as nonconstitutional, but he vehemently argued that *Stone v. Powell* was decided incorrectly in the first place. Disagreement among these four justices was contained, however, by Chief Justice Rehnquist's written decision. The majority opinion would contain discussion regarding *Stone v. Powell* by declaring the issue nonjurisdictional. Because none of the litigants had raised the issue of *Stone v. Powell* on *certiorari*, the Supreme Court was not bound to render any decision regarding extending that decision to contain constitutional Miranda rights appeals at state level. Thus, by not rendering a decision regarding *Stone,* the Court "chose" to reemphasize the importance of preserving federal litigation on federal *habeas corpus* of all Miranda rights cases.

Related Cases

Miranda v. Arizona, 384 U.S. 436 (1966).
Stone v. Powell, 428 U.S. 465 (1976).
California v. Prysock, 453 U.S. 355 (1981).

Bibliography and Further Reading

Biskupic, Joan, and Elder Witt, eds. *Congressional Quarterly's Guide to the U.S. Supreme Court,* 3rd ed. Washington, DC: Congressional Quarterly, Inc., 1996.

Hall, Kermit L., ed. *The Oxford Companion to the Supreme Court of the United States.* New York: Oxford Press, 1992.

MINNESOTA V. OLSON

Legal Citation: 495 U.S. 91 (1990)

Petitioner
State of Minnesota

Respondent
Robert Darren Olson

Petitioner's Claim
It was not unreasonable under the Fourth Amendment for police officers to enter a home without a warrant to arrest a murder suspect if the suspect does not have a sufficient connection with the home.

Chief Lawyer for Petitioner
Anne E. Peek

Chief Lawyer for Respondent
Glenn P. Bruder

Justices for the Court
William J. Brennan, Jr., Anthony M. Kennedy, Thurgood Marshall, Sandra Day O'Connor, Antonin Scalia, John Paul Stevens, Byron R. White (writing for the Court)

Justices Dissenting
Harry A. Blackmun, William H. Rehnquist

Place
Washington, D.C.

Date of Decision
18 April 1990

Decision
It was unconstitutional under the Fourth Amendment for police to enter, without a warrant, a house where a murder suspect was hiding; even though it was not the home of the suspect, the suspect had an expectation of privacy that is recognized and permitted by society.

Significance
The *Olson* case was remarkable because it flatly refused to grant expanded rights to police, a rare occurrence in the Rehnquist Court.

In the early morning of Saturday, 18 July 1986, a lone gunman robbed a gas station in south Minneapolis, killing the station manager in the process. An officer who heard the report over the police radio suspected one Joseph Ecker as the perpetrator, and the officer and his partner drove to Ecker's home. The police officers arrived at Ecker's home just as Ecker was returning home with another person in an Oldsmobile car. Ecker and his friend fled from police; Ecker was captured, but the other person in the Oldsmobile escaped.

Police found money and the murder weapon inside the Oldsmobile. Based on this evidence, the police determined that they had caught the shooter in the killing, and they set about finding the second party involved in the crime. On the title to the car, the name Rob Olson had been crossed out as the secured party. The police tracked down the lead and confirmed that Rob Olson lived at 3151 Johnson Street in the northeast part of the city.

In the morning following the robbery and killing, police received a call from a Dianna Murphy, who stated that a man by the name of Rob had driven the car that was involved in the holdup, and that Rob was planning to leave town by bus. Murphy called a short time later and told police that Rob had admitted to two other women, Louanne Bergstrom and Bergstrom's daughter Julie, that he had driven the car for the robbery. Police visited the Bergstrom's duplex on Fillmore Street in the northeast neighborhood but no one was home in Bergstrom's upper level unit. However, Helen Niederhoffer was at home in the lower level unit, and police spoke to her. Niederhoffer, Bergstrom's mother, confirmed to police that a man named Rob Olson was in fact staying upstairs but was not home. Minneapolis police issued a probable cause arrest bulletin calling for Olson's arrest at 2:00 p.m that day and Niederhoffer promised to call the police when Olson returned home. That call came at approximately 2:45 p.m. The detective in charge of the case ordered police to surround the house on Fillmore Street. The detective then placed a phone call to the Bergstrom home and informed Julie that the house was surrounded and that Olson should come out and surrender. The detective heard a male voice in the background say "tell them

I left," and Julie told the detective that Olson was not home. Minutes later, Minneapolis police stormed the upper unit on Fillmore Street and found Olson hiding in a closet. Olson was taken to jail, where he made inculpatory statements within an hour after his arrest.

Olson was charged with various crimes for his part in the armed robbery and killing. Prior to trial, Olson asked the court to exclude from trial the statements he made after he was arrested. According to Olson, the police did not have a right to storm into the house without a warrant, even if he was suspected of participating in a murder. The trial court disagreed and denied Olson's request. Olson was convicted of first-degree murder, three counts of armed robbery, and three counts of second-degree assault.

On appeal, the Minnesota Supreme Court reversed the convictions and remanded the case for a new trial. The state's highest court held that Olson had a right to challenge the legality of the warrantless arrest in the Bergstrom home because he had a sufficient interest in maintaining his privacy in the home, and that the arrest was illegal because no exigent circumstances existed to justify the failure to obtain a warrant. The state of Minnesota asked the U.S. Supreme Court to review the case, and the Court granted the request.

In a 7-2 decision, the Court held that the warrantless arrest of Olson in Bergstrom's home was illegal, and that the Minnesota Supreme Court was correct in ordering the exclusion of Olson's inculpatory statements. Justice White began the analysis of the case by citing *Payton v. New York* (1980), where the Court held that a suspect should not be arrested in his house without an arrest warrant, even if police have probable cause to make the arrest. The only exceptions to this rule are cases in which exigent circumstances exist. Exigent circumstances, as recognized by the Supreme Court, consist of cases where the police are in hot pursuit of a fleeing suspect, incidents in which the police must prevent the destruction of evidence, and emergency situations in which the police need to take immediate action to prevent injury to persons. In Olson's case, the Minnesota Supreme Court had ruled that there were no exigent circumstances: police already had the suspected shooter detained and the murder weapon in their custody, there was no indication that Olson was ready to harm someone inside the house, and the police were not in hot pursuit. The U.S. Supreme Court was "not inclined to disagree with this fact-specific application of the proper legal standard." Quoting the Minnesota court, the Court noted that three or four Minneapolis police squads had the house surrounded, and that "'[i]t was evident the suspect was going nowhere. If he came out of the house he would have been promptly apprehended.'" Under these facts, the failure of police to obtain a warrant from a magistrate before entering the Bergstrom apartment was unreasonable and therefore illegal under the Fourth Amendment.

The state of Minnesota argued that police had a right to enter and arrest Olson because he did not have sufficient connections to the house to claim the protection from warrantless arrests that persons in homes receive under the Fourth Amendment. The state listed a number of characteristics that, in its opinion, made a dwelling a home, and Olson fit none of them. Olson did not, for example, own the house, pay rent at the house, stay at the house for a long time prior to the arrest, or receive mail at the house.

The Court rejected the state's argument, ruling that none of the factors listed by the state deprived Olson of a rightful expectation of privacy. According to the High Court, Olson's case was on point with *Jones v. United States* (1960), a case in which the Court held that a man who used a friend's apartment for one night had the right to claim Fourth Amendment protection within the apartment. The man in *Jones* had a key to the apartment while its owner was away, his usual home was elsewhere, and he had not paid for the apartment. The *Jones* Court stated that under the circumstances the defendant was legitimately on the premises and that he therefore could challenge the warrantless intrusion of police into the apartment. In a later case, *Rakas v. Illinois* (1978), the Court rejected the "legitimately on the premises" standard as too broad, but it reaffirmed the "unremarkable proposition" stated in *Jones* that a person can have an interest in maintaining protection from governmental intrusion in a place other than his or her own home.

The Court dismissed as insignificant the factual differences between the *Jones* case and Olson's case. To the Court, it was of no importance that Olson's host was not away from the apartment or that he did not have a key. "Staying overnight in another's home," the Court explained, "is a longstanding social custom that serves functions recognized as valuable by society" because it provides the guest "with privacy, a place where he and his possessions will not be disturbed by anyone but his host and those his host allows inside." Nor was the power to permit and exclude others a deciding factor in determining whether Olson had the right to claim Fourth Amendment protection from warrantless arrest in Bergstrom's apartment. "If the untrammeled power to admit and exclude were essential to Fourth Amendment protection," the Court instructed, "an adult daughter temporarily living in the home of her parents would have no legitimate expectation of privacy because her right to admit or exclude would be subject to her parents' veto." Ultimately, the Court affirmed the judgment of the Minnesota Supreme Court.

Justices Stevens and Kennedy concurred and wrote short opinions. Stevens questioned whether the Court should have accepted the case in the first place. In Stevens' opinion, the power of the Court to review decisions of state courts to protect constitutional rights of their citizens "should be used sparingly. Only in the most unusual case," Stevens maintained, "should the Court volunteer its opinion that a state court has imposed standards upon its own law enforcement officials that are too high." In his concurring opinion, Justice Kennedy stated that he understood the majority opinion as merely deferring to a state court's application of the exigent circumstances test, "and not as an endorsement of that particular application of the standard." Justices Rehnquist and Blackmun both dissented, but neither wrote an opinion.

Impact

The *Olson* decision was a stunning affirmation of privacy rights by a Court that usually sided with law enforcement rights. The case was decided on the same day as an identical case in which the Court reached a contrary conclusion. In *New York v. Harris* (1990) police officers made a warrantless arrest of a man in a home and the man made inculpatory statements shortly after the arrest. According to a majority of the Court in *Harris,* the arrest was not unreasonable and the statements were admissible at trial. In the *Olson* opinion, the majority distinguished the *Harris* case by noting that the state of Minnesota had insisted that the statements made by Olson were fruits of the arrest. In the *Harris*

case, the state of New York argued that the statements made by the defendant were not the result of the warrantless arrest. This is an expression of the "fruit of the poisonous tree" doctrine, a rule that prohibits the use of evidence that is obtained as a result of an illegal search and seizure. Thus, when police officers, without a warrant, enter the home of a person whom they have probable cause to believe has committed a crime, statements later made by that person can in fact be used in court: the only difference between the *Olson* case and the *Harris* case was the failure of Minnesota's lawyers to claim that the statements made by Olson were not actually fruits of the warrantless arrest.

Related Cases

Jones v. United States, 326 U.S. 257 (1960).
Rakas v. Illinois, 439 U.S. 128 (1978).
Payton v. New York, 445 U.S. 573 (1980).
New York v. Harris, 495 U.S. 14 (1990).

Bibliography and Further Reading

Biskupic, Joan, and Elder Witt, eds. *Congressional Quarterly's Guide to the U.S. Supreme Court,* 3rd ed. Washington, DC: Congressional Quarterly, Inc., 1996.

Steiker, Carol S. "Counter-Revolution in Constitutional Criminal Procedure? Two Audiences, Two Answers." *Michigan Law Review,* August 1996, p. 2466.

PENNSYLVANIA V. MUNIZ

Legal Citation: 496 U.S. 582 (1990)

Petitioner
State of Pennsylvania

Respondent
Inocencio Muniz

Petitioner's Claim
That videotaped evidence should not be suppressed although Miranda warnings were not given.

Chief Lawyer for Petitioner
J. Michael Eakin

Chief Lawyer for Respondent
Richard F. Maffett, Jr.

Justices for the Court
Harry A. Blackmun, William J. Brennan, Jr. (writing for the Court), Anthony M. Kennedy, Sandra Day O'Connor, William H. Rehnquist, Antonin Scalia, John Paul Stevens, Byron R. White

Justices Dissenting
Thurgood Marshall

Place
Washington, D.C.

Date of Decision
18 June 1990

Decision
The Fifth Amendment privilege against self-incrimination relates only to evidence of a testimonial or communicative nature, not physical evidence.

Significance
This decision established the routine booking exception which exempts from the Miranda rule questions designed to gather biographical data from a suspect in order to complete booking.

On 30 November 1986, a patrol officer stopped Inocencio Muniz, who was driving down a Pennsylvania highway. The officer asked Muniz to perform three sobriety tests, which Muniz performed poorly. The officer arrested Muniz and took him to a booking center. At the center the booking procedures were videotaped, as they routinely were. Although the officer told Muniz that his actions and voice were being recorded, Muniz was not read his Miranda rights. Officer Hosterman asked Muniz his name, address, height, weight, eye color, date of birth, and age. Muniz stumbled over his address and age. The officer next asked Muniz the date of his sixth birthday, to which Muniz replied that he did not know. The officer then again administered the sobriety tests that Muniz had performed earlier on the highway. Muniz had difficulty with these tests and attempted to explain his problems. Next, Officer Deyo asked Muniz to take a breathalyzer test, which measures the alcohol content of a person's breath. The officer read Muniz the Commonwealth's Implied Consent Law. Muniz asked questions regarding the law and made comments about his drunkenness. He finally refused to take the test. At this point, the officer read Muniz his Miranda rights. Miranda rights inform a suspect that he has the right to remain silent and that anything said can be used in court as evidence. Muniz signed a statement waiving his rights and admitted that he had been driving drunk.

The video and audio parts of the videotape were used as evidence at Muniz's bench trial, as was the arresting officer's testimony that Muniz failed the roadside sobriety tests and made incriminating remarks. Muniz was convicted of drunk driving. He then filed a motion for a new trial, stating that the court should have excluded the testimony and the videotape because they were completed before Muniz had been read his Miranda rights. The trial court denied the motion, stating that physical tests did not violate his right not to incriminate himself because the evidence from the tests was physical, not testimonial. Therefore, no Miranda warnings were required.

The Superior Court of Pennsylvania reversed this ruling. The court held that when a physical test "begins to yield testimonial and communicative statements . . .

the protections afforded by *Miranda* are invoked. The court stated that Muniz's videotaped confusion and slurred speech indicated his drunkenness. The court noted that Muniz's answer to the question regarding the date of his sixth birthday and the statements he made while performing the physical tests revealed his thought processes. The court believed that none of Muniz's statements were voluntary but were compelled by the questions being asked. Because Muniz made the statements before he received his Miranda warnings, the court felt they should have been excluded as evidence. The court concluded that the audio part of the tape should have been entirely suppressed (not used in court) and reversed Muniz's conviction. The Pennsylvania Supreme Court denied the state's application for review.

Exception from Miranda's Coverage

Justice Brennan, writing for the majority noted that the Self-Incrimination Clause of the Fifth Amendment states that no one shall be compelled to be a witness against himself. This does not mean that a suspect may not be compelled to produce physical evidence. It refers to a suspect providing evidence of a testimonial or communicative nature, meaning that it relays a factual assertion or discloses information.

Brennan noted that in the case *Miranda v. Arizona* (1966) the Court held that the privilege against self-incrimination protects people not only from testifying against themselves in a criminal courtroom, but also from informal compulsion exerted by law-enforcement officers during in-custody questioning. Before any questioning, a person must be given the Miranda warnings. Because Muniz was not read his Miranda rights until after the videotaped proceedings, any verbal statements that were both testimonial and elicited during interrogations should have been suppressed. The Commonwealth of Pennsylvania argued that because Muniz's statement about his sixth birthday was not testimonial and the answers to the prior questions were not elicited by custodial interrogation his Fifth Amendment rights were not violated. The Supreme Court agreed that slurred speech is not a testimonial. The answer to the sixth birthday question was incriminating because it could be inferred from it that Muniz's mental state was confused. The Commonwealth argued that this incriminating inference does not invoke the Fifth Amendment because the inference concerns the physiological functioning of Muniz's brain.

The Court noted that the correct question to ask here was whether the incriminating inference was drawn from a testimonial act or from physical evidence. To be testimonial a communication must explicitly or implicitly relate a factual assertion or disclose information. The Fifth Amendment is invoked to spare the accused from having to reveal his knowledge relating him to the offense. The privilege of the Fifth Amendment

reflects the Court's unwillingness to subject suspects to the cruel "trilemma" of self-accusation, perjury, or contempt. If a suspect is asked a question forcing him to confront the "trilemma" of truth, falsity, or silence, the suspect's response contains a testimonial component. The sixth birthday question asked of Muniz required a testimonial response because the inherently coercive environment precluded the option of remaining silent. Muniz could therefore only incriminate himself by admitting that he did not know the date or answer untruthfully by guessing. His answer, that he did not know, allowed an incriminating inference that his mental faculties were impaired. Thus the answer to this question, since it was testimonial, should have been suppressed.

The Commonwealth argued that the questions asked regarding name, address, etc. were not custodial interrogation. The Court noted that any words or actions on the part of the police that the police should know are reasonably likely to elicit an incriminating response from the suspect are subject to the Miranda warning. The perceptions of the suspect, rather than the intent of the police, is the focus here. Custodial interrogation includes express questioning and words or actions that, given the officer's knowledge of any special susceptibilities of the suspect, the officer knows are likely to have the force of a question and are likely to elicit an incriminating response. Thus Officer Hosterman's first seven questions were custodial interrogation. However, the answers to these questions are still admissible in court because the questions fall within a routine booking question exception which exempts from *Miranda*'s coverage questions about biographical data needed to complete the booking process. As a result, the answers to these questions did not need to be suppressed.

The Court noted that Muniz's incriminating statements during the videotaping were voluntary and not elicited in response to custodial interrogation. Brennan summed up by stating that *Miranda* requires suppression of Muniz's response to the question regarding the date of his sixth birthday, but not the entire audio portion of the videotape. The lower court's judgment reversing the conviction was vacated and the case was remanded for further proceedings.

Chief Justice Rehnquist concurred in part and dissented in part. His dissent noted that the sixth birthday question does not subject the suspect to the "trilemma." The officer asked the question to check how well Muniz could do a simple math problem. If the police may require Muniz to use his body in order to demonstrate the level of his physical coordination, there is no reason why they should not be able to require him to speak or write in order to determine his mental coordination. . . . Muniz's responses to the videotaped booking questions were not testimonial and do not warrant application of the privilege."

Exceptions Undermine Miranda

Justice Marshall also concurred in part and dissented in part. Marshall concurred with the majority that the sixth birthday question required a testimonial response and should have been suppressed. Marshall disagreed with the others regarding a "routine booking question" exception to *Miranda*. "Such exceptions undermine *Miranda's* fundamental principle that the doctrine should be clear so that it can be easily applied by both police and courts." The police should be required to preface all direct questioning of a suspect with Miranda warnings if they want his responses to be admissible in court. The police should have known that the seven booking questions were reasonably likely to elicit incriminating answers from a drunken suspect. Thus a Miranda warning should have been given.

Marshall felt that the "booking questions" sought testimonial responses because the answers would show Muniz's state of mind. The questions required him to either answer correctly, indicating lucidity, answer incorrectly, implying that his faculties were impaired, or say he did not know, also implying impairment. Because the police did not inform him of his Miranda rights before asking these questions, Marshall thought his answers should have been suppressed.

Impact

Prior to the *Muniz* decision, a routine booking question exception to *Miranda* had gained widespread accep-tance among lower courts. The justification for the exception was that an arrestee is not subjected to the coercive atmosphere of custodial interrogation that *Miranda* was intended to prevent. The *Muniz* decision stated that routine booking questions, not testimonial in nature, regarding the arrestee's name, address, height, weight, eye color, date of birth, and current age, which are aimed at securing "biographical data neces-sary to complete booking or pretrial services," and which are asked in that context are exempt from the requirements of *Miranda,* unless they are "designed to elicit incriminating admissions." This case confirmed that requiring a person in custody to stand or walk in a police lineup, to speak prescribed words, to model particular clothing, or to give samples of handwriting, fingerprints, or blood does not compel him to incrim-inate himself within the rights of the Fifth Amendment privilege against self-incrimination.

Related Cases

Holt v. United States, 218 U.S. 245 (1910).
Miranda v. Arizona, 384 U.S. 436 (1966).
Schmerber v. California, 384 U.S. 757 (1966).
Rhode Island v. Innis, 446 U.S. 291 (1980).
Doe v. United States, 487 U.S. 201 (1988).

Bibliography and Further Reading

Biskupic, Joan, and Elder Witt, eds. *Congressional Quar-terly's Guide to the U.S. Supreme Court,* 3rd ed. Wash-ington, DC: Congressional Quarterly, Inc., 1996.

ILLINOIS V. RODRIGUEZ

Legal Citation: 497 U.S. 177 (1990)

Petitioner
State of Illinois

Respondent
Edward Rodriguez

Petitioner's Claim
It was a violation of the Fourth Amendment when police officers used the consent of a third party to enter his apartment and arrest him without a search warrant or arrest warrant.

Chief Lawyer for Petitioner
Joseph Claps

Chief Lawyer for Respondent
James W. Reilley

Justices for the Court
Harry A. Blackmun, Anthony M. Kennedy, Sandra Day O'Connor, William H. Rehnquist, Antonin Scalia (writing for the Court), Byron R. White

Justices Dissenting
William J. Brennan, Jr., Thurgood Marshall, John Paul Stevens

Place
Washington, D.C.

Date of Decision
21 June 1990

Decision
A warrantless entry by police officers into a person's home is not invalid under the Fourth Amendment if the police officers reasonably—but mistakenly—believe that a third party has the authority to give consent for the entry.

Significance
The *Rodriguez* case was important because it seemed to flatten Fourth Amendment analysis of search and seizure cases into one question: whether the actions of the police officers were reasonable.

On 26 July 1985, Chicago police were summoned to Dorothy Jackson's residence on South Wolcott. There the officers met Gail Fischer, who appeared to have suffered a recent beating. Fischer said that she had been assaulted by Edward Rodriguez earlier that day in an apartment located on South California. Fischer indicated several times that she shared the apartment with Rodriguez, so the officers asked Fischer if she would come with them to the apartment and use her key to open the door. Fischer consented, and the police drove her to the apartment on South California.

At the apartment, Fischer unlocked the door with her key and the officers entered. At no time prior to their entry had the police paused to obtain a search warrant from a magistrate to enter the home. Instead, the police relied on their belief that Fischer lived at the apartment and that she had the authority to consent to their entry. Inside the apartment, the police officers found Rodriguez asleep amid containers of cocaine and related paraphernalia.

Rodriguez was arrested and charged in state court with possession of a controlled substance with intent to deliver. Before trial, Rodriguez asked the court to exclude the cocaine evidence, arguing that the warrantless entry into his apartment was unconstitutional under the Fourth Amendment's prohibition of unreasonable searches and seizures. According to Rodriguez, Fischer had moved out of the apartment several weeks prior to the incident and she did not have authority to give consent for the entry. The trial court agreed with Rodriguez, finding that Fischer was not a "'usual resident'" but "an 'infrequent visitor,'" and it rejected the state's contention that it was reasonable for the officers to believe that Fischer had authority to give consent for the entry and that therefore the Fourth Amendment was not violated. The trial court decided to exclude the cocaine evidence against Rodriguez, effectively thwarting the prosecution, and the state appealed that decision. The Appellate Court of Illinois affirmed the ruling, and the Illinois Supreme Court rejected the state's appeal.

The U.S. Supreme Court, however, took the case and reversed. In 6-3 decision, the High Court ruled that Rodriguez's Fourth Amendment rights were not violated by the warrantless entry because the police officers reasonably believed that Fischer was a resident of the apartment. In an opinion written by Justice Scalia, the Court agreed with the appeals court that the police officers did not, in fact, have the right to enter Rodriguez's apartment based on Fischer's consent because Fischer was not a resident of the apartment and she did not have the authority to give consent.

Rodriguez had argued that permitting officers to enter a dwelling based only on their reasonable belief in the authority of a third party would create a vicarious waiver of his Fourth Amendment rights. The Court had, in the past, held that a person could not vicariously waive his or her Sixth Amendment right to an attorney, and Rodriguez had maintained that Fourth Amendment rights deserved the same protection. There were, however, differences between Fourth and Sixth Amendment rights. Quoting *Schneckloth v. Bustamonte* (1973), the Court noted that there was "a vast difference" between the waiver of trial rights and the waiver of Fourth Amendment rights, and that nothing in the purpose or application of such protection of trial rights "suggest[ed] that it ought to be extended to the constitutional guarantee against unreasonable searches and seizures."

In arguing for the exclusion of the cocaine evidence, Rodriguez had relied on the "exclusionary rule." This was the rule that forbids the introduction of evidence that is obtained in violation of a person's Fourth Amendment rights. The Fourth Amendment itself, though, did not guarantee "that no government search of his house will occur unless he consents." Instead, the Court declared, all that the Fourth Amendment guaranteed was "that no search will occur that is 'unreasonable.'" The determination of what was "reasonable," the Court posited, depended on various elements.

The Court concluded that nothing in the construction of the word "reasonable" required that the government "be not only responsible but correct" in its assessments. Indeed, it had not defined reasonable government behavior on such terms in the past, and it was not inclined to use this standard for the warrantless entry of dwellings. All that the Fourth Amendment required was that law enforcement officers act reasonably in applying their judgment. The Court acknowledged that a warrant was an "ordinary requirement" for entry to a dwelling under the Fourth Amendment. However, the warrant requirement was "sometimes supplanted by other elements that render[ed] the unconsented search 'reasonable.'"

In making its decision, the Court had to fend off *Stoner v. California* (1964). In *Stoner,* the Court held that police officers, relying on the consent of a hotel clerk, did not have the right to enter the defendant's hotel room without a warrant. Justice Scalia carefully parsed various statements made by the *Stoner* Court and con-

cluded that the meaning of the case was unclear and ambiguous. Like most other search and seizure cases, this one had to be decided by looking at the conduct of the police officers: specifically, by asking whether "the facts available to the officer at the moment" would cause a person "of reasonable caution" to believe that Fischer had authority over Rodriguez's premises. (quoting *Terry v. Ohio* [1968]) In the Court's opinion, the officers' belief was reasonable, and the warrantless entry into Rodriguez's home did not violate his Fourth Amendment rights. The reversal of the appeals court's decision meant that the cocaine evidence would not be excluded from Rodriguez's trial, and the state of Illinois could continue in its prosecution of Rodriguez.

Justices Brennan and Stevens joined a dissenting opinion written by Justice Marshall. According to the dissent, the Court had misconstrued the rationale behind allowing third-party consent searches. Such searches were constitutional not because they were considered "'reasonable' under the Fourth Amendment." Rather, insisted the dissent, the constitutionality of such searches rested on the "premise that a person may voluntarily limit his expectation of privacy by allowing [an]other to exercise authority over his possessions." If a person does not so limit his or her expectation of privacy, "the police may not dispense with the safeguards established by the Fourth Amendment."

The dissent reminded that Court that it had "tolerated departures from the warrant requirement only when an exigency makes a warrantless search imperative to the safety of the police and of the community." The need for the police to search and seize without a warrant, the dissent insisted, had to be balanced against the targeted person's Fourth Amendment right to privacy. There was, in fact, no exigency in Rodriguez's case, and the police officers had plenty of time to obtain a warrant for the purpose of entering Rodriguez's apartment and arresting him. The dissent was not persuaded by the majority's use of prior cases to support its position. The holding and reasoning in the *Stoner* case, for example, were quite clear, but the majority had "manufacture[d] the ambiguity." The Court's opinion, wrote Marshall, interpreted prior case law in a "glib" and "superfluous" way, creating a "free-floating" rule on warrantless entries into the home that erased "some of the liberty that the Fourth Amendment was designed to protect."

Impact

The *Rodriguez* decision made it possible for police to enter a person's home without a warrant, even if they are relying on the consent of a person who does not have authority to give consent for the entry. The decision has been criticized by many legal analysts for diluting Fourth Amendment protections against invasion by police

Related Cases

Stoner v. California, 376 U.S. 483 (1964).
Terry v. Ohio, 392 U.S. 1 (1968).
Schneckloth v. Bustamonte, 412 U.S. 218 (1973).

Bibliography and Further Reading

Israel, Jerold H., Yale Kamisar, and Wayne R. LaFave. "Consent Searches." *Criminal Procedure and the Constitution: Leading Supreme Court Cases and Introductory Text.* St. Paul, MN: West Publishing, 1992

Wieber, Michael C. "The Theory and Practice of *Illinois v. Rodriguez:* Why An Officer's Reasonable Belief About a Third Party's Authority To Consent Does Not Protect A Criminal Suspect's Rights." *Journal of Criminal Law and Criminology,* fall 1993, p. 604.

ARIZONA V. EVANS

Legal Citation: 514 U.S. 1 (1995)

Petitioner
State of Arizona

Respondent
Isaac Evans

Petitioner's Claim
That a computer error in law-enforcement files did not result in an unlawful search, and that contraband obtained in that search may be admitted in court.

Chief Lawyer for Petitioner
Gerald Grant

Chief Lawyer for Respondent
Carol Carrigan

Justices for the Court
Stephen Breyer, Anthony M. Kennedy, Sandra Day O'Connor, William H. Rehnquist (writing for the Court), Antonin Scalia, David H. Souter, Clarence Thomas

Justices Dissenting
Ruth Bader Ginsburg, John Paul Stevens

Place
Washington, D.C.

Date of Decision
1 March 1995

Decision
The Court ruled in favor of the state of Arizona's appeal to admit evidence obtained in a search that was underway as a result of computer error.

Significance
By the time *Arizona v. Evans* reached the U.S. Supreme Court in 1994, a succession of lower courts had reversed one another's decisions as to whether marijuana found in a search could be admitted as evidence against the suspect. The respondent, however, had been first placed under arrest because of an error by a court clerk. The Court had to consider whether an error in a law-enforcement database be valid reason for declaring an arrest erroneous, and for suppressing evidence obtained against a citizen as a result of that arrest. It was a new twist in search-and-seizure law, and found the High Court deciding for the first time whether the exclusionary rule could be applied in the event of computer error.

Tempting Arrest

Isaac Evans drove the wrong way down a one-way Phoenix street in front of a police station in January of 1991. He was stopped by a Phoenix police officer, who asked for Evans's driver's license. Evans told the officer that it had been suspended, and the officer verified this on the computer terminal in his patrol car. That database also showed an outstanding warrant for Evans's arrest on a misdemeanor charge. The warrant was originally issued when he failed to appear in court the previous month to answer to a number of traffic tickets. Evans did eventually appear before the justice court on 19 December 1990, and a note was made in his file to "quash warrant." At that point, the clerk of the justice court should have notified the Arizona Sheriff's Office that the warrant was to be removed from the computer database; this is usually done with a phone call to the records clerk at the sheriff's office. The call was not made, and for this reason the warrant for Evans's arrest was still present in the database that the officer checked.

The officer arrested Evans; despite any protestations from a citizen that the matter of the court date had been rectified, such a cursory arrest would constitute proper police procedure. When the officer handcuffed Evans, however, he dropped a hand rolled marijuana cigarette. A search of Evans's car turned up a bag of marijuana under the seat. Evans was charged with possession, and shortly afterward the Phoenix police were informed by the justice court that the warrant should have been quashed.

Evans's lawyer requested a hearing to suppress the evidence. The trial court found for Evans, on the basis of his claim that the drugs found were the result of an unlawful search, and thus could be excluded as evidence under the "exclusionary rule." An Arizona court of appeals reversed this decision, but then when the case appeared before the Arizona Supreme Court, it was once again reversed in Evans's favor. The state of Arizona appealed to the U.S. Supreme Court, and the case was argued in December of 1994.

The Exclusionary Rule

Evans's case hinged on the Fourth Amendment, which states that:

The right of the people to be secure in their persons, houses, papers, and effects, against unreasonable searches and seizures, shall not be violated, and no warrants shall issue, but upon probable cause, supported by oath or affirmation, and particularly describing the place to be searched, and the persons or things to be seized.

The exclusionary rule holds that evidence obtained as the result of an illegal search cannot be admitted in court. At the trial level, a formal arrest warrant obtained from a magistrate can be invalidated if it can be shown that the police lacked probable cause in obtaining it. Any evidence obtained in that search is not allowable in court for use in prosecuting the respondent. The use of the exclusionary rule in state courts, especially in regard to criminal cases, dates back to the U.S. Supreme Court's decision in *Mapp v. Ohio* (1961).

The Arizona Court of Appeals reversed the first court's decision in *Evans* and moved to allow the marijuana into the case against Evans. It did so after deciding that the exclusionary rule did not apply in this situation, since "the purpose of the exclusionary rule was to deter police officers," and "was not intended to deter justice court employees" or other support staff.

But the Arizona Supreme Court reversed that decision. Its justices spoke of a clear distinction between police officers and office support staff. The state court decided in Evans's favor, declaring that the application of the exclusionary rule in this case would make clerks and other support personnel more diligent about record-keeping.

Reagan-Era Reversal

There is, however, the "good faith" exception to the exclusionary rule, the legality of which was affirmed in a 1984 U.S. Supreme Court decision, the *United States v. Leon*. It allowed for evidence to be admitted in the prosecutor's case against the respondent if it is shown that the law enforcement personnel were acting on good faith—in other words, that they had reasonable cause. With this line of reasoning, the state of Arizona argued, the evidence found against Evans should indeed be admitted into the case against him. Its attorneys asserted that the exclusionary rule applies only when the police officer knows that an arrest violates the search-and-seizure tenets of the Constitution. The state also pointed out to the Supreme Court justices that such computer errors were rare, and occurred once every few years.

Evans and his lawyers claimed the "good faith" exception did not apply, that only simple police error was behind his arrest and the subsequent discovery of contraband. Their case in this regard was strong: courts in other states (California, New York, and Maryland) had declared evidence obtained for criminal trials as

the result of computer error inadmissible under the exclusionary rule. In a related case, *United States v. Mackey* (1975) the respondent's name was in the Federal Bureau of Investigation's National Crime Information Center database, but should not have been. It was not cleared from the records, and Mackey was arrested in Nevada on an outstanding California warrant. Law enforcement authorities found a firearm, for which Mackey did not have a permit.

The Ninth Circuit Court ruled in Mackey's favor, noting that he had been deprived of his liberty without due process of law. There were similar cases in subsequent years. "Each state addressing the issue held that a computer error was a correctable mistake by the police, and that the state should not profit from its own mistakes thereby depriving a respondent of his liberty," explained C. Maureen Stinger in the *Richmond Journal of Law & Technology*. Furthermore, a 1985 FBI study found that computerized criminal databases may have up to 12,000 invalid or inaccurate reports transmitted on a daily basis.

The Decision

The U.S. Supreme Court reversed the Arizona Court of Appeals decision, ruling in favor of the state of Arizona and allowing the evidence to be admitted into the case against Evans. Chief Justice Rehnquist wrote the Court's opinion. It noted that the exclusionary rule had been designed to curb police misconduct, and found no police misconduct in this situation. Secondly, the Court's decision took into account that office clerks are not willfully trying to violate the Fourth Amendment rights of citizens when clerical errors are made. This was taken into consideration in contrast with the potential for abuse of power in an arrest situation. Lastly, the Court noted that to allow the exclusionary rule in this case on the basis of computer error would not deter future errors by office personnel.

"The evidence in this case strongly suggests that it was a court employee's departure from established record-keeping procedures that caused the record of the respondent's arrest warrant to remain in the computer system after the warrant had been quashed," wrote Justice O'Connor in a concurring opinion. Furthermore, she concluded:

Prudently, then, the Court limits itself to the question whether a court employee's departure from such established procedures is the kind of error to which the exclusionary rule should apply. The Court holds that it is not such an error, and I agree . . . The Court's holding reaffirms that the exclusionary rule imposes significant costs on society's law enforcement interests and thus should apply only when its deterrence purposes are most efficaciously served.

The Contract with America

In 1994 Republicans gained a majority in the House of Representatives for the first time in four decades. Early in 1995, the new Republican majority issued their "Contract with America," a legislative "agenda for national renewal." Most significant of the planned bills were two constitutional amendments requiring a balanced budget and term limits for legislators, which they were unable to enact. Also significant were a bill capping punitive damage awards, which President Clinton vetoed, and a welfare reform bill, which was passed by Congress and signed by the president. Legislation permitting a "line-item veto," which would enable the president to strike specific parts from appropriations bills, passed and was signed into law but was later declared unconstitutional by the Supreme Court.

Source(s): http://www.gopac.org
Congressional Quarterly Digest. Washington, DC: CQ Press, 1997.

Justices Stevens and Ginsburg dissented. Stevens wrote in his dissent that such an arrest due to computer error violated the dignity of a citizen as much as an arrest made without probable cause; Ginsburg noted that computer technology is still developing and that the Court should be wary of making hasty decisions in such matters.

A Growing Movement to Rescind the Exclusionary Rule

The Fourth Amendment's protection against unreasonable search and seizure is seen by many historians as perhaps the most important item in the Bill of Rights. They theorize that the abuse of power by agents of the British crown in this area was probably the impetus for the American Revolution itself.

The exclusionary rule was a relatively recent development in constitutional law, and the law-enforcement and prosecuting arms of the criminal justice system have found much fault with it. It has been claimed that criminals often go free when their lawyers successfully argue to suppress evidence against them by claiming police misconduct. As Nat Hentoff pointed out in a 1996 *Village Voice* column, even New York City Mayor Rudolph Giuliani has called the exclusionary rule "a terrible mistake." However, studies had found that less than 1 to 2.35 percent of cases are dismissed as a result of it.

The issue did make for good political maneuvering, since most Americans have a fear of the roaming criminal, and it became part of Republican Speaker of the House Newt Gingrich's "Contract with America" legislative package. The bill HR 666 contained the "Exclusionary Rule Reform Act of 1995," sponsored by Florida Republican Bill McCollum. It was designed to tighten what conservatives saw as a "loophole" by expanding the good-faith exception. The bill stated that law-enforcement personnel with "an objectively reasonable belief" that they are abiding by the terms of the Fourth Amendment can search without a warrant. This would technically allow police to simply enter any ordinary citizen's house and argue later that they had probable cause.

HR 666 passed in the House, and was still held up in the Senate Judiciary Committee three years later. Critics of the bill noted that such sweeping police powers were characteristic of fascist or otherwise authoritarian governments, where police or the military had wide range to infringe upon the rights of citizens to be secure in their own homes. "This is the heart of the [Fourth] Amendment—forcing police to convince a neutral magistrate that the totality of the circumstances indicates that evidence of a crime exists," wrote Robert Bauman in the *National Review.*

Related Cases
Mapp v. Ohio, 367 U.S. 643 (1961).
United States v. Mackey, 387 F.Supp. 1121 (1975).
United States v. Leon, 468 U.S. 897 (1984).

Bibliography and Further Reading
Bauman, Robert E. "Congress and the Exclusionary Rule." *National Review,* May 15, 1995, pp. 58-59.

Hentoff, Nat. "Fruits of the Poisonous Tree." *Village Voice,* March 12, 1996, p. 10.

Jackson, Heather A. "Expanding Exclusionary Rule Exceptions and Contracting Fourth Amendment Protection." *Journal of Criminal Law and Criminology,* summer 1996, p. 1201.

LaFave, Wayne R. "Computers, Urinals, and the Fourth Amendment: Confessions of a Patron Saint." *Michigan Law Review,* August 1996, p. 2553.

Richardson, L. Anita. "Exceptions to the Rule; Computer Error Sparks Latest Challenge to Evidentiary Exclusion." *ABA Journal,* December 1994, p. 48.

Stinger. C. Maureen. "*Arizona v. Evans*: Adapting the Exclusionary Rule to Advancing Computer Technology." *Richmond Journal of Law & Technology,* Vol. 2, no. 1, 1996.

DAMAGES

Damages are a civil judicial remedy used to monetarily compensate a party for injuries caused by the wrongful conduct of another, resulting in loss, injury, or other detriment to one's person, property, or rights. Damages are awarded to a plaintiff for losses caused either by a defendant's conduct or to provide a remedy for the breach of a contractual relationship. Damages are sometimes also used to punish outrageous conduct and deter future misconduct. Damages are only one category of remedies; other remedies include *restitution* (restoring something to its rightful owner); *injunctive relief* (forbidding a party to do an act); *mandamus* (requiring a party to do an act); and *declaratory relief* (a judicial decision setting forth the legal rights of respective parties even when no further relief is ordered).

Damages are traditionally awarded in American dollars and are generally made in a single lump-sum payment. The one-time payment is meant to compensate for both past harms as well as those anticipated in the future. Although making only one payment simplifies administration, the amount of the judgement may prove insufficient in six months or ten years. Not only must the award accurately reflect compensation for future harm, it must also include calculations for future inflation and make reductions to present value for payments made now.

Damages are categorized depending upon their purpose. The most commonly employed categories are *compensatory, nominal, liquidated,* and *punitive.* Compensatory damages are intended to compensate a party for injury sustained or make good or replace a loss caused by a wrong. Their purpose is to put the plaintiff in the same situation she would have been in had the harm not occurred. Compensatory damages are not intended to enrich a plaintiff. Nominal damages are damages in name only, a trifling sum awarded to recognize an infringement of rights without resulting substantial loss or injury. Punitive damages are a penalty used where a defendant's conduct has been particularly egregious, vindictive, or malicious; they are not compensation for injury. Liquidated damages are those specified in a contract in the event of a breach.

Compensatory Damages: General Damages

Compensatory damages, also called actual damages, are typically broken down into two categories: general and special. General damages arise naturally and logically from a defendant's conduct or breach of contract. They are the immediate, direct, and proximate result of an injury or breach of contract. General damages are not used to hold a defendant liable for remote consequences flowing from an act or omission. Moreover, they cannot be based upon mere speculation or conjecture, but must be established with reasonable certainty. They do not have to be pleaded specially, merely proven at trial. A plaintiff's medical expenses caused by defendant's negligent operation of a motor vehicle is an example of general damages.

In cases involving tortious conduct, foreseeability of harm is generally not a limitation on recovery for general damages. For example, suppose the plaintiff in the above example suffers from some rare condition that significantly worsens his condition and hampers his recovery. The *tortfeasor* "takes the victim as he finds him," and is responsible for the extraordinary medical costs. In breach of contract cases, the injured party is entitled to the amount of compensation that will leave her as well off as if the contract had been fully performed.

Compensatory damages that are capable of being estimated in and compensated by money are called pecuniary damages. In assessing general damages in a breach of contract action, a plaintiff might use market reports, expert testimony, comparable sales, or other methods to establish the economic value that has been lost, i.e., the "loss of expectancy" or "loss of bargain." An award for doctor and hospital expenses for an plaintiff in a personal injury case is also a pecuniary award.

Consequential Damages

Consequential damages (also known as special damages) are another form of compensatory damages. Special damages do not flow directly and immediately from the defendant's act, but from some of the consequences of the act. They must be causally related to the injury and provable with a reasonable degree of certainty. For example, suppose a plaintiff suffered two broken legs as a result of a defendant's negligence. The plaintiff's medical expenses would constitute the general damages. If the plaintiff was a truck driver who was thereafter unable to work for several months, consequential damages would compensate him for his lost income.

As with general damages, the goal of consequential damages is to make the plaintiff whole, and no more. In a tort action, a defendant is liable for all damages, foreseen or unforeseen, which naturally flowed from the misconduct. In contrast, in a breach of contract case generally the damages must have been foreseeable at the time the contract was made.

Nonpecuniary Damages for Pain and Suffering and Other Emotional Trauma

Compensatory damages may be imposed for a person's pain and suffering. These are called *nonpecuniary damages* because they are difficult to quantify, but they are nevertheless viewed as legitimate compensation for a legally recognized harm. The trier of fact (the jury or the judge in a non-jury case) employs general experience and a knowledge of the economic and social affairs of life to determine an appropriate award. A plaintiff generally is not limited to recovery for present pain and suffering. Where a plaintiff establishes a reasonable likelihood of experiencing future pain, he may be awarded prospective damages as well. A jury is given significant latitude in determining damages for pain and suffering, and an award will only be overturned in cases where the jury has abused its discretion.

Historically, physical injury had to accompany mental suffering, but now most jurisdictions allow recovery even without physical injury if a defendant's conduct was malicious or willful. Mental pain and suffering, including fright, anxiety, grief, emotional trauma, and other forms of mental suffering may be compensable. It is particularly challenging to measure the injury caused by a defendant's intentional infliction of emotional distress, to determine the economic harm caused by a vicious and unlawful slander, or to determine an appropriate amount to compensate someone for a loss of memory or other mental impairment resulting from wrongful conduct.

The judicial system permits recovery of nonpecuniary damages because recovery of such damages funds attorney fees in contingency cases, where a plaintiff might otherwise be unable to afford to bring suit. Moreover, it is a way for society to express a sense of public sympathy for a grievously injured person. Finally, it is one way for the legal system to set standards of behavior.

Punitive Damages

Punitive damages are a non-compensatory type of damages used to penalize or deter behavior. They are used to punish a defendant who has acted in a willful, wanton, malicious, abusive or other outrageous manner. Punitive damages are also known as exemplary damages because they make an example of the defendant in order to deter others. Punitive damages are never mandatory and are only awarded in addition to an award for compensatory damages. Punitive damages are rarely permitted in breach of contract cases.

Determining an award of punitive damages involves a careful examination of the defendant's conduct and state of mind at the time of the misconduct. Unlike compensatory damages, evidence of a defendant's worth may be presented when determining a punitive damages award. Sometimes, statutes authorize double or treble damages as a punitive measure. For example, vehicle dealers who alter an automobile's odometer reading must pay treble damages. Other areas where a damages multiplier is used include antitrust, trademark, patent, and consumer protection statutes.

The constitutionality of punitive damages has been challenged in recent years on grounds that it violates the Eighth Amendment prohibition against excessive fines or the Fourteenth Amendment's Due Process clause. However, relief from punitive damages via a constitutional challenge has thus far proven to be an elusive avenue of relief. In one case, the Supreme Court upheld a punitive damages award that was more than 500 times the compensatory award.

When a judge determines that a damages verdict is excessive or inadequate, the judge may reconsider the award without ordering a new trial or the necessity of an appeal. If a judge determines that an award is inadequate, she may order additur, whereby the defendant is ordered to pay a greater sum. Remittitur is a reduction of a jury verdict deemed excessive by the trial judge.

Nominal Damages

Where a plaintiff has suffered an injury caused by defendant's wrongful conduct, but where the plaintiff is unable to establish proof of a compensable loss, nominal damages may be awarded. This is typically a very small sum such as a dollar, and is meant to be symbolic. Nominal damages are usually awarded only after a plaintiff tries but fails to prove compensatory damages in a case where a real injury occurred, or where there has been a technical invasion of rights or a breach of duty but no substantial loss or injury.

Liquidated Damages

Liquidated damages are sometimes written into a contract by the parties as a method for assessing damages in the event of a breach. The parties stipulate to the amount, or a formula to determine the amount in situations where precise damages would be difficult to ascertain. Liquidated damages provisions are permitted only where prospective damages are uncertain or very difficult to establish; if the parties simply made no attempt to determine the amount of possible damages, a liquidated damages provision may be unenforceable. In addition, a liquidated damages provision will be stricken as void if a court determines that it is in fact penal in nature.

Rules Regarding Avoidable Consequences and Collateral Sources

The plaintiff generally has a duty to minimize special damages, i.e., she cannot recover for damages that could have been avoided by reasonable acts or expenditures. For example, a plaintiff who has been wrongfully discharged from employment by the defendant employer has a duty to seek similar employment after the discharge, rather than to sit idly by and allow damages to accumulate. The plaintiff may have a duty to accept similar employment, thereby mitigating her damages. Likewise, a person who suffers personal injury generally has a duty to seek reasonable medical care.

The collateral source rule means that a defendant shall not be enriched because the plaintiff has received benefits from a source other than the defendant as compensation for injury or breach. For example, a plaintiff injured because of defendant's negligence is entitled to recover from the defendant the full cost of medical services, even if the bills were paid by the plaintiff's relatives or provided free of charge.

Tort Damages Reform and Caps on Damages

Many jurisdictions enacted statutory damages caps on personal injury cases during a tort reform movement in the 1980s. In general, three different types of statutes have been enacted. One type allows full recovery of pecuniary damages, but limits recovery of nonpecuniary losses such as loss of consortium, pain and suffering, or mental distress. Other statutes limit actual pecuniary damages. These statutes typically apply only to specific categories of defendants, such as health care providers, governmental entities, or alcohol providers. Finally, some jurisdictions impose dual caps, that is, some combination of the first and second types of statutes.

Some damages caps have been successfully challenged on constitutional grounds as being a denial of due process and equal protection, particularly where damages were capped in favor of an interest group, such as health care providers, and where the statute provided for no substitute manner of compensation.

Bibliography and Further Reading

Dobbs, Dan B. *Dobbs Law of Remedies*. 2nd ed. St. Paul, MN: West Publishing Co. 1993.

O'Connell, John F. *Remedies in a Nutshell*. St. Paul, MN: West Publishing Co. 1985.

West's Encyclopedia of American Law (various sections). St. Paul, MN: West Publishing Co. 1997.

SWIFT V. TYSON

Legal Citation: 41 U.S. 1 (1842)

Petitioner
John Swift

Respondent
George W. Tyson

Petitioner's Claim
In a federal case based on diversity jurisdiction, the common law of the locus state should govern the tender of a negotiable instrument, not common law developed by a federal court.

Chief Lawyer for Petitioner
Fessenden

Chief Lawyer for Respondent
Dana

Justices for the Court
Henry Baldwin, John Catron, Peter Vivian Daniel, John McKinley, John McLean, Joseph Story (writing for the Court), Roger Brooke Taney, Smith Thompson, James Moore Wayne

Justices Dissenting
None

Place
Washington, D.C.

Date of Decision
January 1842

Decision
In a federal case based on diversity jurisdiction, a federal court has the power to make its own decisions, in the absence of a controlling state statute.

Significance
The decision allowed federal courts hearing civil cases based on diversity jurisdiction to create their own body of common law. Diversity jurisdiction is a special way for a federal court to gain jurisdiction over a case. Generally, federal courts hear only matters of federal concern. However, they can preside over a case that concerns state law if the parties to the case live in different states and the controversy involves a dollar figure that exceeds a minimum threshold amount.

The Need For a Uniform System of Commerce

In the mid-1800s, the United States was still a young country in the process of developing and expanding. One of the major economic problems the United States was encountering was the lack of a uniform system of commercial laws, including the laws on negotiable instruments—any document in which one party promises to pay either money or goods to another party. When a negotiable instrument is issued in a commercial situation, it is called "commercial paper." In the 1830s, the laws on commercial paper varied from state to state, so that commercial paper valid in one state might be worthless in a different state.

On 1 May 1836, George W. Tyson bought land in Portland, Maine, from Jairus S. Keith and Nathaniel Norton. Tyson drew up a bill of exchange worth $1,540.30 and gave it to Norton. Norton later assigned the bill of exchange to John Swift to satisfy a debt that he owed to Swift. When Swift tried to redeem the bill of exchange, Tyson refused to pay, claiming that he had been defrauded by Keith and Norton, who did not own the property they had sold to him. Swift sued Tyson in a federal court in New York.

The common law (law of the courts rather than statutory law created through legislation) of the day prohibited the assignment of a bill of exchange, that is to say an order for a third party to pay a debt between two others. Statutory law is the primary authority in any case because a democratic system requires that laws be made by elected officials. However, not all disputes are covered by statutes, and statutes often must be amplified and construed: in such cases, the opinions of courts create laws that fill in the blanks left by statutes. At the time of the *Swift* case, a federal court sitting in diversity jurisdiction was, under judicial interpretation of Section 34 of the Judiciary Act of 1789, obliged to follow the statutory and common laws of the state in which it was sitting.

At trial, Swift argued that Tyson was liable for the bill of exchange, and that such a bill should be considered assignable. Tyson countered that, under New York common law, the assignment of the bill of exchange by Norton was invalid. The federal court,

Tyson argued further, was obliged under Section 34 of the Judiciary Act of 1789 to follow the laws of New York and invalidate the assignment.

At the time, New York City was fast developing into the country's financial hub. Although Swift did not have the law of New York on his side, he did enjoy the support of business leaders concerned with growing the nation's economy. If New York insisted on retaining its strict laws prohibiting the assignment of negotiable instruments, the argument went, interstate transactions would cease and the national economy would suffer. The federal judges in New York were divided on the issue, and they certified the matter to the U.S. Supreme Court, which unanimously sided with Swift.

Prior to the *Swift* decision, under the Judiciary Act, federal courts were to use the law of the state when they were sitting on a case involving state law. At the heart of the *Swift* case was the definition of the word "laws." Tyson argued that "laws" included common law made by a state's courts. Swift countered that "laws" was only meant to describe statutory laws. Since the New York law forbidding the assignment of a bill of exchange was a law made by the New York courts, Swift maintained, the federal court was not obliged to enforce it. The High Court agreed. Common laws "are, at most, only evidence of what laws are, and are not, of themselves, laws," declared Justice Story, writing for the majority.

Having decided that the federal courts may create their own federal common law in the absence of a controlling state statute, the Court proceeded to hold for Swift in the case. Specifically, the Court held that federal common law allowed the assignment of commercial papers. The Court observed that England followed a similar course on negotiable instruments, noted the benefits to both commercial debtors and commercial creditors, and found no reason to take a different approach. Justice Story wrote,

> It is for the benefit and convenience of the commercial world, to give as wide an extent as practicable to the credit and circulation of negotiable paper, that it may pass not only as security for new purchases and advances, made upon the transfer thereof, but also in payment of, and as security for, preexisting debts.

Impact

The *Swift* case made it possible for federal courts to attempt to create a uniform set of laws for commercial papers. The decision made it safe for persons engaged in interstate commerce to assign commercial paper, and the national economy grew. However, the decision had drastic, unintended consequences on the U.S. court system. The notion that a federal common law on commercial paper existed was illusory, as federal judges sitting on such cases merely decided cases based on their own particular views. Moreover, the decision encouraged "forum shopping," which is a search for the most favorable court to hear a case. For example, in *Black & White Taxicab & Transfer Co. v. Brown & Yellow Taxicab Transfer Co.* (1928), a taxi company wanted to contract with a bus company to provide exclusive service for the bus company's terminal. Realizing that such a contract was illegal under Kentucky law but not illegal under the law created by the area's federal courts, the company moved to Tennessee for the sole purpose of gaining diversity jurisdiction and ensuring that the case went to federal court. Such maneuvers allowed businesses to circumvent state laws. In 1938, after enduring years of criticism, the *Swift* decision was reversed and laid to rest by the High Court in *Erie R. Co. v. Tompkins.* The *Swift* decision's highest purpose—encouraging the formation of a uniform set of laws governing commercial transactions—was realized one-half century later by the National Conference of Commissioners on Uniform States Laws (NCCUSL). The first set of uniform rules crafted by the NCCUSL and intended for adoption by all the states was the Uniform Negotiable Instruments Act, published in 1896.

Related Cases

Black & White Taxicab & Transfer Co. v. Brown & Yellow Taxicab & Transfer Co., 276 U.S. 518 (1928).
Erie R. Co. v. Tompkins, 304 U.S. 64 (1938).

Bibliography and Further Reading

Johnson, John W., ed. *Historic U.S. Court Cases, 1690–1990: An Encyclopedia.* New York: Garland Publishing, 1992.

Rehnquist, William H., *The Supreme Court: How It Was, How It Is.* New York: Morrow, 1987.

West's Encyclopedia of American Law. St. Paul, MN: West Group, 1998.

PALSGRAF V. LONG ISLAND RAILROAD COMPANY

Legal Citation: 248 N.Y. 339 (1928)

Appellant
Long Island Railroad Company

Appellee
Helen Palsgraf

Appellant's Claim
That Ms. Palsgraf failed to establish that her injuries resulted from the defendant's negligence, and that her case should have been dismissed by the State Circuit Court in Kings County, New York.

Chief Lawyer for Appellant
William McNamara

Chief Lawyer for Appellee
Matthew W. Wood

Justices for the Court
Benjamin N. Cardozo, Henry T. Kellogg, Irving Lehman, Cuthbert W. Pound

Justices Dissenting
William S. Andrews, Frederick E. Crane, Denis O'Brien

Place
New York, New York

Date of Decision
29 May 1928

Decision
That Ms. Palsgraf's injuries were not the result of negligence on the part of the Long Island Railroad Company or its employees.

Significance
Legal action for negligence can only arise if the plaintiff's own right is violated, not if the plaintiff incurred injury due to a wrong against someone else.

This case arose from a bizarre accident. As Helen Palsgraf was waiting to buy a ticket to Rockaway, New Jersey on a platform operated by the Long Island Railroad Company, another train stopped at the station, and two men raced to catch it as it began to pull away. The first man reached the train without incident but the second, who was carrying what appeared to be a bundle of newspapers, stumbled as he boarded the train. A conductor on the train reached out to pull the passenger on board, while a second railway employee pushed the passenger from behind. During this awkward boarding the passenger dropped his parcel, which in fact contained fireworks. The package exploded upon hitting the rails and the shock created by the explosion caused a heavy scale to topple over and injure Ms. Palsgraf.

Ms. Palsgraf successfully sued the Long Island Railroad Company for compensation for her injuries in the Kings County, New York State Circuit Court. The Long Island Railroad Company appealed this decision to the Appellate Division of the State Supreme Court, Second Department, which upheld the lower court's ruling. The company appealed once more to the New York Court of Appeals, which agreed to hear the case.

Attorneys for the Long Island Railroad Company argued that no negligence had been proven, and that Ms. Palsgraf's claim should have been dismissed by the lower courts. Palsgraf's lawyers countered that negligence had been proven and the earlier decisions justified.

On 29 May 1928 the New York Court of Appeals found in favor of the Long Island Railroad Company by a margin of 4-3, ruling that "the basis of an action for negligence must be a violation of the plaintiff's own right, and not merely a wrong against someone else." Therefore, although the company's employees were negligent in making the passenger drop his parcel, their negligence affected only him, and not Ms. Palsgraf, who was standing at least 20 to 30 feet away from the spot where the package fell. An ambiguity in the decision makes this case particularly interesting while also reducing its legal impact. The wording of the decision strongly implies that had the railroad employees known that the parcel contained explosives, they would have been negligent with regard to Ms. Palsgraf's safety, and the railroad would have been liable to compensate her for her injuries. Thus, liability is not involved in a case where an injury results from consequences of negligence that could not have been reasonably foreseen. The decision also implied that had the man carrying the explosive parcel been the one injured, he would have been entitled to compensation for his injuries. Dissenting Justices Andrews, Crane, and O'Brien were particularly troubled by the latitude for interpretation in individual cases allowed for by this decision.

Ms. Palsgraf entered a final petition for a rehearing of the case, claiming that she might have been standing closer to the explosion than she had previously indicated, but her motion was denied on 9 October 1928. This case served to clarify the legal definition of actionable negligence by stating that such negligence must be directed against the plaintiff personally.

Related Cases

Derdiarian v. Felix Contracting Corp., 51 N.Y.2d 308 (1980).

Goodwin v. James, 595 A.2d 504 (1991).

Broin v. Philip Morris, Inc., 641 So.2d 888 (1997).

Bibliography and Further Reading

Johnson, John W., ed. *Historic U.S. Court Cases, 1690–1990: An Encyclopedia.* New York: Garland Publishing, 1992.

WIENER V. UNITED STATES

Legal Citation: 357 U.S. 349 (1958)

Petitioner
Myron Wiener

Respondent
United States

Petitioner's Claim
That the court of claims erred by dismissing his suit for back salary, in the wake of his improper dismissal by the president.

Chief Lawyer for Petitioner
T. H. Wachtel

Chief Lawyer for Respondent
J. Lee Rankin, U.S. Solicitor General

Justices for the Court
Hugo Lafayette Black, William J. Brennan, Jr., Harold Burton, Tom C. Clark, William O. Douglas, Felix Frankfurter (writing for the Court), John Marshall Harlan II, Earl Warren, Charles Evans Whittaker

Justices Dissenting
None

Place
Washington, D.C.

Date of Decision
30 June 1958

Decision
Wiener was improperly dismissed by the president.

Significance
The decision held that a president does not have the power to arbitrarily remove a "quasi-judicial" commissioner from office.

A "Quasi-Judicial" Body

In 1948, Congress passed the War Claims Act to provide a means of settling limited claims by internees, prisoners of war, religious organizations, and others who suffered personal injury or property damage at the hands of the enemy during World War II. To adjudicate these claims, a three-member commission, including two attorneys, was to be appointed by the president and confirmed by the U.S. Senate for the task. The appointees were to serve until the commission had finished its work. Myron Wiener was among those chosen for the commission by President Harry S. Truman. Wiener took office shortly after being confirmed by the Senate on 2 June 1950.

When Dwight D. Eisenhower succeeded Truman as president in 1953, he intended to replace the commission with one of his own choosing. When Eisenhower asked for the resignation of the existing commissioners, however, Myron Wiener refused, stating that he had been appointed for the life of the commission. President Eisenhower persisted, dismissing Wiener on 10 December 1953. The War Claims Commission itself lasted for less than six more months, disbanding on 1 July 1954. Ironically, none of President Eisenhower's appointees took office before the commission was dissolved.

Feeling that he had been improperly removed from the commission, Wiener filed a suit with the court of claims, asking for back pay between the date of his dismissal and the day the commission was abolished. His petition was denied.

When Wiener pressed his case before the U.S. Supreme Court on 18 November 1957, his appeal hinged not on the nature of his dismissal itself, but rather on maintaining the independence of special commissions. Reviewing the Constitution and the terms of the War Claims Act, the Court could find nothing to support President Eisenhower's claim to have the power to arbitrarily remove members of "quasi-judicial" bodies. On 30 June 1958, the Court decided unanimously in Wiener's favor.

Shifting Precedents

Justice Frankfurter's written opinion cited the *Wiener* case's close similarity to the *Humphrey's Executor v. United*

Justice Felix Frankfurter

Justice Felix Frankfurter (1882-1965) was among the most highly regarded jurists ever to sit on the Supreme Court. As a professor at Harvard Law School from 1914 to 1939, he taught a number of notable figures in the next generation, including future Secretary of State Dean Rusk. He also pioneered the study of federal courts' jurisdiction. Even before his appointment by President Franklin D. Roosevelt to the nation's highest bench in 1939, he was known as a champion of liberal causes: one of the founding members of the American Civil Liberties Union (ACLU) in 1920, Frankfurter became a prominent national figure with his critique of the Sacco and Vanzetti trial in the 1920s.

Frankfurter strongly supported Roosevelt's New Deal programs in economics, jurisprudence, and other areas; therefore his appointment to the Supreme Court on the eve of World War II was no surprise. He served on the Court for the next 23 years, until 1962, a period that spanned from the latter years of Charles Evans Hughes's chief justiceship to the early days of the Earl Warren Court. During that time, he became known for his opposition to the view of Justices Hugo Black and William O. Douglas, that protection of free speech rights should be absolute.

Source(s): Hurwitz, Howard L. *An Encyclopedic Dictionary of American History.* New York: Washington Square Press, 1974.

States (1935) decision. Prior to 1935, the president enjoyed unrestricted power to remove any executive branch official at will. The constitutionality of this unlimited power was upheld by the Court in *Myers v. United States* (1926). In 1935, however, a later court reversed this position when President Franklin D. Roosevelt attempted to replace William Humphrey, a Federal Trade Commission member opposed to Roosevelt's "New Deal" economic policies. Just as Eisenhower would do later, Roosevelt cited the "national interest" as his main reason for wanting commissioners of his own choice. The Court ruled against Roosevelt on the ground that a commissioner could only be removed for "good cause."

Frankfurter pointed out that Congress had specified regulations for removing any Federal Trade Commission official. Reasons for expulsion from the FTC included inefficiency, neglect of duty, or malfeasance while in office. No such charges were leveled by President Roosevelt in his attempt to remove Humphrey from office. In the *Wiener* case, no such rules even existed.

Just because Congress had not defined any terms of dismissal for the war claims commissioners, however, did not mean that such power automatically fell to the president. The lack of a clause delegating removal power to the president, Frankfurter wrote, indicated that Congress wanted commissioners to be immune from presidential pressure. "Congress did not wish to have hang over the commission the Damocles sword of removal by the President for no reason other than that he preferred to have on that commission men of his own choosing."

Frankfurter recalled the distinction the 1935 Court had drawn between executive branch officials and "quasi-judicial" officers, who were not to be subject to any outside hindrances in the performance of their

duties. It was true that Wiener was appointed by a head of the executive branch; however, as soon as he took office and began to adjudicate legal matters, he was no longer subject to any executive control while fulfilling his commission.

J. Lee Rankin, U.S. Solicitor General, 1963. © AP/Wide World Photos.

Justice Felix Frankfurter, 1956. © Photograph by Harris and Ewing. Collection of the Supreme Court of the United States.

The Court reversed the court of claims dismissal of Wiener's suit, entitling him to his back pay and establishing that he had been improperly removed from office. While the case reflected the subtleties of the doctrine of the separation of powers between judicial and executive government bodies, it demonstrated a limit to absolute presidential control over the executive branch.

Related Cases

Myers v. United States, 272 U.S. 52 (1926).
Humphrey's Executor v. United States, 295 U.S. 602 (1935).

Bibliography and Further Reading

Baker, Russell. "Dismissal Ruling Curbs President." *New York Times,* July 1, 1958, p. 20.

Davis, Kenneth S. *F.D.R.—The New Deal Years 1933-1937.* New York: Random House, 1979.

Hall, Kermit, ed. *The Oxford Companion To The Supreme Court Of The United States.* New York: Oxford University Press, 1992.

MATHEWS V. ELDRIDGE

Legal Citation: 424 U.S. 319 (1976)

Petitioner
Forrest D. Mathews, U.S. Secretary of Health, Education, and Welfare

Respondent
George Eldridge

Petitioner's Claim
That an evidentiary hearing prior to the termination of Social Security disability benefits is not a requirement of due process.

Chief Lawyer for Petitioner
Robert H. Bork, U.S. Solicitor General

Chief Lawyer for Respondent
Donald E. Earles

Justices for the Court
Harry A. Blackmun, Warren E. Burger, Lewis F. Powell, Jr. (writing for the Court), William H. Rehnquist, Potter Stewart, Byron R. White,

Justices Dissenting
William J. Brennan, Jr., Thurgood Marshall (John Paul Stevens did not participate)

Place
Washington, D.C.

Date of Decision
24 February 1976

Decision
The lack of an evidentiary hearing prior to cutting off George Eldridge's disability benefits did not violate the Due Process Clause of the Fifth Amendment.

Significance
Mathews v. Eldridge established the basic test for deciding if a particular procedure satisfied the demands of due process. The Court also noted that due process was flexible.

George Eldridge began receiving Social Security disability benefits in June of 1968 because of chronic anxiety and back strain. He was later found to have diabetes. A few years later, Eldridge filled out a questionnaire from the state agency that monitored the benefits. The agency also obtained reports from Eldridge's doctor and an independent medical consultant. The agency wrote to Eldridge that it had tentatively decided that his disability had ceased in May 1972. In his reply letter, Eldridge noted that he had arthritis of the spine, not a strained back, and that he felt the agency had enough information to establish his disability. The agency reaffirmed its tentative decision. This decision was accepted by the Social Security Administration (SSA), which notified Eldridge in July that his benefits would end after that month and that he had a right to reconsideration by the state agency within six months. Eldridge did not request reconsideration, but instead brought his case to the district court, challenging the constitutionality of the termination of his benefits. He felt that not receiving an evidentiary hearing before his benefits were cut off violated his right to due process in accordance with the Fifth Amendment. Eldridge sought the reinstatement of his benefits pending a hearing.

The district court decided that the termination violated procedural due process. It held that prior to the termination of benefits, Eldridge was entitled to an evidentiary hearing. The court based this decision in part on *Goldberg v. Kelly* (1970). In that case, it was decided that a welfare recipient was entitled to a hearing prior to the termination of payments. The court of appeals agreed with the district court.

Due Process is Flexible

The secretary of health, education, and welfare contended that the district court should not have heard the case because district courts do not have jurisdiction over an action seeking the review of the secretary. District courts can only review a final decision of the secretary. The secretary based his claim on *Weinberger v. Salfi* (1975). In that case, the Supreme Court decided that judicial review in an action challenging the denial of claimed benefits was possible only after exhausting all of the administrative remedies, including a final decision by the secretary. When *Mathews v. Eldridge* was brought before the Supreme Court, however, it held that in the instant case, Eldridge satisfied the requirement that a claim must be presented to the secretary by filling out the questionnaire and writing a letter to the state agency. Although Eldridge did not exhaust the secretary's internal review procedures, the denial of his claim was enough of a "final decision" to satisfy the exhaustion requirement. Thus Eldridge had the right to present the case to the district court.

The Fifth Amendment states that no person shall "be deprived of life, liberty, or property without due process of law." The secretary contended that the existing administrative procedures provided all the process that is constitutionally due before someone can be deprived of benefits. Eldridge contended that the existing review procedures would be adequate if the disability benefits were terminated after the evidentiary hearing, not before it. Justice Powell, writing for the majority, quoted *Cafeteria Workers v. McElroy* (1961) "Due process, unlike some legal rules, is not a technical conception with a fixed content unrelated to time, place and circumstances." Powell also quoted *Morrissey v. Brewer* (1972), "Due process is flexible, and calls for such procedural protections as the particular situation demands." Powell listed the three factors that must be considered when looking into the specific dictates of due process: 1) the private interest that the official action will affect; 2) the risk of mistakenly depriving someone of benefits, and the probable value of additional procedural safeguards; 3) the Government's interest, including the financial and administrative costs that additional procedures would bring about.

Powell described the procedures in place for terminating Social Security disability benefits. The disability insurance program is jointly administered by state and federal agencies. State agencies determine if a person has a disability, when it began, and when it ceased. The worker must show, using medical tests, that he cannot work. The main reason for terminating someone's benefits is that the worker is no longer disabled or has returned to work. A team determines if a person continues to be eligible for benefits. The team consists of a doctor and a nonmedical person trained in disability evaluation. The agency asks the worker, through questionnaires, about his current condition, treatments, and restrictions. The agency also gets information from the worker's doctor. If the agency and the beneficiary disagree about his condition, the agency informs him that his benefits may be terminated, provides a summary of the evidence, and offers the opportunity to review the medical reports and other evidence in his file. He may also respond in writing and send in additional evidence. At that point, the state agency makes its final

decision, which is reviewed by an examiner from the SSA Bureau of Disability Insurance. The SSA then notifies the recipient of the decision and the reasons for it and tells him that he has the right to seek reconsideration from the state agency. The benefits end two months after the person's recovery has taken place. If the person seeks reconsideration from the state agency, and the determination goes against him, the SSA reviews the decision. The person then has a right to an evidentiary hearing in front of an SSA administrative law judge. After that, the claimant is entitled to request discretionary review by the SSA Appeals Council. Finally, he may obtain a judicial review.

Powell noted that despite the elaborate procedures provided, the district court and court of appeals considered them to be constitutionally inadequate. Those courts concluded that due process required an evidentiary hearing before the benefits were terminated. Powell disagreed with that conclusion, believing that a hearing after termination of benefits was sufficient. Powell reasoned that disability benefits were not based on financial need. "Indeed, it is wholly unrelated to the worker's income or support from many other sources."

The Court recognized that the length of time a person is wrongfully deprived of benefits is important in assessing the impact of the government's action on the person's interests. The secretary conceded that the delay between the cutoff of benefits and the final decision after a hearing is over one year. Powell noted that "the hardship imposed upon the erroneously terminated disability recipient may be significant. Still the disabled worker's need is likely to be less than that of a welfare recipient. In addition to the possibility of access to private resources, other forms of government assistance will become available" if the worker falls below the subsistence level. Something less than an evidentiary hearing is sufficient prior to terminating disability benefits.

Powell pointed out that a medical assessment is a more sharply focused and easily documented decision than one involving the termination of welfare benefits. It is based on routine, standard, and unbiased medical reports by specialists. The disability benefits entitlement assessment provides an effective means for the recipient to communicate to the decision-maker, mainly by way of the questionnaire. Also, before the termination of benefits, the person is given full access to the information relied on by the state agency.

Powell noted that the administrative burden must be weighed against requiring, as a constitutional right, an evidentiary hearing upon demand in all cases prior to the termination of disability benefits. "The ultimate additional cost in terms of money and administrative burden would not be insubstantial." He also noted that the judicial model of an evidentiary hearing is neither a required, nor even the most effective, method of decision making in every circumstance. The essence of due process is that a person facing a serious loss be given notice of the case and the opportunity to present his side of it. The procedures must be tailored to the capacities and circumstances of the person to make sure he or she has a meaningful opportunity to present his case. In determining what process is due in this case, substantial weight must be given to the good faith judgments of the people who work in the administration of social welfare programs. The prescribed procedures provide the claimant with an effective process for asserting his or her claim prior to any administrative action. The claimant is also assured a right to an evidentiary hearing and subsequent judicial review before the denial of his claim becomes final.

Powell summed up his opinion by stating that an evidentiary hearing is not required before disability benefits are ended. The current administrative procedures "fully comport with due process."

Hearing Should Come Before Termination of Benefits

Justices Brennan and Marshall dissented. Brennan felt that Eldridge must be given an evidentiary hearing of the type required for welfare recipients. He noted that since disability benefits are provided without a determination of need, a need is presumed. In this case, because disability benefits were terminated, the Eldridge home was foreclosed on and the family's furniture was repossessed, forcing everyone to sleep in one bed. "Finally, it is also no argument that a worker, who has been placed in the untenable position of having been denied disability benefits may still seek other forms of public assistance."

Impact

Mathews v. Eldridge was often quoted in later opinions regarding the definition of due process. Powell's three factors for resolving the issue involving the constitutional sufficiency of administrative procedures before the initial termination of benefits have been relied on in other cases of this sort.

Cases challenging the termination of benefits have tried to rely on *Mathews v. Eldridge*. They have cited this case when desiring judicial review. This case differed from many others in that it dealt with a constitutional issue. In *Califano v. Sanders* (1977) the Supreme Court noted that a decision denying judicial jurisdiction in *Eldridge* would effectively have closed the federal forum to the adjudication of reasonable constitutional claims. Thus *Eldridge* merely adhered to the well-established principle that when constitutional questions are in issue, the availability of judicial review is presumed.

Related Cases

Cafeteria Workers v. McElroy, 367 U.S. 886 (1961).
Goldberg v. Kelly, 397 U.S. 254 (1970).
Richardson v. Perales, 402 U.S. 389 (1971).
Morrissey v. Brewer, 408 U.S. 471 (1972).
Weinberger v. Salfi, 422 U.S. 749 (1975).
Califano v. Sanders, 430 U.S. 199 (1977).

Bibliography and Further Reading

Encyclopedia of the American Constitution, Vol 3. New York: Macmillan, 1986.

TRIMBLE V. GORDON

Legal Citation: 430 U.S. 762 (1977)

Appellants
Deta Mona Trimble, et al.

Appellees
Sherman Gordon, et al.

Appellants' Claim
That Chapter 12 of the Illinois State Probate Act, which allowed illegitimate children to inherit property only from their mother in the event of their parents' death without a will, violated the Equal Protection Clause of the Fourteenth Amendment.

Chief Lawyer for Appellants
James D. Weil

Chief Lawyer for Appellees
Miles N. Beermann

Justices for the Court
William J. Brennan, Jr., Thurgood Marshall, Lewis F. Powell, Jr. (writing for the Court), John Paul Stevens, Byron R. White

Justices Dissenting
Harry A. Blackmun, Warren E. Burger, Potter Stewart, William H. Rehnquist

Place
Washington, D.C.

Date of Decision
26 April 1977

Decision
Reversed the decision of the Illinois Supreme Court and ruled Chapter 12 of the Illinois State Probate Act unconstitutional.

Significance
The ruling marked a reversal of the Court's view of the right of illegitimate children to inherit, which had been set forth in *Labine v. Vincent* (1971). While *Trimble v. Gordon* seemed to guarantee equal protection for illegitimate children with regard to inheritance, this position was once again altered by the Court's judgement in *Lalli v. Lalli*, (1978).

A Small but Contentious Estate

Sherman Gordon, a resident of Chicago, Illinois, was a victim of homicide at the age of 28 without a will. The sole asset of his estate was an automobile valued at $2500. While alive, Gordon had led a complicated personal life. He fathered an illegitimate child, Deta Mona Trimble, with Jessie Trimble in 1970, and Gordon and Trimble lived together from the time of Deta Mona's birth until Gordon's death. Gordon was legally acknowledged as Deta Mona's father, having a paternity order entered against him by the Circuit Court of Cook County on 2 January 1973 which required him to pay Trimble $15 per week for support of the child.

Shortly after Gordon's death Jessie Trimble filed with the Probate Division of the Circuit Court to determine Deta Mona's status as one of Gordon's heirs. The Probate Court found that Gordon's only heirs were his father, mother, siblings, and half siblings. Deta Mona was excluded as an heir under the terms of Chapter 12 of the Illinois State Probate Act, which held that, in the case of parents' death intestate (without a will), "an illegitimate child is heir of his mother and of any maternal ancestor, and of any person from whom his mother might have inherited, if living." Chapter 12 also stipulated that "a child who was illegitimate whose parents intermarry and who is acknowledged by the father as the father's child is legitimate." This latter clause is the crux of the case, in that had Deta Mona been legitimate she would have been first among Gordon's heirs. However, her status as an illegitimate child, noted under the terms of Chapter 12, left her ineligible to inherit any part of Gordon's estate.

Trimble appealed the case to the Illinois Supreme Court, which heard arguments on the matter on 24 September 1975. The state supreme court had already sustained the constitutionality of Chapter 12 in *In re Estate of Karas* (1975), however, so its affirmation of the decision of the circuit court in *Trimble* came as no surprise on 15 October 1975. Following this reversal, Trimble appealed her case to the U.S. Supreme Court, which heard arguments on 7 December 1976.

Heirs and Inheritance Laws

If a person dies intestate—that is, without a will, which provides for the distribution of property after death—his or her heirs have few protections regarding their inheritance. According to most state laws, the government will distribute the property purely according to other people's legal relation to the deceased.

A deceased person who has left a will is called a testator. There are a number of legal safeguards to protect the testator's heirs not only from the state, but from harmful provisions in the will. An example of the latter is the abundance of state statutes which establish a limit to the amount that a testator can leave to charity.

If an heir has reason to believe that the testator was not competent at the time of making the will, or that the will is a forgery or an otherwise faulty document, or that the testator did not intend the document to be a legally binding will, he or she may challenge the will in a probate court. On the other hand, the testator may disinherit a child in the will. In some states, children born or adopted after the making of the will may receive an intestate portion according to *pretermitted heir* statutes.

Source(s): *West's Encyclopedia of American Law.* St. Paul, MN: West Group, 1998.

Discrimination Based on Legitimacy?

The Illinois Supreme Court, in sustaining the ruling of the circuit court, based its decision on its own ruling in *Karas,* which itself had been based on the U.S. Supreme Court's opinion in *Labine v. Vincent.* In *Labine,* the Court allowed to stand a state law preventing acknowledged illegitimate children from inheriting from their fathers if they died intestate. The Court reasoned that striking down the law would represent undue interference with state sovereignty, and that, in any case, a father wishing to bequeath property to his illegitimate offspring could either legitimize them or simply write them into his will. Thus the Court's decision rested in large measure on a reevaluation of its ruling in *Labine.* After applying renewed scrutiny to *Labine,* the Court reversed itself and, by a 5-4 margin found Chapter 12 unconstitutional on 26 April 1977.

Justice Powell, writing for the majority, pointed out that although states could legally "classify" the illegitimate to some degree, such classification must, "at a minimum, bear some rational relationship to a legitimate state purpose." The state of Illinois had maintained that its prohibitions against inheritance by illegitimate children, such as that contained in Chapter 12, served to discourage people from having children out of wedlock. The Supreme Court rejected this reasoning, since the punishment inflicted was directed at the children, who were innocent parties to their own illegitimacy. The Court also backed away from its own reasoning in *Labine,* in that it now believed that "the fact that appellant's father could have provided for her by making a will does not save Chapter 12 from invalidity under the Equal Protection Clause." Finally, the Court decided that Chapter 12 was overly broad, in that

it barred illegitimate children from inheriting from their fathers even if, in life, the fathers had acknowledged them (as was the case with Gordon).

Impact

Trimble v. Gordon represents a reversal of earlier Court positions with regard to the rights of inheritance of the illegitimate. The Court changed directions on this issue again, however, ruling in *Lalli v. Lalli,* that illegitimate children had no rights to inheritance from their fathers unless they were acknowledged by their fathers. The Court has also allowed other distinctions in the inheritance rights of legitimate and illegitimate children, ruling in *Mathews v. Lucas* (1976) that illegitimate children must prove dependency upon a deceased parent in order to inherit from that parent. In the final analysis, the Court appears to view Equal Protection Clause cases involving illegitimate children on a case-by-case basis, thus creating the impression of a willingness to change course on such issues with each successive decision.

Related Cases

Labine v. Vincent, 401 U.S. 532 (1971).
In re Estate of Karas, 61 Illinois 2d 40, 329 N.E. 2d 234 (1975).
Mathews v. Lucas, 427 U.S. 495 (1976).
Lalli v. Lalli, 439 U.S. 259 (1978).

Bibliography and Further Reading

Biskupic, Joan, and Elder Witt, eds. *Guide to the U.S. Supreme Court.* Washington, DC: Congressional Quarterly Inc., 1993.

SILKWOOD V. KERR-McGEE

Legal Citation: 667 F.2d 908 (1979)

Plaintiff
Estate of Karen Silkwood

Defendant
Kerr-McGee Nuclear Company

Plaintiff's Claim
Damages for negligence leading to the plutonium contamination of Karen Silkwood.

Chief Lawyers for Plaintiff
Gerald Spence, Arthur Angel, James Ikard

Chief Defense Lawyers
Elliott Fenton, John Griffin, Jr., Larry D. Ottoway, William Paul, L. E. Stringer, Bill J. Zimmerman

Judge
Frank G. Theis

Place
Oklahoma City, Oklahoma

Date of Decision
18 March 1979

Decision
Defendant was found negligent and was ordered to pay $505,000 actual damages, $10 million punitive damages.

Significance
This precedent-setting action between the estate of a dead woman and a giant industrial conglomerate sparked a public uproar about the issue of safety at nuclear facilities and held a company liable for negligence.

Karen Silkwood, a young lab technician and union activist at an Oklahoma plutonium plant, operated by the Kerr-McGee Nuclear Company, uncovered evidence in 1974 of managerial wrongdoing and negligence. On 13 November, three months after providing the Atomic Energy Commission (AEC) with a detailed list of violations, she was en route to deliver documents to a *New York Times* reporter when her car crashed under mysterious circumstances and she died. An autopsy revealed plutonium contamination, confirming the results of tests taken when she was alive. Speculation among her opponents at that time, was that she had deliberately contaminated herself to embarrass Kerr-McGee, an assertion that Silkwood bitterly denied. When the Silkwood estate announced its intention to sue, Kerr-McGee insisted that its Cimarron plant met federal guidelines and that any contamination Silkwood sustained must have come from elsewhere.

After more than four years of delay, on 6 March 1979, Karen Silkwood's family finally had their day in court against Kerr-McGee. Actually they had three months, the longest civil trial in Oklahoma history. Leading off for the Silkwood estate, attorney Gerry Spence put Dr. John Gofman, a physician and an outspoken critic of lax nuclear regulation, on the stand. In answer to a Spence question about the dangers of plutonium, Gofman replied, "The license to give out doses of plutonium is a legalized permit to murder."

"Was Karen in danger of dying from the plutonium inside her?" asked Spence.

"Yes, she was."

Pressed on Kerr-McGee's skimpy employee training program, Gofman responded: "My opinion is that it is clearly and unequivocally negligence."

The only member of the Kerr-McGee management team to testify against his former employers was ex-supervisor James Smith. While conceding little affection for Silkwood as a person—as a union organizer she had been prickly and combative—Smith corroborated her findings about safety violations at Kerr-McGee. Most alarming was his assertion that there were 40 pounds of Material Unaccounted For (MUF), meaning deadly plutonium that was missing. He dismissed com-

Commercial Nuclear Energy

In 1953, President Dwight D. Eisenhower helped usher in the age of commercial nuclear energy when he called for the use of "Atoms for Peace" in a speech before the United Nations. Just eight years before, "atoms for war" had been used in a dramatic way when the United States dropped nuclear bombs on the Japanese cities of Hiroshima and Nagasaki, thus ending World War II.

In 1957, the first commercial nuclear plant was opened at Shippingport, Pennsylvania, and over the course of the next 35 years, some 109 plants were opened in the United States. The latter number, however, represented a significant shortfall compared to the projec-

tions of nuclear-power proponents in the early 1970s, who believed that the country would have 500 nuclear plants by the year 2000. One of the chief reasons for this shortfall was the increase in public fears concerning nuclear power following an accident in a nuclear power plant at Three Mile Island in Pennsylvania in 1979. Concerned by the growth of nuclear waste, the disposal of which is extremely problematic, Congress in 1982 passed the Nuclear Waste Policy Act.

Source(s): Paehlke, Robert, ed. *Conservation and Environmentalism: An Encyclopedia.* New York: Garland, 1995.

pany claims that the MUF was still at the plant. "Let me put it this way," said Smith, who had been in charge of flushing out the system pipes, "if there's 40 pounds still at Cimarron, I don't know where it is."

Another ex-Cimarron employee, now a highway patrol officer, Ron Hammock, told of defective fuel rods, packed full of plutonium pellets, knowingly being shipped to other facilities. "Who told you to ship them?" Spence asked. "My supervisor," the officer calmly replied.

Near Disaster

Three weeks into the trial something happened that raised the question of nuclear safety throughout the United States. A nuclear reactor in Pennsylvania had a near meltdown. For most Americans, the disaster at Three Mile Island was their first experience of the potential for nuclear calamity. The incident cast an inevitable pall over the Silkwood suit, enough for Kerr-McGee chief attorney Bill Paul to move for a mistrial. After careful consideration, Judge Frank Theis denied the request. On hearing this decision, the Silkwood team heaved a vast sigh of relief. Lacking the limitless financial resources of Kerr–McGee, they were fighting this action on a shoestring; any delay would only play into the hands of the $2-billion giant.

Disgruntled, Bill Paul called Kerr-McGee's star witness, Dr. George Voelz, health director at the prestigious Los Alamos Scientific Laboratory. Voelz testified that, in his opinion, the level of contamination displayed by Karen Silkwood fell within AEC standards. Spence thought otherwise. In a cross-examination lasting two days, he drew one embarrassing retraction after another from the frazzled scientist. Central to Voelz's theme was a model used to arrive at the standards. Spence showed how Karen Silkwood in no way conformed to the average person used for the mode, as she

had been less than 100 pounds and a heavy smoker, both factors that influence the chances of contamination. Also, Spence extracted from Voelz the grudging admission that he really did not know the level of plutonium exposure necessary to cause cancer.

In his final instructions to the jury, Judge Theis spelled out the law: "If you find that the damage to the person or property of Karen Silkwood resulted from the operation of this plant . . . Kerr-McGee . . . is liable."

On 18 May 1979, after four days of deliberation, the jury decided that Kerr-McGee had indeed been negligent and awarded $505,000 in damages. A gasp swept the courtroom when the jury added on their assessment for punitive damages: $10 million.

It was a huge settlement, one obviously destined for the appeal courts. The litigation dragged on until August of 1986, when, in an out-of-court settlement, Kerr-McGee agreed to pay the Silkwood estate $1.38 million, which amounted to less than one year's interest on the sum originally awarded.

Many regarded Karen Silkwood as a nuclear martyr. To this day, the circumstances surrounding her death remain shrouded in mystery. It may never be known if she was killed to be silenced. What is known is that the Silkwood estate's victory, modest though it may have ultimately been, sent the nuclear industry a clear message: Dangerous sources of energy demand unusually vigilant regulation.

Related Cases
Gertz v. Robert Welch, Inc., 418 U.S. 323 (1973).
Pacific G&E Co. v. State Energy Res. C&D Com., 461 U.S. 190 (1983).

Bibliography and Further Reading
Kohn, Howard. *Who Killed Karen Silkwood?* New York: Summit, 1981.

Rashke, Richard. *The Killing of Karen Silkwood.* New York: Houghton Mifflin Co., 1981.

"*Silkwood* Settlement." *Science News,* August 8, 1986, p. 134.

Spence, Gerry. *With Justice for None.* New York: Times Books, 1989.

Stein, J. "The Deepening Mystery." *Progressive,* January 1981, pp. 14-19.

NIXON V. FITZGERALD

Legal Citation: 457 U.S. 731 (1982)

Petitioner
President Richard M. Nixon

Respondent
Ernest Fitzgerald

Petitioner's Claim
That a president should not be held liable for civil damages resulting from the termination of a Pentagon employee.

Chief Lawyer for Petitioner
Herbert J. Miller, Jr.

Chief Lawyer for Respondent
John E. Nolan, Jr.

Justices for the Court
Warren E. Burger, Thurgood Marshall, Sandra Day O'Connor, Lewis F. Powell, Jr. (writing for the Court), William H. Rehnquist, John Paul Stevens

Justices Dissenting
Harry A. Blackmun, William J. Brennan, Jr., Byron R. White

Place
Washington, D.C.

Date of Decision
24 June 1982

Decision
That a president possesses absolute immunity from civil lawsuits for actions taken in the course of his official duties.

Significance
Nixon v. Fitzgerald established the principle of "absolute immunity" for actions taken by a president in the course of his official duties. The Court decided that the presidency was a special office worthy of special protections against civil lawsuits.

Ernest Fitzgerald was a cost analyst employed by the U.S. Air Force. In the final months of the Johnson administration, Fitzgerald testified before Congress about serious cost overruns on the C-5A transport plane. Officials at the Defense Department grew angry over Fitzgerald's "whistleblowing" and worked to devise a plan to eliminate his position. When President Nixon came into office in 1969, Fitzgerald was in fact removed—ostensibly as part of a money saving reorganization plan. In a news conference, however, President Nixon publicly admitted responsibility for Fitzgerald's removal—a statement he later retracted. Fitzgerald complained to the Civil Service Commission, claiming his dismissal came in retaliation for his embarrassing testimony on Capitol Hill. The commission did not find evidence of a political plot, but reinstated Fitzgerald on the grounds that he was removed for personal reasons. In 1982, Fitzgerald proceeded to sue former President Nixon for damages.

The Lower Court Decisions

The lower federal courts dismissed Fitzgerald's action on the grounds that the president is immune from such suits. However, the court of appeals rejected Nixon's claim of immunity. Nixon then appealed this decision to the U.S. Supreme Court.

Nixon v. Fitzgerald raised many important questions about the nature and extent of presidential immunity: questions concerning whether a president should be immune from actions taken in the course of performing his or her official duties, and whether this immunity should be absolute, or if there should be limits to when and if a president can be sued. Moreover, there were questions as to whether the claim to immunity was to be derived from the office of the president itself or from the functions the president performs. That is, whether some actions could be considered immune and others not immune, or whether a president simply should be shielded from all suits simply because of the distraction they might create. These were the questions the Supreme Court wrestled with in *Nixon v. Fitzgerald*.

The Court's Decision

On 24 June 1982 the Supreme Court handed down its decision. By a 5-4 decision, the Court sided with Nixon, ruling that a president is immune from all civil suits deriving from his actions as president. Justice Powell wrote the majority opinion, in which he was joined by Chief Justice Burger, Justice Rehnquist, Justice Stevens, and Justice O'Connor.

The majority rested its decision not on the text of the Constitution but on "the constitutional tradition of the separation of powers" and U.S. history. It afforded the president a unique status that distinguishes him from all other executive officials. The president must often deal with matters that are highly sensitive and sure to arouse passions among citizens. It is for just this reason, Justice Powell contended, that he must be shielded from lawsuits:

> Because of the singular importance of the President's duties, diversion of his energies by concern with private lawsuits would raise unique risks to the effective functioning of government.

In keeping with the theme of the "special" nature of the office of the presidency, Powell argued that the prominence of the president's office made him an unusually easy target for lawsuits:

> In view of the visibility of his office and the effect of his actions on countless people, the President would be an easily identifiable target for suits for civil damages. Cognizance of this personal vulnerability frequently could distract a President from his public duties, to the detriment not only of the President and his office but also the Nation that the Presidency was designed to serve.

Finally, the majority rejected the argument that a president's immunity should derive from the functions he or she performs and not from the office itself. If this rule were adopted, the majority argued, every action a president takes would be subject to allegations that it was unlawful. As a result, "absolute immunity" would have no practical meaning.

The President Above the Law?

The majority opinion in *Nixon v. Fitzgerald* provoked an especially strong dissent. Justice White, joined by Justice Marshall, Justice Blackmun, and Justice Brennan, attacked the Court's opinion for placing "the President above the law":

> A President acting within the outer boundaries of what Presidents normally do may, without liability, deliberately cause serious injury to any number of citizens even though he knows his conduct violates a statute or tramples on the constitutional rights of those who are injured.

Justice Powell anticipated this argument and countered it by listing the many other ways—besides civil lawsuit—that a president may be held accountable for his or her actions. These included impeachment, scrutiny by the press, Congressional oversight, and incentives to avoid misconduct such as the desire to win reelection or secure one's historical reputation.

In a separate case, *Harlow and Butterfield v. Fitzgerald* (1982), the Court refused to extend the immunity to Nixon's aides, who had carried out his orders to remove Fitzgerald from his position.

Albert Bussking (left) and A. E. Fitzgerald (center) speak before a joint congressional subcommittee on contracting procedures, 1968. © AP/Wide World Photos.

Related Cases

United States v. Nixon, 418 U.S. 683 (1974).
Butz v. Economou, 438 U.S. 478 (1978).
Harlow v. Fitzgerald, 457 U.S. 800 (1982).
Clinton v. Jones, 520 U.S. 681 (1997).

Bibliography and Further Reading

Chandler, Ralph C. *The Constitutional Law Dictionary.* Santa Barbara, CA: ABC-Clio, Inc., 1987.

Cushman, Robert F. *Cases in Constitutional Law.* Englewood Cliffs, NJ: Prentice-Hall, Inc., 1986.

Ducat, Craig R., and Harold W. Chase. *Constitutional Interpretation.* St. Paul, MN: West Publishing Company, 1988.

Grossman, Joel B., and David A. Yalof. "The 'Public' versus the 'Private' President." *Presidential Studies Quarterly,* fall 1998, p. 821.

Rabkin, Jeremy A. "Double Immunity." *American Spectator,* August 1994, p. 47.

FIRST ENGLISH EVANGELICAL LUTHERAN CHURCH OF GLENDALE V. COUNTY OF LOS ANGELES, CALIFORNIA

Legal Citation: 482 U.S. 304 (1987)

Appellant
First English Evangelical Lutheran Church of Glendale

Appellee
County of Los Angeles, California

Appellant's Claim
The "interim ordinance" adopted by the County of Los Angeles denied the appellant's right to use of his property and violated the Just Compensation Clause of the Fifth Amendment.

Chief Lawyer for Appellant
Michael M. Berger

Chief Lawyer for Appellee
Jack R. White

Justices for the Court
William J. Brennan, Jr., Thurgood Marshall, Lewis F. Powell, Jr., William H. Rehnquist (writing for the Court), Antonin Scalia, Byron R. White

Justices Dissenting
Harry A. Blackmun, Sandra Day O'Connor, John Paul Stevens

Place
Washington, D.C.

Date of Decision
9 June 1987

Decision
The Court found in favor of the appellant. The county of Los Angeles had, in effect, engaged in a regulatory taking because the appellant was denied use and economic viability of its property. Thus, the effect of the county ordinance was held excessive and subject to the Just Compensation Clause of the Fifth Amendment of the U.S. Constitution. The Court ordered just compensation must be paid, even for "the time before determination that [the] regulation effected [a] taking." The U.S Supreme Court reversed the decision of the lower court and remanded the case further proceedings.

Significance
The ruling of the U.S. Supreme Court clarified criteria which defined differences and actions in temporary and permanent takings.

First English Evangelical Lutheran Church of Glendale bought a parcel of land in 1957. The parcel consisted of 21 acres of which 12 acres were flat land in a valley of the Middle Fork of Mill Creek in the Angeles National Forest. Later, the appellant, used this ground to build up a camp called "Lutherglen," which was used as a resort and recreation center for handicapped children. The camp was situated on both sides of Mill Creek. In July of 1977, a large forest fire destroyed a vast area of woods upstream from Lutherglen; unfortunately, the fire increased the possibility of flooding in Mill Creek Canyon. In February of 1978, a heavy storm poured 11 inches of rain, and the prognosis became reality. Destruction of vegetation on the hillsides of Mill Creek meant that runoff from the rain overflowed river banks and destroyed the buildings in Lutherglen.

Subsequently, in January 1979, Los Angeles County approved "interim ordinance" No. 11855. It was a legislative act that regulated new construction and reconstruction of real estate in Mill Creek Canyon. This regulation prohibited such actions in an area the county of Los Angeles believed was dangerous and sensitive to flooding. To preserve public health and safety, the county ordered that the ordinance had to be strictly, immediately enforced.

Within a month after the interim ordinance was adopted, First English Evangelical Lutheran Church of Glendale brought suit in a California court. The suit maintained two claims against the County Flood Control District and the County of Los Angeles, and under each claim, the appellant demanded just compensation for loss caused through denial of access and use of Lutherglen. The argument supporting the first claim cited section 835 of the California Government Code that stipulated "a governmental entity may be liable for injury caused by a dangerous condition of its property." The second part of their claim maintained that the ordinance denied the appellant use of church property. The appellant demanded "inverse condemnation" (an action that a property owner can claim when government has allegedly taken property without use of formal "eminent domain" proceedings). However, Los Angeles County's counter argument cited what they believed was precedence set by the Supreme Court of California in *Agins*

v. *Tiburon* (1979). In that ruling, the court held that a landowner could not use inverse condemnation as a legal remedy in a "regulatory taking" in the state of California. Further, any form of compensation was not appropriate so long as an ordinance or regulation was not ruled as excessive in proceedings of action for declaratory relief or a writ of *mandamus* and only if the government persisted in enforcing the regulation. The county argued that as long as the ordinance in question was not judged as extreme and the government regulation was a temporary measure, then compensation was not obligatory. The California court ruled consistently with *Agins* and found "irrelevant" the claim of First English Evangelical Lutheran Church of Glendale.

On appeal filed by the appellant in the California Court of Appeals, the court also responded favorably to Los Angeles County's arguments and reliance on *Agins*. Believing the appellant wanted both compensation for loss of use for all property and affirming precedence set by the California Supreme Court ruling, the court of appeals ruled against the church because, according to *Agins,* compensation "was limited to nonmonetary relief." Unsatisfied with the ruling, the church appealed to the U.S. Supreme Court. Their writ invited the Supreme Court to overrule the California Supreme Court's decision in *Agins* which held that the state was not obliged to compensate for property that had been taken by "temporary" regulations.

In presenting the case for the appellant to the U.S. Supreme Court, counsel for the appellant requested a review of *Agins* due to the reliance of the California courts on that decision to make their rulings. However, counsel also pointed out that another, consistent objection of the lower courts was that the appellant's conduct in filing their complaint was in collision with required legal procedure according to *Agins*. Counsel also pointed out that neither court questioned that a taking had actually occurred nor that the owners had been deprived of total use of their property. Notwithstanding, the appellant's attorney claimed the state had the right to enact flood safety regulations, but such action was subject to the Just Compensation Clause of the Fifth Amendment of the U.S. Constitution. Moreover, even if Los Angeles County withdrew the ordinance at issue, the church should be compensated for value loss during the period after the ordinance went into effect. Counsel reasoned that because almost nine years elapsed since the ordinance went into effect, the "temporary" taking in the owner's view was not much different from a permanent taking.

In presenting arguments for Los Angeles County, the appellee's attorney questioned whether the U.S. Supreme Court had jurisdiction. Conceding that the Court could find the case within its legal mandate, counsel argued that precedence set by the California Supreme Court in the *Agins* decision was consistent

with the U.S. Supreme Court's rulings in similar cases, *MacDonald, Sommer & Frates v. Yolo County* (1986), *Williamson County Regional Planning Commission v. Hamilton Bank* (1985), and *San Diego Gas & Electric Co. v. San Diego* (1981). Accordingly, the Supreme Court of California held that the remedy for the alleged temporary property taking was limited to non-monetary relief. Counsel also stipulated that there existed a difference between permanent and temporary taking because the temporary ordinance did not deny use of the total property nor was the ordinance (hence the taking) intended to be permanent. Neither was the means by which First English Evangelical Lutheran Church of Glendale sought redress proper legal remedy according to *Agins*. The appellant's inverse condemnation claim should have taken the form of a declaratory relief or writ of *mandamus* to satisfy proper legal protocol. Furthermore, when (as Los Angeles County claimed) public health and safety were at stake, government had the legal power to prohibit dangerous use of land. Thus the county should not be penalized for the action undertaken to preserve population from the risk from the continued use of Lutherglen.

The Court ruled that the matter did belong within its mandate and jurisdiction. In writing for the majority, Chief Justice Rehnquist saw no similarity in the cases cited by the appellee, (*MacDonald, Williamson County,* and *San Diego*) and thus could not uphold the rule set forth in the *Agins* case. Further, the alleged taking deprived the owner of all use of their property, and the issue was a subject to the Just Compensation Clause. Justice Rehnquist held that the Fifth Amendment of the U.S. Constitution did not prohibit a state from exercising its right of eminent domain, but that such takings had to be balanced with the rights of an owner whose property had been taken and thus entitled to just compensation even if only for the period "before the courts finally determine that the regulation effects a taking of property."

The Court went on to define the nature of permanent and temporary takings. The decision ruled that if a temporary taking denied an owner of all use of property, then such a taking could not be considered different from a permanent taking. Moreover, even if government decided to withdraw its challenged regulation or ordinance, just compensation had to be paid for the time the challenged ordinance was effective and for the period of time the owner was denied total use of the property. Specifically, the Court held that withdrawal of the regulation, without just compensation, would not be a just remedy for a property taking.

In writing the dissenting opinion, Justice Stevens did not agree that the challenged regulation represented "an unconstitutional taking of Lutherglen;" the action, therefore, was not subject to the limitations of the Just Compensation Clause. The minority opinion expressed alarm that the Court's ruling could inspire a spate of litigation because, in effect, the majority ruling suggested that all ordinances could conceivably be interpreted as a taking even if the regulation was only in effect for a limited time. Stevens felt that the appellant should have used all legal avenues and means available in the state of California to attempt to get the objectionable ordinance rescinded. Furthermore, such actions were mandatory before submitting the case to the U.S. Supreme Court to determine if the state proceedings constitute "a temporary taking of property without just compensation." (Interestingly, this view was also supported by majority Justices Blackmun and O'Connor.) Ultimately, Stevens flatly disagreed with the majority opinion that the Just Compensation Clause was applicable to the case as it was presented before the Court. He felt that an ordinance or regulation did not constitute a taking protection if there remained value for most of the property in question. Thus, "improperly motivated, unfairly conducted, or unnecessarily protracted governmental decision-making" taken to regulate the use of private property, as Lutherglen's property, should be decided by applying the Due Process Clause.

Impact

The significance of the case is the Court's ruling itself. In a later case, *Lucas v. South Carolina Coastal Council* (1992), the U.S. Supreme Court ruled that a regulatory taking was justifiable if it prevented a nuisance, was not unnecessarily restrictive, and was consistent with a state's common law practices regarding property nuisances. However, the regulatory taking in which Los Angeles County engaged permitted further clarification as to the limitations of such takings. The Court held that even in a nuisance taking, the public had a right to expect that the government did not inflict harm to health, safety, or property. Los Angeles County's ordinance negated the viability of First English Evangelical Lutheran Church property, thus, such loss (to the innocent parties) permitted compensation for damages for the period during which the regulation amounted to a taking of property. Thus, the Court refined its position in *Lucas*, on one hand, reemphasizing that the government is not absolutely limited to interference regarding private property but, conversely, that just compensation must be granted when such interference, in effect, constituted a taking.

Related Cases

Agins v. Tiburon, 24 Cal. 266 (1979).
San Diego Gas & Electric Co. v. San Diego, 450 U.S. 621 (1981).
Williamson County Regional Planning Commission v. Hamilton Bank, 473 U.S. 172 (1985).
MacDonald, Sommer & Frates v. Yolo County, 477 U.S. 340 (1986).
Lucas v. South Carolina Coastal Council, 505 U.S. 1003 (1992).

Bibliography and Further Reading

Katz, David M. "Pool Uses One Form for Many Liabilities." *National Underwriter Property & Casualty-Risk & Benefits Management*, July 6, 1998, p. 17.

Wise, Charles R., and Kirk Emerson. "Regulatory Takings: The Emerging Doctrine and Its Implications for Public Administration." *Administration & Society*, November 1994, p. 305.

CIPOLLONE V. LIGGETT GROUP

Legal Citation: 858 F2d 775 (1988)

Plaintiff
Estate of Rose Cipollone

Defendant
Liggett Group

Plaintiff's Claim
That the defendant, a cigarette company, was liable for Rose Cipollone's death from cancer because it failed to warn consumers about the dangers of smoking.

Chief Lawyers for Plaintiff
Alan Darnell, Marc Z. Edell, and Cynthia Walters

Chief Defense Lawyer
H. Bartow Farr III

Judge
H. Lee Sarokin

Place
Newark, New Jersey

Date of Decision
13 June 1988

Decision
Jury awarded plaintiff damages of $400,000; reversed on appeal, lawsuit later dropped.

Significance
Despite encouraging early victories, the lesson of the *Cipollone* case is that smokers face very burdensome legal difficulties in suing cigarette companies.

Rose Cipollone of Little Ferry, New Jersey was born in 1926. Like many people of her generation, she took up smoking at an early age. Although medical studies examining evidence of a link between smoking and cancer began to appear as early as the 1920s, they were not widely read, and the U.S. Surgeon General did not look into the issue until 1962. In 1966 the first federal law on cigarette warning labels law went into effect, and in 1969 Congress passed a stricter law requiring that the label, "Warning: The Surgeon General Has Determined That Cigarette Smoking Is Dangerous to Your Health," be printed on all cigarette packs.

Decade after decade, the cigarette industry spent billions of dollars on advertising. Newspaper, magazine, radio, and television ads extolled the pleasures of smoking. There was no mention of any risk, and the tobacco companies vigorously fought government regulation in the 1960s and 1970s with studies of their own that denied any health risk from smoking. Meanwhile, Cipollone had been smoking since 1942. Her favorite brands were Chesterfields and L&M, manufactured by Liggett Group, Inc., one of the smaller tobacco companies.

In 1981, Dr. Nathan Seriff diagnosed Cipollone as having lung cancer, caused by smoking cigarettes. Cipollone filed a lawsuit against Liggett on 1 August 1983 in the U.S. District Court for the District of New Jersey in Newark. Early in the litigation, Cipollone won an important victory when Judge Sarokin refused to dismiss the case on the grounds that Liggett's compliance with the federal warning-label law absolved Liggett from further legal liability:

> This case presents the issue of whether cigarette manufacturers can be subjected to tort liability if they have complied with the federal warning requirements. In effect, the cigarette industry argues that such compliance immunizes it from liability to anyone who has chosen to smoke cigarettes notwithstanding the warning, that federal legislation has created an irrebuttable presumption that the risk of injury has been assumed by the consumer.

The court rejected that contention.

Joe Camel and the Advertising Controversy

In 1987 Camel revived its sagging image with what would become one of the most controversial ad campaigns of the twentieth century. Joe, the cartoon Camel, was a suave, witty figure who played pool and often found himself surrounded by beautiful women. His image helped Camel win consumers; but he also acquired enormous name recognition among children—a 1991 survey, for instance, found that six-year-olds were as likely to recognize Joe Camel as they were Mickey Mouse. On 10 July 1997, manufacturer R. J. Reynolds ended the campaign amidst growing pressure.

Though the appeal to children certainly is a serious matter, Barbara Dority, in a January, 1997 *Humanist* article

raised a number of First Amendment objections to the current wave of campaigns against cigarette advertising. Like other commentators who took a similar position, Dority did not defend smoking, but rather the right of individuals to do it, and of companies to promote it. Besides, Joe Camel's stateside campaign may not be the worst offender where children are concerned: the September 1998 issue of *Sales & Marketing Management* reported that Camel ads had been posted in classrooms in Poland, and that an ad for Marlboro in Cambodia featured eight-year-old girls.

Source(s): *Encyclopedia of Major Marketing Campaigns.* Detroit, MI: Gale, 1999.

Cippolone Dies, But Her Case Proceeds

Sarokin's decision was issued on 20 September 1984, and generated enormous publicity about the case. The prospect of successful smokers' litigation sent tobacco company stocks into a tailspin. Unfortunately for her, Cipollone died shortly thereafter, on 21 October 1984. Her husband, Antonio Cipollone, continued the case on behalf of her estate. After years of foot dragging and delays by Liggett's attorneys, the *Cipollone* case finally went to trial on 1 February 1988. Just getting the case to trial was an accomplishment: of the 300 lawsuits on record against tobacco companies in the previous 40 years, fewer than 10 actually went to trial.

Edell, the senior attorney in the *Cipollone* legal team, described Liggett's legal defenses to the jury as basically a statement to all smokers:

> If you trusted us, if you thought we would test, if you thought we would warn, if you believed our statement in the press, if you believed our advertisements, if you were stupid enough to believe us, then you deserve what you got.

Cipollone's attorneys introduced documents showing that the cigarette companies were aware of smoking-related health risks before the government took any action but failed to disclose these risks to the consumer. For example, one Liggett report from 1961 described certain ingredients in cigarettes as "(a) cancer-causing, (b) cancer-promoting, (c) poisonous, (d) stimulating, pleasurable, and flavorful."

On 13 June 1988 the jury returned its verdict. It was a very conservative mostly based on Liggett's failure prior to the 1966 law to warn smokers like Cipollone about the dangers of smoking. Further, the jury found that Cipollone was 80 percent responsible for her death by smoking, and Liggett only 20 percent responsible.

Nevertheless, the jury assessed $400,000 in damages against Liggett, the first such award in tobacco-litigation history.

Liggett appealed, and the case ultimately reached the U.S. Supreme Court on 8 October 1991. During the lengthy appellate process, however, Antonio Cipollone died in 1990. His son, Thomas Cipollone of Grass Valley, California, carried on the case on behalf of both his parents' estates. The Supreme Court required the parties to reargue the case on 13 January 1992 and issued its opinion on 24 June 1992. Although the Court ruled in a 6-3 decision that health warnings on cigarette packs do not shield cigarette companies like Liggett from personal-injury lawsuits, the Court did impose tougher evidentiary requirements concerning the companies' advertising and promotions. The case would have to be retried.

Thomas Cipollone and the attorneys had enough. After nine years of expensive litigation, they were back at square one, facing even more time-consuming hurdles resulting from the Supreme Court's decision. To make matters worse, Judge Sarokin had been removed from the case for public comments he had made on his belief that the tobacco industry was hiding evidence. On 5 November 1992, the Cipollone family dropped their case against Liggett. While the initial jury verdict was the first of its kind in American legal history, the ultimate lesson is that the tobacco companies can delay and delay in court until their victims die or give up in despair.

Related Cases

Gills v. Ford Motor Co., 829 F.Supp. 894 (1993).
Jenkins v. Amchem Products, Inc., 886 P.2d 869 (1994).
Myrick v. Freuhauf Corp., 13 F.3d 1516 (1994)
Askenazi v. Hymil Mfg. Co., Inc., 648 N.Y.S.2d 895 (1996).

Hernandez-Gomez v. Leonardo, 917 P.2d 238 (1996).

Broin, et al. v. Philip Morris Incorporated, et al., 641 So.2d 888 (1997).

Toole v. Brown and Williamson Tobacco Corp., 980 F.Supp. 419 (1997).

Drattel v. Toyota Motor Corp., 699 N.E.2d 376 (1998).

Bibliography and Further Reading

Crudele, John. "The Smoke Clears; Tobacco Liability Suits Decline." *New York,* November 14, 1988, p. 28.

Gostin, Larry O. "Tobacco Liability and Public Health Policy." *Journal of the American Medical Association,* December 11, 1911, pp. 3178-3182.

Spencer, Leslie. "Just Smoke." *Forbes,* December 23, 1991, pp. 41-42.

The Editors. "For the First Time Ever." *The New Republic,* July 4, 1988, p. 10-11.

The Editors. "Where There's Smoke . . . " *Time,* April 8, 1991, p. 55.

PACIFIC MUTUAL LIFE INSURANCE CO. V. HASLIP ET AL.

Legal Citation: 499 U.S. 1 (1991)

Petitioner
Pacific Mutual Life Insurance Co.

Respondent
Cleopatra Haslip, et al.

Petitioner's Claim
That the punitive damages awarded by an Alabama State jury were excessive, and the decision was unconstitutional because it violated Fourteenth Amendment's guarantee of due process.

Chief Lawyer for Petitioner
Bruce A. Beckman

Chief Lawyer for Respondent
Bruce J. Ennis, Jr.

Justices for the Court
Harry A. Blackmun (writing for the Court), Anthony M. Kennedy, Thurgood Marshall, William H. Rehnquist, Antonin Scalia, John Paul Stevens, Byron R. White

Justices Dissenting
Sandra Day O'Connor (David H. Souter did not participate)

Place
Washington, D.C.

Date of Decision
4 March 1991

Decision
Upheld the decision of the Alabama trial jury and the Alabama Supreme Court, that the punitive damages awarded were not excessive or unconstitutional.

Significance
This was the one of several cases heard by the Court which addressed the constitutionality of large awards of punitive damages by juries. The ruling denied the accusation that these extremely large awards granted by juries were in violation of the due process clause of the Fourteenth Amendment. But the decision in this case did not rule out limitations on the amounts of punitive damages juries could award; this case was one discussion in an ongoing conversation about the function of juries and punitive damages in civil law suits.

During the 1980s and 1990s, public concern over the use of juries in civil law suits grew, especially in the matter of punitive damages awarded by these juries. Some punitive awards reached seven digits or more, and civil suits themselves came to be seen as largely frivolous. The court heard several cases in which the defendant in a civil case appealed the judgement on the grounds that the punitive award was so extraordinarily high that it violated the Constitution, either under the Eighth Amendment's prohibition of excessive fines, or under the Fourteenth Amendment's clause guaranteeing the right to due process.

In *Pacific Mutual Life Insurance Co. v. Haslip et al.*, Cleopatra Haslip and her coworkers sued the insurance company—along with Lemmie L. Ruffin Jr., an agent of that company—because the agent defrauded them as employees of Roosevelt City, misappropriating the premiums they paid for their health insurance. The employees' health insurance policies were cancelled without their knowledge, a fact which Ms. Haslip discovered only when she was hospitalized. The civil case was brought before a jury, and the jury awarded compensatory damages to all the plaintiffs, and punitive damages of $1,000,000 to Ms. Haslip.

Compensatory damages are awarded, literally, to compensate a party for losses or damages incurred because of actions of another. Punitive damages, though, are not linked directly to specific loss; rather, they are intended to act as punishment for inappropriate behavior on the part of the payer. The idea behind punitive damages is that if a company or individual is charged a large enough sum, it would act as a deterrent to repeating the behavior being punished. The question for the Supreme Court was not whether punitive damages could be awarded by juries, as this had been established over time by other courts according to common law. Rather, the question addressed was whether damages considered exorbitant were, in fact, legal.

Because the Court had already decided, in *Browning-Ferris Industries of Vermont, Inc. v. Kelco Disposal, Inc.*, that the Eighth Amendment's Excessive Fines Clause could not be applied to private parties in a civil suit, it did not further consider the argument in this case. Instead, the relevant amendment was the Fourteenth,

---

Punitive Damages

A plaintiff who wins a judgment in a tort case is usually awarded compensatory damages, which normally cover the injury he or she has received, along with the legal costs incurred. But in cases where the plaintiff's legal counsel is able to demonstrate aggravated wrongdoing on the part of the defendant, the judge may also award punitive damages. Whereas the dollar figures for compensatory damages tend to range from the thousands to the tens of thousands, for punitive damages they often run from the hundreds of thousands to multiple millions.

Punitive damages, as their name implies, are indeed often used to punish a defendant for the negligence or intentional wrongdoing that occasioned the lawsuit. But they may also be intended as a deterrent, or to "make an example of" the defendant. For these reasons, punitive damages are a subject of controversy, and in the popular imagination sometimes become almost the stuff of urban legend, as in the 1990s when widespread outrage followed the awarding of millions of dollars to a woman who had burned herself on hot coffee purchased from a fast-food chain.

Source(s): Levy, Leonard W., ed. *Encyclopedia of the American Constitution.* New York: Macmillan, 1986.

---

which guarantees individuals the right to the due process of law. This right includes a trial which is free from undue bias, or prejudiced treatment. As the Court made clear in *Browning-Ferris Industries of Vermont, Inc. v. Kelco Disposal, Inc.,* "The parties agree that due process imposes some limits on jury awards of punitive damages, and it is not disputed that a jury award may not be upheld if it was the product of bias or passion," but it did not decide in that case whether "the Due Process Clause places outer limits on the size of a civil damages award."

While the Court did not find that in the *Browning-Ferris* case—nor in the related *TXO Production Co. v. Alliance Resources,* involving a $10,000,000 award over drilling rights—that the punitive award was in opposition to the right to due process, it did not rule out the possibility that another, more outrageous award might do so. In 1994, for example, the Court held that the state of Oregon could not prevent the careful review of jury-awarded punitive damages, as decided in *Honda Motor Co. Ltd. v. Oberg.* And in 1996, the Court finally found a punitive damages case which exceeded the limits of the Due Process Clause. In *BMW of North America, Inc. v. Gore* the jury's award of $4,000,000 to a man whose new BMW had been repainted by the car company without his knowledge was reduced to $2,000,000 on appeal, but was still called "grossly out of proportion to the severity of the case" by the Court, and was seen to violate the Due Process Clause. Even this finding, though, did not set up hard and fast rules for courts and juries to follow in civil cases.

Justice Blackmun wrote in the Court's opinion for the *Pacific Mutual* case,

> unlimited jury or judicial discretion in the fixing of punitive damages may invite extreme

results that are unacceptable under the Due Process Clause. Although a mathematical bright line cannot be drawn between the constitutionally acceptable and the constitutionally unacceptable that would fit every case, general concerns of reasonableness and adequate guidance from the court when the case is tried to a jury properly enter into the constitutional calculus.

According to these standards, the Court found that the punitive damages charged to Pacific Mutual were acceptable. While even after the *BMW* case there was still no consensus, there stood the Court's assertion that some form of fairness, including considering the nature and degree of the wrongdoing and the need for deterrence, must be applied in individual civil cases.

Related Cases
Browning-Ferris Industries of Vermont v. Kelco Disposal, 492 U.S. 257 (1989).
TXO Production Corp. v. Alliance Resources, 509 U.S. 443 (1993).
Honda Motor Co. Ltd. v. Oberg, 512 U.S. 415 (1994).
BMW of North America, Inc. v. Gore, 517 U.S. 559 (1996).

Bibliography and Further Reading
Biskupic, Joan, and Elder Witt, eds. *Guide to the U.S. Supreme Court.* Washington, DC: Congressional Quarterly, Inc., 1997.

"Two Key Liability Cases Before Supreme Court This Week." *Liability Week,* March 29, 1993.

Witt, Elder, ed. *The Supreme Court A to Z.* Washington, DC: Congressional Quarterly, Inc., 1993.

DAUBERT V. MERRELL DOW PHARMACEUTICALS, INC.

Legal Citation: 509 U.S. 579 (1993)

Petitioners
William Daubert, et ux.

Respondent
Merrell Dow Pharmaceuticals, Inc.

Petitioners' Claim
The standard for determining the admissibility of expert testimony in court set by *Frye v. United States* was superseded by Rule 702 of the Federal Rules of Evidence. Under Rule 702, the expert testimony that was excluded from trial by the trial court should have been included.

Chief Lawyer for Petitioners
Michael H. Gottesman

Chief Lawyer for Respondent
Charles Fried

Justices for the Court
Harry A. Blackmun (writing for the Court), Anthony M. Kennedy, Sandra Day O'Connor, Antonin Scalia, David H. Souter, Clarence Thomas, Byron R. White

Justices Dissenting
William H. Rehnquist, John Paul Stevens

Place
Washington, D.C.

Date of Decision
28 June 1993

Decision
The standard for admission at trial of expert testimony is not whether the expert's proffered testimony is based on science that is generally accepted in the expert's particular scientific community. Instead, the question of whether expert testimony should be admitted must be decided according to Rule 702 of the Federal Rules of Evidence.

Significance
The holding rejected the old standard for the admission at trial of expert testimony and replaced it with a less stringent standard.

In 1923, a Washington, D.C. court held in *Frye v. United States* that expert testimony is admissible only if the science testified to by the expert is generally accepted within the scientific community. Most courts followed this standard until 1993, when the Supreme Court made its ruling in *Daubert*.

When Jason Daubert and Eric Schuller were born with serious birth defects, William and Joyce Daubert and Anita DeYoung suspected that the cause of the defects was Bendectin, a drug made by Merrell Dow Pharmaceuticals, Inc. DeYoung and the Dauberts sued Merrell Dow in state court for Daubert and Schuller. The plaintiffs alleged that the children had been born with reduced limbs because the mothers had ingested a Merrell Dow drug during pregnancy to alleviate nausea and vomiting.

Merrell Dow removed the case to federal court and denied that Bendectin caused the birth defects. In the preliminary stages of the civil case, Merrell Dow moved the court for summary judgment. Summary judgment is a judgment delivered by a judge prior to trial. It may be ordered by a court if a party does not show that there is a genuine issue of material fact involved in the claim. Merrell Dow produced Steven H. Lamm, an epidemiologist and a respected expert on the risks of exposure to various chemical substances. Lamm testified that, according to the public record, the use of Bendectin during the first trimester of pregnancy had not been proven to produce birth defects.

The plaintiffs did not dispute Dr. Lamm's testimony regarding publicly recorded tests of Bendectin. They did, however, maintain that Bendectin was harmful and that this could be proven by other experts. Although these experts had respectable credentials, they offered to testify to evidence culled from tests that were less established than those cited by Dr. Lamm. Specifically, the plaintiffs' experts were prepared to testify to "in vitro" or test tube tests, "in vivo" or live animal studies, pharmacological studies on drug structure, and reanalysis of previously published epidemiological studies. The trial court, however, refused to let the plaintiffs' experts testify. As the plaintiffs lacked testimony to rebut the testimony of Dr. Lamm, no genuine

Expert Witnesses—Are They Really Experts?

Anyone who watched the O. J. Simpson trial, or any number of other high-profile 1990s cases such as the trial of brothers Lyle and Erik Menendez for the murder of their parents, is familiar with the use of "expert witnesses." These are specialists, usually in the natural or social sciences, brought in by one or both sides (whether prosecution or defense, plaintiff or defendant) in civil and criminal trials to bolster the position of that side by offering an informed opinion.

But are they really experts? James Q. Wilson in the *Chronicle of Higher Education* takes issue with that idea, particularly as applied to social sciences such as psychology. Many of these, he wrote, "provide paid testimony in which they inflate their own scientific credentials" to offer their clients the benefit of what Wilson called "'pretend' science." Yet Ivar Roth, former president and board member of the Forensic Consultants Organization of Orange County, California, told *USA Today*, "Contrary to popular belief, expert witnesses are required to be truthful. Professional engineers in particular can't give half truths, but must give the complete truth, revealing the negatives as well as the positives on each case."

Source(s): "Expert Witnesses Often Are Keys to Trial." *USA Today*, April 1998.

Wilson, James Q. "Keep Social-Science 'Experts' Out of the Courtroom." *Chronicle of Higher Education*, June 6, 1997.

issue of material fact had been created by the plaintiffs, and the trial court awarded summary judgment to Merrell Dow.

The plaintiffs lost on appeal to the U.S. Court of Appeals for the Ninth Circuit. Citing the *Frye* standard, the appeals court held that the trial court was correct in its decision to exclude the testimony of the plaintiffs' experts because the techniques they were prepared to testify to were not generally accepted in the scientific community. Arguing that the *Frye* standard was no longer valid, the plaintiffs petitioned the U.S. Supreme Court for a writ of *certiorari*, and the High Court agreed to hear the case. In a nearly unanimous decision (Justices Rehnquist and Stevens concurred in part and dissented in part), the High Court vacated the appeals court ruling and sent the case back to the lower courts.

Writing for the Court, Justice Blackmun acknowledged that the standard set by *Frye* had been hotly debated over the years. However, the petitioners were not, noted Blackmun, basing their challenge on the content of the *Frye* standard, but on the "continuing authority of the rule." In 1975, Congress enacted the Federal Rules of Evidence to govern evidence issues in federal court, and among these was Rule 702, which covered the admissibility of expert testimony. The petitioners argued that this rule displaced the *Frye* standard, and the High Court agreed.

The Court analyzed the federal rules as it would analyze any other legislation and held that they superseded the *Frye* test. In prior cases, the Court had examined court-made, "common law" rules that were put in question by the enactment of the federal rules. In those cases, the Court found that the common law rule was superseded by the new federal rule if the common law rule had not been incorporated into the federal rule.

The drafters of the Federal Rules of Evidence had not included language about "general acceptance in the scientific community" for Rule 702, so the Court held that the *Frye* standard had been superseded by Rule 702.

Under Rule 702 of the Federal Rules of Evidence, an expert witness may testify about scientific and technical matters and other areas of specialized knowledge if it "will assist the trier of fact to understand the evidence or to determine a fact in issue." This was a more permissible standard for the admission of expert testimony, but, the Court warned, that did not mean that the rules placed "no limits on the admissibility of purportedly scientific evidence." The Court reminded the parties that scientific evidence and testimony must be reliable and relevant to the case before it can be admitted.

The relevancy requirement came from Rule 402 of the Federal Rules of Evidence, which commands that all evidence that is not relevant to the case may not be introduced in court. The reliability requirement, according to the Court, came from the language of Rule 702, which requires that an expert's testimony be related to scientific, technical, or other specialized knowledge. Scientific knowledge, opined the Court, meant that the proposed testimony had to be "supported by appropriate validation—i.e. 'good grounds,' based on what is known."

The Court recognized another requirement for the admissibility of expert testimony: it must "assist the trier of fact to understand the evidence or to determine a fact in issue." This "'helpfulness' standard" also required that expert testimony would be inadmissible in court unless it had "a valid scientific connection to the pertinent inquiry." Unlike other witnesses, expert witnesses may give opinions on topics of which they have no firsthand knowledge, so it was important, stressed the Court, to ensure that an expert's opinion would have "a reliable basis in the knowledge and experience of his discipline."

Although the Court was "confident that federal judges possess the capacity" to undertake the new expert witness analysis, it proceeded to offer advice to the lower federal courts. In determining whether a theory or technique is scientific knowledge that will be helpful to the judge or jury, the Court stated that important factors would be whether it could be tested and whether it had in fact been tested. Another factor would be "whether the theory or technique has been subjected to peer review and publication." Still another factor in the analysis would be whether there was a known rate of potential error, and the extent of any identifiable rate of error. The Court added that the Frye test of general acceptance in the scientific community would continue to be a factor in determining the admissibility of expert testimony. However, it could not be the only factor.

The Court dismissed Merrell Dow's claims that the new standard would result in a testimonial "free-for-all" that would confuse juries and subject the legal process to "pseudoscientific assertions." Other rules were in place to ensure that such havoc would not occur in court. Under Rule 706 of the Federal Rules of Evidence, a court may procure an expert of its own choosing. Under Rule 403, a court may exclude evidence if it will unfairly prejudice a party, confuse the issue, or mislead the jury. Rule 703 protects against inadmissible hearsay given by experts. Furthermore, questionable expert testimony, like any questionable testimony, is open to attack through cross-examinations and the presentation of contrary evidence.

Chief Justice Rehnquist and Justice Stevens concurred in part and dissented in part. In an opinion written by Chief Justice Rehnquist, the two justices agreed with the majority that the standard in Frye was replaced by the Federal Rules of Evidence. However, the justices felt that the Court was in no position to give a lecture on science to the lower courts. The general observations on the helpfulness of scientific evidence offered by the Court were, to Rehnquist and Stevens, unnecessary, "vague and abstract."

Rehnquist and Stevens objected to the Court's compendium on good and bad science because, although it was written by justices with no scientific background, it would be considered gospel by the lower courts. The majority had referred to the "falsifiability" of a scientific theory as a factor in determining its admissibility, but Rehnquist confessed that he was "at a loss to know what is meant when it is said the scientific status of a theory depends on its 'falsifiability,'" and he expressed concern that federal judges would be at a similar loss. Rehnquist conceded that Rule 702 required federal judges to know something of science to make informed judgments on the admissibility of expert testimony. However, he did not think that the rule imposed on federal judges "the obligation or the authority to become amateur scientists in order to perform that role."

Impact

The Daubert ruling made it easier for parties to introduce expert testimony at trial. Before Daubert, parties could only use expert testimony that was considered by the judge to be generally accepted in the scientific community. Daubert made it possible for parties to introduce experts in newer, less traditional disciplines, which consequently expanded the amount of information available to judges and juries in their fact-finding duties.

Related Cases

Frye v. United States, 54 App.D.C. 46 (1923).

Bibliography and Further Reading

Berkman, Harvey. "High Court Defers to Judges on Scientific Evidence." National Law Journal, December 29, 1997, p. A10.

Brewer, Scott. "Scientific Expert Testimony and Intellectual Due Process." Yale Law Journal, April 1998, p. 1535.

Capra, Daniel J. "Evidence; Amendments." The National Law Journal, October 5, 1998, p. B11.

"Evidence." West's Encyclopedia of American Law. St. Paul: West Group, 1998.

Green, Michael D. "Judging Science: Scientific Knowledge and the Federal Courts." Science, November 28, 1997, p. 1574.

Johnson, Lynn R., Stephen N. Six, and Patrick A. Hamilton. "Deciphering Daubert." Trial, November 1997, p. 71.

McDonald, James J., Jr. "Daubert in Employment Litigation: A Potent Weapon Against Dubious Science." Employee Relations Law Journal, summer 1998, p. 35.

McMurry, Kelly. "Fifth Circuit Extends Daubert to Physicians' Causation Testimony." Trial, November 1998, p. 108.

"When is an 'Expert' Not Really an 'Expert'?" National Underwriter Property & Casualty-Risk & Benefits Management, September 14, 1998, p. 36.

White, Jeffrey Robert. "Experts and Judges." Trial, September 1998, p. 91.

"Whose Body of Evidence." The Economist, July 11, 1998, p. 78.

BMW OF NORTH AMERICA, INC. V. GORE

Legal Citation: 517 U.S. 559 (1996)

Petitioner
BMW of North America, Inc.

Respondent
Dr. Ira Gore, Jr.

Petitioner's Claim
That a $2 million punitive damages award imposed on it by an Alabama jury was grossly excessive, and violated the company's rights to due process under the Fourteenth Amendment.

Chief Lawyers for Petitioner
Michael C. Quillen, Samuel M. Hill

Chief Lawyers for Respondent
Andrew L. Frey, Evan M. Tager

Justices for the Court
Stephen Breyer, Anthony M. Kennedy, Sandra Day O'Connor, David H. Souter, John Paul Stevens (writing for the Court)

Justices Dissenting
Ruth Bader Ginsburg, William H. Rehnquist, Antonin Scalia, Clarence Thomas

Place
Washington, D.C.

Date of Decision
20 May 1996

Decision
That the punitive damages award was grossly excessive, and therefore exceeded the constitutional limit.

Significance
As Justice Scalia would note in his dissenting opinion, the Court's judgment in *BMW* was in part a response to a glut of cases against businesses involving large punitive damage awards. The Court's decision, in spite of the fact that it was by a narrow 5-4 margin, signalled a shift toward placing a limit on such actions, which many in the country had come increasingly to view as excessive.

In January of 1990, Dr. Ira Gore, Jr., purchased a black BMW sports sedan for $40,750.88 from a Birmingham, Alabama BMW dealer. Nine months later, he took the car to a detailing salon, where he was informed that the vehicle had been previously repainted. Gore, who had purchased the car new, took action against the American distributor for the German car manufacturer, BMW of North America, Inc. In his suit, he demanded $500,000 in compensatory and punitive damages, plus costs.

BMW, in the ensuing trial, noted that it had a nationwide policy, which it had adopted in 1983, regarding vehicles that were damaged in transport and thus required repainting. If the cost of the damage were greater than 3 percent of the suggested retail price, the company sold the car as used; if it were less than 3 percent, however, as in Gore's case, they sold the vehicles as new and did not advise dealers that they had repainted them. Gore presented the testimony of a former BMW dealer, who estimated the damage as about 10 percent of the retail cost, or some $4,000. Gore further produced evidence indicating that since 1983, BMW had sold 983 similarly repainted cars as new—14 of them in Alabama—and that therefore the company's penalty should be the alleged cost of his own damages multiplied by the number of cars, a figure of $4 million.

The jury determined that the company's policy of nondisclosure constituted "gross, oppressive, or malicious fraud," and found BMW liable not only for Gore's compensatory damages of $4,000, but for the $4 million in punitive damages as well. BMW subsequently filed a post-trial motion to set aside the punitive damages award, and in this latter action it produced evidence showing that its policy was in line with the laws of roughly half the states in the Union. Furthermore, the company's legal counsel pointed out, its nondisclosure policy had not been found unlawful up to the time Gore filed his action. (In the months preceding the Gore trial, however, another Alabama jury, in the case of *Yates v. BMW of North America, Inc.* [1993] found that the policy constituted fraud.)

The post-trial motion was denied by the trial judge, who did not find the punitive damages award excessive. BMW appealed the case to the Alabama Supreme Court, which affirmed the judgment of the lower court. But the court did reduce the level of punitive damages to $2 million after it found that the jury had improperly computed the figure.

Three "Indicums of Excessiveness"

The Supreme Court ruled, 5-4, that even the lowered punitive damages figure was excessive. Speaking for the Court in an opinion joined by Justices O'Connor, Kennedy, Souter, and Breyer, Justice Stevens outlined a three-part test whereby the determination of excessiveness was made.

The economic penalties imposed by the state, Stevens began, must be justified by an interest in protecting its citizens and economy. Therefore Gore's reference to events that occurred outside Alabama—the repainting of cars other than the 14 within his own state—was not relevant to the case at hand. What was relevant, Justice Stevens said, was whether BMW had been given fair notice of the severity of the damages it might incur for its action in repainting the cars without notifying dealers or customers. By the three "guideposts" or indicums of excessiveness applied by the Court, it was found that the company had not been given such fair notice.

First was "the degree of reprehensibility of the defendant's conduct," which the Court found lacking. Repainting the car may have constituted economic harm to Gore, but it in no way threatened his safety. In the second test—of the ratio between compensatory damages and punitive damages—the Court found that Gore was making an excessive demand, since the $2 million punitive damage claim exceeded the $4,000 in compensatory damages by a factor of 500. Last came the test of the difference between the punitive damage award and the civil or criminal punishment that BMW could incur for its alleged misconduct. The maximum fine in Alabama in this instance was only $2,000, which further highlighted the excessiveness of the punitive damages claim.

Therefore the Court reversed the ruling of the lower court. As to whether or not "the appropriate remedy" would require a new trial, the High Court expressly left that matter up to the Alabama Supreme Court. Justice Breyer, in a concurring opinion, examined the standards applied by the Alabama courts, and found that

they were vague and "provided no significant constraints or protection against arbitrary results."

Punitive Damages Running Wild

Justice Scalia filed a dissenting opinion, in which Justice Thomas joined. "Today," he said, "we see the latest manifestation of the Court's recent and increasingly insistent "concern about punitive damages that 'run wild.'" This, however, was not a matter of the Court's concern, the justice stated, since the Constitution makes no reference to that particular manner. Furthermore, Scalia found the Court's precedent for its judgment lacking. Such precedents were relatively recent, and had occurred in rapid succession over a short period of time such that they were "too shallowly rooted to justify the Court's recent undertaking."

Nor did the Court offer anything useful, in Scalia's words, to lower courts whereby they might make more fair judgments of punitive damages in the future. Alabama was acting fully within its powers in the judgment, and the case did not properly warrant the Court's attention. Scalia concluded by stating, "By today's logic, every dispute as to evidentiary sufficiency in a state civil suit poses a question of constitutional moment, subject to review in this Court. That is a stupefying proposition."

Justice Ginsburg likewise dissented, in an opinion in which Chief Justice Rehnquist joined. In her view, the Court was "unwisely ventur[ing] into territory traditionally within the States' domain." The states themselves already had measures in place to deal with such matters, and as evidence she produced a long list of state regulations of punitive damage awards. In the case of Alabama, its own supreme court had put still further controls on the levels of punitive damages, and therefore its judgment should be allowed to stand.

Related Cases

Pacific Mutual Life Insurance Co. v. Haslip, 499 U.S. 1 (1991).
TXO Production Corp. v. Alliance Resources Corp., 509 U.S. 443, 454 (1993).
Yates v. BMW of North America, 642 So. 2d 937 (1993).
Honda Motor Co. v. Oberg, 512 U.S. 415 (1994).

Bibliography and Further Reading

Biskupic, Joan, and Elder Witt, eds. *Congressional Quarterly's Guide to the U.S. Supreme Court,* 3rd ed. Washington, DC: Congressional Quarterly, Inc., 1996.

BROIN, ET AL. V. PHILIP MORRIS INCORPORATED, ET AL.

Legal Citation: 641 So.2d 888 (1997)

Plaintiffs
Norma R. Broin, Major Mark L. Broin, and 60,000 airline flight attendants

Defendant
Philip Morris Inc. and 14 other United States tobacco companies

Plaintiffs' Claim
That the United States tobacco companies through conspiracy and fraud withheld from the pubic critical information on the health hazards of secondhand cigarette smoke.

Chief Lawyers for Plaintiffs
Stanley and Susan Rosenblatt

Chief Defense Lawyers
David L. Ross, Norman A. Coll, Robert L. Burlington, Edward A. Moss, Daniel Donahue

Judge
Robert P. Kaye

Place
Miami, Florida

Date of Decision
10 October 1997

Decision
The tobacco companies agreed to settle the injury claim before going to jury, funding a $300 million research foundation and paying $49 million in attorney fees and court costs, but not admitting to wrongdoing.

Significance
The case was the first against the tobacco industry for damages claimed from secondhand smoke. The trial served to greatly increase public awareness of the potentially serious health effects of secondhand smoke. The trial also provided surprising testimony by one tobacco company for the first time publicly admitting the health hazards of smoking tobacco. Efforts were increased in limiting exposure of the public, and particularly children, to secondhand smoke exposure.

Tobacco is a plant long used by humans in North America. American Indians smoked tobacco, a plant native to the New World, well before contact with European cultures. Commercial production of tobacco, which contains small amounts of the stimulant substance nicotine, began in the American colony of Virginia in 1612 where it quickly became an important cash crop. Cigarettes became popular in the 1880s as production technologies came of age. Early during European use of tobacco, health controversies grew. In the sixteenth century some physicians claimed tobacco use should be restricted for medicinal purposes only. The Puritans of New England banned its use. Finally, in 1964 the U.S. Surgeon General released the first official scientific findings highlighting the health hazards of smoking. The tobacco industry was suddenly on the defensive. In 1966, tobacco companies had to place warnings on cigarette packages. In 1971, advertising on radio and television was banned. By the 1980s, concerns over the breathing of the cigarette smoke of others, secondhand smoke, greatly increased. Smoking began to be prohibited in various public places including United States commercial airline flights in 1988.

Secondhand smoke is a mixture of smoke given off by the burning end of a cigarette, pipe, or cigar, and smoke exhaled by smokers. This mixture contains more than 4,000 substances, over 40 of which are known to cause cancer in humans or animals. Exposure to secondhand smoke, also referred to as environmental tobacco smoke (ETS), constituted involuntary smoking. The Environmental Protection Agency (EPA) in a 1993 report estimated 3,000 lung cancer deaths a year due to smoke exposure in American nonsmokers. According to the report, ETS exposure increased the risk of lower respiratory tract infections, including bronchitis and pneumonia. The EPA estimated ETS exposure affected between 150,000 and 300,000 infants less than 18 months of age resulting in hospitalization of between 7,500 and 15,000 infants.

Involuntary Smoking in Airline Cabins

Norma R. Broin was an airline stewardess for American Airlines since 1976. She did not smoke cigarettes, but at age 32 contracted lung cancer. Her story, unfortu-

Lawsuit Awards

There are numerous varieties of injury lawsuits, some of which may be class-action suits, others of which are clearly individual in nature. Among these varieties are suits resulting from automobile accidents, fraud, libel, medical malpractice, personal injury, product liability, professional malpractice, and property damage. In 1992, the type of lawsuit for which juries awarded the lowest median monetary award was for automobile accidents, in which the median award was about $20,000. The highest-paying were product liability suits, for which the median award was more than $200,000.

After having one settlement proposal between the states and tobacco industry fall through in 1997, a $206 billion settlement was reached between the industry and 46 states in November of 1998. Purpose of the settlement was to compensate states for the medical expenses associated with treating smoking-related diseases. Four states had previously settled individually.

Tobacco industry opponents criticized the settlement as soft on industry, since most of the monies would come from increased costs of cigarettes to the public. As a confirmation of those concerns, tobacco companies stock soared in value upon announcement of the settlement. Payments would be made by the Big Four of the tobacco industry: Philip Morris, R. J. Reynolds, Lorillard, and Brown & Williamson. The industry agreed to greatly curtail marketing efforts in return for immunity from all state and local government class action lawsuits. The settlement also contained provisions for financing a research foundation focused on youth smoking issues.

Source(s): Fast, Julius, and Timothy Fast. *The Legal Atlas of the United States.* New York: Facts on File, 1997.

"The Ifs and Buts of the Tobacco Settlement." *The New York Times,* November 29, 1998.

---

nately, was not unique among airline attendants in general, with many experiencing various forms of cancer and serious respiratory illnesses in the prime of life. In October of 1991, Norma Broin and her husband, Major Mark L. Broin of the U.S. Marine Corps, and over 25 other flight attendants and family members, filed a federal class action lawsuit. The suit was filed in the Eleventh Judicial Circuit in Dade County, Florida, against Philip Morris, several other cigarette makers, and two tobacco trade groups. All were involved in the manufacturing, distributing, and selling of cigarettes throughout the United States. The complaint was initially dismissed in May of 1992 but was reinstated after appeal by the attendants.

In May of 1994, Broin filed another revised complaint charging that exposure to secondhand tobacco smoke in airline cabins caused flight attendants to suffer from various diseases and health disorders. Broin contended the companies made dangerous and poisonous products that seriously harmed innocent bystanders. In essence, the companies, Broin charged, were guilty of conspiracy and fraud in withholding and suppressing important scientific information from the public. For over 25 years important health information had been known to the companies, yet, according to Broin, they continued to market their dangerous products through numerous popular merchandising programs. The tobacco companies denied any wrongdoing, and asserted the lawsuit was inappropriate under Florida civil law procedures.

However, in December of 1994 Judge Robert P. Kaye certified the case a class action status. The class con-

sisted of all nonsmoking flight attendants, approximately 60,000 individuals, currently or formerly employed by airline companies based in the United States who suffered from diseases and disorders attributed to their exposure to secondhand cigarette smoke in airline cabins. Health conditions listed in the claim included various cancers, including of the lung, larynx, oral cavity, esophagus, bladder, kidney, pancreas, stomach, cervix, and breast, in addition to various respiratory problems, pregnancy complications, infant mortality, and infertility. Major Broin claimed the loss of comfort and companionship of his wife.

The tobacco companies appealed the class action status but the Third District Court of Appeal affirmed the status in January of 1996. The companies then sought to block the suit by appeal to the Florida Supreme Court, but a review was denied.

Judge Kaye split the trial into two stages. Stage I would concentrate on questions common to the airline employees such as the general connection between smoking and diseases experienced by nonsmokers and general conduct of the tobacco companies. Stage II would focus on individual attendants and their proof of injury. To ultimately receive damage awards, the airline attendants would have to personally present specific evidence in the Miami court, then wait until all other attendants had presented their cases and final rulings were issued, and all appeals were completed.

Stage I proceedings began in June of 1997 with jury selection. The flight attendants then presented their arguments and evidence to the jury until late September. Testimony for the defendants included appearances by two former U.S. Surgeons General and top physicians, researchers, and aircraft designers. Testimony claimed cigarette smoke contained lead, formaldehyde, benzene, and numerous other known cancer-causing chemicals. The tobacco companies then began their response claiming the attendants suffered diseases no more frequently than the general public and the amount of secondhand smoke they inhaled was minor. The companies contended that flight attendants spent only around 12 hours a week closed in airline cabins. A surprising acknowledgment of the harm of cigarettes came during the trial when cigarette manufacturer Liggett admitted that smoking was addictive and causes lung cancer and many other diseases. Such admission was the first historically from a member of the tobacco industry. But, before completing their presentations a settlement was unexpectedly reached with the attendants on 10 October 1997. Settlement had been reached before any interim court decisions as a request by both sides had been made by Kaye. Kaye found the proposed settlement agreement fair and reasonable pending further discussions at a final settlement hearing.

A Landmark Settlement

Four of the tobacco companies, Philip Morris, R. J. Reynolds, Lorillard, and Brown & Williamson agreed to pay $300 million over three years to establish and fund a nonprofit research foundation. The foundation would support scientific research on the early detection and cure of diseases associated with cigarette smoking. Ultimately, the research was hoped to benefit flight attendants suffering such diseases. The foundation, free from all active tobacco company control, was to be managed and directed by a board of trustees partly composed of selected flight attendants. The four companies also agreed to support federal legislation prohibiting smoking on all nonstop regularly scheduled international flights originating or terminating in the United States. The companies, asserting they merely wanted to avoid the expense of a long trial, denied any wrongdoing or violation of law.

As a key part of the settlement, individual flight attendants of the class action suit and their survivors retained the right to pursue separate lawsuits for damage awards from the four companies. The settlement agreement dismissed all other claims against all of the other tobacco companies involved in the case, including Liggett, the Tobacco Institute, Inc., and the Council for Tobacco Research-U.S.A. The settlement agreement, of course, did not affect the attendants' rights to make claims against any other parties not a part of the case.

An attendant could choose to bring a lawsuit in her home jurisdiction or the Eleventh Judicial Circuit of Dade County, Florida. A concern of the companies was how the court would apply the various laws of the 50 states to the individual attendants. The amount of recoverable damages for the individual attendants would vary from state to state. For example, in Florida damages were not subject to dollar restrictions for physical injury in addition to less tangible damages including pain and suffering, disfigurement, loss of enjoyment of life, and disability. Some states had limits for the intangible damages. As a key part of the settlement, the companies waived all relevant statutes of limitations throughout the United States for any potential individual lawsuits filed by class attendants and their survivors for past injury, but the lawsuits had to be filed within a year after the settlement. The class included flight attendants employed back to the 1930s.

The tobacco companies also agreed to a significant shift in legal responsibility for the potential individual lawsuits. The companies assumed the burden of proof to demonstrate a lack of connection between secondhand smoke and the specific cases of cancer and other chronic respiratory ailments. Normally such responsibility would be the attendant's for proving particular diseases or medical conditions resulted from secondhand cigarette smoke in airline cabins. Numerous law firms offered their availability to represent the attendants with continuing technical assistance from the *Broin* lawyers. Also, any evidence presented to the jury in *Broin* would be treated as live witness testimony.

Lastly, the four tobacco companies also agreed to reimburse the attendants for all their legal and other expenses as part of *Broin* which involved over six years of activity. The amount was over $46 million.

Impact

Under the settlement, individual attendant received no monetary compensation. But the tobacco industry pledged to establish the Broin Research Foundation with a goal of seeking cures for diseases attributed to tobacco smoke and to develop methods of early detection. A verdict against the tobacco industry could have been used as evidence at future trials. Instead, the companies chose a settlement, which rarely includes admissions of wrongdoing.

Broin was the first case in which nonsmokers claimed injury against the tobacco industry and was the first tobacco class action case to reach trial. A common defense argument by tobacco companies in death and injury claims brought by smokers was that the individuals freely chose to use the product and be exposed to the smoke. However, *Broin* solely involved nonsmokers exposed to secondhand smoke in the work place. The nation's leading cigarette makers for the first time lacked their usual key defense. Prior to *Broin*, the tobacco industry had never paid damages in a product-liability case.

Potential settlements between industry and states dominated the news in 1997 and 1998. An initial effort at a settlement for industry to compensate states for medical costs associated with smoking fell through when Congress refused to approve the deal which called for federal legislation. Later state settlement proposals avoided involving Congress and potential legislation that would begin regulating nicotine as a drug. Finally, the states and the tobacco industry reached a settlement in November of 1998. Even in light of this, private parties continued to take the tobacco companies to task for their roles in the failing health of smoking Americans. In February of 1999, a San Francisco jury awarded $50 million in punitive damages to a former Marlboro smoker who blamed Philip Morris for the lack of serious warning both when she started smoking at 15 and all throughout her "smoking career." While many of these cases have been appealed and later lost or settled out of court, the *Washington Post* quoted legal analysts who predicted the California appeals courts would be "reluctant to overrule" the decision.

Despite a heightened public awareness of health hazards resulting from tobacco use and increased initiatives to eliminate cigarette smoking from public places, a 1998 study by the Harvard School of Public Health indicated smoking among college students increased by 28 percent between 1993 and 1997. In reaction, President Bill Clinton in his 1999 State of the Union address vowed to fight the industry through federal lawsuits.

Related Cases

State of Mississippi et al. v. American Tobacco Co. et al., Cause No. 94-1429 (1991).

State of Florida et al. v. American Tobacco Co. et al., Civil Action No. 95-1466 AH, 15th Judicial Cir. (1997).

Bibliography and Further Reading

Glantz, Stanton A. *The Cigarette Papers.* Berkeley: University of California Press, 1996.

Kluger, Richard. *Ashes to ashes : America's Hundred-Year Cigarette War, the Public Health, and the Unabashed Triumph of Philip Morris.* New York: Alfred A. Knopf, 1996.

Koven, Edward L. *Smoking: The Story Behind the Haze.* New York: Nova Science Publishers, 1998.

Mollenkamp, Carrick. *The People vs. Big Tobacco: How the States Took on the Cigarette Giants.* Princeton: Bloomberg Press, 1998.

DRUG LAWS

Drugs: A Simple Definition

The term "drugs" is an extraordinarily broad one, which can encompass such a great variety of items that the meaning of the word almost becomes lost. Even *Webster's Dictionary* offers a variety of definitions which distinguish between (usually legal) medications intended to treat a specific physiological or psychological problem and (usually illegal) substances which are used recreationally, and whose use may lead to addiction.

A simple, all-encompassing definition of a drug would be "a substance containing chemicals which result in a specific physical or psychological reaction or reactions." This, at least, is as much true of penicillin, a drug which has saved millions of lives, as it is of cocaine—a drug which, especially in the latter part of the twentieth century, has claimed a death toll in the hundreds of thousands if not the millions.

Drugs, Culture, and Death

Of course, it is worth noting in this context that the body count created by cocaine is at least partially composed of persons who die as a result of illegally trafficking of the substance. There are the drug lords, the pushers, and the dealers, who enter into ultimately fatal encounters with each other or with law enforcement officers; and there are the law enforcement personnel themselves who die in shootouts with their counterparts on the other side of the law. Besides these, there are also "mules," persons low on the dealing hierarchy, who die as the result of foolhardy smuggling schemes—for instance, by swallowing a condom filled with cocaine, which bursts in the intestinal tract and results in an instantaneous overdose.

Cocaine makes a particularly useful example of the human cost created by an illegal substance. Not only is it exceedingly harmful and addictive, its use has remained high in the United States since the 1970s, and it crosses class and racial lines. In the 1970s, cocaine use was associated with a hedonistic urban lifestyle, yet as fashions changed in the much more serious-minded 1980s, the character of cocaine use changed without any diminishment in the degree of prevalence. If anything, its use increased among upwardly mobile "Yup-pies," who enjoyed the drug because it seemingly gave them more energy, creativity, and vitality.

These promises, of course, were illusory. Hence a public service commercial of the era depicted a well-dressed Yuppie type—someone who could easily have been a Wall Street broker—in a tiny, box-like room, much like a rat in a cage; as he moved around and around the room, from wall to wall, a voice-over stated that "Cocaine helps you work harder, so you can earn more money, so you can buy more cocaine, so you can work harder. . . ." Perhaps even more disturbing was the spread of the drug's use among the urban underclass, facilitated by the adaptation of a cheap cocaine derivative called crack in the mid-1980s. Crack was instantly addictive, or very nearly so, and its spread resulted in a massive upsurge in crime.

The War on Drugs

By the time crack appeared on the scene, the federal government had long been engaged in a massive "War on Drugs." The cause came increasingly to public attention during the 1980s, when First Lady Nancy Reagan took it up, and promoted it with the slogan "Just Say No." The latter injunction was geared mostly toward children, who were often vulnerable not only to peer pressure, but to the persuasion of dealers eager to gain more customers. The "Just Say No" campaign did not, however, address another and perhaps equally insidious inducement, the lure of the drug trade itself, which offered instant wealth to young people from disadvantaged backgrounds, who saw little or no hope of attaining comparable rewards by legal means.

At the law enforcement level, the War on Drugs—which had actually begun in the mid-1960s, when recreational drug use began to increase dramatically—involved enormous efforts on the part of numerous federal and local agencies. Most notable among these was the Drug Enforcement Agency (DEA), whose energies were primarily directed toward intercepting drug shipments to the United States. Federal officials had identified south Florida as a principal gateway for cocaine and marijuana from the South American nation of Colombia, which was virtually dominated by drug lords such as Pablo Escobar. In the 1980s and 1990s, millions of kilos of illegal drugs were intercepted and destroyed, and thousands of persons involved in the drug trade were captured and incarcerated. These included Escobar himself, reputed to be the richest man in the world; Panamanian dictator Manuel Noriega, captured in a raid directed by President Bush in 1989; and other prominent figures such as Colombian narcotics kingpin Carlos Lehder.

Despite these successes, critics of U.S. policy pointed out that for every kilo that the DEA captured, many more made it in via plane or boat, or by some other means. Likewise they noted that for every Escobar, there were hundreds of "mules," far less culpable figures drawn into the drug trade by poverty, who paid for their transgressions with life sentences. By the early 1990s, the War on Drugs more or less came to an end: though the government remained committed to stopping the importation, sale, or use of illegal drugs, the days of fervent crusading were over. After the 1993 inauguration of President Bill Clinton, who claimed he had smoked marijuana in college but "didn't inhale," there was little further suggestion that the federal government intended to "win" a war against the drug trade.

Earlier Wars and Racial Questions

This was not the first or only "War on Drugs": "The late 1800s," as James Bovard noted in *Lost Rights: The Destruction of American Liberty,* "saw a national panic over opium, orchestrated in part by U.S. labor unions fearful of low-wage Chinese competition." In fact a number of these drug wars, in the view of Bovard and other critics of federal policy, have had a racial or xenophobic component. *Insight* magazine in the 1980s ran a cover story on "The First War on Drugs," a campaign against cocaine use in the 1910s. At that time, the drug had many prominent advocates, including Sigmund Freud, who promoted its potential for medicine. Likewise the original formula of Coca-Cola contained cocaine, and it may be remembered that Sir Arthur Conan Doyle's fictional creation, the great detective Sherlock Holmes, enhanced his crime-solving ability with regular doses of the drug. But as Bovard wrote, "A backlash against cocaine arose partly because of the drug's popularity with blacks." Hence in 1910, a report presented by a Presidential commission referred to cocaine as "a potent incentive in driving the humbler negroes all over the country to abnormal crimes."

These fears led to the passage of the Harrison Act in 1914, the first significant anti-drug measure by the federal government. The act also spawned the first arguments against the criminalization of drugs on the grounds that it created new crimes: thus a commentary in a 1915 medical journal listed among "the really serious results of this legislation" the fact that "There will be the failures of promising careers, the disrupting of happy families, the commission of crimes which will

never be traced to their real cause, and the influx of many who would otherwise live socially competent lives into hospitals for the mentally disoriented." The Harrison Act, according to Robert Schess in a 1925 *American Mercury* article, "made the drug peddler, and the drug peddler makes drug addicts."

Meanwhile, the federal government had entered into yet another war on drugs, perhaps larger in relative proportions than the one in the late twentieth century. It was called Prohibition, and it began with the adoption of the Eighteenth Amendment, forbidding the manufacture, sale, and consumption of alcohol, in 1919. During the 14 years that followed, ending with the adoption of the Twenty-first Amendment—the only constitutional amendment which directly nullifies a preceding one—in 1933, many people continued to drink alcohol, only they did so now illegally. As many people know, this led to a large crime wave made particularly memorable by colorful figures on both sides of the law: bootleggers and crime bosses such as Al Capone, and law-enforcement officials such as Elliot Ness.

Less well-known, however, is the impact Prohibition may have had with regard to another drug: marijuana. The latter was still legal in the 1920s, when the federal Department of Agriculture encouraged farmers to grow it for its use in making rope; thus Prohibition resulted in an unusual situation whereby it was (by default, at least) legal to smoke marijuana, but illegal to consume alcohol. Yet again, however, racial fears played a part in anti-drug legislation. The Great Depression brought an influx of Mexican immigrants, and according to Bovard and others, "Hostility toward the immigrants"—who often worked for much lower wages than American citizens—led to the passage of the Marijuana Tax Act of 1937. Many of these immigrants smoked marijuana, and in any case their homeland was and is a major producer of the drug. Likewise marijuana use was associated in the popular mind with African Americans; hence a Yale professor later observed that the Marijuana Tax Act "mostly put a lot of jazz bands in jail."

Continuing Legal Questions

A more recent chapter in the saga of drugs and race came in the mid-1990s, with proposals to make penalties for crack sales and usage much higher than those for cocaine. Civil Rights leaders decried this initiative as racist, citing the fact that whereas most cocaine users are white and middle class, the majority of crack users are poor and African American. Advocates of the sentencing laws, by contrast, held that race had nothing to do with it: crack is even more dangerous than cocaine, and therefore its manufacture, sale, and use should be treated with even greater seriousness. Whereas opponents demanded that crack penalties be reduced to the same level as those for cocaine, few suggested a third alternative: *raising* the cocaine penalties to be equal with those for crack.

Clearly not all drugs are the same, and this principle is embodied in the Controlled Substance Act, passed in 1970 in response to the growth of recreational drug use. The act separates drugs into five "schedules" based on a number of criteria that include the drug's potential for abuse, its pharmacological effects, current scientific knowledge regarding it, and other factors. LSD, heroin, and marijuana belong to Schedule I, drugs which have a high potential for abuse, a "lack of accepted safety," and no currently accepted medical use. By contrast, PCP, cocaine, morphine, and methamphetamine belong to Schedule II, because they do have currently accepted medical uses. By the late 1990s, a number of states had passed initiatives allowing medical use of marijuana, which is useful in treatment of glaucoma and other diseases, but the drug was not moved to Schedule II. The remaining three schedules consist of legal drugs, and are based on increasingly diminishing abuse potential, with the lowest level, Schedule V, consisting of such items as over-the-counter cough medicine containing codeine.

Among the constitutional issues relating to drug use that remained in the forefront during the 1980s and 1990s were Fourth and Fifth Amendment questions regarding drug testing and search and seizure. Particularly potent topics included mandatory urinalysis and drug testing, and "knock and announce" rules requiring police to knock and announce their authority and purpose before entering a home with the intent to seize drugs, as in *Richards v. Wisconsin* (1997), for instance. Government power to seize the assets of persons convicted of drug sale or manufacture was on the rise, a fact evidenced by the Supreme Court's rulings in the 1996 cases of *United States v. Ursery* and *Bennis v. Michigan*. These rulings have in turn raised an outcry from civil libertarians, who hold that anti-drug policy is abused as a means of increasing government control over the citizenry.

The debate over legalization continues. Advocates come from the left, including a number of civil liberties groups, and from the right: conservative pundit William F. Buckley, whose magazine, the *National Review*, devoted its February 12, 1996, issue to the topic, is among the most outspoken proponents of legalization. U.S. Superior Court Judge James P. Gray, in a Spring 1994 *Police News* article, presented logic that echoed that of Schess nearly 70 years before: criminal-

ization, he wrote, did nothing to address the desire for drugs on the part of its users, and the difficulty of obtaining illegal substances greatly increased the economic inducements to engage in the drug trade. According to Gray, if drugs were legalized, "Without a doubt, some people will continue to buy and abuse drugs. . . . However, since there would be no incentive to 'push' these drugs . . . the usage should not be above the present rate, and probably, after a possible initial surge, would be materially reduced."

But just as there are compelling arguments for legalization, likewise there are persuasive ones against it, particularly where "hard drugs" such as heroin, cocaine, and crack are concerned. Under the present situation, a recovering drug addict would undoubtedly find it relatively easy to remove him or herself from an environment in which drugs are readily available, whereas if he or she could obtain cocaine at the local drug store, the temptation to relapse might be much higher. In any case, all sides generally agree on two points: recreational drug use is not going away, and most of the government's initiatives to stop it have failed to produce a substantial and lasting decrease in the drug trade.

See also: Search and Seizure

Bibliography and Further Reading
Boire, Richard Glen. *Marijuana Law*. Berkeley, CA: Ronin Publishing, 1993.

Bovard, James. *Lost Rights: The Destruction of American Liberty*. New York: St. Martin's, 1994.

Buckley, William F. "Abolish the Drug Laws? 400 Readers Give Their Views." http://turnpike.net/~jnr/nr0796.htm.

"Controlled Substance Act." http://www.mninter.net/~publish/csa2.htm.

Gray, James P. "Our Drug Laws Have Failed." *Police News*, Spring 1994.

Grosshandler, Janet, and Ruth Rosen. *Drugs and the Law*. Rosen Publishing Group, 1997.

Shulgin, Alexandra T. *Controlled Substances: A Chemical and Legal Guide to the Federal Drug Laws*, 2nd ed. Berkeley, CA: Ronin Publishing, 1992.

Uelmen, Gerald F., and Victor G. Haddox. *Drug Abuse and the Law*. New York: Clark Boardman, 1990.

DRAPER V. UNITED STATES

Legal Citation: 358 U.S. 307 (1959)

Petitioner
James Draper

Respondent
United States

Petitioner's Claim
That the search of petitioner and seizure of heroin following his warrantless arrest by a federal narcotics agent violated the Fourth Amendment because the arrest was based solely on information from a paid informant.

Chief Lawyer for Petitioner
Osmond K. Fraenkel

Chief Lawyer for Respondent
Leonard B. Sand

Justices for the Court
Hugo Lafayette Black, William J. Brennan, Jr., Tom C. Clark, John Marshall Harlan II, Potter Stewart, Charles Evans Whittaker (writing for the Court)

Justices Dissenting
William O. Douglas (Felix Frankfurter and Earl Warren did not participate)

Place
Washington, D.C.

Date of Decision
26 January 1959

Decision
Upheld the lower courts' ruling that petitioner's arrest and the subsequent search of petitioner which turned up heroin were lawful, and affirmed his conviction.

Significance
This decision authorized a warrantless arrest by a federal narcotic agent under the federal narcotics laws based solely on information from a paid informant. Because the informant was employed by the agent to provide such information and his information had always been reliable in the past, the informant's statements to the agent, once verified by the agent's personal observations, gave the agent probable cause and reasonable grounds to believe that petitioner was violating the narcotics law. Since the arrest of petitioner was lawful, the subsequent search which turned up heroin was also valid as incident to the lawful arrest.

In 1791, the states ratified the Fourth Amendment to the U.S. Constitution, prohibiting unreasonable searches and seizures and requiring probable cause for warrants. The newly independent states had learned through their experience with English law that the power to make arrests, searches, and seizures was open to abuse. English writs of assistance and general warrants, which allowed police to search and arrest based on mere suspicion without evidence of unlawful acts, had been exercised by English authorities arbitrarily and for political reasons. "Probable cause" is not defined in the Fourth Amendment, and its meaning has been the subject of numerous U.S. Supreme Court rulings. In 1959, the Supreme Court was asked to decide whether information from a paid informant was sufficient to show "probable cause" for a warrantless arrest.

In 1956, petitioner was arrested by a federal narcotics agent based on information given to the agent by a paid informant. A subsequent search of petitioner uncovered heroin. Petitioner was charged in federal district court with knowingly concealing and transporting narcotic drugs in violation of federal law. The district court overruled the petitioner's motion to suppress, or exclude from evidence, the heroin taken from him during the search. The motion claimed that the arrest and subsequent search were unlawful. At trial, the heroin was allowed into evidence over petitioner's objection, and he was convicted. The Court of Appeals for the Tenth Circuit affirmed the conviction. Petitioner sought a writ of *certiorari* from the U.S. Supreme Court, a method by which the Supreme Court is asked to review a lower court decision. The Supreme Court agreed to review the case.

Informant Provided "Reasonable Grounds"

The Supreme Court affirmed the lower courts' rulings that the search of petitioner and seizure of the heroin were valid as incident to a lawful arrest and that the heroin was properly admitted at trial. The Fourth Amendment requires "probable cause" for an arrest. Under the federal Narcotic Control Act of 1956, agents of the Bureau of Narcotics were permitted to "make arrests without warrant for violations of any law of the United States relating to narcotic drugs . . . [if the arrest-

Marijuana Use and Drug Legalization

In 1973, on the heels of the drug-culture explosion that attended the late 1960s and early 1970s, the National Opinion Research Center asked a sampling of the population, "Do you think the use of marijuana should be made legal or not?"

- Eighteen percent answered that it should, 80 percent that it should not.

- The percentage who wanted to legalize marijuana increased for each year up to and including 1978, when the ratio stood at 30:67.

- Then the number in favor began to decrease, and from 1986 until 1991 it remained at or below the 1973 levels.

- From 1991 the percentage in favor began to rise again, and by 1996 it was at 26 percent, the highest number since the high of 1978.

Interestingly, the Department of Health and Human Services' National Household Survey on Drug Abuse (NHSDA), found an overall decrease in drug use between 1985 and 1996.

- In 1985, 16.3 percent of respondents claimed to have used an illicit drug during the preceding year, and 13.6 percent had smoked marijuana or hashish.

- Eleven years later, however, only 10.8 percent in 1996 claimed to have used illicit drugs in the past year, and just 8.6 percent had smoked marijuana.

Source(s): *Bureau of Justice Statistics Sourcebook of Criminal Justice Statistics-1996.* Washington, DC: U.S. Government, 1997.

---

ing person] has reasonable grounds to believe that the person to be arrested has committed or is committing such violation." Thus, the "crucial question" for the Court was whether knowledge of the related facts and circumstances gave the agent who arrested petitioner "probable cause" within the meaning of the Fourth Amendment, and "reasonable grounds" within the meaning of the Narcotic Control Act, to believe that petitioner had committed or was committing a violation of the narcotic laws. According to the Court, if "probable cause" and "reasonable grounds" existed, the arrest, though without a warrant, was lawful and the subsequent search of petitioner's person and the seizure of the heroin were validly made incident to a lawful arrest. Moreover, if the arrest, search, and seizure were valid, the motion to suppress was properly overruled and the heroin was competently received in evidence at trial.

The petitioner did not dispute this analysis of the issue, but instead asserted that the information from the paid informant was "hearsay," meaning that the information did not reflect the direct personal observations of the agent, but was obtained secondhand from the informant. The petitioner claimed that "hearsay" information could not be considered in determining "probable cause" or "reasonable grounds." The petitioner also argued that, even if hearsay could be considered, the information given to the agent in this case was insufficient to show "probable cause" or "reasonable grounds." The Supreme Court first determined that "probable cause" and "reasonable grounds" had substantially the same meaning. The Court then ruled, as to petitioner's first contention, that *Brinegar v. United States* (1949), had conclusively determined that evi-

dence that is inadmissible to show guilt at trial, such as hearsay, may nonetheless be used to determine probable cause. Quoting from *Brinegar*, the Court explained that "[t]here is a large difference between . . . [guilt and probable cause], as well as between the tribunals which determine them, and therefore a like difference in the quanta and modes of proof required to establish them."

The Court also disagreed with petitioner's second contention that the information given to the agent by the informant was insufficient to show "probable cause" and "reasonable grounds" to believe that petitioner had violated or was violating the narcotic laws and to justify his arrest without a warrant. The informant identified petitioner by name and told the agent that the petitioner was peddling narcotics, had gone to Chicago to obtain a supply, and would return on a certain train on a certain day or the day after. The informant also gave the agent a detailed physical description of petitioner and of the clothing he was wearing and said that he would be carrying "a tan zipper bag," and that he habitually "walked real fast." The agent met the train on both days identified by the informant and on the second day saw a person, having the exact physical attributes and wearing the precise clothing described by [the informant], alight from an incoming Chicago train and start walking "fast" toward the exit. He was carrying a tan zipper bag in his right hand.

The Court concluded that, although the informant's information may have been "hearsay" to the agent, the agent would have been derelict in his duties had he not pursued it since the informant was employed for that purpose and his information had always been found accurate and reliable. Moreover, by the time of the arrest, the agent had personally verified through his own observations every facet of the information given to him by the informant except whether petitioner had narcotics. The Court concluded that "surely, with every other bit of [the informant's] information being thus personally verified, [the agent] had 'reasonable grounds' to believe that the remaining unverified bit of [the informant's] information—that [petitioner] would have the heroin with him—was likewise true." The Court stated that, "In dealing with probable cause, . . . as the very name implies, we deal with probabilities. These are not technical; they are the factual and practical considerations of everyday life on which reasonable and prudent men, not legal technicians, act."

The Supreme Court upheld the state courts' rulings that the agent had probable cause and reasonable grounds to believe that petitioner was violating drug laws at the time he arrested petitioner, that the arrest was therefore lawful, and that the subsequent search and seizure were likewise valid, as incident to that lawful arrest. The Court also affirmed the trial court's denial of petitioner's motion to suppress and the use of the seized heroin to convict petitioner.

Dissent Says Arrest Unlawful

Justice Douglas issued a lengthy dissent in which he concluded that the arrest made on the mere word of an informer violated the spirit of the Fourth Amendment and the requirement of the law governing arrests in narcotics cases. According to Douglas, "apart from those cases where the crime is committed in the presence of the officer, arrests without warrants, like searches without warrants, are the exception, not the rule in our society." Justice Douglas considered the majority's ruling a break from America's long history of opposition to arrests based on "whispered charges and accusations . . . in lieu of evidence of unlawful acts." Douglas stated, "[d]own to this day . . . [s]o far as I can ascertain the mere word of an informer, not bolstered by some evidence that a crime had been or was being committed, has never been approved by this Court as 'reasonable grounds' for making an arrest without a warrant."

Although Justice Douglas agreed with the majority that "proof of 'reasonable grounds' for believing a crime was being committed need not be proof admissible at the trial," he nonetheless concluded that "[m]ere suspicion is not enough; there must be circumstances represented to the officers through the testimony of their senses sufficient to justify them in a good-faith belief that the defendant had violated the law." According to Douglas,

[n]othing but suspicion is shown in the instant case—suspicion of an informer, not that of the arresting officers. Nor did they seek to obtain from the informer any information on which he based his belief. The arresting officers did not have a bit of evidence that the petitioner

had committed or was committing a crime before the arrest. The only evidence of guilt was provided by the arrest itself.

Douglas contended that had the arresting officers gone to a

magistrate to get a warrant of arrest and relied solely on the report of the informer, it is not conceivable . . . that one would be granted . . . [because] they could not present to the magistrate any of the facts which the informer may have had. They could swear only to the fact that the informer had made the accusation.

Douglas concluded that, "[w]e are not justified in lowering the standard when an arrest is made without a warrant and allowing the officers more leeway than we grant the magistrate."

Also, this arrest could not be sanctioned based on the heroin that was uncovered during the search of petitioner after the arrest. "[A] search is not to be made legal by what it turns up. In law it is good or bad when it starts and does not change character from its success."

Impact

Police use of informants to obtain information on criminal activity has become common practice in the United States since *Draper*. The *Draper* decision encouraged the use of paid informants by allowing police to use information obtained from such informants as the basis for making arrests as long as police take time to personally verify or corroborate the information to the extent possible. *Draper* also established a definition of "probable cause" based on common sense, rather than technical rules, a definition still in use in the 1990s.

Related Cases

Nathanson v. United States, 290 U.S. 41 (1933).
United States v. Di Re, 332 U.S. 581 (1948).
Brinegar v. United States, 338 U.S. 160 (1949).
Ker v. California, 374 U.S. 23 (1963).
Aguilar v. Texas, 378 U.S. 108 (1964).
Spinelli v. United States, 393 U.S. 410 (1969).
United States v. Chadwick, 433 U.S. 1 (1977).
Illinois v. Gates, 462 U.S. 213 (1983).

Bibliography and Further Reading

Criminal Justice Legal Foundation. http://www.cjlf.org.

Criminal Law Links-Reference Desk. http://dpa.state.ky.us/~rwheeler/libarch.htm.

National Archive of Criminal Justice Data. http://www.icpsr.umich.edu/nacjd.

National Archives and Records Administration. http://www.nara.gov.

National Association of Criminal Defense Lawyers. http://www.criminaljustice.org.

ROBINSON v. CALIFORNIA

Legal Citation: 370 U.S. 660 (1962)

Petitioner
Lawrence Robinson

Respondent
State of California

Petitioner's Claim
That the state violated his Eighth and Fourteenth Amendment rights, which protect him from cruel and unusual punishment, because the state of California sentenced him to 90 days in jail for having a drug addiction.

Chief Lawyer for Petitioner
S. Carter McMorris

Chief Lawyer for Respondent
William E. Doran

Justices for the Court
Hugo Lafayette Black, William J. Brennan, Jr., William O. Douglas, John Marshall Harlan II, Potter Stewart (writing for the Court), Earl Warren

Justices Dissenting
Tom C. Clark, Byron R. White (Felix Frankfurter did not participate)

Place
Washington, D.C.

Date of Decision
25 June 1962

Decision
The Court decided to reverse the lower courts' rulings, holding that the sentence violated Robinson's Eighth and Fourteenth Amendment rights to be free from cruel and unusual punishment. The Court reasoned that Robinson's sentence was like imprisoning people for having a mental illness, a venereal disease, or leprosy and maintained that drug laws should strive to prevent the sale, use, and possession of illegal drugs, but not punish people with the status of having a drug addiction.

Significance
Initially with this case, the U.S. Supreme Court took a strong stand on what constituted a crime and what did not. Here the Court in effect said that states cannot punish people for behavior stemming from a condition beyond their control. However, after subsequent decisions such as *Powell v. Texas* (1968) the Court moved away from this position, reducing the *Robinson* decision to simply a ban that prohibits states from punishing people for having a status or condition. Nonetheless, the decision helped eliminate status-based crimes such as vagrancy and homelessness.

Under California law, the state could convict people for having a narcotic addiction and a jury in the Municipal Court of Los Angeles convicted Lawrence Robinson of having an illegal drug addiction in 1962. The evidence against Robinson came from reports by two Los Angeles police officers, including an unorthodox search of him on a street in Los Angeles by one of the officers. The first police officer greeted Robinson and proceeded to question and search him without any provocation or apparent suspicion. During the course of this incident, the police officer examined Robinson's arm and noticed scars and discoloration on the inside of his arm as well as what the officer took to be multiple needle marks. The officer also testified that Robinson admitted he used narcotics on occasion. He eventually arrested him and held him in jail.

The second police officer testified that he also observed the scabs and discoloration on Robinson's arm the morning after his arrest. In addition, this officer identified photographs taken of Robinson's arm, which showed the scabs and discoloration. As a ten-year veteran of the Narcotics Division of the Los Angeles Police Department, this officer argued that "these marks and the discoloration were the result of the injection of hypodermic needles into the tissue of the vein that was not sterile." Furthermore, he told the jury that Robinson was not intoxicated by narcotics when he examined him and that he did not seem to be experiencing any withdraw symptoms.

However, Robinson testified that he had not admitted to using narcotics to the police and argued that he never used or was addicted to any drugs. He attributed the scabs and discoloration to an allergic condition he got while in the military. Moreover, two witnesses confirmed Robinson's testimony.

The judge in the trial explained to the jury that California law considered it a misdemeanor to use narcotics or to be addicted to the use of narcotics. The law distinguished between the act of using narcotics and the status or condition of being addicted to the use of narcotics. The state viewed a charge of use as a one time offense, but a charge of addiction as a continuous offense until the user reformed. The judge also instructed the jury that it could convict Robinson under

The Anti-Drug Abuse Act of 1986

The Anti-Drug Abuse Act of 1986 would, during the 1990s, attract controversy due to the wide disparity between the penalties it placed on the distribution of crack cocaine as compared with those for powder cocaine. Because crack is less expensive than cocaine, and thus more popular among inner-city youths, critics charged that the establishment of the same penalty for selling one gram of crack as for selling 100 grams of cocaine was inherently racist.

At the center of the act were two tiers of mandatory prison terms for first-time drug traffickers. For what Congress called "serious offenders," or "the managers of the retail-level traffic," there was a mandatory minimum of five years. For "major traffickers," that is "the manufacturers or the heads of organizations who are responsible for creating and delivering very large quantities," the mandatory minimum was ten years. Differentiation between the levels of offense was based on quantity and type of drug being sold.

Though the act clearly seems to be imbalanced with regard to the penalties for crack and cocaine, there is little reason to believe that its sponsors were motivated by racism. Rather, the act happened to come to Congress's attention at a high point of national concern over drugs in general, crack in particular.

Source(s): "Report on Cocaine and Federal Sentencing Policy." United States Sentencing Commission, http://www.ussc.gov.

a general verdict, if it determined that Robinson either had the condition of being addicted to narcotics or he used narcotics while in Los Angeles. The jury ultimately convicted Robinson under the general verdict and he was sentenced to 90 days in prison.

Robinson appealed the decision to the Los Angeles County Superior Court, which although it had some reservations about the constitutionality of narcotics addiction as crime, nonetheless upheld Robinson's conviction. The Los Angeles County Superior Court based its decision on two previous state cases that questioned the constitutionality of the law where the court had also upheld it.

Cruel and Unusual Punishment

Robinson then petitioned the U.S. Supreme Court, arguing that the law violated his Eighth and Fourteenth Amendment rights, because it punished him for having a drug addiction. In a 6-2 decision, the Court made it clear that it did not want to interfere with the regulation of illegal drugs in the states, because it felt the states could control the traffic of illegal drugs by a host of valid methods. Writing for the majority, Justice Stewart urged that despite the states' independence in deciding on appropriate methods to control the spread and addiction to narcotics, the states had to respect the rights provided by the Constitution made applicable to the states through the Fourteenth Amendment.

The majority reasoned that because the court could have convicted Robinson even if it did not have evidence that he used narcotics while in Los Angeles, the law could punish him for merely having the addiction. Since the jury convicted him under the general verdict, which did not separate the use from the addiction, the majority believed that the jury could have found Robinson guilty for having the signs of a drug addiction alone. The Court argued that the law violated Robinson's rights, because it could convict him for having the status or condition of being a drug addict, and not for using, possessing, selling, or manufacturing drugs. Furthermore, the majority contended that punishing people for simply having a drug addiction was tantamount to punishing them for having a mental illness or a disease.

However, Justices Clark and White dissented, maintaining respectively that the California law actually provided treatment, not punishment, under the appropriate interpretation and that the states have the power to imprison people for illegal drug use and addiction through the criminal justice system. Justice Clark felt that in the proper context the law did not punish people for drug addictions, because the state felt the confinement was a time for the addict to break the addiction. Moreover, he argued that the state has another statute for more serious addicts where sentences range from three months to two years in a state hospital. Justice White, on the other hand, argued that Robinson's sentence was not a punishment for his status, but for being a regular, habitual user of narcotics right before his arrest, which California law prohibits. Justice White supported the conviction because Robinson had to use and possess narcotics in order to use them repeatedly or to be an addict.

The Consequences

This decision began to pave the way for the elimination of status based crimes and reduced prosecution of people for conduct caused by a condition out of their control, according to Ronald J. Allen in *Journal of Crim-*

inal Law and Criminology. However, *Powell v. Texas* put an end to the latter kind of interpretation, leaving the *Robinson* case with only one common reading: the ban on the punishment for and the criminalization of a status or condition. In this case, the Court found that even though chronic alcoholism is a disease that destroys the will power of the afflicted, alcoholism cannot be used as a defense against a charge, because the compulsion to drink is not completely overpowering. Nonetheless, this decision rendered laws that punished vagrants and homeless people invalid in the 1970s, but as homelessness escalated in the 1980s and 1990s some states tried to bypass the *Robinson* ruling by outlawing activities that accompany homelessness such as sleeping in doorways and public places.

Related Cases

Jacobson v. Massachusetts, 197 U.S. 11 (1905).
Whipple v. Martinson, 256 U.S. 41 (1921).
Powell v. Texas, 392 U.S. 514 (1968).

Bibliography and Further Reading

Allen, Ronald J. "Montana v. Egelhoff—Reflections on the Limits of Legislative Imagination and Judicial Authority." *Journal of Criminal Law & Criminology,* spring 1997, p. 633.

Balkin, J. M. "The Constitution of Status." *Yale Law Journal,* June 1997, p. 2313.

Walters, Edward J. "No Way Out: Eighth Amendment Protection for Do-or-Die Acts of the Homeless." *The University of Chicago Law Review,* fall 1995, p. 1619.

MICHIGAN V. LONG

Legal Citation: 463 U.S. 1032 (1983)

Petitioner
State of Michigan

Respondent
David Long

Petitioner's Claim
That the Michigan Supreme Court had erred in overturning Long's conviction for possession of marijuana, after finding police had used an illegal search to obtain the evidence.

Chief Lawyer for Petitioner
Louis J. Caruso

Chief Lawyer for Respondent
James H. Geary

Justices for the Court
Warren E. Burger, Sandra Day O'Connor (writing for the Court), Lewis F. Powell, Jr., William H. Rehnquist, Byron R. White

Justices Dissenting
Harry A. Blackmun, William J. Brennan, Jr., Thurgood Marshall, John Paul Stevens

Place
Washington, D.C.

Date of Decision
6 July 1983

Decision
Upheld the petitioner's claim and ordered the lower court to reconsider its decision.

Significance
The ruling had two results. First, it allowed police to search a detainee's car without first obtaining a warrant or placing the driver under arrest, if the officers had a reasonable fear of physical harm. Second, the Court defined a new standard for when it would review a lower court's decisions. If the lower court clearly stated it had based its decision on "adequate and independent state grounds," the Supreme Court would not take the case.

The U.S. Supreme Court had long held that its jurisdiction applies only to cases involving points of federal law. Over the years, however, some state supreme courts have based their decisions on a mixture of state and federal law, subsequently blurring the High Court's jurisdiction. When the state of Michigan asked the Supreme Court to review *Michigan v. Long,* the respondent, David Long, asserted the case did not belong in the Supreme Court. The Court disagreed, and in its decision it spelled out when it would hear such cases in the future.

Long's case involved his Fourth Amendment rights against unreasonable search and seizure, stemming from his conviction for possession of marijuana. Late one night, two police officers observed Long's car swerving along a Michigan country road. Long then careened off the road into a ditch, and the police investigated the scene. Long got out of his car, and the officers determined he was intoxicated. Looking inside the car, the officers saw a hunting knife. They then searched Long for weapons and looked inside the car again. One officer saw a leather pouch containing marijuana. Long was arrested, and the police then found more marijuana in the trunk.

At his trial, Long tried to suppress the marijuana as evidence, claiming the officers had made an unreasonable search of his car. Both the circuit and appeals court denied Long's claim, extending the Supreme Court's ruling in *Terry v. Ohio* (1968). In that case, the Court held that police can search a detainee's body for weapons before an arrest, if the officers have a reasonable fear for their safety. Now, the so-called "Terry search" was applied to a detainee's car as well.

The Michigan Supreme Court, however, agreed with Long and overturned his conviction. It cited both the Fourth Amendment and the Michigan State Constitution in defending Long's right to be free from unreasonable search and seizure. The state of Michigan then asked the Supreme Court to consider the case and it agreed, wanting to rule on the use of the Terry search on a detainee's car.

Deciding the Court's Jurisdiction
Long argued that the Supreme Court had no reason to hear the case. The Michigan Supreme Court had fol-

lowed an accepted precedent, basing its decision on "adequate and independent state grounds," i.e., the protection provided by the state's constitution. Before addressing the constitutional issues of the case, the Supreme Court looked at Long's claim.

Writing for the 5-4 majority, Justice O'Connor asserted that the state court had not relied on state grounds. The lower court, she wrote, had relied almost exclusively on federal cases, especially *Terry*, in its decision: "The references to the State Constitution in no way indicate that the decision below rested on grounds in any way *independent* from the state court's interpretation of federal law."

O'Connor had previously set forth the new, general standard the Court would apply when deciding to hear similar cases:

> If a state court chooses merely to rely on federal precedents as it would on the precedents of all other jurisdictions, then it need only make clear by a plain statement in its judgment or opinion that the federal cases are being used only for the purpose of guidance, and do not themselves compel the result that the court has reached . . . If the state court decision indicates clearly and expressly that it is . . . based on bona fide separate, adequate, and independent grounds, we, of course, will not undertake to review the decision.

The Court then proceeded to address the validity of a Terry search on a car and upheld it as constitutional. Officers could search the areas of a car where a weapon could be hidden, if they believed the suspect was dangerous and might gain control of a hidden weapon.

Reaction to the "Plain Statement" Rule

In his dissent, joined by Justice Marshall, Justice Brennan criticized the Court's extension of the Terry search. Quoting Justice Robert H. Jackson, Brennan wrote that Fourth Amendment rights "are not mere second-class rights but belong in the category of indispensable freedoms." Brennan thought the Court had gone too far in its new definition of reasonable search and seizure.

To other justices, however, and some legal observers, the most controversial part of the *Michigan* decision was the Court's new standard for hearing state cases, the so-called "plain statement" rule. Although he concurred with the bulk of the majority decision, Justice Blackmun dissented from the section that defined this new approach to the Court's jurisdiction. In a separate

dissent, Justice Stevens offered a lengthy attack on the new rule.

In the past, Stevens noted, the Supreme Court had agreed to hear cases in which a state court denied a citizen a right guaranteed by federal law or the U.S. Constitution. In *Michigan*, on the contrary, the state of Michigan was asking the Court to hear a case in which the state court defined a citizen's rights "too broadly" by overturning Long's conviction, based on the state Constitution. Stevens was uncomfortable with this new precedent. He went on:

> . . . the final outcome of the state processes offended no federal interest whatsoever. Michigan simply provided greater protection to one of its citizens than some other State might provide, or, indeed, than this Court might require throughout the country. I believe that in reviewing the decisions of state courts, the primary role of this Court is to make sure that persons who seek to *vindicate* federal rights have been fairly heard . . . Finally, I am thoroughly baffled by the Court's suggestion that it must stretch its jurisdiction and reverse the judgment of the Michigan Supreme Court in order to show "[r]espect for the independence of the state courts."

Despite Stevens' concerns, the Court had now shown it would hear cases where a state court had granted broader rights than those guaranteed in the U.S. Constitution, as long as the plain statement rule had been met.

Related Cases
Miranda v. Arizona, 384 U.S. 436 (1966).
Terry v. Ohio, 392 U.S. 1 (1968).

Bibliography and Further Reading

Biskupic, Joan, and Elder Witt. *Guide to the U.S. Supreme Court*. Washington, D.C.: Congressional Quarterly, Inc., 1997.

Hall, Kermit L., ed. *The Oxford Companion to the Supreme Court of the United States*. New York: Oxford Press, 1992.

Jackson, Heather A. "Expanding Exclusionary Rule Exceptions and Contracting Fourth Amendment Protection." *Journal of Criminal Law and Criminology*, summer 1996, p. 1201.

Nowak, John E., Ronald D. Rotunda, and J. Nelson Young. *Constitutional Law*, 2nd ed. St. Paul: West Publishing Company, 1984.

UNITED STATES V. URSERY

Legal Citation: 516 U.S. 1070 (1996)

Petitioner
United States

Respondent
Guy Ursery

Petitioner's Claim
That "*in rem*" civil property forfeiture proceedings, combined with a prison sentence for "manufacturing" marijuana, did not constitute double jeopardy in violation of the Fifth Amendment.

Chief Lawyer for Petitioner
Drew S. Days III, U.S. Solicitor General

Chief Lawyers for Respondent
Lawrence Robbins, David Michael, Jeffry K. Finer

Justices for the Court
Stephen Breyer, Ruth Bader Ginsburg, Anthony M. Kennedy, Sandra Day O'Connor, William H. Rehnquist (writing for the Court), Antonin Scalia, David H. Souter, Clarence Thomas

Justices Dissenting
John Paul Stevens

Place
Washington, D.C.

Date of Decision
24 June 1996

Decision
That, according to a two-part test which found that the property forfeiture was civil and remedial, not criminal and punitive, the seizure of property did not constitute a "punishment" as such; hence, this was not a case of double jeopardy.

Significance
United States v. Ursery, along with other cases in the mid-1990s such as *Bennis v. Michigan* (1996), served notice that the Supreme Court was willing to marshal every bit of constitutional firepower that it could against drug dealers and people involved in criminal activity—even, in the case of *Bennis*, people unknowingly or unwillingly involved in that activity. Many had cause to applaud this move to uphold law and order and the power of the states against criminals; others questioned the government's ability to seize property from a citizen, even a lawbreaker.

Guy Ursery Grows His Own

Guy Ursery grew his own marijuana, but this Flint, Michigan, auto worker was not a drug dealer. "The most you could say was he was giving it to friends," his attorney later told the *Los Angeles Times*. On his property, Ursery had some 142 marijuana plants, none more than two feet tall, according to police who raided his place on a tip from the former girlfriend of Ursery's son. Inside the house, authorities found marijuana seeds, stems, stalks, and a "grow light" for enhancing plant growth. The federal government instituted forfeiture proceedings against the house, because it had been used to facilitate the processing of a controlled substance. Ursery settled the forfeiture claim with the federal government, paying $13,250; but just before the settlement, he was indicted for manufacturing marijuana and sentenced to five years, three months in jail.

The question before the Court of Appeals for the Sixth Circuit was whether, by seizing his property and sending him to prison, the federal government had violated the Fifth Amendment's Double Jeopardy Clause. The latter states that no person may be tried twice for the same crime: ". . . nor shall any person be subject for the same offence to be twice put in jeopardy of life or limb . . ." Even though Ursery had not ultimately forfeited his property, he had paid what amounted to a sizeable fine, and had then been subjected to imprisonment. In the eyes of the court, this constituted double jeopardy.

Around the same time, a case with some similarities to Ursery's came to the attention of the government. Charles Wesley Arlt and James Wren had been convicted of conspiracy to aid and abet the manufacture of methamphetamine, a stimulant, in violation of federal law. They were also convicted on conspiracy to launder money, and on various money-laundering counts. Arlt received a life sentence plus ten years of supervised release, along with a fine of $250,000. Wren got a life sentence and a five-year term of supervised release. Before the end of the criminal trial, the United States filed an *in rem*, or civil property forfeiture, action against Arlt, Wren, and Payback Mines, a corporation controlled by Arlt. According to 18 U.S.C. 981(a)(1)(A), "Any property . . . involved in a transaction or attempted trans-

Criminal Cases v. Civil Cases

In a typical civil case, a person files suit against another person or group of persons, claiming that he or she has suffered some kind of harm or injury. The case is tried to determine if such injury has in fact occurred and to provide a legal remedy. Although the remedy sought may involve forcing the defendant to perform a certain act, or to cease certain activities, the usual remedy sought is a money settlement, and if found guilty the defendant is not imprisoned.

Criminal cases are initiated by the state against an individual or group for conduct deemed offensive to society, such as theft or murder. Defendants found guilty in criminal cases may be imprisoned as well as fined.

Since severe penalties, including death, may be imposed in criminal cases, criminal procedure is distinguished from civil procedure by the greater emphasis on the rights of the defendant. Further, the standard of proof is more stringent in criminal cases—the defendant must be proved guilty "beyond a reasonable doubt," whereas in civil cases the defendant may be found guilty by a "preponderance of the evidence."

Source(s): Carp, Robert A. *Judicial Procedure in America.* Washington, DC: CQ Press, 1998.

action in violation of [money-laundering statutes] is subject to forfeiture to the United States." Furthermore, 21 U.S.C. 881(a)(6) provides that "All . . . things of value furnished or intended to be furnished by any person in exchange for illegal drugs . . . all proceeds traceable to such an exchange . . . [and] all moneys, negotiable instruments, and securities used or intended to facilitate" a federal drug felony, shall be forfeited.

The various parties in the Arlt-Wren matter agreed to defer litigation over the civil forfeiture action until the end of the criminal case. More than a year after the conclusion of that trial, by which time Arlt and Wren were behind bars, the district court granted the federal government's motion for summary judgment. Arlt and Wren appealed, and the Court of Appeals for the Ninth Circuit reversed on the double-jeopardy grounds. Given the similarities to the *Ursery* case—although there were crucial differences, including the fact that Ursery was manufacturing drugs for his own use, not to mention the serious differences in potency between marijuana and methamphetamines—the U.S. Supreme Court agreed to review them together.

Various Items, Emerald Cut Stones, and 89 Firearms

The Court ruled by an 8-1 vote that *in rem* civil forfeiture proceedings were neither "punishment" nor criminal in nature; hence the seizure of property, combined with prison sentences, did not constitute double jeopardy. Chief Justice Rehnquist, writing for the majority, noted that federal authorities had Congress's authorization to conduct parallel civil and criminal actions, a history that went back at least to *The Palmyra* (1827). Citing cases such as *Various Items of Personal Property v. United States* (1931), *One Lot Emerald Cut Stones v. United States* (1972), and *United States v. One Assortment of 89 Firearms* (1984), Rehnquist observed that the Double Jeopardy Clause did not apply to forfeiture because it did not impose "punishment." Most recently, in *89 Firearms,* the Court had applied a two-part test in considering whether a forfeiture was barred by prior criminal proceedings. It asked itself first "whether Congress intended the particular forfeiture to be a remedial civil sanction or a criminal penalty"; and second "whether the forfeiture proceedings are so punitive in fact as to establish that they may not legitimately be viewed as civil in nature," regardless of Congress's intent. If the action was a civil sanction that could not be judged "punitive," then it did not constitute double jeopardy.

Chief Justice Rehnquist wrote that in analysis of various of the above-mentioned cases, "the conclusion was the same in each case: *in rem* civil forfeiture is a remedial civil sanction, distinct from potentially punitive *in personam* civil penalties such as fines . . ." *In personam* penalties punish the person; *in rem* penalties "punish" the property, which is no punishment at all. Rather, it is a remedial action, or one aimed at remedying a situation. The courts of appeals, Rehnquist wrote, had misunderstood the Supreme Court's rulings in *United States v. Halper* (1989), *Austin v. United States* (1993), and *Department of Revenue of Montana v. Kurth Ranch* (1994). They read them to imply that civil forfeitures did constitute double jeopardy when combined with imprisonment. "It would have been remarkable," he wrote, "for the Court both to have held unconstitutional a well-established practice, and to have overruled a long line of precedent, without having even suggested that it was doing so." Those cases were different, involving respectively *in personam* civil penalties, civil forfeitures, and a punitive state tax on marijuana. *Halper* and *Kurth Ranch* at least involved the Double Jeopardy Clause, and *Austin* addressed civil forfeitures under the Excessive Fines Clause of the Eighth Amendment, but only the present case was concerned with *in rem* civil forfeitures under the Fifth Amendment Double Jeopardy Clause.

The War on Drugs

The expression "War on Drugs" was popularized by President Ronald Reagan in the 1980s, but it was President Richard M. Nixon who first described federal antidrug efforts as a "war." Between 1969, when Nixon became president, and 1983, the third year of Reagan's administration, annual federal spending on drug eradication grew from $37 million to $1.06 billion.

The government's "war," waged chiefly by the Drug Enforcement Administration (DEA) with help from a variety of federal and local agencies, was aimed at stopping drugs from entering the United States. These law-enforcement initiatives were augmented by the "Just Say No" public-relations campaign, whose spokesperson was First Lady Nancy Reagan. The private sector responded in 1986, when a group of advertising exec-

utives formed the nonprofit Partnership for a Drug-Free America. The latter launched a series of memorable antidrug advertising campaigns that included a spot comparing the brain of a drug user to an egg frying in a pan ("this is your brain on drugs").

The drug war has not been generally judged a success, and appraisals have been less than glowing: according to one estimate, in the years between 1987 to 1992, when the federal government put $10 billion into the War on Drugs, drug use declined by one-tenth of one percent.

Source(s): "Report on Cocaine and Federal Sentencing Policy." United States Sentencing Commission, http://www.ussc.gov.

(*Austin,* to which several justices would refer in concurrence or dissent, involved an attempt by the federal government to seize a mobile home and auto body shop from a man convicted of selling two grams of cocaine. The Court overruled the lower court on the grounds that the Eighth Amendment limited federal power to seize assets.)

Finally, the chief justice applied the *89 Firearms* test to the present case. First, Sections 881 and 981, he wrote, had clearly been intended by Congress to serve civil functions. And second, there was little evidence to suggest that the forfeiture actions were punitive enough to earn them the label of criminal, rather than civil, proceedings. *Austin, Halper,* and *Kurth Ranch* did not have as much bearing on the present case as the petitioners had hoped. However, the statutes in question in the present case were not substantially different from those upheld in *Various Items, Emerald Cut Stones,* and *89 Firearms.* Four other factors gave further support to the understanding of 881 and 981 as non-punitive. First, *in rem* civil forfeiture had not been historically viewed as punishment. Second, the government was not required by the statute to demonstrate scienter (criminal intent), which further distinguished the statutes from criminal ones. Third, the seizure could serve civil goals in addition to its criminal deterrent aims. And fourth, the fact that 881 and 981 were "tied to criminal activity is insufficient in itself to render them punitive."

Concurrence and Dissent: Standing *Austin* on Its Head

Justice Kennedy issued a concurring opinion in which he reviewed the history of past cases and showed why the Court's holding in the present action was consistent with its judgment not only in *Austin,* but also in

Libretti v. United States (1995). "Forfeiture," he wrote, ". . . punishes an owner by taking property involved in a crime, and it may happen that the owner is also the wrongdoer charged with a criminal offense. But the forfeiture is not a second *in personam* punishment for the offense." Justice Scalia, joined by Justice Thomas, concurred in the judgment, holding that "the Double Jeopardy Clause prohibits successive prosecution, not successive punishment." In other words, one could receive more than a single punishment for a crime, but should not be tried twice for the same offense.

Justice Stevens concurred in part of the judgment-with regard to Arlt and Wren—and dissented in part of the judgment involving Ursery. "Because the numerous federal statutes authorizing forfeitures cover such a wide variety of situations," he wrote, "it is quite wrong to assume that there is only one answer to [the] question" of whether the actions against Ursery and the two others constituted double jeopardy. Justice Stevens then went on to establish crucial differences between Ursery's case and that of the two other men. The $405,089.23 seized from Arlt and Wren had come directly from criminal activity; whereas "none of the property seized in No. 95-345 [Ursery] constituted proceeds of an illegal activity."

Looking closely at the facts, Justice Stevens noted a number of problems with the case against Ursery. "Respondent Ursery," who "cultivated marijuana in a heavily wooded area not far from his home in Shiawassee County, Michigan," did so purely for the purpose of supplying his family with marijuana: "there is no evidence, and no contention by the Government, that he sold any of it to third parties." Acting on the basis of the incorrect assumption that the marijuana plants were on respondent's property, the Michigan

State Police executed a warrant to search the premises." The fact that they seized the grow light and other items used in the actual criminal activity, Justice Stevens suggested, was lawful. But the government overstepped the bounds when it attempted to seize Ursery's house, because "There is no evidence that the house had been purchased with the proceeds of unlawful activity[,] and the house itself was surely not contraband." Justice Stevens then proceeded to address the government's four arguments supporting the seizure of the home, first establishing in his view that the forfeiture was punitive in nature.

After reviewing *Austin,* a decision which he held that the Court "today stands . . . on its head," Justice Stevens wrote, "Even if the point had not been settled by prior decisions, common sense would dictate the result in this case. There is simply no rational basis for characterizing the seizure of this respondent's home as anything other than punishment for his crime." He further questioned the majority's view that "There is some mystical difference between *in rem* and *in personam* proceedings, such that only the latter can give rise to double jeopardy concerns." He further took issue with the government's view "that the word 'jeopardy' refers only to a criminal proceeding." Justice Stevens concluded by referring to *Various Items* and other Prohibition-Era decisions cited by the Court in the present ruling. "Consider how drastic the remedy would have been," he observed, "if Congress in 1931 had authorized the forfeiture of every home in which alcoholic beverages were consumed."

Impact

Justice Stevens may have been the only dissenter on the Supreme Court in *Ursery,* but he was far from the only American alarmed by the Court's ruling in the case. The decision reflected a law-and-order trend which, while it may have responded to genuine threats to the public order posed by drug dealers, appeared to catch relatively innocent people in its snares as well. Thus, in a related 1996 decision, *Bennis v. Michigan,* the Court held that a car used for an illegal act—sex with a prostitute, could be seized even if the co-owner of the car had no knowledge of the illegal activities. This was a new trend, a change from the civil-libertarian stance of *Austin,* noted both by Justice Stevens and David G. Savage of the *Los Angeles Times,* who wrote, ". . . Monday's decision is something of a surprise. Three years ago, the justices moved to rein in the aggressive use of civil forfeiture." William R. Schroeder in *The FBI Law Enforcement Bulletin* noted "A decline in the use of asset forfeiture by federal law enforcement over the past 2 years" which had "prompted this reinvigoration effort." Mark Feldman, a former federal prosecutor, likewise told National Public Radio just after the ruling, "I think the government will be enormously embold-

ened, relieved, as a result of this opinion, and you'll see—we will all see the number of seizures and forfeiture cases increase substantially." In an *ABA Journal* article, John Gibeaut used the title of a popular 1960s song whose protagonist has smoked too much marijuana— "One Toke Over the Line"—to suggest that the federal government's *Ursery* ruling would have far-ranging implications for civil liberties. The decision could be used to defeat double-jeopardy challenges by drunk drivers and sex offenders, as Gibeaut indicated; but it was quite possible that in future cases it could be wielded against more mainstream elements of society as well.

Related Cases

The Palmyra, 12 Wheat. 1 (1827).
Various Items of Personal Property v. United States, 282 U.S. 577 (1931).
One Lot Emerald Cut Stones v. United States, 409 U.S. 232 (1972).
United States v. One Assortment of 89 Firearms, 465 U.S. 354 (1984).
United States v. Halper, 490 U.S. 435 (1989).
Austin v. United States, 509 U.S. 602 (1993).
Department of Revenue of Montana v. Kurth Ranch, 511 U.S. 767 (1994).
Libretti v. United States, 516 U.S. 29 (1995).

Bibliography and Further Reading

Brand, Rachel. "Civil Forfeiture as Jeopardy." *Harvard Journal of Law & Public Policy,* fall 1996, pp. 292-309.

Costigan, Matthew. "Go Directly to Jail, Do Not Pass Go, Do Not Keep House." *Journal of Criminal Law and Criminology,* spring 1997, pp. 719-50.

"Criminal Law—Double Jeopardy—Sixth Circuit Overturns Criminal Conviction of Drug Manufacturer After Settlement of Civil Forfeiture as Violation of the Double Jeopardy Clause." *Harvard Law Review,* February 1996, pp. 852-57.

Gibeaut, John. "One Toke Over the Line: A Pot Grower's Supreme Court Loss Scuttles Double Jeopardy Challenges by Drunk Drivers, Sex Abusers." *ABA Journal,* September 1996, p. 28.

"Prisoners, Defendants Get a 1-2 Punch from the Justices." *The National Law Journal,* July 8, 1996, p. A12.

Savage, David G. "Asset Seizure Is Not Double Jeopardy, High Court Rules." *Los Angeles Times,* June 25, 1996, p. A1.

Schroeder, William R. "Civil Forfeiture: Recent Supreme Court Cases." *The FBI Law Enforcement Bulletin,* October 10, 1996, pp. 28-32.

Witt, Elder. *Congressional Quarterly's Guide to the Supreme Court,* 2nd ed. Washington, DC: Congressional Quarterly Inc., 1990.

JURIES

History

A jury is a group of persons selected from the community that is charged with hearing a legal case and delivering a verdict on it. Juries are used in both civil and criminal cases, and they base their decisions on testimony and other evidence that is presented at trial. In death penalty cases, they may be charged with imposing a sentence on a criminal defendant.

The concept of the jury system can be traced to Athens, Greece, around 400 B.C. These earliest juries heard arguments in legal cases but did not apply law. According to author John Guinther, quoting Aristotle, juries in Athens instead decided cases based on their "understanding of general justice." The vast empire of ancient Rome rejected the idea of juries, opting instead for a professional court system in which ordinary citizens had no role. The dark ages that followed the fall of the Roman empire had little use for law, not to mention juries, and the jury system of justice lay dormant until the twelfth century. Around that time, Italian scholars revived the rule of law in Europe with the force of their arguments.

In Great Britain, the jury system was not used until the twelfth century. Prior to that time, the Catholic Church dominated the legal system with its ecclesiastical courts. Judgment and punishment were carried out by the Church through the "ordeal," a form of torture in which a wide variety of physical pains could be inflicted on an accused criminal. Random crimes could be resolved with the "hue and cry," a process in which a person publicly called for a posse to hunt down and thrash a suspected criminal. Civil disputes often were solved by "compurgation," a method that required each party in the case to bring several friends, or "compurgators," for verbal support; the party with the most compurgators won the case. In the twelfth century, English monarch Henry II formulated the earliest British version of the jury system when, after a struggle with the Papacy in Rome, he ordered that a group of regular citizens would decide disputes over land in secular courts. However, Henry II also utilized inquisitions and ordeals and the hue and cry remained the foremost system of justice. It was under the reign of Henry's son, King John, that the

first example of the western world's modern jury system was created.

King John was a rather ruthless monarch who was unpopular with landowners, or "barons." The king was accustomed to seizing the land and families of barons who could not pay their debts on time. The barons, dissatisfied with years of abuse at the hands of King John, banded together and in May of 1215, they confronted King John at Runnymede, a meadow on the bank of the Thames river. At knifepoint, the barons forced King John to sign the Magna Carta, a document which declared that no person was above the law, including the king. Under Chapter 39 of the Magna Carta, "[n]o freeman, shall be taken or imprisoned or seized or exiled or in any way destroyed . . . except by the lawful judgment of his peers and by the law of the land." The barons intended that juries would be composed of other barons, and not of commoners, but this did not come to pass. At first, juries in England were comprised partly of noblemen and partly of commoners, but, as the system evolved, jurors were picked without regard to their economic status.

The case against William Penn and William Mead in the late seventeenth century illustrated the importance of the jury and its rise to power within the judicial system. Penn and Mead were religious dissenters who were given to preaching in public. Around this time, Brits were so suspicious of King Charles II's Catholic leanings that they passed laws against preaching in public. Penn and Mead were arrested, and opponents of the king sought to have Penn and Mead prosecuted and imprisoned, which would have embarrassed the king. The court impaneled a jury and, after both sides presented their case, they retired to deliberate, knowing full well that they were expected to deliver verdicts of guilty. Around this time, the judge had a tremendous amount of power over jurors. A judge could keep jurors until they delivered a verdict desired by the judge, and in some cases, a judge could lock the jury in a room and deprive the jurors of food and water and other amenities until they delivered the desired verdict. Several members of the jury led by Edward Bushell, refused to deliver a unanimous guilty verdict. The jury was sent off to deliberate again and again, without food, drink, fire, or tobacco, but it still could not deliver a guilty verdict. It did absolve Mead, but the judge ruled that Mead could not be released because he was charged with conspiring with Penn. Penn, from his cage in the courtroom (Mead likewise was kept in a cage), bellowed that "[i]f not guilty be not a verdict, then you make of the jury and Magna Carta but a mere nose of wax." The Lord Mayor of London threatened to cut Bushell's throat and the jury was sent away for another night without food or drink. The next morning, it returned with not guilty verdicts again, and the judge imposed a fine on each juror. The jurors refused to pay the fine and were sent to jail. Eight jurors eventually relented, but four did not, and they eventually brought their own case against the court from jail. In what became known as *Bushell's Case,* the Court of Common Pleas declared that the punishment of the jurors was illegal and that no jury could be punished for its verdict. Penn and Mead, both of whom were sent to jail after the fiasco, were released when Penn's father paid their fines. The four jurors were released from jail after the decision in *Bushell's Case,* and their ultimate success helped to establish the power of the jury system in England.

The Jury System in America

The English jury system migrated to colonial America, but the English did not allow juries in all cases. The denial of the right to a jury trial in all cases inflamed the colonists, and it was one of the many reasons for the revolt against England's rule. During the American Revolution, many states included the right to a jury trial in their state constitutions. After the United States won the war, the framers of the U.S. Constitution inserted the right to a jury trial in several places: in Article III, Section 2, the right to a trial by jury in criminal cases; in the Fifth Amendment, which provided for grand juries in criminal cases; in the Sixth Amendment, which guaranteed the right to a trial by jury in serious federal criminal cases; and in the Seventh Amendment, which provided for a jury trial in civil cases where the amount in controversy exceeded $20.

The basic characteristics of juries have changed slightly over the years. Originally, in England, juries were inquisitorial. That is, they could ask questions of the parties. Additionally, the early juries were chosen for their knowledge of the facts of the case. Over time, as populations increased, it became too difficult for courts to insist that a juror have knowledge of the facts of the case, and juries became comprised of persons who were, until the trial, ignorant of the case facts. Under contemporary law, the parties in a case generally prefer jurors who do not know the circumstances and facts of a case. In today's mass communication society, however, it is not always possible to find jurors who have not heard of a particularly infamous case. If those persons can promise to keep an open mind about the case, they may serve on a jury.

Modern Juries

The rules and laws surrounding juries are numerous and varied. Generally, federal and state courts follow the same process in impaneling a jury. First, a pool of jurors, called the *venire,* is selected from the community's driver license lists or voter registration lists to come to court. Before trial, the lawyers for the parties put the venire through *voir dire. Voir dire* is the examination of jurors to see if they are competent and suitable to sit on a jury. The lawyers for each side may excuse a potential juror from the case "for cause," which can be anything that impairs the person's ability to perform the duties of a juror. Lawyers may challenge an unlimited number of prospective jurors for cause. The lawyers also have a limited number of "peremptory challenges," or challenges to prospective jurors that are unsupported by a reason.

One important issue is concerned with precisely who may serve on a jury. Women were excluded from juries in some states as late as the 1940s. In many states, women could serve on juries, but the right of women to serve on a jury was not confirmed by the Supreme Court until 1975. That year, after decades of stops and starts, the High Court held in *Taylor v. Louisiana* that the Sixth Amendment prohibited excluding from jury duty whole identifiable segments of the community, including women.

African Americans historically were prevented from serving on juries, even after passage of the Civil Rights Act of 1866 and the Fourteenth Amendment of 1868, both of which purported to protect the rights of all American citizens. As early as 1880, the U.S. Supreme Court had held in *Strauder v. West Virginia* that exclusion of black persons from a jury violated the equal protection clause of the Fourteenth Amendment. Subsequent High Court decisions confirmed that a jury should be a cross-section of the community, but the practice of excluding whole racial groups from juries continued as lawyers clung to the benefits of racially homogenous juries. In 1986, the Supreme Court attempted to stop such maneuvering with its decision in *Batson v. Kentucky.* In *Batson,* the High Court held that a party may question the removal of a juror if the party believes that the opposing party removed the juror solely on the basis of race or gender.

There are differences in the juries of civil trials and the juries in criminal trials. Under the Seventh Amendment, a party to a civil case is entitled to a jury trial, but the U.S. Supreme Court has not held that the same rule applies to the states. Nevertheless, most states give parties the right to choose a jury trial in most civil cases. On the federal level, Congress may deny the right to a jury trial in a civil case, provided the case deals with public rights (i.e. the right to safe working conditions), and provided Congress creates an administrative body to be the sole arbiter of the disputes. (*Atlas v. Occupational Safety and Health Review Commission*)

The right to a jury trial in a criminal case is slightly more important than the right in a civil case. This is because a person's liberty is at risk in a criminal case. If a criminal defendant does not face jail time of more than six months, the defendant does not have a right to a jury trial. Trials held without a jury are called "bench trials," and are tried solely before the judge, who hears the evidence and makes the decision herself.

See also: **Criminal Procedure**

Bibliography and Further Reading

Guinther, John, *The Jury In America.* New York: Facts On File Publications, 1988

Hans, Valerie P., Vidmar, Neil, *Judging the Jury.* New York: Plenum Press, 1986

"Jury," *West's Encyclopedia of American Law,* Volume 6, p. 301. St. Paul: West Group, 1998

Summer, Lila E., *The American Heritage History of the Bill of Rights: The Seventh Amendment.* New Jersey: Silver Burdett Press, Inc., 1991

Wolf, Robert V., *The Jury System.* Philadelphia: Chelsea House Publishers, 1998

STRAUDER V. WEST VIRGINIA

Legal Citation: 100 U.S. 303 (1879)

Appellant
Taylor Strauder

Appellee
State of West Virginia

Appellant's Claim
That a West Virginia statute allowing only whites to serve on juries prevented Strauder from enjoying due process and full protection under the law.

Chief Lawyers for Appellant
George O. Davenport; Charles Devens, U.S. Attorney General

Chief Lawyers for Appellee
Robert White; J. W. Green

Justices for the Court
Joseph P. Bradley, John Marshall Harlan I, Ward Hunt, Samuel Freeman Miller, William Strong (writing for the Court), Noah Haynes Swayne, Morrison Remick Waite

Justices Dissenting
Nathan Clifford, Stephen Johnson Field

Place
Washington, D.C.

Date of Decision
1 March 1880

Decision
In favor of Strauder, the appellant.

Significance
The *Strauder* decision established the right of African Americans to be seated as jurors.

"A Brand Upon Them"

In its decision handed down on 1 March 1880, the Court agreed with Strauder that the state's jury system was discriminatory. Writing for the majority, Justice Strong wondered how West Virginia could not be considered to discriminate against a "colored" defendant on trial for his life when all other African Americans were expressly prevented from serving as jurors on the basis of race alone. The Court ruled that exclusion from juries on the basis of race violated the Fourteenth Amendment, which specifically forbid states from withholding equal protection under the law:

> The statute of West Virginia which, in effect, singles out and denies to colored citizens the right and privilege of participating in the administration of the law as jurors because of their color, though qualified in all other respects, is, practically, a brand upon them, and a discrimination against them which is forbidden by the amendment.

Despite a dissent by Justices Clifford and Field, the Court ordered the West Virginia court decision reversed and the case remitted. Field and Clifford cited the position they had taken in *Ex Parte Virginia,* a similar case in 1879 involving the racial composition of juries. The two justices felt that the Fourteenth Amendment stopped short of implying that all persons should be allowed to participate in the administration of state laws or hold public office. Field wrote that the Court should restrict itself to ruling on the correctness of verdicts meted out by state courts and order new trials only if errors were found.

Related Cases
Ex Parte Virginia, 100 U.S. 339 (1879).
United States ex rel. Krueger v. Kinsella, 137 F.Supp. 806 (1956).
Murphy v. Garrett, 729 F.Supp. 461 (1990).

Bibliography and Further Reading
Bergman, Peter. *The Chronological History of the Negro In America.* New York: Harper & Row, 1969.

Kurland, Phillip B., and Gerhard Casper, eds. *Landmark Briefs and Arguments of the Supreme Court of the United*

African Americans and the Jury System

Although many people perceive a summons to jury duty as a burden, the opportunity to serve on a jury is in fact a right. As such, it was denied to many African Americans until 1968.

The Supreme Court had ruled as early as 1808, in *United States v. Mullany*, that African Americans could act as competent witnesses in court, but most jurisdictions (particularly in the South) either flatly denied African Americans the right to testify, or subjected the testimony of a black person to extraordinary suspicion and scrutiny. The right to serve as a juror was closely tied with that of acting as a witness, and states found loopholes for withholding both of these civil rights from African Americans despite court rulings that deemed

unconstitutional any systematic efforts at eliminating blacks from juries.

Provisions for enforcement came only with the Civil Rights movement of the 1960s, whose victories included the passage by Congress of the Jury Selection and Service Act. The act, passed in 1968, established specific provisions for inclusion of all citizens in the jury pool, and the Court's decision in *Duncan v. Louisiana* that year extended Sixth Amendment jury-trial provisions to the states.

Source(s): Bradley, David, and Shelley Fisher Fishkin, eds. *The Encyclopedia of Civil Rights in America.* Armonk, NY: Sharpe, 1998.

States. Arlington: University Publications of America, 1975.

Fairman, Charles. *History of the Supreme Court of the United States.* New York: Macmillan, 1987.

Witt, Elder, ed. *The Supreme Court and Its Work.* Washington, DC: Congressional Quarterly, 1981.

MAXWELL V. DOW

Legal Citation: 176 U.S. 581 (1900)

Appellant
Charles L. Maxwell

Appellee
George N. Dow, Warden of the Utah State Prison

Appellant's Claim
That he had been wrongfully convicted of robbery, based on violation of his rights under the Fifth, Sixth, and Fourteenth Amendments.

Chief Lawyer for Appellant
J. W. N. Whitecotton

Chief Lawyer for Appellee
Alexander C. Bishop

Justices for the Court
David Josiah Brewer, Henry Billings Brown, Horace Gray, Melville Weston Fuller, Joseph McKenna, Rufus Wheeler Peckham (writing for the Court), George Shiras, Jr., Edward Douglass White

Justices Dissenting
John Marshall Harlan I

Place
Washington, D.C.

Date of Decision
26 February 1900

Decision
Upheld the appellant's conviction.

Significance
The Court reaffirmed the notion that due process, as guaranteed under the Fourteenth Amendment, did not necessarily apply to the rights spelled out in the Bill of Rights, and that state governments should be the primary defenders of most rights.

When Congress drafted the Fourteenth Amendment, its major goal was to provide citizenship to the newly freed slaves and to guarantee their rights as citizens of both the United States and the individual states. But two parts of the Fourteenth Amendment soon took on a larger meaning.

The amendment said no state government could deny "privileges and immunities" guaranteed to citizens of the United States. They also could not "deprive any person of life, liberty or property, without due process of law." These words echoed the Fifth Amendment, which held the federal government to the same standard.

At first, the Supreme Court ruled the Fourteenth Amendment was only meant to protect ex-slaves. But in his dissent to the Slaughterhouse Cases (1873), Justice Stephen J. Field said the Fourteenth Amendment gave the federal government the authority to strike down state laws that affected anyone, not just ex-slaves. That idea soon became accepted, giving people like Charles Maxwell a chance to have his day in the Supreme Court.

Maxwell's Claim

In June of 1898, Maxwell had been charged with robbery in Utah. State law allowed the county's prosecuting attorney to bring charges against Maxwell without a grand jury first determining if there was enough evidence to try the case. In September, an eight-member jury found Maxwell guilty and he was sentenced to 18 years in prison.

The following year, Maxwell petitioned the Utah State Supreme Court, asserting his conviction was unlawful and violated his rights under the Fifth, Sixth, and Fourteenth amendments. The Fifth Amendment requires a grand jury to bring charges in federal cases; Maxwell argued the amendment should apply to state trials as well. Maxwell also disputed the legality of using a trial jury with only eight members, instead of the 12 recognized under English common law and used in U.S. federal courts. Finally, he claimed that the Utah state laws regarding the grand jury and number of jurors abridged his privileges and immunities and denied him due process, both illegal under the Fourteenth Amendment.

The Utah Supreme Court denied all of Maxwell's arguments. He remained in prison as he appealed his case to the U.S. Supreme Court, which heard arguments on 4 December 1899. Unfortunately, Maxwell did not fare any better at the federal level. The Supreme Court ruled 8-1 that the conviction was lawful and the Utah laws were valid.

In his opinion, Justice Peckham noted that in a previous case, *Hurtado v. California* (1884), the Court ruled that due process under the Fourteenth Amendment did not require a state to use a grand jury to bring an indictment in a murder case tried under state law. The Court now applied the same standard to Maxwell's circumstance.

Peckham went on to say that, in general, a citizen's privileges and immunities do not necessarily apply to the Bill of Rights. States have the right to use an eight-member trial jury instead of 12, or to pass other laws that might conflict with Congress's desires or the Constitution. Peckham trusted the states to usually do what was right. "There can be no just fear that the liberties of the citizens will not be respected by the states respectively," Peckham wrote. "It is a case of self-protection, and the people can be trusted to look out for and care for themselves."

Justice Harlan, however, had major disagreements with the majority decision. He asserted that privileges and immunities did include the rights spelled out in the Bill of Rights, an idea known as "total incorporation," and a state could not take them away. He believed Maxwell should have had a trial with 12 jurors, as should every citizen accused of a crime in a state court.

Harlan went on to attack how the Court interpreted due process under the Fourteenth Amendment. In previous cases, he said, the Court had ruled that due process required a state government to provide just compensation if it took a person's private property. "It would seem that the protection of private property is of more consequence than the protection of life and liberty of the citizen."

After *Maxwell*

The Court's verdict in *Maxwell* allowed states to use fewer than 12 jurors in a criminal case. But, in a broader sense, the verdict highlighted the narrow definition of privileges and immunities held by many justices for a number of years. In a 1908 case, *Twining v. New Jersey,* the Court said that some of the rights protected under the first eight amendments "may also be safeguarded against state action, because a denial of them would be a denial of due process." But a more liberal view of protecting privileges and immunities from state laws did not fully develop until after World War II.

Maxwell remained the law of the land until the 1968 decision in *Duncan v. Louisiana.* In that case, the justices ruled 7-2 that states had to use 12 jurors when trying serious criminal cases, though it left the definition of "serious" undefined.

Related Cases

Slaughterhouse Cases, 83 U.S. 36 (1873).
Hurtado v. California, 110 U.S. 516 (1884).
Twining v. New Jersey, 211 U.S. 78 (1908).
Duncan v. Louisiana, 391 U.S. 145 (1968).

Bibliography and Further Reading

Biskupic, Joan, and Elder Witt. *Guide to the U.S. Supreme Court.* Washington, DC: Congressional Quarterly, Inc., 1997.

Choper, Jess H., Yale Kasimir, and William B. Lockhart. *Constitutional Rights and Liberties.* St. Paul: West Publishing Company, 1975.

Cushman, Robert F. *Cases in Constitutional Law,* 5th ed. Englewood Cliffs, NJ: Prentice Hall, 1984.

Hall, Kermit L., ed. *The Oxford Companion to the Supreme Court of the United States.* New York: Oxford Press, 1992.

New York Times, May 27, 1968.

Witt, Elder, ed. *The Supreme Court A to Z.* Washington, DC: Congressional Quarterly, Inc., 1993.

PATTON V. UNITED STATES

Legal Citation: 281 U.S. 276 (1930)

An accused person's right to a trial by jury predates the Constitution, with deep roots in American and English common law. Sometimes, however, defendants might agree to waive that right, or to accept a jury with fewer than 12 members. That is what John Patton, Harold Conant, and Jack Butler did, and when they later changed their minds, the Supreme Court upheld a right the men wished they had not exercised.

During the days of Prohibition, the three men were involved in bootlegging alcohol. After conspiring to bribe a federal Prohibition agent, Patton and his associates were arrested and tried in an Oklahoma Federal District Court. The three defendants pleaded not guilty. The trial began on 19 October 1927 with 12 jurors. A week later, however, one juror fell seriously ill and could no longer serve on the panel. Patton, Conant, and Butler, along with their attorneys, agreed to let the trial continue with just 11 jurors. The government and the trial judge also agreed. The next day the jury found the defendants guilty.

Patton and the other men then appealed their conviction to the Eighth Circuit Court of Appeals, claiming they had no power to waive their right to a jury trial with fewer than 12 jurors. The circuit court, not sure how to decide the case, asked the Supreme Court for instruction.

Trial by Jury and the Constitution

Patton's lawyer, Charles Nowlin, filed a brief to the Supreme Court citing cases in which the Court suggested a defendant was not entitled to waive the right to trial by jury. But in this case, the Court voted 4-3 to explicitly give defendants in federal criminal cases the power to waive their right to a trial by jury. Justice Sutherland noted that the issue was an important one, as lower courts had differed on the question and the Supreme Court had never directly ruled on it.

Sutherland began his decision by examining the constitutional rights to trial by jury, as contained in Article III Section 2 and the Sixth Amendment. Sutherland defined what constituted a trial by jury: a jury of 12 people, a judge with the power to instruct jurors on points of law and advise them on facts, and a unanimous verdict. These three components, Sutherland wrote, rested on common law principles that were beyond the reach of any legislative tampering. The elimination of any one of the three elements violated a defendant's constitutional rights.

Sutherland then came to the crux of the issue in *Patton,* as the Court saw it: was the right to trial by jury "a part of the frame of government" or just a "guarantee to the accused the right to such a trial"? After exploring several state and federal cases on the topic, Sutherland reached this conclusion:

> The record of English and colonial jurisprudence antedating the Constitution will be searched in vain for evidence that trial by jury in criminal cases was regarded as part of the structure of government, as distinguished from a right or privilege of the accused. On the contrary, it uniformly was regarded as a valuable privilege bestowed upon the person accused of crime for the purpose of safeguarding him against the oppressive power of the king and the arbitrary or partial judgment of the court . . . Article III Section 2 . . . was meant to confer a right upon the accused which he may forego at his election. To deny his power to do is to convert a privilege into an imperative requirement.

Sutherland again referred to English Common Law, acknowledging that it might seem to contradict the power the Court just granted to a defendant to waive a trial by jury. Under common law, the accused was not permitted to waive that right "as generally he was not permitted to waive any right which was intended for his protection." But in earlier times, the accused did not have the other legal protections guaranteed by the U.S. Constitution. These protections included the right of a defendant to testify on his own behalf, the right to an attorney, and the protection from cruel and unusual punishment. With those guarantees in place, it was fair to let a defendant waive the right to a trial by jury.

The Court did set some limits on the right to waive a trial by jury, or by a jury with fewer than 12 members. The defendant had to give "express and intelligent consent" to the waiver, and both the government's counsel and the judge had to agree as well. The pre-

Justice George Sutherland. © Photograph by Harris and Ewing. Collection of the Supreme Court of the United States.

siding judge was obligated to use "sound and advised discretion" before granting the right to waive, "with caution increasing as the offenses dealt with increase in gravity."

Related Cases
In re Debs, 158 U.S. 564 (1895).
Schick v. United States, 195 U.S. 65 (1919).

Bibliography and Further Reading
Hall, Kermit L, ed. *The Oxford Companion to the Supreme Court of the United States.* New York: Oxford Press, 1992.

Witt, Elder, ed. *The Supreme Court and Individual Rights.* Washington, DC: Congressional Quarterly, Inc., 1979.

PATTERSON V. ALABAMA

Legal Citation: 294 U.S. 600 (1935)

Petitioner
Haywood Patterson

Respondent
State of Alabama

Petitioner's Claim
That the exclusion of blacks from a jury list should invalidate the conviction of a black defendant.

Chief Lawyer for Petitioner
Walter H. Pollak

Chief Lawyer for Respondent
Thomas E. Knight, Jr.

Justices for the Court
Louis D. Brandeis, Pierce Butler, Benjamin N. Cardozo, Charles Evans Hughes (writing for the Court), Owen Josephus Roberts, Harlan Fiske Stone, George Sutherland, Willis Van Devanter

Justices Dissenting
None (James Clark McReynolds did not participate)

Place
Washington, D.C.

Date of Decision
1 April 1935

Decision
Hayward Patterson's conviction was overturned based on evidence of the systematic exclusion of blacks from jury duty.

Significance
The Supreme Court's decision in *Patterson v. Alabama* was the second of two important rulings it would issue in the Scottsboro rape case. The controversial trials galvanized the country and highlighted the problem of racial justice in the American South. The Scottsboro trials became emblematic of judicial miscarriage and a rallying cry for civil rights leaders for years to come.

The Scottsboro Case

The Scottsboro case, one of the most racially charged criminal trials in American history, began in March of 1931, when nine black youths ranging in age from 13 to 21 were arrested and charged with raping two white girls, Ruby Bates and Victoria Price, near Scottsboro, Alabama. The "Scottsboro boys" pleaded not guilty to the 20 indictments brought against them. Despite a spirited defense led by a coalition of Communists and civil rights leaders, an all-white jury rejected their pleas. Eight of the boys were found guilty, while a mistrial was declared in the case 13-year-old Roy Wright. The eight convicted defendants were sentenced to death on 9 April 1931.

Given a racial climate overwhelmingly hostile to blacks, the verdicts came as little surprise. The jury ignored a great deal of evidence that tended to exonerate the defendants. Further complicating the defense was the appointment by the court of Milo Moody, an inexperienced lawyer, as defense attorney in the case. A crowd of some 10,000 whites gathered outside the courthouse during the critical days of the trial, demonstrating and calling for vigilante justice.

The convictions likewise generated a passionate reaction worldwide. Labor leaders and radical organizations held rallies to protest the jury's verdict. Demonstrations were held as far away as Germany. Many of the leading intellectuals of the day, including Albert Einstein, signed a petition calling for the release of the defendants. Eventually, these supporters were joined by one of the alleged victims, Ruby Bates, who recanted her testimony that she had been raped by the defendants. In November of 1932, the U.S. Supreme Court, in the case of *Powell v. Alabama*, overturned the convictions. The Court ruled that the Scottsboro boys had been denied due process of the law because the judge had been unacceptably casual in appointing their defense lawyer. New trials were set for all nine defendants.

Patterson's Case

Haywood Patterson was tried first. His defense attorneys asked that the case be thrown out on the grounds that no blacks had been on the first jury. The judge dis-

Jury Nullification

Jury nullification takes place when a jury acquits a defendant even though the prosecution has proven the defendant's guilt beyond all reasonable doubt. The jury acquits the defendant because they disagree with the law whereby he or she is charged, and their acquittal serves as a form of protest.

The idea of jury nullification originated in England and gained popularity among rebellious American colonists, who used it as a means of registering their dissatisfaction with British rule. In the years leading up to the Civil War, jury nullification became popular with Abolitionists, who likewise used it to protest what they saw as an unjust system: the Fugitive Slave Law, which

required the return of runaway slaves. During the late 1800s and early 1900s, white Southern juries, by refusing to convict white men guilty of killing blacks, used jury nullification for less idealistic purposes.

Despite its long and varied past, jury nullification did not gain popular attention until 3 October 1995, when a mostly African American jury in the O. J. Simpson murder case issued a "not guilty" verdict, an act which many saw as an attempt to address past racial injustices.

Source(s): Fully Informed Jury Association (FIJA). http://www.primenet.com/~slack.

missed this objection, and an all-white jury was chosen a second time. Again, despite substantial evidence that suggested otherwise, Patterson was found guilty. Dismayed by this seemingly willful disregard for the evidence, the judge set aside the jury's verdict and ordered a new trial. For a third time, and again with a jury picked from a list that did not include blacks, Patterson was found guilty as charged. On 6 December 1933, Haywood Patterson was once again sentenced to death. He appealed the verdict to the Supreme Court of Alabama, which affirmed. Patterson then took his case before the U.S. Supreme Court.

In presenting his case, Patterson contended that there was a long-standing, systematic, and arbitrary exclusion of qualified blacks from jury service, based solely on their race, in violation of the Fourteenth Amendment of the U.S. Constitution. The state of Alabama argued on technical legal grounds that the Supreme Court had no jurisdiction over the case. Complicating matters further was the disposition of a second Scottsboro case, *Norris v. Alabama* (1935), argued purely on the merits and without the technical controversies.

Norris Case Decided

The case of Clarence Norris was decided first. On 1 April, Chief Justice Hughes delivered the opinion of the High Court, which held that the exclusion of blacks from jury service was pervasive and deliberate. In rendering its decision, the Court relied on overwhelming evidence of tampering with jury rolls to indicate that blacks had been considered for jury service—when in fact they had not been. Hughes rejected the state of Alabama's contention that many blacks simply were not qualified for jury service. He wrote:

> In the light of the testimony given by the defendant's witnesses, we find it impossible to

accept such a sweeping characterization of the lack of qualifications of Negroes in Morgan County. It is so sweeping; and so contrary to the evidence . . . that it destroys the intended effect on the commissioner's testimony.

He ordered the judgment of the appeals court reversed and a new trial ordered.

The decision in *Norris v. Alabama* was to prove pivotal for Haywood Patterson's case as well. While the Supreme Court agreed with the state of Alabama that Patterson's case should have been thrown out for technical legal violations, it was reluctant to send a man to death on the same evidence that had been relied upon to grant Norris a new trial. "We cannot ignore the exceptional features of this case," Chief Justice Hughes wrote in his majority opinion. He concluded that the Alabama State Supreme Court should be given another chance to rule on the matter in light of the new evidence. Hughes also strongly hinted that the U.S. Supreme Court would take another look at the case if Patterson's conviction were not overturned and a new trial granted.

In the end, Haywood Patterson was granted a new trial. But the result was the same. In 1936, a jury composed of 13 whites and one black found him guilty. He was sentenced to 75 years in prison. He pursued another appeal, but this time the Supreme Court refused to hear his case. Patterson died in prison in 1952.

Impact

In the case of *Patterson v. Alabama* the Supreme Court attempted to correct what it perceived to be a gross injustice. In overlooking the technical defects of Patterson's case, the Court signaled that it would not let fidelity to arcane legal protocols prevent it from exonerating an individual from execution.

A crowd gathers to demonstrate against the verdict in the trial of Haywood Patterson, one of the Scottsboro boys. © Photograph by Underwood & Underwood. Corbis-Bettmann.

Related Cases

Norris v. Alabama, 294 U.S. 599 (1935).
Villa v. Van Schaick, 299 U.S. 152 (1936).
People v. Wilson, 318 U.S. 688 (1943).
Tinder v. United States, 345 U.S. 565 (1953).

Bibliography and Further Reading

Carter, Dan T. *Scottsboro: A Tragedy of the American South.* Baton Rouge, LA: Louisiana State Press, 1979.

Chandler, Ralph C. *The Constitutional Law Dictionary.* Santa Barbara, CA: ABC-Clio, Inc., 1987.

DUNCAN V. LOUISIANA

Legal Citation: 391 U.S. 145 (1968)

Petitioner
Gary Duncan

Respondent
State of Louisiana

Petitioner's Claim
That the state denied him his Sixth Amendment right to a trial by jury, which the Fourteenth Amendment guarantees at the state level.

Chief Lawyer for Petitioner
Richard B. Sobol

Chief Lawyer for Respondent
Dorothy D. Wolbrette

Justices for the Court
Hugo Lafayette Black, William J. Brennan, Jr., William O. Douglas, Abe Fortas, Thurgood Marshall, Earl Warren, Byron R. White (writing for the Court)

Justices Dissenting
John Marshall Harlan II, Potter Stewart

Place
Washington, D.C.

Date of Decision
20 May 1968

Decision
The Court found that the state of Louisiana denied Duncan his basic right to a trial by jury. The Court maintained that this right constitutes a fundamental component of the country's justice system, which the Fourteenth Amendment guarantees at the state level and the Sixth Amendment guarantees at the federal level. The Court also held that "a crime punishable by two years of imprisonment is considered a serious crime, not a petty crime, which does not need a jury trial."

Significance
This case represented a key movement of the U.S. Supreme Court to make the states comply with the amendments of the U.S. Constitution under the Fourteenth Amendment, which applied the first eight amendments to the states, according to the Supreme Court majority in this case. In *Duncan v. Louisiana* the Court held that the state must honor the Fourteenth Amendment's guarantee of a jury trial.

Background Amendments and the History of Trial by Jury

Trial by jury has a long history not only in the United States, but also in England where references appear as far back as the Magna Carta (1215), a charter of rights for English subjects. English colonists transplanted the custom to the United States, where it received robust support. The First Congress of the American Colonies held on 19 October 1765 "[t]hat trial by jury is the inherent and invaluable right of every British subject in these colonies." In addition, the Declaration of Independence protested against the king's wish to make judges decide cases based on the crown's will alone, not allowing trials by jury. Hence, when drafting the Constitution, the authors guaranteed this right for all federal trials in the Sixth Amendment. Later, the Fourteenth Amendment granted this right to citizens in all state trials, according to some scholars and justices.

The Allegations Against Gary Duncan

On 18 October 1966, Gary Duncan, an African American teenager, saw two of his younger cousins talking to four white boys, while driving through Plaquemines Parish in Louisiana. Because his cousins had told him of racial incidents that occurred at the predominantly white high school to which they transferred, Duncan stopped the car and got out to see what was happening. The testimony of the various witnesses conflicts after this point, however. Nonetheless, they all agreed that Duncan spoke to the four white boys and told his cousins to get in the car. But the white witnesses testified in trial that before getting into his car, Duncan slapped one of the four boys, Henry Landry, on the elbow, whereas the Duncan's cousins testified that he only touched him. Despite the inconsistencies in the testimonies, the trial court believed the state of Louisiana had proven beyond a reasonable doubt that Duncan had assaulted Landry and convicted him of simple battery.

Duncan appealed the decision to the Louisiana Supreme Court, but it refused to hear the case, maintaining that the trial court made no error in its ruling and violated no constitutional rights of Duncan's. The Louisiana Constitution granted trials by jury only in

Felonies and Misdemeanors

Most types of crime lend themselves to easy analysis as to whether they are felonies or misdemeanors: public drunkenness is a misdemeanor, rape is a felony; vandalism is a misdemeanor, murder a felony. Given their greater seriousness, the number of types of felony is smaller than that for misdemeanors, and indeed the federal government and most states classify as misdemeanors any crimes which are not felonies.

Rather than by the types of crimes which fall under each heading, misdemeanors and felonies are defined by the processes and penalties which attend each. In terms of penalties, length and type of incarceration are the primary factors separating the two. A misdemeanor can be punishable by fine, or by incarceration for a period less than a year. Likewise the place of incarceration—jail for the former, prison for the latter—also separates misdemeanors from felonies. As for process, all accused felons have a right to trial by jury, whereas the Supreme Court found in *Baldwin v. New York* (1970) that only misdemeanants accused of crimes which carry a sentence of six months or more enjoy the same right.

Source(s): Levy, Leonard W., ed. *Encyclopedia of the American Constitution.* New York: Macmillan, 1986.

cases where capital punishment and hard labor may be imposed. Louisiana law also considered simple battery a misdemeanor carry the maximum penalty of two years in prison and a $300 fine.

The Supreme Court's Reversal

Noticing possible violations of Duncan's Sixth and Fourteenth Amendment rights, the U.S. Supreme Court decided to hear the case and arguments began on 17 January 1968. Since the majority held that the Fourteenth Amendment guaranteed all citizens the first eight amendment rights, including the Sixth Amendment's, in state criminal trials and proceedings, it considered whether the right to a jury trial constituted "a fundamental right, essential to a fair trial" as it held in *Gideon v. Wainwright* and other cases.

Having established that the right to trial by jury existed prior to the Constitution and was an important consideration in the authoring of the Constitution with an amendment devoted to it, the Court concluded that trial by jury was an essential component of the country's justice system. Furthermore, the Court noted that all state constitutions, including Louisiana's, granted trials by jury for all serious offenses.

The majority next attempted to determine if Duncan's deed constituted a serious or petty offense under Louisiana law. The state argued that Duncan's crime—simple battery—was only a petty offense in that the judge sentenced him to 60 days in prison. However, the Court noted that the Louisiana Legislature set the maximum penalty for simple battery at two years plus a fine. Consequently, Duncan faced a two-year prison sentence at the time of the trial. The Court compared the sentences for petty crimes in different states and at the federal level and found that many state—as well as federal—petty crimes carry a maximum six-month prison sentence and that 49 states impose no more than a one-year prison sentence for petty offenses. Therefore, in the 7-2 decision, the Court concluded that the state charged Duncan with a serious offense and denied him a jury trial, which the Fourteenth Amendment and the Louisiana Constitution guaranteed, and reversed Duncan's conviction. The Court stated:

> It is sufficient for our purposes to hold that a crime punishable by two years in prison is, based on past and contemporary standards in this country, a serious crime and not a petty offense. Consequently, appellant was entitled to a jury trial and it was [an] error to deny it.

The two justices who dissented, however, maintained that the Constitution did not ban a judge alone from trying and sentencing someone for simple battery. Justices Harlan and Stewart felt the history and role of the jury trial was not at stake in the case, but the responsibility of running state criminal justice systems was. They held that the Fourteenth Amendment mandates that trials must be fair in all respects, but not that the states must uniformly provide jury trials. These justices argued that Fourteenth Amendment did not simply apply the first eight amendments to the states and that a jury trial was not necessary for a fair trial.

Despite the straightforward opinion of the Court in *Duncan v. Louisiana* that the Fourteenth Amendment guarantees the right to jury trials for all serious crimes, later Court decisions strayed from the thrust of the majority's argument, upholding decisions where judges denied jury trials and jury participation in sentencing. For example, in *Spaziano v. Florida* the Court ruled that a judge, not a jury, may impose a death sentence under Florida law.

Related Cases

Maxwell v. Dow, 176 U.S. 581 (1900).
District of Columbia v. Clawans, 300 U.S. 617 (1937).

Palko v. Connecticut, 302 U.S. 319 (1937).
Singer v. United States, 323 U.S. 338 (1945).

Bibliography and Further Reading

Biskupic, Joan, and Elder Witt, eds. *Congressional Quarterly's Guide to the U.S. Supreme Court,* 3rd ed. Washington, DC: Congressional Quarterly, Inc., 1996.

Brody, David C. " *Sparf* and *Dougherty* Revisited: Why the Court Should Instruct a Jury of Its Nullification Right." *American Criminal Law Review,* fall 1995, p. 89.

Butler, Jeff E. "Petty Offenses, Serious Consequences: Multiple Petty Offenses and the Sixth Amendment Right to Jury Trial." *Michigan Law Review,* December 1995, p. 872.

Cushman, Robert F. *Cases in Constitutional Law,* 7th ed. Englewood Cliffs, NJ: Prentice-Hall, Inc., 1989.

Cushman, Robert F. *Leading Constitutional Decisions.* Englewood Cliffs, NJ: Prentice-Hall, Inc., 1982.

Friedman, Barry. "Dialogue and Judicial Review." *Michigan Law Review,* February 1993, p. 577.

Grant, Paul. "Nullified Jurors=Nullified Justice." *The National Law Journal,* Vol. 19, no. 43, June 23, 1997.

Kerper, Hazel B. *Introduction to the Criminal Justice System,* 2nd ed. Minneapolis: West Publishing Co., 1979.

JOHNSON V. LOUISIANA

Legal Citation: 406 U.S. 356 (1972)

Appellant
Frank Johnson

Appellee
State of Louisiana

Appellant's Claim
Louisiana's constitutional provisions, which allowed less-than-unanimous guilty verdicts in criminal cases, violated the Due Process and Equal Protection Clauses of the Fourteenth Amendment.

Chief Lawyer for Appellant
Richard A. Buckley

Chief Lawyer for Appellee
Louise Korns

Justices for the Court
Harry A. Blackmun, Warren E. Burger, Lewis F. Powell, Jr., William H. Rehnquist, Byron R. White (writing for the Court)

Justices Dissenting
William J. Brennan, Jr., William O. Douglas, Thurgood Marshall, Potter Stewart

Place
Washington, D.C.

Date of Decision
22 May 1972

Decision
The reasonable doubt standard contained in the Due Process Clause of the Constitution's Fourteenth Amendment was not violated by nonunanimous jury verdicts.

Significance
Appellant, Frank Johnson, was convicted by a split decision of 12 jurors: nine voted to convict and three to acquit. He contended that provisions under the Louisiana law violated the Constitution because the jury verdict was not unanimous. The U.S. Supreme Court, however, held that a "split-verdict" system was constitutionally "inoffensive" and reasoned that less-than-unanimous jury verdicts did not deprive defendants in criminal prosecutions of their rights under the due process of law. They concluded that the Fourteenth Amendment did not require unanimity in state criminal cases.

Frank Johnson was charged with larceny after being identified from photographs that had recorded his crime. He was also identified in a police lineup as the perpetrator of another, unrelated robbery. At the time Johnson's case went to trial, Louisiana's jury system required a 12-person jury in cases that carried a sentence of hard labor, but a unanimous verdict was not required. Since nine members of Johnson's jury voted guilty, he was convicted. On appeal to the Supreme Court of Louisiana, Johnson challenged provisions of the Louisiana statute that permitted less-than-unanimous jury verdicts to convict. He believed that, under the Constitution, Louisiana's practice violated the reasonable-doubt standard contained in the Due Process Clause of the Fourteenth Amendment. His appeal was denied.

When Johnson's case came before the U.S. Supreme Court on appeal, his attorney argued that the reasonable-doubt standard in criminal cases (so long as there exists a reasonable doubt, a defendant should not be convicted) obligated the state of Louisiana to require a unanimous jury verdict. Because three members of the appellant's jury did not vote to convict Johnson, his attorney asserted the "reasonable-doubt standard has not been satisfied and his conviction is therefore infirm." His attorney further argued that "nine individual jurors will be unable to vote conscientiously in favor of guilt beyond a reasonable doubt when three of their colleagues are arguing for acquittal." However, his most impassioned argument was "that guilt cannot be said to have been proved beyond a reasonable doubt when one or more of a jury's members at the conclusion of deliberation still possesses such doubt." The case pointed out that if Louisiana requires unanimous verdicts in capital cases and in trials where punishment involves hard labor, then "less-than-unanimous" verdicts in other kinds of trials represented an disparate application of the Equal Protection Clause.

U.S. Supreme Court majority justices noted that the Court had never adhered to unanimity of the jury as "requisite of due process of law." They did not believe that three dissenting (jury) votes assumed an inaccurate decision. They pointed out that, in reaching a verdict, the reasonable doubt criterion was fully satisfied by nine jurors. The Court felt it unlikely that jurors could "vote to convict" without taking into account the views of the three jurors who remained unconvinced by the evidence presented at trial. Minority jurors were not obstructed or prohibited from presenting their doubts and a decision could only have been reached after discussing and arguing about all elements involved in deliberation. The justices did not find it reasonable to believe that nine jurors brought their decision without reasonable consideration of all evidence and opinions. The Court disagreed with appellant's contention that "majority jurors simply ignore[d] the reasonable doubts of their colleagues." When nine of 12 jurors voted to convict there could be no doubts about the legitimacy of their findings—a "substantial majority of the jury were [sic] convinced by the evidence." In an apparent reference to previous findings by the Court, Justice White wrote that "jury verdicts finding guilt beyond a reasonable doubt are regularly sustained even though the evidence was such that the jury would have been justified in having a reasonable doubt." He pointed out that a nonunanimous jury did not evidence reasonable doubt about a guilt. Thus, "inharmonious findings" by a jury should not be considered an indicator of deprivation of rights under the due process of law.

The appellant's main objection in presenting his case before the U.S. Supreme Court was Louisiana's law governing conduct of trials. According to the state's statutes, a system of trial classifications determined the number of jurors and verdict requirements that pertained to the gravity of crimes being adjudicated. Unanimous five-person juries were required for crimes that mandated hard labor punishment, and nine to 12 jurors for more serious crimes, but unanimity of 12-person juries for capital offenses.

The Court found that Louisiana's statutory scheme was not discriminatory or offensive. The Court believed that the state's established procedure was practical, efficient and permissible. The system categorically operated with no intention to diminish or to infringe rights of defendants. Justices for the majority pointed out that "the States are free under the Federal Constitution to try defendants with juries of less than twelve men."

Justice Powell, in a separate, concurring opinion, stated that the right to jury trial (the Sixth Amendment) did not require unanimity as a necessary premise of due process. He pointed out that in *Apodaca v. Oregon* (1972), litigants unsuccessfully argued that unanimity should have been a requirement of the state jury system because the Fourteenth Amendment "incorporates" the Sixth Amendment's provision that everyone has the right to a trial by jury. The Court then held that noncapital state criminal cases did not require jury unanimity. Justice Powell also pointed out that requirements for state criminal trials should be distinguished

from requirements for federal courts to have jury unanimity and harmonized verdicts. Justice Powell emphasized that when *Duncan v. Louisiana* (1968) was concluded, that federal practice and its requirements for unanimity of the jury under the due process of law did not create a similar obligation for states. He also cited Justice Peckham's words in *Maxwell v. Dow* (1900), "The States should have the right to decide for themselves what shall be the form and character of the procedure in such trials . . . whether there shall be a jury of twelve of a lesser number, and whether the verdict must be unanimous or not . . ." Justice Powell further supported the majority's ruling in citing *Jordan v. Massachusetts* (1912) wherein the Court declared that "in criminal cases, due process of law is not denied by a state law which dispenses with . . . the necessity of a jury of twelve, or unanimity of the verdict." Justice Powell found no rational precedents, therefore, which supported the appellant's claim that only 12, unanimously agreeing jurors could guarantee principles of fairness and justice. He said jury trial procedure was not debased by "less-than-unanimous" jury provision and that innovations in jury trial procedure should not be considered unconstitutional especially if the law "is the product of a constitutional amendment, approved by a vote of the people in the State, and appears to be patterned on a provision of the American Law Institute's Code of Criminal Procedure." Thus, in rendering a lengthy concurring opinion Justice Powell thoroughly presented a rationale, supported by ample example, that only the notion of jury trial should have been considered fundamental rather than concluding that less-than-unanimous verdicts provided due process protection.

Four dissenting justices disagreed, finding it inappropriate that unanimous jury decisions were required in federal prosecutions and did not apply in state trials. The dissenters believed that unanimity was established as a clear practice through the history of American jurisprudence. In writing for the minority, Justice Douglas cited *Andres v. United States* (1948), wherein "unanimity in jury verdicts is required where the Sixth and Seventh Amendment apply. In criminal cases this requirement of unanimity extends to all issues—character or degree of the crime, guilt and punishment—which are left to the jury."

Dissenting justices criticized the Court's apparent unequal application of the Sixth Amendment. Douglas explained that equal treatment of cases with respect to the Self-Incrimination Clause applied at federal and state levels, and he found it disturbing the Court derived two different approaches from the Sixth Amendment. Justice Douglas disapproved of any provision that enabled states to jeopardize civil rights. He wrote: "If we construe the Bill of Rights and the Fourteenth Amendment to permit States to experiment with the basic rights of people, we open a veritable Pandora's box."

Dissenting justices reasoned that approval of procedures, which did not require unanimous verdicts could decrease a jury's sense of responsibility because non-unanimous juries were placed in position where they did not have to "debate and deliberate as fully as most unanimous juries." Provisions that enabled less-than-unanimous decisions lessened chances of dissenting jurors presenting arguments and provided a disincentive that the majority might be dissuaded. Conversely, a unanimous jury verdict required more discussion and deliberation which, in turn, encouraged better and finer reasoning required when considering questions about reasonable doubt (which could remain open if verdict was not unified). The dissenting justices considered Louisiana law an inadmissible departure from the principles of unanimity that had been constitutionally recognized. Douglas summarized the minority position saying, "proof beyond a reasonable doubt and unanimity of criminal verdicts and the presumption of innocence are basic features of the accusatorial system."

Impact

Although at odds with arguments made by the dissenting justices, the majority opinion ruled that due process of law with respect to the Fourteenth Amendment was served regardless of whether a conviction was obtained by a unanimous jury decision. They held that a "reasonable doubt standard" was not violated by verdicts rendered by a split jury. Justices upheld a Louisiana state law which set in motion a trial system that varied according to severity of crime committed and severity of punishment. In finding Louisiana's statute constitutional, the Court specifically held that a split jury did not indicate that deliberations were indicative of reasonable doubt. Instead they reasoned that a majority of jurors were resolute in their conviction that a crime had been committed by the accused. While instructions to a jury warn that a vote to convict must be accompanied by belief that a defendant's guilt is evidenced by proof beyond a reasonable doubt, the Court ruled that only a majority of jurors need assure that a defendant's right to due process and equal protection is maintained. The decision opened a window of opportunity for other states to engage in trial reform that, like Louisiana's statute, would serve to, in the Court's opinion, "facilitate, expedite, and reduce expense in the administration of justice."

Related Cases

Maxwell v. Dow, 176 U.S. 581 (1900).
Jordan v. Massachusetts, 225 U.S. 167 (1912).
Andres v. United States, 333 U.S. 740 (1948).
Duncan v. Louisiana, 391 U.S. 145 (1968).
Apodaca v. Oregon, 406 U.S. 404 (1972).

Bibliography and Further Reading

Hall, Kermit L., ed. *The Oxford Companion to the Supreme Court of the United States.* New York: Oxford University Press, 1992.

Northwestern University. *Oyez, oyez, oyez-A U.S. Supreme Court Database.* http://court.it-services.nwu.edu/oyez/cases

APODACA V. OREGON

Legal Citation: 406 U.S. 404 (1972)

Petitioners
Robert Apodaca, Henry Morgan Cooper, Jr., and James Arnold Madden

Respondent
State of Oregon

Petitioners' Claim
That conviction by a less than unanimous jury verdict, permitted under Oregon state law, violated the right to trial by jury as guaranteed under the Sixth and Fourteenth Amendments of the Constitution.

Chief Lawyer for Petitioners
Richard B. Sobol

Chief Lawyer for Respondent
Jacob B. Tanzer, Solicitor General of Oregon

Justices for the Court
Harry A. Blackmun, Warren E. Burger, Lewis F. Powell, Jr., William H. Rehnquist, Byron R. White (writing for the Court)

Justices Dissenting
William J. Brennan, Jr., William O. Douglas, Thurgood Marshall, Potter Stewart

Place
Washington, D.C.

Date of Decision
22 May 1972

Decision
That the Fourteenth Amendment does not require jury unanimity.

Significance
As a result of the Court's decision in *Apodaca v. Oregon* state court juries were able to convict defendants on the basis of a less than unanimous vote.

In 1969, an Oregon jury convicted Robert Apodaca for assault with a deadly weapon. Likewise two other juries convicted Henry Morgan Cooper, Jr., of burglary in a dwelling, and James Arnold Madden of grand larceny. But there was something unusual about these juries: in none of the trials was the vote unanimous. It was 11-1 in both Apodaca's and Madden's cases; and in Cooper's situation, the margin was 10-2, the minimum vote whereby a conviction could be obtained under Oregon state law.

At one time, it had been assumed that unless a jury could fully agree to convict a defendant, he or she could not be found guilty. This was thought necessary in order to ensure that the 12 members of the jury made their conviction "beyond all reasonable doubt." Presumably if one or two people could not agree with the majority, this suggested that reasonable doubt was possible. The Supreme Court itself had upheld this position in *Duncan v. Louisiana* (1968), when the majority took the position that criminal charges must be "confirmed by the unanimous suffrage of twelve jurors."

However, by the time Apodaca and the others brought their case before the U.S. Supreme Court, having been denied appeal by the Supreme Court of Oregon, the concept of jury unanimity was no longer a given. Already the Court, in *Williams v. Florida* (1970) had called into question the commonly accepted notion that a jury should consist of 12 people. Now it was about to consider the assumption that to be fair, a jury's verdict must be unanimous. It was a question that would be decided in two 1972 cases, *Johnson v. Louisiana* and *Apodaca v. Oregon*.

The Sixth and Fourteenth Amendment Cases

The appellants' legal counsel made a case under both the Sixth and the Fourteenth amendments, seeking to prove that the use of a verdict obtained by a nonunanimous jury violated a defendant's constitutional rights. The two amendments both concern the conduct of courts in handling criminal trials, but the similarity ends there. The Sixth Amendment was ratified, along with the other nine amendments that make up the Bill of Rights, in 1791, and it applies chiefly to the federal government, ensuring that federal courts do not violate the rights of American citizens. The Fourteenth, on the other hand, became a part of the American legal environment on the heels of the Civil War. It was, along with the amendments that directly preceded and followed it, a part of the "Reconstruction Amendments," and was directed chiefly at the states, to ensure that courts in the former slave-holding states of the South did not violate the civil rights of former slaves.

In fact, as Justice White observed, writing for the plurality that upheld the Oregon court's judgment in *Apodaca,* the Fourteenth Amendment ensured that the Sixth Amendment was applied to the states. But where White disagreed with the appellants was in their claim that the Sixth Amendment *required* jury unanimity in order to protect the standard of reasonable doubt, and to uphold the "due process of law" mandated in the Fourteenth Amendment. The reasonable doubt standard, in fact, is not an actual part of the Constitution; rather, it is implied in the Fourteenth Amendment. And, White noted, the reasonable doubt argument for a unanimous jury had recently been rejected by the Court in the companion case of *Johnson v. Louisiana.*

The petitioners had further argued that, because the Fourteenth Amendment requires jury panels which represent the community as a whole, a jury which votes to convict by a less than unanimous decision has automatically excluded the community's minority elements. White, again speaking for the plurality, rejected that claim on two bases. First of all, he said, the Constitution does not state that "every distinct voice in the community has a right to be represented on every jury"; rather, it merely forbids "systematic exclusion of identifiable segments of the community from jury panels and from the juries ultimately drawn from those panels." Also, White and the other justices voting with him (Chief Justice Burger and Justices Blackmun and Rehnquist) rejected the petitioners' implied assumption that the majority elements of a community would necessarily vote on the basis of ethnic prejudice, or that the jury majority's ability to outvote the minority in itself implied such prejudice.

A Less Than Unanimous Court

It is ironic that this case concerning unanimous jury decisions should itself have been decided by a far from unanimous Court. On the one side was White's faction, which ultimately won; on the other side were Justices Stewart, Brennan, Marshall, and Douglas. Justice Powell's decision was the deciding vote.

The dissenters held, in Justice Stewart's words, that "Until today, it has been universally understood that a unanimous verdict is an essential part of a Sixth Amendment jury trial." Citing an array of cases, the dissenting justices established the necessity for a unanimous jury as a key element in a fair trial. They followed what might be considered a common-sense line of reasoning, based on the idea that lifting the unanimity requirement makes it easier for a jury to convict a defendant— and thus increases the chance that an innocent person may be convicted.

Justice Powell agreed with parts of both arguments. He sided with Stewart's group in holding that the Sixth Amendment required federal juries to be unanimous. But Apodaca's case concerned a state court, and thus the Fourteenth Amendment appeared to be a more significant element of the argument. And on that issue, Powell agreed with White's group, that the Fourteenth Amendment did not prevent states from allowing nonunanimous juries. Like White, he did not believe that permitting a jury majority of 11-1 or 10-2 necessarily meant that ethnic minorities' constitutional rights would be violated.

At the time, *Apodaca v. Oregon* raised fears among some, suggesting a future in which states would be able to alter their standards to permit juries with 9-3 or even smaller margins to convict defendants. But twenty-five years after *Apodaca,* few states had adopted the nonunanimity rule, and the Supreme Court itself had further questioned the idea in *Ballew v. Georgia* (1978).

Related Cases

Duncan v. Louisiana, 391 U.S. 145 (1968).
Williams v. Florida, 399 U.S. 78 (1970).
Johnson v. Louisiana, 406 U.S. 356 (1972).
Ballew v. Georgia, 435 U.S. 223 (1978).

Bibliography and Further Reading

Chandler, Ralph C., et al. *The Constitutional Law Dictionary,* Volume I: *Individual Rights.* Santa Barbara, CA: ABC-Clio, 1985.

Hall, Kermit L., ed. *The Oxford Companion to the Supreme Court of the United States.* New York: Oxford University Press, 1992.

Levy, Leonard W., ed. *Encyclopedia of the American Constitution.* New York: Macmillan, 1986.

Witt, Elder, ed. *The Supreme Court A to Z.* Washington, DC: Congressional Quarterly, 1993.

TAYLOR V. LOUISIANA

Legal Citation: 419 U.S. 522 (1975)

Appellant
Billy Jean Taylor

Appellee
State of Louisiana

Appellant's Claim
That Louisiana's jury selection system violated his right to trial by an impartial jury under the Sixth and Fourteenth Amendments.

Chief Lawyer for Appellant
William M. King

Chief Lawyer for Appellee
Kendall L. Vick

Justices for the Court
Harry A. Blackmun, William J. Brennan, Jr., Warren E. Burger, William O. Douglas, Thurgood Marshall, Lewis F. Powell, Jr., Potter Stewart, Byron R. White (writing for the Court)

Justices Dissenting
William H. Rehnquist

Place
Washington, D.C.

Date of Decision
21 January 1975

Decision
Louisiana's jury selection process, which excluded women who failed to register, violated Taylor's Sixth and Fourteenth Amendment rights.

Significance
By overturning gender-based provisions of state laws governing the selection of jurors, the Court opened the way for women throughout the nation to serve on juries equally with men.

On 28 September 1971, police arrested Billy Jean Taylor, a 25-year-old former convict, in the St. Tammany Parish of Louisiana. They charged him with aggravated kidnapping, armed robbery, and rape. Despite having made seven suicide attempts in jail, Taylor was found competent to stand trial.

Jury Concerns

His trial was going to begin at the 22nd Judicial District of Louisiana on 13 April 1972. The day before his trial was to begin, Taylor asked the court to throw out the list of available jurors. The law had systematically excluded women from that summoned group, Taylor claimed, by Article 402 of the Louisiana Code of Criminal Procedure, which provided: "A woman shall not be selected for jury service unless she has previously filed with the clerk of court of the parish in which she resides a written declaration of her desire to be subject to jury service."

Because of this requirement, few jurors in St. Tammany Parish were women, even though 53 percent of the people who met eligibility requirements were female. More specifically, there were no women among the 175 people drawn for jury service during the criminal term in which Taylor's case would be tried, a situation he claimed violated his right to an impartial jury by a jury of his peers—made up of both women and men.

The court rejected Taylor's motion on the same day he made it and the trial continued. Convicted of aggravated kidnapping by the all-male jury, the court sentenced Taylor to death. Taylor then appealed to the state's supreme court to review whether his motion to quash the list of jurors summoned should have been granted. When Louisiana's Supreme Court ruled that the jury list had been selected by constitutional means, Taylor appealed to the U.S. Supreme Court.

For All Intents and Purposes . . .

Two years later, the case came before the U.S. Supreme Court. Taylor's lawyer, William M. King, argued that his client's constitutional right to "a fair trial by jury of a representative segment of the community . . ." was violated as a result of Louisiana's consideration of only those women who expressly registered their desire to serve as jurors.

He pointed out that from 8 December 1971, to 3 November 1972, there were only 12 women among the 18,000 people drawn for jury service in St. Tammany Parish, and that there had been no women among the 175 people drawn to fill the list for the criminal term during which Taylor's case was tried. In short, whether the intent to eliminate women from the jury was there or not, the fact was that women were excluded.

The state of Louisiana claimed that Louisiana's jury selection system was constitutional and that, in any event, "Taylor, a male, has no standing to object to the exclusion of women from his jury." In other words, since he was not female, he could not object to the lack of women on the jury.

A Fair Cross-Section

Effective 1 January 1975, Louisiana repealed the gender-based provision challenged by Taylor. A decision was nonetheless issued three weeks later, with Justice White pointing out in a footnote to his majority opinion that the repeal "has no effect on the conviction obtained in this case."

White briefly outlined the history of Taylor's case and the Court's jurisdiction "to consider whether the Louisiana jury-selection system deprived appellant of his Sixth and Fourteenth Amendment right to an impartial jury." He then offered the Court's conclusion: "We hold that it did and that these amendments were violated . . . In consequence, appellant's conviction must be reversed."

Explaining the Court's reasoning, White began by agreeing that Louisiana's "jury-selection system . . . operates to exclude from jury service an identifiable class of citizens constituting 53 percent of eligible jurors in the community . . ."

White disagreed with the state's claim that the male Taylor lacked standing to challenge a lack of female jurors, writing that "there is no rule that claims such as Taylor presents may be only by those defendants who are members of the group excluded from jury service." Citing earlier court decisions and the Federal Jury Selection and Service Act of 1968, White emphasized that "the requirement of a jury's being chosen from a fair cross section of the community is fundamental to the American system of justice." That requirement, he wrote, "is violated by the systematic exclusion of women . . ."

White acknowledged that the Court had let stand a similar jury-selection system as recently as 1961, in its decision in *Hoyt v. Florida*. He also acknowledged that "the first Congress did not perceive the Sixth Amendment as requiring women on criminal jury panels . . ." Nonetheless, he wrote:

> We think it is no longer tenable to hold that women as a class may be excluded or given automatic exemptions based solely on sex if the consequence is that criminal jury venires are almost totally male. To this extent we cannot follow the contrary implications of the prior cases, including *Hoyt v. Florida*. If it was ever the case that women were unqualified to sit on juries or were so situated that none of them should be required to perform jury service, that time has long since passed. If at one time it could be held that Sixth Amendment juries must be drawn from a fair cross-section of the community but that this requirement permitted the almost total exclusion of women, this is not the case today.

Taylor v. Louisiana guaranteed that the states would call women and men to jury service on an equal basis.

Related Cases
Hoyt v. Florida, 399 U.S. 524 (1970).
United States v. Townsley, 856 F.2d 1189 (1988).
Leichman v. Secretary, Louisiana Dept. of Corrections, 939 F.2d 315 (1991).

Bibliography and Further Reading
Cary, Eve, and Kathleen Willert Peratis. *Woman and the Law*. Skokie, IL: National Textbook Company in conjunction with the American Civil Liberties Union, 1981.

Goldstein, Leslie Freidman. *The Constitutional Rights of Women: Cases in Law and Social Change*, rev. ed. Madison: The University of Wisconsin Press, 1989.

Hoff, Joan. *Law Gender & Injustice: A Legal History of U.S. Women*. New York: New York University Press, 1991.

St. Tammany Farmer, September 30, 1971, October 7, 1971, November 4, 1971, December 30, 1971, February 17, 1972, April 20, 1972.

BALLEW V. GEORGIA

Legal Citation: 435 U.S. 223 (1978)

Petitioner
Claude Davis Ballew

Respondent
State of Georgia

Petitioner's Claim
That a Georgia law providing for juries of only five persons was in violation of the right to trial by jury guaranteed in the Sixth Amendment to the Constitution, and that by depriving the petitioner of his rights, this law further violated the Due Process Clause of the Fourteenth Amendment.

Chief Lawyer for Petitioner
Michael Clutter

Chief Lawyer for Respondent
Leonard W. Rhodes

Justices for the Court
Harry A. Blackmun (writing for the Court), William J. Brennan, Jr., Warren E. Burger, Thurgood Marshall, Lewis F. Powell, Jr., William H. Rehnquist, John Paul Stevens, Potter Stewart, Byron R. White

Justices Dissenting
None

Place
Washington, D.C.

Date of Decision
21 March 1978

Decision
That by depriving the petitioner of his right to trial by jury, the state of Georgia had violated his Sixth and Fourteenth Amendment rights.

Significance
Ballew v. Georgia followed several significant cases regarding jury size, and helped to establish guidelines in this area. Though for centuries 12 had been considered the magic number for juries, that idea was challenged in *Williams v. Florida* (1970), when the Court ruled that a state could allow juries of only six persons. With *Colegrove v. Battin* in 1973, it extended this provision to federal courts. As Justice Powell would later write in an opinion concurring with the Court's *Ballew* decision, "a line has to be drawn somewhere if the substance of jury trial is to be preserved." *Ballew* set that line at six members, and no fewer.

Fulton County Looks Behind the Green Door

Claude Davis Ballew was the manager of the Paris Adult Theatre at 320 Peachtree Street in Atlanta, Georgia, on 9 November 1973, when two men appeared at his theatre to purchase tickets. The movie they were going to see was *Behind the Green Door,* a pornographic film, and the men were investigators from the Fulton County Solicitor General's Office. In order to let them in to the theatre, Ballew, as manager, had to push a button to allow them access. Following their viewing, they obtained a warrant for the seizure of the film. Later they returned to the theatre, watched the movie a second time, seized it, and arrested both Ballew and the cashier. On 26 November the investigators came back, watched the movie a third time, and secured a second warrant. The next day, they saw *Green Door* a fourth time and seized a second copy of the film.

Some ten months later, on 14 September 1974, Ballew was charged on two misdemeanor counts for

> distributing obscene materials in violation of Georgia Code Section 26-2101 in that the said accused did, knowing the obscene nature thereof, exhibit a motion picture film entitled 'Behind the Green Door' that contained obscene and indecent scenes . . .

Ballew was brought to trial in the Criminal Court of Fulton County before a jury of five persons.

After the swearing in of the jury, however, Ballew moved that the court impanel a jury of 12, as was the custom under common law. The rules of that particular court under a variety of Georgia statutes, however, allowed it to try misdemeanor cases with juries of five. Ballew's counsel contended that since this was an obscenity trial, a jury of just five members was inadequate to assess the community's standards with regard to its definition of indecency. Furthermore, under the guarantees of trial by jury in the Sixth Amendment, and of due process of law in the Fourteenth, Ballew's counsel held that he should be allowed a jury of at least six members.

The judge overruled the motion, and the trial proceeded with the five-member panel. After 38 minutes

The Savings and Loan Scandal

After the savings and loan debacle, Congress created the Resolution Trust Corporation in 1989 to cleanup the mess. The RTC was charged with taking over more than 700 failing thrifts, and trying to refund the losses to depositors, who were stuck with the failed loans. Lincoln Savings & Loan, lost $3.4 billion, the most expensive savings and loan crash in the nation's history.

In January of 1995, the RTC closed its doors, but the fallout from the savings and loan crisis continues. The latest wrinkle is a series of lawsuits charging the federal government with breach of contract over its alleged failure to help failed thrifts rebuild through "favorable regulatory treatment." In *United States v. Winstar Corp.* the Supreme Court ruled that the government defaulted on its promise to the thrift. That decision generated hundreds of other lawsuits making the same charges against the government. The Justice Department estimates that damages could eventually reach as high as $32 billion.

Source(s): Grunwald, Michael. "Lawsuit Surge May Cost U.S. Billions; 125 Claims Allege Breach of Contract." *The Washington Post,* August 10, 1998.

---

of deliberation, they found Ballew guilty on both counts. For each of the two counts, he was sentenced to one year in jail and a fine of $1,000. The sentences were to run concurrently and the incarceration was to be suspended upon payment of the fine. At a later hearing, the court denied an amended motion for retrial.

Ballew took the case to the court of appeals, who rejected his claims. Like the Fulton County investigators before them, the judges, too, subjected the film to a thorough viewing and pronounced it "hard-core pornography" that was "obscene as a matter of constitutional law and fact." This ruling supported the conclusion of the jury that Ballew possessed the necessary scienter, or criminal intent, to be convicted. As manager of the Paris Adult Theatre, he had, among other activities, advertised the movie, sold tickets, and pressed the button to let customers in to the viewing area. As for the issue of the five-person jury, the court noted that in *Williams v. Florida* (1970), the Supreme Court had not set a constitutional minimum for the number of jurors in a panel. Instead, the lower court used the standard of *Sanders v. Georgia* (1976), another pornography-related case, in which the constitutionality of a five-member jury had been upheld.

When Ballew took the case to the Supreme Court, Citizens for Decency Through Law Inc. filed an *amicus curiae* brief urging affirmance of the lower court's ruling. One of the two men filing that brief was Charles Keating, Jr., who in the 1980s would be associated with the savings and loan scandal, and who in 1990 would himself be indicted. The issue of pornography, however—presumably the cause for the Citizens for Decency brief—hardly entered into the Court's discussion of *Ballew v. Georgia*. As petitioner, Ballew raised three issues: the constitutional question regarding the jury size, the constitutional sufficiency of the instructions the jury had received regarding scienter and "constructive knowledge" of the film's contents, and the question of obscenity. Since the Court found that the five-member jury did not satisfy the jury-trial guarantee in the Sixth Amendment, however, it did not even consider the other issues.

The Court's Social-Science Approach

The Court's opinion was unanimous, though several of the justices filed concurring opinions in which they cited aspects other than those raised by Justice Blackmun, who wrote for the Court. The petitioner had the right to a trial by jury, Blackmun wrote, a right guaranteed under the Sixth Amendment and reinforced by the Fourteenth. The right to trial by jury is further bolstered by the Court's ruling in *Duncan v. Louisiana* (1968), when it found that "trial by jury in criminal cases is fundamental to the American scheme of justice." Because the maximum penalty for violating Georgia 26-2101 carried with it a sentence of more than six month's imprisonment, Ballew's could not be considered a "petty" crime—that is, a crime for which it might be reasonably said a jury was not required. In *Williams,* the Court had reflected on its *Duncan* opinion to note that trial by a jury of peers protects a defendant from "oppression by the Government."

As for the size of the jury, the Court in *Williams* found that the number 12 was a "historical accident, unrelated to the great purposes which gave rise to the jury in the first place." The Sixth Amendment did not require 12 jurors but, in Blackmun's words, "a jury only of sufficient size to promote group deliberation, to insulate members from outside intimidation, and to provide a representative cross-section of the community." The Court in *Williams* reserved judgment on whether a jury smaller than six members is unconstitutional. However, a number of legal scholars, spurred on by the questions raised in that case, conducted research on the subject. Blackmun turned to those sources to address a number of concerns.

The practice of consulting social-science evidence had long been controversial in the Court, starting with the presentation of a psychological paper as evidence in *Brown v. Board of Education* (1954). Still controversial when Blackmun applied it in *Ballew,* he would be subjected to criticism, both from his brethren on the Court and from others.

Using a variety of studies, including *Jury Verdicts* (1977) by Michael J. Saks, a 1975 *Michigan Law Review* article by Richard Owen Lempert, and scores of other sources, Blackmun made five points regarding jury size. First, the data showed that larger juries were more likely to spend a longer amount of time deliberating on a case. Larger juries' collective memory of the facts was better when it had more heads to remember all the information and a smaller jury was less able to overcome the biases of its various members. Second, he cited a number of studies which showed small juries as more likely to convict an innocent person (Type I error) whereas larger juries were more likely to let off a guilty one (Type II). These facts suggested to many researchers that the optimal jury would consist of six to eight persons. Third, the evidence seemed to show that the smaller the jury, the more likely it was to rule against the defense. Fourth, smaller juries were less likely to represent minority groups: statistically, if a group constituted ten percent of the community, fifty-three percent of randomly selected six-member juries would have no members of that group, and eighty-nine percent would have no more than one. Fifth, the errors attributed to small juries, when multiplied throughout the nation as they would be if such juries became a widespread practice, would result in large numbers of incorrect judgments.

Blackmun then turned to the arguments Georgia used in its favor. First, its interpretation of *Johnson v. Louisiana* (1968) as establishing the Court's approval of five-person juries was "misplaced" because the Court did not consider the issue of five-person juries in that case. Second, Georgia's argument that five-member juries were sufficient to hear misdemeanor cases, if not felony trials, was invalidated by the Court's ruling in *Baldwin v. New York* (1970) that the right to trial by jury was just as strong in the case of misdemeanor as of felony. Third, Georgia's requirement that its five-member panel reach a unanimous decision did not address the issues of "meaningful deliberation," the jury's memory, or its ability to represent the community as a whole. Fourth, it was not enough to claim, as Georgia did, that the five-member jury represented the community simply because there was no overt effort to exclude a minority opinion or ethnic group: given the data cited earlier, it was easy to see that such exclusion could happen inadvertently. Fifth and finally, Georgia also had attempted to use empirical data, citing two studies presented in the *University of Michigan Journal of Law Reform,* but Blackmun questioned those particular studies, as well as the state's interpretation of these and other sources.

Blackmun devoted the remainder of the Court's opinion to Georgia's claim that a smaller jury saved it time and money. Though six members cost the state less money than 12, in that it had to pay jurors a daily stipend, the evidence did not show that six members saved any time in the selection process. In any case, the difference in savings for five-member juries, as opposed to juries composed of six people, were bound to be minuscule.

Concurrence: "A Line Has to Be Drawn Somewhere"

Ballew represented a rare instance of agreement among the nine justices on the Supreme Court, four of whom filed concurring opinions. Justice Stevens joined the Court's opinion, he said, though apparently for different reasons: "I have not altered the views I expressed in *Marks v. United States,*" he wrote, referring to a case concerned with pornography and not jury-trial issues. Justice White wrote that a jury of fewer than six members would fail to satisfy the "cross-section requirement" of the Sixth and Fourteenth Amendments, because it would not properly represent the community. Justice Brennan, joined by Justices Stewart and Marshall, agreed with the Court but held that Ballew should not be subjected to a new trial since in his view the Georgia statute was "overbroad and therefore facially unconstitutional."

Justice Powell, joined by Chief Justice Burger and Justice Rehnquist, agreed with Justice Blackmun that "the line between five and six-member juries is difficult to justify." But, he wrote, "a line has to be drawn somewhere if the substance of jury trial is to be preserved." He expressed differences with Blackmun over issues raised in *Apodaca v. Oregon* (1972), a case concerned with jury unanimity. Then he came to the apparent heart of his disagreement with Blackmun, which related to methods—specifically, his colleague's "heavy reliance on numerology derived from statistical studies"—rather than results. Not only did he consider the social-science approach unnecessary, Justice Powell questioned its wisdom and further expressed concern over the fact that the data could not be subjected to the "traditional testing mechanisms" applied to constitutional, statutory, or legal material.

Impact

Two decades after *Ballew,* its establishment of a six-person minimum for jury size remained. Questions about jury decisions themselves, however, have been raised often, particularly in the cases resulting from the beating of motorist Rodney King by Los Angeles police in 1991, and from the murder indictment of O. J. Simpson in 1994. On 9 January 1998, Michael J. Saks and Richard Owen Lempert, authors whose studies Justice Blackmun had quoted heavily in *Ballew,* participated in an Association of American Law Schools symposium entitled "Is It Time to Replicate *The American Jury?*" The latter was a study undertaken in the 1950s by Kalven and Zeisel, two other researchers to whom Blackmun referred several times in *Ballew.* "Once again," the announcement of the University of Iowa symposium read,

> the jury system seems to be under wide-ranging attack. Whether many or some of these criticisms are valid and point to needed changes in the jury system or whether they are largely new myths, would seem to require new, large-scale, empirical research on the functioning of the jury system. Has the time come for such work?

Related Cases

Duncan v. Louisiana, 391 U.S. 145 (1968).
Baldwin v. New York, 399 U.S. 66 (1970).
Williams v. Florida, 399 U.S. 100 (1970).
Johnson v. Louisiana, 406 U.S. 356 (1972).
Apodaca v. Oregon, 406 U.S. 404 (1972).
Colegrove v. Battin, 413 U.S. 149 (1973).
Sanders v. Georgia, 424 U.S. 931 (1976).

Bibliography and Further Reading

Biskupic, Joan, and Elder Witt. *Guide to the U.S. Supreme Court,* 3rd ed. Washington, DC: Congressional Quarterly Inc., 1997.

Grofman, Bernard. "Jury Decision Making Models and the Supreme Court: The Jury Cases from *Williams v. Florida* to *Ballew v. Georgia.*" *Policy Studies Journal,* Vol. 8, spring 1980, pp. 749-72.

Hall, Kermit L., ed. *The Oxford Companion to the Supreme Court of the United States.* New York: Oxford University Press, 1992.

"Is It Time to Replicate *The American Way?*" http://www.aals.org.

Lempert, Richard Owen. "Uncovering 'Nondiscernible' Differences: Empirical Research and the Jury-Size Cases." *Michigan Law Review,* Vol. 73, 1975, p. 643.

Levy, Leonard W., ed. *Encyclopedia of the American Constitution.* New York: Macmillan, 1986.

Saks, Michael J. *Jury Verdicts: The Role of Group Size and Social Decision Rule.* Lexington, MA: D.C. Heath, 1977.

Witt, Elder. *Congressional Quarterly's Guide to the Supreme Court,* 2nd ed. Washington, DC: Congressional Quarterly Inc., 1990.

BATSON V. KENTUCKY

Legal Citation: 476 U.S. 79 (1986)

Petitioner
James Kirkland Batson

Respondent
State of Kentucky

Petitioner's Claim
That the state acted improperly in selecting a jury for Batson's trial.

Chief Lawyer for Petitioner
J. David Niehaus

Chief Lawyer for Respondent
Rickie L. Pearson, Assistant Attorney General of Kentucky

Justices for the Court
Harry A. Blackmun, William J. Brennan, Jr., Thurgood Marshall, Sandra Day O'Connor, Lewis F. Powell, Jr. (writing for the Court), John Paul Stevens, Byron R. White

Justices Dissenting
Warren E. Burger, William H. Rehnquist

Place
Washington, D.C.

Date of Decision
30 April 1986

Decision
That the case must return to the lower court, and the prosecutor shall have to provide to the judge valid, nondiscriminatory reasons for his dismissal of four African American potential jurors.

Significance
Limited the use of the peremptory challenge, which had given attorneys on both sides the right to strike potential jurors without providing a valid reason. Sex-based peremptory challenges were extended to include those based on race, making it illegal to dismiss a juror based on race.

In 1981, James Kirkland Batson went to trial in Jefferson County, Kentucky, on burglary charges. Batson was an African American. During the jury selection process, the prosecutor used the "peremptory challenge" to dismiss four African Americans from the panel, and an all-white jury was selected. The peremptory challenge had been a cornerstone of the American jury selection process since the late eighteenth century, and had become particularly entrenched in the legal system since the mid-1960s. In essence, it allowed a prosecutor to object to potential jurors without providing a reason for their unsuitability, and dismiss them from having to serve. In legal terminology, "peremptory" means "precluding further debate or action;" another definition implies "authoritarian, mandatory."

Selecting the Jury

Peremptory-challenge rules often resulted in all-white juries in criminal cases for African American defendants, on the assumption that an African American might not vote to convict another African American. In a more extreme case, it was used to exclude African American jurors from the trial of a member of the Ku Klux Klan charged with the murder of an African American. One significant Supreme Court ruling upholding the peremptory challenge came in 1965 in *Swain v. Alabama,* which asserted that a very obvious pattern of bias on the part of the prosecutor—that he had a long history of keeping African Americans off juries—had to be proven in court. This had occurred only twice since 1965; five states then passed legislation amending their state constitution to overrule *Swain.* Peremptory challenges were still common, however, primarily because they were seen as assuring that an unbiased and qualified jury was selected from the pool. Likewise, a lawyer for an African American defendant would be allowed to dismiss white jurors.

Batson's attorneys filed a motion to dismiss the jury on the grounds that an all-white jury violated Batson's Sixth and Fourteenth Amendment rights to a fair trial, but the judge denied the motion. He was convicted, and his lawyers appealed. Kentucky's State Supreme Court upheld the lower court's decision. The NAACP Legal Defense and Education Fund became involved, and arguments before the U.S. Supreme Court began in December of 1985. On 30 April 1986, the Court announced its decision in favor of James Batson.

The Decision

Batson v. Kentucky reversed the 1965 *Swain* ruling. (The case gained added impact because of the fact that perhaps only once a year does the High Court reverse its prior decisions.) Justice Powell delivered the opinion of the 7-2 majority vote. Justice White, who had written the 1965 decision, sided with the majority to overturn it. The Court ruled that peremptory challenges, in effect, deny a defendant the right to trial by jury of a cross-section of the community. This right is guaranteed by the Sixth Amendment to the U.S. Constitution, which holds that citizens have the right to a trial by jury in the community where the crime allegedly took place.

More importantly, the Powell opinion declared that peremptory challenges were in violation of the first section of Fourteenth Amendment, also known as the Equal Protection Clause, which reads, in part:

> . . . No State shall . . . deprive any person of life, liberty, or property, without due process of law; nor deny to any person within its jurisdiction the equal protection of the laws.

Thus, according to the Court, equal protection prohibited the selection of jury members based on their race. With *Batson*, the Court affirmed the principle it upheld in an 1880 decision that ruled it unfair to force a defendant to stand trial before a jury from which members of his race were purposefully excluded. Such exclusions, the Court said further, assumed that African Americans were incapable of making an impartial decision when considering the case of an African American defendant, as if they were not qualified to serve on a jury.

Broadened in Scope

After sending *Batson v. Kentucky* back to the lower judicial body, the High Court set forth new rules for peremptory challenges to be used there. If a defendant does not approve of the selected jury, he or she must indicate that there were grounds to "infer" that a juror was excluded because of race—for instance, that both are members of a cognizable minority group. Next, the judge must demand a "neutral" explanation from the prosecutor, shifting the burden of proof to the state. The prosecutor's reasons for rejecting the juror must be based on impartial grounds. The High Court also ruled that either the defense lawyer or the trial judge can object to the peremptory challenge, but it must be raised at the initial trial (not in an appeals case) and before the jury is sworn in.

Justices Burger and Rehnquist dissented from the majority opinion. They deemed it unwise to overturn an established legal precedent, and Rehnquist noted that when peremptory challenges were used broadly— that is, to exclude white jurors from cases involving white defendants, for example, they seemed to be within the law. Other opponents, the most vocal of whom was the National District Attorneys Association, asserted that the *Batson* ruling provided the defendant in a criminal trial more rights than it did the average citizen. Some legal analysts contended that *Batson v. Kentucky* would spell the eventual death of the peremptory challenge completely. Indeed, though it originally applied only to criminal cases, it was later expanded to civil trials, and then broadened to include ethnicity and gender discrimination.

Related Cases

Swain v. Alabama, 380 U.S. 202 (1965).
Powers v. Ohio, 499 U.S. 400 (1991).
J.E.B. v. State ex rel. T.B., 511 U.S. 127 (1994).
State v. Bryant, 662 N.E.2d 846 (1995).

Bibliography and Further Reading

Barton, Benjamin Hoorn. "Religion-Based Peremptory Challenges after *Batson v. Kentucky* and *J.E.B. v. Alabama.*" *Michigan Law Review,* October 1995, p. 191.

Breck, David F. "Peremptory Strikes after *Batson v. Kentucky.*" *ABA Journal,* April 1, 1988, pp. 54-60.

Dripps, Donald A. "I Didn't Like the Way He Looked." *Trial,* July 1995, p. 94.

Press, Aric, with Ann McDaniel. "Integrating the Jury Box." *Newsweek,* May 12, 1986, p. 70.

Reidinger, Paul. "Rainbow Juries." *ABA Journal,* May 1989, pp. 100-104.

Shoop, Julie Gannon. "High Court Bans Sex-based Jury Strikes." *Trial,* June 1994, p. 91.

LOCKHART V. MCCREE

Legal Citation: 476 U.S. 162 (1986)

Petitioner
A. L. Lockhart

Respondent
Ardia V. McCree

Petitioner's Claim
That the removal of prospective jurors who oppose the death penalty is a violation of a defendant's constitutional rights.

Chief Lawyer for Petitioner
John Steven Clark

Chief Lawyer for Respondent
Samuel R. Gross

Justices for the Court
Harry A. Blackmun, Warren E. Burger, Sandra Day O'Connor, Lewis F. Powell, Jr., William H. Rehnquist (writing for the Court), Byron R. White

Justices Dissenting
William J. Brennan, Jr., Thurgood Marshall, John Paul Stevens

Place
Washington, D.C.

Date of Decision
5 May 1986

Decision
That the removal of prospective jurors who oppose capital punishment is not unconstitutional.

Significance
The Supreme Court held that a court's decision to remove potential jurors before a trial because they state their opposition to the death penalty does not violate the requirement that juries represent a fair cross section of the community.

Ardia V. McCree was on trial for murder in Arkansas. He faced a capital charge, meaning he would be executed if convicted. Before the trial started, the judge removed from the pool of potential jurors all those who stated that they could not under any circumstance vote to impose the death penalty. The jury that did see the trial voted to convict McCree and sentenced him to life in prison without parole. McCree appealed the conviction in a state appeals court, but his appeal was denied.

McCree then took his case to federal district court. He claimed that the "death qualification" imposed on the jurors had resulted in an impartial jury, thus denying him his right to a fair trial under the Sixth and Fourteenth Amendments to the U.S. Constitution. These amendments state that a jury must be composed of a fair representation of the community.

The Lower Courts Rule

The U.S. District Court for the Eastern District of Arkansas ruled in favor of McCree. The U.S. Court of Appeals for the Eighth Circuit affirmed this ruling. In its decision, it concluded that there was enough evidence to suggest that excluding anti-death penalty persons from jury pools makes the resulting jury more likely to convict a defendant. A.L. Lockhart, the director of the Arkansas Department of Correction, appealed this decision to the U.S. Supreme Court.

The Majority's Argument

The majority rejected McCree's claim that the "death qualification" results in impartial juries, pointing to flaws in the evidence used by the lower courts to assert the opposite. The majority went on to point out that the same jury would have been chosen even had no "death qualifying" questions been asked of them. Besides, both parties in the case had conceded that the individual jurors in this case had been impartial.

On the question of the Sixth Amendment, the majority ruled that the constitutional rule that a jury must represent a "fair cross section" of the community did not apply in this case. Furthermore, even if it had, the majority refused to categorize death penalty opponents as the kind of "distinctive group" that cannot be excluded from juries. According to the majority, the term "distinctive groups" was meant to indicate race, gender, or national origin, not groups of people with shared opinions or political beliefs. It would be wildly impractical, according to the majority, for judges to spend time and energy balancing out different viewpoints and backgrounds on a jury.

Finally, there was the issue of the "two stage" jury. Here, the majority ruled that state prosecutors have a proper interest in making sure they can get a single jury to decide on both the evidence in the case and on whether to seek the death penalty if the defendant is convicted. Therefore, it is permissible for them to exclude opponents of the death penalty from the panel.

The Dissent

Three justices disagreed with the Court's ruling. Justice Marshall wrote the dissent, joined by Justice Brennan and Justice Stevens. In their opinion, the exclusion of death penalty opponents from a jury gave the prosecution an unfair advantage in the trial. They agreed with the lower courts' determination that juries which have been "death qualified" are more likely to convict.

The dissenters raised some other important issues as well. For one, they argued that "death qualification" results in a disproportionate number of minorities on juries, since minorities are more inclined to oppose the death penalty. Also, the dissenters refused to accept the majority's argument that the state has a right to obtain one jury for both the "guilt" and "penalty" phases of a capital trial. In the dissenters' view, this interest cannot be deemed more important than the right of the defendant to a fair trial under the Sixth and Fourteenth Amendments.

The Court seemed to be switching gears in regard to its views on the allowance of death qualification for prospective jurors, as *Lockhart v. McCree* represented a modification of an earlier Supreme Court decision—the 1968 case of *Witherspoon v. Illinois*. In that case, the Court ruled that courts cannot select juries that are unusually willing to sentence a defendant to death. Thus, *Lockhart v. McCree* represents an important shift of direction in the appointing of jury members on murder trials.

Related Cases
Hoyt v. Florida, 368 U.S. 57 (1961).
Duncan v. Louisiana, 391 U.S. 145 (1968).
Witherspoon v. Illinois, 391 U.S. 510 (1968).
Bumper v. North Carolina, 391 U.S. 543 (1968).
Peters v. Kiff, 407 U.S. 493 (1972).
Gregg v. Georgia, 428 U.S. 153 (1976).
Jurek v. Texas, 428 U.S. 262 (1976).
Castaneda v. Partida, 430 U.S. 482 (1977).
Lockett v. Ohio, 438 U.S. 586 (1978).
Duren v. Missouri, 439 U.S. 357 (1979).

Bibliography and Further Reading
Chandler, Ralph C. *The Constitutional Law Dictionary.* Santa Barbara, CA: ABC-Clio, Inc., 1987.

Haney, Craig, and Deana Dorman Logan. "Broken Promise: The Supreme Court's Response to Social Science Research on Capital Punishment." *Journal of Social Issues,* summer 1994, p. 75.

BOOTH V. MARYLAND

Legal Citation: 482 U.S. 496 (1987)

Petitioner
John Booth

Respondent
State of Maryland

Petitioner's Claim
According to the Eighth Amendment, the petitioner's rights were violated because the jury was allowed to read a victim impact statement (VIS) during the sentencing phase of the trial. By allowing additional, unrelated information about how the crime impacted the family of the victim, the state had introduced prejudicial, inflammatory information which prompted the jury to impose extraordinarily severe punishment.

Chief Lawyer for Petitioner
George E. Burns, Jr.

Chief Lawyer for Respondent
Charles O. Monk II

Justices for the Court
Harry A. Blackmun, William J. Brennan, Jr., Thurgood Marshall, Lewis F. Powell, Jr. (writing for the Court), John Paul Stevens

Justices Dissenting
Sandra Day O'Connor, William H. Rehnquist, Antonin Scalia, Byron R. White

Place
Washington D.C.

Date of Decision
15 June 1987

Decision
Presentation of a victim impact statement (VIS) during the sentencing phase of a capital murder trial violated the Eighth Amendment, therefore, the case was remanded back to the lower court.

Significance
Under the Eighth Amendment, the Supreme Court held that states cannot allow juries to consider a "victim impact statement" (VIS) during the sentencing phase of a trial where a guilty conviction may impose the death penalty on the defendant.

In May of 1984, John Booth and Willie Reid entered the home of Irvin and Rose Bronstein for the purpose of stealing money to buy heroin. Booth, who lived only three houses away in the same neighborhood, was aware that the Bronsteins could identify him, so he and Reid stabbed the elderly couple to death. He was found guilty of two counts of first-degree murder, two counts of robbery, and conspiracy to commit robbery. After the trial, Booth opted to let the jury determine his sentence instead of the judge.

Before the sentencing phase began, the State Division of Parole and Probation presented a report that was required by state statute. Information required in the report included a victim impact statement (VIS) that described the affect of the crime on the victims and the victims' family. The VIS was either read to the jury, or the family members offered their views orally by appearing in court. In this case, the VIS was based on a statement by the victims' son, daughter, son-in-law, and granddaughter. The Bronstein family told about the warmness of Irvin and Rose and about all the problems that members of the family suffered due to their loss. In their VIS, the family also offered opinions and characterizations of the crimes and their opinions about the persons who committed the crime. In one part of the VIS, the Bronsteins' daughter said "I don't feel that the people who did this could ever be rehabilitated and I don't want them to be able to do this again."

The state trial court denied the petitioner's request to suppress the VIS, rejecting the argument that information in the VIS was "irrelevant, unduly inflammatory, and therefore its use in a capital case violated the Eighth Amendment." After considering the state's presentencing report, including the victim impact statement, the jury gave Booth the death penalty.

On appeal, the Maryland Court of Appeals affirmed the lower court's decision, finding that the VIS "serves an important interest by informing the sentence of the full measure of harm caused by the crime." The petitioner again appealed to the U.S. Supreme Court where the lower court's sentencing (but not the conviction) was vacated and remanded back for further proceedings.

Victim Impact Statements

According to a study cited by the National Victim Center, 66 percent of crime victims described themselves as "satisfied with the criminal justice system" if they were given the opportunity to present a written victim impact statement (VIS) in court. By contrast, only 25 percent identified themselves as satisfied if they were not given the opportunity to present such a statement.

Few people who witness a criminal trial, particularly a death-penalty case, can fail to be moved by the plight of the victim. Even the acclaimed 1995 motion picture *Dead Man Walking*, which was clearly written from an anticapital punishment viewpoint, makes a compelling presentation of the terror suffered by the victims of the killer, and of the parents' continuing anguish over their murdered children. So who could be opposed to victim impact statements?

The American Civil Liberties Union (ACLU), though it has not made a clear stance with regard to VIS, has presented testimony in opposition to a proposed Victim's Rights Amendment to the Constitution. From the ACLU perspective, everything must be done to protect the rights of the accused—even after the accused becomes the convicted, at which point a VIS may result in an unfairly harsh sentence.

Source(s): "Testimony on S.J. Res. 44." American Civil Liberties Union, http://www.aclu.org.
"Victim Impact Statements: Key Findings." National Victim Center, http://www.

In presenting arguments before the Supreme Court, the chief attorney for the petitioner argued that when making a decision about the death penalty, juries should only consider two criteria: the defendant's background and the circumstances of the crime. He pointed out that neither criterion was part of the VIS presented during his client's sentencing phase. Counsel also pointed out that, typically, persons who gave statements in a VIS were not witness to the crime, so their testimony should not be considered admissible as "aggravating circumstances." Moreover, the petitioner's attorney maintained that information collected and presented in a VIS was individual and therefore not of consistent value in all cases. Each family has a different ability to show grief, thus, VIS presentations varied greatly. In fact, he maintained that some victims were without families and, therefore, a "family-less" VIS would likely impact a jury's deliberations differently than a VIS containing the personal statements of a victim's family. Finally, counsel posited that a VIS that contained emotionally-charged opinions by family members would be inconsistent with reasoned decision making required in capital cases.

Conversely, the attorney for the respondent claimed that a VIS was important precisely because it referred to the emotional state of a victims' family. Counsel conceded that any grief or emotional trauma a family expressed in a VIS was not considered an aggravating factor under Maryland law. (Before the death penalty can be imposed, Maryland requires that a crime must meet at least one of ten possible aggravating circumstances such as was present in the robbery and murder of the Bronsteins.) But, he contended that the VIS was critical in the sentencing phase of a murder trial because there was a direct connection between a murder and the harm that murder caused to a victim's family. Because a perpetrator of murder can assume that the victim leaves a family behind, the perpetrator must also know that the death of the victim must also affect the victim's family too. Thus, in order to have better insight into aggravating circumstances (as an outcome of a murder), a jury needed to read or hear a VIS before imposing the death penalty.

The majority decision of the Supreme Court found that introducing a VIS into jury deliberations during the sentencing phase of a capital murder trial posed a risk of overly prejudicing a jury and thus violated the Eighth Amendment. Writing for the majority, Justice Powell observed that in a capital case, the jury's sentencing task is based on consideration of a defendant as a unique individual. The focus of a VIS, however, was not on the defendant but on the victim's character and reputation and the effect of the crime on a victim's family. Justices agreed with Booth's attorney—the potential for admission of emotionally-charged opinions that might be presented in a VIS was irrelevant to sentencing deliberations because each family possesses a differing ability to show grief. Although the murder of the Bronsteins was a heinous crime, the Court held that, at the time of the crime, Booth was nonetheless unaware of potential consequences on the victims' family (or that the victims had a family) and such information would have been irrelevant in his decision to kill. Thus, such factors as contained in a VIS were inappropriate to consider during sentencing. The majority opinion further reasoned that the presentation of a VIS could cause a jury to divert from the relevant evidence of the crime. Ultimately, the Court held that admission of a VIS created a constitutionally unacceptable risk that the jury might impose the death penalty "in an arbitrary and capricious manner."

In writing the dissenting opinion, Justice Scalia reflected what would, in later years, become an increasing social bias in favor of victim's rights over those of the accused. Dissenting justices felt that if punishment could be enhanced in noncapital cases on the basis of the harm caused (such as information of the kind provided in a VIS), then there was no reason why the majority opinion should have found the same unconstitutional in capital cases. Moreover, justices felt that if the defendant was entitled to be considered as an individual, so too, the victim should have been considered an individual whose death represented a unique loss to family and society. Thus, the dissenting opinion concluded that the only proper basis for setting punishment was not merely the perpetrator's circumstances or frame of mind, but also the amount of harm inflicted on the victim.

In the intervening years since the Court's decision, state legislatures began to reconsider the balance of victims' and defendants' rights. In 1991, the state of New Jersey passed legislation that was considered an important step toward a more equal balance, giving a victim the ability to give an oral statement at the time of sentencing. In the same year, when *Payne v. Tennessee* was appealed to the Supreme Court, the decision of the lower court to admit testimony by the victim's grandmother was affirmed; the decision specifically refuted the defendant's claim that, considering the ruling in *Booth v. Maryland,* his Eighth Amendment rights were violated.

In 1996, a scant decade after the Court rendered their decision in this case, American sensibilities veered towards the rights of victims and away from unconditionally protecting the rights of offenders. Responding to the perceived increase of violent crimes in U.S cities, an alarmed public demanded and received attention from legislative representatives in Congress. In hearings concerning the Victim's Bill of Rights Amendment, the impact of the Court's decision in *Booth v. Maryland* was

examined for its negative impact on the conduct of trials for violent crimes. Speaking before the Committee on the Judiciary of the U.S. Senate, Paul G. Cassell, an associate professor of law from the University of Utah, spoke about the manner in which the adjudication of *Booth v. Maryland* prompted a judge to exclude a victim's mother from capital proceedings lest her presence predispose the jury to the death penalty. Similar Supreme Court decisions concerning rights of perpetrators of violent crimes, resulted in the enactment of legislation that protected the victims of crime and enhanced punishment for offenders. And while *Booth v. Maryland* did not single-handedly change the way legislatures sought to redraft violent crime legislation, it was nonetheless an important, contributing factor in legislative deliberations.

Related Cases
Woodson v. North Carolina, 428 U.S. 280 (1976).
People v. Levitt, 156 Cal. App. 3d 500 (1984).
Lodowski v. State, 302 MD 691 (1985).
Reid v. State, 305 ND 9 (1985).
Payne v. Tennessee, 501 U.S. 808 (1991).

Bibliography and Further Reading
Cassell, Paul G. "Statement of Paul G. Cassell Associate Professor of Law University of Utah College of Law Before The Committee on the Judiciary, United States Senate, Concerning The Victims' Bill of Rights Amendment." http://www.nvc.org/nvcan/Cassell2.htm

Luginbuhl, James, and Michael Burkhead. "Sources of Bias and Arbitrariness in the Capital Trial." *Journal of Social Issues,* summer 1994, p. 103.

Phillips, Amy K. "Thou Shalt Not Kill Any Nice People: The Problem of Victim Impact Statements in Capital Sentencing." *American Criminal Law Review,* fall 1997, p. 93.

Sandel, Michael J. "Crying for Justice." *New Republic,* July 7, 1997, p. 25.

JUVENILE COURTS

A System in Place for Children

A juvenile court is a special court that handles cases of delinquent, dependent, or neglected children under the age of 18. These courts are often a division of the state or county court system so each state follows separate mandates in the administration of juvenile courts. The same offense committed by youths in different states is subject to different rules and punishment. Some states only deal with youths up to age 17. Others allow serious cases, such as murder or armed robbery, to be transferred to adult courts involving youths as young as 11 years old. In most states, however, the juvenile courts have concurrent jurisdiction with adult courts for youths between the ages of 15 and 18. Youths adjudicated delinquent and who have been judged guilty of unlawful acts receive both a juvenile and adult sentence. The juvenile sentence is served first and adult sentence goes into effect in one of two circumstances: an incarcerated juvenile turns 21 and is sent to an adult prison to complete his or her sentence; or the juvenile is not responding to rehabilitation so the adult sentence goes into effect.

Though each state administers juvenile courts differently, all children's courts are dedicated to protecting the child's privacy and best interests. Rather than determining the guilt of a child in court cases, emphasis is placed on the best course of action to rehabilitate the child. A child comes before a juvenile court in one of three circumstances: delinquency, status offenses, or abuse or neglect. Depending on the circumstances, the procedures of the juvenile court differ slightly.

Types of Cases Handled in Juvenile Court

Delinquency cases involve a child entering the juvenile court system because of criminal charges such as robbery, murder, assault, or other felonies. Since the late 1960s, youths charged with delinquency have the right to counsel, notice of charges, and protection against self-incrimination as well as the right to appeal the court's decision. A hearing determines whether the child will be released or held until a trial date. If the involved parties fail to work out a plea arrangement, the case goes to trial. A trial in juvenile court is called an adjudication hearing but is similar in proceedings

to a trial in adult court. The prosecuting attorney must prove the charges, otherwise the youth is acquitted and goes free.

When a youth is convicted, a dispositional hearing is scheduled which is similar to a sentencing in adult court. Rather than punishment of the juvenile offender, the disposition focuses on rehabilitation and the needs of the child. Juvenile court judges have a wide range of alternatives available in determining the best course of action to take with the child. The most common action is probation, but the child can be incarcerated in a juvenile detention center, sent to "boot" camp or special training schools, or the case may be dismissed by the court. The evaluations of psychologists and social workers are crucial in these decisions as is input from lawyers and counselors.

While offenders in delinquency cases have many rights, these rights are often missing for status offenders. Status offenses are cases involving a juvenile charged with an act that would not be criminal if committed by an adult. Status offenses are sometimes termed "pre-delinquency" cases meaning the juvenile is on the road to repeatedly breaking the law and being labeled a "juvenile delinquent." Running away, truancy from school, malevolence or aggressive behavior are examples of status offenses. Proceedings for status offenders do not involve proof beyond a reasonable doubt, a requirement in most other court proceedings, nor does the offender have a right to counsel or protection against self-incrimination. Cases are often diverted from the court system into a social program such as educational or training classes, foster care, family counseling programs, or community-based involvement directed by a social worker.

Children may also enter the juvenile court system not as respondents to the court, but as victims to be protected by the court under *parens patriae* or "the state as parent." In abuse and neglect proceedings, the court files a petition against the parent or adult caregiver of the child. Abuse involves cruelty, mental and/or physical, toward the child or inappropriate physical or sexual contact. Neglect involves the failure to care for, or provide the basic needs of, the child or to protect them from abuse by others.

The adult defendant has the right to an attorney. Depending on the jurisdiction of the juvenile court, the child may have no counsel, may have counsel appointed for the child, or the court may appoint an "interim" guardian or other representative to act in the best interest of the child.

Unlike adult courts, all juvenile court sessions are closed to the public and all files are sealed. Often, the children's initials are used in court records and paperwork instead of full names to protect their identity from the public and the press. A major criticism of the juvenile court system is related to this issue of privacy. When juveniles are transferred to adult courts for trial, their files and past history of delinquency remain protected under the provisions of the juvenile justice system. Some states make this information available to the judge only during arraignment or pre-trial hearings when the future of the case is determined.

Development of Juvenile Courts

Children have not always been afforded the rights and privileges they now have through a juvenile court system. During the early years of America, children were considered miniature adults at the age of seven and therefore responsible for their actions. Crimes committed by a child were handled in the same manner as if the crime were committed by an adult. Children were arrested, detained, tried, and sentenced in criminal court and sent to prison with adults. All prisoners were housed together, whether male or female, child or adult, murderer or pickpocket.

A wave of social consciousness enveloped the country during the early decades of the nineteenth century. Opinions about children changed. Childhood became an important transition between infancy and adulthood. Social activists fought for the protection of children. While some worked to remove children from the drudgery of day-long labor, others saw children victimized by a judicial system that placed impressionable children under the influence of hardened criminals. During the 1820s two groups emerged which helped shape the early juvenile justice system. The Society for the Prevention of Juvenile Delinquency advocated the separation of adult and juvenile criminals. The Society for the Reformation of Juvenile Delinquents worked on reforming children convicted of crimes. Rather than imprisonment, the children went to work schools. They lived in a dormitory, were trained for factory work, and jobbed out to manufacturers. The children were soon exploited by both the manufacturers and the school directors working long hours with all wages turned over to the directors and many boys ran away.

It was apparent that juvenile justice needed to address the hardship and troubles delinquent children faced and to work to mold them into responsible future adults. The home environment of young lawbreakers was often troubled with abuse, neglect, and poverty. If the state became the parent under the *parens patriae* provision, delinquent children could be reformed.

Special juvenile courts were established as an informal alternative to criminal court for children. The first court of this type was organized in Cook County, Illinois in 1899. By 1925 all but two states had followed Illinois' example. Early juvenile courts advocated using a combination of punishment and counseling to reform delinquent youths. For extremely serious crimes, the juvenile court could waive their right to jurisdiction over the youth and the criminal justice system would take the case.

Because juvenile courts were concerned with reforming the child rather than determining guilt, lawyers and official court proceedings were deemed unnecessary. Children had no lawyers or representatives, nor did they have a true trial. Instead, a judge, magistrate, or social worker reviewed the complaint against the child and determined what the child needed as far as punishment and/or training to turn his or her life onto a positive course of growth.

A child's "needs" were often met by sending him to reform school until "rehabilitated" or reaching the age of 21. Children were also brought into the system because their parents could not control them. They might run away from home, miss too much school, or become unruly. These acts were termed "status offenses" and viewed by the juvenile court as pre-delinquent behavior. Status offenders were often placed in reform or training schools, just as juvenile delinquents were. As juvenile courts continued to evolve, differences in how each state handled these special courts also grew.

Regulating and Setting Standards

Though the social reformers who helped establish juvenile courts were fighting for the rights of children, juveniles entering the juvenile justice system had no legal rights. Three cases helped restore legal rights to children and establish some standards in the juvenile courts across the country. *Kent vs. United States* (1966), and *In re Gault* (1967) restored to accused juveniles the right to a fair trial and the right to counsel. Kent, a 16-year-old on probation through juvenile court, was accused of robbery and rape. His case was waived from juvenile court to adult court and in so doing, Kent should have been afforded the privileges given any adult accused of a crime.

In re Gault was a landmark case altering the procedures and rights of the accused within the juvenile court system. Gault, a 15-year-old with no previous juvenile record, was accused and sentenced for making obscene phone calls to a neighbor. He was provided with no attorney, the witnesses and complainant did not appear at his hearing, and he was presumed guilty without proof and sent to reform school until the age of 21. His parents appealed the decision, and the Supreme Court ruled that juveniles had the right to due process of law, including representation and the right to cross-examine witnesses, even in juvenile court.

In re Winship (1970) determined that when juveniles were accused of offenses that would be crimes if committed by an adult, proof of guilt beyond a reasonable doubt had to be established before conviction. Thanks to these three cases, when a juvenile appears in a juvenile court or his case is waived to adult court, he has the right to counsel, to be informed of his offense, to cross-exam witnesses, to receive a transcript of the proceedings, to appeal the decision, and to be protected from self-incrimination. His accuser must provide a preponderance of evidence against him. In juvenile court, however, he does not have the right to a jury trial as long as the presiding judge is fair, impartial, and due process is served, according to *McKeiver v. Pennsylvania* (1976).

In an effort to provide guidelines to state juvenile courts, and aid in reducing juvenile delinquency, two programs were established in 1974 within the United States Justice Department. The Office of Juvenile Justice and Delinquency Prevention assists state and local governments in improving the juvenile court system and preventing delinquency. The Juvenile Justice and Delinquency Prevention Act provides grants for reforming juvenile court procedures and providing counseling and educational programs to prevent delinquency.

Criticisms and Conflicts

Despite efforts by the federal government to help curb juvenile crime rates, the 1980s experienced an increase in serious crimes committed by youths. "Between 1985 and 1995, the juvenile arrest rate for violent crimes rose 69 percent. For murders it rose 96 percent," according to Dan Carney reporting in the *Congressional Quarterly.*

Critics of the juvenile court system blame the rise of drug use, specifically crack cocaine which triggered turf drug wars, an increase in handguns available on the streets and to youths, and the juvenile justice system for not making children aware of the consequences of their crimes.

Reforms are demanded of the system, especially by victims of juvenile criminals who express frustration with the way young criminals are handled. When a child is charged with robbery and assault or attempted murder, but is placed on probation and in the custody of parents who fail to supervise the child, victims see a great injustice being served. More and more opponents of the juvenile court system are calling for waiver of serious crimes to the adult court system. Others disagree saying this will stigmatize the youth as a lost cause and encourage continued criminal behavior. They argue that youths tried in adult courts do not necessarily receive longer or tougher sentences because it is a first offense in criminal court, despite the number of appearances for the same or similar offenses in juvenile court. Still others argue the entire juvenile court system should be abolished and all juveniles sentenced in adult courts. Individual states continue to try different methods to curb the high rate of juvenile delinquency. Where one state finds success, others implement the same procedure all in an effort to best protect and meet the needs of America's children.

See also: **Juvenile Law and Justice**

Bibliography and Further Reading

Carney, Dan. "Experts and Lawmakers Disagree . . . on Stemming Juvenile Crime." *Congressional Quarterly,* April 12, 1997, p. 846.

Gest, Ted, with Victoria Pope. "Crime Time Bomb." *U.S. News & World Report,* March 25, 1996, p. 28.

"Juvenile Injustice." *America,* September 28, 1996, p. 3.

KENT V. UNITED STATES

Legal Citation: 383 U.S. 541 (1966)

Petitioner
Morris A. Kent, Jr.

Respondent
United States

Petitioner's Claim
That the juvenile court order that sent Kent's case to trial in regular criminal court was invalid.

Chief Lawyers for Petitioner
Myron G. Ehrlich, Richard Arens

Chief Lawyer for Respondent
Theodore George Gilinsky

Justices for the Court
William J. Brennan, Jr., Tom C. Clark, William O. Douglas, Abe Fortas (writing for the Court), Earl Warren

Justices Dissenting
Hugo Lafayette Black, John Marshall Harlan II, Potter Stewart, Byron R. White

Place
Washington, D.C.

Date of Decision
21 March 1966

Decision
That the waiver was indeed invalid, and the case was sent back to district court for a rehearing on its validity.

Significance
The Court's ruling ushered in an era of reform in the juvenile legal system that granted increasing constitutional protections to minors.

The first mention of District of Columbia resident Morris A. Kent, Jr., in that city's juvenile court records came in 1959. At the age of 14 Kent had been arrested for several incidents of housebreaking and one of robbery. The juvenile court judge placed him on probation. Two years later, a woman was raped and robbed by an intruder in her home. Fingerprints taken from the scene matched those provided by Kent in 1959 at the time of his first arrest. He was taken into custody and questioned.

A Social Ill

The problem with Kent's case, however, was that it was technically less a "crime" than a "social problem" under the formative guidelines of the juvenile court system. The early twentieth century heralded the formal creation of a separate judicial system for youthful offenders in the United States. Its aim was rehabilitation rather than punishment, and the juvenile courts were designed to provide a framework of support with this in mind. Social workers, probation officers, and psychologists—ruled over by a trained and sympathetic judge—would provide the offender with the necessary assistance to improve himself and stay out of trouble. Juvenile offenses were considered a social problem, not an infraction against society. The juvenile justice system was designed as an exchange of sorts: minors did not enjoy the same rights as adult defendants, but were treated more leniently. To grant them the equal protection dictated by the Constitution would have hindered the system's ability to provide rehabilitation.

Kent's mother obtained a lawyer, and a caseworker from juvenile court met with the attorney and advised him that they were considering "waiving" the case—that is, passing it over to the U.S. district court. There, Kent would be tried as an adult for all the offenses. The lawyer requested a hearing on the waiver, and also filed a request for access to the Social Services file that had been kept on Kent during his probation period. Meanwhile, Kent remained in the District of Columbia's Receiving Home for Children for a week, without being formally arraigned on any charges. For adults, such detention without arraignment is considered unlawful under the Constitution.

Juvenile Justice; or How a Survey Can Influence an Act of Congress

In 1966, the National Council on Crime and Delinquency (NCCD) conducted a survey of juvenile and adult facilities, as well as aspects of juvenile probation and aftercare. From this pivotal study emerged, eight years later, elements of the Juvenile Justice and Delinquency Prevention (JJDP) Act of 1974.

At the time the NCCD conducted its survey, only seven percent of the nation's juvenile court jurisdictions possessed juvenile facilities. Within the existing facilities, the study found overcrowding and abusive conditions. A number of other concerns emerged over the course of the survey, and at its completion the NCCD made several recommendations for "a revised philosophy of the juvenile court," as well as for the correctional system and other aspects of juvenile justice.

Congress in 1974 built four of the NCCD's specific recommendations into the JJDP. A quarter of a century later, most U.S. states and territories were in compliance with these four: deinstitutionalization of status offenders (54 states and territories in full compliance); separation of juveniles from adults in confinement (53 states and territories); jail and lockup removal (53 states and territories); and reduction in the disproportionate confinement of minorities (28 states are nearing full compliance, and others are at various stages.)

Source(s): Howell, James C. "NCCD's Survey of Juvenile Detention and Correctional Facilities." *Crime & Delinquency*, January 1998.

Emotionally Ill

Kent's counsel also asked that his client be moved to another facility for psychiatric evaluation, and this was done. Staff at two hospitals wrote reports describing Kent as severely emotionally ill. However, instead of the waiver hearing his attorney had requested, the juvenile court judge issued an order waiving jurisdiction on the basis of a "full investigation," and the case moved to district court.

At the regular criminal court Kent faced the charges of housebreaking, robbery and rape as an adult. His counsel motioned to dismiss the charges, claiming the waiver that landed him in district court was invalid, since it did not encompass a "full investigation" as dictated by the Juvenile Court Act. The motion was denied, and Kent was found guilty on the housebreaking and robbery charges and sentenced to 30 to 90 years. The case was appealed and the U.S. Court of Appeals for the District of Columbia Circuit found the waiver and the judge's waiver order valid, and upheld the convictions. It was appealed again and came before the U.S. Supreme Court in 1966 as *Kent v. United States*.

In a 5-4 decision delivered on 21 March 1966 by Justice Fortas, the Supreme Court reversed the lower courts' rulings. It found that proper procedure had not been followed when the juvenile court judge waived jurisdiction. Furthermore, whether or not an offender should be tried as an adult—a portentous possibility—could not be determined without some representation on behalf of the youth present.

A System Ill

More importantly than just ruling that juvenile offenders had the right to a waiver hearing, as well as access to their Social Service records, Fortas's opinion brought a new era of change to the juvenile justice system in the United States. The ruling, in essence, allowed that certain due-process procedures must still be followed even though a juvenile court case is technically a civil case, not a criminal one. The denial to Kent of certain safeguards normally allowed adult criminal defendants—evidenced by his week-long detention before arraignment—and then the arbitrary ruling that placed him in the much more severe realm of the adult criminal courts—seemed a definite factor in the decision. Fortas wrote of the abysmal state of the juvenile court system on the whole, and maintained that trade-off had not worked, and in effect, youthful offenders received neither constitutional protection nor the rehabilitative, lenient treatment that prevented them from growing into adult offenders. Justice Stewart and three of his colleagues on the bench dissented, asserting the case should have been sent to a court of appeals.

The *Kent* case was one of several significant Supreme Court decisions that granted minors charged with crimes the same guarantees as adult defendants. In essence, it began to treat an entire group as citizens, after several decades of denying them constitutional protections. This trend was reversed with *McKeiver v. Pennsylvania* (1971), which denied the right to a jury trial for minors.

Related Cases

In Re Gault, 387 U.S. 1 (1967).
McKeiver v. Pennsylvania, In re burrus, 403 U.S. 528 (1971).
Goss v. Lopez, 419 U.S. 565 (1975).

Bibliography and Further Reading

"Criminal Law . . . Juvenile Courts." *American Bar Association Journal,* May 1966, p. 476.

Gardner, Robert. "The *Kent* Case and the Juvenile Court: A Challenge to Lawyers." *American Bar Association Journal,* October 1966, pp. 923-925.

Harvard Law Review, November 1966, pp. 124-129.

Kramer, Donald T. *Legal Rights of Children,* 2nd ed. New York: McGraw-Hill, 1994.

McLean, Daniels. "An Answer to the Challenge of *Kent.*" *American Bar Association Journal,* May 1967, pp. 456-457.

IN RE GAULT

Legal Citation: 387 U.S. 1 (1967)

Appellants
Paul L. Gault and Marjorie Gault, parents of Gerald Francis Gault, a minor

Appellee
State of Arizona

Appellants' Claim
That the Fourteenth Amendment requires states to accord juvenile criminal defendants the same due process rights given to adults accused of criminal offenses.

Chief Lawyer for Appellants
Norman Dorsen

Chief Lawyer for Appellee
Frank A. Parks, Attorney General of Arizona

Justices for the Court
Hugo Lafayette Black, William J. Brennan, Jr., Tom C. Clark, William O. Douglas, Abe Fortas (writing for the Court), John Marshall Harlan II, Earl Warren, Byron R. White

Justices Dissenting
Potter Stewart

Place
Washington, D.C.

Date of Decision
15 May 1967

Decision
Most of the guarantees of procedural due process given to adult defendants at state criminal trials were extended to juveniles.

Significance
In re Gault was an important part of the "due process revolution" that took place during the 1960s, during which many of the rights guaranteed by the first ten amendments to the Constitution—the Bill of Rights—were seen to apply at the state as well as the federal level.

Gerald Gault had his first serious brush with the law early in 1964 when he was picked up by police for having been in the company of another boy who had stolen a wallet from a woman's purse. As a result of this incident, a six-month order of probation was entered against him on 25 February 1964. It was still in effect on 8 June 1964, when Gault was taken into custody by Gila County, Arizona, police for having, together with a friend, made an allegedly obscene phone call to a neighbor.

Both of Gerald Gault's parents were at work when he was taken into custody. They were not notified of his detention. Nor were they served with the petition for a preliminary hearing filed by a probation officer. At the hearing, which was held the next day, Gerald Gault was accompanied by his mother and older brother, but was not represented by counsel. He was still without a lawyer when, a week later, he appeared at a hastily scheduled sentencing hearing. Without an attorney and deprived of an opportunity to confront or cross-examine his accuser, who was not present at either hearing, Gault was convicted almost entirely on the basis of his admission that he had taken part in the phone call. At 15, he was declared a juvenile delinquent and committed to the State Industrial School for a period of up to six years. Arizona permitted no appeals in juvenile cases.

A petition for *habeas corpus,* requesting that Gault be released on grounds that he had been illegally detained, was filed in the state supreme court, which referred it to the trial court. When Gault's petition was rejected, this decision was appealed to the Arizona Supreme Court, which likewise declined to release Gault. His parents then appealed to the U.S. Supreme Court, which considered the matter "in re," that is, in a nonadversarial proceeding requiring only a legal decision, not full litigation.

From the beginning of the twentieth century, juvenile defenders had been subjected to *parens patriae,* that is, a paternalistic, ostensibly protective attitude towards unruly children. As a result, an entirely separate juvenile justice system had developed. Aiming for flexibility and informality, too often this system resulted in a failure of due process for the defendants who were subjected to it. The Supreme Court first addressed this problem in *Kent v. United States* (1966), in which the legal process for juvenile offenders—who were often handed lengthy sentences in informal proceedings where they were deprived of due process guarantees—faced what the Court called "the worst of both worlds."

Supreme Court Declares Juvenile Justice System Delinquent as to Due Process

Gerald Gault had clearly been victimized by this system. Had he been an adult, his maximum punishment would have been a $50 fine or two months in jail. Instead, he faced the prospect of 6 years of incarceration. Writing for the Court, Justice Fortas attacked the whole notion of *parens patriae:*

> The right of the state, as *parens patriae,* to deny to the child procedural rights available to his elders was elaborated by the assertion that a child, unlike an adult, had a right "not to liberty but to custody" . . . On this basis, proceedings involving juveniles were described as "civil" not "criminal" and therefore not subject to the requirements which restrict the state when it seeks to deprive a person of his liberty . . . The constitutional and theoretical basis for this peculiar system is—to say the least—debatable . . . Juvenile Court history has again demonstrated that unbridled discretion, however benevolently motivated, is frequently a poor substitute for principle and procedure.

Seven other justices agreed with Fortas that most of the rights guaranteed adult criminal defendants by the Due Process Clause of the Fourteenth Amendment should be extended to juvenile delinquents facing the prospect of losing their liberty. The only dissenter was Justice Stewart, who voiced the concern that soon the rules governing juvenile and adult criminal procedures would be indistinguishable, with the effect that children would be accorded no special treatment by a harsh and adversarial justice system. In fact, juvenile courts continued to function, although their job was made more difficult by *Gault,* which did not provide any real guidelines as to how a special—but not too special—justice was to be meted out to juvenile defendants. Like many of the landmark cases that constituted part of the Court's "due process revolution," *Gault* attempted to resolve difficult substantive problems in the criminal justice system with not always adequate procedural remedies.

Related Cases

Kent v. United States, 383 U.S. 541 (1966).
McKeiver v. Pennsylvania, In re Burrus, 403 U.S. 528 (1971).
Goss v. Lopez, 419 U.S. 565 (1975).

Bibliography and Further Reading

Houlgate, Laurence D. *The Child and the State: A Normative Theory of Juvenile Rights.* Baltimore, MD: Johns Hopkins Press, 1980.

Kramer, Donald T., ed. *Legal Rights of Children,* 2nd ed. Colorado Springs, CO: Shepard's/McGraw-Hill, 1994.

Mezey, Susan Gluck. *Children in Court: Public Policymaking and Federal Court Decisions.* Albany: State University of New York Press, 1996.

IN RE WINSHIP

Legal Citation: 397 U.S. 358 (1970)

Appellant
Samuel Winship

Appellee
State of New York

Appellant's Claim
That his conviction of a crime in a juvenile delinquency proceeding was unconstitutional because the state did not prove that he committed the crime beyond a reasonable doubt

Chief Lawyer for Appellant
Rena K. Uviller

Chief Lawyer for Appellee
Stanley Buchsbaum

Justices for the Court
Harry A. Blackmun, William J. Brennan, Jr., (writing for the Court), William O. Douglas, John Marshall Harlan II, Thurgood Marshall, Byron R. White

Justices Dissenting
Hugo Lafayette Black, Warren E. Burger, Potter Stewart

Place
Washington, D.C.

Date of Decision
31 March 1970

Decision
That the criminal law standard requiring proof of a crime beyond a reasonable doubt is a constitutional requirement, and it applies equally to adults and juveniles.

Significance
The Court's decision made clear that juveniles accused of crimes are entitled to the same constitutional protections as adults facing criminal convictions. The Court's decision also elevated the general criminal law rule that the prosecution must prove every element of a crime beyond a reasonable doubt to a rule of constitutional law. Thus, following the Court's decision, the prosecutor in the criminal case bears a heavy burden in proving that the defendant committed the crime.

The 1950s and 1960s were a time of great activity for the U.S. Supreme Court. During this era, generally referred to as the "Rights Revolution," the Court expanded greatly the constitutional rights of criminal defendants. Decisions during this time recognized that a defendant has the right to a court appointed attorney, to be informed of his right to remain silent, and to be questioned by the police only in the presence of an attorney. In *Winship*, the Court added to these rights the right to be convicted only where the prosecution proves each element of the criminal offense beyond a reasonable doubt, and expanded this right to juveniles accused of a crime in a juvenile delinquency proceeding.

In 1967, Samuel Winship, who was 12 years old at the time, stole $112 from a purse in a locker. He was charged in the New York Family Court as being a juvenile delinquent. Under New York law at the time, a juvenile delinquent included any person between the ages of seven and 16 who committed an act which, if done by an adult, would be a crime. Any juvenile found to be delinquent could be placed in a juvenile detention center until his eighteenth birthday. Relying on the New York law, the family court judge found that Winship was a juvenile delinquent by a "preponderance of the evidence." The "preponderance of the evidence" standard is much easier to meet than the reasonable doubt standard, and requires only that it is more likely than not that the defendant committed the crime. Put another way, under the preponderance of the evidence standard, the jury need only be 51 percent sure that the defendant committed the crime, whereas under the reasonable doubt standard the jury would have to be a least 95 percent sure that the defendant committed the crime.

Winship then appealed his conviction to the New York Court of Appeals, arguing that the Due Process Clause of the Fourteenth Amendment required the prosecution to prove that he committed the crime he was charged with beyond a reasonable doubt. The Due Process Clause provides that a state may not deprive a person of "life, liberty or property without due process of law." The Supreme Court has interpreted the Due Process Clause to require a state to afford a number of protections to criminal defendants. The New York

Court of Appeals rejected Winship's argument that one of these protections is the right to proof beyond a reasonable doubt before being convicted. Winship appealed this decision to the U.S. Supreme Court.

Due Process Requires Proof Beyond a Reasonable Doubt

The central question before the Court was whether the Constitution required that a defendant be convicted only upon proof beyond a reasonable doubt that he committed the crime. In the 1967 case *In re Gault,* the Court held that when a juvenile is accused of a crime in a juvenile delinquency proceeding, he need not be given all the rights that an adult has in a criminal trial. However, a juvenile must be given "the essentials of due process and fair treatment." Thus, the question in *Winship* was whether the requirement of proof beyond a reasonable doubt is essential to "due process and fair treatment." The Court concluded that it is an integral part of due process.

The Court first noted that the reasonable doubt standard in criminal cases had been followed by nearly every state, the federal government, and England since the 1700s. The Court reasoned that such a long-standing practice reflects an historical judgment that the reasonable doubt standard is an integral part of conducting a fair trial. The Court also reasoned that the reasonable doubt standard is important because it is better to have a potentially guilty person go free than to have an innocent person deprived of his liberty:

> The requirement of proof beyond a reasonable doubt has this vital role in our criminal procedure for cogent reasons. The accused during a criminal prosecution has at stake interest of immense proportions, both because of the possibility that he may lose his liberty upon conviction and because of the certainty that he would be stigmatized by the conviction. Accordingly, a society that values the good name and freedom of every individual should not condemn a man for commission of a crime when there is a reasonable doubt about his guilt.

Thus, the Court held that the reasonable doubt standard is an element of due process required under the Constitution to insure that a defendant receives a fair trial.

Having concluded that the reasonable doubt standard is a constitutional requirement to obtaining a valid conviction, the Court went on to hold that the standard also applies in juvenile delinquency proceedings where the juvenile is charged with a crime. The Court found that the same reasons which support applying the reasonable doubt standard in adult criminal trials also support applying the standard to juveniles accused of a crime.

Creating Rights

In a dissenting opinion, Justice Black accused the Court of creating rights which do not exist in the Constitution. He reasoned that many of the amendments in the Bill of Rights provide for certain rights to criminal defendants, "but nowhere in that document is there any statement that conviction of crime requires proof beyond a reasonable doubt." Justice Black thought that the Court should be guided by the language of the Constitution itself, and should not interpret "due process" to require whatever the Supreme Court decides is "fair." He concluded that it was up to the state and federal legislatures, and not the Court, to determine what is the appropriate standard of proof in criminal trials, and that due process only requires that the prosecution meet that level of proof chosen by the legislature.

Impact

The Court's decision in *Winship* was important in two respects. First, it reaffirmed the Court's earlier decision in *Gault* that juveniles accused of a crime are entitled to the same constitutional protections provided to adults accused of a crime. Second, it clarified that whether in the state or federal courts, a criminal defendant cannot be convicted unless the prosecution proves his guilt beyond a reasonable doubt.

Related Cases
Davis v. United States, 160 U.S. 469 (1895).
In re Gault, 387 U.S. 1 (1967).
Cupp v. Naughten, 414 U.S. 141 (1973).
Mullaney v. Wilbur, 421 U.S. 684 (1975).
Jackson v. Virginia, 443 U.S. 307 (1979).

Bibliography and Further Reading
Cross, Sir Alfred R. N. *The Golden Thread of the English Common Law: The Burden of Proof.* New York: Cambridge University Press, 1976.

Davis, Samuel M. *Rights of Juveniles: The Juvenile Justice System.* New York: Clark Boardman Co., 1974.

Hahn, Paul H. *The Juvenile Offender and the Law,* 3rd ed. Cincinnati, OH: Anderson Publishing Co., 1984.

Hall, Kermit L., ed. *The Oxford Companion to the Supreme Court of the United States.* New York: Oxford University Press, 1992.

Katkin, Daniel, Drew Hyman, and John Kramer. *Juvenile Delinquency and the Juvenile Justice System.* North Scituate, MA: Duxbury Press, 1976.

LaFave, Wayne R., and Austin W. Scott, Jr. *Substantive Criminal Law,* 2 vols. St. Paul, MN: West Publishing Co., 1986.

MCKEIVER V. PENNSYLVANIA

Legal Citation: 403 U.S. 528 (1971)

In 1968, 16-year-old Philadelphian Joseph McKeiver was charged with three felony counts. The charges against McKeiver were robbery, larceny, and receiving stolen goods for his role in an action in which a group of 20 to 30 other youths pursued three other youths and robbed them of 25 cents. McKeiver requested a jury trial, but the request was denied. He had no previous record and the two victims' testimony was described as flimsy. A judge in the Juvenile Branch of Philadelphia's Family Court found McKeiver a "delinquent child" and placed him under probation.

The Due Process Clause

A citizen's right to a trial by jury is covered in the Fourteenth Amendment, which states, in part:

> . . . No State shall . . . deprive any person of life, liberty, or property, without due process of law; nor deny to any person within its jurisdiction the equal protection of the laws.

The "due process" in this case refers to a fair and speedy trial; a trial by a jury composed of members of one's general community is another tenet of the American justice system. Such constitutional rights, however, were generally not accorded to minors within the separate legal sphere of the juvenile courts.

The Rehabilitation of Youthful Offenders

The juvenile justice system in the United States had its origins in Chicago at the onset of the twentieth century, and its reform-minded tenets and goals of rehabilitation rather than punishment had gradually taken hold and become the law of the land. Individual states administered juvenile courts. The courts were considered a support system designed to enfold the juvenile within a framework of social workers, probation officers, and psychologists—and guided by a trained and fair judge—in order to correct the flaws that had led to criminal actions, and prevent them from occurring in the future. The juvenile legal system was designed as a trade-off: in exchange for forgoing some protections usually given to criminal defendants, minors would receive special treatment and would not be subject to the harsh criminal sentences accorded to adults for similar crimes.

Plaintiffs
Joseph McKeiver, Edward Terry

Defendant
State of Pennsylvania

Plaintiffs' Claim
That minors had the constitutional right to a jury trial in criminal proceedings against them.

Chief Lawyer for Plaintiff
Daniel E. Farmer

Chief Defense Lawyer
Arlen Specter

Justices for the Court
Hugo Lafayette Black, Harry A. Blackmun (writing for the Court), William J. Brennan, Jr., Warren E. Burger, John Marshall Harlan II, Thurgood Marshall, Potter Stewart, Byron R. White

Justices Dissenting
William O. Douglas

Place
Washington, D.C.

Date of Decision
21 June 1971

Decision
Trial by jury is a constitutional right that does not apply to minors.

Significance
The Court reversed a trend that had granted increasing constitutional protections to minors accused of crimes.

The Rights of Minors

The definition of "minor" has changed from time to time and place to place in American history. Before the passage in 1971 of the Twenty-sixth Amendment, which gave the the right to vote to 18-year-olds, 21 was considered the age of majority. Differing laws have created odd situations: in some states people can get married—perhaps the greatest commitment in life, aside from having children—at 14, but they have to wait until 16 to drive a car. At 17 they can join the military and die for their country, but they have to wait a year to vote, four years to drink, and (in many states) eight years to rent a car.

Equally inconsistent are ideas about the rights of minors. Some legal scholars treat "rights" in terms of

alleged obligations on the part of adults to provide children with food, clothing, or education, or to otherwise satisfy their needs. Generally, the American legal system gives children fewer rights, but also holds them less accountable for their actions, than it does adults. Thus courts typically defer to parents, if not school authorities, in legal disputes over autonomy; but on the other hand juveniles—either as offenders, victims, or witnesses—often enjoy anonymity in criminal situations.

Source(s): Levy, Leonard W., ed. *Encyclopedia of the American Constitution.* New York: Macmillan, 1986.

Yet as juvenile crime rose, its legal system came to be viewed as underfunded, understaffed, overtaxed, and ultimately ineffective. A 1967 Presidential Task Force on Juvenile Delinquency found major flaws. These included overcrowding in juvenile facilities, which were also understaffed and offered little "rehabilitative" activities or opportunities to the incarcerated youths. Sometimes youths were even held in maximum-security jails due to lack of space in juvenile detention centers.

Courts Granting More Rights

In the years prior to McKeiver's case, the American courts had made a number of benevolent decisions aimed at protecting youths within the system. This culminated in the 1967 *In re Gault* case, which secured for juvenile defendants the right to an attorney, the right to cross-examine witnesses, and protection against self-incrimination, which were already firm tenets of the adult criminal system. Still, in theory juvenile proceedings remained closed hearings, to protect the minor. Only about ten states allowed jury trials for youths under certain circumstances.

McKeiver appealed to the state courts for a new trial, but the lower court's judgment was upheld. The case appeared before the U.S. Supreme Court in December of 1970. At this time, the suit requesting a new trial with a jury was joined by two similar cases. One coplaintiff was Edward Terry, another 15-year-old from Philadelphia, who was facing a charge of assaulting a police officer in 1969. His request for a trial by jury was also denied. Their arguments were combined with that of three North Carolina teenagers. The African American youths were arrested in a civil rights demonstration, and convicted in a closed juvenile court hearing on the testimony of one police officer. Like McKeiver,

the others lost on appeal in the state courts, and appealed finally to the High Court.

Reversed Trend

In the 6-3 vote on *McKeiver v. Pennsylvania* announced on 21 June 1971, the Court tried to reaffirm its faith in juvenile legal system, though admitting it did suffer serious flaws. It asserted that the constitutional right to a trial by jury did not extend to minors, but did not bar the practice in the ten or so states that occasionally allowed it. Though the vote was 6-3, five separate opinions were delivered, showing certain dissension among the justices. The majority opinion was written by Justice Blackmun, and it contended that allowing jury trials for minors would turn proceedings into an "adversarial" situation and in effect reverse the last two decades of benevolent-minded decisions and laws that had aimed at protecting youths within the system.

Furthermore, Blackmun wrote, jury trials for minors would be costly, time-consuming, and force the trial into the public realm. This last effect would rob the juvenile delinquent of the protection the closed hearings granted to him; notoriety from a trial might follow him or her for life, even though the criminal record was expunged upon reaching the age of 21. Blackmun also argued that a juvenile trial court was a "fact-finding" body, fulfilling the same function as a jury in a regular criminal case. Finally, if a minor was allowed a trial by jury, it would blur the distinction between the juvenile and adult court systems, and hasten the dissolution of that line completely.

In a dissenting opinion, Justice Douglas maintained that the police often treated minors as adult criminals, and they should thus be afforded the same rights. Critics of the decision also pointed out that the Supreme

Court had recently ruled that in adult criminal cases, any offense punishable by six or more months of incarceration required a jury trial. In some cases juvenile delinquents faced sentences of five or six years, and legal analysts maintained that in light of this, youths were entitled to the same rights as an adult facing confinement. Others in support of minors' right to a jury trial pointed out that such a formal and risky court procedure might instill a respect of the court in juveniles and deter repeat offenses.

Related Cases

In re Gault, 387 U.S. 1 (1967).

Bibliography and Further Reading

Herbers, John. "Court, 6-3, Says Jury Trial Is Not Required for Youths." *New York Times,* June 22, 1971, p. 1.

Kramer, Donald T. *Legal Rights of Children,* 2nd ed. New York: McGraw-Hill, 1994.

Michigan Law Review, Vol. 70, November 1971, pp. 171-194.

Oelsner, Leslie. "Would They Do Better with a Jury Trial?" *New York Times,* June 27, 1971, sec. IV, p. 8.

THE RIGHTS OF THE ACCUSED BEFORE TRIAL

An Emphasis on the Rights of the Accused

Among the phrases from American legal language that have entered the common usage are "burden of proof" and "presumption of innocence." In legal actions against someone accused of a crime, the burden of proof is on the state to prove its case, not on the accused to prove his innocence—and certainly not for the accused to prove his guilt. Closely tied with this is the presumption of innocence: the defendant is always innocent until proven guilty, and never the other way around. These ideas are usually associated with the system of trials, but they are in fact associated with the entire cycle of criminal procedure that begins at the point when a law enforcement officer makes an arrest.

Hand in hand with these principles go a number of others, embodied either in the Constitution or in its amendments. Article III guarantees that the accused has a right to appear before a judge to determine whether he is being held illegally (writ of *habeas corpus*); likewise it forbids bills of attainder, laws declaring a person guilty without trial; and *ex post facto* laws, or retroactive laws that attempt to punish someone for something that was not a crime when they did it. Article III also directs that "The trial of all Crimes, except in cases of Impeachment, shall be by Jury."

These provisions alone would make the U.S. legal system far more liberal than most others in the world. In many countries, people can be held for years, or even executed, without trial, and many other nations offer only a semblance of the rule of law, vesting all power of judgement in a ruler or his appointed officials. This reality has been made painfully clear in the twentieth century, under totalitarian systems such as those in Nazi Germany; Soviet Russia, particularly under Stalin; and Communist China during and since the years of Chairman Mao Zedong. Hitler, Stalin, and Mao are long gone, but systems of law which favor the state over the individual, and treat the accused as guilty until proven innocent, are not.

The framers of the Constitution had no concept of such brutal repression; their example of injustice—the example they wished to avoid duplicating—was far more liberal, and indeed served as the model for many aspects of American government. This was English com- mon law, which had evolved over the preceding centuries to place limits on the power of the sovereign over his/her citizens. But a number of the framers were not satisfied with the guarantees of liberty embodied in the Constitution itself, and in 1791 Congress passed the first ten amendments to it, commonly known as the Bill of Rights. Modelled on the English Bill of Rights (1689), these guaranteed additional liberties, and a number of them addressed the rights of citizens accused of crimes.

Primary among the Bill of Rights amendments addressing the rights of the accused are the Fifth, Sixth, and Eighth, which will be discussed below; as well as the Fourth, which protects against unreasonable search and seizure. The Fourteenth Amendment, ratified in 1868, extended the Fifth Amendment's guarantee of due process to the states; and later rulings of the Supreme Court, often formed by an interpretation of the Fourteenth, further expanded the rights of the accused. The Court, and indeed the American legal system, also assumes certain rights which are stated neither in the Constitution nor in its amendments, but which are generally agreed to derive from them. Most notable among these is the requirement that guilt must be proven beyond a reasonable doubt.

The Right Against Self-Incrimination

The Sixth Amendment contains a key provision to which the government must abide at the beginning of the criminal justice process, arrest: the right to be informed of the accusation. Under the authoritarian or totalitarian systems referred to above, persons can simply be arrested without even knowing the crime they have supposedly committed. By contrast, the U.S. system requires, under Rule 7 of the Federal Rules of Criminal Procedure, a "plain, concise, and definite written statement of the essential facts constituting the offense charged."

Closely tied to this Sixth Amendment right are several rights embodied in the Fifth. The latter provides, among other things, that persons outside the armed forces must be indicted, or formally accused, by a grand jury. As its name implies, a grand jury is larger than an ordinary, or petit, jury, which is present at the actual trial; a grand jury, composed of as many as 23 persons drawn from the citizenry, evaluates the government's case against the criminally accused, and determines whether or not the state has sufficient cause to bring the case to trial.

Also guaranteed under the Fifth Amendment is the right against self-incrimination, which applies just as much before trial as it does during. In its application before trial, it has often been closely associated with the Fourth Amendment's prohibition against unreasonable search and seizure. For instance the Supreme Court in *Boyd v. United States* (1886) held that "[T]he seizure of a man's private books and papers to be used in evidence against him [would not be] substantially different from compelling him to be a witness against himself." In practical terms, this means that the police cannot come to a person's house and say, "We know you've committed a crime—now show us the evidence"; likewise it means that a person under arrest will not be compelled to sit down and write out a confession, as often happened in Stalinist Russia.

These are both examples of coercion, an issue addressed by the Court in *Bram v. United States* (1897) and extended to state courts in *Malloy v. Morgan* (1964). Under coercion, the police in effect become the court, wresting confessions from the accused. Whereas in an authoritarian system police might beat a confession out of the suspect, even in considerably less dramatic circumstances, an officer could unlawfully obtain incriminating evidence against the suspect simply by asking him leading questions. Concern for this possibility led to the Court's most well-known decision involving Fifth Amendment rights before trial, *Miranda v. Arizona* (1966). As a result of the *Miranda* ruling, law enforcement officers are required to inform persons under arrest of their right to remain silent.

The Right to Counsel

Of course the accused—assuming he pleads "not guilty" in a hearing—will eventually have to speak in his defense, either personally or, as is more likely, through legal counsel. The right to representation by an attorney is guaranteed in the Sixth Amendment, but the Court did not begin to explore the implications of this guarantee until 1932, with *Powell v. Alabama*. In this, the celebrated case of the Scottsboro boys, a group of young black men accused of raping two white women in Alabama, the Court found that the accused had been denied the right to legal counsel, and its ruling extended the application of this right from the federal government to the states. As Justice George Sutherland wrote for the majority in *Powell*, "The right to be heard would be, in many cases, of little avail if it did not comprehend the right to be heard by counsel. . . . Without it [the accused] though he be not guilty . . . faces the danger of conviction because he does not know how to establish his innocence."

As with other rights discussed here, the right to counsel is as important prior to trial as it is when the trial commences; indeed, in *Powell*, the Court described the pre-trial phase as "the most critical." There is an old saying that "he who speaks in his own defense has a fool for a lawyer," and this would seem to be true even if the accused is himself an attorney. But it is perhaps particularly so when the accused lacks education, as is often the case with economically disadvantaged defendants—precisely the people who cannot afford to pay legal counsel. For years, it was generally believed that the Sixth Amendment implied that the court should appoint legal counsel to indigent, or poor, defendants in federal cases, and *Gideon v. Wainwright* (1963) opened the way for making court-appointed legal counsel a practice in the states as well.

Among the areas in which legal counsel is most helpful in the pre-trial phase is during interrogation, or questioning by police following arrest. The Court upheld the right to have counsel present during interrogation in *Escobedo v. Illinois* (1964), and reinforced its holding two years later with the *Miranda* ruling. The presence of a lawyer at a police lineup is also extremely important. In a lineup, the accused is required to stand alongside other persons, often of similar description, while a witness or witnesses attempt to identify the person they saw committing the crime. The 1992 film *The Player* contains a memorable scene in which police officers attempt to influence the recollections of a witness in order to compel identification of a suspect they believe to be the guilty party—a dramatic example of the need for legal counsel at the lineup.

The (Implied) Right to Bail

The Eighth Amendment is much shorter than the Fifth and Sixth, and its importance with regard to the pre-trial phase lies in its first six words: "Excessive bail shall not be required." This is the only mention of bail in the Constitution, but it has long been understood to imply that the accused has a right to bail—not a right to pretrial release, but a right to have bail set.

Under the system of bail, the judge determines an amount of money which the accused, or persons associated with him, must turn over to the court in order to secure his release from incarceration prior to trial. This money will be refunded at trial, but if he fails to show up in court, a warrant will be issued for his arrest, and the money will be forfeited. Bail is an extremely old idea, as can be seen from the story of Damon and Pythias in ancient Syracuse. Pythias was accused of a crime and sentenced to death, but wished to be temporarily released in order to settle his affairs. His friend Pythias put up the ultimate form of security: himself. When Pythias returned to face his sentence, the king was so moved by this example of friendship that he freed both men.

In the modern system of bail, the security requirement is not nearly so dramatic as in the case of Damon and Pythias. Usually it is a sum in the thousands of dollars, but nonetheless this is, like the fees of legal counsel, often beyond the ability of indigent detainees to provide. This has led to a system of bail bonds, which are purchased from a private company for a fee much smaller than the bail requirement, usually ten percent of the total. The bail-bond company in turn presents the court with the money for security.

Although the Court in *Stack v. Boyle* (1951) referred to the "traditional right to freedom before conviction," there has been much debate over whether bail is in fact a right to be guaranteed in all situations. If the court judges the accused to be dangerous, or deems him a particular risk for flight ("jumping bail"), it may refuse to release him, or it may set bail so high as to be prohibitive. In some cases, the accused may be released on recognizance—that is, the honor system.

In any case, where bail can be obtained, it affords the accused the opportunity, with the help of legal counsel, to prepare his defense for the pending trial. As for the trial itself, it must be "speedy," as guaranteed in the Sixth Amendment, meaning that the accused cannot simply be left to languish in a jail cell for months upon months without trial. Nonetheless, the defense may choose to forestall the trial for many reasons, including the opportunity to gain further evidence.

See also: **Criminal Law, Criminal Procedure, Juries, Rights of the Accused During Trial, Rights of the Accused Following Trial, Search and Seizure**

Bibliography and Further Reading

Beaney, William A. *The Right to Counsel in American Courts.* Ann Arbor: University of Michigan Press, 1955.

Cook, Joseph G. *Constitutional Rights of the Accused: Pretrial Rights.* Rochester, NY: Lawyers Co-Operative, 1972.

Farnsworth, E. Allan. *An Introduction to the Legal System of the United States.* New York: Oceana Publications, 1975.

Flemming, Roy B. *Punishment Before Trial: An Organizational Perspective of Felony Bail Processes.* New York: Longman's, 1982.

Harvard Law Review Staff. *Uniform System of Citation: The Bluebook.* Cambridge, MA: Harvard Law Review Association, 1996.

Lafave, Wayne R., and Jerold H. Israel. *Criminal Procedure.* St. Paul, MN: West Publishing, 1984.

Lewis, Peter W., and Kenneth D. Peoples. *Constitutional Rights of the Accused: Cases and Comments.* Philadelphia: Saunders, 1979.

Nagel, Stuart S., ed. *The Rights of the Accused in Law and Action.* Beverly Hills, CA: Sage Publications, 1972.

CHARLES GUITEAU TRIAL

Prosecutor
United States

Defendant
Charles J. Guiteau

Crime Charged
Murder.

Chief Prosecutors
George Corkhill, Walter Davidge, John K. Porter, Elihu Root, E. B. Smith

Chief Defense Lawyers
Leigh Robinson, George Scoville

Judge
Walter Cox

Place
Washington, D.C.

Date of Decision
13 January 1882

Decision
Defendant was found guilty and sentenced to death by hanging.

Significance
Guiteau's trial was one of the first murder trials in which the defendant's claim of insanity was subjected to the modern legal test: namely, whether or not Guiteau understood that his actions were wrong.

Less than 20 years after Abraham Lincoln was shot by John Wilkes Booth, the United States would see another president assassinated. James A. Garfield, a Union major general, had a distinguished military career, which he capitalized on even before the war ended, getting elected to the House of Representatives in 1863. Garfield was a successful politician, becoming the House Republican leader in 1876. Garfield was known for his opposition to President Ulysses S. Grant, a Republican whose scandal-ridden administration and flawed policies had alienated many of his fellow party members such as Garfield. In 1880, Garfield was the Republican candidate for president and won the election.

Unfortunately for Garfield, his presidency had attracted the obsessive interest of one Charles Guiteau. Guiteau claimed to be a lawyer, and specialized in taking small claims court cases for an unheard-of 75 percent contingency fee. Guiteau's legal career never amounted to much, and he was frequently on the run from creditors seeking payment on overdue bills. He also toyed with various political causes, joining the Oneida Community and other experimental religious living communities that were springing up in the 1860s and 1870s. Guiteau tired of the communal life, and moved to Washington, D.C. where he joined the Garfield election campaign as a lowly staff member.

Guiteau Takes Revenge on Garfield for an Imaginary Insult

Guiteau never had any position of importance in the Garfield campaign except in his own mind. Guiteau's behavior had always been erratic, and it is possible that he contracted venereal diseases that further aggravated his mental problems. He was inspired to write a speech, which he hoped that Garfield would use in a debate with the Democratic presidential candidate, W. S. Hancock. Garfield never even read the speech, much less used it in the debate, but Guiteau was convinced that Garfield won the election thanks to his speech. Guiteau demanded to be appointed Ambassador to France, and even personally accosted Secretary of State James G. Blaine several times. Blaine tried to put Guiteau off politely, but eventually lost patience and on their final

Insanity Plea

The insanity defense has been mounted by criminal defendants for several centuries. In fourteenth century England, the insanity plea was available to a person who was "deprived of and memory so as not to know what he [was] doing, no more than an infant, a brute, or a wild beast." England later fashioned the M'Naghten rule, which allowed the insanity defense if the defendant did not know what she was doing or did not know that what she was doing was wrong.

The M'Naghten rule migrated to the United States, but it has since been modified. Some states made the insanity defense available to defendants who acted under an "irresistible impulse," allowing for a form of physi-

cal insanity to supplement M'Naghten's recognition of mental insanity. Many states now allow the insanity defense if the defendant lacked "substantial capacity" to appreciate his or her conduct. On the federal level, the "irresistible impulse" test has been abolished. On the federal level and in some states, defendants on the federal level must prove their insanity. A few states require the prosecutor to prove the defendant's sanity. A successful claim of insanity does not set a defendant free: insane defendants are sent to secure mental health facilities.

Source(s): *West's Encyclopedia of American Law*, Vol. 6. St. Paul: West Group, 1998.

---

encounter pushed Guiteau away and told him never to bother him again.

Guiteau was bitter with resentment, and decided to take revenge against Garfield. Guiteau trailed Garfield throughout the month of June of 1881, waiting for the right opportunity. On 2 July, Guiteau got his chance. The Washington newspapers had reported Garfield's plans to go on a trip with his family, and Guiteau waited for the president at the train station he was to leave from. In the station's lobby, Guiteau came from behind Garfield and shot the president in the back. Station police rushed to arrest Guiteau, who offered no resistance. Meanwhile, Garfield was taken away for medical attention.

Guiteau's shot did not immediately kill Garfield. The president survived only to be diagnosed as having a fatal wound. The bullet had grazed Garfield's spine and lodged in his stomach, where it came to rest in such a position that blood continued to circulate, but the bullet could not be removed without killing Garfield. The doctors therefore did not operate, and they could do nothing for Garfield except try to make him comfortable until the inevitable happened. Garfield was a strong man, and he lived for almost three months before he died on 19 September 1881. The American public was outraged by the murder, and one of the soldiers that guarded Guiteau's prison even tried unsuccessfully to shoot him before trial.

Was Guiteau Insane?

Once Garfield was dead, the government could finally try Guiteau for murder. The trial opened on 14 November 1881, in the District of Columbia. The U.S. attorney general, Wayne MacVeagh, determined to secure a conviction, named five lawyers to the prosecution

team, including E. B. Smith and George Corkhill, who was also the District of Columbia's district attorney. Corkhill summed up the prosecution's opinion of Guiteau's insanity defense in a pretrial press statement that also mirrored public opinion on the issue:

> He's no more insane than I am . . . There's nothing of the madman about Guiteau: he's a cool calculating blackguard, a polished ruffian, who has gradually prepared himself to pose in this way before the world . . . he was a deadbeat, pure and simple . . . Finally he got tired of the monotony of dead-beating. He wanted excitement of some other kind and notoriety, and he's got it.

Unfortunately for his attorneys, Guiteau not only fought their attempt to assert an insanity defense, but insisted on asserting some bizarre legal defenses of his own. For example, he wrote a plea to Judge Cox arguing that the cause of Garfield's death was the doctors' failure to properly treat the bullet wound and therefore Guiteau was not guilty of murder. Of course, Guiteau's argument had no legal support. Any chance of acquitting Guiteau rested with his attorneys' efforts to prove that he was insane.

There is still some debate over what constitutes legal insanity, but most authorities generally agree that the basic test is whether or not the defendant knew that his or her actions were wrong. At the time of the *Guiteau* trial, however, the prevailing test of legal insanity was whether or not the defendant knew that his or her actions were criminal. Therefore, even though someone like Guiteau might be considered insane because he or she did not think it was wrong to shoot the president, he or she could be convicted if the judge determined that he or she understood that the law made it

Charles J. Guiteau. © Corbis-Bettmann.

illegal to shoot people. By the 1880s, courts were beginning to apply the less harsh "was it wrong" test, which also gave the jury rather than the judge the task of determining insanity.

Influenced by this trend in the law, Judge Cox allowed both sides to argue their case directly to the jury, and intervened only occasionally. Despite strong evidence of his insanity, Guiteau insisted he was sane, so his attorneys simply let him ramble on and hoped that the jury drew the right conclusion. For example, they let Guiteau explain that he shot Garfield not only out of revenge, but also because God had told him that Garfield was ruining the Republican Party and must be killed in order to save the country from the Democrats. Guiteau testified that God had promised to protect him if he shot Garfield:

> I want to say right here in reference to protection, that the Deity himself will protect me; that He has used all these soldiers, and these experts, and this honorable court, and these counsel, to serve Him and protect me. That is my theory about protection. The Lord is no fool, and when He has got anything to do He uses the best means He can to carry out His purposes.

Judge Cox and the prosecutors agreed that Guiteau's sanity or insanity had to be measured by whether he knew his actions were wrong, but they were also determined not to let Guiteau escape the hangman. Cox instructed the jury that any minimal amount of understanding on Guiteau's part would be enough to support a guilty verdict:

> When you come . . . to consider . . . such a crime as we have here, murder most foul and unnatural, the law requires a very slight degree of intelligence indeed.

The way was thus paved for the prosecutors, led by Davidge, to make an emotional appeal to the jurors in their closing argument for Guiteau's conviction:

> A man may not have intelligence enough to be made responsible, even for a less crime; but it is hard, it is very hard to conceive of the individual with any degree of intelligence at all, incapable of comprehending that the head of a great constitutional republic is not to be shot down like a dog.

The defense was paralyzed, and their efforts to portray Guiteau as not guilty by reason of insanity were brushed aside. Davidge asserted that Guiteau's erratic behavior could be explained by his overweening ego:

> Such is the indescribable egotism of this man that he put himself on the same plane as the Savior of mankind and the prophets. There you have the explanation of his applying for the mission at Paris. For this man, in his indescribable egotism, seems to have thought all along that there was nothing in the world too high for him.

On 13 January 1882, the jury rendered its verdict. They found Guiteau guilty of murdering President Garfield. Guiteau leaped to his feet and screamed at the jurors "you are all low, consummate jackasses." Guards took Guiteau back to his cell, to await execution. On 30 June 1882, Guiteau went to the scaffold, ranting about the "Almighty" and was hanged. Guiteau had been given the benefit of a new and more liberal legal definition of insanity, but like many criminal defendants to come he found out that public opinion influences judges and juries alike.

Bibliography and Further Reading

Gray, John Purdue. *The United States v. Charles J. Guiteau. Review of the Trial.* Utica: Unknown Publisher, 1882.

Ogilvie, John Stuart. *The Life and Death of James A. Garfield From the Tow Path to the White House.* Cincinnati, OH: Cincinnati Publishing Co., 1881.

Porter, John Kilham. *Guiteau Trial.* New York: J. Polhemus, 1882.

Rosenberg, Charles E. *The Trial of the Assassin Guiteau: Psychiatry and Law in the Gilded Age.* Chicago: University of Chicago Press, 1968.

The Editors. *The United States vs. Charles J. Guiteau.* New York: Arno Press, 1973.

BROWN V. MISSISSIPPI

Legal Citation: 297 U.S. 278 (1936)

Petitioners
Ed Brown, et al.

Respondent
State of Mississippi

Petitioners' Claim
That their confessions to crimes they had committed, obtained during and after torture at the hands of police officers and the general citizenry, were invalid in court.

Chief Lawyers for Petitioners
Earl Brewer, J. Morgan Stevens

Chief Lawyers for Respondent
W. D. Conn, W. H. Maynard

Justices for the Court
Louis D. Brandeis, Pierce Butler, Benjamin N. Cardozo, Charles Evans Hughes (writing for the Court), James Clark McReynolds, Owen Josephus Roberts, Harlan Fiske Stone, George Sutherland, Willis Van Devanter

Justices Dissenting
None

Place
Washington, D.C.

Date of Decision
17 February 1936

Decision
Upheld the petitioners' claim and overturned the decisions of the trial court and Mississippi Supreme Court, ruling that the use of coerced confessions violated the Due Process Clause of the Fourteenth Amendment.

Significance
Brown v. Mississippi marked the development of the test of voluntariness as the means used by the Court to evaluate the constitutionality of criminal confessions. The ruling was the first of a series of cases heard over the next three decades through which the Court restricted the means available to law enforcement personnel seeking to obtain confessions from criminal suspects. This series of cases culminated in the Court's landmark decision in *Miranda v. Arizona* (1966), which mandated that suspects be made aware of their constitutional rights before being questioned by police.

True Confessions

The Fifth Amendment of the U.S. Constitution states that no suspect "shall be compelled in any criminal case to be a witness against himself." This statutory protection of the rights of the individual creates legal problems for authorities seeking to use confessions as evidence in court. Traditionally, the Supreme Court applied the common law test of voluntariness to determine the legality of criminal confessions in federal cases. This test required that a confession be "an essentially free and unconstrained choice by its maker" to be legally admissible, and denied the use in court of any confession that was coerced from a suspect by the authorities. The states, however, were free to develop their own rules regarding the legality of confessions.

Although the states were free to make their own rules regulating criminal procedure, they were limited by their need to adhere to the Constitution's guarantee of Due Process as set forth in the Fourteenth Amendment. *Snyder v. Massachusetts* (1934), confirmed the ability of federal judiciary to invalidate state criminal procedures if they were judged to "offend some principle of justice so rooted in the traditions and conscience of our people as to be ranked as fundamental."

A Travesty of Justice

On 30 March 1934 Raymond Stewart, a white farmer from Mississippi, was murdered. His body was discovered at approximately 1:00 p.m. that same day. Law enforcement authorities thought they knew the perpetrator, and arrested a Mr. Ellington, a local man of African descent. They also detained Ed Brown and Henry Shields, two other African American men who would become petitioners in this case. Ellington was taken to the scene of the murder and asked to confess to the crime, but he professed his innocence. Upon hearing this, a group of white men who had gathered at the crime scene joined the police to encourage Ellington to confess. They threw a rope over a nearby tree limb, made a noose, seized Ellington, and hung him until his neck bore distinct rope marks that lasted for several days. After being let down Ellington still refused to confess, whereupon he was hung once again. When Ellington continued to maintain his innocence after his second hanging, he was savagely whipped by Deputy Sheriff Dial. Ellington still would not confess, and the mob allowed him to return home. Brown and Shields were taken to the county jail and detained overnight.

The following morning Dial and several white citizens returned to Ellington's home and arrested him. They then took him to the county jail after first making a detour through Alabama. While in Alabama, Dial and his colleagues whipped Ellington yet again, whereupon he agreed at last to confess to whatever his tormentors accused him.

On the night of 1 April 1934 deputy Dial and a number of white citizens returned to the county jail. Shields and Brown were forced to disrobe and lie over chairs. They were then beaten with a leather strap bearing metal buckles. During the beating deputy Dial made the men understand that, if they would confess involvement in Stewart's murder, the whipping would stop. Eventually both men confessed, and agreed to every detail of the scenario for the murder concocted by the local police and the mob.

Wasting no time, the authorities convened a grand jury comprising two sheriffs and eight white citizens to hear the "free and voluntary" confessions of Brown, Ellington, and Shields to the murder of Stewart. The suspects duly confessed. Although the accused still bore many visible marks of their ordeals and many of those present had knowledge of their treatment, three of the men watching this charade agreed to testify to the voluntary nature of the confessions in the upcoming trial.

On 4 April 1934 the grand jury indicted Brown, Ellington, and Shields for the murder of Stewart. The suspects were arraigned later in the day, but their guilty pleas were not accepted by the trial court. It was also determined at the arraignment that the suspects had not had access to legal counsel, which was duly appointed for them. Their trial was set for the following morning.

The trial lasted just two days, during which the prosecution offered no evidence of the guilt of the suspects other than their confessions. There was no attempt to disguise the manner in which those confessions were obtained. Deputy Dial even admitted participating in beating Ellington, and offered that the beating was "[n]ot too much for a negro; not as much as I would have done if it were left to me." On 6 April 1934, all three defendants found guilty of Stewart's murder and sentenced to death.

The petitioners then appealed their case to the Mississippi Supreme Court, which upheld their conviction and sentencing on the grounds that: "exemption from compulsory self-incrimination in the courts of the states is not secured by any part of the Federal Constitution" [quoting from *Snyder v. Massachusetts*]. Moreover, the Mississippi Supreme Court held that the petitioner's court-appointed counsel, by not moving to exclude the confessions from the trial, had simply made a legal error that could not be rectified. Two state supreme court justices dissented from this ruling, however, and the U.S. Supreme Court agreed to hear the case on *certiorari*.

Due Process

The Court heard arguments in the case on 10 January 1936, and ruled unanimously in favor of the petitioners, reversing their convictions and removing their sentences. The basis for the decision lay in the Due Process Clause of the Fourteenth Amendment which states that "state action, whether through one agency or another, shall be consistent with the fundamental principles of liberty and justice which lie at the base of all our civil and political institutions." Writing for the majority, Chief Justice Hughes rejected both arguments advanced by the Mississippi Supreme Court. With regard to the state's first contention, that federal courts had no jurisdiction in state criminal proceedings, Hughes responded that "the freedom of the state in establishing its policy is the freedom of constitutional government and is limited by due process of law." Hughes also noted the special circumstances of this case with biting language: "Because a state may dispense with a jury trial, it does not follow that it may substitute trial by ordeal. The rack and torture chamber may not be substituted for the witness stand." Hughes did not refute the right of states to ignore constitutional provisions against self-incrimination in their criminal procedures. The Court then dismissed the state's second contention, that an error by counsel had resulted in the failure to exclude the confessions from the trial. "It is a contention that proceeds upon a misconception of the nature of the petitioners' complaint. That complaint is not of the commission of mere error, but of a wrong so fundamental that it made the whole proceeding a mere pretense of a trial and rendered the conviction and sentence null and void."

Impact

Brown v. Mississippi established the jurisdiction of the federal judiciary to regulate state criminal law procedures when these violate constitutional guarantees of due process. The case was one of the first in a long line that gradually restricted the means available to law enforcement authorities seeking to obtain confessions and evidentiary statements from criminal suspects.

Related Cases

Snyder v. Massachusetts, 291 U.S. 97 (1934).
McNabb v. United States, 318 U.S. 332 (1943).
Ashcraft v. Tennessee, 322 U.S. 143 (1944).

Mallory v. United States, 354 U.S. 449 (1957).
Miranda v. Arizona, 384 U.S. 436 (1966).

Bibliography and Further Reading
Biskupic, Joan, and Elder Witt, eds. *Guide to the U.S. Supreme Court,* 3rd ed. Washington: Congressional Quarterly Inc., 1990.

Elliott, Stephen P., ed. *A Reference Guide to the U.S. Supreme Court.* New York: Facts on File Publications, 1986.

Hall, Kermit L., ed. *The Oxford Companion to the Supreme Court of the United States.* New York: Oxford University Press, 1992.

ASHCRAFT V. STATE OF TENNESSEE

Legal Citation: 322 U.S. 143 (1944)

Petitioners
Ashcraft, Ware

Respondent
State of Tennessee

Petitioners' Claim
That the confessions used to convict the defendants were extorted from them by state law enforcement officers in violation of the Fourteenth Amendment.

Chief Lawyer for Petitioners
James F. Bickers

Chief Lawyer for Respondent
Nat Tipton

Justices for the Court
Hugo Lafayette Black (writing for the Court), William O. Douglas, Frank Murphy, Stanley Forman Reed, Wiley Blount Rutledge, Harlan Fiske Stone

Justices Dissenting
Felix Frankfurter, Robert H. Jackson, Owen Josephus Roberts

Place
Washington, D.C.

Date of Decision
1 May 1944

Decision
Reversed Ashcraft's conviction and remanded the case to the Supreme Court of Tennessee because if Ashcraft made a confession, it was compelled in violation of the Due Process Clause of the Fourteenth Amendment.

Significance
Not until 1940, in *Chambers v Florida*, did the Supreme Court acknowledge that psychological coercion could lead to involuntary confessions. Soon after that in *Ashcraft v. State of Tennessee*, the Court acknowledged that some situations were so inherently coercive that confessions gained from them were inadmissible because they were not voluntary. This case reflected the Court's desire to curb police abuse by refusing to admit coerced confessions, no matter how relevant the confession might be.

On 5 June 1941, Zelma Ida Ashcraft left her home in Memphis, Tennessee, to visit her mother in Kentucky. Mrs. Ashcraft set out about 3:00 a.m. Her car was discovered in the late afternoon a few miles outside of Memphis and her body was found in a slough nearby. At about 6:00 p.m. officers first talked to Mr. Ashcraft, the deceased's husband. He identified the body and was taken to the county jail, where he conferred with officers until about 2:00 a.m.; the officers got no clues from him. The officers also held and interrogated Ashcraft's maid and her friends. During the following week the officers investigated and spoke with Ashcraft several times, but they turned up no evidence.

On Saturday evening, 14 June, officers took Ashcraft into custody. They brought him to a fifth floor room of the Shelby County jail equipped with high-powered lights and other devices used in homicide investigations. The officers sat Ashcraft at a table with a light over his head and began to quiz him. They questioned him in relays until Monday morning, 16 June. From 7:00 p.m. on Saturday until 9:30 a.m. Monday, Ashcraft had no rest from questioning, totaling 36 hours of continuous grilling. At a hearing before a magistrate on Monday morning, Ashcraft pleaded not guilty. Ashcraft's version of the questioning contradicted the officers' version. Ashcraft stated that he was threatened and abused, that his eyes became blinded by the light, he became weary, and his nerves unbearably strained. He also stated that he never admitted knowledge of the crime or accused Tom Ware of the murder. The officers stated that they were kind and considerate and that Ashcraft was cool, calm, normal and that his eyes were not bloodshot and he did not appear tired. They also stated that after 28 hours of constant questioning, Ashcraft said that Ware overpowered him at his home, abducted Mrs. Ashcraft, and was probably the killer. The officers picked up Ware, a 20 year old African American, at about midnight. According to the officers, Ware made a self-incriminating statement early Monday morning and signed by mark a written confession saying that Ashcraft had hired him to commit the murder. The officers stated that this confession was read to Ashcraft, who admitted its truth in a detailed statement taken down by a reporter. The officers stated that when the statement was read to him at 9:30 a.m., Ashcraft affirmed its truth but refused to sign it, saying he wanted to consult his lawyer. The last episode was witnessed by several people brought in by the police.

Dr. McQuiston, the Ashcraft family doctor, was called in to examine Ashcraft and Ware. Ashcraft told the doctor he had been treated all right and did not complain about his eyes. The doctor testified that Ashcraft appeared normal. He also testified that Ashcraft told him that he had not been getting along with his wife for some time, that he had offered her a property settlement and that he offered Ware money to "make away with his wife." The doctor testified that Ashcraft's statement to him was entirely voluntary.

During the trial, the court noted that people might differ as to whether the confessions were voluntary and that it was a matter for the jury to decide. The jury was told that "if the verbal or written statements made by the defendants freely and voluntarily without fear of punishment or hope of reward, have been proven to you in this case, you may take them into consideration." The state supreme court stated that it was "unable to say that the confessions were not freely and voluntarily made." Tom Ware was found guilty of the murder in state court. Ashcraft was convicted as an accessory before the fact. Both men were sentenced to 99 years in the state penitentiary. The Supreme Court of Tennessee affirmed the convictions.

The Constitution Bars Coerced Confessions

The Supreme Court agreed to hear the case because Ware and Ashcraft believed that the alleged confessions used at their trial had been extorted from them in violation of the Fourteenth Amendment and that they had been convicted solely on the basis of the confessions. Justice Black wrote the opinion for the majority. He noted that the dispute over what actually happened to Ashcraft during the 36 hours of questioning is an "inescapable consequence of secret inquisitorial practices. And always evidence concerning the inner details of secret inquisitions is weighted against an accused." The majority concluded that if Ashcraft made a confession it was not voluntary but compelled. Black noted that the situation was so inherently coercive that its very existence was irreconcilable with the possession of mental freedom. The Constitution has stood as a bar against the conviction of anyone in an American court by means of a coerced confession. Black mentioned that there were certain foreign nations whose governments convict individuals with testimony obtained by police organizations with unrestrained power to seize people, hold them in secret custody, and wring confessions from them using physical or mental torture. "So long as the Constitution remains the basic law of our Republic, America will not have that kind of government." The Court vacated the judgment of the

Tennessee Supreme Court affirming Ware's conviction and remanded his case to that court. Ashcraft's conviction was reversed and remanded.

Supervisory Power

Justice Jackson wrote the dissent. He noted that before this case, a confession was admissible unless it was proved that the will of the confessor had been overcome by torture, mob violence, fraud, trickery, threats, or promises. Even where there was excess and abuse of power by the police, the state could still use the confession if it was found that the accused had not lost his freedom of action.

> Respect for the sovereign character of the states has always constrained the Court to give great weight to findings of fact of state court. The Supreme Court has no supervisory power over state courts and may not lay down rules of evidence for them or revise their decision because the Court feels it is wiser. The Court has no power to discipline the police of the State of Tennessee or to reverse its convictions in retribution for conduct that the Court may personally disapprove. The burden of protecting society from most crimes against persons or property falls upon the state.

Justice Jackson felt that the Court was establishing a new doctrine that examination in custody of this duration is inherently coercive. American courts hold that a confession obtained by brutality, torture, beating, starvation, or physical pain is involuntary. "Actual or threatened violence have no place in eliciting the truth and it is fair to assume that no officer of the law will resort to cruelty if truth is what he is seeking." However, a confession obtained by questioning is different because questioning is an indispensable instrumentality of justice. Saying that mere interrogation is unconstitutional would unduly hinder the states from protecting society from criminals. Justice Jackson noted that the majority did not quite say this, but he felt it was moving far and fast in that direction. "The step it now takes is to hold this confession inadmissible because of the time taken in getting it." The duration and intensity of an examination or inquisition has always been regarded as relevant in estimating its effect on the will of the individual. Some people can withstand for days pressure that others can only withstand for hours. Before this case, the ultimate question was whether the confessor was in possession of his own will and self-control at the time of the confession. "For its bearing on this question the Court always has considered the confessor's strength or weakness, whether he was educated or illiterate, intelligent or moronic, well or ill, Negro or white." The majority, instead of finding that Ashcraft's freedom of will was impaired, substituted the doctrine that the situation was inherently coercive. If the constitutional admissibility of a confession is no longer measured by the mental state of the confessor but by the length of the questioning, the Court should give a definite number of permissible hours of questioning. Justice Jackson summed up his dissent by stating that "The use of the due process clause to disable the states in protection of society from crime is quite as dangerous and delicate a use of federal judicial power as to use it to disable them from social or economic experimentation."

After the Supreme Court remanded this case to the Tennessee Supreme Court, that court remanded it to the Criminal Court of Shelby County. Again Ashcraft and Ware were convicted and the state supreme court affirmed. The case returned to the Supreme Court in 1946. Justice Black once again delivered the Court's opinion. He noted that the trial judge construed the Supreme Court's mandate as prohibiting only the admission of the written unsigned confession. Thus the trial judge allowed the jury to hear testimony relating everything else that happened during the 36 hours of questioning. Black pointed out that the testimony used in the last trial might well have had the same practical effect on the jury that the written unsigned confession might have had. The state of Tennessee claimed that Ashcraft's statement that he knew who killed his wife was exculpatory (showed that he was innocent). Black saw no relevant distinction between the introduction of this statement and the unsigned alleged confession. The Court reversed the decision against Ashcraft and vacated that of Ware. Both cases were remanded to the state supreme court.

Impact

In 1940, in *Chambers v. Florida* the Supreme Court acknowledged that psychological coercion, as well as physical torture, could produce involuntary confessions. The use of such confessions violated the Due

Process Clause of the Fourteenth Amendment. In later decisions, such as *Ashcraft v. State of Tennessee,* the Court acknowledged that some situations were so inherently coercive that the confessions produced by them were inadmissible in court. The factor determining admissibility was voluntariness, not veracity. The Court did not reject Ashcraft's confession because it was unreliable. In fact, evidence suggested that Ashcraft was responsible for his wife's murder. But the 36 hours of questioning was unacceptable police conduct, and the Court sought to deter this behavior. The Court used this "police conduct" rationale to condemn and deter abusive police interrogation methods. The Court excluded confessions obtained by offensive means regardless of how credible the confession might be. The "voluntary" test, however, was difficult to apply because the terms "voluntariness" and "coercion" were not used analytically, but merely as conclusions. Not until the mid 1960s did the Court develop a definite rule regarding the admissibility of prolonged questioning of a suspect in custody. This rule emphasized the right to counsel and the new requirements were based on the Fifth and Sixth Amendments.

Related Cases

Palko v. Connecticut, 302 U.S. 319 (1937).
Chambers v. Florida, 309 U.S. 227 (1940).
Lisbena v. California, 314 U.S. 219 (1941).
McNabb v. United States, 318 U.S. 332 (1943).
Ashcraft v. State of Tennessee, 327 U.S. 274 (1946).

Bibliography and Further Reading

Biskupic, Joan, and Elder Witt, eds. *Congressional Quarterly's Guide to the U.S. Supreme Court,* 3rd ed. Washington, DC: Congressional Quarterly, Inc., 1996.

Hall, Kermit L., ed. *The Oxford Companion to the Supreme Court of the United States.* New York: Oxford Press, 1992.

BUTE V. ILLINOIS

Legal Citation: 333 U.S. 640 (1948)

Petitioner
Roy Bute

Respondent
State of Illinois

Petitioner's Claim
By not being advised of the right to legal counsel nor being asked if he desired legal counsel, petitioner was denied a fair, impartial trial under the provisions of the Due Process Clause of the Fourteenth Amendment.

Chief Lawyer for Petitioner
Victor Brudney

Chief Lawyer for Respondent
William C. Wines

Justices for the Court
Harold Burton (writing for the Court), Felix Frankfurter, Robert H. Jackson, Stanley Forman Reed, Fred Moore Vinson

Justices Dissenting
Hugo Lafayette Black, William O. Douglas, Frank Murphy, Wiley Blount Rutledge

Place
Washington D.C.

Date of Decision
19 April 1948

Decision
Failure to advise the petitioner of his right to legal counsel did not invalidate his sentences; the Fourteenth Amendment due process clause did not require a state court to ask a defendant if he desired counsel nor was a state court required to offer counsel.

Significance
Although this decision was later reversed in 1963 by *Gideon v. Wainwright*, it provided lower courts with guidance regarding the rights of defendants in noncapital criminal proceedings. Hence, for a period of 15 years, noncapital criminal defendants were adjudicated even if the accused was not aware of the right to counsel and sometimes without being offered the opportunity to be assigned a court-appointed attorney.

In 1938, the petitioner, Roy Bute, was twice-charged with a noncapital felony—taking indecent liberties with children. He pleaded guilty and was sentenced to 20 years in prison for each indictment. Eight years later, while serving his sentence in the Illinois State Penitentiary, he filed an appeal in the Supreme Court of Illinois asking for a review of proceedings and circumstances related to his trial. Bute's argument was that he was unfairly sentenced because he was denied representation by counsel—the court did not appoint an attorney to represent him. He was, therefore, rushed to trial without proper preparation and was not able to mount an adequate defense in court.

At the time he was indicted, Roy Bute, decided to represent himself in the Circuit Court of La Salle County, where the hearing took place. He was charged with taking indecent liberties with children under the age of 15, first with an 8-year-old girl and then with an 11-year-old girl. When Bute entered a guilty plea, the court explained the consequences and penalties which might proceed from his plea. Although the judge admonished that sentencing would proceed immediately if Bute remained steadfast in his guilty plea, Bute nonetheless indicated he understood that proceedings and wanted to continue. Unknowingly, by submitting to the immediate decision and sentencing of the court, Bute effectively waived his right to counsel. The court sentenced him to 20 years for each indictment and he was sent to the Illinois State Penitentiary to serve his sentence.

Eight years later, while serving his first 20-year term, Bute made an appeal to the Supreme Court of Illinois and asked for a rehearing for each one of the charges and sentences adjudicated in the Illinois Supreme Court. Because the justice presiding over the lower court had not advised him of his right to legal assistance, his petition claimed that he was rushed to trial and deprived of a fair, impartial hearing of his case. The right to representation by legal counsel, the petitioner claimed, was a guarantee to which he was entitled according to state and federal constitutions. The Supreme Court of Illinois, however, found no merit in his claim and denied a rehearing.

In preparing their decision, the Supreme Court justices reviewed the statutory provisions under which the

Self Representation

- Sixty-one percent of middle-income people with legal problems have had no interaction with the country's judicial system.

- More than half of couples going through a divorce received it without legal representation.

- In 88 percent of divorce cases at least one party was self-represented or defaulted.

- People earning less than $50,000 a year are more likely to represent themselves in court.

- At least 20 percent of litigants who represent themselves in court can afford legal representation, but do not want professional help.

- People who represent themselves in court tend to more satisfied with the judicial system than those who obtain legal representation.

- Nearly 75 percent of individuals who have represented themselves in court say they would do so again.

Source(s): *1991 Study of Self-Represented Litigants.* American Bar Association.

state of Illinois administered due process of law and traced the progression and procedural development of the case through Illinois courts. During the period of time in which Bute's trial was adjudicated, criminal case procedure for the state of Illinois was based on 1937 Illinois Revised Statues. Under those provisions, all litigants (especially the accused) were entitled to a specific set of rights: to be heard either in person or through legal counsel; to meet with witnesses; to bring witnesses who would provide supporting testimony; to have a speedy, public trial by jury; and to not be forced into self-incrimination.

The Code of Criminal Procedures for the state of Illinois stipulated that assignment of counsel was at the option of the accused. The Court thus held that a free interpretation of the Illinois code meant the state was not obligated to assign counsel unless a defendant petitioned the court with a specific request for representation. Further, no evidence in the records of the petitioner's case led the justices to believe the petitioner did not have the ability to understand what was being said in court. They concluded that, at the time the trial took place, Roy Bute was fully aware of the crime he committed, was aware of all the facts presented at trial, was cognizant of the proceedings, and fully understood the gravity of the charges/sentences. (In a separate concurring opinion, Justice Vinson further supported the majority's conviction that the petitioner had not been denied due process but had been fairly dealt with under provisions of state law. Roy Bute had appeared before the Illinois court on his own behalf, entered his plea of guilty and "persisted in his desire to do so," even after he had been advised by the court regarding the consequences and penalties which might result.)

The Court found that statutory provisions for criminal case procedure in Illinois courts were consistently applied to the petitioner's case. In comparing and contrasting court protocol of the (Illinois) state and federal

courts, the justices found appropriate corollary. From the Sixth Amendment, federal courts derived the practice that in all criminal procedures, the accused had the right to be assisted by legal counsel. While Illinois, at the time of Bute's trial, exercised criminal court procedure uniquely apart from federal practice, the Court found the state, like federal courts, embraced consistent, legal protocol. Cases in which the accused pleaded guilty were labeled "instant cases" according to Illinois statute. Instant cases required that a guilty plea not be entered until the court fully explained the consequences of such a plea. If the accused still persisted in pleading guilty, only then would the plea be accepted and recorded. The court rendered immediate judgment and execution in the same way as if the defendant's case had been presented before a jury and they had rendered a guilty verdict.

Because majority justices felt that Illinois followed consistent procedure in criminal cases, they ruled that the Fourteenth Amendment did not require the courts of Illinois to apply the same practice applied in federal courts. The due process clause of the Fourteenth Amendment did not require counsel for Roy Bute's defense because state courts are not obligated by the procedures that federal courts are obligated to follow. Although the justices acknowledged that federal courts were subject to strict guidelines regarding due process and, specifically, the right of legal representation, the justices held that the Fourteenth Amendment did not necessarily require states to provide legal counsel if a defendant did not specifically so request. Neither were state courts (unlike federal courts) even bound to inform a defendant about the right to legal counsel. Moreover, under the provisions of the Tenth Amendment, because each state was entitled to exercise jurisdiction over their own police powers and to control procedure undertaken in criminal trials in their own courts, the majority opinion reasoned that differences

Justice Harold Burton. © Photograph by Oscar White. Corbis Corporation.

could concurrently exist between court protocol and conduct of criminal cases at state and federal level.

Minority Opinion

The dissenting justices questioned the logic of Illinois court criminal procedure. Justice Douglas voiced the opinion of dissenting justices that if Bute's trial had been held in a federal court, it would have been mandatory to appoint counsel for him even if he did not ask for an attorney. Believing that the constitutional standards of fairness did not depend on what court conducted a trial, Justice Douglas opined that "the Bill of Rights was applicable to all courts at all times." Further, he reasoned, the main purpose of the Fourteenth Amendment was to further safeguard basic provisions contained in the Bill of Rights, specifically protection against infringement of personal rights whether that be at federal or state level. Thus, minority justices failed to see how an accused defendant could be denied counsel in the Illinois state court if, according to the U.S. Constitution, that benefit could not been taken away from him in a federal court.

Impact

The Supreme Court confirmed that state courts were not bound to follow federal court criminal procedure. Provisions of the Tenth Amendment gave states great latitude in the exercise of jurisdiction over judicial procedure undertaken in state courts. Unlike federal courts, which had to assign legal counsel for defendants who did not have an attorney, state courts were under no such obligation so long as the state's judicial protocol provided for appointment of counsel if specifically requested by a defendant. The Court also made clear that states were not obliged to assign counsel automatically; neither were they obligated to inform the accused of any right to request counsel if the accused committed a noncapital crime. Thus, for the 15 years before this ruling was struck down by *Gideon v. Wainwright,* the decision in *Bute v. Illinois* established that appointment of an attorney for the accused was not necessarily a fundamental right for defendants in state courts.

Related Cases

Powell v. Alabama, 287 U.S. 45 (1932).
Betts v. Brady, 316 U.S. 455 (1942).
Uveges v. Pennsylvania, 335 U.S. 437 (1948).
Reid v. Covert, 354 U.S. 1 (1957).
Kinsella v. United States, 361 U.S. 234 (1960).
Gideon v. Wainwright, 372 U.S. 335 (1963).

Bibliography and Further Reading

Biskupic, Joan, and Elder Witt, eds. *Congressional Quarterly's Guide to the U.S. Supreme Court,* 3rd ed. Washington, DC: Congressional Quarterly, Inc., 1996.

MALLORY V. UNITED STATES

Legal Citation: 354 U.S. 449 (1957)

Petitioner
Andrew R. Mallory

Respondent
United States

Petitioner's Claim
That being arrested without probable cause and held for a prolonged period without being formally charged invalidated his confession.

Chief Lawyer for Petitioner
William B. Bryant

Chief Lawyer for Respondent
Edward L. Barrett, Jr., Special Assistant to the U.S. Attorney General

Justices for the Court
Hugo Lafayette Black, William J. Brennan, Jr., Harold Burton, Tom C. Clark, William O. Douglas, Felix Frankfurter (writing for the Court), John Marshall Harlan II, Earl Warren, Charles Evans Whittaker

Justices Dissenting
None

Place
Washington, D.C.

Date of Decision
24 June 1957

Decision
Mallory's confession was ruled inadmissible and his conviction reversed.

Significance
Mallory, together with *McNabb v. United States* (1943) resulted in the so-called McNabb-Mallory rule, which made confessions inadmissible in federal court if they were obtained from a criminal suspect being held in violation of federal rules requiring that such a suspect be quickly charged.

On the night of 7 April 1954, a woman was raped in the basement of her apartment house in the District of Columbia. She had gone down there to do her laundry, with which she experienced some difficulty. She sought help from the janitor, who lived in the basement with his wife, three sons, and 19-year-old half-brother, Andrew Mallory. Mallory was the only one at home at the time, and he helped the women. Shortly thereafter, she was raped by a masked man who seemed to resemble him.

Mallory and one of his grown nephews then disappeared from the apartment, but Mallory was picked up by police the next afternoon. He was taken with his adult nephew to police headquarters, where they were questioned for nearly two hours before they submitted to lie detector tests. Mallory was the last to be tested, and the test was not administered until 8:00 p.m. He had not been given anything to eat or drink since being taken into custody.

After another 90 minutes of questioning, Mallory admitted to the crime. After several more hours of questioning, he finally signed a written confession, sometime after midnight. He was not formally charged until the next morning, when he was brought before a magistrate judge. His trial was delayed for nearly a year owing to doubts about his ability to understand the proceedings against him. Finally, on the basis of his signed confession, Mallory was convicted in U.S. District Court for the District of Columbia. He then appealed his conviction to the U.S Supreme Court.

Supreme Court Formulates McNabb-Mallory Rule

In 1943, the Supreme Court held, in *McNabb v. United States* that a confession—even one given voluntarily—obtained while a criminal suspect is unlawfully detained (i.e., held for a prolonged period without being formally charged) is inadmissible in federal court. In *Mallory*, this rule was reaffirmed. Writing for a unanimous Court, Justice Frankfurter, the author of the *McNabb* opinion, stated:

> The scheme for initiating a federal prosecution is plainly defined. The police may not arrest

Omnibus Crime Control and Safe Street Acts of 1968

Generally viewed as legislation passed by Congress to curtail the impact of *Miranda v. Arizona*, this act states that a confession is admissible as evidence if voluntarily given by the suspect.

It is up to the trial judge to determine if the confession was voluntary after considering the amount of time that elapsed between the arrest and arraignment of the defendant making the confession, if the confession was made after arrest and before arraignment; if the suspect was clearly aware of the nature of the criminal offense at the time the suspect was charged or while making the confession; if the suspect realized he was not compelled to make a statement, and if he did, that the statement could be used against him in court; if the suspect was aware of his right to counsel; and finally, whether the suspect made the confession without the presence of counsel.

Source(s): Legal Information Institute. http://www.law.cornell.edu/uscode/18/3501.html

upon mere suspicion but only on "probable cause." The next step in the proceeding is to arraign the arrested person before a judicial officer as quickly as possible so that he may be advised of his rights and so that the issue of probable cause may be promptly determined. The arrested person may, of course, be "booked" by the police. But he is not to be taken to police headquarters in order to carry out a process of inquiry that lends itself . . . to eliciting damaging statements to support the arrest and ultimately his guilt.

The Supreme Court can only overturn criminal convictions in state courts if they violate the due process rights guaranteed by the Fourteenth Amendment. The Court can, however, formulate rules of evidence that go beyond due process when exercising its power to supervise criminal trials in federal court. The so-called McNabb-Mallory rule imposed strict limitations on the admissibility of confessions in federal criminal trials, and many feared that the Court might succeed in making the rule applicable to the states through the Fourteenth Amendment. In 1968, Congress severely limited the reach of the McNabb-Mallory rule with legislation that spelled out the circumstances under which a voluntary confession can be admitted in federal court.

The Supreme Court, in the meantime, approached the problem of coerced confessions by focusing on the issue of the Fifth Amendment privilege against self-incrimination and the Sixth Amendment right to counsel. These efforts culminated in the landmark *Miranda v. Arizona* (1966) case, which required that criminal suspects be given "Miranda warnings" outlining their Fifth and Sixth Amendment rights before they are even taken into custody.

Related Cases
McNabb v. United States, 318 U.S. 332 (1943).
Miranda v. Arizona, 384 U.S. 436 (1966).

Bibliography and Further Reading
Garcia, Alfredo. *The Sixth Amendment in Modern American Jurisprudence: A Critical Perspective.* New York, NY: Greenwood Press, 1992.

Grano, Joseph D. *Confessions, Truth, and the Law.* Ann Arbor: University of Michigan Press, 1993.

Inbau, Fred E., John E. Reid, and Joseph P. Buckley. *Criminal Interrogation and Confessions,* 3rd ed. Baltimore, MD: Williams & Wilkins, 1986.

GIDEON V. WAINWRIGHT

Legal Citation: 372 U.S. 335 (1963)

Appellant
Clarence Earl Gideon

Appellee
Louie L. Wainwright, Director, Division of Corrections

Appellant's Claim
That the Sixth Amendment requires states to provide legal counsel for impoverished criminal defendants charged with serious offenses.

Chief Lawyer for Appellant
Abe Fortas

Chief Lawyer for Appellee
Bruce R. Jacob

Justices for the Court
Hugo Lafayette Black (writing for the Court), William J. Brennan, Jr., Tom C. Clark, William O. Douglas, Arthur Goldberg, John Marshall Harlan II, Potter Stewart, Earl Warren, Byron R. White

Justices Dissenting
None

Place
Washington, D.C.

Date of Decision
18 March 1963

Decision
Declaring that the Due Process Clause of the Fourteenth Amendment makes the Sixth Amendment right to counsel binding on the states, the Supreme Court unanimously voted to order that Gideon be assigned a court-appointed lawyer and retried.

Significance
Gideon v. Wainwright made an enormous contribution to the so-called "due process revolution" going on in the Court led by Chief Justice Warren. Because of the ruling in this case, all indigent felony defendants—like many others charged with misdemeanors—have a right to court-appointed attorneys.

Clarence Earl Gideon was a drifter who occasionally worked at the Bay Harbor Poolroom in Panama City, Florida. On the morning of 3 June 1961, after a patrol officer discovered that the pool hall had been burglarized, eyewitnesses led police to arrest Gideon. He professed his innocence, but two months later, Gideon was put on trial for burglary. A 1942 U.S. Supreme Court ruling, *Betts v. Brady*, which held that states need appoint counsel only to those indigent criminal defendants facing the death penalty, was still the law of the land. Gideon defended himself without benefit of legal counsel. Predictably, he was found guilty. He was sentenced to five years in prison.

Gideon applied to the Florida Supreme Court for a writ of *habeas corpus*, asking to be freed because he had been denied his right to counsel. When the state supreme court denied Gideon's petition, he submitted a five-page handwritten appeal to the U.S. Supreme Court. The Warren Court had been looking for an opportunity to overturn *Betts v. Brady*, and it agreed to hear Gideon's appeal. The Court appointed Abe Fortas, one of the best-known appellate lawyers in the country (and later a Supreme Court justice himself) to argue the case.

Court Unanimously Votes to Overturn *Betts v. Brady*

Writing for the unanimous Court, Justice Black stated the rationale for overturning *Betts* in simple terms. This was for him—and apparently for the rest of the Court—a straightforward decision:

> [R]eason and reflection require us to recognize that in our adversary system of justice, any person haled into court, who is too poor to hire a lawyer, cannot be assured a fair trial unless counsel is provided for him. This seems to us an obvious truth.

The Due Process Clause of the Fourteenth Amendment, which had been the vehicle for applying other Bill of Rights guarantees at the state level, again saw service in the ongoing "due process revolution" being led by Justice Black. After *Gideon*, every indigent defendant charged with a serious crime in state court (criminal tri-

The Warren Court

Earl Warren, the former governor of California, served as chief justice of the Supreme Court from 1953 to 1969. Warren's tenure as chief justice is widely viewed as a period of extraordinary judicial activism, which resulted in landmark Supreme Court cases.

One of the most important cases Warren ever presided over was also one of the first cases he presided over as chief justice. The case was *Brown v. Board of Education,* which overturned segregated public schools as "inherently unequal" and in violation of the Equal Protection Clause of the Fourteenth Amendment.

The Warren Court was also responsible for two landmark decisions that protected the rights of the accused in *Gideon v. Wainwright* and *Miranda v. Arizona.* In *Griswold v. Connecticut,* the Court threw out a Connecticut law that banned the circulation of birth control information. That ruling would prove critical for the post-Warren Court ruling of *Roe v. Wade,* which upheld a woman's right to have an abortion.

Source(s): *West's Encyclopedia of American Law,* Volume 10. Minneapolis, MN: West Publishing, 1998.

als are almost invariably heard in state courts) would be appointed legal counsel as required by the Sixth Amendment's guarantee of the right to a fair trial. The Court soon extended this right, in *Argersinger v. Hamlin* (1972) to misdemeanor defendants sentenced to imprisonment. In 1984, in *Strickland v. Washington,* the principle first enunciated by the Supreme Court in *Gideon* was elaborated to include a right to effective legal representation.

Clarence Earl Gideon, c. 1961. © UPI/Corbis-Bettmann.

Clarence Gideon was retried on 5 August 1963, in the Panama City Courthouse. This time an experienced trial lawyer, W. Fred Turner, argued his case, and this time Gideon was found innocent. A book about Clarence Gideon's pursuit of his constitutional rights, Anthony Lewis' *Gideon's Trumpet,* was made into a Hollywood film. But the true measure of Gideon's victory is not that it makes a compelling narrative, but that its effects are so far-reaching. Most large cities now maintain public defender offices that serve indigent clients like Gideon. In other parts of the country, judges appoint private attorneys to serve as representatives for criminal defendants who cannot afford to pay for their own lawyers. In 1984, the Justice Department estimated that two-thirds of the American population is served by the public defender system.

Related Cases

Betts v. Brady, 316 U.S. 455 (1942).
Argersinger v. Hamlin, 407 U.S. 25 (1972).
Strickland v. Washington, 466 U.S. 668 (1984).

Bibliography and Further Reading

Johnson, John W., ed. *Historic U.S. Court Cases, 1690–1990: An Encyclopedia.* New York: Garland Publishing, 1992.

Kurland, Philip B., ed. *The Supreme Court and the Constitution: Essays in Constitutional Law from the Supreme Court Review.* Chicago, IL: University of Chicago Press, 1965.

Lewis, Anthony. *Gideon's Trumpet.* New York: Random House, 1964.

Smith, Christopher E. *Courts and the Poor.* Chicago, IL: Nelson-Hall, 1991.

ESCOBEDO V. ILLINOIS

Legal Citation: 378 U.S. 478 (1964)

Petitioner
Danny Escobedo

Respondent
State of Illinois

Petitioner's Claim
That once a person detained by police for questioning about a crime becomes a suspect, his Sixth Amendment right to counsel becomes effective.

Chief Lawyer for Petitioner
Barry L. Kroll

Chief Lawyer for Respondent
James R. Thompson

Justices for the Court
Hugo Lafayette Black, William J. Brennan, Jr., William O. Douglas, Arthur Goldberg (writing for the Court), Earl Warren

Justices Dissenting
Tom C. Clark, John Marshall Harlan II, Potter Stewart, Byron R. White

Place
Washington, D.C.

Date of Decision
22 June 1964

Decision
By a vote of 5-4, the Supreme Court ruled that because Escobedo's request to consult with his attorney had been denied and because he had not been warned of his constitutional right to remain silent, his confession was inadmissible and his conviction was reversed.

Significance
Escobedo is less important in and of itself than as part of a movement led by the Court to liberalize due process in criminal procedure.

On the night of 19 January 1960, Danny Escobedo's brother-in-law was fatally shot. Shortly thereafter, police arrested Escobedo without a warrant. He was taken into custody and interrogated. Escobedo did not, however, give police a statement, and he was released that afternoon after his lawyer filed a writ of *habeas corpus* in state court alleging that there was not enough evidence to hold his client. On 30 January, Escobedo was rearrested, together with his sister, after Benedict DiGerlando, another individual being questioned about the murder, told police that Escobedo had fired the shots that killed his brother-in-law.

Escobedo was handcuffed and, as he was driven to the police station, the arresting officers told him repeatedly that he had been fingered as the culprit and might as well confess. They did not warn him of his Fifth Amendment right to remain silent. Escobedo repeatedly asked to consult with his attorney, but even after his lawyer arrived at the station, police refused to permit him to speak with his client. Told by an officer that he and his sister would be released if he made a statement incriminating DiGerlando, Escobedo did so, and on the basis of his statement he was tried and found guilty of murder. His appeal was rejected by the Supreme Court of Illinois, and Escobedo then petitioned the U.S. Supreme Court for review of his conviction.

The Supreme Court Confirms a Criminal Suspect's Right to Have an Attorney

Earlier that year, in *Massiah v. United States* (1964), the Court had thrown out a criminal confession obtained without benefit of counsel. But the outcome in *Massiah* rested on the fact that the confession had been obtained after criminal proceedings had begun but before the accused had retained a lawyer. Now the Court was confronted with a situation that involved a confession obtained without benefit of counsel before the suspect had been indicted. Justice Goldberg, writing for the Court, held that under the circumstances in *Escobedo*, a confession was equally inadmissible:

> [W]here, as here, the investigation is no longer a general inquiry into an unsolved crime but has begun to focus on a particular suspect, the

The Right to Counsel

The Sixth Amendment guarantees that in all criminal prosecutions the "accused shall enjoy the right . . . to have compulsory process for obtaining Witnesses in his favor, and to have Assistance of Counsel for his defense."

Yet, courts have struggled with deciding exactly when this right begins, especially in cases where the accused confesses during interrogation and then recants. In Crooker v. California the defendant confessed after he refused to be appointed counsel. The court ruled that the confession was voluntary and dismissed the defen-dant's argument that he had a right to counsel at the police station.

Later in Cicencia v. La Gay when the defendant was found guilty after having been denied access to his attorney at the police station, the Court upheld the conviction. In White v. Maryland the absolute right to counsel in a capital case was held applicable to a pretrial proceedings, such as preliminary arrangements.

Source(s): West's Encyclopedia of American Law, Vol. 3. Minneapolis, MN: West Publishing, 1998.

suspect has been taken into police custody, the police carry out a process of interrogations that lends itself to eliciting incriminating statements, the suspect has requested and been denied an opportunity to consult with his lawyer, and the police have not effectively warned him of his absolute constitutional right to remain silent, the accused has been denied "the Assistance of Counsel" in violation of the Sixth Amendment . . .

Escobedo enlarged the Court's holding in Massiah, but the particularity of Justice Goldberg's opinion left some doubt as to just how to apply the new ruling. On the one hand, the Escobedo Court provided little clear guidance as to when the Sixth Amendment right to counsel is triggered; on the other, the circumstances laid out in the opinion seemed so specific that the Court seemed only to be addressing Danny Escobedo's case.

The sub-text of Escobedo, the Fifth Amendment prohibition against compulsory self-incrimination, became the focus two years later of another right-to-counsel case, Miranda v. Arizona (1966). Miranda proved to be an even more controversial decision, in part because it clearly stated that in order to avoid Fifth Amendment problems, criminal suspects must be alerted not only to their right to remain silent, but to their right to be represented by a lawyer. And instead of waiting until some rather ill-defined moment when a detainee becomes a primary suspect, as in Escobedo, after Miranda police were on notice that the right to counsel is activated when an individual is taken into custody. Miranda clarified the import of Escobedo by stating plainly that the only way to preserve a criminal suspect's privilege against self-incrimination was to provide him or her with the opportunity to retain a lawyer as soon as possible.

Related Cases
Crooker v. California, 357 U.S. 433 (1958).
Cicenia v. Lagay, 357 U.S. 504 (1958).
Gideon v Wainwright, 372 U.S. 335 (1963).
Massiah v. United States, 377 U.S. 201 (1964).
Miranda v. Arizona, 384 U.S. 436 (1966).

Bibliography and Further Reading
Baker, Liva. Miranda: Crime, Law and Politics. New York, NY: Atheneum, 1983.

Garcia, Alfred. The Sixth Amendment in Modern Jurisprudence: A Critical Perspective. New York, NY: Greenwood Press, 1992.

Grano, Joseph D. Confessions, Truth and the Law. Ann Arbor, MI: University of Michigan Press, 1993.

Johnson, John W. Historic U.S. Court Cases, 1690–1990: An Encyclopedia. New York: Garland Publishing, 1992.

MIRANDA V. ARIZONA

Legal Citation: 384 U.S. 436 (1966)

Petitioner
Ernesto Miranda

Respondent
State of Arizona

Petitioner's Claim
That a failure to inform the petitioner of his constitutional right to an attorney made his confession inadmissible in court.

Chief Lawyer for Petitioner
John Flynn

Chief Lawyer for Respondent
Gary K. Nelson, Assistant Attorney General of Arizona

Justices for the Court
Hugo Lafayette Black, William J. Brennan, Jr., William O. Douglas, Abe Fortas, Earl Warren (writing for the Court)

Justices Dissenting
Tom C. Clark, John Marshall Harlan II, Potter Stewart, Byron R. White

Place
Washington, D.C.

Date of Decision
13 June 1966

Decision
The Court extended a defendant's constitutional right to counsel to include pretrial questioning and required police to advise defendants of their rights.

Significance
Few events have altered the course of American jurisprudence more than the 1963 rape conviction of Ernesto Miranda. The primary evidence against him was a confession he made while in police custody. How that confession was obtained exercised the conscience of a nation and prompted the landmark U.S. Supreme Court decision.

In the early hours of 3 March 1963, an 18-year-old Phoenix, Arizona, movie theater attendant was accosted by a stranger while on her way home from work. He dragged her into his car, drove out to the desert, and raped her. Afterwards he dropped the girl off near her home. The story she told police, often vague and contradictory, described her attacker as a bespectacled Mexican, late twenties, who was driving an early 1950s car, either a Ford or a Chevrolet.

By chance, one week later, the girl and her brother-in-law saw what she believed was the car, a 1953 Packard, license plate DFL-312. Records showed that this plate was actually registered to a late model Oldsmobile, but DFL-317 was a Packard, registered to a Twila N. Hoffman; and her boyfriend, Ernesto Miranda, 23, fit the attacker's description almost exactly.

Miranda had a long history of emotional instability and criminal behavior, including a one-year jail term for attempted rape. At police headquarters, he was placed in a lineup with three other Mexicans of similar height and build, though none wore glasses. The victim did not positively identify Miranda but said he bore the closest resemblance to her attacker. Detectives Carroll Cooley and Wilfred Young then took Miranda into an interrogation room. He was told, inaccurately, that he had been identified, and asked him if he wanted to make a statement. Two hours later Miranda signed a written confession. There had been no blatant coercion or brutality, and included in the confession was a section stating that he understood his rights. When the detectives left interrogation room 2, they were pleased, not realizing the legal repercussions that would result from their efforts.

Tainted Evidence

As an indigent, Miranda was granted a court-appointed defender, Alvin Moore. Moore studied the evidence. The state had an apparently unassailable case, buttressed by Miranda's confession. And yet there was something about that confession that Moore found troubling. Convinced that it had been obtained improperly, he intended to move for its inadmissibility.

Miranda Rights

In *Miranda v. Arizona* the Court established unequivocal protections that the accused was entitled to during interrogation "while in custody at the station or otherwise deprived of his freedom of action in any significant way."

Miranda established that the accused must be informed that he or she has the right to remain silent and that if the suspect chooses not to remain silent that anything said can be used against the suspect in court. Before being interrogated the suspect must also be informed of the right to consult with an attorney, and to have legal counsel present during interrogation.

Additionally, the Miranda rule also requires that if the suspect is indigent that he or she be informed that the court will provide counsel. If the suspect decides to remain silent, then the interrogation must end. Any statements obtained in violation of the suspects' Miranda rights are inadmissible as evidence in court. If the suspect decides to speak without consulting with an attorney then the prosecutor must prove that the suspect willingly waived Miranda rights.

Source(s): Biskupic, Joan, and Elder Witt. *Congressional Quarterly's Guide to the U.S. Supreme Court.* Washington, DC: Congressional Quarterly, Inc., 1997.

Only four witnesses appeared for the prosecution: the victim, her sister, and Detectives Cooley and Young. After their testimony, Deputy County Attorney Laurence Turoff told the jury that the victim "did not enter into this act of intercourse with him [Miranda] willfully, but in fact she was forced to, by his own force and violence, directed against her."

Moore responded by highlighting inconsistencies in the victim's story. She claimed to have been a virgin prior to the attack, an assertion discounted by medical examiners, and could not remember the exact chronology of the night's events. Neither did she exhibit any bruising or abrasions after the attack; reason enough for Moore to thunder the jury, "You have in this case a sorrowful case, but you do not have the facts to require that you send a man to prison for rape of a woman who should have resisted and resisted and resisted, until her resistance was at least overcome by the force and violence of the defendant" (an essential requirement under Arizona law at the time; anything less was regarded as compliance).

But it was not until cross-examination of Carroll Cooley that Moore struck:

Question: Officer Cooley, in the taking of this statement, what did you say to the defendant to get him to make this statement?

Answer: I asked the defendant if he would . . . write the same story that he just told me, and he said that he would.

WARNING

The constitution requires that I inform you of your rights:

You have a right to remain silent. If you talk to any police officer, anything you say can and will be used against you in court.

You have a right to consult with a lawyer before you are questioned, and may have him with you during questioning.

If you cannot afford a lawyer, one will be appointed for you, if you wish, before any questioning.

If you wish to answer questions, you have the right to stop answering at any time.

You may stop answering questions at any time if you wish to talk to a lawyer, and may have him with you during any further questioning.

Rev. 9-79

Miranda rights must be read each time an arrest takes place.
© Connecticut State Police.

Question: Did you warn him of his rights?

Answer: Yes, sir, at the heading of the statement is a paragraph typed out, and I read this paragraph to him out loud.

Question: I don't see in the statement that it says where he is entitled to the advice of an attorney before he made it.

Answer: No, sir.

Question: Is it not your practice to advise people you arrest that they are entitled to the services of an attorney before they make a statement?

No, sir.

This admission prompted Moore to object to the confession as evidence, but he was overruled by Judge Yale McFate, who favored the jury with a well-balanced and eminently fair account of the law as it stood at the time. In 1963, the constitutional right to silence was not thought to extend to the jailhouse.

Consequently, on 27 June 1963, Ernesto Miranda was convicted and sentenced to two concurrent terms of 20 to 30 years imprisonment.

But Alvin Moore's arguments about the confession had touched off a legal firestorm. Miranda's conviction was appealed all the way to the U.S. Supreme Court. On 13 June 1966, Chief Justice Earl Warren, speaking for a 5-4 majority, for the first time established unequivocal guidelines about what is and what is not permissible in the interrogation room:

> Prior to any questioning, the person must be warned that he has a right to remain silent, that any statement he does make may be used as evidence against him, and that he has the right to the presence of an attorney, either retained or appointed . . .

Conviction Overturned

With Miranda's conviction overturned, Arizona glumly faced the prospect of having to free its most celebrated prison inmate. Without the confession, the chances of winning a retrial were negligible. Ironically, it was Miranda himself who brought about his own downfall. Expecting to be released after retrial, he had begun a custody battle with his common-law wife, Twila Hoffman, over their daughter. Hoffman, angry and fearful, approached the authorities and revealed to them the content of a conversation she had with Miranda after his arrest, in which he had admitted the rape.

The fresh evidence was all Arizona needed.

Miranda's second trial began 15 February 1967. Much of the case was argued in the judge's chambers. At issue was whether a common-law wife could testify against her husband. Yes, said County Attorney Robert

Ernesto Miranda. © AP/Wide World Photos.

Corbin. Defense counsel John Flynn, who had pleaded Miranda's case before the Supreme Court, bitterly disagreed. After considerable legal wrangling, Judge Lawrence K. Wren ruled such evidence admissible, and Twila Hoffman was allowed to tell her story to the jury. It proved decisive. Miranda was again found guilty and sentenced to 20 to 30 years in jail.

On 31 January 1976, four years after being paroled, Ernesto Miranda was stabbed to death in a Phoenix bar fight. The killer fled but his accomplice was caught. Before taking him to police headquarters, the arresting officers read the suspect his rights. In police vernacular, he had been "Mirandized."

Impact

The importance of this case cannot be overstated. Denounced by presidents from Richard Nixon to Ronald

Reagan, the *Miranda* decision has withstood all attempts to overturn it. Framed originally to protect the indigent and the ignorant, the practice of "reading the defendant his rights" has become standard operating procedure in every police department in the country. The practice is seen so frequently in television police dramas that today the so-called "Miranda Warnings" are as familiar to most Americans as the Pledge of Allegiance.

Related Cases
Chambers v. Florida, 309 U.S. 227 (1940).
Mapp v. Ohio, 367 U.S. 643 (1961).
Escobedo v. Illinois, 378 U.S. 478 (1964).
Harris v. New York, 401 U.S. 222 (1971).

Michigan v. Tucker, 417 U.S. 433 (1974).
Rhode Island v. Innis, 446 U.S. 291 (1980).

Bibliography and Further Reading

Baker, Liva. *Miranda: Crime, Law and Politics.* New York: Atheneum, 1983.

Graham, Fred P. *The Self-Inflicted Wound.* New York: Macmillan Co., 1970.

Johnson, John W., ed. *Historic U.S. Court Cases, 1690–1990: An Encyclopedia.* New York: Garland Publishing, 1992.

Skene, Neil. "The *Miranda* Ruling." *Congressional Quarterly,* June 6, 1991, p. 164.

Tucker, William. "The Long Road Back." *National Review,* October 18, 1985, pp. 28–35.

SCHMERBER V. CALIFORNIA

Legal Citation: 384 U.S. 757 (1966)

Petitioner
Armando Schmerber

Respondent
State of California

Petitioner's Claim
That the blood test administered during his hospital stay for injuries suffered from a traffic accident violated his Fifth Amendment right against providing self-incriminating evidence as well as his Fourth and Fourteenth Amendment rights against unreasonable searches and seizures.

Chief Lawyer for Petitioner
Thomas M. McGurrin

Chief Lawyer for Respondent
Edward L. Davenport

Justices for the Court
William J. Brennan, Jr. (writing for the Court), Tom C. Clark, John Marshall Harlan II, Potter Stewart, Byron R. White

Justices Dissenting
Hugo Lafayette Black, William O. Douglas, Abe Fortas, Earl Warren

Place
Washington, D.C.

Date of Decision
20 June 1966

Decision
The Court found that the Fifth Amendment did not prohibit blood tests to determine intoxication levels, because the Fifth Amendment applies to only interrogation and testimony and because the results of blood tests constituted neither testimony nor evidence of a confession or other communicative act. In addition, the Court concluded that the blood test did not a constitute an unreasonable search and seizure given the circumstances.

Significance
Schmerber v. California brought about a period of increased pro-government decisions concerning the Fourth and Fourteenth Amendments' prohibition of unreasonable and arbitrary searches and seizures, undermining the previous trend of pro-individual decisions dating back to 1886 in *Boyd v. United States*. The Court's decision also provided law enforcement agents, especially police and prosecutors, with a strong scientific method for determining intoxication. Furthermore, courts used this case as a starting point for rulings on compulsory employee drug testing in later decades.

The Accident, Arrest, and Conviction

The Los Angeles police found Schmerber at an accident scene and smelled alcohol on his breath. The police also noticed other symptoms of intoxication both at the scene and at the hospital and decided to arrest him for drunk driving. They informed him of his right to have a lawyer present, to remain silent, and to have a lawyer appointed, if he could not afford one. While Schmerber was in the hospital, the police ordered a blood test to determine if Schmerber was intoxicated, even though Schmerber refused based on advice from his lawyer. The test revealed Schmerber was drunk at the time of the accident and the trial court admitted the test as evidence.

Schmerber was convicted and appealed the decision. Citing numerous constitutional right violations, he arguing that the blood test was administered against his will and its use as evidence obstructed due process of law granted by the Fourteenth Amendment. He contended that it also violated his right to refuse to provide self-incriminating evidence under the Fifth Amendment, and subjected him to unreasonable searches and seizures, violating his Fourth and Fourteenth Amendment rights. The Appellate Department of the California Superior Court agreed with the lower court, rejecting Schmerber's arguments and upholding his conviction. Finally, Schmerber petitioned the U.S. Supreme Court, still maintaining the police violated numerous constitutional rights.

A Difficult Decision

Since the Court had made several new decisions related to the issue of blood tests after it initially considered the issue, it decided to hear the case, which began on 25 April 1966. Writing for the majority, Justice Brennan first addressed the due process claim. He pointed out that in a similar case, *Breithaupt v. Abram,* the Court upheld the conviction even though the doctor took the blood test under police orders while the driver was unconscious and could not refuse the test. Therefore, the Court rejected Schmerber's claim of violated due process, finding no injustice.

Next the Court explored Schmerber's claim of Fifth Amendment right violations. The Fifth Amendment

Justice Abe Fortas

Born on 19 June 1910 in Memphis to a Jewish immigrant, Abe Fortas was a gifted scholar at a very early age. Fortas started his law career as a professor, under the tutelage of William O. Douglas (also a Supreme Court justice). He excelled in his profession, becoming a prominent Washington attorney before being appointed to the Supreme Court in 1965. Fortas was well-known and revered for was the amount of *pro bono* work which he did. One of his *pro bono* clients was Clarence Gideon. Gideon was convicted in a Florida state court of breaking into a poolroom and taking the money from a vending machine. Gideon was unable to afford an attorney and the court refused to appoint one. He successfully prepared his own appeal to the U.S. Supreme Court, claiming that the state's refusal to provide legal counsel was illegal. The Court agreed to hear his case and Fortas was appointed his attorney.

That case *Gideon v. Wainwright* resulted in the landmark ruling that every person, regardless of financial means, was entitled to an attorney in a criminal case.

Source(s): Paddock, Lisa. *Facts About the Supreme Court of the United States.* New York: H. W. Wilson and Company, 1996.

states that no one "shall be compelled in any criminal case to be a witness against himself," which Schmerber and his attorney argued included using blood samples and presumably other medical reports against the accused unless they authorize it. The Court disagreed, holding that though the police required Schmerber to submit to the blood test and its results were used against him, the evidence obtained from the blood test and the chemical analysis did not constitute self-incriminating testimony. The Court noted the potential for a constitutional right violation in that the police did not obtain their own evidence, but the Court reasoned that the Fifth Amendment did not exclude the body of the accused as evidence. Just as state and federal courts generally agree that this amendment allows compulsory fingerprinting, photographing, measuring, and so forth, so it also can allow tests, according to the majority. The Court concluded that the taking of the blood test never forced Schmerber to give any statement or testimony or personally communicate guilt in any way and hence fell outside of the Fifth Amendment's scope.

Schmerber also felt the police denied him his Sixth Amendment right to legal representation. However, since the Court decided that the police can order blood tests whether or not the accused consent to them, it held that Schmerber's argument that the police denied him his right to counsel did not apply to this situation, because he had no choice and the police were not interrogating him. Consequently, the majority rejected this claim, too.

Justice Brennan then tackled the most complicated claim made by Schmerber: that the blood test violated his Fourth Amendment right not to be subjected to unreasonable searches and seizures. The majority argued that although the Fourth Amendment and the Fourteenth Amendment, which applied the Fourth Amendment to the state level, protects citizens from unreasonable and arbitrary searches and seizures, it

does not prevent the police from ordering blood tests. Because the Court decided that the Fifth Amendment allowed the police to obtain blood tests and to use them as evidence without trespassing on the right not to provide self-incriminating testimony, it reasoned that the Fourth Amendment can allow the police to obtain blood tests in certain circumstances, just as the Fourth Amendment permits the police to search homes in certain circumstances. Furthermore, the Court noted that under California law, the police may arrest suspects without a warrant for felonies, if they have probable cause. In Schmerber's case, the majority agreed that the police had probable cause because he smelled of liquor and displayed other symptoms associated with drunkenness. The Los Angeles police arrested Schmerber in this manner while in he was in the hospital before they ordered the blood test.

Since Schmerber was under arrest at the time of the test, the Court concluded that the police can continue to examine a suspect after arrest, such as when searching for weapons. In the same way, the Court reasoned the police could require a blood test once they arrested a suspect. Finally, the majority argued that since the evidence of Schmerber's intoxication could disappear from his blood in a few hours, the need to preserve the evidence overrode the need to obtain a search warrant, as the Court decided in *Preston v. United States*.

Nonetheless, the case drew mixed opinions from the justices. Four of them dissented, because the case addressed some difficult legal questions concerning the rights of the accused. Justice Warren felt that the decision broke the Fourteenth Amendment's guarantee to due process of law. Justices Black and Douglas contended that the blood test did indeed force Schmerber to provide self-incriminating testimony. In a separate opinion, Justice Douglas also argued that the blood test violated Schmerber's right to due process as well as his right to be free from arbitrary searches and seizures under the Fourth and Fifth Amendments. Finally, Justice Fortas disagreed because he believed the blood test amounted to self-incriminating evidence and a state cannot extract blood from anyone unless voluntarily allowed under the due process of law clause.

Impact

This case helped introduce a new era of Fourth Amendment U.S. Supreme Court decisions, replacing an older era that followed *Boyd v. United States*. In the *Boyd* case, the Court called for the broad application of the Fourth Amendment's ban on unreasonable searches and seizures, extending to "all invasions on the part of the government and its employees of the sanctity of a man's home and the privacies of his life." The Court's decision in the *Schmerber* case, however, limited its application and granted a new exception under certain conditions.

Schmerber v. California also became an important case for later hearings on mandatory employee drug testing. Since the Court decided that blood tests or other extractions of bodily fluids constituted searches and seizures, some courts held that urine tests also were searches by analogy. Consequently, various other cases—*Skinner v. Railway Labor Executives' Assn.* and *Carroll v. United States*—had to decide under what conditions these tests were reasonable in order not to violate the Fourth Amendment.

We thus conclude that the present record shows no violation of petitioner's right under the Fourth and Fourteenth Amendments to be free of unreasonable searches and seizures. It bears repeating, however, that we reach this judgment only on the facts of the present record. The integrity of an individual's person is a cherished value of our society. That we today hold that the Constitution does not forbid the States minor intrusions into an individual's body under stringently limited conditions in no way indicates that it permits more substantial intrusions, or intrusions under other conditions.

Related Cases

Boyd v. United States, 116 U.S. 616 (1886).
Breithaupt v. Abram, 352 U.S. 432 (1957).
Mapp v. Ohio, 367 U.S. 643 (1961).
Malloy v. Hogan, 378 U.S. 1 (1964).

Bibliography and Further Reading

Dees, Rusch O. "An Employer 'Quick Fix.'" *Management Solutions,* November 1986, p. 12.

Dripps, Donald A. "The Brennan Legacy." *Trial,* October 1997, p. 77.

Wall, Patricia S. "Drug Testing in the Workplace: An Update." *Journal of Applied Business Research,* spring 1992, p. 127.

ORZOCO V. TEXAS

Legal Citation: 394 U.S. 324 (1969)

Petitioner
Reyes Arias Orozco

Respondent
State of Texas

Petitioner's Claim
That incriminating statements made to police were inadmissible at his murder trial because the police did not give Miranda warnings.

Chief Lawyer for Petitioner
Charles W. Tessmer

Chief Lawyer for Respondent
Lonny F. Zwiener, Assistant Attorney General of Texas

Justices for the Court
Hugo Lafayette Black, (writing for the Court), William J. Brennan, Jr., William O. Douglas, John Marshall Harlan II, Thurgood Marshall, Earl Warren

Justices Dissenting
Potter Stewart, Byron R. White, (Abe Fortas did not participate)

Place
Washington, D.C.

Date of Decision
25 March 1969

Decision
Reversed the state courts' ruling that petitioner's incriminating statements to police were admissible at the murder trial despite the lack of Miranda warnings, and reversed petitioner's conviction.

Significance
This decision extended the application of the Miranda rule to in-custody interrogations occurring outside of a police station. The Miranda rule, originally adopted by the Supreme Court in a case involving a station house interrogation, requires police to inform a suspect prior to questioning of the right to remain silent and the right to counsel. Any confession or incriminating statement made by a suspect without these warnings is presumed involuntary and is inadmissible at trial. The case also established the proposition that a suspect arrested and questioned in his home is "in custody," for Miranda purposes. The effect of *Orozco* was to require law enforcement officers to give Miranda warnings to suspects who are "in custody" regardless of where the questioning takes place.

The Fifth Amendment right against self-incrimination and right to representation have their roots in English law. In the 1600s, The English Parliament abolished the infamous inquisitorial Court of Star Chamber after John Lilburn, a vocal opponent of the Stuarts who occupied the British throne, resisted the Star Chamber oath, which would have required him to answer all questions posed to him on any subject. Lilburn resisted the oath on the grounds that no man ought to be required to answer questions concerning himself in criminal matters. The Lilburn principle made its way to the English colonies in America and was implanted in the Fifth Amendment to the U.S. Constitution.

In the 1930s, a presidential commission's report revealed that, despite the protections of the Fifth Amendment, use of police violence and the "third degree" to extract criminal confessions flourished in the United States. In 1961, the Commission on Civil Rights found evidence that policemen resorted to physical violence to obtain confessions. Police manuals and texts in use in the 1960s documented interrogation procedures that relied on psychological or mental coercion through isolation, relentless questioning, cajolery, and trickery. In 1966, the U.S. Supreme Court issued *Miranda v. Arizona,* which required police to inform in-custody suspects prior to interrogation of their right to remain silent, to have a lawyer's advice before making a statement, and to have a lawyer appointed if the suspect could not afford to hire one. This decision was an attempt to place limits on custodial interrogation in hopes of eradicating the use of physical violence or the "third degree" to coerce a confession.

In 1966, Orzoco was convicted of murder in a Texas state court and sentenced to two to ten years in prison following a midnight shooting outside of a restaurant. Four hours after the shooting, police went to Orzoco's boarding house and questioned him in his bedroom. During police questioning, he admitted to having been at the restaurant and produced a pistol, which was subsequently proved to be the weapon used in the shooting. At trial, the court allowed one police officer to relate Orzoco's statements concerning the gun and his presence at the restaurant, despite objections by Orzoco's lawyer that the statements were inadmissible because police failed to give the petitioner the warnings required by *Miranda v. Arizona*. On appeal, the Texas Court of Criminal Appeals held, with one judge dissenting, that *Miranda* did not apply to interrogations occurring outside a police station and that the failure to give Miranda warnings did not preclude the admission of police testimony concerning the statements the petitioner had made in his own home. The Texas Court of Criminal Appeals affirmed the conviction, rejecting the petitioner's contention that a material part of the evidence against him was obtained in violation of the self-incrimination provision of the Fifth Amendment to the U.S. Constitution that: "No person . . . shall be compelled in any criminal case to be a witness against himself." The petitioner's sought a writ of *certiorari* from the U.S. Supreme Court. A writ of *certiorari* is a means whereby the Supreme Court obtains the case from the lower court for appellate review. The U.S. Supreme Court granted the writ.

A Significant Reversal

In a 5-2 decision, the U.S. Supreme Court reversed Orzoco's conviction. The Supreme Court disagreed with the state courts' conclusion that *Miranda* did not apply to bar admission of incriminating statements made by a suspect to police during questioning in the suspect's home. The Supreme Court held that *Miranda* applied to the questioning of Orzoco in his own home because the petitioner was "in custody," and that the use of statements obtained in the absence of the required Miranda warnings was a "flat violation of the Self-Incrimination Clause of the Fifth Amendment as construed in *Miranda*."

Acknowledging that some of the language in the *Miranda* decision suggested that the Court had viewed interrogation of a suspect in a police station as particularly susceptible to police intimidation or trickery, the Supreme Court refused to limit the Miranda rule to questioning of suspects by police in police stations. The Court instead emphasized the language of the *Miranda* opinion which "iterated and reiterated the absolute necessity for officers interrogating people 'in custody' to give the described warnings." According to the Supreme Court, *Miranda* declared that the warnings were required when the person being interrogated was "in custody at the station or otherwise deprived of his freedom of action in any significant way." In this case, the record was clear that the petitioner was under arrest and not free to leave from the time the police officers entered his boarding house bedroom at 4:00 A.M.

Justice Harlan wrote a concurring opinion in which he disagreed with, but reluctantly acquiesced in the majority's reversal of the conviction. Justice Harlan had dissented in *Miranda v. Arizona* and still found the *Miranda* decision unpalatable. However, he felt compelled by the principle of stare decisis to concur in the reversal. *Stare decisis* refers to the principle of precedent, which requires judges to decide their cases by following the principles that previous judges have established in similar cases, even if they disagree with the established principles. To emphasize his reluctance in agreeing with the reversal, Justice Harlan stated in his concurrence that "the constitutional condemnation of this perfectly understandable, sensible, proper, and indeed commendable piece of police work highlights the unsoundness of *Miranda*."

In a dissenting opinion, Justices White and Stewart opposed the extension of *Miranda* to instances of in-custody questioning outside of police stations. Justices White and Stewart had dissented in the original *Miranda* ruling and viewed it as a "constitutional straitjacket" on law enforcement "which was justified neither by the words or history of the Constitution, nor by any reasonable view of the likely benefits of the rule as against its disadvantages." However, even accepting the original Miranda rule, the justices concluded that the *Orozco* majority had taken the rule to a "new and unwarranted extreme" by applying the rule to questioning outside of police stations. The dissenting justices believed that the purpose of the Miranda rule was to guard against "incommunicado interrogation of individuals in a police-dominated atmosphere" using such techniques as extended periods of isolation, repeated interrogation, cajolery, and trickery. The dissenting justices criticized the majority for ignoring the question "whether similar hazards exist or even were possible when police arrest and interrogate on the spot, whether on the street corner or in the home." Moreover, the dissent concluded that, in this case, there was "no prolonged interrogation, no unfamiliar surroundings, no opportunity for the police to invoke those procedures which moved the majority in *Miranda*."

Impact

Miranda warnings have become a standard part of police interrogation procedure. "You have the right to remain silent—anything you say can and will be used against you in a court of law" is a familiar litany. However, debate continues as to the parameters of *Miranda* and its application in specific instances. Cases subsequent to *Orozco* interpreted *Miranda* in a manner that attempted to curtail its potentially broad holding and tip the balance of interests in favor of effective law enforcement. Nonetheless, in the 1990s, failure to properly advise suspects of their Miranda rights still caused charges to be dismissed and convictions overturned. Legal experts do not agree as to what, if any, effect *Miranda* and the subsequent cases have had on law enforcement and the rate of confessions and convictions.

Related Cases
Miranda v. Arizona, 384 U.S. 436 (1966).
Beckwith v. United States, 425 U.S. 341 (1976).

New York v. Quarles, 467 U.S. 649 (1984).
Berkemer v. McCarty, 468 U.S. 420 (1984).
Oregon v. Elstad, 470 U.S. 298 (1985).

Bibliography and Further Reading

Cassell, Paul G. and Bret S. Hayman. "Police Interrogation in the 1990s: An Empirical Study of the Effects of Miranda." *UCLA Law Review,* Vol. 42, 1996, p. 839.

Faulkner, Jane M. "So You Kinda, Sorta, Think You Might Need a Lawyer?: Ambiguous Requests For Counsel After Davis v. United States." *Arkansas Law Review,* Vol. 49, no. 2, 1996.

HARRIS V. NEW YORK

Legal Citation: 401 U.S. 222 (1971)

Petitioner
Viven Harris

Respondent
State of New York

Petitioner's Claim
That Harris's constitutional rights had been violated, and thus his narcotics conviction should be overturned.

Chief Lawyer for Petitioner
Joel Martin Aurnou

Chief Lawyer for Respondent
James J. Duggan

Justices for the Court
Harry A. Blackmun, Warren E. Burger (writing for the Court), John Marshall Harlan II, Potter Stewart, Byron R. White

Justices Dissenting
Hugo Lafayette Black, William J. Brennan, Jr., William O. Douglas, Thurgood Marshall

Place
Washington, D.C.

Date of Decision
24 February 1971

Decision
That statements considered inadmissible in convicting a defendant could be used to attack his or her credibility on the witness stand.

Significance
Narrowed suspects' rights in an attempt by a new conservative majority on the High Court to redress past liberal decisions.

Alleged Heroin Sale

On two occasions in early January of 1966, Viven Harris of New Rochelle, New York, was involved in the sale of heroin to undercover police. He claimed to have acted as a middleman in both transactions, and for the second sale was promised part of the heroin. After Harris was arrested on 7 January, he admitted to police that he had made both sales, but asserted that the undercover officer had instructed him to do so. He also mentioned that he thought he should talk to a lawyer before answering any more questions. At his jury trial, the police officer was the chief witness for the prosecution, and provided evidence that Harris had sold him drugs. Harris took the stand in his own defense, and made statements that contradicted what he had said while in police custody, in which he admitted to both sales. Under oath, he denied making the first sale, and said that the second sale had merely been a scam, that the packet contained only baking powder.

When Harris was cross-examined by the prosecution, he was asked whether or not he had made confessional statements on 7 January. He claimed he could not remember what he had said to police after his arrest, nor what the questions were. Later, his lawyer would argue that at the time, Harris was suffering from heroin addiction withdrawal symptoms and had a host of other medical problems affecting his judgement and memory. The cross-examination that challenged Harris's assertions did not become part of the transcript upon which the jury would decide his guilt or innocence. The statements initially made in police custody were inadmissible to convict him, since they qualified as evidence not obtained within proper legal guidelines. This was a recent development in American criminal law known as the *Miranda* warnings.

Miranda v. Arizona

In a significant Supreme Court decision of 1966, the Court ruled that evidence, such as confessional statements made to police, could not be used in court if the defendant had not been informed of his right to a lawyer, as well as instructed that anything he or she said could be used against them in court. It gave suspects the option of remaining silent and let them know that if they could not afford a lawyer, one would be provided free of charge. These admonitions came to be known as the *Miranda* warnings and were designed to curb potential police misconduct. Harris's interrogation happened before *Miranda* rule went into effect, but the rules governing whether or not statements had been "coerced" still applied in his case.

Miranda was a controversial Supreme Court decision at the time, issued by the Warren Court, a liberal-leaning majority led by Chief Justice Earl Warren. During the 1968 presidential campaign, Republican candidate Richard M. Nixon condemned the Warren Court and its liberal slant. During his first term in office, Nixon was able to appoint replacements for retiring justices, naming Burger chief justice and sending the conservative Blackmun to the bench. By the time *Harris v. New York* reached the High Court in 1971, these two, along with the three justices who had dissented in the *Miranda* case, formed a conservative "law-and-order" voting block.

Testifying Against Oneself

Harris's case tested whether statements made while in police custody—though considered legally inadmissible as a confession—could, however, be used to "impeach" (in this sense, to attack or discredit) a defendant's statements under oath. During that first trial, the judge instructed the jury that the statements Harris may or may not have made after his arrest should not be used to determine evidence of his guilt, but rather to judge his credibility. The jury found him guilty of the second sale. Harris appealed to New York's state appellate court, claiming that the use of his earlier statements violated several rights guaranteed him by the U.S. Constitution, most importantly the Fifth Amendment, which holds that a person shall not be compelled to be a witness against himself in a criminal trial. The appellate court rejected his argument as well, and it appeared before the U.S. Supreme Court in 1971.

Decision on *Harris*

In an opinion written by Chief Justice Burger, the Court ruled in a 5-4 decision that a defendant's statements, even though made without the obligatory *Miranda* warnings, were admissible in court to impeach his or her testimony. They cited other cases as legal precedent, specifically a 1954 Supreme Court decision that deemed knowledge of narcotics evidence taken in an illegal search (but not used to convict the person) was permitted to contradict a defendant's testimony in which he asserted that he had never been in possession of drugs. Furthermore, Burger's opinion on *Harris v. New York* asserted that exposing perjurious statements was a far more grave concern to the American justice system than any unsupported claim that this ruling might encourage police misconduct.

Opponents of the *Harris v. New York* decision criticized the ruling for its murky language and its reversal of all lower court decisions. They asserted that it gave little incentive for law-enforcement authorities to comply with the *Miranda* rules—for example, if police officers knew they might obtain some sort of admissible statement, they might delay the moment in which they were compelled to ask the suspect if he wished to contact a lawyer. Criminal-rights advocates also pointed out that the *Harris* ruling, allowing such questioning, would discourage defendants from taking the stand in their own defense, a tactic that greatly improved their chances for acquittal in a jury trial.

Related Cases

Walder v. United States, 347 U.S. 62 (1954).
Blackburn v. Alabama, 361 U.S. 199 (1960).
Townsend v. Sain, 372 U.S. 293 (1963).
Miranda v. Arizona, 384 U.S. 436 (1966).
Lego v. Twomey, 404 U.S. 477 (1972).
Colorado v. Connelly, 479 U.S. 157 (1986).

Bibliography and Further Reading

Dershowitz, Alan M. and John Hart Ely. "*Harris v. New York:* Some Anxious Observations on the Candor and Logic of the Emerging Nixon Majority." *Yale Law Journal,* Vol. 80, May 1971, pp. 1198-1227.

Graham, Fred P. "Justices Narrow a Crime Decision by Warren Court." *New York Times,* February 25, 1971, p. 1.

Harvard Law Review, Vol. 85, November 1971, pp. 44-64.

ARGERSINGER V. HAMLIN

Legal Citation: 407 U.S. 25 (1972)

Petitioner
Jon Richard Argersinger

Respondent
Raymond Hamlin, Leon County Sheriff, Florida

Petitioner's Claim
That being sentenced to jail after a trial where he was not represented by counsel violated the Sixth Amendment.

Chief Lawyers for Petitioner
J. Michael Shea, Bruce S. Rogow

Chief Lawyer for Respondent
George R. Georgieff

Justices for the Court
Harry A. Blackmun, William J. Brennan, Jr., Warren E. Burger, William O. Douglas (writing for the Court), Thurgood Marshall, Lewis F. Powell, Jr., William H. Rehnquist, Potter Stewart, Byron R. White

Justices Dissenting
None

Place
Washington, D.C.

Date of Decision
12 June 1972

Decision
Finding that defendants facing a jail sentence of any length have a right to counsel, the Supreme Court by a unanimous decision reversed a lower court's refusal to grant Argersinger's *habeas corpus* petition.

Significance
Argersinger extended the holding of the landmark case, *Gideon v. Wainwright* (1963), in which the Supreme Court had ruled that all accused felons must be represented by counsel at trial. Now, the Court held, the state must appoint a lawyer to represent even misdemeanor defendants facing the prospect of incarceration if they are too poor to afford one.

Jon Richard Argersinger was arrested and charged in Florida with carrying a concealed weapon, a misdemeanor offense punishable by imprisonment for up to six months, a $1,000 fine, or both. After a trial before a judge, where Argersinger was not represented by counsel because he could not afford one, he was sentenced to 90 days in jail. Argersinger then filed a *habeas corpus* action before the Florida Supreme Court, challenging his confinement on grounds that his conviction without benefit of counsel violated the Sixth Amendment's right to a fair trial. After the state supreme court denied Argersinger's petition, he applied to the U.S. Supreme Court for review of this decision.

The Florida court had based its decision on a U.S. Supreme Court case, *Duncan v. Louisiana* (1968), in which the Court had ruled that the right to a court-appointed attorney only extended to indigent defendants charged with non-petty offenses punishable by more than 6 months imprisonment. The issue in *Duncan* had been the Sixth Amendment right to trial by jury, so now the Court turned to another precedent, *Gideon v. Wainwright* (1963), to address the issue of incarceration of criminal defendants without representation. The holding there—that indigent defendants in felony cases have a right to appointed counsel—was now extended to include misdemeanor defendants facing prison sentences. As Justice Douglas wrote for the Court: "We hold, therefore, that absent a knowing and intelligent waiver, no person may be imprisoned for any offense, whether classified as petty, misdemeanor, or felony, unless he was represented by counsel at his trial."

Although the vote to overturn the lower court ruling in *Argersinger* was unanimous, Justice Powell wrote a concurring opinion in which he voiced doubts about the sweeping rule this case established, which he believed would cause difficulties in the administration of criminal justice:

> The flat six-month rule of the Florida court and the equally inflexible rule of the majority opinion apply to *all* cases within their defined areas regardless of circumstances. It is precisely because of this mechanistic application that I find these alternatives unsatisfactory. Due

Justice William O. Douglas. © Photograph by Harris and Ewing. Collection of the Supreme Court of the United States.

process, perhaps the most fundamental concept in our law, embodies the principles of fairness rather than immutable line drawing as to every aspect of a criminal trial. While counsel is often essential to a fair trial, this is by no means a universal fact.

Instead, Powell wrote:

I would hold that the right to counsel in petty offense cases is not absolute but is one to be determined by the trial courts exercising a judicial discretion on a case-by-case basis. The determination should be made before the accused formally pleads . . .

And indeed, 16 years later, the Supreme Court limited the implication of *Argersinger* that all criminal defendants who cannot afford to hire an attorney be appointed counsel. In *Scott v. Illinois* (1979), the Court held that only those indigent criminal defendants who are actually confronting jail time—not those for whom it is only a theoretical possibility—have a Sixth Amendment right to a court-appointed lawyer.

Related Cases
Gideon v Wainwright, 372 U.S. 335 (1963).
Duncan v. Louisiana, 391 U.S. 104 (1968).
Scott v. Illinois, 440 U.S. 367 (1979).

Bibliography and Further Reading
Garcia, Alfredo. *The Sixth Amendment in Modern American Jurisprudence: A Critical Perspective.* New York: Greenwood Press, 1992.

Latzer, Barry. *State Constitutional Criminal Law.* Deerfield, IL: Clark Boardman Callaghan, 1995.

Right to Counsel in Criminal Cases: The Mandate of Argersinger v. Hamlin. Cambridge, MA: Ballinger Publishing, 1976.

SIELING V. EYMAN

Legal Citation: 478 F.2d 211 (1973)

Petitioner
Gilbert F. Sieling, Sr.

Respondent
Frank A. Eyman, Warden, Arizona State Prison

Petitioner's Claim
The trial court committed a reversible error when it failed to conduct an inquiry into his mental capacity to enter a plea of guilty.

Chief Lawyer for Petitioner
Dennis J. Skarecky

Chief Lawyers for Respondent
William P. Dizon, Gary K. Nelson

Judges
Duniway, Koelsch (writing for the majority), Merrill

Place
Los Angeles, California

Date of Decision
23 April 1973

Decision
Where a U.S. District Court in the Ninth Circuit inquires into the mental capacity of a defendant to stand trial, it also must conduct an inquiry into that defendant's mental capacity to plead guilty. Furthermore, when a questionably competent defendant pleads guilty, the standard for determining competency is higher than when the court is determining a defendant's mental capacity to stand trial.

Significance
The decision made the Ninth Circuit the first federal circuit to require that its trial courts look further into a defendant's competency to plead guilty than it looks into a defendant's capacity to stand trial.

Gilbert F. Sieling, Sr., was charged in an Arizona state court with three counts of assault with a deadly weapon and five counts of assault to commit murder. Sieling pleaded not guilty at his arraignment, and the court granted his lawyer's motion for an examination of Sieling's mental health to see if he was competent to stand trial. The two psychiatrists who examined Sieling disagreed on the question, and the court ordered a third psychiatric evaluation. At a pretrial hearing, all three psychiatrists testified that they believed Sieling was legally insane at the time he allegedly committed the crimes. On the question of Sieling's mental capacity to stand trial, the psychiatrists were split: only one believed that Sieling might be incapable of understanding the proceedings and assisting in his own defense. The finding of competency is important in a criminal trial because it decides whether the government will try to incarcerate the accused or, in the case of a mentally challenged person, commit the person to a secure mental health facility.

The court ruled that Sieling was mentally competent to stand trial and set a trial date. Shortly before trial, Sieling notified the court that he wished to change his not guilty plea to guilty. After a brief inquiry into Sieling's understanding of the charges and the consequences of the guilty plea, the court dismissed the charges of assault to commit murder, but found Sieling guilty on the counts of assault with a deadly weapon. The court ordered Sieling to serve consecutive terms of 8 to 10 and 4 to 6 years for the crimes.

Sieling later tried and failed to reverse his conviction in state court. He then filed a *habeas corpus* petition in a federal district court for the Ninth Circuit, arguing that his guilty pleas were invalid because the state trial court had not inquired into his competency to make the pleas. In the short colloquy that preceded his guilty plea, the trial court had only inquired into the usual matters that precede all guilty pleas: whether Sieling's plea was voluntary, whether there was any coercion from any party, and whether Sieling understood the nature of his plea. According to Sieling's attorneys, that inquiry was not enough to resolve the question of Sieling's competency to make his own plea of guilty. Indeed, the court had never made a finding on the issue of Sieling's competency to plead guilty. The district court denied his request for outright release or a rehearing, but, in April of 1973, the U.S. Court of Appeals for the Ninth Circuit reversed.

The appeals court cited the U.S. Supreme Court case of *Westbrook v. Arizona* (1966) as support for Sieling's argument. In that case, the trial court had found that the defendant was competent to understand the proceedings and assist his lawyer in his own defense, but the High Court held that such a finding could not stand in for a finding that the defendant was competent to proceed without a lawyer. To the Supreme Court, there was a difference between a defendant's mental competency to stand trial and a defendant's mental competency to waive a right to counsel at trial. So too, said the appeals court, was there a difference between a defendant's mental competency to stand trial and mental competency to plead guilty.

The constitutional rights involved in pleading guilty, explained the appeals court, were legion. Citing Supreme Court precedent, the appeals court noted that in pleading guilty a defendant waived the Fifth Amendment right to be free from compulsory self-incrimination and the Sixth Amendment rights to confrontation of witnesses and a trial by jury. Because so many important constitutional rights were at stake in a guilty plea, a court should, as the Supreme Court said in *Boykin v. Alabama,* (1969) "exercise the utmost solicitude" to ensure that a defendant who may be mentally challenged knows what he or she is doing. In a case where the defendant's mental capacity is an issue, "it is logically inconsistent to suggest that his waiver can be examined by mere reference to those criteria we examine in cases where the defendant is presumed competent."

Although the *Westbrook* case dealt with a defendant's waiver of counsel, which was not the specific issue in *Sieling*, the appeals court considered the Supreme Court's *Westbrook* decision ample support for its holding. The High Court did not articulate a standard for determining whether a person has enough mental capacity to intelligently waive a right to counsel, but, said the appeals court, "it is reasonable to conclude from the Court's language that the degree of competency required to waive a constitutional right is that degree which enables him to make decisions of very serious import."

Having decided that the usual inquiry into a criminal defendant's understanding and awareness were insufficient for criminal defendants who may lack sufficient mental capacity to understand the proceedings, the court needed to set a higher standard. It found the standard in the words of Judge Hufstedler in *Schoeller*

v. Dunbar, (1970) a prior Ninth Circuit case. In *Schoeller*, the Ninth Circuit appeals court ruled that a defendant was competent to plead guilty at the time he was sentenced. Hufstedler, who dissented, proposed that "'[a] defendant is not competent to plead guilty if a mental illness has substantially impaired his ability to make a reasoned choice among the alternatives presented to him and to understand the nature of his plea.'" Such a standard, said that court, takes into account "the gravity of the decisions with which the defendant is faced."

The court observed that no such inquiry had taken place in Sieling's case, and that the determination was "a deficient basis for upholding a plea of guilty." It then remanded the case back to the state trial court for a determination of whether Sieling was competent to plead guilty. Before making this determination, the appeals court advised, the trial court should review the existing information from the three psychiatrists and determine whether additional information was needed to make the determination.

Impact

The federal appeals court decision made the Ninth Circuit the first to adopt a higher standard for determining competency to plead guilty than the competency standard for standing trial. Only the District of Columbia Circuit followed the Ninth Circuit's lead. In many jurisdictions, the standard remained the same: a person was competent to plead guilty if the person was competent to stand trial. Generally, a person is competent to stand trial if he understands the nature and the objective of the proceedings and is capable of assisting his lawyer in his defense. Other jurisdictions crafted slightly different standards. In 1993, the U.S. Supreme Court put an end to the confusion. By a vote of 7-2, the High Court held in *Godinez v. Moran* (1993) that the standard for competency to plead guilty should be the same as the standard for competency to stand trial.

Related Cases
Westbrook v. Arizona, 384 U.S. 150 (1966).
Boykin v. Alabama, 395 U.S. 238 (1969).
Schoeller v. Dunbar, 423 F. 2d 1183 (1970).
Godinez v. Moran, 509 U.S. 389 (1993).

Bibliography and Further Reading
Boch, Brian R. "Fourteenth Amendment—The Standard of Mental Competency to Waive Constitutional Rights Versus the Competency Standard to Stand Trial." *Journal of Criminal Law and Criminology*, winter/spring 1994.

"Competence To Plead Guilty and to Stand Trial: A New Standard When a Criminal Defendant Waives Counsel." *Virginia Law Review*, May 1982.

SCOTT V. ILLINOIS

Legal Citation: 440 U.S. 367 (1979)

Petitioner
Aubrey Scott

Respondent
State of Illinois

Petitioner's Claim
That the state of Illinois's failure to supply him with legal counsel for his trial on a shoplifting charge violated his Sixth and Fourteenth Amendment rights to due process of law.

Chief Lawyer for Petitioner
John S. Elson

Chief Lawyer for Respondent
Gerri Papushkewych

Justices for the Court
Warren E. Burger, Lewis F. Powell, Jr., William H. Rehnquist (writing for the Court), Potter Stewart, Byron R. White

Justices Dissenting
Harry A. Blackmun, William J. Brennan, Jr., Thurgood Marshall, John Paul Stevens

Place
Washington, D.C.

Date of Decision
5 March 1979

Decision
Upheld the decisions of the Illinois Intermediate Appellate Court and the Illinois Supreme Court, denying the petitioner's claim and holding that the right of due process does not extend to criminal cases in which no prison term is imposed.

Significance
The ruling clarified the Court's reasoning with regard to provision of legal counsel to indigent criminal defendants as outlined in *Argersinger v. Hamlin,* (1972). In *Argersinger* the Court had ruled that a state must provide legal counsel to indigent criminal defendants potentially subject to prison terms of not greater than six months. *Scott v. Illinois* limited a state's obligation to provide legal counsel to indigent defendants to those cases in which a sentence of imprisonment was imposed.

An Open-and-Shut Case?

Aubrey Scott was found guilty of shoplifting merchandise with a value of greater than $50, a misdemeanor. The verdict was announced during a bench trial in the Circuit Court of Cook County, Illinois, at which he was not provided with free legal counsel by the state of Illinois. Under Illinois state law he faced a sentence of up to one year in prison, a fine of up to $500, or both for his conviction. Scott was merely fined $50. Despite the relative lightness of his sentence Scott appealed his case to the Illinois Intermediate Appellate Court, which upheld the circuit court ruling. He then took his case to the Illinois Supreme Court, which affirmed the lower court holdings in the case, stating that the legal precedent set in *Argersinger v. Hamlin* did not apply to this case since Scott did not receive a sentence of imprisonment for his crime. Scott disagreed with this position, and appealed the case to the U.S. Supreme Court, which heard arguments in the matter on 4 December 1978.

Legal Precedents

It is generally agreed that the Sixth Amendment to the U.S. Constitution, which guarantees due process of law to those accused of crimes, was not intended by its writers to demand provision of legal counsel to the accused, but rather only to bar the state from denying individuals the right to legal representation in court. Nevertheless, since the 1930s the U.S. Supreme Court has consistently held that the Sixth Amendment does guarantee legal counsel to those accused of crimes. In *Powell v. Alabama* (1932) the Court overturned the sentences of eight black youths who were convicted and sentenced to death in an abbreviated trial without the benefit of legal counsel. The Court continued to broaden its interpretation of the Sixth Amendment guarantee of due process in *Johnson v. Zerbst* (1938), ruling that federal criminal defendants who lacked the financial means to retain legal counsel must be provided with an attorney by the court. In each of these cases the Court reasoned that due process could only be guaranteed by the presence of counsel, and, in *Johnson,* that an individual's financial means should not unduly impact upon their legal status.

The Court failed to extend the same guarantee of counsel to individuals accused of felonies by the states. In *Betts v. Brady* (1942), the Court held that states were free to judge the circumstances under which felony defendants facing state charges need be provided with counsel. This ruling was overturned in *Gideon v. Wainwright* (1963), however, when the Court ruled that all state felony defendants must be provided with legal counsel if unable to obtain it for themselves. Finally, in *Argersinger,* the Court held that a defendant charged with a misdemeanor was entitled to state appointed counsel.

Interpreting *Argersinger*

In reaching its decision to affirm the findings of the Illinois Intermediate Appellate Court and Illinois Supreme Court, the Supreme Court made a very narrow interpretation of the ruling in *Argersinger.* Writing for the majority, Justice Rehnquist stated that *Argersinger* applied only to cases in which a defendant was actually sentenced to time in prison, and was inapplicable in cases where imprisonment was either not part of the sentencing guidelines or merely a sentencing option. This reflects a very literal reading of the majority opinion in *Argersinger,* which stated that "every judge will know when the trial of a misdemeanor starts that no imprisonment may be imposed, even though local law permits it, unless the accused is represented by counsel." Rehnquist went on to conclude that "the central premise of *Argersinger* that actual imprisonment is a penalty different in kind from fines or the mere threat of imprisonment—is eminently sound and warrants adoption of actual imprisonment as the line defining the constitutional right to appointment of counsel." Finally, to extend the guarantee of legal counsel to all misdemeanor defendants would cause "confusion and impose unpredictable, but necessarily substantial, costs" on the states.

The four dissenting justices disagreed strongly with the majority's reasoning. In their view, the Sixth Amendment clearly delineated the right of defendants to legal counsel regardless of the circumstances of their trial or the potential sentences they faced. The dissent also maintained that *Argersinger* extended the right to counsel to all defendants facing a possible prison term, regardless of their actual sentence.

Impact

Scott v. Illinois marked a stepping back from the trend established by the Court in the 1930s to expand the right of the accused to legal counsel under the Sixth Amendment. The ruling narrowed the scope of *Argersinger v. Hamlin,* which had guaranteed state appointed counsel for misdemeanor defendants facing possible prison sentences, by mandating appointment of counsel only in cases where a sentence of imprisonment was sought. Practically, the ruling enabled the state to forgo appointment of counsel in cases where the prosecution did not seek a prison sentence for the accused.

Related Cases

Powell v. Alabama, 287 U.S. 45 (1932).
Johnson v. Zerbst, 304 U.S. 458 (1938).
Betts v. Brady, 316 U.S. 455 (1942).
Gideon v. Wainwright, 372 U.S. 335 (1963).
Argersinger v. Hamlin, 407 U.S. 25 (1972).

Bibliography and Further Reading

Biskupic, Joan, and Elder Witt, eds. *Guide to the Supreme Court of the United States.* Washington, DC: Congressional Quarterly Inc., 1997.

RHODE ISLAND V. INNIS

Legal Citation: 446 U.S. 291 (1980)

Petitioner
State of Rhode Island

Respondent
Thomas J. Innis

Petitioner's Claim
That a conversation between two police officers with a murder suspect within earshot did not constitute an interrogation in violation of the suspect's Miranda rights.

Chief Lawyer for Petitioner
Dennis J. Roberts II

Chief Lawyer for Respondent
John A. MacFadyen III

Justices for the Court
Harry A. Blackmun, Warren E. Burger, Lewis F. Powell, Jr., William H. Rehnquist, Potter Stewart (writing for the Court), Byron R. White

Justices Dissenting
William J. Brennan, Jr., Thurgood Marshall, John Paul Stevens

Place
Washington, D.C.

Date of Decision
12 May 1980

Decision
Suspect Thomas J. Innis was found to have not been interrogated by the police.

Significance
In *Rhode Island v. Innis,* the Supreme Court clarified the definition of interrogation as it relates to the Miranda rule, which prohibits police officers from interrogating suspects if they have requested legal representation.

The events in this case follow the death of a Providence, Rhode Island, taxi driver in a shotgun murder. Shortly after this murder, a second taxi driver was robbed by a man wielding a sawed-off shotgun. The taxi driver identified a photograph of Thomas J. Innis as the man who attacked him. Soon after, a police officer spotted Innis, who was unarmed, on the street near a school for handicapped children. The officer arrested Innis and advised him of his Miranda rights. A group of other police officers arrived at the scene. Innis was advised of his Miranda rights two more times. He stated that he understood his rights and wanted to speak with an attorney. The police captain had Innis placed in a police car to be driven to the central station. The captain instructed the three patrolmen in the car not to interrogate or intimidate Innis in any way.

On the way to the station, two of the patrolmen, Officers Gleckman and McKenna, began talking to each other about the missing shotgun. They expressed concern about whether one of the children might find the weapon the next morning. "God forbid one of them might find a weapon with shells and they might hurt themselves," said one of the officers. Innis interrupted the conversation, telling the officers he could lead them to the missing shotgun. The patrol car returned to the scene of the arrest where Innis was once again advised of his Miranda rights. He replied that he understood his rights and proceeded to show the policemen where the shotgun was located. Innis was subsequently put on trial for kidnapping, robbery, and murder. In court, he tried to have the evidence of the shotgun and his statements to the police suppressed. The court denied this motion and convicted Innis. Upon his conviction, Innis appealed.

On appeal, the Rhode Island Supreme Court set aside the conviction. It held that the police officers in the patrol car had indeed interrogated Innis without first getting him to waive his right to a lawyer. This constituted a violation of the *Miranda* requirement that, in the absence of counsel, all "custodial interrogation" of a suspect must cease. The Court ordered a new trial. The state of Rhode Island appealed this decision and in 1979 the U.S. Supreme Court agreed to hear the case.

The Supreme Court Ruling

On 12 May 1980 the Supreme Court issued its decision. In a 6-3 vote, it vacated the ruling of the Rhode Island Supreme Court. Justice Stewart wrote the majority opinion, in which he was joined by Justices Blackmun, Rehnquist, Powell, and White. Chief Justice Burger concurred with the judgment but did not sign on with the majority opinion. Justices Marshall, Brennan, and Stevens dissented. Since all participants agreed that Innis had been read his Miranda rights, both the majority opinion and the dissents rested on the one central issue in the case, as stated by Justice Stewart:

> The issue, therefore, is whether the respondent was "interrogated" by the police officers in violation of the respondent's undisputed right under *Miranda* to remain silent until he had consulted with a lawyer.

In making its decision, the Court majority first had to establish a definition of "interrogation":

> [T]he term "interrogation" under *Miranda* refers not only to express questioning, but also to any words or actions on the part of the police (other than those normally attendant to arrest and custody) that the police should know are reasonably likely to elicit an incriminating response from the suspect.

The Court then subjected the facts in the case to the legal test to determine whether what happened to Innis was, in fact, an interrogation:

> It is undisputed that the first prong of the definition of "interrogation" was not satisfied, for the conversation between Patrolmen Gleckman and McKenna included no express questioning of the respondent. Rather, that conversation was, at least in form, nothing more than a dialogue between the two officers to which no response from the respondent was invited.

The Court went on to conclude that Innis was not even subjected to the "functional equivalent" of an interrogation because there was no way the officers could have known that he would respond to their conversation in the way that he did:

> The case thus boils down to whether, in the context of a brief conversation, the officers should have known that the respondent would suddenly be moved to make a self-incriminating response. Given the fact that the entire conversation appears to have consisted of no more than a few offhand remarks, we cannot say that the officers should have known that it was reasonably likely that Innis would so respond.

Rhode Island v. Innis was an important case in the clarification of the Miranda rule first set down in 1966. The majority opinion contained the Court's clearest definition of interrogation to date. To the dissenters, however, this decision represented an unnecessary narrowing of Miranda rights that rendered them all but meaningless.

Related Cases

Miranda v. Arizona, 384 U.S. 436 (1966).
United States v. Henry, 447 U.S. 264 (1980).
Edwards v. Arizona, 451 U.S. 477 (1981).
Maine v. Moulton, 474 U.S. 159 (1985).
Kuhlmann v. Wilson, 477 U.S. 436 (1986).

Bibliography and Further Reading

Cassell, Paul G. "Protecting the Innocent from False Confessions and Lost Confessions—and from *Miranda.*" *Journal of Criminal Law and Criminology,* winter 1998, p. 497.

Choper, Jesse H., Yale Kamisar, and Laurence H. Tribe. *The Supreme Court: Trends and Developments.* Minneapolis, MN: National Practice Institute, Inc., 1979.

Goldman, Sheldon. *Constitutional Law: Cases and Essays.* New York, NY: Harper and Row, 1987.

Leo, Richard A. "The Impact of *Miranda* Revisited." *Journal of Criminal Law and Criminology,* spring 1996, p. 621.

Steiker, Carol S. "Counter-Revolution in Constitutional Criminal Procedure? Two Audiences, Two Answers." *Michigan Law Review,* August 1996, p. 2466.

Thomas, George C., III. "Confessions, Truth, and the Law." *Journal of Criminal Law and Criminology,* winter 1995, p. 807.

LASSITER V. DEPARTMENT OF SOCIAL SERVICES

Legal Citation: 452 U.S. 18 (1981)

Petitioner
Abby Gail Lassiter

Respondent
Department of Social Services of Durham County, North Carolina

Petitioner's Claim
Because she was indigent, the Fourteenth Amendment's Due Process Clause dictated that the state provide her with counsel.

Chief Lawyer for Petitioner
Leowen Evans

Chief Lawyer for Respondent
Thomas Russell Odom

Justices for the Court
Warren E. Burger, Lewis F. Powell, Jr., William H. Rehnquist, Potter Stewart (writing for the Court), Byron R. White

Justices Dissenting
Harry A. Blackmun, William J. Brennan, Jr., Thurgood Marshall, John Paul Stevens

Place
Washington, D.C.

Date of Decision
1 June 1981

Decision
Refusing to appoint counsel for an indigent parent in proceedings terminating parental status was found not to violate the Due Process Clause of the Fourteenth Amendment.

Significance
The decision in this case helped establish that the Court did not have to appoint counsel for an indigent parent as long as no criminal charges were involved.

One of the rights guaranteed under the Fourteenth Amendment is that of due process. In a general way it implies a procedure. A person cannot go to jail without a trial. A trial must contain a certain amount of elements and procedures to be considered within a citizen's constitutional right. This, however, is the concept's general meaning. Its specific meaning has changed through the years, evolving even into the twentieth century.

Originally, due process only referred to federal proceedings, but through the years, the Supreme Court reversed more and more convictions due to unfair state court proceedings. Beginning in 1897, the Supreme Court ruled that when a state takes private property from a person without just compensation to that person, due process is violated (*Chicago, Burlington and Quincy Railroad Company v. Chicago*).

This is a specific form of due process—procedural due process. When the question of procedural due process arises in a Supreme Court case, it refers to the fairness of a case in a lower court. Fairness is the issue at hand in the case of *Lassiter v. Department of Social Services*.

In May of 1975, a social worker took William Lassiter to the hospital because he was suffering from difficulty in breathing, malnutrition, and scarring that showed he had an untreated severe infection. After hearing that Abby Gail Lassiter had not provided the infant, William, with proper medical attention, the District Court of Durham County, North Carolina, ruled that William was a neglected child and he was transferred to the custody of the Durham County Department of Social Services. The child died.

A year after this, the state charged Lassiter with first degree murder and convicted her of second-degree murder. Her sentence was to be imprisonment for 25 to 40 years.

In 1978, the Social Services Department asked the court to take away Lassiter's parental rights because she had not had any contact with her son since December 1975. Also, she had left her son in foster care longer than two consecutive years without making virtually any attempt to correct the conditions which originally led to the department removing the child. Furthermore, she had not responded at all to the department's attempts at improving her relationship with her son, nor had she engaged in any dialogue with the department regarding her son's future.

In an effort to repeal her murder conviction, Lassiter had her mother engage the services of an attorney. When she met with this attorney, Lassiter apparently never mentioned the pending custody hearing. In fact, except to someone in prison with her, she never mentioned it to anyone.

On 31 August 1978, at the hearing, to which she had been brought from prison, the judge questioned whether Lassiter should have more time to obtain counsel. The court determined that she had had sufficient time to procure an attorney. Since Lassiter did not claim she was indigent, the court did not offer to appoint an attorney for her.

The judge established that when the Department of Social Services had served her with papers, she responded by saying she would not come. Also, it was brought out that on 8 May 1975, Lassiter's mother had filed a complaint with the department, stating that her daughter had left her children with her for days, providing no money or food during her absences. The result of the hearing was that Lassiter's relationship as mother to her son William was terminated because she had "willfully failed to maintain concern or responsibility for the minor," and because it was in her son's best interests.

In the course of an appeal, Lassiter's only argument was that since she was indigent, the Fourteenth Amendment's Due Process Clause guaranteed an attorney for her and the state had been mistaken in not providing her with counsel. The Court of Appeals of North Carolina ruled that even though terminating her status as William's mother invaded a "protected area of individual privacy," it was not serious enough, nor was it so unreasonable, as to believe it was "constitutionally correct to appoint counsel for indigent parents."

In a 5-4 decision, the U.S. Supreme Court affirmed the court's ruling. In Justice Stewart's opinion, he said, essentially, that the Court's tradition had been to rule

that the more an indigent person's liberty was threatened, the more likely it was that the Court would rule in favor of a right to appointed counsel. In fact, the Court had refused, in the past, to grant the right of appointed counsel even in criminal cases, if the outcome did not involve defendants losing their personal liberty.

Summing up, Stewart emphasized that Supreme Court precedents clearly indicate that, in this context, "fundamental fairness" means that an indigent defendant only has a right to an appointed counsel if the consequences include possible loss of personal liberty. On the other hand, said Stewart's opinion, circumstances may dictate otherwise, in other custody questions, but in this case, it was evident that Lassiter was disinterested in her child. She had not discussed the case with an attorney when she had the opportunity. It was obviously in the child's best interests that the relationship be dissolved. Considering all of these things, the Court ruled that the presence of counsel would not have made a substantive difference.

Related Cases

Chicago, Burlington and Quincy Railroad Company v. Chicago, 166 U.S. 226 (1897).
Betts v. Brady, 316 U.S. 455 (1942).
Gideon v. Wainwright, 372 U.S. 335 (1963).
Argersinger v. Hamlin, 407 U.S. 25 (1972).
Goss v. Lopez, 419 U.S. 565 (1975).
Scott v. Illinois, 440 U.S. 367 (1979).

Bibliography and Further Reading

Brandes, Joel R. "The Custody Rights of Parents." *New York Law Journal,* Vol. 220, no. 58, September 22, 1998.

Lieberman, Jethro K. *The Evolving Constitution.* Random House, 1992.

Patterson, Charlotte J., and Richard E. Redding. "Lesbian and Gay with Children: Implications of Social Research for Policy." *Journal of Social Issues,* Vol. 52, no. 3, September 27, 1996.

Woodhouse, Barbara Bennett. "Mad Midwifery: Bringing Theory, Doctrine, and Practice to Life. *Michigan Law Review,* August 1993, p. 1977.

NEW YORK V. QUARLES

Legal Citation: 467 U.S. 649 (1984)

Petitioner
State of New York

Respondent
Benjamin Quarles

Petitioner's Claim
A police officer's failure to provide Miranda warnings before questioning the respondent about incriminating evidence did not violate Fifth Amendment rights, as the delay was justified in the interest of public safety.

Chief Lawyer for Petitioner
Steven J. Rappaport

Chief Lawyer for Respondent
Steven A. Hyman

Justices for the Court
Harry A. Blackmun, Warren E. Burger, Lewis F. Powell, Jr., William H. Rehnquist (writing for the Court), Byron R. White

Justices Dissenting
William J. Brennan, Jr., Thurgood Marshall, Sandra Day O'Connor, John Paul Stevens

Place
Washington, D.C.

Date of Decision
12 June 1984

Decision
The U.S. Supreme Court held that an officer's immediate concern with protecting the safety and welfare of the public represented a justified exception to the Miranda rule.

Significance
The most important issue addressed by this case was whether an incriminating statement regarding information about where the respondent hid his gun, could be accepted as testimonial evidence at trial if a police officer failed to provide a Fifth Amendment Miranda rights warning before questioning his suspect. The U.S. Supreme Court reversed judgments of lower courts and explained that an exception to the Miranda rule was justified because the officer believed he needed to ensure public safety. In ruling as acceptable a departure from the required, very precise instructions of the Miranda rule, which ensured a suspect would not be subject to self-incrimination if Miranda warnings were not given, the U.S. Supreme Court gave guidance that in circumstances where public safety was at risk, it may be necessary and correct to forego Miranda warnings.

On 11 September 1980, shortly after midnight, two police officers, Frank Craft and Sal Scarring, were on patrol when a woman came to their car and told them she had been raped. She provided a description of an black male, six feet tall, armed, and wearing a black jacket. She also told officers he fled into a supermarket. Officer Craft rushed in to apprehend the suspect while his partner called for assistance. He recognized a man who matched the description and gave chase. Craft ordered his suspect to stop and put his hands over his head. Other officers convened and surrounded the suspect in back of the store, but Officer Kraft was the first to reach the man. Handcuffing the suspect, the officer noticed the man's empty shoulder holster and asked him where the gun was. The suspect nodded his head toward some empty boxes answering, "The gun is over there." Officer Craft secured the weapon then returned to inform the suspect, Benjamin Quarles, of his Miranda rights. Quarles decided to waive his Miranda rights and answer the officer's questions without an attorney's presence. He stated that he bought the revolver in Miami, Florida, and it was his.

Miranda Warnings Inadequate

Benjamin Quarles was charged with criminal possession of a gun. (Under New York Penal Law, "any person who possesses a loaded firearm outside of his home or place of business is guilty of criminal possession of a weapon in the third degree.") The trial court elected to exclude the respondent's evidential testimony, "The gun is over there," and the physical evidence, a .38 caliber revolver, because Miranda warnings were not given to Quarles before the officer asked him the location of the gun. The New York Appellate Division of the New York Supreme Court and the New York Court of Appeals affirmed the lower court's decision to suppress Quarles's statements. Because Officer Kraft failed to advise Quarles of his rights before asking any questions, the court believed the Miranda warning was inappropriately omitted. The court of appeals did not accept the state of New York's contention that the police officer was in a situation where the safety of himself, fellow officers, and the public had to be protected. The appellate court held that any interrogation before giving

---

Self-Incrimination Clause

The Fifth Amendment guarantees that "no person shall be held to answer for a capital, or otherwise infamous crime, unless on a presentment or indictment of a Grand Jury . . . nor shall be compelled in any criminal case to be witness against himself . . ."

In criminal cases the prosecution must prove the guilt of the defendant without forcing the accused to confess or testify. Only individuals, and not businesses or corporations, can use the privilege against self-incrimination. This privilege also extends to witnesses, who can refuse to answer questions that may incriminate them in a civil or criminal proceeding. The privilege against self-incrimination extends to all judicial proceedings including grand jury transactions, legislative investigations and administrative hearings.

In order to claim this privilege, a witness must first appear in court. Failure to appear can result in a contempt of court citation. Defendants in criminal cases have the same privileges as witnesses. Unless the accused has been given their Miranda rights any statement made is considered involuntary and cannot be used against them.

Source(s): *West's Encyclopedia of American Law*, Vol. 4. Minneapolis, MN: West Publishing, 1998.

Miranda warnings, such as questioning about the location of the gun, was in violation of Fifth Amendment rights, which states that "No person shall be compelled in any criminal case to be a witness against himself." Consequently, because due process was violated, lower court rulings were affirmed.

A Compelling Exception

The U.S. Supreme Court reversed the decision of the lower courts. The Court found that the use of the Miranda warnings could be avoided when public safety was at issue. They explained the "immediate necessity of ascertaining the whereabouts of the gun" to ensure the safety of the public was important enough to justify an exception to *Miranda v. Arizona* (1966). Justices for the majority opinion reasoned that a suspect's associates "might make use" of the weapon or shoppers or employees might later find it. They pointed out that if officers were required to give Miranda warnings in such circumstances, it might deter the suspect from responding. Consequently, while the constitutional Miranda rights of a suspect would be secured, the risk of potential danger could be substantial. Justice Rehnquist wrote, "Officer Kraft needed an answer to his question not simply to make his case against Quarles but to insure that further danger to the public did not result from the concealment of the gun in a public area."

The Court conceded that its decision would have the impact of reducing the "explicitness" of the Miranda rule. On the other hand, it believed that in order to ensure safety to life and limb, police officers had to retain the ability to instinctively judge the conditions in any given situation. The majority opinion went on to suggest that although Miranda safeguards against self-incrimination were abandoned, in certain situations when swift action is needed officers may have to decide whether it was appropriate to "ask nec-

essary questions without the Miranda warnings." Such a decision could "render whatever probative evidence they uncover inadmissible." Or an officer may decide to "give the warnings in order to preserve admissibility of evidence they might uncover but possibly damage or destroy their ability to obtain that evidence and neutralize the volatile situation confronting them." Thus, in light of its findings, the Court reversed and remanded the case for readjudication by a lower court.

Justice O'Connor concurred in part and dissented in part. She opined that the Court's arguments did not justify making a departure from the clear prospect of the Miranda rule. The Self-Incrimination Clause should have been considered a safeguard against interrogations that could implicate involuntary confessions or disclose evidence connected with a crime. Justice O'Connor thus maintained that unequivocal application of Miranda warnings should be exercised. She reasoned that "society's need for interrogation" (e.g., Officer Craft's question about the gun) should not usurp the guards assumed in *Miranda*. Thus, to accurately enforce Miranda warnings, it is only necessarily to prevent an "admission of testimonial self-incriminations." However, Justice O'Connor agreed with the majority opinion that the lower courts incorrectly suppressed the gun as evidence. Incrimination with non-testimonial evidence could not be considered a violation of privilege against self-incrimination. Justice O'Connor regarded the gun as physical evidence, and finding that the gun could not be categorized as testimonial evidence, she held that suppression of the gun was unjustified.

The dissenting justices pointed out that the respondent, Quarles "had been reduced to a condition of physical powerlessness" when he was asked about the gun. Justices found it difficult, therefore, to believe Quarles, who did not have any accomplices, was a significant danger to anybody. The dissenting justices rejected the petitioner's assertion that interrogation without Miranda warnings was appropriate because of a risk to public safety. The supermarket was almost empty. Quarles was apprehended around midnight, and police could have easily conducted a search after arresting their suspect. The dissenting justices reasoned that because the weapon was out of sight it "did not pose a risk either to the arresting officers or to the public."

In writing the dissenting opinion, Justice Marshall voiced the minority view that majority justices made assumptions which seemed to represent an "abuse of the facts." They could not conceive any reason to justify any departure from *Miranda.* They did not agree that the police officers were faced with the dilemma of having to choose between "establishing the suspect's guilt and safeguarding the public from danger." *Miranda v. Arizona* (1966) was established to address procedural safeguards when suspects were taken into custody; its explicit purpose was to provide law enforcement with definitive protocol which would protect a suspect's rights during while she was being questioned. It was unacceptable to deviate from due process of law and to nullify the years of explicitness represented by *Miranda.* The minority justices thus felt their position voiced resolute support of the Fifth Amendment in finding fault with allowing an invalid concern for "public safety" to justify departure from the common explicitness of the Miranda rule.

The minority justices believed that under *Miranda,* "coerced confessions were simply inadmissible in criminal prosecutions." To do otherwise interfered with due process. Thus, it was especially disturbing to the justices that although Quarles was handcuffed and surrounded by officers in the back of the store, the majority did not find such circumstances to be coercive. (Justice Marshall's opinion apparently was referring to the manner in which the majority opinion characterized circumstances of Quarles' arrest as "instinctive.") The minority justices felt the arresting officer's conduct did not correctly adhere to Miranda "safeguards" which would have ensured an untainted gathering of criminal evidence. By not reading the suspect his rights prior to questioning, the officer's conduct had to be viewed as unacceptably coercive. Thus, the gun, obtained as a direct product of forcible, improper inquiry, represented inadmissible evidence because, in direct violation of the Miranda rule, it was "derived from an illegally obtained source."

Impact

The dissenting justices pointed out that the Miranda rule did not represent a "decision about public safety; it was decision about coerced confessions." They questioned how, given the majority opinion's exception to the Miranda rule, police officers could avoid future misunderstandings when apprehending suspects. Nonetheless, the majority of justices believed their ruling to be an expression of clarification which extended the Miranda rule to allow law enforcement more latitude in instances where there appeared to be a risk to the safety of officers or the public. Thus, the Court ruled that an individual's Fifth Amendment rights could be superseded in specific circumstances. In an apparent departure from years of upholding an explicit, resolute, and persistent interpretation of *Miranda,* the U.S. Supreme Court made a precedent-setting decision in rationalizing that when security concerns were involved, police offers were justified in delaying Miranda warnings. Justice Rehnquist wrote:

> The exception will not be difficult for police to apply because in each case it will be circumscribed by the exigency which justifies it. We think police officers can and will distinguish almost instinctively between questions necessary to secure their own safety or the safety of the public and questions designed solely to elicit testimonial evidence from a suspect.

Related Cases
Miranda v. Arizona, 384 U.S. 436 (1966).
Schmerber v. California, 384 U.S. 757 (1966).
Orzoco v. Texas, 394 U.S. 324 (1969).

Bibliography and Further Reading
Hall, Kermit L., ed. *The Oxford Companion to the Supreme Court of the United States.* 1992.

OREGON V. ELSTAD

Legal Citation: 470 U.S. 298 (1985)

Petitioner
State of Oregon

Respondent
Michael James Elstad

Petitioner's Claim
The police obtained two confessions from a suspect. The first one was a voluntary admission obtained without Miranda warnings, and the second was a written confession made in full compliance with Miranda warnings. Petitioner claimed that the earlier voluntary admission made his subsequent, written confession inadmissible evidence.

Chief Lawyer for Petitioner
David B. Frohnmayer

Chief Lawyer for Respondent
Gary D. Babock

Justices for the Court
Harry A. Blackmun, Warren E. Burger, Sandra Day O'Connor (writing for the Court), Lewis F. Powell, Jr., William H. Rehnquist, Byron R. White

Justices Dissenting
William J. Brennan, Jr., Thurgood Marshall, John Paul Stevens

Place
Washington, D.C.

Date of Decision
4 March 1985

Decision
There was no question that the respondent's first confession was illegal since it was obtained without Miranda warnings. Nevertheless, because his admission of guilt was voluntary and because his second, written confession was preceded by properly administered Miranda warnings, the Court ruled that the second confession was admissible as evidence.

Significance
The Miranda rule dictates that failure to inform a suspect in custody of Miranda warnings creates a presumption of compulsion. The U.S. Supreme Court found that if a confession given without Miranda warnings was voluntary, then subsequent confessions are not tainted because the first was illegal. This decision provided law enforcement with more latitude when faced with an accommodating suspect who volunteers evidence or confession prior to waiving Miranda rights.

Miranda Warnings

In *Miranda,* the right to remain silent and a continuous opportunity to exercise that right was viewed as critical to the question of voluntariness and coercion regarding confessions. To secure the privilege against self-incrimination, several procedural safeguards were established: persons who were in custody, prior to any questioning, must be warned of their right to remain silent, must be told that any statement they made might be used as evidence against them, that they had a right to the presence of an attorney, either retained or appointed, and that they might waive these rights, provided the waiver was made voluntarily, knowingly and intelligently. The right to interrupt the conversation and refrain from answering any further inquiries until consultation with an attorney was also included. Subsequently, the U.S. Supreme Court recognized that Miranda warnings were not constitutional rights, but were instead protective measures created to ensure that the right against compulsory self-incrimination was protected. The basis for establishing Miranda warnings was the conviction that police interrogation itself was inherently coercive and that this coercion conflicted with the privilege of self-incrimination protection. Statements or confessions made without the benefit of Miranda warnings were presumed to be given under compulsion. As a result, they were excluded from evidence. The matter of voluntariness and coercion in giving confessions was thus resolved, and courts and the police were furnished with useful means to secure the admissibility of evidence.

Inadmissible Confessions?

Michael James Elstad was suspected of committing a burglary in his neighborhood in December of 1981, and was picked up by two police officers at his home in Salem, Oregon. He was not given Miranda warnings before making a voluntary confession to one of the officers. Elstad was then transported to the police station and advised of his rights. He waived his Miranda rights and executed a written confession. No threats or promises were involved in making his confessions either at his home or at the sheriff's office.

Elstad was tried in an Oregon trial court. The defendant tried to suppress both his oral statement and signed confession saying that his first, illegally obtained confession tainted his second confession as, in Elstad's defense, "fruit of the poisonous tree." The U.S. Supreme Court, in *United States v. Bayer* (1947), remarked that after an accused had once "let the cat out of the bag" by confessing, no matter what the inducement, he was never thereafter free of the psychological and practical disadvantages of having confessed. The Court also held that making a confession under circumstances that preclude its use did not perpetually disable the confessor from making a usable confession after those conditions had been removed. *Wong Sun v. United States* (1963) was a case in which the Supreme Court held that evidence and witnesses discovered as a result of a search in violation of the Fourth Amendment must be excluded from evidence. This doctrine also applied to whether an illegal confession and the admissibility of that confession was "sufficiently an act of free will to purge the primary taint of the unlawful invasion." Thus, Elstad's first incriminating statement—made at the defendant's home—was excluded from evidence because he had not been advised of his Miranda rights. The circuit court judge ruled that the other, written confession made at the Sheriff's office, in full compliance with *Miranda,* was given freely, voluntarily, and knowingly after waiving Miranda rights, and that it was not tainted in any way by the previous brief statement. The second confession was admitted in evidence, and Elstad was found guilty of burglary in the first degree.

Elstad then appealed to the Oregon Court of Appeals. The state of Oregon as respondent recognized that the first incriminating statement was inadmissible as evidence because Elstad was in custody and was not given Miranda warnings when he first confessed. The state claimed that the second confession was not tainted, because of the careful administration of Miranda warnings. The court of appeals found that the main constitutional inquiry was whether there had been a sufficient break in the stream of events between the inadmissible statement and the written confession to insulate the latter statement from the effect of the previous. The court concluded that the period separating the two incidents was brief and therefore the "cat was sufficiently out of the bag to exert a coercive impact on latter admissions." The state trial court's decision was reversed. The state of Oregon petitioned to the Oregon Supreme Court for review, but the court declined to review the case. The U.S. Supreme Court then granted *certiorari,* a written order to a lower court to forward the proceedings of a case for review, and subsequently, the case was heard before the U.S. Supreme Court.

The Second Confession is Admissible

In a 6-3 vote, the U.S. Supreme Court reversed the decision of the Oregon Court of Appeals, and remanded the case for further proceedings. Delivering the major-

ity opinion, Justice O'Connor pointed out that a procedural Miranda violation differed in significant respects from violations of the Fourth Amendment invoked by the "fruit of the poisonous tree" metaphor. O'Connor emphasized that Miranda warnings were not a constitutional provision, but rather a protective measure to reinforce the Fifth Amendment right against self-incrimination. In this case there was no constitutional violation. Earlier precedents established that evidence obtained in violation of Miranda rights, though it was "fruit of the poisonous tree," could be used for purposes of impeachment or cross-examination. The Court concluded that it was an unwarranted extension of *Miranda* to hold that a simple failure to administer the warnings, unaccompanied by any actual coercion or undermining of the suspect's ability to exercise his free will, so tainted the investigatory process that a subsequent voluntary and informed waiver was ineffective for some indeterminate period.

The Court reasoned that the failure of the police to administer Miranda warnings did not mean that the statements received had actually been coerced, but that it should be presumed the privilege against compulsory self-incrimination had not been intelligently exercised. In this case, the Court held that the first confession was clearly voluntary. In such circumstances, the Court held, a careful and thorough administration of Miranda warnings served to cure the condition that had made the unwarned statement inadmissible. O'Connor also emphasized that the psychological effects of voluntary unwarned admissions should not have constitutional implications because they would practically immunize a suspect against the effect of statements made and disable the police from obtaining informed cooperation.

Referring to the issue of holding a suspect in custody without benefit of Miranda warnings, the U.S. Supreme Court felt that whatever the reason for the police officers' "oversight," the incident had no earmarks of coercion. O'Connor also noted that the police officers had not used the unwarned admission to pressure the respondent into waiving his right to remain silent. The respondent's attorney argued that Elstad had been unable to give a fully informed waiver of his rights because he had been unaware that his prior statement could not have been used against him. The attorney suggested that an additional warning should have been given when his client had been informed of Miranda warnings. The Court found that such a requirement was not constitutionally necessary.

The U.S. Supreme Court found no rationale for presuming coercive effect where the suspect's initial inculpatory statement, though technically in violation of *Miranda,* had been voluntary (although *Miranda* dictates that failure to administer its warnings creates a presumption of compulsion). The Court held that the relevant inquiry was whether the second statement had also been made voluntarily. Concluding the decision, Justice O'Connor wrote that the Court that day in no way retreated from *Miranda*'s "bright-line" rule (a simple, practicable and effective rule). In this case it was enough to bar use of the unwarned statement pursuant to a voluntary and knowing waiver.

Dissenting Opinions

Justice Brennan, joined by Justice Marshall, claimed that there was a refutable presumption that a confession obtained in violation of *Miranda* tainted subsequent confessions, and that the taint could not be dissipated solely by giving Miranda warnings. He argued that to resolve this case the practice of state courts should be examined. His view was that the practice justified application of the "cat out of the bag" presumption to this case, and therefore there had been a causal connection between the confession obtained in violation of *Miranda* and the subsequent confession preceded by the usual Miranda warnings. (Justice O'Connor, writing for the majority, referred to these arguments of the dissenting justices, and noted that their reasoning did not include the fact that there had obviously not been any compulsion present in obtaining either of the two statements.) Justice Brennan also wrote that the police officers should have given an additional warning while they had been informing the suspect of his Miranda rights. They should have clarified that Elstad's prior confession could not have been used against him, and that would have sufficed to dissipate the taint from the subsequent confession. Brennan concluded that the Court's decision undermined the rights protected by Miranda warnings.

In a separate dissenting opinion, Justice Stevens objected to the Court's finding that there was no presumption of coercion in obtaining both confessions. It was an ill-founded conclusion, since *Miranda* regulated that both the state of custody and failure to administer Miranda warnings presumed presence of compulsion. He reasoned that the Court intended its holding to apply only to a narrow category of cases in which the first statement was obtained in uncoercive setting and had no influence on the second. He concluded that even such an exception was discordant with prior cases,

and the attempt to identify its boundaries in future cases would breed confusion and uncertainty in the administration of criminal justice.

Impact

The right to remain silent as a privilege against self-incrimination is one of the core components of the notion of freedom in the American society. The key element for judging admissibility of confessions was the question of coercion and voluntariness. In *Oregon v. Elstad,* the Supreme Court found that the issue of voluntariness was essential for a confession to be admitted in evidence. The Court also ruled that an incriminating confession might be voluntary even though it was obtained without Miranda warnings. Though dissenting justices opposed this point of jurisprudence, the Court affirmed the importance of voluntariness in obtaining confessions despite the presumption of compulsion and the "bright-line" rule of *Miranda* was upheld.

Related Cases

Bram v. United States, 168 U.S. 532 (1897).
United States v. Bayer, 311 U.S. 532 (1947).
Wong Sun v. United States, 371 U.S. 471 (1963).
Miranda v. Arizona, 384 U.S. 436 (1966).
Michigan v. Tucker, 417 U.S. 433 (1974).
Edwards v. Arizona, 451 U.S. 477 (1981).

Bibliography and Further Reading

Crawford, Kimberly A. *International Violations of Miranda: A Strategy for Liability,* 1997. http://www.fbi.gov/leb/aug976.htm

Kamisar, Yale. "On the 'Fruits' of *Miranda* Violations, Coerced Confessions, and Compelled Testimony." *Michigan Law Review,* March 1995, p. 929.

Latzer, Barry. "Toward the Decentralization of Criminal Procedure: State Constitutional Law and Selective Disincorporation." *Journal of Criminal Law and Criminology,* fall 1996, p. 63.

Steiker, Carol S. "Counter-Revolution in Constitutional Criminal Procedure? Two Audiences, Two Answers." *Michigan Law Review,* August 1996, p. 2466.

UNITED STATES V. SALERNO

Legal Citation: 481 U.S. 739 (1987)

Petitioner
United States

Respondents
Anthony Salerno, Vincent Cafaro

Petitioner's Claim
That the federal court can order someone who presents a danger to others or the community to be held without bail before trial.

Chief Lawyer for Petitioner
Charles Fried, U.S. Solicitor General

Chief Lawyer for Respondents
Anthony M. Cardinale

Justices for the Court
Harry A. Blackmun, Sandra Day O'Connor, Lewis F. Powell, Jr., William H. Rehnquist (writing for the Court), Antonin Scalia, Byron R. White

Justices Dissenting
William J. Brennan, Jr., Thurgood Marshall, John Paul Stevens

Place
Washington, D.C.

Date of Decision
26 May 1987

Decision
The Supreme Court reversed the court of appeals decision that pretrial detention violated the right to due process of the arrested. The Court found that holding a potentially dangerous person without bail did not violate the right to due process or constitute excessive bail, if the government can supply sufficient evidence to warrant such detention.

Significance
The ruling provided the federal government with a tool for reducing threats posed by dangerous people who are arrested and likely to commit further crime, if the government can produce clear and convincing evidence to support pretrial detention, such as the criminal history and background of the arrested. With this decision, the Supreme Court decision resolved ongoing controversy of the right of the arrested to due process and a reasonable amount of bail, resulting from the Bail Reform Act of 1984.

Background

In the mid-1980s, the Reagan administration began pushing for legislation that would reduce crime, especially crime by previously convicted felons and crime lords. The Reagan administration also sought to eradicate organized crime and began targeting Mafia leaders for prosecution through investigation by various government agencies. The Racketeer Influenced and Corrupt Organizations Act of 1970 (RICO) provided prosecutors with an effective method of charging crime chiefs, by authorizing the convictions based on crime patterns instead of completely on individual crimes. Furthermore, the administration allowed the use of phone taps for obtaining evidence and offered witness protection programs to Mafia members who provided information on crime bosses.

Resulting from the Reagan administration's initiatives, the Bail Reform Act of 1984 required courts to conduct a special hearing to decide whether to hold those accused of serious felonies, such as murder and racketeering, without bail before their trial. Under the act, in order for the court to detain the accused in this manner, the government must offer ample evidence to demonstrate that the accused presents a danger to particular people or to the community. At the same time, the accused has a right to legal representation, to testify, to cross examine witnesses, and to offer evidence.

Following these procedures, the District Court of Southern New York ordered the respondents, Anthony Salerno and Vincent Cafaro, to remain in jail until after their trial, because of their extensive criminal charges: 35 counts of racketeering, including fraud, extortion, and conspiracy to commit murder. Moreover, Salerno, know as "Fat Tony," was the boss or leader of the Genovese Crime Family of La Cosa Nostra, a crime organization that operated throughout the Northeast. In addition, Salerno controlled several Teamsters union officials and used his power to influence the International Brotherhood of Teamsters' elections. *Fortune* magazine recognized him as the wealthiest and most powerful gangster in the country in 1986. The other respondent, Vincent Cafaro, held the important position of captain in the organization.

Racketeering-Influenced and Corrupt Organizations Act of 1970

Congress passed The Racketeering Influenced and Corrupt Organizations Act, more commonly referred to as RICO, in 1970 to help prosecute rapidly expanding organized criminal activity. To that end, a wide array of criminal activities fall under RICO, once a pattern of repeated criminal activity can be established. Racketeering activity requires that such acts must occur within a ten-year period of the first criminal act. Crimes that display a pattern of racketeering include any act or threat of murder, kidnapping, gambling, arson, robbery, bribery, and/or extortion.

Other criminal acts that can be prosecuted under RICO include embezzlement of pension funds, welfare fraud,

sports bribery, interstate transportation of stolen vehicles, sexual exploitation of children, obstruction of justice and mail fraud.

Conviction under the RICO statute could result in a maximum 20 year sentenced for each violation. Additionally, the accused, if convicted, must forfeit any profits from the criminal enterprise and can be liable for damages in civil court.

Source(s): *West's Encyclopedia of American Law*, Vol. 7. Minneapolis, MN: West Publishing, 1998.

The respondents used their rights under the Bail Reform Act to appeal their pretrial detention, arguing that it violated their Fifth Amendment right to a fair and speedy trial or due process. The court of appeals reversed the district courts decision, finding the pretrial detention of the respondents unconstitutional. The appeals court found that denial of bail applies only to circumstances where the accused is apt to disrupt the trial by intimidating witnesses and fleeing before trial, not to the mere suspicion of danger. Elsewhere, other courts of appeals considered the act and also found it unconstitutional.

Rights of the Community v. Rights of the Individual

The government petitioned the U.S. Supreme Court, which began hearing the case on 21 January 1987. At stake in the case was whether people could lose some of their constitutionally granted rights if they were repeat offenders or posed a potential danger to society. While reviewing the decision of the court of appeals, the Supreme Court majority noticed a misunderstanding and misinterpretation of the Bail Reform Act as well as the amendments in question in the previous trials and in the respondents' view. The act called not for the indiscriminate application of its policies, but for the application in very specific circumstances where the accused committed extremely serious felonies, following a specific set of procedures by the government and by the accused.

Hence, by a 6-3 vote the Supreme Court reversed the lower court's ruling. Chief Justice Rehnquist delivered the opinion that the Bail of Reform Act of 1984 did not violate the constitutional rights of the accused under the bail provision of the Eighth Amendment and Due Process Clause of the Fifth Amendment, providing the federal government could clearly demonstrate the likely

danger posed by the accused. He contended that the act is "regulatory in nature, and does not constitute punishment before trial," as the respondents and others argued.

The Court believed that the respondents failed in their attempt to demonstrate the Bail Reform Act amounted to punishment before trial and to excessive bail. The Supreme Court viewed the pretrial detention as a method of controlling crime, not as punishment, reasoning that holding someone before trial does not necessarily constitute punishment in any straightforward way. Moreover, Chief Justice Rehnquist showed that the Constitution does permit denial of certain rights in special circumstances, as in times of war when the government can hold people considered dangerous. In addition, the Supreme Court already gave lower federal courts this power for holding juvenile offenders if they posed a demonstrable risk to society in *Schall v. Martin* (1984). In such cases, the rights of society outweigh the rights of the individual. Chief Justice Rehnquist concluded that since the Court previously upheld these kinds of exceptions to individual rights, the Bail Reform Act in no way violated the tenor of the Constitution given the carefully delineated policies and procedures of the act.

The Court also found no evidence to support the respondents' second claim: that the Bail Reform Act violated the Eighth Amendment's ban on excessive bail. Though the respondents reasoned that denial of bail equaled setting bail at an infinitely high level even when there was no apparent risk of flight, the Court held that this clause does not guarantee bail in all cases. Instead it states that when there is bail, the court may not set it at an unreasonable amount. Again, the Court noted numerous circumstances when courts can deny bail such as in capital offense and deportation trials. "On the other side of the scale, of course, is the individual's strong interest in liberty. We do not minimize the importance and fundamental nature of this right. But, as our cases hold, this right may, in circumstances where the government's interest is sufficiently weighty, be subordinated to the greater needs of society."

Further Resistance to the Bail Reform Act

Not only did three Supreme Court justices voice dissent after hearing the case, but lawyers around the country took issue with the finding, in particular members of the American Civil Liberties Union (ACLU). Justices Marshall and Brennan sided largely with the court of appeals, asserting that provisions of the Bail Reform Act of 1984 violated portions of the Fifth and Eighth Amendments, as the respondents claimed. Justice Stevens dissented separately, expressing the view that though the government could detain people accused of crimes briefly in special circumstances, the act was unconstitutional and the government was using *United States v. Salerno* as a test case, not trying to protect the community. In *United States v. Salerno*, the district court tried to use criminal allegations against respondents as proof of their dangerousness, but that violated their right to be treated as innocent until proven guilty, according to the dissenting justices. Furthermore, ACLU lawyer David Goldstein argued that, "What the court has done is to reverse the 200-year assumption of innocence and replace it with this vague notion of

dangerousness." The ACLU disputed the finding, asserting that the provisions of the act gave the government the authority to impose punishment before trial and conviction.

Related Cases

Schall v. Martin, 467 U.S. 253 (1984).
United States v. Portes, 786 F.2d 758 (1985).
United States v. Rodriguez, 803 F.2d 1102 (1986).
United States v. Walker, 805 F.2d 1042 (1986).

Bibliography and Further Reading

Chaze, William L. "How Teamsters High Command May Be Unhorsed." *U.S. News & World Report,* June 22, 1987, p. 12.

Fagan, Jeffrey, and Martin Guggenheim. "Preventative Detention and the Judicial Prediction of Dangerousness for Juveniles: A Natural Experiment." *Journal of Criminal Law and Criminology,* winter 1996, p. 415.

"N.Y. Crime Boss 'Fat Tony' Salerno Dies at Age 80." *The Washington Post,* July 30, 1992, p. B6.

Wermiel, Stephen. "High Court Upholds Law Denying Bail To Accused Who Are Deemed Dangerous." *The Wall Street Journal,* May 27, 1987, p. 62.

Witkin, Gordon. "Drawing A Bead on the Big-Time Bosses." *U.S. News & World Report,* March 23, 1987, p. 25.

JAMES V. ILLINOIS

Legal Citation: 493 U.S. 307 (1990)

Petitioners
Darryl James, et al.

Respondents
State of Illinois, et al.

Petitioners' Claim
That the state should be allowed to use illegally obtained evidence to impeach the credibility of defense witnesses.

Chief Lawyer for Petitioners
Martin S. Carlson

Chief Lawyer for Respondents
Terence M. Madsen

Justices for the Court
Harry A. Blackmun, William J. Brennan, Jr., (writing for the Court), Thurgood Marshall, John Paul Stevens, Byron R. White

Justices Dissenting
Anthony M. Kennedy, Sandra Day O'Connor, William H. Rehnquist, Antonin Scalia

Place
Washington, D.C.

Date of Decision
10 January 1990

Decision
Upheld the inadmissibility of illegally obtained evidence.

Significance
Maintained the exclusionary rule should not be compromised in the context of the courtroom setting.

On 30 August 1982, Darryl James was reported to have killed one youth and critically injured another with a gun. James allegedly told detectives, when he was taken into questioning the day after the murder as a suspect, that he had deliberately altered his hair style since the shooting. Because it was determined that James was arrested without a warrant or probable cause, his statements about changing his hair were deemed inadmissible in his subsequent trial. Once the case did go to trial, five witnesses from the original group accosted during the shooting testified that one member of the group who had committed murder, allegedly James, had, in fact, "slicked back, shoulder-length, reddish hair." James wore black curly hair during police questioning, as well as at trial where he preferred to remain silent. A witness, however, Jewel Henderson, was called on his behalf, testifying that James's hair the day of, and prior to the shooting, was black and curly—just as it appeared in the courtroom. At that point, the court permitted the state to introduce James's illegally obtained statements to impeach Henderson's testimony. James was convicted on both counts.

In 1987 the Illinois Appellate Court turned over James's conviction because of the exclusionary rule which states, "The rule of constitutional law that evidence secured by the police by means of an unreasonable search and seizure, in violation of the Fourth Amendment, cannot be used as evidence in a criminal prosecution." In 1989 the Illinois Supreme Court followed, reversing on the premise that the "impeachment exception to the exclusionary rule should be expanded to include the testimony of other defense witnesses in order to deter the defendant from engaging in perjury 'by proxy.'" Supporters of the ruling noted that the decision would discourage a witness from committing perjury. Detractors noted that police misconduct would be encouraged in such situations, ultimately strengthening the prosecution's case.

The U.S. Supreme Court agreed to review the decision. Justice Brennan delivered the opinion of the Court majority on 4 June 1990. Brennan noted "We believe that this proposed expansion would frustrate rather than further the purposes underlying the exclusionary rule." He went on to say, "Thus, the truth-seeking rationale supporting the impeachment . . . does not apply to other witnesses with equal force." Brennan added ". . . much if not most of the time, police officers confront opportunities to obtain evidence illegally after they have already legally obtained . . . sufficient evidence to sustain a prima facie case." The opinion of the Court noted that ". . . Expanding the impeachment exception to encompass the testimony of all defense witnesses likely would chill some defendants from presenting their best defense . . . through the testimony of others." Finally, Brennan stated, "So long as we are committed to protecting the people from the disregard of their constitutional rights during the course of criminal investigations, inadmissibility of illegally obtained evidence must remain the rule, not the exception."

Justice Kennedy gave the dissenting opinion of the minority. He stated, ". . . the line drawn by today's opinion grants the defense in a criminal case broad immunity to introduce whatever false testimony it can produce from the mouth of a friendly witness." He went on to explain that the "exclusionary rule does not apply where the interest in pursuing truth or other important values outweighs any deterrence of unlawful conduct that the rule might achieve." Specifically, Kennedy believed that James's statements to the police about the appearance of his hair should have been admissible, thus, agreeing with the Illinois State Supreme Court's decision. The U.S. Supreme Court's majority decision, however, furthered the trend of erring in favor of the accused in order to avoid potential transgressions by law enforcement.

Related Cases
Walder v. United States, 347 U.S. 62 (1954).
Mapp v. Ohio, 367 U.S. 643 (1961).
Harris v. New York, 401 U.S. 222 (1971).
Arizona v. Hicks, 480 U.S. 321 (1987).

Bibliography and Further Reading
Forde, Michael K. "The Exclusionary Rule at Sentencing." *American Criminal Law Review,* winter 1996, p. 379.

Schwartz, Bernard. *A History of the Supreme Court.* New York: Oxford University Press, 1993.

Steiker, Carol S. "Counter-Revolution in Constitutional Criminal Procedure? Two Audiences, Two Answers." *Michigan Law Review,* August 1996, p. 2466.

THE RIGHTS OF THE ACCUSED DURING TRIAL

The Adversarial System

American justice is based on the adversarial, or accusatory, system, as opposed to the inquisitional system. Under the latter, a magistrate—or a king or religious official—takes an active role in determining facts and making judgments, while defense lawyers (assuming any are allowed) remain in the background, only speaking when asked to speak. This description calls forth a number of images, none of them pleasant: the Spanish Inquisition or various other religious witch hunts, France under Louis XIV, the "kangaroo courts" of Nazi Germany and Stalinist Russia, or the Islamic fundamentalist system in Iran under the Ayatollah Khomeini. It is almost by definition a method in which the accused is guilty until proven innocent.

Under the adversarial system, the roles are reversed: lawyers, both for the defense and the state, take an active part in the proceedings, while the magistrate assumes the passive position of a referee. In both situations, the magistrate maintains control over the courtroom, but in the adversarial scenario, he or she acts merely as the servant of the law, not as its source. Again, almost by definition, it is a system in which the accused is innocent until proven guilty. Thus the burden of proof is on the government, and guilt must be proven beyond all reasonable doubt.

The Burden of Proof

The "beyond all reasonable doubt" phrase, though it is not found in the Constitution, nonetheless remains a bedrock principle of the American legal system. It does not mean, however, that guilt must be proven beyond *all* doubt. This would be not be possible, any more than it would be possible to prove beyond the shadow of a doubt that the sun will rise in the morning and go down in the evening. The requirement of proving guilt beyond a reasonable doubt, by contrast, is considered to be implied by the Constitution, as the Supreme Court held in *In re Winship* (1970).

As part of its burden of proof, the prosecution must do a number of things. The Sixth Amendment requires that it inform the accused of the crime for which he is charged, and this is interpreted to mean that the accusation must be as explicit as possible. Likewise the

notion of due process in the Fifth Amendment is held to imply that the state must provide evidence to the defense—even, or rather especially, if that evidence helps the case of the accused. For instance if a prosecutor knows that a key witness has provided evidence which may exonerate the accused, he or she is compelled by law to inform the defense.

By contrast, the accused is not compelled to provide the prosecution with evidence which may help its case against him. On the contrary, the Fifth Amendment guarantees the right against self-incrimination. Not only is the accused not compelled to provide evidence, he is free to withhold it under questioning by "taking the Fifth." This does not mean that he is free to lie; it simply means that he is not compelled to take the witness stand, or if he does, he is not compelled to answer questions.

The Right to Counsel

The Sixth Amendment makes a number of guarantees affecting the rights of the accused both before and during trial, among them the right to legal counsel. The accused may choose to represent himself, though this is seldom advisable. Aside from the obvious fact that a lawyer knows much more about the law than a layman does, there is the simple reality that a person often lacks perspective in matters that relate to him or herself. In most aspects of life, this lack of perspective seldom carries a worse penalty than embarrassment—as for instance if one were to adopt a new hairstyle that one's friends thought looked ridiculous—but in a legal context, its consequences are far more dire.

If the accused cannot afford a lawyer, one will be appointed for him by, and at the expense of, the state. This was not always so. In *Betts v. Brady* (1942), the Supreme Court upheld the ruling of a lower court denying legal assistance to an unemployed laborer accused of robbery. In 1963, however, the Court reversed this ruling in *Gideon v. Wainwright,* and since then, it has been common practice for indigent (poor) defendants to receive court-appointed counsel even in state trials. Nonetheless, questions concerning this practice remain, particularly since a lawyer appointed by the court may present disadvantages when compared with his or her counterpart on the prosecution. Usually such lawyers are overworked and underpaid, and whereas an attorney paid by a client usually takes a case willingly, the assistance of a court-appointed lawyer is compelled by law.

The O. J. Simpson murder trial of 1994, in which a wealthy defendant was able to pay a fleet of extremely capable lawyers, and an even larger number of experts on various types of evidence, highlights the fact that not all forms of legal defense are the same. No court could ever provide a defendant with a degree of legal assistance even approaching the levels of Simpson's "Dream Team" and their expert witnesses; nonetheless, the state is required, in addition to supplying legal counsel, to provide funds necessary for the indigent defendant's counsel to gather evidence for his or her case.

Witnesses and the Right of Confrontation

The Sixth Amendment directs that the accused must "be confronted with the witnesses against him" and must "have compulsory process for obtaining witnesses in his favor." The first of these provisions, often called the right of confrontation, is closely tied with another Sixth Amendment right, that of being informed of the accusation. It means that any witness whose testimony plays a part in the prosecution's case must personally appear in court, so that the defendant can hear from that person's mouth the evidence against him.

There may be exceptions, of course, as when a witness has died before the case goes to court. Likewise a number of Supreme Court cases such as *Coy v. Iowa* (1988) and *Maryland v. Craig* (1990) have addressed cases of child abuse in which the accuser is a minor, and in which the child's advocates claim that the child's appearance in court would compound the psychological damage already incurred in the alleged abuse.

The second of the provisions mentioned above means that the defense has the right to require that anyone who can testify in favor of the accused must appear in court. Allied with this is the idea that the defendant may present any evidence that he may reasonably use in aid of his case.

Trial by Jury and Other Rights

The Constitution provides for trial by jury not only in the Eighth Amendment, but in Article III. In addition, the Seventh Amendment provides for jury trial in civil cases. Petit juries, as opposed to the grand juries which conduct the hearings to hand down an indictment earlier in the legal process, are usually composed of 12 people chosen from the citizenry at large—thus the oft-quoted phrase "a jury of his peers."

Juries are selected by a process called *voir dire,* in which both the prosecution and the defense have an opportunity to question prospective jurors. On the basis of a prospective juror's answer, one side or the other may arrange to have that person stricken from the list, as a defense lawyer might do if a prospective juror in a capital case states that she favors the death penalty. Prosecution and defense lawyers may also exercise a limited number or peremptory challenges. Under peremptory challenge, for instance, a lawyer defending a man accused of rape may learn from the record that a prospective juror was herself a victim of rape, and may ask that she be kept off the panel for this reason. Peremptory challenges are sometimes controversial when used to shape the jury by race or gender or other characteristics, as many observers believe the Simpson defense team did.

The size of the jury has been established by tradition, though states have used juries consisting of as few as six members. With *Ballew v. Georgia* (1978), however, the Court held that a jury of only five members was too small to create a proper atmosphere of deliberation. Indeed, deliberation is one of the central issues surrounding the operation of the jury: to be effective, its members must spend a sufficient amount of time reviewing the facts in order to reach a verdict. Hand in hand with this idea is the requirement that juries reach a unanimous verdict: according to this logic, serious deliberation is virtually guaranteed in the long process of thought and discussion required for twelve people to agree. Though unanimity is required at a federal level, many states allow "super majorities" of ten or more members, and in *Apodaca v. Oregon* (1972), the Court upheld a conviction of a defendant by an 11-1 majority.

In some cases the jury reaches a verdict. If a verdict is not reached, a "hung jury" is declared. Such a situation may lead to another trial before a new jury, or it may lead to the case being dismissed. Or at any stage leading up to the jury's deliberation, the judge may declare a mistrial if one of the parties to the case fails to act in accordance with the law—e.g., if a defendant were to claim that their interests were not being protected by their lawyer. A mistrial could also result if a juror were to suddenly stand up in the middle of the trial and say "I think he's guilty." In the case of a mistrial, as with a hung jury, the defendant may be tried again.

But if the conviction is overturned by the court due to insufficiency of evidence resulting in a verdict of "not guilty," the defendant cannot be tried again for the same crime. To do so would constitute "double jeopardy," forbidden under the Fifth Amendment; however, the double jeopardy provision does not mean that a defendant cannot be tried by a different "sovereign"—e.g., by a state court as opposed to a federal court, though this seldom happens in practice. And even if the accused is convicted of the crimes as charged, he is guaranteed the right to appeal his case.

Thus, ideally at least, the American system of law allows the accused every possible opportunity to defend himself against the charges against him.

See also: **Juries, The Rights of the Accused Before Trial, The Rights of the Accused Following Trial**

Bibliography and Further Reading

Brewster, Stanley Farrar. *Twelve Men in a Box.* Chicago: Callaghan and Company, 1934.

Busch, Francis Xavier. *Law and Tactics in Jury Trials.* Indianapolis, Bobbs-Merrill, 1959.

Cook, Joseph G. *Constitutional Rights of the Accused: Post-Trial Rights.* Rochester, NY: Lawyers Co-Operative, 1976.

Decof, Leonard. *Jury Trial and the Independent Bar.* Los Angeles, CA: International Academy of Trial Lawyers, 1981.

The Fifth Amendment and Self Incrimination (motion picture). Jefferson Productions/McGraw-Hill Book, 1955.

Heller, Francis Howard. *The Sixth Amendment to the Constitution of the United States: A Study in Constitutional Development.* Lawrence: University of Kansas Press, 1951.

Hook, Sidney. *Common Sense and the Fifth Amendment.* New York: Criterion Books, 1957.

The Jury Trial. St. Paul, MN: Hamline University School of Advanced Law, 1985.

Levy, Leonard W. *Origins of the Fifth Amendment: The Right Against Self-incrimination.* New York: Oxford University Press, 1968.

TWINING V. STATE OF NEW JERSEY

Legal Citation: 211 U.S. 78 (1908)

Appellants
Albert C. Twining, David C. Cornell

Appellee
State of New Jersey

Appellants' Claim
That New Jersey's Court of Errors & Appeals erred in upholding a conviction obtained in a trial during which the appellants' Fourteenth Amendment rights to due process under the law were violated.

Chief Lawyers for Appellants
James Johnson, William Gooch, Herbert Smyth, Frederick Scofield (for Twining), Marshall Van Winkle (for Cornell)

Chief Lawyers for Appellee
H.M. Nevious, Robert McCarter

Justices for the Court
David Josiah Brewer, William Rufus Day, Melville Weston Fuller, Oliver Wendell Holmes, Joseph McKenna, William Henry Moody (writing for the Court), Rufus Wheeler Peckham, Edward Douglass White

Justices Dissenting
John Marshall Harlan I

Place
Washington, D.C.

Date of Decision
9 November 1908

Decision
In favor of appellee, affirming the sentences of the appellants.

Significance
The 1908 Court's narrow interpretations of the Fifth and Fourteenth Amendments in the *Twining* decision limited the right of individuals to remain silent in courtroom proceedings to avoid self-incrimination.

An Inference of Guilt

Few clauses of the U.S. Constitution are as familiar as the Fifth Amendment prohibition against being forced to give testimony which might be self-incriminatory. It might surprise many Americans to learn that such protection was an incomplete privilege for nearly two centuries after the amendment's ratification in 1791.

When the Monmouth Trust and Safety Deposit Company of Asbury Park closed its doors in February of 1903, Albert Twining's and David Cornell's troubles began. New Jersey bank examiner Larue Vreedenburg promptly arrived to inspect the defunct bank's records. Among other things, President Twining and Treasurer Cornell gave the inspector the minutes of a meeting at which several bank directors, including Twining and Cornell, had approved a payment of $44,875 for 381 shares of First National Bank stock. When inspector Vreedenburg finished his investigation of the transaction, he had Twining and Cornell arrested under a New Jersey statute forbidding bank officials from intentionally providing false information or documents to state examiners.

In January of 1904, Twining and Cornell were convicted and sentenced to three years imprisonment for falsifying bank records relating to an estate account. They were out on bail when they returned to court to face the Vreedenburg charge. Although another bank director, whose name appeared on the questionable minutes approving the stock transfer, testified that he never signed the document and that the meeting never took place, neither Twining nor Cornell took the stand.

The presiding judge spoke at length about the fact that while the signatures of both defendants appeared on the fraudulent document, both refused to speak about the nonexistent meeting. He also spoke about their choice not to testify in their own defense. "Because a man does not go on the stand, you are not necessarily justified in drawing an inference of guilt," concluded the judge. "But you have a right to consider the fact that he does not go on the stand where a direct accusation is made against him." The jury took one hour to find Twining and Cornell guilty. The two men were sentenced to six and four years imprisonment respectively.

Twining and Cornell appealed their sentences to the New Jersey Supreme Court, without success. Their luck was no better at New Jersey's Court of Errors and Appeals, which affirmed the state supreme court's decision to uphold the convictions. Twining's and Cornell's appeal of their sentences on constitutional grounds, however, resulted in their argument being heard by the U.S. Supreme Court on 19 and 20 March 1908.

State Citizens, American Citizens

In Justice Moody's majority opinion of 9 November, the Court affirmed the decisions of New Jersey's courts, allowing the convictions to stand. The Court's decision was unconcerned with the merits of the case against Twining and Cornell. The judge's instructions to the jury in the criminal case were entered as a matter of record, but the Court was more concerned with delineating the rights of defendants in state versus federal trials.

Twining and Cornell were convicted of breaking a state law. The Court found no reason to reverse the decisions of that state's courts just because state statutes did not include an exemption from self-incrimination. It was true that federal law provided such an exemption within the Fifth Amendment. All but two states included the exemption in their own laws. One state which did not specifically include the principles of the Fifth Amendment in its own constitution was Iowa. Unfortunately for Twining and Cornell, the other was New Jersey.

The two defendants were American citizens, but they were also citizens of the state of New Jersey. Citing the 1872 Slaughterhouse Cases, Justice Moody stated that citizenship of the United States and citizenship of a state were distinct from each other. The Court ruled that the first eight amendments to the U.S. Constitution applied only to action by federal authorities. However fundamental they might be, privileges found within the amendments were not specifically protections against action in state courts. The Court declared that the Fifth Amendment was reserved for use in federal trials only.

Twining's and Cornell's attorneys were aware that appealing the convictions by claiming the protection of the Fifth Amendment would be ineffective. Instead, all of their appeals were grounded in the argument that the judge's comments in the criminal trial violated an immunity from self-incrimination, not under the Fifth Amendment, but under the Fourteenth Amendment's guarantee of "due process" under the law. This strategy was equally unsuccessful. Justice Moody pointed out that the framers of the Constitution had seen fit to enumerate the guarantees of the Fifth Amendment as a distinct and separate right, not as part of the general legal framework known as "due process."

William Henry Moody. © Photograph by Pach Brothers. The Library of Congress/Corbis.

Only Justice Harlan dissented from this opinion. Justice Harlan chided his associates for skirting the issue of whether or not Twining's and Cornell's rights had been infringed by the judge's comments in their trial. Harlan also differed from the majority in his belief that "exemption from testimonial compulsion" was protected by both the Fifth and Fourteenth Amendments. Finally, Harlan adamantly rejected the distinction the other justices made between individual privileges under state and federal law, which allowed differing interpretations of the right to silence.

"The declaration of the Court, in the opinion just delivered, that immunity from self-incrimination is of great value, a protection to the innocent, and a safeguard against tyrannical prosecutions, meets my cordial approval," Harlan wrote. But, he added, in view of the Court's long-held view that forcing defendants to testify against themselves "was in violation of universal American law, was contrary to the principles of free government and a weapon of despotic power which could not abide the pure atmosphere of political liberty and personal freedom, I cannot agree that a State may make that rule a part of its law and binding on citizens despite the Constitution of the United States."

Regardless of Justice Harlan's foresight in the matter, the majority decision in the *Twining* decision remained the policy of the Court for decades. In 1947, the decision's principles were reaffirmed in *Adamson v. California*. Not until the Court's 1964 *Malloy v. Hogan* decision did the guarantee against self-incrimination extend to defendants in both state and federal trials.

Related Cases
Slaughterhouse Cases, 83 U.S. 36 (1873).
Adamson v. California, 332 U.S. 46 (1947).
Malloy v. Hogan, 378 U.S. 1 (1964).

Bibliography and Further Reading

Biskupic, Joan, and Elder Witt. *Congressional Quarterly's Guide to the U.S. Supreme Court,* 3rd ed. Washington, DC: Congressional Quarterly, Inc., 1996.

Cushman, Robert F. *Leading Constitutional Decisions.* Englewood Cliffs, NJ: Prentice-Hall, Inc., 1982.

Hall, Kermit L., ed. *The Oxford Companion to the Supreme Court of the United States.* New York: Oxford University Press, 1992.

Kurland, Phillip B., and Gerhard Casper, eds. *Landmark Briefs and Arguments of the Supreme Court of the United States,* Vol. 16. Arlington: University Publications of America, 1975.

POWELL V. ALABAMA

Legal Citation: 287 U.S. 45 (1932)

Petitioners
Ozie Powell, et al.

Respondent
State of Alabama

Petitioners' Claim
That the group had been denied due process when they were convicted of rape.

Chief Lawyer for Petitioners
Walter H. Pollak

Chief Lawyer for Respondent
Thomas E. Knight, Jr.

Justices for the Court
Louis D. Brandeis, Benjamin N. Cardozo, Charles Evans Hughes, Owen Josephus Roberts, Harlan Fiske Stone, George Sutherland (writing for the Court), Willis Van Devanter

Justices Dissenting
Pierce Butler, James Clark McReynolds

Place
Washington, D.C.

Date of Decision
7 November 1932

Decision
That the petitioners' rights to due process had been violated.

Significance
No one knows how many cases like the one triggering *Powell* occurred in Southern states before this one. With its large number of defendants, their youth, their brief and almost cursory trials and severe sentences, the Scottsboro cases demanded the entire country's attention. The trials, and their appeals, gave America harsh and unforgettable lessons in the procedures of Southern courts, the opportunism of American communists, the prejudice against blacks and Jews in the South, and the hypocrisy then rampant among Southern whites.

On a March morning in 1931, seven bedraggled white youths appeared in a railroad station master's office in northern Alabama and announced that, while riding as hoboes, they had been thrown off a freight train by a "bunch of Negroes" who picked a fight. The station master phoned ahead and, near Scottsboro, a deputy sheriff deputized every man who owned a gun. When the train stopped, the posse rounded up nine black boys and two white girls—the latter dressed in men's caps and overalls.

While the white girls chatted with townspeople, the deputy sheriff tied the blacks together and quizzed them. Five were from Georgia. At 20, Charlie Weems was the eldest. Clarence Norris was 19, Ozie Powell, 16. Olin Montgomery, 17, looked "sleepy-eyed," for he was blind in one eye and had only 10 percent vision in the other. Willie Roberson, 17, suffering from syphilis and gonorrhea, walked unsteadily with a cane. Four were from Chattanooga, Tennessee. Haywood Patterson and Andy Wright were 19. Eugene Williams was 13. And Wright's brother Roy was 12.

When the deputy sheriff had loaded his prisoners onto an open truck, one of the girls, Ruby Bates, from Huntsville, Alabama, told him that she and her friend Victoria Price had been raped by the nine blacks. In Scottsboro, the sheriff sent the women off to be examined by two doctors. In the meantime, word of the rape charge spread through Jackson County. By nightfall, a mob of several hundred, promising to lynch the prisoners, stood before the little jail. The sheriff, barricaded with 21 deputies, phoned the governor. But by the time 25 National Guardsmen arrived, the mob had cooled down and most had drifted away.

As the trial began on 6 April 1931, 102 guardsmen held a crowd of several thousand at a distance of 100 feet from the courthouse.

Ready to appoint defense counsel, Judge Alfred E. Hawkins offered the job to any lawyer in the county who would take it. He accepted Chattanooga attorney Stephen R. Roddy, who admitted he did not know Alabama law, when local attorney Milo Moody offered to help. Roddy, who had a jail record for drunkenness, was already inebriated at 9:00 a.m.

NAACP Defense Teams

Founded in 1909 by both black and white civil rights activists, the National Association for the Advancement of Colored People (NAACP) has fought to curtail and eliminate discrimination through legal action. Since its inception, the NAACP used the court system to quash discriminatory codes and statutes so that African Americans could exercise their constitutional rights. The organization's key early court victories include: *Guinn v. United States* in 1915, which removed grandfather clauses that restricted voting rights; *Moore v. Dempsey* in 1923, which held that excluding African Americans from juries was unconstitutional; and *Shelley v. Kraemer* in 1948, which barred racially restrictive land agreements.

Thurgood Marshall become the special counsel for the NAACP in 1936 and later became the U.S. Supreme Court's first African American justice in 1967. In 1940, the organization established a separate legal branch, the NAACP Legal Defense and Educational Fund, which Marshall headed. The NAACP won one of its greatest Supreme Court victories in 1954's *Brown v. Board of Education.* In this case, the Court held that segregation in public schools was unconstitutional.

Source(s): *West's Encyclopedia of American Law.* St. Paul, MN: West Publishing, 1998.

Circuit Solicitor H. G. Bailey tried Weems and Norris first. Victoria Price described how she and Ruby Bates had hopped freight trains to Chattanooga to look for jobs and, finding none, were returning when the black boys, after throwing the whites off the train, turned on them. She described how she was "beaten up" and "bruised up" by rape after rape, then "lost consciousness" and next found herself on her way to the jail in Scottsboro.

Dr. R. R. Bridges testified he saw no evidence of violence when he examined the girls. Victoria Price, he said, "was not lacerated at all. She was not bloody, neither was the other girl." A second doctor agreed that while both girls showed evidence of recent sexual intercourse, the semen found was "non-motile," or inactive, whereas semen is normally viable for 12 to 48 hours.

By Thursday afternoon, all defendants except 12-year-old Roy Wright had been found guilty. Because of his age, the state had asked for life imprisonment for him, but the jury was deadlocked—seven jurors insisted on death. The judge declared a mistrial for Roy Wright and sentenced the eight others to electrocution.

"Victims of 'Capitalist Justice'"

Liberals and radicals nationwide reacted. The Central Committee of the Communist Party of the United States called the sentences "legal lynching" of "the victims of 'capitalist justice.'" Its International Labor Defense (ILD) wing pushed the National Association for the Advancement of Colored People (NAACP) to champion the case to the U.S. Supreme Court. In Harlem, 300,000 blacks and whites marched to the slogan "the Scottsboro Boys Shall Not Die."

The ILD hired prominent Chattanooga attorney George W. Chamlee. Requesting a new trial, he and the ILD's chief lawyer, Joseph Brodsky, produced affidavits

from Chattanooga blacks stating that they had seen Victoria Price "embracing Negro men in dances in Negro houses," that Ruby Bates had bragged that she could "take five Negroes in one night," that a boardinghouse operator had let Victoria use a room for prostitution and that she turned down a white man one night because it was "Negro night." The local press denounced the statements as slander, but a Huntsville detective confirmed that the girls were common prostitutes.

"You Can't Mix Politics With Law"

The motion for a new trial was denied. The defendants switched allegiance constantly from the NAACP to the ILD and back again. Prominent attorney Clarence Darrow declined the NAACP's request that he steer the case through the Supreme Court. "You can't mix politics with law," he said, adding that the cases would have to be won in Alabama, "not in Russia or New York." The NAACP then withdrew its support.

In March, the Alabama Supreme Court upheld the convictions of all except Eugene Williams; as a juvenile, he was granted a new trial.

In November, the U.S. Supreme Court ruled that the seven boys had been denied "due process" under the Fourteenth Amendment when Judge Hawkins treated the appointment of defense counsel so casually.

As the state ordered a new trial, the ILD turned to Samuel Leibowitz, a noted criminal lawyer in New York. He argued successfully for a change of venue to Decatur, Alabama, where townspeople welcomed the hordes of reporters, and Western Union brought in extra operators.

Haywood Patterson was tried first. Leibowitz produced several revelations: Ruby Bates recanted, saying she and Price had invented the rape story to avoid arrest for vagrancy (but she damaged her credibility by testifying in smart "New York clothes" bought for her by the ILD during a trip they provided to the big city); the boys had been seized from several points all over the 42-car train; Willie Roberson's painful, raging syphilis made him incapable of sexual activity; Olin Montgomery's blindness was equally limiting; and Victoria Price, who was married, had served time for adultery and fornication.

After Dr. Bridges repeated his testimony that the girls had not been raped, the second doctor—Marvin Lynch—spoke privately with Judge James Edward Horton during a recess. "I told the women they were lying, that they knew they had not been raped," said the doctor, "and they just laughed at me." But, he added, if he testified for the boys, "I'd never be able to go back into Jackson County." The judge, believing the defense would prove Patterson's innocence, said nothing.

Defense attorney Leibowitz himself now lived with National Guard protection against threats of lynching. County Solicitor Wade Wright added to the incendiary atmosphere: "Show them," he told the jury, "that Alabama justice cannot be bought and sold with Jew money from New York."

The jury found Patterson guilty. The sentence was death. When the defense filed a motion for a new trial, Judge Horton reviewed the medical testimony about the women, the lack of physical evidence of sexual activity on the part of the boys, and the unreliable testimony of Victoria Price and Ruby Bates. He set aside the jury's judgment and ordered a new trial. Then, under pressure from Attorney General Thomas Knight and the chief justice, he withdrew from the case.

No More Picture Snappin' Around Here"
Opening the new trial, Judge William Washington Callahan, 70, dismissed the National Guard. Declaring, "There ain't going to be no more picture snappin' around here," he banned cameras inside or outside the courtroom. He dismissed Leibowitz's motion to quash the indictment because blacks had been systematically excluded from the jury lists—despite testimony by a handwriting expert that names had been fraudulently added to the jury book to make it appear that blacks were listed. He ran a 12-hour day in the courtroom. He destroyed Leibowitz's defense plan by refusing to permit testimony on Victoria Price's busy sexual activity during the two nights before the train ride. And when he made his charge to the jury, he told them any intercourse between a black man and a white woman was rape. He also omitted—until Leibowitz darted up to the bench and reminded him—the instructions on how to render an acquittal.

Again Patterson was found guilty and the sentence was death. Clarence Norris was next found guilty. But now Leibowitz faced an unexpected challenge: Two ILD

lawyers were caught trying to bribe Victoria Price, who had hinted that money could help her change her story. Brodsky told Leibowitz the changed story would have been "good propaganda for the cause." Furious, Leibowitz announced he would withdraw "unless all Communists are removed from the defense." Brodsky capitulated.

Now the U.S. Supreme Court overturned the convictions on the evidence of exclusion of blacks from jury duty. Alabama Governor Bibb Graves responded, "We must put the names of Negroes in jury boxes in every county."

In November 1935, a grand jury of 13 whites and one black brought new indictments. At the fourth trial,

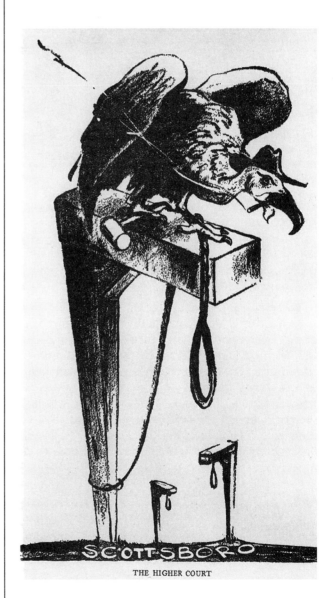

THE HIGHER COURT

A cartoon from the Scottsboro trials depicts a judge holding a gavel and a noose. The cartoon infers that the state was like a vulture trying to string up the defendants in an unfair trial. © The Library of Congress.

Sam Leibowitz with the Scottsboro boys. © UPI/Corbis-Bettmann.

in January 1936, Patterson was again found guilty, with the sentence this time 75 years in prison "I'd rather die," he said.

The next trial was delayed until July 1937. Then Clarence Norris was found guilty and sentenced to death, followed by Andy Wright (99 years) and Charlie Weems (75 years). The rape charge against Ozie Powell was dropped when he pleaded guilty to stabbing a deputy sheriff (during a jail transfer) and received 20 years. Abruptly, prosecutor Thomas Lawson, who had succeeded Knight, proposed *nol pros,* or dropping of charges, for Olin Montgomery, Roy Wright, Willie Roberson, and Eugene Williams. The Scottsboro trials were over.

"All Were Guilty Or All Should Be Freed"

The U.S. Supreme Court refused to review Patterson's conviction. Alabama Governor Bibb Graves listened to

a clemency appeal and agreed that "all were guilty or all should be freed." He officially set a date to pardon all four, then reneged. While Graves said he changed his mind after personally interviewing the Scottsboro boys, those close to the governor said he realized public opinion had not changed and simply got cold feet.

Weems was freed in November 1943, Andy Wright and Clarence Norris in January 1944—but Wright and Norris broke parole by moving North and were sent back to prison. Wright was paroled again in 1950. Patterson escaped from prison in 1948 and was arrested in Detroit, but Michigan Governor G. Mennen Williams refused to sign extradition papers. Later convicted of manslaughter, Patterson died of cancer in prison in 1952. Norris, the last surviving Scottsboro boy, was pardoned at age 64 by Alabama Governor George C. Wallace in 1976.

Victoria Price worked in a Huntsville cotton mill until it closed in 1938, then moved to nearby Flintsville, Tennessee. Ruby Bates toured briefly as an ILD speaker, then worked in a New York state spinning factory until 1938, when she returned to Huntsville. Both women died in 1961.

Related Cases

Norris v. Alabama, 294 U.S. 487 (1935).
Patterson v. Alabama, 294 U.S. 600 (1935).
Gideon v. Wainwright, 372 U.S. 335 (1963).
Miranda v. Arizona, 384 U.S. 436 (1966).
Argersinger v. Hamlin, 407 U.S. 25 (1972).

Bibliography and Further Reading

Carter, Dan T. *Scottsboro: A Tragedy of the American South.* Baton Rouge: Louisiana State University Press, 1969.

Chalmers, Allan Knight. *They Shall Be Free.* Garden City, NY: Doubleday & Co., 1951.

Crenshaw, Files, and Kenneth A. Miller. *Scottsboro: The Firebrand of Communism.* Montgomery, AL: Brown Printing Co., 1936.

Hays, Arthur Garfield. *Trial by Prejudice.* New York: Covici, Friede Publishers, 1933.

Jordan, J. Glenn. *The Unpublished Inside Story of the Infamous Scottsboro Case.* Huntsville, AL: White Printing Co., 1932.

Patterson, Haywood. *Scottsboro Boy.* Garden City, NY: Doubleday & Co., 1950.

JOHNSON V. ZERBST

Legal Citation: 304 U.S. 458 (1938)

Appellant
John A. Johnson

Appellee
Fred G. Zerbst, Warden, U.S. Penitentiary, Atlanta, Georgia

Appellant's Claim
That the court must appoint lawyers to represent indigent defendants in federal criminal cases.

Chief Lawyer for Appellant
Elbert P. Tuttle

Chief Lawyer for Appellee
Bates Booth

Justices for the Court
Hugo Lafayette Black (writing for the Court), Pierce Butler, James Clark McReynolds, Stanley Forman Reed

Justices Dissenting
Louis D. Brandeis, Charles Evans Hughes, Owen Josephus Roberts, Harlan Fiske Stone (Benjamin N. Cardozo did not participate)

Place
Washington, D.C.

Date of Decision
23 May 1938

Decision
The Supreme Court held that counsel must be appointed for all defendants in federal criminal trials who cannot afford to hire their own attorneys.

Significance
Johnson raised the standard set in 1932 by *Powell v. Alabama,* in which the Court held that counsel must be appointed to all indigent criminal defendants facing the possibility of the death sentence in federal court.

On 21 November 1934, John Johnson was arrested in Charleston, South Carolina, for possessing and passing four counterfeit $20 bills—a federal offense. At the time, he was enlisted in the Marine Corps. He was indicted on 21 January 1935 and tried and sentenced two days later to four and one-half years in prison. He began to serve his sentence two days later, when he was transported to the federal penitentiary in Atlanta, Georgia.

While he was serving his sentence, Johnson filed a petition for *habeas corpus*—a request to be released on the grounds that he had been illegally detained—with the federal distinct court. Johnson cited as the basis for his petition the fact that he had been tried, convicted, and sentenced without benefit of counsel. Johnson, who lacked the funds to hire his own attorney, had asked the district attorney to appoint a lawyer to represent him at his trial. But after the district attorney told him that South Carolina only appointed counsel to indigent defendants when they were facing the possibility of capital punishment, the issue was dropped. Asked by the court if he had a lawyer, Johnson merely answered no and agreed that he was ready for trial.

Now, in his *habeas corpus* petition, Johnson claimed that he had been deprived of his right to counsel under the Sixth Amendment, which reads: "In all criminal prosecutions, the accused shall enjoy the right . . . to have the Assistance of Counsel for his defence." When the district court denied his petition, he appealed to the U.S. Fifth Circuit Court of Appeals, which affirmed this decision. Johnson's next step was to appeal to the U.S. Supreme Court.

Supreme Court Requires That Counsel Be Appointed

The Supreme Court agreed with Johnson. For much of the nation's history, the right to counsel meant that everyone who could afford to hire a lawyer had a right to do so. Then, in *Powell v. Alabama* (1932), the Supreme Court had ruled that state courts were obliged—under the Fourteenth Amendment's Due Process Clause—to provide counsel for those indigent defendants facing the death penalty. Now, writing for

Federal Court of Appeals

The U.S. court of appeals is the second level of the federal court system where parties dissatisfied with the U.S. district court's decisions can have them reviewed. The U.S. Supreme Court is the third level of the federal judicial system where parties can have the decisions by the courts of appeals reviewed. The federal courts of appeals also hear and review decisions by the U.S. Tax Court and some federal administrative agencies. Judges for the courts of appeals receive life appointments by the president with help and approval of the Senate and each court has at least six judges.

This branch of the federal court system includes 12 regional courts of appeals as well as the U.S. Court of Appeals for the Federal Circuit. These regional courts are divided into circuits and the First through Eleventh Circuits consist of three or more states each. In addition, there is the U.S. Court of Appeals for the District of Columbia, which handles appeals in the District of Columbia and has jurisdiction over many departments of the federal government.

Source(s): The Federal Judiciary Home Page. http://www.uscourts.gov.

the Court, Justice Black spelled out a more expansive interpretation of procedural due process under the Constitution:

> [The right to counsel] is one of the safeguards of the Sixth Amendment deemed necessary to insure fundamental human rights of life and liberty . . . It embodies a realistic recognition of the obvious truth that the average defendant does not have the professional legal skill to protect himself when brought before a tribunal with the power to take his life or liberty, wherein the prosecution is represented by experienced and learned counsel . . . The ". . . right to he heard would be, in many cases, of little avail if it did not comprehend the right to be heard by counsel."

Black added that Johnson's failure to request a lawyer directly from the trial court did not amount to a waiver of his right. Rather, in order to waive the right to counsel intelligently, a defendant must first be told that he has the right, then deliberately choose to waive it

The right to counsel in state courts was later expanded in *Gideon v. Wainwright* (1963), which granted indigent defendants the right to appointed counsel in all felony cases, and in *Argersinger v. Hamlin* (1972), which extended this guarantee to cover misde-

meanor offenses and all crimes of a lesser order. The issue of informed right to counsel came to the forefront most prominently in *Miranda v. Arizona* (1966), in which the Court determined that the right begins at the time a criminal suspect becomes subject to police interrogation. *Miranda* was perhaps the high-water mark of the Court's "due process revolution," in which criminal procedure was radically overhauled to ensure that state criminal defendants received the benefits of the Bill of Rights. *Johnson v. Zerbst* was an important step along the way.

Related Cases
Powell v. Alabama, 287 U.S. 45 (1932).
Gideon v. Wainwright, 372 U.S. 335 (1963).
Miranda v. Arizona, 384 U.S. 436 (1966).
Argersinger v. Hamlin, 407 U.S. 25 (1972).

Bibliography and Further Reading
Bradley, Craig M. *The Failure of the Criminal Procedure Revolution.* Philadelphia: University of Pennsylvania Press, 1993.

Galloway, John. *The Supreme Court & The Rights of the Accused.* New York, NY: Facts on File, 1973.

Garcia, Alfredo. *The Sixth Amendment in Modern American Jurisprudence: A Critical Perspective.* New York, NY: Greenwood Press, 1992.

ADAMSON V. CALIFORNIA

Legal Citation: 332 U.S. 46 (1947)

Appellant
Dewey Adamson

Appellee
The State of California

Appellant's Claim
That the state prosecutor who drew the jury's attention to Adamson's refusal to testify at his own murder trial violated the Fifth Amendment's ban on self-incrimination.

Chief Lawyer for Appellant
Morris Lavine

Chief Lawyer for Appellee
Walter L. Bowers

Justices for the Court
Harold Burton, William O. Douglas, Felix Frankfurter, Robert H. Jackson, Stanley Forman Reed (writing for the Court), Wiley Blount Rutledge, Fred Moore Vinson

Justices Dissenting
Hugo Lafayette Black, Frank Murphy

Place
Washington, D.C.

Date of Decision
23 June 1947

Decision
Finding that the Due Process Clause of the Fourteenth Amendment did not make all aspects of the Bill of Rights applicable at the state level, the Supreme Court declined to rule that the prosecutor had committed a crucial error and upheld Dewey's conviction.

Significance
Although the Court later overruled *Adamson* with *Griffin v. California* (1965), in which it held that the Fourteenth Amendment does not permit prosecutors to call attention to defendants' failure to testify, in *Adamson* the Court declined—as it continues to decline—to endorse the notion that all parts of the Bill of Rights apply to the states.

After Admiral Dewey Adamson, a career criminal apparently named after the naval hero, was convicted of murder in the first degree in California Superior Court and sentenced to death, he sought a review of his trial from the U.S. Supreme Court. In particular, the appellant challenged provisions of the state constitution and penal code that permitted a state prosecutor to draw a jury's attention to a defendant's failure to deny or explain the evidence presented against him in court. Adamson had not wanted to take the witness stand in his own defense because to do so would subject him to cross-examination about his former crimes that would undermine his credibility and, in all probability, contribute to his conviction. Through his attorney, Adamson argued that the Due Process Clause of the Fourteenth Amendment makes the Fifth Amendment prohibition on such compelled self-incrimination applicable at the state level.

At the time, a debate was raging in the American judicial system about the so-called "incorporation doctrine," that is, the incorporation of the guarantees of the Bill of Rights into the Fourteenth Amendment. As the Fourteenth Amendment extends the concept of due process to the states, the incorporation doctrine was especially significant for criminal defendants, who are customarily tried in state courts. At the time *Adamson* came before the Court, the justices had adopted, in *Palko v. Connecticut* (1937), only a philosophy of selective incorporation, whereby only those Bill of Rights guarantees "implicit in the concept of ordered liberty" were binding on the states. Citing this precedent, the Court reasoned that because the prosecutor's actions had not resulted in an unfair trial, Adamson's conviction should stand.

Justice Black Argues for Total Incorporation

The *Adamson* court divided 5-4. Both Justices Murphy and Black wrote dissenting opinions. Black, who was emerging as the leader of the "due process revolution" that would eventually see most of the Bill of Rights incorporated into the Fourteenth Amendment, argued powerfully for a "total incorporation" approach to due process:

Due Process of Law

Dating back to the Magna Carta (1215), due process of law was part of England's first written code of law. Later the authors of the U.S. Constitution included the notion of due process in the Fifth and Fourteenth Amendments to limit the power of the federal government and the state governments, respectively. Legal scholars interpreted the Due Process Clause of these amendments to cover procedure or process in court and to refer to a basic right of "all persons within the territory of the United States that protects them from unfair treatment from the legislative, executive, and judicial branches of the government," according to Justice Curtis in 1855.

The U.S. Supreme Court has interpreted the Due Process Clause to guarantee fair trials, non-arbitrary action, reasonable bail and fines, and adequate compensation for property seized by the federal and state governments. The Supreme Court also has ruled that the Due Process Clause requires the accused to receive advanced notice of legal proceedings and that they have an opportunity to defend themselves before any branch of the government restricts their liberty or seizes their property.

Source(s): *West's Encyclopedia of American Law.* Minneapolis, MN: West Publishing, 1998.

The first 10 amendments were proposed and adopted largely because of fear that Government might unduly interfere with prized individual liberties. The people wanted and demanded a Bill of Rights written into their Constitution. The amendments embodying the Bill of Rights were intended to curb all branches of the Federal Government in the fields touched by the amendments—Legislative, Executive, and Judicial. The Fifth, Sixth, and Eighth Amendments are pointedly aimed at confining exercise of power by courts and judges within precise boundaries, particularly in the procedure used for the trial of criminal cases . . . My study of the historical events that culminated in the Fourteenth Amendment . . . persuades me that one of the chief objects that the provisions of the Amendment's first section, separately, and as a whole, were intended to accomplish was to make the Bill of Rights, applicable to the states.

Justice Black would always remain a constitutional fundamentalist, but towards the end of his tenure on the Supreme Court, convinced that the Courts headed by Justices Earl Warren and Warren Burger had gone too far in their judicial activism, he grew more conservative. Black's early commitment to the due process revolution, however, led to significant changes in the administration of criminal justice, such as the administration of the Miranda warning to individuals arrested to inform them of their right to remain silent and their right to be represented by an attorney, and the exclusionary rule, which prevents improperly obtained evidence from being introduced at a trial.

Related Cases
Palko v. Connecticut, 302 U.S. 319 (1937).
Griffin v. California, 380 U.S. 609 (1965).

Bibliography and Further Reading
Cortner, Richard C. *The Supreme Court and the Second Bill of Rights.* Madison: University of Wisconsin Press, 1981.

The Fourteenth Amendment and the Bill of Rights: The Incorporation Theory. New York: Da Capo Press, 1970.

Nelson, William E. *The Fourteenth Amendment: From Political Principle to Judicial Doctrine.* Cambridge, MA: Harvard University Press, 1988.

ULLMANN V. UNITED STATES

Legal Citation: 350 U.S. 422 (1956)

On 3 November 1954, William Ludwig Ullmann put in an appearance in the Federal District Court for the Southern District of New York. Ullmann had been subpoenaed to appear before a grand jury that had been convened to investigate espionage and other threats against the federal government. When the grand jury asked him a series of questions about his own or others' activities and Communist Party affiliations, Ullmann refused to answer, citing his Fifth Amendment privilege against self-incrimination.

The U.S. attorney for the district filed an application under the Immunity Act of 1954 for an order requiring Ullmann to testify. The Immunity Act provided witnesses with immunity from criminal prosecution for matters revealed by the compelled testimony. Ullmann in turn challenged the constitutionality of the act, claiming that the so-called "transactional" immunity it afforded would not protect him from other serious harm, such as job loss and social ostracism. The district court upheld the statute and ordered Ullmann to testify. When he again refused to answer questions put to him by a grand jury, he was convicted of contempt of court and sentenced to six months in jail. When his appeal to the Court of Appeals for the Second Circuit failed, Ullmann petitioned the U.S. Supreme Court for review of his case.

Court Holds That the Privilege Against Self-Incrimination Only Protects Against Criminal Prosecution

Writing for the Court, Justice Frankfurterheld that the Fifth Amendment privilege only protects a witness from being compelled to give testimony that could result in criminal prosecution:

> [T]he immunity granted need only remove those sanctions which generate the fear justifying invocation of the privilege: "the interdiction of the 5th Amendment operates only where a witness is asked to incriminated himself,—in other words, to give testimony which may possibly expose him to a criminal charge. But if the criminality has already been taken away, the amendment ceases to apply." [Quoting *Hale v. Henek* (1906)].

Petitioner
William Ludwig Ullmann

Respondent
United States

Petitioner's Claim
That the Immunity Act of 1954, making it a criminal offense to refuse to testify about matters of national security, violates the Fifth Amendment privilege against self-incrimination.

Chief Lawyer for Petitioner
Leonard B. Boudin

Chief Lawyer for Respondent
Charles F. Barber

Justices for the Court
Harold Burton, Tom C. Clark, Felix Frankfurter (writing for the Court), John Marshall Harlan II, Sherman Minton, Stanley Forman Reed, Earl Warren

Justices Dissenting
Hugo Lafayette Black, William O. Douglas

Place
Washington, D.C.

Date of Decision
26 March 1956

Decision
The Supreme Court upheld the Immunity Act.

Significance
Ullmann clarified the meaning of the privilege against self-incrimination.

Prima Facie Evidence

The Latin phrase *prima facie* means on first appearance and prima facie evidence refers to the apparent truth of a piece evidence on initial inspection that supports a case or an argument in a case that requires support. Both civil and criminal law rely on the notion of prima facie evidence.

Prima facie evidence comes into play, for example, when a prosecutor in an assault case offers letters in which the defendant threatens the victim. Here, the prosecutor presents prima facie evidence that the defendant intended to harm the victim, which the prosecutor must demonstrate before the defendant can be convicted. In addition, statutes also determine what counts as prima facie evidence. For instance, an appropriately verified copy of a criminal record can be used against a defendant in court as prima facie evidence.

Source(s): *West's Encyclopedia of American Law.* Minneapolis, MN: West Publishing, 1998.

Since the Immunity Act removed the threat of prosecution for actions revealed by the compelled testimony, the privilege did not apply in Ullmann's case. The Fifth Amendment was not designed by the framers of the Constitution to protect against the kinds of harms Ullmann cited. Always a proponent of judicial restraint and an advocate of legislative prerogatives, Frankfurter added that the Constitution could not be changed except by the formal amendatory process. The Immunity Act was upheld.

Ullmann had good reason to fear testifying before the grand jury. During the red-baiting period that followed World War II, those who refused to testify before investigative bodies like the notorious House Committee on Un-American Activities (HUAC) became known as "Fifth Amendment Communists." For them, an invocation of the privilege might as well have been an admission of guilt. Many lost jobs, families, friends, and all social status. When the Red Scare abated, cooling off to the point it became a Cold War with the Soviet Union, domestic persecution of suspected communists also eased. But in 1954, transactional immunity could not really protect William Ullmann adequately.

In the 1970s, Congress enacted a law providing for "use immunity." This type of immunity offers even less coverage than transactional immunity, in that it only protects a witness from use in a subsequent prosecution of the compelled testimony and any evidence obtained because of it. Unlike transactional immunity, it does not protect a witness from being prosecuted for the same offense if evidence is independently obtained. Use immunity, like transactional immunity, has been upheld as constitutional. The purpose of the Fifth Amendment privilege against self-incrimination has been interpreted as a support for the fundamental proposition that under the American system of laws, the prosecution has to carry the burden of proof. If witnesses are granted immunity—of either sort—in exchange for their testimony, they will not be doing the prosecution's work for them.

Related Cases
Twining v. New Jersey, 211 U.S. 78 (1908).
Slochower v. Board of Higher Education of New York City, 350 U.S. 551 (1956).
Kastigar v. United States, 406 U.S. 441 (1972).

Bibliography and Further Reading
Bodenhamer, David J. *Fair Trial: Rights of the Accused in American History.* New York: Oxford University Press, 1992.

Maguire, John MacArthur. *Evidence of Guilt: Restrictions Upon Its Discovery or Compulsory Disclosure.* Boston, MA: Little, Brown, 1959.

Meltzer, Milton. *The Right to Remain Silent.* New York: Harcourt Brace Jovanovich, 1972.

MALLOY V. HOGAN

Legal Citation: 678 U.S. 1 (1964)

William Malloy was initially arrested during a gambling raid in 1959 by Hartford, Connecticut, police. He pleaded guilty to the lesser crime of misdemeanor, and was sentenced to a year in jail and a fine of $500. After he had served 90 days, his sentence was suspended, and he was placed on probation for two years.

About a year later, Malloy was ordered to testify at a state inquiry into gambling and other crimes. When he was asked several questions about his arrest and conviction, Malloy refused to answer "on the grounds it may tend to incriminate [him]." The Connecticut Superior Court ruled him in contempt of court and sent him to prison until he was willing to answer the questions put to him. Malloy petitioned the superior court for a writ of *habeas corpus*—a request to be released on grounds that he had been unlawfully detained. The court rejected his petition, and this rejection was upheld on appeal. Malloy then petitioned the U.S. Supreme Court for review of this decision.

The Court had long held, in decisions such as *Twining v. State of New Jersey* (1904) and *Adamson v. California* (1947), that the Fifth Amendment privilege against self-incrimination did not apply in state courts. In *Twining* and *Adamson*, the issue was that the prosecution drew attention to the defendant's failure to testify in his own defense. In both cases, the defendant's appeal of his conviction failed. The Supreme Court reasoned, even as late as 1961, in *Cohen v. Hurley*, that state courts were only obliged to show fundamental fairness to criminal defendants.

Right to Remain Silent

In cases like *Mallory v. United States* (1957), however, the Warren Court had been moving towards a policy of overturning convictions obtained in state court through the use of confessions acquired through improper means, such as prolonged detention without arraignment. Writing for the five-member majority in *Malloy*, Justice Brennan made a connection between the prohibition against coerced confessions and the privilege against self-incrimination:

> [T]oday the admissibility of a confession in a state criminal prosecution is tested by the

Transactional Immunity

Because the Fifth Amendment protects people from giving self-incriminating evidence, state and federal courts sometimes trade immunity from prosecution for testimony that will help them convict offenders who are more detrimental to society. Rather than prosecute a prostitute, for instance, an agency may use testimony from a prostitute to break an entire prostitution ring. Transactional immunity, or full immunity, is one of the two kinds of prosecutorial immunity offered by state prosecutors to witnesses. Transactional immunity exempts witnesses not only from providing self-incriminating evidence, but also from being prosecuted for any wrongdoings admitted even when the prosecution obtains evidence outside of and not stemming from the witness's testimony. Although controversial, Congress passed a statute in 1893 that allowed transactional immunity in exchange for testimony

and the Supreme Court sustained the statute by a 5-4 vote.

Use immunity, on the other hand, offers the same protection against any admittance of wrongdoing during the testimony. If, however, prosecutors obtain outside evidence outside of the scope of the testimony, they can still use it to prosecute a witness. Congress has found use immunity consistent with the Fifth Amendment. Congress also replaced all previous immunity statutes with a use-immunity statute. The Supreme Court agreed, arguing in 1972 that "[t]ransactional immunity . . . affords the witness considerably broader protection than does the Fifth Amendment privilege." Nevertheless, federal and state prosecutors continue to grant transactional immunity.

Source(s): FindLaw. http://www.findlaw.com.

---

same standard applied in federal prosecutions . . . Under this test, the constitutional inquiry is not whether the conduct of state officers in obtaining the confession was shocking, but whether the confession was "free and voluntary" . . . In other words the person must not have been compelled to incriminate himself.

The reason the *Malloy* Court was shifting to the federal standard concerning compelled testimony was the "recognition that the American system of criminal prosecution is accusatory, not inquisitional, and that the Fifth Amendment privilege is its essential mainstay." After *Malloy*, state prosecutors had to shoulder the entire burden of proof when witnesses proved unwilling to testify.

This decision was an important part of the "due process revolution" that reached its highest point during the tenure of Chief Justice Warren. During this revolution, most of the guarantees of the Bill of Rights—which had previously been thought to apply only to the federal government—were made to apply to the states through the Due Process Clause of the Fourteenth Amendment. The due process revolution affected many areas of the law, but criminal defendants—most of whom are tried in state courts—were among the primary beneficiaries of this shift in constitutional interpretation. The closeness of the vote in *Malloy* is one

indication of how hard fought some of the battles were during the revolution. In fact, Justices White and Stewart, although concurring with the majority's view that the Fourteenth Amendment incorporated the privilege against self-incrimination, nevertheless dissented from the decision to apply the privilege to William Malloy. They did not believe that there had been any risk that he might incriminate himself.

Related Cases
Twining v. State of New Jersey, 211 U.S. 78 (1904).
Gitlow v. New York, 268 U.S. 652 (1925).
Palko v. Connecticut, 302 U.S. 319 (1937).
Cantwell v. Connecticut, 310 U.S. 296 (1940).
Adamson v. California, 332 U.S. 46 (1947).
Mapp v. Ohio, 367 U.S. 643 (1961).
Gideon v. Wainwright, 372 U.S. 335 (1963).

Bibliography and Further Reading
Levy, Leonard W. *Origins of the Fifth Amendment: The Right Against Self-Incrimination.* New York: Oxford University Press, 1968.

Meltzer, Milton. *The Right to Remain Silent.* New York: Harcourt Brace Jovanovich, 1972.

Mykkeltvedt, Roald Y. *The Nationalization of the Bill of Rights: Fourteenth Amendment Due Process and the Procedural Rights.* Port Washington, NY: Associated Faculty Press, 1983.

POINTER V. TEXAS

Legal Citation: 380 U.S. 400 (1965)

Petitioner
Bob Granville Pointer

Respondent
State of Texas

Petitioner's Claim
That the use of transcribed testimony in a criminal prosecution deprived the defendant of his Sixth Amendment right to confront and cross-examine witnesses against him.

Chief Lawyer for Petitioner
Orville A. Harlan

Chief Lawyer for Respondent
Gilbert J. Pena

Justices for the Court
Hugo Lafayette Black (writing for the Court), William J. Brennan, Jr., Tom C. Clark, William O. Douglas, Arthur Goldberg, John Marshall Harlan II, Potter Stewart, Earl Warren, Byron R. White

Justices Dissenting
None

Place
Washington, D.C.

Date of Decision
5 April 1965

Decision
Reversed Pointer's conviction.

Significance
Although in 1965 most states recognized the right of confrontation guaranteed in federal trials by the Sixth Amendment, Texas did not. *Pointer* emphasized that the standard for upholding this right must be uniform throughout the states.

Bob Granville Pointer and an accomplice were arrested in Texas and charged with robbing Kenneth W. Phillips of $375. Pointer and his accomplice were then taken before a state judge for a preliminary hearing. At the hearing, an assistant district attorney examined witnesses, but neither of the accused men was represented by a lawyer. As the chief witness against them, Phillips gave his version of events, identifying Pointer as the one who had robbed him at gunpoint. Although Pointer's accomplice tried to cross-examined Phillips, Pointer did not. Pointer was subsequently indicted on robbery charges.

Before the trial began, Phillips moved to California. After submitting evidence that Phillips did not intend to return to Texas, the prosecution offered the transcript of his testimony at the preliminary hearing as evidence against Pointer. Pointer was by this time represented by counsel, but although his lawyer objected to the admission of the transcript, the trial judge overruled him. Pointer was convicted of armed robbery. After his appeal to the Texas Court of Criminal Appeals failed, he took his case to the U.S. Supreme Court.

In *Gideon v. Wainwright* (1963), the Supreme Court ruled that the Due Process Clause of the Fourteenth Amendment made the Sixth Amendment's guarantee of a right to counsel in criminal cases applicable in state trials. The issue in *Pointer* was whether or not the Fourteenth Amendment also made the Confrontation Clause of the Sixth Amendment applicable to the states. The Confrontation Clause guarantees that "In all criminal prosecutions, the accused shall enjoy the right . . . to be confronted with the witnesses against him." Although the right to confront one's accusers in a criminal prosecution had long been recognized by the laws of most states, the circumstances in *Pointer* made it clear that there was a lack of uniformity in the state standards for satisfying this right.

Supreme Court Holds that States Must Allow Criminal Defendants to Confront and Cross-Examine Witnesses Against Them

Writing for a unanimous Court, Justice Black stated unequivocally that states must permit criminal defendants to confront and cross-examine witnesses against them in all cases where the federal standard for observing the Confrontation Clause applies:

> [T]he right of cross-examination is included in the right of an accused in a criminal case to confront the witnesses against him . . . There are few subjects . . . upon which this Court and other courts have been more nearly unanimous than in their expressions of belief that the right of confrontation and cross-examination is an essential and fundamental requirement for the kind of fair trial which is this country's constitutional goal. Indeed, we have expressly declared that to deprive an accused of the right to cross-examine the witnesses against him is a denial of the Fourteenth Amendment's guarantee of due process of law.

In other words, the right of the accused to confront his accusers is grounded in the necessity for cross-examination. And because cross-examination of witnesses requires some legal skill, criminal defendants must be represented by counsel. The Court did recognize that there are some practical limitations on this rule: where a key witness has died, for example, admission of his or her earlier testimony must be admitted at trial. Following *Pointer*, however, the exceptions to the rule are the same both in federal and state criminal prosecutions.

Pointer, with its unanimous decision, proved to be one of the least controversial cases in the so-called due process revolution of the 1940s through the 1960s. Led by Justice Black, this "revolution" succeeded in making most of the guarantees of the Bill of Rights applicable at the state level through the Fourteenth Amendment. Both civil rights and criminal procedure were radically altered as a result of this expansion of individual liberties, giving rise to a backlash. *Pointer*, however, was never challenged.

Related Cases
Palko v. Connecticut, 302 U.S. 319 (1937).
Mapp v. Ohio, 367 U.S. 643 (1961).
Gideon v. Wainwright, 372 U.S. 335 (1963).
Malloy v. Hogan, 678 U.S. 1 (1964).

Bibliography and Further Reading

Cortner, Richard C. *The Supreme Court and the Second Bill of Rights: The Fourteenth Amendment and the Nationalization of Civil Liberties*. Madison: University of Wisconsin Press, 1981.

Garcia, Alfredo. *The Sixth Amendment in Modern American Jurisprudence: A Critical Perspective*. New York, NY: Greenwood Press, 1992.

Mykkeltvedt, Roald Y. *The Nationalization of the Bill of Rights: Fourteenth Amendment Due Process and the Procedural Rights*. Port Washington, NY: Associated Faculty Press, 1983.

GRIFFIN V. CALIFORNIA

Legal Citation: 380 U.S. 609 (1965)

Petitioner
Griffin

Respondent
State of California

Petitioner's Claim
That a prosecutor's comment on the fact that the defendant, Griffin, did not take the stand in a state criminal trial violated the Self-Incrimination Clause of the Fifth Amendment.

Chief Lawyer for Petitioner
Morris Lavine

Chief Lawyer for Respondent
Albert W. Harris

Justices for the Court
Hugo Lafayette Black, William J. Brennan, Jr., Tom C. Clark, William O. Douglas (writing for the Court), Arthur Goldberg, John Marshall Harlan II

Justices Dissenting
Potter Stewart, Byron R. White (Earl Warren did not participate)

Place
Washington, D.C.

Date of Decision
28 April 1965

Decision
State laws allowing adverse comment on the failure of a defendant to take the witness stand to deny or explain evidence violates a defendant's right not to incriminate himself.

Significance
The decision to forbid comments by prosecutors or judges on the failure of a defendant to testify at his own trial preserved the presumption of innocence to which a defendant is constitutionally entitled.

On the night that Essie Mae was found dead, she had been seen by a Mr. Villasenor in an alley with petitioner Griffin. Griffin was later convicted of the first degree murder of Essie Mae, after a jury trial in a California court. He did not testify at his trial, and while the trial court instructed the jury on the issue of guilt, stating that a defendant has a constitutional right not to testify, it also told the jury that they may take into consideration the fact that the defendant did not testify as tending to indicate the truth of the evidence and that of the inferences drawn from the evidence those unfavorable to the defendant are the more probable. The court also stated that the failure of a defendant to deny or explain the evidence of which he had knowledge does not create a presumption of guilt nor by itself warrant an inference of guilt nor relieve the prosecution of any of its burden of proof. During the trial, the prosecutor drew a great deal of attention to the fact that Griffin did not testify with such statements as, "Essie Mae is dead, she can't tell you her side of the story. The defendant won't." Griffin received the death penalty and the California Supreme Court affirmed this sentence.

A Remnant Of The Inquisitorial System

The Supreme Court agreed to hear the case to decide if comment on the failure to testify violated the Self-Incrimination Clause of the Fifth Amendment. The Supreme Court had ruled in *Malloy v. Hogan* (1964) that this clause was applicable to the states by reason of the Fourteenth Amendment. *Malloy v. Hogan* was decided after the Supreme Court of California had affirmed Griffin's conviction.

Justice Douglas, in his opinion for the majority stated that the "comment rule" violated the Fifth Amendment. He noted that the comment rule is a rule of evidence that allowed the state the privilege of offering to the jury for its consideration the failure of the accused to testify. The prosecutor's comments and the court's acquiescence are the equivalent of an offer of evidence and its acceptance. In *Wilson v. United States* (1893), the Court stated "the failure of the defendant in a criminal action to request to be a witness shall not create any presumption against him."

Federal Circuit Court

The term "circuit court" originally referred to the route a judge rode to hold trials in each district in a designated circuit. In sparsely populated areas, the circuit court system alleviated the costs associated with setting up a court in every small town or village.

The U.S. Federal Circuit Court system consists of 12 circuits. The First through Eleventh Circuits contain three or more states each. Territories such as the Virgin Islands and Guam are also included in these circuits. The twelfth circuit is the court for the District of Columbia. Federal circuit courts have jurisdiction over only the states or counties within their circuits. The decisions made by federal district courts can be reviewed by the court of appeals in each circuit.

Source(s): *West's Encyclopedia of American Law*. Minneapolis, MN: West Publishing, 1998.

Commenting on the refusal to testify is a remnant of the inquisitorial system of criminal justice, which the Fifth Amendment outlawed. Such commenting is "a penalty imposed by court for exercising a constitutional privilege. It cuts down on the privilege by making its assertion costly . . . .What the jury may infer, given no help from the court, is one thing. What it may infer when the court solemnizes the silence of the accused into evidence against him is quite another." Justice Douglas summed up by stating that the Fifth Amendment forbids either comment by the prosecution on the accused's silence or instructions by the court that such silence is evidence of guilt.

Justice Harlan concurred "with great reluctance." He felt that the decision exemplified the "creeping paralysis with which this Court's recent adoption of the 'incorporation' doctrine is infecting the operation of the federal system." Justice Harlan noted that *Malloy v. Hogan* put forth the argument that "It would be incongruous to have different standards determine the validity of a claim of privilege . . . , depending on whether the claim was asserted in a state or federal court. Therefore, the same standards must determine whether an accused's silence in either a federal or state proceeding is justified." Justice Harlan responded to this statement in *Malloy,* incongruity within the limits of fundamental fairness is at the heart of the federal system. The powers and responsibilities of the state and federal governments are not congruent and the Constitution did not intend them to be. Justice Harlan suggested that the way to eliminate friction between the state and federal systems is to attempt a working harmony, not for the federal system to override the states altogether.

Unwarranted Inferences

Justice Stewart wrote the dissent. He stated that the question in this case was whether Griffin had been "compelled . . . to be a witness against himself." Justice Stewart felt that compulsion was the key here. "I think that the Court in this case stretches the concept of compulsion beyond all reasonable bounds, and that

whatever compulsion may exist derives from the defendant's choice not to testify, not from any comment by court or counsel." Justice Stewart, referring to the majority's opinion, did not understand what penalty was imposed here.

Justice Stewart did not feel that the defendant would be at more of a disadvantage under the California comment rule than in a court where no comment on a suspect's failure to take the witness stand was allowed. The inferences drawn by the jury under the limiting and carefully controlling language of instruction might be less detrimental than if the jury were "left to roam at large with only its untutored instincts to guide it, to draw from the defendant's silence broad inferences of guilt."

A prosecutor will seek to encourage the drawing of inferences unfavorable to the defendant, but the defendant's counsel has an equal opportunity to explain why a defendant may not wish to take the stand. The California comment rule "is not a coercive device which impairs the right against self-incrimination, but rather a means of articulating and bringing into the light of rational discussion a fact inescapably impressed on the jury's consciousness." The rule protects the defendant against unwarranted inferences that an uninformed jury might draw. It also attempts to recognize and articulate what the state believes to the natural probative force of certain facts.

Justice Stewart stated that the formulation of procedural rules governing the administration of criminal justice in the states should be a matter of local concern; the Supreme Court's function is to prevent violations of the Constitution. California has not compelled anyone to be a witness against himself. Whenever a defendant in a criminal trial exercises this constitutional right, the jury is bound to draw inferences. "No constitution can prevent the operation of the human mind. Without limiting instruction, the danger exists that the inferences drawn by the jury may be unfairly broad."

Impact

The decision in *Griffin v. California* overruled *Twining v. State of New Jersey* (1908) and *Adamson v. California* (1947). Not only may a prosecutor not comment to the jury about a defendant's refusal to take the stand, but a prosecutor may not tell the jury that a defendant who has given an alibi at trial originally refused to speak to the police. If the defense requests it, the judge must tell the jury to give no weight whatsoever to the fact that the defendant chose not to take the stand.

Related Cases

Wilson v. United States, 149 U.S. 60 (1893).
Twining v. State of New Jersey, 211 U.S. 78 (1908).

Adamson v. California, 332 U.S. 46 (1947).
Malloy v. Hogan, 378 U.S. 1 (1964).

Bibliography and Further Reading

FindLaw *Internet Legal Resources.* http://www.findlaw. com.

Hall, Kermit L., ed. *The Oxford Companion to the Supreme Court of the United States.* New York: Oxford Press, 1992.

Levy, Leonard W., ed. *Encyclopedia of the American Constitution.* Vol. 4. New York: Macmillan, 1986.

Lieberman, Jethro K. *The Evolving Constitution.* New York: Random House, 1992.

ALBERTSON V. SUBVERSIVE ACTIVITIES CONTROL BOARD

Legal Citation: 382 U.S. 70 (1965)

Petitioner
William Albertson

Respondent
Subversive Activities Control Board

Petitioner's Claim
That the requirement of the Internal Security Act of 1950 (the McCarran Act) that members of the Communist Party register with the attorney general violates the Fifth Amendment privilege against self-incrimination.

Chief Lawyer for Petitioner
Kevin T. Maroney

Chief Lawyer for Respondent
John J. Abt

Justices for the Court
Hugo Lafayette Black, William J. Brennan, Jr. (writing for the Court), Tom C. Clark, William O. Douglas, Abe Fortas, John Marshall Harlan II, Potter Stewart, Earl Warren

Justices Dissenting
None (Byron R. White did not participate)

Place
Washington, D.C.

Date of Decision
15 November 1965

Decision
This registration requirement of the McCarran Act was struck down as an infringement on a citizens Fifth Amendment rights.

Significance
Albertson marked the beginning of the end of the Subversive Activities Control Board. A remnant of the McCarthy era, it was eventually allowed to lapse in 1973 for lack of congressional appropriation.

In 1950, during the era of the Red Scare, the heyday of Senator Joseph McCarthy and of the House Un-American Activities Committee, Congress passed the Internal Security Act, also known as the McCarran Act. The statute required communist organizations to register with the attorney general, with the registration process to be managed by the Subversive Activities Control Board (SACB). Registered groups were also required to provide a list of their members, who were in turn required to register individually. Members of registered organizations were denied passports, as well as the opportunity to work in defense plants. Each day that an individual failed to register could cost as much as $1,000 or five years in prison, or both.

Not surprisingly, most organizations, including the Communist Party of the United States of America, declined to register. The attorney general then petitioned the SACB for an order requiring party member William Albertson and others to register. They, in turn, sought review of the order from the Court of Appeals of the District of Columbia Circuit, which affirmed the order. Albertson and others then applied directly to the U.S. Supreme Court for a final review of the legitimacy of the registration requirement, claiming among other things, that it violated the Fifth Amendment privilege against self-incrimination.

Registration Requirement Struck Down

Writing for a unanimous Court, Justice Brennan argued that while the registration requirement itself might not amount to mandatory self-incrimination, being listed as a member of a subversive organization might be used as the basis for some future criminal prosecution. In the superheated atmosphere of paranoia that gave rise to the SACB and which was furthered by it, mere association with such an organization as the Communist Party was damning in and of itself. If nothing else, it cast suspicion over the registered person, who was required to supply information such as date and place of birth, which could provide leads for investigators trying to collect evidence for a criminal action. The immunity clause attached to the McCarran Act, which purportedly protected against prosecution based on the act of registering was, therefore, no protection:

Senator Joseph McCarthy

Senator Joseph McCarthy became notorious for leading a witch hunt in the form of trials of alleged Communists in the 1950s. After practicing law in Wisconsin and serving in the Marine Corp during World War II, McCarthy was elected to the Senate as a Republican in 1946. McCarthy served his first three years quietly, until his explosive 1950 speech where he claimed that 205 Communists had infiltrated the State Department. In response, a Senate committee ordered McCarthy to provide evidence to support his allegations. Although McCarthy failed to produce any evidence, he became a vocal leader of the anti-Communist movement and his message resonated with citizens who feared the spread of Communism.

Senator McCarthy chaired the Senate's Government Committee on Operations and headed its subcommittee on investigations beginning in 1953. McCarthy used his position to continue his attack on Communism and accused many people of being Communists or Communist sympathizers through the Committee's trials. When the Democrats took control of the Senate in 1954, Senator John L. McClellan replaced McCarthy as chair of the investigating committee. Senator McClellan criticized McCarthy's tactics and pushed to have him censured, which occurred in 1955. McCarthy's censure led to the decline of his political influence. McCarthy died in 1957.

Source(s): *West's Encyclopedia of American Law.* Minneapolis, MN: West Publishing, 1998.

The judgment as to whether a disclosure would be "incriminatory" has never been made dependent on an assessment of the information possessed by the Government at the time of interrogation; the protection of the privilege [against self-incrimination] would be seriously impaired if the right to invoke it was dependent on such an assessment, with all its uncertainties. The threat to the privilege is no less present where it is proposed that this assessment be made in order to remedy a shortcoming in the grant of immunity. The representation that the information demanded is of no utility is belied by the fact that the failure to make the disclosure is so severely sanctioned . . .

Although the Court had upheld the registration requirement per se in *Communist Party of the United States v. Subversive Activities Control Board* (1961), it postponed a decision on the sanctions attached to the requirement until they were at issue. After *Albertson* did away with registration under the McCarran Act, subsequent cases, such as *United States v. Robel* (1967), which threw out the ban on defense department employment, succeeded in gutting the act. In 1973, it was allowed to expire altogether for lack of appropriation.

Related Cases

Communist Party of the United States v. Subversive Activities Control Board, 367 U.S. 1 (1961).
United States v. Robel, 389 U.S. 258 (1967).

Bibliography and Further Reading

Belfrage, Cedric. *The American Inquisition, 1945-1960: A profile of the "McCarthy Era."* New York, NY: Thunder's Mouth Press, 1989.

Schrecker, Ellen. *The Age of McCarthyism: A Brief History with Documents.* Boston: Bedford Books, 1994.

Senator Joseph McCarthy. © The Library of Congress/Corbis.

KASTIGAR V. UNITED STATES

Legal Citation: 406 U.S. 441 (1972)

Petitioners
Charles Joseph Kastigar, Michael Gorean Stewart

Respondent
United States

Petitioners' Claim
That the petitioners were correct to refuse to testify because only transactional immunity, which was not granted, would satisfy the Fifth Amendment with respect to self-incrimination.

Chief Lawyer for Petitioners
Hugh R. Manes

Chief Lawyer for Respondent
Erwin N. Griswold

Justices for the Court
Harry A. Blackmun, Warren E. Burger, Lewis F. Powell, Jr. (writing for the Court), Potter Stewart, Byron R. White

Justices Dissenting
William O. Douglas, Thurgood Marshall (William J. Brennan, Jr., and William H. Rehnquist did not participate)

Place
Washington, D.C.

Date of Decision
22 May 1972

Decision
The U.S. Supreme Court affirmed the decision of the court of appeals.

Significance
The case of *Kastigar v. United States* raised many important questions concerning the extent and application of Fifth Amendment protection against self-incrimination, levels of immunity, refusal of a witness to testify on the grounds of inadequate immunity, and the historical precedents for compulsory testimony.

Case Background

The case of *Kastigar v. United States* arose from a situation in a California district court in 1971 where the petitioners were to appear before a grand jury. Believing that the petitioners would plead the Fifth Amendment, the district court issued an order to give them a grant of immunity that directed them to answer questions and turn over any evidence to the grand jury. Even though they were granted immunity, the petitioners appeared in court but refused to answer questions, "asserting their privilege against compulsory self-incrimination." Both Kastigar and Stewart were found in contempt. The court of appeals affirmed, "rejecting the petitioners' contention that it violated their constitutional privilege against self-incrimination to compel them to testify without granting them transactional immunity from prosecution for any offense to which the compelled testimony might relate." Because of the important question as to what level of testimony was necessary to compel testimony, the U.S. Supreme Court granted *certiorari*, and the case of *Kastigar v. United States* was argued on 11 January 1972.

How Comprehensive Must the Offered Immunity Be?

Hugh R. Manes, representing the petitioners Kastigar and Stewart, argued that his clients declined to testify because they believed that only transactional immunity would afford them an appropriate level of protection against self-incrimination, as promised by the Fifth Amendment. He also implied that having to testify before a grand jury is unfair because although one would be faced with a lawyer, that person would not be allowed to have a lawyer in the room with him, and that having to decide between jail or incriminating oneself would be a "choice between a rock and a whirlpool."

The chief lawyer for the respondent, Erwin N. Griswold, pointed out that no compelled testimony can be used against a witness if a guarantee of immunity has been given. When using any testimony or evidence derived by a witness under immunity, the burden is placed upon the prosecution to show that such information came from a completely independent source.

Griswold maintained that the extended immunity that was offered to Kastigar and Stewart met all of the requirements of the Fifth Amendment.

Justice Powell delivered the opinion of the Court, which affirmed the ruling of the court of appeals. The Supreme Court found that a witness "who invokes the Fifth Amendment privilege against compulsory self-incrimination" can be compelled to testify if given immunity "as such immunity from use and derivative use is coextensive with the scope of the privilege and is sufficient to compel testimony over a claim of privilege." While transactional immunity offers broader protection, it "is not constitutionally required."

Historically, many governments have been known to have the power to compel testimony from witnesses, as this information was important to the protection of their public. The Fifth Amendment of the U.S. Constitution is an exception that protects an individual from having to incriminate himself. Justice Powell noted that the petitioners' first point of contention, that the Fifth Amendment's protection of a witness from self-incrimination may allow that witness to decline to testify, would require that the cases of *Brown v. Walker* (1896) and *Ullmann v. United States* (1956) be overruled, to which the Court found no merit, and reaffirmed them. The petitioners' second contention was that the scope of the offered immunity was not coextensive with what the Fifth Amendment offers, which in their opinion would be transactional immunity, the most extensive available, pointing to *Counselman v. Hitchcock* (1892). The Court found that "transactional immunity, which accords full immunity from prosecution from the offense to which the compelled testimony relates, affords the witness considerably broader protection than does the Fifth Amendment privilege." The Court decided that transactional immunity was not required

in this case, and that the immunity offered was "sufficient to compel testimony over a claim of the privilege." The Court affirmed the decision of the court of appeals.

Two justices offered dissenting views. Justice Douglas did not believe that the "use" immunity offered to the petitioners in this case was coextensive compared to making a person "be a witness against himself," saying that he "would adhere to *Counselman v. Hitchcock* and hold that this attempt to dilute the Self-Incrimination Clause is unconstitutional." Justice Marshall, also dissenting, believed that the Fifth Amendment gives the right to withhold testimony, unless such a broad grant of immunity was offered so that there was no "possibility that the testimony will in fact operate to incriminate him." He concluded that "it is clear to me that an immunity statute must be tested by a standard far more demanding than that appropriate for an exclusionary rule fashioned to deal with past constitutional violations. Measured by that standard, the statute approved today by the Court fails miserably."

Related Cases
Counselman v. Hitchcock, 142 U.S. 547 (1892).
Brown v. Walker, 161 U.S. 591 (1896).
Ullmann v. United States, 350 U.S. 422 (1956).
Speiser v. Randall, 357 U.S. 513 (1958).
Malloy v. Hogan, 378 U.S. 1 (1964).

Bibliography and Further Reading
Biskupic, Joan, and Elder Witt, eds. *Congressional Quarterly's Guide to the U.S. Supreme Court,* 3rd ed. Washington, DC: Congressional Quarterly, Inc., 1996.

Hall, Kermit L., ed. *The Oxford Companion to the Supreme Court of the United States.* New York: Oxford University Press, 1992.

ZICARELLI V. THE NEW JERSEY STATE COMMISSION OF INVESTIGATION

Legal Citation: 406 U.S. 472 (1972)

Petitioner
Joseph Arthur Zicarelli

Respondent
The New Jersey State Commission of Investigation

Petitioner's Claim
That a state commission's requirement that Zicarelli answer questions under a grant of immunity from prosecution was inconsistent with his constitutional rights under the Fifth Amendment.

Chief Lawyer for Petitioner
Michael A. Querques

Chief Lawyer for Respondent
Andrew F. Phelan

Justices for the Court
Harry A. Blackmun, Warren E. Burger, Lewis F. Powell, Jr. (writing for the Court), Potter Stewart, Byron R. White

Justices Dissenting
William O. Douglas, Thurgood Marshall (William J. Brennan, Jr., and William H. Rehnquist did not participate)

Place
Washington, D.C.

Date of Decision
22 May 1972

Decision
The Commission could compel Zicarelli to answer questions under a grant of immunity without violating his constitutional rights.

Significance
Zicarelli v. The New Jersey State Commission of Investigation clarified the conditions under which a witness can be compelled to give testimony.

The Fifth Amendment to the U.S. Constitution grants a witness the privilege to refuse to answer questions on the grounds that they might incriminate him. In certain situations, however, courts or investigative bodies can force a witness to testify when they grant the witness immunity from prosecution. This case revolves around one such situation.

On 8 July 1969, the New Jersey State Commission of Investigation subpoenaed Joseph Arthur Zicarelli to appear and testify about organized crime, racketeering, and political corruption in the city of Long Branch. Zicarelli appeared before the commission on numerous occasions, several times invoking his privilege under the Fifth Amendment and refusing to answer the commission's questions. In response, the commission granted him immunity "from having such responsive answer given by him or such responsive evidence produced by him, or evidence derived therefrom used to expose him to criminal prosecution or penalty or to a forfeiture of his estate." In other words, the commission promised it would not use Zicarelli's testimony to prosecute him, not that it would not prosecute him entirely. It then ordered him to answer the questions. Still Zicarelli refused to answer. The commission then took its grievance to the Superior Court of Mercer County. At a hearing on the matter, Zicarelli challenged the order to testify on several grounds. Chiefly he argued that full immunity from prosecution for any offense to which he might testify was required for him to be compelled to answer questions. The Superior Court of Mercer County found Zicarelli to be in contempt and ordered him incarcerated until he testified as ordered. On appeal, the Supreme Court of New Jersey affirmed this judgment. Zicarelli then took his case to the U.S. Supreme Court.

The Supreme Court Ruling

On 22 May 1972 the Supreme Court issued its decision. By a vote of 5-2, it affirmed the ruling of the Supreme Court of New Jersey. Justice Powell wrote the majority opinion, in which he was joined by Chief Justice Burger, and Justices White, Blackmun, and Stewart. Justices Douglas and Marshall filed dissenting opinions. The remaining justices, Brennan and Rehnquist, did not participate in the consideration or the decision of this case. The majority opinion held on three key points.

The Issue of Immunity

Contrary to Zicarelli's contention, the Court decided that the type of immunity granted in this case—"immunity from use and derivative use" of Zicarelli's testimony—was entirely consistent with the Fifth Amendment's privilege against self-incrimination. Therefore, even though the commission had not promised not to prosecute Zicarelli for the events about which he was being asked to testify, it could force him to testify without violating his constitutional rights. In making this determination, the Court relied on a previous decision, in the case of *Kastigar v. United States*. As Justice Powell wrote:

> Appellant . . . contends that while immunity from use and derivative use may suffice to secure the protection of the privilege from invasion by jurisdictions other than the jurisdiction seeking to compel testimony, that jurisdiction must grant the greater protection afforded by transactional immunity. In *Kastigar,* we held that immunity from use and derivative use is commensurate with the protection afforded by the privilege, and rejected the notion that in our federal system a jurisdiction seeking to compel testimony must grant protection greater than that afforded by the privilege in order to supplant the privilege and compel testimony. Our holding in *Kastigar* is controlling here.

Vagueness of the Statute

Next, the Court addressed Zicarelli's contention that the term "responsive" in the commission's grant of immunity was unconstitutionally vague and would allow the commission to decide which of Zicarelli's answers would be subject to immunity. The Court rejected this claim:

> The term "responsive" in ordinary English usage has a well-recognized meaning. It is not,

as appellant argues, "so vague that men of common intelligence must necessarily guess at its meaning and differ as to its application" . . . The responsiveness limitation is not a trap for the unwary; rather it is a barrier to those who would intentionally tender information not sought in an effort to frustrate and prevent criminal prosecution.

Finally, the Court dismissed Zicarelli's claim that he could not be compelled to testify because his testimony would expose him to prosecution under foreign law:

> [W]e agree with the conclusion of the Supreme Court of New Jersey that appellant was never in real danger of being compelled to disclose information that might incriminate him under foreign law. Even if appellant has international Cosa Nostra responsibilities, he could have answered this question truthfully without disclosing them. Should he have found it necessary to qualify his answer by confining it to domestic responsibilities in order to avoid incrimination under foreign law, he could have done so. To have divulged international responsibilities would have been to volunteer information not sought, and apparently not relevant to the Commission's investigation. We think that in the circumstances of the questioning this was clear to appellant and his counsel.

Related Cases

Kastigar v. United States, 406 U.S. 441 (1972)

Bibliography and Further Reading

Brune, Susan E. "The Fifth Amendment and Fear of Foreign Prosecution." *New York Law Journal,* Vol. 219, no. 38, February 27, 1998.

Heller, Gerald W. "Invoking the 5th in Civil Cases: Awareness of Self-Incrimination Risks in Non-Criminal Forums Can Prevent a Waiver of the Privilege." *The National Law Journal,* Vol. 17, no. 23, February 6, 1995.

DOYLE V. OHIO

Legal Citation: 426 U.S. 610 (1976)

Thanks to film and television shows on crime, most people are familiar with the term "Miranda rights." This refers to the case of *Miranda v. Arizona* (1966) in which the rights of a person to due process under the law were established. According to these rights, when an individual is arrested, he must be advised immediately that he has the right to remain silent, that anything he says may be used against him, and that he has a right to legal counsel before answering questions. In the case of *Doyle v. Ohio* and a corresponding case, *Wood v. Ohio*, these rights were under review by the courts.

In Tuscarawas County, Ohio, Jefferson Doyle and Richard Wood were arrested and charged with selling ten pounds of marijuana to a local narcotics bureau informant. Upon arrest, they were both given Miranda warnings and stayed silent after receiving them. However, during their trial, the two men both testified that they had been framed by the narcotics agents. The state's accounts of the transaction differed from the defendants in that the state alleged that the defendants were selling the marijuana to the informant, whereas the defendants alleged that the informant was selling marijuana to the defendants. The defense argued that because there was a limited view of the parking lot where the transaction supposedly took place, the narcotics agents did not actually see the transaction take place. Both stories were plausible, without direct evidence to contradict it.

In both cases, the prosecutor, in order to cast doubt on their testimony, questioned them as to why they did not provide this account at the time of their arrest. Although their defense attorneys objected to the prosecutor's line of questioning, the trial court judge overruled them and Doyle and Wood admitted that they had remained silent. The two men were both convicted in the Common Pleas Court of Tuscarawas County.

Both cases were appealed to the Court of Appeals of the Fifth District, Tuscarawas County on the basis that the trial court should not have allowed the prosecutor's line of questioning. The appeals court agreed with the trial court's decision, noting that the questioning "was not evidence offered by the state in its case . . . as confession by silence or as substantive evidence of guilt but

Petitioner
Jefferson Doyle

Respondent
State of Ohio

Petitioner's Claim
That the prosecutor's use of Doyle's post-arrest silence during his trial for the purpose of casting doubt on Doyle's testimony violated the due process clause of the Fourteenth Amendment.

Chief Lawyer for Petitioner
James R. Willis

Chief Lawyer for Respondent
Ronald L. Collins

Justices for the Court
William J. Brennan, Jr., Warren E. Burger, Thurgood Marshall, Lewis F. Powell, Jr. (writing for the Court), Potter Stewart, Byron R. White

Justices Dissenting
Harry A. Blackmun, William H. Rehnquist, John Paul Stevens

Place
Washington, D.C.

Date of Decision
23 February 1976

Decision
Jefferson Doyle's right to due process was violated when a state prosecutor challenged the validity of his testimony through questions about his post-arrest silence after receiving the Miranda warning.

Significance
A person's right to due process, including the right to remain silent after arrest without later penalty, was preserved in this case.

rather cross examination of a witness as to why he had not told the same story earlier at his first opportunity." The defendants then appealed to the Ohio Supreme Court which refused to review the case further. Finally, the appellants asked the U.S. Supreme Court to review the case, also known as taking the case on *certiorari*.

On 17 June 1976, the Supreme Court reversed the men's convictions and returned the cases to the Ohio State courts for further action. In a 6-3 decision, Justice Powell delivered the opinion for the majority. The relatively brief decision stated that the prosecutor's use of the defendants' silence following their arrest violated their right to due process. The support for this argument was that silence following arrest was only the individual's exercise of their Miranda rights which makes its intent or meaning indefinite. In addition, although the Miranda rights do not say explicitly that

a person's silence will not be penalized later, that assurance is implicit. Because of this, it is a violation of due process to allow the person's silence to be used to question an explanation later offered at the trial. In essence, the Court preserved an individual's right to due process under the law.

Related Cases
Bruno v. United States, 308 U.S. 287 (1939).
Griffin v. California, 380 U.S. 609 (1965).
Miranda v. Arizona, 384 U.S. 436 (1966).
United States v. Hale, 422 U.S. 171 (1975).
Wood v. Ohio, 427 U.S. 610 (1976).

Bibliography and Further Reading
Alschuler, Albert W. "A Peculiar Privilege in Historical Perspective: The Right to Remain Silent." *Michigan Law Review*, August 1996, p. 2625.

GANNETT CO. V. DEPASQUALE

Legal Citation: 443 U.S. 368 (1979)

Petitioner
Gannett Co., Inc.

Respondent
Daniel A. DePasquale, Seneca County Court Judge

Petitioner's Claim
That exclusion of the press from a pretrial hearing was tantamount to denying a public right of access to trials and violated the First, Sixth, and Fourteenth Amendments of the U.S. Constitution.

Chief Lawyer for Petitioner
Robert C. Bernius

Chief Lawyer for Respondent
Bernard Kobroff

Justices for the Court
Warren E. Burger, Lewis F. Powell, Jr., William H. Rehnquist, Potter Stewart (writing for the Court), John Paul Stevens

Justices Dissenting
Harry A. Blackmun, William J. Brennan, Jr., Thurgood Marshall, Byron R. White

Place
Washington, D.C.

Date of Decision
2 July 1979

Decision
Closure of pretrial hearings to journalistic media was held acceptable.

Significance
The essential issue debated in this case was whether public interest in open criminal proceedings should take precedence over individual rights to request temporary suppression of proceedings. The U.S. Supreme Court upheld the lower court's decision to close the pretrial hearing, and found that unrestricted access to trials was not, as claimed by the petitioner, a provision of the First, Sixth and Fourteenth Amendments. They ruled the Sixth Amendment provides a measure of common law that permits open court proceedings in the interest of defendants' rights, but does not extend to provide an unrestricted right to access by journalistic media or public scrutiny.

After fishing in Seneca Lake near Rochester, New York, 42 year-old Wayne Clapp never returned home. A publisher of the two Rochester newspapers, Gannett Co., Inc., assigned a reporter to follow the police investigation and subsequent capture of two suspects: Greathouse and Jones. Reports and articles described the circumstances of Clapp's disappearance—three men were seen on the lake; a few witnesses testified to "having heard five or six shots;" and, after an examination of Clapp's boat, the police theorized his death was violent. Police arrested the suspects in Jackson County, Michigan, after they noticed a truck matching the description of Clapp's stolen vehicle parked at a local motel. At the time of his arrest, Greathouse revealed to the police where he had hidden Clapp's revolver; police also found matching ammunition at the motel.

News stories reported that the case would be prosecuted even though a body was not found. Although police found incriminating evidence in the possession of the suspects that included Clapp's 357 Magnum revolver, credit card, and truck, police could not find the body. During the three months before their pretrial hearing, the suspects tried to suppress statements given to the police. They alleged that statements were given involuntarily, primarily with respect to admissions regarding the gun and the subsequent entry of the gun as physical evidence. In the time that ensued, newspapers continued covering details of the arraignments, reported the indictment of the suspects by the Seneca County grand jury, and reported the "not guilty" plea entered by both men.

Motions to suppress reporting of the pretrial hearing were presented to Judge DePasquale. Defense attorneys felt exclusion of the public and press from the hearing was warranted because media coverage had been quite extensive; they considered that "adverse publicity" could diminish their clients' right to have a fair trial. The district attorney concurred with their request and the presiding judge granted an exclusionary order which permitted a closed, pretrial hearing.

Although in attendance at the proceedings, a reporter for Gannett Co. failed to voice objections to the ruling. The day after the hearing, she submitted a letter that demanded permission for the press to cover

Guarantee to a Public Trial

The Sixth Amendment guarantees that "in all criminal prosecutions, the accused shall enjoy the right to a speedy and public trial." The difficulty for courts has been with balancing the requirements of the Sixth Amendment with the First Amendment—ensuring that the rights of the defendant are protected and that the rights of the press are equally protected.

As British novelist Arnold Bennett once noted, "The price of justice is eternal publicity." At one point, it appeared that the Court disagreed with this notion.

Yet, more recently the Court has come to the view that both the press and the public are both equally entitled to a public trial, even at the expense of the defendant's wishes. In the groundbreaking decision, *Chandler v. Florida*, the Court ruled that television cameras could be placed in the courtroom, even if the defendant felt it intruded upon his right to a fair trial.

Source(s): *Congressional Quarterly's Guide to the Supreme Court*, Vol. 1. Washington, D.C.: Congressional Quarterly, Inc., 1997.

---

the pretrial hearing. Gannett Co., the reporter's publisher, subsequently petitioned for abrogation of the exclusionary order; however, Judge DePasquale denied the motion simply noting that "the suppression [of the] hearing had concluded and that any decision on immediate release of the transcript had been reserved." He further stated that there existed no constitutional right of the press to attend a court trial and report about the evidence presented. Further, he found that granting the defendants a closed hearing provided a significant safeguard against negative public reaction that could influence the impending trial.

Gannet Co. challenged DePasquale's ruling before the Appellate Division of the New York Supreme Court. Their petition considered the exclusion of the public as violation of the provision for a public trial as guaranteed by the First, Sixth, and Fourteenth Amendments. The Appellate Division found DePasquale's order unlawful believing that the lower court's decision denied the "public's vital interest in open judicial proceedings." On appeal to the New York Court of Appeals, however, Judge DePasquale's decision was upheld. The Court of Appeals pointed out that because the defendants pleaded "guilty to lesser included offenses," that a "transcript of the suppression hearing was made available to petitioner." The higher court seemed to suggest the issue was therefore rendered moot.

In contrast to the decision of the appellate division, the U.S. Supreme Court majority decision held that under the Constitution there was no "affirmative right of access to the pretrial proceeding" and confirmed Judge DePasquale's original ruling. First, they reasoned that a trial judge had the right to bar public scrutiny that might negatively influence court proceedings or jeopardize the right of due process for the accused. The Court reasoned that unrestrained media reporting may, at times, adversely shape public opinion and therefore threaten to render a jury unreliable or prejudiced by misinformed opinion. As such, Judge DePasquale's ruling, supported by both defense and prosecuting attorneys,

seemed to appropriately exclude the public *vis-a-vis* journalistic coverage in the interest of fairness and to avoid "effects of prejudicial pretrial publicity." The U.S. Supreme Court went on to explain that the right to a public trial under the Sixth Amendment "is for the protection of all persons accused of crime" and that openness of criminal trials did not entitle the public and press to unrestricted access to courtrooms. Justices pointed out that the public desire to be informed about the proceedings of trials must be balanced with "other constitutional guarantees extended to the accused as well." The Court did not underestimate the social interest served by media coverage of court proceedings, but they held that none of the petitioner's rights were infringed upon under the Sixth Amendment. The majority opinion further pointed out that although history showed that the Sixth Amendment presumes the "common-law rule of open civil and criminal proceedings," that did not necessarily mean that trials could not be closed from the public to ensure fairness of process. If, as in the case presided over by Judge DePasquale, all participants agreed to have a closed hearing for "efficient administration of justice," press members have no right to demand access for the purpose of public scrutiny. Neither did the Court find evidence of constitutional violations under the First and Fourteenth Amendment. The petitioner's reporter attended the hearing but made no objection to the judge's decision at that time. Moreover, denial of information about the pretrial hearing was only temporary since transcripts were later made available after the risks of prejudicial danger had expired. Finally, the U.S. Supreme Court's decision denied the validity of the petitioner's claim because the Court was not asked to evaluate the importance of social desirability for open trials. Instead, the issue at stake was whether barring the petitioner from a pretrial hearing was unconstitutional if all participants in the litigation had agreed to a closed proceeding. In that respect, the Court found that respecting the due process rights of the defendants outweighed the right of public access to judicial proceedings.

In principle, Chief Justice Burger, Justice Powell, and Justice Rehnquist agreed with the Court's majority opinion but all chose to deliver separate, concurring opinions. Notwithstanding a public interest to attend court proceedings, Burger noted that "interest alone does not create a constitutional right." Justice Powell further pointed out that the "right of access to [the] courtroom is not absolute" because there existed a possibility that press reports could stir up wrongful and deceptive public opinion and thus inappropriately prejudice a jury. Powell also pointed out that because the two defendants were so young, press coverage of the case was greatly extended and, in fact, represented a credible threat to their right to have fair trial. Justice Rehnquist further held that courts could exercise a perfectly acceptable practice by freely determining "whether to open or close the proceeding."

Conversely, dissenting justices agreed that there were no significant reasons to justify the exclusion of publicity for pretrial hearings. The minority view was that press reports of the defendant's trial presented a factual, objective review of events; neither did the minority opinion believe that public opinion necessarily manifested danger to fair judicial proceedings. They explained that Sixth Amendment constraints to have open trials should be considered as a "restraint on possible abuse of judicial power." Thus, they emphasized the need to allow public presence in courtrooms because, historically, the public interest serves as a safeguard in the administration of justice. They further opined that Sixth Amendment rights did not enable defendants to have "private" court proceedings if they waived their Sixth Amendment rights to have open public trials. Instead, they felt that public trials increase "effectiveness of the trial process" by scrutinizing the system of justice applied in a courtroom. Moreover, before excluding public scrutiny of a trial, substantial proof must be provided to show that public conduct could "irreparably damage fair trial right" and that other alternatives could not protect defendant's due process rights. The minority opinion felt that to exclude public access to a pretrial hearing, the court and trial participants must provide precise reasons that "demonstrate inescapable necessity for closure of proceedings."

Impact

In a close, 5-4 decision, the U.S. Supreme Court ruled that trial judges could close criminal proceedings despite an apparently conflicting public interest and right to have open access to courtrooms. Although dissenting justices provided convincing rationale to support the petitioner's claim that media publishers do indeed represent a viable public right, the Court held that, in order to have fair, lawful proceedings, lower courts could close trials. The rights of defendants under due process took precedence over public access. The Sixth Amendment right to a public trial was designed to protect defendants and enable them to enjoy benefits of public presence. The Court found it acceptable, therefore, that Judge DePasquale ruled to grant defendants a closed pretrial hearing in order to avoid prejudicial influence of press and public. All participants at court agreed to a closed hearing, and a transcript from the pretrial hearing was soon delivered to the press after the hearing. Thus, the U.S Supreme Court found no constitutional public (or journalistic media) right to attend criminal trials. The interests of justice to provide fair, impartial trials to defendants prevailed over the social, public interest to have unrestricted access to trials.

Related Cases

Estes v. Texas, 381 U.S. 532 (1965).
Sheppard v. Maxwell, 384 U.S. 333 (1966).
Nebraska Press Assn. v. Stuart, 427 U.S. 539 (1976).
United States v. Cianfrani, 573 F.2d 835 (1978).
Richmond Newspapers Inc. v. Virginia, 448 U.S. 555 (1980).
Press-Enterprise Co. v. Superior Court, 464 U.S. 501 (1984).

Bibliography and Further Reading

Lassiter, Christo. "TV or Not TV—That is the Question." *Journal of Criminal Law and Criminology,* spring 1996, p. 928.

LIDB Online (Louisiana Indigent Defender Board Online Information Center) "Controlling Prejudicial Publicity." *JLAMANUAL,* 1997. http://www.lidb.com/manuals/jlamanua.htm

WALLER V. GEORGIA

Legal Citation: 467 U.S. 39 (1984)

Petitioner
Guy Waller

Respondent
State of Georgia

Petitioner's Claim
That the state's closure of a hearing to the public constituted a violation of the right to a public trial guaranteed under the Sixth and Fourteenth Amendments.

Chief Lawyer for Petitioner
Herbert Shafer

Chief Lawyer for Respondent
Mary Beth Westmoreland, Assistant Attorney General of Georgia

Justices for the Court
Harry A. Blackmun, William J. Brennan, Jr., Warren E. Burger, Thurgood Marshall, Sandra Day O'Connor, Lewis F. Powell, Jr. (writing for the Court), William H. Rehnquist, John Paul Stevens, Byron R. White

Justices Dissenting
None

Place
Washington, D.C.

Date of Decision
21 May 1984

Decision
That the conditions of the hearing closure failed justification under a set of tests developed in *Press-Enterprise Co. v. Superior Court of California* (1984); and that the closure would not withstand Sixth Amendment scrutiny.

Significance
On one level, *Waller v. Georgia* involved Sixth Amendment issues. However, as Justice Powell stated in the unanimous opinion, the Court had "not recently" considered a Sixth Amendment case, and instead it turned to recent rulings with regard to reporting of trial proceedings—a concern more properly addressed under the First Amendment. *Waller* thus further established and solidified the tests developed by the Court earlier in the 1984 term, in its *Press-Enterprise Co. v. Superior Court of California* decision. The latter defined the limits of the government's power to suppress trial proceedings on the one hand, and of the public's right to know on the other. Both cases belonged to a larger trend in the 1980s toward allowing the public as much knowledge of trial proceedings as was constitutionally possible.

Seven Days' Suppression for Two-and-a-Half Hours of Evidence

In the latter half of 1981, Georgia police began tapping the phones of individuals they suspected of involvement in an illegal lottery operation. This was long before that state had a legal, state-run lottery, and the particular scheme operated by the individuals in this case involved gambling on the volume of stocks and bonds traded on the New York Stock Exchange. In early January of 1982, state law enforcement officials executed search warrants simultaneously at a number of locations, including the homes of the individuals who would become the petitioners in *Waller v. Georgia*. Along with 35 others, these individuals were indicted and charged under the Georgia Racketeer Influenced and Corrupt Organizations (Georgia RICO) Act of 1982, as well as under Georgia statutes regarding illegal gambling.

Before the trial, the petitioners, who were set to be tried separately in a series of cases that involved 13 other defendants, moved to suppress the police wiretaps and other evidence seized during the searches. The reason for this was that the warrants authorizing the wiretaps were not supported by probable cause, normally required by police to conduct such surveillance, and were based instead on vague and overly general information. Furthermore, the petitioners held that these taps were not conducted under appropriate supervision, and that the searches following them were indiscriminate, as well as "exploratory and general." The state of Georgia then moved to close the hearing on the motion to suppress, meaning that the public would not be able to witness the proceedings. In its closure motion, the state held that in order to justify its seizure of evidence derived from the wiretaps, it would have to introduce evidence which could infringe on the privacy of individuals other than the defendants.

The state made its reasoning more clear when on 21 June 1982, the court—having impaneled and then excused a jury—heard the closure and suppression motions. Under the Georgia wiretap statute, the state's attorney argued any use of information that was not "necessary and essential" would constitute inadmissible evidence. More specifically, the wiretaps would "involve" individuals already indicted but not on trial

Surveillance

Electronic surveillance includes the secret monitoring of people and places while using devices such as cameras, tape recorders, video recorders, and wiretaps. State and federal investigators use this equipment to gather evidence on suspected criminals or criminal activity. The three main types of electronic surveillance are wiretapping, bugging, and videotaping. Wiretaps intercept telephone calls by directly tapping into telephone lines, while bugs transmit telephone conversations to investigators after being hidden in a suspected place of criminal activity. Video surveillance equipment records and/or submits recorded images after video cameras are set up in a suspected place of criminal activity.

Investigators must, however, respect the right of people under the Fourth Amendment to secure themselves and their property against unreasonable searches and seizures. The Fourth Amendment also prohibits judges from issuing warrants without probable cause. Although the Supreme Court held in 1928 that electronic surveillance techniques such as wiretapping did not constitute a search and seizure, the Court ruled in 1967 that electronic surveillance did constitute a search and seizure and therefore it requires a warrant to be constitutional.

Source(s): *West's Encyclopedia of American Law.* St. Paul, MN: West Publishing, 1998.

at that point, as well as others who had not been indicted at all. The state's purpose was not to protect the indicted individuals' right to a fair trial, or the unindicted persons' right to privacy; rather, Georgia's prosecutor noted that the presentation of these wiretaps in open court would cause the evidence to be "tainted," and thus unavailable for use in future prosecution cases. The trial court agreed and, over objection from the petitioners, ordered the suppression hearing closed to persons other than the parties involved, the lawyers, court personnel, and witnesses.

The hearings that followed lasted seven days, but less than two-and-a-half hours of that time was devoted to playing the tapes of intercepted phone conversations. As it turned out, the voices recorded on the tapes included those of some who were not then on trial, but had been indicted. Though a single unindicted individual was mentioned by the others in one phone call, there was no one not currently under indictment. Throughout the remainder of the trial, the court's attention was directed to an examination of the procedures used to obtain and execute the search warrants and wiretap authorizations, as well as those used in preserving the tape recordings, and to the petitioners' allegations of misconduct on the part of police and prosecutors. All of these proceedings could, therefore, have been attended by the public without impinging on the matter addressed with regard to the tapes and the various indicted and unindicted individuals included on them. The court having agreed with the state's admission that ten boxes of papers it had seized during the searches were personal in nature, and unrelated to the crime in question, it ordered them suppressed, but refused to suppress other files.

Following trial by jury in an open court, the petitioners were acquitted of charges under the Georgia

RICO statute, but not the charges of commercial gambling and communicating gambling information. Just before the trial of the other indicted individuals, the court released the transcript of the suppression hearing to the public.

On appeal to the Georgia Supreme Court, the convictions were upheld in 1983. With regard to the issue of an open trial, that court ruled that the trial court had properly balanced rights under Georgia law and the Sixth Amendment—the right to a fair trial on the one hand, and the right to privacy on the other. The petitioners then took the case to the U.S. Supreme Court, at which time briefs of *amici curiae* urging affirmance were filed by the U.S. solicitor general, the Arizona attorney general, and individuals representing Americans for Effective Law Enforcement, Inc., et al.

The Presumption of Openness

A unanimous Court reversed the ruling of the lower court. Justice Powell, who delivered the opinion, first identified a series of tests for justifying closure of a suppression hearing. The tests, derived from the Sixth Amendment and the Court's *Press-Enterprise Co. v. Superior Court of California* ruling earlier in the 1984 term, included the following:

> the party seeking to close the hearing must advance an overriding interest that is likely to be prejudiced; the closure must be no broader than necessary to protect that interest; the trial court must consider reasonable alternatives to closing the hearing; and it must make findings adequate to support the cause.

Press-Enterprise, of course, addressed First Amendment, not Sixth Amendment concerns, and Powell noted this fact. "Nevertheless," he wrote, "there can be little doubt that the explicit Sixth Amendment right of the accused is no less protective of a public trial than the implicit First Amendment right of the press and public." In essence, Justice Powell noted, a public trial keeps everyone honest: it helps to ensure that judge and prosecutor undertake their duties as prescribed by law, it encourages witnesses to come forward, and it discourages the latter from perjury—presumably because it is easier to advance a falsehood in front of a small group of people than a large one. "These aims and interests," Powell wrote, "are no less pressing in a hearing to suppress wrongfully seized evidence."

Addressing the question of whether Georgia had met these criteria, the Court found that it had not. The state had not been specific enough in its proffer with regard to

> whose privacy interests might be infringed if the hearing were open to the public, what portions of the wiretap tapes might infringe those interests, and what portion of the evidence consisted of the tapes.

Due to the state's failure to answer those specifics, the findings of the trial court were "broad and general," and did not support the move to close the entire hearing. Clearly, as Justice Powell noted, "the closure was far more extensive than necessary," given the fact that "The tapes lasted only 2 1/2 hours of the seven-day hearing, and few of them mentioned or involved parties not then before the court." Furthermore, the court had not considered alternatives to closure.

Thus the Court reversed the lower court's judgment, and the only remaining issue to be addressed was where to go from there with regard to the case at hand. The petitioners had asked for a new trial on the merits, but the Court did not think this necessary. "If, after a new suppression hearing, essentially the same evidence is suppressed," Powell wrote, "a new trial presumably would be a windfall for the defendant, and not in the public interest." Unless "a new, public suppression hearing results in the suppression of material evidence not suppressed at the first trial," the Court concluded, "or in some other material change in the positions of parties," a new trial did not need to be held.

Impact

On its own, the impact of *Waller v. Georgia* was slight. An informal review of Supreme Court cases over a

period of nearly 15 years following the Court's 1984 decision, for instance, found only five cases that referred to *Waller* specifically. Considered as part of a larger trend, however, the results of *Waller* were powerful indeed. This trend relates at least as much to the First Amendment as to the Sixth: together with *Press-Enterprise* and the earlier cases of *Gannett Co. v. DePasquale* (1979), *Richmond Newspapers, Inc. v. Virginia* (1980), and *Globe Newspaper Co. v. Superior Court for the County of Norfolk* (1982), it helped to usher in an era of increased public awareness of trial proceedings. The introduction of cameras into the courtroom, which materially increased this awareness manifold, helped enhance public interest in the 1995 trial of O. J. Simpson and other legal actions. This in turn spawned a veritable industry of "courtroom entertainment" in the 1990s, symbolized by the creation of the Court TV network, which put a new spin on the idea of a "public trial" by broadcasting courtroom proceedings to millions of homes.

Related Cases

Gannett Co. v. DePasquale, 443 U.S. 368 (1979).
Richmond Newspapers, Inc. v. Virginia, 448 U.S. 555 (1980).
Globe Newspaper Co. v. Superior Court for the County of Norfolk, 457 U.S. 596 (1982).
Press-Enterprise Co. v. Superior Court of California, 464 U.S. 501 (1984).
Press-Enterprise Co. v. Superior Court of California, 478 U.S. 1 (1986).

Bibliography and Further Reading

Biskupic, Joan, and Elder Witt. *Guide to the U.S. Supreme Court,* 3rd ed. Washington, DC: Congressional Quarterly Inc., 1997.

Hall, Kermit L., ed. *The Oxford Companion to the Supreme Court of the United States.* New York: Oxford University Press, 1992

"Sixth Amendment—Public Trial Guarantee Applies to Pretrial Suppression Hearings—*Waller v. Georgia.*" *The Journal of Criminal Law & Criminology,* Vol. 75, fall 1984, pp. 802–812.

Witt, Elder. *Congressional Quarterly's Guide to the Supreme Court,* 2nd ed. Washington, DC: Congressional Quarterly Inc., 1990.

NIX V. WHITESIDE

Legal Citation: 475 U.S. 157 (1984)

Petitioner
Crispus Nix, Warden

Respondent
Emanuel Charles Whiteside

Petitioner's Claim
That even though Emanuel Whiteside's attorney dissuaded him from giving false testimony and warned him that he would withdraw if Whiteside insisted on perjuring, Whiteside nonetheless received a fair trial and effective legal representation, suffering no violation of his the Sixth Amendment right to counsel.

Chief Lawyer for Petitioner
Brent R. Appel

Chief Lawyer for Respondent
Patrick Reilly Grady

Justices for the Court
Harry A. Blackmun, William J. Brennan, Jr., Warren E. Burger (writing for the Court), Thurgood Marshall, Sandra Day O'Connor, Lewis F. Powell, Jr., William H. Rehnquist, John Paul Stevens, Byron R. White.

Justices Dissenting
None

Place
Washington, D.C.

Date of Decision
26 February 1986

Decision
The Court ruled that Whiteside's lawyer did not violate Whiteside's Sixth Amendment right to counsel by refusing to allow him to present perjured testimony.

Significance
In conjunction with *Strickland v. Washington* and *Harris v. New York*, this case determined and emphasized that the right to effective counsel guaranteed by the Sixth Amendment does not force an attorney to assist a client in perjury. In fact, the codes of ethics adopted by states and legal associations prohibit such conduct and require attorneys to make a full disclosure when a client threatens or actually has committed perjury. The decision sent a clear message to attorneys that they must take appropriate action if clients intend to or do commit perjury and to the accused that the right to effective counsel does not include the right to perjure.

Overview

The Sixth Amendment protects the rights of the accused by allowing everyone the right to legal representation at trial. However, this amendment does not specify exactly how an attorney must provide effective counsel. Consequently, when Emanuel Whiteside faced murder charges, he tried to present a fabricated account of the events or perjure as part of his defense, he expected his lawyer to assist him in presenting the kind of defense he wanted. However, the attorney refused and warned Whiteside not to present false testimony at trial. Whiteside agreed and was convicted of second-degree murder. Afterwards, Whiteside began to protest, arguing that his right to effective counsel had been violated. Whiteside petitioned courts in Iowa to hear his case, which several courts denied, but the U.S. Court of Appeals for the Eighth District sided with Whiteside. However, the U.S. Supreme Court reached a unanimous decision to reverse the ruling by the court of appeals.

Whiteside's Crime and Defense

The crime occurred on 8 February 1977 in Iowa, when Whiteside and two friends stopped by Calvin Love's residence to purchase marijuana. When they arrived, Love was sleeping and an argument between Whiteside and Love broke out over the marijuana. Throughout the course of the argument, Love asked his girlfriend to get his "piece" or gun and began reaching under his pillow at another point. Whiteside saw Love reaching under the pillow and fatally stabbed him.

Confronted with murder charges, Whiteside objected to his first appointed lawyer, because he had been a prosecutor. Gary L. Robinson was assigned to defend Whiteside and questioned him about the incident. Whiteside said that he stabbed Love because he saw him, "pulling a pistol from underneath the pillow on the bed." However, when Robinson questioned this statement, Whiteside admitted that he had not actually seen a gun, but that he was sure Love was retrieving a pistol when he was slain. Despite Whiteside's insistence that Love had a gun, no police evidence supported his claim. The police searched Love's apartment after the murder, but found no gun. Furthermore, Robinson learned from interviewing Whiteside's com-

Federal District Court

The country's court system includes a state and local court system as well as a federal court system. The federal district court is the first of three levels in the federal system, which also includes U.S. court of appeals and the U.S. Supreme Court. Federal cases begin at the district level, where they are heard and decided. If a party disagrees with the ruling by a federal district court, it can petition the federal court of appeals and if still dissatisfied the party can petition the Supreme Court.

All district court judges receive life appointments by the president with approval from the Senate, except for territorial courts. Congress determines the number of judges per district based on caseloads. In the late 1990s, there were 646 district court judges serving the country's 94 district courts.

Source(s): The Federal Judiciary Home Page.
http://www.uscourts.gov.

panions who accompanied him that they had not seen a gun either.

Therefore, Robinson advised Whiteside not to testify that he had actually seen a gun, because he could make a self-defense argument based solely on the reasonable belief that Love was getting a gun. Although Whiteside repeatedly said he had not seen a gun, about a week before his trial he told Robinson that he had seen Love holding a "metallic" object. Robinson questioned the statement and Whiteside replied that "in Howard Cook's case there was a gun" and said "If I don't say I saw a gun, I'm dead." Robinson once again assured him that seeing a gun was not necessary for his defense and warned him that giving a false statement constituted perjury. Robinson also informed Whiteside that he would withdraw from the case if he insisted on giving false testimony.

At the trial, Whiteside testified that he knew Love had a gun, which he was trying to get at the time of the stabbing, and that he stabbed Love quickly in self-defense. During cross examination, Whiteside conceded that he had not seen a gun, however. But Robinson presented evidence to demonstrate Whiteside had strong reason to believe Love had a gun and was getting it at the time of the stabbing. Robinson argued that Love carried a sawed-off shotgun at other times, that the police search of Love's place may not have been thorough enough, and that Love's family removed all of his belongings immediately after the police search.

Nonetheless, a jury convicted Whiteside of second-degree murder, so Whiteside filed a motion for a new trial, arguing that Robinson prevented him from having a fair trial because he warned him not to say he saw a gun or something "metallic." The trial court heard statements by both Whiteside and Robinson and decided to deny Whiteside a new trial, holding that the facts of the case corresponded to Robinson's account. The Supreme Court of Iowa upheld Whiteside's conviction, noting that the right to effective counsel did not mean the right to an attorney who would assist in presenting perjured testimony.

Whiteside did not give up, however, and filed for a writ of *habeas corpus*—a legal document granting relief from improper imprisonment—from the U.S. District Court for the Southern District of Iowa. The district court denied Whiteside the writ, agreeing with the trial court that the accused have no right to present a perjured defense. However, the U.S. Court of Appeals for the Eighth Circuit reversed the district court's decision, granting Whiteside a writ of *habeas corpus*. Though court of appeals agreed with the other courts that Robinson had strong reason to believe Whiteside would commit perjury and that Whiteside has no constitutional right to give false testimony, it argued that since Robinson threatened to inform the court of Whiteside's intention to commit perjury and withdraw his services, he failed to preserve the confidence of his client. The court of appeals felt that by having intent to testify falsely, Whiteside did not forfeit his right to effective counsel.

A Unanimous Decision

However, Warden Crispus Nix and the Iowa correctional system petitioned the U.S. Supreme Court to hear the case, maintaining that Whiteside received a fair trial and effective legal counsel and was convicted through a fair legal process. The Court set out on 5 November 1985 to determine if Robinson's conduct violated Whiteside's Sixth Amendment right to fair and effective legal representation. The Court examined the decision in *Strickland v. Washington* (1984) where it laid down a number guidelines for judging the appropriateness of defense attorney conduct for cases of alleged Sixth Amendment rights violations. Writing for the majority, Justice Burger noted that the Court called for defense attorneys' "duty of loyalty" and "overarching duty to advocate the defendant's cause" but not for attorneys to aid in testifying falsely or any activity that obstructs the truth.

Furthermore, the American Bar Association's Code of Ethics also prohibits such conduct, demanding that the attorney "must . . . observe and advise his client to observe the statute law." Although attorneys maintain a policy of confidentiality with their clients under the American Bar Association, they cannot uphold this policy when clients inform them of their intentions to commit a crime, including presenting perjured testimony. The Iowa Code of Professional Responsibility for Lawyers also allows an exception to attorney/client confidentiality for cases where clients have committed or announce their intentions to commit crimes. Moreover, the Iowa code not only gives attorneys the option of revealing that their clients plan to commit perjury, it requires that they reveal this information. Justice Burger also pointed out that Robinson could have faced felony charges and disbarment for aiding in Whiteside's false testimony, if he passively allowed Whiteside to offer it.

Given these standards of the American Bar Association and the state of Iowa, the Court concluded that Robinson's conduct clearly remained consistent with commonly held ethical practices of lawyers and that his conduct in no way violated Whiteside's right to effective counsel. The Court argued that Robinson's conduct did not deprive Whiteside of due process of law or effective counsel as the court of appeals maintained. Instead, the Court held that at most Robinson deprived Whiteside of an opportunity to present perjured testimony, but nothing to undermine Whiteside's argument that he believed Love owned a gun and was reaching for one when the stabbing occurred. The Court reiterated that no one has a constitutional right to testify falsely and that no Supreme Court case set a precedent for such a right or expectation.

Although all the justices agreed that Whiteside failed to demonstrate a constitutional violation or an ethical violation by Robinson under *Strickland v. Washington,* some disagreed with the Court's stance on ethical conduct by lawyers. Justice Brennan argued that "the Court cannot tell the states or the lawyers in the states how to behave in their courts, unless and until federal rights are violated." Justice Blackmun, joined by Justices Brennan, Marshall, and Stevens also balked at the Court's adoption of a code of ethics for lawyers, maintaining that the states have that responsibility, not the federal government.

> Whiteside's attorney treated Whiteside's proposed perjury in accord with professional standards, and since Whiteside's truthful testimony could not have prejudiced the result of his trial, the Court of Appeals was in error to direct the issuance of a writ of *habeas corpus* and must be reversed.

Related Cases
Harris v. New York, 401 U.S. 222 (1971).
Wilcox v. Johnson, 555 F. 2d 115 (1977).
Strickland v. Washington, 466 U.S. 668 (1984).

Bibliography and Further Reading
Hirsch, Alan. "The Gladiators of the Courtroom." *Washington Times,* January 31, 1997, p. A19.

Pope, Daniel J., and Stephanie J. Kim. "Client Perjury: Should a Lawyer Defend the System or the Client?" *Defense Counsel Journal,* July 1997, p. 447.

UNITED STATES V. SCHEFFER

Legal Citation: 118 S.Ct. 1261 (1998)

The *United States v. Scheffer* ruling came, as legal writer Joan Biskupic noted in the *Washington Post,* "at a time when [polygraph] machines are increasingly being used outside the courtroom"—and inside as well. Prosecutors were using polygraph results "to extract confessions from suspects," Biskupic observed, and defense lawyers were using "them for leverage in plea bargains"; likewise polygraph tests were being subjected to greater and greater use in the workplace. Employers were using them to test job applicants with regard to past wrongdoing, and to monitor present jobholders as well. While the latter practice might raise Fourth Amendment questions of its own, the use of polygraph results in the courtroom had become a battleground for opposing factions of evidentiary experts.

Airman Scheffer Claims "Innocent Ingestion"

In March of 1992, when he volunteered to work as an informant with the Air Force Office of Special Investigations (OSI), Edward Scheffer was serving as an airman at March Air Force Base in California. At that time he was advised of the fact that the OSI would require him to submit to periodic drug testing and polygraph examinations to ensure that he remained drug-free in spite of the repeated exposure to drugs that his undercover work would entail. Accordingly, he was given a urinalysis test in early April, and soon afterward—before the results of his urinalysis were known—he was administered a polygraph examination. In the latter test, the OSI examiner asked Scheffer three relevant questions: (1) "Since you've been in the [Air Force], have you used any illegal drugs?"; (2) "Have you lied about any of the drug information you've given OSI?"; and (3) "Besides your parents, have you told anyone you're assisting OSI?" Scheffer answered "No" to each of these, and in the opinion of the OSI examiner, who evaluated his polygraph test, his pulse rate while answering these questions "indicated [that] no deception" was taking place.

But starting on 30 April 1992, a bizarre series of events began to unfold. Scheffer failed to show up for work, and could not be found anywhere on the air base. In an ordinary context, this would undoubtedly have

Petitioner
United States

Respondent
Edward Scheffer

Petitioner's Claim
That *per se* exclusion of polygraph evidence offered by the accused in a military court does not violate the Sixth Amendment right to present a defense.

Chief Lawyer for Petitioner
Michael D. Dreeben

Chief Lawyer for Respondent
Kim L. Sheffield

Justices for the Court
Stephen Breyer, Ruth Bader Ginsburg, Anthony M. Kennedy, Sandra Day O'Connor, William H. Rehnquist, Antonin Scalia, David H. Souter, Clarence Thomas (writing for the Court)

Justices Dissenting
John Paul Stevens

Place
Washington, D.C.

Date of Decision
31 March 1998

Decision
That Military Rule of Evidence 707, which makes polygraph evidence inadmissible in court-martial proceedings, does not unconstitutionally abridge the right of accused members of the military to present a defense.

Significance
This case marked the first occasion on which the Supreme Court issued a ruling with regard to the highly controversial matter of polygraph, or "lie-detector," testing.

gotten him fired, but due to the fact that he was an enlisted member of the U.S. armed forces, Scheffer's disappearance had considerably more severe consequences. He remained AWOL (absent without leave) until 13 May when he turned up in Iowa, nearly 2,000 miles away from the California air base. An Iowa state patrolman, making a routine traffic stop, became aware of the fact that Scheffer was an AWOL serviceman, and arrested him. Meanwhile, OSI agents learned that Scheffer's urinalysis had rendered a positive result for the presence of methamphetamine—this despite the fact that his polygraph tests seemed to indicate that he was not lying when he said he had used no illegal drugs. Scheffer was subjected to a general court-martial on four charges, including an unrelated matter involving his issuance of 17 bad checks. The facts relevant to the case that brought him before the Supreme Court included charges of using methamphetamine, an illegal stimulant consumed recreationally; failure to report for duty; and wrongfully absenting himself from his place of duty for 13 days.

At his trial, Scheffer claimed that he had been in the process of investigating two civilians allegedly selling drugs, a fact of which he had made the OSI investigators aware just before they administered the urine and polygraph tests. He testified that, in the course of his undercover work, he had visited the home of one of the civilians under suspicion. After leaving the residence of the alleged drug dealer, he indicated, he had lost all memory for some time. Thus he claimed "innocent ingestion," holding that he had unwittingly ingested drugs, which his host (or some other guest at the home of the alleged dealer) had presumably slipped into a drink or otherwise secreted into his bloodstream. The prosecution said of Scheffer, "He lies. He is a liar. He lies at every opportunity he gets and he has no credibility. He knowingly used methamphetamine, and he is guilty . . ." To counter these claims, and to prove his innocence, Scheffer sought to introduce the exculpatory results of the earlier polygraph examination.

But the military judge refused to allow that evidence before the court, citing Military Rule of Evidence 707, which states in part that "Notwithstanding other provisions of law, the results of a polygraph examination, the opinion of a polygraph examiner, or any reference to an offer to take, failure to take, or taking of a polygraph examination, shall not be admitted into evidence." Thus use of polygraph evidence was denied not only in situations where such evidence would serve to exonerate the accused, but likewise in situations where it would serve the government's case. The military judge cited three reasons to support the constitutionality of his ruling: that "the President may, through the Rules of Evidence, determine that credibility is not an area in which a factfinder needs help"; that "the polygraph is not a process that has sufficient scientific acceptability to be relevant"; and that disputes over the relevance or reliability of a polygraph test would take up "an inordinate amount of time and expense."

The military court found Scheffer guilty, and sentenced him to a bad-conduct discharge, as well as 30 months' imprisonment, forfeiture of all pay and allowances, and reduction to the lowest enlisted grade. On appeal, the sentence was reversed by a 3-2 vote of the U.S. Court of Appeals for the Armed Forces. The majority held that *per se* exclusion of polygraph results violates the Sixth Amendment right to a legal defense, though it did not cite specific language in the amendment.

A Question of Legitimate Interests

Justice Thomas's opinion stated that "legitimate interests" were served by excluding polygraph evidence—namely that "there is simply no consensus that polygraph evidence is reliable." He offered two other "legitimate interests" ("the jury's core function of making credibility determinations in criminal trials" and "avoiding litigation over issues other than the guilt or innocence of the accused"). Thomas was joined by a plurality.

These "legitimate interests" were essentially those cited by the military judge in the court-martial, whose ruling the Court upheld inasmuch as it reversed the decision of the appeals court. In presenting his response to the three "legitimate interest" questions, Justice Thomas noted that "A defendant's right to present relevant evidence is subject to reasonable restrictions to accommodate other legitimate interests in the criminal trial process." For this reason, there are rules governing the introduction or exclusion of evidence, and as long as they cannot be deemed "arbitrary" or "disproportionate to the purposes they are designed to serve," they do not infringe on the defendant's Sixth Amendment rights. Only when a rule excluding evidence denies "a weighty interest of the accused," Justice Thomas wrote, can it be considered arbitrary or disproportionate. In the present instance, Rule 707 "serves the legitimate interest of ensuring that only reliable evidence is introduced." Justice Thomas then cited the great body of literature which questions the validity of polygraph results, as well as the view that, unlike other expert witnesses, a polygraph examiner in effect supplants the jury by offering simply one more opinion. Addressing the third "legitimate interest," he mentioned some of the ancillary (and time-consuming) disputes that would inevitably arise if polygraph evidence were allowed into the courtroom.

"A Serious Undervaluation" of Constitutional Rights

Justice Kennedy, joined by Justices Breyer, Ginsburg, and O'Connor, filed an opinion concurring in part and concurring in the judgment. In Justice Kennedy's view, only one of the three "legitimate interests" cited—that of strongly differing views regarding the validity of polygraph examinations—was necessary to invalidate the introduction of such evidence to a courtroom. As for the second "legitimate interest," the view that the use of polygraph evidence diminished the jury's role in determining the credibility of the accused, Justice Kennedy wrote that "With all respect . . . it seems the principal opinion overreaches when it rests its holding on [this] additional ground." To prevent the jury from hearing "a conclusion about the ultimate issue at trial" was, Justice Kennedy held, a "tired argument," and one which demeaned jurors. This was particularly so, he noted, quoting the military's court-martial manual, due to "The statutory qualifications for military court members [which] reduce the risk that . . . [jurors] will be unduly influenced by the presentation of ultimate opinion testimony from psychiatric experts."

Justice Stevens filed a dissenting opinion, in which he attacked the Court's ruling as a "serious undervaluation of the importance of the citizen's constitutional right to present a defense." He stated that rather than approaching Rule 707 simply from a constitutional standpoint, as the Court of Military Appeals had done, he would have also invalidated it on the basis that it violated Article 36(a) of the Uniform Code of Military Justice (UCMJ). Rule 707 was a blanket rule of exclusion, Justice Stevens held, and thus "categorically denies the defendant any opportunity to persuade the court that the evidence should be received for any purpose." Taking the view that the use of polygraph evidence is not nearly as questionable as the Court would make it appear, Justice Stevens suggested that the very fact that polygraphs are used more regularly in the military than in private life ought to justify their use in a military court. Thus it was particularly ironic that Rule 707, as he noted, "has no counterpart" in federal civilian rules either for evidence or criminal procedure.

Justice Stevens then turned to the three sets of interests cited by the military court, and by the present majority opinion. In an observation cited by Justice Kennedy, he noted that given the special qualifications of the jurors who hear court-martial cases, as well as those of military polygraphers, "those interests pose less serious concerns in the military than in the civilian context." As for the question of what specific language in the Sixth Amendment would justify the use of polygraph evidence, Justice Stevens wrote that it was not necessary to point to specific language, since the

Court's holding represented a clear abridgement of the right to a fair trial. In *Washington v. Texas,* he suggested, the Court had rejected a blanket rule of inadmissibility, but its current ruling tended to uphold just such a "potential injustice." In the latter part of his opinion, Justice Stevens approached the three cited interests—reliability, the role of the jury, and collateral litigation—and in each instance found arguments against the majority ruling.

Impact

Even before *Scheffer,* the use of polygraph evidence was on shaky ground. Thus Biskupic in the *Washington Post* noted that some 30 states already prohibited the introduction of polygraph evidence in court, "and some legal experts said [the *Scheffer* decision] may prompt the states that do not have outright prohibitions to consider imposing them." On the other hand, an official with the American Polygraph Association told Biskupic that the Court's opinion "represents an ongoing debate," and Biskupic herself noted that the Kennedy opinion suggested "that perhaps in the future another dispute might offer a more compelling case for the introduction of polygraph testimony." With regard to the other issue addressed in *Scheffer,* the less prominent but ultimately more significant question regarding exclusionary rules of evidence, future directions on the Court's part are less clear.

Related Cases

Frye v. United States, 293 F. 1013 (1923).
Washington v. Texas, 388 U.S. 14 (1967).
Chambers v. Mississippi, 410 U.S. 284 (1973).
Rock v. Arkansas, 483 U.S. 44 (1987).
Daubert v. Merrell Dow Pharmaceuticals, 509 U.S. 579 (1993).

Bibliography and Further Reading

Biskupic, Joan. "High Court to Rule on Defendant's Right to Present Polygraph Rules as Evidence." *Washington Post,* May 20, 1997, p. A06.

———. "Justices Allow Ban on Polygraph Use." *Washington Post,* April 1, 1998, p. A01.

Dripps, Donald A. "Polygraph Evidence After *United States v. Scheffer.*" *Trial,* June 1998, pp. 75-77.

Kaye, D. H. "The Evidence Site: D. H. Kaye on Scientific Evidence Cases Pending in the U.S. Supreme Court." University of Michigan Law School. http://www.law.umich.edu/thayer/kaye.htm

The Rights of the Accused Following Trial

The rights of the accused after trial are many and varied. Criminal defendants who are convicted at trial must go through the process of sentencing, but they have the right to argue for a certain sentence. They then have the right to appeal the guilty verdict and the sentence. Should all available appeals fail, they have the right to attack the conviction again through a civil proceeding against the prison warden called a writ of *habeas corpus*. Finally, defendants have the right to ask the state's governor or the president of the United States (depending on whether the conviction was in federal or state court) for clemency. The sources of these rights can be found in federal and state constitutions and statutes.

Sentencing

Conduct at trial can affect a defendant's sentence. For example, under the Federal Sentencing Guidelines, a defendant may receive an increased penalty (usually a longer prison term) if the defendant "willfully impeded or obstructed, or attempted to impede or obstruct the administration of justice during the investigation or prosecution." In other words, if, in the estimation of the judge, the defendant "testif[ied] untruthfully" at trial, the defendant may receive a harsher-than-normal sentence.

The sentencing phase follows a criminal conviction. Between the day of conviction and the day of sentencing, the court has the option of jailing the defendant or releasing the defendant into the community until the sentencing date. If the court decides to release the defendant, the defendant may be required to post a security bond with the court to ensure his or her return to court for sentencing.

Convicted criminal defendants have the right to present a case for themselves at the sentencing phase. In most states, if the conviction was a violation or petty misdemeanor and the defendant is not being sentenced to jail or prison, the court conducts no hearing and simply imposes a sentence on the defendant immediately after the verdict is reached. In any case, the judge gives the defendant an opportunity to make a statement in his or her defense before the judge hands down the sentence.

In most states, the court holds a sentencing hearing for felony convictions and convictions that can lead to incarceration. This hearing is usually held several days or weeks after delivery of the verdict and can consist of oral testimony, cross-examination of witnesses, evidence, and arguments to the sentencing authority (either the judge or the jury). Sentencing options for judges include fines, imprisonment, restitution to victims, probation, and a variety of lesser penalties.

Probation is a status of conditional liberty. That is, the defendant is free only so long as he fulfills certain conditions and refrains from certain conduct. A judge may order a probationer to do or refrain from doing a number of things for the length of the probationary period. The length of a probationary period can depend on a variety of factors, most significantly the seriousness of the crime.

On the federal level and in most states, sentences are formulated from "sentencing guidelines." Sentencing guidelines set forth a presumptive sentence for a conviction based on factors that relate to the defendant and the crime involved. Such factors include the nature of the defendant's crime or crimes and the defendant's criminal history. The judge may depart from the sentencing guidelines, and if the sentence stays within the minimum and maximum allowed under the guidelines, the judge does not have to state the reasons for the departure on the record. If, however, a judge decides to increase or decrease a defendant's sentence beyond the maximum and minimum sentences allowed under the guidelines, the judge must clearly state the reasons for the departure on the record.

For years, the general rule on sentencing under U.S. Supreme Court decisions was that the Eighth Amendment prohibited punishments that were grossly disproportionate to the offense committed. However, this rule was officially questioned by the Supreme Court in *Harmelin v. Michigan* (1991). In that case, the Court upheld the life sentence of Ronald Harmelin. Although Harmelin did not have any prior felony convictions, the trial court was compelled by the sentencing guidelines in Michigan to impose a life sentence after Harmelin was convicted of selling more than 650 grams of cocaine.

Capital defendants are entitled to a full sentencing hearing before a sentencing authority. The sentencing authority is either the judge or jury or both. In most cases, the sole sentencing authority in a capital case is the jury that delivered the verdict. At the hearing, the sentencing authority must be given sufficient guidance to make an informed decision. If the prosecution argues to the jury that a capital defendant should be put to death because he presents a future danger to the community, the defendant has the right to inform the sentencing authority that he would be ineligible for parole and would die in prison if it decides to reject the death penalty.

Sentences may be appealed. The standards for sentencing review vary from state to state. Approximately half of all states allow appeals courts to review all sentences, even sentences that are within statutory guidelines. Other states allow appellate review only of sentences that fall below or above the state's sentencing guidelines.

Appeals

The federal government and all states provide the opportunity to appeal a criminal conviction. However, on the federal level and in most states, there is no constitutional right to appeal a criminal conviction. Instead, the right is provided by statute. This means that a legislature may retract the privilege of an appeal. In the appeals statutes, legislatures declare that defendants are entitled to information necessary to appeal, such as a transcript of the trial and instructions on how to file an appeal with the appropriate reviewing court.

All jurisdictions provide the right to appeal a criminal conviction, and so all must make sure the right is available to all defendants. Where appeal is available as a matter of right (in most cases this is only the first appeal), the court must appoint a lawyer, free of charge, for persons who are unable to afford their own attorney. Where the appeal is discretionary (i.e. a second appeal, usually to the state's highest court), no such right to a free attorney exists. A person who is on probation or parole and is accused of violating the terms of his probation or parole may be faced with revocation of that status. In such cases, if the probationer or parolee cannot afford an attorney, he may be entitled to free legal counsel. This depends on a number of factors, but generally, if the defendant denies committing the act and faces imprisonment, the court will appoint an attorney.

Capital defendants in state court are entitled to a review of the death sentence in a court with state-wide jurisdiction. On the federal level, capital defendants are entitled to one appeal: to the U.S. Court of Appeals for the particular circuit in which the district court sits. An appeal to the U.S. Supreme Court is not automatic, even for capital defendants. In most situations, state court criminal defendants must appeal first to the state's highest court (usually called the Supreme Court) before asking the U.S. Supreme Court to hear the case.

Habeas Corpus

A defendant who has filed all possible appeals may thereafter petition the courts for *habeas corpus* relief. *Habeas corpus* relief can consist of a new trial, a new sentence, or outright release from incarceration. *Habeas corpus* relief is available only to defendants who are incarcerated.

A *habeas corpus* petition is a civil suit filed against the prisoner's jailer. In the suit, the prisoner must allege that she was deprived of a constitutional right in the case, and that continued incarceration is unlawful. Typical bases for *habeas corpus* petitions include complaints about the trial, including ineffective assistance of counsel, discrimination in the jury selection, juror misconduct, prosecutorial misconduct, violation of the right to be free from self-incrimination, and similar issues pertaining to constitutional rights. Notably, a prisoner may not challenge a Fourth Amendment (unreasonable search and seizure) violation in a *habeas corpus* petition. Furthermore, a claim of actual innocence based on newly discovered evidence is not a basis for *habeas corpus* relief.

State court defendants may file a round of *habeas corpus* petitions in the state courts and, if a federal constitutional question is involved, another round in the federal courts. Many states limit the number of times that a prisoner may file *habeas corpus* petitions to one round. In most states, this means one petition at the trial court level, one petition to an appeals court, and one petition to the state's highest court. Some states have only trial courts and a high court, which effectively limits the possible number of *habeas corpus* petitions in state court to two.

A prisoner whose conviction came from federal court may file *habeas corpus* petitions only in the federal court system. In 1996, Congress passed restrictions on *habeas corpus* petitions in federal court. The statutes created strict filing deadlines for state prisoners filing *habeas corpus* petitions in federal court, limited the time that a court may spend on petitions, limited the opportunities for evidentiary hearings, limited the capacity to challenge facts determined at trial, required federal courts to give deference to the legal conclusions of the state courts, and made it more difficult for prisoners to file successive *habeas corpus* petitions.

Under the federal act, the filing deadlines for state prisoners filing in federal court are determined beginning with the date of the last direct review by a court. For prisoners who come from states that provide counsel to prisoners, the filing deadline is six months after the date of the "direct review" of the state court's final judgment. The term "direct review" is not defined in the legislation, but commentators believe that it refers to the date of the last review in state court. For prisoners petitioning from states that do not provide free counsel, the filing deadline is one year. The statute of limitations, or limited amount of time during which actions can be brought or rights enforced, is tolled (overwritten), however, by certain events, including the discovery of new evidence for a constitutional claim.

Prison

By and large, prisoners are entitled to only a "minimal civilized measure of shelter." Prisoners have a modicum of rights, but most of them may be curtailed in the interests of security. Established rights of prisoners include: the right to sufficient nourishment; the right to be free from arbitrary punishment on the basis of beliefs, religion, or racial and ethnic origin; the right to be free from constant physical restraint; the right to access to the courts and to legal materials; the right to a minimal amount of exercise; the right to adequate medical care; the right to essential personal hygiene; and the right to adequate heat, cooling, ventilation, and light. Other rights, such as the right to see visitors, the right to send and receive mail, the right to free speech, the right to practice religion, the right to privacy, and the right to personal property all may be infringed upon to the point necessary to preserve safety and security within the prison.

Bibliography and Further Reading

Bright, Stephen. "Does the Bill of Rights Apply Here Any More? Evisceration of Habeas Corpus and Denial of Counsel to Those Under Sentence of Death." *Champion*, November 1996.

Kochan, Andrea A. "The Antiterrorism and Effective Death Penalty Act of 1996: Habeas Corpus Reform?" *Washington University Journal of Urban and Contemporary Law*, Vol. 52, no. 399, 409-410, 417 (1997).

Miller, Frank W., Robert O. Dawson, George E. Dix, and Raymond I. Parnas. *Prosecution and Adjudication*, 4th Ed. Westbury, NY: The Foundation Press, Inc., 1991.

West's Encyclopedia of American Law. St. Paul, MN: West Publishing, 1998.

TROP V. DULLES

Legal Citation: 356 U.S. 86 (1958)

Appellant
Albert L. Trop

Appellee
John Foster Dulles, U.S. Secretary of State

Appellant's Claim
That taking away his American citizenship amounted to cruel and unusual punishment in violation of the Eighth Amendment.

Chief Lawyer for Appellant
Osmond K. Fraenkel

Chief Lawyer for Appellee
J. Lee Rankin, U.S. Solicitor General

Justices for the Court
Hugo Lafayette Black, William J. Brennan, Jr., William O. Douglas, Earl Warren (writing for the Court), Charles Evans Whittaker

Justices Dissenting
Harold Burton, Tom C. Clark, Felix Frankfurter, John Marshall Harlan II

Place
Washington, D.C.

Date of Decision
31 March 1956

Decision
The Supreme Court reversed Trop's expatriation.

Significance
Although the cruel and unusual punishment argument made in this case was not developed in subsequent expatriation cases, it became the crucial element in debate over the constitutionality of the death penalty in cases such as *Gregg v. Georgia* (1976).

Albert L. Trop was a native-born American. In 1944, he was a private in the U.S. Army, serving in French Morocco during World War II. Imprisoned there for a disciplinary offense, he escaped on 22 May. The next day he was picked up by an army truck and turned over to military police. Although Trop never offered any resistance and had been gone only one day, he was tried before a court-martial and convicted of desertion. He was sentenced to three years at hard labor, forfeiture of all pay, and given a dishonorable discharge.

In 1952 Trop, by then a free man, applied for a passport. The State Department refused to issue one, citing a provision of the Immigration and Nationality Act of 1940 which made a conviction for wartime desertion and dishonorable discharge punishable by loss of American citizenship. In 1955, Trop sued in federal district court seeking a declaratory judgment that he was still a citizen. The district court ruled against him, as did the Court of Appeals for the Second Circuit, and Trop then took his case to the U.S. Supreme Court.

Court Rules That Denaturalization Is Cruel and Unusual Punishment

Trop was decided the same day as another denaturalization case, *Perez v. Brownell*, in which the Court voted 5-4 in favor of supporting Congress's power to strip American citizenship from someone who had voted in a foreign election. Chief Justice Warren had dissented in *Perez*, arguing that Congress had no power to deprive an American of his citizenship without his consent. In *Trop*, Warren announced the judgment of the Court and delivered an opinion which was joined by only three other members. Warren's opinion reflected his view that however reprehensible wartime desertion might be, it did not signify allegiance to a foreign state. To deprive Trop of his citizenship was to impose upon him cruel and unusual punishment in violation of the Eighth Amendment. The prohibition was just as applicable here as in cases involving excessive physical punishment:

> [T]he words of the Amendment are not precise, and . . . their scope is not static. The Amendment must draw its meaning from the evolving standards of decency that mark the progress of a maturing society . . . We believe . . . that

Rescinding American Citizenship

A United States citizen may, under certain circumstances, be stripped of her or his citizenship. A leading case on the loss of citizenship is *Trop v. Dulles* (1958). In that case, the U.S. Supreme Court held that the loss of citizenship for desertion—without allegiance to a foreign power by the deserter—was cruel and unusual punishment under the Eight Amendment to the Constitution and beyond the war powers of Congress. In *Kennedy v. Mendoza-Martinez* (1963), the High Court held that a person who leaves the country during time of war to avoid military service may be deprived of his citizenship, but not without a hearing.

There are many actions that can lead to the loss of citizenship. These include obtaining naturalization in a foreign state, entering into the armed forces of another state, accepting employment in the government of another state, formally renouncing one's United States nationality before a diplomat or consular officer in a foreign state, committing treason against the United States, and attempting to overthrow or bear arms against the United States.

Source(s): *West Encyclopedia of American Law*, Vol. 2. Minneapolis, MN: West Publishing, 1998.

the use of denaturalization as a punishment is barred by the Eighth Amendment. There may be no physical mistreatment, no primitive torture. There is instead the total destruction of the individual's status in an organized society.

Although in the end the Court voted to overturn the Immigration and Nationalization Act, it did so as a plurality. Justice Brennan voted with the majority, but he wrote a separate opinion in which he detailed his own reasons for doing so. While Justice Brennan did not agree that denaturalization amounted to cruel and unusual punishment, he concluded that it was not an appropriate exercise of Congress's war powers to punish wartime desertion with expatriation.

In *Afroyim v. Rusk* (1967), the Court overturned *Perez*, using Warren's argument in *Trop* as its rationale. This line of reasoning received its greatest attention, however, during the great debate among the justices over the death penalty. In *Furman v. Georgia* (1972), the Court for the first time struck down capital punishment as cruel and unusual punishment. Then four years later, in *Gregg v. Georgia*, the Court declared that capital punishment was not *per se* cruel and unusual, that "evolving standards of decency" did not hold that a death sentence was always unconstitutional. Under certain tightly controlled circumstances, the Court concluded, states could impose the death sentence for crimes so heinous that they offended civilized society.

Related Cases
Perez v. Brownell, 356 U.S. 44 (1958).
Afroyim v. Rusk, 387 U.S. 253 (1967).
Furman v. Georgia, 408 U.S. 238 (1972).
Gregg v. Georgia, 428 U.S. 153 (1976).

Bibliography and Further Reading
Karst, Kenneth L. *Belonging to America: Equal Citizenship and the Constitution*. New Haven, CT: Yale University Press, 1989.

Meltsner, Michael. *Cruel and Unusual: The Supreme Court and Capital Punishment*. New York, NY: Random House, 1973.

Sigloer, Jay A. *American Rights Policies*. Homewood, IL: Dorsey Press, 1975,

John Foster Dulles, U.S. Secretary of State.

RUMMEL V. ESTELLE

Legal Citation: 445 U.S. 263 (1980)

Petitioner
William James Rummel

Respondent
Estelle, Corrections Director for the State of Texas

Petitioner's Claim
That Article 63 of the Penal Code of the state of Texas, which mandated that a person convicted of three felonies would receive a life sentence as a recidivist criminal, violated Eighth and Fourteenth Amendment protections against cruel and unusual punishment.

Chief Lawyer for Petitioner
Scott J. Atlas

Chief Lawyer for Respondent
Douglas M. Becker

Justices for the Court
Harry A. Blackmun, Warren E. Burger, William H. Rehnquist (writing for the Court), Potter Stewart, Byron R. White

Justices Dissenting
William J. Brennan, Jr., Thurgood Marshall, Lewis F. Powell, Jr., John Paul Stevens

Place
Washington, D.C.

Date of Decision
18 March 1980

Decision
Upheld the state of Texas and affirmed the opinion of the U.S. Court of Appeals for the Fifth Circuit, finding that Article 63 of the Texas Penal Code did not violate the constitutional prohibitions against cruel and unusual punishment of criminals.

Significance
Established that a severe penalty for repeat offenders was not a violation of the protection against cruel and unusual punishment.

Three-Time Loser

Texas resident William James Rummel plead guilty to a charge of fraudulent use of a credit card to obtain $80 in goods or services in 1964. The penalty for this offense, classified as a felony under Texas law, was two to ten years imprisonment. Rummel received a sentence of three years in prison which he served without incident. Upon release from confinement, Rummel's run-ins with the law continued. In 1969 he pled guilty to passing a bad check in the amount of $28.26, a crime punishable by two to five years imprisonment, and received a four year prison sentence. Finally, in 1973, Rummel faced prosecution on the charge of obtaining $120.75 through false pretenses. This crime qualified as a "felony theft" under Texas law, and was punishable by two to ten years imprisonment. The prosecutors of the case decided to proceed against Rummel using the state's so-called recidivist statute, Article 63 of the Texas State Penal Code. Under Article 63, criminals with three felony convictions of any type are subjected to a mandatory sentence of life imprisonment. Rummel decided on a jury trial, but was convicted and sentenced to life in prison on 26 April 1973 by the trial court.

Cruel and Unusual?

Following his conviction and sentencing, Rummel attempted to appeal his case to the Texas Court of Appeals. The court rejected his appeal, however, and Rummel subsequently filed a petition for a writ of *habeas corpus* to the U.S. District Court for the Western District of Texas. Rummel claimed in his petition that a life sentence was so out of proportion to the damage done by his crimes, which were nonviolent and involved a total property value of $229.01, that it violated Eighth and Fourteenth Amendment prohibitions against cruel and unusual punishment of criminals. The district court rejected Rummel's constitutional claims, pointing out that he would be eligible for parole in approximately 12 years, regardless of the initial length of his sentence. Rummel then brought his case before a panel of the U.S. Court of Appeals for the Fourth Circuit. The circuit court overruled the district court, ruling that Rummel's punishment was "grossly dispro-

---

Legal Malpractice

Legal malpractice occurs when a lawyer fails to honor the interests of his or her client or commits an ethical or procedural transgression that results in injury to the client.

Most claims of legal malpractice can be placed into one of four categories: negligent court-related mistakes by the lawyer, such as the failure to file documents on time; negligence or misconduct in the professional relationship with the client, such as mishandling of client funds or representation of interests that are adverse to the client; misconduct related to arrangements with the client, such as the overcharging of fees; and transgres-

sions identified by parties other than the client. This last category consists of errors that are based on the manner in which the attorney represented the client, and includes such claims as defamation, intentional infliction of emotional distress, malicious prosecution, filing of court documents in bad faith, and abuse of process. Such claims generally are not as successful as claims based on fees, negligent mistakes, and negligent dealings with the client.

Source(s): *West's Encyclopedia of American Law,* Vol. 7. Minneapolis, MN: West Publishing, 1998.

---

portionate" to his crimes. Following this ruling, the court of appeals reheard the case, vacating the opinion of the circuit court panel's decision and reaffirming their earlier decision and agreeing with a dissenting circuit court panel judge that "no neutral principle of adjudication permits a federal court to hold that in a given situation individual crimes are too trivial in relation to the punishment imposed." The court of appeals also affirmed the district court's denial of Rummel's petition for a writ of *habeas corpus*. In reaching its conclusions, the court of appeals relied heavily on the probability that Rummel's sentence would actually turn out to be considerably less than life, due to the probability of his parole after an approximately 12-year period. Significantly, six members of the court of appeals dissented in the final decision, noting that Rummel had no guarantee of parole and therefore the constitutionality of his sentence should be determined on its face, and not on the basis of perceived probabilities. With such deep disagreement within the court of appeals, the case was sent to the U.S. Supreme Court, which heard arguments on 7 January 1980.

The Nature of Proportionality

The Supreme Court upheld the finding of the court of appeals, ruling that Article 63 of the Texas State Penal Code did not violate constitutional prohibitions against the cruel and unusual punishment of criminals. Justice Rehnquist, writing for the majority, noted that most sentences struck down for lack of proportionality to the offense committed had been in capital cases. Of noncapital sentences challenged for constitutionality, those of *Weems v. United States* (1910) and *Graham v. West Virginia* (1912) were among the very few to be struck down. In *Weems,* the Court invalidated the sentence of a man convicted of falsifying a public document. This sentence included a 12-year prison term, the wearing of ankle and wrist chains, hard labor, and continual

surveillance by prison authorities. Rummel had cited *Weems* as a precedent for his own case, and the court of appeals had accepted his argument that the length of his sentence had been the most disproportionate portion of Weems's punishment. The Supreme Court rejected the comparison, however, with Justice Rehnquist observing that the Court's opinion in *Weems* "consistently referred jointly to the length of imprisonment and its 'accessories' or 'accompaniments.'" At no time in his case had Rummel claimed to be mistreated by Texas penal authorities. In *Graham,* the Court had decided that West Virginia's recidivist statute was constitutional in the case of a man convicted three times of stealing horses. The Court also compared Texas penal codes to those of other states and found that they did not vary appreciably in the length or severity of the sentences mandated for Rummel's crimes. Finally, the Court agreed with the district court that Rummel's sentence could not reasonably be viewed as a life sentence, given the probability of his parole within approximately 12 years. In the final analysis, the Court held that the constitutionality of criminal sentencing should be questioned on thoroughly objective grounds, such as the severity of a sentence. The assessment of the length of sentencing for various crimes was deemed completely subjective, and, as such, properly a matter for legislative decision. Dissenting justices observed that noncapital sentences should be analyzed on the same basis as capital cases and that the possibility of parole should not be considered in assessing the proportionality of the length of sentencing.

Impact

The ruling made it exceedingly difficult to argue the proportionality of sentencing in noncapital cases. The Court subsequently showed flexibility on this issue, however, ruling in *Solem v. Helm,* (1983) that a recidivist statute in South Dakota which called for mandatory life sentencing without possibility of parole for repeat felons was unconstitutional. The Court has since further complicated its position regarding mandatory felony sentencing, ruling in *Harmelin v. Michigan,* (1991) that the state of Michigan's statute mandating life sentencing without possibility of parole for first-time felony drug offenders was constitutional.

Related Cases

Weems v. United States, 217 U.S. 367 (1910).
Graham v. West Virginia, 224 U.S. 616 (1912).
Solem v. Helm, 463 U.S. 277 (1983).
Harmelin v. Michigan, 501 U.S. 294 (1991).

Bibliography and Further Reading

Biskupic, Joan, and Elder Witt, eds. *Guide to the Supreme Court of the United States.* Washington, DC: Congressional Quarterly Inc., 1997.

SOLEM V. HELM

Legal Citation: 463 U.S. 277 (1983)

Petitioner
Herman Solem, Warden

Respondent
Jerry Buckley Helm

Petitioner's Claim
That according to South Dakota law repeat felons must serve life in prison without parole. Helm had been convicted of six crimes prior to his conviction for writing a bad check for $100.

Chief Lawyer for Petitioner
Mark V. Meierhenry

Chief Lawyer for Respondent
John J. Burnett

Justices for the Court
Harry A. Blackmun, William J. Brennan, Jr., Thurgood Marshall, Lewis F. Powell, Jr. (writing for the Court), John Paul Stevens

Justices Dissenting
Warren E. Burger, Sandra Day O'Connor, William H. Rehnquist, Byron R. White

Place
Washington, D.C.

Date of Decision
28 June 1983

Decision
The U.S. Supreme Court upheld the court of appeals' decision that life imprisonment without parole for passing a bogus check constituted a disproportionate punishment, which the Eighth Amendment prohibits given the crime.

Significance
This case along with a host of others helped the Supreme Court define which punishments fit which crimes. The case also calls into question blanket "three strikes and your out" laws where states impose life sentences on anyone with three or more felonies as well as "petty with a prior" laws where anyone previously convicted of a felony is charged with a felony for committing a petty theft.

The Origins of Proportional Punishment

Dating back to the Magna Carta (1215), early English law expressed deep concern for proportionate punishment. Later the English Bill of Rights included the ban on cruel and unusual punishment, which the United States adopted for its Eighth Amendment. The prohibition of cruel and unusual punishment includes sentences disproportionate to the offense as well as barbaric punishment.

For over a century, the Supreme Court recognized the ban on extreme forms of punishment that significantly outweighed the crime. For example, in *Weems v. United States,* (1910) the Court opposed a disproportionate sentence issued by the lower court. In this case a defendant received a 15-year sentence to hard labor for falsifying a public document.

The Case of Jerry Helm

Under South Dakota state law, habitual felons with more than three felonies can face life imprisonment without parole. The respondent, Jerry Helm, had six prior felonies to his record: three convictions of third-degree burglary in 1964, 1966, and 1969 as well as one count each of grand larceny in 1973, drunk driving in 1975, and obtaining money under false pretenses in 1972. However, Helm had committed no violent crimes and his seventh conviction for the "no account" check also was nonviolent. The state typically issued a five-year sentence and a $5000 fine for this crime. Nonetheless, the South Dakota district court gave Helm a life sentence, explaining to Helm: "I think you certainly earned this sentence, and certainly proven that you're an habitual criminal, and that would indicate that you're beyond rehabilitation and that the only prudent thing to do is lock you up for the rest of your natural life . . ." Helm began his sentence in 1979.

After serving two years of his sentence, Helm asked the governor of South Dakota to reduce his sentence to one with a definite number of years—his only option for a reduced sentence, but the governor denied his request. Subsequently, Helm petitioned the U.S. District Court for the District of South Dakota, arguing that his sentence amounted to cruel and unusual punishment

Magna Carta

The Magna Carta (Latin for "Great Charter") is the document that forms the foundation of English government. Concerned with establishing limits on the tyrannical powers of the English monarchy, the Magna Carta is considered the first great assertion of political liberties in the history of western civilization. The Magna Carta provided the inspiration for the U.S. Constitution and the constitutions of other democratic nations.

King John (1199-1216) signed the Magna Carta on 15 June 1215. That day, having recently suffered defeat at the hands of the French, King John was surrounded by sword-wielding English lords and noblemen in a battlefield near Runnymede. The barons, angry over the various financial extractions and court-related abuses by the Crown, forced King John to sign a document

that contained a long list of rights. King John believed that the document would be worthless, and he signed it only as a way to postpone his bad fortunes. However, the document lived on and later became known as the Magna Carta.

The Magna Carta established various rights for English citizens and curbed the Crown's powers. For example, the Magna Carta pronounced the right of a person to be free from exile, imprisonment, and other punishments "except by the judgment of his peers, or by the law of the land."

Source(s): *West Encyclopedia of American Law*, Vol. 7. Minneapolis, MN: West Publishing, 1998

---

in violation of his Eighth Amendment right; however, the district court also refused to reduce the sentence citing *Rummel v. Estelle* (1980). The court did acknowledge that the penalty was extreme. In *Rummel v. Estelle,* the court in Texas sentenced Rummel to life in prison for his third offense: obtaining $120.75 under false pretenses, because he had two prior felonies. Helm then took his case to the court of appeals, which reversed the district court's decision.

Mixed Messages

The warden of South Dakota petitioned the Supreme Court to hear the case and in 1983 the Court began reviewing it. Although the court of appeals had overturned the district court's ruling, *Rummel v. Estelle* did set the stage for decisions such as the district court's concerning repeat felons. Consequently, the majority's decision prevailed only by a slim margin, in the 5-4 ruling on 28 June 1983. Justice Powell and the justices in the majority argued for some objective measures in determining whether a sentence matched a crime and formulated three criteria for making this determination: Courts should first consider the seriousness of the offense and the severity of the sentence, second weigh their sentences against others in the jurisdiction for the same crime, and third compare their sentences with those of other jurisdictions for the same crime.

Using these criteria, the Court decided to uphold the ruling by the court of appeals. Helm's crimes ranked less serious than other crimes punishable by life imprisonment without parole—the state's maximum penalty—and the crimes did not involve violence or the threat of violence. According to the majority opinion, society generally views Helm's crimes, especially

his last, as less serious than other felonies such as murder, assault, and rape. The Court concluded that Helm's sentence was equal or more severe than the sentences of people in the state who committed much more serious crimes and more severe than in any other state, except Nevada for similar crimes.

The majority's decision relied on a subtle distinction between the *Rummel* and *Helm* cases: Rummel received a sentence with the possibility of parole, whereas Helm receive a life sentence without that possibility. After 12 years, Rummel could be eligible for parole for good behavior, but Helm would not have that option. The Court also noted that Helm had an alcohol addiction and that his crimes stemmed from this addiction. With proper treatment, Helm could arguably be rehabilitated. However, his sentence prevented such rehabilitation, according to the majority. Therefore, they upheld the ruling by the court of appeals.

On the other hand, the dissenting justices argued that given the recent decision in *Rummel v. Estelle* the life sentence did not constitute cruel and unusual punishment. They reasoned that because Rummel committed only three felonies: fraudulently using a credit card, passing a forged check, and obtaining money under false pretenses, all of which were nonviolent, his sentence certainly was no more severe than Helm's. Moreover, since the majority made no effort to overturn this ruling, the dissenting justices questioned the consistency of the majority's opinion when the Court had deemed a life sentence for a man convicted of three felonies acceptable and not in violation of the Eighth Amendment ban on cruel and unusual punishment. In addition, the five justice majority in *Rummel v. Estelle* agreed that states had the right to impose the length of prison sentences at their discretion.

Lingering Problems

Controversy still surrounds repeat offender laws as more states adopt these policies. With two separate decisions in two similar cases: *Rummel v. Estelle* and *Solem v. Helm,* states continue to grapple with the problem of what to do with habitual felons. In California, for example, the "three strikes" law sent a man to prison for life for stealing two packs of cigarettes as well as a man who stole a slice of pizza, because they were previously convicted of multiple felonies. *Solem v. Helm* remains the case cited to reduce these kinds of sentences, while *Rummel v. Estelle* remains the case cited to issue such sentences.

The court of appeals noted that *Rummel v. Estelle* was distinguishable. Helm's sentence without parole was qualitatively different from Rummel's life sentence with the prospect of parole because South Dakota has rejected rehabilitation as a goal of the criminal justice system.

Related Cases

Weems v. United States, 217 U.S. 349 (1910).
Rummel v. Estelle, 445 U.S. 263 (1980).

Bibliography and Further Reading

DiSpoldo, Nick. "Three-Strikes Laws." *Commonweal,* June 14, 1996.

Finkel, Norman J., Stephen T. Maloney, et al. "Recidivism, Proportionalism, and Individualized Punishment." *The American Behavioral Scientist,* February 1996.

Mathews, Gordon. "Bad Check Conviction Not Worth Life Sentence." *American Banker,* June 30, 1983, p. 16.

HUDSON V. MCMILLIAN

Legal Citation: 503 U.S. 1 (1992)

Petitioner
Keith J. Hudson

Respondent
Jack McMillian, et al.

Petitioner's Claim
Proof of serious injury is not required to prove a claim under the Eighth Amendment of cruel and unusual punishment.

Chief Lawyer for Petitioner
Alvin J. Bronstein

Chief Lawyer for Respondent
Harry McCall, Jr.

Justices for the Court
Harry A. Blackmun, Anthony M. Kennedy, Sandra Day O'Connor (writing for the Court), William H. Rehnquist, David H. Souter, John Paul Stevens, Byron R. White

Justices Dissenting
Antonin Scalia, Clarence Thomas

Place
Washington, D.C.

Date of Decision
25 February 1992

Decision
A petitioner claiming that excessive force constituted cruel and unusual punishment does not have to suffer a serious injury to prevail in the case.

Significance
The decision extended Eighth Amendment protection against cruel and unusual punishment to prisoners who are beaten, even if the prisoner does not suffer a serious injury.

Prison Inmate Claims Beating Violated his Civil Rights

In the early morning hours of 30 October 1983, Keith J. Hudson, an inmate at the Angola state penitentiary in Louisiana, got into an argument with corrections security officer Jack McMillian. With the help of coworker Marvin Woods, McMillian placed Hudson in handcuffs and shackles, removed him from his cell, and took him to an "administrative lockdown" area. According to Hudson, as he was being led to the administrative lockdown area, Woods held Hudson while McMillian punched Hudson in the mouth, eyes, chest, and stomach. Hudson also claimed that Woods also kicked and punched him from behind and that Arthur Mezo, the supervisor on duty, watched the beating and told the officers "not to have too much fun." Hudson suffered minor bruises on his body, facial swelling, loosened teeth, and a cracked dental plate.

Hudson sued Mezo, McMillian, and Woods in a federal district court. Hudson asked for damages, claiming that he had been subjected to cruel and unusual punishment and that his civil rights had been violated. The parties agreed to try the case before a magistrate, who found that the use of force was unnecessary and that Mezo had condoned the actions of McMillian and Woods. The magistrate awarded Hudson $800, and the correctional officers appealed. The Court of Appeals for the Fifth Circuit reversed, holding that Hudson had no claim because his injuries were minor and did not require medical attention. Hudson applied to the U.S. Supreme Court for a writ of *certiorari,* and the High Court agreed to take the case.

In a 7-2 decision, the High Court reversed the appeals court, holding that Hudson's claim of cruel and unusual punishment did not hinge on whether he had suffered a serious physical injury. Justice O'Connor, writing for the majority, cited the case of *Whitley v. Albers* (1986) as precedent. In that case, an inmate was shot by a guard in a prison riot, and the Court ruled that "the unnecessary and wanton infliction of pain . . . constitutes cruel and unusual punishment." The *Whitley* Court added that "unnecessary and wanton infliction of pain" varies according to the constitutional violation alleged by the prisoner. In a case where the

Sandra Day O'Connor, First Female Justice

Sandra Day O'Connor was the first female U.S. Supreme Court Justice in the United States. Appointed in 1981 by President Ronald Reagan, O'Connor replaced Justice Potter Stewart, who had retired.

O'Connor was born Sandra Day on 26 March 1930 in El Paso, Texas. At Stanford Law School, she graduated third in her class, which included future colleague and chief justice, William H. Rehnquist. After marrying John O'Connor, also an attorney, O'Connor sought work in private law firms but none would hire a female as anything other than a legal secretary. She found work as a deputy county attorney in San Mateo, California and

then embarked on a public and private legal career that landed her a seat by appointment in the Arizona Senate. After winning an election and a reelection, O'Connor was elected to a judgeship in the Maricopa County Superior Court. Thus O'Connor began an ascension up the judicial ladder that continued with her appointment by Governor Bruce Babbitt to the Arizona Court of Appeals and culminated in her historic appointment to the highest court in the land.

Source(s): *West's Encyclopedia of American Law,* Vol. 7, p. 373. St. Paul, MN: West Publishing, 1998.

---

prisoner alleges that officials have failed to give medical attention, for example, the proper inquiry is whether the officials exhibit "deliberate indifference" to the medical needs of the prisoner.

High Court Defines Force Used on Inmates

In a case such as Hudson's, where the prisoner alleges that he or she has been beaten by prison officials during a "prison disturbance," O'Connor wrote, the Court must balance the need of prison officials to maintain order against the harm that inmates might suffer from the force used by the officials. Under *Whitley,* the Court must ask whether "the force was applied in a good faith effort to maintain or restore discipline or maliciously and sadistically for the very purpose of causing harm" when it examines a claim that a prison official inflicted unnecessary and wanton infliction of pain and suffering. In determining whether the use of force by a prison official was applied in good faith or whether it was malicious, the Court must look at several factors. These factors, said the majority, included the need for the force, the connection between the need for force and the amount of force used, the threat that was reasonably perceived by the prison officials, and efforts made to minimize the severity of the force.

The majority acknowledged that the extent of the injury suffered by the inmate is another factor in deciding an Eighth Amendment claim based on the use of excessive force. McMillian, Mezo, and Woods claimed that under the Court's decision in *Wilson v. Seiter* (1994) the Court had inserted an objective requirement into the analysis by preventing an Eighth Amendment claim unless the inmate has suffered a significant physical injury. In *Wilson,* a prison inmate made a claim of cruel and unusual punishment based on the horrific conditions of his confinement. In that case, the Court ruled that in making an Eighth Amendment claim based on conditions of confinement, the prisoner had to prove

that he or she had suffered a serious physical injury as a result of the confinement conditions. The respondents argued that Hudson's claim of cruel and unusual punishment could not succeed because Hudson had not suffered a serious physical injury.

The respondents' understanding of the *Wilson* case was flawed, the majority wrote, because under *Whitley* the analysis for Eighth Amendment claims varies according to the nature of the claim. The analysis varies, the majority instructed, for two reasons: first, because of the differences in the kind of conduct that comprises Eighth Amendment claims, and second, because the Eighth Amendment prohibitions draw their meaning "from the evolving standards of decency that mark the progress of a maturing society," an approach that forecloses most "absolute limitations." In the context of health care, for example, the Court had observed in *Estelle v. Gamble* (1976) that society does not expect that prison inmates will have completely unfettered access to health care. However, society does expect that prison officials will not be deliberately indifferent to the serious medical needs of prison inmates. In *Rhodes v. Chapman* (1981), a case dealing with conditions of confinement, the Court had stated that society expects prisoners to experience "routine discomfort" as part of the incarceration experience. At the same time, though, society does not condone depriving prisoners of a "minimal civilized measure of life's necessities." These cases, the majority maintained, demonstrated how standards of decency were derived from societal mores.

Excessive Use of Force Against Inmates Violates Societal Standards

The majority declared that, in a case of excessive force, if the officials "maliciously and sadistically use force to cause harm, contemporary standards of decency always are violated." This was true even if significant injury was not evident. "Otherwise," the majority explained,

Sandra Day O'Connor was the first woman to be appointed the U.S. Supreme Court.
© Photograph by Keith Meyers. Archive Photos.

"the Eighth Amendment would permit any physical punishment, no matter how diabolic or inhuman, inflicting less than some arbitrary quantity of injury. Such a result would have been as unacceptable to the drafters of the Eighth Amendment as it is today."

The majority reminded readers that the holding was not intended to prevent prison officials from using force to maintain order, nor was its purpose to protect overly sensitive prison inmates. "[E]very malevolent touch by a prison guard" does not constitute a federal case, the Court cautioned. Disagreeing with the Fifth Circuit Court's factual findings, the majority concluded that the "bruises, swelling, loosened teeth, and cracked dental plate" were not insignificant, and that they provided "no basis" for the dismissal of his claim. O'Connor rebutted the arguments of the dissenting Justices, Scalia and Thomas, noting differences in interpretation of precedent, and she dismissed the respondents' argument that their acts were "isolated and unauthorized" and therefore could not constitute an Eighth Amendment violation. The majority refused to consider the argument because it was not presented in the question to the Court, because a supervisor had authorized the alleged beating, and because the record in the case indicated that the alleged actions of the accused officials were not, in fact, isolated.

Justices Stevens and Blackmun wrote concurring opinions. Stevens disagreed with the majority over its use of the "malicious and sadistic" standard. Such a high standard of proof for an inmate is appropriate, Stevens maintained, when the force under question was used to protect visitors, guards, other prisoners, and other people. Because no such threat existed in Hud-son's case as Hudson was in shackles, Stevens felt that the majority should have used the lesser standard and examined whether the guards inflicted unnecessary and wanton pain.

Blackmun wrote an entirely different concurring opinion. In it, Stevens described the real-life torture of prisoners that would go unpunished if significant physical injury was required for Eighth Amendment excessive force claims: "lashing prisoners with leather straps, whipping them with rubber hoses, beating them with naked fists, shocking them with electric currents, asphyxiating them short of death, intentionally exposing them to undue heat or cold, or forcibly injecting them with psychosis-inducing drugs." Citing various cases, Blackmun noted that "[t]hese techniques, commonly thought to be practiced only outside this Nation's borders, are hardly unknown within this Nation's prisons." Blackmun agreed with the majority that significant physical injury was not required in Hudson's case, but he went even further and suggested that psychological injury should not be foreclosed in other Eighth Amendment cases. As support for this proposition, Blackmun cited the case of *Wisniewski v. Kennard* (1990) in which a prison guard was accused of placing a gun in a prisoner's mouth and threatening to kill him.

Dissenting Justices Assert Eighth Amendment Not Intended to Regulate Prisons

Justice Thomas, joined by Justice Scalia, wrote a long dissent. The dissent concentrated on the Court's prior cases on the Eighth Amendment, arguing that the majority's holding extended them too far. Thomas noted that the Court's first application of the Eighth Amendment to a prisoner's suffering in prison did not come until 1976, and the holding in that case, *Estelle v. Gamble,* gave the Eighth Amendment only "a very limited role in regulating prison administration." The dissent argued that the Court's cases since *Estelle* gave the Court no room to extend the Eighth Amendment to cover insignificant harm. The Court had synthesized its Eighth Amendment jurisprudence in *Wilson,* a case decided the previous term. In that case, the dissent argued, the Court had indeed established two basic issues in Eighth Amendment analysis: whether the deprivation was sufficiently serious (the objective component), and whether the officials act with a sufficiently culpable state of mind (the subjective component).

The *Whitley* opinion, the dissent asserted, did not endorse the elimination of the objective component. Thomas noted that while the majority had eliminated the objective component, it had heightened the standard of proof on the subjective component for prisoners claiming excessive force, from wanton infliction of pain and suffering to malicious and sadistic. "The Court's unwarranted extension of *Whitley,* I can only suppose," mocked Thomas, "is driven by the implausibility of saying that minor injuries imposed upon prisoners with anything less than a 'malicious and sadistic' state of mind can amount to cruel and unusual punishment."

Thomas decried the violence in the case, but he emphasized that the lower court had found that the injuries suffered by Hudson were minor. The dissent felt that the Court should not have disturbed the finding of that court. Furthermore, the High Court should not have taken the case in the first place: it was a matter of state law, not the law of the federal Constitution. "The Eighth Amendment is not," Thomas averred, "and should not be turned into, a National Code of Prison Regulation."

Impact

The *Hudson* decision made it possible for incarcerated persons to make Eighth Amendment claims of excessive force without alleging the infliction of a serious physical injury. This gave prisoners with such claims another avenue into the federal court system, giving them an option between state and federal court. A prisoner may decide to forego suing in state court if the laws in federal court are more favorable.

Related Cases

Estelle v. Gamble, 429 U.S. 97 (1976).
Rhodes v. Chapman, 452 U.S. 337 (1981).
Whitley v. Albers, 475 U.S. 312 (1986).
Wisniewski v. Kennard, 901 F.2d 1276 (1990).
Wilson v. Seiter, 501 U.S. 294 (1994).

Bibliography and Further Reading

Call, Jack E. "The Supreme Court and Prisoners' Rights." *Federal Probation,* March 1995, p. 36.

New York Times, February 26, 1992.

Simon, James F. *The Center Holds: The Power Struggle Inside the Rehnquist Court.* New York: Simon & Schuster, 1995.

Smolla, Rodney A. *A Year In the Life of the Supreme Court.* Durham, NC: Duke University Press, 1995.

KANSAS V. HENDRICKS

Legal Citation: 521 U.S. 346 (1997)

Petitioner
State of Kansas

Respondent
Leroy Hendricks

Petitioner's Claim
That the Kansas Sexually Violent Predator Act, which provides for civil commitment of persons convicted of crimes of sexual violence to be civilly committed to a mental institution for treatment, did not violate the Constitution.

Chief Lawyer for Petitioner
Carla J. Stovall

Chief Lawyer for Respondent
Thomas J. Weilert

Justices for the Court
Anthony M. Kennedy, Sandra Day O'Connor, William H. Rehnquist, Antonin Scalia, Clarence Thomas (writing for the Court)

Justices Dissenting
Stephen Breyer, Ruth Bader Ginsburg, John Paul Stevens, David H. Souter

Place
Washington, D.C.

Date of Decision
23 June 1997

Decision
That the Kansas Sexually Violent Predator Act did not violate the defendant's rights to due process, and was not a criminal penalty which violated the Double Jeopardy and Ex Post Facto Clauses of the Constitution.

Significance
The Court's decision granted wide latitude to the states to fashion measures for protecting society from repeated crimes by violent sexual predators.

In the early 1990s, a number of states enacted tough laws to deal with the rising problem of violent sexual crimes, particularly those against children. States imposed harsher sentences on those convicted of violent sexual crimes and required sexual offenders to register their address with the police following their release from prison. In 1994, Kansas took an innovative approach by enacting the Kansas Sexually Violent Predator Act. This law allowed the state to confine sexual offenders that suffered from a "mental abnormality" to a mental institution through a process known as civil commitment. Civil commitment is a process apart from the criminal justice process in which a person can be committed involuntarily to a mental facility. Civil commitment generally is used only for people who are a danger to themselves or to others.

The Kansas law provided a detailed procedure for committing violent sexual offenders. First, the prison was required to notify the prosecuting attorney who handled the case 60 days before the sexual offender was to be released from prison. The prosecutor then had 45 days in which to file a petition in the state court asking that the person be involuntarily committed. If such a petition was filed, the state court was then required to determine whether there was sufficient evidence that the person was a "sexually violent predator." Under the law, "sexually violent predator" was defined as a person suffering from a mental abnormality which makes the person likely to commit sexually violent acts and who is convicted of or charged with a sexually violent offense. If the court determined that there was sufficient evidence, the person was evaluated by a psychological professional. After the evaluation, a trial was held, and if the person was found to be a sexually violent predator beyond a reasonable doubt, he was committed to a mental facility for care and treatment. Finally, after a person's commitment, the trial court was required to conduct an annual review to determine whether the person should remain committed. Also, the person could petition the court for release at any time.

Kansas Law Applied to Hendricks

One of the first people to be committed under the Kansas law was Leroy Hendricks. In 1984, Hendricks, a pedophile, was convicted of sexually abusing two 13-year-old boys. This was his sixth conviction for sexually abusing children. After serving 10 years of his sentence, Hendricks was scheduled to be released from prison. Before his release, however, the state sought to have Hendricks committed as a sexually violent predator under the newly enacted law. The jury unanimously found that Hendricks was a sexually violent predator, and the court determined that Hendricks's pedophilia was a "mental abnormality" covered by the law. Accordingly, the state court committed Hendricks to a mental institution.

Hendricks appealed to the Kansas Supreme Court. He argued that the Kansas law violated his right to "substantive" due process of law. He also argued that the law actually imposed a criminal penalty, and was thus unconstitutional under the Ex Post Facto and Double Jeopardy Clauses of the Constitution. The Kansas Supreme Court did not address the ex post facto or double jeopardy arguments, but did find that the law violated Hendricks's right to due process of law. The state appealed the decision to the U.S. Supreme Court.

Court Upholds Law

The Supreme Court reversed the Kansas Supreme Court's decision and upheld the law. Under the Fourteenth Amendment to the Constitution, a state may not deprive a person of life, liberty, or property without due process of law. Although it is written in terms of "process," the Supreme Court has interpreted the amendment to protect various substantive rights, not just procedural rights. This is known as "substantive due process." Based on earlier U.S. Supreme Court cases, the Kansas court concluded that substantive due process required that the state prove, before imposing civil commitment, that the person to be committed suffers from a mental illness, not merely a mental abnormality, and that the person is a danger to himself or others. The Supreme Court concluded that its earlier cases do not require "mental illness," and that it is sufficient if the state shows that the person suffers from a "mental abnormality" which makes the person unable to control his behavior and which makes him a danger to others. Because the Kansas law required such a showing, the Court concluded that it did not violate Hendricks rights to substantive due process.

The Supreme Court also rejected Hendricks's argument that the Kansas law imposed a criminal penalty which violated both the Ex Post Facto and Double Jeopardy Clauses of the Constitution. The Ex Post Facto Clause prohibits a state from imposing a criminal penalty on conduct which occurred before the law was enacted, while the Double Jeopardy Clause prohibits a state from punishing a person twice for the same conduct. Hendricks claimed that the Kansas law, as applied to him, violated these clauses because his crime

occurred in 1984, ten years before the law was passed, and because he had already been punished for his crime by being sent to prison. The Court rejected these arguments because the Ex Post Facto and Double Jeopardy Clauses apply to only criminal penalties, and the Kansas law regarded only civil proceedings. In order to be a criminal penalty, a law must have either the purpose or effect of punishing a person. The Court concluded that the purpose of the Kansas law was not to punish violent sex offenders, but to treat them so that they can safely re-enter society. Justice Breyer, who was joined by three other justices, disagreed with the majority. Justice Breyer concluded that the real purpose of the Kansas law was to permanently confine violent sex offenders, and therefore the law violated the Ex Post Facto Clause as applied to Hendricks.

Importantly, however, all nine justices agreed that the law did not violate a sex offender's right to substantive due process. Thus, the Court's decision effectively validated the civil commitment laws in 16 other states which provided for civil commitment of violent sexual offenders. Also, the Court's decision opened the door for more legislative experimentation by the states in dealing with the problems posed by violent sexual assaults by repeat offenders.

Related Cases

Jacobson v. Massachusetts, 197 U.S. 11 (1905).
Minnesota ex rel. Pearson v. Probate Court of Ramsey City, 309 U.S. 270 (1940).
Baxstrom v. Herold, 383 U.S. 107 (1966).
Schall v. Martin, 467 U.S. 253 (1984).
Allen v. Illinois, 478 U.S. 364 (1986).
Heller v. Doe, 509 U.S. 312 (1993).
California Department of Corrections v. Morales, 514 U.S. 499 (1995).

Bibliography and Further Reading

Dority, Barbara. "Shades of the Gulag." *The Humanist,* January-February 1998, p. 39.

Dripps, Donald A. "Civil Commitment for Convicted Criminals." *Trial,* August 1997, p. 62.

Kaihla, Paul. "Sex Offenders: Is There a Cure?" *MacLeans,* February 3, 1995, pp. 56-57.

Lally, Stephen. "Steel Beds vs. Iron Bars; New Laws Muddle How to Handle Sex Offenders." *Washington Post,* July 27, 1997, p. C1.

Leo, John. "Dealing with Career Predators." *U.S. News & World Report,* April 11, 1994, p. 19.

Planty, Michael G., and Louise van der Does. "Megan's Laws Aren't Enough." *Wall Street Journal,* July 17, 1997, p. A22.

Rollman, Eli M. "'Mental Illness': A Sexually Violent Predator is Punished Twice for One Crime." *Journal of Criminal Law and Criminology,* spring 1998, p. 985.

"Serve a Sentence and Stay On." *Washington Post,* June 25, 1997, p. A18.

"Sex Offenders: Double Jeopardy?" *The Economist,* September 2, 1995, pp. 24-25.

Steiker, Carol S. "The Limits of the Preventative State." *Journal of Criminal Law and Criminology,* spring 1998, p. 771.

"The Court and the Predators: Approval of Civil Commitment of Violent Sexual Offenders Has Its Dangers, but Adds Protection for Endangered Children." *Cleveland Plain Dealer,* June 27, 1997, p. 10B.

Zonana, Howard. "The Civil Commitment of Sex Offenders." *Science,* November 14, 1997, p. 1248.

OHIO ADULT PAROLE AUTHORITY V. WOODARD

Legal Citation: 118 S.Ct. 1244 (1998)

Petitioners
Ohio Adult Parole Authority, et al.

Respondent
Eugene Woodard

Petitioners' Claim
That Ohio clemency procedures violated a death-row inmate's Fourteenth Amendment right to due process and his Fifth Amendment right to remain silent.

Chief Lawyer for Petitioners
Jeffrey S. Sutton

Chief Lawyer for Respondent
David H. Bodiker

Justices for the Court
Stephen Breyer, Ruth Bader Ginsburg, Anthony M. Kennedy, Sandra Day O'Connor, William H. Rehnquist (writing for the Court), Antonin Scalia, David H. Souter, Clarence Thomas

Justices Dissenting
John Paul Stevens

Place
Washington, D.C.

Date of Decision
25 March 1998

Decision
Reversed the judgment of the Court of Appeals for the Sixth Circuit. Held that neither the Fifth Amendment nor the Due Process Clause were violated by the state of Ohio's clemency procedures.

Significance
With this ruling, the Supreme Court allowed the states more freedom in deciding when and how they grant pardons to convicted death row inmates. In reaching the conclusion that an inmate's Fourteenth and Fifth Amendment rights were not violated by Ohio's clemency procedures, the Court sharply restricted the role of the judiciary in clemency issues. The justices were divided over exactly how much constitutional protection states must include in their clemency practices, but upheld Ohio's existing procedures.

Background

Ever since the establishment of the British colonies North America, the concept of clemency has been an integral part of the American justice system. Clemency can mean the granting of a pardon, or commutation, meaning the changing of a death sentence to life imprisonment. It has long been put to use as a fail-safe way to protect the innocent from wrongful execution. At the end of the twentieth century, the American states that allowed the death penalty also authorized their governors to grant clemency to death row inmates.

The state of Ohio reinstituted its death penalty in 1981. The Ohio State Constitution gives its governor the power to grant clemency after a "thorough investigation" of the inmate's case. Although the power to grant clemency is the governor's, the authority to regulate the application and investigation process belongs to the Ohio General Assembly. The Ohio Adult Parole Authority (APA) has had the responsibility for carrying out those investigations since 1965. It holds interviews and hearings, completes clemency reviews, and makes nonbinding recommendations to the governor.

A Protected Life Interest on Death Row

In 1990, Eugene Woodard was convicted in Ohio of aggravated murder and sentenced to die on 7 October 1994. In 1993 and 1994, his conviction and his death sentence were affirmed by the Ohio Court of Appeals and the Ohio Supreme Court. The U.S. Supreme Court denied *certiorari* in 1994. The Ohio Supreme Court, however, on 24 August 1994 stayed the execution date so that Woodard could seek post-conviction relief. APA regulations required that clemency hearings must be scheduled 45 days prior to the execution. Because the Ohio Supreme Court's stay was granted less than 45 days before execution, however, Woodard's clemency review and his post-conviction litigation were to continue concurrently. The APA notified Woodard two weeks after his stay was granted that his clemency hearing had been scheduled in ten days, on 16 September 1994. The APA also informed Woodard that he could have a pre-hearing interview on 9 September 1994. Woodard protested the short notice. Because he also had post-conviction litigation in process, he requested,

Statistics on Clemency

Generally, clemency is an act of mercy or leniency. Clemency includes pardons, reprieves, and commutations of criminal sentences, and it is given to a criminal defendant by the president on the federal level, and, in most instances, by the governor on the state level.

There is no single source for data on the granting of clemency in the United States, but the National Association for the Advancement of Colored Persons and Amnesty International began gathering data on the issue in the late twentieth century. The general trend is to grant clemency in fewer cases.

Between 1972 and 1993, at least 70 prison inmates who were sentenced to death had their death sentences commuted to prison terms. Approximately 58 percent of the clemencies were granted because the government believed that it would lose on appeal, and clemency was less expensive than challenging the appeal in court. All of the 38 states that allow the death penalty have given the governor and/or the parole board the power to grant clemency to death row inmates.

Source(s): Radelet, Michael L., and Barbara A. Zsembik. "Executive Clemency in Post-*Furman* Capital Cases." *University of Richmond Law Review*, Vol. 27, winter 1993.

contrary to APA regulations, that his lawyer be present at both the interview and hearing. His request was denied, and Woodard filed suit in the U.S. District Court disputing the constitutionality of the APA's clemency process. He claimed that the process breached both his Fifth Amendment right to remain silent and his Fourteenth Amendment right to due process.

The case later went before the Court of Appeals for the Sixth Circuit. That court stated that Woodard had failed to establish ". . . out of the clemency proceeding itself . . . a protected life or liberty interest." It did find, however, that the Fourteenth Amendment protected his "original" life and liberty interest when the clemency process was regarded as part of the "entire punitive scheme." The court held that at any particular stage of this scheme, the amount of process due was proportional to how integral that stage was to the entire judicial process. Because the clemency process, the court said, "was far removed from trial, the process due could be minimal." The court then remanded the decision on what the actual process should be to the district court. The court, in conclusion, agreed with Woodard's claim that the process violated his Fifth Amendment right to remain silent. It held that the interview procedure presented him with a choice between asserting that right and taking part in the clemency procedure. This choice, it said, might well give rise to an unconstitutional situation.

The U.S. Supreme Court granted *certiorari,* or ordered the lower court to forward the record of its proceedings for review, to consider the case's constitutional implications more closely. The Court had two issues before it, each dealing with how the Constitution limits state clemency procedures. The first was whether or not an inmate has a constitutionally-protected life or liberty interest in those procedures. The second issue was whether the option given inmates to voluntarily participate in a clemency interview violates that inmate's Fifth Amendment right to silence.

On the first question Chief Justice Rehnquist, delivering the Court's opinion, responded to Woodard's argument that inmates preserve an original, or pretrial, life interest which continues until the moment of execution and requires due process until then. Justice Rehnquist rested his response on the Supreme Court's reasoning in the *Connecticut Board of Pardons v. Dumschat* (1981) case. In that case, the Court held that an inmate had

> no constitutional or inherent right to commutation of his sentence . . . [because] the individual's interest in release or commutation [of his sentence had] already been extinguished by the conviction and sentence.

Justice Rehnquist asserted that the reasoning in *Dumschat* "did not depend on the fact that it was not a capital case" and so the same reasoning should be applied in Woodard's case. He conceded that an inmate, justly tried and convicted, retains an "interest in not being executed." However, he reasoned, the inmate cannot use that interest to challenge clemency procedures and thus possibly change the outcome of his or her clemency decision.

In analyzing the nature of the clemency mechanism, Justice Rehnquist drew a clear distinction between the adjudicatory and clemency processes. He called a petition for clemency in effect merely a

> unilateral hope. [The inmate] . . . accepts the finality of death for purposes of adjudication, and appeals for clemency as a matter of [executive] grace.

Thus, he reasoned, clemency procedures were free from the kind of due process requirements which bind the judicial system. Because this executive discretion was not constrained by the type of protections sought by Woodard, he concluded, Ohio's clemency procedures did not violate his Fourteenth Amendment right to due process.

Justice Rehnquist addressed the Fifth Amendment right to silence issue by noting that the amendment only protected against compelled self-incrimination. He compared the inmate's participation in the voluntary interview to a defendant who chooses to take the stand in his or her own defense, thus giving up his or her right against self-incrimination. He found it "difficult to see how a voluntary [clemency] interview could 'compel' [Woodard] to speak." Thus, he held, Ohio's clemency interview was not in violation of the Fifth Amendment. The court of appeals judgment was reversed on both questions.

Safeguarding Against Irresponsible Clemency

Justice O'Connor concurred in part with the judgment. She took some exception, however, with the idea that a death-row inmate's interest in life had been extinguished. She felt that although clemency had always been an executive privilege, and not the business of the judiciary, some "minimal procedural safeguards apply to clemency proceedings." She reasoned that the courts may be correct in intervening, for example, when the clemency procedure involved "a state official [flipping] a coin." She believed that Ohio's clemency process violated Woodard's rights and was joined by Justices Souter, Ginsburg and Breyer in that finding.

In his lone dissent Justice Stevens, in agreement with Justice O'Connor, differed with the Chief Justice's reasoning and conclusions on the due process question. He agreed with Woodard that *Dumschat* was not the proper controlling precedent since that case was concerned with only a liberty interest, not a life interest.

He further contended that a death-row inmate does retain a "continuing life interest" which should be protected by the Due Process Clause. He agreed with the majority that Woodard's Fifth Amendment protections against self-incrimination were not violated by the clemency interview process.

Impact

By limiting the involvement the judiciary can have in questions concerning the executive power to grant clemency, the Court gave more autonomy to the states. Charles Hobson of the conservative Criminal Justice Legal Foundation stated,

> This decision makes it clear that a state's clemency process is essentially unavailable for scrutiny by federal courts. Had the court adopted . . . [Woodard's] claims, every state would have had to choose between abandoning clemency altogether or having it dictated to them by federal judges.

Yet others, such as the American Civil Liberties Union, argue that without authoritative framing of

> basic procedural standards by [the Supreme] Court, clemency can no longer be relied on to fulfill its historical role in state schemes of capital punishment.

Related Cases

Greenholtz v. Nebraska Penal Inmates, 442 U.S. 1 (1979).
Connecticut Board of Pardons v. Dumschat, 452 U.S. 458 (1981).
Evitts v. Lucey, 469 U.S. 387 (1985).
Ford v. Wainwright, 477 U.S. 399 (1986).
Herrera v. Collins, 506 U.S. 390 (1993).

Bibliography and Further Reading

American Civil Liberties Union. http://www.aclu.org/court/ohiovwoodard.html

USA Today, December 8, 1997; March 26, 1998.

SEARCH AND SEIZURE

Fourth Amendment Protections

Many issues in criminal procedure have complicated roots, and though the questions surrounding the issue of search and seizure are themselves complex, the Constitution's primary regulations regarding it can be found in a single amendment, the Fourth. The amendment states that "The right of the people to be secure in their persons, houses, papers, and effects, against unreasonable searches and seizures, shall not be violated, and no Warrants shall issue, but upon probable cause, supported by Oath or affirmation, and particularly describing the place to be searched, and the persons or things to be seized."

The wording of the Fourth Amendment may seem fairly straightforward, but it has given rise to endless debate about such key issues as the exact definition of probable cause. Nor does it address the myriad other questions which arise in the ordinary course of law enforcement: does the law officer have to obtain the warrant *before* the arrest? What if this makes it impossible to catch the suspect, who might have a chance to flee while the officer is busy obtaining a warrant? What if the officer sees something without even having to search—for example, he or she stops someone for speeding and notices a bag of cocaine sitting on the passenger seat? What happens to evidence obtained by less-than-legal means? These are some questions that have been addressed in cases testing the Fourth Amendment; likewise changes in society and technology have required examination of issues such as automobile searches, mandatory drug testing, and electronic wiretapping.

Search and Seizure Before the 1960s

Like books or songs, some constitutional amendments are more "popular"—i.e., they have been the subject of more Supreme Court cases—than others; and likewise amendments enjoy periods of greater or lesser attention from the legal community. The Fourteenth Amendment, for instance, has had several periods of enormous "popularity" since its adoption in 1868: in the late 1800s, it was used to protect corporate interests, and in the 1960s and 1970s, it was wielded on behalf of civil rights and civil liberties. As for the Fourth Amendment, it had been all but ignored until the 1880s. It did not become a pressing matter until the 1960s, and it was subjected to a significant challenge in the 1980s.

In its first important search and seizure case, *Boyd v. United States* (1886), the Court read the Fourth and Fifth Amendments together and linked the right against unreasonable search and seizure with the right against self-incrimination. "[T]he seizure of a man's private books and papers to be used in evidence against him," the Court held, would not be "substantially different from compelling him to be a witness against himself." Almost an entire generation passed until the Court again addressed a significant search and seizure issue, and in *Adams v. New York* (1904) it proved less vigilant with regard to Fourth Amendment protections. In the latter ruling, it held that only when the defendant is required to undertake a "positive act"—e.g., to actually show a law enforcement officer his private books and papers—would this constitute unlawful search and seizure.

The issue of unlawfully obtained evidence came to the forefront with *Weeks v. United States* (1914), in which the Court held that such evidence would be inadmissable in a federal court. This was the "exclusionary rule," providing for the exclusion of evidence obtained illegally. Yet this restriction, as the ruling in *Wolf v. People of the State of Colorado* in 1949 indicated, did not apply to the states, and would not until 1961.

One of the primary requirements for lawful search and seizure, of course, is the issuance of a warrant according to constitutional guidelines. For instance, the magistrate who issues the warrant must be "neutral and detached," as the Court stated in a 1948 ruling—i.e., the judge must not have any vested interest in the arrest or conviction of the suspect. In *Brinegar v. United States* (1949), the Court noted that a warrant balanced the "often opposing interests" of individual liberty on the one hand, and public safety on the other. But warrants have to be followed strictly: as was stated in the opinion for *Gouled v. United States* (1921), which held that law officers could only seize "instrumentalities" of crime, as well as the products of crime, but not "mere evidence." Hence officers could seize an illegal drug lab or the products thereof, but they could not simply go on a hunt for anything to corroborate their case against the suspect.

The Exclusionary Rule and Other Holdings of the Warren Court

The Fourth Amendment first came to prominence in an era of high regard for property rights, when a largely conservative Court in the late 1800s and early 1900s tended to rule in favor of business interests. Concerns over search and seizure entered a second phase during the 1960s, and this time the issue's champions were much further to the left politically. Perhaps the most important Fourth Amendment ruling of that decade came in 1961, with *Mapp v. Ohio,* in which the Court overturned its earlier holding in *Wolf,* and applied the exclusionary rule to state governments as well as to the federal government. To do otherwise, the Court ruled, would be to render the Fourth Amendment "'a form of words,' valueless and undeserving of mention in a perpetual charter of inestimable human liberties."

In *Wong Sun v. United States* (1963), the Court addressed the issue of a warrantless search and seizure. The Court held that when an officer apprehends a criminal in the middle of committing a crime, there are certain types of search and seizure that may be permissible. Nonetheless, with its holding in *Wong Sun,* the Court made it clear that "the requirements of reliability and particularity of the information on which an officer may act . . . surely cannot be less stringent [in cases of warrantless arrest] than where an arrest warrant is obtained. Otherwise, a principal incentive now existing for the procurement of arrest warrants would be destroyed." In other words, a law officer would be tempted to violate Fourth Amendment requirements in order to obtain evidence, and then claim that no warrant was required.

Decisions such as that in *Wong Sun* tended to suggest, in the wake of *Mapp,* a tightening of possible government loopholes for violation of Fourth Amendment rights. In *Aguilar v. Texas* (1964), the Court established stricter standards with regard to the use of information provided to police by informants, and in *Katz v. United States* (1967), it ruled that electronic eavesdropping by means of a recording device on the outside of a telephone booth constituted illegal search and seizure.

With *Katz,* once again Fourth Amendment issues seemed to be merging with Fifth Amendment concerns regarding self-incrimination. Yet even as Fourth Amendment protections were increasing on some fronts, they were decreasing on others. *Terry v. Ohio* (1968), nicknamed the *Stop and Frisk Case,* provided for situations in which police could stop and frisk a suspect on the street, a measure which the Court deemed a positive alternative to arrest as a means of

short-term detention. Some rulings seemed like plain common sense: thus in *Camara v. Municipal Court* (1967), the Court allowed safety inspections of dwellings even when there was no evidence of existing building code violations. But with such 1970s cases as *United States v. Robinson* (1973), authorizing search of anyone under lawful custodial arrest, and *Delaware v. Prouse* (1979), which permitted law officers to stop vehicles to check license and registration even without evidence of any violation, the Court signalled a growing trend toward favoring police interests in Fourth-Amendment cases.

Search and Seizure vs. Law and Order: the 1980s and 1990s

In the early 1990s, President Bill Clinton raised hackles among civil libertarians for his advocacy of routine searches of public housing, as well as "roving wiretaps"—the use of a warrant as a basis to tap all of a suspect's phones, rather than the one on which police had probable cause to believe they would obtain information of criminal activity. But reaction to these abrogations of Fourth Amendment rights was relatively limited. There were a number of reasons for this lack of outcry, not least of which was the fact that escalating concerns regarding crime had overtaken the preoccupation with constitutional liberties which had animated a more carefree era.

Times had changed: the drug culture of the 1960s had spawned a much more sinister version, surrounding cocaine and its derivative, crack, in the 1980s and 1990s. Public housing, much of it established during the wave of optimism that characterized the 1960s "War on Poverty," had long since ceased to be regarded as a solution to poverty. People tended to regard housing projects as breeding grounds for crime and drugs, and with the very idea of the welfare state on the decline, sweeping searches of public housing projects seemed justified. Likewise in the area of wiretapping, advocates of law and order could point to the FBI's enormous success in gathering evidence against the Gambino crime family during the late 1980s and early 1990s, an effort which led to the downfall of crime boss John Gotti.

Perhaps typical of the attitude toward search and seizure cases in the 1980s and 1990s was the Court's ruling in *Richards v. Wisconsin* (1997). The case involved a "no knock entry" into a suspect's hotel room, which represented a departure from the "knock and announce" requirement implied in the Court's 1995 *Wilson v. Arkansas* ruling. In the case of suspected drug dealer Steiney Richards, the Madison, Wisconsin, police asserted that if they had "knocked and announced" prior to their 1992 arrest of the suspect in his hotel room, he would have had time to flush the evidence down the toilet. The Court agreed, thus limiting its earlier *Wilson* holding in light of what Justice John Paul Stevens referred to as "today's drug culture."

The "knock and announce" requirement had its roots, like much of U.S. constitutional law, in British common law. By the time of *Wilson,* the federal government as well as thirty-four states and the District of Columbia had their own "knock and announce" rules. Likewise there were exceptions, as noted in *Richards.* These included the "Apprehension of Peril" exception, which pertains when officers have reason to believe that announcing their presence would bring harm to themselves or to others (e.g., a shootout); the "Useless Gesture" exception, triggered when the occupants of a dwelling already know that the officer is coming in, and why; and the "Destruction of Evidence" exception, which applied in *Richards.*

In light of the government's competing needs to support public safety while protecting individual liberties, it is understandable why such exceptions should be made. Nonetheless, the ruling in *Richards* highlights—at least, in the view of some civil libertarians—the toll which may be taken on individual rights because of "today's drug [and crime] culture." Some proposed legislation resulting from the decision includes mandatory drug testing, which came to the forefront during the 1980s "War on Drugs"; and one of the bills introduced by the then-new Republican majority in Congress in 1995, the Exclusionary Rule Reform Act of 1995—nicknamed the "Take Back Our Streets Act." It reflected the disgust many citizens felt with the continued spread of crime, which many attributed to the lax judicial attitude that had followed in the wake of the Warren Court.

See also: **The Rights of the Accused, Privacy, Drug Laws, Criminal Procedure**

Bibliography and Further Reading

Bulzomi, Michael J., J.D. "Knock and Announce: A Fourth Amendment Standard." *Federal Bureau of Investigation.* http://www.fbi.gov/leb/may976.htm (September 8, 1998).

Ladynski, Jacob W. *Search and Seizure and the Supreme Court.* Baltimore, MD: Johns Hopkins University Press, 1966.

LaFave, Wayne R. *Search and Seizure: A Treatise on the Fourth Amendment,* three volumes. St. Paul, MN: West Publishing, 1978.

"Search and Seizure." *Court TV.* http://www.courttv.com/legalcafe/home/search/search_background.html (September 8, 1998).

Wetterer, Charles M. *The Fourth Amendment: Search and Seizure.* Springfield, NJ: Enslow, 1998.

LEISY V. HARDIN

Legal Citation: 135 U.S. 100 (1890)

Appellants
Gus Leisy & Co., et al.

Appellee
A. J. Hardin

Appellants' Claim
That the laws under which property was seized from the appellants were unconstitutional, as they assumed powers reserved only for Congress.

Chief Lawyer for Appellants
James C. Davis

Chief Lawyers for Appellee
H. Scott Howell, William B. Collins, John Y. Stone

Justices for the Court
Samuel Blatchford, Joseph P. Bradley, David Davis, Stephen Johnson Field, Melville Weston Fuller (writing for the Court), Lucius Quintus C. Lamar

Justices Dissenting
David Josiah Brewer, Horace Gray, John Marshall Harlan I

Place
Washington, D.C.

Date of Decision
28 April 1890

Decision
Overturned the decision of the Iowa Supreme Court, ruling for the return of the appellants' property, which had been confiscated by the state under laws that were declared unconstitutional.

Significance
The ruling made clear that commerce between the states was within the domain of Congress, and that no state could confiscate property that Congress recognized as legally imported. The Court's decision reinforced Congress's control over interstate trade, and paved the way for legislation which surrendered that right under certain conditions.

During the mid- and late-1800s, the United States witnessed an increase in temperance groups, who called for the prohibition of alcohol. Their perception of drinking liquor as a detriment to society was also held by Supreme Court justices. In *Mugler v. Kansas* (1887), for example, the Court said, "statistics accessible to every one [show] that the idleness, disorder, pauperism, and crime existing in the country are, in some degree at least, traceable to this evil." In response to the grass-roots temperance movements, many states began passing legislation limiting the sale of liquor, while making exceptions for its production and sale for medicinal, mechanical, and religious purposes. Because of this nationwide trend, several cases concerning the prohibition of alcohol, and the confiscations relating to that prohibition, came before the Court.

In this particular case, the question centered around whether an individual state could control imports from other states. Gus Leisy & Co., made up of Christiana, Edward, Lena, and Albert Leisy, was a brewing company based in Peoria, Illinois. This brewing company brought into Keokuk, Iowa, barrels and cases of beer, all of which were sealed with metallic IRS seals. They were stilled sealed in this way on 30 June 1888, when they were confiscated by authority of a search warrant by A.J. Hardin, the marshal for the city of Keokuk. The state of Iowa had outlawed the production and sale of "intoxicating liquors," except "for pharmaceutical and medicinal purposes, and alcohol for specified chemical purposes, and wine for sacramental purposes," for which permits had to be secured. Because the Leisy beer was to be sold without such a permit indicating it was for one of these exempted purposes, the actions of Gus Leisy & Co. were seen as illegal, and the beer was confiscated. Gus Leisy & Co. then brought suit against Hardin to recover the confiscated property. The state court ruled that the laws under which the property were confiscated were unconstitutional, and therefore void; the ruling was for the company, calling for the return of the property. The state supreme court reversed this ruling, and the case was then heard by the U.S. Supreme Court.

While the U.S. Supreme Court acknowledged in this and other cases the rights of states to pass legislation which would protect its citizens (including the right to restrict access to alcohol, considering its negative effects), the question specifically to be answered was whether states could usurp powers normally reserved for Congress. In *Brown v. Maryland* (1827), for example, consideration was given to states' powers to tax imports, and to restrictions requiring imports to be sold in their original packaging. In that case, the Court ruled that "the right to sell any article imported was an inseparable incident to the right to import it;" i.e., if states allow the importation of an article, they cannot make the sale of that article illegal. In *Bowman v. Railway Co.* (1888), the Court also considered the ability of states to restrict interstate trade, and rejected any authority except that of Congress: a certificate Iowa required for interstate transport "was declared invalid, because essentially a regulation of commerce among the states, and not sanctioned by the authority, express or implied, of Congress." In view of these precedents, then, and the constitutional designation of power over interstate trade to Congress, the U.S. Supreme Court overturned the ruling of the Iowa Supreme Court, and ruled for Gus Leisy & Co. As the opinion of the Court stated, ". . . in the absence of congressional permission to do so, the State had no power to interfere by seizure, or any other action, in

prohibition of importation . . . we cannot hold that any articles which Congress recognizes as subjects of interstate commerce are not such."

But this decision did not affect the possibility of Congress passing legislation which would specifically allow states to control the importation of liquor. In fact, the Court made it clear that Congress retained control over interstate trade only until it gave up that control by enacting legislation. This did eventually occur, with Congress passing laws allowing states to ban all sales and importation of liquor, such as the Wilson Act, and later, the Eighteenth Amendment to the Constitution which brought in the era of Prohibition.

Related Cases
Brown v. Maryland, 12 Wheat. 419 (1827).
Mugler v. Kansas, 123 U.S. 623 (1887).
Bowman v. Railway Co., 125 U.S. 465 (1888).

Bibliography and Further Reading
Biskupic, Joan, and Elder Witt, eds. *Guide to the U.S. Supreme Court.* Washington, DC: Congressional Quarterly, Inc., 1997.

Witt, Elder, ed. *The Supreme Court A to Z.* Washington, DC: Congressional Quarterly, Inc., 1993.

WEEKS V. UNITED STATES

Legal Citation: 232 U.S. 383 (1914)

Petitioner
Fremont Weeks

Respondent
United States

Petitioner's Claim
That his house was searched and his papers seized without a search warrant and thus the papers should not be admissible in court as evidence against him.

Chief Lawyer for Petitioner
Martin J. O'Donnell

Chief Lawyers for Respondent
Denison, U.S. Assistant Attorney General; John William Davis, U.S. Solicitor General

Justices for the Court
William Rufus Day (writing for the Court), Oliver Wendell Holmes, Charles Evans Hughes, Joseph Rucker Lamar, Horace Harmon Lurton, Joseph McKenna, Mahlon Pitney, Willis Van Devanter, Edward Douglass White

Justices Dissenting
None

Place
Washington, D.C.

Date of Decision
24 February 1914

Decision
Reversed the decision of a district court and held that evidence obtained by unreasonable searches and seizures could not be used against a person in federal court.

Significance
Weeks v. United States marked the creation of the exclusionary rule, which originally stated that evidence obtained in violation of the Fourth Amendment's protection against unreasonable search and seizure could not be used against a person in federal court.

Before the decision in *Weeks v. United States,* the courts admitted illegally seized material as evidence to avoid allowing guilty parties to go free. The rights of the individual were considered less important than the administration of justice. This case marked a turning point in the Court's thinking. With the introduction of the exclusionary rule, the Court devised a way of enforcing the Fourth Amendment, which prohibited unreasonable searches and seizures. Since evidence seized unlawfully could no longer be used in federal court against a defendant, a prosecutor might lose or drop a case for lack of evidence. Thus, in theory, the police would be careful to obtain search warrants and make sure their searches and seizures were legal.

On 21 December 1911, a police officer arrested Fremont Weeks, without a warrant, at his place of employment. Other police officers went to his house and searched Weeks's room, without a search warrant. The officers seized books, letters, money, papers, stocks, deeds, candies, clothes, and other property, which they turned over to the U.S. marshal. Later the same day, the police returned with the marshal, who seized letters and envelopes found in a drawer. The marshal did not have a search warrant. The material was given to the district attorney. Weeks asked for the return of his property, so the court ordered those things which were not pertinent to the case to be returned. The district attorney returned some of the property, but kept what was pertinent to the alleged sale of lottery tickets. After the jury had been sworn in, but before any evidence had been given, Weeks asked for the rest of his property to be returned. The court denied this request. When Weeks's papers were introduced as evidence at the trial, he objected on the ground that the papers had been obtained without a search warrant and by breaking into his home, violating the Fourth and Fifth Amendments. The court overruled the objection. The lottery tickets and letters regarding the lottery were used as evidence against Weeks.

Great Principles Must Not Be Sacrificed

Justice Day wrote the unanimous opinion of the Court. Day reviewed the history of the Fourth Amendment, noting that it was based on the premise that a man's

The Silver Platter Doctrine

Weeks in 1914 established not only the exclusionary rule, but also an exception to the exclusionary rule called the "Silver Platter Doctrine." This exception covered situations in which federal law-enforcement officers had evidence "handed to them on a silver platter"—Justice Felix Frankfurter's phrase—by state authorities.

The key idea here was the participation of state law-enforcement personnel, who usually worked under less strict requirements regarding search and seizure laws; if federal authorities became involved, the Court ruled in *Byars v. United States* (1927)—no matter how slight the degree of involvement—improperly obtained evidence would then have to be subjected to the exclusionary rule.

In its application to criminal cases, the Silver Platter Doctrine had a life span of 44 years, until *Elkins v. United States* (1960). In the meantime, the Court had begun to apply Fourth Amendment principles to the states, and a number of the states themselves had adopted exclusionary rules. But for civil proceedings, the Court held in *Janis v. United States* (1976), the Silver Platter Doctrine remains valid.

Source(s): Levy, Leonard W., ed. *Encyclopedia of the American Constitution.* New York: Macmillan, 1986.

---

house was his castle and thus should not be invaded. This feature of the Constitution was written to prevent the kind of general warrants issued by the government in colonial times. Based on the case, *Ex parte Jackson,* the prohibition against unreasonable searches and seizures was applicable to letters and sealed packages in the mail.

Day quoted Justice Joseph P. Bradley in *Boyd v. United States,* "It is not the breaking of his doors and rummaging of his drawers that constitutes the essence of the offense; but it is the invasion of his indefeasible right of personal security, personal liberty, and private property." Day noted that the effect of the Fourth Amendment was to place the courts under limitations regarding their power. The courts should not sanction the tendency of law enforcement to obtain convictions by using unlawful seizures. It is the duty of all those in law enforcement to make sure the Fourth Amendment has force.

Day felt that the guarantees of the Fourth Amendment would be useless without the enforcement power of the exclusionary rule. He stated that,

> If letters and private documents can thus be seized and held and used in evidence . . . the protection of the Fourth Amendment . . . is of no value and . . . might as well be stricken from the Constitution. The efforts of the courts . . . are not to be aided by the sacrifice of those great principles established by years of endeavor and suffering.

Thus Day placed individual rights before the needs of law enforcement.

Day summed up his opinion by stating that Weeks's letters were taken and not returned, in direct violation of his constitutional rights. Day also noted

that "the Fourth Amendment is not directed to individual misconduct of such officials. Its limitations reach the Federal government and its agencies." This statement meant that the exclusionary rule applied only to the federal government and not to states or cities.

A Personal Right of the Defendant?

The Court's opinion in this case left some points unclarified. Was the exclusionary rule required by the Constitution? Or was the rule the product of the Court's power to supervise the lower federal courts? Was it subject to negation by Congress? The *Weeks* opinion seemed to endorse the belief that the exclusionary rule was a personal right of the defendant. More recent decisions dealing with the exclusionary rule favored the belief that the rule was primarily a deterrent against unlawful searches, and not a personal right.

Impact

The *Weeks* case attracted little notice until Prohibition, when issues surrounding federal government searches and seizures often arose. In 1961, the Supreme Court applied the exclusionary rule to the states, in *Mapp v. Ohio.* This application became one of the Court's most controversial rulings. It formed part of the "Warren Revolution," lead by Chief Justice Warren. With Warren as its leader, the Supreme Court became the guardian of individual rights, part of which meant restricting the power of government regarding searches and seizures. Under the leadership of Chief Justice Burger, the Supreme Court leaned in the opposite direction, finding many exceptions to the exclusionary rule. Justice William H. Rehnquist led the crusade against the exclusionary rule in the 1980s and 1990s, substantially broadening the exceptions to the rule.

Related Cases
Ex parte Jackson, 96 U.S. 727 (1877).
Boyd v. United States, 116 U.S. 616 (1886).
Bram v. United States, 168 U.S. 532 (1897).
Holt v. United States, 218 U.S. 245 (1910).
Mapp v. Ohio, 367 U.S. 643 (1961).

Bibliography and Further Reading
Bernstein, Richard B., and Jerome Agel. *Into the Third Century: The Supreme Court.* New York: Walker, 1989.

Biskupic, Joan, and Elder Witt, eds. *Guide to the U.S. Supreme Court.* Washington, DC: Congressional Quarterly, Inc., 1997.

Hall, Kermit L., ed. *The Oxford Companion to the Supreme Court of the United States.* New York: Oxford University Press, 1992.

Irons, Peter. *Brennan vs. Rehnquist: The Battle for the Constitution.* New York: Alfred A. Knopf, 1994.

Johnson, John W., ed. *Historic U.S. Court Cases, 1690–1990: An Encyclopedia.* New York: Garland Publishing, 1992.

CARROLL V. UNITED STATES

Legal Citation: 267 U.S. 132 (1925)

Appellants
George Carroll, John Kiro

Appellee
United States

Appellants' Claim
That since there was no basis for the search of their car, the evidence resulting from the search should have been excluded from trial, their arrest and seizure were unlawful, and the use of the liquor as evidence violated their constitutional rights.

Chief Lawyer for Appellants
Thomas E. Atkinson

Chief Lawyers for Appellee
John G. Sargent, Attorney General; James M. Beck

Justices for the Court
William Howard Taft (writing for the Court), Joseph McKenna, Willis Van Devanter, Louis D. Brandeis, Pierce Butler, Edward Terry Sanford

Justices Dissenting
James Clark McReynolds, George Sutherland

Place
Washington, D.C.

Date of Decision
2 March 1925

Decision
Upheld the warrantless search of a car, noting that probable cause existed and the mobility of the automobile made it impracticable to get a search warrant.

Significance
The ruling in this case created the automobile exception to the general rule that searches require warrants. Evidence from warrantless automobile searches is admissible in court as long as the officer had probable cause to search.

In January of 1920 the Eighteenth Amendment went into effect, prohibiting the manufacture, sale, or transportation of intoxicating liquors. Congress passed the Volstead Act to implement the Eighteenth Amendment. The act forbade any person to manufacture, sell, barter, transport, import, export, deliver, furnish, or possess liquor. The commissioner of internal revenue enforced the act with fewer than 2,000 agents to police the entire country. Because Congress never granted enough money for more than token enforcement of the act, gangs took control of the illegal liquor trade, bootlegging, smuggling, and running speakeasies.

On 15 December 1921, Fred Cronenwett, chief prohibition officer, and other officers, saw George Carroll and John Kiro driving towards Grand Rapids, Michigan. Cronenwett recognized the occupants and the automobile and decided to follow them. After stopping the car, Cronenwett asked the occupants to get out. He searched the car and discovered 69 quarts of whisky hidden in the upholstery. He did not have a search warrant.

Warrantless Automobile Searches Valid

Chief Justice Taft, formerly president of the United States, wrote the opinion for the majority in this case. He noted that the Stanley Amendment called for the punishment of any officer who searches a private dwelling without a warrant or who searches any other building or property where the search without a warrant is done maliciously and without probable cause. "In other words, it left the way open for searching an automobile or vehicle of transportation without a warrant, if the search was not malicious or without probable cause." Taft stated that Congress intended to make a distinction between the necessity for a search warrant for private dwellings and for automobiles, in the enforcement of the Prohibition Act. Taft believed that this distinction was consistent with the Fourth Amendment because the amendment does not denounce all searches or seizures, but only unreasonable ones. ". . . If the search and seizure without a warrant are made upon probable cause, that is, upon a belief, reasonably arising out of circumstances known to the seizing officer, that an automobile or other vehicle contains that which by law is subject to seizure and destruction, the search and seizure are valid." Taft stated that the Fourth Amendment should be understood in light of what was considered an unreasonable search and seizure when the amendment was adopted. It should be construed in a manner which conserves public interests as well as the interests and rights of individuals. Almost since the beginning of our government, the Fourth Amendment guarantee of freedom from unreasonable search and seizure has recognized a necessary difference between the search of a building and the search of a method of transportation, where it is not practical to get a warrant because the vehicle can be moved quickly.

Taft noted that people have the right to freely use the highways unless an official has probable cause to believe that a vehicle is carrying illegal goods. The appellants argued that common law states that a police officer may arrest without a warrant a person that the officer believes upon reasonable cause to have committed a felony. The officer may only arrest without a warrant if the person is guilty of a misdemeanor committed in the officer's presence. The appellants argued that since a misdemeanor must be committed in the officer's presence to justify arrest without a warrant, unless the officer can detect with his senses that the liquor was being transported, the offense was not committed in his presence. Taft felt this distinction was unsatisfactory since the main object is to forfeit and suppress the liquor. The arrest of the individual is only incidental.

The appellants based one argument on *Weeks v. United States* (1914), asserting that when someone is legally arrested for an offense, whatever is found upon his person or in his control that it is unlawful for him to have and which may be used to prove the offense may be seized and held as evidence in the prosecution. The appellants argued that the seizure in this case can only be justified if it were based on a valid arrest, without a seizure. Taft countered that "the right to search and the validity of the seizure are not dependent on the right to arrest. They are dependent on the reasonable cause the seizing officer has for belief that the contents of the automobile offend against the law." The nature of the offense for which, after the liquor is found and seized, the driver can be prosecuted does not affect the validity of the seizure. Taft felt that this conclusion satisfied the Fourth Amendment.

Taft next discussed the question of probable cause in this case. The prohibition agents were engaged in a regular patrol of the highways from Detroit to Grand Rapids, Detroit being one of the most active centers for smuggling liquor into the country. Their patrol involved stopping cars and seizing liquor carried in them. The officers "knew or had convincing evidence" that the "Carroll boys" were bootleggers in Grand Rapids. The officers recognized the car driven by the suspects because it was the same car they had been in when they tried to furnish whisky to the officers. The car was heading from Detroit, a major source of whisky, to Grand Rapids, where the men plied their trade. "That the officers, when they saw the defendants, believed that they were carrying liquor, we can have no doubt, and we think it is equally clear that they had reasonable cause for thinking so." The defendants had argued that the officers were not looking for the defendants when they spotted them. Taft felt this argument had no weight. When the defendants did appear, "the officers were entitled to use their reasoning faculties upon all the facts of which they had previous knowledge in respect to the defendants." The officers in this case were justified in their search and seizure because a man of reasonable caution and with their knowledge would have believed that liquor was being transported in the automobile.

What Becomes Of The Fourth And Fifth Amendments?

Justice McReynolds wrote the dissent. As McReynolds saw the case, George Carroll and John Kiro "while quietly driving an ordinary automobile along a much frequented public road . . . were arrested by federal officers without a warrant and upon mere suspicion— ill-founded, as I think."

Justice McReynolds noted that the Volstead Act indicates that probable cause is not always enough to justify a seizure and that suspicion that the law is being violated does not justify an arrest. Noting that the Fourth Amendment denounces only unreasonable seizures, McReynolds felt that unreasonableness often depends upon the means adopted. In this case, the seizure followed an unlawful arrest and therefore became unlawful. "The validity of the seizure under consideration depends on the legality of the arrest . . . If an officer, upon mere suspicion of a misdemeanor, may stop one on the public highway, take articles away from him and thereafter use them as evidence to convict him of crime, what becomes of the Fourth and Fifth Amendments?" McReynolds summed up his dissent by stating that the arrest of George Carroll and John Kiro was unauthorized, illegal, and violated the due process guarantee of the Fifth Amendment. The liquor taken as evidence was obtained in a search that followed the arrest and was therefore obtained in violation of the men's constitutional rights.

Impact

The decision in *Carroll v. United States* was the first time that the Supreme Court recognized the car search exception to the warrant requirement. The Court continued to articulate the position it took with the *Carroll* case, that privacy interests in a car have constitutional protection, but a car's mobility justifies less broad protection and is thus exempt from traditional warrant requirements. In 1931, the Court upheld the search of a parked car because police could not know when the car might be moved. A 1948 decision appeared to limit the automobile exception to vehicles suspected of violating federal laws. But in 1949, the Court upheld warrantless searches of cars as long as the police had probable cause to believe the vehicle was involved in illegal activity.

In the 1960s, the Supreme Court applied the same limits to state police as to federal authorities regarding warrantless automobile searches. The Court upheld the warrantless search of a car as long as a week after the owner's arrest, since the car was subject to government forfeiture. The Court has permitted law enforcement officers to search cars after they have been towed to a police garage from an arrest site. Evidence obtained in a routine warrantless search of an impounded vehicle was deemed admissible in court. They have also ruled that a warrant is not necessary when taking paint samples from a car parked in a public lot.

In the 1977 *United States v. Chadwick* trial, the Court brought up the concept of a person's expectations of privacy being less in an automobile than in other things, such as a locked piece of luggage. Since the *Chadwick* ruling, the Supreme Court has continued to enlarge the automobile exception begun with *Carroll*. In 1978, the Court decided that passengers could not object to a warrantless search of a car. This ruling linked the Fourth Amendment rights of passengers more closely to property concepts than to privacy interests. In the 1980s, the Court ruled that law enforcement officers, with probable cause to search a car, could also search closed containers in that car. In the 1990s, the Court found that the police could search an entire car when they had probable cause only to search a container in the car. Over the decades the Court has moved away from Taft's reasoning about the mobility of cars making warrantless searches a necessity to a concept of the limited expectations of privacy that people have regarding their automobiles.

Related Cases
Boyd v. United States, 116 U.S. 616 (1886).
Weeks v. United States, 232 U.S. 383 (1914).
United States v. Chadwick, 433 U.S. 1 (1977).

Bibliography and Further Reading
FindLaw, Inc. *Internet Legal Resources.* http://www. findlaw.com

Hall, Kermit L., ed. *The Oxford Companion to the Supreme Court of the United States.* New York: Oxford Press, 1992.

Witt, Elder, ed. *The Supreme Court A to Z. CQ's Encyclopedia of American Government.* Washington, DC: Congressional Quarterly, Inc., 1993.

UNITED STATES V. LEE

Legal Citation: 274 U.S. 559 (1927)

Petitioner
United States

Respondent
Lee, et al.

Petitioner's Claim
That the Coast Guard's search and seizure of an American vessel on the high seas more that 12 miles from land and the subsequent arrest of persons on the vessel for violations of the Tariff Act and the National Prohibition Act was lawful.

Chief Lawyer for Petitioner
John G. Sargent, U.S. Attorney General

Chief Lawyer for Respondent
None

Justices for the Court
Louis D. Brandeis (writing for the Court), Pierce Butler, Oliver Wendell Holmes, James Clark McReynolds, Edward Terry Sanford, Harlan Fiske Stone, George Sutherland, William Howard Taft, Willis Van Devanter

Justices Dissenting
None

Place
Washington, D.C.

Date of Decision
31 May 1927

Decision
The search and seizure of the vessel on the high seas and the arrest of persons on the vessel was lawful because probable cause existed to believe that revenue laws were being violated.

Significance
The ruling resolved the question of whether the U.S. Coast Guard could board and search American vessels on the high seas and arrest persons on the vessels for violations of the Tariff Act of 1922 and the National Prohibition Act. The Court concluded that if probable cause existed to believe that the vessel and persons in it were violating U.S. revenue laws, the Coast Guard could seize, board, and search the vessel beyond the U.S. territorial waters and the high seas 12 miles outward from the coast. The case was also significant for its ruling that the Coast Guard's use of a searchlight to view the contents of the vessel on the high seas did not constitute a search and thus did not warrant Fourth Amendment protections. The ruling allowed the U.S government to intensify its effort to enforce prohibition by preventing the smuggling of liquor.

In the early twentieth century, individual states and the U.S. government made numerous attempts to control the sale and consumption of alcoholic beverages by its citizens. The most ambitious and well-known attempt was the passage in 1919 of the Eighteenth Amendment, establishing nationwide prohibition. The Eighteenth Amendment prohibited the manufacture, sale, transportation, importation, and exportation of intoxicating liquors for beverage purposes and authorized both Congress and the states to enact enforcing legislation. Congress subsequently passed the National Prohibition Act to prevent the use of intoxicating liquor as a beverage. The act made it unlawful to have or possess any liquor intended for beverage use and provided that a person possessing such liquor had no property rights to the liquor. The act also authorized issuance of search warrants under which such liquor could be seized and destroyed. A subsequent amendment to the act, the Stanley Amendment, allowed warrantless searches of automobiles or vehicles of transportation, as opposed to private dwellings, if the search was not malicious or without probable cause. The passage of the Eighteenth Amendment and the National Prohibition Act did not, however, stop commerce in liquor, but simply drove it underground.

In 1925, the U.S. Coast Guard seized, boarded, and searched a motorboat 24 miles off the coast of Massachusetts, and after finding cans of alcohol on the boat, arrested the persons on board for violation of the Tariff Act and the National Prohibition Act. Two of those arrested were convicted. One of the convicted respondents sued via a writ of error complaining that the seizure, boarding, and search of the motorboat on the high seas violated the Fourth Amendment, and, consequently, that the evidence found during the search—including the liquor—could not be used to convict him. The circuit court of appeals, with one judge dissenting, agreed with the respondents and vacated or cancelled the conviction. The circuit court held that the Coast Guard was not authorized to visit, search, and seize an American vessel on the high seas more than 12 miles from the coast. The circuit court also held that the failure of the government to ratify the seizure by instituting legal forfeiture proceedings against the boat and liquor rendered the seizure illegal, barring use in evidence of any knowledge gained as a result of the search. The United States petitioned for a writ of *certiorari* seeking review by the U.S. Supreme Court, which the Supreme Court granted.

Search on High Seas Lawful

The Supreme Court, in a decision authored by Justice Brandeis, reversed the circuit court of appeals. In the Supreme Court, the government argued that the Coast Guard has authority to visit, search, and seize an American vessel on the high seas beyond the 12-mile limit when probable cause exists that a U.S. law is being violated. The government also argued that the Coast Guard has authority to arrest persons on such vessels when reason exists to believe that a felony is being committed. The government argued further that, in this case, probable cause existed that the Tariff Act and National Prohibition Act were being violated, justifying the seizure of the boat and arrest of the respondents. Regarding the subsequent search of the boat, the government argued that any search made before the boat reached port was valid as an incident of a lawful arrest. However, the government also claimed that the Coast Guard did not search the boat.

The Supreme Court agreed with the government's contentions. Referring to its holding in *Maul v. United States* (1927), decided on the same day, the Court stated that Coast Guard officers are authorized by federal statute to seize on the high seas beyond the 12-mile limit any American vessel subject to forfeiture for violation of any law respecting the revenue. From that power, Justice Brandeis inferred that Coast Guard officers were also "authorized to board and search such vessels when there is probable cause to believe them subject to seizure for violation of revenue laws, and to arrest persons thereon engaged in such violation." Justice Brandeis drew a distinction between authority based on probable cause and the "belligerent right to visit and search even without probable cause."

The Supreme Court found probable cause to believe that the revenue laws were being violated by the American vessel and the persons on it in such a manner as to render the vessel subject to forfeiture. Comparing the motorboat to an automobile, the Court stated, "search and seizure of the vessel and arrest of the persons thereon, by the Coast Guard on the high seas, is lawful, as like search and seizure of an automobile and arrest of the persons therein, by prohibition officers on land is lawful." The Court also rejected the respondents' contention that the government's subsequent failure to institute proceedings for forfeiture of the motorboat and liquor rendered the seizure and the search illegal.

Justice Brandeis was known as a liberal jurist who tended to oppose big business and uphold individual rights. © Corbis-Bettmann.

Was There a High Seas Search?

The Supreme Court further concluded that if the Coast Guard conducted a search of the vessel on the high seas, the search was constitutional because it was an incident of a lawful arrest. However, the Court agreed with the government's contention that the evidence did not establish that the Coast Guard had, in fact, conducted a 'search' on the high seas that would trigger the protections of the Fourth Amendment. The Coast Guard boatswain testified that he used a searchlight to view the motorboat and no testimony was given that exploration below decks or under hatches took place. It appeared to the Court that the cases of liquor may have been on deck and may have been discovered when the boatswain shone the searchlight on the motorboat before it was boarded. The Court stated, "[s]uch use of a searchlight is comparable to the use of a marine glass or a field glass. It is not prohibited by the Constitution."

Impact

The Court's ruling in this case and in *Maul v. United States,* legalized expansion of the U.S. Coast Guard's jurisdiction to enforce the Tariff Act and the National Prohibition Act beyond the territorial waters and the high seas 12 miles outward from the coast. The ruling reflected the government's efforts to intensify the pressure against "rum-runners" who circumvented the prohibition laws by smuggling liquor into and out of the United States. Despite the broad powers given the government, prohibition was ultimately unsuccessful. In 1933, ratification of the Twenty-first Amendment repealed the Eighteenth Amendment and rendered the National Prohibition Act inoperative. Other courts subsequently agreed that the use of artificial means to illuminate a darkened area does not constitute a search under the Fourth Amendment. The ruling has also been used to support the proposition that an arresting officer may look around at the time of the arrest and seize evidence of crime or contraband articles that are in plain sight and in his immediate and discernible presence. This proposition is the basis for what is commonly known as the "plain view" exception to the general requirement of a valid search warrant to legitimize a search or seizure.

Related Cases

Hamilton v. Kentucky Distilleries & Warehouse Co., 251 U.S. 146 (1919).
Rhode Island v. Palmer, 253 U.S. 350 (1920).

Dillon v. Gloss, 256 U.S. 368 (1921).
Maul v. United States, 274 U.S. 501 (1927).
United States v. Chambers, 291 U.S. 217 (1934).
United States v. Frankfort Distilleries, 324 U.S. 293 (1945).
Katz v. United States, 389 U.S. 347 (1967).
Texas v. Brown, 460 U.S. 730 (1983).
United States v. Dunn, 480 U.S. 294 (1987).

Bibliography and Further Reading

Clark, Norman. "A Booze Barons' Flamboyant Reign." *Seattle Magazine,* September 1964, pp. 14–18.

Levine, Harry Gene, and David C. Smith, comp. *A Selected Bibliography on Alcohol Control, Particularly before and at Repeal.* California: University of California, Berkeley, 1977.

Mortenson, Lynn Ove. "Black Nights and Bootleg Booze." *Peninsula Magazine,* summer 1993, pp. 40–43.

Richardson, David. "The Noble Disaster." *Pig War Islands.* Eastsound: Orcas Publishing Company, 1971, pp. 308–325.

U.S. Senate Committee on the Judiciary. *The National Prohibition Law: Hearings before the Committee on the Judiciary.* U.S. Senate. 69th Cong., 1st sess. 1926.

WOLF V. PEOPLE OF THE STATE OF COLORADO

Legal Citation: 338 U.S. 25 (1949)

Petitioner
Julius A. Wolf

Respondent
People of the State of Colorado

Petitioner's Claim
That evidence, obtained illegally, should not have been used against Wolf at his state trial for a state offense because it violated his constitutional rights.

Chief Lawyer for Petitioner
Philip Hornbein

Chief Lawyer for Respondent
James S. Henderson

Justices for the Court
Hugo Lafayette Black, Harold Burton, Felix Frankfurter (writing for the Court), Robert H. Jackson, Stanley Forman Reed, Fred Moore Vinson

Justices Dissenting
William O. Douglas, Frank Murphy, Wiley Blount Rutledge

Place
Washington, D.C.

Date of Decision
27 June 1949

Decision
Affirmed the decision of the Supreme Court of Colorado to let stand Wolf's conviction on the ground that, although the Fourth Amendment applied to the states, the states were not required to exclude evidence obtained unlawfully.

Significance
The decision in *Wolf v. People of the State of Colorado* advised that states should exclude evidence from trial if it was illegally obtained, but left the ultimate decision for such exclusion in the hands of the state.

Wolf was convicted of conspiracy to commit abortion in Colorado. He challenged this conviction on the ground that the seizure and use of the evidence against him violated his constitutional rights. The Supreme Court of Colorado affirmed the conviction.

The U.S. Supreme Court agreed to hear the case to decide if the Fourth Amendment guarantee against unreasonable search and seizure was incorporated by the Due Process Clause of the Fourteenth Amendment and thus applied both to the states and the federal government. The Court also looked at whether the exclusionary rule, which prohibited the use of unlawfully gathered evidence by the federal government, also applied to the states.

Due Process Represents A Living Principle

Justice Frankfurter wrote the opinion for the majority. In considering the restrictions which the Due Process Clause imposed on the states regarding the enforcement of criminal law, Frankfurter noted that "this clause exacts from the States for the lowliest and the most outcast all that is implicit in the concept of ordered liberty." Frankfurter felt that the requirements of due process of law are neither formal nor fixed nor narrow. Due process is all the rights which the courts must enforce because they are basic to our free society; they are eternal verities. A free society advances in its ideas what is reasonable and right. Thus due process represents a living principle and is not confined by what may be considered fundamental rights at any given time. Trying to define a fundamental right ignores the movements of a free society. The Court should not be asked to draw a line delimiting due process once and for all, but it should draw that line by the "gradual and empiric process of inclusion and exclusion."

Being secure against arbitrary intrusion by the police is basic to a free society and is at the core of the Fourth Amendment. Because this is implicit in the concept of ordered liberty it is enforceable against the states through the Due Process Clause. "The knock at the door . . . as a prelude to a search, without authority of law but solely on the authority of the police, did not need the commentary of recent history to be condemned as inconsistent with the conception of human rights enshrined in the history and the basic constitutional documents of English speaking peoples."

If a state sanctioned police incursion into privacy, it would run counter to the guarantee of the Fourteenth Amendment. The question of enforcing this basic right has many possible answers. In *Weeks v. United States* (1914), the Court held that in a federal prosecution, the Fourth Amendment barred the use of evidence obtained through an illegal search and seizure. This ruling was a matter of judicial implication. In 1949, 30 states rejected the Weeks doctrine and 17 agreed with it. Excluding from trial evidence illegally obtained only protects a person on whose premises something incriminating has been found. Such people, and innocent people, have private action and the internal discipline of the police as remedies. Excluding evidence may be an effective deterrent against unreasonable searches, but the states may use other methods equally effective. Excluding evidence unreasonably obtained by federal police is more compelling than excluding such evidence obtained by state or local authorities because the public opinion of a community can be more effectively exerted at the local level, than at the federal level.

Frankfurter concluded that "in a prosecution in a State court for a State crime the Fourteenth Amendment does not forbid the admission of evidence obtained by an unreasonable search and seizure."

Justice Black wrote in his concurring opinion that "the federal exclusionary rule is not a command of the Fourth Amendment but is a judicially created rule of evidence which Congress might negate." Black felt that the Fourteenth Amendment was intended to make the Fourth Amendment in its entirety applicable to the states. He stated that "I am unable to agree that the protection of people from overzealous or ruthless state officers is any less essential in a country of 'ordered liberty' than is the protection of people from overzealous or ruthless federal officers."

Only Exclusion Will Deter Violations

Justice Douglas wrote a dissenting opinion. He felt that the Fourth Amendment was applicable to the states and that evidence obtained in violation of it must be excluded from state as well as federal prosecutions. Without the exclusionary rule, the amendment would have no effective sanction.

Justice Murphy also wrote a dissenting opinion. He noted that there were three remedies possible in the enforcement of the search and seizure clause: judicial exclusion of the illegally obtained evidence; criminal prosecution of violators; and civil action against violators for trespassing.

Concerning criminal prosecutions for those violating the clause, Murphy noted that "Self-scrutiny is a lofty ideal, but its exaltation reaches new heights if we expect a District Attorney to prosecute himself or his associates for well-meaning violations of the search and seizure clause during a raid the District Attorney or his associates have ordered." Regarding a trespass action, a person can only receive the amount equal to the damage to physical property. If the officer searches carefully there will be no damage. Where punitive damages are permitted the plaintiff must show real ill will or malice to the defendant. "Surely it is not unreasonable to assume that one in honest pursuit of crime bears no malice toward the search victim." Murphy concluded that only the exclusion of illegally obtained evidence will deter violations of the search and seizure clause. Without judicial action, there are no effective sanctions available. Murphy felt that "Today's decision will do inestimable harm to the cause of fair police methods in our cities and states. Even more important, perhaps, it must have a tragic effect upon public respect for our judiciary." Murphy felt that the Court was now allowing lawlessness by officers of the law.

Justice Rutledge also wrote a dissent. He felt that unless the Fourth Amendment was enforced, it was a dead letter. He noted that "the version of the Fourth Amendment today held applicable to the states hardly rises to the dignity of a form of words; at best it is a pale and frayed carbon copy of the original, bearing little resemblance to the Amendment . . . I had heretofore thought to be an indispensable need for a democratic society."

Impact

The 12 years following the decision in *Wolf v. People of the State of Colorado* showed that states without exclusionary rules had not found an effective means of deterring unlawful searches. Suits in tort proved to be a paper remedy rather than a useful sanction. In fact, during that time, several states adopted state exclusionary rules. In *Mapp v. Ohio* (1961), the Court accepted the minority position, overturned its decision in *Wolf v. People of the State of Colorado* and imposed the exclusionary rule on the states.

Related Cases

Weeks v. United States, 232 U.S. 383 (1914).
Palko v. California, 302 U.S. 319 (1937).
McNabb v. United States, 318 U.S. 332 (1943).
Adamson v. California, 332 U.S. 46 (1947).
Mapp v. Ohio, 367 U.S. 643 (1961).

Bibliography and Further Reading

Hall, Kermit L., ed. *The Oxford Companion to the Supreme Court of the United States.* New York: Oxford University Press, 1992.

Levy, Leonard W., ed. *Encyclopedia of the American Constitution.* Vol. 4. New York: Macmillan, 1986.

ROCHIN V. CALIFORNIA

Legal Citation: 342 U.S. 165 (1952)

Petitioner
Antonio Richard Rochin

Respondent
State of California

Petitioner's Claim
That the police violated his Fifth and Fourteenth Amendment rights to not give self-incriminating testimony and his right to due process of law when they induced vomiting to obtain two capsules of morphine, which they used as evidence to convict him.

Chief Lawyers for Petitioner
Dolly Lee Butler, A. L. Wirin

Chief Lawyer for Respondent
Howard S. Goldin

Justices for the Court
Hugo Lafayette Black, Harold Burton, Tom C. Clark, William O. Douglas, Felix Frankfurter (writing for the Court), Robert H. Jackson, Stanley Forman Reed, Fred Moore Vinson

Justices Dissenting
None (Sherman Minton did not participate)

Place
Washington, D.C.

Date of Decision
2 January 1952

Decision
The Court found that the police violated Rochin's right to due process of law by ordering a doctor to induce vomiting to obtain two capsules of morphine and therefore reversed his conviction.

Significance
The Court's decision that the Fourteenth Amendment's guarantee of due process of law prohibits any "conduct that shocks the conscience" by the government established a standard for judging the constitutionality of police tactics for obtaining evidence. However, the Court's justification for its decision faced criticism from legal scholars and from other justices, including Justice Black, who concurred with the decision. Critics argued that standards such as "shocking to the conscience" were too vague and lacked real content.

Key Amendments in the Case

This case examined the Fifth Amendment's privilege against providing self-incriminating evidence as well as the Fourteenth Amendment's application of the Fifth and other amendments to the state level. The Fifth Amendment guarantees that no one "shall be compelled in any criminal case to be witness against himself." Arguably, the capsules pumped from Rochin amounted to a self-incriminating testimony forced from him by the arresting officers. Furthermore, the Fourteenth Amendment grants this right to all citizens in all states, prohibiting any state from depriving "any person of life, liberty, or property, without the due process of law." Rochin contended that the police confiscated his property without due process of law or without any legal proceeding, forcing self-incriminating evidence from his body.

The Arrest and Conviction of Rochin

With information that Antonio Rochin was peddling drugs, three police officers from Los Angeles went to his home on 1 July 1949. On arrival they noticed the front door open, so they entered and went upstairs, forcing their way into Rochin's room where they found Rochin and his wife. They also noticed two capsules on the night stand and asked, "Whose stuff is this?" Rochin quickly grabbed and swallowed the capsules, and the police began wrangling with him in an effort to retrieve the capsules. In the course of the struggle, they jumped on him and attempted to force the capsules out of him. After realizing they had failed, the police handcuffed Rochin and took him to a hospital, where they ordered a doctor to pump a solution into his stomach to induce vomiting. In Rochin's vomit, the police found the two capsules, which they confirmed contained morphine.

The police charged Rochin with possession of morphine and a California Superior Court convicted him, sentencing him to 60 days in prison. The two capsules the police forced from Rochin constituted the crucial evidence against him, even though Rochin objected to its admission in court. Upon appeal the district court upheld his conviction, though it did admit that the evidence was obtained by "unlawfully breaking into and entering defendant's room" and by "unlawfully assaulting, battering, torturing, and falsely imprisoning the defendant at the alleged hospital." The California Supreme Court also rejected Rochin's arguments, although two justices felt that they should hear the case and severely criticized the police abuses and the lower court's decision.

The Supreme Court Hears the Case

With support from the American Civil Liberties Union (ACLU), Rochin petitioned the U.S. Supreme Court, which granted *certiorari* or review of the lower courts' decisions and began hearing the case on 16 October 1951. The Supreme Court felt the case raised questions about the way California enforced its penal codes concerning the Fourteenth Amendment's call for due process at the state level. The Court set out to determine whether the arrest and conviction of Rochin "offend[ed] those canons of decency and fairness which express the notions of justice" as Justice Frankfurter, writing for the majority, quoted from *Malinski v. New York* (1945).

The Court likened the police's method of obtaining evidence from Rochin to coercing a confession from him. The Court reasoned that just as testimony forced by police brutality would not be admitted in court, likewise evidence forcibly extracted from a suspect's body should not be admitted. Though Justice Frankfurter conceded that the concept of due process of law was vague and changed over time, he nonetheless contended that the police clearly overstepped the boundaries of their job and human decency, bringing about the conviction of Rochin in a manner that violated a general sense of justice and fair play.

Although they agreed with Justice Frankfurter's conclusion, other justices argued that the due process of law line of reasoning carried too little constitutional weight, remaining murky and difficult to apply. Instead, they turned to more concrete constitutional right violations to order the reversal of the lower courts' decisions. Unconvinced by the majority's reliance on due process, Justice Black argued that the Fifth Amendment prohibits the method used by the police to obtain the evidence from Rochin. Justice Black cited the Court's decision in *Boyd v. United States* (1886), reasoning "I think a person is compelled to be a witness against himself not only when he is compelled to testify, but also when as here, incriminating evidence is forcibly taken from him by a contrivance of modern science."

Furthermore, Justice Black also criticized the reasoning of the majority, maintaining that the Bill of Rights protects individual liberties much more effectively and permanently than recourse to vague notions of due process. Moreover, Justice Black argued that not only did the majority bypass the Bill of Rights, but also weakened it by basing its decision on the somewhat arbitrary concept of what shocks the conscience.

Justice Douglas also argued for the reversal of the lower courts' decisions, but felt that the majority's rea-

sons were invalid. Instead, Justice Douglas agreed with Justice Black that the Fifth Amendment ban on compulsory self-incriminating testimony covered both forced confessions as well as forced evidence from the body. In addition, he warned that similar decisions would lead to the erosion of citizens' rights at the state level, resulting from the Court's refusal to uphold the basic rights guaranteed by the Constitution and relying on fleeting and subjective Ideas.

Aftermath of *Rochin v. California*

Perhaps as a consequence of the vague subjective constitutional violation in the *Rochin* case, later cases involving clearly illegal tactics for obtaining evidence did not result in conviction reversals. For example, in *Irvine v. California* (1954) the police broke into the suspect's home multiple times and illegally tapped his telephone. However, the U.S. Supreme Court upheld the conviction. Hence, William Stuntz argued in *The Yale Law Journal* that "the justices' consciences would be shocked only where some grossly improper use of physical force was involved. Stealth and snooping, even when plainly illegal, would not be enough to violate due process." Stuntz also contended that since these notions of voluntariness and shocking to the conscience are vague, they have no real content and therefore the police can ignore them and get around them.

> This is conduct that shocks the conscience. Illegally breaking into the privacy of the petitioner, the struggle to open his mouth and remove what was there, the forcible extraction of his stomach's contents—this course of proceeding by agents of government to obtain evidence is bound to offend even hardened sensibilities.

Related Cases

Boyd v. United States, 116 U.S. 616 (1886).
Malinski v. New York, 324 U.S. 401 (1945).
Adamson v. California, 332 U.S. 46 (1947).
Irvine v. California, 347 U.S. 128 (1954).

Bibliography and Further Reading

Biskupic, Joan, and Elder Witt. *Congressional Quarterly's Guide to the U.S. Supreme Court,* 3rd ed. Washington, DC: Congressional Quarterly, Inc., 1996.

Cushman, Robert F. *Cases in Constitutional Law,* 7th ed. Englewood Cliffs, NJ: Prentice-Hall, Inc., 1989.

———. *Leading Constitutional Decisions.* Englewood Cliffs, NJ: Prentice-Hall, Inc., 1982.

Hall, Kermit L., ed. *The Oxford Companion to the Supreme Court of the United States.* New York: Oxford University Press, 1992.

Kerper, Hazel B., *Introduction to the Criminal Justice System,* 2nd ed. Minneapolis: West Publishing Co., 1979.

Stuntz, William J. "The Substantive Origins of Criminal Procedure." *Yale Law Journal,* November 1995.

MAPP V. OHIO

Legal Citation: 367 U.S. 643 (1961)

Petitioner
Dollree Mapp

Respondent
State of Ohio

Petitioner's Claim
That the state is barred from using evidence at trial that was obtained through an unlawful search and seizure.

Chief Lawyer for Petitioner
A. L. Kearns

Chief Lawyer for Respondent
Gertrude Bauer Mahon

Justices for the Court
Hugo Lafayette Black, William J. Brennan, Jr., Tom C. Clark (writing for the Court), William O. Douglas, Potter Stewart, Earl Warren

Justices Dissenting
Felix Frankfurter, John Marshall Harlan II, Charles Evans Whittaker

Place
Washington, D.C.

Date of Decision
19 June 1961

Decision
The Court held that the exclusionary rule, which prevents unconstitutionally obtained evidence from being introduced at trial, applies to states as well as to the federal government.

Significance
After *Mapp*, state police as well as state courts, where most criminal prosecutions take place, were obliged to follow the Fourth Amendment prohibition against illegal search and seizure.

On 23 May 1957, officers from the Cleveland, Ohio, police department came to the home of Dollree Mapp, seeking entry. They had information that a person wanted for questioning in connection with a bombing was hiding inside. They also believed that the house contained gambling equipment. After calling her lawyer, Mapp refused to let them in without a warrant.

Police continued to watch the house. Three hours later, they again sought entrance. When Mapp did not immediately come to the door, they forced their way inside. Meanwhile, Mapp's lawyer had arrived, but the police, who had begun to search the premises, would not let him in and would not allow him to see his client. Encountering officers on the stairs, Mapp again demanded to see a warrant. She was shown a piece of paper (not a warrant), which she grabbed. She struggled as police tried to retrieve it, and as a result she was handcuffed because she had been "resisting arrest."

Police never did find what they supposedly were looking for, but in the course of their search they happened across some allegedly obscene books and photographs. Mapp was convicted of possessing obscene material and put in prison. The Ohio Supreme Court upheld her conviction, even while conceding that the search that had netted the evidence used against her was "unlawful." The state's highest court concluded that the evidence could be used against Mapp because of a 1949 U.S. Supreme Court ruling, *Wolf v. People of the State of Colorado*. Although in *Wolf* the Court ruled that states are bound by the due process requirements of the Fourth Amendment, the majority opinion in that case also stated that the exclusionary rule—preventing improperly obtained evidence from being introduced in court—need not be applied in state court proceedings.

When Mapp took her case to the U.S. Supreme Court, her lawyers appealed her conviction primarily on First Amendment grounds. They argued that the state of Ohio had violated Mapp's right to freedom of thought and expression by making the mere possession of obscene material illegal. However, the American Civil Liberties Union also filed an *amicus* ("friend of the court") brief in which it argued for a reconsideration of *Wolf*.

The Exclusionary Rule

According to the exclusionary rule governing search and seizure, evidence obtained illegally cannot be used to convict a suspect in a criminal case. There are a number of exceptions to the exclusionary rule, not least of which is the "good faith" exception. Thus when officers conduct a search that turns out to be illegal but which they believed in good faith to be legal while they were doing it—e.g., with an expired warrant, as in *United States v. Leon* (1984)—the evidence is still permissible. Illegally obtained evidence may be used to impeach the testimony of a defendant who testifies in their own defense; and a private citizen may use illegally obtained evidence, as long as he or she did not obtain it on orders from law-enforcement personnel. Moreover, the exclusionary rule applies only to criminal trials: evidence obtained illegally is not forbidden in civil cases, or in grand jury proceedings.

Source(s): *West's Encyclopedia of American Law.* St. Paul, MN: West Group, 1998.

Dollree Mapp is escorted into 105th precinct in New York. © AP/Wide World Photos.

Court Applies Exclusionary Rule to States

The Court had long been looking for an opportunity to overturn *Wolf.* Just a year earlier, in *Elkins v. United States* (1960), the Court had found that the Due Process Clause of the Fourteenth Amendment afforded criminal suspects protections against unlawful searches and seizures at the state level that were equivalent to those that the Fourth Amendment made binding on the federal government. But because *Elkins* did not involve a state criminal prosecution, the Court could not use it as an opportunity to revisit *Wolf.* Now, with *Mapp,* the Supreme Court seized the opportunity to do so.

Writing for the Court, Justice Clark found ample reason to apply the exclusionary rule at the state level. Noting that without it the Fourth Amendment prohibition on unreasonable search and seizure becomes merely "a form of words." In *Elkins* he went on to elaborate on the practical reasons for implementing the exclusionary rule across the board:

> There are those who say . . . that under our constitutional exclusionary doctrine '[t]he criminal is to go free because the constable has blundered.' . . . The criminal goes free if he must, but it is the law that sets him free. Nothing can destroy a government more quickly than its failure to observe its own laws, or worse, its disregard of the character of its own existence . . . Nor can it lightly be assumed that, as a practical matter, adoption of the exclusionary rule fetters law enforcement. Only last year this

Court expressly considered that contention and found that 'pragmatic evidence of a sort' to the contrary was not wanting.

Stewart, who wrote the majority opinion in *Elkins* now refused to join the Court's opinion. Although he voted with the majority to reverse Dollree Mapp's conviction, he wrote his own opinion laying out his rationale for doing so. Because Mapp's lawyers had not, in his view, properly addressed the issue of overturning *Wolf* in their legal papers or in their oral argument before the Court, the Court had no business using this opportunity to do so of its own volition.

In the end, the opinion of the Court expressed only a four-vote plurality that favored overturning *Wolf.* Justice Black turned out to be the swing vote. Although he joined the Court's opinion, he did so for his own reasons. Black was perhaps the most ardent supporter of the incorporation doctrine, making most of the guarantees of the Bill of Rights applicable to the states via the Fourteenth Amendment. Now, however, he found that it was a combination of the Fourth and Fifth Amendments—rather than the Fourteenth Amendment—that required state courts to honor the exclusionary rule. He wrote a separate concurring opinion that was not joined by any other justice.

The three dissenters, Harlan, Frankfurter, and Whittaker—all of whom had dissented in *Elkins*—continued to disapprove of the incorporation doctrine. Following that logic, they refused to apply the exclusionary rule to the states.

Despite the confused pattern of voting and opinions in *Mapp,* it soon became the law of the land—and remains so. State police and state courts continue to be required to observe Fourth Amendment guidelines when gathering and assessing evidence in criminal matters.

Related Cases

Wolf v. People of the State of Colorado, 338 U.S. 25 (1949).
Elkins v. United States, 364 U.S. 206 (1960).
Schmerber v. California, 384 U.S. 757 (1966).

Bibliography and Further Reading

Everson, David H., ed. *The Supreme Court as Policy-Maker: Three Studies on the Impact of Judicial Decisions,* 2nd ed. Carbondale: Public Affairs Research Bureau, Southern Illinois University, 1972.

Johnson, John W., ed. *Historic U.S. Court Cases, 1690–1990: An Encyclopedia.* New York: Garland Publishing, 1992.

Stewart, Potter. "The Road to *Mapp v. Ohio* and Beyond: The Origins, Development and Future of the Exclusionary Rule in Search and Seizure Cases." *Columbia University Law Review,* Vol. 83, pp. 1365-1404.

Swigert, Victoria L., ed. *Law and Legal Process.* Beverly Hills, CA: Sage Publications, 1982.

WONG SUN V. UNITED STATES

Legal Citation: 83 U.S. 407 (1963)

Petitioners
Wong Sun, James Wah Toy

Respondent
United States

Petitioners' Claim
That use of evidence illegally obtained by police in criminal proceedings violates the petitioners' constitutional rights under the Due Process Clause of the Fourteenth Amendment.

Chief Lawyer for Petitioners
Edward Bennett Williams

Chief Lawyer for Respondent
J. William Doolittle

Justices for the Court
Hugo Lafayette Black, William J. Brennan, Jr. (writing for the Court), William O. Douglas, Arthur Goldberg, Earl Warren

Justices Dissenting
Tom C. Clark, John Marshall Harlan II, Potter Stewart, Byron R. White

Place
Washington, D.C.

Date of Decision
14 January 1963

Decision
Upheld Wong Sun's claim and overturned two lower courts' decisions allowing use in criminal trials of evidence illegally obtained without warrants.

Significance
The ruling established the "fruits of the poisonous tree" doctrine. In conformance with the Due Process Clause, the doctrine directs that any evidence resulting from illegal search and seizure, no matter how remotely connected can not be introduced in court. After a court finding of illegality, the government is charged with the responsibility to show that any evidence introduced did not result from knowledge of the illegal evidence. The decision significantly expanded the exclusionary rule which excludes the use of certain evidence in trials. Later Court decisions weakened the rule by creating more exceptions where evidence could be appropriately used. This decision, and others by the Warren Court protecting defendants' rights, led to creation of the public defender system in the United States.

The Fourth Amendment is perhaps one of the most important provisions protecting human liberty in the Constitution. The amendment prohibits "unreasonable" search and seizure by requiring police to obtain a search warrant only after showing "probable cause" to an impartial neutral magistrate. The warrants must describe the particular place to be searched and items to be seized as evidence. Probable cause requires the government to demonstrate that the evidence would lead a person of reasonable caution to the belief that a felony was committed. The Court in the 1948 *Johnson v. United States* case reaffirmed the role of "a neutral and detached magistrate" to assess probable cause and issue warrants rather than relying solely on the instantaneous judgement of "zealous officers . . . engaged in the often competitive enterprise of ferreting out crime." Because the Fourth Amendment did not provide remedies for violations, the Court in the 1914 *Weeks v. United States* case created the exclusionary rule to deter police misconduct. The rule excluded from trials evidence gained through illegal searches and seizures.

Early on a June morning in 1959, after six weeks of surveillance, federal narcotics agents in San Francisco arrested Hom Way for heroin possession. Upon arrest, Way stated he had purchased heroin from a person known as "Blackie Toy," owner of a laundry elsewhere in town. The police proceeded promptly to a laundry in the vicinity indicated by Way. When a street-clothed agent announced at the door of the closed laundry that he was a narcotics agent, James Wah Toy slammed the door and fled to a rear residence room with his family. The agents broke through the door and pursued Toy through the laundry and residence. A search uncovered no narcotics. Upon arrest, Toy denied selling narcotics but indicated another person named "Johnny" did and described where "Johnny" could be found. The agents then proceeded promptly to the residence described, which they entered, and where they discovered Johnny Yee in a bedroom. A search revealed less than an ounce of heroin. Upon his arrest Yee stated the heroin was obtained from Toy and another person named "Sea Dog" who Toy identified as Wong Sun. The agents next proceeded to Sun's residence which they entered and where they found Sun still sleeping. A search uncovered no narcotics. Toy, Yee, and Sun were arraigned on violation of federal narcotics laws and released. Several days later they returned for interrogation. No attorneys were present during the questioning. An agent prepared written statements based on comments made by the three and each reviewed them for accuracy. They, however, refused to sign the statements though admitting to their accuracy.

At the resulting trial without a jury in the U.S. District Court for the Northern District of California, Way did not testify and Yee, the principal witness, repudiated his own unsigned statement. The court excused Yee to avoid self-incrimination. Four items of evidence were therefore introduced to support the government's case: (1) statements by Toy in his bedroom while being arrested; (2) heroin taken from Yee; (3) Toy's unsigned pretrial statement; and (4) Sun's pretrial statement. The defense objected to the use of these "fruits" of their alleged unlawful arrests and searches. Yee and Sun were found not guilty of conspiracy charges, but convicted "of fraudulent and knowing transportation and concealment of illegally imported heroin."

An appeal to the Court of Appeals for the Ninth Circuit resulted in affirmation of the conviction. Though the appeals court held that the arrests violated the Fourth Amendment's requirement of warrants based on "probable cause" and "reasonable grounds," the court ruled the four items of evidence "were not the fruits of the illegal arrests," and, therefore, were properly admitted as evidence. The court found neither Way nor Yee to be proven reliable informants to justify the arrests of Toy and Sun without warrants. The Supreme Court then granted *certiorari* to hear the case. The Court's interest in the case focused on the trial judge's acceptance of the four items of evidence.

Fruits of the Poisonous Tree

By a 5-4 vote, the Court reversed and remanded the appeals court decision. In addressing Toy's connection, Justice Brennan, writing for the majority, first agreed with the court of appeals finding that neither reasonable grounds nor probable cause existed to support Toy's arrest. Brennan wrote, "It is basic that an arrest with or without a warrant must stand upon firmer ground than mere suspicion." In the case of Toy, insufficient evidence existed to justify issuing a warrant, even if sought, since Hom Way was not a previously established reliable informant. Brennan asserted that agents cannot "roam" the streets of San Francisco following the lead of an unproven informant. The government argued Toy's flight from the front door justified the use of Way's information. However, Brennan found the narcotics agent at Toy's door initially misrepresented his intent by neither readily identifying his purpose nor making an effort to confirm that Toy was the "Blackie Toy" described by Way. Brennan believed

Toy's flight could easily have been "a natural desire to repel an apparently unauthorized intrusion." To accept the government's argument "would mean that a vague suspicion could be transformed into probable cause for arrest by reason of ambiguous conduct which the arresting officers themselves [had] provoked." Brennan added that the Court has "consistently rejected that a search unlawful at its inception may be validated by what it turns up." Therefore, since the agent's uninvited entry into Toy's residence was illegal, the resulting arrest was illegal. Similarly, Toy's statements at the time of arrest cannot be used as evidence since they resulted from illegal police activity. Brennan rejected the government argument that Toy's statements at the time of his arrest were admissible as evidence and not subject to the exclusionary rule because they were spoken at "free will" and were not incriminating.

Brennan continued that if Toy's statements about Yee were unlawfully obtained and excluded as evidence, then narcotics taken from Yee must also be excluded. Since the narcotics seizure resulted from illegal police action, it was also "fruit of the poisonous tree." Lastly, Sun's unsigned statement offered no corroborating evidence about Toy's activity. Information in Toy's statement, being directly connected with the illegal arrest, could not stand alone and be lawfully used as evidence. Brennan concluded Toy's conviction must be reversed based on the lack of submissible evidence not associated in some way with illegal police actions.

Regarding Wong Sun's conviction, Brennan agreed with the court of appeals that Sun's arrest was without probable cause or reasonable grounds. However, Brennan found that Sun's unsigned statement was not fruit of the illegal arrest. That Sun returned voluntarily several days after his initial release to provide the statement indicated to Brennan the statement was sufficiently disconnected from the illegal arrest. Also, though Toy's statement did not sufficiently support Sun's statement, the heroin seized from Yee did serve as independent corroboration. Hence, Sun's statement was legally acceptable evidence. Brennan was not certain as to whether the lower court based its decision on Yee's narcotics alone, or the inadmissible confession of Toy. Therefore, Brennan reversed the court of appeals decision and ruled that Sun be retried.

Justice Clark, joined by Justices Harlan, Stewart, and White, offered the dissenting opinion. Clark wrote that the Court made a "Chinese puzzle" out of basically simple facts and "dashed to pieces . . . standards of probable cause necessary to secure an arrest warrant or to make an arrest without one." Clark asserted this decision placed a much greater burden on officers carrying out duties often involving split-second decisions in uncertain situations. Clark saw efficient police work in the case facts, demonstrated by the swiftness of the four contacts that early June morning. Toy's flight from officers when being informed they were narcotics agents constituted probable cause for further action in Clark's mind. The combination of Way's statements concerning Toy, Toy's flight, Toy's statement at the time of arrest, and the discovery of narcotics subsequently at Yee's residence did not construct a "poisonous tree" and were admissible evidence. As a result, Clark saw no reason to overturn the consistent decisions of the two lower courts regarding Toy's conviction. Regarding Sun, Clark maintained the Court applied too high a standard by dismissing Toy's confession about Sun. Clark wrote, "corroboration merely fortifies the truth of the confession, without independently establishing the crime charged." He believed the two confessions provided key details of their acquisition and use of heroin the day prior to the arrest.

Impact

This landmark decision established the "fruit of the poisonous tree" doctrine and affirmed the constitutional prohibition against unreasonable search and seizure. The *Wong* case added to the exclusionary rule by holding that unless the government can clearly demonstrate that secondary evidence was discovered independently of the "tainted," illegal, primary evidence, then the secondary evidence must be excluded as "fruit of the poisonous tree."

The *Wong* decision was one of a series of key findings made by the Warren Court in the 1960s, during what was perceived as a "revolution" in the development of criminal procedure. Another landmark case was the *Miranda v. Arizona* decision in 1966 requiring police to advise suspects of their rights prior to questioning. The Court, by limiting police powers to investigate and prosecute crimes, sought to balance the need to gather evidence against invasion of privacy.

More conservative Supreme Courts since the 1960s sought to limit the exclusionary rule by narrowing the range of evidence considered "fruit" of a Fourth Amendment violation. In *United States v. Leon* (1984) the Court held that if officers acted with a reasonable belief their conduct did not violate the Fourth Amendment then the search was legal. This amounted to a generalized "good faith" or "reasonableness" exception to the exclusionary rule. In *Nix v. Williams* (1984), the Court recognized the "inevitable-discovery" exception by holding that illegally gathered evidence could still

be used if the government could demonstrate that such evidence would have been "inevitably" discovered through other lawful sources anyhow. The Court further expanded the exception to the "independent source" exception in *Murray v. United States* in 1988.

With the *Wong* decision the exclusionary rule became perhaps the most contentious issue associated with the Fourth Amendment. Many believed punishment for Fourth Amendment violations should more appropriately consist of civil or criminal lawsuits or disciplinary actions against police officers responsible for unlawful searches. In 1995, as part of the "Contract with America" war on crime, the newly Republican-controlled 104th Congress introduced the Exclusionary Rule Reform Act. The bill expanded on the Court's "good faith" exception to the exclusionary rule, made electronic search and seizure easier, and suspended the need for search warrants in many situations. The proposed standards only required that law enforcement demonstrate "good intent" instead of obtaining a warrant before searching a business or residence.

Increased emphasis on defendants' constitutional rights by the Court in the 1960s led to a rapid increase in the number of public defender offices by the early 1970s. Defense lawyers were no longer considered a luxury, but instead were constitutionally required to protect defendants' rights. By the 1980s public defender offices were a major part of the criminal justice system.

Related Cases

Weeks v. United States, 232 U.S. 383 (1914).
Johnson v. United States, 333 U.S. 10 (1948).
Miranda v. Arizona, 387 U.S. 436 (1966).
Nix v. Williams, 467 U.S. 431 (1984).
Unites States v. Leon, 468 U.S. 897 (1984).
Murray v. United States, 487 U.S. 533 (1988).

Bibliography and Further Reading

American Civil Liberties Union. http://www.aclu.org

Bodenhamer, David J., and James W. Ely, Jr., eds. *The Bill of Rights in Modern America: After 200 Years.* Washington, DC: Congressional Quarterly, 1993.

"Congress and the Exclusionary Rule: Would Killing the Exclusionary Rule Repeal the Fourth Amendment or Restore It?" *National Review,* May 15, 1995.

LINKLETTER V. WALKER

Legal Citation: 381 U.S. 618 (1965)

Petitioner
Victor Linkletter

Respondent
Victor G. Walker

Petitioner's Claim
Evidence obtained as a result of unreasonable search and seizure should be found inadmissible under the Fourth Amendment under *Mapp v. Ohio*.

Chief Lawyer for Petitioner
Euel A. Screws, Jr.

Chief Lawyer for Respondent
Teddy W. Airhart, Jr.

Justices for the Court
William J. Brennan, Jr., Tom C. Clark (writing for the Court), Arthur Goldberg, John Marshall Harlan II, Potter Stewart, Earl Warren, Byron R. White

Justices Dissenting
Hugo Lafayette Black, William O. Douglas

Place
Washington, D.C.

Date of Decision
7 June 1965

Decision
In the Constitution there are no circumstances that require retroactive implementation of the exclusionary rule.

Significance
The most important question of this case was whether provisions of the exclusionary rule, as developed in *Mapp v. Ohio*, should be applied retroactively. The *Linkletter* ruling served to instruct lower courts that the decision in *Mapp* was authoritative only for future cases and that no previously adjudicated cases should be reconsidered.

The petitioner, Victor Linkletter, was arrested on suspicion of burglary. At the time he was arrested, the police suspected that he was involved in other "breaking and entering" crimes. In the police station, officers confiscated his keys during a search of his person. Without a warrant, police officers subsequently entered Linkletter's home and appropriated some of his personal effects. Police officers also confiscated Linkletter's personal effects during a search of his work place. These intrusions were justified according to the District Court of Louisiana; police officers had "reasonable cause for the arrest under Louisiana law" and therefore "probable cause" for search and seizure. Based on evidence seized, Victor Linkletter was found guilty of burglary by the Louisiana District Court. The decision was affirmed, nine months later, by the Supreme Court of Louisiana.

Two years later, in *Mapp v. Ohio* (1961), the U.S. Supreme Court held that "all evidence obtained by searches and seizures in violation of the Constitution is, by (the Fourth Amendment), inadmissible in a state court." The *Mapp* decision thus set a precedent which ordered that all illegally obtained evidence must be excluded during trial. Although the exclusionary rule was established in *Weeks v. United States* (1914), the *Mapp* decision extended and clarified application of the exclusionary rule in federal courts *and* state courts. This extension of Fourth Amendment rights met with great controversy because police officers were restrained and precluded from collecting illegal, improper evidence in prosecutions.

Victor Linkletter applied for a reconsideration of his case on the basis of the exclusionary rule that was recognized and extended to all the levels of the government by the *Mapp* decision. He invoked a writ of *habeas corpus* (a petition claiming discretionary, unlawful arrest/detention) but his claim was rejected by the Louisiana courts and the U.S. district court. Linkletter's appeal to the U.S. court of appeals yielded a finding that admitted that the search and seizure in his case was unlawful, but also reasoned that "the constitutional requirement of exclusion of the evidence under *Mapp* was not retrospective."

Retroactivity

The term "retroactive" means something that refers to facts or events in the past, and a retroactive law is one that applies to past events. The Omnibus Budget Reconciliation Act of 1993 (OBRA), for instance, retroactively raised 1993 taxes on a number of individuals in the newly created 36 percent and 39.6 percent tax brackets.

Is this fair? The retroactivity provisions in OBRA were legal if not necessarily "fair", but generally, common law has tended to hold retroactive laws in disfavor. As for criminal law, the Constitution renders retroactivity illegal through its prohibition of *ex post facto* laws.

There would seem to be little to justify retroactivity, at least from the perspective of the individual and not the government. It is conceivable, that a retroactive tax law could benefit an individual by lowering taxes in a certain category for a certain year. Retroactive application of a civil-rights law could help members of a minority group subjected to past discrimination.

In any case, judicial decisions are, unlike sentences in criminal law, retroactive. This retroactivity is almost always at the legal rather than the practical level, however, because actual attempts to change a past condition would most likely lead to violation of someone's rights.

Source(s): *West's Encyclopedia of American Law.* St. Paul, MN: West Group, 1998.

On *certiorari,* Linkletter's attorney presented two main arguments to the U.S. Supreme Court. He maintained the appellate court made a mistake in finding that the *Mapp* decision was not retrospective. Further, Linkletter was empowered by the ruling in *Mapp* to ask for the same approach in his case because his offense occurred more than one year later after Mapp's crime, (but because he was convicted before the *Mapp* decision, he maintained his case should be adjudicated in the same way.

The majority justices upheld the rulings of the lower courts. In their opinion, presented by Justice Clark, they declared that "subsequent rulings" were not directly applicable to past events. They emphasized that previous cases could not be automatically affected because of the application of a new set of legal criteria. Historically, the justices found various interpretations of the law concerning compatibility of new approaches to the law *vis-a-vis* prior decisions, but they warned that the "past cannot be always erased by a new judicial declaration." They pointed to a diversity of circumstances that had to be taken into account before rendering "determination of unconstitutionality." The justices for the majority reasoned that facts pertaining to any previous finding had to be contemplated before any employment of judicial standard. They pointed out all the elements involved in every particular case (police conduct, claimed depreciated and deprived rights, final character of announced decisions, consequences) that had to be reconsidered. Considering past events, the Court also found that changes in law could have efficacy only on cases in direct review. Majority opinion actually found that new extensions of the law could not be applied on prior final rulings. The majority opinion also held that although Linkletter rightly contended that there were former judgments which

showed applicability of "new constitutional rules" on previously closed cases, they did not feel obliged to treat Linkletter's conviction in the same manner. There was no absolute rule which required the Court to apply changes in the Constitution to previously adjudicated cases retroactively. The justices believed "that the Constitution neither prohibits nor requires retrospective effect." Accordingly, they concluded that they must only "weigh the merits and demerits in each case by looking to the prior history of the rule in question, its purpose and effect, and whether retrospective operation will further or retard its operation." The majority justices found that this perspective did not diverge from Fourth Amendment provisions.

The Court stressed that the main purpose of extending the exclusionary rule in the *Mapp* ruling was to prevent violation of Fourth Amendment rights. Thus, *Mapp* was never intended to correct or repair previously adjudicated cases. Although erroneous findings in *Wolf v. People of the State of Colorado,* which rejected the exclusionary rule, resulted in a great number of unreasonable searches and seizures, the Court's new ruling issued in *Mapp* was not reversionary. Justice Clark summed up the Court's position simply: "reparation comes too late." He also pointed out that the purpose of more effective application of Fourth Amendment rights "will not at this late date be served by the wholesale release of the guilty victims." The Court also asserted that retroactive relitigation based on *Mapp* would not be appropriate because rehearings would be impractical to hold after so much time had passed and much of the evidence was probably destroyed or removed. In further explaining their ruling in *Mapp,* the Court reasoned that the petitioner's reliance on *Fay v. Noia* (1963) and *Reck v. Pate* (1961) was inappropriate. Although the exclusionary rule in these cases was applied retroactively, they found that the cases had no similarity because they were issues about coerced confessions. The majority pointed out that: "all that [the] petitioner attacks is the admissibility of evidence, the reliability and relevancy of which is not questioned, and which may well have had no effect on the outcome." Furthermore, that the date evidence was illegally seized in *Mapp v. Ohio* was irrelevant because legal application of the ruling became valid only from the date of judgment, not from the day of the seizure.

In contrast to the majority decision, two dissenting justices reasoned that the *Mapp* decision was applicable to Linkletter's case. As in *Mapp,* Linkletter's conviction was upheld after evidence was illegally obtained. Unreasonable search and seizure also occurred; therefore, like *Mapp* "all evidence obtained by searches and seizures in violation of the Constitution is, by that same authority, inadmissible in a state court." The minority justices felt that Linkletter was convicted by evidence illegally obtained; they found it unacceptable to keep him in jail simply because his case was decided before the *Mapp* decision was rendered. The minority opinion pointed out that Mapp's crime occurred before Linkletter was arrested and accused and if the courts of Ohio had been as expeditious in adjudicating as Louisiana courts, Linkletter would have been automatically entitled to demand relief on direct review. Dissenting justices felt the majority opinion represented a discriminating approach between two very similar cases and therefore, were promoting unequal protection under the Fourth Amendment. Further, the minority opinion maintained it would be appropriate to provide a "new trial in conformity with the Constitution" for all convicts who were imprisoned due to unconstitutionally seized evidence.

Dissenting justices found the Court's reasoning that there was no equity among the cases *Fay v. Noia, Reck v. Pate* and Linkletter's case to be improper. They explained that, in those cases, even more than 20 years after adjudication, the Court recognized that the litigants were unlawfully convicted because of coerced confessions used against them. Thus, evidence collected in Linkletter's case, after an apparent infringement of his Fourth Amendment rights, should also be treated in a different way. Unlike the justices for the majority, they reasoned that circumstances merited full protection under the Constitution and, consequently, a new fair trial.

Impact

The findings of the U.S. Supreme Court did not depreciate the legitimacy of the exclusionary rule as set forth in *Mapp v. Ohio,* but it held that the Constitution "neither prohibits nor requires retrospective effect." Conclusions in *Mapp v. Ohio* were significant because they established more stringent application of the exclusionary rule (defendants were not to be convicted based on evidence seized as the result of an illegal search). However, the justices for the majority held that there were no essential rationale which made the *Mapp* decision one which had to be automatically, retroactively applied to cases adjudicated before that ruling. Instead, the *Mapp* ruling was intended to give lower courts a measure of understanding of how to enforce the exclusionary rule as set forth in that decision. Nothing in *Mapp* obliged the Court to apply its conclusions retroactively.

Related Cases

Weeks v. United States, 232 U.S. 383 (1914).
Wolf v. People of the State of Colorado, 338 U.S. 25 (1949).
Reck v. Pate, 367 U.S. 433 (1961).
Mapp v. Ohio, 367 U.S. 643 (1961).
Fay v. Noia, 372 U.S. 391 (1963).

Bibliography and Further Reading

Hall, Kermit L., ed. *The Oxford Companion to the Supreme Court of the United States.* New York: Oxford University Press, 1992.

WARDEN, MARYLAND PENITENTIARY V. HAYDEN

Legal Citation: 387 U.S. 294 (1967)

Petitioner
Warden, Maryland Penitentiary

Respondent
Bennie Joe Hayden

Petitioner's Claim
A police officer may seize mere evidence—evidence that is not an instrumentality of a crime, the fruits of a crime, or contraband—found in the course of a valid warrantless search conducted in a criminal suspect's home immediately after a hot pursuit of the suspect.

Chief Lawyer for Petitioner
Franklin Goldstein, Assistant Attorney General of Maryland

Chief Lawyer for Respondent
Albert R. Turnbull

Justices for the Court
Hugo Lafayette Black, William J. Brennan, Jr. (writing for the Court), Abe Fortas, John Marshall Harlan II, Thurgood Marshall, Potter Stewart, Earl Warren, Byron R. White

Justices Dissenting
William O. Douglas

Place
Washington, D.C.

Date of Decision
29 May 1967

Decision
A police officer may seize, and the prosecution may introduce at trial, mere evidence that is found during a valid, warrantless search of a home.

Significance
The case shifted the focus in Fourth Amendment cases from property rights to privacy rights.

In the morning of 17 March 1962, the Diamond Cab Company in Baltimore, Maryland was robbed by an armed man dressed in a light-colored cap and a dark jacket. Two cab drivers followed the robber to 2111 Cocoa Lane, and police officers arrived at the house within minutes. An officer knocked on the door to announce their arrival, and, according to the officers, Mrs. Hayden did not object when they asked if they could search the house for the robber.

The police officers found Bennie Joe Hayden in an upstairs bedroom pretending to sleep. When the officers determined that there was no other male in the house, they arrested Hayden. Meanwhile, other officers were searching and encountering evidence. One officer found a shotgun and pistol hidden in a toilet flush tank, another officer found ammunition for the guns, and another officer found a jacket and trousers similar to those reportedly worn by the robber.

Hayden was charged with armed robbery and convicted in a trial without a jury, or a "bench trial." Hayden did not object to the introduction of the clothing evidence found in the house, and he was convicted. After further state court proceedings went against him, Hayden filed a *habeas corpus* petition in federal court. He was denied at the district court level, but a divided panel of the Court of Appeals for the Fourth Circuit reversed that decision.

The appeals court held that the search of the home was valid under the Fourth Amendment, but that the introduction at trial of the clothing evidence was improper. According to rulings in similar Fourth Amendment cases, the officers had no right to seize items of mere evidential value when they were in Hayden's home. Because they had entered without a warrant, the officers were authorized to do no more than arrest Hayden and seize instrumentalities of the crime, fruits of the crime, and any contraband in plain view. The state of Maryland, through the respondent in Hayden's case, the warden of Hayden's penitentiary, asked the U.S. Supreme Court to review the case, and the High Court consented.

Upending its own precedent, the High Court reversed the appeals court and held for the warden and the state by a vote of 8-1. In an opinion written by Justice Brennan, the Court confessed that the distinction it had created in prior cases between "mere evidence" of a crime and other evidence—contraband and instrumentalities or fruits of a crime—was no longer valid. It was, said the Court, "based on premises no longer accepted as rules governing the application of the Fourth Amendment."

The legal premises that created the distinction between mere evidence and other evidence, Brennan explained, was based on an incorrect analysis of the Fourth Amendment. In these early Fourth Amendment cases, such as *Gouled v. United States* (1921) and *Silverthorne Lumber Co. v. United States* (1920), the Court had analyzed the Fourth Amendment right against unreasonable searches and seizures from a property standpoint, as opposed to a privacy standpoint. If, for example, the government asserted that it sought the fruits of a crime, it was deemed to have asserted a superior property interest and was therefore entitled to seize it. Such interest was extended in later cases to the instruments used in a crime and contraband, or articles that are illegal to own or possess. But this analysis, noted Brennan, was "discredited." The Court had begun to base its Fourth Amendment analyses on the protection of personal privacy in recent cases such as *Jones v. United States* (1960) and *Silverman v. United States* (1961). The question had become, then, whether a person's reasonable expectation of privacy was violated, and, opined Brennan, "[p]rivacy is no more disturbed by a search directed to a purely evidential object than it is by a search directed to an instrumentality, fruit, or contraband."

The Court agreed with the appeals court that the search was legal under the Fourth Amendment. However, the introduction of the clothing evidence did not, said the Court, constitute a violation of Hayden's Fourth Amendment rights. In *Schmerber v. California* (1966) the Court held that it is not unreasonable under the Fourth Amendment for government to conduct searches to obtain evidence (i.e. blood from a suspected drunk driver) that can help secure an arrest or conviction of a criminal. Brennan emphasized that there must be a connection between the items sought and the criminal behavior. In Hayden's case, the clothes found to be inadmissible by the federal appeals court were connected to proving the robbery because the robber's clothing had been identified by witnesses. Thus, the introduction of the evidence did not violate Hayden's Fourth Amendment rights.

Ultimately, the Court not only held for the warden, it went on to specifically reject the mere evidence rule. The majority said that the "mere evidence" rule had "spawned exceptions so numerous and confusion so great" that it did not afford meaningful protection.

There was, therefore, "no viable reason" to observe the distinction.

Justices Black, Fortas, and Warren concurred in the judgment. In an opinion joined by Justice Warren, Justice Fortas agreed that the Fourth Amendment should not prevent the introduction of the clothing evidence in Hayden's case. However, Fortas and Warren believed that the majority had gone too far in striking down the mere evidence rule.

Fortas reviewed long-standing Fourth Amendment rules to explain his position. A general requirement of the Fourth Amendment is that a search should not be carried out without a warrant from a magistrate. A warrant may not be issued by a magistrate unless the police officer seeking the search warrant possesses probable cause to believe that the search will yield evidence of a crime, and the officer must specify what places are to be searched and what items are sought. One exception to the requirement of a warrant is where police officers are in hot pursuit of a fleeing felon. In such a case, officers need not obtain a warrant prior to conducting a search. Nevertheless, Fortas lectured, such searches "have, until today, been confined to those essential to fulfill the purpose of the exception: that is, we have refused to permit use of articles the seizure of which could not be strictly tied to and justified by the exigencies which excused the warrantless search." Instrumentalities and fruits of crime and contraband, said Fortas, are always sufficiently connected to a search that follows a hot pursuit of a criminal. Other evidence is not connected to the extraordinary circumstance of hot pursuit, and, Fortas argued, police should not be able to seize such evidence, nor should prosecutors be allowed to use such evidence at trial.

The Fourth Amendment does not, Fortas wrote, allow police to "search an entire building" in which an arrest occurs, or "to rummage through locked drawers and closets, or to search at another time and place." In Hayden's case, the clothing discovered was in fact related to the exigency that created the exception to the warrant requirement. The clothes worn by Hayden were "pertinent to identification of the person hotly pursued as being, in fact, the person whose pursuit was justified by connection with the crime." Unlike the majority, Fortas would not "drive an enormous and dangerous hole in the Fourth Amendment" to accommodate another exception to the mere evidence rule. Fortas closed by echoing the fears of dissenting Justice Douglas, ominously describing the majority's opinion as destroying "root and branch, a basic part of liberty's heritage."

In a long, strong dissent, Justice Douglas wrote passionately about the evils of the general warrant, which the Fourth Amendment was designed to thwart. The general warrant was used in England prior to the American Revolution, and it let police search around unfettered for evidence of crime and subsequently use the evidence as testimonial evidence in a prosecution. The framers of the Constitution found the practice repugnant to basic liberty, and argued for "the sanctity of one's home and his personal belongings, even the clothes he wore." Patrick Henry, for example, warned that government officers, if they were not restrained, would "go into your cellars and rooms, and search, ransack, and measure, everything you eat, drink, and wear." In Boston, colonists complained that their houses and bedrooms were "'exposed to be ransacked, our boxes, chests, and trunks broke open, ravaged and plundered by wretches, whom no prudent man would venture to employ even as menial servants.'"

Douglas insisted that the case of *Entick v. Carrington* (1765), decided in England, was in the forefront of the founding fathers' minds when they fashioned the Fourth Amendment. In *Entick,* Douglas lectured, England's high court not only outlawed the use of the general warrant, it created "a zone of privacy which no government official may enter." Douglas noted that the Court had recently shrunk that zone of privacy in *Schmerber,* but he had objected to that decision and he renewed his objection in Hayden's case, arguing that the holding not only violated Hayden's Fourth Amendment rights but his Fifth Amendment right against self-incrimination. "That which is taken from a person without his consent and used as testimonial evidence," Douglas maintained, "violates the Fifth Amendment."

Douglas conceded that the Fourth Amendment does not make homes and offices "sanctuaries where the law can never reach." However, Douglas believed that individuals "should have the freedom to select for himself the time and circumstances when he will share his secrets with others and decide the extent of that sharing." Without such a zone of privacy, Douglas predicted that the Fourth and Fifth Amendments would become "ready instruments for the police state that the Framers sought to avoid."

Impact

The decision in *Hayden* adopted privacy as the measure of an individual's interest protected by the Fourth Amendment. This proposition was solidified mere months later, when the Court in *Katz v. United States* (1967) again based its analysis of a questionable police search on privacy principles rather than property principles. The effect of this shift has not led to more predictability in Fourth Amendment analyses, but it has fostered analyses that the Court believes comports with the basic intent of the Fourth Amendment—the protection against unreasonable searches and seizures.

Related Cases

Entick v. Carrington, 95 Eng. Rep. 807 (K.B. 1765).
Silverthorne Lumber Co. v. United States, 251 U.S. 385 (1920).
Gouled v. United States, 255 U.S. 298 (1921).
Jones v. United States, 362 U.S. 257 (1960).
Silverman v. United States, 365 U.S. 505 (1961).
Schmerber v. California, 384 U.S. 757 (1966).
Katz v. United States, 389 U.S. 347 (1967).

Bibliography and Further Reading

Biskupic, Joan, and Elder Witt. *Congressional Quarterly's Guide to the U.S. Supreme Court,* 3rd ed. Washington, DC: Congressional Quarterly, Inc., 1996.

Kerper, Hazel B., *Introduction to the Criminal Justice System,* 2nd ed. Minneapolis: West Publishing Co., 1979.

New York Times, May 30, 1967.

Witt, Elder, ed. *Search and Seizure.* Washington, DC: Congressional Quarterly, 1990.

SEE V. CITY OF SEATTLE

Legal Citation: 387 U.S. 541 (1967)

Appellant
See

Appellee
City of Seattle

Appellant's Claim
That the city of Seattle Fire Department must have a search warrant consistent with the safeguards against unreasonable search offered by the Fourth Amendment to perform a fire code inspection of a locked private warehouse.

Chief Lawyer for Appellant
Norman Dorsen

Chief Lawyer for Appellee
A. L. Newbould

Justices for the Court
Hugo Lafayette Black, William J. Brennan, Jr., William O. Douglas, Abe Fortas, Earl Warren, Byron R. White (writing for the Court)

Justices Dissenting
Tom C. Clark, John Marshall Harlan II, Potter Stewart

Place
Washington, D.C.

Date of Decision
5 June 1967

Decision
Upheld See's claim and overturned two lower courts' decisions allowing entry by the fire department over the owner's objections without a warrant.

Significance
The ruling established an administrative warrant system to conduct health and safety inspections at private business properties not open to the public. To avoid violating the Fourth Amendment, a city must demonstrate reasonableness by submitting its formal procedures for conducting such inspections to a magistrate. Since the *See* ruling, the Court identified several exceptions not requiring warrants including inspections of liquor and firearms businesses, aerial surveillance, search of students in public schools, and airline security screenings.

Fundamental protection of an individual's right to privacy is provided by the Fourth Amendment to the Constitution. The amendment established the 'right of the people to be secure in their persons, houses, papers, and effects, against unreasonable searches and seizures.' The amendment further stipulates that warrants may only be issued when supported by 'probable cause, supported by Oath and affirmation, and particularly describing the place to be searched, and the persons or things to be seized.' The Fourth Amendment grew directly from experiences with British authorities in the American colonies in the 1700s.

With rapid population growth and urban expansion following World War II, governmental regulation of businesses grew as well. Assuring compliance with city health and safety standards required inspections on a regular basis. Such inspections commonly focused on the condition of electrical wiring, rodent infestation, plumbing, trash accumulation, zoning ordinances, fire codes, and job safety. The Supreme Court had not addressed the application of Fourth Amendment protections to such "administrative" inspections until 1959. The Court held in *Frank v. Maryland* (1959) that city health officials did not need warrants to inspect private dwellings even when owners opposed entry. The Court distinguished between administrative needs to obtain entry to private properties and criminal investigatory needs. The inspections required less rigorous protection of the individual's privacy and were not held to traditional Fourth Amendment standards.

Accordingly, the city of Seattle Fire Department contacted See regarding a routine city-wide inspection to assess compliance with Seattle fire codes. See would not allow the city access to his locked commercial warehouse without a warrant showing probable cause that a violation was expected. The city arrested See for violating the Seattle Fire Code. See argued in his trial that the warrantless inspection violated his rights under the Fourth and Fourteen Amendments. The city argued that such administrative searches were automatically restricted by the ordinance and regulations directing the inspection. See, who was convicted of the violation and fined $100, appealed the conviction to the Washington State Supreme Court which upheld the lower court's decision. The U.S. Supreme Court issued *certiorari* to hear this case concurrently with a similar challenge, *Camara v. Municipal Court* (1967), involving an inspection of a private residence.

Protection from Administrative Searches

The Court found in favor of See by a 6-3 vote. Justice White, writing on behalf of the majority, wrote that the Court saw no reason to distinguish between the need for administrative entry for enforcement of commercial property standards and police entry. Both need Fourth Amendment safeguards. Similarly, the Court found in *Camara* that inspection of a private dwelling also required a warrant. These two decisions, announced on the same day by the Court, reversed the earlier *Frank* decision.

In *See,* White found that the "businessman, like the occupant of a residence, has a constitutional right to go about his business free from unreasonable official entries upon his private commercial property." The Court disagreed with Seattle by finding that the ordinance actually provided few restrictions leaving much discretion to the inspectors on how to conduct their searches. White concluded "that warrants are a necessary and a tolerable limitation on the right to enter upon and inspect commercial premises. Such warrants should be limited in scope, well defined in purpose, and specifically targeted to what is to be inspected. The need for individual privacy must be weighed against the public need for effective enforcement of the regulation." White did recognize that "surprise may often be a crucial aspect of routine inspections of business establishments." Therefore, warrants may be reasonably obtained in some situations prior to initially approaching the owner of the business. As for See, he could "not be prosecuted for exercising his constitutional right to insist that the fire inspector obtain a warrant authorizing entry" to his locked warehouse.

Justice Clark, joined in dissent by Justices Harlan and Stewart, favored the previous *Frank* decision. Inspection of private properties for purposes of protecting public health and safety should not be hampered by the same "blanket requirement of the safeguards necessary for a search of evidence of criminal acts." Clark feared that reversing *Frank* would greatly cripple enforcement of city ordinances throughout the country "jeopardizing . . . the health, welfare, and safety of literally millions of people." Worst of all, wrote Clark, the local government must now show probable cause for wishing to inspect an establishment under this "newfangled" warrant system. Enforcement of health and safety codes should automatically satisfy the Fourth Amendment's test of reasonableness, not necessitating individual property justifications. Like many other inspections publicly accepted over the previous 150 years of enforcing such standards, nothing in this case suggested to

Clark "that the inspection was unauthorized, unreasonable, for any improper purpose, or designed as a basis for a criminal prosecution; nor is there any indication of any discriminatory, arbitrary, or capricious action." The anticipated lack of individual uniqueness for such administrative warrants, unlike in criminal searches, would lead to "boxcar" warrants being identical for each dwelling in a given area. To Clark such a system would create a false appearance of protecting rights, degrade the issuing magistrate and the judicial process, and be time consuming and costly.

Impact

The rulings of *See* and *Camara* broadened application of Fourth Amendment protection. They established that fire, health, and building inspections were "searches." Therefore, government officials must obtain warrants for administrative entry for both private residences and commercial properties not open to the public. However, the Court also created substantially new and different standards for obtaining such warrants. The warrants required something less than the normal probable cause and "particularity" associated with criminal investigations. First, "probable cause" was redefined to simply mean "reasonableness" of routine inspections, rather than requiring a detailed level of knowledge about the condition of the property. The lesser degree of proof was required since inspections were considered by the Court neither personal in nature nor focused on a crime and involved limited invasion of privacy. Secondly, the "particularity" requirement of the amendment was also altered since the desire was to inspect a large number of properties rather than targeting any specific one. In essence, suspicionless searches were recognized.

Following the *See* decision, the Court identified several exceptions to the warrant requirements. Businesses subject to pervasive government regulation did not enjoy the same Fourth Amendment protections. These included establishments covered by liquor laws as decided in *Colonnade Catering Corp. v. United States* (1970) and gun dealers in *United States v. Biswell* (1972). Operating such businesses posed an "implied consent" to warrantless inspections. In *Michigan v. Tyler* (1978) the Court ruled that fire investigators and firefighters did not need warrants to investigate a fire during or immediately after a fire, including efforts to fight a fire. However, any further entries at the site of a fire would require warrants if access was not granted. On the other hand like *See,* the Court found in *Marshall v. Barlow, Inc.* (1978) that when owners object to occupational health and safety inspections in nonpublic work areas warrants are required.

Prior to the 1960s, concepts of protecting privacy under the Fourth Amendment required warrants only when government officials were physically intruding actual property. The Court, later in 1967 after *See,* significantly expanded Fourth Amendment protections once again in the *Katz v. United States* decision. The Court transformed the Fourth Amendment from a property-based to a privacy-based system. Warrants became necessary if the individual had a reasonable expectation of privacy from government surveillance and confrontation. Even if a person was in a public place they may be constitutionally protected.

Implications for administrative inspections were substantial. For example, use of drug sniffing dogs for random searches in public schools and airport luggage areas called forth issues of safeguarding the privacy of persons from arbitrary invasions by government officials. However, in 1979 the Court ruled the Fourth Amendment had only limited application in public schools since school officials act as surrogate parents. Such warrantless searches were lawful. In 1995 the Court in *Vernonia School District 47J v. Acton* upheld random, suspicionless drug testing of athletes by finding that a school's interest in deterring drug abuse outweighed students' rights. Young students did not have adult rights. Regarding other public places, President Bill Clinton in 1994 pressed for warrantless searches of apartments in public housing projects to fight crime.

Airline safety led to two applications of search. One, clearly warrantless, involved the screening and possible search of passengers prior to boarding airlines. Later in the 1990s concerns increased regarding the sale of unsafe "counterfeit" airplane parts to airlines. In 1995 the Federal Aviation Administration began escalating its search and seizure activities.

Another issue focused on police aerial surveillance. Legal scholars contended that if persons had a reasonable expectation of privacy, then governmental aerial surveillance should be subject to warrants. In *Dow Chemical Co. v. United States* (1986) the Court ruled that aerial photographs used to detect possible Clean Air Act violations did not constitute a search under the Fourth Amendment when no effort was made to protect against the aerial surveillance. The use of heat imagery techniques for environmental regulatory compliance in the 1990s faced similar concerns.

Critics claimed the primary purpose of administrative inspections was not to apprehend violators of laws or to compile information for prosecution, but to improve the health and safety of the nation's citizens. However, the Court found the threat of prosecution was still present if compliance with regulation did not result. The Court commonly found that laws addressing public health and safety merely expressed public interest in conducting related compliance inspections. They normally did not state such inspections should occur without warrants.

Related Cases

Frank v. Maryland, 359 U.S. 360 (1959).
Camara v. Municipal Court, 387 U.S. 523 (1967).
Katz v. United States, 389 U.S. 347 (1967).
Colonnade Catering Corp. v. United States, 397 U.S. 72 (1970).
United States v. Biswell, 406 U.S. 311 (1972).
Michigan v. Tyler, 436 U.S. 499 (1978).
Dow Chemical Co. v. United States, 476 U.S. 227 (1986).
Vernonia School District 47J v. Acton, 515 U.S. 646 (1995).

Bibliography and Further Reading

Biskupic, Joan, and Elder Witt. *Guide to the U.S. Supreme Court.* Washington, DC: Congressional Quarterly, 1997.

"FAA Plans Tough Action Against Illegal Parts." *Aviation Week & Space Technology,* October 23, 1995.

New York Times, April 17, 1994.

"The Heat Seekers—Use of Thermal Imagery in Law Enforcement." *The Nation,* October 16, 1995.

TERRY V. OHIO

Legal Citation: 392 U.S. 1 (1968)

Petitioner
Terry

Respondent
State of Ohio

Petitioner's Claim
That the "stop and frisk" actions of police officer Martin McFadden constituted an unreasonable search and seizure.

Chief Lawyer for Petitioner
Louis Stokes

Chief Lawyer for Respondent
Reuben M. Payne

Justices for the Court
Hugo Lafayette Black, William J. Brennan, Jr., Abe Fortas, John Marshall Harlan II, Thurgood Marshall, Potter Stewart, Earl Warren (writing for the Court), Byron R. White

Justices Dissenting
William O. Douglas

Place
Washington, D.C.

Date of Decision
10 June 1968

Decision
A police officer may stop a person and perform a limited weapons patdown if the officer has observed suspicious behavior which would justify making such an examination.

Significance
Terry v. Ohio expanded the right of police officers to "stop and frisk" individuals whom they deem to be suspicious. At the same time, it set limits on the conditions under which such a stop could take place.

Martin McFadden, a veteran Cleveland detective, was walking his beat one afternoon when he observed two strangers on a street corner. He saw them proceed alternately back and forth along an identical route and pausing to stare in the same store window, which they did over a dozen times. At some point, they were joined by a third man. Suspecting the trio of "casing" the store for a potential burglary, McFadden followed them. The officer approached the three, identified himself as a policeman, and asked their names. The men "mumbled something," at which point McFadden grabbed one of the men, Terry, spun him around, and patted down his outside clothing—a common police tactic known as "stop and frisk." He found a pistol in Terry's overcoat pocket but was unable to remove it. McFadden then ordered the three men into the store and removed Terry's overcoat. He removed the gun and ordered the three to face the wall with their hands raised. He then patted down the outer clothing of the other two men and seized another revolver. McFadden asked the store's proprietor to call the police, at which point they were placed under arrest for carrying concealed weapons.

Terry and his companions were convicted of carrying concealed weapons and sentenced to one to three years in prison. They appealed the conviction on the grounds that McFadden's actions were an unreasonable search and seizure under the Fourth and Fourteenth Amendments. If that were true, the evidence that was seized—the pistols—should not have been admitted in court. At Terry's trial, the court denied his motion to suppress this evidence on the grounds that McFadden had cause to believe the men were acting suspiciously, and that he had the right to pat down their outer clothing if he had reasonable cause to believe that they might be armed. The court made a distinction between a "stop" and an arrest, and between a "frisk" of the outer clothing for weapons and a full-blown search for evidence of crime. An appellate court affirmed the guilty verdict, and the state supreme court dismissed Terry's appeal. The case then came before the U.S. Supreme Court

The Supreme Court Decision

By an 8-1 vote, the Supreme Court upheld the validity of the stop and frisk practice. Though it was determined

Stop and Frisk Searches

The question of "stop and frisk" searches hinges on that most eternal of issues in American jurisprudence: civil liberties on the one hand, and law and order on the other. According to the doctrine articulated by the Supreme Court in *Terry*, a police officer may stop someone on the basis of a reasonable suspicion that the person is engaged in wrongdoing; and may on a similarly reasonable basis—i.e., one that will hold up to scrutiny in the courtroom—"frisk" or search the subject.

In order to meet standards, police making a "stop" must witness unusual conduct which arouses suspicions that can be justified according to specific facts. In order to justify a "frisk" search, the officer must have reason to believe that the individual in question is armed and dangerous.

In extreme cases, stop and frisk searches are clearly justified, but many fall into a gray area that gives rise to questions regarding the justification for searching. For example, there have been numerous cases of black males wrongly subjected to suspicion; on the other hand, there have been situations in which fear of a civil-liberties violation kept officers from preventing a crime. As always, there is tension between the polarities of safeguarding the public's property and safeguarding its liberties.

Source(s): Levy, Leonard W., ed. *Encyclopedia of the American Constitution.* New York: Macmillan, 1986.

---

that Officer McFadden did not in fact have "probable cause" for a full search, the Court made an important distinction between a "stop and frisk" search and a full search. A frisk was deemed to be "an intrusion upon the sanctity of the person" and bound by Fourth and Fourteenth Amendment protections. However, it was ruled to be justified in an attempt to locate concealed weapons. Chief Justice Warren wrote the opinion for the majority:

> We conclude that the revolver seized from Terry was properly admitted in evidence against him. At the time he seized petitioner and searched him for weapons, Officer McFadden had reasonable grounds to believe that petitioner was armed and dangerous, and it was necessary for the protection of himself and others to take swift measures to discover the true facts and neutralize the threat of harm if it materialized. The policeman carefully restricted his search to what was appropriate to the discovery of the particular items which he sought. Each case will, of course, have to be decided on its own facts. We merely hold today that where a police officer observes unusual conduct which leads him reasonably to conclude in light of his experience that criminal activity may be afoot and that the persons with whom he is dealing may be armed and presently dangerous, where in the course of investigating this behavior he identifies himself as a policeman and makes reasonable inquiries, and where nothing in the initial stages of the encounter serves to dispel his rea-

sonable fear for his own or other's safety, he is entitled for the protection of himself and others in the area to conduct a carefully limited search of the outer clothing of such persons in an attempt to discover weapons which might have been used to assault him.

In his dissent, Justice Douglas argued that McFadden had to have had probable cause to believe that Terry was carrying a weapon before performing the stop and frisk. Despite his objections, however, the "Terry type search" became the standard by which police officers could measure the lawfulness of searches performed without obtaining a warrant.

Related Cases
Weeks v. United States, 232 U.S. 383 (1914).
Mapp v. Ohio, 367 U.S. 643 (1961).
Miranda v. Arizona, 384 U.S. 436 (1966).
Katz v. United States, 389 U.S. 347 (1967).
Michigan v. Long, 463 U.S. 1032 (1983).

Bibliography and Further Reading
Chandler, Ralph C. *The Constitutional Law Dictionary.* Santa Barbara, CA: ABC-Clio, 1987.

Cushman, Robert F. *Cases in Constitutional Law.* Englewood Cliffs, NJ: Prentice-Hall, 1986.

Ducat, Craig R., and Harold W. Chase. *Constitutional Interpretation.* St. Paul, MN: West Publishing Company, 1988.

Encyclopedia of the American Constitution. New York: Macmillan, 1986.

CHIMEL V. CALIFORNIA

Legal Citation: 395 U.S. 752 (1969)

Petitioner
Ted Chimel

Respondent
State of California

Petitioner's Claim
That the warrantless search of Chimel's entire house, incident to arrest, was not justifiable under the Fourth Amendment.

Chief Lawyer for Petitioner
Keith C. Monroe

Chief Lawyer for Respondent
Ronald M. George

Justices for the Court
William J. Brennan, Jr., Warren E. Burger, William O. Douglas, John Marshall Harlan II, Thurgood Marshall, Potter Stewart (writing for the Court)

Justices Dissenting
Hugo Lafayette Black, Byron R. White (Abe Fortas retired)

Place
Washington, D.C.

Date of Decision
23 June 1969

Decision
Reversed the lower courts' rulings and held that searches incident to arrest are limited to the area within the immediate control of the suspect in order to prevent the grabbing of a weapon or the destruction of evidence.

Significance
For sixty years the Supreme Court struggled with the issue of how extensive a warrantless search conducted at the time of an arrest could be. The rulings over the years ranged from a search only of the arrestee to a search of the suspect and the entire premises. The *Chimel* ruling settled the controversy over what could be searched without a search warrant, pursuant to an arrest. The "Chimel rule" limited such a search to the suspect and the area within his reach. This limit allowed the officers to guard against a suspect grabbing a weapon or destroying evidence, but continued to protect the suspect's right to privacy. The decision also served to prevent the police from rummaging through an entire house without a search warrant, during the course of an arrest.

On 13 September 1965 three police officers arrived at the Santa Ana, California home of Ted Chimel with a warrant for his arrest, based on information that he had been involved in the robbery of a coin shop. Chimel's wife let the officers in to wait for her husband to return home from work. When Chimel arrived home, one officer gave him the arrest warrant and asked for permission to look around. Although Chimel objected to the search, the officers stated that "on the basis of the lawful arrest," they would search the house, even though they had no search warrant. Chimel's wife objected to the search, but accompanied the officers as they searched the three-bedroom home, including the attic, garage, and workshop. In the master bedroom and sewing room, the officers told Mrs. Chimel to open drawers and move things so they could look for items from the coin shop. After the search, the officers seized numerous items, including coins, medals, and tokens.

At Chimel's state trial, the items found in the search were used as evidence against him. Chimel objected to this on the grounds that the items were seized unconstitutionally and thus should be excluded. His plea was rejected, and he was convicted. The California Court of Appeals and the California Supreme Court affirmed the conviction. Both courts held that although the arrest warrant was invalid, the arrest was lawful because the officers had obtained the warrant in good faith and had probable cause for the arrest. The courts agreed that the search of Chimel's house was justified because it was incident to a valid arrest, even though the officers did not have a search warrant.

The California courts relied on the case *United States v. Rabinowitz* for their decision. In this case, a one-room business office was searched at the time of the occupant's arrest, although the officers had only an arrest warrant, but not a search warrant. The Court held that a warrantless search "incident to a lawful arrest" may be made of the area that is in the possession or under the control of the arrested person. Because of *United States v. Rabinowitz* (1950), the California courts upheld the search of Chimel's entire house.

Before the *Chimel* decision, courts relied on the Harris-Rabinowitz rule for their decisions regarding searches incident to arrest. In *Harris v. United States* (1947), officers arrested Harris with an arrest warrant and then searched his entire four-room apartment, without a search warrant. This search was considered acceptable by the Supreme Court as being "incident to arrest."

Setting the Standard

Justice Stewart wrote the opinion for the majority in *Chimel v. California*. He stated that the decision in *United States v. Rabinowitz* "at least in the broad sense in which it was applied by the California courts in this case, can withstand neither historical nor rational analysis." Stewart explained that when an arrest is made, it is reasonable for the officer to search the person to remove weapons that might be used to resist arrest or to make an escape. If the officer did not search the person, the officer might be in danger. It is also reasonable for the officer to search for and seize evidence on the arrestee to prevent its concealment or destruction. The area in reach of the arrestee—within his immediate control—may also be searched to prevent the person from grabbing a weapon or evidence.

No justification exists for routinely searching any room, except for the one where the arrest occurs. Even there, no reason exists to search desk drawers or other closed or concealed places in the room. Such searches require a search warrant. That principle was used to decide *Preston v. United States*. In that case, a car towed after arrest was searched without a warrant. The Court held the search to be unlawful under the Fourth Amendment although it was contended that the search was incidental to a valid arrest. Because the search was remote in time and place from the arrest, it was not valid.

The defense contended that the search of Chimel's house was reasonable because he had been arrested in the house. Stewart felt that that "argument is founded on little more than a subjective view regarding the acceptability of certain sorts of police conduct and not on considerations relevant to Fourth Amendment interests. Under such an unconfined analysis, Fourth Amendment protection in this area would approach the evaporation point." Stewart pointed out that it would be hard to explain why it is less reasonable to search a person's house when he is arrested on the front lawn or just down the street. The necessary distinction must be made between a search of the arrestee and the area in his reach versus more extensive searches.

Stewart summed up his opinion by noting that the search of Chimel's house went far beyond a search of the arrestee and the area from which he could have gotten a weapon or evidence. "There was no constitutional justification, in the absence of a search warrant, for extending the search beyond that area. The scope of the search was, therefore, 'unreasonable' under the Fourth and Fourteenth Amendments, and the petitioner's conviction cannot stand."

Warrantless Emergency Search

Justice White wrote the dissent, in which Black joined. The dissenters felt that the Harris-Rabinowitz rule should remain in place. White felt that when the circumstances are urgent and probable cause exists, an emergency search may be a reasonable one. "It seems to me unreasonable to require the police to leave the scene in order to obtain a search warrant when they are already legally there to make a valid arrest." If the police did leave the scene to get a search warrant, the accomplices of the arrestee could remove evidence. The protection of privacy must be weighed against the risk of destruction of evidence.

Impact

Chimel v. California was the Court's most important decision regarding warrantless searches conducted while making a valid arrest. Prior to the *Chimel* decision, the Harris-Rabinowitz rule, permitting searches of a premises incident to arrest, gave police a broad opportunity for abuse. The police made warrantless searches while arresting a suspect on the grounds that they did not have time to get a search warrant. But in the case of *Chimel*, the crime was committed a month before the arrest. After the police obtained the arrest warrant, they waited several days before serving the warrant. The police never explained why they could not get a search warrant.

The *Chimel* decision was important because it said that evidence seized during unlawful searches may not be used in court, a concept known as the exclusionary rule. Since *Chimel* limited the area of warrantless searches, it opened up the possibility that evidence seized outside of the immediate area of the suspect would be excluded and inadmissible in court, thus aiding the defendant. When Chief Justice Warren extended the use of the exclusionary rule to the states in *Mapp v. Ohio* (1961), the Warren Court was accused of coddling criminals. Warren resigned from the Court on 23 June 1969, the same day the *Chimel* case was decided. President Richard Nixon chose as his replacement a strong critic of the exclusionary rule, Warren E. Burger.

In 1971, in *Williams v. United States,* the Court decided that the "Chimel rule," limiting a search area to within a person's immediate control incidental to an arrest, could not be applied retroactively and should not affect searches conducted prior to the date of the *Chimel* decision.

Through the 1980s, the Supreme Court permitted law enforcement officers to search anything in the suspect's immediate control, meaning anywhere from which the arrestee might obtain a weapon. This included his person, the room in which he was located, and drawers. In 1990, the Court ruled that officers may make a "protective sweep" of the premises where the arrest took place. But they may only do this if they have a "reasonable belief" that a dangerous person might be there. The police may also inventory a suspect's effects without a search warrant, including a shoulder bag. Any evidence found in this manner may be used in a criminal trial.

Related Cases

Weeks v. Ohio, 232 U.S. 383 (1914).
Harris v. United States, 331 U.S. 145 (1947).
United States v. Rabinowitz, 339 U.S. 56 (1950).
Mapp v. Ohio, 367 U.S. 643 (1961).
Preston v. United States, 376 U.S. 364 (1964).
Williams v. United States, 401 U.S. 646 (1971).
State v. Thomas, 318 N.C. 287 (1986).

Bibliography and Further Reading

Bessette, Joseph M., ed. *American Justice,* Vol. 1. Pasadena, CA: Salem Press, Inc., 1996.

FindLaw Internet Legal Resources. http://www.find-law.com.

Hall, Kermit L., ed. *The Oxford Companion to the Supreme Court of the United States.* New York: Oxford University Press, 1992.

Lieberman, Jethro K. *The Evolving Constitution.* New York: Random House, 1992.

Northwestern University. *Oyez Oyez Oyez: A U.S. Supreme Court Database.* http://oyez.nwu.edu/.

COOLIDGE V. NEW HAMPSHIRE

Legal Citation: 403 U.S. 443 (1971)

Petitioner
Edward H. Coolidge, Jr.

Respondent
State of New Hampshire

Petitioner's Claim
The petitioner stated that the warrant authorizing the seizure and subsequent search of his automobile should be considered invalid on the ground that it was a violation of the Fourth and Fourteenth Amendments of the U.S. Constitution.

Chief Lawyer for Petitioner
Archibald Cox

Chief Lawyer for Respondent
Alexander Kalinski

Justices for the Court
William J. Brennan, Jr., William O. Douglas, John Marshall Harlan II, Potter Stewart (writing for the Court), Thurgood Marshall

Justices Dissenting
Hugo Lafayette Black, Harry A. Blackmun, Warren E. Burger, Byron R. White

Place
Washington, D.C.

Date of Decision
21 June 1971

Decision
The Court determined that the searches and seizures of Coolidge's property were unconstitutional.

Significance
Coolidge v. New Hampshire opened a debate concerning the proper use of a warrant for search and seizure, as well as what actually constituted "plain view" evidence and the proper means of obtaining evidence that is incident to an arrest.

The Investigation of a "Particularly Brutal Murder" and the Trial that Followed

On the evening of 13 January 1964, 14-year-old Pamela Mason left her home in Manchester, New Hampshire. It was snowing heavily that night and she had received a call from a man in need of a babysitter. Eight days later, her body was found many miles away by the side of a north-south highway. The police immediately began a large-scale investigation into the murder.

Police inquiries led to the questioning of Edward Coolidge. He was cooperative throughout the entire process. When asked if he owned any guns he responded that he did and produced three—a rifle and two shotguns. He agreed to participate in a polygraph test the following Sunday, his day off from work. Coolidge's wife was present for the entire interview.

Police contacted Coolidge the following Sunday and asked him to come to the police station where he would be taken to Concord, New Hampshire for the lie-detector test. That evening, as Mrs. Coolidge waited with her mother-in-law for her husband to return, two plainclothes policemen called on the Coolidge residence. It is important to note that these were not the same officers who had questioned Coolidge in front of his wife earlier in the week; indeed these officers were not even aware that Coolidge had readily provided three guns for inspection to the previous officers. The plainclothes policemen stated that her husband was in "serious trouble" and would not be returning home that night. Coolidge was being held in jail overnight for an unrelated charge; during the polygraph test he had confessed to stealing money from his employer. They then asked the mother-in-law to leave and began questioning Mrs. Coolidge. At one point during the questioning they asked to see Coolidge's guns and the clothes that Mrs. Coolidge believed her husband had been wearing on the night of Pamela Mason's disappearance. Mrs. Coolidge produced four guns (not three) and the clothing in question.

The state used the next two-and-a-half weeks to gather evidence supporting the theory that Coolidge had murdered Pamela Mason. On 19 February 1964 the results of the investigation were exhibited to the state

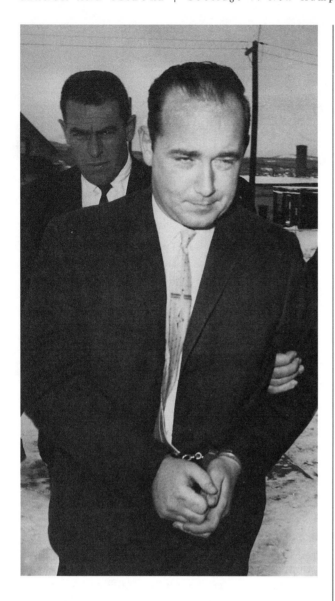

Edward H. Coolidge, Jr., is led into Hillsborough County Jail, Manchester, New Hampshire, 1964. © AP/Wide World Photos.

attorney general—who had not only taken charge of the case, but would later also act as chief prosecutor at the trial. It was decided that the murder charge, along with a search of his residence and two cars, would provide enough evidence to support the arrest of Coolidge. The chief of the Manchester police applied, under oath, for arrest and search warrants, which were subsequently signed and issued by the attorney general himself—in the role of acting justice of the peace. The procedure allowing a justice of the peace to authorize and issue search warrants was allowed under New Hampshire law at the time of this case.

The police wasted no time in arresting Coolidge on the same day that the warrant was issued. Mrs. Coolidge was told that she could not stay in the house and that the police would provide transportation for her as they

were impounding both of Coolidge's vehicles. It is extremely important to note that the vehicles were parked in Coolidge's driveway in plain sight from both the street and the inside of the house.

Several items of evidence were presented in Coolidge's murder trial to indicate that he was guilty. The New Hampshire Supreme Court turned down motions to suppress all evidence. Vacuum sweepings from one of his vehicles included particles of gunpowder. The gun, not presented by Coolidge during the initial police interview, was a .22-caliber Mossberg rifle—claimed by the prosecution to be the murder weapon (although ballistics tests were conflicting). The prosecution then attempted to show via microscopic analysis that there was a strong chance that the clothes obtained at Coolidge's residence had been in contact with the body of Pamela Mason. The jury found Coolidge guilty and sentenced him to life imprisonment. The New Hampshire Supreme Court confirmed the judgement.

The Improper Use of a Warrant

At this point the U.S. Supreme Court granted *certiorari* to take into account a multitude of constitutional issues raised by the admission of the evidence against Coolidge. Although Coolidge challenged the manner in which the police obtained the guns and clothing from his wife (it was later concluded that no police coercion was involved and that she had volunteered her assistance in hopes of clearing her husband of the charges), the primary concern of the Supreme Court stemmed from the manner in which the search warrant was issued and used.

Primarily, the justices delved into the determination of probable cause—ascertained by none other than the state attorney general. While this in itself was not considered a problem, the fact that the same individual was in charge of the Pamela Mason murder investigation was viewed as a conflict of interest and an infringement on the right to privacy.

> . . . it is enough to answer that there could hardly be a more appropriate setting than this for a *per se* rule of disqualification rather than a case-by-case evaluation of all the circumstances. Without disrespect to the state law enforcement agent here involved, the whole point of the basic rule . . . is that prosecutors and policemen simply cannot be asked to maintain the requisite neutrality with regard to their own investigations—the "competitive enterprise" that must rightly engage their single-minded attention.

Justice Robert H. Jackson (in *Johnson v. United States* [1948]) summarized this type of situation quite succinctly: "When the right of privacy must reasonably yield to the right of search is, as a rule, to be decided by a judicial officer, not by a policeman or government enforcement agent." The New Hampshire method of issuing search warrants was found to be a violation of the Fourth and Fourteenth Amendments of the U.S. Constitution.

The state of New Hampshire developed three theories in an attempt to explain the warrant's validity, or at least to cover the legal issues involving a warrantless search. The first theory stated that the search and seizure of Coolidge's automobile were "incident" to the arrest. In order for this to have been the case, it would have been necessary for Coolidge to be in possession or control of the vehicle. As noted in *United States v. Rabinowitz*, a search could be considered incident to an arrest ". . . only if it is substantially contemporaneous with the arrest and is confined to the *immediate* vicinity of the arrest . . ." Coolidge was arrested inside of his house while the Pontiac rested in the driveway—outside. Other cases were cited to back this contention, including *Vale v. Louisiana, Shipley v. California, Stoner v. California*, and *Agnello v. United States*. It was also noted in *Rabinowitz* that even after an accused person is arrested and in police custody, a search of the person's property after the arrest was "simply not incident to the arrest."

The second theory postulated by the state maintained that probable cause allowed for a warrantless search of an automobile. As stated in previous cases (primarily involving the transportation of contraband), there was a considerable difference between the search of a house or a store and the search of a vehicle simply because a vehicle could be moved out of the jurisdiction covered by a specific warrant. It was deemed that this "automobile exception" was not applicable to the *Coolidge* case. Coolidge was arrested without resistance in his own house; the car remained untouched throughout this event, as he made no attempt to escape. Since the police had suspected the role of the car in the crime for some time, it became apparent that the warrantless search was illegal due to the lack of exigent circumstances.

The state's final theory supporting a warrantless seizure and search relied on the Pontiac as being an "instrumentality of the crime" that could be seized because it was in plain view. However, an item of evidence discovered in plain view could not be considered as such unless it was discovered while the search was in progress—and the discovery itself must be considered inadvertent. The Supreme Court rightly believed that the police had a sufficient amount of time in which to obtain a valid warrant as the description and the location of the Pontiac were known in advance of the arrest.

None of these theories validated the warrant provided by the state attorney general; nor did they justify a warrantless search. It was found that the seizure

and subsequent search of Coolidge's automobile was unconstitutional. As the evidence obtained in this search was permitted at the murder trial, the U.S. Supreme Court deemed that the judgement of this trial must be reversed and remanded the case to the New Hampshire Supreme Court.

Incident to Arrest or Breach of the Fourth Amendment?

Although this case was reversed by the U.S. Supreme Court, many of the justices expressed dissenting opinions concerning specific issues. Justice White strongly argued that a warrantless entry into a man's house in order to arrest him is a legitimate enough cause for search and seizure of the man's property. In examining this argument and cases in which this issue had arisen before (such as *Chimel v. California* [1969] and *Trupiano v. United States* [1948]) the Court came to a disturbing conclusion.

> If we were to agree with Mr. Justice White that the police may, whenever they have probable cause, make a warrantless entry for the purpose of making an arrest, and that seizures and searches of automobiles are likewise *per se* reasonable given probable cause, then by the same logic *any* search or seizure could be carried out without a warrant, and we would simply have read the Fourth Amendment out of the Constitution.

Chief Justice Burger and Justice Black concurred on the overall ruling, but dissented on the grounds that the Fourth Amendment did not contain any statement that would quantify the disqualification of the state attorney general to act as a magistrate. They also believed that the seizure and search of the automobile were constitutional for a variety of reasons. Since the automobile was visible not only from outside of the house, but inside as well, they felt it should be considered incident to Coolidge's arrest. The subsequent search of the Pontiac could be justified by citing *Chambers v. Maroney* in which it was held legal for the police to seize and search the petitioner's car based on probable cause that the vehicle had been used in the commission of a murder. Numerous other cases, such as *Ker v. California* and *Marron v. United States* were also mentioned to support the seizure of evidence incident to arrest. It was felt that the seizure of Coolidge's car "was valid under the well-established right of the police to seize evidence in plain view at the time and place of the arrest."

Chief Justice Burger stated that the *Coolidge* case was an excellent example of what happens when the legal system traps itself in its own creation of an "exclusionary rule"—in this case the nuances of plain view and the definition of evidence that is incident to arrest. He felt that the Court was able to distort rules as a result of this, and therefore could reverse a ruling on a case that simply did not merit such a decision.

Impact

The *Coolidge v. New Hampshire* case clearly demonstrated the gray area that exists in the use of warrants and the acts of search and seizure, as shown by the multiple opinions expressed by many of the justices. The proper issuance and use of search warrants with respect to the Fourth Amendment remains a topic of great concern to law officials. As late as 1987, in *Arizona v. Hicks,* the definition of plain view and the questioning of warrant validity were once again brought before the U.S. Supreme Court. It seems that the contradictions argued in *Coolidge* still allow for varying interpretations of what, in many respects, can be viewed as the same scenario of "warrantless" search and seizure.

Related Cases

Agnello v. United States, 269 U.S. 20 (1925).
Marron v. United States, 275 U.S. 192 (1927).
Trupiano v. United States, 334 U.S. 699 (1948).
Ker v. California, 374 U.S. 23 (1963).
Katz v. United States, 389 U.S. 347 (1967).
Chimel v. California, 395 U.S. 752 (1969).
Arizona v. Hicks, (1987).

Bibliography and Further Reading

Biskupic, Joan, and Elder Witt, eds. *Congressional Quarterly's Guide to the U.S. Supreme Court,* 3rd ed. Washington, DC: Congressional Quarterly, Inc., 1996.

ADAMS V. WILLIAMS

Legal Citation: 407 U.S. 143 (1972)

Petitioner
Frederick E. Adams

Respondent
Robert Williams

Petitioner's Claim
That a police officer does not violate the Fourth Amendment by reaching in to a car window and removing a gun from the waistband of a driver when the officer has reason to believe that the suspect is armed and dangerous.

Chief Lawyer for Petitioner
Donald A. Browne

Chief Lawyer for Respondent
Edward F. Hennessey III

Justices for the Court
Harry A. Blackmun, Warren E. Burger, Lewis F. Powell, Jr., William H. Rehnquist (writing for the Court), Potter Stewart, Byron R. White

Justices Dissenting
William J. Brennan, Jr., William O. Douglas, Thurgood Marshall

Place
Washington, D.C.

Date of Decision
12 June 1972

Decision
As long as an officer is permitted to make a forcible traffic stop to investigate evidence of wrongdoing, the Fourth Amendment does not prohibit the officer from conducting a limited search for weapons so that he may safely pursue his investigation when the officer has reason to believe that the suspect is armed and dangerous.

Significance
The Court's decision gave officers significantly increased powers in pursuing investigations and frisking suspects for weapons. It extended the circumstances in which police officers may stop and frisk a person for weapons. More importantly, the Court's decision was the first step in a series of cases expanding the situations in which a police officer may conduct a search of a person without first obtaining a search warrant.

In the 1968 case *Terry v. Ohio*, the Supreme Court held that a police officer may "stop and frisk" a person whom the officer has a reasonable suspicion to believe is carrying a weapon. This reasonable suspicion standard is a less rigorous standard than the "probable cause" requirement ordinarily required to support a search under the Fourth Amendment. In *Adams*, the Court considered the scope of its holding in *Terry*.

Early in the morning, while patrolling a high crime area in Bridgeport, Connecticut, police officer John Connolly was approached by an informant he knew and was told that Williams, who was sitting in a parked car nearby, was carrying narcotics. The informant also told officer Connolly that Williams had a gun tucked into his waistband. Connolly approached the car, knocked on the window, and asked Williams to open the car door. When Williams rolled down the window, the officer reached in and removed the gun from Williams' waistband, which was exactly where the informant had indicated. Based on his seizure of the handgun, the officer arrested Williams for unlawful possession of a pistol. As part of the arrest, Williams' car was also searched, and the police discovered heroin and additional weapons.

Williams was tried and convicted of charges of possessing both a handgun and narcotics in the state court, and his convictions were affirmed by the state appellate courts. Williams then filed a petition for a writ of *habeas corpus* in the U.S. District Court for the District of Connecticut. *Habeas corpus*, a Latin phrase meaning literally "you have the body," is a procedure in which a state prisoner asks a federal court to order his release from a state prison because his imprisonment in some way violates the U.S. Constitution. Williams claimed that the officer's reaching into his car and grabbing his gun was unreasonable, and thus violated the Fourth Amendment. Thus, he argued, the subsequent search of his vehicle which was based on the officer finding the gun was also illegal, and the evidence seized in the search should have been suppressed. The district court denied the writ of *habeas corpus*. However, the U.S. Court of Appeals for the Second Circuit reversed the district court and granted the writ of *habeas corpus*. The state then sought to appeal the case to the Supreme Court by petitioner for a writ of *certiorari*, which the Court granted.

Protective Searches for Weapons Are Permissible

On appeal, the Supreme Court reversed the court of appeals, concluding that the police officer's search of Williams was a reasonable protective search under its decision in *Terry v. Ohio*. As the Court explained, *Terry* held that a police officer may stop a person to investigate if the officer has a reasonable suspicion to believe that the person is committing a crime. The Fourth Amendment, which protects people against unreasonable searches and seizures, generally requires that a police officer have probable cause to believe that a search will recover evidence of a crime or contraband. However, in *Terry* the Court reasoned that a police officer should be able to protect himself from attack by a hostile suspect he has stopped to investigate. Thus, the officer is permitted to conduct a limited search of the suspect for weapons if he has a reasonable suspicion (which is less than probable cause) to believe that the suspect is armed.

Applying the Terry rule to the facts of the case, the Court concluded that the police officer had reasonable suspicion to believe that Williams was armed and dangerous, and thus he was justified in reaching into the car to seize the gun. The Court reasoned that the tip by the informant that Williams was carrying a gun in his waistband, the fact that Williams was suspected of carrying narcotics and a concealed weapon, and the fact that Williams was sitting alone in a parked car in the early morning in a high crime area all gave the officer "ample reason to fear for his safety." Further, this reasonable fear was increased when Williams failed to comply with the officer's request to get out of his car, but rather rolled down the window. Thus, the Court concluded: "Under these circumstances the policeman's action in reaching to a spot where the gun was thought to be hidden constituted a limited intrusion designed to insure his safety, and we conclude it was reasonable."

Having found the limited search for the weapon in Williams' waistband to be reasonable, the Court concluded that he was properly arrested for unlawful possession of the weapon. At this point, the police were justified in searching the remainder of the vehicle, because under the Fourth Amendment, as interpreted by the Supreme Court, the police may search a person and his automobile incident to a lawful arrest. Thus, the Court concluded that the evidence was properly admitted in Williams' trial, and that he was therefore not entitled to a writ of *habeas corpus* from the federal courts.

A Dangerous Extension of *Terry*

Justices Douglas, Brennan, and Marshall, dissenting from the Court's opinion, decried the Court's extension of *Terry*. The dissenting justices first thought that the informant's uncorroborated tip was insufficient to give the officer a reasonable suspicion that Williams was in possession of a gun. Justice Marshall distinguished the search allowed in *Terry* because, in that case, the officer acted based on his own observations after careful scrutiny of the suspects. On the contrary, in this case, Justice Marshall argued, the officer relied only upon "unreliable, unsubstantiated, conclusory hearsay to justify an invasion of liberty."

More importantly, in Justice Marshall's view, the Court was extending *Terry* too far. As he reasoned, *Terry* struck a delicate balance between the rights of citizens to be free from unreasonable searches and the need for police officers to be safe when conducting reasonable investigations of criminal wrongdoing. In Justice Marshall's view, the Court's opinion tipped this balance too far in favor of police officers:

> As a result of today's decision, the balance struck in *Terry* is now heavily weighted in favor of the government. And the Fourth Amendment, which was included in the Bill of Rights to prevent the kind of arbitrary and oppressive police action involved herein, is dealt a serious blow. Today's decision invokes the specter of a society in which innocent citizens may be stopped, searched, and arrested at the whim of police officers who have only the slightest suspicion of improper conduct.

Impact

In a limited sense, the Court's decision was significant in granting police additional powers to stop and frisk suspects. More importantly, however, the *Adams* decision was the first step in a series of decisions in which the Court has continued to expand the situations in which police officers may conduct searches without first obtaining a search warrant. In the years since the *Adams* decision, the Court has extended *Terry* to allow police to stop a person based only on reasonable suspicion in order to fingerprint the person, to determine whether that person is wanted for another crime, or to detain the person for a reasonable time while further investigation is conducted. Thus, *Adams* signaled a drastic step in the interpretation of the Fourth Amendment.

Related Cases

Terry v. Ohio, 392 U.S. 1 (1968).
Michigan v. Summers, 452 U.S. 692 (1981).
Minnesota v. Dickerson, 508 U.S. 366 (1993).

Bibliography and Further Reading

Dressler, Joshua. *Understanding Criminal Procedure.* New York: Matthew Bender & Co., 1991.

LaFave, Wayne R. *Search and Seizure: A Treatise on the Fourth Amendment,* 3rd ed. St. Paul, MN: West Publishing Co., 1996.

Project on Law Enforcement Policy and Rulemaking. *Stop and Frisk.* Tempe, AZ: Arizona State University College of Law, 1974.

SCHNECKLOTH V. BUSTAMONTE

Legal Citation: 412 U.S. 218 (1973)

Petitioner
Merle R. Schneckloth, Superintendent, California Conservation Center

Respondent
Robert Clyde Bustamonte

Petitioner's Claim
The appeals court erred when it held that the state had to prove that the person who gave consent to the police for a search had knowledge of the right to refuse consent.

Chief Lawyer for Petitioner
Robert R. Granucci

Chief Lawyer for Respondent
Stuart P. Tobisman

Justices for the Court
Harry A. Blackmun, Warren E. Burger, Lewis F. Powell, Jr., William H. Rehnquist, Potter Stewart (writing for the Court), Byron R. White

Justices Dissenting
William J. Brennan, Jr., William O. Douglas, Thurgood Marshall

Place
Washington, D.C.

Date of Decision
29 May 1973

Decision
When the state seeks to justify a warrantless police search based on a person's consent, it need not prove that the person knew that the request to search could be refused.

Significance
Although the Court heard Bustamonte's Fourth Amendment claim, a decision that was roundly criticized by three justices, the Court ruled against him. In the process, the Court established that police officers do not have to tell people that they can refuse an officer's request to search their person or their belongings.

On the morning of 19 January 1967, in the town of Mountain View, California, Speedway Car Wash owner Charles Kehoe discovered that he had been burglarized. A check-writing machine (a "check protector") and blank checks had been taken from Kehoe's office. Two days later, Robert Bustamonte, with the assistance of Joe Alcala and Joe Gonzalez, made out one of the stolen checks to a "Joe Garcia" for $63.75 and cashed it to buy a carton of cigarettes.

The three men made several other attempts to cash the checks at private businesses, but they were unsuccessful. On 30 January 1967, the men traveled to San Jose to find three other men for help in cashing the checks. Riding in a black 1958 Ford 4-door sedan with only one functioning headlight and a burnt-out license plate light, the six men set out to cash the checks. At approximately 2:40 a.m. on 31 January, Officer James Rand of the Sunnyvale Department of Public Safety spotted the sedan and stopped them. Gonzalez, who was driving, did not produce a driver's license for Officer Rand; only Alcala could produce a license, and Alcala stated that the car belonged to his brother. Officer Rand ordered the men out of the vehicle, and two more police officers arrived. Officer Rand then asked Alcala if he could search the car, and, according to Officer Rand, Alcala said "'Sure, go ahead.'" Officer Rand and another officer searched the car and they found three Speedway Car Wash checks wadded up under the left rear seat.

The officers arrested the six men. Thereafter, Sunnyvale police obtained a search warrant to search Bustamonte's cars. In the cars, the police found Speedway Car Wash checks and a check protector. Bustamonte was prosecuted in California state court on a charge of possessing a check with intent to defraud, and prosecutors gave Gonzalez a plea bargain in exchange for his testimony against Bustamonte. Bustamonte moved the trial court to exclude, or suppress, the evidence found in the car, arguing that the evidence was obtained in violation of his Fourth Amendment right to be free from unreasonable searches and seizures. Specifically, Bustamonte argued that Alcala's consent was the result of police coercion. In a suppression hearing conducted before trial, Gonzalez supported Officer Rand's version of events, testifying that Alcala had given his consent to a search of the car and even helped by opening the trunk and the glove compartment. The trial court denied Bustamonte's motion to suppress the evidence, and Bustamonte was convicted after a trial. The conviction was upheld on appeal. According to the state appeals court, the consent given by Alcala to the search was not invalidated by any "express or implied assertion of authority."

The California Supreme Court refused to review the case, and Bustamonte filed a *habeas corpus* petition against his jailer in federal district court. That court denied the petition, but the Court of Appeals for the Ninth Circuit reversed, holding that the state had to prove not only the absence of police coercion, but that Alcala knew that he could withhold his consent. The federal district court had not analyzed whether Alcala knew of his right to reject Officer Rand's request to search, so the appeals court remanded the case to the district court for further proceedings. The state of California, through prison Superintendent Merle R. Schneckloth, appealed that decision to the U.S. Supreme Court.

By a vote of 6-3, the U.S. Supreme Court reversed. In an opinion written by Justice Stewart, the plurality identified the issue in the case: "what must the prosecution prove to demonstrate that a consent was 'voluntarily' given." Upon a thorough review of the Court's precedent and a thorough analysis of the term "voluntariness," the plurality concluded that the prosecution did not have to prove that a person knew of the right to refuse consent.

The Court acknowledged the competing interests in the case. On one hand, society must be protected from unfair and brutal police tactics. On the other hand, society needs "police questioning as a tool for the effective enforcement of criminal laws." In other cases where voluntariness was questioned, such as cases involving criminal confessions, the Court had looked at a number of factors and all of the circumstances surrounding the consent to determine whether the confession was voluntary. The Court believed that the determination of whether consent to search was voluntary should be subjected to the same type of analysis.

The plurality believed that a person's knowledge of the right to refuse was a factor in determining whether a person's consent to search was voluntarily given. However, it was not the only factor, and it was not the deciding factor. Voluntariness was, the plurality emphasized, a vital aspect to a consent to search. However, it would be a "near impossibility" for the prosecution to prove that a person knew of the right to refuse consent because the person could "simply fail to testify that he in fact knew he could refuse to consent."

The plurality rejected the requirement that the police warn a person of his or her rights regarding consent to search. Most courts had refused to create such a requirement, and the Court did the same. "[I]t would be thoroughly impractical," declared the plurality, "to impose on the normal consent search the detailed requirements of an effective warning." The plurality noted that consent searches "are part of the standard investigatory techniques of law enforcement agencies," that they normally take place in public or at home "under informal and unstructured conditions." The request for consent to search may be "a logical extension of investigative police questioning," and the police may wish to follow up leads. "These situations are a far cry," reasoned the Court, "from the structured atmosphere of a trial, where, assisted by counsel if he chooses, a defendant is informed of his trial rights." There was, announced the Court, "a vast difference between those rights that protect a fair criminal trial and the rights guaranteed under the Fourth Amendment."

Consent searches, opined the plurality, also were different from police interrogations. In *Miranda v. Arizona*, a 1966 case, the High Court had held that police officers had to apprise arrested persons of the right to remain silent and the right to an attorney. However, in that case, the Court had stated that police did not have to give such warnings to persons during "'[g]eneral on-the-scene questioning.'"

Instead of requiring the government prove that a person had knowledge of the right to refuse consent to a search, the Court had to engage in a "careful sifting of the unique facts and circumstances of each case." In prior consent cases, the Court had reversed convictions where the consent to search was "coerced by threats or force, or granted only in submission to a claim of lawful authority." In no case had the Court held that knowledge of the right to refuse consent was a prerequisite to finding voluntary consent. The Court had upheld strict standards on waivers of rights at trial, such as the right to counsel and the right to a jury trial, but such standards were necessary to prevent the "severe injustice risked by confronting an untrained defendant with a range of technical points of law, evidence, and tactics familiar to the prosecutor but not to himself."

The Fourth Amendment, by contrast, had nothing to do with promoting a fair trial. Consent searches occurred outside the controlled setting of the courthouse, and "it was unrealistic to expect that in the informal, unstructured context of a consent search, a policeman, upon pain of tainting the evidence obtained, could make [a] detailed type of examination." The Court disagreed with the appeals court that such an examination was required, and Bustamonte continued to languish in prison.

Justice Blackmun filed a short concurring opinion. According to Justice Blackmun, the Court should not have reconsidered its opinion in a precedent-setting case, *Kaufman v. United States* (1969), in deciding Bustamonte's case. Chief Justice Burger and Justice Rehnquist joined a separate concurring opinion authored by Justice Powell. Justice Powell agreed with the judgment of the Court, but he believed that the issue in the case should have been limited to the following: whether Bustamonte "was provided a fair opportunity to raise and have adjudicated the question in state courts." In Justice Powell's opinion, Bustamonte should not have been allowed to base his *habeas corpus* petition on a Fourth Amendment claim unless he was arguing that the state courts had unfairly denied him an opportunity to raise and argue the claim. In *Kaufman v. United States,* the Court had held that a *habeas corpus* petitioner could base the petition on a Fourth Amendment violation that had been fully litigated in state court. In Powell's opinion, *Kaufman* should have been overruled.

Justice Powell conducted a thorough examination of the history of the *habeas corpus* petition. The *habeas corpus* petition was an exception to the general rule of "due regard for the finality of the judgment of the committing court." *Habeas corpus* petitions essentially constituted another round of appeals for a convicted criminal defendant. However, the range of issues that a *habeas corpus* petitioner could raise was limited to questions about the trial court's jurisdiction and questions that concerned the Constitution. Justice Powell, concerned about the abuse of state court decisions through the use of *habeas corpus* petitions in federal court, felt that the issues in such a petition should not be expanded to include claims of Fourth Amendment violations that had already been litigated. Other constitutional claims, though, could be placed in a *habeas corpus* petition even if they had been fairly litigated in state court.

Fourth Amendment claims, Justice Powell argued, were different from other constitutional claims. Specifically, they had little to do with guilt or innocence. The exclusionary rule, which forbade the use of evidence that had been obtained in violation of Fourth Amendment rights, had benefits and "liabilities." The rule was a prophylactic for the right of persons to live free from unreasonable searches and seizures, but it also deprived the criminal justice system of the opportunity to use evidence that, in most cases, clearly established guilt. "Prisoners raising Fourth Amendment claims [in a *habeas corpus* petition] usually are quite justly detained," Powell declared. Powell maintained that the *habeas corpus* petition should be reserved for cases where the issue is "whether the prisoner was innocent of the crime," and not "whether some evidence of undoubted probative value has been admitted in violation of an exclusionary rule ritualistically applied without due regard for whether it has the

slightest likelihood of achieving its avowed prophylactic purpose."

Justices Douglas, Brennan, and Marshall each filed separate dissenting opinions. Justice Douglas supported the federal appeals court's decision, and would have denied review of Bustamonte's petition and let the petition go forward in the district court. Justice Brennan decried the plurality's treatment of the Fourth Amendment. "It wholly escapes me," Justice Brennan confessed, "how our citizens can meaningfully be said to have waived something as precious as a constitutional guarantee without ever being aware of its existence."

Justice Marshall, in a long dissenting opinion, objected to "the curious result that one can choose to relinquish a constitutional right—the right to be free of unreasonable searches—without knowing that he has the alternative of refusing to accede to a police request to search." The Court had "always scrutinized with great care" other cases in which a person had failed to assert a constitutional right, and Marshall "saw no reason" to treat the Fourth Amendment differently. The Court's opinion, Marshall maintained, had "sanction[ed] a game of blindman's bluff, in which the police always have the upper hand, for the sake of nothing more than the convenience of the police."

Impact

The *Bustamonte* decision confirmed that the police do not have to inform people of their right to refuse a police request to search. However, the *Bustamonte* decision could not have been made after 1976. That year, the High Court held in *Stone v. Powell* that a *habeas corpus* petitioner may not base the petition on a Fourth Amendment search and seizure claim unless the state had failed to provide an opportunity for full and fair litigation of the issue. The *Stone* decision provided redemption for Justice Powell's concurring opinion in *Bustamonte.*

Related Cases

Miranda v. Arizona, 384 U.S. 436 (1966).
Kaufman v. United States, 394 U.S. 217 (1969).
Stone v. Powell, 428 U.S. 465 (1976).

Bibliography and Further Reading

Yanofsky, Carole J. "*Withrow v. Williams:* The Supreme Court's Surprising Refusal to Stone Miranda." *American University Law Review,* October 1994.

Barrio, Adrian J. "Rethinking *Schneckloth v. Bustamonte:* Incorporating Obedience Theory Into the Supreme Court's Conception of Voluntary Consent." *University of Illinois Law Review,* 1997.

UNITED STATES V. ROBINSON

Legal Citation: 414 U.S. 218 (1973)

Petitioner
United States

Respondent
Willie Robinson

Petitioner's Claim
That a conviction for a drug offense should not have been overturned on the ground that the search during which the drugs were discovered violated the suspect's Fourth Amendment rights.

Chief Lawyer for Petitioner
Allan A. Tuttle

Chief Lawyer for Respondent
Joseph V. Gartlan, Jr.

Justices for the Court
Harry A. Blackmun, Warren E. Burger, Lewis F. Powell, Jr., William H. Rehnquist (writing for the Court), Potter Stewart, Byron R. White

Justices Dissenting
William J. Brennan, Jr., William O. Douglas, Thurgood Marshall

Place
Washington, D.C.

Date of Decision
11 December 1973

Decision
Reversed the court of appeals decision and held that a search incident to a lawful arrest is not limited to a frisk of the outer clothing for the removal of weapons.

Significance
In *United States v. Robinson* the Court reaffirmed its views that a suspect under valid arrest may be subjected to a full search of his person, without a search warrant, and that a search incident to arrest is reasonable under the Fourth Amendment. The Court also reaffirmed that evidence found during such a search should not be excluded from court.

On 23 April 1968, Officer Richard Jenks of the District of Columbia Metropolitan Police Department saw Willie Robinson driving a 1965 Cadillac. Because of a previous investigation four days earlier, Jenks believed that Robinson was driving a car after his driver's license had been revoked. Jenks pulled Robinson over and all three occupants got out of the car. Jenks arrested Robinson for "operating after revocation and obtaining a permit by misrepresentation." Jenks searched Robinson in accordance with police department rules. During the patdown, Jenks felt something in the left breast pocket of Robinson's coat but could not tell what it was. He then reached into the pocket and pulled out a crumpled cigarette package. Jenks felt objects in the package, but did not know what they were. Upon opening the package, Jenks found 14 gelatin capsules of white powder, which turned out to be heroin. This heroin was used as evidence in a district court trial, in which Robinson was convicted of a drug offense.

The court of appeals reversed this conviction on the ground that the heroin had been found during a search that violated the Fourth Amendment, which prohibits unreasonable searches and seizures and requires a search warrant. The Supreme Court ruled that even after a police officer lawfully places a suspect under arrest for the purpose of taking him into custody, he may not ordinarily proceed to fully search the prisoner. Instead, he must make a limited frisk of the outer clothing and remove any weapons found. This decision was based on *Terry v. Ohio* (1968), a decision that frisking for weapons is a reasonable search even without a warrant or probable cause.

In the instant case, because this was a traffic stop, no further evidence of the crime could be obtained in a search of the arrestee. Thus, only a search for weapons could be justified. The court of appeals also felt that case-by-case adjudication was necessary to decide if a search of a person incident to a lawful arrest is justified.

A Traditional Exception To The Warrant Requirement

Justice Rehnquist, in his opinion for the majority, noted that a search incident to a lawful arrest is a traditional exception to the warrant requirement of the Fourth Amendment. This is based on two propositions. The first is that a search of a person may be made during a lawful arrest. The second is that a search may be made of the area within the control of the arrestee. The authority to search incident to a valid arrest has been repeatedly affirmed in decisions by the Court since *Weeks v. United States* was decided in 1914. These cases do not simply speak in terms of an exception to the warrant requirement, but in terms of an affirmative authority to search. Thus, they clearly imply that such searches also meet the Fourth Amendment's requirement of reasonableness.

Justice Rehnquist noted that early authorities are sketchy on the issue of search incident to arrest, but they tend to support the broad statement of the authority to search incident to arrest found in later Court decisions, rather than the restrictive one used by the court of appeals in this case. The reason for this authority rests both on the need to disarm a suspect and on the need to preserve evidence on his person. The police should not assume that a person arrested for driving with a revoked license is less likely to have dangerous weapons than a person arrested for some other crime. In taking a suspect into custody and transporting him to the police station, the officer is exposed to a certain amount of danger. This justifies treating all custodial arrests alike for the purposes of searching a suspect.

Justice Rehnquist's main argument with the court of appeals decision was that case-by-case adjudication was not necessary. "A police officer's determination as to how and where to search the person of a suspect whom he has arrested is necessarily a quick ad hoc judgment which the Fourth Amendment does not require to be broken down in each instance into an analysis of each step in the search." The authority to search does not depend on what a court might later decide was the likelihood that weapons or evidence might have been found on the suspect. Since a custodial arrest based on probable cause is a reasonable, lawful intrusion under the Fourth Amendment, a search incident to the arrest needs no further justification. The fact of the lawful arrest establishes the authority to search. In the case of a lawful custodial arrest a full search of the person is an exception to the warrant requirement of the Fourth Amendment and is also a reasonable search under that amendment.

Justice Rehnquist summed up his remarks by noting that the search conducted by Officer Jenks was permissible under the Fourth Amendment. Although thorough, the search was not extreme or abusive. Since custodial arrest gives the authority to search, the fact that Jenks was not afraid of Robinson and did not suspect that he was armed makes no difference to his authority to search. Because Jenks found the crumpled cigarette package during the course of a lawful search, he

was entitled to search it. When he found the heroin, he was entitled to seize it as "fruits, instrumentalities, or contraband" that furnished evidence of a crime.

Justice Powell, in a concurrence, stated, "I believe that an individual lawfully subjected to a custodial arrest retains no significant Fourth Amendment interest in the privacy of his person." Custodial arrest is a significant intrusion of state power into the privacy of one's person. During a lawful arrest one's privacy interest is subordinated to a legitimate and overriding governmental concern.

A Long Tradition Of Case-By-Case Adjudication

Justice Marshall wrote the dissent. He noted that the majority's decision represented a clear and marked departure from the long tradition of case-by-case adjudication of the reasonableness of searches and seizures under the Fourth Amendment. Justice Marshall believed that the Fourth Amendment has meaning only when the conduct of law enforcement can be subjected to the detached, neutral scrutiny of a judge who evaluates the reasonableness of a particular search or seizure, taking into account the particular circumstances. The function of the Fourth Amendment is to ensure that the "quick ad hoc" judgments of police officers are subject to review and control by the judiciary. There are some situations that require exceptions to the warrant requirement, such as moving vehicles, but those exceptions do not justify precluding further judicial inquiry into the reasonableness of that search. "It is the role of the judiciary, not of police officers, to delimit the scope of exceptions to the warrant requirement."

Justice Marshall noted that several states and federal courts have held that, absent special circumstances, a police officer has no right to conduct a full search of the person incident to a lawful arrest for violation of a motor vehicle regulation. Marshall felt that the majority's attempt to avoid case-by-case adjudication of Fourth Amendment issues "is not only misguided as a matter of principle, but is also doomed to fail as a matter of practical application." The possibility always exists of a police officer using a traffic stop as a pretext to conduct a search in the absence of probable cause. Case-by-case adjudication will always be necessary to determine whether a full arrest was made for legitimate reasons or as a pretext for a search.

An individual's interest in remaining free from unnecessarily intrusive invasions of privacy and society's interest that police officers not take unnecessary risks in the performance of their duties are competing interests that deserve the Court's most serious attention. Justice Marshall was not convinced that it is reasonable for police officers to conduct more than a Terry-type frisk for weapons when seeking to disarm a traffic offender who is taken into custody. He saw no justification consistent with the Fourth Amendment that authorized Jenks to open the package he found in Robinson's pocket and to look inside. Opening the package served no purpose because even if it had contained a small weapon, Robinson could not have gotten a hold of it once Jenks took it. "The mere fact of an arrest should be no justification, in and of itself, for invading the privacy of the individual's personal effects."

Justice Marshall felt that the only reasoned distinction that should be made in cases like this is between warrantless searches which serve legitimate protective and evidentiary functions and those that do not. Jenks's search went beyond what was reasonably necessary to protect him from harm or to ensure Robinson would not escape. This search fell outside the scope of a properly drawn "search incident to arrest" exception to the Fourth Amendment's warrant requirement.

Impact

The Supreme Court's ruling in *Whren v. United States* (1996), which gave police broad power to use even minor traffic violations as justification for pulling over motorists and searching their cars for drugs cited *United States v. Robinson* as a precedent. Under *Whren's* unanimous ruling, once a car is stopped because of a traffic violation, police may ask the driver questions and visually search the passenger compartment. If officers suspect a weapon is in the car, they can physically search the entire car. Justice Antonin Scalia wrote in that opinion:

> We flatly dismissed the idea that an ulterior motive might serve to strip the agents of their legal justification. In *United States v. Robinson* . . . we held that a traffic-violation arrest (of the sort here) would not be rendered invalid by the fact that it was "a mere pretext for a narcotics search," and that a lawful post-arrest search of the person would not be rendered invalid by the fact that it was not motivated by the officer-safety concern that justifies such searches.

Scalia quoted from the *Robinson* case: "Since it is the fact of custodial arrest which gives rise to the authority to search, it is of no moment that [the officer] did not indicate any subjective fear of the [arrestee] or that he did not himself suspect that [the arrestee] was armed."

Related Cases
Weeks v. United States, 232 U.S. 383 (1914).
Carroll v. United States, 267 U.S. 1320 (1925).
Terry v. Ohio, 392 U.S. 1 (1968).
Chimel v. California, 395 U.S. 752 (1969).
Scott v. United States, 436 U.S. 128 (1978).
Whren v. United States, 517 U.S. 806 (1996).

Bibliography and Further Reading
Biskupic, Joan, and Elder Witt. *Congressional Quarterly's Guide to the U.S. Supreme Court,* 3rd ed. Washington, DC: Congressional Quarterly, Inc., 1996.

Cushman, Robert F. *Leading Constitutional Decisions.* Englewood Cliffs, NJ: Prentice-Hall, Inc., 1982.

Witt, Elder, ed. *Congressional Quarterly's Guide to the U.S. Supreme Court.* Washington, DC: Congressional Quarterly, Inc., 1979.

UNITED STATES V. CALANDRA

Legal Citation: 414 U.S. 338 (1974)

Petitioner
United States

Respondent
John Calandra

Petitioner's Claim
A witness summoned before a grand jury should not be excused from testifying because the questions are based on evidence gathered during an unlawful search and seizure.

Chief Lawyer for Petitioner
Louis F. Claiborne

Chief Lawyer for Respondent
Robert J. Rotatori

Justices for the Court
Harry A. Blackmun, Warren E. Burger, Lewis F. Powell, Jr. (writing for the Court), William H. Rehnquist, Potter Stewart, Byron R. White

Justices Dissenting
William J. Brennan, Jr., William O. Douglas, Thurgood Marshall

Place
Washington, D.C.

Date of Decision
8 January 1974

Decision
Reversed the decisions of a district court and court of appeals and held that a grand jury witness may not refuse to answer questions on the grounds that they are based on evidence gained through unlawful search and seizure.

Significance
In *United States v. Calandra*, the Supreme Court made it clear that the exclusionary rule was not a personal constitutional right, but was simply meant as a remedy to safeguard Fourth Amendment rights through its deterrent effect.

In connection with an extensive investigation into suspected illegal gambling, the police obtained a search warrant for the Royal Machine & Tool Co. in Cleveland, Ohio. This business was owned by John Calandra. The warrant specified that the objects of the search were bookmaking records and wagering paraphernalia. The warrant was based on information from informants to the FBI and surveillance by the FBI. On 15 December 1970, federal agents spent four hours searching the premises. The agents did not find any gambling paraphernalia, but they did find a card indicating that Dr. Walter Loveland was making periodic payments to Calandra. The agents seized the card along with books, records, stock certificates, and address books.

On 1 March 1971, a special grand jury convened in the Northern District of Ohio to investigate possible loan sharking activities. The grand jury subpoenaed Calandra to question him. Their questions were based on the material seized in the search of his business. On 17 August 1971 Calandra appeared before the grand jury but refused to testify, invoking the Fifth Amendment, which states that people may not be compelled to be a witness against themselves. The government asked the district court to grant Calandra immunity. Calandra got a postponement of the immunity hearing so he could prepare a motion to suppress the evidence seized in the search.

Calandra asked that the evidence be suppressed and returned because the warrant was insufficient and the search went beyond the scope of the warrant. The district court ordered the evidence suppressed and returned and said that Calandra did not need to answer any grand jury questions based on the suppressed evidence. The court agreed that the search warrant had been issued without probable cause, and the search had exceeded the scope of the warrant. The Court of Appeals for the Sixth Circuit agreed with the district court. The case next went to the Supreme Court.

Exclusionary Rule's Prime Purpose

Justice Powell wrote the opinion for the majority. A grand jury hearing is an investigation to determine if a crime has been committed and whether criminal proceedings should take place. If a grand jury feels that criminal proceedings should occur, it will present to the court an indictment, a written accusation made upon oath. Powell noted that the operation of a grand jury is generally unrestrained by the technical, procedural, and evidentiary rules that are used in criminal trials. An indictment is not subject to a challenge that the grand jury acted on inadequate evidence or on information obtained in violation of a defendant's Fifth Amendment privilege against self-incrimination. Powell explained that the exclusionary rule was adopted to guard against unreasonable searches and seizures, which are forbidden by the Fourth Amendment. Powell noted that the "rule's prime purpose is to deter future unlawful police conduct." The rule is a remedy designed to safeguard Fourth Amendment rights through its deterrent effect, "rather than a personal constitutional right of the party aggrieved." The exclusionary rule has never been interpreted to forbid the use of illegally seized evidence at all times.

Regarding grand juries and the exclusionary rule, Powell explained that "we must weigh the potential injury to the historic role and functions of the grand jury against the potential benefits of the rule." Extending the exclusionary rule to grand jury proceedings would seriously impede grand juries. Suppression hearings would halt the progress of a grand jury investigation. Extending the exclusionary rule to grand jury evidence would deter police investigation that was directed toward finding evidence only for grand jury use. Since evidence obtained unlawfully would not be admissible in a criminal trial, a prosecutor would probably not ask for an indictment in a case where a conviction could not be gained.

Calandra claimed that the grand jury's questions invaded his privacy and because the questions were based on illegally obtained evidence, they violated his Fourth Amendment rights. Powell disagreed. The wrong done to Calandra took place during the original search and seizure. Grand jury questions based on evidence from that incident "involve no independent governmental invasion . . . , but rather the usual abridgment of personal privacy common to all grand jury questioning." Grand jury questions based on unlawfully obtained evidence are only a "derivative use" of that evidence. Powell summed up by stating that the damage to grand juries that would be done by extending the use of the exclusionary rule would outweigh the benefit as a deterrent to police misconduct.

Better For Some Guilty People To Go Free

Justice Brennan wrote the dissent. Brennan indicted that the purpose of the exclusionary rule was "to fashion an enforcement tool to give content and meaning to the Fourth Amendment's guarantees" against

unlawful searches and seizures. The rule accomplished the goals of helping the judiciary avoid the taint of partnership in official lawlessness and it assured the people that the government would not profit from its lawless behavior. This would help people trust their government. Brennan accused the majority of the Supreme Court of discounting, "to the point of extinction, the vital function of the rule to insure that the judiciary avoid even the slightest appearance of sanctioning illegal government conduct." The judges who established the rule knew that it implied that it was better for some guilty people to go free than for the police to engage in illegal behavior. Brennan expressed concern that the decision in the case indicated that a majority of justices wanted to abandon the exclusionary rule altogether in search and seizure cases. Brennan called the decision in *United States v. Calandra* a "long step toward the abandonment of the exclusionary rule."

Even Larger Exceptions To The Exclusionary Rule

United States v. Calandra was the most important exclusionary rule case decided in the 1970s. The concept of the rule being a deterrent to police misconduct and the idea of weighing the costs of the rule against its benefits formed the basis of judicial thinking on the matter. The ruling in *United States v. Calandra* reflected the views of President Richard Nixon's appointee, Chief Justice Burger, who had serious reservations about the usefulness of the exclusionary rule.

In the 1980s the Supreme Court created even larger exceptions to the exclusionary rule, severely limiting its application. In *United States v. Leon* (1984) the Court created the "good faith" exception, stating that if officers acted in good faith, the evidence they unlawfully gathered would still be admissible in court. In the *Leon* case, the opinion quoted *United States v. Calandra*, stating that using the fruits of a past unlawful search or seizure "works no new Fourth Amendment wrong." In 1995, the Supreme Court revisited the good faith exception in *Arizona v. Evans* and used the same quotation from *Calandra*. In *Evans*, the Court decided that evidence gathered illegally due to a clerk's error need not be excluded.

The exclusionary rule has many critics. Some have criticized the Court for limiting the rule by creating the good faith exception. Others have suggested that the rule be abolished because it hinders law enforcement. Members of Congress have proposed legislation to do away with the rule in federal court, but such legislation has not yet been adopted.

Related Cases

Weeks v. United States, 232 U.S. 383 (1914).
Gelbard v. United States, 408 U.S. 41 (1972).

United States v. Leon, 468 U.S. 897 (1984).
Arizona v. Evans, 514 U.S. 1 (1995).

Bibliography and Further Reading
Johnson, John W., ed. *Historic U.S. Court Cases, 1690–1990: An Encyclopedia.* New York: Garland Publishing, 1992.

Lieberman, Jethro K. *The Evolving Constitution.* New York: Random House, 1992.

Schwartz, Herman, ed. *The Burger Years: Rights and Wrongs in the Supreme Court, 1969–1986.* New York: Viking, 1987.

UNITED STATES V. MATLOCK

Legal Citation: 415 U.S. 164 (1974)

Petitioner
United States

Respondent
William Matlock

Petitioner's Claim
That out-of-court statements should not have been excluded from evidence at a suppression hearing and that a third party who had common authority over a premises may give permission for a search.

Chief Lawyer for Petitioner
Wallace, U.S. Deputy Solicitor General

Chief Lawyer for Respondent
Donald S. Eisenberg

Justices for the Court
Harry A. Blackmun, Warren E. Burger, Lewis F. Powell, Jr., William H. Rehnquist, Potter Stewart, Byron R. White (writing for the Court)

Justices Dissenting
William J. Brennan, Jr., William O. Douglas, Thurgood Marshall

Place
Washington, D.C.

Date of Decision
20 February 1974

Decision
A third party with control over a property may give permission for a warrantless search of the property. Also, no automatic rule exists against receiving hearsay evidence during a suppression hearing.

Significance
The decision clarified when a third party can give permission for a warrantless search of a property. When a prosecutor seeks to justify a warrantless search by showing voluntary consent was given, that consent is not limited to the defendant, but can be given by a third party who had common authority over the premises.

On 12 November 1970, William Matlock was arrested, on charges of bank robbery, in the front yard of the house where he lived in Pardeeville, Wisconsin. The arresting officers did not ask him if they could search the house, and they did not have a search warrant. Gayle Graff, with whom Matlock shared a room in the house, admitted three of the arresting officers into the house. They told Mrs. Graff that they were looking for money and a gun and asked if they could search the house. She said they could. They did not tell her that she had a right to refuse to consent to the search. The officers searched the bedroom where they found $4,995 in a diaper bag in the closet.

Matlock asked that the evidence seized from the bedroom be suppressed (deemed inadmissible). The district court held that when a third person gives consent for a search, the government must show that it reasonably appeared to the searching officers that the person had authority to consent and that the person had actual authority to permit the search. The district court concluded that the government had failed to prove that Mrs. Graff had actual authority to consent to the search. Although Mrs. Graff had told the officers that she and Matlock shared the bedroom, proving the good faith of the officers, her statement failed to prove that what she said was true. At various times and places Gayle Graff and William Matlock had told people they were married, which they were not. The district court felt that the evidence was insufficient to prove that at the time of the search the two were living together in the east bedroom. The court also rejected the government's claim that it only had to prove that the officers could reasonably have concluded that Gayle Graff's consent was binding on Matlock. The district court excluded the out-of-court statements Mrs. Graff made regarding her and Matlock's joint occupancy and use of the bedroom and their claim that they were married. The court of appeals affirmed the judgment of the district court. The case then went to the Supreme Court.

Rules Of Evidence Applicable In A Criminal Trial

Justice White wrote the opinion of the majority. Various state courts and courts of appeal have applied the basic proposition that the voluntary consent of any joint occupant of a residence to search the premises is valid and permits evidence discovered in the search to be used against a co-occupant in a criminal trial. The consent of a person who has common authority over a premises is valid against the absent, nonconsenting person who shares that authority. Other co-occupants have assumed the risk that one of their number might permit the common property to be searched.

White questioned why the district court ruled inadmissible Matlock's own out-of-court statements that he and Mrs. Graff were married. White noted that regarding Mrs. Graff's statements to the officers, the rules of evidence applicable in a criminal trial do not apply with full force at hearings to determine admissibility of evidence, known as a suppression hearing. In a proceeding where the judge is considering the admissibility of evidence, the exclusionary rules should not be applicable. The judge should receive the evidence and decide using his judgment and experience whether it should be admitted. White stated that the trial judge should not have excluded Mrs. Graff's statements in this case. No apparent reason existed for the judge to distrust the evidence and to exclude her statements while resolving the issues raised at the suppression hearing. The judge should have admitted her statements at the suppression hearing, even if they would not have been admitted at the criminal trial.

White noted that Mrs. Graff was a witness for Matlock at the suppression hearing. Because she was available for cross examination, the use of hearsay was reduced. At the hearing, she denied that she gave consent to the search or made the statements to the officers that the court excluded. When asked if she and Matlock lived together, she declined to answer on the grounds that she might incriminate herself. Byron stated that given the admissibility of Mrs. Graff's out-of-court statements, the government proved, by the preponderance of the evidence, that her voluntary consent to search the bedroom was sufficient to admit the money as evidence.

Police Acting On Their Own
Justice Douglas dissented because he believed that "the absence of a search warrant in this case, where the authorities had opportunity to obtain one, is fatal." He noted that at no time did the officers attempt to get a search warrant. Also, the search of the house was not incidental to the arrest of Matlock.

Douglas explained that a search warrant provided judicial intervention as a restraint of police conduct before a search. A neutral and detached magistrate, not law enforcement agents, should decide if a home must be searched. Douglas quoted from *McDonald v. United*

States (1948), "The right of privacy was deemed too precious to entrust to the discretion of those whose job is the detection of crime and the arrest of criminals. Power is a heady thing; and history shows that the police acting on their own cannot be trusted."

Douglas noted that Mrs. Graff's permission to the police to invade the house provided a sorry and wholly inadequate substitute for a search warrant. The police commanded all the authority that they had during colonial times when general warrants were used, the hatred of which led to the passage of the Fourth Amendment. This amendment prohibits warrantless searches and seizures. Douglas summed up by stating, "Government agents are now free to rummage about the house, unconstrained by anything except their own desires . . . Since the Framers of the Amendment did not abolish the hated general warrants only to impose another oppressive regime on the people, I dissent."

Justices Brennan and Marshall also dissented. Brennan wrote that it was necessary to determine if Mrs. Graff consented to the search knowing that she was not required to do so. An individual cannot waive this right if he or she is totally ignorant of the fact that, without consent, the invasion of privacy would be unconstitutional. Brennan quoted his own dissent in *Schneckloth v. Bustamonte* (1973), "It wholly escapes me how our citizens can meaningfully be said to have waived something as precious as a constitutional guarantee without ever being aware of its existence."

Impact
In *United States v. Matlock,* the Supreme Court determined that third party consent to search a premises without a warrant was sufficient if the person "possessed common authority over or other sufficient relationship to the premises or effects sought to be inspected." The Court ruled in *Illinois v. Rodriguez* (1990) that actual common authority over a place is not required. It is sufficient if the officer had a reasonable but mistaken belief that the third party possessed common authority and could consent to the search. *United States v. Matlock* and *Illinois v. Rodriguez* illustrate the Supreme Court's growing interest in upholding warrantless searches as not "unreasonable" under the Fourth Amendment.

Related Cases
Trupiano v. United States, 334 U.S. 699 (1948).
McDonald v. United States, 335 U.S. 451 (1948).
Brinegar v. United States, 338 U.S. 160 (1949).
Frazier v. Cupp, 394 U.S. 731 (1969).
Schneckloth v. Bustamonte, 412 U.S. 218 (1973).
Illinois v. Rodriguez, 497 U.S. 177 (1990).

UNITED STATES V. EDWARDS

Legal Citation: 415 U.S. 800 (1974)

Petitioner
United States

Respondents
Eugene H. Edwards, William T. Livesay

Petitioner's Claim
The Fourth Amendment was not violated when, ten hours after a suspected burglar was placed in jail, police officers took the clothes of the suspected burglar without first obtaining a search warrant.

Chief Lawyer for Petitioner
Edward R. Korman

Chief Lawyer for Respondents
Thomas R. Smith

Justices for the Court
Harry A. Blackmun, Warren E. Burger, Lewis F. Powell, Jr., William H. Rehnquist, Byron R. White (writing for the Court)

Justices Dissenting
William J. Brennan, Jr., William O. Douglas, Thurgood Marshall, Potter Stewart

Place
Washington, D.C.

Date of Decision
26 March 1974

Decision
The Fourth Amendment was not violated when, without a search warrant, police officers took the clothes of a suspected burglar ten hours after the suspect had been placed in jail.

Significance
The holding in *Edwards* is significant because it effectively expands the length of time that police officers have to make warrantless searches and seizures after the time of arrest, but while the suspect is still detained.

On 21 May 1970, at around 10:15 p.m., Patrolman Ashley of the Lebanon, Ohio Police Department received a report that a suspicious tan car with out-of-town license plates was parked near the city's post office. Three men had been seen leaving the car, and two persons had been seen at a meat locker on the street corner. After examining the car and the meat locker and finding nothing amiss, Ashley decided to check the post office, where he spotted two men walking along the sidewalk and then crossing the street. About three minutes later, Ashley received a radio report that the silent burglar alarm at the post office had sounded in the home of a nearby resident.

Ashley overtook, apprehended, and arrested the two men, Eugene H. Edwards and William T. Livesay. While the two men were being processed in jail, Lebanon police officers investigated the post office and found that someone had tried to get into a window. An officer took paint samples from the window sill and the wire mesh screen as evidence. The next morning, Lebanon police officers took Edward's clothes from him and gave him some new clothes because they wanted to compare the paint chips found in Edwards's clothes to the paint chips at the post office window. The officers had to wait ten hours to seize Edwards's clothes because they did not have any other clothing to give to Edwards.

Edwards and Livesay were tried in federal court on a charge of attempted breaking and entering of a U.S. Post Office. Before trial, Edwards challenged the seizure of his clothes, claiming that they were obtained in violation of his Fourth Amendment right to be free from unreasonable searches and seizures, and that the clothes and the paint chips from his clothes should be excluded from the trial. According to Edwards, the officers should have obtained a search warrant from a judge or magistrate before seizing his clothes. The trial court disagreed, the evidence was admitted, and Edwards and Livesay were convicted. The two appealed their convictions to the U.S. Court of Appeals for the Sixth Circuit, which reversed. Because the arrest and booking process had come to a halt, reasoned the appeals court, the officers had no right to seize Edwards's clothes without a warrant.

The federal government appealed the reversal to the U.S. Supreme Court. In the meantime, Livesay died, leaving Edwards as the sole defendant. A divided Court voted 5-4 to reverse the appeals court, effectively reinstating Edwards's conviction.

Justice White wrote the majority's opinion. The Court cited the general rule that searches and seizures should be conducted pursuant to a search warrant. A search warrant may be obtained by a police officer from a judge or magistrate after the police officer has offered enough information to support a probable cause belief that the search or seizure will uncover criminal activity. There are, however, exceptions to the search warrant requirement. One of these exceptions is the search of a person, the person's possessions, and the immediate area of the person at the time of arrest. It also was well settled from prior decisions, noted the Court, that police officers have the right to seize the clothing and belongings of an arrestee upon arriving at jail after the arrest.

The appeals court nevertheless had held that the seizure of Edwards's clothes was illegal under the Fourth Amendment because the "administrative mechanics of arrest" had been completed. Once that procedure was complete, the appeals court had opined, the police officers should have obtained a search warrant for any seizures of evidence. There was, in fact, no extraordinary circumstance that required immediate attention and made an application for a search warrant impracticable. The High Court, however, disagreed with the appeals court's analysis. "[I]t seems to us," Justice White declared for the majority, "that the normal processes incident to arrest and custody had not been completed when Edwards was placed in his cell."

The appeals court had conceded that the police officers had probable cause to believe that Edwards's clothing would yield evidence, and that they were justified in taking the clothes from him when they arrived at jail. The appeals court had held, though, that the long period between arrival at jail and the actual seizure of the clothes was not justified without a warrant. According to the High Court, though, the police officers had a right to take Edwards's clothing as soon as they could find another set of clothing to wear in jail. It would have been quite unreasonable, observed the Court, if the police officers had "stripped [Edwards] of his clothing and left him exposed in his cell throughout the night." Because they made the exchange of clothing as soon as they could, the seizure "was no more than taking from [Edwards] the effects in his immediate possession that constituted evidence of crime."

Since the police already had lawful custody of Edwards and his possessions, the Court pondered how the seizure could have been unreasonable. "[I]t is difficult to perceive what is unreasonable," wondered the Court, "about the police's examining and holding as evidence those personal effects of the accused that they already have in their lawful custody as the result of a lawful arrest." In prior cases, other federal appeals courts had approved of such seizures, and the Court was inclined to agree with those courts. The majority conceded that it was possible for a warrantless, post-arrest search or seizure to violate the warrant requirement of Fourth Amendment. However, citing the First Circuit Court of Appeals, the Court closed its opinion by describing the shift in the constitutional balance between the rights of accused persons and the rights of police officers after an arrest has been made: "'While the legal arrest of a person should not destroy the privacy of his premises, it does—for at least a reasonable time and to a reasonable extent—take his own privacy out of the realm of protection from police interest in weapons, means of escape, and evidence.'"

Justices Stewart, Douglas, Brennan, and Marshall dissented. In an opinion written by Justice Stewart, the dissenters deplored the majority's understanding of the Fourth Amendment. The issue was not, as the majority claimed, "'whether the Fourth Amendment should be extended'" in the case. To the dissenters, the question was "whether the Fourth Amendment is to be ignored." Citing the Court's own precedent, Stewart observed that "'the most basic constitutional rule'" in Fourth Amendment jurisprudence was that a warrant was required for all searches and seizures unless the search or seizure was one of "'a few specifically established and well-delineated exceptions.'" The burden was on the government to show that the circumstances of the seizure brought it "within one of the 'jealously and carefully drawn' exceptions to the warrant requirement," and, in the opinion of the dissenters, the government had failed to do so.

The dissent acknowledged that a warrantless search or seizure is valid when it is conducted incident to a valid arrest. Under the Court's precedent, though, such searches should be limited in space and time. In Edwards's case, the dissent felt that a time span of ten hours was too remote from the time of arrest, and that the failure to obtain a search warrant prior to the seizure was not justified.

The dissent disagreed also with the Court's philosophical approach to the Fourth Amendment. The majority was analyzing the reasonableness of searches according to "'the acceptability of police conduct, and not on considerations relevant to Fourth Amendment interests.'" This was flawed because, according to dissenting Justice Felix Frankfurter in *Chimel v. California* (1969), the test of reason that makes a search reasonable "'is the reason underlying and expressed by the Fourth Amendment: the history and the experience which it embodies and the safeguards afforded by it against the evils to which it was a response.'"

The dissent conceded that the seizure in Edwards's case "was not a shocking one," and that the officers had not acted in bad faith. Nonetheless, the dissent warned, such seemingly innocuous transgressions should not be ignored because "'illegitimate and unconstitutional practices get their first footing in that way, namely, by silent approaches and slight deviations from legal modes of procedure.'" (quoting *Boyd v. United States* [1886])

Impact

The *Edwards* decision resolved a split between federal courts and established that police do not need a search warrant to seize articles from arrested persons after the booking process is completed. Depending on the facts of the case, a warrantless search or seizure of a jailed person might still be ruled unconstitutional. However, the *Edwards* Court omitted any specific guidelines for time limitations on the right of police officers to seize the clothes of a person who has been arrested and jailed.

Related Cases

Boyd v. United States, 116 U.S. 616 (1886).
Abel v. United States, 362 U.S. 217 (1960).
Cooper v. California, 386 U.S. 58 (1967).
Chimel v. California, 395 U.S. 752 (1969).

Bibliography and Further Reading

Biskupic, Joan, and Elder Witt, eds. *Congressional Quarterly's Guide to the U.S. Supreme Court,* 3rd ed. Washington, DC: Congressional Quarterly, Inc., 1996.

New York Times, March 27, 1974.

UNITED STATES V. SANTANA

Legal Citation: 427 U.S. 38 (1976)

Petitioner
United States

Respondents
Mom Santana, et al.

Petitioner's Claim
That Santana's arrest for possession of heroin with intent to distribute was legally admissible, despite the fact that the arrest occurred within her home and without benefit of a search or arrest warrant.

Chief Lawyer for Petitioner
Frank H. Easterbrook

Chief Lawyer for Respondents
Dennis H. Eisman

Justices for the Court
Harry A. Blackmun, Warren E. Burger, Lewis F. Powell, Jr., William H. Rehnquist (writing for the Court), John Paul Stevens, Potter Stewart, Byron R. White

Justices Dissenting
William J. Brennan, Jr., Thurgood Marshall

Place
Washington, D.C.

Date of Decision
24 June 1976

Decision
Reversed the finding of the court of appeals, ruling that the respondents' arrest was legal given the fact that Santana was first confronted in the vestibule of her home, and the actual arrest occurred during "hot pursuit."

Significance
The ruling confirmed the Court's view that warrantless searches and arrests may be conducted in public places as long as police can show probable cause for their actions as developed in *United States v. Watson* (1976) and *Katz v. United States* (1967). Dissenting justices maintained that police could manipulate circumstances to create the conditions necessary for warrantless search and arrest given the latitude for action that this decision allows them in pursuing criminal investigations and detentions.

A Drug Bust

In August 1974 undercover police officer Michael Gilletti of the Philadelphia narcotics squad set up a purchase of heroin from a woman named Patricia McCafferty. Officer Gilletti had purchased illegal drugs from McCafferty in the past, and when he approached her to set a time for his buy, McCafferty told him to meet her at a set location, and to bring $115 with him. After obtaining $110 in marked bills from his commanding officer, Gilletti met McCafferty and the pair drove to the home of Mom Santana, to purchase the heroin.

McCafferty took Gilletti's money and entered the house, pausing first to speak with a man named Alejandro (who became one of the respondents in this case), and emerged shortly thereafter bearing several envelopes containing heroin, which she handed over to Gilletti. At this point Gilletti identified himself as a police officer, placed McCafferty under arrest, informed her the police would be raiding Santana's house shortly, and asked her what had happened to the money he had given her. McCafferty informed him that she had given the money to Mom Santana, and Gilletti passed this information along to Sergeant Pruitt, who would lead the raid.

When Pruitt and his team arrived, they saw Santana standing in the doorway of her house with a brown paper bag in her hand. As the officers got out of their vehicles and approached Santana, she attempted to withdraw into her house, but was apprehended in the vestibule. As she tried to elude the officers, Santana dropped several "glazed paper packets" containing a "white powder" (subsequently identified as heroin). Alejandro picked up the packets and attempted to make off with them, but was apprehended before he could leave the premises. Santana was then ordered to empty her pockets, and was found to be in possession of $70 of the marked bills given to McCafferty by Gilletti.

Charges and Preliminary Trials

Santana and Alejandro were charged with possession of heroin with intent to distribute, and McCafferty was charged with distribution of heroin, in the U.S. District Court for the Eastern District of Pennsylvania. McCafferty pled guilty to the charges against her, but Santana and Alejandro moved that the heroin and money seized from them in the arrest be suppressed since it had been obtained without benefit of a warrant. The district court upheld the respondents' contention, stating that although probable cause existed to suspect Santana of participating in the drug buy made by McCafferty, one of the police officers involved in the operation testified that its true objective was the arrest of Santana, while another officer testified that the true objective was the recovery of the money planted by Gilletti. If either of these were the true objective of the raid, a warrant would have been required for its execution. The circuit court also found that Santana's retreat into her house did not constitute a flight from the police, and, as such, that the police did not have the right to follow her into the house without possessing a warrant, on the grounds of being in "hot pursuit" of a suspect. The case was then heard by the state court of appeals, which upheld the ruling of the district court in all its parts. The U.S. Attorney General's office then asked the U.S. Supreme Court to consider the case, and the Court heard arguments in the matter on 27 April 1976.

Search and Seizure

The Fourth Amendment of the Constitution prohibits unreasonable search and seizure of individuals and their property. The Amendment defines reasonable searches and seizures as those which are conducted under legal warrant issued due to the existence of probable cause that wrongdoing will be uncovered by them. Throughout its history, the Supreme Court has wavered in its interpretation of the Fourth Amendment. This wavering has centered around a fundamental question: are only searches and seizures conducted under legal warrants admissible, or are there some occasions when a search or seizure may be undertaken without a warrant. During the decade of the 1970s, the Court considered this issue on several occasions, and established precedents which were applied to its ruling in *United States v. Santana*.

The Court handed down its decision in the case on 24 June 1976, reversing the lower court rulings and holding that the actions of the Philadelphia police were legal and the evidence obtained in the raid against Santana was admissible in court. Justice Rehnquist, writing for the majority, identified two questions as being crucial to the Court's view of the case. The Court considered if Santana was in a public place when the police attempted to arrest her and if were the police were justified in following Santana into her home to achieve her arrest. With regard to the first question, the Court relied on its rulings in *United States v. Watson* and *Katz v. United States,* as precedents. In *Watson* the Court ruled that a warrantless arrest of a person in a public area, given the existence of probable cause, did not violate the Fourth Amendment. In *Katz,* the Court held that "what a person knowingly exposes in public, even in his own house or office, is not a subject of Fourth Amendment protection." In the Court's opinion Santana, by standing

in her doorway where she was as "exposed to public view, speech, hearing, and touch as if she had been standing completely outside her house," had been in a public place when the police began their attempt to apprehend her. This view also answered the second question, in that Santana's retirement into her house constituted an attempt to flee police pursuit, making the entry by the police into her house legally admissible as a result of their "hot pursuit" of a fleeing suspect. The right of police to pursue suspects into their homes, given probable cause, had been established by the Court in *Warden, Maryland Penitentiary v. Hayden* (1967). The Court did not question the existence of probable cause for police action in the case. In summarizing the majority opinion, Justice Rehnquist stated: "a suspect may not defeat an arrest which has been set in motion in a public place, and is therefore proper under *Watson,* by the expedient of escaping to a private place." The dissenting justices in the case did not dispute the issue of the existence of probable cause, and only mildly disagreed with the majority's opinion that Santana had been in a public place when the attempt to arrest her began. Instead, they were troubled by the possibility that the police were really seeking to arrest Santana from the start, and merely used McCafferty's heroin purchase as a ruse to establish circumstances under which a warrantless search and seizure would be possible.

Impact

United States v. Santana represented a less rigorous definition of the Fourth Amendment than the Court had maintained earlier in the decade. In the years since this decision, the Court has identified many new circumstances under which warrantless searches and seizures may be made. Familiar examples of such searches include metal detection searches of individuals entering public schools and federal government buildings, drug testing of public and transportation employees, and various searches conducted within prisons by penal authorities. The Court also ruled, subsequent to *Santana,* that police officers who had a "reasonable" belief that circumstances justified a warrantless search or seizure could proceed with such action, and that any evidence obtained by such a search would be admissible in court.

Related Cases
Warden, Maryland Penitentiary v. Hayden, 387 U.S. 294 (1967).
Katz v. United States, 389 U.S. 347 (1967).
United States v. Watson, 423 U.S. 411 (1976).

Bibliography and Further Reading
Biskupic, Joan, and Elder Witt, eds. *Congressional Quarterly's Guide to the U.S. Supreme Court,* 3rd ed. Washington, DC: Congressional Quarterly, Inc., 1996.

Findlaw, Inc. *Supreme Court Cases Online.* http://www.findworld.com

MINCEY V. ARIZONA

Legal Citation: 437 U.S. 385 (1978)

Petitioner
Rufus Junior Mincey

Respondent
The State of Arizona

Petitioner's Claim
That a search of his home conducted by police officers who did not first obtain a search warrant violated his Fourth Amendment protection against unreasonable searches, and therefore his criminal conviction based on evidence seized during the search was invalid.

Chief Lawyer for Petitioner
Richard Oseran

Chief Lawyer for Respondent
Galen H. Wilkes

Justices for the Court
Harry A. Blackmun, William J. Brennan, Jr., Warren E. Burger, Thurgood Marshall, Lewis F. Powell, Jr., William H. Rehnquist (writing for the Court), John Paul Stevens, Potter Stewart, Byron R. White

Justices Dissenting
None

Place
Washington, D.C.

Date of Decision
21 June 1978

Decision
That there is no "murder scene" exception to the requirement that police obtain a warrant before searching someone's home, and thus the appellant's conviction was invalid because it was based on evidence seized by the police during a warrantless search of his home.

Significance
The Court severely limited the ability of police officers to conduct searches of murder scenes without first obtaining a search warrant.

The Fourth Amendment to the Constitution provides that the government may not subject a person to an unreasonable search or seizure of their "persons, houses, papers, and effects." Generally, to be reasonable, a search must be based on "probable cause," that is, the police officers must have some reason to believe that the search will find contraband, evidence of a crime, or similar items. Also, prior to conducting a search, the police generally have to obtain a warrant from a judge authorizing the search. The requirements are strictly applied to cases in which police officers enter a private home. In certain situations, however, the Supreme Court has determined that the police do not need to obtain a warrant to conduct a search supported by probable cause. These situations, referred to as exceptions to the warrant requirement, typically involve scenarios where the police do not have time to obtain a warrant, or where obtaining a warrant would be useless. One such situation in which police officers are justified in conducting a search without a warrant is where so-called "exigent," or emergency, circumstances exist. The most important exigent circumstance is where a search is necessary to find an injured person or to otherwise prevent the death or injury of a person.

In the case of *Mincey v. Arizona*, the state of Arizona asked the Supreme Court to recognize a new category of exigent circumstances for which a search warrant is not required. On 28 October 1978, undercover police officers in Tucson, Arizona, conducted a raid at an apartment occupied by Rufus Mincey. Shots were fired by Mincey, and one officer was killed. Mincey was also wounded in the exchange. Police officers rushed into the apartment to search for other possibly injured people. They conducted a quick search of the living room, bedroom, and bedroom closet, but refrained from conducting any further investigation. However, about ten minutes later homicide detectives arrived on the scene and conducted a thorough, four-day search of the apartment.

Mincey was charged in the Arizona state trial court with the murder of the police officer, assault, and possession of narcotics. Mincey filed a motion in the trial court to exclude the evidence seized by the homicide officers during the search of his apartment. He claimed that the officers should have obtained a warrant to search the premises. The trial court disagreed and allowed the prosecution to introduce the evidence. Mincey was convicted, and he raised the same argument on appeal to the Arizona Supreme Court. The Arizona Supreme Court concluded that the search was valid based on a so-called "murder scene" exception to the warrant requirement. According to the Arizona Supreme Court, the search did not violate the Fourth Amendment because police officers may search the scene of a homicide without a warrant as long as the search is "limited to determining the circumstances of death."

Mincey then sought to appeal his conviction to the U.S. Supreme Court through a procedure known as a petition for writ of *certiorari*. The Court granted the petition and heard the case on 21 February 1978.

The Court unanimously rejected the argument that the search was proper because of the injured victims, concluding that the four-day search conducted by the homicide officers exceeded the scope of the emergency. The Court also rejected Arizona's request that the Court recognize a murder scene exception to the warrant requirement. According to Arizona, such an exception was necessary due to the public's interest in quickly investigating and solving murder cases. The Court found this argument unpersuasive:

> [T]he State points to the vital public interest in the prompt investigation of the extremely serious crime of murder. No one can doubt the importance of this goal. But the public interest in the investigation of other serious crimes is comparable. If the warrantless search of a

homicide scene is reasonable, why not the warrantless search of the scene of a rape, a robbery, or a burglary?

Mincey was retried in the Arizona courts and was convicted despite the fact that the prosecution was unable to introduce the evidence seized in Mincey's apartment. He was sentenced to life imprisonment. The Court's decision in *Mincey* did have a rather profound impact on the ability of police to conduct a warrantless search of a murder scene. Up to the time of the decision, most lower courts had allowed the police to conduct such searches without a warrant. Following *Mincey*, however, the police may do no more than search for possible victims at the scene until they have obtained a search warrant.

Related Cases
United States v. Rabinowitz, 339 U.S. 56 (1950).
Mapp v. Ohio, 367 U.S. 643 (1961).
Ker v. California, 374 U.S. 23 (1963).
Chimel v. California, 395 U.S. 752 (1969).
Payton v. New York, 445 U.S. 573 (1980).

Bibliography and Further Reading
Dressler, Joshua. *Understanding Criminal Procedure.* New York: Matthew Bender & Company, 1991.

"Killer of Tucson Police Officer Denied Request for Early Parole." *Tucson Citizen,* July 20, 1995, p. 1C.

LaFave, Wayne R. *Search and Seizure: A Treatise on the Fourth Amendment,* 3rd edition. Volume 3. St. Paul, MN: West Publishing Co., 1996

DELAWARE V. PROUSE

Legal Citation: 440 U.S. 648 (1979)

Petitioner
State of Delaware

Respondent
William J. Prouse III

Petitioner's Claim
Random vehicle stops by state patrolmen are justified by a compelling state interest to promote traffic safety.

Chief Lawyer for Petitioner
Charles M. Oberly III

Chief Lawyer for Respondent
David M. Lukoff

Justices for the Court
Harry A. Blackmun, William J. Brennan, Jr., Warren E. Burger, Thurgood Marshall, Lewis F. Powell, Jr., John Paul Stevens, Potter Stewart, Byron R. White (writing for the Court)

Justices Dissenting
William H. Rehnquist

Place
Washington, D.C.

Date of Decision
27 March 1979

Decision
The U.S. Supreme Court upheld the decision of the Delaware Supreme Court—that it was unconstitutional for state police to randomly stop vehicles at a check stop unless there was a justifiable reason for a motorist to be stopped. Unwarranted stops represented unreasonable seizure under the Fourth Amendment.

Significance
The Court's mandate was to determine if discretionary spot checks by police officers on a public highway constituted unreasonable seizure. In reaching their decision, justices depended on guidance rendered in previous decisions regarding constitutionally legal, random spot checks conducted by U.S. Border Patrol officers. Essentially, in citing from precedence set in those cases, states were given clear guidance as to what circumstances merited random spot checks. Thus, while the state of Delaware's law enforcement agencies were held to have conducted unwarranted, arbitrary, and (therefore) constitutionally unreasonable seizure through random spot checks, the Court nonetheless gave states needed guidance by which law enforcement could legally engage in measures which promoted traffic safety.

In rendering their decision, the Supreme Court reiterated previous decisions that defined what constituted appropriate measure and protocol for random vehicular stops. In so doing, they ruled that the state of Delaware's support of random spot checks—made without pre-established protocol and at an officer's individual discretion—constituted unreasonable seizure which violated the Fourth and Fourteenth Amendments. Unless there was a reasonable cause or suspicion that a vehicle and its occupants should be stopped and detained such as might be justified by a driver's violation of traffic regulations or any other law, police officers could not randomly stop and detain a driver. However, the Court's decision did not preclude the state of Delaware, or any other state, from crafting measures that would promote traffic safety so long as such measures did not intrude on a driver's privacy. The discretionary spot check on a public highway represented a constitutional violation because such stops were undertaken without probable cause or reasonable suspicion. Moreover, in specifying that random stops were not an effective method of preventing traffic accidents but, rather, an invasion of privacy, the Supreme Court's ruling served to provide states with guidance which would guide law enforcement from committing an intrusive and unreasonable assault on the individual rights of drivers.

Even though there was no probable cause to stop his vehicle, William Pouse was pulled over by a patrol officer in New Castle County, Delaware. Walking toward the stopped vehicle, the patrolman smelled marijuana smoke. When the officer looked into the vehicle, marijuana was in plain view. Four occupants were in the car, and Prouse was not driving. Nonetheless, the vehicle was registered to Prouse so he was arrested and, subsequently, indicted for illegal possession of a controlled substance.

When the case came to trial, Prouse submitted a motion to suppress the evidence (marijuana) seized as a result of the stop. At the hearing, the police officer testified that he stopped the car in order to check the driver's operating permit and the vehicle registration; it was what the officer referred to as a "routine stop." When asked to define what constituted such a stop, the patrolman replied, "I saw the car in the area and I was-

Drunk Driving and Drug Use

- In 1992, there were 1,319,583 reported arrests for drunk driving in the United States.

- Leading the nation was California, with 255,856 arrests, or about 19 percent of the whole. This means that an average of one Californian out of 123—a staggering number—was arrested for drunk driving.

- Texas came in second, with 109,956 (8.33 percent), and North Carolina third, with 72,889 (5.5 percent).

- Drug-abuse violations accounted for a much smaller (but still substantial) number of arrests: 920,424 across the United States in 1992.

- Again, California had the dubious distinction of taking the lead, with 227,784—almost one-quarter of all drug arrests nationwide.

- New York was second, with 101,348, a little more than 11 percent.

- Texas took third place with 69,835, or approximately 7.5 percent.

- Delaware was in 47th place with 525 arrests, or 0.06 percent, placing it ahead of only Montana, North Dakota, and Vermont. It should be noted that among the states, Delaware ranks 46th in population, but even so, the proportion of drug arrests is small—an average of one in every 1,345 Delawareans.

Source(s): Morgan, Kathleen O'Leary, et al., eds. *Crime State Rankings.* Lawrence, KS: Morgan Quitno, 1994.

n't answering any complaints, so I decided to pull them off." Further questioning revealed that the officer did not undertake any procedural protocol related to documentation of his spot check. Moreover, the spot check he subjected Prouse to was not part of a preplanned procedure scheduled by his superiors. Accordingly, the trial court granted Prouse's motion to suppress the evidence seized. The Court felt that unwarranted, non-scheduled, and irregular random stopping of Prouse's vehicle constituted an unreasonable seizure and, therefore, violated the Fourth Amendment. The Court further emphasized that random vehicle stops without reasonable suspicion or cause violated not only the Fourth and the Fourteenth Amendments but also provisions of the Delaware Constitution. The Supreme Court affirmed the lower court's decision on appeal.

Arguments on behalf of the petitioner, the state of Delaware, sought to justify random vehicle stops as essential to the state's interest in promoting traffic safety. The state felt its police officers should have a means at their disposal which, in accordance with each officer's judgment, gave visible evidence of the state's vigilance with respect to safe conduct on the roads and highways. The state supported random stops because they represented a "brief opportunity" in which detention of a vehicle "for a minute" constituted nothing more than a simple check of a driver's operating license and car registration rather than a major intrusion of privacy. Moreover, counsel for Delaware reasoned that the state's interest in increasing traffic safety on its roadways outweighed any intrusion of privacy imposed during any kind of spot check.

Prouse's attorney not only refuted the state's arguments, but (as a preliminary matter) questioned if the

U.S. Supreme Court had appropriate jurisdiction. Prouse's attorney voiced misgivings as to whether the Delaware Supreme Court relied on the U.S. Constitution to render its decision or on provisions of the state constitution. If the Court's decision rested solely on the state constitution, the U.S. Supreme Court would not have jurisdiction in the matter. Additionally, Prouse's attorney argued that because the officer's unwarranted, random spot check occurred at night, there existed an increased level of intrusion. In a less esoteric argument, Prouse's counsel responded directly to the state's presentation by reasoning that if a police officer was allowed to stop any car at any time without any reason, that constituted an abuse of a police officer's authority. Moreover, even if the state saw a compelling interest to promote public safety by allowing law enforcement to engage in spot checks of vehicles, there should be special guidelines provided which identified exactly what constituted appropriate conduct and protocol during random checks.

The U.S. Supreme Court's decision was nearly unanimous (only one justice dissented). As a preliminary matter, the Court resolved the question of jurisdiction. The Delaware Supreme Court rendered its decision, in part, on the state constitution and the federal constitution (by specifically citing the Fourth and Fourteenth Amendments as bases for its ruling). Therefore, the justices held that the Supreme Court had appropriate jurisdiction. In directly addressing arguments presented before the Court, they reasoned that stopping a vehicle without any reasonable suspicion or cause, even if only to check a driver's license and registration, constituted a violation of the Fourth and Fourteenth Amendment—it was unreasonable search and seizure. Citing precedence from *United States v. Brignoni-Ponce*

(1995), the Court explained that only under specific circumstances could random stops be justified such as when the U.S. Border Patrol conducted spot checks in the interest of preventing aliens from illegally entering the country. In that case, officers were further justified because there existed the additional possibility of interdicting illegal smuggling trade over the international border. The Court also found precedence in *United States v. Martinez-Fuerte* (1976). Following a specific protocol, Border Patrol officers established a checkpoint through which all traffic slowed and was channeled through a highway roadblock where some vehicles were singled out and directed to an area designated for secondary inspection. The Court recognized that not only did there exist a governmental interest in such roadblock stops but that the protocol maintained was, itself, less intrusive than merely engaging in random stops of vehicles in moving traffic. Both decisions provided guidance for weighing a public interest against an individual's Fourth Amendment rights. Thus, the Court objected to the random stopping of Prouse by the Delaware police officer because, unlike roadblock stops of all vehicles, a random stop of a single vehicle carried the stigma of intrusiveness without reasonable cause. Further, it was the opinion of the Court that at the least Prouse's stopping constituted interference in his freedom of movement.

Although the Court recognized the state's interest in fostering traffic safety, "discretionary spot checks" appeared arbitrary and thus did not validate an intrusion on a driver's privacy. The Court agreed that, as counsel for the petitioner pointed out, reckless drivers represent endangerment to life and property. But the justices found it difficult to believe that, given a random choice of drivers on a street, a police officer could be able to randomly select which drivers might be operating a vehicle without a license or proper registration. In a large number of stopped vehicles, the Court reasoned there would probably only be a small number of drivers who did not have valid driving documents. Instead, the majority opinion went on to explain, it seemed preferable to rely on routine police procedures such as those undertaken when police officers stop vehicles for traffic violations; at that time officers could easily identify individuals operating a vehicle without a driving license or proper registration. Moreover, annual inspection of cars, car registration, and a driver's insurance coverage seemed better designed to keep dangerous automobiles and/or drivers off the roadways and better served to protect citizens who might otherwise become involved in traffic accidents with irresponsible drivers. Therefore, the Court held that, at best, random stops seemed marginally helpful in promoting traffic safety.

The Court concluded, too, that while an automobile and its use are subject to governmental regulation, a driver who is operating or traveling in that vehicle had the right to expect that his privacy not be violated. Justice White, in writing the decision for the majority, observed that "people are not shorn of all Fourth Amendment protection when they step from the sidewalks into their automobiles." This viewpoint was supported by findings in *Terry v. Ohio* (1968). Justice White further pointed out that privacy is the reason why many people choose to go by car rather than utilize public transportation or walk. However, the majority decision also observed that their decision in no way prevented a state from developing measures which would serve to increase traffic safety and, at the same time, not interfere with the privacy of drivers.

Impact

In rendering their decision, the Supreme Court reiterated previous decisions that defined what constituted appropriate measure and protocol for random vehicular stops. In so doing, they ruled that the state of Delaware's support of random spot checks—made without preestablished protocol and at an officer's individual discretion—constituted unreasonable seizure which violated the Fourth and Fourteenth Amendments. Unless there existed a reasonable cause or suspicion that a vehicle and its occupants should be stopped and detained such as might be justified by a driver's violation of traffic regulations or any other law, police officers could not randomly stop and detain a driver. However, the Court's decision did not preclude the state of Delaware, or any other state, from crafting measures that would promote traffic safety so long as such measures did not intrude on a driver's privacy. The discretionary spot check on a public highway represented a constitutional violation because such stops were undertaken without probable cause or reasonable suspicion. Moreover, in specifying that random stops were not an effective method of preventing traffic accidents but, rather, an invasion of privacy, the Supreme Court's ruling served to provide states with guidance which would discourage law enforcement from committing an intrusive and unreasonable assault on the individual rights of drivers.

Related Cases

Terry v. Ohio, 392 U.S. 1 (1968).
Adams v. Williams, 407 U.S. 143 (1972).
United States v. Brignoni-Ponce, 422 U.S. 873 (1975).
United States v. Martinez-Fuerte, 428 U.S. 543 (1976).
Michigan Department of State Police v. Sitz, 496 U.S. 444 (1990).

Bibliography and Further Reading

Anderson, Sean. "Individual Privacy Interests and the 'Special Needs' Analysis for Involuntary Drug and HIV Tests." *California Law Review*, January 1998, p. 119.

Biskupic, Joan, and Elder Witt, eds. *Congressional Quarterly's Guide to the U.S. Supreme Court,* 3rd ed. Washington, DC: Congressional Quarterly, Inc., 1996.

Cushman, Robert F. *Leading Constitutional Decisions.* Englewood Cliffs, NJ: Prentice-Hall, Inc., 1982.

Donahoe, Diana Roberto. "'Could Have,' 'Would Have': What the Supreme Court Should Have Decided in Whren v. United States." *American Criminal Law Review,* spring 1997, p. 1193.

Glantz, Craig M. "'Could' This Be the End of Fourth Amendment Protections for Motorists?" *Journal of Criminal Law and Criminology,* spring 1997, p. 864.

Mendelsohn, Aaron H. "The Fourth Amendment and Traffic Stops: Bright-Line Rules in Conjunction with the Totality of the Circumstances Test." *Journal of Criminal Law and Criminology,* spring 1998, p. 930.

ARKANSAS V. SANDERS

Legal Citation: 442 U.S. 753 (1979)

Petitioner
State of Arkansas

Respondent
Lonnie James Sanders

Petitioner's Claim
That a warrantless search of the respondent's private luggage did not constitute unreasonable search under the Fourth and Fourteenth Amendments.

Chief Lawyer for Petitioner
Joseph H. Purvis

Chief Lawyer for Respondent
Jack T. Lassiter

Justices for the Court
William J. Brennan, Jr., Warren E. Burger, Thurgood Marshall, Lewis F. Powell, Jr. (writing for the Court), John Paul Stevens, Potter Stewart, Byron R. White

Justices Dissenting
Harry A. Blackmun, William H. Rehnquist

Place
Washington, D.C.

Date of Decision
20 June 1979

Decision
Absent of urgent or critical circumstances, a police search of personal luggage requires a warrant under the provisions of the Fourth Amendment. Therefore, the U.S. Supreme Court affirmed the judgment of the Arkansas Supreme Court.

Significance
The Supreme Court accepted *Arkansas v. Sanders* to clarify and extend *United States v. Chadwick* (1977) regarding the matter of warrantless searches of luggage or containers seized during searches of lawfully detained vehicles. As with any personal, private, closed container not being transported but seized during the course of a normal police investigation, a search could only be undertaken with a warrant if a vehicle had been stopped. While exigent circumstances permit police to conduct warrantless searches, a stopped automobile did not qualify as exigent circumstances where evidence was in danger of being destroyed or lost.

Little Rock police received a tip from an informant that the respondent, Lonnie Sanders, would arrive at the local municipal airport carrying a green suitcase which contained marijuana. Because of the tip and their knowledge of Sanders's criminal activity, police set up a three-man surveillance team at the airport. When passengers departed from the afternoon flight into the Little Rock Municipal Airport, surveillance officers witnessed Sanders retrieve a green suitcase from the airline baggage service and, after meeting David Rambo, pass the suitcase to him. Both men were detained after police stopped the taxi they were in several blocks from the airport. When officers asked the taxi driver to open the trunk of the cab, the police discovered an unlocked green suitcase containing 9.3 pounds of marijuana. Sanders and Rambo were arrested and charged with possession of marijuana with intent to deliver.

Before his trial was adjudicated in the Arkansas court, Sanders moved to suppress the evidence obtained from the suitcase; he believed he had been subjected to an unreasonable search. Since the police did not have a warrant to open the green suitcase, Sanders felt his rights were violated under the Fourth and Fourteenth Amendments. This motion was denied without comment by the trial court, and, after conviction by a jury, the court sentenced Sanders to ten years in prison and a fine of $15,000. On appeal, the Supreme Court of Arkansas reversed the conviction, ruling that the trial court should have suppressed the marijuana as evidence because it was obtained through an unlawful search of the suitcase. The U.S. Supreme Court affirmed.

In the majority opinion, delivered by Justice Powell, the question posed by the case centered about whether, in absence of urgent need or critical circumstances, the police were obliged to conduct a warrantless search of personal luggage taken from an automobile even if the vehicle was properly stopped. The Court ruled that Fourteenth Amendment protection from unreasonable search extended to personal luggage. Justice Burger, joined by Stevens, concurred in the judgment but expressed the view that the case did not invoke the "automobile" exception. Because the Court established in earlier rulings—*United States v. Chadwick, Chambers v. Maroney* (1970), and *Carroll v. United States* (1925)—

that the "inherent mobility of automobiles often makes it impracticable to obtain a warrant," police are not required to obtain a warrant if a motorist is legally stopped and subsequently "searched on the street." Furthermore, Justice Blackmun joined by Justice Rehnquist, dissented from the Court's opinion. Their view was that personal property could be seized and searched without a warrant if it was found in an automobile that was lawfully seized and searched.

Rights guaranteed under the Fourth Amendment protect the privacy and property of individuals by ensuring "the right of the people to be secured in their persons, houses, papers and effects, against unreasonable searches and seizures." By the late 1970s, the Court had also established that Fourth Amendment rights included the requirement that searches of private property had to be performed pursuant to a search warrant issued in compliance with the Warrant Clause. The Warrant Clause of the Fourth Amendment provides that warrants cannot be issued unless there is probable cause and if evidence of a criminal act may only be obtained through search and seizure. However, there are permissible exceptions: if there exists the potential of danger to law enforcement officers or if the risk of loss or destruction of evidence, as determined by a neutral magistrate, outweighs the rationale for prior recourse. In *Arkansas v. Sanders,* such reasons were not in evidence. The Court believed Little Rock police should have obtained a warrant before searching Sanders' luggage even though the suitcase was taken from an automobile that had been properly stopped and searched for contraband. Police had already detained the individuals suspected of criminal activity and had already secured the suitcase; there appeared to be no danger of loss of evidence or risk to law enforcement.

The attorney for the state of Arkansas argued that the search and seizure by Little Rock police did not require a warrant because their conduct was consistent with legal exceptions to search and seizure rights delineated in the Fourth Amendment. One legally permissible deviation, the "automobile exception," permitted police to stop an automobile if they had probable cause to believe it contained contraband or evidence of a crime. Counsel explained that police acted in accordance with that exception based on a reliable tip from an informant which provided an exact description of Sanders, his arrival time and location, the appearance of the suitcase, and its contents. Nevertheless, the Court held that officers were required to secure a warrant to search Sanders' luggage since there was nothing in the circumstances that made obtaining a search warrant impractical. The Court expressed that the warrantless search of Sanders' suitcase was also improper because the rationale pertaining to the automobile exception (the risk of losing evidence due to the mobility of an automobile) did not apply to searches of personal luggage already taken out from an automobile and secured by police. The majority opinion also reasoned that Fourth Amendment warrant requirements apply to personal luggage taken from an automobile to the same degree they apply to luggage in other locations. (The only notable exception is when the contents of containers and packages can be inferred from their outward appearance and are found by police during normal conduct of their duty.)

In a separate, concurring opinion, Chief Justice Burger and Justice Stevens pointed out that the Court's opinion was unnecessarily broad and obscured because the facts of the case did not invoke the automobile exception. Minority justices agreed that the police officers, acting under probable cause, should have obtained a search warrant; however, the fact that the suitcase was in an automobile was completely irrelevant to the case. The security of the luggage being transported by Sanders at the time of his arrest was at issue, not the automobile in which it was being carried. Burger stressed that, as in *United States v. Chadwick,* the relationship between contraband and the automobile was purely coincidental. The crux of the *Sanders* decision should, therefore, have addressed Sanders's right to privacy. His expectation of privacy was not diminished since the arrest happened in a public place where his right to privacy mandated a search warrant. Sanders had a right to expect that his luggage would not, without his approval, be exposed to the demands of police in public.

Justice Blackmun also argued that the Court has not distinguished between the lesser intrusion of a seizure and the greater intrusion of a search with respect to automobiles or persons subject to custodial arrest. The minority opinion reasoned that the Court's judgment should have distinguished between a case in which there was probable cause to search the car and its contents as a whole and a case in which there was probable cause to search for a specific item within the car, such as Sanders's luggage. Thus, the dissenting justices concluded that the automobile exception did not apply. The intrusion of privacy (and consequently the need for protection under the Fourteenth Amendment's Warrant Clause) was greater when police searched the entire interior area of the car than when they confined their search to a single suitcase. The dissenting opinion went on to explain that a police officer, when approaching an automobile, must understand that, in three distinct ways, an individual has possession rights with respect to personal property. If there was probable cause to arrest the occupant, then according to the Court's decision in *Chimel v. California* (1969), an officer may search for objects within immediate control of the vehicle's occupants, with or without probable cause. Secondly, if there was probable cause to search the automobile itself, the officer may be entitled to do so, with or without a warrant. And finally, the criteria specified by the Court in the *Chadwick* decision applied. Any object found in the car outside the immediate control of the occupants, such as Sanders's suitcase, in the absence of exigent circumstances, could not be searched without a warrant.

Impact

In rendering a decision in *Sanders,* the Court concerned itself with aspects of the case comparable to *United States v. Chadwick* where evidence was illegally obtained under similar circumstances. As in *Chadwick,* police acting on probable cause opened luggage found in the trunk of a parked car and searched it without a warrant. The majority justices reasoned that in both cases there was no danger of law enforcement losing the luggage or its contents since the containers were under the exclusive control of the arresting officers. Thus, the Court concluded the state failed to demonstrate a need for warrantless search of property stored in the trunk of a stopped automobile; like the vehicle in which it rode, the luggage was no longer mobile. Arresting offi-

cers had to assess the likelihood of an automobile leaving the scene at the point immediately before a search commenced. In circumstances where police had already seized the object of their interest and held it directly under their control, a search could not be conducted without a warrant. Thus, in rendering the Court's decision, the justices provided specific guidance for law enforcement and the lower courts. The Warrant Clause contained in the Fourth Amendment applies to personal luggage taken from an automobile to the same degree it applies to luggage seized in other locations.

Related Cases

Carroll v. United States, 267 U.S. 132 (1925).
Chimel v. California, 395 U.S. 752 (1969).
Chambers v. Maroney, 399 U.S. 42 (1970).
United States v. Chadwick, 433 U.S. 1 (1977).

Bibliography and Further Reading

Bradley, Craig M. "The Court's 'Two Model' Approach to the Fourth Amendment: Carpe Diem." *Journal of Criminal Law and Criminology,* fall 1993, p. 429.

PAYTON V. NEW YORK

Legal Citation: 445 U.S. 573 (1980)

Appellants
Theodore Payton, Obie Riddick

Appellee
State of New York

Appellants' Claim
That a New York statute authorizing police to enter a home without a warrant to make an arrest violates the Fourth Amendment.

Chief Lawyer for Appellants
William E. Hellerstein

Chief Lawyer for Appellee
Peter L. Zimroth

Justices for the Court
Harry A. Blackmun, William J. Brennan, Jr., Thurgood Marshall, Lewis F. Powell, Jr., John Paul Stevens (writing for the Court), Potter Stewart

Justices Dissenting
Warren E. Burger, William H. Rehnquist, Byron R. White

Place
Washington, D.C.

Date of Decision
15 April 1980

Decision
That the Fourth Amendment prohibits police from making a warrantless entry into a person's home in order to make a routine arrest, and thus New York's statute was unconstitutional.

Significance
The Court's ruling reiterated the strong privacy protection people enjoy in their homes, and reaffirmed that the police may not enter a person's home without consent except when they obtain a warrant, or in other very narrow circumstances.

The Fourth Amendment to the Constitution provides that the "right of the people to be secure in their persons, houses, papers, and effects, against unreasonable searches and seizures, shall not be violated, and no Warrants shall issue, but upon probable cause . . ." The Fourth Amendment is based, in large part, on English common law. Thus, as early as 1886, in the case of *Boyd v. United States,* the Supreme Court noted that the Fourth Amendment protects people against "all invasions on the part of the government and its employees of the sanctity of a man's home and the privacies of life." In *Payton,* the strengths and limits of this theory were put to the test before the Supreme Court.

The *Payton* case involved two separate criminal prosecutions in the state of New York. In the first case, Theodore Payton was suspected of murder by New York City detectives. After investigating Payton for two days, the police decided that they had probable cause to believe that Payton had committed the murders, and went to his apartment to arrest him. The police entered the apartment based on a New York state statute which permitted officers to enter a home without a search or arrest warrant to arrest a person if they had probable cause to believe that the person committed a felony. Although Payton was not at home, the police discovered a bullet shell casing, which was used against Payton in his trial.

In the second case, Obie Riddick was suspected of two armed robberies. The police, acting pursuant to the New York statute, arrested Riddick in his home without obtaining a warrant. During the arrest, the police discovered narcotics and narcotics paraphernalia. Riddick was tried and convicted on narcotics charges.

Both Payton and Riddick moved to suppress the evidence against them discovered by the police, arguing that the police violated their Fourth Amendment right to be free from unreasonable seizures by entering their homes without a warrant. The state trial courts denied their motions, and both were convicted. They each appealed their convictions to the New York Court of Appeals which, in a single opinion, agreed with the trial courts that the Fourth Amendment does not require a police officer to obtain a warrant before entering a home to arrest a person for committing a felony.

Warrant Required for Entry of a Home

Payton and Riddick asked for the New York Court of Appeals decision to be reviewed by the U.S. Supreme Court. Noting that both state and federal courts have disagreed over whether the Fourth Amendment prohibits a warrantless arrest in a person's home, the Supreme Court decided to hear the case. In the 1976 case *United States v. Watson,* the Court held that a police officer need not obtain an arrest warrant before arresting a person suspected of a felony in a public place. However, the Court refused to extend the rule of *Watson* to arrests occurring within the home.

In an opinion written by Justice John Paul Stevens, the Court concluded that, absent special or "exigent" circumstances, the Fourth Amendment prohibits police officers from entering a person's home to make an arrest without first obtaining an arrest warrant.

The Court began by noting that the Fourth Amendment was designed to protect the privacy of individuals in various settings, and that in no setting "is the zone of privacy more clearly defined than when bounded by the unambiguous physical dimensions of an individual's home." The Court then rejected New York's argument that, because warrantless arrests in the home were allowed in common law England, the founders did not intend the Fourth Amendment to prohibit such arrests. Examining old English cases and the works of English legal commentators, the Court concluded that there was no general common law rule regarding whether a police officer needed to obtain a warrant before entering a home to make an arrest at the time the Fourth Amendment was adopted.

The Court also rejected New York's argument that requiring a warrant before entering a home to make an arrest would have practical consequences for law enforcement. The Court noted that several states had already required a warrant, and there was no evidence that law enforcement was hampered in making arrests in any of these states. Thus, the Court concluded that "neither history nor this Nation's experience requires us to disregard the overriding respect for the sanctity of the home that has been embedded in our traditions since the origins of the Republic," and held that the Fourth Amendment requires an officer to obtain an arrest warrant before entering a person's home to make an arrest, in the absence of exigent circumstances.

A Common Law Rule

Justice White, Chief Justice Burger, and Justice Rehnquist dissented from the Court's decision. Justice White disagreed with the Court's conclusion that there was no common law rule relating to warrantless arrests in the home. On the contrary, Justice White

argued that the English common law at the time of the Fourth Amendment allowed such arrests provided that four circumstances were met: (1) the crime committed was a felony; (2) the officers knocked and announced their presence; (3) the entry was made during the daytime; and (4) there was probable cause to believe that the person who committed the felony was in the home at the time of the entry. Justice White thus concluded that the drafters of the Fourth Amendment did not intend to prohibit such arrests. He also reasoned that these four restrictions were adequate to protect the privacy interests protected by the Fourth Amendment. Finally, noting both that such warrantless arrests were allowed under the common law and that a number of states had long allowed such arrests, Justice White concluded: "Our cases establish that the ultimate test under the Fourth Amendment is one of 'reasonableness' . . . I cannot join the Court in declaring unreasonable a practice which has been thought entirely reasonable for so long." Thus, Justice White would have found the warrantless entries into the homes of both Payton and Riddick to be constitutional because they met the four requirements of the common law rule.

Impact

A few years prior to the *Payton* decision, the Supreme Court held in *United States v. Watson* that the police may arrest a felony suspect in a public place without obtaining an arrest warrant. The Court's decision in *Payton* made clear that this rule does not extend to arrests which occur in the home, due to the Fourth Amendment's particular protection of the home, where a person's privacy interest is nearly absolute. Thus it is clear after *Payton* that in the absence of certain emergency, or "exigent," circumstances such as where there is a possibility that the suspect will escape, destroy evidence, or harm the police or others, the police must obtain a warrant from a judge before entering a person's home to make a felony arrest. Further, the holding of *Payton* has been extended to prohibit warrantless entry into a home to arrest a guest in the home.

Related Cases

Boyd v. United States, 116 U.S. 616 (1886).
Coolidge v. New Hampshire, 403 U.S. 443 (1971).
United States v. Watson, 423 U.S. 411 (1976).
Michigan v. Summers, 452 U.S. 692 (1981).
Welsh v. Wisconsin, 466 U.S. 740 (1984).
Maryland v. Buie, 494 U.S. 325 (1990).
New York v. Harris, 495 U.S. 14 (1990).

Bibliography and Further Reading

Dressler, Joshua. *Understanding Criminal Procedure.* New York: Matthew Bender & Co., 1991.

Hall, Kermit L., ed. *The Oxford Companion to the Supreme Court of the United States.* New York: Oxford University Press, 1992.

LaFave, Wayne R. *Search and Seizure: A Treatise on the Fourth Amendment,* 3rd ed. St. Paul, MN: West Publishing Co., 1996.

Malooly, Daniel J. "Physical Searches Under FISA: A Constitutional Analysis." *American Criminal Law Review,* winter 1998, p. 411.

Steiker, Carol S. "Counter-Revolution in Constitutional Criminal Procedure? Two Audiences, Two Answers." *Michigan Law Review,* August 1996, p. 2466.

UNITED STATES V. PAYNER

Legal Citation: 447 U.S. 727 (1980)

Petitioner
United States

Respondent
Jack Payner

Petitioner's Claim
That although gathered using an illegal search, the evidence against Jack Payner for falsifying a federal income tax return should not be suppressed and the conviction should not be set aside.

Chief Lawyer for Petitioner
Wade H. McCree, U.S. Solicitor General

Chief Lawyer for Respondent
Bennet Kleinman

Justices for the Court
Warren E. Burger, Lewis F. Powell, Jr. (writing for the Court), William H. Rehnquist, John Paul Stevens, Potter Stewart, Byron R. White

Justices Dissenting
Harry A. Blackmun, William J. Brennan, Jr., Thurgood Marshall

Place
Washington, D.C.

Date of Decision
23 June 1980

Decision
Overturned two lower courts' rulings that a federal court could use its supervisory power to exclude evidence seized illegally from a third party.

Significance
The ruling settled the question of whether the supervisory power of the federal court could be substituted for established Fourth Amendment doctrines. Since only the victim of an illegal search, not a third party, can claim that his Fourth Amendments rights were violated, the federal courts cannot suppress evidence against the third party by using its supervisory power. This decision served to limit the uses to which the federal courts could put their supervisory power.

In 1965, the Internal Revenue Service (IRS) began investigating the financial activities of American citizens in the Bahamas. This investigation, called "Operation Trade Winds," was headquartered in Florida. In 1972, the IRS became suspicious of the Castle Bank when investigators discovered that a suspected drug trafficker had an account there. Special Agent Richard Jaffe asked Norman Casper, a private investigator and informant, to learn more about the Castle Bank. Casper was already an acquaintance of Castle Bank vice president Michael Wolstencroft. Casper introduced Wolstencroft to Sybol Kennedy, a private investigator. Casper devised the so-called "briefcase caper" when he learned that Wolstencroft would be spending a few days in Miami in January of 1973. On 11 January, Casper told Special Agent Jaffe that he planned to enter an apartment and take Wolstencroft's briefcase. Jaffe told him he would have to clear the plan with his supervisor, Troy Register, Jr., chief of the IRS Intelligence Division in Jacksonville, Florida. Register cleared the plan and Jaffe told Casper to proceed. Casper asked Jaffe for the name of a locksmith who could be "trusted." Wolstencroft arrived on 15 January and went straight to Kennedy's apartment. When the couple left to go out to dinner, Casper entered the apartment using a key that Kennedy had given him. He stole the briefcase and met with the locksmith in a parking lot nearby. The locksmith made a key to fit the lock. Casper took the briefcase and the key to the home of an IRS agent. There Jaffe, Casper, and an IRS photography expert photographed over 400 documents. A lookout called Casper when the couple had finished dinner. Casper returned the briefcase to the apartment one and one-half hours after he had taken it.

During the following two weeks, Jaffe asked Casper to get more information on Castle Bank. Casper sent Kennedy to the Bahamas, where she stole a rolodex file from Wolstencroft's office. The IRS paid Casper $8,000 for his services, and Casper paid Kennedy $1,000 for hers.

The documents in the briefcase indicated a relationship between Castle Bank in the Bahamas and the Bank of Perrine in Florida. Subpoenas issued to the Bank of Perrine revealed the loan guarantee agreement which was the main evidence against Payner at his trial. In this agreement, Payner pledged the money in his Castle Bank account as security for $100,000 loan. Payner was indicted in September of 1976 on a charge of falsifying his 1972 income tax return by denying that he had a foreign bank account.

Payner waived his right to a jury trial and asked that the loan guarantee agreement be suppressed (found inadmissible as evidence). The U.S. District Court for the Northern District of Ohio found Payner guilty. However, the court also found that the government got its evidence by using a flagrantly illegal search. The court thus suppressed all the evidence except the 1972 tax return. Since the tax return alone did not show that he had falsified the return, the district court set aside Payner's conviction. The district court found that the government "knowingly and willfully participated in the unlawful seizure of Michael Wolstencroft's briefcase . . ." The court also noted that the government tells its agents that the Fourth Amendment standing limitation permits them to intentionally conduct an unconstitutional search and seizure of one person to get evidence about another. The standing rule states that "a court may not exclude evidence under the Fourth Amendment unless it finds that an unlawful search or seizure violated the defendant's own constitutional rights."

The district court also found that the documents taken from the briefcase led to the discovery of the loan guarantee agreement. Although the search did not violate Payner's Fourth Amendment rights, the district court felt that the Due Process Clause of the Fifth Amendment required it to exclude the evidence. Another factor in excluding the evidence was the inherent supervisory power of the federal courts to police the administration of justice in the federal system. This supervisory power serves to deter illegality and protect judicial integrity. This concept of supervisory power also persuaded the District Court to exclude evidence tainted by the government's "knowing and purposeful bad faith hostility to any person's fundamental constitutional rights." The district court concluded that society's interest in deterring law enforcement misconduct by excluding tainted evidence outweighed society's interest in furnishing the court with all of the relevant facts. The Court of Appeals for the Sixth Circuit agreed with the district court's use of its supervisory power.

Illegal Actions

Regarding the use of supervisory power in this case, the Supreme Court, as stated by Justice Powell, felt that it "upsets the careful balance of interests embodied in the Fourth Amendment decisions of this Court . . . Such an extension of the supervisory power would enable federal courts to exercise a standardless discretion in their application of the exclusionary rule to enforce the Fourth Amendment." Although stating that no court should condone the "briefcase caper," Powell noted that this type of illegal conduct does not command the exclusion of evidence in every case where it was gathered illegally. The illegal actions of law enforcement "must be weighed against the considerable harm that would flow from indiscriminate application of an exclusionary rule." Using the exclusionary rule to enforce proper behavior on the part of law enforcement would impede the functions of the courts. The Court held that the supervisory power does not authorize a federal court to suppress evidence on the ground that it was seized unlawfully from a third party.

Federal Courts

In his dissent Justice Marshall noted that the Court's decision turned the standing rule "into a sword to be used by the Government to permit it deliberately to invade one person's Fourth Amendment rights in order to obtain evidence against another person." If the federal court permits evidence gathered in this illegal way to be admissible at a trial, it gives its stamp of approval to lawlessness and taints its own integrity. It becomes "the accomplice of the Government lawbreaker . . . for without judicial use of the evidence the 'caper' would have been for naught. Such a pollution of the federal courts should not be permitted."

Marshall noted that the government deliberately used illegal means to gain evidence against people like Payner. No claim can be made that the illegal actions are only slightly connected to Payner's case. "The Government misconduct is at the very heart of this case. . . . The District Court refused to be made an accomplice to illegal conduct by the IRS by permitting the agency to use the proceeds of its crimes for the very purpose for which they were committed—to convict persons such as Payner." The Court should prevent the government from using evidence deliberately acquired illegally using bad-faith hostility to constitutional rights. Marshall would have suppressed the fruits of the government's illegal action under the Court's supervisory powers.

Impact

The refusal to exclude evidence gained through flagrantly illegal means illustrated the majority of the Court's dislike of the exclusionary rule. The early 1980s was a time when the Supreme Court began chipping away at the exclusionary rule, developing many exceptions to its application. Many of the justices wanted the rule abolished. Some members of Congress have proposed abolishing the exclusionary rule in federal court, but this has not yet occurred.

Related Cases

Olmstead v. United States, 277 U.S. 438 (1928).
Rakas v. Illinois, 439 U.S. 128 (1978).
United States v. Caceres, 440 U.S. 741 (1979).

Bibliography and Further Reading

Bloom, Robert M. "Judicial Integrity: A Call for Its Re-Emergence in the Adjudication of Criminal Cases." *Journal of Criminal Law and Criminology,* fall 1993, p. 462.

Steiker, Carol S. "Counter-Revolution in Constitutional Criminal Procedure? Two Audiences, Two Answers." *Michigan Law Review,* August 1996, p. 2466.

MICHIGAN V. SUMMERS

Legal Citation: 452 U.S. 692 (1981)

Petitioner
State of Michigan

Respondent
George Summers

Petitioner's Claim
That a valid warrant to search a person's home also allows the police officers conducting the search to detain the homeowner while the search is being conducted.

Chief Lawyer for Petitioner
Timothy A. Baughman

Chief Lawyer for Respondent
Gerald M. Lorence

Justices for the Court
Harry A. Blackmun, Warren E. Burger, Lewis F. Powell, Jr., William H. Rehnquist, John Paul Stevens (writing for the Court), Byron R. White

Justices Dissenting
William J. Brennan, Jr., Thurgood Marshall, Potter Stewart

Place
Washington, D.C.

Date of Decision
22 June 1981

Decision
That a warrant to search a home carries with it an implicit authority on the part of the officers executing the warrant to detain the occupants of the home while the search is being conducted.

Significance
The Court's decision made it much easier and safer for police officers to conduct searches of homes. The decision allows officers to detain the occupants of the home while a search is being conducted so that the occupants cannot interfere with the search, destroy evidence, or threaten the safety of the officers.

The Fourth Amendment to the United States Constitution provides that the "right of the people to be secure in their persons, houses, papers, and effects, against unreasonable searches and seizures, shall not be violated, and no Warrants shall issue, but upon probable cause." Ordinarily, police may not search a person or his property without having "probable cause" to believe that the search will reveal contraband or evidence of a crime. Likewise, the police may not seize a person, that is arrest or detain the person, without probable cause to believe that the person is committing a crime. Nevertheless, the Supreme Court has recognized certain exceptions to the probable cause requirement. In the watershed 1968 case *Terry v. Ohio,* the Court held that a police officer may stop a person and search him if the officer has a "reasonable suspicion" (which is a much lower standard than probable cause) that the person is armed with a weapon. In such a situation, the officer may "stop and frisk" the person for weapons. Since that decision, the Court has expanded the *Terry* rule to a number of other situations.

In *Michigan v. Summers,* the Court expanded the *Terry* rule to allow police to detain the occupants of a home while the home is being searched pursuant to a valid search warrant. Detroit police officers, having probable cause to believe that a house contained narcotics, secured a search warrant for the house. As the police officers arrived at the house to execute the warrant, they encountered George Summers on the front steps. The officers detained Summers while they searched the house. The officers discovered narcotics in the basement of the house and, having ascertained that he owned the house, arrested Summers. Incident to his arrest, the officers searched Summers himself, and discovered 8.5 grams of heroin in his coat pocket.

Summers was charged with possession of the heroin the police discovered in his coat pocket. Summers moved to have the evidence suppressed because his original detention by the police, from which all of the evidence discovered by the police flowed, violated the Fourth Amendment. The trial court, Michigan Court of Appeals, and Michigan Supreme Court all agreed with Summers's argument and dismissed the charges against him. The state appealed this decision to the U.S. Supreme Court.

Detention While Search Is Conducted Is Reasonable

The Supreme Court reversed the decision of the Michigan courts, concluding that the Fourth Amendment allows the police to detain a person while they search his house. The Court began its analysis by noting that its decision in *Terry* recognized that, in certain situations, the police do not need probable cause to detain a person for a limited amount of time. The Court also noted that, since its decision in *Terry,* the Court had expanded the *Terry* rule to allow limited detentions in a number of circumstances. As the Court explained, "[t]hese cases recognized that some seizures admittedly covered by the Fourth Amendment constitute such limited intrusions on the personal security of those detained and are justified by such substantial law enforcement interests that they may be made on less than probable cause." Relying on these cases, the Court concluded that the detention of Summers was limited and was justified by substantial law enforcement interests.

First, the Court found that the detention was limited because the police had secured a search warrant for the home, which was supported by probable cause. The Court reasoned that detaining Summers was less intrusive than the search of his home, which the police had authority to conduct. The Court also reasoned that police are unlikely to abuse the power to detain someone while the home is being searched by prolonging the detention to gain information because the information sought by the police will be obtained through the search itself. Finally, the Court reasoned that the detention was of a limited nature because most citizens will choose to be present to witness the search of their homes, unless they intend to flee in order to avoid arrest following the search. Also, the Court concluded that substantial law enforcement interests justified the police officers' detention of Summers while they searched his home. The Court noted that allowing officers to detain the owner while the search is being conducted allows the officers to prevent attempts to flee the scene if the search reveals evidence of wrongdoing. Also, detention of the homeowner while the home is searched protects the officers' safety, and allows the police to search the home in a more orderly fashion because the owner may be asked to open locked doors or containers.

Having concluded that Summers could be detained while the search was conducted on less than probable cause, the Court also concluded that the existence of the search warrant itself provided sufficient reasonable suspicion, as required under the *Terry* rule, to allow the officers to detain Summers. Thus, the Court held that "a warrant to search for contraband founded on probable cause implicitly carries with it the limited authority to detain the occupants of the premises while a proper search is conducted."

An Unwarranted Extension of *Terry*

Justice Stewart, writing an opinion joined by Justices Brennan and Marshall, dissented from the Court's decision and concluded that the decision was an unwarranted extension of the *Terry* rule. Justice Stewart noted that the Court allowed a detention based on less than probable cause in only two situations: where the officers had reason to believe that the person detained was carrying a weapon and thus posed a threat to the safety of the officers; and brief stops of vehicles near international borders to question the occupants about their citizenship. Justice Stewart reasoned that "[t]he common denominator of [these] cases is the presence of some governmental interest independent of the ordinary interest in investigating crime and apprehending suspects." Justice Stewart found that the interests supporting the officers' detention of Summers—preventing flight from the scene and the orderly conduct of the search—represent "nothing more than the ordinary police interest in discovering evidence of crime and apprehending wrongdoers."

Justice Stewart also disagreed with the majority's conclusion that the detention of a person while his home is searched is only a limited type of detention. He reasoned that a search of a home can take several hours, which is much longer than the brief one or two minute detentions involved in *Terry*-type "stop and frisk" cases and the border patrol cases. He also noted that the police could prolong the detention, because "[i]f the purpose of the detention is to help the police make the search, the detention can be as long as the police find it necessary to protract the search." Finally, Justice Stewart disagreed with the majority's conclusion that most citizens will choose to remain in their homes during the search, noting that Summers apparently did not want to do so. Thus, Justice Stewart concluded that the majority's decision was an extension of *Terry* which was not justified by the reasons underlying that rule or subsequent cases applying the rule.

Impact

The Court's decision in *Summers* constituted a significant expansion of the situations in which police officers may detain a person even though they do not have probable cause to do so. The Court has continued this expansion after *Summers,* in conjunction with recognizing more exceptions to the warrant requirement of the Fourth Amendment. Thus, the Court's decision in *Summers* fostered a growing number of situations in which police may conduct searches of property and seizures of persons outside of the requirements of the Fourth Amendment.

Related Cases

Terry v. Ohio, 392 U.S. 1 (1968).
Adams v. Williams, 407 U.S. 143 (1972).

Payton v. New York, 445 U.S. 573 (1980).

Maryland v. Wilson, 519 U.S. 408 (1997).

Bibliography and Further Reading

Dressler, Joshua. *Understanding Criminal Procedure.* New York: Matthew Bender & Co., 1991.

LaFave, Wayne R. *Search and Seizure: A Treatise on the Fourth Amendment,* 3rd ed. St. Paul, MN: West Publishing Co., 1996.

Riggs, Jenny L. "Excluding Automobile Passengers from Fourth Amendment Protection." *Journal of Criminal Law and Criminology,* spring 1998, p. 957.

NEW YORK V. BELTON

Legal Citation: 453 U.S. 454 (1981)

Petitioner
State of New York

Respondent
Roger Belton

Petitioner's Claim
During a lawful arrest of persons riding in an automobile, it is constitutional for the arresting police officer to conduct a warrantless search of the passenger compartment of the arrested person's vehicle and any containers contained therein, and it is constitutional for the arresting officer to search, without a warrant, through an arrestee's jacket.

Chief Lawyer for Petitioner
James R. Harvey

Chief Lawyer for Respondent
Paul J. Cambria, Jr.

Justices for the Court
Harry A. Blackmun, Warren E. Burger, Lewis F. Powell, Jr., William H. Rehnquist, John Paul Stevens, Potter Stewart (writing for the Court)

Justices Dissenting
William J. Brennan, Jr., Thurgood Marshall, Byron R. White

Place
Washington, D.C.

Date of Decision
1 July 1981

Decision
During a lawful arrest, it is constitutional for an officer to conduct a warrantless search of the immediate vicinity, including closed containers and zipped pockets.

Significance
The holding in *Belton* seemed to increase the permissible scope of warrantless police searches that are conducted as part of an arrest. Prior to the decision, officers generally were required to limit such searches to the person and the area immediately surrounding the person. In *Belton*, the Court confirmed that law enforcement personnel have the right to conduct warrantless searches of enclosed places that may be outside of the arrestee's immediate vicinity.

On 9 April 1978, New York State Trooper Douglas Nicot noticed a speeding automobile on the New York State Thruway. Nicot stopped the car and asked to see the driver's license and registration. Neither the driver nor his companions had a driver's license or registration for the vehicle, and no one was related to the vehicle's owner. Nicot smelled an odor of burnt marijuana emanating from the car, and he spotted an envelope marked "Supergold." Suspecting that there was marijuana in the car, Nicot ordered the occupants out of the car, informed them that they were under arrest, read them their Miranda rights, and ordered them to stand apart from each other around his squad car. Nicot opened the suspicious envelope and discovered marijuana. He then searched a jacket that had been left in the vehicle by one of the occupants, Roger Belton. Nicot unzipped a pocket of the jacket and found cocaine.

Belton subsequently was indicted for criminal possession of cocaine. At trial, Belton asked the trial court to exclude the cocaine evidence, arguing that the search of his jacket was illegal under the Fourth Amendment. According to Belton, Officer Nicot should have obtained a search warrant before searching his jacket. The trial court denied the request, and Belton pleaded guilty to criminal possession of a controlled substance. However, in a special plea, Belton preserved a right to appeal the trial court's decision.

Belton lost his first appeal, but the New York Court of Appeals reversed the decision, holding that because Belton was not in a position to gain access to his jacket, Nicot had no right to search it at that time because he did not have a warrant issued by a magistrate. One of the first principles of search and seizure law is that law enforcement personnel must have a warrant before they conduct a search of a person or place. A warrant is issued by a magistrate only after a police officer has persuaded the magistrate that probable cause exists to believe that the person or place to be searched will turn up evidence of a crime. Sometimes an officer does not need a warrant to conduct a search, but the New York Court of Appeals did not consider this one of those times.

The U.S. Supreme Court disagreed. In a 6-3 decision, the Court held that the Fourth Amendment does not prohibit the warrantless search of a car's backseat and closed containers in the backseat when the search is incident to a lawful arrest of the car's occupants. The majority opinion, written by Justice Stewart, began its analysis by quoting a law review article written by Professor Wayne R. LaFave. In "Case-By-Case Adjudication Versus Standardized Procedures: The Robinson Dilemma," LaFave posited that the Fourth Amendment "is primarily intended to regulate the police in their day-to-day activities," and that the amendment did not require a "highly sophisticated set of rules, qualified by all sorts of ifs, ands, and buts and requiring the drawing of subtle nuances and hairline distinctions."

Having advanced the notion that rules on warrantless searches by police officers should be simplified, the Court then declared that Fourth Amendment jurisprudence on warrantless searches also needed to be simplified. Various courts around the United States were in disagreement on what constituted an illegal warrantless search, and this was having a detrimental impact on police and the general public. "When a person cannot know how a court will apply a settled principle to a recurring factual situation," Stewart observed, "that person cannot know the scope of his constitutional protection, nor can a policeman know the scope of his authority." The Court acknowledged that *Chimel v. California* (1969) had established that a warrantless search contemporaneous to an arrest may not "stray beyond the immediate control of the arrestee," but it also noted that courts around the country could not agree on a definition of "beyond the immediate control of the arrestee."

The Court decided that since Belton was seated in the passenger compartment of the vehicle, the passenger compartment of the vehicle was within Belton's immediate control. Thus, it was not unlawful for Nicot to search the passenger compartment. Furthermore, it was not unlawful for Nicot to search any enclosed containers that he found in the passenger compartment. Citing *United States v. Robinson* (1973) and *Draper v. United States* (1959), the High Court reasoned that since the passenger compartment was within Belton's reach, so too were any enclosed containers in the passenger area. Since the closed containers also were within Belton's reach, Nicot was justified in opening and searching them.

The New York Court of Appeals held that the warrantless search of Belton's jacket was illegal because Nicot had gained exclusive control over the jacket by seizing it. Such reasoning was "fallacious," wrote Justice Stewart in a footnote, because under such a theory "no search or seizure incident to a lawful custodial arrest would ever be valid; by seizing an article even on the arrestee's person, an officer may be said to have reduced that article to his 'exclusive control.'"

Justices Stevens and Rehnquist concurred in the opinion, while Justices Brennan, White, and Marshall

dissented. In a dissenting opinion joined by Marshall, Brennan criticized the ruling for creating a rule "that fails to reflect *Chimel's* underlying policy justifications." Quoting *Chimel*, Brennan maintained that the real reason for allowing the warrantless search of the area within the immediate control of an arrestee was to permit police officers to conduct a warrantless search of areas "within which [an arrestee] might gain possession of a weapon or destructible evidence." Quoting more Supreme Court precedents, Brennan argued that there is a "temporal and a spatial limitation of searches incident to arrest," and that the formality of a warrant may be excused only when the search is conducted at the same time as the arrest and is confined to the immediate vicinity of the arrest. As Belton was already arrested and had been placed by Nicot some distance away from the car when Nicot conducted the warrantless search, the High Court's approval of the search "ignore[d] both precedent and principle."

The Court's decision, according to Brennan, also failed to create a more understandable set of rules for warrantless police searches that are conducted incident to an arrest. "Would a warrantless search incident to arrest be conducted five minutes after the suspect left his car?" Brennan wondered. "Thirty minutes? Three hours? Does it matter whether the suspect is standing in close proximity to the car?" Brennan offered a dozen-odd questions that were raised by the majority's decision and then insisted that *Chimel* "provides a sound, workable rule for determining the constitutionality of a warrantless search incident to arrest." "Unlike the Court's rule," Brennan chided, "it would be faithful to the Fourth Amendment."

Finally, in his own footnote, Brennan ridiculed the majority's claim that all warrantless police searches would be invalid under the analysis employed by the New York Court of Appeals. The majority had set up a "strawman," or a false danger, with such rhetoric. Quoting *Chimel* and *United States v. Chadwick* (1977), Brennan complained that the High Court had chosen to ignore its own case precedent that gave the term "exclusive control" a clear definition: "sufficient control such that there is not significant risk that the arrestee or his confederates might gain possession of a weapon or destructible evidence."

In a shorter dissenting opinion also joined by Justice Marshall, Justice White called the ruling "an extreme extension of *Chimel* and one to which I cannot subscribe." The Court had ignored its own Fourth Amendment jurisprudence, said Justice White, and "[t]his calls for more caution than the Court today exhibits."

Impact

The decision in *Belton* increased the police authority to conduct warrantless searches of automobiles incident to an on-the-spot arrest. Prior to the ruling, it was unclear how extensively a police officer could search the vehicle of an arrested motorist or arrested passenger. The ruling did not specifically define everything associated with warrantless searches of vehicles incident to arrest, but it clearly gave police officers in the field more breathing room. The Supreme Court finally brought its basic analysis on the issue to a conclusion in *California v. Acevedo* (1991), where the Court held that police may search an automobile and all the containers within the automobile if the search is supported by probable cause to believe that contraband or evidence of a crime is contained therein.

Related Cases

Draper v. United States, 358 U.S. 307 (1959).
Chimel v. California, 395 U.S. 752 (1969).
United States v. Robinson, 414 U.S. 218 (1973).
United States v. Chadwick, 433 U.S. 1 (1977).
California v. Acevedo, 500 U.S. 565 (1991).

Bibliography and Further Reading

Schwartz, Herman, ed. *The Burger Years: Rights and Wrongs In the Supreme Court, 1969-1986.* Nation Enterprises, 1987.

WASHINGTON V. CHRISMAN

Legal Citation: 455 U.S. 1 (1982)

Petitioner
State of Washington

Respondent
Chrisman

Petitioner's Claim
That evidence seized during a warrantless search of the respondent's dormitory room was legally obtained and admissible in court.

Chief Lawyer for Petitioner
Ronald R. Carpenter

Chief Lawyer for Respondent
Robert F. Patrick

Justices for the Court
Harry A. Blackmun, Warren E. Burger (writing for the Court), Sandra Day O'Connor, Lewis F. Powell, Jr., William H. Rehnquist, John Paul Stevens

Justices Dissenting
William J. Brennan, Jr., Thurgood Marshall, Byron R. White

Place
Washington, D.C.

Date of Decision
13 January 1982

Decision
Upheld the state of Washington and overturned the verdict of the Washington Court of Appeals, holding that the warrantless search of the respondent's dormitory room did not violate his Fourth Amendment right to protection against unreasonable search and seizure, and that the evidence obtained in that search was legally admissible.

Significance
The ruling represents an early example of the Court's willingness to interpret the Fourth Amendment in such a way as to allow great discretion on the part of law enforcement authorities in conducting searches, particularly in cases involving the use of, or trafficking in, illegal substances. In *Washington v. Chrisman*, the Court interpreted the so-called "plain view rule" broadly and allowed police officers to presume that every arrest presents a risk to the arresting officer, thus freeing police officers from "reviewing courts' after-the-fact assessment of the particular arrest situation."

Call for Action

In the 1970s and 1980s public concern over the use of, and traffic in, illegal drugs rose to new levels. With drug use among youth at all time highs during the late 1970s, popular opinion demanded that some action be taken by authorities to curb the illegal drug trade. The Supreme Court was not immune to such public pressure, embarking on a consistent trend toward interpreting Fourth Amendment prohibitions against unreasonable search and seizure in such a way as to allow maximum freedom of action among law enforcement officers investigating drug cases.

A Bad Time for a Party

On the night of 1 January 1978 Washington State University student Carl Overdahl left his dormitory building carrying a half-gallon bottle of gin in plain view. His timing and his judgement were seriously flawed, given that his university prohibited the possession of alcohol on campus, and that his movements were being observed by Officer Daugherty of the university's police department. Daugherty immediately approached Overdahl and asked him to present his identification. When Overdahl responded that he would have to return to his dorm room to retrieve it, Daugherty informed him that he could go get it, but that Daugherty would have to accompany him. The two men then proceeded to Overdahl's room, which was located on the eleventh floor of the dormitory building. Upon reaching his room, Overdahl entered and began searching for his identification. Overdahl's roommate, respondent Chrisman, was in the room. While he waited, Daugherty stood in the room's doorway and glanced inside. Daugherty spotted what he believed to be marijuana seeds and a pipe sitting in plain view in Overdahl's room, and entered the room to confirm his suspicions. Daugherty was immediately satisfied that he had discovered illegal drugs on the premises, and informed Overdahl and Chrisman of their rights as criminal suspects under *Miranda v. Arizona* (1966).

Daugherty then informed the suspects that he intended to search their room, and that, although they had a right to demand that he obtain a warrant to do so, they could also voluntarily allow the search to com-

---

Increased Sentencing for Drug Offenders?

With its five- and ten-year minimum sentences, the Anti-Drug Abuse Act of 1986 is a leading example of the stiff sentencing for drug offenders that became the norm during the 1980s. In 1979, New York became the first state to pass a law authorizing mandatory sentencing for drug offenders.

Nearly two decades later, however, New York and other states began to roll back the most stringent of their anti-drug measures. An example of the reason why is the case of Thomas Eddy, one of the first New Yorkers sentenced under the new laws in 1979. A National Merit Scholar attending the State University of New York at Binghamton, he was arrested for selling two ounces of cocaine. He expected to receive a

few years in jail; instead, his sentence was fifteen years to life.

Not only have minor offenders such as Eddy received disproportionate punishments, but often the stiff penalties have evaded powerful drug kingpins who can trade information for reduced sentences. Prison overcrowding and other issues—not the least of which is the fact that the mandatory sentences have not significantly reduced the rate of drug-related crimes—have led Michigan, Connecticut, Oklahoma, Arizona, and a dozen other states to reconsider their minimum-sentencing guidelines.

Source(s): Marks, Alexandra. "Rolling Back Stiff Drug Sentences." *Christian Science Monitor*, 8 December 1998.

---

mence forthwith. Overdahl and Chrisman elected to allow Daugherty to proceed with his search, which uncovered three small bags of marijuana, $112 in cash, and some lysergic acid diethylamide (LSD), another controlled substance.

Legal Proceedings

Chrisman was charged with possession of more that 40 grams of marijuana and possession of LSD, both felonies under Washington state law. He entered a pretrial motion to suppress the evidence obtained by Daugherty's warrantless search. Chrisman maintained that, since Daugherty had no reasonable suspicion that Overdahl would attempt to escape or destroy evidence while searching for his identification, his entrance into the dorm room violated Chrisman's Fourth Amendment right to freedom from unreasonable search and seizure. This motion was denied and Chrisman was convicted on both counts. He appealed the case to the Washington Court of Appeals, which affirmed the legality of Daugherty's search. Upon further appeal to the Washington State Supreme Court, however, Chrisman met with success. The state supreme court ruled that, because Daugherty's visual scanning of the dorm room was not triggered by "exigent circumstances," his spotting of the marijuana seeds represented an unreasonable search, and all evidence obtained by this spotting and subsequent searches was legally inadmissible. The ruling was not unanimous, however. Three justices maintained that it was reasonable for a police officer to keep an arrested person in sight at all times and that on this basis Daugherty was justified in looking into the room, and, having spotted illegal drugs, taking his subsequent actions. Given the implications of this case for future law enforcement actions against the trade in

illegal drugs, the Supreme Court took the case on *certiorari* and heard arguments on 3 November 1981.

The Plain View Rule

On 13 January 1982 the Supreme Court reversed the verdict of the Washington State Supreme Court, finding by a margin of 6-3 that Daugherty's search was reasonable and the evidence he obtained legally admissible. Justice Burger, writing for the majority, noted two main issues in the case.

First, the Court determined that it was reasonable under the Fourth Amendment for a police officer to monitor the movements of an arrested person. Citing *Pennsylvania v. Mimms* (1977) and *United States v. Robinson* (1972), the Court noted that the "absence of affirmative indication that an arrested person might have a weapon available or might attempt to escape does not diminish the arresting officer's authority to maintain custody over the arrested person." In so finding they validated Daugherty's having kept Overdahl in his sight at all times, and thereby also validated Daugherty's having found the marijuana seeds and pipe under the plain view rule. This rule, established in the cases of *Coolidge v. New Hampshire* (1971) and *Harris v. United States*, (1968), states that authorities may seize evidence that is in plain view when evidence is discovered in a place where authorities have a constitutional right to be without a warrant.

Having found Daugherty's initial search and seizure to be constitutionally valid under the Fourth Amendment, the Court turned to the issue of the other contraband found in the more thorough search agreed to by the respondent. The Court ruled, once again, that Daugherty had not violated the respondent's constitutional rights with his second search. Because he had informed the respondent and Overdahl of their rights as suspects per *Miranda,* and had also informed them of their right to refuse an immediate search and demand a search warrant before further searching could occur, Chrisman and Overdahl's voluntary submission to a second search was constitutionally valid.

Impact

Washington v. Chrisman marks an early example of the Court's tendency throughout the 1980s and 1990s to interpret the Fourth Amendment in such a way as to allow maximum freedom of action for law enforcement personnel investigating the use of, and trafficking in, illegal drugs. The implications of the Court's decision are plain for law enforcement officers who now may:

accompany an arrested person to a location of that person's choosing; demand to take an arrested person to some place where that person may be keeping their identification; look around for evidence in plain view at whatever location the arrested person takes them.

Related Cases

Miranda v. Arizona, 384 U.S. 346 (1966).
Katz v. United States, 389 U.S. 347 (1967).
Harris v. United States, 390 U.S. 234 (1968).
Coolidge v. New Hampshire, 403 U.S. 443 (1971).
United States v. Robinson, 414 U.S. 218 (1973).

Bibliography and Further Reading

Strickland, Ralph P. Jr., North Carolina Justice Academy. http://www.state.nc.us/Justice/NCJA/legap94.html

UNITED STATES V. ROSS

Legal Citation: 456 U.S. 798 (1982)

Petitioner
United States

Respondent
Albert Ross, Jr.

Petitioner's Claim
That police officers, who had properly stopped an automobile and who had probable cause to believe that there were illegal substances in the car, did not violate the Constitution by searching a container in the car without first obtaining a search warrant.

Chief Lawyer for Petitioner
Andrew L. Frey

Chief Lawyer for Respondent
William J. Gerber

Justices for the Court
Harry A. Blackmun, Warren E. Burger, Sandra Day O'Connor, Lewis F. Powell, Jr., William H. Rehnquist, John Paul Stevens (writing for the Court)

Justices Dissenting
William J. Brennan, Jr., Thurgood Marshall, Byron R. White

Place
Washington, D.C.

Date of Decision
1 June 1982

Decision
That when the police properly stop and search an automobile, the police may search any container within the automobile which could hold the illegal substance which is the subject of the search.

Significance
The Court's decision was the first in a series of decisions which led to broad powers on the part of the police to search closed containers in automobiles without first obtaining a search warrant.

The Fourth Amendment to the Constitution provides that the government may not subject a person to an unreasonable search or seizure of their "persons, houses, papers, and effects." Generally, to be reasonable, a search must be based on "probable cause," that is, the police officers must have some reason to believe that the search will find contraband, evidence of a crime, or similar items. Also, prior to conducting a search, the police generally have to obtain a warrant from a judge authorizing the search. In certain situations, however, the Supreme Court had determined that the police do not need to obtain a warrant to conduct a search supported by probable cause. These situations, referred to as exceptions to the warrant requirement, typically involve scenarios where the police do not have time to obtain a warrant, or where obtaining a warrant would be useless. Thus, for example, the police may search a person for weapons upon arresting the person.

One such exception to the warrant requirement is the search of an automobile. In a 1925 case, *Carroll v. United States,* the Supreme Court held that the police may search an automobile without first obtaining a warrant because an automobile may be quickly moved while the warrant is sought. In later cases, the Court has also justified such searches on the basis that people do not have an expectation of privacy in their cars because they are designed to travel on public streets and are subject to public scrutiny. However, the Supreme Court had not, through much of the 1960s and 1970s, been clear on whether the police may also search closed containers within the car. In previous cases, the Court held that where the intention of the police was to search the container itself and not the car, and where the police had the opportunity to seize the container before it was put into the car, the police must obtain a warrant before searching the container. The Court also suggested that the police are always required to obtain a warrant before searching a container in a car.

On 27 November 1978, Albert Ross was pulled-over in his automobile by Washington, D.C. police officers. Based on information obtained from an informant, the police believed Ross to be in possession of heroin. The police stopped Ross and searched the vehicle. In the trunk, an officer discovered a closed brown paper bag and a zippered leather pouch. The officer opened both and found heroin in the paper bag and $3,200 in cash in the leather pouch. Ross was arrested and placed on trial for possession of a narcotic.

At his trial, Ross asked the trial court to prevent the prosecution from introducing the evidence seized by the police. Ross claimed that the police should have obtained a search warrant before opening the paper bag and leather pouch. The trial court disagreed, and Ross was convicted. However, Ross appealed to the U.S. Court of Appeals, which agreed with his argument and reversed his conviction. The prosecution then appealed to the Supreme Court, which agreed with the original decision of the trial court and reinstated Ross' conviction. The Court concluded that, when the police rightfully conduct a warrantless search of an automobile, the police may search anywhere in the car, including separate containers, in which the item for which the police are searching may be stored: "If probable cause justifies the search of a lawfully stopped vehicle, it justifies the search of every part of the vehicle and its contents that may conceal the object of the search." Thus, for example, the police would not be justified in opening a paper bag which was too small to hold the item being searched for. However, because the paper bag in Ross' car was capable of holding the heroin for which the police were searching, the search of the bag and leather pouch were proper.

Three justices, Marshall, Brennan, and White, disagreed with the Court's decision. These justices thought that the reasons the Court has allowed warrantless searches of automobiles did not apply to containers within automobiles. Justice Marshall, writing for the dissenters, concluded that "the traditional rationales for the automobile exception plainly do not support extending it to the search of a container found inside a vehicle." For example, although automobiles are mobile and may be driven away while the police try to obtain a warrant, there is no similar problem with a container seized by the police and kept in the possession of the police. Also, although people may have less of an expectation of privacy in their cars, they still expect that closed containers in their cars,

such as purses and briefcases, will provide some level of privacy.

The *Ross* decision had a significant impact on the power of police officers to search containers inside of automobiles without having to first obtain a warrant. The decision itself provided two separate rules for such containers. Under *Ross*, a container that coincidentally happens to be in a car subject to a warrantless search may itself be searched without a warrant. However, under the Court's previous decisions, if the police seek to search the container itself, the mere fact that it is placed in the automobile does not allow the police to search the container without first obtaining a warrant. In *California v. Acevedo*, a 1991 decision also involving the search of a paper bag stored in a car's trunk, the Court abolished this distinction and ruled, relying on its decision in *Ross*, that whenever the police have probable cause to believe evidence or illegal items are in an automobile, whether or not in a container, the police may conduct a search without obtaining a search warrant. Thus *Ross* has had a profound impact on the power of police to search automobiles without first obtaining a search warrant.

Related Cases
Carroll v. United States, 267 U.S. 132 (1925).
Katz v. United States, 389 U.S. 347 (1967).
Mincey v. Arizona, 437 U.S. 385 (1978).
California v. Acevedo, 500 U.S. 565 (1991).

Bibliography and Further Reading
Dressler, Joshua. *Understanding Criminal Procedure*. New York: Matthew Bender & Company, 1991.

LaFave, Wayne R. *Search and Seizure: A Treatise on the Fourth Amendment*, 3rd edition, Volume 2. St. Paul, MN: West Publishing Co., 1996.

Marcus, Ruth. "Supreme Court Permits Warrantless Car Search; Ruling Addresses Longtime Legal Problem." *Washington Post*, May 31, 1991, p. A8.

Shepard, Catherine A. "Search and Seizure: From *Carroll* to *Ross*, the Odyssey of the Automobile Exception." *Catholic University Law Review*, Vol. 32, fall 1982, pp. 221-60.

HORTON V. GOOSE CREEK INDEPENDENT SCHOOL DISTRICT

Legal Citation: 693 F.2d 524 (1982)

Appellants
Robert Horton, Heather Horton, Sandra Sanchez, on their own behalf and on behalf of all other students in the Goose Creek School District

Appellee
Goose Creek Independent School District

Appellants' Claim
That drug-sniffing dogs violated the students' Fourth Amendment rights.

Chief Lawyers for Appellants
Arthur Val Perkins, Stefan Presser

Chief Lawyer for Appellee
Richard A. Peebles

Judges
John M. Wisdom, Carolyn Dineen Randall, Albert Tate, Jr.

Place
U.S. Court of Appeals, Fifth Circuit, New Orleans, Louisiana

Date of Decision
14 December 1982

Decision
The dogs could sniff students' cars and lockers, but could not sniff the students themselves for drugs.

Significance
Searches conducted of students by school officials made without a reasonable suspicion were unconstitutional.

School officials and teachers have a duty to ensure that their students are safe and in an atmosphere conducive to learning. Increasingly, however, school officials find that these two goals are difficult to carry out. Students in schools across the nation have been known to bring alcohol, drugs, and even guns into schools, which threaten not only the learning environment, but also the safety of everyone within the school. School officials need to balance their desire to maintain a healthy and safe environment, however, with the fact that students are protected by the Constitution. As ruled in *Tinker v. Des Moines Independent Community School District* (1969), students do not "shed their constitutional rights . . . at the schoolhouse gate."

In *Horton v. Goose Creek Independent School District*, the efforts of school officials to maintain a healthy and safe learning environment, against the backdrop of drug and alcohol abuse, were weighed against the students' constitutional rights. The decision of the Fifth Circuit Court of Appeals illustrates that the students' Fourth Amendment rights could not be violated simply because they were on school property, despite the sympathy the court showed for school officials trying to deal with a growing alcohol and drug problem.

In 1978 the Goose Creek Independent School District in Texas brought in drug-sniffing dogs in an attempt to deal with a rampant drug and alcohol problem. The dogs were trained to detect more than 60 different controlled and over-the-counter substances. On an unannounced and random basis, dogs were taken to all of the schools in the district to sniff the students' lockers and cars and were brought into the classrooms to sniff the students themselves. If a dog indicated that a car or locker had an illegal substance, the student was required to open the locker or vehicle for a search. If the dog indicated a student was carrying an illegal substance, he or she was brought into the school office to be searched.

Three students, Robby Horton, Heather Horton, and Sandra Sanchez, speaking for all of the students, sued the school district. They claimed that the dog searches violated their Fourth Amendment rights to be free from illegal searches and seizures, as well as their Fourteenth

Search and Seizure in the Schools

Fourth Amendment requirements differ, depending on whether the place in which a search and seizure occurs is a private or a public locale. And within public venues, schools present a special situation, in part because both law and judicial practice tend to grant lesser rights (but also a lesser degree of culpability) to minors.

A pivotal case in the development of law regarding school search and seizure is *New Jersey v. T.L.O.* (1985), in which a unanimous Supreme Court applied the Fourth Amendment prohibition against unreasonable search and seizure to public schools. But in the same case, a 6-3 majority held that probable cause is not needed to justify, or a search warrant to legalize, a search of a student by a school authority. Rather than probable cause, Justice White established a two-pronged test of "reasonableness" as a basis for searches.

Thus under *T.L.O.*, the legality of school locker searches is predicated on the student's expectation of privacy. Searches of vehicles in the school parking lot are not considered unreasonable, and the California Attorney General in 1992 likewise applied the reasonableness standard to justify the placement of metal detectors as part of a generalized search for weapons.

Source(s): "School Searches of Students and Seizures of Their Property." http://eric-web.tc. columbia.edu.

Amendment rights that assured they would not be deprived of their liberty and property without due process.

All three of the students had been subjected to searches and claimed that they were disruptive and embarrassing. For example, Heather Horton described what happened when a dog entered her classroom to sniff for drugs and alcohol:

> Well, we were in the middle of a major French exam and the dog came in and walked up and down the aisles and stopped at every desk and sniffed on each side all around the people, the feet, the parts where you keep your books under the desk.

Horton described her fear of large dogs and how it interrupted her concentration for her test. Although the dog did not indicate that Heather Horton was carrying any illegal substances, the dogs did react to both Sandra Sanchez and Robby Horton. School officials searched Sanchez's purse without her consent and searched Horton's pockets, socks, and pant legs. No illegal substances were found on either person, and they were deeply embarrassed by the search.

Initially, the case was decided in favor of the school district. The case was appealed, however, to the Fifth Circuit Court of Appeals. With the facts of the case laid out before them, the court divided their decision into two parts. First, they would decide whether the dogs could sniff the students' cars and lockers for drugs, and second, whether they could sniff the students themselves. The judges would decide whether either of these actions violated the students' Fourth Amendment rights—the right to be free from unreasonable searches.

The court ruled that the dogs could sniff the students' lockers and cars without violating their Fourth Amendment rights. Because the lockers and cars were unattended and in public view, the court ruled that it was not a search to have the dogs sniff these objects. If the dogs were not conducting a technical search, the students could not possibly have their Fourth Amendment rights broken.

The court ruled, however, that the dogs could not sniff the students. First, the judges found that the dogs "sniffing around each child, putting his nose *on* the child and scratching and manifesting other signs of excitement in the case of an alert—is intrusive." Because the dogs intruded on the students' bodies, the judges ruled that the case was a search according to the Fourth Amendment.

Second, the judges found that not only was it a search to have the dogs sniff the students, but it was also unreasonable. The officials conducting the search did not have any individual suspicion that a particular student was carrying drugs or alcohol. As such, it was unreasonable to search all of the students and subject them to an intrusive, and even offensive experience, with no cause.

In the case of *Horton v. Goose Creek Independent School District* the court upheld the constitutional rights of the students. But in the years that followed many decisions were made in favor of school officials. As in the case of *Smith v. McGlothilin* (1997), a vice principal made a group of students caught smoking on school grounds empty their pockets and purses. When the search of one girl yielded three knives, she was turned over to the police. Ultimately the actions of the vice principal were upheld. Clearly, when administrators are able to substantiate a "reasonable suspicion" and keep the scope of the search limited, courts rule in favor of the schools.

Related Cases

Tinker v. Des Moines Independent Community School District, 393 U.S. 503 (1969).

New Jersey v. T.L.O., 469 U.S. 325 (1985).

Arizona v. Hicks, 480 U.S. 321 (1987).

Veronia School District 47J v. Acton, 515 U.S. 646 (1995).

Smith v. McGlothlin, 119 F.3d 788 (1997).

Bibliography and Further Reading

Delahoyde, Patricia Lenore. "Drug Use in Schools." *Journal of Juvenile Law,* Vol. 7, no. 2, 1983, pp. 222-226.

O'Connell, Tom. "*Horton v. Goose Creek Independent School District*: Canine Searches at the School." *South Texas Law Journal,* Vol. 24, no. 3, pp. 931-938.

"Public Schools, Canine Sniffing." *ABA Journal,* Vol. 68, October 1982, p. 1311.

Trosch, Louis A., Robert G. Williams, and Fred W. Devore III. "Public Searches and the Fourth Amendment." *Journal of Law and Education,* Vol. 11, no. 1, January 1982, pp. 41-63.

FLORIDA V. ROYER

Legal Citation: 460 U.S. 491 (1983)

Petitioner
State of Florida

Respondent
Mark Royer

Petitioner's Claim
Dade County detectives did not violate Royer's Fourth Amendment rights when they detained him in an airport and opened his luggage to find illegal drugs.

Chief Lawyer for Petitioner
Calvin L. Fox

Chief Lawyer for Respondent
Theodore Klein

Justices for the Court
William J. Brennan, Jr., Thurgood Marshall, Lewis F. Powell, Jr., John Paul Stevens, Byron R. White (writing for the Court)

Justices Dissenting
Harry A. Blackmun, Warren E. Burger, Sandra Day O'Connor, William H. Rehnquist

Place
Washington, D.C.

Date of Decision
23 March 1983

Decision
The detectives violated Royer's Fourth Amendment rights by exceeding the legal limits of the encounter.

Significance
The *Royer* decision approved of a police stop but disapproved of the detention that followed, reinforcing the concept that there are limits to the things that police officers can do when they stop a person based on a level of belief that does not rise to the level of probable cause.

Mark Royer was in the Miami International Airport on 3 January 1978, preparing to take a flight to New York City. To plain clothes detectives of the Dade County, Florida, Public Safety Department, Royer's appearance, luggage, and actions fit the profile of a drug courier. Specifically, Royer was young, casually dressed, seemed pale and nervous, looked around at other people, paid for his ticket with a large number of bills, failed to complete his luggage identification tag, and used luggage that appeared to be heavy.

The detectives approached Royer and asked if he had a "'moment'" to speak with them. Royer responded "'Yes.'" The detectives asked for Royer's driver's license and his airline ticket, and Royer, without giving his oral consent, handed them over. The airline ticket, like Royer's luggage tickets, bore the name "Holt." When he was questioned about the discrepancy, Royer responded that a friend had made the reservation for him. Royer became nervous, and the detectives informed him that they were investigating illegal drug violations and that they had reason to believe that Royer was transporting illegal drugs.

The detectives retained possession of Royer's airline ticket and identification and asked Royer to accompany them to a small room adjacent to the concourse. Saying nothing, Royer went with the detectives. One of the detectives retrieved Royer's luggage and brought it to the room without asking for Royer's consent. The detectives asked Royer if they could open the suitcases and search inside, and Royer, again without verbally responding, handed the detectives a key. Without asking for Royer's consent, a detective tried the key on one of the suitcases and opened it and found marijuana. The second suitcase, fastened by a combination lock and opened with a screwdriver, yielded more marijuana. While he had not given his oral consent, Royer also had not verbally objected to the uncovering of 65 pounds of marijuana in his possession. Later, Royer would testify that he did not object because "'[t]hey were police officers'" and he "'thought [he] had to.'"

Royer was charged with felony possession of marijuana in Florida state court. At trial, he moved the court to suppress, or exclude, the marijuana evidence because it was obtained in violation of his Fourth Amendment rights. The trial court denied the motion, ruling that Royer had consented to the search. Royer changed his not guilty plea to a no contest plea, reserving the right to appeal the court's ruling on the suppression motion. On appeal, the district court of appeal first affirmed, and then, after a hearing, reversed the decision. According to the appeals court, because Royer had been confined involuntarily without probable cause and because the detention had gone beyond the boundaries established by the Supreme Court's decision in *Terry v. Ohio* for such detentions, and any consent given by Royer was invalid. The encounter was like an arrest, explained the appeals court, and Royer was justified in his belief that he was not free to leave. Such a detention can only be justified by the presence of probable cause to believe that Royer was guilty of a crime, and the detectives did not have enough evidence to support that.

The state of Florida appealed to the U.S. Supreme Court, which voted to affirm the appeals court's ruling by a narrow 5-4 margin. Justice White, writing for the plurality, began the opinion by observing the general rules that guided the case. Under the Fourth Amendment to the U.S. Constitution and the Court's prior case law, a police officer had to have probable cause to believe that a person had committed a crime before the officer could seize the person. One exception to this rule, under the Court's decision in *Terry v. Ohio,* was the temporary detention of a criminal suspect. If a police officer had a reasonable, articulable suspicion that a person was guilty of a crime or was about to commit a crime, the officer could stop the person and briefly detain the person for questioning and perform a limited pat-down search for weapons.

The plurality listed six "observations" about Fourth Amendment jurisprudence that guided the case. "[I]f the events in this case amounted to no more than a permissible police encounter in a public place or a justifiable *Terry*-type detention," the Court surmised, "Royer's consent, if voluntary, would have been effective to legalize the search of his two suitcases." The appeals court had concluded that Royer's consent was tainted by the illegality of the detention, and so the question was "whether the record warrant[ed] that conclusion."

The state of Florida had argued that Royer was not detained. In the state's view, the entire encounter was consensual, so there was no detention of Royer. Even if the encounter was not consensual, the state maintained, the police had a reasonable, articulable suspicion that Royer was transporting drugs, and this belief justified the detention. Furthermore, claimed the state, the police had probable cause to arrest Royer, and so he was not being illegally held. To the High Court, the argument that the encounter was consensual was "untenable" because the detectives used "a show of

authority" that would have made a reasonable person feel detained.

The Court gave more attention to the argument that the police officers had reasonable suspicion to stop Royer. They conceded that the officers had reasonable suspicion, but believed that "at the time Royer produced the key to his suitcase, the detention to which he was then subjected was a more serious intrusion on his personal liberty than is allowable on mere suspicion of criminal activity." What may have been a permissible stop at first "escalated into an investigatory procedure in a police interrogation room, where the police, unsatisfied with previous explanations, sought to confirm their suspicions . . . [a]s a practical matter, Royer was under arrest." Moreover, the actions of the detectives were too intrusive to qualify as a limited *Terry* stop. The detectives did not return Royer's driver's license and ticket, they removed him from the immediate area, and the detectives may have been able to "investigate the contents of Royer's bags in a more expeditious way." The plurality mentioned the use of trained dogs as a less intrusive alternative to the kind of methods employed by the detectives.

To justify Royer's arrest, the police had to have probable cause, a standard of belief that is stronger than reasonable suspicion and requires more supporting information. The state of Florida argued that the police had enough information to support probable cause, but the Court disagreed. The Court could not agree that "every nervous young man paying cash for a ticket to New York City under an assumed name and carrying two heavy bags may be arrested and held to answer for a serious felony charge." Ultimately, the Court affirmed the appeals court's decision and the prosecution of Royer was over.

Justice Powell wrote a concurring opinion to emphasize that despite the Court's holding, "the public has a compelling interest in identifying by all lawful means those who traffic in illicit drugs for personal profit." However, in Royer's case, the actions of the detectives went beyond lawful means. Powell noted that Royer "found himself in a small, windowless room—described as a "'large closet'"—alone with two officers who, without his consent, already had obtained possession of his checked baggage." Royer clearly was not free to leave and, in Powell's opinion, Royer's surrender of the luggage key could not be seen as consensual.

Justice Brennan concurred in the result of the case, but he felt that the plurality had decided more issues than was necessary. The plurality did not have to hold that the stop of Royer was legal; it could have merely affirmed the ruling of the appeals court on the basis that the stop exceeded the bounds of such a stop delineated in *Terry*. Brennan believed that the stop itself was illegal because the detectives did not have enough information to support a reasonable suspicion that

Royer was committing a crime. The observations made by the detectives (Royer was young, nervous, pale, paid with cash, looked around at other people, and used heavy luggage) were "perfectly consistent with innocent behavior and [could not] possibly give rise to any inference supporting a reasonable suspicion of criminal activity." Brennan admitted that "traffic in illicit drugs is a matter of pressing national concern," but he warned that the nation's "zeal for effective law enforcement" should not obscure "the peril to our free society that lies in this Court's disregard of the protections afforded by the Fourth Amendment."

Chief Justice Burger and Justices Blackmun, Rehnquist, and O'Connor dissented. In his own dissenting opinion, Justice Blackmun expressed his view that, in light of the threats posed by illegal drug traffic, the actions of the police officers were reasonable and therefore not violative of the Fourth Amendment. Justice Rehnquist, joined by Chief Justice Burger and Justice O'Connor, offered a more pointed dissent. "The plurality's meandering opinion," Rehnquist wrote, "contains in it a little something for everyone." Although much of its opinion indicated that it was not indifferent to the dangers of drug trafficking, the plurality managed to affirm the reversal of conviction, all of which reminded Rehnquist of an old nursery rhyme: "'The King of France/With forty thousand men/Marched up the hill/And then marched back again.'" Rehnquist compared the plurality's "mind-set" to that of shuffleboard officials, more "concerned with which particular square the disc has landed on" than administering criminal justice.

Rehnquist mocked the plurality's assessment of the detectives' conduct. The plurality had mentioned that Royer was kept in a small room with two chairs; this left Rehnquist wondering whether the encounter would have been constitutional if the detectives had searched the luggage in the busy concourse, or "[i]f the room had been large and spacious, rather than small, if it had possessed three chairs rather than two." Rehnquist compared the plurality's vague opinion to an Impressionist painting, and insisted that the Court's holding was foreclosed by the Court's decision in *United States v. Mendenhall*. In that case, the Court had upheld the stop, detention, and strip search of a woman who was suspected of possessing drugs. The search of the woman in *Mendenhall* had been upheld on the basis that the woman had consented to the search. Rehnquist believed that Royer, who went on to gain a college degree in communications, also had consented, and that the detectives had done nothing to warrant invalidation of that consent.

Impact

Although the *Royer* case has not been reversed, subsequent decisions by the Court have eroded its importance. In 1991, for example, the Court upheld the warrantless, random stop and search of bus passengers for drugs. In 1996, Justice Rehnquist enjoyed some vindication for his dissent in *Royer* from the Court's decision in *Ohio v. Robinette*. In that case, the Court held that a police officer's subjective intentions have no bearing on the legality of a continuing detention, and that a police officer need not advise a detained person that he or she is free to go before the person's consent to a search will be deemed voluntary.

Related Cases

Terry v. Ohio, 392 U.S. 1 (1968).
United States v. Mendenhall, 446 U.S. 544 (1980).
Florida v. Bostick, 501 U.S. 429 (1991).
Ohio v. Robinette, 519 U.S. 33 (1996).

Bibliography and Further Reading

Choi, Jin S., and Ernest Kim. "The Constitutional Status of Photo Stops: The Implications of *Terry* and Its Progeny." *Asian Pacific American Law Journal*, fall 1994.

Owens, John B., "Judge Baer and the Politics of the Fourth Amendment: An Alternative to Bad Man Jurisprudence." *Stanford Law & Policy Review*, winter 1997.

KOLENDER V. LAWSON

Legal Citation: 461 U.S. 352 (1983)

Petitioner
William Kolender, et al.

Respondent
Edward Lawson

Petitioner's Claim
It is not a violation of constitutional due process rights to require that persons who loiter or wander on the streets account for their presence and provide a "credible and reliable" identification when requested by a police officer.

Chief Lawyer for Petitioner
A. Wells Petersen

Chief Lawyer for Respondent
Mark D. Rosenbaum

Justices for the Court
Harry A. Blackmun, William J. Brennan, Jr., Warren E. Burger, Thurgood Marshall, Sandra Day O'Connor (writing for the Court), Lewis F. Powell, Jr., John Paul Stevens

Justices Dissenting
William H. Rehnquist, Byron R. White

Place
Washington, D.C.

Date of Decision
2 May 1983

Decision
The California statute requiring persons to produce identification and explain their presence on the street is unconstitutional under the Fourteenth Amendment due process clause.

Significance
The decision surprised legal observers because it demanded greater specificity in the language of a loitering statute than it had required in the language of other criminal statutes in prior cases.

Edward Lawson, a self-described "walker by temperament," was arrested or detained by police approximately 15 times between March of 1975 and January of 1977 for violating a California disorderly conduct statute. The statute made it a crime—disorderly conduct—for a person to loiter on the street and refuse to identify himself and provide an account for his presence to a police officer "if the surrounding circumstances are such as to indicate to a reasonable man that the public safety demands such identification." After being prosecuted twice and convicted once, Lawson brought a civil suit in a California federal court seeking a judgment from the court declaring the statute unconstitutional and an injunction to keep law enforcement from enforcing the statute. Lawson also sought damages from the various police officers who detained him.

The district court held for Lawson, but refused to award any damages. Both Lawson and the defendants appealed to the U.S. Court of Appeals for the Ninth Circuit. The appeals court affirmed the holding in favor of Lawson and reversed the ruling on the damages and sent the case back to the trial court for a jury trial. According to the appeals court, the statute was unconstitutional under the Fourth Amendment's prohibition of unreasonable searches and seizures, the statute contained an unconstitutionally vague enforcement standard that could lead to arbitrary enforcement by police, and it failed to give persons fair and adequate notice of the kind of conduct that was prohibited by the statute. The police officers, through the state of California, appealed the ruling on the constitutionality of the statute and the injunction against the statute's enforcement to the U.S. Supreme Court.

By a vote of 7-2, the High Court upheld the ruling. In analyzing Lawson's claim, the Court, quoting legal analyst M. Cherif Bassiouni, pronounced that the U.S. Constitution was "designed to maximize individual freedoms within a framework of ordered liberty." Courts had to look at statutes to make sure that both the form and substance of the statutory limitations on individual freedoms did not violate the Constitution. Lawson had claimed that the statute was facially invalid under the Due Process Clause of the Fourteenth Amendment because it was too vague. This caused the Court to look at the "void-for-vagueness" doctrine, which, according to prior case law, required that a criminal statute define the criminal offense "with sufficient definiteness" so that ordinary people and law enforcement personnel would know what conduct was proscribed or mandated. Furthermore, in passing a criminal statute, a legislature had to create "'minimal guidelines'" to govern police officers and prevent police sweeps that allow "'policemen, prosecutors, and juries to pursue their personal predilections.'"

The loitering provision in the California disorderly conduct statute, observed the Court, contained "no standard for determining what a suspect ha[d] to do in order to satisfy the requirement to provide a 'credible and reliable' identification." This being the case, the statute vested too much discretion in police officers to determine whether someone has satisfied the identification and account requirements and is free to walk away in the absence of any probable cause to believe that the person has committed a crime. Even if police officers did not have probable cause to make an arrest, a person was entitled to walk the public streets under California's loitering statute "'only at the whim of any police officer'" who happened to find the person suspicious (*Shuttlesworth v. City of Birmingham* [1965]).

The Court expressed concern about the arbitrary suppression of First Amendment liberties and "the constitutional right to freedom of movement." In the past, the Court had approved of statutes that required persons to stop and identify themselves. In this case, though, the challenged statute required persons to actually carry "'credible and reliable' identification that carries a 'reasonable assurance' of its authenticity, and that provides 'means for later getting in touch with the person who has identified himself.'" Moreover, the suspect also could be required to account for his presence "'to the extent it assists in producing credible and reliable identification.'" If a police officer was not satisfied with the reliability of the identification provided by the suspect, then the suspect was considered in violation the statute and was guilty of misdemeanor disorderly conduct.

To avoid punishment under the loitering statute, the state explained that a person had only to recite his or her name and address to the questioning officer. In the alternative, the person could answer a series of questions about the route the person took to arrive at the point where he or she was detained. The High Court acknowledged that police officers have the right to stop people and ask them questions, and the Court admitted that the initial detention under the statute was justified. However, the state had failed to establish guidelines for the police officers to determine if a suspect had complied with the identification requirement. Quoting *Papachristou v. City of Jacksonville* (1972) and *Thornhill v. Alabama* (1940), the Court considered the

Edward Lawson at the steps of the U.S. Supreme Court, 1982.
© AP/Wide World Photos.

California statute "a convenient tool for 'harsh and discriminatory enforcement by local prosecuting officials, against particular groups deemed to merit their displeasure.'" Ultimately, the High Court held that the statute was unconstitutionally vague because it "encourage[d] arbitrary enforcement by failing to describe with sufficient particularity what a suspect must do in order to satisfy the statute." In a footnote closing the majority opinion, Justice O'Connor noted that the Court had struck down the loitering provision in the statute on the first possible constitutional question; there were several other constitutional questions about the statute with which the Court had not even bothered.

Justice Brennan wrote a lengthy concurring opinion. Brennan agreed with the majority's decision that the statute was unconstitutionally vague. However, he would have gone farther to hold that even if the statute were not unconstitutionally vague, it would be invalid under the Fourth Amendment prohibition against unreasonable searches and seizures. Brennan reminded the Court of the well settled proposition that under Fourth Amendment jurisprudence, a police officer must have probable cause to believe that a person has committed a crime before seizing, detaining, or searching that person. However, there are exceptions to this basic rule. Citing *Terry v. Ohio* (1968) and its progeny, Brennan allowed that, in the context of the seizure of a person, a police officer may stop a person and question that person for a brief period of time and conduct a brief frisk of that person. An officer may do this only when the officer has a reasonable suspicion, based on articulable facts, that criminal activity is afoot.

The stop-and-frisk exception to the requirement of probable cause was, said Brennan, "a powerful tool for the investigation and prevention of crimes." The exception allowed police to do "far more" than "direct[ing] a question to another person in passing." Police officers can have a coercive effect on a person with such devices as "an official 'show of authority,' the use of physical force to restrain him, and a search of the person for weapons." Indeed, Brennan noted, in most of the cases that the Court had seen that dealt with police stops, few people felt "free not to cooperate fully with the police by answering their questions," even when cooperation risked their liberty. Because they intrude on individual interests protected by the Fourth Amendment, such seizures must be "strictly circumscribed, to limit the degree of intrusion they cause." The length of time for the stop must be brief, unless evidence of criminal activity is detected; the suspect must not be moved more than a short distance; physical searches must be a limited pat-down for weapons; and, "most importantly, the suspect must be free to leave after a short time and to decline to answer the questions put to him . . . Should a police officer fail to observe these limitations," Brennan lectured, "the stop becomes an encounter that is justified only if the police officer has probable cause to believe a crime has been committed, as opposed to a mere reasonable belief that criminal activity is afoot."

The intrusion into persons' lives authorized by the loitering statute, Brennan surmised, had not been justified by the state. A pedestrian who asserted his or her Fourth Amendment rights under the statute could look forward to "new acquaintances among jailers, lawyers, prisoners, and bail-bondsmen, first-hand knowledge of local jail conditions, a 'search incident to arrest,' and

the expense of defending against a possible prosecution." Brennan concluded that "[m]ere reasonable suspicion does not justify subjecting the innocent to such a dilemma."

Justice Rehnquist joined a dissenting opinion written by Justice White. The dissenters attacked the majority's application of the void-for-vagueness doctrine, arguing that it had held the state of California's loitering statute to a higher standard of clarity than it had set for other criminal statutes it had examined. The dissenters disagreed with the majority's interpretation of the cases that the majority had cited in support of its holding, and objected to the invalidation of "a statute that is clear in many of its applications but which is somehow distasteful to the majority." The majority's decision, according to the dissent, left California "in a quandary as to how to draft a statute that will pass constitutional muster."

Impact

The *Kolender* decision struck down the California law because it required a person to produce "credible and reliable" identification at the request of a police officer. The net result of this holding was that California simply deleted the provision referring to "credible and reliable identification." California, like other states, retained its disorderly conduct law requiring persons to account for their presence and identify themselves to a police officer whose suspicion is aroused.

Related Cases
Thornhill v. Alabama, 310 U.S. 88 (1940).
Shuttlesworth v. City of Birmingham, 382 U.S. 87 (1965).
Terry v. Ohio, 392 U.S. 1 (1968).
Papachristou v. City of Jacksonville, 405 U.S. 156 (1972).

Bibliography and Further Reading
New York Times, May 3, 1983.

Trosch, William. "The Third Generation of Loitering Laws Goes to Court: Do Laws that Criminalize 'Loitering with the Intent to Sell Drugs' Pass Constitutional Muster?" *North Carolina Law Review*, January 1993.

ILLINOIS V. GATES

Legal Citation: 462 U.S. 213 (1983)

Under the Fourth Amendment to the United States Constitution, citizens are guaranteed certain rights regarding criminal prosecution. The Amendment states, in full, that

> The right of the people to be secure in their persons, houses, papers, and effects, against unreasonable searches and seizures, shall not be violated, and no warrants shall issue, but upon probable cause, supported by Oath of affirmation, and particularly describing the place to be searched, and the persons or things to be seized.

The Exclusionary Rule

Law-enforcement authorities need a valid warrant, or, in legal terms, a judicial writ, to search a citizen's home or person. Such guarantees, enshrined by the Constitution, are considered cornerstones of a free, non-totalitarian society. In some instances, searches and seizures do occur without a proper writ, or have been granted under spurious grounds by judges, but any evidence obtained with such invalid warrants is not admissible in a trial. This is called the "exclusionary rule," for it excludes any evidence of a crime from being presented by prosecutors, no matter how damaging.

In May of 1978, a letter arrived at the police department of Bloomingdale, Illinois. The anonymous writer alleged that Bloomingdale residents Lance and Sue Gates were selling drugs from their home. The letter also provided a date on which the couple would travel to and return from Florida separately in order to ferry another shipment of contraband to their home for resale. Police investigated the Gates and their whereabouts, and confirmed that Lance Gates had flown to Florida and stayed in a motel room registered to his wife. Further inquiries revealed that Gates and an unidentified woman left the motel in a car with license plates registered to Gates, but for a different vehicle. With these details, Bloomingdale police obtained a warrant to search both the Gates residence as well as the car upon its arrival. They found 350 pounds of marijuana in the trunk of the car, and inside the house, more drugs and an unregistered firearm.

Petitioner
State of Illinois

Respondent
Lance Gates

Petitioner's Claim
That evidence obtained via a search warrant that was later declared invalid could still convict.

Chief Lawyer for Petitioner
Paul J. Biebel, Jr., Assistant Attorney General of Illinois

Chief Lawyer for Respondent
James W. Reilley

Justices for the Court
Harry A. Blackmun, Warren E. Burger, Sandra Day O'Connor, Lewis F. Powell, Jr., William H. Rehnquist (writing for the Court), John Paul Stevens, Byron R. White

Justices Dissenting
William J. Brennan, Jr., Thurgood Marshall

Place
Washington, D.C.

Date of Decision
8 June 1983

Decision
Reversed the Illinois Supreme Court's decision that prevented evidence seized from being presented at a criminal trial.

Significance
Provided law-enforcement authorities and prosecutors with a new and less restrictive set of rules to abide by in obtaining search warrants.

Invalid Warrant

Prior to Gates's trial, the respondent filed a motion to suppress the evidence, asserting the warrant that procured it had been obtained without "just cause." In legal terms, an anonymous tip is considered insufficient evidence for granting a search warrant. They were successful in this, and an appellate court upheld this decision suppressing all evidence. The Illinois Supreme Court also upheld the exclusion of evidence. All of these courts used two legal precedents in determining that the Bloomingdale police's search warrant was not valid. In the first, *Aguilar v. Texas* (1964), the courts had ruled that an informant's tip is enough to obtain a warrant if the police can determine the reliability of the source of this knowledge (for example, that the informant was a firsthand witness to it), and if the police can prove the informant's veracity in other areas. The Bloomingdale police's affidavit had neither.

Spinelli v. United States (1969) was another case used by courts to determine if a warrant was valid if it had not passed the requirements set forth in *Aguilar v. Texas*. *Spinelli* holds that there is "probable cause" to grant a warrant if some details provided by the tip are corroborated by police investigation, but if the informant presents evidence that may just be hearsay or rumor, this is not considered trustworthy. This was also a significant factor in barring evidence seized at the Gates home from incriminating them at their trial.

Hints of New Stance on Exclusionary Rule

The U.S. Supreme Court had ruled consistently in matters concerning the exclusionary rule since 1914. Again and again, it confirmed that evidence obtained outside proper legal means could not be used in a criminal trial. Yet by the early 1980s, some conservatives had argued for exceptions to this rule. President Ronald Reagan asserted that the American people had lost faith in the legal system, viewing it as constrained by constitutional loopholes and unable to protect citizens from crime. He urged the granting of greater powers to law enforcement authorities to fight crime.

The State of Illinois asked the High Court to allow the drugs seized to be presented as evidence under a "good-faith" exception to the exclusionary rule. This exception took into account that the officers had acted in "good faith" that a crime had been committed; in other words, they believed they were operating within the law. Liberals, on the other hand, argued that granting a "good-faith" exception to the exclusionary rule would invent two separate realms of the Constitution: one for citizens, who must abide by it, and another for law-enforcement authorities and the state, who were allowed to defy it. In other words, to adopt a good-faith exception to the exclusionary rule would endorse unconstitutional police behavior.

Decision, "With Apologies"

When *Illinois v. Gates* first appeared before the Supreme Court in October of 1982, the state of Illinois had requested that the High Court decide whether "probable cause" was present in the police affidavit that requested the warrant. The Illinois assistant attorney general later requested to enlarge the question to include whether or not such evidence was admissible in court, based on the "reasonable belief" that the search was valid under the Fourth Amendment—even though it was later found not to be. After a few weeks, the Supreme Court motioned to return *Illinois v. Gates* to the docket, and it was re-argued in March of 1983.

On June 8 of that year, the Court issued its decision, with apologies. The good-faith clause had *not* been present in petitions to the lower courts, and the Supreme Court's task was to review the cases as they existed. It did, however, reverse the Illinois Supreme Court ruling barring the evidence against the Gates from trial. Justice Rehnquist's majority decision rejected the Aguilar and Spinelli tests, and asserted that courts should abide by a "totality of circumstances" rule. This holds that a magistrate, presented with a police affidavit and request for warrant, should consider whether or not there is a "fair probability" that evidence of a crime will be found at a specific place, and found that the issuing judge and Bloomingdale police had acted within these precepts. Rehnquist also promised to look into modifying the exclusionary rule in three cases scheduled for the following term. Justices Brennan and Marshall dissented from the majority.

Related Cases

Aguilar v. Texas, 378 U.S. 108 (1964).
Spinelli v. United States, 393 U.S. 410 (1969).
Kolendar v. Lawson, 461 U.S. 352 (1983).

Bibliography and Further Reading

Garbus, Martin. "Excluding Justice." *New York Times*, April 4, 1983, p. 19.

Silverberg, Marshall H. "Anonymous Tips, Corroboration, and Probable Cause: Reconciling the *Spinelli/Draper* Dichotomy in *Illinois v. Gates*." *American Criminal Law Review*, Vol. 20, summer 1982, pp. 99-126.

Welsh, Robert C., and Ronald K. Collins. "A Matter of Evidence." *New York Times*, January 7, 1983, p. 25.

Young, Rowland L. "Exclusionary Rule Stands, But Warrant Requirements Eased." *American Bar Association Journal*, Vol. 69, August 1983, p. 122.

ILLINOIS V. LAFAYETTE

Legal Citation: 462 U.S. 640 (1983)

Petitioner
State of Illinois

Respondent
Ralph Lafayette

Petitioner's Claim
The Fourth Amendment does not prohibit the search of an arrestee's personal knapsack and closed containers contained therein as part of a routine inventory search conducted while as the arrestee is being booked into jail.

Chief Lawyer for Petitioner
Michael A. Ficaro

Chief Lawyer for Respondent
Peter A. Carusona

Justices for the Court
Harry A. Blackmun, William J. Brennan, Jr., Warren E. Burger (writing for the Court), Thurgood Marshall, Sandra Day O'Connor, Lewis F. Powell, Jr., William H. Rehnquist, John Paul Stevens, Byron R. White

Justices Dissenting
None

Place
Washington, D.C.

Date of Decision
20 June 1983

Decision
When an arrestee is being jailed, the Fourth Amendment does not prevent police officers from searching, without a warrant, the knapsack or purse of the arrestee.

Significance
The decision was one of many made by the Burger Court that rolled back the Fourth Amendment protections given to persons by the Warren Court of the 1950s and 1960s. Most notably, the ruling reinforced the notion that law enforcement officers who are conducting a search need not resort to the least intrusive means in carrying out the search.

On 1 September 1980, Officer Maurice Mietzner of the Kankakee City Police Department in Kankakee, Illinois, responded to a call about a disturbance at the Town Cinema, a local movie theatre. At the theatre, Mietzner encountered Ralph Lafayette, who was embroiled in a dispute with the theatre manager. Mietzner arrested Lafayette for disturbing the peace and Mietzner took Lafayette away in handcuffs. En route to the station, Lafayette remained in possession of his shoulder bag.

In the booking room at the police station, Mietzner removed the handcuffs from Lafayette's wrists and ordered Lafayette to empty his pockets. Mietzner then searched through the contents of Lafayette's shoulder bag and found ten amphetamine pills. Lafayette was charged with possession of a controlled substance.

Before trial, Lafayette moved the court to exclude the amphetamine evidence, arguing that Mietzner had the opportunity to obtain a warrant for the search of the shoulder bag. It is, in fact, a general rule of law under the Fourth Amendment that police should obtain a warrant from a magistrate before they conduct a search. Mietzner conceded at the pre-trial hearing that the bag could have been placed in a locker for safekeeping until he obtained a warrant from a magistrate, but he also testified that it was standard procedure to conduct an inventory of everything in the possession of an arrested person. After the hearing, the state submitted a brief in which it argued, for the first time, that the search was conducted incident to Lafayette's arrest and that Mietzner merely delayed the search. The trial court decided to exclude the evidence.

The state of Illinois appealed the decision to the Illinois Appellate Court, which affirmed. The appeals court reviewed similar cases argued before the U.S. Supreme Court to come to their decision. In *South Dakota v. Opperman* (1976), the High Court held that an inventory search of an arrestee's locked vehicle, impounded for parking violations, was not unreasonable under the Fourth Amendment since the inventory search was conducted to prevent theft of the articles. Additionally, the search of the arrestee's unlocked glove compartment in *Opperman* was not unreasonable because vandals would have the same access to the glove compartment as they would to the rest of car's interior. Using the reasoning employed by the High Court in *Opperman,* the Illinois appeals court ruled that the search of Lafayette's shoulder bag was illegal under the Fourth Amendment. "[T]he postponed warrantless search of [Lafayette's] shoulder bag was neither incident to his lawful arrest," the Illinois court pronounced, "nor a valid inventory of belongings, and thus, violated the Fourth Amendment."

The Illinois Supreme Court refused to hear the appeal by the state of Illinois, so the state appealed to the U.S. Supreme Court, which unanimously reversed. After recounting the case history and facts, Chief Justice Burger, writing for the Court, framed the issue: whether it is "reasonable for police to search the effects of a person under lawful arrest as part of the routine administrative procedure at a police station house incident to booking and jailing the suspect." Since the justification for such searches is not probable cause, Burger wrote, "the absence of a warrant is immaterial to the reasonableness of the search." Rather than probable cause, an inventory search is justified by the need to protect both the arrestee and the officer. By conducting an inventory searching of an arrestee and the arrestee's belongings prior to jailing the arrestee, an officer ensures that the arrestee has no devices that may cause injury to someone. Also, such a search is necessary to prevent theft by police or false claims of theft by jailed arrestees. "[E]very consideration of orderly police administration benefiting both police and the public," Burger stated, "points toward the appropriateness of [Lafayette's] shoulder bag prior to his incarceration."

According to the Court, prior cases supported the decision to reverse. In *Opperman,* the Court did not consider whether there existed a less intrusive means of protecting police and an arrestee's property. Using the Illinois court's own words, the Court declared that "the real question is not what 'could have been achieved,' but whether the Fourth Amendment requires such steps . . . [I]t is not our function to write a manual on administering routine, neutral procedures of the station house," Burger lectured. "Our role is to assure against violations of the Constitution."

Justices Marshall and Brennan concurred in the judgment. In a short concurring opinion, Marshall wrote that "[a] very different case would be presented if the State had relied solely on the fact of arrest to justify the search of [Lafayette's] shoulder bag." According to Marshall and Brennan, Mietzner would not have been able to search the bag at the theatre. The offense—disturbing the peace—was not a charge that required evidence from the bag, nor was it a charge that could have been thwarted by a destruction of evidence. Furthermore, a search of the bag justified by a concern about the possible presence of weapons in the bag would have been illegal because seizure of the bag itself would have accomplished the goal of depriving Lafayette of any weapons in the bag. Thus, according to the concurring justices, the only reason Mietzner's search was legal was because he waited until he reached the police station to conduct it.

Impact

The decision confirmed that a police officer may conduct a warrantless search of the personal possessions of an arrestee who is about to be jailed. The most important principle that emerged from the case was the notion that the U.S. Supreme Court would not require police officers to use the least intrusive means possible in carrying out a warrantless search. Following the decision, the *Lafayette* case was, and still is, frequently cited for that proposition.

Related Cases

South Dakota v. Opperman, 428 U.S. 364 (1976).
United States v. Chadwick, 433 U.S. 1 (1977).

Bibliography and Further Reading

Bradley, Craig M. "The Court's 'Two Model' Approach to the Fourth Amendment: Carpe Diem." *Journal of Criminal Law and Criminology,* fall 1993, p. 429.

Epstein, Lee, and Thomas G. Walker. *Constitutional Law for a Changing America: Rights, Liberties, and Justice,* 2nd ed. Washington, DC: Congressional Quarterly, 1995.

Harris, David A. "'Driving While Black' and All Other Traffic Offenses." *Journal of Criminal Law and Criminology,* winter 1997, p. 544.

Stover, Carl P. "The Old Public Administration is the New Jurisprudence." *Administration & Society,* May 1995, p. 82.

UNITED STATES V. PLACE

Legal Citation: 462 U.S. 696 (1983)

Petitioner
United States

Respondent
Raymond J. Place

Petitioner's Claim
That the government should be allowed to perform search and seizure of baggage without needing to provide probable cause.

Chief Lawyer for Petitioner
Alan I. Horowitz

Chief Lawyer for Respondent
James D. Clark

Justices for the Court
Harry A. Blackmun, William J. Brennan, Jr., Warren E. Burger, Thurgood Marshall, Sandra Day O'Connor (writing for the Court), Lewis F. Powell, Jr., William H. Rehnquist, John Paul Stevens, Edward Douglass White

Justices Dissenting
None

Place
Washington, D.C.

Date of Decision
20 June 1983

Decision
The Court ruled that the respondent should not be prosecuted, but noted that searches of baggage are allowable when reasonable suspicion is raised.

Significance
The decision gave latitude to the government in situations involving the search and seizure of baggage.

On Friday, 17 August 1979, Raymond J. Place was in the Miami International Airport at the National Airlines ticket counter, preparing to board a flight to LaGuardia Airport in New York City. As four Dade County detectives surveilled the National Airlines ticket counter, Place waited in line and scanned the airport lobby, looking closely at every person in his immediate area. This aroused the suspicion of one of the detectives, Robertson McGavock, who was in line in front of Place. Place watched McGavock as McGavock left the line to speak with another detective, John Facchiano. Place continued to watch McGavock as he moved about the area, but Place looked away whenever McGavock looked at him.

As Place left for the concourse for his flight, McGavock checked the tags on Place's luggage and noticed that they were headed for LaGuardia Airport. At this point, in the subsequent words of the trial court, "a curious ballet" began. McGavock followed Place to the concourse, but Place changed directions en route and headed in the direction from which he had come. McGavock continued on and Place, after circling around the lobby area, went in the restroom. Less than a minute later, Place emerged from the restroom and proceeded to pass through the security gates.

Before Place boarded the plane, Facchiano and McGavock approached Place and displayed their credentials. A brief conversation ensued in which Place asked the detectives if anything was wrong and the detectives responded that they had "a big problem with contraband going out of here in the airport." At Facchiano's request, Place produced his airline ticket and his driver's license. The detectives explained that they were looking specifically for narcotics, and Place responded that he did not "use any stuff like that." The detectives asked Place if they could search inside his suitcase and Place gave his consent, whereupon the detectives decided to let Place go. As he walked toward his plane, Place turned back to the detectives and said "Hey, I knew you guys were cops when I saw you down in the lobby." The detectives asked how many cops he had seen; Place said that he had seen four or five, and then he boarded the plane.

Their curiosity renewed, the detectives did some more checking on Place. They found that there were

Unabomber Caught

The search for the Unabomber was one of the longest, most expensive criminal manhunts in the United States. Despite the massive amount of data collected by federal authorities and a million hours of work by federal agents, Theodore Kaczynski was found out not through the effort of law enforcement, but because his younger brother turned him in to authorities upon recognizing phrases of the Unabomber's 35,000 word anti-technology manifesto, which had been published in the *Washington Post*.

Kaczynski's nearly 18 year bombing spree resulted in three deaths, 29 injuries, and permanently heightened security by the U.S. Postal Service and airports. Many mailboxes now bear signs stating that mail over 16 ounces or parcels with stamps may not be placed in

the mailbox, but must be mailed from a post office. Security at airports has been raised and passengers must show picture identification, walk through metal detectors, and have their luggage x-rayed. As the U.S. Secretary of Transportation Frederico Pena stated at a news conference in Los Angeles after the Unabomber threatened to blow up an airplane in June of 1995, "Because of the past history of this individual, we take this threat very seriously. All of us as Americans are beginning to understand we live in a changed society. We realize that our lives are going to be inconvenienced because of the changing nature of the world."

Source(s): Knappman, Edward W., ed. *Great American Trials.* Detroit, MI: Visible Ink Press, 1994.

---

two different addresses on Place's luggage tags and that, according to police, neither of the addresses existed. Based on Place's nervousness and constant scanning, the discrepancies in the luggage tags, and the conversation he and Facchiano had with Place, McGavock decided to call Drug Enforcement Agency (DEA) officials in New York to alert them about Place.

The "ballet" that had begun in Miami resumed in New York City. Two DEA agents observed Place meet another male after exiting the plane and nervously look about as they walked and talked. Place waited outside the baggage claim area until his luggage appeared, watching people in the area. When his bags appeared, Place took hold of them and then, after waiting a few more minutes, he left the baggage claim area and began to walk down a corridor. At one point, Place stopped in his tracks and turned around to stare at the DEA agent who was tailing him. The agent kept walking past Place, but when Place stopped at a pay phone, both agents made contact with him.

Again Place informed the police that he was aware of their presence. The detectives told Place that, based on their information from the Miami detectives, they believed he was carrying narcotics. Place said that he had already been searched in Miami, and that the search was embarrassing. The detectives told Place that they had information to the contrary and asked Place if they could search his luggage. Place refused, and the detectives said they would keep his luggage until Monday morning, when they would see a federal judge about obtaining a search warrant to search the luggage. Place could either follow the agents to the magistrate or leave.

After some "hysterics" by Place, the agents took the bags to John F. Kennedy Airport (JFK). At JFK, "Honey,"

a drug-sniffing dog, lighted on the smaller of Place's two bags. On Monday, the agents obtained a search warrant to search the smaller bag. Inside the bag, the DEA agents found 1,125 grams of cocaine. Place was arrested, indicted, and charged in New York with a federal offense of possession of cocaine with an intent to distribute.

Before trial, Place moved the district court to exclude, or "suppress," the cocaine evidence from trial, arguing that it was seized in violation of the Fourth Amendment to the U.S. Constitution. According to Place, the Miami detectives violated the Fourth Amendment when they questioned him in the Miami International Airport, and the subsequent search by the agents in New York City was a continuation of the constitutional violation. The district court rejected Place's argument and deemed the cocaine evidence admissible, and Place pleaded guilty. However, he reserved the right to appeal the denial of his motion to suppress the evidence.

The U.S. Court of Appeals for the Second Circuit reversed the district court's decision. According to the appeals court, the stopping of Place and seizure of Place's luggage was not unconstitutional. However, the lengthy detention of Place's bags did constitute a violation of Place's Fourth Amendment right to be free from unreasonable searches and seizures. The Supreme Court agreed to hear the federal government's appeal and, in a subtly divided unanimous opinion, the High Court affirmed the appeals court's ruling.

In an opinion written by Justice O'Connor, the Court began its analysis by trotting through the jurisprudential rules created by the Court under the Fourth Amendment. Generally, a police officer must have obtained a search warrant from a judge or magistrate before conducting a search of a person or place. A judge or magistrate may issue a search warrant if the police officer seeking the warrant produces enough information to show that probable cause exists. In a criminal case, probable cause is a reasonable belief that the person targeted in the warrant has committed a crime. There are many exceptions to this general rule, though, and one is known as the "investigative stop." Under this exception to the warrant requirement, created by the Court in *Terry v. Ohio* (1968) a police officer, acting on mere reasonable suspicion of criminal activity—a level of belief that is less than probable cause—may stop a person and ask the person questions. In addition, the officer may perform a limited pat-down search for weapons to ensure his or her own safety. Police may seize property belonging to a person, provided that they have developed probable cause to believe the property is contraband or contains evidence of a crime, and also provided that "the exigencies of the circumstances demand it or some other recognized exception to the warrant requirement is present."

In Place's case, the police officers had something less than probable cause to believe that Place had committed, or was committing, a crime. The level of belief on the part of the law enforcement personnel was more like reasonable suspicion. The government acknowledged this and asked the Court to hold, for the first time, that the warrantless seizure and detention of a person's luggage based on mere reasonable suspicion does not violate the Fourth Amendment. Six of the nine justices agreed to this expansion of law enforcement powers. The Court concluded that the Fourth Amendment did not prohibit the detention of a person's luggage, "[g]iven the enforcement problems associated with the detection of narcotics trafficking and the minimal intrusion that a properly limited detention would entail."

In determining whether a particular exception to the warrant requirement makes a search unreasonable, the Court recognized in *Terry* that it must conduct a balancing test. Specifically, the Court must balance "the nature and quality of the intrusion on the individual's Fourth Amendment interests against the importance of the governmental interests alleged to justify the intrusion." Where a warrantless seizure is based on less than probable cause, the Court declared, the law enforcement interests will win out if "the nature and extent of the detention are minimally intrusive of the individual's Fourth Amendment interests."

On the facts in Place's case, the Court continued, the dog sniffing of the luggage by Honey did not even constitute a search in Place's case. "We know of no other investigative procedure that is so limited in both the manner in which the information is obtained and in the content of the information revealed by the procedure." However, the detention of Place's luggage was

an entirely different matter. Although it was legal for the DEA agents to seize and detain Place's luggage, "the police conduct here exceeded the permissible limits of a Terry-type investigative stop."

The very length of the detention of Place's luggage, the Court explained, "precludes the conclusion that the seizure was reasonable in the absence of probable cause." It made no difference in the analysis that the seizure was of Place's property, and not Place's person. When a person has luggage seized, that person's itinerary is disrupted and the person is deprived of his or her possessory interest in his luggage. "[S]uch a seizure can effectively restrain the person since he is subjected to the possible disruption of his travel plans in order to remain with his luggage or to arrange for its return." The Court declined to put any specific time limitation on so-called "Terry stops," but it had never "approved a seizure of the person for the prolonged 90-minute period involved here" and it could not do so on the facts in Place's case. The police, the Court added, could have been more diligent in their investigation; this comment seemed to suggest that the DEA agents in New York should have stopped Place as he came off the plane and questioned him further to develop probable cause for the lengthy detention of Place's luggage. Ultimately, the Court held in favor of the government on the issue of warrantless searches and seizures based only on reasonable suspicion. However, on the particular case before it, the Court ruled that the seizure of Place's luggage "went beyond the narrow authority possessed by police to detain briefly luggage reasonably suspected to contain narcotics."

Justices Brennan, Marshall, and Blackmun concurred only in the judgment in favor of Place; all three disagreed with the Court's holding on the issue of warrantless seizures of luggage based only on reasonable suspicion. In a long concurring opinion joined by Justice Marshall, Justice Brennan maintained that the Court should have held merely that the officers had the reasonable suspicion necessary to conduct a Terry stop, and that the principles set forth in the *Terry* case should govern seizures of property. As it turned out, the Court saw fit to reach "issues unnecessary to the judgment," and Brennan did not agree with the Court's analysis of the issues. The decision, Brennan insisted, represented "a radical departure from settled Fourth Amendment principles." According to Brennan and Marshall, nothing in the *Terry* case or any of its progeny could support the expansion of police search powers to allow the detention of a person's luggage on mere reasonable suspicion. "[E]ven when the Court finds that an individual's Fourth Amendment rights have been violated," Brennan complained, "it cannot resist the temptation to weaken the protections the Amendment affords."

Justice Blackmun wrote a separate concurring opinion, which Justice Marshall also joined. Blackmun could not fault the Court for wanting to make guidelines on the seizure of luggage, but he was concerned with "an emerging tendency on the part of the Court to convert the *Terry* decision into a general statement that the Fourth Amendment requires only that any seizure be reasonable." Blackmun and Marshall also objected to the Court's approval of dog-sniffs, an issue that was not raised by the parties. A decision on that issue, the two justices insisted, should have had "a full airing . . . in a proper case."

Impact

Although the Court held the Place should not be prosecuted, the Court's analysis favored the government. The decision allowed police officers to seize a person's luggage based on the police officer's reasonable suspicion that the luggage contains evidence of a crime. Prior to the *Place* decision, police officers had to have probable cause to believe that the luggage contained evidence of a crime before seizing it. Furthermore, under the *Place* decision, once the luggage is seized, a police

officer may examine the luggage, without opening it, to detect the presence of contraband. Police officers may use various methods and technology to determine the content of the luggage without actually opening the luggage. If they subsequently develop probable cause to believe that the luggage contains contraband or evidence of a crime and some extraordinary circumstance exists that requires the police to act on the spot, they may search inside the luggage without obtaining a search warrant.

Related Cases

Terry v. Ohio, 392 U.S. 1 (1968).
Commissioners v. Johnston, 530 A2d 74 (1987).
United States v. Letsinger, 93 F.3d 140 (1996).
People v. Evans, 689 N.E.2d 142 (1997).

Bibliography and Further Reading

New York Times, June 21, 1983.

"Terry v. Ohio," *West's Encyclopedia of American Law.* St. Paul: West Group, 1998.

HAWAII HOUSING AUTHORITY V. MIDKIFF

Legal Citation: 467 U.S. 229 (1984)

Appellant
Hawaii Housing Authority

Appellee
Frank E. Midkiff

Appellant's Claim
That the Hawaii Land Reform Act of 1967, which uses condemnation procedures to redistribute landholdings, violates the Fifth Amendment requirement that government takings must be for public use.

Chief Lawyer for Appellant
Lawrence H. Tribe

Chief Lawyer for Appellee
Clinton R. Ashford

Justices for the Court
Harry A. Blackmun, William J. Brennan, Jr., Warren E. Burger, Sandra Day O'Connor (writing for the Court), Lewis F. Powell, Jr., William H. Rehnquist, John Paul Stevens, Byron R. White

Justices Dissenting
None (Thurgood Marshall did not participate)

Place
Washington, D.C.

Date of Decision
30 May 1984

Decision
Finding that there needs only to be a rational relationship between the taking and some purpose that will benefit the public, the Supreme Court unanimously upheld the act.

Significance
In *Midkiff*, the Court essentially threw out the requirement that a government taking of property must be for public use; the state's power to condemn property, said the Court, is as broad as its extensive police power.

Hawaii was at one time a monarchy, in which a few major landholders owned most of the property in the islands. After Hawaii became a U.S. territory, and even after it gained statehood in 1959, landholdings remained concentrated in a few hands. In order to redistribute real estate, the Hawaiian legislature passed the Land Reform Act of 1967, which allowed the state to transfer land from lessors to lessees by using condemnation procedures. The Fifth Amendment to the Constitution authorizes government "takings" of private property so long as they are instituted for public use and the original owners receive just compensation.

The statute in question gave lessees of single family homes the right to invoke the state's power of eminent domain, or condemnation, in order to purchase the property they leased, even if the owner did not want to sell. After an initial public hearing to determine whether or not such a taking would "effectuate the public purposes" of the act, the Hawaii Housing Authority (HHA) would then purchase the land in question at a price set by condemnation trial or by a negotiation between the lessor and the lessee. The HHA would then sell the property to the lessees at the agreed price. If the lessors refuse to negotiate, the HHA was empowered to order that they submit to compulsory arbitration to determine the price at which the land would be sold.

When Frank E. Midkiff, as a land trustee, was ordered to participate in such arbitration, he declined, opting instead to file suit in federal district court. He asked that the land reform act be declared unconstitutional and the state prevented from proceeding to acquire his property. Instead, the district court granted HHA summary judgment, essentially throwing Midkiff's case out of court. Midkiff appealed to the U.S. Court of Appeals for the Ninth Circuit, which agreed with his claim that the act violated the Fifth Amendment's Public Use Clause, made applicable to the states by the Fourteenth Amendment. HHA in turn appealed this ruling to the U.S. Supreme Court.

Supreme Court Rules that Public Purpose, Not Public Use, Determines Constitutionality of a Government Taking of Land

By a vote of 8-0, the Court upheld the constitutionality of the act. Writing for the Court, Justice O'Connor

The Public Use Clause

The Public Use Clause limits eminent domain powers on the part of government in order to prevent the kind of abuses that might take place in a monarchy or other authoritarian state, where a king might simply desire a piece of property and seize it from the owner.

In 1897 the Supreme Court extended the application of the Public Use Clause to the states, through the Fourteenth Amendment. A number of cases since then have broadened the meaning of "public" so as to include anything that would provide the greatest good for the greatest number. Thus in *Berman v. Parker* (1954), for instance, the acquisition of private property, which was then sold to private individuals to redevelop for a com-

munity rehabilitation project, was justified because it served a sufficiently "public" interest.

The loosening of standards with regard to the Public Use Clause heralded an overall erosion of respect for property rights. *Midkiff* seemed to sound the death knell for property rights, but the Court's decision in *Nollan v. California Coastal Commission* (1987)—in which the justices split 5-4, more or less along ideological lines—reaffirmed the idea that taking of property is justified only if to do so "substantially furthered governmental purposes."

Source(s): Levy, Leonard W., ed. *Encyclopedia of the American Constitution.* New York: Macmillan, 1986.

stated that even when land is turned over to private hands under the act, without ever having been used by the public, the requirement of the Public Use Clause is met. What matters, she stated, is not the use of the property, but the purpose of the taking:

To be sure, the Court's cases have repeatedly stated that "one person's property may not be taken for the benefit of another private person without justifying public purpose, even though compensation be paid." . . . But where

Floyd Dotson (left) swears in Frank Midkiff as High Commissioner of the trust territory of Pacific Islands. In the center is Secretary of Interior Douglas McKay, 1953. © AP/Wide World Photos.

the exercise of eminent domain power is rationally related to a conceivable public purpose, the Court has never held a compensated taking to be proscribed by the Public Use Clause.

O'Connor added that the state's power of eminent domain is so broad that its scope equals that of the state police power, which permits states and localities to restrict individual rights in order to promote the public welfare. And courts should defer to legislative determinations of what constitutes a public use of land unless there is no rational relationship between the taking and the government purpose that motivated it. *Midkiff* was a unanimous decision by the Court, which spoke with one voice through Justice O'Connor. Because of this rare unanimity and because of the clear language of the opinion, *Midkiff* seems to have done away with the concept of public use as a limitation on government takings.

Related Cases

United States v. Gettysburg Electric R. Co., 160 U.S. 668 (1896).

Missouri Pacific R. Co. v. Nebraska, 164 U.S. 403 (1896).

Block v. Hirsch, 256 U.S. 135 (1921).

Rindge v. Los Angeles, 262 U.S. 700 (1923).

Old Dominion Co. v. United States, 269 U.S. 55 (1925).

Thompson v. Consolidated Gas Corp., 300 U.S. 55 (1937).

United States ex rel. TVA v. Welch, 327 U.S. 546 (1946).

Berman v. Parker, 348 U.S. 26 (1954).

Exxon Corp. v. Governor of Maryland, 437 U.S. 117 (1978).

Vance v. Bradley, 440 U.S. 93 (1979).

Minnesota v. Clover Leaf Creamery Co., 449 U.S. 456 (1981).

Western and Southern Life Insurance Co. v. State Board of Equalization, 451 U.S. 648 (1981).

Bibliography and Further Reading

Ely, James W., Jr. *The Guardian of Every Other Right: A Constitutional History of Property Rights.* New York, NY: Oxford University Press, 1992.

"Institute on Law and Planning." *The Private Property and Public-Interest Conflict: Proceedings.* Urbana: University of Illinois at Urbana-Champaign, Bureau of Community Planning and College of Law, 1969.

Kanner, Gideon. "Do-Gooders' Designs Twist Takings Clause." *National Law Journal,* January 8, 1996, p. A19.

Nedelsky, Jennifer. *Private Property and the Limits of American Constitutionalism: The Madisonian Framework and Its Legacy.* Chicago, IL: University of Chicago Press, 1990.

NIX V. WILLIAMS

Legal Citation: 467 U.S. 431 (1984)

Petitioner
Crispus Nix

Respondent
Robert Anthony Williams

Petitioner's Claim
That evidence pertaining to the discovery of a body was properly admitted because it would have ultimately been discovered, even if the defendant's right to counsel had not been violated. Also that the state need not prove the absence of bad faith in securing the evidence.

Chief Lawyer for Petitioner
Brent R. Appel

Chief Lawyer for Respondent
Robert Bartels

Justices for the Court
Warren E. Burger (writing for the Court), Harry A. Blackmun, Sandra Day O'Connor, Lewis F. Powell, Jr., William H. Rehnquist, John Paul Stevens, Byron R. White

Justices Dissenting
William J. Brennan, Jr., Thurgood Marshall

Place
Washington, D.C.

Date of Decision
11 June 1984

Decision
Reversed the court of appeals and held that unlawfully obtained evidence is admissible if it would inevitably have been discovered lawfully. Also held that to establish the admissibility of such evidence, the prosecution does not have to prove the absence of bad faith.

Significance
The ruling settled controversy over whether evidence gained in violation of an arrestee's constitutional rights could still be admissible in court. When that evidence would inevitably have been discovered by lawful means, it would be admissible. This ruling is one example of the Burger Court's broadening of the exceptions to the exclusionary rule.

On 24 December 1968 a ten year old girl was abducted from a YMCA in Des Moines and subsequently found dead. Iowa authorities suspected Robert Anthony Williams, who was observed placing what appeared to be a human body wrapped in a blanket into his car the same evening at the YMCA. Williams was arrested at a rest stop the next day in Davenport, Iowa. The police found clothes belonging to Pamela Powers, the missing girl, clothing of Williams, and a blanket at a rest stop between Des Moines and Davenport. They presumed that Williams must have hidden the body somewhere between Des Moines and Grinnell, where they found clothes and blanket.

State law enforcement officials of Iowa, along with 200 volunteers, began to search the area between Grinnell and Des Moines in an effort to recover the body. When Williams surrendered to police in Davenport, the search had been well under way. Williams called an attorney in Des Moines who arranged to have a Davenport attorney escort Williams back to Des Moines with the police. The law enforcement officials to whom Williams surrendered in Davenport agreed not to question Williams on the ride back to Des Moines. This agreement precluded the need for a Davenport attorney to escort Williams back to Des Moines.

On the return trip to Des Moines, however, Detective Leaming broke the agreement and began questioning Williams. Leaming told Williams, in effect, that they would be driving past the general vicinity where the body had been hidden and, because snow was forecast for that evening, he could save the family and community additional pain and suffering by showing them where the body was. In addition, Leaming told Williams that the least he could do is enable the family to provide a "Christian burial for the little girl who was snatched away from them on Christmas Eve." Williams ultimately agreed to show the police where the body was and made self incriminating statements in the process. The search was then called off and the body was recovered. At the time the search was called off one of the search parties was closing in on where the body had been discovered; they were two and one half miles away from the body.

The important aspect of the case, in essence, the reason it was ultimately reviewed by the Supreme Court, centered around the legal ramifications of admitting evidence that has been illegally obtained. In the original trial, Williams had been found guilty by an Iowa state court despite his efforts to have key evidence, the girl's body and the autopsy, suppressed. The defense argued that the police learned of the location of the body by the "fruit" of an illegal interrogation. The Iowa state court disagreed, and the Iowa Supreme Court upheld the decision. Upon being sentenced to life in prison for first degree murder, Williams took his case to the U.S. District Court for the Southern District on the grounds that he had been unlawfully imprisoned, *habeas corpus* relief. The district court ruled that the evidence in question, the body of the young girl, should not have been admitted. By a 5-4 margin, the Court of Appeals for the Eighth Circuit upheld the decision.

In *Brewer v. Williams* (1977) the Supreme Court reviewed the case. The Court ruled that, indeed, the Iowa police had violated Williams's Sixth Amendment right to counsel by interrogating him in the car. However, the Court also held that although Williams's self incriminating statements could not be admitted in a second trial, the body "might well be admissible" on the grounds that it would have ultimately been found in the same condition.

In Williams's second trial in Iowa state court, the prosecution adhered to the U.S. Supreme Court's ruling, and refrained from offering Williams's statements, including his pointing out where the body was, as evidence. The prosecution relied on the location of the body, the autopsy report, and the clothing that was found to support their arguments. The state court ruled that the body would have inevitably been found by the search party and was therefore admissible as evidence. Williams again was found guilty of first degree murder and sentenced to life in prison. Williams subsequently appealed to the Iowa Supreme Court where it was ruled that the body was admissible on the basis of what is known as the "independent source doctrine." The independent source doctrine simply means that evidence can be allowed if it is discovered independent of a constitutional violation. The Iowa Supreme Court also ruled that the evidence cannot be suppressed on the basis that it had been obtained by the police in "bad faith."

Williams and his defense, however, did not surrender their position. After being denied a writ of *habeas corpus* in district court in 1980, Williams once again took his case to the Court of Appeals for the Eighth Circuit. Here the appeals court reversed the district court's decision. The court of appeals ruled that in order for an inevitable discovery exception to the exclusionary rule to be considered valid, the state first must prove that the police did not act in bad faith, then prove that the evidence would have been "inevitably discovered." The

appeals court concluded that Iowa did not meet the first condition—proving that the police did not act in bad faith. The appeals court agreed with the district court that the state did prove, by a preponderance of the evidence, that the body would have been found. However, this, in their opinion, was irrelevant because the state failed to show that the police acted in good faith.

Supreme Court Approves Inevitable Discovery Exception

On 18 January 1984 the Supreme Court granted *certiorari* to review the second Williams case. When the Supreme Court grants *certiorari* it means that it has agreed to review a case on the basis of its appellate jurisdiction. Chief Justice Burger wrote the opinion of the Court, which reversed the decision made by the Court of Appeals for the Eighth Circuit. To this point, most state supreme courts acknowledged the merit of an inevitable discovery exception to the exclusionary rule. The matter was now before the U.S. Supreme Court whose ruling would have considerable bearing on the way future cases involving the exclusionary rule would be decided.

In his opinion, Burger cited *Silverthorne Lumber Co. V. United States* (1920) and *Wong Sun v. United States* (1963) both of which strengthened the exclusionary rule. He also astutely pointed out that in both rulings the Court had allowed room for exceptions to the exclusionary rule. More importantly, Burger noted that in *Wong Sun*, the Court held that the state does not have to prove "good faith" in order for evidence to be admitted. This was the basis upon which the appeals court had reversed the district court's ruling in the Williams case. In the opinion Burger reiterated that the reasoning behind the exclusionary rule was to prohibit law enforcement officials from violating constitutional rights in their pursuit of criminals. He noted, however, that not all evidence, or "fruit," obtained by unlawful interrogations, is inadmissible. This, he emphasized, is the point of the independent source doctrine. In simple terms, evidence that is found independent of a constitutional violation should not be thrown out.

Burger also addressed the argument made by Williams' defense which maintained that the exclusionary rule applies differently to the Fourth and Sixth Amendments. Williams argued that, with respect to the Fourth Amendment, the exclusionary rule is designed to prohibit unlawful police conduct. With respect to the Sixth Amendment, the defense argued, the exclusionary rule is designed to purify the "fact-finding process." On this basis, the defense claimed that the Court should not decide the case on the basis of competing values—the social cost of excluding or admitting the evidence—but rather, the Court should merely address whether the evidence was lawfully obtained. Burger rejected the argument on the grounds that excluding evidence that would have inevitably been found has no bearing on an individual's Sixth Amendment rights—whether one has been granted a "fair trial."

Justice White offered a concurring opinion which was designed to temper some of the observations offered by Justice Stevens in his reluctant concurrence. Justice White restated an opinion he had made in the Courts ruling in *Brewer v. Williams*. In that case Justice White was of the opinion that Detective Leaming had done nothing wrong, and that the issue of "bad faith" was completely irrelevant. He added that there is no need to promote the view that Detective Leaming behaved improperly in his investigation. Justice Stevens concurred with the decision, however, he added that Detective Leaming could have saved the state of Iowa considerable time and money had he behaved properly, and refrained from interrogating the suspect.

Dissenters Feel Exclusionary Rule is Undermined

Justices Brennan and Marshall offered a joint dissenting opinion arguing that the Court undermined the exclusionary rule by blurring the difference between the inevitable discovery doctrine and the independent source exception. The independent source doctrine, they stressed, applies only to evidence that was, in fact, found. Brennan and Marshall cautioned that allowing evidence to be admitted, which would have inevitably been discovered, could potentially impose on constitutionally protected rights. They therefore argue that the inevitable discovery exclusion, though sound in principle, should be subjected to a "heightened burden of proof."

Exclusionary Rule Offends Law and Order Supporters

Some politicians and judges take exception to the principle of excluding evidence from a trial because it was gathered in violation of an individual's constitutional rights. President Richard Nixon nominated two Supreme Court justices who reputedly opposed the exclusionary rule, Warren Burger and William Rehnquist. Burger was appointed in 1971 and Rehnquist in 1971. The majority of the Warren Court believed that law enforcement officials should not have investigations negated by technicalities. The Rehnquist Court has promoted the view in their decisions that the "good faith" test should be employed to determine whether evidence should ultimately be admitted.

In 1981, President Ronald Reagan denounced the exclusionary rule at a police convention. He stated that the exclusionary rule relies on the "absurd proposition that a law enforcement error, no matter how technical, can be used to justify throwing out an entire case" regardless of the nature of the crime and the clarity of a persons guilt. Decisions offered by the Warren, Burger, and Rehnquist Courts have generally aligned with this view, by broadening the exceptions to the exclusionary rule.

The exclusionary rule still survives, but the exceptions to it are growing. *Nix v. Williams* reflects the Burger-Rehnquist distaste for the exclusionary rule and provides an example of an exception to it, that of the "inevitable discovery" of evidence.

Related Cases

Spano v. New York, 360 U.S. 315 (1959).
Wong Sun v. United States, 371 U.S. 471 (1963).
Chapman v. California, 386 U.S. 18 (1967).
United States v. Wade, 388 U.S. 218 (1967).
Brewer v. Williams, 430 U.S. 387 (1977).

Bibliography and Further Reading

Irons, Peter. *Brennan vs. Rehnquist: The Battle for the Constitution.* New York: Alfred A. Knopf, 1994.

Schwartz, Herman, ed. *The Burger Years: Rights and Wrongs in the Supreme Court, 1969–1986.* New York: Viking, 1987.

HUDSON V. PALMER

Legal Citation: 468 U.S. 517 (1984)

Petitioner
Ted S. Hudson

Respondent
Russel Thomas Palmer, Jr.

Petitioner's Claim
Privacy rights and protection against unreasonable search and seizure under the Fourth and Fourteenth Amendment cannot be extended to prison inmates. Such expectations are inconsistent with effective prison administration in correctional centers.

Chief Lawyer for Petitioner
William G. Broaddus

Chief Lawyer for Respondent
Deborah C. Wyatt

Justices for the Court
Warren E. Burger (writing for the Court), Sandra Day O'Connor, Lewis F. Powell, Jr., William H. Rehnquist, Byron R. White

Justices Dissenting
Harry A. Blackmun, William J. Brennan, Jr., Thurgood Marshall, John Paul Stevens

Place
Washington, D.C.

Date of Decision
3 July 1984

Decision
Prison guards act of unreasonable search, seizure and deprivation of prisoners property did not violate the Fourth and Fourteenth Amendment rights of the respondent.

Significance
Although a ward of the prison system, the respondent, Russel Palmer, claimed that his personal rights were infringed after an "unreasonable" and cruel "shakedown" by prison guard Ted Hudson. He also contended that the guard's intentional search and seizure was conducted solely as harassment and that there existed no reason to suspect Palmer harbored contraband. The U.S. Supreme Court, however, judged that a prison inmate's rights under the Fourth Amendment could not be standardized (equalized) with personal rights outside penal institutions; thus, damage to a prisoner's personal property, if sustained in custody, did not usurp due process of law under the Fourteenth Amendment so long as a post-deprivation remedy was provided by the state.

Prison guard Ted. S. Hudson conducted a "shakedown" of Russel Thomas Palmer, an inmate in a state penitentiary. He searched Palmer's personal area and, in the process, discovered a torn pillow case. Although no contraband was uncovered, the disciplinary commission of the prison charged Palmer with damaging state property and ordered that he pay for the damaged property. Believing his constitutional right to due process was violated under the Fourth and Fourteenth Amendments, Palmer took his case to the U.S. District Court for the District of Virginia. His claim alleged the prison officer intentionally destroyed his non-contraband personal effects; intentionally sought to humiliate and harass him; the "shakedown" search was conducted without proper authorization; and the search was unconstitutional because it was not part of a prison-wide protocol.

The U.S. district court found that Palmer had available to him established state tort remedies which enabled him to recover from deprivation of his property. Quoting from *Parratt v. Taylor* (1981), the district court maintained that "negligent deprivation of a prison inmate's property does not violate the Due Process Clause of the Fourteenth Amendment if an adequate post-deprivation state remedy exists." The U.S. district court found there were no grounds for Palmer to claim that Hudson's conduct violated his constitutional rights. On appeal, the U.S. Court of Appeals reversed the district court's decision in part, finding that prisoners should have a "limited expectation of privacy" because a "prisoner retains at least (a) minimal degree of Fourth Amendment protection in his cell," and that the guard's "shakedown" was, therefore, unreasonable. The appellate court reasoned that the guard should not have searched Palmer's cell in a manner that did not respect established, random search procedures unless he had strong reason to suspect contraband. Although the court of appeals categorically disapproved of searches which served only to harass inmates, it affirmed part of the district court's decision holding that deprivation of prisoner's property was not conducted with disregard to due process.

In presenting his case before the U.S. Supreme Court, Palmer's attorney claimed that "because searches and

Do Prison Inmates Have Rights?

Common sense would seem to dictate that prisoners should have fewer rights than people on the outside; otherwise prison would not be prison. Lack of freedom of movement, for instance, is a defining factor of prison. Likewise prisoners forfeit certain civil rights, such as the right to vote; a number of property rights (e.g. the warden might prevent a prisoner from receiving a gift of a gold watch for fear that his wearing the watch might encourage theft); the right to privacy with regards to his mail (though unreasonable censorship or restriction is unconstitutional); free speech (e.g., the prisoner cannot call for protests against the prison administration); and other rights.

Prisoners do have some rights, particularly under the Eighth Amendment prohibition of cruel and unusual punishment. They have a right to food, medical care, proper hygiene facilities, and adequate shelter. They also have a right to practice their own religion. Prison rules govern the administration of discipline and punishment in accordance with the Eighth Amendment.

Source(s): *West's Encyclopedia of American Law.* St. Paul, MN: West Group, 1998.

seizures to harass are unreasonable, a prisoner has reasonable expectation of privacy not to have his cell, locker, personal effects, person invaded for such a purpose." He contended that a "shakedown" search (such as was administered by Hudson) was an intentional and unreasonable action by a state officer. Palmer believed that the officer's intention was only to demonstrate his authority and that his action was without necessary, justified rationale. He asserted that the guard did not have an appropriate reason to search his cell and that he issued a false charge (concerning the torn pillowcase) in order to harass Palmer. Citing findings of the U.S. court of appeals, Palmer's attorney argued that because Palmer expected a certain level of privacy in his prison cell it was therefore especially violative that his personal effects were damaged during the shakedown. He conceded the necessity of routine "shakedowns" in prisons, but pointed out that unreasonable harassment should be barred under the provisions of the Fourth Amendment. Palmer's attorney argued that his client's rights were violated under the Due Process Clause of the Fourteenth Amendment because unauthorized searches and seizures did not fit procedural requirements and intentional deprivation of a prisoner's personal property infringed on an inmate's rights. The "shakedown" was not conducted as a random search; it was an unauthorized violation of the Palmer's privacy. Moreover, Palmer's attorney pointed out that since noncontraband items must not be of interest to prison authorities, the unauthorized, irregular search constituted malicious, destructive action motivated only by the wish to demonstrate force. Furthermore, Palmer's attorney contended that the state's post-deprivation remedy could not adequately compensate for damaged property because items seized by the guard "may have contained things irreplaceable, and incompensable" or "may also have involved sentimental items which are of equally intangible value."

Finally, Palmer's attorney argued that Virginia's state relief law was inapplicable (Hudson enjoyed "sovereign immunity" from liability as a state employee). The Court found this argument insignificant holding that "liability for intentional tort (remedy)" for state employees was instituted under Virginia law.

In providing a counterargument, Hudson's attorney contended that imprisonment normally means prisoners must be aware they possess only a limited, legitimate expectation of privacy. He argued that inmates in prison could not expect the same level of privacy rights guaranteed by the Constitution against unreasonable searches as people who are not incarcerated. Hudson's attorney further argued that Palmer's rights under the Fourteenth Amendment with respect to due process of law were not violated by Hudson's search nor confiscation of personal property. Moreover, there existed a mandate of order required in penal institutions that could justify such actions even if performed outside of certain routine.

The U.S. Supreme Court decided in favor of Hudson. The opinion of the Court was that with regard to the Due Process Clause, Palmer had no sustainable arguments to support the claim that his rights under the Fourteenth Amendment were violated by illegal search and seizure. The justices for the majority pointed out that the expectation of privacy in prison is incompatible with internal security and safety measures. Consequently, a reasonable or legitimate expectation of privacy could not be extended to a prison cell. They also held that prison officers had to be empowered to detect, without any obstacles, all illegal activities that could be done by prisoners in order to ensure safety and prevent possible accidents. Accordingly, the Court found no violation of the Fourth Amendment.

The justices for the majority explained that the concept of due process of law was satisfied since the state's post-deprivation remedy was made available to Palmer when his property was destroyed during the unexpected, "shakedown" search. Consequently, there was no reason to invoke Fourteenth Amendment rights. (Moreover, the justices agreed that the adequacy of the state's post-deprivation remedy was not at issue.)

In addressing Palmer's argument that random searches had to be performed in accordance with pre-established protocol, the justices for the majority found that such procedures could undermine the effectiveness of prison security. They sustained Hudson's claim that unplanned and spontaneous "shakedowns" serve a viable purpose in prison. Chief Justice Burger concluded that "prisoners have no legitimate expectation of privacy," so the Fourth Amendment's prohibition on unreasonable searches did not apply in prison cells. Further, the justices emphasized that the state's interest in preserving and maintaining order in incarceration centers provided substantial, valid reasons which superseded a prisoner's expectation of privacy.

Justice Stevens, in representing the dissenting minority opinion, wrote that unrestrained and unreasonable search and seizure should not be considered correct. Since Palmer was deprived of his property after having been searched, his personal privacy rights were violated (albeit, he conceded, minimally.) The dissenting justices did not agree that "the interest of society in the security of its penal institutions precludes prisoners from having any legitimate possessory interest." Justice Stevens went further stating that Palmer had a right to possess all the things of which he had been deprived—items like letters, family photos, and diaries could not be considered contraband. Under the Due Process Clause of the Constitution, Palmer had a "legitimate possessory interest" in his seized and destroyed personal materials. Stevens questioned the reasonableness of the prison guard's actions and the destruction of evidently noncontraband items. After the officer had examined Palmer's possessions (which were not found dangerous to prison security), he destroyed Palmer's property without reason. Accordingly, Stevens wrote: "When, as here, the material at issue is not contraband, it simply makes no sense to say that its seizure and destruction serve 'legitimate institutional interest.'" The minority justices believed that if rights under the Fourth Amendment could not be extended and respected in prison, then all searches and seizures, no matter how intrusive or destructive, might be considered reasonable.

Impact

In *Hudson v. Palmer,* the Supreme Court sought to define the limits of the constitutional rights of prisoners. Toward that end, its decision tacitly served to instruct states and penal authorities in the constitutionally acceptable administration of justice in detention facilities. The Court ruled prisoners must be aware that incarceration reduces and limits applicability of personal rights. Although a certain level of constitutional rights cannot be denied to the inmates, the risk of contraband and violence in prisons enabled prison officers to search and seize randomly in order to maintain order and prevent accidents. Moreover, the Court supported the notion that planned programs of inspection would only serve to weaken prison security measures. Finally, the justices reasoned that if state law provided post-deprivation remedies as compensation for harmful conduct by state officials, there could be no question as to the violation of constitutional rights of incarcerated prisoners. Dissenting opinions showed that the Court relied on the argument that all actions of prison officers could not be taken as "reasonable" and "indispensable," especially because Palmer's seized and destroyed property was not prohibited or contraband. It means that while the rights of convicts are minimal, guards are not entitled to act just to harass them. Diminishing the value of the Fourth Amendment rights inside reformatory centers may also "undermine the rehabilitation function of the institution."

Related Cases

Lanza v. New York, 370 U.S. 139 (1962).
Wolff v. McDonell, 418 U.S. 539 (1974).
Bell v. Wolfish, 441 U.S. 520 (1979).
Parratt v. Taylor, 451 U.S. 527 (1981).

Bibliography and Further Reading

Call, Jack E. "The Supreme Court and Prisoners' Rights." *Federal Probation,* March 1995, pp. 36–46.

Emory University School of Law. *Criminal Procedures-Cases, Statutes, & Executive Materials.* "Chapter Four: Searches in Recurring Places and Contexts," 30 September 1997. http://www.law.emory.edu/CRIMPRO/notes/ch4notes.html

UNITED STATES V. LEON

Legal Citation: 468 U.S. 897 (1984)

Petitioner
United States

Respondent
Alberto Antonio Leon

Petitioner's Claim
Evidence obtained through use of a search warrant subsequently judged to be defective should be admissible in court.

Chief Lawyer for Petitioner
Rex E. Lee, U.S. Solicitor General

Chief Lawyers for Respondent
Barry Tarlow, Roger L. Cossack

Justices for the Court
Harry A. Blackmun, Warren E. Burger, Sandra Day O'Connor, Lewis F. Powell, Jr., William H. Rehnquist, Byron R. White (writing for the Court)

Justices Dissenting
William J. Brennan, Jr., Thurgood Marshall, John Paul Stevens

Place
Washington, D.C.

Date of Decision
5 July 1984

Decision
Evidence obtained under a search warrant subsequently ruled defective may still be admissible in court.

Significance
Defendants must establish that either the magistrate issuing a search warrant, or the police officers that submit an affidavit establishing probable cause to obtain a search warrant, did not act in good faith to make evidence obtained under a warrant subsequently deemed defective inadmissible in court.

Public concern over the use of, and traffic in, illegal drugs reached new levels in the early 1980s. Perceptions of increases in violent crime linked to substance abuse led to political support for laws and policies making it easier for police to obtain convictions for drug traffickers. Amid this climate of popular support for aggressive law enforcement, Burbank, California police began investigating a suspected drug ring in August of 1981.

Police officers observed the activities of a group of individuals suspected of trafficking in drugs, and in due course applied to a neutral magistrate for a warrant to search their residences and automobiles. The warrant application was reviewed by a number of deputy district attorneys, and the warrant was granted by a state court judge. In the ensuing search, large quantities of drugs were recovered.

The case continued to district court, where an evidentiary hearing concluded that the officers' affidavit based on initial surveillance of the respondents was insufficient to establish probable cause, and that on this basis the search warrant used was invalid. This ruling was upheld on appeal by the state court of appeals, whereupon the government petitioned for *certiorari* on the question of "whether the Fourth Amendment exclusionary rule should be modified so as not to bar the admission of evidence seized in reasonable, good-faith reliance on a search warrant that is subsequently held to be defective." The Supreme Court agreed to hear the case, and arguments were presented on 17 January 1984.

Attorneys for Leon argued that the Fourth Amendment should be interpreted to preclude the use of evidence obtained under a defective warrant in a court of law. The government countered that the use of a warrant granted in good faith by neutral magistrates, and found to be defective only after the fact, should not constitute an impediment to law enforcement.

The Court overturned the judgement of the court of appeals by a vote of 6-3, allowing evidence obtained under the defective warrant to be used in court. Justice White delivered the Court's opinion. Central to the Court's thinking was the fact that the government did not ask for review of the lower courts' determinations that the search warrant was unsupported by probable cause, but rather for a ruling on the pliability of the Fourth Amendment exclusionary rule:

> Although it undoubtedly is within our power to consider the question whether probable cause existed . . . that question has neither been briefed nor argued . . . and it is also within our authority, which we choose to exercise, to take the case as it comes to us.

The Court also made it clear that it believed the lower court decisions in this case to have been correct given the interpretation of the Fourth Amendment then in effect, stating that "the Court of Appeals understandably declined to adopt a modification of the Fourth Amendment exclusionary rule that this Court had not previously sanctioned." Finally, the Court ruled that the Fourth Amendment's intent would rarely be served by warrants invalidated after the fact, and that a modification of the amendment's interpretation should be allowed, as follows:

> In the absence of an allegation that the magistrate abandoned his detached and neutral role, suppression is appropriate only if the officers were dishonest or reckless in preparing their affidavit or could not have harbored an objectively reasonable belief in the existence of probable cause.

Justices Brennan, Marshall, and Stevens dissented from the decision. Brennan and Marshall argued that evidence obtained under a defective warrant is always legally inadmissible, regardless of when the warrant is judged to be defective. Stevens offered that without probable cause all searches are unreasonable and therefore prohibited by the Fourth Amendment.

United States v. Leon marked a fundamental shift in the interpretation of the U.S. Constitution. By putting the onus of proof on defendants wishing to invalidate evidence obtained under defective search warrants, the Court radically altered the traditional interpretation of the Fourth Amendment and greatly increased the capabilities of law enforcement agencies at the expense of the rights of the individual.

Related Cases

Olmstead v. United States, 277 U.S. 438 (1928).
Mapp v. Ohio, 367 U.S. 643 (1961).
Aguilar v. Texas, 378 U.S. 108 (1964).
Spinelli v. United States, 393 U.S. 410 (1969).
Harris v. New York, 401 U.S. 222 (1971).
Illinois v. Gates, 462 U.S. 213 (1983).

Bibliography and Further Reading

Biskupic, Joan, and Elder Witt. *Congressional Quarterly's Guide to the U.S. Supreme Court,* third ed. Washington, DC: Congressional Quarterly, Inc., 1996.

Deegan, Paul J. *Search and Seizure.* Minneapolis: Abdo & Daughters, 1987.

Hall, Kermit L., ed. *The Oxford Companion to the Supreme Court of the United States.* New York: Oxford University Press, 1992.

Jackson, Heather A. "Expanding Exclusionary Rule Exceptions and Contracting Fourth Amendment Protection." *Journal of Criminal Law and Criminology,* summer 1996, p. 1201.

Jost, Kenneth. "Exclusionary Rule Reforms Advance; Opponents Claim Proposals Unconstitutional, Encourage Police Misconduct." *ABA Journal,* May 1995, p. 18.

LaFave, Wayne R. "Computers, Urinals, and the Fourth Amendment: Confessions of a Patron Saint." *Michigan Law Review,* August 1996, p. 2553.

McWhirter, Darien A. *Search, Seizure, and Privacy.* Phoenix: Oryx Press, 1994.

MASSACHUSETTS V. SHEPPARD

Legal Citation: 468 U.S. 981 (1984)

Petitioner
State of Massachusetts

Respondent
Osborne Sheppard

Petitioner's Claim
That evidence found and used against Osborne Sheppard should not be suppressed because it was gathered using a defective warrant.

Chief Lawyer for Petitioner
Barbara A. H. Smith

Chief Lawyer for Respondent
John Reinstein

Justices for the Court
Harry A. Blackmun, Warren E. Burger, Sandra Day O'Connor, Lewis F. Powell, Jr., William H. Rehnquist, John Paul Stevens, Byron R. White (writing for the Court)

Justices Dissenting
William J. Brennan, Jr., Thurgood Marshall

Place
Washington D.C.

Date of Decision
5 July 1984

Decision
Reversed the decision of the Supreme Court of Massachusetts and held that evidence is admissible, even if gathered under a defective search warrant, as long as the police acted in good faith in executing what they believed was a valid warrant.

Significance
The ruling settled controversy over whether evidence gathered with a defective warrant should be suppressed, even if the police officers acted in good faith. Because the exclusion of evidence gathered by unreasonable search and seizure was designed to prevent police misconduct, the Court determined that excluding evidence obtained in good faith would not serve the purpose of deterring police misbehavior. This ruling assures that criminals will not benefit from clerical errors in search warrants.

On Saturday, 5 May 1979, the burned body of Sandra Boulware was found in an empty lot in the part of Boston, Massachusetts, known as Roxbury. Boulware had died from multiple blows to the head. On investigating, the police questioned one of Boulware's boyfriends, Osborne Sheppard. He claimed to have last seen Boulware on Tuesday night. Sheppard stated that he had been in a gaming house from 9:00 p.m. on Friday until 5:00 a.m. on Saturday. Witnesses agreed that he had been there, but that he had borrowed a car at 3:00 a.m. to give two men a ride home. The trip should have taken 15 minutes, but Sheppard did not return until almost 5:00 a.m.

The police searched the borrowed car and found bloodstains, hair, and wire similar to that found near Boulware's body. Based on this evidence, Detective Peter O'Malley drafted an affidavit in order to get an arrest warrant and a search warrant so he could search Sheppard's residence. The affidavit listed what the police intended to look for: a bottle of amaretto liquor, two nickel bags of marijuana, a woman's jacket, wire and rope like those found near the victim, a blunt instrument, and clothing with blood, gasoline, or burns on them.

O'Malley showed the affidavit to the district attorney, the district attorney's first assistant, and a sergeant. They all agreed that probable cause existed for a search and arrest. The local court was closed because it was Sunday, and O'Malley had trouble locating a warrant application form. He finally found one that had been used in the Dorchester District regarding a controlled substance. O'Malley deleted the subtitle "Controlled Substance," substituted "Roxbury" for "Dorchester," and added Sheppard's name and address. The words "controlled substance" were not deleted from the part of the form that would become the warrant itself, once signed.

O'Malley brought the affidavit and the warrant form to the home of a judge who agreed to authorize the search. The detective explained that the present form dealt with controlled substances and he showed the judge where he had crossed out the subtitles. The judge told O'Malley that he would make the changes necessary for a proper search warrant. The judge then took the form, made some changes, and signed and dated the warrant. He had not, however, changed the part of the warrant that authorized a search for controlled substances. He also did not alter the form to incorporate the affidavit. The judge gave the affidavit and warrant back to O'Malley, stating that the warrant was sufficient to carry out the requested search.

O'Malley and other officers took the documents to Sheppard's residence, which they proceeded to search. While looking for the items listed in the affidavit, they found several pieces of incriminating evidence—bloodstained boots, bloodstains on the floor, a woman's earring with blood on it, bloody clothing, and three types of wire. They then charged Sheppard with first-degree murder.

A suppression hearing was held before the trial itself. This type of hearing is used to determine what evidence will be suppressed, or excluded, from a trial. Excluding evidence is possible because of the exclusionary rule, which states that evidence gathered during an unreasonable search and seizure cannot be used in a criminal prosecution. At the suppression hearing in the *Sheppard* case, the judge decided that the warrant did not conform to the Fourth Amendment because it did not describe the items to be seized. The Fourth Amendment forbids unreasonable searches and seizures and states that probable cause must exist for a warrant to be issued and that the warrant must describe the place to be searched and the persons or things to be seized. However, the judge ruled that although the warrant was inaccurate, the evidence could still be admitted because the police had acted in good faith. They thought they were executing a valid warrant.

Sheppard was convicted, but appealed on the grounds that the evidence seized with the defective warrant should have been suppressed. The Supreme Court of Massachusetts agreed with this decision. The justices decided that although the police had conducted the search in good faith, the evidence should have been excluded because the Supreme Judicial Court of Massachusetts had not recognized a good faith exception to the exclusionary rule.

The Court Applies the Good Faith Rule

The Supreme Court created the "good faith" rule in *United States v. Leon*. The rule states that evidence gathered in violation of the Fourth Amendment's guarantee against unreasonable search and seizure will still be admissible in a trial if the police acted reasonably, although mistakenly. The good faith exception was deemed necessary because the exclusionary rule was designed to prevent police misconduct. Suppressing evidence gathered without police misconduct occurring would not serve the purpose of the exclusionary rule and would benefit criminals.

The Supreme Court agreed to hear *Massachusetts v. Sheppard* to determine if the officers reasonably believed that the search of Sheppard's residence was authorized by a valid warrant. The trial court and the majority of the Massachusetts Supreme Court felt that there was an objectively reasonable basis for the officers' mistaken belief that the warrant authorized the search they conducted. The majority of the Supreme Court justices agreed with these lower courts.

The attorney for Sheppard argued that since O'Malley knew the warrant form was defective he should have examined it to see if the necessary changes had been made.

Justice White wrote the opinion for the majority stating, "The officers in this case took every step that could reasonably be expected of them . . . We refuse to rule that an officer is required to disbelieve a judge who has just advised him, by word and by action, that the warrant he possesses authorizes him to conduct the search . . ." White pointed out that in most jurisdictions, the determinations of a judge are valid and binding, even if erroneous, until they are set aside through recognized procedure. White noted that there is little reason why an officer "should be expected to disregard assurances that everything is all right especially when he has alerted the judge to the potential problems."

White summed up by noting that the police conduct in this case was objectively reasonable. The judge, not the police officers, made the mistake. Since the exclusionary rule was designed to deter unlawful searches by police, not to punish clerical errors by judges, suppressing the evidence would not serve a deterrent purpose. The decision of the Supreme Judicial Court was reversed and the case sent back for further proceedings.

Justices Brennan and Marshall dissented in this case, stating that under the Fourth Amendment, illegally obtained evidence cannot be admitted. Their dissent in this case appeared in *United States v. Leon*. There they stated that the main deterrent function of the exclusionary rule goes beyond just the prevention of police misconduct. They felt that if a search warrant was defective for any reason, including an honest mistake, the evidence in the case should be suppressed. Brennan and Marshall stated that this strict interpretation would preserve the integrity of law enforcement and the Fourth Amendment. They summed up their dissent by noting that the majority's viewpoint "robbed the [exclusionary] rule of legitimacy."

Excluded Evidence Can Still Be Used In Court

Massachusetts v. Sheppard involved the application of the good faith exception to the exclusionary rule, articulated in *United States v. Leon* on the same day that *Massachu-*

setts v. Sheppard was decided. In *Massachusetts v. Sheppard*, the Supreme Court held that although a warrant was found invalid after a search, the exclusionary rule did not apply. In *United States v. Leon*, the Court redefined the test for applying the exclusionary rule and narrowed the scope of Fourth Amendment protection for defendants. In *Leon*, the Court allowed evidence obtained in a search with a mistakenly issued warrant to be admitted because the police were acting in good faith. To determine whether the exclusionary rule should be applied, the Court used a cost-benefit analysis. The benefits of deterring police misconduct were weighed against the costs of suppressing the evidence. The purpose of the rule is to prevent the police from overstepping constitutional bounds. In *Leon*, the police did not overstep their bounds, so the Court concluded that there would be little benefit in applying the rule. Releasing a law breaker was a cost outweighing any benefit from attempting to prevent outrageous police behavior.

Decisions prior to *Leon* and *Massachusetts v. Sheppard* failed to create a good faith exception to the exclusionary rule. The Court finally created the good faith exception with *Leon* and applied it immediately in *Massachusetts v. Sheppard*, pointing out the possibilities of excluded evidence still being used in court, then noting the purposes of the exclusionary rule.

The Supreme Court revisited the good faith exception to the exclusionary rule in *Arizona v. Evans* (1995). A court employee mistakenly identified Isaac Evans as the subject of an arrest warrant. When a police officer stopped Evans for a traffic violation and searched him, using the incorrect warrant information, he found marijuana. The Supreme Court ruled that evidence seized in violation of the Fourth Amendment because of a clerk's error does not have to be excluded from the defendant's trial. The Court once again emphasized that the Fourth Amendment's purpose is to prevent unreasonable searches and seizures by the police.

Related Cases

Stanford v. Texas, 379 U.S. 476 (1965).
United States v. Johnson, 459 U.S. 1214 (1983).
Illinois v. Gates, 462 U.S. 213 (1983).
United States v. Leon, 468 U.S. 897 (1984).

Bibliography and Further Reading

Bessette, Joseph M., ed. *American Justice*, Vol. 2. Pasadena, CA: Salem Press, Inc., 1996.

West's Encyclopedia of American Law. St. Paul, MN: West Group, 1998.

WINSTON V. LEE

Legal Citation: 470 U.S. 753 (1985)

Petitioners
Andrew J. Winston, County Sheriff; Aubrey M. Davis, Jr.

Respondent
Rudolph Lee, Jr.

Petitioners' Claim
It is unconstitutional for a state to authorize surgery under general anesthesia on a person to retrieve evidence for a criminal prosecution.

Chief Lawyer for Petitioners
Stacy F. Garrett III

Chief Lawyer for Respondent
Joseph Ryland Winston

Justices for the Court
Harry A. Blackmun, William J. Brennan, Jr. (writing for the Court), Warren E. Burger, Thurgood Marshall, Sandra Day O'Connor, Lewis F. Powell, Jr., William H. Rehnquist, John Paul Stevens, Byron R. White

Justices Dissenting
None

Place
Washington, D.C.

Date of Decision
20 March 1985

Decision
It is a violation of the Fourth Amendment for a state to conduct a surgical intrusion into a robbery suspect for the purpose of retrieving a bullet when the surgery requires general anesthesia, the medical risks are in dispute, and there is no compelling need to recover the bullet in light of the availability of other evidence.

Significance
The unanimous decision established a limit to the physical intrusions that criminal defendants must endure.

At around one o'clock in the morning on 18 July 1982, Ralph E. Watkinson was closing the Lombardy Market in Richmond, Virginia, when he was approached by an armed stranger. Watkinson drew his own gun and the stranger told Watkinson to freeze. Watkinson fired his gun and the stranger returned fire; Watkinson was shot in the legs, but he managed to wound the stranger in the left side.

Watkinson's attacker fled from the scene. A short time later, police officers found Rudolph Lee, Jr. approximately eight blocks from the shooting. Lee, who was suffering from a chest wound to this left chest area, told the police that he had been the victim of an attempted robbery. Officers escorted Lee to a hospital emergency room where Watkinson was receiving treatment for his leg wounds. When he saw Lee, Watkinson pointed and stated "that's the man that shot me." Upon further investigation, the officers arrested Lee and charged him with attempted robbery, malicious wounding, and two counts of using a firearm during a felony.

Before trial, the Commonwealth of Virginia asked the court for permission to extract the bullet that was lodged in Lee's left chest area. The Commonwealth initially represented that the bullet was lodged under the left collarbone, that such a surgery would require general anesthesia, and that there were minor chances of nerve damage or death. Later the Commonwealth produced testimony from an expert who stated that the bullet was located just beneath the skin, and that a surgery to remove it would require only local anesthesia. On the basis of this testimony, the court ordered Lee to submit to surgery. Seeking to avoid the surgery, Lee petitioned the Virginia Supreme Court, but the court denied the petitions. Lee then brought the case to federal court, but the U.S. District Court for the Eastern District of Virginia rejected Lee's pleas.

On 18 October 1982, as Lee was being prepared for surgery, the surgeon discovered through X-rays that the bullet was in fact approximately one inch deep into Lee's muscle, and that the surgery would require general anesthesia. Another hearing followed, but the trial court refused to change its decision. The Virginia Supreme Court affirmed that decision, and Lee went back to federal court, still trying to avoid the surgery. After hearing all the evidence, the federal court put a stop to the surgery. The Commonwealth appealed, and a divided Court of Appeals for the Fourth Circuit affirmed. The Commonwealth turned to the U.S. Supreme Court, which agreed to hear arguments on the issue.

A unanimous High Court held for Lee, affirming the federal appeals court. In a majority opinion written by Justice Brennan, the Court held that the Fourth Amendment, with its prohibition of unreasonable searches, forbid the surgery on Lee. The Court began its analysis by citing the proposition that the Fourth Amendment protects a person's legitimate expectations of privacy and, as the Court said in *Olmstead v. United States* (1928), "the right to be let alone—the most comprehensive of rights and the right most valued by civilized men." At the same time, the Court acknowledged, persons must give up some measure of privacy and submit to searches that are supported by probable cause to believe that the search will turn up evidence of a crime. Such searches are reasonable and "advance the community's vital interests in law enforcement."

Lee's case, the Court continued, was different from the ordinary search and seizure case. The surgery proposed "implicate[d] expectations of privacy and security of such magnitude that the intrusion may be 'unreasonable' even if likely to produce evidence of a crime." In examining case precedent, the Court cited *Schmerber v. California* (1966), the Court's first case dealing with the state's intrusion into the human body. In *Schmerber,* the Court had held that police may draw blood from a suspected drunk driver. Although the *Schmerber* Court held in favor of the state's police interests, the analysis provided in that precedent-setting case provided a framework that, in the Court's opinion, called for a different result in Lee's case.

The *Schmerber* Court noted the general rule that police must have probable cause to believe that evidence of a crime will be found in a search before conducting the search. *Schmerber* established additional factors for courts to consider on occasions when police seek to surgically intrude into a person's body. One consideration is whether the procedure would threaten the safety or health of the person. Another factor established by *Schmerber* was "the extent of intrusion upon the individual's dignitary interests in personal privacy and bodily integrity." These things had to be weighed against the community's interest in criminal law enforcement and the ability of police to use other evidence. Thus, *Schmerber* fashioned a balancing test that courts were to apply on a case-by-case basis. In Lee's case, the Court opined, the balance weighed in favor of Lee.

The Court noted that the two sides differed in their opinions over the risks the surgery posed to Lee's health and safety. Considering the medical testimony, the Court concluded that the federal appeals court was right in determining that the surgery would be an "'extensive'" intrusion on Lee's privacy and bodily integrity. Such a surgery, requiring general anesthesia, would not be intrusive if performed on a consenting person. However, in Lee's case, the Commonwealth sought to "take control of [Lee's] body, to 'drug this citizen—not yet convicted of a criminal offense—with narcotics and barbiturates into a state of unconsciousness'" in order to search beneath the skin for evidence of a crime.

Furthermore, in the Court's opinion, the Commonwealth and its police had little need to intrude in such a way on Lee's body. The Commonwealth had plenty of evidence establishing that Lee was the man who accosted Watkinson, and no one had suggested that Watkinson's identification of Lee in the hospital emergency room would be inadmissible at Lee's trial. In weighing all the relevant factors, the Court determined that the Commonwealth had "failed to demonstrate that it would be 'reasonable' under the terms of the Fourth Amendment" to gain the bullet evidence through forced surgery.

Justices Blackmun, Rehnquist, and Burger concurred in the judgment, but only Justice Burger filed an opinion. In an attempt to avoid a misunderstanding about the Court's opinion, Burger declared that the holding in Lee's case should not prevent the "detention of an individual if there are reasonable grounds to believe that natural bodily functions will disclose the presence of contraband materials secreted internally."

Impact

The *Lee* decision established a limit to the power of a state to intrude into a person's body in the course of a criminal prosecution. Many intrusions are routine for criminal defendants and suspects. Depending on the case, a person may be ordered to relinquish hair, blood, saliva, or urine samples and submit to a complete physical examination. Just a few weeks after the High Court decided Lee's case, it heard a case dealing with an issue anticipated by Justice Burger: the detention of a criminal suspect for the purpose of extracting contraband from a normal bodily function. In *United States v. Montoya de Hernandez* (1985), the High Court upheld the 16-hour detention of a person suspected of smuggling drugs by swallowing them.

Related Cases

Olmstead v. United States, 277 U.S. 438 (1928).
Schmerber v. California, 384 U.S. 757 (1966).
United States v. Montoya de Hernandez, 473 U.S. 531 (1985).

Bibliography and Further Reading

Biskupic, Joan, and Elder Witt. *Congressional Quarterly's Guide to the U.S. Supreme Court,* 3rd ed. Washington, DC: Congressional Quarterly, Inc., 1996.

"Search and Seizure." *West's Encyclopedia of American Law.* St. Paul: West Group, 1998.

Steiker, Carol S. "Counter-Revolution in Constitutional Criminal Procedure? Two Audiences, Two Answers." *Michigan Law Review,* August 1996, p. 2466.

CALIFORNIA V. CARNEY

Legal Citation: 471 U.S. 386 (1985)

Petitioner
State of California

Respondent
Charles R. Carney

Petitioner's Claim
That the Fourth Amendment to the U.S. Constitution is not violated when a police officer conducts a warrantless search of a mobile home.

Chief Lawyer for Petitioner
Louis R. Hanoian

Chief Lawyer for Respondent
Thomas F. Homann

Justices for the Court
Harry A. Blackmun, Warren E. Burger (writing for the Court), Sandra Day O'Connor, Lewis F. Powell, Jr., William H. Rehnquist, Byron R. White

Justices Dissenting
William J. Brennan, Jr., Thurgood Marshall, John Paul Stevens

Place
Washington, D.C.

Date of Decision
13 May 1985

Decision
The warrantless search of a motor mobile home does not violate the Fourth Amendment to the U.S. Constitution.

Significance
The decision established that motor mobile homes may not receive the heightened protection from warrantless police searches to which stationary homes are entitled. Instead, motor mobile homes are more akin to automobiles, which police may search without a warrant and with probable cause.

Is It a Car or a Home?

The Fourth Amendment to the U.S. Constitution protects persons from unreasonable searches and seizures by the government. The U.S. Supreme Court has held that the amendment generally requires police to obtain a search warrant from a magistrate before conducting a search, and that state governments, in addition to the federal government, must follow the amendment. There are many exceptions to the warrant requirement for police searches, and one of the issues that arises in the context of police searches is precisely what may be searched without a warrant.

The premises of a dwelling is a place that receives the most Fourth Amendment protection. Generally, law enforcement personnel must obtain a search warrant from a magistrate before conducting a search of a home. By contrast, a police officer need not obtain a search warrant before searching an automobile. This rule, created by courts shortly after the invention of the automobile and commonly called the automobile exception, is in place because motorized vehicles are mobile and can be quickly moved from jurisdiction to jurisdiction, thwarting the enforcement of criminal laws. Prior to the U.S. Supreme Court's decision in *California v. Carney*, the question remained as to whether mobile dwellings, such as a boat, camper, or motor home, should be afforded the same protection as stationary homes, or whether they should be treated as automobiles.

On 31 May 1979, in San Diego, California, Robert Williams, an agent for the Drug Enforcement Agency, observed Charles Carney escort a boy into a Dodge Mini Motor Home. The mobile motor home was parked in a parking lot, and Williams was watching the motor home because he had received information that the home was being used as a site for exchanging sex for marijuana. After 75 minutes, Williams saw the boy leave the home. A short time later, DEA agents stopped the boy, who told them that he had received marijuana from Carney and that he had, in return, allowed Carney to engage in sexual contact with him.

The agents and the boy returned to the camper and the agents instructed the boy to knock on the door. Carney answered the door and then stepped outside. With-

Warrantless Searches

The issue of warrantless searches has most often come up in relation to searches of automobiles. The Supreme Court treats cars in a special category with regard to the Fourth Amendment, and has allowed law-enforcement officers greater latitude in searches of automobiles than for other types of personal property. Justifications for this view include the fact that a car can easily be moved, and that the expectation of privacy is lower when one is in one's car.

Opponents of warrantless searches hold that such searches constitute an unduly lax regard of the Fourth Amendment, which may lead to increased police power to search other types of property—including one's home.

Is this as it should be? On the one hand, smoking marijuana while driving a vehicle is clearly more dangerous than when one is sitting at home. On the other hand, the right of police officers to stop a car for perceived violations of the law does not in itself imply that the driver should expect a lesser degree of privacy. After all, police can also see evidence of a violation at one's home—e.g., watering one's grass on a day when such is restricted due to drought—and this does not give officers the right to search for evidence of other violations.

Source(s): *West's Encyclopedia of American Law.* St. Paul, MN: West Group, 1998.

out obtaining Carney's consent or a search warrant from a magistrate, an agent went inside Carney's mobile home. When the agent spotted marijuana, plastic baggies, and a weight scale, Carney was placed under arrest and charged with possession of marijuana for sale.

At a preliminary hearing in the case, Carney asked the court to suppress the marijuana evidence, arguing that it had been obtained in violation of his Fourth Amendment right against unreasonable searches. The search was illegal, Carney maintained, because the motor home was his dwelling and the law enforcement officers had failed to obtain a warrant or his permission. Carney also claimed that there were no exigent circumstances requiring quick action, an exceptional circumstance that allows law enforcement officers to conduct warrantless searches of homes. Carney's motion was denied by the magistrate. Just prior to trial, Carney renewed his request to the judge in Superior Court, but the request was again denied. Carney proceeded to plead no contest, to the charges, and the superior court judge placed him on probation for three years.

Carney appealed the probation order to the California Court of Appeals, arguing that the trial judge should have declared the search illegal and excluded the marijuana evidence. The appeals court disagreed with Carney, but the California Supreme Court agreed. California's highest court found the search to be illegal, because the primary use for mobile homes is "to provide the occupant with living quarters." Because it was Carney's home, the court declared, the officers should have obtained a warrant from a magistrate, or Carney's permission, before searching the mobile home.

It Is a Car

The state of California appealed the decision to the U.S. Supreme Court, which reversed the decision by

a vote of 6-3. Chief Justice Burger, writing for the majority, noted at the outset the long-standing rule allowing warrantless searches of motorized vehicles. Citing U.S. Supreme Court precedent, *Carroll v. United States* (1925) Burger stated that a vehicle's "capacity to be 'quickly moved'" was the reason for allowing warrantless searches of automobiles. Burger went on to observe that the mobility of the automobile was only the initial justification for the rule. Since the *Carroll* case, the Court also had decided in *South Dakota v. Opperman* (1976) that another reason for the rule was because persons have a lesser expectation of privacy in motorized vehicles. This result in *Opperman*, Burger explained, stemmed from long-standing, widely known government regulations of the automobile, "which necessarily lead to reduced expectations of privacy."

Applying these rules to Carney's case, the majority found that Carney's motor home was "readily mobile," that the motor home had a valid license to operate on public roads, and that it was subject to government regulations. Furthermore, Carney's motor home "was so situated [in a parking lot] that an observer would conclude that it was being used not as a residence, but as a vehicle." These factors contributed to the Court's conclusion that the privacy afforded to a mobile home under the Fourth Amendment did not prohibit warrantless searches. Allowing police to conduct warrantless searches on mobile homes that are being used for transportation "ensure[s] that law enforcement officials are not unnecessarily hamstrung in their efforts to detect and prosecute criminal activity, and that the legitimate privacy interests of the public are protected." By determining first whether a mobile home is in fact mobile and whether it is being used for transportation, law enforcement personnel may fulfill the "essential purposes" of the automobile exception, "while assuring that the exception will acknowledge legitimate privacy interests."

As a final matter, the Court addressed the issue of whether the particular search conducted in Carney's case was reasonable. Citing the "fresh, direct, uncontradicted evidence" that Carney was dispensing marijuana from his motor home, Burger declared that the agents "had abundant probable cause to enter and search the vehicle . . . notwithstanding its possible use as a dwelling place."

It Is a Home

Justice Stevens, joined by Justices Brennan and Marshall, dissented. Stevens observed that the Court had two recent, applicable precedents that tugged it in different directions: *Payton v. New York* (1980) and *United States v. Ross* (1982). In *Payton,* the Court decided that searches of the home generally must be accompanied by a search warrant. In *Ross,* the Court affirmed the right of police to conduct warrantless searches of vehicles, provided the search was supported by probable cause. By opting to use the *Ross* case as its most relevant precedent, Stevens wrote, the Court had "abandoned the limits on the [automobile] exception imposed by prior cases."

Not only was the case wrongly decided, Stevens insisted, it was not worthy of the Court's review. Stevens decried the Court's increased interest in Fourth Amendment cases. "Unless an order suppressing evidence is clearly correct," Stevens lamented, "a petition for *certiorari* is likely to garner the four votes required for a grant of plenary review." In the face of an ever-expanding Court docket, the Court had decided to accept the case to establish "a rule for searching motor homes that is to be followed by the entire Nation" when it could have let stand a single state high court decision.

Stevens opened the dissent's analysis by stating the general rule on search warrants: unless the circumstances fit an exception recognized by the Court, police must obtain a search warrant before conducting a search. On the discrete topic of the expectation of privacy in mobile motor homes, Stevens said that the owners of motor homes have "a substantial and legitimate expectation of privacy when they dwell within."

Having established an expectation of privacy, Stevens examined the facts of the case and concluded that the circumstances did not justify the failure of the police to secure a search warrant. The motor home was parked in a lot with its windows covered by curtains, and when the agents entered the motor home the window blinds were drawn, making it unlikely that the occupant was preparing to drive it away. Moreover, it was parked in a parking lot just a few blocks away from a courthouse "where dozens of magistrates were avail-

able to entertain a warrant application." All of these factors, combined with a lack of exigent circumstances, left Stevens wondering "why [the agents] eschewed the safe harbor of a warrant."

Stevens rejected the argument that the bare mobility of a motorized vehicle excuses a warrantless search that is supported by probable cause. Citing *United States v. Chadwick* (1977), Stevens argued that the simple mobility of a vehicle is not sufficient justification for a warrantless search. In *Chadwick,* the Court held that the warrantless search of luggage was illegal. "If 'inherent mobility' does not justify warrantless searches," Stevens declared, "it cannot rationally provide a sufficient justification for the search of a person's dwelling place."

Stevens closed the dissenting opinion by analyzing the characteristics of the mobile home. The motor home "was designed to accommodate a breadth of ordinary living," and "the mode of construction should have indicated to the officers that it was a vehicle containing mobile living quarters." Stevens refused to believe that law enforcement officers would not be able to determine whether a particular vehicle contained living quarters. "Although it may not be a castle," Stevens lectured,

> a motor home is usually the functional equivalent of a hotel room, a vacation and retirement home, or a hunting and fishing cabin. These places may be as spartan as a humble cottage when compared to a majestic mansion, but the highest and most legitimate expectations of privacy associated with these temporal abodes should command the respect of this Court.

Impact

From a legal perspective, the *Carney* case was remarkable for its decisiveness. The majority of the Court placed motor mobile homes in the same legal category as passenger vehicles, giving them minimal protection from warrantless searches. As a result of the holding, a law enforcement officer may, without a search warrant, enter and search a mobile home. However, the officer must have probable cause to believe that the home contains evidence of a crime or a suspected criminal.

The *Carney* ruling put motor homes outside the protections offered by *Payton v. New York*. In that case, the Court held that police must have a warrant to enter a dwelling to make a routine felony arrest. Thus, if a person living in a camper or motor home is wanted for a felony, the police may enter the abode at will.

Related Cases

Carroll v. United States, 267 U.S. 132 (1925).
South Dakota v. Opperman, 428 U.S. 364 (1976).
United States v. Chadwick, 433 U.S. 1 (1977).

Payton v. New York, 445 U.S. 573 (1980).
United States v. Ross, 456 U.S. 798 (1982).

Bibliography and Further Reading

Bradley, Craig M. "The Court's 'Two Model' Approach to the Fourth Amendment: Carpe Diem." *Journal of Criminal Law and Criminology,* fall 1993, p. 429.

Hall, Kermit L., ed. *The Oxford Companion to the Supreme Court of the United States.* New York: Oxford University Press, 1992.

Nation, May 25, 1985, p. 612.

Newsweek, May 27, 1985, p. 89.

CALIFORNIA V. CIRAOLO

Legal Citation: 476 U.S. 207 (1986)

Petitioner
State of California

Respondent
Ciraolo

Petitioner's Claim
The respondent's Fourth Amendment rights were not violated when law enforcement conducted aerial observation of his home and backyard which, in turn, resulted in his arrest and conviction for cultivating marijuana.

Chief Lawyer for Petitioner
Lawrence K. Sullivan

Chief Lawyer for Respondent
Marshall Warren Krause

Justices for the Court
Warren E. Burger (writing for the Court), Sandra Day O'Connor, William H. Rehnquist, John Paul Stevens, Byron R. White

Justices Dissenting
Harry A. Blackmun, William J. Brennan, Jr., Thurgood Marshall, Lewis F. Powell, Jr.

Place
Washington, D.C.

Date of Decision
19 May 1986

Decision
Although conducted without a search warrant, aerial observation of the respondent's fenced-in backyard by law enforcement did not violate his Fourth Amendment rights.

Significance
The important focus of this case revolved around determining the impact of technological advancement on the ability of law enforcement to conduct search and seizure. The court ultimately decided that open airspace constituted a public place and, therefore, citizens have no Fourth Amendment protection from any overflight made by law enforcement. However, the dissenting opinion nonetheless presented compelling rationale and admonition for the Court to remain mindful that continuing technological advancement requires constant review of how Fourth Amendment jurisprudence is applied.

After receiving an anonymous tip that the respondent was cultivating marijuana in his garden, police rented a small aircraft and conducted an overflight in order to determine if there was sufficient evidence to obtain a warrant to search the property. The two officers that flew over the site were trained in recognition of marijuana crops via aerial reconnaissance. The photographs of the suspect's garden from the air, strongly suggested the presence of a marijuana crop on the property. Based on a sworn affidavit attesting to their expert opinion that there was a presence of marijuana plants, officers obtained a search warrant. The ensuing search of the premises resulted in seizure of 73 marijuana plants.

The local court found the accused guilty of illegal cultivation of marijuana, but the California Court of Appeals reversed that decision. It found the judgment violated the Fourth Amendment because the flight, which ultimately resulted in gaining evidence that convicted the respondent, illegally invaded the respondent's privacy. The state of California appealed the ruling to the U.S. Supreme Court which reversed the decision of the lower, appellate court. The Court was split by divided opinions: five justices held the opinion that the respondent's Fourth Amendment rights were violated, and four justices held the dissenting opinions. Neither the majority or dissenting justices questioned whether the respondent illegally cultivated marijuana; rather, at issue was whether the flight over the respondent's house constituted a search and seizure that was prohibited by the Fourth Amendment.

Unreasonable Search and Seizure

In presenting the case to the Supreme Court, the respondent's attorney argued that police really did not have a warrant when they flew over his client's home and his curtilage (a small piece of ground next to a house that is usually considered within a person's private domain). The respondent expected to have absolute privacy at his home; his fenced-in home was an obvious sign that he did not want to expose his activities to public scrutiny. He had been subjected to deliberate, unreasonable search and seizure because, the respondent's attorney contended, police officers conducted their fly-over without just cause and with specific intent to collect information about the respondent's activities. In effect, law enforcement had intruded on his privacy.

The arguments presented for the respondent were persuasive and four of the nine justices joined to write an equally compelling dissenting opinion. Writing for the dissenting opinion, Justice Powell expressed great concerned over the possibility that the sanctity of citizens' privacy would be threatened if the Fourth Amendment was strictly interpreted to define unlawful search and seizure as only pertaining to actual, physical entry onto a person's private property. He pointed out that as technology advanced (even beyond air travel), the possibility for authorities to violate the Fourth Amendment without physical entry increased when "reasonable expectations of privacy may be defeated by electronic as well as physical intrusion." Citing *Katz v. United States* (1967), Justice Powell went on to maintain that when a person shows expectations of privacy, it is reasonable to expect to remain protected from public scrutiny. Further, if there were obvious signs that someone wanted privacy in his yard (for example, fencing in and enclosing a home), society should understand and respect those signs as evidence of a "reasonable" expectation of privacy. Justices, therefore, felt that even though the respondent took precautions to show he had expectations of privacy, police jeopardized that privacy not through direct, physical entry, but indirectly by using a product of modern technology—an airplane. Powell pointed out that the respondent did not "knowingly" expose his curtilage to public scrutiny and that there really was no equity between accidentally noticing illegal activity and gathering photographs during an official, planned air surveillance. Essentially, dissenting justices maintained that people's rights under the Fourth Amendment should be protected whether those rights were jeopardized from the ground or air.

The Liability of Open Airspace

Although the opinion of dissenting Supreme Court justices made a compelling argument, a slim majority of justices elected to rule that the police had not conducted an unreasonable search and seizure and had not violated the respondent's Fourth Amendment rights. In direct disagreement with their colleagues and the written opinion of the California Court of Appeal, the majority disagreed that there was a significant distinction between regular police patrol and focused observations on the respondent's home. In his written opinion, Chief Justice Burger reasoned that like any other person who had flown over the respondent's home, police officers saw an obvious violation of the law. The Fourth Amendment could, therefore, not protect the respondent even if the respondent made clear that he wanted to remain "untouchable" in his pri-

vacy. As with all public places, air space is open for everybody; police could not neglect the obvious fact that the respondent was breaking the law by illegally cultivating marijuana. That the police officers who conducted the aerial observation had been trained in drug search and seizure was irrelevant because they simply had seen an illegal act that could have been seen by anybody else during an overflight. Regardless of whether the respondent erected a six-foot fence around his property and another ten-foot fence around the marijuana, the majority opinion agreed with the state of California's argument that, in effect, the respondent had "knowingly" exposed his yard to public view.

Chief Justice Burger agreed that the Fourth Amendment of U.S. Constitution was written to protect people and their privacy. However, citing precedent in *Hester v. United States* (1924), he pointed out that the Fourth Amendment did not protect "open fields" and that an individual could not expect outdoor privacy except in the area immediately surrounding the home. Further, privacy could not be expected if activities were visible from the outside even if the area was enclosed with a high fence in order to restrict ground-level view. There was still no reasonable expectation of privacy from naked eye inspection if taken from open, navigable airspace—an airplane could not be considered a device of advancing technology because the fact of air flight is routine.

Impact

The decision of the Supreme Court to uphold the lower court's conviction was, by no means, unanimous. Only by one vote, did the majority opinion prevail. The majority opinion held that a citizen's right to privacy in the home and its curtilage did not include ability to engage in unlawful conduct. The opinion of dissenting justices, however, also expressed serious reservations as to whether the Court had failed to enforce Fourth Amendment rights pertaining to personal security, liberty and private property. Dissenting justices strongly believed that open air space should not deprive citizens of either their private interest inside the home or intrude on their activities around private property. Non-routine, warrantless flight over the homes of private citizens broke the basic principles of the right to privacy under the Fourth Amendment. In an opinion appending the dissenting justices' arguments, Justice John Marshall Harlan II accurately predicted that developing technology would always require the court to continuously reexamine the possibility that constitutional rights could be subverted through technology. He observed that interpretation of privacy rights protected by the Fourth Amendment "should not be limited to prescribing only physical intrusions onto private property" because "it is, in the present day, bad physics as well as bad law, for reasonable expectations of privacy may be defeated by electronic as well as physical invasion."

Related Cases

Hester v. United States, 265 U.S. 57 (1924).
Katz v. United States, 389 U.S. 347 (1967).
United States v. Knotts, 460 U.S. 276 (1983).

Oliver v. United States, 466 U.S. 170 (1984).
Dow Chemical Co. v. United States, 476 U.S. 227 (1986).
Florida v. Riley, 488 U.S. 445 (1989).

Bibliography and Further Reading

Biskupic, Joan, and Elder Witt, eds. *Congressional Quarterly's Guide to the U.S. Supreme Court,* 3rd ed. Washington, DC: Congressional Quarterly, Inc., 1996.

MARYLAND V. GARRISON

Legal Citation: 480 U.S. 79 (1987)

Petitioner
State of Maryland

Respondent
Garrison

Petitioner's Claim
That evidence taken from Garrison's apartment should not be suppressed even though the police officers used an overbroad warrant.

Chief Lawyer for Petitioner
Stephen H. Sacks, Attorney General of Maryland

Chief Lawyer for Respondent
Gerald A. Kroop

Justices for the Court
Sandra Day O'Connor, Lewis F. Powell, Jr., William H. Rehnquist, Antonin Scalia, John Paul Stevens (writing for the Court), Byron R. White

Justices Dissenting
Harry A. Blackmun, William J. Brennan, Jr., Thurgood Marshall

Place
Washington, D.C.

Date of Decision
24 February 1987

Decision
Reversed the Maryland Court of Appeals ruling and held that the search warrant was valid and the execution of the warrant did not violate Garrison's rights under the Fourth Amendment, since the mistake made by the officers was understandable and reasonable.

Significance
The ruling provided another good faith exception to the exclusionary rule. The use of an overly broad warrant did not justify the exclusion of evidence from trial because the officers made a reasonable effort to identify the place intended for search.

On 21 May 1982 Baltimore police officers obtained a warrant to search Lawrence McWebb and a 2036 Park Avenue third floor apartment. Although there were actually two apartments, the police believed that only one apartment existed on the third floor of that building. They concluded this through listening to an informant, examining the exterior of the building, and questioning the utility company. Six police officers executed the warrant. They encountered McWebb in front of the building and used his key to get into the building and onto the third floor. As they entered the vestibule on the third floor, the officers encountered Garrison, clad in pajamas and wearing a half body cast. The doors to both apartments were open and police could see inside both areas. The officers entered Garrison's apartment, still thinking that only one apartment stood on that floor, and found heroin, cash, and drug paraphernalia. At that point, the officers realized that two apartments existed and they were in Garrison's. They discontinued the search.

Garrison was convicted of possession of a controlled substance. Although Garrison made a motion to suppress the evidence and make it inadmissible in court, the trial court denied this motion. The Maryland Court of Special Appeals agreed with this, indicating that the warrant was intended to authorize a search of the entire third floor of the building. The Maryland Court of Appeals reversed that decision because it felt that the warrant authorized the search of McWebb's apartment only, and not the entire third floor. The court of appeals concluded that the police should not have entered Garrison's apartment without a warrant.

Latitude For Honest Mistakes Made By Officers

The Supreme Court agreed to hear the case, noting that it involved two separate constitutional issues—the validity of the warrant and the reasonableness of its execution. In his written opinion, Justice Stevens noted that the warrant clause of the Fourth Amendment prohibits the issuance of a general warrant. Instead, the warrant must describe the place to be searched and the persons or things to be seized. This is known as the particularity requirement. This requirement serves to care-

The Good Faith Exception

The exclusionary rule was developed to enforce Fourth Amendment search and seizure requirements in its exclusion from the criminal courtroom of evidence obtained by other than legal means. The good faith exception to the exclusionary rule, on the other hand, offers law-enforcement officers an area of leeway—opponents would call it a loophole—within the legal confines of the exclusionary rule. Thus when a search turns out to be illegal, but while conducting it the police officers believed in good faith that they were operating within the law, the evidence obtained in such a search is deemed admissible.

Such was the situation in *United States v. Leon* (1984), in which Justice Byron White articulated the good faith

exception as a modification of the exclusionary rule to uphold the admissibility of "evidence seized on a search warrant issued by a detached and neutral magistrate but ultimately found to be unsupported by probable cause."

Views on the good faith exception that, like the exclusionary rule, applies to criminal proceedings, vary depending on whether the commentator is a civil libertarian or someone whose primary emphasis is on law and order.

Source(s): Levy, Leonard W., ed. *Encyclopedia of the American Constitution.* New York: Macmillan, 1986.

fully tailor the search to its justification and to prevent wide-ranging exploratory searches, which the framers of the Constitution wanted to prohibit. In the current case, the description of the place to be searched was broader than appropriate because of the mistaken belief that only one apartment was on the third floor. The constitutionality of the officers' actions must be judged based on the information that they had at the time. The discovery of facts showing that a valid warrant was unnecessarily broad does not make that warrant invalid.

Stevens next discussed whether the execution of the warrant violated Garrison's right to be secure in his home. If the officers had known that the third floor contained two apartments, they would have had to limit their search to McWebb's apartment. Once they realized they were in the wrong apartment they ended the search. Their conduct and the search limits were based on information that became available as the search proceeded. Although the purpose of a search strictly limits the extent of a search, "the Court has also recognized the need to allow some latitude for honest mistakes that are made by officers in the dangerous and difficult process of making arrests and executing search warrants."

Stevens quoted *Hill v. California,* a case in which the officers arrested the wrong man. "Sufficient probability, not certainty, is the touchstone of reasonableness under the Fourth Amendment . . . the officers' mistake was understandable and the arrest a reasonable response to the situation . . ." Stevens felt the same principle applied in *Maryland v. Garrison.* The validity of the search of Garrison's apartment, using a warrant for the search of the entire third floor, depends on whether the officers' failure to recognize the over-

breadth of the warrant was understandable and reasonable. The objective facts show that the officers had never suggested two apartments existed. Thus, their belief that only one apartment existed and that they could search the whole third floor was reasonable. The Supreme Court reversed the court of appeals' decision that the warrant did not authorize the search and that the police were not justified in entering Garrison's apartment.

Evidence Against the Victim of Police Error Should Not Be Used

Justice Blackmun wrote the dissent. Blackmun believed that the search violated the Fourth Amendment and that the evidence should have been suppressed. Regarding the search of apartments in multi-unit buildings, courts have found invalid those warrants that do not describe the targeted unit with enough specificity to prevent a search of all the units in the building. Blackmun and the court of appeals both felt that the warrant specified only the search of McWebb's apartment, not Garrison's. Therefore the search was warrantless and unreasonable and the evidence gathered in the search should have been excluded.

Blackmun noted that it might make sense to excuse a mistake that produced evidence against a person being investigated based on probable cause, but it does not follow that a mistake should be excused when evidence is collected on someone not singled out and who was the victim of an error.

Detective Marcus, who obtained the search warrant, did not make reasonable efforts to verify the layout of the third floor. He should have noted that the building had seven mailboxes, and he should have asked his informant if McWebb's was the only apartment on the third floor. Blackmun expressed doubt about whether the warrant was executed with reasonableness. Only when they were well into their search and had discovered incriminating evidence, did the police realize their "mistake." They should have realized they were in a separate apartment well before they discovered the evidence. When they first encountered Garrison, they asked him who he was, but not where he lived. The officers should have realized their error when they made their security sweep since each apartment had a bathroom, a kitchen, a living room, and a bedroom. "Even if a reasonable error on the part of police officers prevents a Fourth Amendment violation, the mistakes here, both with respect to obtaining and executing the warrant, are not reasonable and could easily have been avoided."

The decision in this case was an example of the good faith exception to the exclusionary rule. The exclusionary rule states that evidence gathered unlawfully should be excluded from a trial. Since the 1980s, the Supreme Court has established many exceptions to this rule. The majority of the Court felt that the exclusionary rule was not a personal right, but was created to deter police misconduct. Excluding evidence that the police gathered through an honest mistake would not deter misconduct and would allow a guilty person to go free. Justices Brennan and Marshall maintained that if a search warrant is faulty, the evidence should be excluded from trial, even if the problem with the warrant was due to an honest mistake. This would preserve the integrity of the Fourth Amendment.

Related Cases

Steele v. United States, 267 U.S. 498 (1925).
Brinegar v. United States, 338 U.S. 160 (1949).
Hill v. California, 401 U.S. 797 (1971).
Coolidge v. New Hampshire, 403 U.S. 443 (1971).

Bibliography and Further Reading

Biskupic, Joan, and Elder Witt. *Congressional Quarterly's Guide to the U.S. Supreme Court,* 3rd ed. Washington, DC: Congressional Quarterly, Inc., 1996.

West's Encyclopedia of American Law, Vol. 4. St. Paul, MN: West Group, 1998.

Wieber, Michael C. "The Theory and Practice of Illinois v. Rodriguez." *Journal of Criminal Law and Criminology,* fall 1993, p. 604.

ARIZONA V. HICKS

Legal Citation: 480 U.S. 321 (1987)

Petitioner
State of Arizona

Respondent
Hicks

Petitioner's Claim
That a search of Hicks's apartment was legal under the Fourth Amendment.

Chief Lawyer for Petitioner
Linda A. Akers

Chief Lawyer for Respondent
John W. Rood III

Justices for the Court
Harry A. Blackmun, William J. Brennan, Jr., Thurgood Marshall, Antonin Scalia (writing for the Court), John Paul Stevens, Byron R. White

Justices Dissenting
Lewis F. Powell, Jr., William H. Rehnquist, Sandra Day O'Connor

Place
Washington, D.C.

Date of Decision
3 March 1987

Decision
Upheld two lower courts' decisions that the search was a violation of the Fourth Amendment.

Significance
The decision set a requirement that "probable cause" operates as a separate limitation on the application of the "plain view" doctrine. The "plain view" doctrine, which was established in *Coolidge v. New Hampshire*, allows police to seize incriminating evidence that is found during a warrantless search, if the material is in plain view. *Arizona v. Hicks* changed this significantly, by requiring the police to have "probable cause" to suspect criminal activity in order to be allowed to seize material in plain view. The ruling could be considered a victory for privacy advocates, and a loss for those who advocate stronger law enforcement.

On 18 April 1984, in Arizona, a bullet was fired through the floor of Hicks's apartment, injuring a man in the apartment below. Police officers entered Hicks's apartment to search for the gunman, for other victims, and for weapons. During the search, the police discovered a .25 caliber automatic pistol, a .45 caliber automatic, a .22 caliber sawed-off rifle, and a stocking-cap mask. The apartment was also littered with drug paraphernalia.

One of the police officers, Officer Nelson, noticed two sets of expensive stereo components, which seemed out of place in the otherwise squalid four-room apartment. Suspecting that they had been stolen, he read and recorded their serial numbers—moving some of them, including a turntable, to do so.

Nelson phoned in the numbers to the National Crime Information Center to check them against the center's computerized listing of stolen property. The listing confirmed his suspicion that the turntable had been taken during an armed robbery, and therefore Nelson seized it. Later, it was determined that some of the other stereo equipment had been stolen in the same armed robbery. A warrant was obtained and executed to seize that equipment as well.

Hicks was subsequently indicted for the robbery. However, the state trial court granted his motion to suppress the evidence that had been seized, and the Arizona Court of Appeals affirmed. The court of appeals based its decision on a statement in *Mincey v. Arizona* (1977), that a warrantless search must be "strictly circumscribed by the exigencies which justify its initiation." The shooting was considered to be an exigency, or emergency, and therefore the police were justified in entering Hicks's apartment without a warrant.

However, police had not entered Hicks's apartment to look for stolen merchandise, and therefore the policeman had violated Hicks's Fourth Amendment rights when he obtained the serial numbers of the stereo equipment. Both courts rejected the state of Arizona's contention that the policeman's actions were justified under the "plain view" doctrine, which had been established in *Coolidge v. New Hampshire*. The Arizona Supreme Court denied review, and the state eventually petitioned the Supreme Court, which agreed to hear it. The case was argued on 8 December 1986 and decided on 3 March 1987. Two groups filed "friend of the court" briefs in the case: the American Civil Liberties Union Foundation urged that the lower courts' decisions should be affirmed, while Americans for Effective Law Enforcement urged reversal.

The state of Arizona argued that Officer Nelson's actions constituted neither a "search" nor a "seizure" within the meaning of the Fourth Amendment. The Court agreed with the state that the mere recording of the serial numbers did not constitute a seizure. However, moving of the equipment did constitute a "search" separate and apart from the search for the shooter, victims, and weapons that was the lawful objective of his entry into the apartment.

Responding to a question on cross-examination, Officer Nelson explained that his suspicion was "based on 12 years worth of police experience. I have worked in different burglary crimes throughout that period of time and . . . I'm just very familiar with people converting stolen stereos and TVs into their own use" (quoted in a footnote in Justice Powell's dissenting opinion). Nevertheless, the state conceded that Nelson had only a "reasonable suspicion," not "probable cause," to believe that the stereo equipment was stolen—and therefore the search was invalid.

The Court had not previously ruled on the question of whether probable cause is required in order to invoke the "plain view" doctrine. In its decision in this case, the Court ruled for the first time that probable cause is required. "To say otherwise would be to cut the 'plain view' doctrine loose from its theoretical and practical moorings," asserted Justice Scalia, writing for the majority.

In a dissenting opinion, Justice Powell asked what the Court would have had Officer Nelson do in these circumstances. He asserted that the officers' suspicion that the stereo components were stolen was both reasonable and based on the facts of the case. "Indeed, the State was unwise to concede the absence of probable cause," he wrote.

For Powell, the distinction between "merely looking at" an object in plain view and "moving" or "disturbing" the object to investigate a reasonable suspicion was an arbitrary one. He cited a hypothetical example in which one possibly stolen watch was lying face up and another lying face down: reading the serial number on one would not constitute a search, but turning over the other to read its serial number would. "With all respect, this distinction between looking at a suspicious object in plain view and moving it even a few inches trivializes the Fourth Amendment," Powell wrote.

Justice Antonin Scalia. © Photograph by Joseph Lavenburg, National Geographic. Collection of the Supreme Court of the United States.

Justice O'Connor also dissented, arguing that Nelson's actions be upheld because they constituted a "cursory inspection" rather than a "full-blown search," and could therefore be justified by reasonable suspicion instead of probable cause. "The overwhelming majority of both state and federal courts have held that probable cause is not required for a minimal inspection of an item in plain view," she wrote. However, the majority opinion was that the Court was unwilling to create a subcategory of "cursory" searches under the Fourth Amendment, because nothing in the prior opinions of the Court would support such a distinction.

Impact

"Today the Court holds for the first time that the requirement of probable cause operates as a separate limitation on the application of the plain-view doctrine," Powell wrote in his dissenting opinion. In Powell's view, the Court's new rule would cause uncertainty, making law enforcement less effective without enhancing privacy interests. "Unfortunately, in its desire to establish a 'bright-line' test, the Court has taken a step that ignores a substantial body of precedent and that places serious roadblocks to reasonable law enforcement practices," O'Connor agreed. In his majority opinion, Scalia acknowledged their opinions, but nevertheless asserted that in this case, protecting privacy had to take precedence over law enforcement: "There is nothing new in the realization that the Constitution sometimes insulates the criminality of a few in order to protect the privacy of us all."

Related Cases

Stanley v. Georgia, 394 U.S. 557 (1969).
Coolidge v. New Hampshire, 403 U.S. 443 (1971).
Mincey v. Arizona, 434 U.S. 1343 (1977).
Texas v. Brown, 460 U.S. 730 (1983).
Illinois v. Andreas, 463 U.S. 765 (1983).
Maryland v. Macon, 472 U.S. 463 (1985).

Bibliography and Further Reading

Biskupic, Joan, and Elder Witt, eds. *Congressional Quarterly's Guide to the U.S. Supreme Court,* 3rd ed. Washington, DC: Congressional Quarterly, Inc., 1996.

MacIntosh, Susanne M. "Fourth Amendment-The Plain Touch Exception to the Warrant Requirement." *Journal of Criminal Law and Criminology,* winter-spring 1984, p. 743.

Steiker, Carol S. "Counter-Revolution in Constitutional Criminal Procedure?" *Michigan Law Review,* August 1996, p. 2466.

Stuntz, William J. "Privacy's Problem and the Law of Criminal Procedure." *Michigan Law Review,* March 1995, p. 1016.

CALIFORNIA V. GREENWOOD

Legal Citation: 486 U.S. 35 (1988)

Petitioner
State of California

Respondent
Billy Greenwood

Petitioner's Claim
That a warrantless search and seizure of garbage placed at the curb for pickup does not violate the Fourth Amendment.

Chief Lawyer for Petitioner
Michael J. Pear

Chief Lawyer for Respondent
Michael Ian Garey

Justices for the Court
Harry A. Blackmun, Sandra Day O'Connor, William H. Rehnquist, Antonin Scalia, John Paul Stevens, Byron R. White (writing for the Court)

Justices Dissenting
William J. Brennan, Jr., Thurgood Marshall (Anthony M. Kennedy did not participate)

Place
Washington, D.C.

Date of Decision
16 May 1988

Decision
Reversed the California Court of Appeal decision and ruled that the Fourth Amendment does not prohibit the warrantless search and seizure of garbage placed on the curb for collection.

Significance
The ruling settled the question of whether a person's trash, placed on the curb for collection, could be searched without a warrant. The expectation of privacy does not guarantee protection by the Fourth Amendment unless society considers that expectation to be reasonable. It is not reasonable to believe that trash placed at the curb will remain private.

In February of 1984, a criminal suspect informed a federal drug enforcement agent that a shipment of illegal drugs was on its way to the home of Billy Greenwood. Also, a neighbor had complained that numerous cars arrived at Greenwood's home late at night and stayed only a few minutes. Acting on this information, Investigator Jenny Stracner of the Laguna Beach Police Department observed vehicles making brief stops at the house at night. She followed a truck from Greenwood's house to a suspected drug dealing location.

On 6 April 1984, Stracner asked the trash collector to bring her Greenwood's plastic garbage bags, which Greenwood had left for pick-up on the curb. The trash collector did so. Stracner searched through the garbage and found items associated with drug use—razor blades, straws with cocaine residue, and phone bills noting calls to people with drug records. Listing her finds in an affidavit, Stracner obtained a search warrant. The police searched the house, found quantities of hashish and cocaine, and arrested Greenwood and Dyanne Van Houten on felony narcotics charges. Greenwood posted bail and was soon free. Once again, the police received complaints about frequent late-night visits to the house.

On 4 May 1984, Investigator Robert Rahaeuser got Greenwood's trash bags from the garbage collector. A search of the rubbish revealed evidence of illegal drug use. Rahaeuser obtained a search warrant, and the police found more drugs and evidence of drug dealing. They again arrested Greenwood.

The Superior Court of Orange County dismissed the charges against Greenwood because *People v. Krivda* (1971) held that trash searches without a warrant violated the Fourth Amendment and the California Constitution. The court felt that without the search of the trash, the police would not have had probable cause to search the home. The California Court of Appeals agreed with the Superior Court. The California Supreme Court declined to review the case.

The Fourth Amendment forbids unreasonable searches and seizures and states that probable cause must exist for a warrant to be issued. The Fourth Amendment was added to the Constitution to guard against arbitrary police intrusions, such as the colonists had frequently experienced under British rule, and which had come to represent governmental oppression. Like many parts of the Constitution, this amendment could be interpreted in many different ways. Until the twentieth century, the Fourth Amendment was of no help to criminal defendants because evidence seized during an unreasonable search was still admissible in court. Not until *Weeks v. United States* (1914) was evidence seized in an unreasonable search deemed inadmissible. Thus was created the exclusionary rule, which states that evidence obtained in violation of a suspect's Fourth Amendment rights cannot be used in a criminal prosecution.

A Reasonable Expectation of Privacy

On 11 January 1988, the case was argued before the Supreme Court and was decided on 16 May 1988. Greenwood's lawyer, Michael Ian Garey, argued that Greenwood had an expectation of privacy regarding the trash that he had placed on the curb in opaque plastic bags, and had assumed would be collected, mixed with other trash, and taken to the dump. In theory, the Fourth Amendment protects people's rights to privacy. Justice White, writing for the majority of six, stated that the expectation of privacy does not guarantee protection by the Fourth Amendment unless society considers that expectation to be reasonable. White explained, "It is common knowledge that plastic garbage bags left on or at the side of a public street are readily accessible to animals, children, scavengers, snoops, and other members of the public." Greenwood had placed the bags on the curb in order to convey them to the trash collector, who could have sorted through them or allowed the police to do so. Because the bags of trash were deposited in an area particularly suited for public inspection, the expectation of privacy was not objectively reasonable.

Greenwood's lawyer also argued that the expectation of privacy should be considered reasonable because under the *Krivda* ruling, searches and seizures of trash, done without warrants, were illegal under California law. He also argued that a California constitutional amendment eliminated the exclusionary rule for evidence seized in violation of state, but not federal, law. Garey claimed that the California amendment violated the Due Process Clause of the Fourteenth Amendment, meaning that the government may not deprive anyone of life, liberty, or property without a fair trial or hearing.

White countered that California could amend its constitution to negate the decision in the *Krivda* case. He stated that "at the federal level, we have not required that evidence obtained in violation of the Fourth Amendment be suppressed in all circumstances." White noted that decisions made about excluding evidence, based on the Fourth Amendment, have weighed the benefits of preventing police misconduct against the costs of excluding reliable evidence. The Court has declined to apply the exclusionary rule when law officers have acted in good faith and when the benefit to the guilty defendant would go against the basic concepts of the criminal justice system. White suggested that the states could take a similar position balancing the benefits of excluding relevant evidence of criminal activity against the costs, as long as the police have not violated federal law. Based on these opinions, the majority ruled to reverse the decision of the California Court of Appeals, deciding, along with the "vast majority of lower courts that have addressed the issue," that the Fourth Amendment does not prohibit the warrantless search and seizure of garbage left for collection.

Should the Fourth Amendment Protect Garbage?

Justice Brennan wrote the dissenting opinion, in which Justice Marshall joined. Brennan noted, "Scrutiny of another's trash is contrary to commonly accepted notions of civilized behavior . . . Society will be shocked to learn that the Court, the ultimate guarantor of liberty, deems unreasonable our expectation that the aspects of our private lives that are concealed safely in a trash bag will not become public." He held that a container that can support a reasonable expectation of privacy may not be searched without a warrant and that a package closed against inspection is protected by the Fourth Amendment. It should make no difference what type of package it is, as long as its contents are concealed. Brennan also pointed out that it should make no difference that Greenwood used the bags to throw away, rather than to transport, his belongings. Greenwood's decision to throw away the trash does not lessen his expectation of privacy. "A single bag of trash testifies eloquently to the eating, reading and recreational habits of the person who produced it."

Brennan held that, "Most of us, I believe, would be incensed to discover a meddler—whether a neighbor, a reporter, or a detective—scrutinizing our sealed trash containers to discover some detail of our personal lives." However, since occasional intrusions into trash containers do happen, the police cannot be expected to look away from evidence of criminal activity that anyone could have seen. They must simply adhere to norms of privacy that are generally accepted by society. Just because someone may rummage through a person's trash does not mean a person cannot expect privacy. And even though Greenwood was getting rid of the trash, it does not follow that he was giving up his expectation of privacy.

Brennan summed up his dissent by stating:

In holding that the warrantless search of Greenwood's trash was consistent with the Fourth Amendment, the Court paints a grim picture of our society . . . The American society with which I am familiar . . . is more dedicated to individual liberty and more sensitive to intrusions on the sanctity of the home than the Court is willing to acknowledge.

Impact

The FBI, the Drug Enforcement Administration, and many police departments regularly search trash. The decision in *California v. Greenwood* was welcomed by law enforcement agencies and led to even more detectives looking for evidence in this manner.

Civil libertarians objected to the decision. Arthur Spitzer of the American Civil Liberties Union stated in a *Time* magazine interview, *California v. Greenwood* "is one more step in squeezing the right to privacy to the point where Americans will no longer feel secure against the prying eye of Big Brother."

The decision did not surprise many legal scholars, since the Supreme Court had been taking a narrow view of the right to privacy. People have no reasonable expectation of privacy regarding banking records, vehicle location, handwriting, and land visible from public places. Law enforcement officers may inspect these things without a warrant.

In the mid-1990s, the Supreme Court's decision in *California v. Greenwood* was still being used as the basis for opinions regarding the warrantless searching of trash. The Supreme Court of North Carolina, in *State v. Hauser* (1976) held that a search of a defendant's garbage did not violate the Fourth Amendment, even though the garbage was taken from the backyard. Because it was removed during the normal course of trash collection, the defendant lost his expectation of privacy because he knew that the trash collector would take it, and could possibly look through it or give it to someone else. To maintain his privacy interest in his trash, the defendant needed to deliver the trash to the dump personally or burn it.

Related Cases

People v. Krivda, 5 Cal.3d 357 (1971).
United States v. Calandra, 414 U.S. 338 (1974).
State v. Hauser, 342 N.C. 382 (1976).
United States v. Leon, 468 U.S. 897 (1984).

Bibliography and Further Reading

Sanders, Alain L. "Lifting the Lid on Garbage." *Time,* May 30, 1988.

Shanoff, Barry. "Garbage is Public Property on Curb." *World Wastes,* June 1998, p. 74.

Uviller, H. Richard. "The Fourth Amendment: Does it Protect Your Garbage?" *The Nation,* October 10, 1988.

SKINNER V. RAILWAY LABOR EXECUTIVES' ASSN.

Legal Citation: 489 U.S. 602 (1989)

Petitioner
Samuel K. Skinner, U.S. Secretary of Transportation

Respondents
Railway Labor Executives' Association, et al.

Petitioner's Claim
That regulations requiring the testing of bodily fluids after a train accident do not violate the Fourth Amendment rights of railroad employees.

Chief Lawyer for Petitioner
Richard Thornburgh, U.S. Attorney General

Chief Lawyer for Respondents
Lawrence M. Mann

Justices for the Court
Harry A. Blackmun, Anthony M. Kennedy (writing for the Court), Sandra Day O'Connor, William H. Rehnquist, Antonin Scalia, John Paul Stevens, Byron R. White

Justices Dissenting
William J. Brennan, Jr., Thurgood Marshall

Place
Washington, D.C.

Date of Decision
21 March 1989

Decision
Upheld regulations that required railroads to test blood, urine, and breath of employees involved in train accidents, deciding that such tests did not violate the Fourth Amendment.

Significance
Although done without a warrant, probable cause, or individualized suspicion, mandatory drug testing of railroad employees was held not to violate the Fourth Amendment prohibition against unreasonable searches because of the "special need" to ensure the public's safety.

In 1985 the Federal Railroad Administration (FRA) adopted regulations addressing the problem of alcohol and drug use among railroad employees. This was the direct result of at least 21 significant train accidents involving alcohol or drug use between 1972 and 1983. These accidents resulted in 25 deaths. Subpart C of the regulations, called "Post-Accident Toxicological Testing," is mandatory. It states that all railroad employees directly involved in an accident must provide blood and urine samples for testing. These samples must be obtained at an independent medical facility and then shipped to the FRA laboratory for analysis. The FRA relies primarily on the blood sample analyses because they note the presence of alcohol and drugs and their current impairment effects. Urine samples are also necessary because traces of drugs remain longer in the urine than in the blood and a delay in taking the samples could mean the drugs could be eliminated from the blood stream. The urine tests are important because a positive test could help determine the cause of an accident. The regulations require the FRA to notify employees of the test results and to allow them an opportunity to respond in writing before the final report on the accident is prepared.

Subpart D, called "Authorization to Test for Cause," authorized railroads to require employees to take breath or urine tests after an accident where a supervisor had a "reasonable suspicion" that an employee's acts contributed to an accident. The tests could also be required after certain rule violations or if supervisors suspect an employee is under the influence of drugs or alcohol.

The Railway Labor Executives' Association filed a lawsuit in the U.S. District Court for the Northern District of California to forbid these regulations. The judge granted summary judgment in the petitioner's favor and against the railway association. The judge stated that the railroad employees "have a valid interest in the integrity of their own bodies." This interest deserved protection under the Fourth Amendment, which prohibits unreasonable searches and seizures. The court held, however, that this interest was outweighed by the competing interest of railway safety.

A divided panel of the Court of Appeals for the Ninth Circuit reversed the district court's decision. The court of appeals ruled that particularized suspicion is essential for the searches (the blood, urine, and breath testing) to be reasonable. The court invalidated the parts of the regulations that did not require "reasonable suspicion." The court of appeals also noted that "blood and urine tests intended to establish drug use other than alcohol . . . cannot measure current drug intoxication or degree of impairment."

A "Special Need," Ensuring Railway Safety, Makes A Warrant Impractical

The Supreme Court agreed to hear the case to decide if the invalidated regulations violated the Fourth Amendment. The Court noted that the collection and testing of biological samples required by the regulations are searches, subject to the Fourth Amendment. This amendment requires that searches be reasonable. This is determined by balancing the intrusion on the individual's Fourth Amendment interests against the promotion of legitimate governmental interests. Usually a search is not reasonable unless a warrant is obtained, based on probable cause. However, the Court has recognized "special needs" beyond the normal need for law enforcement, which make a warrant impractical. The government's interest in ensuring railway safety is a "special need." These regulations were not formulated to help prosecute employees for drug use, but rather to prevent accidents.

The main purpose for requiring a warrant is to protect people's privacy by making sure that intrusions are not random acts of government agents. A warrant is issued by a detached, neutral magistrate to ensure an objective decision regarding the validity of a search. Since in the present case "there are virtually no facts for a neutral magistrate to evaluate," a warrant is not required. This is especially so because taking the time to obtain a warrant might result in the destruction of valuable evidence, since alcohol and drugs are eliminated from the bloodstream at constant rate.

Usually searches, with or without a warrant, must be based on probable cause, which means a reasonable belief that a person has committed a crime. In this case however, Justice Kennedy noted, "In limited circumstances, where the privacy interests implicated by the search are minimal, and where an important governmental interest furthered by the intrusion would be placed in jeopardy by a requirement of individualized suspicion, a search may be reasonable despite the absence of such suspicion."

Relying on *Schmerber v. California*, Kennedy noted that the intrusion occasioned by a blood test is not significant. Breath tests are even less intrusive. Kennedy noted that although urination is traditionally shielded by great privacy, the regulations try to reduce the intrusiveness of the collection process since the samples do not have to be furnished under direct observation and are collected in a medical environment. He stated that the expectations of privacy of these employees, in a highly safety-regulated industry, are diminished. Therefore, the testing procedures in Subparts C and D "pose only limited threats to the justifiable expectations of privacy . . ."

The government has a strong interest in testing without having to demonstrate individualized suspicion. These employees can cause a great loss of life before any signs of impairment are noticeable. The regulations would help deter alcohol and drug use on the job since employees know that through testing they would be discovered. The testing procedures would also help obtain information about the causes of accidents. Negative test results would eliminate drug use as a cause of an accident and would help establish the actual cause. If particularized suspicion were required before testing, the railroads would be impeded in gathering important information about accidents. Since the scene of train accidents is chaotic, obtaining evidence that a particular employee might be impaired is impractical. Attempting to pinpoint particular employees for testing would result in the loss of evidence. "It would be unrealistic, and inimical to the Government's goal of ensuring safety in rail transportation, to require a showing of individualized suspicion in these circumstances."

Urine testing, if it showed recent use of a controlled substance, would provide information for further investigative work. However, principal reliance is placed on blood tests, which can identify very recent drug use. The urine tests are a secondary source of information. Taken together they form a highly effective means of determining on the job impairment and they serve to deter drug use by railroad employees.

Kennedy summed up by stating that compelling government interests would be hindered if railroads were required to show a reasonable suspicion of impairment before testing anyone. Since the testing is not an undue infringement on the justifiable expectations of privacy of these employees, the government's interests outweigh privacy concerns. "It is reasonable to conduct such tests in the absence of a warrant or reasonable suspicion that any particular employee may be impaired . . . The tests are reasonable within the meaning of the Fourth Amendment." Thus the majority of the Supreme Court reversed the decision of the court of appeals, which had invalidated the testing regulations.

Justice Stevens, concurring in part and concurring in judgment, noted that it is doubtful that the regulations deter alcohol and drug use on the job. ". . . If the risk of serious personal injury does not deter their use of these substances, it seems highly unlikely that the additional threat of loss of employment would have any effect on their behavior."

Highly Intrusive Searches Should Be Based On Probable Cause

Justices Marshall and Brennan dissented. Marshall called the government's compulsory collection and testing of blood and urine "a particularly Draconian weapon" in the war on drugs. "Precisely because the need for action against the drug scourge is manifest, the need for vigilance against unconstitutional excess is great." Marshall noted that times of urgency are times of grave threats to liberty, such as during World War II when Japanese Americans were place in relocation camps and during the 1950s when Senator Joseph McCarthy led an effort to identify and ostracize Communist sympathizers. Marshall observed that when fundamental freedoms are sacrificed in the name of a threat, we later regret it.

Marshall contended that in allowing drug testing without evidence of wrongdoing, "the majority today joins those shortsighted courts which have allowed basic constitutional rights to fall prey to momentary emergencies." Highly intrusive searches should be based on probable cause, not on the "evanescent cost-benefit calculations of agencies or judges." The majority trivialized the intrusiveness of the testing and overlooked flaws in the testing program. ". . . Dragnet blood and urine testing ensures that the first, and worst, casualty of the war on drugs will be the precious liberties of our citizens."

Marshall criticized the concept of a "special need" making probable cause impracticable and felt that the Court in its decision took "its longest step yet toward reading the probable-cause requirement out of the Fourth Amendment." The amendment should not be subject to shifting judicial majorities who are worried about the problems of the day. The requirements of the Constitution are not "fair-weather friends, present when advantageous, conveniently absent when 'special needs' make them seem not." The Court recognized "special needs" exceptions to the probable clause rule since 1985 and since that time has badly distorted the clarity of Fourth Amendment doctrine, according to Marshall. But until the decision in *Skinner v. Railway Labor Executives' Assn.*, individualized suspicion was still a requirement. The majority in this case has completed "the process . . . of eliminating altogether the proba-

ble-cause requirement for civil searches." In its place is a manipulable balancing inquiry. This balancing approach can be justified only on the basis of policy results; the special needs rationale is dangerous.

In Marshall's opinion, although the urgency of needing to collect samples before the drug or alcohol disappeared from the body justified waiving the warrant requirement for *collecting* the evidence, there was no reason for railroad officials to not get a warrant before *testing* the samples.

Marshall found the majority's characterization of the privacy interests in this case as minimal, "nothing short of startling." The framers of our Constitution "would be appalled by the vision of mass governmental intrusions upon the integrity of the human body . . . The immediate victims of the majority's constitutional timorousness will be those railroad workers whose bodily fluids the government may now forcibly collect and analyze. But ultimately, today's decision will reduce the privacy all citizens may enjoy . . ."

Impact

Since *Skinner v. Railway Labor Executives' Assn.*, the Supreme Court has refused to hear other challenges to random drug testing. Many aspects of this issue have yet to be resolved including the degree of allowable intrusiveness, the validity of other government drug testing programs less related to safety, and the relative privacy expectations of employees.

Related Cases

Schmerber v. California, 384 U.S. 757 (1966).
United States v. Jacobsen, 466 U.S. 109 (1984).
New Jersey v. T.L.O., 469 U.S. 325 (1985).
United States v. Montoya de Hernandez, 473 U.S. 531 (1985).

Bibliography and Further Reading

Hall, Kermit L., ed. *The Oxford Companion to the Supreme Court of the United States*. New York: Oxford Press, 1992.

Witt, Elder, ed. *The Supreme Court A to Z. CQ's Encyclopedia of American Government*. Washington, DC: Congressional Quarterly, Inc., 1993.

UNITED STATES V. SOKOLOW

Legal Citation: 490 U.S. 1 (1989)

Petitioner
United States

Respondent
Andrew Sokolow

Petitioner's Claim
That agents of the United States Drug Enforcement Agency had probable cause to suspect that Sokolow was in possession of an illegal substance, and were legally justified under the Fourth Amendment in detaining Sokolow and searching his belongings.

Chief Lawyer for Petitioner
Paul J. Larkin, Jr.

Chief Lawyer for Respondent
Robert P. Goldberg

Justices for the Court
Harry A. Blackmun, Anthony M. Kennedy, Sandra Day O'Connor, William H. Rehnquist (writing for the Court), Antonin Scalia, John Paul Stevens, Byron R. White

Justices Dissenting
William J. Brennan, Jr., Thurgood Marshall

Place
Washington, D.C.

Date of Decision
3 April 1989

Decision
Upheld the position of the United States, overturning the ruling of the court of appeals and holding that law enforcement officers can detain an individual if they have a "reasonable suspicion" that the individual is engaging or about to engage in criminal activity, even without probable cause to believe that any criminal action has or will occur.

Significance
The ruling demonstrated the willingness of the Court to define Fourth Amendment prohibitions against unreasonable search and seizure narrowly in cases involving the transportation or sale of illegal drugs. In upholding the government's case, the Court ruled admissible the detention of suspects who merely fit a police profile for illegal activity. Prior to *Sokolow*, authorities were required to show evidence of "ongoing criminal activity" when using profiling to identify potential criminal suspects.

Throughout the 1970s and 1980s public concern over the use of and trafficking in illegal drugs remained at a high level. Many people came to believe that constitutional guarantees of the rights of the individual served in large measure to protect criminals, and political sentiment ran toward allowing greater latitude in police work involving the illegal drug trade, and toward more stringent sentencing of convicted drug offenders. Amid this political climate, law enforcement techniques for identifying potential suspects, including profiling and the use of electronic eavesdropping devices and drug-detecting dogs, improved greatly and began to run afoul of Fourth Amendment prohibitions against unreasonable search and seizure by state authorities. During this time the U.S. Supreme Court used the precedent established in *Terry v. Ohio* (1968), which allowed authorities to briefly detain an individual if they "have a reasonable suspicion supported by articulable fact that criminal activity 'may be afoot,' even if they lack probable cause under the Fourth Amendment," to broaden the scope of allowable activities for law enforcement officers and investigators.

A Brief and Unusual Trip

In July of 1984 Andrew Sokolow, using the assumed name Andrew Kray, booked airline flights from Honolulu, Hawaii, to Miami, Florida, for himself and his girlfriend, Janet Norian. He paid cash for their tickets, bringing out a substantial roll of $20 bills and peeling off the requisite $2100 in front of a rather surprised airline ticket agent. The ticket agent found Sokolow's manner of payment for his tickets unusual, and thought that Sokolow was "acting nervous." Accordingly, the agent alerted Officer John McCarthy of the Honolulu Police Department to the situation. McCarthy investigated by attempting to telephone "Kray" at the phone number Sokolow had left with the ticket agent, but was only able to reach a message machine at the number. The ticket agent listened to the message on the tape and confirmed that it was Sokolow's voice on the recording. McCarthy then found that "Kray" and Norian had booked a return flight from Miami to Honolulu just three days hence, making their stay in Florida exceedingly short given the

20 hours of flying time required for the round-trip journey. He also determined that "Kray" and Norian would make stopovers in Denver, Colorado, and Los Angeles, California, on their return flight.

A Successful Police Operation

During his stopover in Los Angeles, "Kray" was shadowed by agents of the federal Drug Enforcement Administration (DEA). These agents confirmed that "Kray" seemed highly nervous, and was unwilling to check any of his baggage. When "Kray" and Norian arrived in Honolulu, they immediately left the airport and were attempting to hail a cab when they were detained by DEA Agent Richard Kempshall and three of his colleagues. Kempshall asked "Kray" for his airline ticket and identification, and "Kray" responded that he possessed neither, and revealed his true name, explaining that he was travelling using his mother's maiden name. Sokolow and Norian were then escorted to the DEA offices in the Honolulu airport, where their luggage was examined by Donker, a narcotics-sniffing police dog. Donker responded positively to Sokolow's shoulder bag, and the agents arrested Sokolow forthwith. Sokolow was advised of his constitutional rights and declined to make any statements. The DEA agents then acquired a warrant to search Sokolow's bag, which contained no illegal substances, but did hold business papers indicating his involvement in drug trafficking. Donker then sniffed the rest of Sokolow's luggage, and responded positively to another piece, but it was too late in the day for the DEA agents to acquire a second search warrant. Sokolow was thus allowed to leave for the night, but his luggage was impounded pending acquisition of a new warrant in the morning. The warrant was duly obtained, and 1063 grams of cocaine were uncovered in the second bag identified by Donker.

An Invasion of Privacy

Sokolow was indicted for intent to distribute cocaine, and filed a motion to suppress the evidence obtained against him by the DEA in the U.S. District Court for Hawaii. The district court denied Sokolow's motion, ruling that DEA agents had "reasonable suspicion" that he was involved in drug trafficking when they stopped him outside the Honolulu airport. Sokolow then appealed for the suppression of the DEA's evidence to the U.S. Court of Appeals for the Ninth Circuit and entered a conditional guilty plea in his criminal trial. The court of appeals reversed the district court's ruling, holding that DEA agents did not have sufficient evidence to justify detaining Sokolow and searching his possessions. In reaching this verdict the court applied a two-pronged test for determining validity of evidence leading to reasonable suspicion on the part of the authorities: evidence of ongoing criminal activity, such as the use of an alias and evasive behavior around law

enforcement personnel; and personal characteristics "shared by drug couriers and the public at large." The court of appeals found that evidence of the former type should carry far more weight than the latter, and in this case, that DEA agents had relied more on Sokolow's behavior, such as the paying of cash for his tickets and his nervousness, than on his use of an alias or any other evidence. The U.S. Supreme Court than granted *certiorari* to review the case, given its obvious implications for the investigation of trafficking in illegal drugs, and heard arguments on 3 April 1989.

Reasonable Suspicion and Probable Cause

The court of appeals had ruled that Sokolow was seized by the authorities when they stopped him from hailing a cab outside the Honolulu airport, so the Supreme Court examined whether or not a reasonable suspicion existed that he was engaging in a criminal activity at that time. The Court had already ruled, in case of *Terry v. Ohio*, that police officers could briefly detain a person given a reasonable suspicion that the person was engaged or preparing to engage in a criminal activity. Furthermore, in *Illinois v. Gates* (1983), the Court had defined probable cause as: "a fair probability that contraband or evidence of crime will be found" if a search is conducted. While admitting that definitions of reasonable suspicion were highly subjective, the Court believed that the two-pronged evaluation of evidence used by the court of appeals to be even less useful. Writing for the majority, Justice Rehnquist stated that while reasonable suspicion must consist of something more than an "inchoate and unparticularized suspicion," it need not adhere to as strict a scrutiny as the probable cause required to obtain a warrant. In the Court's opinion, the Fourth Amendment required only that authorities show "some minimal level of objective justification" for making a stop, and that this minimal level of justification existed in Sokolow's case. As such, the decision of the court of appeals was reversed and the evidence obtained against Sokolow deemed admissible in court.

Impact

United States v. Sokolow continued the Court's tendency to interpret the Fourth Amendment prohibition against unreasonable search and seizure in such a way as not to unduly hamper law enforcement officials, particularly those engaged in curtailing the illegal drug trade. The ruling had the effect of giving legal credence to the use of profiles of "typical" behavior and appearance of various types of criminals to identify potential offenders. It was this point which most troubled the dissenting justices, who noted that none of the behaviors exhibited by Sokolow that were used to put the authorities on his trail were illegal. Especially troubling to the dissenters was the use made by authorities of Sokolow's nervousness in various airports, noting that many individuals who are innocent of any wrongdoing are anxious about flying aboard commercial airlines.

Related Cases

Terry v. Ohio, 392 U.S. 1 (1968).

Illinois v. Gates, 462 U.S. 213 (1983).

INS v. Delgado, 466 U.S. 210 (1984).

United States v. Montoya de Hernandez, 473 U.S. 531 (1985).

Bibliography and Further Reading

Burnett, Arthur L. "Permeation of Race, National Origin, and Gender Issues from Initial Law Enforcement Contact Through Sentencing." *American Criminal Law Review,* summer 1994, p. 1153.

"25th Annual Review of Criminal Procedure." *Georgetown Law Journal.* Washington, DC: Georgetown University Press, April 1996.

FLORIDA V. WELLS

Legal Citation: 495 U.S. 1 (1990)

Petitioner
State of Florida

Respondent
Martin Leslie Wells

Petitioner's Claim
It is not a violation of the Fourth Amendment for a police officer to open a locked suitcase that is found in the trunk of an arrestee's vehicle, even if the police station has no clear policy on the opening of locked containers during an inventory search.

Chief Lawyer for Petitioner
Michael J. Neimand

Chief Lawyer for Respondent
Huntley Johnson

Justices for the Court
Harry A. Blackmun, William J. Brennan, Jr., Anthony M. Kennedy, Thurgood Marshall, Sandra Day O'Connor, William H. Rehnquist (writing for the Court), Antonin Scalia, John Paul Stevens, Byron R. White

Justices Dissenting
None

Place
Washington, D.C.

Date of Decision
18 April 1990

Decision
Absent a policy on the opening of closed containers found by police officers during an inventory search, an inventory search that involves the opening of a locked suitcase is not sufficiently regulated under the Fourth Amendment and is therefore illegal.

Significance
The case was a rare example of the Rehnquist Court enforcing Fourth Amendment privacy rights at the expense of law enforcement. In an interesting sleight of hand, however, the majority of the Court used the case to broaden police rights in inventory searches while holding against the police action in the case.

On 11 February 1985, during routine patrol, Trooper Rodney Adams of the Florida Highway Patrol stopped Martin Wells for speeding. Adams determined that Wells was intoxicated, and he arrested him for drunk driving. Wells agreed to go with Adams to the police station to take a breathalyzer test, and Adams impounded Wells' car. Adams also obtained Wells' permission to perform an inventory search on the car. Such searches are designed to guard against theft while the car is impounded and to prevent a false claim of theft when the arrestee regains the car. Police officers also conduct inventory searches to protect against potential dangers posed by the car or its contents.

Adams had the car towed to nearby K & S Automotive. With the assistance of Grover Bryan, a K & S employee, Adams searched Wells' vehicle and discovered two marijuana cigarette butts in the ashtray and a locked suitcase in the trunk. His interest piqued, Adams and Bryan forced open the lock on the suitcase with two knives and discovered more marijuana.

Wells was charged with possession of a controlled substance. Prior to trial, Wells moved the court to exclude the marijuana evidence, arguing that the search of his suitcase violated the Fourth Amendment to be free from unreasonable searches. The trial court denied the motion and Wells pleaded no contest to the charges. However, he preserved his right to appeal the judge's ruling on his motion, and the Florida District Court of Appeal for the Fifth Circuit reversed the trial court. The Supreme Court of Florida affirmed, and the state of Florida appealed to the U.S. Supreme Court.

In a unanimous decision, the High Court sided with Wells, holding that the search of Wells' suitcase was illegal. Although the Court arrived at the same decision as Florida's High Court, it utilized different reasoning. The Florida court was right when it held that law enforcement personnel must follow a clearly stated policy in conducting inventory searches, and that if no policy exists then the inventory search is illegal under the Fourth Amendment. However, the Florida court went on to state that a policy on inventory searches must be created by police departments that either forbids or requires the opening of closed containers found in the course of an inventory search.

The U.S. Supreme Court allowed that police must create and follow a policy on inventory searches. This was true because the Court had already determined in *Illinois v. Lafayette* (1983) that an inventory search of an arrestee's vehicle "must not be a ruse for a general rummaging in order to discover incriminating evidence." Because Adams had searched Wells' suitcase without the benefit of a guiding departmental policy on inventory searches, the search was illegal and the Court declared that the marijuana evidence found in the suitcase would be unavailable to prosecutors. This effectively ended the prosecution against Wells, but the Court continued its opinion to correct a mistake made by the Florida court.

According to the High Court, police should be allowed to retain discretion to decide whether to open a closed container encountered in an inventory search. Quoting *Colorado v. Bertine* (1987), the Court stated that such searches "'serve to protect an owner''s property while it is in the custody of the police, to insure against claims of lost, stolen, or vandalized property, and to guard the police from danger.'" It is not, maintained the Court, a violation of the Fourth Amendment to allow police officers "the exercise of judgment based on concerns related to the purposes of an inventory search." Ultimately, the Court affirmed the judgment of the Supreme Court of Florida, holding for Wells.

Justices Brennan, Marshall, Blackmun, and Stevens concurred with the majority opinion but wrote separate opinions to express their concerns about it. In an opinion joined by Marshall, Brennan recounted many facts that did not appear in the majority opinion. According to the trial transcript, Adams stated that he deferred to his superior on the matter of the inventory search and that his superior had given Adams discretion to do as he wished. Adams' boss, however, did not find anything suspicious about the car. Bryan, the K & S employee, testified that Adams told him that "'he wanted to go through it real good because he felt that there was drugs in it.'" Adams had discovered a large sum of cash on the floor of the car when he arrested Wells, and, according to Bryan, Adams believed that "'[t]here ain't nobody runs around with that kind of money in the floorboard unless they're dealing drugs or something like that.'"

Brennan placed the additional facts about the case into his opinion to lay the groundwork for his objection. In Brennan's opinion, the Court had gone too far in announcing that police officers have discretion to open any and all containers they find in a vehicle during an inventory search. Brennan noted that the Court's rule on discretion was "pure dictum," or outside the scope of the issue at hand, but he feared that lower courts might rely on the statements when they determine the constitutionality of inventory searches. Supreme Court precedent, argued Brennan, actually counseled against giving

police officers discretion in deciding what to do in an inventory search. Under *South Dakota v. Opperman* (1976), inventory searches should be conducted "in accordance with standard procedures that limit the discretion of the police." Brennan believed that *Bertine* had been misapplied by the majority. The reference to police discretion in that case was made in response to arguments on whether police should have discretion to decide whether to impound a car. The *Bertine* case did not, Brennan pointed out, stand for the proposition that police officers have the discretion to search all closed containers in an inventory search. "I continue to believe," Brennan wrote, "that in the absence of consent or exigency, police may not open a closed container found during an inventory search of an automobile."

Justices Blackmun and Stevens wrote separate concurring opinions. In his opinion, Blackmun stated that he agreed with the majority in its decision, but that its dicta on discretion was "problematic." The question of what constituted a proper inventory police was not presented in the lower courts and was not presented by the case. "I see no reason," declared Blackmun, "for the Court to say anything" on the topic.

In a third concurring opinion, Stevens added to Blackmun's criticism. Stevens wondered why the Court took the case in the first place. Stevens decried the tendency of the Court "to become self-appointed editors of state-court opinions in the criminal law area." Had the Court left the Florida court's ruling untouched, the ruling may have provided Florida citizens with more protection from inventory searches than the minimal protection required on the federal level, but, Stevens argued, there was no suggestion that the extra protection would hamper law enforcement. To Stevens, the Court's actions constituted "unabashed judicial activism" of the highest order. "Apparently the mere possibility of a minor burden on law enforcement," Stevens growled, "is enough to generate corrective action by this Court."

Impact

The *Wells* decision put police departments across the country on notice that they had to craft a general policy on inventory searches in addition to rules to implement the policy. At the same time, the opinion paved the way for broader police powers in vehicle inventory searches by proclaiming that police have the discretion to open whatever containers they may find during an inventory search.

Related Cases

South Dakota v. Opperman, 428 U.S. 364 (1976).
Illinois v. Lafayette, 462 U.S. 640 (1983).
Colorado v. Bertine, 479 U.S. 367 (1987).

Bibliography and Further Reading

West's Encyclopedia of American Law, Volume 9. St. Paul: West Group, 1998.

HORTON V. CALIFORNIA

Legal Citation: 496 U.S. 128 (1990)

Petitioner
Terry Brice Horton

Respondent
State of California

Petitioner's Claim
That the court must suppress the evidence Sergeant LaRault discovered in plain view while conducting a lawful search, because his search warrant did not mention these items and because LaRault did not find them inadvertently.

Chief Lawyer for Petitioner
Juliana Drous

Chief Lawyer for Respondent
Martin S. Kaye

Justices for the Court
Harry A. Blackmun, Anthony M. Kennedy, Sandra Day O'Connor, William H. Rehnquist, Antonin Scalia, John Paul Stevens (writing for the Court), Byron R. White

Justices Dissenting
William J. Brennan, Jr., Thurgood Marshall

Place
Washington, D.C.

Date of Decision
4 June 1990

Decision
Found that the Fourth Amendment does not prohibit seizure of belongings not specifically listed in a warrant found in plain sight during a legal search for other items, even though the discovery was not inadvertent, as *Coolidge v. New Hampshire* (1971) mandated.

Significance
This case removed the inadvertence requirement from one of the exceptions to the Fourth Amendment's call for a search warrant that specifies the items to be searched for and seized. Previously, the U.S. Supreme Court held that in order for the police to seize evidence not mentioned in a warrant, they must find it inadvertently and it must be in plain view. However, in *Horton v. California* the Court argued that the inadvertence requirement was unnecessary and that the other warrant requirements would prevent police abuse of the warrant, even though the Fourth Amendment requires the warrant to describe all items on some interpretations. Furthermore, this decision granted police greater freedom for obtaining evidence, as long as they met the conditions imposed by the Constitution and the Supreme Court's rulings.

Background Laws and Decisions

As a safeguard against random searches unsupported by strong evidence, the Fourth Amendment prohibits the police and other government agents from searching a person's home and possessions without a warrant. The warrant must be issued by a neutral judge for a search based on probable cause, and the warrant must specify the places to be searched and items to be confiscated.

However, the U.S. Supreme Court also acknowledges some exceptions to the Fourth Amendment's search and seizure clause, including finding evidence while in "hot pursuit" of a suspect, obtaining evidence when there is a strong possibility of its destruction, finding evidence during a frisk as part of an arrest, and discovering evidence in plain view while lawfully searching for items mentioned in a warrant. Items seized in such circumstances do not need to be listed in a warrant.

Coolidge v. New Hampshire and other cases helped define the "plain view" doctrine, which allows police to seize items they discover inadvertently because they are in plain view. The *Coolidge* ruling established three conditions that must be met in order for the seizure of evidence in this manner to be permissible. First, a warrant must authorize the initial search in the first place. Second, the incriminating character of the items must be immediately apparent. Third, the discovery of such items must be inadvertent. *Arizona v. Hicks* (1987) later reaffirmed that with probable cause, the police may seize evidence under the "plain view" doctrine.

The Crime and the Evidence

The treasurer of the San Jose Coin Club, Erwin Wallaker, was robbed one day after returning from the club's yearly show. Armed with a machine gun and a stun gun, the two attackers approached Wallaker in his garage and stunned him using the electrical shocking device. Then they tied and handcuffed him, before stealing his cash and jewelry. While investigating the armed robbery of the San Jose Coin Club's treasury, Sergeant LaRault found probable cause to search Terry Horton's home for the stolen property and weapons used in the crime. The warrant the officer obtained to search his home, however, specified searching only for stolen property. When the officer executed the search warrant, he discovered weapons used in the robbery—an Uzi machine gun, a .38 caliber revolver, and two stun guns—in plain view, but no stolen property. The officer confiscated the weapons as well as a few other items, including clothing described by Wallaker, a handcuff key, and an advertisement for the club's show.

LaRault testified that in addition to looking for the stolen property specified in the warrant, he also sought further evidence that would link the suspect with the robbery, hence making his discovery of the weapons deliberate, not inadvertent. The trial court deemed this evidence admissible, even though the LaRault's warrant did not authorize seizing it. A jury convicted Horton of armed robbery and sentenced him to prison. Horton asked the California Court of Appeals to hear his case, arguing that the court must suppress all evidence not specified in the warrant, because LaRault did not find it inadvertently. However, the court denied his request, relying on a view that if the evidence was in plain sight, then the police could seize it. Horton next petitioned the California Supreme Court, but it also rejected his petition.

The Case of Terry Horton

Since the California court's interpretation of the "plain view" ruling conflicted with other courts' interpretations, the U.S. Supreme Court decided to hear the case, which began 21 February 1990. While the Court had established the previously mentioned exceptions to the Fourth Amendment's ban on warrantless searches and seizures, it had to sharpen its view on finding and confiscating of conspicuous belongings not inadvertently found and not listed on a search warrant.

The Court had previously ruled that the item must not only be in plain view but also must be obviously incriminating in character. In addition, the Court found that the search warrant must authorize the police to search a specific place and area from where the evidence is conspicuous and the police must discover it inadvertently. However, Justice Stevens, writing for the majority, disputed this last condition, that the discovery must be inadvertent, for two reasons. First, the majority argued that just because the police expect to find more evidence during a search than the warrant specifies should not invalidate the search, providing that the search remained confined to the area and the duration specified in the warrant or constituted a valid exception to the warrant.

Second, the Court reasoned that other requirements of the Fourth Amendment safeguard against the police using specific warrants as general warrants, thus ren-

dering the inadvertence requirement unnecessary. Because the police must always have a warrant specifying the person, the place, and the items, they can only search a limited area for a limited amount of time, as authorized by the warrant. The Court felt that if the police followed these rules, the inadvertence policy did not provide any further protection of Fourth Amendment rights, because once the police strayed outside of the specified area of search, they would already have violated the Fourth Amendment and any evidence they obtained would be inadmissible, whether found advertently or inadvertently. The Court hoped this requirement would replace attempts to judge the admissibility of evidence based on trying to determine what a police officer's expectations were while performing a lawful search.

However, Justices Brennan and Marshall dissented, maintaining that the Fourth Amendment explicitly requires search warrants to describe the specific contents to be seized, which the majority overlooked. Nonetheless, despite the apparent liberties taken with the Fourth Amendment, Justice Stevens's view received the most support, and *Horton v. California* eliminated the inadvertence requirement. The majority argued that the new "plain view" doctrine relied on objective grounds for judging whether evidence not mentioned in a warrant can be permissibly seized, instead of on subjective grounds of trying to read the minds of the police to determine if the discovery of such evidence was truly inadvertent.

> In this case the items seized from petitioner's home were discovered during a lawful search authorized by a valid warrant. When they were discovered, it was immediately apparent to the officer that they constituted incriminating evidence. He had probable cause, not [only] to search for the stolen property, but also to believe that the weapons and handguns had been used in the crime he was investigating.

Related Cases

Weeks v. United States, 232 U.S. 383 (1914).
Terry v. Ohio, 392 U.S. 1 (1968).
Coolidge v. New Hampshire, 403 U.S. 443 (1971).
Arizona v. Hicks, 480 U.S. 321 (1987).

Bibliography and Further Reading

MacIntosh, Susanne M. "Fourth Amendment—The Plain Touch Exception to the Warrant Requirement." *Journal of Criminal Law & Criminology,* winter-spring 1994, p. 743.

"Review and Outlook: Common Sense, Uncommon Source." *Wall Street Journal,* June 5, 1990, p. A24.

MICHIGAN DEPARTMENT OF STATE POLICE V. SITZ, ET AL.

Legal Citation: 496 U.S. 444 (1990)

Petitioners
Michigan Department of State Police, et al.

Respondents
Rick Sitz, et al.

Petitioners' Claim
That the lower court had erred in ruling roadside sobriety checkpoints were unconstitutional under the Fourth Amendment.

Chief Lawyer for Petitioners
Thomas L. Casey

Chief Lawyer for Respondents
Mark Granzotto

Justices for the Court
Harry A. Blackmun, Anthony M. Kennedy, Sandra Day O'Connor, William H. Rehnquist (writing for the Court), Antonin Scalia, Byron R. White

Justices Dissenting
William J. Brennan, Jr., Thurgood Marshall, John Paul Stevens

Place
Washington, D.C.

Date of Decision
14 June 1990

Decision
That sobriety checkpoints do not violate constitutional rights.

Significance
The ruling gave state authorities a powerful tool for curbing drunk driving, as it allowed police to stop all cars at checkpoints and look for drunken drivers. This stop is a "reasonable" seizure under the Fourth Amendment, since the checkpoints are an effective way to reduce drunk driving, reducing drunk driving is a legitimate state concern, and the sobriety checks are not intrusive on drivers.

In May of 1986, Michigan State Police set up a sobriety checkpoint along a stretch of Saginaw County highway in a publicized campaign to combat drunk driving. It was the state's first and only such action, and had been prompted by Michigan Governor James J. Blanchard, who had suggested adoption of the program a few months earlier in his State of the State address. Nationwide, alcohol-related fatalities topped 23,000 annually during the 1980s, though these figures were steadily declining as anti-drunk-driving campaigns and other deterrent programs, such as MADD (Mothers Against Drunk Driving), became more commonplace.

Sobriety checkpoints had been used in other states with mixed results. Opponents argued that the rate of arrest was insignificant compared to the inconvenience presented to motorists, not to mention the tax dollars used. Supporters of the program asserted that if a checkpoint found just one percent of a hundred drivers detained to be driving under the influence, that might yield at least one innocent life saved from a fatal collision. Checkpoint advocates also argued that the program's true effectiveness lay in deterring intoxicated people from getting behind the wheel of a car. Such programs had been challenged in other state courts, with varied outcomes: some judges had declared them unconstitutional on the basis that unreasonable search and seizure violated Fourth Amendment rights; other courts upheld them.

One Checkpoint Attempt

In Michigan's case, an advisory committee consisting of both law enforcement and civilian transportation experts met to set specific guidelines for the location, techniques used, and advance publicity about a sobriety checkpoint program. These were cautiously devised parameters that tried to follow constitutional precedents, after the committee members had examined the elements of others states' sobriety checkpoints that had been declared illegal by the courts. A computer was utilized to pinpoint state roads with high alcohol-related accident statistics, and on a rainy night in May of 1986 the State Police conducted a 75-minute checkpoint on Dixie Highway in Saginaw County.

Drunk Driving Statistics

- In 1982, 43,945 people in the United States died in car crashes, less than 11,000 deaths short of the entire American body count for the Vietnam War. In 1988, the death toll climbed to a high of 47,087, and in 1992 it dropped to 39,250; by 1995, it was at 41,798.

- The number of annual traffic fatalities caused by alcohol has decreased by nearly 32 percent, from 25,165 in 1982 to 17,274 in 1995. As a percentage of traffic fatalities, alcohol-related crashes dropped from 57 percent in 1982 to 41 percent in 1995.

- Transportation Department figures also show that whereas the numbers of alcohol-related traffic fatalities have decreased for persons in younger age groups, they have generally increased for older people.

- Almost 3,000 drivers in the 75 and older category caused fatal crashes while intoxicated behind the wheel in 1995.

Source(s): *Bureau of Justice Statistics Sourcebook of Criminal Justice Statistics—1996.* Washington, DC: U.S. Government, 1997.

For the 126 vehicles that came through the checkpoint, the average delay was 25 seconds. Drivers were briefly appraised for signs of intoxication by means of innocuous conversation. If a driver was suspected of intoxication, he or she was directed to another nearby spot off the highway, where their license and registration were requested and examined by another officer; this officer could also conduct further sobriety tests. Of the 126 drivers, two were detained, and one of those two was found to be driving under the influence of alcohol. A third driver attempted to drive through the checkpoint, but was pursued and found to be intoxicated.

Challenged Immediately

The day before the checkpoint program was initiated, the American Civil Liberties Union filed suit in Wayne County Circuit Court on behalf of a group of licensed Michigan drivers opposed to sobriety checkpoints. The "Sitz" name in the case belonged to Rick Sitz, a state representative in Michigan's House. The petitioners sought an injunction against such checkpoints, and Wayne County Circuit Court Judge Michael L. Stacey granted it. Stacey questioned whether checkpoints were effective in deterring drunk drivers, and asserted that their power to strike fear in law-abiding citizens far outweighed any effectiveness factor. Still other opponents of the checkpoints argued that they were too costly; they required several officers and patrol cars in order to slow down, then stop drivers, and then more officers to conduct off-road sobriety tests; a similar detention rate of 1 percent could also be accomplished by two officers merely sitting in a parked patrol car observing traffic.

Brown v. Texas

The Michigan State Police then filed an appeal with the Michigan State Court of Appeals. Like the lower court, this judicial body used the *Brown v. Texas* balancing

test. *Brown,* named after a U.S. Supreme Court decision, provided guidelines for establishing the constitutionality of intrusions onto citizens' rights against unreasonable search and seizure. (It had already been determined that stopping an automobile constituted "seizure," and courts had ruled that a person inside a car does not have the same privacy rights as someone inside a house.) *Brown* asked if the gravity of public concerns justified the seizure. In this case, alcohol-related traffic deaths were described as a cause for public concern, and the sobriety checkpoints were designed to keep all citizens safe on the road. *Brown* also queried to what degree the seizure advanced the public interest—whether sobriety checkpoints actually worked. Finally, the third question of the balancing test dealt with just how far an intrusion, or inconvenience, a sobriety checkpoint presented to the normal, law-abiding motorist.

In 1988, the Michigan State Court of Appeals decided in favor of upholding Stacey's decision banning checkpoints. State Attorney General Frank Kelley appealed to the U.S. Supreme Court to overturn the ruling and allow reinstatement of the checkpoints. It would be the first such case dealing with sobriety checkpoints heard before the Court. Since the Michigan program had been carefully conceived to circumvent legal challenges, other states anticipated the decision—if the High Court declared Michigan's program unconstitutional, it was unlikely any other version of the checkpoint would ever be allowed. Twenty-eight other state attorney generals filed briefs in support of the Michigan State Police's appeal, as did an insurance-industry group and the grass-roots organization Mothers Against Drunk Driving.

What About Airport Checkpoints?

The Court's position was to determine whether the sobriety checkpoint program violated the Fourth

Amendment—outlawing unreasonable search and seizure—as well as the Fourteenth Amendment—which prevents states from enacting laws that violate citizens' other constitutional rights. Challenges against unreasonable search and seizure had been argued before. For instance, a person who enters the United States at a border crossing can expect to be briefly detained and questioned; the same holds true for those passing through security gates into airport boarding areas. Such controls—to deter the entry of illegal aliens, and to prevent firearms or explosives from being carried onto planes—are considered valid since their ultimate goal in advancing the public interest outweighs their inconvenience to the average citizen thusly detained.

The Decision

The Court, ruling on 14 June 1990, overturned the Michigan courts' decisions by a vote of 6-3. In his majority opinion, Chief Justice Rehnquist opined that such "seizures" were indeed reasonable, even though the one percent detention rate seemed minuscule. Rehnquist noted that the inconvenience presented to motorists was a slight one, and was superseded by the sobriety checkpoint's goal in deterring crime. Furthermore, in the end such statistics, Rehnquist and the other justices noted, were unable to support the argument—the one percent rate could only point up drunk driving arrests, not the number of drivers deterred from operating a vehicle under the influence of alcohol or drugs.

The High Court's decision was the first ever to support the actions of law-enforcement officials to detain individuals without any prior suspicion of wrongdoing. The three dissenting votes came from Justices Marshall, Brennan, and Stevens. In his dissenting brief, Stevens

called sobriety checkpoints "publicity stunts." Brennan and Marshall argued that such tactics, based on instilling elements of fear and surprise in citizens, were the cornerstones of authoritarian governments.

Related Cases

Perez v. Campbell, 402 U.S. 637 (1971).
United States v. Ortiz, 422 U.S. 891 (1975).
Brown v. Texas, 443 U.S. 47 (1979).

Bibliography and Further Reading

Biskupic, Joan, and Elder Witt. *Congressional Quarterly's Guide to the U.S. Supreme Court,* 3rd ed. Washington, DC: Congressional Quarterly, Inc., 1996.

Copacino, John M. "Suspicionless Criminal Seizures After Michigan Department of State Police v. Sitz." *American Criminal Law Review,* winter 1994, p. 215.

Greenhouse, Linda. "Court Approves Sobriety Checkpoints Along the Road." *New York Times,* June 14, 1990, p. A1.

Hall, Kermit L., ed. *The Oxford Companion to the Supreme Court of the United States.* New York: Oxford University Press, 1992.

Steiker, Carol S. "Counter-Revolution in Constitutional Criminal Procedure? Two Audiences, Two Answers." *Michigan Law Review,* August 1996, p. 2466.

Steiker, Carol S. "The Limits of the Preventive State." *Journal of Criminal Law and Criminology,* spring 1998, p. 771.

Willing, Richard. "Sobriety Checkpoint Issue Up for High Court." *Detroit News,* February 25, 1990, p. A3.

CALIFORNIA V. HODARI D.

Legal Citation: 499 U.S. 621 (1991)

Petitioner
State of California

Respondent
Hodari D.

Petitioner's Claim
That police officials' use of materials discarded by a fleeing suspect prior to a warrantless arrest does not violate Fourth Amendment search and seizure standards.

Chief Lawyer for Petitioner
Kenneth Winston Starr, U.S. Solicitor General

Chief Lawyer for Respondent
Paul L. Hoffman

Justices for the Court
Anthony M. Kennedy, William H. Rehnquist (writing for the Court), Antonin Scalia, David H. Souter, Clarence Thomas, Byron R. White

Justices Dissenting
Harry A. Blackmun, Sandra Day O'Connor, John Paul Stevens

Place
Washington, D.C.

Date of Decision
15 June 1992

Decision
Upheld California's claim and overturned a lower court's decision prohibiting use of evidence obtained without a search warrant prior to illegal seizure of the suspect.

Significance
The ruling established that if a person avoids or resists police efforts at apprehension, then seizure of the person has not occurred and Fourth Amendment protections do not apply. Police must apply physical force or the suspect must respond to restraint willingly for a seizure to occur and the person to be under protections of the amendment. The decision gave greater discretion to government officials in approaching suspected individuals and collecting evidence incidental to such encounters. Some feared that, with knowledge of very few actual facts, police could act much more arbitrarily in their efforts to interrogate people on the street, particularly by chasing them if they try to avoid contact.

The Fourth Amendment ensures the "right of the people to be secure in their persons, houses, papers, and effects against unreasonable search and seizures." Such privacy can not be violated and no warrants can be issued unless "probable cause" is shown, supported by an oath or affirmation. The warrant must specifically describe the place to be searched and things to be seized. The amendment only applies to searches and seizures conducted by the government. The Supreme Court in *Katz v. United States* (1967) broadened Fourth Amendment protections by asserting if an individual targeted by the search expects privacy then protections apply.

Fourth Amendment protections also guard against unreasonable governmental seizures of citizens themselves. However, courts normally applied common law standards in upholding the right of police officers to take people into custody without warrants. The police must have probable cause to believe the person seized committed a criminal offense. The probable cause must be satisfied by information discovered prior to the police officer's stop. Information discovered afterward is not sufficient to retroactively establish probable cause. Following the Court's decision in *Terry v. Ohio* (1968), the standard for stopping individuals for investigative purposes evolved into one of "reasonable suspicion of criminal activity." This test allowed some stops and questioning without probable cause in order for police officers to explore the basis of their suspicions. Fourth Amendment protection did not come into effect until a physical "seizure" occurred. The *Terry* Court recognized that "not all personal intercourse between policemen and citizens involves 'seizures' of persons." It suggested that only when the officer, by "means of physical force or show of authority," has in some way restricted the liberty of a citizen that a "seizure" has occurred. Later, in *United States v. Mendenhall* (1980), Justice Stewart proposed a standard stating that a person has been seized "only if, in view of all of the circumstances surrounding the incident, a reasonable person would have believed that he was not free to leave." This standard, adopted by the Court three years later in *Florida v. Royer* (1983), became the *Mendenhall-Royer* test.

Late one evening in April of 1988, two city police officers were on patrol in an unmarked police car in a high-crime area of Oakland, California. A group of black youths, including Hodari D., fled as the police vehicle approached. One officer, wearing a jacket with "Police" written on its front, left the car to give chase on foot.

The officer did not follow Hodari directly, but took a different route bringing the two face to face on the next street. Hodari looking back as he ran, did not turn to see the officer until the officer was almost upon him. At that moment, Hodari tossed away a small rock. The officer tackled Hodari and recovered the rock which proved to be crack cocaine. Hodari was subsequently arrested by the officers and charged with possession of illegal narcotics.

Hodari filed a motion to suppress the cocaine evidence prior to juvenile proceedings. He argued the drugs were the result, the "fruit," of an illegal seizure violating the Fourth Amendment's search and seizure clause. The circuit court denied Hodari's motion to suppress the evidence and found him guilty of the illegal narcotics possession charge.

Hodari appealed the conviction to the California State Court of Appeals. The appellate court reversed the circuit court's verdict by finding that Hodari had been "seized" when he saw the police officer running toward him. Such a seizure was considered "unreasonable" under the Fourth Amendment since the state of California conceded the officer did not have the "reasonable suspicion" required to justify stopping Hodari. Therefore, the evidence of cocaine, being the fruit of an illegal seizure, had to be suppressed as Hodari had argued. The state of California next appealed the court's decision to the California Supreme Court which denied the application. The U.S. Supreme Court then granted *certiorari*, a written order commanding a lower court to forward the proceeding of the case for the Court's review.

When Questioning Is Seizure

On a 7-2 vote, the U.S. Supreme Court reversed and remanded the state court of appeals decision that the drug evidence was the fruit of an illegal seizure. In reaching this conclusion, the Court looked to the common law definition of arrest which required bringing the subject within physical control. Writing for the majority, Justice Scalia explained that in order for a seizure to have occurred there must have been either "the application of physical force, however slight," or submission to an officer's "show of authority" to restrain the person's liberty. Scalia's two-part analysis focused first on whether any physical force occurred at the moment of the officer's show of authority and, second, on the defendant's failure to comply with that show of authority. If no physical force accompanied the show of authority and an individual then chooses

to ignore the show of authority, no seizure exists until the officer does apply physical force. The police had not applied physical force in this case before Hodari tossed the drugs. Scalia wrote that the word "seizure" did not remotely apply to a policeman yelling, "Stop, in the name of the law!" at a fleeing person that continued to flee.

The Court was unwilling to accept Hodari's argument that the officer's pursuit qualified as a "show of authority" constituting a seizure even though Hodari did not submit to that expression of authority. As a result, the Court determined that the drugs abandoned during Hodari's flight were not the fruit of an illegal seizure at all, since no seizure occurred at that time. Thus, his motion to suppress the evidence was properly denied by the circuit court prior to the juvenile proceedings. In fact, any object discarded by the fleeing individual would be considered abandoned and its retrieval would not involve Fourth Amendment concerns.

An Erosion of Fourth Amendment Rights?

In a dissent joined by Justice Marshall, Justice Stevens experienced strong misgivings about the Court's ruling. It seemingly adopted a new definition of "seizure" inconsistent with a long line of Fourth Amendment cases. The Court traditionally had adopted a broad view of the Fourth Amendment protection. The decision in this case clearly narrowed the view of those protections, essentially decreasing citizens' rights to protection from seizures by the government. The previous decisions in *Katz* and *Terry* rejected the notion that the common law of arrest defined the limits of the term "seizure" in the Fourth Amendment. Stevens wrote:

> In *Katz*, the Court abandoned the narrow view that would have limited a seizure to a material object, and instead, held that the Fourth Amendment extended to the recording of oral statements. And in *Terry*, the Court abandoned its traditional view that a seizure under the Fourth Amendment required probable cause, and instead, expanded the definition of a seizure to include an investigative stop made on less than probable cause. Thus, the major premise underpinning the majority's entire analysis today—that the common law of arrest should define the term "seizure" for Fourth Amendment purposes—is seriously flawed. The Court mistakenly hearkens back to common law, while ignoring the expansive approach that the Court has taken in the Fourth Amendment analysis since *Katz* and *Terry*.

The dissenters continued by arguing that the way a citizen responds should not determine the constitutionality of the officer's conduct. Further, they expressed concern that the majority's decision would encourage unlawful displays of force that will frighten innocent citizens into surrendering privacy rights to which they are entitled under the Fourth Amendment.

Impact

The *Hodari* verdict went well beyond the *Mendenhall-Royer* test. This decision along with others in 1991, such as *Florida v. Bostick,* consistently overturned lower court rulings applying Fourth Amendment protections and substantially narrowed those protective boundaries. To some, the Court decisions reflected current public opinion in which anyone expressing concerns about constitutional safeguards were labeled "soft" on crime.

The *Hodari* ruling partially reversed previous findings, such as *Terry,* by establishing that a restraint must be a successful one to invoke constitutional protections. That is, either the citizen the officer is seeking to restrain must submit to the restraint, or the officer must use physical force in order for a seizure to have occurred. An officer could pursue a citizen even without a reasonable suspicion that the citizen had committed a crime. Despite the absence of any apparent wrongdoing, the government could assume the citizen had violated the law and take measures to confirm that assumption. Following *Hodari,* citizens had to trust the government to use its intrusion power wisely rather than the police trusting the citizens as guided by the Constitution regarding assumption of innocence until proven guilty.

Justice Scalia quoted the biblical proverb, "the wicked flee when no man pursueth" to assert that avoidance of police indicates guilt. This perspective directly conflicted with what the Supreme Court recognized long ago in 1896. In *Alberty v. United States* (1896), the Court stated it is "a matter of common knowledge that men who are entirely innocent do sometimes fly from the scene of a crime through fear of being apprehended as the guilty parties, or from an unwillingness to appear as witnesses." Giving police officials unlimited discretion to initiate chases hardly seemed likely to reduce the occasions on which individuals might seek to elude the police or increase the willingness of members of the public in responding to police commands. The *Hodari* ruling allowed police officers to assume guilt on the part of the fleeing person, and give chase without the Fourth Amendment coming into play.

Civil rights activists among others were alarmed by the *Hodari* decision. The Court seemed oblivious to the tensions between police and minority communities, especially regarding street encounters. Scalia's proverb was not considered applicable to young black men who may have many reasons to fear police contact. Studies ignored by the Court had shown that black youths were subjected more frequently to warrantless search and seizures and aggressive police behavior. The case demonstrated clearly that race is not relevant to the Court in considering the circumstances surrounding an incident, which is contrary to reality in dealing with black and white encounters.

Related Cases

Alberty v. United States, 162 U.S. 499 (1896).
Katz v. United States, 389 U.S. 347 (1967).
Terry v. Ohio, 392 U.S. 1 (1968).
Florida v. Royer, 460 U.S. 491 (1983).
United States v. Mendenhall, 446 U.S. 544 (1988).
Florida v. Bostick, 501 U.S. 429 (1991).

Bibliography and Further Reading

Biskupic, Joan, and Elder Witt. *Guide to the U.S. Supreme Court.* Washington, DC: Congressional Quarterly, 1997.

LaFave, Wayne R. *Search and Seizure: A Treatise on the Fourth Amendment,* 3rd Edition. St. Paul, MN: West Publishing Co., 1996.

COUNTY OF RIVERSIDE V. MCLAUGHLIN

Lega2l Citation: 500 U.S. 44 (1991)

Petitioner
County of Riverside

Respondent
Donald Lee McLaughlin

Petitioner's Claim
That the county's providing a probable cause hearing to those arrested without a warrant within 48 hours of the arrest was acceptable.

Chief Lawyer for Petitioner
Timothy T. Coates

Chief Lawyer for Respondent
Dan Stormer

Justices for the Court
Anthony M. Kennedy, Sandra Day O'Connor (writing for the Court), William H. Rehnquist, David H. Souter, Byron R. White

Justices Dissenting
Harry A. Blackmun, Thurgood Marshall, Antonin Scalia, John Paul Stevens

Place
Washington, D.C.

Date of Decision
13 May 1991

Decision
Reversed the decision of the court of appeals and held that a probable cause hearing must take place as soon as is reasonably feasible, but no later that 48 hours after an arrest.

Significance
The ruling settled controversy which arose after *Gerstein v. Pugh* (1975), as to the meaning of "prompt, " when referring to the necessity of providing a prompt probable cause hearing to someone arrested without a warrant. A suspect arrested without a warrant has a Fourth Amendment right to prompt judicial determination of whether probable cause existed for his arrest. Absent extraordinary circumstances, "prompt" means within 48 hours.

Donald Lee McLaughlin was incarcerated in the Riverside County Jail in California. He had been arrested without a warrant and had not yet received a hearing. In August of 1987, Donald Lee McLaughlin filed a complaint in the U.S. District Court for the Central District of California seeking prompt probable cause, bail, and arraignment hearings for himself and other in-custody arrestees who had been arrested without warrants. In November of 1988 the district court certified as a "class" those prisoners in the Riverside County Jail held there from 1 August 1987 to the present and all future detainees denied prompt probable cause, bail, or arraignment hearings. In a class action lawsuit, a named petitioner files a complaint on behalf of himself and others who are similarly situated, meaning suffering from the same problem. A judge must then certify, or approve, these people filing a lawsuit as a group. If they receive certification, they become the petitioners in the lawsuit.

In *County of Riverside v. McLaughlin,* the petitioners asked the district court, in March of 1989, to issue a preliminary injunction (an order) to require the county to provide all those arrested without a warrant a probable cause hearing within 36 hours of their arrest. At this type of hearing, a law enforcement officer must explain to a judge why he arrested a person without a warrant. The officer must show that at the time of the arrest he believed an offense had been committed and that the arrestee likely committed it.

The lawsuit challenged the way that Riverside County provided probable cause hearings to those arrested without a warrant. The county combined the probable cause determination with arraignment procedures. At an arraignment, the suspect is formally charged by the judge and enters a plea of guilty or not guilty. Although county policy was to conduct the arraignment without unnecessary delay—within two days of the arrest—the two-day requirement did not compute in weekends and holidays. Thus someone arrested late in the week might be held for as long as five days before getting a probable cause determination. If the arrest took place around Thanksgiving, a seven day delay may have occurred.

The district court issued the injunction stating that the existing practice of the county violated the Supreme

Court's decision in *Gerstein v. Pugh,* which mandated "prompt" probable cause hearings for people arrested without warrants. The district court adopted a rule that the county must provide such hearings within 36 hours of arrest. The U.S. Court of Appeals for the Ninth Circuit agreed with the district court's decision to grant the preliminary injunction. The court of appeals stated that the county's policy of providing probable cause hearings within 48 hours was not in accordance with the *Gerstein* requirement of a hearing "promptly after arrest" because no more than 36 hours were needed. The Ninth Circuit joined the Fourth and Seventh Circuits in interpreting the *Gerstein* ruling to mean that a probable cause hearing must immediately follow the completion of the administrative procedures that occur after an arrest. The Second Circuit, however, stressed the need for flexibility and the desire of states to combine probable cause hearings with other pretrial proceedings.

The Promptness Requirement

In *Gerstein v. Pugh,* the Supreme Court attempted to reconcile important competing interests in arrests without warrants. States have a strong interest in protecting public safety and individuals have a strong interest in protecting job, income, and family. The Court sought to balance these competing concerns and reach a practical compromise between the rights of individuals and the realities of law enforcement by stating that a probable cause hearing must be held "promptly after arrest." In *Gerstein* the Court noted that "flexibility and experimentation by the States" were desirable. The Court's purpose in *Gerstein* was to clarify that the Fourth Amendment requires the states to hold a prompt probable cause hearing, but the Constitution does not demand a rigid procedural framework compelling an immediate determination of probable cause upon completion of the administrative steps that go along with an arrest. The Fourth Amendment "permits a reasonable postponement of a probable cause determination while the police cope with the everyday problems of processing suspects through an overly burdened criminal justice system."

Writing for the Court, Justice O'Connor noted the importance of providing sufficient guidelines for states and counties to follow. The majority of the Court agreed that providing a probable cause hearing within 48 hours of arrest would satisfy the promptness requirement in *Gerstein.* An arrestee's rights could still be violated if a probable cause hearing was delayed unreasonably, even if it took place within 48 hours of arrest. Some examples of an unreasonable delay are delays used to gather additional evidence to justify the arrest, delays motivated by ill-will, or delays for delays' sake. In determining if a delay is unreasonable, the courts must allow a substantial degree of flexibility. If an

arrestee does not receive a probable cause hearing within 48 hours, the government must demonstrate that a bona fide emergency or extraordinary circumstance prevented it. Consolidating pretrial proceedings or intervening weekends does not qualify as extraordinary circumstances.

No More Than 24 Hours Is Needed

Justice Scalia in his dissent noted that the Bill of Rights (the first ten amendments to the Constitution) had already achieved a "balancing" between the competing concerns of protecting public safety and avoiding prolonged detention. "It is the function of the Bill of Rights to preserve that judgment, not only against the changing views of Presidents and Members of Congress, but also against the changing views of Justices whom Presidents appoint and Members of Congress confirm to this Court."

Scalia noted that in *Gerstein,* the Court relied upon the common law understanding that the period of warrantless detention must be limited to the time necessary to complete the arrest and get a magistrate's review. Scalia felt that the idea of flexibility and experimentation referred to the nature of the hearing and not to its timing. He criticized the majority's idea of "balancing." Scalia noted that the purpose of the Fourth Amendment was "to put this matter beyond time, place, and judicial predilection." A determination to deprive someone of his or her liberty should be made, not according to a schedule that suits the state's convenience, but as soon as an arrest is completed and a magistrate found. Scalia noted that no more than 24 hours is needed for this process and that most federal courts and many state courts have applied a 24-hour limit.

Scalia summed up his dissent by stating, "One hears the complaint, nowadays, that the Fourth Amendment has become constitutional law for the guilty; that it benefits the career criminal (through the exclusionary rule) often and directly, but the ordinary citizen remotely if at all." Scalia felt that the majority's opinion in this case reinforces the public's view of the Fourth Amendment and does not benefit its intended beneficiaries, the innocent. He went on to criticize the exclusionary rule and lament the lack of protection for those presumed innocent. "While in recent years we have invented novel applications of the Fourth Amendment to release the unquestionably guilty, we today [in the majority's decision in this case] repudiate one of its core applications so that the presumptively innocent may be left in jail."

Impact

In 1994, the Supreme Court ruled in *Powell v. Nevada* (1994), that McLaughlin's 48-hour rule must be applied retroactively, noting that a rule for the conduct of criminal prosecutions is to be applied retroactively to all cases, state or federal, not yet final when the rule is announced. In this case the Court also pointed out that the appropriate remedy for a delay in determining probable cause was an issue not resolved by the *McLaughlin* case.

In *United States v. Alvarez-Sanchez,* a respondent asserted that his confession was obtained during an ongoing violation of his Fourth Amendment right to a prompt determination of probable cause. The respondent, however, did not raise a Fourth Amendment claim in the district court or the court of appeals, so the Supreme Court declined to address his Fourth Amendment argument. Not receiving a probable-cause review within 48 hours of confinement has come to be known as a Riverside violation. In a case where the trial court determines that there was a Riverside violation but the respondent never sought to have his confession suppressed as a result of that violation, an alleged Riverside violation is waived unless it is raised before the trial court.

In January of 1998, U.S. District Court Judge Julie E. Carnes ruled that Georgia's system for probable cause hearings provided juveniles less protection than adults. Under the Georgia law, juveniles could be incarcerated for 72 hours, or upwards of one week, if a weekend or holiday intervened, without a probable cause hearing.

Judge Carnes noted that such hearings, "minimize the time a presumptively innocent individual spends in jail" and that such "pretrial detention is an onerous experience, especially for juveniles." Gerry Weber, the Legal Director of the American Civil Liberties Union of Georgia stated that he was pleased that the Court recognized the double standard in giving juveniles fewer due process rights than adults. He stated that "Innocent youth wrongly accused of crimes will no longer have to languish in jail for days awaiting a court's conclusion that they should never have been there in the first place."

Related Cases

Gerstein v. Pugh, 420 U.S. 103 (1975).
Allen v. Wright, 468 U.S. 737 (1984).
Powell v. Nevada, 511 U.S. 79 (1994).
United States v. Alvarez-Sanchez, 511 U.S. 350 (1994).

Bibliography and Further Reading

American Civil Liberties Union. http://www.aclu.org/news.

Legal Information Institute. http://www.law.cornell.edu.

Witt, Elder, ed. *The Supreme Court A to Z. CQ's Encyclopedia of American Government.* Washington, DC: Congressional Quarterly, Inc., 1993.

CALIFORNIA V. ACEVEDO

Legal Citation: 500 U.S. 565 (1991)

Petitioner
State of California

Respondent
Charles Steven Acevedo

Petitioner's Claim
That police may search a container seized from an automobile where there is probable cause to believe that the container holds evidence or an illegal substance.

Chief Lawyer for Petitioner
Robert M. Foster

Chief Lawyer for Respondent
Frederick Westcott Anderson

Justices for the Court
Harry A. Blackmun (writing for the Court), Anthony M. Kennedy, Sandra Day O'Connor, William H. Rehnquist, Antonin Scalia, David H. Souter

Justices Dissenting
Thurgood Marshall, John Paul Stevens, Byron R. White

Place
Washington, D.C.

Date of Decision
30 May 1991

Decision
Marijuana seized from defendant's car could be admitted into evidence at defendant's trial on drug charges. Reversed lower court decision barring admission of marijuana because police had not procured search warrant.

Significance
Established that police need not obtain a search warrant prior to searching a closed container seized from a vehicle so long as they have probable cause to believe that the vehicle or container contains evidence or an illegal substance.

The United States' "War on Drugs" became a major concern in the 1970s and 1980s. As drug arrests increased, a growing number of defendants sought to exclude drugs found in their possession from evidence at trial. Convictions often depended upon the introduction of such evidence. In other criminal cases, defendants sought to exclude from evidence weapons that had been seized in police searches. In *Acevedo* the Supreme Court delineated the circumstances under which evidence seized from a vehicle would be admissible at trial.

The case arose when police officers saw Acevedo place a brown paper bag in the trunk of his car and drive away. The bag appeared to be one of a number of packages of marijuana, which police had observed being brought into the building from which Acevedo was leaving. The police stopped the car, opened the trunk and bag, and found the marijuana. Acevedo was charged with possession of marijuana for sale.

Prior to trial, Acevedo moved to exclude the marijuana from evidence. His attorney argued that the search of the bag was unconstitutional because the police did not first obtain a search warrant. The trial court denied his motion to exclude the evidence, but the California Court of Appeals reversed and ruled that the officers should not have searched the bag without obtaining a warrant. The California Supreme Court denied the state's petition for review of the court of appeals decision, following which the state applied for and was granted a review of the decision by the U.S. Supreme Court.

A Uniform Rule for Vehicle Searches

The Supreme Court ruled in a 6-3 decision that the search of the bag in Acevedo's trunk was constitutional. Therefore, the marijuana found in the trunk was admissible as evidence at trial. In reaching this result, the Court rejected the respondent argument that the police should have obtained a search warrant before opening the bag.

The basis of the respondent challenge was the Fourth Amendment's prohibition of unreasonable searches and seizures. That prohibition has been repeatedly interpreted to require that authorities have "probable

Kids, Drugs, and Crime

According to the U.S. Department of Justice, in 1992 there were 73,981 arrests relating to the possession, sale, use, growing, and manufacture of illegal drugs on the part of youths 17 years or age and younger. Of these, 14,529, or nearly 20 percent, took place in California. New York state came in second, with 8,301 arrests (11 percent), and Texas was third with 6,306 (about 8.5 percent).

A 1996 Justice Department study compared drug use by male juvenile arrestees or detainees—as determined by drug tests—in 12 U.S. cities, including the California jurisdictions of Los Angeles, San Diego, and San Jose.

Other cities included: Birmingham, Alabama in the South; Washington, D.C. in the East; Cleveland, Ohio in the Northeast; Indianapolis, Indiana and St. Louis,

Missouri in the Midwest; Denver, Phoenix, and San Antonio, Texas in the West; and Portland, Oregon in the Northwest.

The average percentage of arrestees using drugs of any kind was 53.8 percent, meaning that San Diego, with 53 percent, was almost exactly at the statistical mean. San Jose was well below, with 46 percent; and Los Angeles was above the average. However, at 57 percent, it was not substantially above, and it was surpassed by Denver (61 percent), Cleveland (63), and Washington (67).

Source(s): Morgan, Kathleen O'Leary, et al., eds. *Crime State Rankings*. Lawrence, KS: Morgan Quitno, 1994.

cause" to conduct a search, just as in an earlier case, *United States v. Ross* (1982). It has also been interpreted to require that in many circumstances police obtain a search warrant prior to conducting a search. Where authorities have conducted an unconstitutional search, the remedy courts have imposed is to exclude evidence obtained from the illegal search from consideration by the judge or jury at trial.

The Supreme Court initially narrowed the issues in *Acevedo* by refusing to review the California Courts' finding that there was probable cause to search the bag. The Supreme Court also did not question the propriety of seizing the bag. Instead, the Court focused exclusively on whether the police should have obtained a search warrant before opening the bag. The legal question addressed was, under what circumstances can a container seized from a vehicle can be searched without first obtaining a search warrant.

The answer to this question was complicated by the existence of different rules for searching vehicles and containers such as bags or suitcases. In cases involving vehicles, the police were allowed to stop a car and conduct a search of the car without first obtaining a search warrant so long as there was probable cause to believe the vehicle contained evidence or an illegal substance. That search could include searching containers found in the vehicle. In contrast, police having probable cause to believe that a container contained evidence or an illegal substance could seize the container, but could not search it without a search warrant. This distinction resulted in confusion in cases involving containers found inside vehicles. More specifically, the Court had to consider whether the rules applied to searches of vehicles or containers.

Previously, in *Arkansas v. Sanders* (1979), the Supreme Court had applied the container rule requiring a warrant where police had probable cause to search a container which had been placed in a car, but lacked probable cause to search the entire auto. The California Court of Appeals followed *Sanders* and applied the container rule to Acevedo's case. The California court concluded that the container rule applied because at the time Acevedo was stopped there was no reason to be suspicious of anything in the car other than the bag itself. Therefore, there was no cause to search the entire automobile, and the California court held the warrantless search invalid.

The Supreme Court rejected the distinction between vehicle searches and searches of containers in vehicles. It emphasized that the result was confusion for courts and police officers trying to decide whether a warrant was necessary in a particular case. The Court simplified the area by announcing one rule governing all searches of containers in vehicles:

> Until today, this Court has drawn a curious line between the search of an automobile that coincidentally turns up a container and the search of a container that coincidentally turns up an automobile. The protections of the Fourth Amendment must not turn on such coincidences . . . We therefore . . . [provide] one rule to govern all automobile searches. The police may search an automobile and the containers within it where they have probable cause to believe contraband or evidence is contained.

Justice Scalia wrote a separate opinion in which he concurred with the majority. He would have gone even further in permitting warrantless searches. In his opinion a warrantless search of a closed container located outside a private building would be permissible so long as the police had probable cause to believe the article contained an illegal substance.

Dissent Finds Warrantless Search Unacceptable

Justices Stevens, Marshall and White disagreed with the majority. Stevens urged in his dissenting opinion that the search of Acevedo's bag without a search warrant was unconstitutional. He reasoned that there was no justification for not requiring a warrant where the container had been seized and was under police control. Thus, there was no risk that the evidence would be destroyed or hidden before a warrant could be obtained. Under such circumstances Stevens found the loss of individual privacy resulting from the warrantless search to be unacceptable.

Impact

The *Acevedo* Court established a clear rule for police to follow when searching containers found in vehicles. At the law enforcement level, the decision has broadened police officers' ability to conduct a search without first obtaining a search warrant. It has prevented defendants challenging an automobile search from arguing that a search warrant was necessary. Instead, the only question they can raise is whether there was probable cause to initiate the search. As a practical matter, since the *Acevedo* decision, evidence obtained in a vehicle search is more likely to be admitted into evidence against a defendant at trial.

Related Cases

United States v. Chadwick, 433 U.S. 1 (1977).
Arkansas v. Sanders, 442 U.S. 753 (1979).
United States v. Ross, 456 U.S. 798 (1982).
United States v. Cook, 938 F.2d 149 (9th Cir. 1991).
United States v. Corral, 970 F.2d 719 (10th Cir. 1992).

Bibliography and Further Reading

Bernheim, David. *Defense of Narcotics Cases.* New York: Matthew Bender, 1997.

Bradley, Craig M. "The Court's 'Two Model' Approach to the Fourth Amendment: Carpe Diem." *Journal of Criminal Law and Criminology,* fall 1993, p. 429.

FLORIDA V. BOSTICK

Legal Citation: 501 U.S. 429 (1991)

Petitioner
State of Florida

Respondent
Terrance Bostick

Petitioner's Claim
Random police searches of the effects of consenting passengers are not *per se* unconstitutional.

Chief Lawyer for Petitioner
Joan Fowler, Assistant Attorney General of Florida

Chief Lawyer for Respondent
Donald B. Ayer

Justices for the Court
Anthony M. Kennedy, Sandra Day O'Connor (writing for the Court), William H. Rehnquist, Antonin Scalia, David H. Souter, Byron R. White

Justices Dissenting
Harry A. Blackmun, Thurgood Marshall, John Paul Stevens

Place
Washington, D.C.

Date of Decision
20 June 1991

Decision
Police sweeps of buses and their passengers are not necessarily unconstitutional.

Significance
The *Bostick* case was significant for what it authorized: police dragnets of buses and bus passengers and searches that are unsupported by suspicion.

Terrance Bostick was on a bus headed from Miami, Florida, to Atlanta, Georgia, when the bus stopped for a layover in Fort Lauderdale. Two police officers wearing casual clothes and jackets clearly marked "raid" boarded the bus and began to eye the passengers. The officers picked out Terrance Bostick, a black man, for questioning. Standing between Bostick and the door with their pistols and badges visible, the officers told Bostick that they were narcotics agents looking for illegal drugs. Upon searching Bostick's luggage, the officers found cocaine and arrested Bostick.

Bostick was charged with trafficking in cocaine. Before trial, Bostick moved the court to exclude the cocaine evidence, arguing that the search was conducted in violation of his Fourth Amendment right to be free from unreasonable search and seizure. The trial court refused to suppress the evidence, and Bostick pleaded guilty but preserved his right to appeal the court's decision on the suppression motion. The Florida District Court of Appeal affirmed the trial court's ruling, but it considered the question important enough to certify to the Florida Supreme Court, which reversed the ruling. According to Florida's high court, "an impermissible seizure result[s] when police mount a drug search on buses during scheduled stops and question boarded passengers without articulable reason for doing so, thereby obtaining consent to search the passengers' luggage." The state of Florida petitioned for *certiorari* to the U.S. Supreme Court, and the High Court agreed to hear the case.

In a 6-3 decision, the High Court held that the search in the case was not *per se* unreasonable. In an opinion written by Justice O'Connor, the majority initially noted two important facts about the case: first, although Bostick disputed the finding, the trial court found that the police officers gave Bostick the right to refuse consent and that the officers never threatened Bostick with their guns. The Court then explained that its reason for taking the case was to see if Florida's high court had created a rule that was inconsistent with the Supreme Court's Fourth Amendment jurisprudence.

The sole issue in Bostick's case was whether a police encounter on a bus, such as the one that Bostick expe-

Random Bus and Train Searches

Legal writer Stuart Taylor, discussing random searches in *Manhattan Lawyer*, would no doubt have taken quite a different view. "It's after midnight," Taylor wrote, setting the scene for his discussion. "You are hurrying through the airport with a carry-on bag, impatient to get home . . . A man keeps pace with you, staying close . . . Another man hovers nearby. You walk faster. The first man closes in from the side. The other circles behind you. Your heart is pounding. 'Excuse me.' He flashes a badge. 'Can I talk to you?' . . . You know you've done nothing wrong. But suddenly you're a suspect. Your hands are shaking." Taylor went on to ask readers if they knew their rights in such a situation, and noted that many courts would not consider such an approach coercive. But in Taylor's view, these random airport, train station, or bus terminal searches are indeed coercive, precisely because no one wants to invoke their rights for fear of raising suspicions that they are carrying something illegal. "And so we have moved into a regime of random police fishing expeditions," he observed, "in which innocent citizens must submit to searches or be branded as drug suspects for refusing."

Source(s): Taylor, Stuart Jr. "Travelers Becoming POWs in Drug War." *Manhattan Lawyer*, May 1990.

rienced, constitutes a seizure by the police under the Fourth Amendment. If such a police encounter does not constitute a seizure, then the Fourth Amendment protections against unreasonable search and seizure do not apply. All parties in the case agreed that if the encounter was found to be a seizure, it was an illegal seizure, unsupported as it was by any reasonable suspicion that Bostick had done anything wrong. In such a ruling the cocaine evidence would have to be thrown out of court, effectively ending the state's prosecution of Bostick.

The state of Florida argued that the encounter did not constitute a seizure, and it compared the case to prior cases in which the Court had held that similar police questioning in an airport did not constitute a seizure. Bostick argued that his case was different because the encounter took place in the cramped confines of a bus. Bostick maintained that his exit route was cut off by the armed officers, and he claimed that the intimidating nature of the confrontation created an atmosphere in which he was effectively seized by the police.

The Court rejected Bostick's arguments. The Court cited some of its earlier cases for the proposition that simple police questioning does not constitute a seizure. That rule is in place because the alternative—preventing police officers from even talking to people without first developing a reasonable suspicion that the person has committed or is about to commit a crime—would be an unnecessary burden on law enforcement. Quoting *California v. Hodari D.* (1991), the Court recited the test for determining whether a police encounter constitutes a seizure: if the person reasonably feels free "to disregard the police and go about his business," the encounter is not a seizure.

In Bostick's case, however, the Florida Supreme Court's emphasis on whether Bostick was free to leave was error. Because Bostick was on a bus, he probably had no desire to leave, so "the degree to which a reasonable person would feel that he or she could leave is not an accurate measure of the coercive effect of the encounter." The majority acknowledged that Bostick's movements were in fact confined, but "this was the natural result of his decision to take the bus; it says nothing about whether or not the police conduct at issue was coercive."

The majority declared this case was similar to that of *Immigration and Naturalization Service v. Delgado* (1984). In that case, Immigration and Naturalization Service (INS) agents, looking for illegal aliens, visited factories at random and questioned employees without reasonable suspicion to believe that any of the employees were illegal aliens. The Supreme Court ruled that the practice was not unconstitutional because there was no seizure of employees by the INS agents. Despite the fact that the factory employees were not free to leave the factory, the Court believed that the agents' conduct gave employees "no reason to believe that they would be detained if they gave truthful answers . . . or if they simply refused to answer."

The majority, however, refused to determine whether the agents in Bostick's case had in fact seized Bostick. That was a factual determination that had not been decided by the Florida courts under the proper standard. The proper standard for determining whether Bostick was seized, the Court pronounced, was the totality of the circumstances. In other words, the courts would have to look at all the factors involved in the encounter from the standpoint of a reasonable person to determine whether Bostick was in fact seized. The majority made it a point, though, to specifically reject Bostick's claim that he must have been seized because no reasonable person would willingly give police officers an opportunity to look through a container that contains illegal drugs. This argument was futile because when judges and juries determine what a reasonable person would feel, they must made that determination from the perspective of an innocent person, not a guilty person. The question remaining for the Florida courts, said the majority, was whether Bostick actually consented to the search of his luggage.

Justice O'Connor spent the rest of the opinion defending the majority's decision against a scathing dissent by Justice Marshall. The dissent claimed that the opinion authorized police to intimidate passengers into "voluntary" cooperation. The opinion authorized no such thing, said O'Connor, noting that the question on remand to Florida's courts was whether Bostick in fact gave the officers consent to search his luggage. The dissent also claimed that the majority opinion decreased constitutional protection for persons on buses, but the opinion merely gave police the same rights that they have on the streets and in airports and trains. O'Connor observed that the dissent objected to the idea of random police questioning, but, she noted, the Court had endorsed the idea in several prior cases.

Striking a conciliatory tone, O'Connor closed the majority opinion by agreeing with the dissent that the Court does not have the power to "suspend constitutional guarantees" as the country fights a "war on drugs." The holding, however, suspended no constitutional guarantees. According to the majority, its holding was in line with precedent and merely corrected the Florida Supreme Court's conclusion that such police sweeps as the one conducted in Bostick's case were not *per se* unconstitutional.

Minority Opinion

Justices Blackmun and Stevens joined Justice Marshall in a blistering dissent. The police sweep conducted in Bostick's case "violate[d] the core values of the Fourth Amendment," wrote Justice Marshall. The sweep was conducted "in 'Dragnet' style" without an articulable suspicion about a specific bus or passenger. In a footnote, Marshall observed that the decision to approach certain passengers was not "completely random." In fact, Marshall noted, black persons were being targeted. To support this proposition, Marshall cited testimony in *United States v. Williams* (1991). In that case, a detective testified that he decided to question three persons because they "were young and black." Thus, the decision "to single out particular passengers during a suspicionless sweep," Marshall opined, "is less likely to be inarticulable than unspeakable."

Marshall sided with the Florida Supreme Court, arguing for deference to its judgment as a court "located at the heart of the 'drug war.'" He quoted *Florida v. Kerwick* (1987), another case involving a police sweep for drugs, at length. In that case, the court compared the police tactics to police tactics

of other days, under other flags, when no man traveled his nation's roads or railways without fear of unwarranted interruption, by individuals who held temporary power in the Government. The spectre of American citizens being asked, by badge-wielding police, for identification, travel papers—in short a *raison d'etre*—is foreign to any fair reading of the Constitution, and its guarantee of human liberties. This is not Hitler's Berlin, nor Stalin's Moscow, nor is it white supremacist South Africa.

Marshall also quoted a District of Columbia court, which stated in a similar case, "[i]n this 'anything goes' war on drugs, random knocks on the doors of our citizens' homes seeking 'consent' to search for drugs cannot be far away."

The majority had "inexplicably" stressed that the police informed Bostick that he was free to withhold his consent to the search of his luggage. This was beside the point, Marshall lectured: If Bostick was actually seized before the police searched his luggage, then the search, as the parties had conceded, was illegal. Thus, under Supreme Court precedent on the topic of such encounters, the real question in the case was whether a reasonable person in Bostick's position, unapprised of his constitutional rights, would have felt free to terminate the encounter with the police. "Unlike the majority," said Marshall, "I have no doubt that the answer to this question is no."

Marshall ridiculed the majority's analysis of Bostick's mode of transportation, calling it borderline "sophism" that "trivializes the values that underlie the Fourth Amendment." The option to leave a bus before a destination without stowed belongings is not an attractive one, and "[i]t is exactly because this 'choice' is no 'choice' at all that police engage this technique." Marshall noted that the majority had kind words for individual rights, but "[t]he actions . . . speak louder than its words."

Impact

The Supreme Court's ruling in *Bostick*, perhaps out of necessity, endorsed the historically vague application of the Fourth Amendment's search and seizure provision. The standard used to determine whether a search or seizure violates an individual's constitutional rights is "objective" reasonableness. Objective reasonableness is a hypothetical guideline used to determine whether the "typical reasonable individual" would consent to a search or seizure given the situation in question. Some contend that such a standard opens the door to perjury by law enforcement officials. There is evidence to suggest that the temptation for law enforcement officials to provide false testimony that a suspect consented to a search or seizure is too great to resist. *Bostick* did little to discourage such eventualities. As with many cases that involve the application of the Fourth Amendment, the central issue that *Bostick* addressed pertains to a citizen's knowledge of their right to deny officers permission to search their belongings or detain them. Previously, the application of the Fourth Amendment operated under the assumption that an individual understood that he or she did not have to consent to a search. O'Connor's opinion shifted the burden of proving this understanding to the person being searched; it is incumbent upon the individual to prove that a law enforcement official made it clear that he or she did not have to consent to the search.

The *Bostick* ruling and subsequent Rehnquist rulings such as *Ohio v. Robinette* (1996) and *Maryland v. Wilson* (1997) tilted the application of the Fourth Amendment further in favor of law enforcement practices. In *Ohio* the Court ruled that the Fourth Amendment does not require police officers to inform defendants that they are "free to go" in order for a consent to search the individual to be considered voluntary. In *Maryland* the Court held that it is not a violation of the Fourth Amendment for an officer to request that a passenger get out of a car that has been lawfully detained.

Related Cases
Immigration and Naturalization Service v. Delgado, 466 U.S. 210 (1984).

Florida v. Kerwick, 512 So.2d 347 (Fla App. 1987).
California v. Hodari D., 499 U.S. 621 (1991).
United States v. Williams, 500 U.S. 901 (1991).

Bibliography and Further Reading

Dripps, Donald A. "Police, Plus Perjury, Equals Polygraphy." *Journal of Criminal Law and Criminology,* spring 1996, p. 693.

Hall, Kermit L., ed. *The Oxford Companion to the Supreme Court of the United States.* New York: Oxford University Press, 1992.

Makau, Josina M., and David Lawrence. "Administrative Judicial Rhetoric: The Supreme Court's New Thesis of Political Morality." *Argumentation and Advocacy,* spring 1994, p. 191.

Savage, David G. *Turning Right: The Making of the Rehnquist Supreme Court.* John Wiley & Sons, Inc., 1992.

Slansky, David A. "Traffic Stops, Minority Motorists, and the Future of the Fourth Amendment." *Supreme Court Review,* annual 1997, p. 271.

Steiker, Carol S. "Counter-Revolution in Constitutional Criminal Procedure? Two Audiences, Two Answers." *Michigan Law Review,* August 1996, p. 2466.

LUCAS V. SOUTH CAROLINA COASTAL COUNCIL

Legal Citation: 505 U.S. 1003 (1992)

Petitioner
David H. Lucas

Respondent
South Carolina Coastal Council

Petitioner's Claim
The South Carolina State Beachfront Management Act deprived the petitioner of profitable use of his property by prohibiting construction of new dwellings on his parcels. Thus, it must compensate the petitioner.

Chief Lawyer for Petitioner
A. Camden Lewis

Chief Lawyer for Respondent
C. C. Harness III

Justices for the Court
Anthony M. Kennedy, Sandra Day O'Connor, William H. Rehnquist, Antonin Scalia (writing for the Court), Clarence Thomas, Byron R. White

Justices Dissenting
Harry A. Blackmun, David H. Souter, John Paul Stevens

Place
Washington, D.C.

Date of Decision
29 June 1992

Decision
The Court ruled that the petitioner suffered a "taking;" his property was rendered "valueless" by South Carolina statute and he was thus entitled to "just compensation."

Significance
Although the South Carolina Supreme Court decided that state regulations "were designed to prevent serious public harm," the U.S. Supreme Court held that when a property owner suffered a "taking," there were no exceptions from common rule (the Takings Clause and the Just Compensation Clause). Furthermore, when the state of South Carolina amended its original statute by including provisions that might permit limited construction, the U.S. Supreme Court held that a property owner must still be compensated. Even when legislation later renders the initial act less restrictive, property owners still suffer from the original effects of a taking, thus, just compensation must be rendered.

In 1972, Congress passed the Coastal Zone Management Act in order to protect the state's shoreline from coastal erosion. After five years, South Carolina issued its own Coastal Zone Management Act in order to protect the shoreline from erosion, preserve the beach/dune system and prevent further coastal damage. The act stipulated that before construction could take place in any designated, environmentally-sensitive "critical area," an owner had to obtain permission from the South Carolina Coastal Council. In 1977, the "critical area" was not large and construction was prohibited only along a narrow zone of the coast. David H. Lucas (the petitioner) bought two residential lots on the South Carolina coast in 1986 (Isle of Palms, Charleston County) for about $900,000. He planned to build single-family homes similar to those on nearby parcels. However, the next year, after a survey gave evidence that beaches of South Carolina were "critically eroding," South Carolina issued the Beachfront Management Act (BMA). The statute placed broad restraints on use along the South Carolina shoreline. Because the "critical area" was extended (on which there was a building ban), Lucas's recently purchased plots were affected. No exceptions were provided. (At the time Lucas bought his parcels, that particular zone was not subject to any construction ban, therefore he was not required to have a permit to build a residential development.

Lucas submitted his suit to the South Carolina Court of Common Pleas. He believed that his property was rendered worthless, hence he required "just compensation" (a constitutionally guaranteed practice that requires proper compensation for property the government obtains in a "taking"). As petitioner, he asserted that the South Carolina Coastal Council action infringed on his constitutional rights according to the Fifth Amendment (the Takings Clause) because no restrictions against building were effective at the time when he purchased his lots. He did not dispute the legitimacy of Coastal Council's efforts to preserve the shoreline from further destruction, but he felt entitled to compensation because his property was rendered "valueless" by what constituted, in effect, a government regulatory "taking."

Coastal Zones and the Law of the Sea

The United States has long been a jealous guardian of its coastal boundaries. Its inaccessibility to foreign invaders has helped keep it safe from outside military forces since the War of 1812. Long before that war, in 1793, Secretary of State Thomas Jefferson formulated a principle that became a legal convention long before it was ever memorialized by statute: that the American "territorial sea" extended to three nautical miles beyond its shoreline. Thus anyone operating a vessel within three miles of America's shores was subject to U.S. law.

The closest America came to foreign invasion after 1812 was during World War II, when cruising Axis vessels on both coasts posed a threat to the nation. After the war was over, President Harry S. Truman in 1945 declared that the territorial sea extended beyond the three-mile limit, all the way to the edge of the continental shelf from which the sea floor rapidly slopes off into deep ocean. Other countries supported this idea—and several asserted their own territorial sea extensions to the continental shelf. This the United States opposed, and over subsequent decades the United Nations would hold three different Conferences on the Law of the Sea (UNCLOS) to adjudicate international disputes about territorial waters and other aspects of maritime law.

Source(s): Jentleson, Bruce W. and Thomas G. Paterson, eds. *Encyclopedia of U.S. Foreign Relations.* New York: Oxford University Press, 1997.

The attorney for the respondent argued that the South Carolina coast was an extremely precious public resource; therefore, there existed a justifiable public interest in prohibiting further construction along natural resources like beach/dune shoreline areas. Because public interest outweighed personal claims to property, the South Carolina Coastal Council opposed the Lucas's claim. Furthermore, previous cases suggested that reimbursement was not necessary when noxious and destructive uses of property were recognized and prohibited by the government. Finally, counsel for the respondent argued that Lucas's claim was not "ripe." Lucas had not petitioned the Coastal Council for permission to use his land and therefore had not exhausted all legal avenues.

The (lower) trial court thought that because "prohibition deprived Lucas of any reasonable economic use of the lots and rendered them valueless," the respondent was obliged to pay more than one million dollars "just compensation." The Supreme Court of South Carolina rescinded that judgment, reasoning that the Beachfront Management Act was intended to preserve South Carolina beaches and that additional construction would imperil the eroding coastal environment. Believing the taking was designed "to prevent serious public harm," the Court cited a U.S. Supreme Court ruling, *Mugler v. Kansas* (1887), stipulating that when government applied its power to preclude "noxious use of property" no owing under the Taking Clause existed.

When the case finally came before the U.S. Supreme Court, the majority opinion rejected the judgment of the Supreme Court of South Carolina. The existence of "constitutional limits" barred deprivation of real estate by irregular "takings." Moreover, the Fifth Amendment established clear procedure outlining circumstances when compensation must be extended. Particularly, compensation was required when a physical confiscation of property occurred and "where regulation denies all economically beneficial or productive use of property."

Finding South Carolina inappropriately took private property without compensation, the Court was particularly disturbed by the inference that a public interest or "common good" rationalized lack of compensation. All appropriations that diminished viable use of belongings constituted a taking. Moreover, the Court found the respondent's reliance on cases where compensation was avoided by practicing a reasonable "state's police power" failed to evidence an "objective conception of noxiousness" in order to exercise an exception from just compensation. The majority justices also emphasized that a thin line separated "harm-preventing" and "benefit-conferring" in order to justify departure from the Fifth and Fourteenth Amendment regulations regarding takings and just compensation. But the "noxious-use logic" was not designed as a way for government to avoid compensation.

Further, the majority stressed "noxious-use justification cannot be the basis for departing from our categorical rule that total regulatory takings must be compensated." Consequently, if "noxious-use logic" was considered a reference point, constitutional constraints under the Fifth and Fourteenth Amendments (that "taking" must be compensated) would be violated. Thus, the justices reasoned that precluding "permanent physical occupation" of property through "confiscatory regulations" (regulations that made all beneficial use of property impossible) as claimed by the petitioner constituted a taking.

The heart of the U.S. Supreme Court's decision held that traditional understandings about private property and its economical, beneficial use should be respected. The state could have an interest, in certain circumstances, to take property or to prescribe regulations that could devalue property or use of belongings; however, American history (dating back to property rights objections voiced in the Declaration of Independence) required just compensation. Ultimately such "common law principles" could not justify infringing on the petitioner's rights—the Court found it inconceivable that the respondent could merely suggest the petitioner's rights were incompatible with public interest and thereby avoid compensation as ordained by the Constitution.

In writing the opinion for dissenting justices, Justice Blackmun pointed out that the state had the authority to uphold South Carolina General Assembly legislation addressing evident coastal ruination and attempts to protect it. The Beachfront Management Act (BMA) clearly underscored the importance of the beach/dune system in "protecting life and property by serving as a storm barrier which dissipates wave energy and contributes to shoreline stability in an economical and effective manner." Thus, the minority reasoned it appropriate to recognize that the continued development in places adjacent to the seashore "jeopardize the stability of the beach/dune system, accelerated erosion, and endanger adjacent property." Accordingly, the noncompensated taking of Lucas's land was reasonable. Justice Blackmun emphasized that, inherently, an owner's use of property had to be unhazardous to the community; therefore regulations which the government used to safeguard the "common welfare" did not require compensation. The state's intent was only to "minimize damage to coastal areas" and to "prevent serious injury to the community"; thus, he concluded that the South Carolina Supreme Court was correct in finding that no taking had occurred. Furthermore, Justice Blackmun pointed out that the council never made a determination as to whether Lucas's lots were in a "critical area" and inappropriate for construction; Lucas had never applied for a "special permit" nor for additional consideration about natural conditions on his parcels that might permit erecting habitation without damaging the environment. (In fact, Lucas had stated that his company produced a study showing the land was "perfectly safe to build on.") The minority opinion, therefore, disagreed that Lucas suffered "total" damage due to restrictions on the use of his property. Moreover, Justice Blackmun reasoned that the state had "full power to prohibit an owner's use of property if it is harmful to the public." Thus, economic loss to an owner could not prevail over the interest of government to restrict harmful use of real estate.

Justice Stevens wrote a separate opinion supporting the dissenting opinion. He ultimately concluded that the BMA had no other intention than to protect the beach/dune system. Further, since the substantial purpose of South Carolina's Legislature was within the limits of restricting land use for general public safety, the BMA did not amount to a property taking and compensation was not appropriate.

Impact

Dissenting opinion notwithstanding, the provisions of the Takings and Just Compensation Clauses of the Constitution's Fifth and Fourteenth Amendments were upheld by the Supreme Court as immutable rules which ensured that property could not be taken without fair market compensation. In this instance, Lucas's property was not physically taken but because it was rendered valueless, Lucas was entitled to compensation. South Carolina thus failed in its ambition to avoid reimbursement by characterizing its actions as a restriction of "public nuisances" to prevent "noxious uses of property." The majority opinion held that takings of property, even if regulatory, must be compensated and that payment could not be avoided even if the state recognized, in some circumstances, that there existed a need to prevent "public harm" or support a public need to preserve the natural environment. In weighing private and public interests in this issue, economic loss (private property rendered idle) could not be justified even if the government found sufficient interest to prohibit activities or specific kinds of use of private land. The Court summarily held that the Takings Clause (of the Fifth Amendment) could not be lawfully applied without the payment of just compensation.

Related Cases

Mugler v. Kansas, 123 U.S. 623 (1887).
Pennsylvania Coal Co. v. Mahon, 260 U.S. 393 (1922).
Agins v. City of Tiburon, 447 U.S. 255 (1980).
First English Evangelical Lutheran Church of Glendale v. County of Los Angeles, 482 U.S. 304 (1987).

Bibliography and Further Reading

FindLaw, Inc. *Supreme Court Cases Online.* http://laws. findlaw.com

Hall, Kermit L., ed. *The Oxford Companion to the Supreme Court of the United States.* Oxford University Press, 1992.

Northwestern University. *Oyez, oyez, oyez-A U.S. Supreme Court Database.* http://court.it-services.nwu.edu/oyez/ cases

SOLDAL V. COOK COUNTY

Legal Citation: 506 U.S. 56 (1992)

Petitioner
Edward Soldal et ux.

Respondent
Cook County, Illinois, et al.

Petitioner's Claim
The seizure and removal of their mobile home by a property manager, overseen by police officers, was a violation of the Fourth Amendment.

Chief Lawyer for Petitioner
John L. Stainthorp

Chief Lawyer for Respondent
Kenneth L. Gillis

Justices for the Court
Stephen Breyer, Anthony M. Kennedy, Sandra Day O'Connor, William H. Rehnquist, Antonin Scalia, David H. Souter, John Paul Stevens, Clarence Thomas, Byron R. White (writing for the Court)

Justices Dissenting
None

Place
Washington, D.C.

Date of Decision
8 December 1992

Decision
The Fourth Amendment protects persons from deprivations of property such as the one that occurred in this case.

Significance
The decision clarified Fourth Amendment jurisprudence, declaring that property rights were still a factor in Fourth Amendment analysis, and that a person's expectation of privacy was not the only thing that the Fourth Amendment protected.

In May of 1987, Terrace Properties, the owner of Willoway Terrace mobile home park in Elk Grove, Illinois, began eviction proceedings against Edward and Mary Soldal. The Soldals lived with their four children in a trailer home at Willoway Terrace. The suit was dismissed on 2 June 1987, but Terrace Properties and its manager, Margaret Hale, brought a second eviction suit in August of 1987, claiming that the Soldals had not paid their rent. The case was set for trial on 22 September 1987, but Hale and Terrace Properties took their own action in early September.

On 4 September 1987, Hale told the Cook County Sheriff's Department that she was preparing to move the Soldal's trailer home away from the mobile home park. Hale asked that sheriff deputies be present at the scene to prevent any resistance by the Soldal family. Two Terrace Properties employees arrived at Willoway Terrace later that day, accompanied by a deputy sheriff. The employees wrenched the sewer and water connections from the trailer, disconnected the phone, tore off the trailer's canopy and skirting, hooked the home to a tractor, and hauled the Soldal's home off the property.

All this time, Edward Soldal was attempting to put a stop to the actions of the Terrace Properties employees. Soldal told two other sheriff's deputies who arrived at the scene that he wanted to file a complaint against the Terrace employees for criminal trespass, and the deputy sheriffs referred Soldal to a Deputy Lieutenant Jones, who was nearby in Hale's office. At Hale's office, Jones told Soldal to remain outside while he conferred with Hale and other Terrace Properties employees for 20 minutes. Jones then spent another 30 minutes talking with a district attorney, who advised Jones that the police could not arrest the Terrace employees for criminal trespass because the matter was between the landlord and tenant. Throughout the incident, the sheriff deputies knew that Terrace Properties did not have an eviction order from any court.

At a hearing held on 9 September, the judge presiding over the eviction proceedings ruled that the eviction was unauthorized and ordered Terrace Properties to return the Soldal's trailer home to the lot. The Soldals were evicted in December of 1987, but

The Plain View Exception

The plain view exception, or plain view doctrine, gives law-enforcement authorities right to conduct a warrantless seizure on probable cause. Thus if a police officer making a routine stop on a traffic violation happens to be talking to a driver and sees a marijuana cigarette on the dashboard, the officer can seize the illegal substance (and make an arrest) without recourse to a warrant.

The Supreme Court first established the plain view doctrine in *Coolidge v. New Hampshire* (1971). The plurality in that case held that law-enforcement officials would be authorized to make a warrantless seizure in accor-

dance with three requirements. First of all, the officer must have entered the place where he makes the seizure legally. Secondly, he must be "inadvertent" in his discovery; that is, it should not be a situation in which he knew about the item beforehand and simply failed to obtain a warrant to search for it. And thirdly, it must be "immediately apparent" that the item to be seized is illegal or incriminating, so that no further search is required to make that determination.

Source(s): Levy, Leonard W., ed. *Encyclopedia of the American Constitution*. New York: Macmillan, 1986.

they had already filed a civil rights suit under 42 U.S.C.A. sec. 1983 against Terrace Properties, Hale, and the Cook County Sheriff's Department. In the complaint, the Soldals alleged that Terrace Properties and Hale had conspired with the police to violate their Fouteenth Amendment right to due process and their Fourth Amendment right to be free from unreasonable seizures.

The defendants quickly moved for summary judgment, and the federal district court granted the motion. According to the district court, the Soldals had offered no proof of a conspiracy with the police. Thus, the Soldals had not supported their claim of "state action," a requirement for civil rights claims that ask for damages from the government. "State action" is a term that describes a connection between government and the unlawful activity. On appeal, the Court of Appeals for the Seventh Circuit disagreed with the district court's conclusion, holding that there was, in fact, state action when Soldal's trailer home was ripped from its moorings and moved. Nevertheless, the appeals court held for the defendants, ruling that the seizure of the Soldal's trailer home did not constitute a seizure within the boundaries covered by the Fourth Amendment; nor did it constitute a deprivation of due process under the Fourteenth Amendment.

The Seventh Circuit appeals court agreed to hear the case again, this time with all the judges weighing in on the case, but a majority within the appeals court came up with the same decision. According to the appeals court, the seizure was not made in the course of public law enforcement and it did not invade the Soldal's privacy. Thus, the seizure was not within the purview of the Fourth Amendment because only privacy is protected by the Fourth Amendment, not a "pure deprivation of property." The only cause of action Soldal could maintain, said the appeals court, was under the

Due Process Clauses of the Fifth and Fourteenth Amendments, and that claim had not been proved by Soldal. Soldal petitioned the U.S. Supreme Court, which agreed to hear the case.

In a unanimous decision, the High Court reversed. Justice White, writing for the Court, opened the analysis by citing Supreme Court precedent and defining the word seizure as a "meaningful interference with an individual's possessory interest." The Court noted that at the heart of the Fourth Amendment is "the right of a man to retreat into his own home" and observed that in Soldal's case, the home "was not only seized, it literally was carried away, giving new meaning to the term 'mobile home.' We fail to see," the Court continued, "how being unceremoniously dispossessed of one's home in the manner alleged here can be viewed as anything but a seizure invoking protection of the Fourth Amendment."

The Court declined to rule on the issue of whether the Fourth Amendment was actually violated in the case because that question had not been presented to the Court. The Court held only that the Fourth Amendment applied to the seizure in Soldal's case, but it went to great lengths to explain its holding. The federal appeals court had explained that unless it held as it did, "every repossession and eviction with police assistance" would be open to a Fourth Amendment claim. Such a holding would, according to the appeals court, "trivialize the amendment and gratuitously shift a large body of routine commercial litigation from the state courts to the federal courts," a fate that could be avoided by recognizing a difference between "possessory and privacy interests."

In response, the Court called attention to the language of the Fourth Amendment, which indicated that "persons, houses, papers, and effects" were protected from unreasonable searches and seizures. This language, as well as the High Court's prior case law, called for a different ruling than the one delivered by the appeals court. In *United States v. Jacobsen* (1984), the Court had examined the search and seizure and chemical testing of suspected narcotics from a privacy standpoint, ruling that the seizure did not violate the defendant's right to privacy. The Court in *Jacobsen* went on, though, to analyze the seizure from a possessory standpoint as well. A similar analysis had been conducted by the Court in *United States v. Place* (1983).

Cook County, the sheriff's officers, Terrace Properties, Hale, and the other respondents argued that the Court's prior case law called for a different result. The Court refuted the arguments advanced by the respondents as misconstructions of its prior case law. The rulings in *Warden, Maryland Penitentiary v. Hayden* (1967) and *Katz v. United States* (1967), for example, did not suggest that privacy was the sole interest protected by the Fourth Amendment. In each case cited by the respondents, the Court found language that contradicted the petitioners' interpretations, and the Court remained "unconvinced that any of the Court's prior cases support the view that the Fourth Amendment protects against unreasonable searches of property only where privacy or liberty is also implicated."

The appeals court had created a difference between seizures that are the outcome of a search and seizures that are the outcome of something other than a search. The High Court found this division "interesting and creative," but it was unconvinced. The reason why an officer might enter a house or seize property was "wholly irrelevant to the threshold question whether the [Fourth] Amendment applies." What really mattered, declared the Court, was "the intrusion on the people's security from governmental interference," and not whether the person is suspected of criminal behavior.

The High Court dismissed the petitioner's prediction—also the appeals court's theory—that a holding for Soldal would make routine matters attended by police into federal cases. Under the Court's opinion, many seizures similar to those in Soldal's case would survive judicial scrutiny. Had Hale and Terrace Properties possessed a valid court order, for example, the seizure of Soldal's home would not have been unreasonable. Calling the case something other than a "garden variety" landlord-tenant or commercial conflict, the Court held in favor of Soldal and sent the case back to the lower courts.

Impact

The decision in *Soldal* made it slightly easier to make civil rights claims against the government under the Fourth Amendment. The ruling also clarified the Court's understanding of the Fourth Amendment. It is not, as it seemed to hint in prior cases such as *Hayden* and *Katz,* an amendment concerned only with the protection of privacy. Instead, the Court instructed, the amendment was designed to protect against "the intrusion on the people's security from governmental interference."

Related Cases

Warden, Maryland Penitentiary v. Hayden, 387 U.S. 294 (1967).
Katz v. United States, 389 U.S. 347 (1967).
United States v. Place, 462 U.S. 696 (1983).
United States v. Jacobsen, 466 U.S. 109 (1984).

Bibliography and Further Reading

New York Times, December 9, 1992.

West's Encyclopedia of American Law. St. Paul: West Group, 1998.

MINNESOTA V. DICKERSON

Legal Citation: 508 U.S. 366 (1993)

Petitioner
State of Minnesota

Respondent
Timothy Dickerson

Petitioner's Claim
A police officer's patdown search of a person on the street and subsequent seizure of a small object does not violate the Fourth Amendment.

Chief Lawyers for Petitioner
Michael O. Freeman, Beverly J. Wolfe

Chief Lawyer for Respondent
Peter W. Gorman

Justices for the Court
Anthony M. Kennedy, Sandra Day O'Connor, Antonin Scalia, David H. Souter, John Paul Stevens, Byron R. White (writing for the Court)

Justices Dissenting
Harry A. Blackmun, William H. Rehnquist, Clarence Thomas

Place
Washington, D.C.

Date of Decision
7 June 1993

Decision
Police may seize contraband that is nonthreatening and detected through the sense of touch during a limited patdown search for weapons, but the search in Dickerson's case was unlawful because it exceeded the lawful bounds of such a search.

Significance
The holding reinforced the limitations on police officers who search persons for weapons before talking to them. It also demonstrated that the Rehnquist Court, a Court renowned for its deference to police activity, was capable of circumscribing police powers.

On 9 November 1989, in Minneapolis, Minnesota, police officers Vernon D. Rose and Bruce S. Johnson were patrolling an area on the city's north side. Officer Rose knew that an apartment that they were passing was notorious for its illegal drug activity. As the officers drove in their marked squad car, Timothy Dickerson emerged from the apartment building. Dickerson saw the officers in their car and headed in the opposite direction to an alley on the other side of the apartment building. With their interest piqued by Dickerson's evasive action, the officers followed Dickerson and stopped him.

The officers ordered Dickerson to submit to a patdown search. Officer Rose did not find weapons on Dickerson, but the officer did encounter a small lump in Dickerson's nylon jacket. Officer Rose felt a small lump in the front pocket and thought that it might be drugs. Rose removed the lump from Dickerson's jacket, determined that the object was in fact crack cocaine, and arrested Dickerson.

Dickerson was charged with possession of a controlled substance. Before trial, he moved to have the cocaine evidence excluded, arguing that the search was conducted in violation of his Fourth Amendment right to be free from unreasonable search and seizure. The trial court denied the request, finding that the officers were justified in stopping Dickerson, that they were justified in frisking Dickerson, and that the seizure of the cocaine did not violate the Fourth Amendment. The court compared the seizure of the cocaine to the seizure of any contraband under the "plain view" doctrine, a judicial rule that allows officers to seize any contraband in their plain view without obtaining a search warrant from a magistrate. According to the trial court, there was "no distinction as to which sensory perception the officer uses to conclude that the material is contraband." Since it was legal for police officers to seize, without a warrant, contraband that is in plain view, the court reasoned, police officers also should be able to seize objects that plainly feel like contraband. This analysis created a "plain feel" exception to the requirement of a search warrant.

Dickerson was found guilty at trial, but the conviction was reversed by the Minnesota Court of Appeals.

Nightwalker Statutes

There is a presumption that when someone is out late, it has to be for a reason, and though not everyone who goes about in the wee hours is a criminal, certainly criminals are apt to be operating at a time when the largest number of people are asleep. The common-law definition of burglary, in fact, used to involve the issue of whether or not the act took place after dark. Though in many jurisdictions, the nighttime aspect is no longer crucial to a definition of the crime, statutes linking burglary with darkness remain on the books in many states.

As Justice Scalia noted, common law documents as old as the Statute of Winchester, enacted in England in

1285, provide for the detention of suspicious nightwalkers. Scalia stated that this was just about as far as the nightwalker statutes should go: thus a 1942 article from the *Virginia Law Review* that stated "At common law, if a watchman came upon a suspiciously acting nightwalker, he might arrest him and then search him for weapons, but he had no right to search before arrest."

Source(s): *West's Encyclopedia of American Law.* St. Paul, MN: West Group, 1998.

The appeals court held that the stop was lawful, but it rejected the plain feel doctrine, holding that the officers did not have the authority to seize the cocaine. The Minnesota Supreme Court also rejected the plain feel doctrine and affirmed, and the state of Minnesota appealed to the U.S. Supreme Court. Noting a conflict between state and federal courts on the topic of warrantless plain feel seizures, the Supreme Court consented to hear the case. By a vote of 6-2, with Chief Justice Rehnquist concurring in part and dissenting in part, the High Court affirmed the reversal of Dickerson's conviction.

Justice White, writing for the majority, began the opinion at the usual starting point in Fourth Amendment analysis: police officers must obtain a warrant before conducting a search unless the circumstances of the search fit one of a few well established and clearly delineated exceptions. One of these exceptions is known as the "Terry stop," a circumstance named after the facts in the 1968 case of *Terry v. Ohio.* In that case, the Court ruled that a police officer may stop and question a person and perform a limited patdown search for weapons if the person is engaged in "unusual conduct which leads [the officer] reasonably to conclude in light of [the officer's] experience that criminal activity may be afoot." The Court held that such a search was not unreasonable because it felt officers have the right, when making contact with suspicious strangers, to discover weapons that might be used to injure the officer or others.

The issue in Dickerson's case was slightly different from the *Terry* case. In *Terry,* the police had discovered a gun on the suspect. The Minneapolis police found no weapons on Dickerson, but they did find an illegal substance. Thus, the issue in Dickerson's case was whether the police have the right to seize "nonthreatening contraband detected during a protective patdown search."

The Court answered that question in the affirmative, but it held that the search and seizure in Dickerson's case had exceeded the bounds of searches conducted during a Terry stop and was therefore unlawful.

The majority opinion cited Supreme Court precedents endorsing the rule that if police "lack probable cause to believe that an object in plain view is contraband without conducting some further search of the object," then the object cannot be made admissible by invoking the plain view doctrine. Because the officer could not determine the contents of the drug packet without further examining it, however, the contraband found through the sense of feel could not be admitted.

The Court agreed with the Minnesota Supreme Court's conclusion, but it disagreed with the state court's analysis. The Minnesota Supreme Court had held that the seizure was unlawful because the sense of touch is less immediate and less reliable than the sense of sight, and because the sense of touch is more intrusive than the sense of sight. Such factors, reasoned the Minnesota court, militated against acceptance of the plain feel doctrine. This kind of reasoning, the Court instructed, did not follow the *Terry* case, which clearly held that a police officer's warrantless use of the sense of touch was not unreasonable under the Fourth Amendment. With the U.S. Supreme Court already having established a police officer's right to feel in *Terry,* the Minnesota court's concerns about privacy were misplaced because "[t]he seizure of an item whose identity is already known occasions no further invasion of privacy."

The real reason that Rose's search of Dickerson was unreasonable under the Fourth Amendment was because it exceeded the lawful bounds of such searches outlined in *Terry.* Citing *Texas v. Brown* (1983), a case that relied on *Terry,* the High Court held that Rose's "continued exploration of [Dickerson's] pocket after having concluded that it contained no weapon was unrelated to '[t]he sole justification of the search [under *Terry*:] . . . the protection of the police officer and others nearby.'" Officer Rose's own testimony revealed that he did not determine the exact nature of the lump until he conducted a search that exceeded the limited frisk for weapons authorized by *Terry*, so Rose's search of Dickerson was unlawful. Although it took a different route, the High Court arrived at the same conclusion as the Minnesota Supreme Court, and the reversal of Dickerson's conviction remained intact.

Justice Scalia wrote a concurring opinion in which he analyzed the constitutional issue from the perspective of the framers' original intent. Scalia believed that Rose's stop of Dickerson should be ruled legal not because it was allowed by the *Terry* case, but because so-called "nightwalker statutes" had allowed police to stop persons at the time the Constitution was written. The *Terry* case, according to Scalia, represented bad law, a product of the "original-meaning-is-irrelevant, good-policy-is-constitutional-law school of jurisprudence." Scalia questioned the legality of the search, doubting as he did that "the fiercely proud men who adopted our Fourth Amendment would have allowed themselves to be subjected, on mere suspicion of being armed and dangerous, to such indignity." Nevertheless, Scalia did not think *Terry* was wrongly decided, so he joined the opinion of the Court.

Justices Rehnquist, Blackmun, and Thomas concurred in part and dissented in part. These justices agreed with the opinion of the majority that Rose's stop of Dickerson was legal. However, they would not have affirmed the judgment of the Minnesota Supreme Court. The factual findings of the Minnesota court were imprecise, noted the justices, because the court had not used the correct Fourth Amendment analysis.

Impact

The holding in *Dickerson* prevented police officers from seizing nonthreatening articles when they conduct a limited patdown search for weapons on suspicious persons, but only if the officers cannot determine whether an article is contraband without removing the article for further examination. Far from rejecting the plain feel doctrine, though, the Court confirmed that police may seize nonthreatening contraband if they know immediately upon feeling an object that the object is illegal.

Related Cases

Terry v. Ohio, 392 U.S. 1 (1968).
Texas v. Brown, 460 U.S. 730 (1983).

Bibliography and Further Reading

Epstein, Lee, and Thomas G. Walker. *Constitutional Law for a Changing America: Rights, Liberties, and Justice.* Washington, DC: Congressional Quarterly, 1995.

Harris, David A. "'Driving While Black' and All Other Traffic Offenses." *Journal of Criminal Law and Criminology,* winter 1997, p. 544.

MacIntosh, Susanne M. "Fourth Amendment—The Plain Touch Exception to the Warrant Requirement." *Journal of Criminal Law and Criminology,* winter-spring 1994, p. 743.

New York Times, June 8, 1993.

Smolla, Rodney A., ed. *A Year In the Life of the Supreme Court.* Durham, NC: Duke University Press, 1995.

WILSON V. ARKANSAS

Legal Citation: 514 U.S. 927 (1995)

Petitioner
Sharlene Wilson

Respondent
State of Arkansas

Petitioner's Claim
That failure of the police to knock and announce their presence prior to a warranted search rendered their entry into her house unconstitutional under the Fourth Amendment.

Chief Lawyer for Petitioner
John Wesley Hall, Jr.

Chief Lawyer for Respondent
Kent C. Holt, Arkansas Assistant Attorney General

Justices for the Court
Stephen Breyer, Ruth Bader Ginsburg, Anthony M. Kennedy, Sandra Day O'Connor, William H. Rehnquist, Antonin Scalia, David H. Souter, John Paul Stevens, Clarence Thomas (writing for the Court)

Justices Dissenting
None

Place
Washington, D.C.

Date of Decision
22 May 1995

Decision
Reversed the decision of the Arkansas State Supreme Court and remanded the case for reconsideration by the trial court, holding that police in possession of a search warrant are justified in entering a person's house without knocking at the door and announcing their presence only in cases where they may be put in danger or stand to lose evidence by doing so.

Significance
The ruling reverses a tendency of the Court in the 1980s to allow law enforcement authorities great latitude for action within Fourth Amendment guidelines. While recognizing this, it is significant that the Court remanded this case to the trial court for reconsideration under its ruling rather than reversing the lower court's decision altogether.

Set Up

Arkansas police were operating undercover in pursuit of Sharlene Wilson during the fall of 1992. During November and December of that year undercover officers made a series of narcotics purchases from Wilson, culminating in a potentially violent marijuana buy on 30 December. At this last meeting, Wilson told the informant that she suspected her of working with the police, and produced a semiautomatic pistol and threatened to kill her if her suspicions turned out to be correct. Judging from this incident that they should proceed with their operation before their informant was discovered, the Arkansas State Police applied for and obtained warrants to search Wilson's house the following day. Wilson lived with another person, Bryson Jacobs, and police noted in their warrant applications that Jacobs had prior convictions for arson and firebombing.

Police officers then proceeded to Wilson and Jacobs' house, finding the front door open and an unlocked screen door closed when they arrived. As they opened the screen door and entered the house, the officers announced themselves and informed the occupants that they possessed search warrants. Officers quickly discovered a quantity of narcotics, including marijuana, methamphetamine, and valium in the house, as well as drug paraphernalia, a gun, and ammunition. They also found Wilson and arrested her in the bathroom as she attempted to flush a quantity of marijuana down the toilet. Jacobs was also taken into custody during the raid.

A Fourth Amendment Violation?

Prior to her trial on narcotics trafficking charges, Wilson filed a motion to suppress evidence seized by police in their raid on her home. She claimed that the failure of the police to knock on her door and announce their presence and intentions before entering her home violated her Fourth Amendment protection from unreasonable search and seizure. The trial court denied her motion and Wilson was found guilty of all charges against her and sentenced to 32 years in prison. Following her conviction, Wilson appealed the case to the Arkansas Supreme Court, which upheld the trial court's ruling. The state supreme court could find "no authority for [the] theory that the knock and announce principle is required by the Fourth Amendment." Wilson then appealed her case to the U.S. Supreme Court, which heard arguments in the matter on 28 March 1995.

Common Law

In examining the petitioner's claim, the Supreme Court was forced to look beyond the Fourth Amendment, which does not mention any requirement for government authorities to identify themselves when making a reasonable search. In this case, the search was reasonable without question since the police had obtained warrants before proceeding. Therefore, the Court was obliged to seek its answer in the English common law, recognized as the foundation upon which U.S. law has been built.

When the United States secured its independence from Britain, the individual states and the union itself were faced with the task of devising their own legal systems. As a practical expedient, the original states decided to retain English common law until their legislatures saw fit to amend it. The language used by the New York legislature is typical: "such parts of the common law of England as did form the law [New York prior to the Revolution] shall be and continue the law of this State, subject to such alterations and provisions as the legislature of this State shall, from time to time, make concerning the same." In fact, the Court had recognized the standing of common law within American courts in many cases, including *Miller v. United States,* (1958).

Although the Fourth Amendment does not mention any requirement for authorities to knock and announce themselves before entering a suspect's home, English common law certainly does. One of its cornerstone principles is that "a man's home is his castle," within which the individual is a kind of monarch. As stated in *Blackstone's Commentaries,* although the authorities may even break down a suspect's door to enter his house if he does not answer or refuses to submit to a search, they must knock and announce themselves first. "But before he [the authorities] breaks it, he ought to signify the cause of his coming, and to make request to open doors." In effect, common law gives the suspect the chance to willingly submit to a search before the authorities are legally able to direct action to conduct it.

Mitigating Circumstances

Given the position of common law on the subject of knocking and announcing before entering, the Court was forced to reverse the decisions of the trial court and state supreme courts. Despite taking this step, the Court did not completely overturn the rulings of the lower courts, remanding the case instead for reconsideration in light of its finding. The Court also added that, although the petitioner had successfully advanced her case for the need for police to knock and identify themselves before entering a suspect's house generally, situations could arise where this procedure could be skipped. Writing for the majority, Justice Thomas noted that common law was less clear with regard to whether or not authorities must knock and announce their intentions before entering the house of a felon: "Although there has been some doubt on the question, the better opinion seems to be that, in cases of felony, no demand of admittance is necessary, especially as, in many cases, the delay incident to it would enable the prisoner to escape." Indeed, the state of Arkansas had argued in this case that because of Jacobs's convictions for arson and firebombing, the police felt that announcing themselves prior to entering the house would have placed them, and the evidence within the house, in jeopardy.

Impact

Wilson v. Arkansas confirmed the common law requirement for authorities to knock and announce themselves before conducting a warranted search. The ruling was less than ironclad, however, as the Court specified that the knock and announce requirement could be ignored in cases where police officers' lives or evidence would be endangered by giving suspects advance notice of the arrival of the authorities. In the final analysis, its chief impact was to clarify the circumstances under which knock and announce requirements could be ignored by authorities.

Related Cases

Miller v. United States, 357 U.S. 301 (1958).
Ker v. California, 374 U.S. 23 (1963).
Sabbath v. United States, 391 U.S. 585 (1968).
Richards v. Wisconsin, 520 U.S. 385 (1997).

Bibliography and Further Reading

Biskupic, Joan, and Elder Witt, eds. *Guide to the U.S. Supreme Court,* 3rd ed. Washington DC: Congressional Quarterly Inc., 1990.

Legal Information Institute and Project Hermes. http://supct.law.cornell.edu/supct/html/94 5707.ZS.html.

VERNONIA SCHOOL DISTRICT 47J V. ACTON

Legal Citation: 515 U.S. 646 (1995)

Petitioner
Vernonia School District 47J

Respondent
Wayne Acton, et al.

Petitioner's Claim
That a school policy mandating random drug testing for participants in interscholastic athletic programs did not violate Fourth Amendment prohibitions against illegal search and seizure.

Chief Lawyer for Petitioner
Timothy R. Volpert, John A. Matterazzo, Davis Wright Tremaine

Chief Lawyer for Respondent
Thomas M. Christ, John A. Wittmayer, Steven R. Shapiro

Justices for the Court
Stephen Breyer, Ruth Bader Ginsburg, Anthony M. Kennedy, William H. Rehnquist, Antonin Scalia (writing for the Court), Clarence Thomas

Justices Dissenting
Sandra Day O'Connor, David H. Souter, John Paul Stevens

Place
Washington, D.C.

Date of Decision
26 June 1995

Decision
Upheld the school district's claim, vacating a judgement by the court of appeals and remanding the case for further proceedings in the court of appeals consistent with a finding that Vernonia's student athlete drug testing policy did not violate Fourth Amendment prohibitions against unreasonable search and seizure.

Significance
The ruling represented another example of the Court interpreting the Fourth Amendment so as to enable authorities to act expeditiously against the use of and trafficking in illegal drugs. Because of the compelling state interest in curbing illegal drug use among youth, and given the special status of both school authorities and student athletes, the Court ruled that random drug testing did not violate the constitutionally guaranteed privacy of participants in interscholastic sports programs.

Stimulus

Throughout the 1980s and early 1990s drug use, violence, and disciplinary problems in the nation's schools captured public attention as never before. During this period schools began routine searches of students for weapons, and confiscated a surprising array of firepower in this manner. Although some analysts reported that drug use among students had fallen from its high in the mid-to-late 1970s, public opinion equated increases in disciplinary problems in the schools with student use of illegal drugs.

The Vernonia, Oregon, school system operated three elementary schools and one high school in the late 1980s. As is the case in many small towns, high school athletes in Vernonia enjoyed elevated social status and served as role models for their fellow students. Beginning in 1988, however, Vernonia school authorities began to notice a disturbing trend among their students. Many students, and particularly student athletes, were heard to discuss and seen to emulate the outward trappings of the "drug culture," and between 1988 and 1989 disciplinary referrals within the schools increased to twice the level seen in the early 1980s. Vernonia's athletic coaches also began to suspect that use of illegal drugs was impairing the performance of their athletes, and had been responsible for several serious injuries.

Response

In an effort to counteract what was perceived as a rise of illegal drug use among its students, the Vernonia School District searched for an effective antidrug policy. Given the high prestige of student athletes, the school district decided to focus its antidrug abuse efforts within its interscholastic athletic programs. After consultation with the district's parents, a Student Athlete Drug Policy was adopted for implementation in the fall of 1989. The policy mandated that all participants in interscholastic athletic programs and their parents agree to submit to a drug search program involving an initial urinalysis at the beginning of the practice season and random urinalyses throughout the competitive year. The school district agreed not to make positive test results public, and any athlete producing a positive

Teenagers and the Availability of Drugs

- According to material cited by the U.S. Department of Justice, for each year from 1984 to 1996, more than 82 percent of high-school seniors answered that it would be "fairly easy" or "very easy" to obtain marijuana if they wanted to.

- About 20 percent of the class of 1984 stated that it would be fairly easy or very easy to obtain heroin, whereas more than 32 percent of the class of 1996 answered the same.

- Another study cited by the Justice Department found that in 1996, almost 55 percent of eighth graders stated that it would be fairly or very easy to obtain marijuana. More than 23 percent said it would be easy to buy LSD, and about 20 percent answered the same for PCP (angel dust) and heroin.

Source(s): *Bureau of Justice Statistics Sourcebook of Criminal Justice Statistics—1996.* Washington, DC: U.S. Government, 1997.

test would be retested before any action was taken. Upon a second positive result, the athlete's parents would be notified and the athlete would be given the choice of entering a treatment program including weekly urinalysis or a two-year suspension from interscholastic athletics. Vernonia's parents were nearly unanimously in favor of the policy.

An Invasion of Privacy?

James Acton, a seventh grade student, expressed his desire to play football for a Vernonia school in the fall of 1991. He and his parents refused to sign the required consent form, however, believing that submission to random drug testing constituted an unreasonable invasion of Acton's privacy as guaranteed in the Fourth and Fourteenth Amendments. The school district therefore forbade Acton from participating in interscholastic athletics, and Acton and his parents filed for an injunction against the school district in the district court. The district court heard the case but dismissed the Acton's claims, and the matter proceeded to the U.S. Court of Appeals for the Ninth Circuit. The court of appeals reversed the ruling of the district court, finding that the Vernonia School District's policy violated both the Fourth and Fourteenth Amendments, as well as provisions of the Oregon State Constitution. The school district then appealed the case to the U.S. Supreme Court, which heard arguments on 28 March 1995.

In Loco Parentis

In deciding this case, the Court noted the special status of students, who are voluntarily put under the authority of school personnel by their parents. As such, school officials function as *de facto* parents while students are in their charge, and there are no constitutional guidelines for nonviolent parental discipline of children to ensure order. The Court also observed that athletes engaged in team sports understand that they must voluntarily give up some rights to privacy, given the communal nature of locker room facilities and team

activities in general. Thus, in the Court's view, students in general, and student athletes in particular, may expect their activities to be subject to more scrutiny and have their behavior more circumscribed by school authorities than other individuals. As such, the Court ruled that Vernonia's policy did not violate the constitutional rights of students, and remanded the case to the court of appeals for reconsideration.

The legal justification for this ruling was quite straightforward. Random drug testing of railroad employees had been deemed constitutional by the Court in *Skinner v. Railway Labor Executives' Assn.* (1989), given the state's compelling interest in maintaining passenger safety by insuring that transportation employees are not working while under the influence of intoxicants. Furthermore, the Court held in *Delaware v. Prouse* (1979), that a particular search's validity under the Fourth Amendment "is judged by its intrusion on the individual's Fourth Amendment interests against its promotion of legitimate governmental interests." In this case the Court judged that the state's interest in discouraging drug abuse among students and maintaining order within the classroom was so compelling as to justify some abridgement of student's Fourth Amendment rights. With regard to Fourteenth Amendment prohibitions against invasion of privacy, the Court ruled that, given the relative lack of privacy accepted by all participants in team sports, the additional intrusion represented by urinalysis was negligible. At any rate, the Court had already established in *New Jersey v. T.L.O.* (1985), that "students within the school environment have a lesser expectation of privacy than members of the population generally." Therefore the policy was deemed reasonable and acceptable under the Fourteenth Amendment.

Impact

Vernonia School District 47J v. Acton at first glance seems to represent another instance of the Court's willingness to deny Fourth Amendment protection to criminals engaged in the illegal use of, or trafficking in, drugs.

James Action with friends and family after his case was heard at the Supreme Court. © AP/Wide World Photos.

This appearance is misleading, however. Justice Scalia, writing for the majority, was careful to point out that the legal status of students, and the equally unique social status and voluntary forfeiture of privacy accepted by student athletes, made this case unique and of limited use as a legal precedent.

Related Cases
Delaware v. Prouse, 440 U.S. 648 (1979).
New Jersey v. T.L.O., 469 U.S. 325 (1985).

Skinner v. Railway Executives' Association, 489 U.S. 602 (1989).

Bibliography and Further Reading
Biskupic, Joan, and Elder Witt, eds. *Guide to the U.S. Supreme Court,* 3rd ed. Washington DC: Congressional Quarterly Inc., 1990.

Legal Information Institute and Project Hermes. http://supct.law.cornell.edu/supct/html/94590.ZS.html.

BENNIS V. MICHIGAN

Legal Citation: 516 U.S. 442 (1996)

Petitioner
Tina B. Bennis

Respondent
State of Michigan

Petitioner's Claim
That she should be allowed to contest the confiscation of the car she jointly owned with her husband because she did not know her husband would use the car to violate Michigan's indecency law.

Chief Lawyer for Petitioner
Stefan B. Herpel

Chief Lawyers for the Respondent
Larry L. Roberts, Richard H. Seamon

Justices for the Court
Ruth Bader Ginsburg, Sandra Day O'Connor, William H. Rehnquist (writing for the Court), Antonin Scalia, Clarence Thomas

Justices Dissenting
Stephen Breyer, Anthony M. Kennedy, David H. Souter, John Paul Stevens

Place
Washington, D.C.

Date of Decision
4 March 1996

Decision
Upheld the state of Michigan's claim that the uncompensated taking of property used as a public nuisance, from an innocent owner, does not violate the Due Process Clause of the Fourteenth Amendment or the Takings Clause of the Fifth Amendment.

Significance
The ruling affirmed the government's right to seize private property, known as forfeiture, if the property was used as a public nuisance. The Supreme Court decided that taking a vehicle did not violate the owner's right to due process because Michigan's nuisance abatement law legally transferred ownership of the car to the state. The Court also decided that the innocent property owner was not entitled to payment for the seized property. This contrasts with the Fifth and Fourteenth Amendments' guarantees of just compensation when property is taken for public use. The ruling assured that law enforcement agencies would be able to use forfeiture laws in their fight against drugs, gambling, and prostitution.

Since 1827, private property has been seized from an innocent owner if the property was used to break the law. A ship, the *Palmyra,* was commissioned by the King of Spain to attack a U.S. vessel. The owner argued that he had not been convicted of privateering, using a privately owned ship to attack an enemy vessel, so the ship should not be confiscated. The court disagreed, stating that the ship was the offender.

Later cases also supported seizure of private property used for illegal purposes, even when respective owners were unaware of illegal use. During Prohibition (1919-1933), when alcohol was illegal, the Court upheld the forfeiture of cars used to transport liquor, even though the owners did not know the car was being used for this purpose. In 1974, the Supreme Court decided that a yacht leasing company should forfeit a yacht after a customer came on board with a marijuana cigarette.

Michigan Courts Disagree on Seizure of Vehicle

In *Bennis v. Michigan,* a married couple, in 1988, purchased a 1977 Pontiac for $600 so the husband could drive to his job at a steel mill. Without Tina Bennis's knowledge, her husband, John Bennis, had oral sex with a prostitute in the front seat of their jointly owned car. Bennis was fined for "gross indecency." A local county prosecutor asked that the car be abated (confiscated) and sold as a public nuisance by the Wayne County Circuit Court under a Michigan "red light abatement" law. The Bennis' car was one of the first confiscated under the Detroit Police Department's policy of cleaning up inner-city prostitution. Tina Bennis, a mother of five, appealed stating she was entitled to half the car's value because she had done nothing wrong and did not know that her husband was committing an illegal act in the family's car.

The judge in the Wayne County Circuit Court, Michael Talbot, who originally ordered the car's abatement, rejected Tina Bennis's arguments. He considered the fact that the couple owned another car and thus had some form of transportation. He also noted that although he had the authority to order that she be paid her half share after costs were deducted, the amount was so small that almost nothing would be left in this situation.

The Michigan Court of Appeals reversed the lower court's decision. The court felt that Bennis's interest in the car should not be abated unless she knew how the car was being used. Also, the court ruled that the husband's act was not a public nuisance because it only happened once, and no proof existed that he had paid for the act.

The Michigan Supreme Court disagreed with the appeals court and reinstated the abatement on the grounds that the act was an abatable nuisance. The Michigan Supreme Court agreed with the lower court's description of the nuisance abatement as an "equitable action." The court also decided that the state did not need to prove that the owner knew how her vehicle was being used in order to confiscate the vehicle without payment. The Michigan Supreme Court found that Michigan did not have to provide an innocent-owner defense, according to the Constitution.

Question of Whether Constitutional Rights Violated

The U.S. Supreme Court agreed to hear the case to determine if Tina Bennis's share of the forfeited car had been denied her without due process, as guaranteed in the Fourteenth Amendment. Due process means that the government may not deprive anyone of life, liberty, or property without a fair trial or hearing. The Supreme Court also wanted to determine if the Fifth Amendment had been violated by taking her property for public use without compensation.

On 29 November 1995, the Court heard the arguments in the *Bennis* case. The Clinton administration argued for the state of Michigan, defending the government's right to seize property used in crimes. The administration's lawyer argued that a property owner's ignorance of illegal activity should not be used as a defense. He added that if a property owner can prove that he or she took "all reasonable steps" to prevent the property from being misused, then the owner should not have the property seized.

Bennis's lawyer, Stefan B. Herpel, argued that in the case of a seized yacht, a passage from the case stated, "It would be difficult to reject the constitutional claim of . . . an owner who proved not only that he was uninvolved in and unaware of the wrongful activity, but also that he had done all that reasonably could be expected to prevent the proscribed use of his property." Chief Justice Rehnquist, in his decision, rejected this statement because it was *obiter dictum* (said in passing), rather than in the holdings of the case, which held that the yacht company should forfeit the yacht used for transporting controlled substances, even though the owners had no involvement in or knowledge of the illegal activity.

Petitioner Asserted Fifth Amendment Rights Violated

Herpel also proposed that a criminal defendant may not be punished for a crime if he is found to be not guilty. Rehnquist noted in his decision that this line of reasoning would require Michigan to show that it was trying to be punitive in denying Bennis her share of the forfeited car.

Herpel argued that seizing the car without paying Bennis for her share violated the Takings Clause of the Fifth Amendment by taking private property for public use without payment. Rehnquist wrote, "The property in the automobile was transferred . . . to the State. The government may not be required to compensate an owner for property which it has already lawfully acquired under the exercise of governmental authority other than the power of eminent domain."

Bennis's claim ultimately rested on the premise that the Michigan forfeiture law was unfair because it did not require a distinction between co-owners who participate in the misuse of property and innocent co-owners. Rehnquist held that this argument did not stand up because the Michigan State Court confirmed the trial court judge's authority to order the payment of half the proceeds after costs, if he saw fit.

A Close Decision

The justices appeared sympathetic to Tina Bennis during the oral arguments presented on 29 November 1995. Justice Ginsburg asked the administration's lawyer, "What was Tina Bennis supposed to do?" Despite this in March of 1996, the Court voted 5-4 to support the administration against Tina Bennis. Writing for the majority, Rehnquist found that the forfeiture did not violate the Due Process Clause. He reasoned that a long line of cases held that property may be forfeited even though the owner did not know it was being put to illegal use. Rehnquist felt the Takings Clause was not violated because of the legal transfer of the car from Bennis to the state. He noted that the government is not required to pay an owner for forfeited property.

In his concurring opinion, Justice Thomas wrote:

> Forfeiture of property simply because it was used in crime has been permitted time out of mind . . . This case is ultimately a reminder that the Federal Constitution does not prohibit everything that is intensely undesirable . . . Improperly used, forfeiture could become more like a roulette wheel employed to raise revenue from innocent but hapless owners whose property is unforeseeably misused . . .

Ginsburg noted that, "Michigan has decided to deter johns from using cars they own (or co-own) to contribute to neighborhood blight, and that abatement endeavor hardly warrants this Court's disapprobation."

Four justices disagreed with the majority. Justice Stevens wrote:

> The logic of the Court's analysis would permit the States to exercise virtually unbridled power to confiscate vast amounts of property where professional criminals have engaged in illegal acts . . . While our historical cases establish the propriety of seizing a freighter when its entire cargo consists of smuggled goods, none of them would justify the confiscation of an ocean liner just because one of its passengers sinned while on board.

Stevens held that confiscating the car would not prevent John Bennis from committing a similar act in another location. Stevens noted that Bennis "had been sighted twice during the previous summer, without the car, soliciting prostitutes in the same neighborhood." Stevens wanted the decision reversed because of a lack of connection between the car and the act, and because Tina Bennis, "is entirely without responsibility for that act. Fundamental fairness prohibits the punishment of innocent people."

Impact

The Court's ruling in the *Bennis* case represented a reversal of what appeared to be a growing concern over the use of forfeitures by the government. In 1993, the Court established a constitutional safeguard when it ruled that forfeitures were subject to the Eighth Amendment's prohibition of excessive fines. The *Bennis* decision appeared to be a dismantling of the protections the Court had erected in forfeiture cases.

The *Bennis* case bolstered government authority to confiscate property used to commit a crime. Prosecutors, who considered forfeiture laws a useful tool in the war against crime, welcomed the apparent change in the Court's attitude toward forfeiture. Prosecutor John O'Hair noted that in seven years the Detroit police had seized 9,000 cars from individuals who patronized prostitutes, and that this was the only program that had any effect in fighting prostitution. Larry L. Roberts, the prosecutor who argued the *Bennis* case, noted that the policy of confiscating johns' cars has spread from the inner city to the suburbs.

Defense attorneys, libertarian conservatives, and the banking industry have expressed concern over the decision in *Bennis v. Michigan.* The American Bankers Association worried that financial institutions might have to inspect property to determine if it was being used properly. A brief filed by the ABA noted that, "The state's assertion of sweeping authority to seize property rights of those who have done nothing wrong is frightening."

Related Cases

Van Oster v. Kansas, 272 U.S. 465 (1926).
United States v. Fuller, 409 U.S. 488 (1973).
Calero-Toledo v. Pearson Yacht Leasing Co., 416 U.S. 663 (1974).
Foucha v. Louisiana, 504 U.S. 71 (1992).
Austin v. United States, 509 U.S. 602 (1993).

Bibliography and Further Reading

Brodey, Jami. "The Supreme Court Rejects Fifth and Fouteenth Amendment Protection Against the Forfeiture of an Innocent Owner's Property." *Journal of Criminal Law and Criminology,* spring 1997, p. 692.

Coyle, Marcia. "Critics: Forfeiture Ruling Certain to Spur Reform." *The National Law Journal,* March 18, 1996, p. A12.

Dripps, Donald A. "Innocence is No Defense." *Trial,* June 1996, p. 67.

Herpel, Stefan B. "A License to Steal: The Forfeiture of Property." *Michigan Law Review,* May 1998, p. 1910.

Jost, Kenneth. *The Supreme Court Yearbook, 1995-1996.* Washington, DC: Congressional Quarterly, Inc., 1996.

Mickenberg, Ira. "Prosecutors Granted Leeway in Forfeitures; Decisions Give the Government Broad Authority to Expropriate Criminal Defendants' Property." *The National Law Journal,* July 29, 1996, p. C6.

Savage, David G. "Innocence Punished; Justice Ginsburg Keys Surprise Ruling in Double Jeopardy Case." *ABA Journal,* May 1996, p. 47.

Spencer, Jerome. "Auspices of Austin: Examining Excessiveness of Civil Forfeitures Under the Eighth Amendment." *American Criminal Law Review,* fall 1997, p. 163.

"Supreme Court OKs Property Seizure Laws." *Today's Realtor,* June 1996, p. 46.

ORNELAS V. UNITED STATES

Legal Citation: 517 U.S. 690 (1996)

Petitioners
Saul Ornelas, Ismael Ornelas-Ledesma

Respondent
United States

Petitioners' Claim
Police lacked probable cause to conduct a search of their vehicle.

Chief Lawyer for Petitioners
Cornelia T. L. Pillard

Chief Lawyers for Respondent
Robert G. LeBell, Brian W. Gleason

Justices for the Court
Stephen Breyer, Ruth Bader Ginsburg, Anthony M. Kennedy, Sandra Day O'Connor, William H. Rehnquist (writing for the Court), David H. Souter, John Paul Stevens, Clarence Thomas

Justices Dissenting
Antonin Scalia

Place
Washington, D.C.

Date of Decision
28 May 1996

Decision
The decision of the lower court was vacated and remanded for a full review of the facts.

Significance
The case established that an appeals court, when reviewing a trial court's conclusions on reasonable suspicions by police and the existence of probable cause for a warrantless police search, must thoroughly review the trial court's factual findings rather than accept them at face value.

In December of 1992, Michael Pautz, a detective with the Milwaukee County Sheriff's Department in Milwaukee, Wisconsin, was downtown, conducting surveillance for drug activity. In the early morning hours, Pautz spotted a 1981 two-door automobile with California license plates parked at a motel. Pautz felt suspicious because California is a "source state" for illegal drugs and because the automobile was of a kind favored by drug couriers for its many secret compartments. A check of the motel registry, the car's registration, and an inquiry to the Narcotics and Dangerous Drugs Information System revealed that the registered operators of the car, Saul Ornelas and Ismael Ornelas-Ledesma were considered by federal law enforcement officials to be known drug traffickers.

Accompanied by Merlin, a drug-sniffing dog, Milwaukee detectives waited outside the motel for the men to exit. When Ornelas and Ornelas-Ledesma approached the Oldsmobile to leave the motel, the detectives confronted them and asked if they had any illegal drugs in the car. Ornelas and Ornelas-Ledesma answered in the negative, so the detectives asked for permission to search. Ornelas and Ornelas-Ledesma consented, and a deputy performed the search. Some time into the search, the deputy noticed a rusty screw holding a door jam adjacent to a loose panel. The deputy removed the panel and found two kilograms of cocaine.

Ornelas and Ornelas-Ledesma were charged in federal court with trafficking in cocaine. Before trial, they moved the court to exclude the cocaine evidence, arguing that it was obtained in violation of their Fourth Amendment rights against unreasonable search and seizure. Ornelas and Ornelas-Ledesma pleaded guilty to the charges, but they reserved the right to challenge the decision to deny their motion. After a series of decisions and appeals between the magistrate judge, the district court, and the U.S. Court of Appeals for the Seventh Circuit ended in the federal government's favor, the men appealed to the U.S. Supreme Court.

The defendants argued that the appeals court committed an error warranting reversal when it conducted a deferential review of the facts in the case. In an 8-1

Drug-Sniffing Dogs

Law-enforcement departments throughout the United States often make use of a canine (often designated as "K-9") unit. Dogs, with their highly developed sense of smell, can sniff out bombs or drugs that a human inspector might miss, and often a search by a dog with its handler can provide evidence that results in a conviction. Thus drug-detection dogs can often be found at airports, bus terminals, and rail stations—that is, in likely places for the transport of drugs—and they are often used on patrols or sweeps, or for inspections of postal packages.

In *United States v. Place* (1983), the Supreme Court ruled that a sniff is not a search, and therefore the Fourth

Amendment requirements governing the use of drug-sniffing dogs are less stringent than those for human law-enforcement personnel. For instance, if a police officer stops someone for a traffic violation, it is permissible for a canine to sniff the exterior of the individual's vehicle—but only the outside. If a drug-sniffing dog is not present and an officer has reasonable suspicion of drug activity, he or she may detain the vehicle and driver while they wait for the dog to be brought to the scene.

Source(s): Wallentine, Ken. "Introductory Canine Search and Seizure." http://www.minn. net/uspca.

decision, the High Court agreed, and it vacated the holding of the appeals court and remanded the case. According to the majority, the appeals court should not have deferred to the factual findings of the trial court. Instead, it should have conducted a full, or *de novo,* review of the facts.

Chief Justice Rehnquist, writing for the majority, discussed the nature of Fourth Amendment claims of unreasonable search and seizure and concluded that it was not standard practice for appeals courts to defer to trial courts in reviewing the facts in such a case. Such a case usually requires a court to determine either: (1) whether a police officer who performed a limited patdown search for weapons without obtaining a warrant from a magistrate had reasonable suspicion to believe that criminal activity was afoot; or (2) whether a police officer who conducted a warrantless search of a person or place had probable cause to believe a crime has been committed. These questions are difficult questions for courts to answer because "[a]rticulating precisely what 'reasonable suspicion' and 'probable cause' mean is not possible." They are "fluid concepts that take their substantive content from the particular contexts in which the standards are being assessed."

In order to achieve a more meaningful jurisprudence on the questions, the majority felt it best to require that appeals courts conduct *de novo* review in cases where the questions arise. The Court cited three main reasons for its decision. First, to hold otherwise would subject Fourth Amendment jurisprudence to the whims of trial court judges. Second, the legal rules for the issues of reasonable suspicion and probable cause "acquire content only through application." If appeals courts are to clarify and control the legal principles that guide those issues, they must be able to give meaning to the principles by thoroughly considering all of the facts on

record. Third, full review by appeals courts unifies precedent, makes law enforcement more predictable, and generally stabilizes the law.

Scalia Dissents

Rehnquist defended the majority's decision against Justice Scalia's dissent. Scalia argued that the Court's holding accomplished nothing because the factual differences between cases will still make the opinions virtually worthless as precedent. The majority maintained, though, that some cases could be considered factually similar to other cases. Finally, the Court listed a number of factors that it thought the appeals court should consider on remand. The majority emphasized that the weather in Milwaukee should be a factor in determining whether the Milwaukee detectives had reasonable suspicion to believe that the defendants were engaged in criminal activity, and whether the deputy's claim of probable cause to open the panel in the Oldsmobile was credible. "What may not amount to reasonable suspicion at a motel located alongside a transcontinental highway at the height of the summer tourist season," Rehnquist instructed, "may rise to that level in December in Milwaukee. That city is unlikely to have been an overnight stop selected at the last minute by a traveler coming from California to points east."

Justice Scalia dissented mainly because he thought that the decision would not provide any benefits. In Scalia's opinion, the *de novo* review of facts surrounding a police officer's reasonable suspicion and probable cause determination was unnecessary, and it would not provide meaningful precedent for future cases. Scalia reminded the majority that the trial court is in a much better position to evaluate the facts of a case than is an appeals court because the trial court has the advantage of presiding over the trial. Appeals courts, by contrast, do not see or hear the witnesses and must confine their review to the trial court record. Scalia mocked the circular nature of the decision: the majority held that the appeals court should not give deference to the trial court's interpretation of the facts, but at the same time the majority strongly suggested that the work of the Milwaukee detectives was reasonable. "This finding of 'reasonableness' is precisely what it has told us the appellate court must review *de novo;* and in *de novo* review, the 'weight due' to a trial court's finding is zero. In the last analysis, therefore, the Court's opinion seems to me not only wrong but contradictory."

Impact

The *Ornelas* holding increased the work load of appeals courts by requiring that they make a full examination of the facts as presented in certain trials, specifically, where a defendant claims that a warrantless search and seizure conducted by police officers was not supported by reasonable suspicion or probable cause. An appeals court, when presented with such a case, must review the entire record. The court should give due weight to the trial court's factual conclusions, but it must conduct a full review.

Related Cases

Terry v. Ohio, 392 U.S. 1 (1968).
New York v. Belton, 453 U.S. 454 (1981).
Nix v. Williams, 467 U.S. 431 (1984).
California v. Acevedo, 500 U.S. 565 (1991).

Bibliography and Further Reading

Lee, Cynthia K. Y. "A New 'Sliding Scale of Deference' Approach to Abuse of Discretion." *American Criminal Law Review,* fall 1997, p. 1.

Reuben, Richard C. "Police Under the Gun: Search and Seizure on the Docket Amid Tensions Over Police Conduct." *ABA Journal,* June 1996, p. 44.

Slansky, David A. "Traffic Stops, Minority Motorists, and the Future of the Fourth Amendment." *Supreme Court Review,* annual 1997, p. 271.

WHREN V. UNITED STATES

Legal Citation: 517 U.S. 806 (1996)

Petitioners
Michael A. Whren, James L. Brown

Respondent
United States

Petitioners' Claim
That evidence discovered and seized by police during a minor traffic stop was inadmissible in court given Fourth Amendment prohibitions against unreasonable search and seizure.

Chief Lawyers for Petitioners
A.J. Kramer, G. Allen Dale, Neil H. Jaffee, Lisa Burget Wright

Chief Lawyers for Respondent
Drew S. Days, U. S. Solicitor General; John C. Kenney, Acting Assistant Attorney General

Justices for the Court
Stephen Breyer, Ruth Bader Ginsburg, Anthony M. Kennedy, Sandra Day O'Connor, William H. Rehnquist, Antonin Scalia (writing for the Court), David H. Souter, John Paul Stevens, Clarence Thomas

Justices Dissenting
None

Place
Washington, D.C.

Date of Decision
10 June 1996

Decision
Denied the petitioners' claim and affirmed the decisions of the trial court and court of appeals, ruling that probable cause to believe that a traffic violation has occurred is sufficient justification for the police to stop a vehicle and conduct a search for objects in plain view within that vehicle.

Significance
The ruling allowed law enforcement officers greater latitude in the investigation and pursuit of individuals engaged in the illegal drug trade. Because a violation of the traffic laws, however minor, justifies the authorities in stopping a vehicle, the Court ruled that any additional evidence obtained by a plain view search during such a stop, regardless of police motives or the existence of probable cause to believe that any crime other than the traffic violation was occurring, was legally admissible.

The War on Drugs

Beginning in the early 1980s, the Court interpreted Fourth Amendment prohibitions against unreasonable search and seizure so as to increase the ability of law enforcement authorities to obtain evidence against criminal suspects. This tendency has been particularly apparent in cases involving the trade in illegal drugs, and has generally mirrored public sentiment.

A Routine Traffic Stop?

On the evening of 10 June 1993 two Washington, D.C. police officers cruised the streets of an area of the city known to be a center of the illegal drug trade. The officers were in plain clothes and drove an unmarked car as they looked for suspicious activity along their route. They soon spotted something that aroused their suspicions: a dark-colored small truck of a type favored by young drug dealers which waited an inordinate amount of time at a stop sign while its driver looked down toward the passenger in the front seat. When the officers made a U-turn to investigate the situation, the small truck made a right turn without using its turn indicator and began to speed off. The officers then followed the truck until it reached a stoplight, whereupon one of the officers stepped out, identified himself to the driver of the truck (petitioner Brown), and directed him to put his vehicle in park.

When the officer approached the driver's window he saw two large bags containing a white substance which turned out to be crack cocaine. Brown and Whren were then arrested and charged with violation of several federal drug laws. The petitioners entered a pretrial motion to suppress the evidence obtained by the police search of their truck, arguing that the authorities had no reasonable suspicion or probable cause to believe that they were engaged in drug trafficking. They also asserted that the traffic stop was a pretext, and that the police had really intended to look for drugs in the truck simply because it was a model favored by drug dealers and was occupied by two young African American men.

Lower Court Rulings

The district court refused to grant the petitioners' motion for suppression of evidence, and Whren and

Brown were convicted of the drug charges brought against them. They then appealed their case to the U.S. Court of Appeals for the District of Columbia. The appeals court affirmed their convictions, stating that "regardless of whether a police officer subjectively believes that the occupants of an automobile may be engaging in some other illegal behavior, a traffic stop is permissible as long as a reasonable officer in the same circumstances would have stopped the car for the suspected traffic violation." Whren and Brown then appealed their case to the U.S. Supreme Court, which heard arguments in the matter on 17 April 1996.

Use of Pretext to Enable a Search

While the petitioners did not contend that they had not violated the traffic laws of the District of Columbia, they did maintain that the arcane nature of traffic laws rendered nearly all motorists guilty of repeated infractions, and that in this case police officers had used a minor traffic violation as a pretext to conduct a visual search of the vehicle. Whren and Brown also maintained that the case represented an instance of selective enforcement of the law based on race, contending that their traffic violation might have gone unnoticed if they had not "fit the profile" for drug dealers in the area in which they were stopped. Although the Court found some merit in this last argument, it chose not to consider whether or not the search represented a selective enforcement based on race, holding that this was more properly a Fourteenth Amendment question of Equal Protection and not germane to the petitioners' Fourth Amendment case. The Court thus implied that this latter argument may have been more efficacious for the petitioners. However, the Court was not as sympathetic to the Fourth Amendment case the petitioners advanced, as it upheld the decisions of the district court and court of appeals by a unanimous vote.

Writing for the Court, Justice Scalia agreed with the court of appeals that when police officers observe a traffic violation, they automatically have probable cause to stop the offending vehicle and to issue a citation or a warning to its driver. With probable cause thus established, any incriminating evidence of the traffic violation or any other criminal activity found by an officer in plain view within the stopped vehicle could legally be seized and used as evidence in court. Scalia also noted the possible validity of the petitioners' Fourteenth Amendment argument, however. He thus proposed that, to avoid selective enforcement based on race, the standard for determining reasonableness of traffic stops be amended from automatic probable cause created by any minor infraction to a test of whether any officer, acting reasonably, would have made the same stop.

The Court also rejected the petitioners' argument that traffic stops used as a pretext for obtaining other evidence should be abolished, noting that such pretext would be impossible to ascertain. In the final analysis the Court ruled that as long as a traffic stop was made following an actual traffic infraction it was reasonable by definition.

Impact

Whren v. United States is an example of the Court's willingness to allow law enforcement authorities engaged in operations against the trade in illegal drugs great latitude under the Fourth Amendment. The ruling allowed evidence of other crimes found in plain view and seized by police officers during routine traffic stops to be used in court. Despite the apparent permissiveness of the decision toward law enforcement officers the Court was quite sensitive to the possibility of selective enforcement of the law based on race, and suggested the slightly more rigorous standard for determining the reasonableness of traffic stops discussed previously.

Related Cases

United States v. Brignoni-Ponce, 422 U.S. 873 (1975).
United States v. Martinez Fuerte, 428 U.S. 543 (1976).
Pennsylvania v. Mimms, 434 U.S. 106 (1977).
Delaware v. Prouse, 440 U.S. 648 (1979).

Bibliography and Further Reading

Biskupic, Joan, and Elder Witt. *Guide to the U.S. Supreme Court.* Washington, DC: Congressional Quarterly Inc., 1997.

Rights, Liberties, and Justice Home Page: Institutional Powers Home Page: Short Course Home Page. http://voter96.cqalert.com/mall/case6.html.

OHIO V. ROBINETTE

Legal Citation: 519 U.S. 33 (1996)

Petitioner
State of Ohio

Respondent
Robert D. Robinette

Petitioner's Claim
Provisions of the Fourth Amendment do not require police officers to warn motorists that they are "free to go" at the end of a traffic stop.

Chief Lawyer for Petitioner
Carley J. Ingram

Chief Lawyer for Respondent
James D. Ruppert

Justices for the Court
Stephen Breyer, Ruth Bader Ginsburg, Anthony M. Kennedy, Sandra Day O'Connor, William H. Rehnquist (writing for the Court), Antonin Scalia, David H. Souter, Clarence Thomas

Justices Dissenting
John Paul Stevens

Place
Washington, D.C.

Date of Decision
18 November 1996

Decision
The respondent's Fourth Amendment rights were not violated when, after being lawfully stopped, the motorist consented to search even though the police officer failed to advise that the motorist had the right to refuse consent, since initial detention was finished. The U.S. Constitution did not specifically stipulate that such searches and seizures were unreasonable.

Significance
Two main issues were outlined in this case. First, whether searches and seizures could be assumed unlawful if police officers, fail to warn drivers that they were "free to go" before engaging in any additional questioning. The second issue addressed concerned whether the "first-tell-then-ask" rule contained in the Ohio State Constitution could be recognized as the "new legal rule" governing adjudication of this case when its language seemingly interpreted the Federal Constitution's Fourth Amendment. The U.S. Supreme Court ruled that consent to search could not be presumed "unvoluntary" if a police officer failed to inform a motorist that he had the right to drive away before answering any further questions.

In 1992, respondent, Robert D. Robinette was speeding in his car just north of Dayton, Ohio when Deputy Roger Newsome stopped him. At the time of stopping, Newsome's primary assignment was as an officer on drug interdiction patrol. After a computer check of Robinette's driving license and registration showed no outstanding warrants, Deputy Newsome asked him to step out of his car, warned Robinette to slow down, and gave him back his documents. Then Deputy Newsome asked one more question. He wanted to know if there were "any weapons of any kind, drugs, anything like that?" When Robinette answered, "No," the deputy requested a car search and asked for and received Robinette's consent. A search of the car resulted in discovery of a small amount of marijuana and methylenedioxymethamphetamin—an "Ecstasy" pill. Robinette was arrested for possessing illicit drugs.

Before trial, Robinette moved that the evidence obtained be suppressed because, at the time, he did not believe the search was absolutely voluntary: he feared that Deputy Newsome's request could not be contested. Robinette's motion was denied by the trial court and he was charged with "knowing possession of a controlled substances" even though Robinette contended that "continued detention" after the initial traffic stop constituted an unlawful seizure. He believed that the deputy's conduct evidenced an unjustified extension of detention, and that the deputy's motivation for further questioning and investigation was substantially different from the original purpose of the stop—speeding. Robinette appealed to the Ohio Court of Appeals where the lower court's decision was reversed. The appellate court found that the "search resulted from unlawful detention." Similarly, the state's appeal to the Supreme Court of Ohio was denied. In its written opinion, the Ohio State Supreme Court stated that its findings were consistent with determined guarantees of the Federal and Ohio Constitutions. After finishing the initial detention of a motorist, officers in traffic control had to inform a "detainee" that he was free to go before police could ask any further questions or request permission for a search. A "consensual interrogation," thus, could not be valid if the detaining officer failed, under the provisions of the Ohio Constitution, to indicate to a stopped driver (either verbally or by gesture) "at this time you legally are free to go."

In an 8-1 vote, the Court overruled the decision of the Ohio Supreme Court. Justice Rehnquist, writing for the majority opinion, first emphasized the Court's certitude that it held jurisdiction over the case. He explained the Supreme Court held jurisdiction because the Ohio Supreme Court judgement was based on previous cases which distinctly relied on federal law and that almost all of the cited cases implemented the U.S. Constitution. He pointed out that it was completely permissible to review Ohio's decision because the general concept of the issue under consideration rested on both Federal and Ohio Constitutions.

The majority opinion found no violation of the Fourth Amendment occurred. Justices held that "once [a] motor vehicle has been lawfully detained for a traffic violation, the police officer may order the driver to get out of the vehicle." They reasoned that "subjective intentions" (such as Officer Newcomb's mission while on drug interdiction patrol) did not transgress the law if objectively viewed circumstances could justify "continued detention." Also, the Court believed that if there existed a reasonable element which justified continuing to detain a stopped motorist, then there would be no violation of the Fourth Amendment protection. Further, justices believed that consideration of all important elements in every case was required to determine the relative unreasonableness or reasonableness of searches and seizures. Cases that centered on a question of Fourth Amendment violations could not be measured only by applying one basic standard and not implicate "totality of the circumstances."

While Justice Ginsburg agreed with the majority, she separately expressed that the findings of the Ohio Supreme Court were not appropriate because upholding the state's "first-tell-then-ask" rule would not be an appropriate practice for the "nation as whole." Instructions by the state supreme court to police officers in Ohio could not be recognized as orders taken from the Federal Constitution. Moreover, neither did the state supreme court independently rely on state law but referred to both Federal and Ohio Constitutions in its ruling. Justice Ginsburg explained that while actions of the state of Ohio could be applied only within the state, sole reliance on state law, excluding provisions of the Federal Constitution, could not be an adequate basis for the ruling of the state's Supreme Court.

Citing an earlier case, *Schneckloth v. Bustamonte* (1973), the Court reasoned that before "consent search," the government did not have to advise an individual that he had "a right to refuse the request." Justices also reasoned that it would be impractical to estab-

lish a plan wherein police officers had to familiarize detainees with all circumstances which might enable a motorist to deny further communication. Justices did not believe that "normal consent searches" could be justified only after detailed warnings. They concluded that because "voluntariness is a question of fact to be determined from all circumstances," there occurred no violation of the Fourth Amendment.

Only Justice Stevens dissented. He conceded that the Federal Constitution did not specify that law enforcement officers were required to advise a "lawfully seized person" that he was "free to go" before asking an individual to submit to a voluntary search. But, Stevens pointed out that detention of the respondent for a traffic violation prepared a backdrop for an unlawful search that was in violation of the Fourth Amendment. The deputy had no reasonable grounds to suspect that there were drugs in the respondent's car. In fact, the deputy did not even issue a speeding ticket. Therefore, in Stevens's opinion, by engaging in further questioning without informing the respondent he was free to leave, the deputy created a situation where all evidence was obtained as a by-product of unlawful detention. Furthermore, circumstances did not seem conducive to give the respondent, or any motorist for that matter, the idea that is was permissible to "simply walk away from the officer, get back in his car, and drive away." As Ohio's Supreme Court found, Justice Stevens observed that "most people believe that they are validly in a police officer's custody as long as the officer continues to interrogate them." He pointed out that because ordinary citizens did not know when they were "free to go," officers should not have the ability to use that ignorance as a means to obtain permission for searches. Neither did Justice Stevens find justification in the deputy's "subjective motivation" that the Court reasoned provided "legality" for "continued detention." The reasonableness of continued detention did not exist for any other purpose than might have been justified on the basis of the initial, lawful traffic stop. Consequently, the deputy had no justifiable reason to assume that the respondent concealed drugs in his car. The questioning which proceeded then was promulgated by an unlawful detention and, therefore, produced an illegal seizure. Stevens also found no reason why the state of Ohio should be restricted from protecting its citizens through a provision in the state constitution that enjoined state police officers to warn drivers about their rights when a traffic stop was concluded.

Impact

The U.S. Supreme Court found that the Ohio Supreme Court did not find adequate and independent grounds apart from the U.S. Constitution to support its decision and its requirements for their police officers to practice a "first-tell-then-ask" rule. They emphasized that the ruling of the Ohio Supreme Court should have been based on the state law, rather than Federal constitutional law. In effect, the Court's rationale served as notice to state courts that the question of jurisdiction was largely determined by the rationale of cases and statutes cited. Reliance on federal statutes and federally adjudicated cases yielded a jurisdictional possibility for the U.S. Supreme Court to intervene.

The dissenting opinion held that continued detention was unlawful beyond the original purpose of detention, a traffic violation, once a traffic stop was complete. However, both majority and minority opinions concluded no requirements existed, under the Fourth Amendment, for police officers to notify drivers when they are "free to go." In differing with the dissenting opinion, the majority ruled that after a vehicle had been stopped, the motivation of a police officer did not have to preclude asking for voluntary consent to search. In such instances, under the "totality of circumstances," consent to search was obligatory, and therefore provisions of the Fourth Amendment did not require police officers to inform motorists that they could refuse additional communication because initial purpose for detention had finished.

Related Cases

Schneckloth v. Bustamonte, 412 U.S. 218 (1973).
Michigan v. Long, 463 U.S. 1032 (1983).
Florida v. Bostick, 501 U.S. 429 (1991).
Whren v. United States, 517 U.S. 806 (1996).

Bibliography and Further Reading

The American Civil Liberties Union. *ACLU News Wire-11/18/96,* " A Search For Justice Ends at the High Court," December 12, 1997. http://www.aclu.org/news/w111896a.html

FindLaw, Inc. *Supreme Court Cases Online.* http://laws.findlaw.com

Hall, Kermit L., ed. *The Oxford Companion to the Supreme Court of the United States.* New York: Oxford University Press, 1992.

National Drug Strategy Network. "Consensual Drug Searches During Traffic Stops Upheld by Supreme Court," April 2, 1998. http://www.ndsn.org/DEC96/CONSENT.html

North Carolina Justice Academy. *Legal Commentary on Recent Judicial Decisions,* April 19, 1998. http://www.state.nc.us/Justice/NCJA/juris.htm

MARYLAND V. WILSON

Legal Citation: 519 U.S. 408 (1997)

Petitioner
State of Maryland

Respondent
Jerry Lee Wilson

Petitioner's Claim
Maryland maintained that passengers of a vehicle should be expected to exit a vehicle when requested by a law officer.

Justices for the Court
Stephen Breyer, Ruth Bader Ginsburg, Sandra Day O'Connor, William H. Rehnquist (writing for the Court), Antonin Scalia, David H. Souter, Clarence Thomas

Justices Dissenting
Anthony M. Kennedy, John Paul Stevens

Place
Washington, D.C.

Date of Decision
16 February 1997

Decision
The Supreme Court held that it was consistent with the Fourth Amendment for an officer making a traffic stop to order passengers to get out of the vehicle until the completion of the stop.

Significance
The ruling determined that a police officer has the right to order the passenger of a vehicle out of the car during a traffic stop. Previously, this law had only extended to the driver of the vehicle, due to probable cause when the driver had committed a traffic violation. The determination to extend this law to cover the passenger as well was primarily based on the added safety risk placed on an officer by passengers of motor vehicles. Justices Stevens and Kennedy dissented, stating that aspects of *Maryland v. Wilson* had not been properly preserved and were therefore not relevant to the Supreme Court. They also stated that the extension of this law to cover passengers of vehicles infringed on Fourth Amendment issues due to lack of evidence that the passenger presented any risk to the officer.

A Maryland state trooper witnessed a car, bearing a torn shred of paper with the name of a car rental agency written on it instead of a license tag, driving over the posted speed limit. After a brief pursuit of one and a half miles, the car finally pulled over. Aside from the driver, two passengers could be seen in the car, each looking repeatedly back at the trooper, then ducking below sight level, only to glance back up moments later. As the trooper approached the car, the driver climbed out and met the trooper halfway, carrying a valid driver's license. The trooper instructed the driver to return to the car and gather the car's rental papers. As the driver sat behind the wheel, looking for the documents, the trooper noticed that the passenger occupying the front seat appeared quite nervous. He asked this passenger to exit the vehicle. As the passenger exited the car, a quantity of crack cocaine fell to the ground. The trooper immediately arrested the passenger, Jerry Lee Wilson, under the charge of "possession of cocaine with the intent to distribute."

The case was brought to trial in the Circuit Court for Baltimore County, Maryland. Before the trial began Wilson moved to suppress the evidence, stating that the trooper's order amounted to an unjustifiable seizure under the Fourth Amendment of the U.S. Constitution. The circuit court granted the motion to suppress. On appeal, the Court of Special Appeals of Maryland declared that a police officer may order the driver of a lawfully stopped car to exit the vehicle (as decided by the U.S. Supreme Court in *Pennsylvania v. Mimms*), but this procedure did not extend to the passengers. On *certiorari* this case was referred to the Supreme Court.

A Bright Line Rule?

The argument surrounding this case became an issue of police officer safety verses a constitutional right. In determining whether or not the *Maryland v. Wilson* case constituted an infringement of Fourth Amendment rights, the Supreme Court studied the case of *Pennsylvania v. Mimms* (1977). In 1977 Harry Mimms was detained during a routine traffic stop due to an expired license plate. The officer asked Mimms to step out of the car, whereupon the officer noticed a bulge in Mimms's jacket that turned out to be a .38-caliber revolver. The officer arrested Mimms for carrying a concealed deadly weapon. Like Wilson, Mimms also called for the suppression of evidence due to unreasonable seizure because of the officer's order to exit the vehicle. And, like as in *Maryland v. Wilson*, the court allowed this suppression. The Supreme Court reversed, stating that the rights provided under the Fourth Amendment were subject to a "reasonableness that depend[ed] on a balance between the public interest and the individual's right to personal security . . ." (*Terry v. Ohio* [1968]). It was noted that Mimms's actions had not been suspicious, but that it was the arresting officer's habit to order all drivers out of their vehicles as a "precautionary measure" to protect the officer's safety.

The Fourth Amendment of the U.S. Constitution proclaims the "right of the people to be secure in their persons, houses, papers, and effects, against unreasonable searches and seizures, shall not be violated, and no Warrants shall issue, but upon probable cause, supported by Oath or affirmation, and particularly describing the place to be searched, and the persons or things to be seized." A fundamental question arose as to what situations would allow probable cause for a legal search and seizure.

In each case the officer was required to rapidly assess the situation and act accordingly. This "unfettered discretion" came under fire by many Supreme Court justices. It was referred to as a bright line rule, a ". . . rule or principle that is simple and straightforward; a rule that avoids or ignores ambiguity." It was feared that if the practice of ordering passengers from vehicles became standard police routine that an unnecessary invasion of the rights of innocent citizens was inevitable.

A Matter of Safety

Attorney General Janet Reno presented what would be the strongest argument in favor of allowing officers to order passengers from lawfully stopped vehicles. Her primary concern revolved around police safety. In 1994, there were 5,762 officers assaulted in traffic stops. It was noted that there had been a 17-percent drop in fatalities of this nature since the *Mimms* decision. Reno essentially stated that an officer was at a reduced risk of danger if he could see the passenger.

At the heart of the case was the issue of passengers always being considered dangerous. It was reasoned that the passenger in an automobile would be quite likely to know the driver in some way, and that only under statistically rare circumstances would the passenger be a stranger to the driver. Under this rationale a certain connection between the passenger and the driver could be predicted. The passenger would be aware of what was happening inside the vehicle and would therefore be aware of any illegal activity on the part of the driver. That the vehicle contained more than

one occupant was enough to create an increase in risk to the officer. With this in mind it was reasoned that the safety of a police officer would be greatly enhanced if the passenger was ordered to stand outside of the vehicle.

The ramifications this would have on personal liberty were considered. Given the situation, it is obvious that the passengers "are already stopped by virtue of the stop of the vehicle." The only difference produced by the officer's order to exit the car was simply that the passenger would now be outside, instead of inside, the vehicle. By placing the passenger(s) outside of the vehicle, the officer would effectively deny access to any concealed weapons hidden in the vehicle. This action also allowed the officer to more easily determine if the passenger posed a threat as he would now be able to see the passenger completely. It was determined by most of the Supreme Court justices that the amount of safety granted by this action significantly outweighed the minor constitutional infringement placed on the passenger.

Differing Opinions

Justices Stevens and Kennedy dissented from this decision. Justice Stevens's primary concern stemmed from the millions of other cases that would be affected by this decision. The ordering of passengers would apply equally to legally stopped traffic vehicles in which there was absolutely no sign of potential risk to the police officer. He pointed out that statistics did not carry the number of how many assaults on officers were carried out by passengers. Likewise, no statistics were found showing that the ratio of assaults was lower in jurisdictions that allowed officers to order passengers out of vehicles. Justice Stevens argued that the sheer volume of annual routine traffic stops (in comparison with the relatively low number of stops that placed an officer at risk) would render the ruling of *Maryland v. Wilson* as a constitutional burden on passengers. "In all events," he stated, "the aggregation of thousands upon thousands of petty indignities has an impact on freedom that I would characterize as substantial, and which in my view clearly outweighs the evanescent safety concerns pressed by the majority [of justices]." He believed that innocent passengers had a constitutional right to decide whether or not to remain in the vehicle. In *Maryland v. Wilson* the evidence as to why the officer ordered the passenger from the vehicle could not be preserved, since it was of a visual, not a physical nature. Therefore, the evidence concerning Wilson's agitated activity was not considered relevant.

Justice Kennedy agreed with Justice Stevens, and added that the discretion of the officer was valid to the success of this ruling. Even with this discretion, Kennedy pointed out that complaints from citizens and possible political intervention could end the practice of ordering passengers from vehicles. "Liberty comes not from officials by grace but from the Constitution by right," he stated in his opinion.

Impact

The ramifications of this case solidified the procedure used by police officers during traffic stops. The issue of officer safety verses the constitutional rights of citizens will most likely remain a hot point of conflict, and not just in the area of traffic stops. Because of the virtually endless possibilities that arise during an event requiring police attention it becomes impossible to avoid. Certain situations demand certain actions and if these actions result in minor constitutional infringements committed in the course of saving a life, it is possible that the Supreme Court will see many more cases similar to *Maryland v. Wilson*.

Related Cases

Terry v. Ohio, 392 U.S. 1 (1968).
United States v. Brignoni-Ponce, 422 U.S. 873 (1975).
Pennsylvania v. Mimms, 434 U.S. 106 (1977).
Michigan v. Long, 463 U.S. 1032 (1983).

Ohio v. Robinette, 433 U.S. 562 (1996).
Whren v. United States, 517 U.S. 806 (1996).

Bibliography and Further Reading

Hansen, Mark. "Rousting Miss Daisy: U.S. Supreme Court Says Police Can Order Passengers Out of Cars During Routine Traffic Stops." *ABA Journal,* May 1997, p. 22.

"Police Group Files Brief to U.S. Supreme Court on Knowles v. Iowa." *PR Newswire,* October 28, 1998, p. 1620.

Riggs, Jenny L. "Excluding Automobile Passengers from Fourth Amendment Protection." *Journal of Criminal Law and Criminology,* spring 1998, p. 957.

Slansky, David A. "Traffic Stops, Minority Motorists, and the Future of the Fourth Amendment." *Supreme Court Review,* annual 1997, p. 271.

Urbonya, Kathryn R. "The Fishing Gets Easier; Police Gain More Latitude in Traffic Stops, and Other Powers Could Be on the Way." *ABA Journal,* January 1997, p. 46.

CHANDLER V. MILLER

Legal Citation: 520 U.S. 305 (1997)

Petitioners
Walker L. Chandler, et al.

Respondent
Zell D. Miller, Governor of Georgia

Petitioners' Claim
That Georgia's requirement for a negative urinalysis to qualify for candidacy violated their constitutional rights under the First, Fourth, and Fourteenth Amendments.

Chief Lawyer for Petitioners
Walker L. Chandler

Chief Lawyer for Respondent
Patricia Guilday

Justices for the Court
Stephen Breyer, Ruth Bader Ginsburg (writing for the Court), Anthony M. Kennedy, Sandra Day O'Connor, Antonin Scalia, David H. Souter, John Paul Stevens, Clarence Thomas

Justices Dissenting
William H. Rehnquist

Place
Washington, D.C.

Date of Decision
15 April 1997

Decision
The Court found that the state of Georgia violated the constitutional rights of the petitioner because the negative drug test constituted a suspicionless search.

Significance
Although the Supreme Court acknowledged that the U.S. Constitution gives states the right to set qualifications and protocol for state elections, the Court viewed Georgia's statute as an unreasonable, suspicionless search. Moreover, this decision definitively stipulated that regardless of purpose, in order for any state to engage in any act that involved suspicionless search there had to exist a viable, compelling government interest or special need to justify infringement on individual rights granted under the U.S. Constitution.

Political Nominees Challenged Mandatory Drug Testing

In 1990, the state of Georgia enacted a statute that required every candidate for a designated state office to submit to a urinalysis drug test. Thus, Georgia became the first and only state that required drug screening for state office nominees. Test results had to be negative and verified by a state approved laboratory at least 30 days before balloting for nomination or election to state offices. (Candidates could choose whether to be tested in a laboratory approved by the state or by their own physician.)

Libertarian Party nominee for the office of lieutenant governor, Walker L. Chandler, and two other nominees of the Libertarian Party, believed that their constitutional right to privacy would be violated. They sought protection from what they felt constituted an unreasonable search. The action, filed in the U.S. District Court for the Northern District of Georgia claimed the "creators" of the statute inappropriately used state power under the U.S. Constitution's Tenth Amendment to enact their statute. Because the petitioners felt that their rights had been constitutionally violated, they requested declaratory and injunctive relief barring implementation and enforcement of the act. The district court, however, refused their request to obtain a preliminary injunction; final judgment of the district court was also delayed until after the election. When the court ultimately rendered its decision, the Georgia statute was upheld.

Chandler appealed the ruling to the Eleventh Circuit Court of Appeals; however, the court affirmed. (Interestingly, the circuit court cited as justification for its ruling the same three cases that the U.S. Supreme Court would claim as precedence which rendered the Georgia statute as unconstitutional.) The court's opinion stated that although drug testing qualified as a search, the state had compelling reason to have nominees for state office submit to drug testing. The circuit panel further reasoned that the import of administrative and policy decision-making in which elected officials engaged rendered the state's rationale as valid. Moreover, the state's "special needs" went beyond the limits of normal law enforcement and so a warrant or reasonable suspicion

Walker Chandler speaks with reporters after arguing his case.
© Photograph by Michael Ryan. Archive Photos.

was not necessarily incident to the "search" (drug tests). Finally, being permitted to take tests in the office of their private physician, nominees could simply forfeit their candidacy if they tested positive; thus, the court felt that there existed no potential that an individual's privacy might be violated. The Eleventh Circuit Court ultimately ruled that the Georgia statute was constitutionally valid because the state's interests outweighed individual expectations of privacy.

State Cited Three Earlier Decisions Involving Drug Testing

When the case was argued before the Supreme Court, the state of Georgia focused on drug testing programs previously upheld by the Supreme Court. These included two cases decided in 1989. The first was *Skinner v. Railway Labor Executives' Assn.* This case involved drug and alcohol tests performed on railway employees involved in train accidents and for those who violated particular safety rules. The second 1989 case was *Treasury Employees v. Von Raab.* The *Treasury Employees* case addressed the use of drug tests for U.S. Customs Service employees who sought transfer or promotion to certain positions. A third case cited as precedence had been decided in 1995, *Vernonia School District 47J v. Acton,* and concerned the use of random drug testing of students who participated in interscholastic sports.

These were the same cases cited and recognized by the Eleventh Circuit Court as the examples of reasonable searches for the purpose of identifying drug abuse. Counsel for the state of Georgia reasoned that these related cases focused on a state's interest to have pro-

grams to prevent drug abuse in special circumstances wherein lack of testing could have a serious, deleterious effect. Counsel pointed out that, as written, the Georgia statute did not have any invasive elements since nominees submitted to testing in the privacy of their own physician's office. Therefore the state could not be faulted for excessive intrusion. Finally, the respondent's attorney maintained that the existence of such a statute was warranted because use of illicit drugs in society was pervasive, and could conceivably involve even candidates who ran for state office.

The U.S. Supreme Court based its decision on four points of law. The Court agreed with petitioners that the Georgia statute's requirements were unconstitutional because respondents failed to prove and justify their reasons for authoring such a statute. Justices did not consider as valid the respondent's claim that requirements for drug testing were reasonable because there was no "individualized suspicion of wrong doing" which justified unwarranted search and seizure (a description which even the lower court applied to the drug testing requirement). Further, the Court reasoned that a state's power under the Tenth Amendment to establish criteria and procedure for state elections did not entitle a state to challenge personal rights under the Fourth Amendment.

Majority of Justices Believed Testing Unnecessary

Justices specifically felt there were no "special needs" that permitted violation of Fourth Amendment rights which protect society against unreasonable searches;

neither was there a proven, compelling necessity to require drug tests for nominees to the ballot. Writing for the majority, Justice Ginsburg observed that personal rights "diminished for a symbol's sake" did not constitute a valid reason to infringe on personal rights of nominees. Justices found the respondent's arguments as spurious that there existed a potential for drug abuse among politicians. Instead, the majority opinion went on to reason, the state's fears seemed more hypothetical than real. Nominees for state office were exposed to the public, their conduct attracted the attention of society and they were thus likely to find such exposure sufficient reason to refrain from drug use. Moreover, the Court felt that "state officials typically do not perform high-risk, safety sensitive tasks, and required certification immediately aids no interdiction effort." Furthermore, the Court reasoned that Georgia's certification requirement did not succeed in its effort to identify drug abusers because tests were given with advance notice. Unlike *Skinner, Treasury Employees,* and *Vernonia School District,* where tests were scheduled without precise timing, users of illegal drugs could thus abstain for a period prior to testing long enough not to be detected. The Supreme Court thus felt that the Georgia statute was not only unconstitutional, but procedurally flawed.

During oral arguments brought before the Court, justices questioned the respondent's attorney as to whether there were real indications that Georgia has special problems with drug abuse among state officeholders. Counsel for the respondent said, "No, there is no such evidence . . . and to be frank, there is no such problem as we sit here today." Accordingly, the justices held that there was no argument showing real need for establishing a suspicionless program of drug testing among nominees for state office. Thus, cases and rationale on which the respondent based its defense were rendered impertinent to the facts of the case. In her final statement, Justice Ginsburg summarized the Court's characterization of Georgia's attempt to require drug testing for nominees running for state office. The justices almost unanimously agreed. Only Justice Rehnquist dissented. The majority of justices held that the existence of the Georgia statute was "symbolic." They asserted that there existed no discernible "special" need that served the state's argument. Additionally, the Court concluded with this commentary: "We reiterate, too, that where the risk to public safety is substantial and real, blanket suspicionless searches calibrated to the risk may rank as 'reasonable.' But where, as in this case, public safety is not genuinely in jeopardy, the Fourth Amendment precludes the suspicionless search, no matter how conveniently arranged."

The only justice who dissented, Chief Justice Rehnquist, thought that the majority opinion, "had been distorted with novelty of the case." Agreeing that the state of Georgia had reason to fear political leaders may succumb to drug abuse, Rehnquist pointed out that drug abuse is one of the most dangerous problems that exists in the United States, and therefore the state was presented with a potential dilemma that could not be ignored. It was not unreasonable to assume that usage of drugs might be extended even to candidates for public office. Rehnquist therefore considered the Georgia statute a correct exercise of a state's legal right, under the Tenth Amendment of the Constitution, to create such a "prophylactic mechanism."

Impact

Although responding to a real, rather than perceived threat—that of illicit drug use—the state of Georgia appeared to the Court as misguided in its attempt to force political nominees to prove their worthiness as candidates by submitting to drug testing. This case demonstrated how personal rights, protected by the Fourth Amendment, could not be infringed upon or overwhelmed even if a state was acting in response to what it perceived to be a justifiable threat. Because drug testing without suspicion qualified as a warrantless search (a fact uncontested among the lower courts as well), the U.S. Supreme Court maintained that the state had no compelling interest or "special needs" which could justify compelling candidates for political office to submit to drug testing. To do so constituted an invasion of reasonable expectations of privacy guaranteed under the Constitution when there existed little or no real threat that such strata of American society were especially prone to drug abuse. Neither was it appropriate to subject individuals to protocol that exceeded the ordinary needs of law enforcement. The public interest did not, under such circumstances, outweigh individual expectations of privacy. In reversing the decisions of the lower courts, the U.S. Supreme Court further defined the limitations which states were compelled to observe when establishing drug testing mechanisms but outlined the constraints under which states could extend their Tenth Amendment right to set and administer electoral balloting within their jurisdiction.

Related Cases

Olmstead v. United States, 277 U.S. 438 (1928).
Skinner v. Railway Labor Executives' Association, 489 U.S. 602 (1989).
Treasury Employees v. Von Raab, 489 U.S. 656 (1989).
Michigan Dept. of State Police v. Sitz, 496 U.S. 444 (1990).
Vernonia School District 47J v. Acton, 515 U.S. 646 (1995).

Bibliography and Further Reading

Anderson, Sean. "Individual Privacy Interests and the 'Special Needs' Analysis for Involuntary Drug and HIV Tests." *California Law Review,* January 1998, p. 119.

Dripps, Donald A. "Drug Testing—Again." *Trial,* June 1997, p. 72.

Savage, David G. "Speaking of Drugs and Deadbeats; Court Says No Testing of Candidates, No Child Support Action Against States." *ABA Journal,* June 1997, p. 46.

Steiker, Carol S. "The Limits of the Preventive State." *Journal of Criminal Law and Criminology,* spring 1998, p. 771.

"Supreme Court Strikes Down Drug Testing of Candidates." *Drug Detection Report,* April 21, 1997.

RICHARDS V. WISCONSIN

Legal Citation: 520 U.S. 385 (1997)

Petitioner
Steiney Richards

Respondent
State of Wisconsin

Petitioner's Claim
That police violated his Fourth Amendment rights by using deception and force to enter his hotel room on a drug-related case.

Chief Lawyers for Petitioner
Henry Schultz, David Karpe, John Wesley Hall, Jr.

Chief Lawyers for Respondent
James E. Doyle, Stephen W. Kleinmaier

Justices for the Court
Stephen Breyer, Ruth Bader Ginsburg, Anthony M. Kennedy, Sandra Day O'Connor, William H. Rehnquist, Antonin Scalia, David H. Souter, John Paul Stevens (writing for the Court), Clarence Thomas

Justices Dissenting
None

Place
Washington, D.C.

Date of Decision
28 April 1997

Decision
That the evidence in this case established the reasonableness of the officers' decision not to knock and announce their presence, and thus there was no Fourth Amendment violation.

Significance
Richards v. Wisconsin clarified the Court's position in *Wilson v. Arkansas* (1995). The Supreme Court affirmed, upholding the common law "knock and announce" rule whereby police are required to knock on the door of a suspect's dwelling and announce their identity and purpose before forcing entry. *Richards* tested the limits of the "no knock" concept, whereby officers were allowed to enter without announcing themselves, on the basis that to do otherwise would give the suspect too much time to destroy evidence.

The Police Knock on Richards's Door

Madison, Wisconsin police had been investigating Steiney Richards for some time before they obtained a warrant to search his hotel room on the last day of 1991. They suspected Richards of conducting illegal drug sales out of his room, and had requested a warrant that would give them authorization for "no knock" entry—that is, a warrant which would permit them to enter the room without knocking on the door. It was an advantage the officers believed they needed, because Richards would otherwise be able to destroy evidence or flee before they could make an arrest. The magistrate, however, denied their request.

Proceeding with an ordinary warrant requiring them to "knock and announce," the officers arrived at Richard's room at 3:40 a.m., presumably on 1 January 1992. Dressed as a maintenance man, Officer Pharo, the team leader, approached the door. Around and behind him stood several others, at least one of them in a police uniform. When Pharo knocked on the door, a voice from inside asked who was there, and Pharo responded that he was the maintenance man. Richards slowly cracked the door, with the chain still on it.

The next sequence of events would be disputed, but apparently as soon as he saw the uniformed officer behind Pharo, Richards slammed the door shut. Two or three seconds later, the officers began kicking the door down, shouting all the while—according to their later testimony—that they were police officers. Finally entering the room after breaking through the door, the officers caught Richards attempting to flee through a window, and a search revealed cash and cocaine hidden above the tiles in the bathroom ceiling.

At the subsequent trial, Richards filed a motion seeking suppression of the evidence from his hotel room on the grounds that the officers had not knocked or announced their presence before forcing their way into his dwelling. The trial court denied the motion, ruling that the strange behavior Richards exhibited in opening and then rapidly closing the door justified the police officers' reaction. Given the disposable nature of the drugs involved, the judge noted, the police were justified in making their way across the threshold as quickly as they could.

Richards appealed to the Wisconsin Supreme Court, which affirmed the ruling of the lower court. They used as their guide the U.S. Supreme Court's holding in *Wilson,* and reviewed this in light of their own decision in *State v. Stevens* (1995). In the latter case, the Wisconsin high court held that "when the police have a search warrant, supported by probable cause, to search a residence for evidence of delivery of drugs or evidence of possession with intent to deliver drugs, they necessarily have reasonable cause to believe exigent circumstances exist." That would justify a no knock entry. *Wilson* did not negate *Stevens;* it was possible to apply exceptions to the knock and announce rule. This is so particularly in light of "today's drug culture," which often involves violence, as well as substances such as cocaine that could be rapidly destroyed by flushing them down the toilet. Felony drug crimes involve "an extremely high risk of serious if not deadly injury to the police as well as the potential for the disposal of drugs by the occupants prior to entry by the police," the court held.

The Supreme Court Strikes a Balance

The U.S. Supreme Court affirmed Wisconsin's decision by a unanimous vote. Justice Stevens, who gave the Court's opinion, began by noting that the ruling did not provide a constitutional justification for a "blanket exception" to the knock and announce requirement in felony drug cases. Rather, exceptions could be made to that requirement on a case-by-case basis in view of certain factors. These included the possibility of physical violence or fears that, if the police took the time to knock and announce, the suspect would use the lead time to destroy evidence or flee—as Richards had apparently attempted to do. Exceptions could be created, Justice Stevens wrote, but they had to be subjected to the scrutiny of courts as needed, and they had to take into account "at least two serious concerns." The first of these was the fact that officers might attempt to include within the special exceptions some drug investigations that did not really involve special risks, and this would place too many such cases outside the watchful eyes of judges. Second, "an exception in one category can, relatively easily, be applied to others." It was not the Court's desire to create a series of exceptions, and the application of exceptions in every situation that posed a threat to officers would simply render the knock and announce requirement meaningless.

Hence, Justice Stevens held, a no knock entry could be justified in situations where the police had reasonable suspicion that announcing their presence would be "dangerous or futile, or that it would inhibit the effective investigation of the crime." To thus permit exceptions, but to forbid blanket exceptions to the knock and announce requirement struck "the appropriate balance between the legitimate law enforcement concerns at issue in the execution of search warrants and the individual privacy interests affected by no knock entries."

Having addressed the general question, Justice Stevens turned to the specific situation involved in *Richards.* The evidence in the present case justified the decision on the part of the officers not to announce their presence, Justice Stevens held, and thus they had not violated the Fourth Amendment. As for the objection that the magistrate had specifically refused a no knock warrant, this meant only "that at the time warrant was requested there was insufficient evidence for a no knock entry. However, the officers' decision to enter the room must be evaluated as to the time of entry."

Impact

Both civil libertarians and upholders of law and order found something to applaud in the balance Justice Stevens had applied in *Richards.* The American Civil Liberties Union (ACLU) and National Association of Criminal Defense Lawyers (NACDL), which had provided Richards's defense, issued a statement on 28 April 1997 calling the Court's decision "a victory for the Fourth Amendment." Despite the fact that their client had not gained the relief he sought, the two organizations expressed pleasure with the Court's decision not to uphold the blanket exception. Certainly police officers and others on the "law and order" side could appreciate the Court's willingness to uphold certain exceptions to the knock and announce rule. In an *FBI Law Enforcement Bulletin* article published prior to the Court's decision in *Richards,* Michael J. Bulzomi made the government's case obliquely by noting the many perils officers face when approaching a suspect's dwelling. "A police officer making a high-risk warrant entry," Bulzomi wrote, "is not on an even playing field with the occupants of the premises . . . [T]he armed occupants know what they intend to do, whereas the officers can only infer whether [they] intend to fight, flee, or surrender." Perhaps because of such perils, "The point of entry into a house, be it a door or a window, is referred to as the fatal funnel." Ira Mickenberg in *The National Law Journal* reviewed the decision as one of several in the 1996-97 term that favored police and prosecutors.

Related Cases

Wilson v. Arkansas 514 U.S. 927 (1995).
State v. Stevens 515 U.S. 1102 (1995).

Bibliography and Further Reading

Bulzomi, Michael J. "Knock and Announce: A Fourth Amendment Standard." *The FBI Law Enforcement Bulletin,* May 1, 1997, pp. 27-31.

"In the Courts: *Richards v. Wisconsin*." American Civil Liberties Union Freedom Network. http://www.aclu.org/court/richards.html.

McCloud, Sheryl Gordon. "Will State or Federal Constitutional Law Save the 'Knock, Announce & Wait' Rule from a Drug Exception?" *The Champion*. National Association of Criminal Defense Lawyers. http://www.criminaljustice.org/CHAMPION.

Mickenberg, Ira. "Criminal Rulings Primarily Benefit the Prosecution." *The National Law Journal*, August 11, 1997, p. B-14.

GLOSSARY

A

Abandonment The surrender, relinquishment, disclaimer, or cession of property or of rights. Voluntary relinquishment of all right, title, claim, and possession, with no intention of reclamation.

The giving up of a thing absolutely, without reference to any particular person or purpose, such as vacating property with no intention of returning it, so that it may be appropriated by the next comer or finder. The voluntary relinquishment of possession of a thing by the owner with intention of terminating ownership, but without vesting it in any other person. The relinquishing of all title, possession, or claim, or a virtual, intentional throwing away of property.

Accessory Aiding or contributing in a secondary way or assisting in or contributing to as a subordinate.

In criminal law, contributing to or aiding in the commission of a crime. One who, without being present at the commission of an offense, becomes guilty of such offense, not as a chief actor, but as a participant, as by command, advice, instigation, or concealment; either before or after the fact of commission.

One who aids, abets, commands, or counsels another in the commission of a crime.

Accessory after the fact One who commits a crime by giving comfort or assistance to a felon, knowing that the felon has committed a crime, or is sought by authorities in connection with a serious crime.

Accomplice One who knowingly, voluntarily, and with common intent unites with the principal offender in the commission of a crime. One who is in some way involved with commission of a crime; partaker of guilt; one who aids or assists, or is an accessory. One who is guilty of complicity in a crime charged, either by being present and aiding or abetting in it, or having advised and encouraged it, though absent from place when it was committed. However, the mere presence, acquiescence, or silence, in the absence of a duty to act, is not enough, no matter how reprehensible it may be, to constitute one an accomplice. One is liable as an accomplice to the crime of another if he or she gave assistance or encouragement or failed to perform a legal duty to prevent it with the intent thereby to promote or facilitate commission of the crime.

Accord An agreement that settles a dispute, generally requiring a compromise or satisfaction with something less than what was originally demanded.

Acquittal The legal and formal certification of the innocence of a person who has been charged with a crime.

Action Conduct; behavior; something done; a series of acts.

A case or a lawsuit; a legal and formal demand for the enforcement of one's rights against another party asserted in a court of justice.

Actual authority The legal power, expressed or implied, that an agent possesses to represent and to bind into agreement the principal with a third party.

Actual damages Compensation awarded for the loss or the injury suffered by an individual.

Adjudication The legal process of resolving a dispute. The formal giving or pronouncing of a judgment or decree in a court proceeding; also the judgment or decision given. The entry of a decree by a court in respect to the parties in a case. It implies a hearing by a court, after notice, of legal evidence on the factual issue(s) involved. The equivalent of a determination. It indicates that the claims of all of the parties thereto have been considered and set at rest.

Administrative agency An official governmental body empowered with the authority to direct and supervise the implementation of particular legislative acts. In addition to *agency*, such governmental bodies may be called commissions, corporations (i.e., FDIC), boards, departments, or divisions.

Administrative law The body of law that allows for the creation of public regulatory agencies and contains all of the statutes, judicial decisions, and regulations that govern them. It is the body of law created by administrative agencies to implement their powers and duties in the form of rules, regulations, orders, and decisions.

Administrator A person appointed by the court to manage and take charge of the assets and liabilities of a decedent who has died without making a valid will.

Admissible A term used to describe information that is relevant to a determination of issues in any judicial proceeding so that such information can be properly considered by a judge or jury in making a decision.

Adultery Voluntary sexual relations between an individual who is married and someone who is not the individual's spouse.

Adversary system The scheme of American jurisprudence wherein a judge renders a decision in a controversy between parties who assert contradictory positions during a judicial examination, such as a trial or hearing.

Affidavit A written statement of facts voluntarily made by an affiant under an oath or affirmation administered by a person who is authorized to do so by law.

Affirmative action Employment programs required by federal statutes and regulations designed to remedy discriminatory practices in hiring minority group members; i.e., positive steps designed to eliminate existing and continuing discrimination, to remedy lingering effects of past discrimination, and to create systems and procedures to prevent future discrimination; commonly based on population percentages of minority groups in a particular area. Factors considered are race, color, sex, creed, and age.

Agent One who agrees and is authorized to act on behalf of another, a principal, to legally bind an individual in particular business transactions with third parties pursuant to an agency relationship.

Age of consent The age at which a person may marry without parental approval. The age at which a female is legally capable of agreeing to sexual intercourse, so that a male who engages in sex with her cannot be prosecuted for statutory rape.

Age of majority The age at which a person, formerly a minor or an infant, is recognized by law to be an adult, capable of managing his or her own affairs and responsible for any legal obligations created by his or her actions.

Aggravated assault A person is guilty of aggravated assault if he or she attempts to cause serious bodily injury to another or causes such injury purposely, knowingly, or recklessly under circumstances manifesting extreme indifference to the value of human life; or attempts to cause or purposely or knowingly causes bodily injury to another with a deadly weapon. In all jurisdictions, statutes punish such aggravated assaults as assault with intent to murder (or rob or kill or rape) and assault with a dangerous (or deadly) weapon more severely than "simple" assaults.

Alien Foreign-born person who has not been naturalized to become a U.S. citizen under federal law and the Constitution.

Alimony Payment a family court may order one person in a couple to make to the other when the couple separates or divorces.

Alimony pendente lite Temporary alimony awarded while separation and divorce proceedings are taking place. The award may cover the preparation for the suit, as well as general support.

Alternative dispute resolution Procedures for settling disputes by means other than litigation; i.e., by arbitration, mediation, or minitrials. Such procedures, which are usually less costly and more expeditious than litigation, are increasingly being used in commercial and labor disputes, divorce actions, in resolving motor vehicle and medical malpractice tort claims, and in other disputes that otherwise would likely involve court litigation.

Amendment The modification of materials by the addition of supplemental information; the deletion of unnecessary, undesirable, or outdated information; or the correction of errors existing in the text.

Amicus curiae [*Latin, Friend of the court.*] A person with strong interest in or views on the subject matter of an action, but not a party to the action, may petition the court for permission to file a brief, ostensibly on behalf of a party but actually to suggest a rationale consistent with his or her own views. Such amicus curiae briefs are commonly filed in appeals concerning matters of a broad public interest; i.e., civil rights cases. They may be filed by private persons or by the government. In appeals to the U.S. courts of appeals, an amicus brief may be filed only if accompanied by written consent of all parties, or by leave of court granted on motion or at the request of the court, except that consent or leave shall not be required when the brief is presented by the United States or an officer or agency thereof.

Amnesty The action of a government by which all persons or certain groups of persons who have committed a criminal offense—usually of a political nature that threatens the sovereignty of the government (such as sedition or treason)—are granted immunity from prosecution.

Annulment A judgment by a court that retroactively invalidates a marriage to the date of its formation.

Answer The first responsive pleading filed by the defendant in a civil action; a formal written statement that admits or denies the allegations in the complaint and sets forth any available affirmative defenses.

Apparent authority The amount of legal power a principal knowingly or negligently bestows onto an agent for representation with a third party, and which the third party reasonably believes the agent possesses.

Appeal Timely resort by an unsuccessful party in a lawsuit or administrative proceeding to an appropriate superior court empowered to review a final decision on the ground that it was based upon an erroneous application of law.

Appeals court *See* Appellate court or Court of appeal.

Appellate court A court having jurisdiction to review decisions of a trial-level or other lower court.

Appellate jurisdiction The power of a superior court or other tribunal to review the judicial actions of lower courts, particularly for legal errors, and to revise their judgments accordingly.

Apportionment The process by which legislative seats are distributed among units entitled to representation. Determination of the number of representatives that a state, county, or other subdivision may send to a legislative body. The U.S. Constitution provides for a census every ten years, on the basis of which Congress apportions representatives according to population. However, each state must have at least one representative. *Districting* is the establishment of the precise geographical boundaries of each such unit or constituency. Apportionment by state statute that denies the rule of one-person, one-vote is violative of equal protection laws.

Arbitration The submission of a dispute to an unbiased third person designated by the parties to the controversy, who agree in advance to comply with the award—a decision to be issued after a hearing at which both parties have an opportunity to be heard.

Arraignment The formal proceeding whereby the defendant is brought before the trial court to hear the charges against him or her and to enter a plea of guilty, not guilty, or no contest.

Arrest The detention and taking into custody of an individual for the purpose of answering the charges against him or her. An arrest involves the legal power of the individual to arrest, the intent to exercise that power, and the actual subjection to the control and will of the arresting authority.

Arrest warrant A written order issued by an authority of the state and commanding the seizure of the person named.

Arson At common law, the malicious burning or exploding of the dwelling house of another, or the burning of a building within the curtilage, the immediate surrounding space, of the dwelling of another.

Assault At common law, an intentional act by one person that creates an apprehension in another of an imminent harmful or offensive contact.

Assumption of risk A defense, facts offered by a party against whom proceedings have been instituted to diminish a plaintiff's cause of action or defeat recovery to an action in negligence, which entails proving that the plaintiff knew of a dangerous condition and voluntarily exposed himself or herself to it.

Attachment The legal process of seizing property to ensure satisfaction of a judgment.

Attempt An undertaking to do an act that entails more than mere preparation but does not result in the successful completion of the act.

Attractive nuisance doctrine The duty of an individual to take necessary precautions around equipment or conditions on his or her property that could attract and potentially injury children unable to perceive the risk of danger, such as an unguarded swimming pool or a trampoline.

Avoidance An escape from the consequences of a specific course of action through the use of legally acceptable means. Cancellation; the act of rendering something useless or legally ineffective.

B

Bail The system that governs the status of individuals charged with committing crimes from the time of their arrest to the time of their trial, and pending appeal, with the major purpose of ensuring their presence at trial.

Bait and switch A deceptive sales technique that involves advertising a low-priced item to attract customers to a store, then persuading them to buy more expensive goods by failing to have a sufficient supply of the advertised item on hand or by disparaging its quality.

Balancing A process sometimes used by the Supreme Court in deciding between the competing interests represented in a case.

Bankruptcy A federally authorized procedure by which a debtor—an individual, corporation, or municipality—is relieved of total liability for its debts by making court-approved arrangements for their partial repayment.

Battery At common law, an intentional unpermitted act causing harmful or offensive contact with the person of another.

Beneficiary An organization or a person for whom a trust is created and who thereby receives the benefits of the trust. One who inherits under a will. A person entitled to a beneficial interest or a right to profits, benefit, or advantage from a contract.

Bigamy The offense of willfully and knowingly entering into a second marriage while validly married to another individual.

Bilateral contract An agreement formed by an exchange of promises in which the promise of one party supports the promise of the other party.

Bill A declaration in writing. A document listing separate items. An itemized account of charges or costs. In equity practice, the first pleading in the action, that is, the paper in which the plaintiff sets out his or her case and demands relief from the defendant.

Bill of attainder A special legislative enactment that imposes a death sentence without a judicial trial upon a particular person or class of persons suspected of committing serious offenses, such as treason or a felony.

Bill of rights The first ten amendments to the U.S. Constitution, ratified in 1791, which set forth and guarantee certain fundamental rights and privileges of individuals, including freedom of religion, speech, press, and assembly; guarantee of a speedy jury trial in criminal cases; and protection against excessive bail and cruel and unusual punishment.

A list of fundamental rights included in each state constitution.

A declaration of individual rights and freedoms, usually issued by a national government.

Bill of sale In the law of contracts, a written agreement, previously required to be under seal, by which one person transfers to another a right to, or interest in, personal property and goods, a legal instrument that conveys title in property from seller to purchaser.

Black codes Laws, statutes, or rules that governed slavery and segregation of public places in the South prior to 1865.

Bona fide [*Latin, In good faith*.] Honest; genuine; actual; authentic; acting without the intention of defrauding.

Bona fide occupational qualification An essential requirement for performing a given job. The requirement may even be a physical condition beyond an individual's control, such as perfect vision, if it is absolutely necessary for performing a job.

Bonds Written documents by which a government, corporation, or individual—the obligator—promises to perform a certain act, usually the payment of a definite sum of money, to another—the obligee—on a certain date.

Booking The procedure by which law enforcement officials record facts about the arrest of and charges against a suspect, such as the crime for which the arrest was made, together with information concerning the identification of the suspect and other pertinent facts.

Breach of contract The breaking of a legal agreement that had been sealed by the signing of a written, legal contractual document.

Bribery The offering, giving, receiving, or soliciting of something of value for the purpose of influencing the action of an official in the discharge of his or her public or legal duties.

Brief A summary of the important points of a longer document. An abstract of a published judicial opinion prepared by a law student as part of an assignment in the case method study of law. A written document drawn up by an attorney for a party in a lawsuit or by a party appearing pro se that concisely states the (1) issues of a lawsuit; (2) facts that bring the parties to court; (3) relevant laws that can affect the subject of the dispute; and (4) arguments that explain how the law applies to the particular facts so that the case will be decided in the party's favor.

Broker An individual or firm employed by others to plan and organize sales or negotiate contracts for a commission.

Burden of proof The duty of a party to prove an asserted fact. The party is subject to the burden of persuasion—convincing a judge or jury—and the burden of going forward—proving wrong any evidence that damages the position of the party. In criminal cases the persuasion burden must include proof beyond a reasonable doubt.

Burglary The criminal offense of breaking and entering a building illegally for the purpose of committing a crime therein.

Bylaws The rules and regulations enacted by an association or a corporation to provide a framework for its operation and management.

C

Capacity The ability, capability, or fitness to do something; a legal right, power, or competency to perform some act. An ability to comprehend both the nature and consequences of one's acts.

Capital punishment The lawful infliction of death as a punishment; the death penalty.

Case law Legal principles enunciated and embodied in judicial decisions that are derived from the application of particular areas of law to the facts of individual cases.

Cause Each separate antecedent of an event. Something that precedes and brings about an effect or a result. A reason for an action or condition. A ground of a legal action. An agent that brings something about. That which in some manner is accountable for a condition that brings about an effect or that produces a cause for the resultant action or state.

A suit, litigation, or action. Any question, civil or criminal, litigated or contested before a court of justice.

Cause in fact The direct cause of an event. Commonly referred to as the "but for" rule, by which an event could not have happened but for the specified cause.

Cause of action The fact or combination of facts that gives a person the right to seek judicial redress or relief against another. Also, the legal theory forming the basis of a lawsuit.

Caveat emptor [*Latin, Let the buyer beware.*] A warning that notifies a buyer that the goods he or she is buying are "as is," subject to all defects.

Cease and desist order An order issued by an administrative agency or a court proscribing a person or a business entity from continuing a particular course of conduct.

Censorship The suppression or proscription of speech or writing that is deemed obscene, indecent, or unduly controversial.

Certiorari [*Latin, To be informed of.*] At common law, an original writ or order issued by the Chancery or King's Bench, commanding officers of inferior courts to submit the record of a cause pending before them to give the party more certain and speedy justice.

A writ that a superior appellate court issues on its discretion to an inferior court, ordering it to produce a certified record of a particular case it has tried, in order to determine whether any irregularities or errors occurred that justify review of the case.

A device by which the Supreme Court of the United States exercises its discretion in selecting the cases it will review.

Challenge for cause Request from a party that a prospective juror be disqualified for given causes or reasons.

Change of venue The removal of a lawsuit from one county or district to another for trial, often permitted in criminal cases where the court finds that the defendant would not receive a fair trial in the first location because of adverse publicity.

Charter A grant from the government of ownership rights in land to a person, a group of people, or an organization, such as a corporation.

A basic document of law of a municipal corporation granted by the state, defining its rights, liabilities, and responsibilities of self-government.

A document embodying a grant of authority from the legislature or the authority itself, such as a corporate charter.

The leasing of a mode of transportation, such as a bus, ship, or plane. A *charter-party* is a contract formed to lease a ship to a merchant in order to facilitate the conveyance of goods.

Chattel An item of personal property that is movable; it may be animate or inanimate.

Circumstantial evidence Information and testimony presented by a party in a civil or criminal action that permit conclusions that indirectly establish the existence or nonexistence of a fact or event that the party seeks to prove.

Citation A paper commonly used in various courts—such as a probate, matrimonial, or traffic court—that is served upon an individual to notify him or her that he or she is required to appear at a specific time and place.

Reference to a legal authority—such as a case, constitution, or treatise—where particular information may be found.

Citizens Those who, under the Constitution and laws of the United States, or of a particular community or of a foreign country, owe allegiance and are entitled to the enjoyment of all civil rights that accrue to those who qualify for that status.

Civil action A lawsuit brought to enforce, redress, or protect rights of private litigants (the plaintiffs and the defendants); not a criminal proceeding.

Civil death The forfeiture of rights and privileges of an individual who has been convicted of a serious crime.

Civil law Legal system derived from the Roman *Corpus Juris Civilis* of Emperor Justinian I; differs from a common-law system, which relies on prior decisions to determine the outcome of a lawsuit. Most European and South American countries have a civil law system. England and most of the countries it dominated or colonized, including Canada and the United States, have a common-law system. However, within these countries, Louisiana, Quebec, and Puerto Rico exhibit the influence of French and Spanish settlers in their use of civil law systems.

A body of rules that delineate private rights and remedies and govern disputes between individuals in such areas as contracts, property, and family law; distinct from criminal or public law.

Civil liberties Freedom of speech, freedom of press, freedom from discrimination, and other natural rights guaranteed and protected by the Constitution, which were intended to place limits on government.

Civil rights Personal liberties that belong to an individual owing to his or her status as a citizen or resident of a particular country or community.

Class action A lawsuit that allows a large number of people with a common interest in a matter to sue or be sued as a group.

Clause A section, phrase, paragraph, or segment of a legal document, such as a contract, deed, will, or constitution, that relates to a particular point.

Closing The final transaction between a buyer and seller of real property.

Closing argument The final factual and legal argument made by each attorney on all sides of a case in a trial prior to a verdict or judgment.

Code A systematic and comprehensive compilation of laws, rules, or regulations that are consolidated and classified according to subject matter.

Coercion The intimidation of a victim to compel the individual to do some act against his or her will by the use of psychological pressure, physical force, or threats. The crime of intentionally and unlawfully restraining another's freedom by threatening to commit a crime, accusing the victim of a crime, disclosing any secret that would seriously impair the victim's reputation in the community, or by performing or refusing to perform an official action lawfully requested by the victim, or by causing an official to do so.

A defense asserted in a criminal prosecution that a person who committed a crime did not do so of his or her own free will, but only because the individual was compelled by another through the use of physical force or threat of immediate serious bodily injury or death.

Cohabitation A living arrangement in which an unmarried couple live together in a long-term relationship that resembles a marriage.

Cohabitation agreement The contract concerning property and financial agreements between two individuals who intend to live together and to have sexual relations out of wedlock.

Collateral Related; indirect; not bearing immediately upon an issue. The property pledged or given as a security interest, or a guarantee for payment of a debt, that will be taken or kept by the creditor in case of a default on the original debt.

Collective bargaining agreement The contractual agreement between an employer and a labor union that governs wages, hours, and working conditions for employees which can be enforced against both the employer and the union for failure to comply with its terms.

Comity Courtesy; respect; a disposition to perform some official act out of goodwill and tradition rather than obligation or law. The acceptance or adoption of decisions or laws by a court of another jurisdiction, either foreign or domestic, based on public policy rather than legal mandate.

Commerce Clause The provision of the U.S. Constitution that gives Congress exclusive power over trade activities between the states and with foreign countries and Native American tribes.

Commercial paper A written instrument or document such as a check, draft, promissory note, or a certificate of deposit, that manifests the pledge or duty of one individual to pay money to another.

Commercial speech Advertising speech by commercial companies and service providers. Commercial speech is protected under the First Amendment as long as it is not false or misleading.

Common law The ancient law of England based upon societal customs and recognized and enforced by the judgments and decrees of the courts. The general body of statutes and case law that governed England and the American colonies prior to the American Revolution.

The principles and rules of action, embodied in case law rather than legislative enactments, applicable to the government and protection of persons and property that derive their authority from the community customs and traditions that evolved over the centuries as interpreted by judicial tribunals.

A designation used to denote the opposite of statutory, equitable, or civil; for example, a common-law action.

Common-law marriage A union of two people not formalized in the customary manner as prescribed by law but created by an agreement to marry followed by cohabitation.

Community property The holdings and resources owned in common by a husband and wife.

Commutation Modification, exchange, or substitution.

Comparable worth The idea that men and women should receive equal pay when they perform work that involves comparable skills and responsibility or that is of comparable worth to the employer; also known as pay equity.

Comparative negligence The measurement of fault in percentages by both parties to a negligence action, so that the award of damages is reduced proportionately to the amount of negligence attributed to the victim. In order to recover, the negligence of the victim must be less than that of the defendant.

Compelling state interest A basis of upholding a state statute, against constitutional challenges grounded on the First and Fourteenth Amendments, due to the important or "compelling" need for such state regulations. Often state laws implemented under a state's police power are deemed to have satisfied a compelling state interest and therefore will survive judicial scrutiny.

Compensatory damages A sum of money awarded in a civil action by a court to indemnify a person for the particular loss, detriment, or injury suffered as a result of the unlawful conduct of another.

Complaint The pleading that initiates a civil action; in criminal law, the document that sets forth the basis upon which a person is to be charged with an offense.

Conclusive presumption The presumption that a fact is true upon proof of another fact. Evidence to the contrary cannot refute the presumed fact. Proof of a basic fact creates the existence of the presumed fact, and that presumed fact becomes irrebuttable.

Concurrent jurisdiction The authority of several different courts, each of which is authorized to entertain and decide cases dealing with the same subject matter.

Concurrent powers The ability of Congress and state legislatures to independently make laws on the same subject matter.

Concurrent resolution An action of Congress passed in the form of an enactment of one house, with the other house in agreement, which expresses the ideas of Congress on a particular subject.

Concurring opinion An opinion by one or more judges that provides separate reasoning for reaching the same decision as the majority of the court.

Conditional Subject to change; dependent upon or granted based on the occurrence of a future, uncertain event.

Conditional acceptance A counter offer. Acceptance of an offer that differs in some respects from the original contract.

Condition precedent A stipulation in an agreement that must be performed before the contract can go into effect and become binding on the parties. In terms of estates, the condition must be performed before the estates can vest or be enlarged.

Condition subsequent A stipulation in a contract that discharges one party of any further liability or performance under an existing contract if the other party fails to satisfy the stipulation.

Confession A statement made by an individual that acknowledges his or her guilt in the commission of a crime.

Conflict of interest A term used to describe the situation in which a public official or fiduciary who, contrary to the obligation and absolute duty to act for the benefit of the public or a designated individual, exploits the relationship for personal benefit, typically pecuniary.

Consent Voluntary acquiescence to the proposal of another; the act or result of reaching an accord; a concurrence of minds; actual willingness that an act or an infringement of an interest shall occur.

Consent decree An agreement by the defendant to cease activities, alleged by the government to be unlawful, in exchange for the dismissal of the case. The court must approve the agreement before it issues the consent decree.

Consideration Something of value given by both parties to a contract that induces them to enter into the agreement to exchange mutual performances.

Consolidation The process of combining two or more parts together to make a whole.

Consolidation of corporations The formation of a new corporate entity through the dissolution of two or more existing corporations. The new entity takes over the assets and assumes the liabilities of the dissolved corporations.

Conspiracy An agreement between two or more persons to engage jointly in an unlawful or criminal act, or an act that is innocent in itself but becomes unlawful when done by the combination of actors.

Constituent An individual, a principal, who appoints another to act in his or her behalf, an agent, such as an attorney in a court of law or an elected official in government.

Constitution of the United States A written document executed by representatives of the people of the United States as the absolute rule of action and decision for all branches and officers of the government, and with which all subsequent laws and ordinances must be in accordance unless it has been changed by a constitutional amendment by the authority that created it.

Consumer An individual who purchases and uses products and services in contradistinction to manufacturers who produce the goods or services and wholesalers or retailers who distribute and sell them. A member of the general category of persons who are protected by state and federal laws regulating price policies, financing practices, quality of goods and services, credit reporting, debt collection, and other trade practices of U.S. commerce. A purchaser of a product or service who has a legal right to enforce any implied or express warranties pertaining to the item against the manufacturer who has introduced the goods or services into the marketplace or the seller who has made them a term of the sale.

Contempt An act of deliberate disobedience or disregard for the laws, regulations, or decorum of a public authority, such as a court or legislative body.

Content neutral The principle that the government may not show favoritism between differing points of view on a particular subject.

Contingent fee Payment to an attorney for legal services that depends, or is contingent, upon there being some recovery or award in the case. The payment is then a percentage of the amount recovered—such as 25 percent if the matter is settled, 30 percent if it proceeds to trial.

Continuance The adjournment or postponement of an action pending in a court to a later date of the same or another session of the court, granted by a court in response to a motion made by a party to a lawsuit. The entry into the trial record of the adjournment of a case for the purpose of formally evidencing it.

Contraband Any property that is illegal to produce or possess. Smuggled goods that are imported into or exported from a country in violation of its laws.

Contract implied in fact *See* Implied contract.

Contracts Agreements between two or more persons that create an obligation to do, or refrain from doing, a particular thing.

Contributing to delinquency A criminal offense arising from an act or omission that leads to juvenile delinquency.

Contributory negligence Negligence on the part of the plaintiff for failure to exercise reasonable care for his or her own safety, and which contributes to the negligence of the defendant as the actual cause of the plaintiff's injury.

Conversion Any unauthorized act that deprives an owner of personal property without his or her consent.

Copyright An intangible right granted by statute to the author or originator of certain literary or artistic productions, whereby, for a limited period, the exclusive privilege is given to the person to make copies of the same for publication and sale.

Corporations Artificial entities that are created by state statute, and that are treated much like individuals under the law, having legally enforceable rights, the ability to acquire debt and pay out profits, the ability to hold and transfer property, the ability to enter into contracts, the requirement to pay taxes, and the ability to sue and be sued.

Cosigner An obligor—a person who becomes obligated, under a commercial paper, such as a promissory note or check—by signing the instrument in conjunction with the original obligor, thereby promising to pay it in full.

Counsel An attorney or lawyer. The rendition of advice and guidance concerning a legal matter, contemplated form of argument, claim, or action.

Counterclaim A claim by a defendant opposing the claim of the plaintiff and seeking some relief from the plaintiff for the defendant.

Counteroffer In contract law, a proposal made in response to an original offer modifying its terms, but which has the legal effect of rejecting it.

Court below The court from which a case was removed for review by an appellate court.

Court of appeal An intermediate federal judicial tribunal of review that is found in thirteen judicial districts, called circuits, in the United States.

A state judicial tribunal that reviews a decision rendered by an inferior tribunal to determine whether it made errors that warrant the reversal of its judgment.

Court of claims A state judicial tribunal established as the forum in which to bring certain types of lawsuits against the state or its political subdivisions, such as a county. The former designation given to a federal tribunal created in 1855 by Congress with original jurisdiction—initial authority—to decide an action brought against the United States that is based upon the Constitution, federal law, any regulation of the executive department, or any express or implied contracts with the federal government.

Court of equity A court that presides over equity suits, suits of fairness and justness, both in its administration and proceedings. Courts of equity no longer exist due to the consolidation of law and equity actions in federal and state courts.

Court of general jurisdiction A superior court, which by its constitution, can review and exercise a final judgment in a case under its authority. No further judicial inspection is conducted, except by an appellate power.

Covenant An agreement, contract, or written promise between two individuals that frequently constitutes a pledge to do or refrain from doing something.

Credit A term used in accounting to describe either an entry on the right-hand side of an account or the process of making such an entry. A credit records the increases in liabilities, owner's equity, and revenues as well as the decreases in assets and expenses.

A sum in taxation that is subtracted from the computed tax, as opposed to a deduction that is ordinarily subtracted from gross income to determine adjusted gross income or taxable income. Claim for a particular sum of money.

The ability of an individual or a company to borrow money or procure goods on time, as a result of a positive opinion by the particular lender concerning such borrower's solvency and reliability. The right granted by a creditor to a debtor to delay satisfaction of a debt, or to incur a debt and defer the payment thereof.

Creditor An individual to whom an obligation is owed because he or she has given something of value in exchange. One who may legally demand and receive money, either through the fulfillment of a contract or due to injury sustained as a result of another's negligence or intentionally wrongful act. The term *creditor* is also used to describe an individual who is engaged in the business of lending money or selling items for which immediate payment is not demanded but an obligation of repayment exists as of a future date.

Criminal law A body of rules and statutes that defines conduct prohibited by the government because it threatens and harms public safety and welfare and that establishes punishment to be imposed for the commission of such acts.

Cross-examination The questioning of a witness or party during a trial, hearing, or deposition by the party opposing the one who asked the person to testify in order to evaluate the truth of that person's testimony, to develop the testimony further, or to accomplish any other objective. The interrogation of a witness or party by the party opposed to the one who called the witness or party, upon a subject raised during direct examination—the initial questioning of a witness or party—on the merits of that testimony.

Cruel and unusual punishment Such punishment as would amount to torture or barbarity, any cruel and degrading punishment not known to the common law, or any fine, penalty, confinement, or treatment so dispro-portionate to the offense as to shock the moral sense of the community.

Custodial parent The parent to whom the guardianship of the children in a divorced or estranged relationship has been granted by the court.

D

Damages Monetary compensation that is awarded by a court in a civil action to an individual who has been injured through the wrongful conduct of another party.

Death penalty *See* Capital punishment.

Debtor One who owes a debt or the performance of an obligation to another, who is called the creditor; one who may be compelled to pay a claim or demand; anyone liable in a claim, whether due or to become due.

In bankruptcy law, a person who files a voluntary petition or person against whom an involuntary petition is filed. A person or municipality concerning which a bankruptcy case has been commenced.

Declaration of rights *See* Bill of rights.

Decree A judgment of a court that announces the legal consequences of the facts found in a case and orders that the court's decision be carried out. A decree in equity is a sentence or order of the court, pronounced on hearing and understanding all the points in issue, and determining the rights of all the parties to the suit, according to equity and good conscience. It is a declaration of the court announcing the legal consequences of the facts found. With the procedural merger of law and equity in the federal and most state courts under the Rules of Civil Procedure, the term *judgment* has generally replaced *decree*.

Decriminalization The passing of legislation that changes criminal acts or omissions into noncriminal ones without punitive sanctions.

Deed A written instrument, which has been signed and delivered, by which one individual, the grantor, conveys title to real property to another individual, the grantee; a conveyance of land, tenements, or hereditaments, from one individual to another.

De facto [*Latin*, In fact.] In fact; in deed; actually.

Defamation Any intentional false communication, either written or spoken, that harms a person's reputation; decreases the respect, regard, or confidence in which a person is held; or induces disparaging, hostile, or disagreeable opinions or feelings against a person.

Defendant The person defending or denying; the party against whom relief or recovery is sought in an action or suit, or the accused in a criminal case.

Defense The forcible repulsion of an unlawful and violent attack, such as the defense of one's person, property, or country in time of war.

The totality of the facts, law, and contentions presented by the party against whom a civil action or criminal prosecution is instituted in order to defeat or diminish the plaintiff's cause of action or the prosecutor's case. A reply to the claims of the other party, which asserts reasons why the claims should be disallowed. The defense may involve an absolute denial of the other party's factual allegations or may entail an affirmative defense, which sets forth completely new factual allegations. Pursuant to the rules of federal civil procedure, numerous defenses may be asserted by motion as well as by answer, while other defenses must be pleaded affirmatively.

De jure [*Latin,* In law.] Legitimate; lawful, as a matter of law. Having complied with all the requirements imposed by law.

Delegation of powers Transfer of authority by one branch of government in which such authority is vested to some other branch or administrative agency.

Deliberate Willful; purposeful; determined after thoughtful evaluation of all relevant factors; dispassionate. To act with a particular intent, which is derived from a careful consideration of factors that influence the choice to be made.

Delinquent An individual who fails to fulfill an obligation, or otherwise is guilty of a crime or offense.

Domestic partnership laws Legislation and regulations related to the legal recognition of non-marital relationships between persons who are romantically involved with each other, have set up a joint residence, and have registered with cities recognizing said relationships.

Demurrer An assertion by the defendant that although the facts alleged by the plaintiff in the complaint may be true, they do not entitle the plaintiff to prevail in the lawsuit.

Denaturalization The deprivation of an individual's rights as a citizen.

Deportation Banishment to a foreign country, attended with confiscation of property and deprivation of civil rights.

The transfer of an alien, by exclusion or expulsion, from the United States to a foreign country. The removal or sending back of an alien to the country from which he or she came because his or her presence is deemed inconsistent with the public welfare, and without any punishment being imposed or contemplated. The grounds for deportation are set forth at 8 U.S.C.A., sec. 1251, and the procedures are provided for in secs. 1252–1254.

Deposition The testimony of a party or witness in a civil or criminal proceeding taken before trial, usually in an attorney's office.

Desegregation Judicial mandate making illegal the practice of segregation.

Desertion The act by which a person abandons and forsakes, without justification, a condition of public, social, or family life, renouncing its responsibilities and evading its duties. A willful abandonment of an employment or duty in violation of a legal or moral obligation.

Criminal desertion is a husband's or wife's abandonment or willful failure without just cause to provide for the care, protection, or support of a spouse who is in ill health or impoverished circumstances.

Detention hearing A proceeding to determine the restraint to be imposed upon an individual awaiting trial, such as bail or, in the case of a juvenile, placement in a shelter.

Deterrent Anything that discourages or obstructs a person from committing an act, such as punishment for criminal acts.

Detriment Any loss or harm to a person or property; relinquishment of a legal right, benefit, or something of value.

Diplomatic immunity A principle of international law that provides foreign diplomats with protection from legal action in the country in which they work.

Directed verdict A procedural device whereby the decision in a case is taken out of the hands of the jury by the judge.

Direct examination The primary questioning of a witness during a trial that is conducted by the side for which that person is acting as a witness.

Direct tax A charge levied by the government upon property, which is determined by its financial worth.

Disaffirm Repudiate; revoke consent; refuse to support former acts or agreements.

Disbar To revoke an attorney's license to practice law.

Discharge To liberate or free; to terminate or extinguish. A discharge is the act or instrument by which a contract or agreement is ended. A mortgage is discharged if it has been carried out to the full extent originally contemplated or terminated prior to total execution.

Discharge also means to release, as from legal confinement in prison or the military service, or from some legal obligation such as jury duty, or the payment of debts by a person who is bankrupt. The document that indicates that an individual has been legally released from the military service is called a discharge.

Disclaimer The denial, refusal, or rejection of a right, power, or responsibility.

Discovery A category of procedural devices employed by a party to a civil or criminal action, prior to trial, to require the adverse party to disclose information that is essential for the preparation of the requesting party's case and that the other party alone knows or possesses.

Discretion Independent use of judgment to choose between right and wrong, to make a decision, or to act cautiously under the circumstances.

Discretion in decision making Discretion is the power or right to make official decisions using reason and judgment to choose from among acceptable alternatives.

Discrimination In constitutional law, the grant by statute of particular privileges to a class arbitrarily designated from a sizable number of persons, where no reasonable distinction exists between the favored and disfavored classes. Federal laws, supplemented by court decisions, prohibit discrimination in such areas as employment, housing, voting rights, education, and access to public facilities. They also proscribe discrimination on the basis of race, age, sex, nationality, disability, or religion. In addition, state and local laws can prohibit discrimination in these areas and in others not covered by federal laws.

Dishonor To refuse to accept or pay a draft or to pay a promissory note when duly presented. An instrument is dishonored when a necessary or optional presentment is made and due acceptance or payment is refused, or cannot be obtained within the prescribed time, or in case of bank collections, the instrument is seasonably returned by the midnight deadline; or presentment is excused and the instrument is not duly accepted or paid. Includes the insurer of a letter of credit refusing to pay or accept a draft or demand for payment.

As respects the flag, to deface or defile, imputing a lively sense of shaming or an equivalent acquiescent callousness.

Disinherit To cut off from an inheritance. To deprive someone, who would otherwise be an heir to property or another right, of his or her right to inherit.

Dismissal A discharge of an individual or corporation from employment. The disposition of a civil or criminal proceeding or a claim or charge made therein by a court order without a trial or prior to its completion which, in effect, is a denial of the relief sought by the commencement of the action.

Disposition Act of disposing; transferring to the care or possession of another. The parting with, alienation of, or giving up of property. The final settlement of a matter and, with reference to decisions announced by a court, a judge's ruling is commonly referred to as disposition, regardless of level of resolution. In criminal procedure, the sentencing or other final settlement of a criminal case. With respect to a mental state, denotes an attitude, prevailing tendency, or inclination.

Disposition hearing The judicial proceeding for passing sentence upon a defendant who was found guilty of the charge(s) against him or her.

Dispossession The wrongful, nonconsensual ouster or removal of a person from his or her property by trick, compulsion, or misuse of the law, whereby the violator obtains actual occupation of the land.

Dissent An explicit disagreement by one or more judges with the decision of the majority on a case before them.

Dissolution Act or process of dissolving; termination; winding up. In this sense it is frequently used in the phrase *dissolution of a partnership*.

Division of powers *See* Separation of powers.

Divorce A court decree that terminates a marriage; also known as marital dissolution.

Domicile The legal residence of a person, which determines jurisdiction for taxation and voting, as well as other legal rights and privileges. Considered to be the permanent residence of an individual, or the place where one intends to return after an absence, such as in the case of the president who physically lives in the White House, but has a domicile in his or her home state.

Double indemnity A term of an insurance policy by which the insurance company promises to pay the insured or the beneficiary twice the amount of coverage if loss occurs due to a particular cause or set of circumstances.

Double jeopardy A second prosecution for the same offense after acquittal or conviction or multiple punishments for the same offense. The evil sought to be avoided by prohibiting double jeopardy is double trial and double conviction, not necessarily double punishment.

Draft A written order by the first party, called the drawer, instructing a second party, called the drawee (such as a bank), to pay money to a third party, called the payee. An order to pay a certain sum in money, signed by a drawer, payable on demand or at a definite time, to order or bearer.

A tentative, provisional, or preparatory writing out of any document (as a will, contract, lease, and so on) for purposes of discussion and correction, which is afterward to be prepared in its final form.

Compulsory conscription of persons into military service.

A small arbitrary deduction or allowance made to a merchant or importer, in the case of goods sold by weight or taxable by weight, to cover possible loss of weight in handling or from differences in scales.

Due process of law A fundamental, constitutional guarantee that all legal proceedings will be fair and that one will be given notice of the proceedings and an opportunity to be heard before the government acts to take away one's life, liberty, or property. Also, a constitutional guarantee that a law shall not be unreasonable, arbitrary, or capricious.

Duress Unlawful pressure exerted upon a person to coerce that person to perform an act that he or she ordinarily would not perform.

Duty A legal obligation that entails mandatory conduct or performance. With respect to the laws relating to customs duties, a tax owed to the government for the import or export of goods.

E

Easement A right of use over the property of another. Traditionally the permitted kinds of uses were limited, the most important being rights of way and rights concerning flowing waters. The easement was normally for the benefit of adjoining lands, no matter who the owner was (an easement appurtenant), rather than for the benefit of a specific individual (easement in gross).

Emancipation The act or process by which a person is liberated from the authority and control of another person.

Embezzlement The fraudulent appropriation of another's property by a person who is in a position of trust, such as an agent or employee.

Eminent domain The power to take private property for public use by a state, municipality, or private person or corporation authorized to exercise functions of public character, following the payment of just compensation to the owner of that property.

Employment at will A common-law rule that an employment contract of indefinite duration can be terminated by either the employer or the employee at any time, for any reason; also known as terminable at will.

Encumbrance A burden, obstruction, or impediment on property that lessens its value or makes it less mar-

ketable. An encumbrance (also spelled incumbrance) is any right or interest that exists in someone other than the owner of an estate and that restricts or impairs the transfer of the estate or lowers its value. This might include an easement, a lien, a mortgage, a mechanic's lien, or accrued and unpaid taxes.

Entitlement An individual's right to receive a value or benefit provided by law.

Entrapment The act of government agents or officials that induces a person to commit a crime he or she is not previously disposed to commit.

Enumerated powers Authority specifically granted to a body of the national government under the U.S. Constitution, such as the powers granted to Congress in Article I, Section 8.

Equal Pay Act Federal law which mandates the same pay for all persons who do the same work without regard to sex, age, race or ability. For work to be "equal" within meaning of the act, it is not necessary that the jobs be identical, but only that they be substantially equal.

Equal protection The constitutional guarantee that no person or class of persons shall be denied the same protection of the laws that is enjoyed by other persons or other classes in like circumstances in their lives, liberty, property, and pursuit of happiness.

Equitable Just; that which is fair and proper according to the principles of justice and right.

Equitable action A cause of action that seeks an equitable remedy, such as relief sought with an injunction.

Equity The pursuit of fairness. In the U.S. legal system, a body of laws that seeks to achieve fairness on an individual basis. In terms of property, the money value of property in excess of claims, liens, or mortgages on the property.

Error A mistake in a court proceeding concerning a matter of law or fact which might provide a ground for a review of the judgment rendered in the proceeding.

Escrow Something of value, such as a deed, stock, money, or written instrument, that is put into the custody of a third person by its owner, a grantor, an obligor, or a promisor, to be retained until the occurrence of a contingency or performance of a condition.

Espionage The act of securing information of a military or political nature that a competing nation holds secret. It can involve the analysis of diplomatic reports, publications, statistics, and broadcasts, as well as spying, a clandestine activity carried out by an individual or individuals working under a secret identity for the benefit of a nation's information gathering techniques. In the United States, the organization that heads most activities dedicated to espionage is the Central Intelligence Agency.

Establishment Clause The provision in the First Amendment which provides that there will be no laws created respecting the establishment of a religion, inhibiting the practice of a religion, or giving preference to any or all religions. It has been interpreted to also denounce the discouragement of any or all religions.

Estate The degree, quantity, nature, and extent of interest that a person has in real and personal property. An estate in lands, tenements, and hereditaments signifies such interest as the tenant has therein. *Estate* is commonly used in conveyances in connection with the words *right, title,* and *interest,* and is, to a great degree, synonymous with all of them.

When used in connection with probate proceedings, the term encompasses the total property of whatever kind that is owned by a decedent prior to the distribution of that property in accordance with the terms of a will, or when there is no will, by the laws of inheritance in the state of domicile of the decedent. It means, ordinarily, the whole of the property owned by anyone, the realty as well as the personalty.

In its broadest sense, the social, civic, or political condition or standing of a person; or a class of persons considered as grouped for social, civic, or political purposes.

Estate tax The tax levied upon the entire estate of the decedent before any part of the estate can be transferred to an heir. An estate tax is applied to the right of the deceased person to transfer property at death. An "inheritance tax" is imposed upon an heir's right to receive the property.

Estoppel A legal principle that precludes a party from denying or alleging a certain fact owing to that party's previous conduct, allegation, or denial.

Euthanasia The merciful act or practice of terminating the life of an individual or individuals inflicted with incurable and distressing diseases in a relatively painless manner.

Eviction The removal of a tenant from possession of premises in which he or she resides or has a property interest, done by a landlord either by reentry upon the premises or through a court action.

Excise tax A tax imposed on the performance of an act, the engaging in an occupation, or the enjoyment of a privilege. A tax on the manufacture, sale, or use of goods or on the carrying on of an occupation activity, or a tax on the transfer of property. In current usage the term has been

extended to include various license fees and practically every internal revenue tax except the income tax (i.e., federal alcohol and tobacco excise taxes).

Exclusionary rule The principle based on federal constitutional law that evidence illegally seized by law enforcement officers in violation of a suspect's right to be free from unreasonable searches and seizures cannot be used against the suspect in a criminal prosecution.

Exclusive jurisdiction The legal authority of a court or other tribunal to preside over a suit, an action, or a person to the exclusion of any other court.

Exclusive power The authority held solely by one individual, such as the President, or one group, such as a regulatory committee.

Exclusive right The privilege that only a grantee can exercise, prohibiting others from partaking in the same.

Executive agreement An agreement made between the head of a foreign country and the President of the United States. This agreement does not have to be submitted to the Senate for consent, and it supersedes any contradicting state law.

Executive orders Presidential policy directives that implement or interpret a federal statute, a constitutional provision, or a treaty.

Executor The individual named by a decedent to administer the provisions of the decedent's will.

Ex parte [*Latin, On one side only.*] Done by, for, or on the application of one party alone.

Expatriation The voluntary act of abandoning or renouncing one's country and becoming the citizen or subject of another.

Expert witness A witness, such as a psychological statistician or ballistics expert, who possesses special or superior knowledge concerning the subject of his or her testimony.

Ex post facto laws [*Latin, "After-the-fact" laws.*] Laws that provide for the infliction of punishment upon a person for some prior act that, at the time it was committed, was not illegal.

Express Clear; definite; explicit; plain; direct; unmistakable; not dubious or ambiguous. Declared in terms; set forth in words. Directly and distinctly stated. Made known distinctly and explicitly, and not left to inference. Manifested by direct and appropriate language, as distinguished from that which is inferred from conduct. The word is usually contrasted with *implied*.

Express contract An oral or written contract where the terms of the agreement are explicitly stated.

Expressed power *See* Enumerated powers.

Express warranty An additional written or oral guarantee to the underlying sales agreement made to the consumer as to the quality, description, or performance of a good.

Extortion The obtaining of property from another induced by wrongful use of actual or threatened force, violence, or fear, or under color of official right.

Extradition The transfer of an accused from one state or country to another state or country that seeks to place the accused on trial.

F

Family court A court that presides over cases involving: (1) child abuse and neglect; (2) support; (3) paternity; (4) termination of custody due to constant neglect; (5) juvenile delinquency; and (6) family offenses.

Federal circuit courts The 12 circuit courts making up the U.S. Federal Circuit Court System. The twelfth circuit presides over the District of Columbia. Decisions made by the federal district courts can be reviewed by the court of appeals in each circuit.

Federal district courts The first of three levels of the federal court system, which includes the U.S. Court of Appeals and the U.S. Supreme Court. If a participating party disagrees with the ruling of a federal district court in its case, it may petition for the case to be moved to the next level in the federal court system.

Felon An individual who commits a crime of a serious nature, such as burglary or murder. A person who commits a felony.

Felony A serious crime, characterized under federal law and many state statutes as any offense punishable by death or imprisonment in excess of one year.

Fiduciary An individual in whom another has placed the utmost trust and confidence to manage and protect property or money. The relationship wherein one person has an obligation to act for another's benefit.

First degree murder Murder committed with deliberately premeditated thought and malice, or with extreme atrocity or cruelty. The difference between first and second degree murder is the presence of the specific intention to kill.

Forbearance Refraining from doing something that one has a legal right to do. Giving of further time for repay-ment of an obligation or agreement; not to enforce a claim at its due date. A delay in enforcing a legal right. Act by which a creditor waits for payment of debt due by a debtor after it becomes due.

Within usury law, the contractual obligation of a lender or creditor to refrain, during a given period of time, from requiring the borrower or debtor to repay the loan or debt that is then due and payable.

Foreclosure A procedure by which the holder of a mortgage—an interest in land providing security for the performance of a duty or the payment of a debt—sells the property upon the failure of the debtor to pay the mortgage debt and, thereby, terminates his or her rights in the property.

Forgery The creation of a false written document or alteration of a genuine one, with the intent to defraud.

Formal contract An agreement between two or more individuals in which all the terms are in writing.

Franchise A special privilege to do certain things that is conferred by government on an individual or a corporation and which does not belong to citizens generally of common right (i.e., a right granted to offer cable television service).

A privilege granted or sold, such as to use a name or to sell products or services. In its simplest terms, a franchise is a license from the owner of a trademark or trade name permitting another to sell a product or service under that name or mark. More broadly stated, a franchise has evolved into an elaborate agreement under which the franchisee undertakes to conduct a business or sell a product or service in accordance with methods and procedures prescribed by the franchisor, and the franchisor undertakes to assist the franchisee through advertising, promotion, and other advisory services.

The right of suffrage; the right or privilege of voting in public elections. Such a right is guaranteed by the Fifteenth, Nineteenth, and Twenty-fourth Amendments to the U.S. Constitution.

As granted by a professional sports association, franchise is a privilege to field a team in a given geographic area under the auspices of the league that issues it. It is merely an incorporeal right.

Fraud A false representation of a matter of fact—whether by words or by conduct, by false or misleading allegations, or by concealment of what should have been disclosed—that deceives and is intended to deceive another so that the individual will act upon it to her or his legal injury.

Freedom of assembly *See* Freedom of association.

Freedom of association The right to associate with others for the purpose of engaging in constitutionally protected activities, such as to peacefully assemble.

Freedom of religion The First Amendment right to individually believe and to practice or exercise one's belief.

Freedom of speech The right, guaranteed by the First Amendment to the U.S. Constitution, to express beliefs and ideas without unwarranted government restriction.

Freedom of the press The right, guaranteed by the First Amendment to the U.S. Constitution, to gather, publish, and distribute information and ideas without government restriction; this right encompasses freedom from prior restraints on publication and freedom from censorship.

Full Faith and Credit Clause The clause of the U.S. Constitution that provides that the various states must recognize legislative acts, public records, and judicial decisions of the other states within the United States.

Full warranty The guarantee on the workmanship and materials of a product. If the product is defective in any way, then the consumer is entitled to corrective action from the manufacturer, at no cost to the consumer, and within a reasonable amount of time.

Fundamental rights Rights which derive, or are implied, from the terms of the U.S. Constitution, such as the Bill of Rights, the first ten amendments to the Constitution.

G

Gag rule A rule, regulation, or law that prohibits debate or discussion of a particular issue.

Garnishment A legal procedure by which a creditor can collect what a debtor owes by reaching the debtor's property when it is in the hands of someone other than the debtor.

General partnership A business relationship with more than one owner where all parties manage the business and equally share any profits or losses.

Gerrymander The process of dividing a particular state or territory into election districts in such a manner as to accomplish an unlawful purpose, such as to give one party a greater advantage.

Good faith Honesty; a sincere intention to deal fairly with others.

Grandfather clause A portion of a statute that provides that the law is not applicable in certain circumstances due to preexisting facts.

Grand jury A panel of citizens that is convened by a court to decide whether it is appropriate for the government to indict (proceed with a prosecution against) someone suspected of a crime.

Grand larceny A category of larceny—the offense of illegally taking the property of another—in which the value of the property taken is greater than that set for petit larceny.

Grounds The basis or foundation; reasons sufficient in law to justify relief.

Guarantee One to whom a guaranty is made. This word is also used, as a noun, to denote the contract of guaranty or the obligation of a guarantor, and, as a verb, to denote the action of assuming the responsibilities of a guarantor.

Guaranty As a verb, to agree to be responsible for the payment of another's debt or the performance of another's duty, liability, or obligation if that person does not perform as he or she is legally obligated to do; to assume the responsibility of a guarantor; to warrant.

As a noun, an undertaking or promise that is collateral to the primary or principal obligation and that binds the guarantor to performance in the event of nonperformance by the principal obligor.

Guardian A person lawfully invested with the power, and charged with the obligation, of taking care of and managing the property and rights of a person who, because of age, understanding, or self-control, is considered incapable of administering his or her own affairs.

Guardian ad litem A guardian appointed by the court to represent the interests of infants, the unborn, or incompetent persons in legal actions.

H

Habeas corpus [*Latin, You have the body.*] A writ (court order) that commands an individual or a government official who has restrained another to produce the prisoner at a designated time and place so that the court can determine the legality of custody and decide whether to order the prisoner's release.

Hate crime A crime motivated by race, religion, gender, sexual orientation, or other prejudice.

Hearing A legal proceeding where issues of law or fact are tried and evidence is presented to help determine the issue.

Hearsay A statement made out of court that is offered in court as evidence to prove the truth of the matter asserted.

Heir An individual who receives an interest in, or ownership of, land, tenements, or hereditaments from an ancestor who had died intestate, through the laws of descent and distribution. At common law, an heir was the individual appointed by law to succeed to the estate of an ancestor who died without a will. It is commonly used today in reference to any individual who succeeds to property, either by will or law.

Homicide The killing of one human being by another human being.

Hung jury A trial jury duly selected to make a decision in a criminal case regarding a defendant's guilt or innocence, but who are unable to reach a verdict due to a complete division in opinion.

I

Immunity Exemption from performing duties that the law generally requires other citizens to perform, or from a penalty or burden that the law generally places on other citizens.

Impeachment A process used to charge, try, and remove public officials for misconduct while in office.

Implied consent Consent that is inferred from signs, actions, or facts, or by inaction or silence.

Implied contract A contract created not by express agreement, but inferred by law, based on the conduct of the parties and the events surrounding the parties' dealings.

Implied power Authority that exists so that an expressly granted power can be carried into effect.

Implied warranty A promise, arising by operation of law, that something that is sold will be merchantable and fit for the purpose for which it is sold.

Imprimatur [*Latin, Let it be printed.*] A licence or allowance, granted by the constituted authorities, giving permission to print and publish a book. This allowance was formerly necessary in England before any book could lawfully be printed, and in some other countries is still required.

Inalienable Not subject to sale or transfer; inseparable.

Inalienable rights Rights (i.e., life, liberty, and the pursuit of happiness) which cannot be ceded or transferred without permission from the individual who possesses them.

Incapacity The absence of legal ability, competence, or qualifications.

Income tax A charge imposed by government on the annual gains of a person, corporation, or other taxable unit derived through work, business pursuits, investments, property dealings, and other sources determined in accordance with the Internal Revenue Code or state law.

Incorporate To formally create a corporation pursuant to the requirements prescribed by state statute; to confer a corporate franchise upon certain individuals.

Indemnity Recompense for loss, damage, or injuries; restitution or reimbursement.

Indeterminate That which is uncertain or not particularly designated.

Indictment A written accusation charging that an individual named therein has committed an act or admitted to doing something that is punishable by law.

Indirect tax A tax upon some right, privilege, or corporate franchise.

Individual rights Rights and privileges constitutionally guaranteed to the people, as set forth by the Bill of Rights, the ability of a person to pursue life, liberty, and property.

Infants Persons who are under the age of the legal majority—at common law, 21 years, now generally 18 years. According to the sense in which this term is used, it may denote the age of the person, the contractual disabilities that nonage entails, or his or her status with regard to other powers or relations.

Information The formal accusation of a criminal offense made by a public official; the sworn, written accusation of a crime.

Inherent Derived from the essential nature of, and inseparable from, the object itself.

Inherent powers Implicit control, which by nature cannot be derived from another.

Inherent rights Rights held within a person because he or she exists. *See also* inalienable rights.

Inheritance Property received from a decedent, either by will or through state laws of intestate succession, where the decedent has failed to execute a valid will.

Inheritance tax A tax imposed upon the right of an individual to receive property left to him or her by a decedent.

Injunction A court order by which an individual is required to perform or is restrained from performing a particular act. A writ framed according to the circumstances of the individual case.

In loco parentis [*Latin, In the place of a parent.*] The legal doctrine under which an individual assumes parental rights, duties, and obligations without going through the formalities of legal adoption.

Inquisitorial system A method of legal practice in which the judge endeavors to discover facts while simultaneously representing the interests of the state in a trial.

Insanity defense A defense asserted by an accused in a criminal prosecution to avoid liability for the commission of a crime because, at the time of the crime, the person did not appreciate the nature or quality or wrongfulness of the act.

Insider In the context of federal regulation of the purchase and sale of securities, anyone who has knowledge of facts not available to the general public.

Insider trading The trading of stocks and bonds based on information gained from special private, privileged information affecting the value of the stocks and bonds.

Insurance A contract whereby, for a specified consideration, one party undertakes to compensate the other for a loss relating to a particular subject as a result of the occurrence of designated hazards.

Intangibles Property that is a "right," such as a patent, copyright, trademark, etc., or one that is lacking physical existence, like good will. A nonphysical, noncurrent asset that exists only in connection with something else, such as the good will of a business.

Intent A determination to perform a particular act or to act in a particular manner for a specific reason; an aim or design; a resolution to use a certain means to reach an end.

Intermediate courts Courts with general ability or authority to hear a case (trial, appellate, or both), but are not the court of last resort within the jurisdiction.

Intestate The description of a person who dies without making a valid will or the reference made to this condition.

Involuntary manslaughter The act of unlawfully killing another human being unintentionally.

Irrevocable Unable to cancel or recall; that which is unalterable or irreversible.

Item veto *See* Line item veto.

J

Joint committee Members of two houses of a state or federal legislature that work together as one group.

Joint resolution A type of measure that Congress may consider and act upon; the other types of measures being bills, concurrent resolutions, and simple resolutions, in addition to treaties in the Senate.

Judicial discretion Sound judgment exercised by a judge in determining what is right and equitable under the law.

Judicial review A court's authority to examine an executive or legislative act and to invalidate that act if it is contrary to constitutional principles.

Jurisdiction The geographic area over which authority extends; legal authority; the authority to hear and determine causes of action.

Jurisprudence From the Latin term *juris prudentia,* which means "the study, knowledge, or science of law;" in the United States, more broadly associated with the philosophy of law.

Jury In trials, a group of people selected and sworn to inquire into matters of fact and to reach a verdict on the basis of evidence presented to it.

Jury nullification The ability of a jury to acquit the defendant despite the amount of evidence against him or her in a criminal case.

Jus sanguinis The determination of a person's citizenship based upon the citizenship of the individual's parents.

Jus soli The determination of a person's citizenship based upon the individual's place of birth.

Just cause A reasonable and lawful ground for action.

Justifiable homicide The killing of another in self-defense or in the lawful defense of one's property; killing of another when the law demands it, such as in execution for a capital crime.

Juvenile A young individual who has not reached the age whereby he or she would be treated as an adult in the area of criminal law. The age at which the young person attains the status of being a legal majority varies from state to state—as low as 14 years old, as high as 18 years old; however, the Juvenile Delinquency Act determines that a youthful person under the age of eighteen is a "juvenile" in cases involving federal jurisdiction.

Juvenile court The court presiding over cases in which young persons under a certain age, depending on the area of jurisdiction, are accused of criminal acts.

Juvenile delinquency The participation of a youthful individual, one who falls under the age at which he or she could be tried as an adult, in illegal behavior. *See also* Delinquent child.

L

Landlord A lessor of real property; the owner or possessor of an estate in land or a rental property, who, in an exchange for rent, leases it to another individual known as the tenant.

Lapse The termination or failure of a right or privilege because of a neglect to exercise that right or to perform some duty within a time limit, or because a specified contingency did not occur. The expiration of coverage under an insurance policy because of the insured's failure to pay the premium.

The common-law principle that a gift in a will does not take effect but passes into the estate remaining after the payment of debts and particular gifts, if the beneficiary is alive when the will is executed but subsequently predeceases the testator.

Larceny The unauthorized taking and removal of the personal property of another by a person who intends to permanently deprive the owner of it; a crime against the right of possession.

Lease A contractual agreement by which one party conveys an estate in property to another party, for a limited period, subject to various conditions, in exchange for something of value, but still retains ownership.

Legal defense A complete and acceptable response as to why the claims of the plaintiff should not be granted in a point of law.

Legal tender All U.S. coins and currencies—regardless of when coined or issued—including (in terms of the Federal Reserve System) Federal Reserve notes and circulating notes of Federal Reserve banks and national banking associations that are used for all debts, public and private, public charges, taxes, duties, and dues.

Legation The persons commissioned by one government to exercise diplomatic functions at the court of another, including the ministers, secretaries, attachés, and interpreters, are collectively called the *legation* of their government. The word also denotes the official residence of a foreign minister.

Legislation Lawmaking; the preparation and enactment of laws by a legislative body.

Legislative intent The history of events leading to the enactment of a law that a court refers to when interpreting an ambiguous or inconsistent statute.

Liability A comprehensive legal term that describes the condition of being actually or potentially subject to a legal obligation.

Libel and slander Two torts that involve the communication of false information about a person, a group, or an entity, such as a corporation. Libel is any defama-

tion that can be seen, such a writing, printing, effigy, movie, or statue. Slander is any defamation that is spoken and heard.

Lien A right given to another by the owner of property to secure a debt, or one created by law in favor of certain creditors.

Limited liability partnership A form of general partnership that provides an individual partner protection against personal liability for certain partnership obligations.

Limited warranty A written performance guarantee that only covers workmanship or materials for a specified period of time.

Line item veto The power that governors in some states have to strike individual items from appropriation bills without affecting any other provisions.

Litigation An action brought in court to enforce a particular right. The act or process of bringing a lawsuit in and of itself; a judicial contest; any dispute.

Living will A written document that allows a patient to give explicit instructions about medical treatment to be administered when the patient is terminally ill or permanently unconscious; also called an advance directive.

Loan shark A person who lends money in exchange for its repayment at an interest rate that exceeds the percentage approved by law and who uses intimidating methods or threats of force in order to obtain repayment.

Lobbying The process of influencing public and government policy at all levels: federal, state, and local.

Lower court The court where a suit was first heard. *See also* Court below.

M

Magistrate Any individual who has the power of a public civil officer or inferior judicial officer, such as a justice of the peace.

Majority Full age; legal age; age at which a person is no longer a minor. The age at which, by law, a person is capable of being legally responsible for all of his or her acts (i.e., contractual obligations), and is entitled to the management of his or her own affairs and to the enjoyment of civic rights (i.e., right to vote). The opposite of minority. Also the *status* of a person who is a major in age.

The greater number. The number greater than half of any total.

Malfeasance The commission of an act that is unequivocally illegal or completely wrongful.

Malice The intentional commission of a wrongful act, absent justification, with the intent to cause harm to others; conscious violation of the law that injures another individual; a mental state indicating a disposition in disregard of social duty and a tendency toward malfeasance.

Malice aforethought A predetermination to commit an act without legal justification or excuse. A malicious design to injure. An intent, at the time of a killing, willfully to take the life of a human being, or an intent willfully to act in callous and wanton disregard of the consequences to human life; but *malice aforethought* does not necessarily imply any ill will, spite, or hatred towards the individual killed.

Malpractice The breach by a member of a profession of either a standard of care or a standard of conduct.

Mandate A judicial command, order, or precept, written or oral, from a court; a direction that a court has the authority to give and an individual is bound to obey.

Manslaughter The unjustifiable, inexcusable, and intentional killing of a human being without deliberation, premeditation, and malice. The unlawful killing of a human being without any deliberation, which may be involuntary, in the commission of a lawful act without due caution and circumspection.

Material Important; affecting the merits of a case; causing a particular course of action; significant; substantial. A description of the quality of evidence that possesses such substantial probative value as to establish the truth or falsity of a point in issue in a lawsuit.

Material fact A fact that is necessary in determining a case, without which there would be no defense. Disclosure of the fact is necessary for the reasonable person to make a prudent decision.

Mediation A settlement of a dispute or controversy by setting up an independent person between two contending parties in order to aid them in the settlement of their disagreement.

Mens rea [*Latin, Guilty mind.*] As an element of criminal responsibility, a guilty mind; a guilty or wrongful purpose; a criminal intent. Guilty knowledge and willfulness.

Merger The combination or fusion of one thing or right into another thing or right of greater or larger importance so that the lesser thing or right loses its individuality and becomes identified with the greater whole.

Minor An infant or person who is under the age of legal competence. A term derived from the civil law, which described a person under a certain age as *less than* so many years. In most states, a person is no longer a minor after reaching the age of 18 (though state laws might still prohibit certain acts until reaching a greater age; i.e., purchase of liquor). Also, less; of less consideration; lower; a person of inferior condition.

Misdemeanor Offenses lower than felonies and generally those punishable by fine, penalty, forfeiture, or imprisonment other than in a penitentiary. Under federal law, and most state laws, any offense other than a felony is classified as a misdemeanor. Certain states also have various classes of misdemeanors (i.e., Class A, B, etc.).

Mistrial A courtroom trial that has been terminated prior to its normal conclusion. A mistrial has no legal effect and is considered an invalid or nugatory trial. It differs from a "new trial," which recognizes that a trial was completed but was set aside so that the issues could be tried again.

Mitigating circumstances Circumstances that may be considered by a court in determining culpability of a defendant or the extent of damages to be awarded to a plaintiff. Mitigating circumstances do not justify or excuse an offense but may reduce the severity of the charge. Similarly, a recognition of mitigating circumstances to reduce a damage award does not imply that the damages were not suffered but that they have been partially ameliorated.

Mitigation of damages The use of reasonable care and diligence in an effort to minimize or avoid injury.

Monopoly An economic advantage held by one or more persons or companies deriving from the exclusive power to carry on a particular business or trade or to manufacture and sell a particular item, thereby suppressing competition and allowing such persons or companies to raise the price of a product or service substantially above the price that would be established by a free market.

Moratorium A suspension of activity or an authorized period of delay or waiting. A moratorium is sometimes agreed upon by the interested parties, or it may be authorized or imposed by operation of law. The term also is used to denote a period of time during which the law authorizes a delay in payment of debts or performance of some other legal obligation. This type of moratorium is most often invoked during times of distress, such as war or natural disaster.

Mortgage A legal document by which the owner (buyer) transfers to the lender an interest in real estate to secure the repayment of a debt, evidenced by a mortgage note. When the debt is repaid, the mortgage is discharged, and a satisfaction of mortgage is recorded with the register or recorder of deeds in the county where the mortgage was recorded. Because most people cannot afford to buy real estate with cash, nearly every real estate transaction involves a mortgage.

Motion A written or oral application made to a court or judge to obtain a ruling or order directing that some act be done in favor of the applicant. The applicant is known as the moving party, or the movant.

Motive An idea, belief, or emotion that impels a person to act in accordance with that state of mind.

Murder The unlawful killing of another human being without justification or excuse.

N

National origin The country in which a person was born or from which his or her ancestors came. It is typically calculated by employers to provide equal employment opportunity statistics in accordance with the provisions of the Civil Rights Act.

Naturalization A process by which a person gains nationality and becomes entitled to the privileges of citizenship. While groups of individuals have been naturalized in history by treaties or laws of Congress, such as in the case of Hawaii, typically naturalization occurs on the individual level upon the completion of the following steps: (1) an individual of majority age, who has been a lawful resident of the United States for five years, petitions for naturalization; (2) the Immigration and Naturalization Service conducts an investigation to establish whether the petitioner can speak English and write English, has a general knowledge of American government and history, especially in regards to the principles of the Constitution, and is in good moral standing; (3) a hearing is held before a U.S. district court, or, when applicable, a state court of record; and (4) a second hearing is held after a period of at least thirty days when the oath of allegiance is administered.

Natural law The unwritten body of universal moral principles that underlie the ethical and legal norms by which human conduct is sometimes evaluated and governed. Natural law is often contrasted with positive law, which consists of the written rules and regulations enacted by government. The term *natural law* is derived from the Roman term *jus naturale*. Adherents to natural law philosophy are known as naturalists.

Necessary and Proper Clause The statement contained in Article I, Section 8, Clause 18 of the U.S. Constitution that gives Congress the power to pass any laws that are "necessary and proper" to carrying out its specifically granted powers.

Necessity A defense asserted by a criminal or civil defendant that he or she had no choice but to break the law.

Negligence Conduct that falls below the standards of behavior established by law for the protection of others against unreasonable risk of harm. A person has acted negligently if he or she has departed from the conduct expected of a reasonably prudent person acting under similar circumstances.

Negligence is also the name of a cause of action in the law of torts. To establish negligence, a plaintiff must prove that the defendant had a duty to the plaintiff, the defendant breached that duty by failing to conform to the required standard of conduct, the defendant's negligent conduct was the cause of the harm to the plaintiff, and the plaintiff was, in fact, harmed or damaged.

No-fault divorce Common name for the type of divorce where "irreconcilable" differences are cited as the reason for the termination of the marriage. Fault by either party does not have to be proven.

Nolo contendere [*Latin, I will not contest it.*] A plea in a criminal case by which the defendant answers the charges made in the indictment by declining to dispute or admit the fact of his or her guilt.

Nominal damages Minimal money damages awarded to an individual in an action where the person has not suffered any substantial injury or loss for which he or she must be compensated.

Nonprofit A corporation or an association that conducts business for the benefit of the general public without shareholders and without a profit motive.

Notary public A public official whose main powers include administering oaths and attesting to signatures, both important and effective ways to minimize fraud in legal documents.

Notice Information; knowledge of certain facts or of a particular state of affairs. The formal receipt of papers that provide specific information.

Nuisance A legal action to redress harm arising from the use of one's property.

Null Of no legal validity, force, or effect; nothing. The phrase "null and void" is used in the invalidation of contracts or statutes.

O

Obscenity The character or quality of being obscene; an act, utterance, or item tending to corrupt public morals by its indecency or lewdness.

Option A privilege, for which a person had paid money, that grants that person the right to purchase or sell certain commodities or certain specified securities at any time within an agreed period for a fixed price.

A right, which operates as a continuing offer, given in exchange for consideration—something of value—to purchase or lease property at an agreed price and terms within a specified time.

Ordinance A law, statute, or regulation enacted by a municipal corporation.

Original jurisdiction The authority of a tribunal to entertain a lawsuit, try it, and set forth a judgment on the law and facts.

Overbreadth doctrine A principle of judicial review that holds that a law is invalid if it punishes constitutionally protected speech or conduct along with speech or conduct that the government may limit to further a compelling government interest.

P

Palimony The settlement awarded at the termination of a non-marital relationship, where the couple lived together for a long period of time and where there was an agreement that one partner would support the other in return for the second making a home and performing domestic duties.

Pardon The action of an executive official of the government that mitigates or sets aside the punishment for a crime.

Parens patriae ["Parent of the country."] The principle that the state should provide for and protect the interests of those who cannot take care of themselves, such as juveniles or the insane. The term also refers to the state's authority to bring legal suits on behalf of its residents, such as antitrust actions.

Parental liability A statute, enacted in some states, that makes parents liable for damages caused by their children, if it is found that the damages resulted from the parents' lack of control over the acts of the child.

Parent corporation An enterprise, which is also known as a parent company, that owns more than 50 percent of the voting shares of its subsidiary.

Parole The conditional release of a person convicted of a crime prior to the expiration of that person's term of imprisonment, subject to both the supervision of the correctional authorities during the remainder of the term and a resumption of the imprisonment upon violation of the conditions imposed.

Parol evidence *Parol* refers to verbal expressions or words. Verbal evidence, such as the testimony of a witness at trial.

Parol evidence rule The principle that a finalized, written contract cannot be altered by evidence of contempo-

raneous oral agreements to change, explain, or contradict the original contract.

Partnership An association of two or more persons engaged in a business enterprise in which the profits and losses are shared proportionally. The legal definition of a partnership is generally stated as "an association of two or more persons to carry on as co-owners of a business for profit" (Revised Uniform Partnership Act sec. 101 [1994]).

Patent Open; manifest; evident.

Patents Rights, granted to inventors by the federal government, pursuant to its power under Article I, Section 8, Clause 8, of the U.S. Constitution, that permit them to exclude others from making, using, or selling an invention for a definite, or restricted, period of time.

Pawnbroker A person who engages in the business of lending money, usually in small sums, in exchange for personal property deposited with him or her that can be kept or sold if the borrower fails or refuses to repay the loan.

Payee The person who is to receive the stated amount of money on a check, bill, or note.

Peremptory challenge The right to challenge a juror without assigning, or being required to assign, a reason for the challenge.

Perjury A crime that occurs when an individual willfully makes a false statement during a judicial proceeding, after he or she has taken an oath to speak the truth.

Personal property Everything that is the subject of ownership that does not come under the denomination of real property; any right or interest that an individual has in movable things.

Personal recognizance *See* Release on own recognizance.

Petition A written application from a person or persons to some governing body or public official asking that some authority be exercised to grant relief, favors, or privileges.

A formal application made to a court in writing that requests action on a certain matter.

Petit jury The ordinary panel of twelve persons called to issue a verdict in a civil action or a criminal prosecution.

Petit larceny A form of larceny—the stealing of another's personal property—in which the value of the property that is taken is generally less than $50.

Plaintiff The party who sues in a civil action; a complainant; the prosecution—that is, a state or the United States representing the people—in a criminal case.

Plain view doctrine In the context of searches and seizures, the principle that provides that objects perceptible by an officer who is rightfully in a position to observe them can be seized without a search warrant and are admissible as evidence.

Plea A formal response by the defendant to the affirmative assertions of the plaintiff in a civil case or to the charges of the prosecutor in a criminal case.

Plea bargaining The process whereby a criminal defendant and prosecutor reach a mutually satisfactory disposition of a criminal case, subject to court approval.

Pleading Asking a court to grant relief. The formal presentation of claims and defenses by parties to a lawsuit. The specific papers by which the allegations of the parties to a lawsuit are presented in proper form; specifically, the complaint of a plaintiff and the answer of a defendant, plus any additional responses to those papers that are authorized by law.

Plurality The opinion of an appellate court in which more justices join than in any concurring opinion.

The excess of votes cast for one candidate over those votes cast for any other candidate.

Pocket veto A method of indirectly vetoing a bill due to a loophole in the Constitution. The loophole allows a bill that is left unsigned by the president or by the governor of a state at the end of a legislative session to be vetoed by default.

Police power The authority conferred upon the states by the Tenth Amendment to the U.S. Constitution which the states delegate to their political subdivisions to enact measures to preserve and protect the safety, health, welfare, and morals of the community.

Poll tax A specified sum of money levied upon each person who votes.

Polygamy The offense of having more than one wife or husband at the same time.

Power of attorney A written document in which one person (the principal) appoints another person to act as an agent on his or her behalf, thus conferring authority on the agent to perform certain acts or functions on behalf of the principal.

Precedent A court decision that is cited as an example or analogy to resolve similar questions of law in later cases.

Precinct A constable's or police district. A small geographical unit of government. An election district created for convenient localization of polling places. A county or municipal subdivision for casting and counting votes in elections.

Preferential treatment Consideration for an individual which is prioritized based on whether the person meets a certain requirement, such as residency. In employment, this type of consideration has been found to be a violation of fair employment practices.

Preliminary hearing A proceeding before a judicial officer in which the officer must decide whether a crime was committed, whether the crime occurred within the territorial jurisdiction of the court, and whether there is probable cause to believe that the defendant committed the crime.

Premarital agreement *See* Prenuptial agreement.

Premeditate To think of an act beforehand; to contrive and design; to plot or lay plans for the execution of a purpose.

Prenuptial agreement An agreement, made prior to marriage, between individuals contemplating marriage, to establish and secure property and other financial rights for one or both of the spouses and their children.

Preponderance of evidence A standard of proof that must be met by a plaintiff if he or she is to win a civil action.

Pre-sentence hearing A hearing commenced after the criminal trial judge examines the pre-sentence report and other relevant materials before passing sentence on the defendant.

Pre-sentence investigation Research that is conducted by court services or a probation officer relating to the prior criminal record, education, employment, and other information about a person convicted of a crime, for the purpose of assisting the court in passing sentence.

Pre-sentence report The written report of the pre-sentence investigation for the judge to evaluate before passing sentence on the defendant. Typically the report covers the following: description of the background, employment history, residency and medical history; information on the environment to which the defendant will return and the resources that will be available to him or her; the probation officer's view of the defendant; full description of the defendant's criminal record; and recommendations on sentencing.

Presentment A grand jury statement that a crime was committed; a written notice, initiated by a grand jury, that states that a crime occurred and that an indictment should be drawn.

In relation to commercial paper, presentment is a demand for the payment or acceptance of a negotiable instrument, such as a check. The holder of a negotiable instrument generally makes a presentment to the maker, acceptor, drawer, or drawee.

Pretrial motion A written or oral request made to the court before the trial to obtain a ruling in favor of the movant, such as a motion to dismiss or a motion to suppress evidence.

Preventive detention The confinement in a secure facility of a person who has not been found guilty of a crime.

Prima facie [*Latin,* On the first appearance.] A fact presumed to be true unless it is disproved.

Prima facie case A case that, because it is supported by the requisite minimum of evidence and is free of obvious defects, can go to the jury; thus the defendant is required to proceed with its case rather than move for dismissal or a directed verdict.

Primary liability In commercial law, the liability of a contract signer.

Principal A source of authority; a sum of a debt or obligation producing interest; the head of a school. In an agency relationship, the principal is the person who gives authority to another, called an agent, to act on his or her behalf. In criminal law, the principal is the chief actor or perpetrator of a crime; those who aid, abet, counsel, command, or induce the commission of a crime may also be principals. In investments and banking, the principal refers to the person for whom a broker executes an order; it may also mean the capital invested or the face amount of a loan.

Prior restraint Government prohibition of speech in advance of publication.

Privacy In constitutional law, the right of people to make personal decisions regarding intimate matters; under the common law, the right of people to lead their lives in a manner that is reasonably secluded from public scrutiny, whether such scrutiny comes from a neighbor's prying eyes, an investigator's eavesdropping ears, or a news photographer's intrusive camera; and in statutory law, the right of people to be free from unwarranted drug testing and electronic surveillance.

Private That which affects, characterizes, or belongs to an individual person, as opposed to the general public.

Private nuisance Anything that creates an unreasonable interference with the use and enjoyment of the property of an individual or small group.

Private property Property that belongs exclusively to an individual for his or her use. This tangible property can be possessed or transferred to another, such as a house or land.

Privilege An advantage, benefit, or exemption possessed by an individual, company, or class beyond those held by others.

Privileges and immunities Concepts contained in the U.S. Constitution that place the citizens of each state on an equal basis with citizens of other states with respect to advantages resulting from citizenship in those states and citizenship in the United States.

Probable cause Apparent facts discovered through logical inquiry that would lead a reasonably intelligent and prudent person to believe that an accused person has committed a crime, thereby warranting his or her prosecution, or that a cause of action has accrued, justifying a civil lawsuit.

Probate The court process by which a will is proved valid or invalid. The legal process wherein the estate of a decedent is administered.

Probate court Called Surrogate or Orphan's Court in some states, the probate court presides over the probate of wills, the administration of estates, and, in some states, the appointment of guardians or approval of the adoption of minors.

Probation A sentence whereby a convict is released from confinement but is still under court supervision; a testing or a trial period. It can be given in lieu of a prison term or can suspend a prison sentence if the convict has consistently demonstrated good behavior.

The status of a convicted person who is given some freedom on the condition that for a specified period he or she acts in a manner approved by a special officer to whom he or she must report.

An initial period of employment during which a new, transferred, or promoted employee must show the ability to perform the required duties.

Procedural due process The constitutional guarantee that one's liberty and property rights may not be affected unless reasonable notice and an opportunity to be heard in order to present a claim or defense are provided.

Product liability The responsibility of a manufacturer or vendor of goods to compensate for injury caused by a defective good that it has provided for sale.

Promissory note A written, signed, unconditional promise to pay a certain amount of money on demand at a specified time. A written promise to pay money that is often used as a means to borrow funds or take out a loan.

Property A thing or things owned either by government—public property—or owned by private individuals, groups, or companies—private property.

Property right A generic term that refers to any type of right to specific property whether it is personal or real property, tangible or intangible; i.e., a professional athlete has a valuable property right in his or her name, photograph, and image, and such right may be saleable by the athlete.

Pro se For one's own behalf; in person. Appearing for oneself, as in the case of one who does not retain a lawyer and appears for himself or herself in court.

Prosecute To follow through; to commence and continue an action or judicial proceeding to its ultimate conclusion. To proceed against a defendant by charging that person with a crime and bringing him or her to trial.

Prosecuting attorney An appointed or elected official in each judicial district, circuit, or county, that carries out criminal prosecutions on behalf of the State or people. Federal crimes are prosecuted by U.S. Attorneys.

Prosecution The proceedings carried out before a competent tribunal to determine the guilt or innocence of a defendant. The term also refers to the government attorney charging and trying a criminal case.

Protective order A court order, direction, decree, or command to protect a person from further harassment, service of process, or discovery.

Provision Anticipated accommodation(s) that may need to be made to fulfill an obligation in the event that something happens.

Proximate cause An act from which an injury results as a natural, direct, uninterrupted consequence and without which the injury would not have occurred.

Proximate consequence or result A consequence or result that naturally follows from one's negligence and is reasonably foreseeable and probable.

Proxy A representative; an agent; a document appointing a representative.

Public forum An open-discussion meeting that takes place in an area which is accessible to or shared by all members of a community.

Public hearing The due process of an individual before a tribunal to hear evidence and testimony in determination of the defendant's guilt or innocence.

Punitive damages Monetary compensation awarded to an injured party that goes beyond that which is necessary to compensate the individual for losses and that is intended to punish the wrongdoer.

Purchase To buy; the transfer of property from one person to another by an agreement, which sets forth the price and terms of the sale. Under the Uniform Commercial Code (UCC), taking by sale, discount, negotiation, mortgage, pledge, lien, issue, reissue, gift, or any voluntary transaction.

Q

Quiet enjoyment A covenant that promises that the grantee or tenant of an estate in real property will be able to possess the premises in peace, without disturbance by hostile claimants.

Quitclaim deed An instrument of conveyance of real property that passes any title, claim, or interest, that the grantor has in the premises but does not make any representations as to the validity of such title.

Quorum A majority of an entire body; i.e., a quorum of a legislative assembly.

Quota A quantitative boundary set for a class of things or people.

R

Rape A criminal offense defined in most states as forcible sexual relations with a person against that person's will.

Ratification The confirmation or adoption of an act that has already been performed.

Reapportionment The realignment in legislative districts brought about by changes in population and mandated in the constitutional requirement of one person, one vote.

Reasonable care The degree of caution that a rational and competent individual would exercise in a given circumstance. It is an subjective test used to determine negligence.

Reasonable person A phrase frequently used in tort and criminal law to denote a hypothetical person in society who exercises average care, skill, and judgment in conduct and who serves as a comparative standard for determining liability.

Rebut To defeat, dispute, or remove the effect of the other side's facts or arguments in a particular case or controversy.

Rebuttable presumption A conclusion as to the existence or nonexistence of a fact that a judge or jury must draw when evidence has been introduced and admitted as true in a lawsuit but that can be contradicted by evidence to the contrary.

Recall The right or procedure by which a public official may be removed from a position by a vote of the people prior to the end of the term of office.

Recognizance A recorded obligation, entered into before a tribunal, in which an individual pledges to perform a specific act or to subscribe to a certain course of conduct.

Redlining A discriminatory practice whereby lending institutions refuse to make mortgage loans, regardless of an applicant's credit history, on properties in particular areas in which conditions are allegedly deteriorating.

Redress Compensation for injuries sustained; recovery or restitution for harm or injury; damages or equitable relief. Access to the courts to gain reparation for a wrong.

Redress of grievances The right to request relief from the government for an injustice or wrong it has committed, as guaranteed by the First Amendment.

Referendum The right reserved to the people to approve or reject an act of the legislature, or the right of the people to approve or reject legislation that has been referred to them by the legislature.

Refugees Individuals who leave their native country for social, political, or religious reasons, or who are forced to leave as a result of any type of disaster, including war, political upheaval, and famine.

Regulation A rule of order having the force of law, prescribed by a superior or competent authority, relating to the actions of those under the authority's control.

Regulatory agency *See* Administrative agency.

Rehabilitation The restoration of former rights, authority, or abilities.

Release A contractual agreement by which one individual assents to relinquish a claim or right under the law to another individual against whom such a claim or right is enforceable.

Release on own recognizance The release of an individual who is awaiting trial without a bail bond. It is used in place of bail when the judge is satisfied that the defendant will appear for trial, given the defendant's past history, his or her roots in the community, his or her regular employment, the recommendation of the prosecutor, the

type of crime, and the improbability that the defendant will commit another crime while awaiting trial.

Remand To send back.

Remedy The manner in which a right is enforced or satisfied by a court when some harm or injury, recognized by society as a wrongful act, is inflicted upon an individual.

Removal The transfer of a person or thing from one place to another. The transfer of a case from one court to another. In this sense, removal generally refers to a transfer from a court in one jurisdiction to a court in another, whereas a change of venue may be granted simply to move a case to another location within the same jurisdiction.

Rent Control The system by which the federal, state, and local governments regulate rent rates by placing ceilings on the amount that private individuals can be charged for rent.

Replevin A legal action to recover the possession of items of personal property.

Replevy In regards to replevin, the return of goods to the original owner pending the outcome of the case. Also, the release of an individual on bail.

Repossession The taking back of an item that has been sold on credit and delivered to the purchaser because the payments have not been made on it.

Reprieve The suspension of the execution of the death penalty for a period of time.

Rescind To declare a contract void—of no legal force or binding effect—from its inception and thereby restore the parties to the positions they would have occupied had no contract ever been made.

Rescission The cancellation of a prison inmate's tentative parole date. The abrogation of a contract, effective from its inception, thereby restoring the parties to the positions they would have occupied if no contract had ever been formed.

Reservation A clause in a deed of real property whereby the grantor, one who transfers property, creates and retains for the grantor some right or interest in the estate granted, such as rent or an easement, a right of use over the land of another. A large tract of land that is withdrawn by public authority from sale or settlement and appropriated to specific public uses, such as parks or military posts. A tract of land under the control of the Bureau of Indian Affairs to which a Native American tribe retains its original title of ownership, or that has been set aside from the public domain for use by a tribe.

Reserve Funds set aside to cover future expenses, losses, or claims. To retain; to keep in store for future or special use; to postpone to a future time.

Residence Personal presence at some place of abode.

Resolution The official expression of the opinion or will of a legislative body.

Restraining order A command of the court issued upon the filing of an application for an injunction, prohibiting the defendant from performing a threatened act until a hearing on the application can be held.

Restrictive covenant A provision in a deed limiting the use of the property and prohibiting certain uses. A clause in contracts of partnership and employment prohibiting a contracting party from engaging in similar employment for a specified period of time within a certain geographical area.

Retainer A contract between attorney and client specifying the nature of the services to be rendered and the cost of the services.

Retribution Punishment or reward for an act. In criminal law, punishment is based upon the theory that every crime demands payment.

Reverse discrimination Discrimination against a group of people that is alleged to have resulted from the affirmation action guidelines applied for a different group of people who were historically discriminated against by the former group.

Revocation The recall of some power or authority that has been granted.

Rider A schedule or writing annexed to a document such as a legislative bill or insurance policy.

Right of legation *See* Legation.

Right-to-work laws State laws permitted by section 14(b) of the Taft-Hartley Act that provide in general that employees are not required to join a union as a condition of getting or retaining a job.

Robbery The taking of money or goods in the possession of another, from his or her person or immediate presence, by force or intimidation.

Rule of law Rule according to law; rule under law; or rule according to a higher law.

S

Sabotage The willful destruction or impairment of, or defective production of, war material or national defense material, or harm to war premises or war utilities. During a labor dispute, the willful and malicious destruction of an employer's property or interference with his or her normal operations.

Sales agreement A present or future covenant that transfers ownership of goods or real estate from the seller to the buyer at an agreed upon price and terms.

Search warrant A court order authorizing the examination of a place for the purpose of discovering contraband, stolen property, or evidence of guilt to be used in the prosecution of a criminal action.

Second degree murder The unlawful taking of human life with malice, but without premeditated thought.

Secured transactions Business dealings that grant a creditor a right in property owned or held by a debtor to assure the payment of a debt or the performance of some obligation.

Security Protection; assurance; indemnification.

Security deposit Money aside from the payment of rent that a landlord requires a tenant to pay to be kept separately in a fund for use should the tenant cause damage to the premises or otherwise violate terms of the lease.

Sedition A revolt or an incitement to revolt against established authority, usually in the form of treason or defamation against government.

Seditious libel A written communication intended to incite the overthrow of the government by force or violence.

Segregation The act or process of separating a race, class, or ethnic group from a society's general population.

Self-defense The protection of one's person or property against some injury attempted by another.

Self-incrimination Giving testimony in a trial or other legal proceeding that could subject one to criminal prosecution.

Sentencing The post-conviction stage of a criminal justice process, in which the defendant is brought before the court for the imposition of a penalty.

Separate but equal The doctrine first enunciated by the U.S. Supreme Court in *Plessy v. Ferguson*, 163 U.S. 537, 16 S. Ct. 1138, 41 L. Ed. 256 (1896), establishing that different facilities for blacks and whites was valid under the Equal Protection Clause of the Fourteenth Amendment as along as they were equal.

Separation of church and state The separation of religious and government interest to ensure that religion does not become corrupt by government and that government does not become corrupt by religious conflict. The principle prevents the government from supporting the practices of one religion over another. It also enables the government to do what is necessary to prevent one religious group from violating the rights of others.

Separation of powers The division of state and federal government into three independent branches.

Settlement The act of adjusting or determining the dealings or disputes between persons without pursuing the matter through a trial.

Sexual harassment Unwelcome sexual advances, requests for sexual favors, and other verbal or physical conduct of a sexual nature that tends to create a hostile or offensive work environment.

Share A portion or part of something that may be divided into components, such as a sum of money. A unit of stock that represents ownership in a corporation.

Shield laws Statutes affording a privilege to journalists not to disclose in legal proceedings confidential information or sources of information obtained in their professional capacities.

Statutes that restrict or prohibit the use of certain evidence in sexual offense cases, such as evidence regarding the lack of chastity of the victim.

Shoplifting Theft of merchandise from a store or business establishment.

Silent partner An investment partner in a business who has no involvement in the management of the business.

Slander *See* Libel and slander.

Small claims court A special court, sometimes called conciliation court, that provides expeditious, informal, and inexpensive adjudication of small claims.

Sole proprietorship A form of business in which one person owns all the assets of the business, in contrast to a partnership or a corporation.

Solicitation Urgent request, plea or entreaty; enticing, asking. The criminal offense of urging someone to commit an unlawful act.

Sovereignty The supreme, absolute, and uncontrollable power by which an independent state is governed and from which all specific political powers are derived; the intentional independence of a state, combined with the right and power of regulating its internal affairs without foreign interference.

Specific performance An extraordinary equitable remedy that compels a party to execute a contract according to the precise terms agreed upon or to execute it substantially so that, under the circumstances, justice will be done between the parties.

Standing committee A group of legislators, who are ranked by seniority, that deliberate on bills, resolutions, and other items of business within its particular jurisdiction.

Stare decisis [*Latin, Let the decision stand.*] The policy of courts to abide by or adhere to principles established by decisions in earlier cases.

State courts Judicial tribunals established by each of the fifty states.

Status offense A type of crime that is not based upon prohibited action or inaction but rests on the fact that the offender has a certain personal condition or is of a specified character.

Statute An act of a legislature that declares, proscribes, or commands something; a specific law, expressed in writing.

Statute of frauds A type of state law, modeled after an old English law, that requires certain types of contracts to be in writing.

Statute of limitations A type of federal or state law that restricts the time within which legal proceedings may be brought.

Statutory Created, defined, or relating to a statute; required by statute; conforming to a statute.

Statutory law A law which is created by an act of the legislature.

Statutory rape Sexual intercourse by an adult with a person below a statutorily designated age.

Steering The process whereby builders, brokers, and rental property managers induce purchasers or lessees of real property to buy land or rent premises in neighborhoods composed of persons of the same race.

Stock A security issued by a corporation that represents an ownership right in the assets of the corporation and a right to a proportionate share of profits after payment of corporate liabilities and obligations.

Strict liability Absolute legal responsibility for an injury that can be imposed on the wrongdoer without proof of carelessness or fault.

Subcontractor One who takes a portion of a contract from the principal contractor or from another subcontractor.

Sublease The leasing of part or all of the property held by a tenant, as opposed to a landlord, during a portion of his or her unexpired balance of the term of occupancy.

Subpoena [*Latin, Under penalty.*] A formal document that orders a named individual to appear before a duly authorized body at a fixed time to give testimony.

Subsidiary Auxiliary; aiding or supporting in an inferior capacity or position. In the law of corporations, a corporation or company owned by another corporation that controls at least a majority of the shares.

Substantive due process The substantive limitations placed on the content or subject matter of state and federal laws by the Due Process Clauses of the Fifth and Fourteenth Amendments to the U.S. Constitution.

Substantive law The part of the law that creates, defines, and regulates rights, including, for example, the law of contracts, torts, wills, and real property; the essential substance of rights under law.

Suffrage The right to vote at public elections.

Summons The paper that tells a defendant that he or she is being sued and asserts the power of the court to hear and determine the case. A form of legal process that commands the defendant to appear before the court on a specific day and to answer the complaint made by the plaintiff.

Suppression or exclusion of evidence The dismissal of evidence put forth by the prosecution by a judge; often due to the unconstitutionality of the method of seizure of said evidence.

Supremacy clause The clause of Article VI of the U.S. Constitution that declares that all laws and treaties made by the federal government shall be the "supreme law of the land."

Supreme court An appellate tribunal with high powers and broad authority within its jurisdiction.

Surrogate mother A woman who agrees under contract to bear a child for an infertile couple. The woman is paid to have a donated fertilized egg or the fertilized egg of the female partner in the couple (usually fertilized by the male partner of the couple) artificially inseminated into her uterus.

Suspended sentence A sentence given after the formal conviction of a crime that the convicted person is not required to serve.

Syllabus A headnote; a short note preceding the text of a reported case that briefly summarizes the rulings of the court on the points decided in the case.

Symbolic speech Nonverbal gestures and actions that are meant to communicate a message.

T

Tenant An individual who occupies or possesses land or premises by way of a grant of an estate of some type, such as in fee, for life, for years, or at will. A person who has the right to temporary use and possession of a particular real property, which has been conveyed to that person by the landlord.

Testator One who makes or has made a will; one who dies leaving a will.

Testify To provide evidence as a witness, subject to an oath or affirmation, in order to establish a particular fact or set of facts.

Testimony Oral evidence offered by a competent witness under oath, which is used to establish some fact or set of facts.

Title In property law, a comprehensive term referring to the legal basis of the ownership of property, encompassing real and personal property and intangible and tangible interests therein; also a document serving as evidence of ownership of property, such as the certificate of title to a motor vehicle.

In regard to legislation, the heading or preliminary part of a particular statute that designates the name by which that act is known.

In the law of trademarks, the name of an item that may be used exclusively by an individual for identification purposes to indicate the quality and origin of the item.

Tortfeasor A wrongdoer; an individual who commits a wrongful act that injures another and for which the law provides a legal right to seek relief; a defendant in a civil tort action.

Tortious Wrongful; conduct of such character as to subject the actor to civil liability under tort law.

Tort law A body of rights, obligations, and remedies that is applied by the courts in civil proceedings to provide relief for persons who have suffered harm from the wrongful acts of others. The person who sustains injury or suffers pecuniary damage as the result of tortious conduct is known as the plaintiff, and the person who is responsible for inflicting the injury and incurs liability for the damage is known as the defendant or tortfeasor.

Trade secret Any valuable commercial information that provides a business with an advantage over competitors who do not have that information.

Trade union An organization of workers in the same skilled occupation or related skilled occupations who act together to secure for all members favorable wages, hours, and other working conditions.

Transfer To remove or convey from one place to another. The removal of a case from one court to another court within the same system where it might have been instituted. An act of the parties, or of the law, by which the title to property is conveyed from one person to another.

Treason The betrayal of one's own country by waging war against it or by consciously or purposely acting to aid its enemies.

Treaty A compact made between two or more independent nations with a view to the public welfare.

Trespass An unlawful intrusion that interferes with one's person or property.

Trial A judicial examination and determination of facts and legal issues arising between parties to a civil or criminal action.

Trial court The court where civil actions or criminal proceedings are first heard.

Truancy The willful and unjustified failure to attend school by one required to do so.

Trust A relationship created at the direction of an individual, in which one or more persons hold the individual's property subject to certain duties to use and protect it for the benefit of others.

Trustee An individual or corporation named by an individual, who sets aside property to be used for the benefit of another person, to manage the property as provided by the terms of the document that created the arrangement.

U

Unenumerated rights Rights that are not expressly mentioned in the written text of a constitution but instead are inferred from the language, history, and structure of the constitution, or cases interpreting it.

Unconstitutional That which is not in agreement with the ideas and regulations of the Constitution.

Uniform commercial code A general and inclusive group of laws adopted, at least partially, by all of the states to further uniformity and fair dealing in business and commercial transactions.

U.S. Constitution *See* Constitution of the United States.

U.S. Court of Appeals *See* Court of appeals.

U.S. Supreme Court *See* Supreme court.

Usury The crime of charging higher interest on a loan than the law permits.

V

Valid Binding; possessing legal force or strength; legally sufficient.

Vandalism The intentional and malicious destruction of or damage to the property of another.

Venue A place, such as the territory, from which residents are selected to serve as jurors.

A proper place, such as the correct court to hear a case because it has authority over events that have occurred within a certain geographical area.

Verdict The formal decision or finding made by a jury concerning the questions submitted to it during a trial. The jury reports the verdict to the court, which generally accepts it.

Veto The refusal of an executive officer to assent to a bill that has been created and approved by the legislature, thereby depriving the bill of any legally binding effect.

Void That which is null and completely without legal force or binding effect.

Voidable That which is not absolutely void, but may be avoided.

Voir dire [*Old French, To speak the truth.*] The preliminary examination of prospective jurors to determine their qualifications and suitability to serve on a jury, in order to ensure the selection of a fair and impartial jury.

Voluntary manslaughter The unlawful killing of a person falling short of malice, premeditation or deliberate intent but too near to these standards to be classified as justifiable homicide.

W

Waive To intentionally or voluntarily relinquish a known right or engage in conduct warranting an inference that a right has been surrendered.

Waiver The voluntary surrender of a known right; conduct supporting an inference that a particular right has been relinquished.

Ward A person, especially an infant or someone judged to be incompetent, placed by the court in the care of a guardian.

Warrant A written order issued by a judicial officer or other authorized person commanding a law enforcement officer to perform some act incident to the administration of justice.

Warranty deed An instrument that transfers real property from one person to another and in which the grantor promises that title is good and clear of any claims.

White collar crime Term for nonviolent crimes that were committed in the course of the offender's occupation, such as commercial fraud or insider trading on the stock market.

Will A document in which a person specifies the method to be applied in the management and distribution of his or her estate after his or her death.

Workers' compensation A system whereby an employer must pay, or provide insurance to pay, the lost wages and medical expenses of an employee who is injured on the job.

Work release program A sentencing alternative designed to permit an inmate to continue regular employment during the daytime but to return to prison at night for lockup.

Writ An order issued by a court requiring that something be done or giving authority to do a specified act.

Writ of assistance A court order issued to enforce an existing judgment.

Writ of certiorari *See* Certiorari.

Writ of habeas corpus *See* Habeas corpus.

Z

Zoning The separation or division of a municipality into districts, the regulation of buildings and structures in such districts in accordance with their construction and the nature and extent of their use, and the dedication of such districts to particular uses designed to serve the general welfare.

Alphabetical List of Court Cases

Volume II

The following list includes the name of each case covered in this volume of *Great American Court Cases* and the page number on which coverage of the case begins. The case names are arranged in alphabetical order. Names not found here might be located within the cumulative index in the back of this volume.

CHRONOLOGICAL LIST OF COURT CASES

Volume II

The following list includes the name of each case covered in this volume of *Great American Court Cases* and the page number on which coverage of the case begins. The case names are arranged in alphabetical order under the year in which the corresponding case took place. Names not found here might be located within the cumulative index in the back of this volume.

CUMULATIVE INDEX

This index cites cases, people, events, and subjects in all four volumes of Great American Court Cases. Roman numerals refer to volumes.

Contract with America, **II:** 129 (box); **IV:** 350

contributions, political. *See* campaigns

Contributors to the Pennsylvania Hospital v. City of Philadelphia, **IV:** 59

Controlled Substance Act, **II:** 171

Cook, Fred J., **I:** 219

Cooley v. Board of Wardens, **IV:** 81, 358-359 (main)

Coolidge v. New Hampshire, **II:** 393-396 (main), 438, 486, 500, 522 (box)

Coolidge, Calvin, **IV:** 134 (box)

Copelon, Rhonda, **III:** 442

Coppage v. Kansas, **IV:** 300-302 (main)

copyright law, **I:** 419, 435 (box)

corporal punishment, **III:** 154-156

corporate law. *See also* employment law; labor law. **III:** 102, 104; **IV:** 2-4, 92-95, 147-149

corporations, **III:** 104; **IV:** 2, 37-38, 42-44, 450-452, 514

government, **I:** 314-316

corruption, **IV:** 263

Cotton Petroleum Corporation v. New Mexico, **IV:** 500

Counselman v. Hitchcock, **II:** 315

County of Allegheny v. ACLU, **I:** 116, 129-130 (main), 160, 326

County of Oneida v. Oneida Indian Nation, **III:** 6; **IV:** 478

County of Riverside v. McLaughlin, **II:** 508-510 (main)

County of Sacramento v. Lewis, **III:** 64-66 (main)

court martial, **IV:** 417, 432

court of claims, **IV:** 228, 327-329

court packing, **I:** 14; **IV:** 8, 56, 104, 138, 141, 145, 313, 321, 380, 538, 541

courts

organization of circuit, **II:** 310 (box); **IV:** 227

organization of federal appellate, **II:** 300 (box); **IV:** 227, 251

organization of federal district, **II:** 327 (box); **IV:** 227

Cox Broadcasting Corp. v. Cohn, **I:** 358, 381-384 (main)

Cox v. Louisiana, **I:** 1, 42, 166, 205-208 (main), 212

Cox v. New Hampshire, **I:** 1, 11-13 (main), 166

Coy v. Iowa, **II:** 290; **III:** 383

Coyle v. Oklahoma, **IV:** 194

Coyle v. Smith, **IV:** 194-195 (main)

Craig v. Boren, **III:** 69, 317, 321, 322-323 (main), 350

Craig v. Harney, **I:** 382

Crawford v. Board of Education of Los Angeles, **III:** 550

Crawford-El v. Britton, **I:** 347-349 (main)

Crazy Horse, **IV:** 510-512

Creationism Act, **I:** 127-128

Creationism theory, **I:** 67-71

creches

display of, **I:** 129-130, 159-161

Creedon v. Cloyd W. Miller Co, **IV:** 386

Crime Act of 1994, **I:** 563

Crime Victims Protection Act, **I:** 384

crimes. *See* specific crimes

Criminal Appeals Act, **III:** 116

criminal law, **II:** 61-80; **IV:** 253-254

criminal procedure, **II:** 81-129

distinction from civil procedure, **II:** 181 (box)

criminal syndicalism, **IV:** 241-242

Criminal Syndicalism Act of California, **I:** 7 (box)

Crockett v. Reagan, **IV:** 459

Crooker v. California, **II:** 254 (box)

cross-examinations, **I:** 532-534; **III:** 382-383

right to, **II:** 307-308

crosses

display of, **I:** 326-327

Crow Dog, Ex Parte, **IV:** 488-490 (main)

cruel and unusual punishment, **I:** 392; **II:** 2, 9-11, 15-23, 31-45, 48-55, 175-177, 333, 336-347; **III:** 154-156, 160-162, 223-225, 265-267, 421, 476

Cruzan v. Director, Missouri Department of Health, **I:** 97; **III:** 39, 46-48 (main), 50

Cubby, Inc. v. CompuServe, Inc., **I:** 421-423 (main), 431

Culombe v. Connecticut, **II:** 110

Cummings v. Missouri, **II:** 68

curfews, **III:** 93-96, 377 (box)

Curran v. Mount Diablo Council of the Boy Scouts of America, **III:** 494-496 (main)

curriculum laws, **I:** 511-513

Curtis Act, **IV:** 472

Curtis, Benjamin, **IV:** 358

Curtis Publishing Co. v. Butts, **I:** 232, 250, 440, 451-453 (main)

Customs Service, U.S., **I:** 465, 549-551

Cyber Promotions, Inc. v. America Online, Inc., **I:** 424-426 (main)

D

DaCosta v. Laird, **IV:** 458

dairy industry, **IV:** 137-139, 374-375, 381-383

Dallas v. Stanglin, **I:** 13

Dalton v. Specter, **IV:** 347

damages, **II:** 131-168; **III:** 33, 55

civil, **II:** 149-151

compensatory, **I:** 413, 443, 451; **II:** 131, 158, 163-164, 167; **IV:** 31

for wrongful death, **III:** 118-120

liquidated, **II:** 131

nominal, **II:** 131

punitive, **I:** 413, 444, 451; **II:** 131, 158-159, 163-164; **III:** 56; **IV:** 31

Dames & Moore v. Regan, **IV:** 151

Dandridge v. Williams, **III:** 129-130 (main)

Danforth v. Planned Parenthood of Central Missouri, **III:** 422

Daniels v. Williams , **III:** 65

Darrow, Clarence, **I:** 67; **II:** 296

Dartmouth College v. Woodward, **IV:** 37

Darwinism, **I:** 67-71

date rape, **III:** 332 (box)

Daubert v. Merrell Dow Pharmaceuticals, Inc., **II:** 91, 160-162 (main)

Davis v. Alaska, **I:** 532-534 (main)

Davis v. Bandemer, **III:** 642-644 (main)

Davis v. Beason, **I:** 64

Davis v. Davis, **III:** 468

Davis v. Massachusetts, **I:** 369

Davis v. N.J. Zinc Co., **III:** 59

Dawes Severalty Act (General Allotment Act), **IV:** 472, 484-487

Day, William Rufus, **II:** 360

De Jonge v. Oregon, **I:** 1, 9-10 (main)

de novo review, **II:** 536

Dean Milk Company v. Madison, **IV:** 375

Dean v. District of Columbia, **III:** 487

death, **III:** 42-54, 64-66

Debs, Eugene V., **IV:** 285-288

Debs, In Re, **IV:** 285-288 (main)

Debs v. United States, **I:** 172; **IV:** 275

debt adjustment, **IV:** 208-209

debts, **IV:** 47-49, 60-62

Decent Interval, **I:** 257

decisions (judicial)

retrospective application of, **II:** 379-381

declaratory relief

definition of, **II:** 131

defamation. *See also* libel. **I:** 385-386, 405, 407, 411-412, 418, 439-441, 535-538, 541-543; **IV:** 510-512

Defense of Marriage Act, **III:** 472

DeFunis v. Odegaard, **III:** 2

Delaware v. Prouse, **II:** 356, 418-421 (main), 530

Delaware v. Van Arsdall, **I:** 534

delinquency, **II:** 219

Dellums v. Bush, **IV:** 168-170 (main)

Democratic National Committee, **I:** 270

Democratic-Republicans, **IV:** 460

demonstrations

against race discrimination, **I:** 224-228

against segregation, **I:** 41-42, 200-201, 205-208, 212-213

at abortion clinics, **I:** 555

at embassies, **I:** 55

nonviolent, **I:** 227 (box), 363, 581, 584-586, 589, 592; **II:** 88; **III:** 509

picketing, **I:** 579-580, 585 (box)

violent, **I:** 389; **IV:** 45, 127

denaturalization, **II:** 336

Dennis v. Sparks, **I:** 230

Dennis v. United States, **I:** 8, 32, 166, 189-191 (main), 195, 198, 222

Dennison, William, **II:** 84-86

Denver Area Educational Consortium v. Federal Communications Commission, **IV:** 26-28 (main)

Department of Agriculture, U.S., **III:** 62

draft, the, **I:** 65, 581; **II:** 68-71; **III:** 358; **IV:** 127-128, 273, 434-436; **IV:** 417
    exclusion of women from, **III:** 329-331
    protestation of, **I:** 587-588
Draft Act, **IV:** 434
draft card burning, **I:** 574, 581-583; **IV:** 436
Draper v. United States, **II:** 172-174 (main), 435
Dred Scott case. *See Scott v. Sandford*
driving while intoxicated, **II:** 106, 121, 259-261, 419 (box), 498, 502-504
drug abuse. *See also* drug use. **I:** 549-551
drug control laws, **I:** 539
Drug Enforcement Agency (DEA), **II:** 169, 456, 496
drug laws, **II:** 169-183, 182 (box), 265-266, 522 (box)
    juveniles, **II:** 512 (box)
    legalization, **II:** 173 (box)
drug possession, **II:** 72, 124, 127, 371, 376, 397, 403, 418, 425, 431, 434, 437-439, 441-447, 451, 453, 456, 468, 480-483, 495-498, 500-501, 505-507, 511-514, 524, 527-528, 535-540, 550-552; **III:** 380-381
drug testing, **II:** 171, 261, 329
    of government officials, **I:** 549-551; **II:** 546-549
    of railroad employees, **II:** 492-494
    of student-athletes, **II:** 529-531
drug trafficking, **I:** 549; **II:** 79, 333, 414, 422, 476; **III:** 219; **IV:** 406
drug use, **II:** 36, 175-177, 221, 330, 356, 371-372, 492; **IV:** 504-506
    teens, **II:** 530 (box)
drug-sniffing dogs, **II:** 442-444, 456, 500-501, 536 (box)
drugs (prescription), **I:** 539-540
Du Bois, W. E. B., **III:** 508
dual system estimation, **III:** 652
Duckworth v. Eagan, **II:** 115-117 (main)
due process of law, **II:** 81
    juveniles, **II:** 220, 225-226; **III:** 384-386
Duffield v. Robertson, Stephens & Co., **III:** 575-577 (main)
Dulles, John Foster, **I:** 23
Duncan v. Louisiana, **II:** 97, 189 (box), 191, 197-199 (main), 201, 203, 208, 267
Dunn v. Blumstein, **III:** 618-619 (main), 624
Duren v. Missouri, **III:** 303
Duro v. Reina, **IV:** 490

E

e-mail, **I:** 418, 424-426
Eakin v. Raub, **IV:** 190-191 (main)
Earth Day, **IV:** 71

easements, **IV:** 66-69
East Bibb Twiggs Neighborhood Association v. Macon-Bibb County Planning and Zoning Commission, **III:** 205-207 (main)
Eastern Railroad Presidents Conference v. Noerr Motor Freight, Inc., **III:** 465
Economic Stabilization Act, **IV:** 338
Eddleman v. Center Township, **III:** 127
education
    compulsory, **I:** 514-515
education law. *See also* colleges and universities; schools; students' rights. **I:** 135-137, 353-354; **III:** 7-9, 141-142, 177-182, 334-336, 528-533, 539-542, 546-548; **IV:** 35-36
Education of All Handicapped Children Act, **III:** 178 (box)
Edwards v. Aguillard, **I:** 127-128 (main)
Edwards v. South Carolina, **I:** 2, 42, 180, 200-201 (main), 205, 225, 321
Edye and Another v. Robertson, Collector, **IV:** 519 (main)
EEOC v. Franklin and Marshall College, **I:** 289
Eighteenth Amendment, **II:** 170, 363, 366; **IV:** 129 (box), 403 (box)
Eighth Amendment, **II:** 2, 9-11, 15-55, 59-60, 215-217, 234, 290, 333, 336-347, 534; **III:** 154-156, 160-162, 223, 421-424, 476, 503-504; **IV:** 219
    bail provision, **II:** 284
Eisenhower, Dwight D., **II:** 138; **IV:** 160
Eisenstadt v. Baird, **I:** 505, 521; **III:** 387, 395, 403, 409-411 (main)
El Paso v. Simmons, **IV:** 58-59 (main)
elections, **I:** 48-49, 60-62, 237-239, 269-272, 292-294, 317-319, 335; **III:** 208, 583-594, 599-602, 613-626, 630-633; **IV:** 392, 409-412
    voting in foreign, **III:** 358-360, 363-364
electrocution, **II:** 9-11, 21-23
Electronic Communications Privacy Act, **I:** 418; **III:** 490-493
Eleventh Amendment, **III:** 160-162, 357; **IV:** 101-103, 219-221, 256, 331, 507-509
Elfbrandt v. Russell, **I:** 198
Elkins v. United States, **II:** 361 (box), 374
Ellsburg, Daniel, **I:** 371
Elrod v. Burns, **I:** 59, 284, 335
Emancipation Proclamation, **IV:** 124 (box)
embassies, **I:** 55-57; **II:** 113 (box)
embezzlement, **II:** 78; **III:** 91
Emergency Planning and Community Right-to-Know Act, **IV:** 73
eminent domain, **II:** 459; **IV:** 389
employment discrimination, **III:** 13-14, 19-20, 197-198, 247-256,

290-291, 559-560; **IV:** 13-15, 291-293
affirmative action, **III:** 27-29, 170-173
    against nonresidents, **III:** 250-252
    gender based, **III:** 304-306, 324-325
    job qualification tests, **III:** 146-147
    mandatory leave, **III:** 309-311
    mandatory retirement, **III:** 208-211
    organized labor, **IV:** 144
    racial quotas, **III:** 191-193
    reverse, **III:** 4-6, 10-12, 15-18, 21-24, 30-32
    sexual harassment, **III:** 567-577
Employment Division v. Smith, **I:** 65, 101, 141; **IV:** 504-506 (main)
employment law, **I:** 167, 289-291, 308-311, 332-337, 418, 558-560; **II:** 492-494; **III:** 4-6, 10-24, 30-32, 58-61, 146-147, 170-173, 191-193, 197-198, 202-204, 208-211, 248-249, 304-306, 309-311, 324-325, 356-357, 497, 564-571, 575-577; **IV:** 13-15, 47-49, 285-320, 323-332, 336-342, 504-506
encryption, **I:** 418
Endangered Species Act, **IV:** 73
Endo, Ex Parte, **III:** 100-101 (main)
energy industry, **III:** 250-252; **IV:** 56-57, 450-452
Engel v. Vitale, **I:** 86-88 (main), 89, 118, 128, 132, 146, 153
Enmund v. Florida, **II:** 27, 37-39 (main)
Entick v. Carrington, **II:** 384
environmental law, **II:** 518-520; **III:** 139-140, 205-207, 212-214; **IV:** 71-95, 198-200
Environmental Protection Agency, **III:** 60; **IV:** 2, 71, 79-80, 93, 247
Epperson v. Arkansas, **I:** 146, 152-153 (main)
Equal Access Act, **I:** 147
Equal Credit Opportunity Act, **III:** 289
Equal Employment Opportunity Act, **III:** 5
Equal Employment Opportunity Commission, **I:** 289-291; **III:** 2, 30, 247, 304-306, 324, 555, 559, 573
Equal Pay Act, **III:** 68, 247, 289; **IV:** 311
Equal Protection Clause, **III:** 68-70
Equal Rights Amendment, **III:** 68, 289; **IV:** 312
equitable estoppel, **I:** 414
Erdman Act, **IV:** 45-46
Erie R. Co. v. Tompkins, **II:** 135; **IV:** 201-203 (main)
Erznoznik v. City of Jacksonville, **I:** 490
Escobedo v. Illinois, **II:** 234, 253-254 (main)
espionage, **I:** 173, 372 (box); **III:** 93, 100
Espionage Act, **I:** 169, 172-175, 373; **IV:** 457